ALSO BY ANTHONY BIANCO

Rainmaker

THE
REICHMANNS

THE
REICHMANNS

Family, Faith, Fortune,

and the Empire

of Olympia & York

ANTHONY BIANCO

TIMES BOOKS

RANDOM HOUSE

Library of Congress Cataloging-in-Publication Data
Bianco, Anthony.
The Reichmanns : family, faith, fortune, and the empire of Olympia & York /
Anthony Bianco.
p.   cm.
Includes index.
ISBN 0-8129-2140-2
1. Reichmann family.   2. Jews—Canada—Biography.   3. Jews,
Hungarian—Canada—Biography.   4. Jews—Hungary—Biography.
5. Orthodox Judaism—Canada.   6. Canada—Biography.   I. Title.
F1035.J5B53   1997   929'.2'0971—dc20   96-24847

Random House website address: http://www.randomhouse.com/
Printed in the United States of America on acid-free paper
Book design by J. K. Lambert
9 8 7 6 5 4 3 2

First Edition

To my grandmother, Amy Walsh Bianco,

and in memory of my grandfather, Dr. Anthony Bianco

Rabbi Weissmandel planned the emigration of several hundred Jewish families to Canada, among them were families from Nitra and Tyrnau, but the plan was never realized. Later, Jews from Nitra and Tyrnau were among the first to be sent to Auschwitz, where they were forced to work in the construction of the crematoria and deal with the bodies of the victims. Ultimately, they too were killed. When they arrived in Auschwitz, instead of Canada, the people of Nitra and Tyrnau made a gruesome joke, "Well, we've arrived in Canada."

Abraham Fuchs,
The Unheeded Cry

Transports of Jews reached Birkenau every day. . . . [Their] packages and suitcases were taken to a part of the camp known as "Canada," the huts in which the Jews of a so-called "Clearing Commando" would unpack them, sort them, and prepare them for dispatch to Germany. Hundreds more Jews, mostly women, were employed in the huts of "Canada," assembly point of the remaining wealth and possessions of more than two million Jews.

Martin Gilbert,
The Holocaust

Acknowledgments

I began work on this book more than four years ago with no assurance of cooperation from my subjects. In the end, I benefited greatly from the participation of numerous family members. Although their participation was often reluctant, never was it grudging.

I owe special thanks to Edward Reichmann, who was exceptionally generous in sharing his time, his own writing, his photographs, and his family papers, and to his wife, Edith, for tolerating my frequent instrusions. Paul Reichmann was far more elusive and yet in the end no less voluble than his older brother. After two years of silence, Paul gave me five meaty interviews in 1995 and 1996, each four to six hours long. I am grateful to him for his belated decision to speak his mind, and to his wife, Lea, for her mediation. I am no less indebted to Louis and Marika Reichmann for a five-hour interview and for the use of several family photographs. Neither Ralph nor Albert Reichmann consented to be interviewed. Philip Reichmann was invaluable as a stand-in for his father and as an interviewee in his own right, as was Frank Hauer. My thanks to Philip and Evelyn Heller in Toronto for the invitation to dinner and to David Gestetner, Netti Morgenstern, and Naomi Heller in London for their hospitality—and to Rachel and Morris Brenick for the late-night ride home to Marylebone.

I would like to thank all of the more than two hundred people I interviewed and single out the following for especially valuable or generous contributions: Robert Abramovici, Messod Bendayan, Bob Canning, Leonie Faludy, Sandy Frucher, Nahum Gelber, Shari Holzer, Lady Jakobovits, Jose Benaim Hachuel, Messody Hadida, Stanley Honeyman, Robert John, Morris Joseph, Isaac Klein, Regina Klein, Moses Lasry, Joe Lebovic, Stuart Lipton, William Minuk, William Mulholland, Tibor Pivko, Albert Reinhard, Keith Roberts, Emile Rooz, Gerald Rothman, Abraham Schreiber, Joel Simon, Morley Sirlin, Israel Singer, Malcolm Spankey, Rabbi Irwin Witty, Frank Wos, Jack and Pearl Zimmerman, John Zuccotti, and others whom I am not at liberty to name.

I am indebted to Peter Osnos, the former publisher of Times Books, whose idea it was that I write a biography of the Reichmanns, and to Geoff Shandler, for his astute and conscientious editing of the manuscript. Paul Golob left Times Books before the book was completed but provided wise early counsel. Copy editor Vicky Macintyre improved the manuscript significantly. My agent, Esther Newberg, was a deft and vigilant champion of my commercial interests throughout.

The research for this book was conducted in nine countries and five languages—at least four of which are alien to me. For Hebrew translations, I relied on Zalman Alpert and Cindy Akiva. I also frequently called on Zalman's encyclopedic knowledge of Judaism. Jill Hamburg and Margo Sugarman contributed solid reporting from Israel. French translations were handled by Fred Katzenberg, a *Business Week* colleague of mine, and by Gillian O'Meara. I am doubly indebted to Gill, who was my translator and guide not only in Paris but in Tangier and whose enthusiasm and savvy were invaluable in both places. I had the luxury of three German translators: Eva Marie Frank, Regine Woznitza, and Katie Hafner, who really did not have time to help but did anyway. Deborah Wise provided research assistance in Berlin. Spanish translations were supplied by Jennifer Napoli and by Angelica de Diego, who also was my guide in Madrid.

In Hungary, Mihaly Benkő of Budapest acted as my translator and exceeded the call of duty in searching the archives and in traveling to Sopron, Beled, and Győr on my behalf. Lorana Sullivan offered astute advice during my long stay in London and also contributed some research.

Steve Sheperd, the editor-in-chief of *Business Week,* and Seymour Zucker, the magazine's senior editor of finance and economics, were kind enough to read the manuscript and offer suggestions for improvement. Ronnie Weil, also of *Business Week,* was a great help in assembling the photos. I got off to a fast start thanks to Tina Brown, who commissioned an article on the Reichmanns for her last issue of *Vanity Fair,* and to Michael Caruso, my editor at *Vanity Fair.*

For assistance of miscellaneous sorts that helped me along my way, I am grateful to Eileen Bashom, Cheryl Brooks, Shulamith Berger, Chaim Bermant, Leopoldo Calvo-Sotello, Val Chapman, Bill Dudley, Linda Eklund, Maile Hulihan, Denise Gluck, David Gold, Mitchell Klein, Rachel Muyal, Peter Rosenthal, Sallyanne Sack, Steven Sharp, Terri Thompson, David Ward, Margo Warnecke, and Suzanne Woolley. I would also like to thank my parents, my brother Dick and his wife, Frances, and, last but never least, Marissa Antonella.

Contents

Introduction

Along the serpentine path its members followed from the Old World to the New, from one generation to the next, and from obscurity to vast wealth and corporate preeminence, the Reichmann family of Toronto did not change its identity one iota. It remained a fixed product of two seemingly opposite traits: vaulting commercial ambition, on one hand, and rock-ribbed piety, on the other.

The Reichmanns' main business vehicle, Olympia & York Development, was the greatest property development company in Western history. Olympia & York's forte was the contrary masterstroke, whether it was putting up one of the world's tallest buildings in Toronto, its home city, at a time when local zoning laws set a maximum height of forty-eight feet, or buying a package of eight skyscrapers in Manhattan at a fraction of their value during the city's mid-1970s brush with bankruptcy, or constructing the grandest addition to the New York City skyline in half a century—the World Financial Center—on a desolate sandbar in the Hudson River. In London, Olympia & York mounted a multibillion-dollar development called Canary Wharf with the aim of transforming a vast stretch of abandoned docklands along the River Thames into a new commercial district to rival the City, the age-old capital of British capital. The credit for all this mastery went mainly to Paul, who was lauded not merely as an astute entrepreneur but as a commercial genius—"an Einstein in a field that usually doesn't produce Einsteins," as a colleague put it. At Olympia & York's peak in the late 1980s, the Reichmanns' fortune exceeded $10 billion, ranking them among the world's ten richest families, just behind the British royal family.

Even as Olympia & York was altering the skylines of some of the world's leading cities, it remained a private company in every sense. No one other than the Reichmanns ever owned stock in Olympia & York or sat on its board of directors. The brothers wrapped their finances in layers of secrecy and artful convolution as impenetrable as the marble cladding on the neoclassical towers in which the firm specialized and shunned the social limelight that lesser moguls craved. Once, during a rare appearance at a country club reception for a visiting Israeli dignitary, Albert managed to evade news photographers by hiding behind a column for two hours and then walking out backwards. And Albert was supposed to be the outgoing one! With his shy, crooked smile, soft-spoken politesse, slightly stooped posture, and elegantly funereal attire, Paul Reichmann was a capitalist daredevil in the guise of an undertaker.

Like generation upon generation of their Hungarian ancestors, Paul and his four brothers—Edward, Louis, Albert, and Ralph—are strictly observant Jews. That is, the Reichmanns are people of the Book—the Torah—in the most exacting sense. The Torah is made up of the Bible and dozens of volumes of ancient Jewish law and holy writ, including 613 mitzvoth, or divine commandments, that regulate in meticulous detail almost every aspect of human conduct. In the lexicon of contemporary Jewry, the Reichmanns and their coreligionists are categorized not merely as Orthodox but as "ultra-Orthodox" Jews. For their part, the devout reject this mildly pejorative label, preferring instead the Hebrew noun "haredim" or the Yiddish terms "Yidn," simply meaning Jews, or "erlicher Yidn," virtuous Jews.

The life of strict observance is isolating in myriad ways. Hence the Reichmanns' brand of Judaism is not only an all-encompassing identity but a fortress against the society of nonbelievers and to some extent against modernity itself. Audacious innovators in real estate, the Reichmanns maintained modest and rigorously insular private lives even as Olympia & York's spectacular growth added zeros to their net worth. Edward and Louis, the eldest brothers, left Canada in the late 1960s and struck out on their own, but Paul, Albert, and Ralph remained in North York, the semifashionable Toronto suburb into which they had first moved as immigrants in the late 1950s, living within a few blocks of one another in homes that were elegantly appointed but quite humble in relation to their means. Over the years, the family transformed its neighborhood into a self-sufficient Orthodox community of a few hundred families, complete with fundamentalist religious schools, synagogues, and kosher suppliers of all sorts. Except to go to work or to visit another, distant haredi enclave, the Reichmanns rarely ventured from their little citadel of Judaic traditionalism or invited in outsiders, whether Jewish or Gentile.

Within the teeming global village of ultra-Orthodoxy, the Reichmanns inspired an extravagance of affection and admiration of a sort that society at large seems to reserve for great athletes or liberating generals. Olympia & York's success was a source of pride—a world-class exception to the rule of low-wage servitude and penny-ante entrepreneurship that has long predominated among the strictly observant. At the same time, the Reichmanns ranked among the most munificent philanthropists of this century, giving away hundreds of millions of dollars, almost all of it to narrowly benefit their coreligionists. At the peak of Olympia & York's prosperity, the family supported a thousand schools and other religious institutions scattered around the world but concentrated in Israel, the haredi capital. Most important, the brothers made no attempt to smooth their ascent in business by compromising or camouflaging their religiosity. To the contrary, they incurred considerable expense in shutting down every Olympia & York construction site from sundown Friday to sundown Saturday in observance of Shabbat, and the menu for the company's receptions remained strictly kosher even when the guest lists came to include presidents and prime ministers.

The Reichmanns' exalted reputation within their circle rested not just on the achievements of Paul and his brothers but on those of their forebears, for they are products of a truly dynastic family—a kind of haredi Rothschilds and Warburgs rolled into one. The brothers' mother, Renée Gestetner Reichmann, was descended from one of the founding families of Hungarian Orthodoxy. With roots in the Oberland region of western Hungary dating back to the 1600s, the Gestetners were a prolific clan that produced august rabbis and accomplished businessmen in roughly equal measure. In Samuel Reichmann, Renée Gestetner married a man of comparatively undistinguished lineage who nonetheless was cast in the Gestetner mold, being as commercially proficient as he was devout. Samuel and Renée Reichmann left Hungary in 1928 to seek—and make—their fortune in Vienna as exporters of fresh eggs and promptly fled to Paris when Germany annexed Austria in 1938. Managing always to stay a step ahead of Hitler's armies, the Reichmanns eventually made their way across the Strait of Gibraltar to Tangier, Morocco. In the multicultural maze of espionage and black market dealing that was wartime Tangier, Samuel Reichmann made a second fortune, this time as a currency dealer.

During World War II, Tangier was occupied by Spain, which, though officially neutral, was both pro-German and fascist. And yet from Tangier, Mrs. Reichmann and her eldest child and only daughter, Eva, organized one of the most improbable and effective rescue campaigns of the Holocaust. Undaunted by their refugee status and lack of official standing, Renée and Eva Reichmann employed an artful mix of feminine charm, amateur diplomacy, bribery, and tenacity to maneuver the government of Francisco Franco into sponsoring the mailing of tens of thousands of food parcels to the inmates of Nazi concentration camps under the aegis of the Spanish Red Cross. In 1944, the Reichmann women outdid themselves in persuading Madrid to issue protective visas to Jews in Nazi-occupied Budapest, helping to save several thousand lives. For the Reichmanns, though, this triumph was the silver lining of overwhelming personal tragedy, for the great majority of the dozens upon dozens of close relatives they had left behind in Hungary were murdered in Auschwitz.

The North American careers of Paul and his brothers recapitulated the accomplishments of their parents on a grander scale, albeit by means less heroic than their mother's in a setting far more benign than Hitler's Europe.

Olympia & York was founded on $100,000 and the deeply held belief that money need not be the currency of transformation (à la the "American dream") but of self-preservation in every sense. Most tellingly perhaps, it was a source of deep satisfaction to the brothers that few of their twenty-one children—all of whom were raised if not born in Canada—ever attended college or, with one exception, married anyone who had; they were in every essential respect as ultra-Orthodox as their parents. Through Olympia & York, Paul, Albert, and Ralph cast themselves in the role of haredi Robin Hoods, taking from the rich—the mighty corporations that were their tenants, competitors, and acquisition targets—and giving to the strictly observant in an effort to rebuild on distant shores the lost world of European Orthodoxy.

Remarkably, the Reichmann brothers were no less esteemed by their business peers than by their coreligionists. Throughout the 1980s, the leading lights of the North American corporate establishment extolled Paul and his brothers as the epitome of old-fashioned integrity in a corrupt, mercenary era. The phrase "their word is their bond" was so frequently intoned in praise of the Reichmann brothers that they might as well have copyrighted it for use as Olympia & York's corporate motto. In straddling the disparate worlds of casino capitalism and Jewish fundamentalism, the Reichmanns performed one of the most singular balancing acts of the century, long maintaining an equipoise so improbable as to seem to confound the biblical command, "Ye cannot serve God and Mammon."

In the end, Paul Reichmann's ambition would ruinously exceed his talent, vast though it was. Nor would all the family always live up to the exalted moral code it espoused and came to epitomize. But if the Reichmanns were never quite the equal of the superhuman myth that grew around them, they did in fact reconcile faith and fortune on a truly epic scale, qualifying them as one of the most remarkable families of the twentieth century. The saga of the Reichmanns speaks to the universal struggle to amass wealth and influence while remaining true to one's most deeply held sense of self and family, but it is also a quintessentially Jewish tale. To understand it, and the family, one must return to a particular place—northwest Hungary—and the golden age of Hungarian Jewry.

PART I

OBERLAND EXODUS

Chapter 1

According to historical tradition, the first Jews settled in Hungary in the second half of the eleventh century, having wandered south from Germany, Bohemia, and Moravia. In Hungary, as elsewhere in Europe, Jews were given scant legal rights, were restricted to peddling, moneylending, and a few other occupations, and were taxed at punitive rates. Gentile toleration waxed and waned over the next few centuries, fluctuating with the predilections of kings and the politics of feudalism. In central Hungary, the status of the Jews improved in 1541 after Turkish armies conquered the region and incorporated it into the Ottoman Empire, but in the Hapsburg-ruled lands of western Hungary, the Jews were scapegoated for the defeat and gradually expelled from most cities and towns. As the Hapsburg kings of Vienna gradually regained dominion over Hungary in the 1600s, many Jews fled with the retreating Turks. By 1700, Hungary had only about four thousand Jews, and few traces remained of its oldest Jewish settlements.

On their mother's side, the brothers Reichmann were descended from the Gestetner family, which was, in every sense, among the first families of Hungarian Orthodoxy. The family tree of the clan dates back to 1665 in Hungary and is festooned both with great rabbis and with devout, prosperous businessmen. Like most Hungarian Jews who outlasted the era of the Turkish Wars, the Gestetners resided in the Burgenland, a verdant swath of rolling farm country that today forms the far northwestern corner of Hungary and originally included lands that are now part of Austria. As the Jews had been banned from the cities of western Hungary, some of the Magyar noblemen of the Burgenland, known to its Jewish inhabitants as the Oberland, had offered them refuge in the villages on their vast estates. Under the protection of the counts Esterhazy, many Jews settled in Eisenstadt and six small neighboring Oberland villages collectively known as the Seven Communities. In exchange for the payment of heavy taxes and "gifts" to the Esterhazys, the Seven Communities were granted charters that gave Jewish residents considerable powers of self-government. These comparatively benign conditions attracted eminent rabbis who founded synagogues and Talmudic academies, or yeshivas, that earned renown throughout Europe and would flourish until the Nazi era.

The Seven Communities held sway over a dozen neighboring villages in which Jews also settled in large numbers. It was in one of these satellite communities—Schlaining—that the first Jew to call himself by the name Gestetner entered recorded history. Born in Schlaining in 1720, Leopold Gestetner was married in 1744 to a great-granddaughter of the famous sage Rabbi Meir Ash—an honor that suggested that Gestetner, a merchant, was a man of some means as well as piety.

Leopold Gestetner and his bride moved to Deutschkreutz, one of the Seven Communities, and settled finally in Csorna, which lay further into Hungary on the far eastern edge of the Esterhazy lands. In hopes of stimulating the development of laggard areas, the Esterhazys encouraged Jews from the villages under their protection to relocate to their outlying properties. The first Jews arrived in Csorna in the first half of the eighteenth century but did not remain long, retreating to more established communities. Leopold and Gittel Gestetner came to Csorna as part of a second, enduring wave of pioneering settlement and put down deep, lasting roots. The first Grunwald arrived in Csorna about the same time, and the first of many Grunwald-Gestetner marriages occurred in 1851, when Amram Grunwald wed Esther Gestetner. Two decades later, their son Emerich Grunwald wedded Esther's niece Netti Gestetner, thus cementing the bond between the two families that together would dominate the communal life of Csorna for a century and a half.

As prolific as they were pious, the Gestetner clan did their bit to spur Jewish repopulation of Hungary. From 1852 to 1861 alone, Gestetner and Grunwald women gave birth to forty-two children, or about one-fifth of all Jewish children born in Csorna. Quite a few Gestetner infants carried a double dose of Gestetner blood, being the product of cousins. In the villages of the Oberland, inbreeding was a common expression of Orthodox exclusivity, and the Gestetner who did not marry a Gestetner cousin was likely to marry a Grunwald.

Whereas male Grunwalds tended to aspire to the rabbinate, Gestetners gravitated toward business, becoming merchants and shopkeepers. Religious families like the Gestetners tended to be large—they took to heart the biblical injunction "Be fruitful and multiply"—and the inevitable result was more sons and sons-in-law than there were positions in the family business—or in the local rabbinate, for that matter. And so as some young Grunwalds left Csorna to accept rabbinical positions in other communities, young Gestetners were endowed with a bit of capital and scattered over the surrounding Oberland landscape and beyond, like seeds from a dandelion.

From its small base, the Jewish population of Hungary grew at a rapid rate throughout the eighteenth and nineteenth centuries. By 1850, 340,000 Jews lived in Hungary, quadrupling the figure of 81,000 recorded in the census of 1787—itself a huge leap from the 4,000 recorded in 1700. Thanks mainly to religious families such as the Gestetners, the Jewish birth rate was exceptionally high. At the same time, large numbers of Jews migrated to Hungary from points north, arriving mainly by two geographically disparate routes. While thousands of German-speaking Jews from Moravia and Bohemia entered Hungary through the Oberland, successive waves of Polish and Galician Jews came cascading over the Carpathians through Slovakia and into northeastern Hungary—a district known as the Maramaros.

The Reichmann brothers' paternal ancestors reached Hungary by the eastern route. Although less numerous and accomplished than the Gestetners, the Reichmanns were no less religious. Little is known about Eliyahu Reichmann, the first forebear to use the surname, other than that he was born in 1834, wed in 1858, fathered four children, and died in 1869 at age thirty-five. Reichmann, whose legal (as opposed to Hebrew) first name was Elias, was buried in Nyírbátor, the northeastern village that was his wife's hometown. Reichmann's own place of birth was listed in the communal Jewish records of Nyírbátor as "Csmerna," which is most likely the magyarized spelling of Czerna, a small Jewish village, or shtetl, in Galicia. Located about thirty miles southwest of Cracow, Czerna was one of many impoverished Galician shtetls that were wholly emptied by emigration and vanished with nary a trace long before the Holocaust.

According to Reichmann family lore, Eliyahu, familiarly known as Eli, was the son of Shmayahu Feldmann and had lived as a boy in Sátoraljaujhély, a Hungarian border town near the Maramaros filled with Galician immigrants. In the early 1800s, Sátoraljaujhély was famed among Jews throughout eastern Europe as the adopted home of Rabbi Moses Teitelbaum, the Galician-born founder of one of the greatest of Hungarian rabbinical dynasties. As the Reichmanns tell it, Shmayahu Feldmann was a merchant who ranked among the most loyal and generous financial contributors to Rabbi Teitelbaum's congregation. When Feldmann died, Rabbi Teitelbaum himself supposedly advised his two sons to change their surname to honor their father's memory. The older son, Yehuda, became Yehuda Grunfeld, while Eli took the name Reichmann; thus the two perpetuated the Feldmann name through the final syllables of the new surnames: "feld" and "mann."

This family account of how the Reichmanns got their name is almost certainly apocryphal. After all, the simplest way for Shmayahu's sons to have preserved his name would have been to keep the surname they presumably had been given at birth: Feldmann. In 1787, long before the birth of Eli and his brother, the Hapsburg emperor Josef II had made German surnames mandatory for Jews throughout his dominion, which then included Galicia. In nineteenth-century Hungary, which also was under Hapsburg rule but had its own monarchy and emphatic national identity, many Jews dropped their German surname and adopted a Hungarian one, ostensibly to signify their patriotism. However, religious Hungarian Jews rarely made the switch; moreover, Reichmann was hardly less Germanic than Feldmann. In any event, Eli Feldmann's transformation into Eli Reichmann was astoundingly prophetic. "Nomen est omen," goes the Latin proverb: "Name is an omen." The name Feldmann, literally translated, means "peasant"; Reichmann means "rich man."

⸻

Although the Reichmann and Gestetner families originated at opposite ends of Hungary, they stood together on the Orthodox side of the great divide opened in the bedrock of European Jewry by the Emancipation. Since time immemorial, the Jews of Europe had been treated as second-class citizens, if citizens at all, and were segregated from and subjugated to the Gentile majority in almost every community in which they were allowed to settle. In 1791, in the wake of the French Revolution, the new Republic of France took a flying leap into the future by granting Jews full legal rights. As waves of populist discontent washed over the rest of Europe in subsequent decades, the Jews were grudgingly emancipated almost everywhere else but Russia. In Hungary, most of the remaining legal restrictions were dismantled in 1859 and 1860, and subsequently Jews were able to live where and to work how they chose. In 1867, the Hungarian Parliament formally adopted a bill of emancipation.

Emancipation visited an identity crisis of epic proportions on European Jewry. Under the old feudal order, Jews had not been permitted the privilege of self-definition. A Jew was a Jew by birth, not choice, and all Jews were governed by rabbinic law, or halakah. Codified most authoritatively as the Shulhan Aruch, the halakah closely regulated every aspect of Jewish behavior and was enforced within the old ghettos by rabbinical councils that wielded the power of excommunication, which was tantamount to banishment. In granting basic civil rights to Jews under secular law, the new nation-states of Europe undermined the traditional authority of Jewish communal leaders. As the emancipated Jew was free to leave the ghetto, he now also had the right to modify his Judaism as he saw fit or, for that matter, to discard it altogether.

In pursuit of new opportunity, many Jews threw off the customs and beliefs of their forebears and blended into Gentile society as best they could. In its most extreme form, assimilation culminated in conversion to Christianity. Other so-called Jews, the maskilim, sought the middle ground of acculturation—that is, they immersed themselves in secular culture while continuing to practice Judaism. To paraphrase a popular aphorism of the day, the maskil considered himself "a person in the street and a Jew at home." As a rule, maskilim preferred their Judaism remolded to suit the rationalist spirit of the age. The most prevalent of these newfangled varieties was Reform Judaism, which began as a modernization of the rituals of worship. Reform rabbis brought organ music, choral singing, and Protestant-style sermonizing into the synagogue. Before long, Reform rabbis were challenging basic precepts of the Talmud, the vast compendium of Jewish law and literature that was integral to Judaism's historical identity. "In the Talmudic age, the Talmud was right," declared one leading Reformer of the mid-1800s. "In my age, I am right."

As the unitary faith of European Jewry's ghetto age fragmented, those Jews who held tight to the faith of their fathers came to be known as Orthodox. In general, Orthodox Jews were "those who accept as divinely inspired the totality of the historical religion of the Jewish people as it is recorded in the written and oral laws and codified in the Shulhan Aruch and its commentaries until recent times, and as it is observed in practice according to the teachings and unchanging principles of the halakah."

In most places in Europe, the Orthodox soon found themselves in the minority. In western Europe, where the interlocking forces of republicanism and industrialism were most powerful, the Orthodox resistance was simply steamrolled; by the late 1800s, it was estimated that only five hundred Orthodox Jews remained in all of France. In central Europe, where feudalism died a slower death, the process of assimilation was more protracted but equally decisive. The only exception was greater Hungary, where strict Orthodoxy survived in two distinctly different forms, the newest of which was Hasidism.

As a religious and social movement, Hasidism was based on the teachings of Rabbi Israel ben Eliezer, better known as the Baal Shem Tov ("the master of the good name"), who was born in 1700 in the Ukraine. He was a highly charismatic leader whose popularity was in large measure a reaction against the pedantic elitism of the rabbinical academies of Lithuania, which long had dominated religious life throughout Europe. The Baal Shem Tov taught that the ignorant and the scholarly man are equal before God—indeed, that devotion and humility are more blessed than intellectual accomplishment. Populist in form as well as content, his teachings were not set down in writing but transmitted orally and embroidered over the years. Hasidism had a pronounced mystical flavor as well, as its founder believed in seeking communion with God in nature. "Directing its appeal to the feelings and emotions, Hasidism injected a new and vital power into Jewish religious life."

The Baal Shem Tov's many disciples spread Hasidism far and wide through the Ukraine, Russia, and Poland. The leading Hasidic rabbis, or "rebbes," inspired a cultlike following whose members, or Hasidim, looked upon these figures not only as tzaddikim—prototypically righteous men—but as intermediaries to God Himself. Each rebbe founded a "court," where his followers pressed round, hanging on his every word and emulating his eccentricities of dress and demeanor. As the Reform movement diluted old-fashioned Judaism, the Hasidim cultivated a theatrically archaic appearance, letting their beards and sidelocks grow to great unkempt lengths. The various Hasidic sects each had their trademark apparel, variously including caftans, knickers, plus-fours, colored sashes, elaborate fur or broad-brimmed hats, and so on. Scorning established synagogues, the Hasidim built their own prayerhouses and rocked them with fundamentalist fervor, praying and singing at the top of their lungs. Many rebbes were able to pass on their exalted position to sons or sons-in-law and thus to give rise to Hasidic dynasties.

Hasidism was imported to Hungary by the Poles who settled in the Maramaros. Shmayahu Feldmann's spiritual mentor, Moses Teitelbaum, was among the first rebbes to spread Hasidism in the northern and central districts of Hungary. It is unclear to what extent Feldmann was himself Hasidic in belief and practice, for Rabbi Teitelbaum was beloved among all segments of the Jewish population of Hungary as a learned and holy man. His son, Eli Reichmann, was "middle-of-the-road Orthodox, not Hasidic, as far as we know," said Louis Reichmann, a great-grandson of Eli. In any event, the evolutionary path taken by the Reichmann family would lead away from Hasidism and the Maramaros.

Throughout Eastern Europe sizable communities of Hasidim took deep root and resisted modernism's onslaught. The only places where strict Orthodoxy remained predominant in its conventional, non-Hasidic mode were Lithuania and the Hungarian Oberland. In the Oberland, the influence of Rabbi Moses Sofer, also known as the Hatam Sofer, was decisive. A Talmudic prodigy born and schooled in Germany, Rabbi Sofer in 1808 was named chief rabbi of Bratislava, which sits on the Danube River in the upper reaches of the Oberland. Now the capital of Slovakia, Bratislava was part of Hungary until the end of World War I. Rabbi Sofer's impassioned, uncompromising leadership made him the undisputed leader of the European rabbis who banded together to combat the early inroads made by the Reform movement in Berlin, Hamburg, and Vienna. While the Hatam Sofer's influence was felt throughout Europe, naturally it was strongest within the Oberland.

Widely admired as a halakic authority, Rabbi Sofer's main weapons in his holy war against the modernizers of Judaism were the responsa, or rabbinical rulings, issued in formal reply to questions that were put to him from every corner of Hungary and beyond. A spellbinding orator, the Hatam Sofer was not above resorting to demagoguery when it served the cause of Judaic traditionalism, at times deriding reformists as heretics and reprobates. Rabbi Sofer was a master of the nineteenth-century equivalent of the sound bite, bedeviling his foes with witty, pointed epigrams. The most famous of these was his application of the Talmudic dictum—"He chodosh osur min ha torah"—to mean that any innovation, even though it may be insignificant in terms of the halakah, is forbidden simply because it is a departure from hallowed tradition.

The Hatam Sofer's extraordinary authority was rooted as much in his integrity as in his scholarship. At a time when abuse of rabbinical office for personal gain was not uncommon, he was a model of rectitude. Early in his career, he had just accepted an appointment as rabbi of Mattersdorf, one of the Seven Communities, when he received a more lucrative offer from the town of Prossnitz. In a letter to the Prossnitz community, he explained why he could not accept their offer: "I have already replied to the holy congregation of Mattersdorf and I have told them that I will come there. I will not, God forbid, deceive them, and I will not search for excuses and pretexts as might normally be done in such a case. For, if I now reversed myself, would they not say in their confusion, 'Every man is deceitful and this man Moses, upon whose shoulders we placed the rabbinical office, is a liar.' "

The Hatam Sofer's influence was undiminished by his passing in 1839. In fact, it was only after his death that his voluminous writings were published and widely distributed. Both of his sons and a half-dozen of his grandsons followed him into the rabbinate, and the exceptionally large yeshiva that he had founded in Bratislava—the most important in all of central Europe—continued to churn out dozens of other rabbis cast in his zealous, combative mold. Sofer's disciples fanned out through the Oberland, establishing yeshivas by the score and stimulating the study of Torah in almost every village, including Csorna, the Gestetner redoubt.

While the Oberlander Orthodox certainly held Rabbi Sofer and other "great Torah personalities" in high esteem, they did not follow them in the cultish way that the Hasidim venerated their rebbes. Oberlanders were altogether more restrained, more Germanic, in their piety. The men generally trimmed their beards and sidecurls, and some even went clean-shaven, though they used a depilatory powder rather than violate the halakic prohibition against the use of razors. Oberlanders of both sexes dressed in somber but contemporary fashion, with the men favoring white shirts, dark jackets, and fedoras or homburgs. As their appearance implied, the Oberlanders may have opposed innovation in Judaism but were not opposed to modernity. While the Hasidim of the Maramaros spoke Yiddish and a broken Hungarian at best, Oberlanders generally mastered both Hungarian and German and were much less resistant to augmenting their religious training with instruction in science, mathematics, and other secular subjects. The branch of the Gestetner family from which the Reichmann brothers were descended was definitively Oberlander.

Hasidism's first flowerings had aroused such an intense backlash among the Lithuanian rabbinate that their criticism came to define them; they were known as misnagdim, which translates literally as "opponents." Many rabbis in Hungary also had disdained Hasidism, though rarely with such vehemence. By the mid-1800s, though, the two strains of Hungarian Orthodox had set aside their ideological differences and joined forces against the common enemy of the Reform movement, which in Hungary was known as Neology. The culture war between Orthodoxy and Neology came to a head in 1868. By the decree of Franz Josef, the reigning Hapsburg monarch, a General Jewish Congress was convened at which Hungary's newly emancipated Jews were to decide for themselves how to reorganize their communal life. Outnumbered 126 to 94, the Orthodox delegates took the offensive by proposing that all Jews be required by law to submit to the authority of the Shulhan Aruch. After this resolution was voted down, the entire Orthodox contingent stomped out in protest. Left to their own devices, the Neologue delegates enacted an ultra-reformist agenda.

After the Hungarian Parliament ratified the Neologue agenda, a delegation of Orthodox rabbis petitioned Franz Josef for exemption. The emperor was amenable. "If your liberal brethren are not interested in the Torah, I will not force them to observe it," he declared. "Nor will they force upon you its non-observance." In 1870, the Hungarian Parliament authorized the Orthodox to organize separate communities throughout Hungary. Hungarian Jewry actually split in three: about 65 percent of practicing Jews affiliated with the Neologue wing, 30 percent joined with the Orthodox, and 5 percent rejected both groups (and became known as Status Quo Ante). In the Oberland and the Maramaros, which bracketed Hungary like mismatched bookends, a large majority of communities departed from the national trend and defined themselves as Orthodox.

That no other country in Europe sanctioned a formal division of Jewry into enemy camps helps explain the remarkably obdurate character of Orthodoxy in Hungary. In much of Europe, Judaism survived the Emancipation as a finely graded continuum of belief and practice: Reform shaded into Conservatism, neo-Orthodoxy, modern Orthodoxy, and ultra-Orthodoxy. But in Hungary, ultra-Orthodoxy was Orthodoxy. The middle ground fell away as traditionalist Jews withdrew en masse into what amounted to a self-imposed internal exile, shunning all contact with the reviled Neologue majority, whose members were considered "worse than goyim." Orthodox families often disowned a son or daughter who crossed the great divide and married into a Neologue or nonreligious family, and in extreme cases cross-marriage brought excommunication. Long after Neology had lost its sting as a movement, the Oberlander Orthodox would remain isolated within the carapace of their traditional beliefs and practices, which would be passed on virtually unchanged from generation to generation until the Hungarian countryside was emptied of Jews in 1944.

———

Unlike Christianity, Judaism does not equate poverty with virtue, or vice versa. To the contrary, moral worthiness and material well-being are closely linked throughout the Torah. In Deuteronomy, for example, Moses stresses the bounty that God will bestow on those who keep his law: "And he will love thee, and bless thee, and multiply thee: he will also bless the fruit of thy womb, and the fruit of thine land, thy corn and thy wine, and thine oil, the increase of thy kine and the flocks of thy sheep." In the Talmud, this theme is less poetically rendered: "Seven characteristics there are which are comely to the righteous and comely to the world. One of them is riches." And again: "In time of scarcity, a man learns to value wealth best."

As a practical matter, however, the multitudinous requirements of observance took precedence over commerce in the daily lives of Orthodox Jews. Judaism involved no less than 613 mitzvot, or divine commandments, governing every aspect of thought and behavior. Most were subsumed within three cardinal societal precepts that largely defined Orthodoxy in practice. The first was the Sabbath, or Shabbat, which begins sundown Friday and ends sundown Saturday. For the Orthodox, the biblical imperative of "resting" on the Sabbath translated into a highly technical code of do's and don'ts. Meanwhile, kashrut, the dietary laws, dictated in mind-numbing detail not only which animals were permissible to eat but how they were to be slaughtered and how food of all kinds was to be prepared and served. Finally, the laws of taharat mahishpacha ("the purity of the family") closely regulated all facets of the interaction between husband and wife and between males and females in general.

Adherence to the regimen of strict observance was time-consuming in countless ways. The most obvious was the imperative of Shabbat rest, which forced the pious businessman to the sidelines of commerce every Saturday. In addition, three daily prayer sessions were mandatory: shaharit, the dawn service, consumed nearly an hour, while mincha, the prelunch prayer, and maariv, said before dinner, took at least twenty minutes apiece. Most important, the obligation to study the Torah (which, states the Talmud, "counts more than all the other mitzvot put together") was open-ended. The Oberland was filled with merchant-scholars who spared no more time for business than that needed to eke out a subsistence living.

Conforming to the mitzvah also tended to restrict the Orthodox businessman's clientele. Every Hungarian village had kosher food suppliers and other Orthodox merchants who made a good living catering to an exclusively Jewish clientele. But Orthodox businessmen with broader ambitions were disadvantaged by the requirements of their faith. The Orthodox, the most visibly Jewish of Jews, bore the brunt of anti-Semitism everywhere in Europe. But even if bigotry somehow could have been factored out of God's plan, it would have remained a feat of great intrinsic difficulty to do business within the economic mainstream while at the same time maintaining a proper distance from the society of nonbelievers.

Emancipation greatly raised the ante on commercial temptation. At about the same time that Franz Josef emancipated the Jews, he liberated Hungary from the yoke of the Hapsburg empire. The formation of the dual monarchy of Austria-Hungary represented the ascendance of liberalism in economics no less than politics, ushering in a period of massive development that lasted half a century and opened a wide range of opportunity for Jews in all the Hapsburg lands of central Europe. For the first time, capital and labor were allowed to move freely within the empire, effectively fusing Austria, Hungary, Bohemia, Moravia, Slovakia, Galicia, Bukovina, and Ruthenia into a single market of fifty million people. As free trade policies led to geographic specialization within the empire, Hungary became Austria-Hungary's granary, with highly advanced flour milling and food-processing industries. From 1867 to the start of World War I in 1914, the Hungarian capital, Budapest, grew faster than any other major European city.

Jews benefited disproportionately from the advent of modern capitalism in Hungary, filling a void left by the Magyar aristocracy and gentry, which had always disdained business as a middle-class pursuit. By the mid-1800s, Jews had replaced Greeks as the dominant middlemen of commerce in the Hungarian countryside. Jews often served as managers of noble estates and virtually monopolized the business of purchasing the agricultural produce of the Magyar elite and conveying it to market. Many wealthy Jewish families accumulated their initial capital in the grain trade and then moved into banking and manufacturing as the economy industrialized in the 1880s and 1890s. In the process, many Jews left the countryside and congregated in Budapest and other industrial centers. By 1910, Jews accounted for 23 percent of the population of Budapest and 53 percent of all residents of the capital engaged in industry, and 65 percent of those employed in trade and finance. Jews were prevalent not only among the bourgeoisie but among the robber baron class. The Hatvany-Deutsch family controlled a quarter of Hungary's sugar production and three of its five largest banks. The Strasser family of Győr, an important Danube port in the Oberland, built Strasser and Koenig into the fifth-largest shipping firm in the world.

For the most part, Hungary's golden age passed the Orthodox by. At a time when Hungarian business as a whole was hell-bent in pursuit of economies of scale, the great majority of religious Jews continued to scratch out a marginal existence in the traditional way as shopkeepers, tradesmen, innkeepers, and the like. The average Orthodox businessman no doubt lacked the drive needed to attempt to straddle the disparate and equally demanding worlds of Judaic traditionalism and cutthroat capitalism.

But this was only part of the story. In Hungary to a greater extent than anywhere else in Europe, the commercially ambitious Jew had to accept a Mephistophelian pact in which he basically exchanged his Jewishness for opportunity. Although Hungary had abolished the legal privileges of the landed aristocracy in 1848, the Magyar nobles retained their estates and the enormous social prestige and political clout derived from them. Increasingly, though, the Magyar elite perceived a demographic threat to its status. The number of Romanians, Slovaks, Ruthenians, and other rival ethnic minorities within Hungary was increasing much faster than the Magyar population, which by 1880 had dwindled to 47 percent. And so in the final decades of the nineteenth century, the Hungarian government embarked on a ruthless policy of "magyarization" intended to intimidate and cajole the nationalities into adopting the Magyar language and culture as their own. To this end, the Magyar elite invited an alliance with the Jews, the one ethnic minority without nationalist aspirations of its own. "The Jews played a singularly important role in the process of magyarization . . . ," observed historian Randolph L. Braham. "The overwhelming majority of Hungarian Jewry realized that complete assimilation and magyarization was the price they had to pay for their emancipation."

Elsewhere in Europe, the self-made moguls of the era, Jewish or otherwise, were loath to forsake the middle class and join the old landed aristocracy, but in Hungary thousands of individual Jews belonging to 346 families acquired noble rank. "Even in imperial Germany and tsarist Russia, where middle class ennoblement was officially encouraged, there does not seem to have been so massive an ennoblement of the century's new economic elite as there was in Hungary." Of those 346 families, only two were Orthodox at the time of ennoblement, and both soon drifted into apostasy. In the provinces, newly ennobled Jews tended to be leading figures in the Neology community. In Budapest, a large percentage converted to Christianity and took pains to disguise their Jewish roots, magyarizing their names, stocking their boards of directors with "paradegoyim"—idle Magyar aristocrats for hire—and even furnishing their homes in Gentile fashion. "In Vienna, Berlin, London or New York the atmosphere and the tone of the drawing room of a Jewish financier was perceptibly different from that of a Gentile magnate. In Budapest and in the Hungarian country, these differences were subdued to the extent of being hardly perceptible."

———

Although many Gestetners prospered in business while remaining true to Orthodoxy, it was telling that the only true industrialist in the family left Hungary as a teenager. Born in Csorna in 1854, David Gestetner left home at thirteen, not to attend yeshiva, as was customary among the Oberlander Orthodox, but to apprentice himself to an uncle who had a sausage-making business in Sopron, the county seat. In 1871, he moved to Vienna to work under another uncle, a broker on the Vienna Stock Exchange. Two years later, a world exhibition came to Vienna and Gestetner's parents temporarily moved to the capital to open a kosher restaurant, which David helped run. But after

Vienna was rocked by financial crisis that same year, nineteen-year-old Gestetner decided to seek his fortune in America and bought a ticket in steerage with funds supplied by his mother, who pawned her jewelry on his behalf.

On his way to Chicago, to stay with a friend who worked in a tannery, Gestetner had his pocket picked. He replenished his funds with a job selling Japanese paper kites and finally made it to Chicago, where he spent two years failing slowly in the laundry business. In 1877, he returned to Vienna and formed a partnership with yet another uncle to make equipment for hectographs, a copying machine utilizing pads of gelatin. When this business fizzled, Gestetner moved to London. While working as a stationer's assistant, he finally found his life's calling. In 1881, Gestetner patented his most important early invention, the cyclostyle—a pen with a toothed wheel at its tip that could be used to cut stencils. Once Gestetner thought to pair the cyclostyle with the sort of Japanese paper used to make the kites he had once sold in America, it became possible to produce a highly legible copy in ten seconds. This "was office duplicating for the first time in quantity, at speed, and of good quality."

With financial backing from his employer, Gestetner began manufacturing the pens, stencils, and ink. Eventually, he became sole proprietor of the Cyclostyle trademarks, opened his own sales outlets in London, and built a large factory at Tottenham. A shrewd, relentless marketer as well as a gifted inventor, Gestetner soon had branches throughout England and crossed the channel to fill the stencil-duplicating void on the continent. As competitors emerged, D. Gestetner Limited maintained an edge by continuously refining and broadening its product line—and by giving no quarter in various legal battles over patent rights. By the late 1920s, the company had circled the world with sales outlets and owned thriving subsidiaries in many countries, among them France, Italy, the United States, Canada, India, South Africa, and Egypt.

In the early stages of D. Gestetner Limited's growth, the founder's hiring practices were blatantly nepotistic and helped impart a cosmopolitan flavor to the Gestetner family. In 1885, David's brother Jacob joined him in London and would remain with the firm until his death in the 1950s. To develop the Austro-Hungarian market, David formed a subsidiary company with two of his other brothers and a brother-in-law, who was stationed in Vienna. In 1893, he hired his uncle Leopold, the failed manufacturer of glue and gelatin, to open an office in Amsterdam. In 1897, Leopold moved on to Paris, where he was joined by his son Arnold, who, in turn, opened an office in Milan. In the early 1900s, the founder dispatched one of his many Hungarian nephews to set up Gestetner sales operations in Budapest, Belgrade, and Bucharest.

A staunchly observant Jew his entire life, David Gestetner was never a very spiritual man. "There can be no doubting the effect that his early training in religious observance and practice had on his daily work and thought and yet any idea that he allowed religion to overstep reasonable defined limits would be off the mark," observed Charles David, Gestetner's longtime private secretary, in an unpublished memoir entitled "The DG I Knew." Mr. David recalled that his boss once reacted angrily when one of the many poorer Gestetner relations he helped support back in Hungary failed to acknowledge the receipt of his quarterly pension, the check having arrived on a religious holiday. "Tell him that unless acknowledgments are prompt," Gestetner commanded, "payments will stop." In the opinion of his secretary, who generally admired him, Gestetner's real religion was work: "Everything else was subservient to it and he felt that honest application to work was as good for the soul as religious practice."

The Reichmann brothers' maternal grandfather, Adolf Gestetner, was the son of a first cousin of David Gestetner. Adolf's father, Isaac Gestetner, had inherited the family's large general store in Csorna and was one of the town's wealthiest merchants. Born in Csorna in 1874, Adolf left the Oberland in the mid-1890s and moved to the Maramaros city of Huzst to complete his religious instruction by studying with his uncle, Rabbi Moses Grunwald, who was one of the greatest rabbis in the modern history of Hungary. Considered the most authoritative halakists among the Hungarian rabbis who followed the Hatam Sofer, Rabbi Grunwald pioneered in incorporating elements of Hasidism into his teachings. In the yeshiva society of Hungary during its golden age, nepotism was irrelevant; the yeshiva in Huzst was among the finest half-dozen in Hungary but was open to anyone with the aptitude and desire to submit to the rigors of Orthodox education. A contemporary of Adolf Gestetner's recorded this description of Rabbi Grunwald and his yeshiva: "He was my master for three semesters, and during that time more than 400 of us listened thirstily to the words of his mouth. We starved on dry bread, we shivered with cold in unheated rooms, only to be able to listen, twice a day, morning and evening to his profound teachings, to be able to enjoy the radiance of his face reflecting the splendor of the Shekhina [Divine Presence]."

In 1897, while still a student in his famous uncle's yeshiva, Adolf Gestetner married Róza Stern, the nineteen-year-old daughter of a lumber dealer in Huzst. Like the overwhelming majority of Orthodox unions, this one was arranged, most likely by Rabbi Grunwald himself. As a rule, wealthy Orthodox businessmen sought to elevate their social standing by marrying their daughters to the most accomplished yeshiva students or to the relatives of esteemed rabbis (often they were one and the same). As a nephew of Rabbi Grunwald, Adolf Gestetner would have been a desirable commodity on the Huzst marriage market, which suggests, in turn, that Róza Stern's father was the richest Orthodox man in town. After finishing at his uncle's yeshiva, Adolf and his wife left Huzst for nearby Tokaj, the center of Hungary's wine country, and later settled in Satu Mare, where one of Moses Grunwald's sons had been installed as chief rabbi of the Orthodox community.

The rapprochement of the Oberlander and Hasidic wings of Hungarian Orthodoxy was the product of two-way traffic. A decade before Adolf Gestetner had begun his tour of northeastern Hungary, David Reichmann, the Reichmann brothers' paternal grandfather, had left the Maramaros to seek his fortune in the Oberland. Born in Nýirbátor in 1862, David was third of the four children of Eli and Lisi Reichmann. He was only six when his father died, probably of tuberculosis. With the help of her own mother, who was relatively well-off, the widow Reichmann saw to it that her children received a proper Orthodox upbringing. "They practically took the food from their own mouths in order to feed us and to strengthen us for Torah," recalled Zvi Reichmann, the youngest of Eli's sons, who would become a rabbi. In the mid-1880s David left home to attend yeshiva in Deutschkreutz, the Oberland town where the first Gestetner had briefly lived more than a century before.

In 1888, David married twenty-three-year-old Lidi Feldmann and settled down with his bride in her hometown, the Oberland village of Beled. The Feldmanns had come to Beled from the Maramaros and might have been related to Shmayahu Feldmann, David Reichmann's grandfather. Reichmann's father-in-law, a Beled merchant, set him up in business as a glazier. Actually, the business was run by his wife, since David continued to devote himself primarily to the study of the Talmud in the classic Oberland manner. Reichmann, who looked every inch the Torah scholar, with his long hair and full, untrimmed beard that covered most of his chest, worked in a study with a window that looked out into the shop. "I spent a lot of time in my grandfather's house," recalled Edward Reichmann, the eldest Reichmann brother, "and I do not remember ever seeing him in bed. He was always up in the morning before everyone else got up and he was always up when everyone else went to bed. Whenever I was going to sleep and whenever I arose in the morning I heard the voice of Torah in my ears."

David and Lidi Reichmann would have ten children, the first of whom, a son, was born in 1889. In conformance with Jewish custom, he was named Eli, after his late grandfather, and followed at regular intervals by Herman, Eszter, Jakob, Regi, and Helena. On February 2, 1898, came Samuel, the son who would transform the family fortunes. The following October 27, in Huzst, Adolf and Róza Gestetner had their first child, a daughter named Renée. Born ten months apart on the eve of the twentieth century, Samuel Reichmann and Renée Gestetner were destined to join together to disprove the unwritten law that a Hungarian Jew could not be as rich as he was pious.

Chapter 2

After returning to Csorna from points east in 1910, Adolf Gestetner went into business for himself making rubber stamps. Unable to keep the shop going at home, in 1911 he moved it twenty miles down the road to Győr, an important port city of 60,000. Strategically located about halfway between Budapest and Vienna, at the confluence of the Danube and three other rivers, Győr had been an important military stronghold of the Magyars for centuries. In the last decades of the nineteenth century, Győr's exceptionally well-preserved Gothic and Baroque core had been encased in a suburban shell of heavy industry. Jewish predominance in the grain trade (Győr was the gateway of wheat exports to Serbia, Romania, and Bulgaria) had given rise to a prosperous Jewish community of some six thousand, which included a half dozen of the richest Jewish families in all Hungary.

The Gestetners were new to Győr but hardly strangers, for their surname was as renowned within its Jewish community as it was throughout the rural precincts of the Oberland. In fact, a Gestetner, also named Adolf, had married the daughter of the chief rabbi of Győr and had served as secretary of the community in the 1860s. The second Adolf was one of five Gestetner cousins who had forsaken the village life of Csorna or Sopron and settled in Győr with their families by the outbreak of World War I. Despite its proximity to Bratislava, the Jerusalem of Oberlander Orthodoxy, the Győr community was predominantly Neologue, as were all major cities in Hungary.

In Győr, Adolf again hung out a shingle as a maker of rubber stamps and also dabbled in retailing kosher wine, a trade he had picked up in Tokaj. To supplement the family income, his wife, Róza, opened a small kosher milk store. The rubber stamp shop occupied the first floor of a three-story building that Adolf leased for a time and then purchased. The Gestetners rented out the top floor to a tenant and occupied the second floor. "They had three or four rooms and a kitchen. At that time, it was nice," recalled Ilonka Eisekovits, who lived next door and would grow up to marry one of Renée's brothers. "They had a bathroom and for that time it was a modern house." It was crowded, however. Adolf and his wife had six children when they moved to Győr: Renée and Henrik, who had been born in Huzst; Sándor, Elza, and Antal, born in Tokaj; and Olga, born in Satu Mare. In Győr, Róza Gestetner gave birth to five more children from 1913 to 1920: Lajos, Dezsö, Klára, Gabriella, and Albert. Although Adolf was able to provide for a family of thirteen—no mean feat in itself—he fell short of the standard of living he had known as a boy in Csorna, where his parents had ranked among the wealthiest Jewish residents.

Despite their modest means, the Gestetners were known for their generosity. "When somebody came to the city and came to the synagogue, they took him home and they gave him a place to sleep, not just a Shabbat dinner," Eisekovits recalled. Adolf was active in the local Orthodox community and, along with several other Gestetners, was instrumental in founding a separate Orthodox burial society in Győr.

Gestetner fitted out the back room of his shop as a study, and there he would remain, bent over a religious text, until a customer entered the front door, tripping the bell that summoned him to the counter. But, in Paul Reichmann's recollection of his two grandfathers, Gestetner was not as cerebral as David Reichmann, who was "totally absorbed in the study of Torah. It was his life. Even after he had his stroke, he would ask us what tractate of the Talmud we were studying and then he'd recite it from memory. My Gestetner grandfather would study but he was also worldly. The Gestetners were a different type altogether, I'd say. They were worldly and strong. My mother [Renée] was the strongest of them all."

Although Renée Gestetner received a strict, old-fashioned upbringing, she was simply too ambitious and forceful a personality to be wholly subsumed in the subservient role Orthodox tradition assigned to women. Piety had nothing to do with it. In fact, according to her sons, Renée was more devout in some small measure than was their father. At the same time, she had a much keener interest in things secular than did Samuel Reichmann. "She was not what you would call an intellectual either, but her curiosity in the larger world was extraordinary," Paul said. "When we arrived in Paris [in 1940] she would not let us rest. We had to see all the sights, go to all the museums, and so on. She read whenever she had time—secular books, not religious ones. My wife says that my mother was the best-read woman she ever met." Renée Gestetner was largely self-taught, for in keeping with the Oberland custom of the day, her formal education ended at age twelve.

Renée's curiosity about the secular world was not of the idle sort; she was as acquisitive as she was inquisitive. Unlike her father, or her future husband, she was a product not of the village but of a booming metropolis of commerce and industry. If, for the Orthodox, the riches of Hungary's golden age were like luxuries glimpsed through the window of a department store window, then Renée had her face pressed right up against the plate glass. "For money," she liked to say after she had accumulated some, "you get honey." Renée's girlhood longings no doubt were intensified by her inclusion among the poorer relations in the extended Gestetner family. Her aspirations were not heroic but incremental. She did not imagine herself the next David Gestetner; all she really wanted was a better life for herself than her parents had made for themselves—but she wanted it intensely. However, young Hungarian women of Renée Gestetner's generation, be they Orthodox or Gentile, had no real outlet for their ambitions until they first had a husband.

In Beled, David Reichmann and his family also were engaged in a continuous struggle to make ends meet. The Reichmanns slept three and four to a room in a sparsely furnished apartment behind the family glazing shop, but still there were funds enough to send Samuel to the local yeshiva after his thirteenth birthday, like his older brothers before him. Samuel did well enough at his studies, being a clever boy, but did not last long as a full-time Talmudic student. Years later, when Samuel had children of his own, he often told them how he had gotten his start in business as a youth of fifteen or sixteen. This story evolved through constant retelling into one of the defining legends of the Reichmann family, a seamless mix of fact and fiction, as recollected here by Edward, the eldest of the Reichmann brothers. (Samuel's Hebrew name was the same as his great-grandfather's—Shmayahu, or Shmaya for short.)

It happened during World War I, when conditions were difficult. Most of the men in the village had been mobilized into the army. There was no construction going on and people did not have the money for new glassware or even to fix a broken window. The cash register in the store was empty and the outlook was bleak.

In our village, as in most, there was a big property owner ("the Poritz"), who lived in a big palace. The Poritz lived mainly in the big city and only came to his palace from time to time. One Thursday morning, he came to our store and said to my grandmother, "Mrs. Reichmann, there are 101 windows broken in the palace. I want you to have them fixed by Sunday, for I am leaving the village then. Otherwise, it must wait until next year."

My grandmother answered, "I'm sorry, but it is impossible. Today is already Thursday. Friday afternoon and all day Saturday we do not do any work."

But my grandfather, who had heard all this from his study, came in and said, "We can do it and we will do it."

As my grandfather was never involved in the business, my grandmother looked at him in amazement and said, "You don't know anything about glazing. It is impossible." But my grandfather kept insisting it could be done. Finally, the Poritz said, "Please settle this between you. If the job can be done, do it. But if it can't, don't start."

My grandfather immediately left the house and went to the yeshiva. He sought out the rosh yeshiva and said, "I have come to pick up Shmaya. He must come home at once. You know, rabbi, how much it hurts me to take my son away from learning but I must do it, so forgive me."

Grandfather brought my father home and told him to take the worker the family employed in the store and go at once to the palace of the Poritz. "It is already 11 o'clock," my grandfather said. "The worker usually finishes at 6 o'clock. Go and buy a crate of beer and get also an equal number of empty bottles. Mix the bottles with half beer and half water so you will have a lot of beer for the worker but he will not get drunk quickly. Promise him more beer once the job is finished."

My father and the worker went to the palace and they worked nonstop. By Friday morning, after almost 24 hours of uninterrupted labor, they had finished. The Poritz was amazed that this young Jewish boy with the sidecurls had been able to complete this tremendous job. "How much do I owe you?" he asked. My father replied, "Six forints per window, 606 forints altogether." The landlord took out 1,000 forints, gave it to my father and said, "Here is your payment. The rest is a tip."

My father went home and put the 1,000 forints on the table. At the time, it was enough to live on for a year. My grandfather began to cry with great emotion, and my father used to tell me that his crying continued for over an hour. Then he turned to my father and said, "Shmaya, you know how much it hurt me to take you away from learning but you must understand that this is wartime and it was essential." Then he struck the table with his fist. "Listen, Shmaya," he said. "I promise that as a result of what you have done today, you will be a successful businessman all your life."

My father went back to the yeshiva but left shortly afterward and went into business, and from then on a lifelong success story began. My father believed firmly that it was his father's blessing that was the reason for his success.

After Austria-Hungary's decisive defeat in World War I, the empire of the Hapsburgs was carved into a half dozen hostile succession states. Vienna, once the imperial city of central Europe, now was the beggared capital of a bankrupt, dwarf republic less than one-eighth the size of Austria-Hungary. Defeated soldiers and furloughed civil servants returned from the lost outposts of empire to find a ruined city of two million people desperately short of life's necessities. As late as 1920, "Milk and butter were still unobtainable. So, for many, was bread, which anyway was black and sour. People still lived on old seedling potatoes and polenta, and 'meat' was often birch bark. Wiener schnitzel had become a mixture of mashed potatoes and carrots fried in rancid fat. Jam was made from decaying vegetables. Tea was a preparation of straw-berry leaves and coffee was based on barley or ground acorns. Thousands were starving."

In 1919, about a year after the fighting ended, Samuel Reichmann traveled the eighty-five miles from Beled to view Vienna's devastation for himself. It could not have been an easy trip. The trains from Hungary into Vienna ran irregularly, and the coaches were filthy and bare, having been stripped right down to the nickel and copper ash trays. At many stops, policemen searched passengers, looking for undeclared caches of flour and potatoes, as well as firearms and drugs. But Samuel was undeterred; he was not traveling to Vienna for pleasure but for business, or rather the hope of business. While con-tinuing to devote most of his working hours to his parents' glazing and glass-ware business, Samuel began taking the occasional day off to develop a sideline. He would rent a truck, load it with fresh produce purchased from farmers in the Beled area, cross the border into Austria and sell his wares on the street in Leopoldstadt, the Jewish quarter of Vienna.

Soon Samuel began specializing in fresh eggs, apparently following in the footsteps of his older brother Herman, an egg merchant who died of tubercu-losis in 1920 at the age of twenty-eight. Samuel's venture was straightforward yet fraught with difficulty, even danger. No record exists of the prices that he charged. But there is no reason to surmise that he demanded less than the going rate, which was astronomical, thanks to the noxious combination of rampant inflation and pervasive profiteering. "People carried bags filled with high-denomination bills, bank notes that were worth several millions, and handed them over to a small shopkeeper as payment for three eggs," observed one chronicler of Vienna's postwar agonies. "An egg," wrote another, "cost the price of a car." When the shelves of the food shops were empty, "Viennese stripped their homes of their treasures and dragged them into the country to hand them over to greedy peasants in exchange for butter and eggs." At a time when a good share of the population was convinced that the Jews were some-how to blame for Austria's resounding defeat, a Jewish produce vendor in Vienna faced double-barreled resentment that could turn the simple selling of an egg into an act of daring.

Reichmann had to cope with even more alarming conditions on the Hun-garian side of the border. In 1919, the Hungarian Soviet Party seized power in a putsch organized by Béla Kun, who, like many of his co-conspirators, was Jewish. The Kun regime proclaimed a series of radical reforms abolishing noble titles, socializing housing and medicine, nationalizing all businesses with at least twenty employees, and confiscating vast tracts of farmland from the old aristocracy. When its Marxist-Leninist program met with resistance, the Kun government imposed a dictatorship so brutal that it alienated even many of its supporters. Within six weeks, Hungary's misguided experiment in Communism collapsed and Kun fled to Austria.

Although an overwhelming majority of Hungarian Jews had opposed Kun, the violent counterrevolution that toppled his short-lived regime—the "White Terror"—was as anti-Semitic as it was anti-Communist in tone. Throughout Hungary, right-wing army units and paramilitary groups roamed from town to town terrorizing Jews and suspected Red sympathizers and inciting the local citizenry to violence. In Beled, the White Terror stopped short of bloodshed, but in many Oberland localities—including Csorna—rampaging army units murdered Jews, often carrying out public executions to encourage civilians to emulate them. By the time moderate forces had wrested political control from the radical right wing in mid-1920, at least three thousand Jews had perished in Hungary.

Like most villagers, young Reichmann had little appreciation of or interest in the machinations of the politicians in Budapest, but as an Orthodox Jew he had no trouble recognizing the hatemongers of the far right as his mortal enemies. At the same time, the political paroxysms that culminated in the White Terror also imprinted on Reichmann a deep loathing of leftist ideology in general and of Soviet Communism in particular. In his politics no less than in his religion, Samuel Reichmann was conservative to the core.

―――

The story of how Renée Gestetner and Samuel Reichmann came to be wed was not one featured in Reichmann family lore. Each of the three brothers interviewed for this book—Edward, Louis, and Paul—claimed not to have any idea of how their parents' marriage was made. This seems odd, if only because it proved a blessed union in every sense.

The great majority of Orthodox marriages in Hungary were not left to romantic accident but were carefully arranged, with parental consideration of the suitability of the prospective partner depending mainly on family pedigree. On the other hand, the boy and girl usually were introduced before a betrothal was sealed, and many fathers were disinclined to force marriage on a reluctant child. By 1920, the Adolf Gestetner and David Reichmann families certainly would have known one another by reputation, if in no other way. Gestetner was a preeminent name in Hungarian Orthodoxy, and by this time the elder Reichmann's renown as a Torah scholar had spread throughout the entire region. Then, too, several branches of the Gestetner family had members living in Beled, which was just a dozen miles from Csorna; in fact, there had been Gestetners in Beled long before David Reichmann had arrived from the east. Although the Gestetners outranked the Reichmanns in the social hierarchy of Oberlander Orthodoxy, the clear superiority of the Gestetner pedigree was offset to some extent by the fact that Adolf Gestetner was not among his extended family's most accomplished members. And Samuel's industry and entrepreneurial leanings no doubt recommended him to both Adolf and his ambitious daughter.

On March 28, 1921, Samuel Reichmann and Renée Gestetner were wed in the Orthodox synagogue in Győr. He had just turned twenty-three; she was twenty-two. Not long before the ceremony, Renée posed alone for a photograph that is quite striking in its utter lack of feminine affect or ornamentation. Attired in the simple blue-and-white striped frock traditional among the Jews of western Hungary, she gazes directly into the camera with the slightest hint of a smile. The photo is enlivened only by her eyes, a set of outsized human headlights beaming intelligence and self-assurance.

The newlyweds settled in Beled in a small house just a few blocks from the house where Samuel had grown up and where his parents still lived. In the mid-1920s, Beled was a bustling village of almost three thousand people, most of whom lived within a block or two of the main thoroughfare, Rákóczi Utca. Like much of the Oberland, this was farm country, with high rainfall and rich clay and loam soil excellent for growing wheat, barley, and other grains. The farmers of the Oberland also kept large numbers of livestock, mainly dairy cattle and hogs. Although more prosperous than the average Hungarian village, Beled was typical in that much of the surrounding countryside was owned by the Magyar nobility and gentry and organized into large, generally efficient, working estates. Like the Poritz, some of the biggest landowners kept large castlelike houses in the village, which they used mainly in the summer months.

Life in Beled in the 1920s was comfortable but primitive in many ways. The village was not supplied with electricity until the 1930s, and even Rákóczi Utca, which was lit by kerosene lamps in the evening, remained unpaved until after World War II. The wealthy made their rounds in horse-drawn carriages, while most townsfolk made do with bicycles and wagons. The village's municipal water system was rudimentary at best (there was no serviceable aqueduct) and outhouses predominated into the 1940s. At his bride's insistence, Samuel Reichmann installed what was reputedly Beled's first indoor toilet.

Jews had lived in Beled continuously since the early 1700s, when the first of them were brought in from a neighboring town by the governing Magyar nobleman in hopes of developing local trade and commerce. By the 1920s the Jewish community of Beled numbered about three hundred and was completely and emphatically Orthodox; Neology never made a dent here. Aside from a few wives who offended propriety by declining to shave their heads and wear wigs, the Jews of Beled generally adhered to a high standard of observance. The community was entirely self-sufficient, with a full complement of institutions, including a synagogue, yeshiva, elementary school (Talmud Torah), ritual bath (mikveh), matzoh baker, kosher butcher, burial society, and a well-tended cemetery.

Like most Oberland villages, Beled was home to a minority of Hasidic families who had arrived from points east over the past few decades. The Beled Hasidim preferred their own prayerhouse to the communal synagogue but were well accepted by the majority and integrated into the community in most respects. In fact, by this time many of the most devout Oberlanders had followed the lead of the Orthodox rabbinate and incorporated elements of Hasidism into their own beliefs, in what amounted to an effort to inoculate themselves against the creeping incursions of secular modernity with a more old-fashioned and robust strain of piety. The chief Orthodox rabbi in Győr termed the resulting amalgam "salon Hasidism," in that it enriched the inner life of its adherents without significantly altering their practices or appearance—except that sidecurls, or payos, became fashionable for boys. Both Adolf Gestetner and David Reichmann exemplified the trend. As boys, Samuel and his brothers sported payos, but not caftans or any other characteristically Hasidic apparel, and had visited the prayerhouse on occasion while mainly worshipping at the synagogue. And they had all attended the local yeshiva, which was strongly Hasidic in flavor, if not content.

The Beled yeshiva was widely known among the Orthodox but was celebrated less for its quality (though it was more than adequate) than its status as the only yeshiva in Hungary run not by a rabbi but by a learned layman. Benjamin Berger, its founder and chief instructor, was a simple but charismatic man who had studied in Moses Grunwald's famous yeshiva in Huzst and then moved to Poland, where he joined the court of one of the great Hasidic rebbes. After World War I, Berger settled in Beled, opened a construction supply business, and used its profits to start a yeshiva for boys from poor families. Like David Reichmann, his close friend and contemporary, Berger considered business an unwelcome distraction from study. An inspiring teacher and devoted guardian of his boarders, he drew students from throughout the Oberland and was credited with raising the level of Torah observance in Beled and the surrounding villages. Reichmann shared importantly in this achievement, for Berger sent both his best and worst students to him for special tutoring.

The social standing of Beled's Jews in the decades before World War II was made manifest by the memorial the village erected after the war to honor the dead. Although nearly every Jewish resident of the village had perished in Auschwitz, their suffering was only briefly and collectively noted: "For the memory of the Jewish martyrs." Meanwhile, every Gentile casualty was listed by name.

The Jewish families lived together in their own neighborhood, and the synagogue, school, and other religious facilities were clustered together adjacent to the Jewish cemetery on the outskirts of the village. Yet the Orthodox were much more closely integrated into the economic life of Beled than their counterparts in Budapest or even Győr. In fact, Beled's Jewish minority dominated the village economy in the 1920s, accounting for perhaps 75 percent of non-agricultural employment and an equivalent share of local commerce. Two dozen of the three dozen stores and shops that lined Rakoczi Utca were Jewish-owned. Most were quite large and well provisioned, for they served a clientele drawn not only from the village and the surrounding estates but from scores of other settlements within a radius of twenty to twenty-five miles. By contrast, the town of Csorna, which was three times Beled's size, supported half the number of Jewish shops. "There were many jobless people in Hungary, but in Beled we never knew unemployment," recalled Gyula Sagi, the village's long-time postman. "In Beled, everyone could work at the Jews."

Fully half of Beled's largest taxpayers, or "virilists," were Jews and, like the major landowners, were automatically entitled to membership on the village council. In the village setting, the symbiosis of Jew and Gentile had its social as well as economic aspects. Beled's Jewish-owned coffeehouse was one of only two such establishments in the Kapuvar district and was as popular with Magyar landowners as with the village Jews. The Jewish merchants of Beled were so ecumenical in their charity that the Christian beggars took Saturdays off and made their rounds on Friday, before the start of Shabbat. However inadvertently, Jewish families even stimulated the Gentile marriage market by bringing scores of teenaged peasant girls in from the countryside to work as housemaids. Beled had undercurrents of anti-Semitism, to be sure, but after the paroxysm of the White Terror, they would remain muted until the late 1930s. It was not uncommon for the younger Jewish and Gentile children to play together in the village or swim together in the Raba River.

Three of Samuel and Renée Reichmann's six children were born in Beled, arriving at regular intervals. Eva, the eldest, was born on October 3, 1923, and was followed by Edward on March 1, 1925, and Ludwig (later known as Louis) on May 5, 1927. Among themselves, the Reichmanns, like most Orthodox families, used their Hebrew names exclusively—a preference that would occasionally test Samuel's memory. (During the family's long stay in Tangier, a policeman investigating a bicycle accident once knocked on the Reichmanns' door and asked Mr. Reichmann if he had a son named Paul. Samuel pondered and then sheepishly summoned Renée. "Do we have a son named Paul?" he asked. To his father, Paul would always be Moishe.) Eva's Hebrew name was Chaya, but she was familiarly known as "Maidie," a customary nickname for an eldest daughter. Edward's was Eliyahu, after his great-grandfather, the first Reichmann, and Ludwig's was Herschel.

———

Emboldened no doubt by his new wife's encouragements, Samuel Reichmann left the family glazing business sometime in the early 1920s and set up a business of his own in partnership with his brother, Simon, who was three years his junior and had also married into the Gestetner family. The brothers named their venture David Reichmann & Sons in honor of their father, though he played no role in it. Samuel held a majority stake and Simon owned the rest. Later, they were joined by a third brother, Izidor, born in 1907.

During the long reign of the Hapsburgs, the Viennese had developed quite an egg habit, eating three times as many eggs per capita as Austria's chickens laid. Ever since the late 1700s the growing gap between production and consumption had been filled in part by eggs imported from the Hungarian Oberland. Even so, the egg trade remained one of the least organized and most inefficient facets of Hungarian agriculture. In Hungary, wheat was king and the land-owning Magyar aristocracy simply could not be bothered with chickens and their leavings. Hungary was rich in poultry just the same, for the peasants employed by the big landowners typically were allowed to keep a pig or a flock of hens for themselves, and many tenant farmers developed a sideline in poultry-rearing. In 1898, the year of Samuel's birth, the Hungarian agricultural ministry had begun a belated effort to organize a poultry export industry. Budapest founded state-owned poultry farms, where the native species of chickens was refined through interbreeding to create a bigger bird, and also encouraged the formation of rural egg-collecting cooperatives similar to those that already existed in the dairy industry. "To foster export, and so to increase the revenue of the small farmers, the policy adopted was to eliminate the superfluous middleman," declared a government promotional pamphlet issued in 1905. Because the brokering of fresh produce long had been a Jewish occupation in Hungary, these innocuous-sounding goals amounted to an attempt to purge Jews from the egg trade.

Throughout the 1920s, Budapest was chronically short of fresh milk even though Hungarian cows produced more than ample volumes. The problem was distribution: a huge quantity of milk spoiled in rural collection stations before it could be hauled to market. Fresh eggs were nearly as perishable as milk and languished in thousands of baskets in hundreds of chicken coops until they were no longer fit for eating. Despite the efforts of the Hungarian governments, the fresh egg market in the Oberland remained both highly fragmented and underdeveloped upon the Reichmanns' entry.

The Hungary in which Samuel Reichmann established himself as a merchant was a virtual test laboratory of adverse conditions. After World War I, Hungary not only was carved out of the Hapsburg Empire and forced to stand on its own but was itself dismembered to satisfy the territorial demands of its neighbors, including Austria, which absorbed that part of the Oberland that included the Seven Communities. In the infamous Trianon Treaty signed in 1920, Hungary was deprived of two-thirds of its territory, three-fifths of its population, and commensurate portions of its manufacturing capacity and natural resources. Crippled by loss, the economy was afflicted into the mid-

1920s by a catastrophic combination of stagnation and hyperinflation. Hungary exacerbated its woes by succumbing to the international vogue of protectionism. That is, tariffs were set high to protect manufacturing and thus invited retaliation against the mainstay of the Hungarian economy, agricultural exports. All in all, Hungary's postwar "economic landscape was perhaps the bleakest in Eastern Europe." Not until 1926 did production reach prewar levels.

In setting themselves up as egg merchants, or eirehandlers, Samuel and his brother chose shrewdly, eggs being one of the few commodities in which the dynamics of post–World War I trade clearly favored Hungary, tariffs notwithstanding. The war and the Communist revolution had combined to decimate the Russian egg industry, which had gained ascendancy in all European export markets. Even in distant England, Russian exporters controlled 50 percent of the market as late as 1910, with the Danes a distant second at 20 percent. In Vienna especially, the ruination of the Russian exporters had left a void that could be most cost-efficiently filled from the Oberland.

Within a few years, the brothers Reichmann appear to have established themselves as the biggest of some one dozen eirehandlers plying the Oberland, which was Hungary's leading egg-exporting district. By the late-1920s, David Reichmann & Sons was handling a significant share of the egg crop of Győr-Moson-Sopron, Vas, and Veszprém counties, an area of about six thousand square miles. The Reichmanns hired field agents who did the purchasing and gathered the eggs in a central location to be picked up by horse-drawn coaches and wagons dispatched from Beled. Since the collectors, most of whom were moonlighting local tenant farmers, were expected to furnish their own transport, the Reichmanns' capital investment was limited to the egg crates their drivers hauled. The typical route took a week or so to complete. Back in Beled, the eggs were sorted by size and weight into three classes and packed into crates. Most eggs of the top and second quality were shipped to Vienna, where they brought higher prices than in Budapest. Every Wednesday or Thursday, Lidi Reichmann, Samuel's mother, walked through the plant, gathering eggs that were cracked and otherwise unsalable and distributing them among the village's poorer Jewish families for use in their Shabbat meals.

On the buy side of their business, the Reichmann brothers inspired a certain loyalty among the peasantry by assuring them of a ready and steady market for their eggs. The price might vary, but David Reichmann & Sons was prepared to buy every egg it was offered. Naturally, this had the effect of stimulating egg production in many local markets, which, in turn, boosted the brothers' productivity, since more wagons returned to Beled with a full load. The egg trade was seasonal, with the period of heaviest collection running from March through August. During periods of peak production, the Reichmanns ranked among Beled's largest employers, with a payroll composed of some two dozen collectors and an equal number of packers and sorters—most of whom were Gentile housewives or Jewish teenagers of both sexes.

Theirs was a simple business, but logistically unforgiving. An egg was not fresh for long, and the necessity of making daily deliveries multiplied the chances of costly error. In the highly competitive Vienna market, an unreliable supplier was quickly punished with a loss of business. The Reichmanns sought advantage wherever they could find it, becoming one of the first eirehandlers in western Hungary to capitalize on advances in techniques for preserving eggs. In Beled, the brothers built a large storage warehouse in which thousands of eggs were immersed in twenty-eight lime-water basins. During the winter, the preserved eggs were retrieved and sold. In all likelihood, David Reichmann & Sons also was the first Oberland eirehandler to invest in automated processing machinery, which sorted eggs into ten size categories instead of the customary three. Samuel may have been an unreconstructed traditionalist in matters religious, but in business he was a committed modernist.

In 1927, not long before the birth of his third child, Samuel Reichmann signaled his arrival as a local man of means by buying a massive brick house at Rakoczi Utca 170. It was in the spacious yard behind this house, which was one of the largest in Beled, that the Reichmanns built their state-of-the-art egg-packing plant and storage facility. Simon bought the house next door and joined with Samuel to build a new house for their parents in one corner of what amounted to a Reichmann family compound in the heart of Beled.

And yet by the end of 1927, just a few months after they moved into their new house, Samuel and Renée decided to leave Beled and move to Vienna. A city girl born and bred, Mrs. Reichmann had never really taken to Beled, which, for all its commercial vibrancy, was about as cosmopolitan as a manure pile. Her dissatisfaction with village life crystallized around the question of where Eva, who would turn five in the fall of 1928, would begin her schooling. Neither Beled's Talmud Torah nor its public elementary school measured up to Mrs. Reichmann's exacting educational standards. While Samuel considered the local school—his alma mater—perfectly adequate, he had outgrown the village, too. By 1927, he was practically commuting between Beled and Vienna as he increasingly concentrated his efforts on building David Reichmann & Son's Viennese clientele while moving the firm into new markets in Germany and Italy. Even in its humbled post-Hapsburg condition, Vienna remained the financial capital of central Europe.

Ever since the mid-1800s, Jews in huge numbers had been abandoning villages throughout eastern Europe for the big city, be it Vienna, Warsaw, Prague, Budapest, Bratislava, or Bucharest. And yet in forsaking Beled for Vienna in February 1928, the Reichmanns also were going against the demographic grain, in a sense. The great majority of Jews who left Galicia, Bukovina, and the other regions of heaviest Jewish population loss in the interwar period were reluctant emigrants driven from their rural enclaves by poverty and persecution. The Reichmanns left Beled eagerly, if not without mixed feelings, compelled not by misery but by ambition. This did not make Samuel and Renée any less observant than their stay-at-home siblings, but it did put their faith at greater risk. For a century or more, the Austrian capital had acted as a kind of supercharged assimilation machine, receiving Orthodox immigrants and gradually leaching the Jewishness from them. In fact, historically Vienna had a higher rate of Jewish conversion to Christianity than any other European capital.

Samuel had been doing business in the Austrian capital for the better part of a decade, and Renée knew the place from her own travels, as well as through the accounts of Gestetner relatives who had lived there over the years. They moved to Vienna with eyes wide open, taking a calculated risk that they would be able to add to their fortune without subtracting from their faith. They were nearly thirty years old and secure in their identities. Their concern lay with the next generation. Could they, in Vienna, succeed in raising children who would be as devoutly observant as they were themselves and thus preserve a familial continuum that reached back centuries?

The Reichmanns hung on to their big house in Beled and would return to it often over the coming decade. In some ways, it was as if they never left. And yet moving to Vienna was perhaps the most fortuitously fateful decision Samuel and Renée Reichmann would ever make. If demography were destiny, the Reichmann family would have ended, literally, on history's ash heap. Six years would elapse between Germany's annexation of Austria in 1938 and its occupation of Hungary in 1944, and yet the great majority of Orthodox Oberlanders—the extended Reichmann and Gestetner families included—would make no attempt to escape until escape was impossible. In moving to Vienna, Samuel and Renée breached the geographic constraints of Orthodox traditionalism. When the time came to flee for their lives, they would not hesitate, for in effect they already had one foot out the door.

Chapter 3

S amuel and Renée Reichmann lived in Leopoldstadt, Vienna's poorest and most populous "bezirk," or district, throughout the ten years they spent in the Austrian capital. First assigned to the Jews in 1622, Leopoldstadt was surrounded by water, with the Danube River on one side and the Donau Kanal on the other. Nicknamed "Die Mazzes Insel" (Matzos Island), Leopoldstadt was connected to the base of the old medieval citadel by a series of bridges. After Emperor Franz Josef abolished all ghettos in 1849, tens of thousands of Jews crossed those bridges into Vienna proper and transformed the ancient metropolis into Europe's greatest civic monument to Jewish overachievement. "Nine-tenths of what the world celebrated as Viennese culture in the nineteenth century was promoted, nourished, and even created by Viennese Jewry," claimed the writer Stefan Zweig, himself a Viennese Jew.

The Jews of Vienna were prolific contributors to business no less than to the arts. Jewish entrepreneurs built Austria's first steel mills; were instrumental in founding the textile, sugar-refining, meatpacking, and other heavy industries; and predominated in the wholesale and retail trades. Jews established most major banks in Vienna and were overrepresented in many professions, including law, journalism, and medicine. As early as 1880, 60 percent of physicians in Vienna, which was the medical capital of Europe, were Jewish. The most famous Viennese doctor of them all, Sigmund Freud, grew up in Leopoldstadt as the son of Galician immigrants and left the district at the earliest opportunity.

Viennese Jewry's secular achievements made the city an early citadel of Reform Judaism and spurred a particularly ardent brand of assimilationism that manifested itself as avid pro-Germanism. Jews joined the German National Union in droves before it became overtly anti-Semitic in the 1930s, adding their voices to group sing-alongs of "Deutschland, Deutschland über Alles." Well-to-do Jews grew so attached to "Vienna Gloriosa" that few would venture farther than the outlying suburbs even on vacation. And yet no Jews were fully accepted in Gentile society—regardless of whether they had converted to Christianity or were the most acclaimed and assimilated of all those in Vienna. The latter led subtly segregated lives in whichever tony bezirk they settled after leaving Leopoldstadt. The frustrated social ambitions of the Jewish haute bourgeoisie fed a particularly nasty brand of Jewish self-loathing, typified by this excerpt from a letter written by Theodor Herzl, the father of Zionism: "Yesterday grand soirée at the Treitels. Thirty or forty ugly little Jews and Jewesses. No consoling sight."

The favorite target of anti-Semites, whether Jew or Gentile, were the Orthodox immigrants—the Ostjuden—who descended on Leopoldstadt from the shtetls of Galicia, Poland, and Russia in great ragged waves. Adolf Hitler, who spent six of the most humiliating years of his early life wandering around the fringes of Leopoldstadt, claimed that it was a sidewalk encounter with an Ostjude in payos and black caftan that knocked the scales from his eyes and revealed to him the pervasiveness of the Jewish menace. "Vienna appeared to me in a new light," he wrote in *Mein Kampf.* "Was there any shady undertaking, any form of foulness, especially in cultural life, in which at least one Jew did not participate?"

The immigrant influx, especially heavy during World War I and its aftermath, pushed Vienna's Jewish population to its historic peak of 180,000 in 1923. By the time the Reichmann family arrived five years later, Leopoldstadt was home to sixty thousand Jewish and an equal number of Gentile inhabitants. Homeless refugees filled the Prater, the park that ran like a green ribbon for two-and-a-half miles along the Donau Kanal, and they were packed by the thousands into squalid, one-room flats in dilapidated tenements. At the same time, Leopoldstadt's main thoroughfares, Taborstrasse and Praterstrasse, were bustling and, in stretches, almost elegant. The Kaffeehausen for which Vienna was famous were no less numerous there than in other biserks and even more heavily patronized. And if parts of Leopoldstadt were slums as squalid as any in Europe, others were solidly middle-class neighborhoods and a few were downright prosperous.

The Reichmanns moved first into a middling section of Leopoldstadt on its back side—that is, the part farthest away from the bridges to the First Bezirk— where they rented a three-room apartment in a newly constructed but plain little building at Herminengasse 6. The apartment's only virtue was location: it was a few blocks from a narrow storefront warehouse leased by David Reichmann & Sons at Tandelmarktgasse 9. Also, eggs could be stored here on those odd occasions when an order could not be immediately delivered to a customer. Mrs. Reichmann commandeered the forward part of the space and started her own business. Every Wednesday and Thursday she sold live chickens, geese, and other kosher birds, supplied through her brother Dezsö, a poultry wholesaler in Győr.

The Reichmanns did not remain long in the apartment on Herminengasse. In November 1928, just after Eva began attending a Jewish kindergarten on Malzgasse, they moved to a more affluent street on the side of the island facing Vienna proper. The new apartment, in a five-story walk-up at Rembrandtstrasse 34, was only a few feet off the tree-lined Donau Kanal.

The fixed axis of the Reichmanns' Vienna orbit was the Adas Israel synagogue on Grosschiffengasse in Leopoldstadt. Better known as the Schiffschul, it was the foremost Orthodox synagogue in the city, with seven hundred members. Decisively stamped in the Oberland mold, the Schiffschul had been founded in 1864 by a group of Hungarian immigrants in protest against the reformism of the "Kultusgemeinde," Vienna's Jewish communal government. Austria never did let the Orthodox take the next step and organize a wholly separate community along Hungarian lines, but the leaders of the Schiffschul went ahead and created a full complement of institutions and acted as a self-contained Orthodox "kehillah" in all but name, becoming, in the words of an in-house historian, "a mighty fortress against reform and assimilation in Vienna."

Although the Reichmanns found the Schiffschul community's brand of Orthodoxy reassuringly familiar, Samuel thought the synagogue itself too grand for routine use, especially in view of the commotion inevitably made by small boys. For daily prayers, he preferred the humbler and altogether less social environment of the Hasidic prayerhouse (shteibel), of which there were dozens in Leopoldstadt. As a rule, Samuel began his weekdays with a visit to a shteibel on Glockengasse. Even on the high holidays, Samuel rarely used his seat in the main Schiffschul synagogue, preferring a smaller, less formal branch facility run by the community.

By the time that the Reichmanns joined the Schiffschul, the Reform movement had long since lost its sting in Vienna (though the stampede to assimilate continued unabated). Instead, Orthodox traditionalists were locked in a bitter struggle with a new internecine enemy: the Zionists. As the home of Herzl, Vienna was the birthplace of Zionism, which coalesced as a political movement around 1900 but did not come into its own until after World War I. Herzl's basic argument was that because of anti-Semitism, Jews could never hope to fully integrate into any Gentile country and instead should be ceded land to form a sovereign Jewish nation, one that would take its place as an equal in the community of nations. Zionist opinion favored Palestine, the original Jewish homeland, as the best location for the Jewish state.

To most devoutly Orthodox Jews, secular Zionism was a blasphemous perversion of one of the most sacred tenets of the Torah: that the Holy Land would be returned to the Jewish people by the Messiah. Politically, Zionism threatened Orthodoxy by offering a novel, less demanding form of Jewish separatism that proved especially palatable to the young. "Quite a number of youngsters in my generation became Zionists," recalled Teddy Kollek, the future mayor of Jerusalem, who grew up in Vienna in the 1920s in a moderately traditionalist home. To coordinate their opposition to Zionism, most of the various factions of European Orthodoxy had joined forces in 1912 to form the organization Agudath Israel. Throughout the 1920s and 1930s, Vienna was no less a stronghold of Agudism than of Zionism. Wolf Pappenheim, Agudath Israel's first president, was a Viennese who belonged to the Schiffschul, as did many leading Agudists. If, like most pious Jews, the Reichmanns were no friend to political Zionism, neither were they defined by anti-Zionism. Samuel and Renée had many friends in the Agudist movement but did not join it or any other group with a political slant.

In the 1920s and early 1930s, Leopoldstadt teemed with sectarian political strife of all sorts. Although the district was popularly identified with socialism, it was in fact a breeding ground for activists and organizers spanning the entire spectrum, from far left to far right. In the face of this partisan tumult, the Reichmanns remained serenely apolitical, joining nothing. All of the Reichmanns' sons (with the conspicuous exception of Edward) inherited this aversion to organizational entanglement. As extraordinarily purposeful people, the Reichmanns had no patience for the partisan wrangling and compromising that inevitably complicates organizational life. To swear allegiance was to interpose a temporal agenda between the family and its divinely ordained destiny, and that, not Zionism, was heresy to a Reichmann.

—

In 1929, Samuel Reichmann became truly rich. During the preceding year, he had gone to Budapest and secured a bank loan of some 500,000 pengos, a substantial sum at the time. Reichmann used part of it to greatly expand his egg storage capacity in Beled. The timing of this project was doubly fortuitous. First, the egg crop that summer was unusually large, and the Reichmann brothers needed to make full use of the added storage capacity; second, the winter that followed was, in Edward Reichmann's words, "a famous horror." Its brutal cold brought a sharp drop in the output of laying hens throughout Central Europe, with the result that the price of an egg in Vienna doubled and then doubled again. Samuel fed his trove of lime-preserved eggs into a hungry market and made a killing.

From this point, the fortunes of the Reichmanns sharply diverged from those of average folk, whether Jew or Gentile. The Great Depression that rolled out of the United States to engulf the industrial world in the 1930s arrived early in the farm regions of central Europe. The year 1929 saw "catastrophe for Hungarian agriculture and the countryside" as a combination of overproduction at home and steep tariff barriers abroad sent prices into a protracted tailspin; the leading index of agricultural prices plunged from a peak of 137 in 1928 to 53 by mid-1932. Meanwhile, Hungarian exports of farm goods—the largest single source of national income—fell precipitously, and industrial production stagnated. When foreign banks began calling their Hungarian loans in mid-1931, the Hungarian National Bank's cash reserves disappeared within weeks. To avoid bankruptcy, the Hungarian government submitted to a humiliating regime of foreign supervision.

If anything, Austria was even harder hit. By the late 1920s, the Austrian economy was finally showing signs of health and stability. Although unemployment was still high at 12 percent, industrial production had nearly reached pre–World War I levels. Then the depression took hold. By 1932, Austria's unemployment had doubled, while industrial production was cut in half. A dozen important banks collapsed, including the two great Rothschild banks in Vienna. The severity of the economic crisis revived doubts about Austria's ability to survive as an independent nation.

Samuel and Simon changed the name of their firm to Reichmann Brothers and managed not only to survive but to thrive. In their favor was the fact that the decline in egg and poultry prices was relatively modest compared with the free fall in wheat, corn, cattle, hogs, and other traditional staples. Because poultry-keeping was still in transition from a farm sideline to a full-fledged industry, the supply of eggs had not yet caught up to demand in much of Europe. This not only buoyed prices but dissuaded large net egg-importing nations like England, France, and Austria from boosting tariffs on eggs as rapidly as on other commodities.

Reichmann Brothers' investment in state-of-the-art equipment also helped maintain its profit margins throughout hard times, as did the monopoly it enjoyed as an egg buyer in much of Sopron country. Not content merely to hold their own, the Reichmann brothers increased their revenues by adding customers in markets other than Vienna. Simon took the lead in developing Budapest, while Samuel ranged farther afield, going to London, Berlin, Munich, and Leipzig. In traveling to Germany, Samuel followed a well-worn path; Germany had long been Hungary's largest foreign market for eggs, accounting for 47 percent of the export total in 1929. Still, for an Orthodox Jew, prospecting for customers in a Germany increasingly agitated by Nazi propaganda could hardly be described as routine. Samuel also braved the rising anti-Semitism of rural Poland to diversify his sources of supply. Most of the eggs Samuel bought in Poland were shipped via Germany to England.

The Reichmann family expanded in parallel with the family business. On January 19, 1929, in the midst of Samuel's cold-weather bonanza, Renée gave birth to Albert, the first of three sons born in Vienna. Mrs. Reichmann soon was pregnant again, and Paul was born on September 27, 1930. Hard-pressed by the demands of mothering five children while running the poultry shop, Mrs. Reichmann hired a teenaged Gentile girl as a full-time nanny and maid.

In August 1932, the Reichmanns moved out of the flat on Rembrandt-strasse into a much larger apartment in a turreted turn-of-the-century building at Hafnergasse number 5, which lay just off the Taborstrasse in one of Leopoldstadt's best neighborhoods. In moving a few blocks across town, the Reichmanns ascended into the nouveau riche, as any visitor could plainly see. Crystal chandeliers hung from the ceilings of the six-room apartment, and fine Persian rugs were draped on the walls, in the style of the day. The sitting room, which Renée called her salon, was furnished in Chippendale and featured a display case in which a large collection of silver tableware glittered. Despite the time and money she invested in her furnishings, Mrs. Reichmann shrugged off the compliments of her friends and indulged no inquiry about the prices she had paid. "Well," she would quip, "they wouldn't sell it any cheaper."

On October 2, 1933, Mrs. Reichmann gave birth to her sixth child, Rudolph (later known as Ralph). The household now totaled nine, including Renée's pretty, exuberant younger sister, Olga, better known as Aunt Dadi, who moved to Vienna after finishing school to help her eldest sister with the children. Aunt Dadi also worked as Samuel Reichmann's secretary. Renée was only thirty-five years old, but her childbearing years were over. "If she could have had more children, I'm sure she would have," said Regina "Rufka" Klein, a close friend of the family during their Vienna years. In her late twenties, Renée had developed a painful stomach ulcer that was aggravated by the stress of pregnancy. "She suffered very badly from it," recalled Klein. "There was always a doctor around."

The new apartment was a few blocks closer to the Malzgasse Talmud Torah, which Eva, Edward, Louis, Paul, and Albert attended in due course. By all accounts, this was a first-rate school that offered its three hundred students both religious training and the secular instruction required under Austrian law. Girls and boys were taught separately, in keeping with Orthodox custom. "The Vienna school was much more demanding than the ones in Beled," recalled Louis, who, along with Albert and Paul, would continue his education in the village after the Reichmanns abruptly pulled out of Vienna in 1938. All six Reichmanns excelled in school, their mother, in particular, having made it clear that she expected no less of them.

Renée Reichmann was the family disciplinarian, ruling with an unyielding but light touch. "My father had certain expectations of our behavior—you could see that," Louis said. "But my mother was the one who gave out the instructions. I don't remember any punishment being handed out. Somehow it was made clear that we were to conduct ourselves respectfully." Added Rufka

Klein: "The children looked up to their parents. They knew how to conduct themselves, so there was no real need to be too strict. It was always a very happy home."

With all five of her sons, Mrs. Reichmann would place unremitting emphasis on the religious aspect of their education. "My mother was absolutely determined to see to it that her children were raised in the same old-fashioned, religious way in which her parents had raised her. She was consumed by it," Paul recalled. "It was ironic because her own self-education had been all secular, and she'd never gotten enough of it, which was something that differentiated her from my father. My mother was much broader in outlook than her own parents, too. I think she was aware of the irony, but this was one thing on which she wouldn't compromise."

All five brothers grew up sporting the long sidecurls, or payos, that had once been a badge of Hasidic affiliation but had long since become a generic symbol of Judaic piety adopted by the Oberlander Orthodox. From an early age, the Reichmann boys were taught that at age thirteen, like both of their grandfathers before them, they would be sent away to one of the major Hungarian yeshivas for four or five years of complete immersion in the Torah. With Edward, Mrs. Reichmann did not wait until his bar mitzvah to start molding her eldest boy into a talmid hacham, or religious scholar. After Edward completed fourth grade in 1935, he was pulled out of the Talmud Torah and sent to a religious school in Vienna that prepared boys for yeshiva. To continue his secular education as required by law, Edward went to a private tutor every day after school. At the end of the year, he underwent about ten days of exams at the Schwarzinger Schule, a private school in Leopoldstadt that not only was non-Jewish but was considered a bastion of anti-Semitism.

The Reichmann children spent their summers in Hungary, splitting their time between Beled and Győr, and during the cold-weather months they often returned with their parents to the Oberland for a long Shabbat weekend or to attend one family event or another. It was an easy trip; Győr was an hour and a half and Beled two hours from Vienna by train. "We all looked forward to trips to Hungary," Louis recalled. "Whenever we had an excuse, we'd go—even for a day."

Even so, to Eva and her brothers, home was Vienna, not Beled or Győr. "As a boy, I never thought of myself as Hungarian; I was Austrian," Louis said. Among themselves, Eva and her brothers spoke German—the language they studied in school and spoke on the street in Vienna. With their parents, they conversed both in German and Hungarian, which they learned to speak fluently during their visits to Hungary but never quite mastered as a written language. (In contrast to Jews from northeastern Hungary and the rest of eastern

Europe, none of the Reichmanns spoke Yiddish.) Louis's sure sense of himself as Austrian would not outlast childhood. Even before he celebrated his bar mitzvah in a bomb shelter in Paris, Louis had come to understand that his fundamental identity was a function not of language or citizenship but of religion—that he was first and foremost an Orthodox Jew.

In Beled, as in Győr, the Reichmann children were engulfed by first cousins. Of Samuel's eight siblings who survived into adulthood, six had remained in Beled and among them would produce nearly fifty children. Samuel and Simon were far and away the most prosperous members of the family. In fact, their brothers and brothers-in-law were by and large on the poor side, mainly because they shared David Reichmann's preference for study over commerce. In addition to helping his parents and other members of his family, Samuel gave generously in support of the synagogue, schools, and other institutions of the Beled community. The combination of Samuel's money and generosity and his father's status as the local Talmudic sage made the Reichmanns the kings of the Beled Jews in all but name. "Most people thought that the Wollsteins [a family of textile manufacturers] were even richer than the Reichmanns," recalled Murray Stern, a prewar resident of Beled, "but somehow the Reichmanns were more respected."

Samuel Reichmann was a most mild-mannered monarch; it was not his style to lord it over anyone. At five feet, ten inches and a square-shouldered 175 pounds, Samuel was an athletic and rather handsome man. His beard, a distinctive strawberry blond, was thick and cropped close, defining the outlines of a strong, resolute jaw. And yet Samuel had inherited his father's gentle, unassuming manner, if not his bookishness. "With my father, the first thing was that his visitor had to have a tea," Paul said. "He got a tea for everyone, especially those who needed his help. He didn't want the people who came to him to feel like beggars." As an older man, Reichmann would always insist on bringing a chair for a visiting grandchild to sit on, inverting standard protocol in the rigidly patriarchal world of traditional Orthodoxy.

Although Reichmann never held office in the Beled community, he wielded effective veto power over major decisions. For years, Samuel had employed an old man named Steiner to tend the team of horses he kept in Beled. This Mr. Steiner had three sons, each of whom developed into a pious, accomplished Talmudist. At one point, Beled was without a rabbi and many leading members of the community were leaning toward one of the Steiner brothers to fill the vacancy. However, Rabbi Steiner's candidacy ended abruptly when Samuel Reichmann was asked his opinion. "I cannot accept as my rabbi the son of my coachman," Reichmann replied.

In his own way, Reichmann tried to make it up to Rabbi Steiner, who was hired as the rabbi in a nearby community that was even smaller than Beled. Reichmann took it upon himself to augment Rabbi Steiner's meager salary by mailing him the occasional packetful of pengos. Years later, Rabbi Steiner's son married the daughter of Eli Reichmann, Samuel's eldest brother. After the ceremony, Rabbi Steiner asked Samuel to come with him into his study. He unlocked his desk drawer and removed every one of the two dozen envelopes that Reichmann had sent over the years. "He didn't want to use the money because he was hurt over his rejection in Beled but didn't want to risk insulting my father by sending it back to him," Edward Reichmann recalled. The two men opened the envelopes and counted out about 5,000 pengos. Samuel took the cash back and made out a check in the same amount to the newlyweds. (At the time, 10,000 pengos bought a nice little house in an Oberland village.)

Life in the Orthodox time capsule that was Beled in the 1930s left a deep imprint on the older Reichmann brothers. More than a half century later, Edward offered this recollection of a typical Shabbat in Beled during the last fading glow of Hungarian Orthodoxy's golden age:

Grandfather and grandmother had six married children in Beled and with all the families, there were over fifty grandchildren. Every Friday evening after candlelighting the men went to synagogue and the women went to grandmother's. After the prayers all men accompanied grandfather home to say happy Shabbas to grandmother and pick up the women. Every Saturday afternoon everyone came to grandfather's house. It was a weekly scene and this is how it went. When they all arrived, grandfather used to go out into the big yard and signal with his hand, boys to the right and girls to the left. And then all the sons and sons-in-law would go to grandfather's room and the daughters and daughters-in-law would go to grandmother's room. My grandfather would go into my grandmother's room and say to the ladies, 'Good Shabbas, have a nice time, but I ask you not to talk any lashon harah [malicious gossip]. Then he would go into the men and teach the Shulhan Aruch [a sixteenth-century code of Jewish law].

In the winter of 1937, Edward spent a month in Beled, sleeping in Uncle Simon's house with four cousins. Every morning at 3:30, Joseph Reichmann, the most pious of Samuel's brothers, would ride over from his house on a bicycle and slip silently into the house. Pulling a hatchet from under his coat, he chopped up some twigs, put them in the stove, poured a little kerosene on them and then left as quietly as he'd entered. A half hour later Uncle Yossi returned to light the fire and waited a few minutes while the stove heated up. Then he turned on the room light, went to each of the boys and gently shook them awake, saying, "Get up to serve God." Joseph sat with his nephews until about 5:30 and then got back on his bike and rode away. Curious to know what his uncle did in the half hour between the preparation and the lighting of the fire, Edward got into bed one night fully dressed. When Joseph left, Edward followed him to the mikveh, the ritual bath, and watched as he broke the surface covering of ice with his hatchet and immersed himself in its pure, frigid waters.

⸻

No one knew the Reichmanns better during their years in Vienna than Rufka Klein, née Fischof, who was descended from a prominent Oberlander family in Bratislava. In the early 1920s, Rufka's older sister, Margit, had married Henrik Gestetner, Renée's eldest brother. Rufka was the same age as Olga Gestetner and the two became fast friends after their siblings had married. When Olga moved to Vienna to help Renée, Rufka often came to visit on weekends. "I went up to their apartment like I was going to my own home," Rufka recalled. "I was one of them."

To the young Rufka, Samuel, or "Shimi," as she called him, was a formidable if somewhat remote presence. "He was a nice guy—handsome, dignified. He had a big business head. Whatever he touched, it turned to gold. I guess the boys took after him, especially Moishe [Paul]. But Shimi was a quiet person. Renée was the tower of strength. Shimi was a strong person, too, but in comparison to her, he was weak. Even in business, he might have better ideas but she was more persuasive. He couldn't present things like she could.

"Mrs. Reichmann was no beauty," she continued. "She wasn't a pretty woman and she was a bit on the heavy side—a bit. But she was elegant. She dressed beautifully and had a lot of diamonds. Her husband showered her. I guess it made her look like what she ain't. The minute she opened her mouth you forgot all about her appearance. She was so smart, pearls came out of her mouth. She could talk you into anything, believe me. What Lola wanted, Lola got."

No doubt the Reichmann brothers would blanch at such testimony. As adults, the brothers would rarely discuss their parents publicly, but when they did were careful to honor each equally. To their parents' contemporaries, though, Mrs. Reichmann's dominance was no less apparent from the male vantage point. Abraham Schreiber, who was descended from the Hatam Sofer himself, first met the Reichmanns in 1928 through the Schiffschul and maintained a relationship with the family that would last into the 1990s (and his nineties). "Mr. Reichmann was very *frum* [pious], very serious—a fine man but simple," Schreiber recalled decades later. "Mrs. Reichmann was exceptionally clever. She was the brains."

Like her husband, Mrs. Reichmann was physically imposing. Even as a young bride, she had been moonfaced and a bit stout, like her mother. Childbearing had thickened her limbs and aged her considerably, though the impression conveyed by photos taken of her in the 1930s is not of decline but of great strength and solidity. For all her loquaciousness, Mrs. Reichmann was really rather reserved. "She never showed her emotions to you," Rukfa said. "She would suppress it when she was excited." She tended to dominate a room as much through wit as through argument. Although her humor was rarely mean-spirited, her commentary could be intimidatingly acute, and she had no patience for self-aggrandizement or self-pity from any quarter. You never knew when she might put you in your place.

Beneath her slightly sardonic exterior, Mrs. Reichmann was a woman of ferocious emotional attachments. Edward, the son to whom she was closest, characterized his mother's feeling for her father as "something almost unbelievable" and the filial equivalent of "religious fanaticism." Renée's feelings for her mother, though less tinged with reverence, were no less powerful. Edward recalled his mother crying night and day for a month after her own mother died. And when Renée learned, toward the end of World War II, that one of her younger brothers had been shot dead by Hungarian fascists, she instantly collapsed to the ground and writhed uncontrollably as if she were suffering an epileptic fit.

Although wifely dominance was unusual in the patriarchal world of Orthodoxy, it was not in itself contrary to strict traditionalism. Although Talmudic law excluded women from important spheres of religious and communal life and made wives subservient to their husbands in certain, precisely defined ways, the great sages of the Torah did not consider women an inferior caste, but rather "a nation apart." In other words, "the distinction between the sexes is based on a fundamental division of tasks which are seen as separate but equal." Renée's dominance was not a product of overstepping the boundaries of her prescribed role—she did not usurp Samuel's seat in the synagogue, his leadership in communal matters, or his status as chief breadwinner—but of the interaction of her personality and his. And the nature of that interaction was that Renée Reichmann prevailed by subtle methods. "She never gave Shimi the impression that she knew more than he did about something," Rufka said.

One day Mrs. Reichmann invited her mother to Vienna, took her to a local furrier for a fitting, and bought her a mink coat. When the coat had been tailored to fit, Renée paid for it out of her poultry earnings and brought it home. When her husband came home, she put on the coat. "She looked like a freak," Klein said. "Her mother was quite a bit shorter and slimmer. So she said, 'Will you look at this. They spoiled my coat. Can I wear this thing?' Shimi said, 'Of course not.' 'Well, what should I do with it then?' she said. 'Why don't you give it to your mother?' Of course, that's what Renée wanted from the beginning but she didn't want to tell him. She was too proud to say to her husband, 'I want my mother to have a fur coat but she can't afford it, so I'll buy it for her.' She just wouldn't do that. So she played a role."

It is entirely possible that Samuel realized that this mishap in mink was no accident and played along to please Renée. By all accounts, he admired his wife no less than did their friends and endured her innate superiority with good humor. When the Communists seized power in Hungary after World War II, Samuel, a confirmed anti-Communist, quipped amid the safety of Tangier: "You know Communism might not be such a bad thing. That way, I could have my say, too."

All in all, Samuel was a man easily underestimated. He may not have been his wife's equal in terms of charisma or drive, but he would prove no less indomitable throughout the family's long exile. Reichmann's gentle manner was genuine, but it amounted to a covering of velvet draped over a core of steel. Schooled in the rock-ribbed certitudes of old-fashioned Orthodoxy and rural poverty, Samuel had supported not only himself but also his parents ever since he was fifteen or sixteen. Before he turned twenty, he had set up a new business of his own, making a success of himself under arduous and occasionally dangerous conditions. In traveling widely throughout Germany and Austria in the 1920s and 1930s, Reichmann continually braved the rising tide of Nazi anti-Semitism. In photographs taken in Paris and Tangier during the war for various official documents, Samuel would show the world a face that his grandchildren would never see. In none of these photos does Reichmann show a hint of deference or shyness as he stares into the camera with laser-beam intensity, his chiseled features hardened into an expression just short of a scowl.

———

Edward, the oldest and most rambunctious of the Reichmann brothers, was the only one given his own room in the Hafnergasse apartment. Eight at the time, Edward went to a signmaker and ordered a little copper nameplate, which, with laborious effort, he proudly mounted on the door to his room. The door had a large keyhole, which Edward enlarged to make it easier to spy on his parents and their guests in the adjoining sitting room. Every now and then, an important-looking rabbi came with an empty briefcase, which his father stuffed full of money. Other times, the same rabbi drew bundles of cash from the case and handed them to Samuel. One such visitor was the Kopitshnitzer Rebbe, who was among the most prominent of the many Hasidic rabbis who settled in Vienna between the world wars. In keeping with ancient Jewish practice, rabbis and other communal leaders borrowed large sums from benefactors such as the Reichmanns and made interest-free loans to the poor, according to the long-standing Jewish custom of free-loan societies.

In Judaism, charity fundamentally is not an expression of noblesse oblige or even of simple human kindness but is considered an aspect of justice and a mitzvah of high priority. "The world stands on three things," says the Mishna. "On Torah, on Worship, and on Charity." The Torah specifies that the wealthy should give 10 percent of their income to the needy. Tithing is a kind of tzedoka, or charity from the pocket. Hesed, on the other hand, is the

Hebrew phrase for nonfinancial giving. In matters of tzedoka, Samuel and Renée considered the 10 percent requirement a floor, not a ceiling. But it was as practitioners of hesed that the Reichmanns—especially Renée—distinguished themselves in the 1930s, establishing a reputation that reached beyond Vienna and the Oberland to encompass the Hasidic strongholds of Hungary and Poland.

By Orthodox standards, the Reichmanns were unusually ecumenical in their philanthropy. Despite cooperating to fight Zionism, the Hasidic and Mitnadic wings of European Orthodoxy remained sharply divided over matters of custom and belief and, in the realm of philanthropy, hardly overlapped at all. In Vienna, the great majority of Hasidic immigrants continued to adhere tightly to their Rebbe and had tangential contact at most with the Schiffschul crowd, which as a rule was content to take care of its own first and last. The Reichmanns took a broader view: need was need, whether it came with or without payos and a caftan.

Mrs. Reichmann's most elaborate hesed evolved from the simple act of putting up out-of-town visitors in the apartment on Hafnergasse. "Rarely did I sleep in my own room," recalled Edward, who usually made do on the floor in a corner of the living room. "From the first day, we always had guests—family or complete strangers. And it was always my room that was first to go." As it happened, many of the Reichmanns' guests were major Hasidic rabbis who came to Vienna from throughout central Europe to avail themselves of the city's high-quality medical care. Often, Mrs. Reichmann pulled Edward from school to assist the ailing visitors. "I did errands for them and accompanied them every morning to synagogue," Edward said. "This was not evidence of mother's indifference to school but her belief in 'leshamesh Talmidei hachamin'—that me serving the Rebbes was a higher calling."

Mrs. Reichmann dedicated herself to helping her guests, many of whom could not speak German, gain access to the best medical care. Quite a number of eminent physicians belonged to the Schiffschul and Mrs. Reichmann persuaded a number of them to offer cut-rate or even free care to the indigent followers of their rabbi patients. In effect, she created her own private system of socialized medicine, printing up vouchers that needy patients could redeem with participating doctors. By the mid-1930s, health care administration was a daily occupation for Mrs. Reichmann, who had to rely increasingly on her oldest children to keep the poultry shop running. Although no records of Mrs. Reichmann's program survived, Edward believes the beneficiaries numbered in the hundreds. By the late 1930s, rabbis throughout Hungary and Poland were telling ailing congregants bound for Vienna to look up Mrs. Reichmann.

Often the distraught relatives of someone who had just died in surgery would appear in the middle of the night at the Reichmanns' apartment, pleading for help to stop an impending autopsy. In strict Orthodox interpretation, the Torah prohibited the dismemberment of a corpse for any reason. This requirement long has created conflict between religious Jews and the medical profession. These days, the main point of contention is the organ transplant, but in the 1930s it was the autopsy, which was still regarded as an indispensable technique of scientific advancement. In fact, in Vienna, a hub of academic and research medicine, an autopsy was de rigueur unless the attending physician signed an affidavit stating that it would serve no scientific purpose. In the case of a beloved rebbe, most physicians realized that to insist on an autopsy was to risk a riot. As an advocate of regular Orthodox folk, though, Mrs. Reichmann often found herself embroiled in postmortem debate.

"Very few people could help in such a case but Mother often did succeed," recalled Edward, who often accompanied his mother on her medical rounds. "In the beginning, it was not due to her connections. She simply would get up, get dressed and go to the doctor at any time of day or night and begin to cry until the doctor finally gave in just to get rid of her. She would not leave until he gave her a note to the hospital authorizing release of the body. Eventually, the doctors came to respect her stubbornness on this issue and would cooperate with her requests without a scene."

Of course, Mrs. Reichmann was not the only ba'alles hesed of Viennese health care. In her work, she met and befriended a similarly inclined Hasidic couple named Simcha and Yachetta Klein. The Kleins, who moved to Vienna from Cracow in 1918, were followers of the Czortkover Rebbe and attended a little Polish shul near their home in the Twentieth Bezirk, which was a good thirty-five- or forty-minute walk from the Reichmanns' Leopoldstadt neighborhood. After he moved to Vienna, Simcha founded a candy wholesaling business, which thrived, especially after Stephen, the oldest of five sons, took charge in 1933.

Isaac, the youngest Klein brother, was a class ahead of Edward at the Talmud Torah on Malzgasse. Martin Klein attended yeshiva in Beled and ate many a Shabbat meal at the home of David Reichmann. The bond between the Reichmanns and the Kleins was cemented by Martin's marriage to Rufka Fischof in 1935. They made an odd couple in some ways, though the difference in their religious background—he was Hasidic, she was not—did not seem as pertinent as the difference in their height. At five feet, eight inches, Rukfa towered over Martin, who was five-two. The Reichmanns offered to throw the engagement party at their apartment because it was bigger than the Kleins' place. Custom dictated that the ceremony be held in Bratislava, but because Simcha and Yachetta Klein did not have passports the wedding was moved to the Austrian border town of Kitsee, one of the famous Seven Communities. The entire Reichmann family down to two-year-old Ralph were in attendance, as were Gestetners too numerous to mention.

The newlyweds moved into an apartment in Leopoldstadt not far from the Reichmanns. "I saw Renée and Olga almost every day," Mrs. Klein recalled. "Oh, it was such a lovely time. Vienna was so beautiful. I had friends who moved there and we got together every day for coffee. It was very nice. But it didn't last too long. After three years, Hitler came."

Chapter 4

Nazi Germany's annexation of Austria in 1938—the "Anschluss"—was the culmination of a decade of mounting Nazi agitation in both countries. The Brownshirts of the Austrian National Socialist Party rose to power roughly in tandem with the German Nazis and by the same brute methods. Although Nazi anti-Semitism did not begin intruding into the Reichmanns' personal realm until the mid-1930s, Nazi violence formed an increasingly unnerving counterpoint to what was generally a happy and productive decade for the family.

With its large Jewish population, Leopoldstadt was a natural stomping ground for provocateurs of the radical right. By the time the Reichmanns moved to Vienna, anti-Semites armed with canes occasionally patrolled the bridges over the Donau Kanal, and small groups of Nazi rabble-rousers staged periodic commando-style attacks on prayerhouses and cafés. The Café Produktenborse, a popular Kaffeehaus derided as "Judencafé" by rightists, was completely demolished in such a raid in 1929, not long after the Reichmanns arrived in Vienna. The violence escalated in lockstep with rising unemployment as Jews were blamed for Austria's economic crisis. In July 1932, Nazis marched through the streets of Vienna shouting "Judah perish!" and vandalized synagogues and Jewish-owned businesses. By the spring of 1933, so many Jewish shops had been bombed that Gentile businessmen began to display swastikas in their windows to ward off attack.

Viennese Jewry found a protector in Chancellor Engelbert Dollfuss, who outlawed the Nazi Party in mid-1933 after a particularly vicious murder of a Viennese jeweler. A year later, Dollfuss himself was assassinated by right-wing extremists encouraged by German intelligence. Under his successor, Kurt von Schuschnigg, the government enacted a series of laws that squeezed

Jews out of Austrian cultural life but neither impeded Jewish commerce nor mandated emigration. The Brownshirts derided von Schuschnigg's policies as "anti-Semitism on rubber-soled shoes" and continued to try to accomplish through terror what the government would not do by statute. "In our circles there is already a great deal of trepidation," Sigmund Freud wrote to a friend in 1934. "People feel that the national extravaganzas in Germany may spread to our little country. I have even been advised to flee already to Switzerland or France."

In a Freudian sense, Vienna Jewry was being held hostage to its own repressed fears. Few Jews—Freud included—could tear themselves away from their beloved Vienna while the going was good. "The Austrian Jews with all the signs of coming catastrophe around them behaved like ostriches," observed a Jewish historian who was himself a prewar resident of Vienna. Many assimilated Jews in Austria and Hungary deceived themselves into believing the increasingly strident bell of Nazi anti-Semitism tolled not for them but for the unredeemably Jewish, for the Ostjuden. Meanwhile, many devout Jews fashioned their piety into a set of blinders and went about their business as if Hitler had never drawn breath. In general, the Orthodox in Vienna "tended to be oblivious of what was going on around them, and their newspaper, *Judische Presse*, only barely noticed the rise of National Socialism."

Samuel Reichmann was an emphatic exception to the rule. He studied Hitler with the same intensity that his father studied Torah, even reading *Mein Kampf.* On his business trips to Berlin, Munich, Leipzig, and other German capitals during the 1920s and 1930s, Samuel had witnessed firsthand the steady deterioration of Jewish life in Germany wrought by Nazism in its rise to power. Indeed, Reichmann happened to have been in Munich in 1923 during the famous beer-hall putsch that marked the start of Hitler's political career. Although most strictly observant men of Reichmann's generation avoided the secular news media as agents of spiritual contamination, Samuel's instinct for self-preservation overwhelmed his Orthodox scruples. He made a habit of stopping in a coffeehouse after his regular morning visit to the prayerhouse to look over the Viennese dailies as well as newspapers from Germany, and he bought a state-of-the-art radio set capable of pulling in news broadcasts from all over Europe. In the evenings after work, he would tune in various German stations, but he listened mainly to foreign-language broadcasts of the British Broadcasting Corporation (BBC) out of London. When Rabbi Levi Grunwald, who was a frequent houseguest of the Reichmanns, first saw the big box radio he gazed upon it with amazement but said nothing. Soon, Rabbi Grunwald's curiosity got the better of his Orthodoxy. "Shmayahu," he would ask, as soon as he set foot in the Reichmann apartment, "what is the latest news?"

After Germany occupied the Rhineland in 1936, Reichmann graduated from a "pessimist" to a "superpessimist," according to his son Edward. Convinced not only that Hitler would continue to rely on military force to realize his dream of a Greater Reich but that Britain and France would prevaricate in opposing him, Reichmann began preaching catastrophe to his friends and relatives. Samuel believed in the coming of the Messiah as ardently as any Jew but did not presume that He would arrive in time to deliver him and his family from the evil of Nazism. That was his job. "My father was absolutely determined never to live under German occupation," Louis recalled. "So he was always one step ahead."

The annexation of the Rhineland prompted Reichmann to travel to Zurich and open an account in the bank of Julius Beer. Over the next few years, he would make frequent trips to Zurich in arranging the transfer of the largest portion of his wealth out of Vienna into secret, numbered Swiss bank accounts. Although Reichmann developed a close relationship with Beer and trusted him, just to be on the safe side he opened a second account in Zurich with Banque Wohl et Landau and a third account with the Swiss Bank Corporation, whose London office had helped finance Reichmann Brothers' export trade between Poland and England.

The Reichmann firm gradually pulled back from the German market as the Hitler regime throttled imports of most agricultural commodities, eggs included. In National Socialist ideology, farms and farming tradition were bulwarks of Germanic racial superiority; this view was put forth in *The Yeomanry as the Life Source of the Nordic Race*, the major work of Hitler's chief agricultural policy maker, Walther Darre. In curbing food imports, Hitler's goals were twofold: to protect the noble German farmer from foreign competition, and to make Germany self-sufficient in food production. Nazi-created Reichsstellen, or state import boards, not only exerted complete control over the volume and prices of imports, but they decided which foreign suppliers would be granted access to German markets. Needless to say, the Nazification of German agricultural trade put Jewish exporters at a competitive disadvantage.

In Vienna, too, anti-Semitism was souring commerce. One afternoon Edward Reichmann accompanied his father in calling on Shmidel & Company, the largest commodity dealer in Vienna, which was quartered in a handsome six-story building. After the business at hand had been transacted, Mr. Shmidel asked Reichmann how many sons he had. "Five," he replied. "Perfect," Shmidel said. "I see already that you will sit here in my office on the sixth floor and each of your sons will be running another floor." Edward left the office bursting with pride but was brought back to earth with a thud when his father explained that his customer was a Jew-hater who spoke out of fear, not admiration. Samuel's beard—a virtual badge of Jewishness in prewar Europe—was becoming a handicap in dealing with government officials. When Reichmann Brothers was required to apply for an export license or make tax payments, increasingly Samuel sent Renée in his stead.

Conditions were no more congenial on the supply side of Samuel's business. The hardships wrought in Hungary by the depression in agriculture had boosted the popularity of the radical right in Budapest and many localities. In 1932, Admiral Miklós Horthy, the Magyar aristocrat who was Hungary's chief of state, ceded significant power to Gyula Gömbös, a radical leader whose brand of ultranationalism came liberally seasoned with hatred of Jews. (Gömbös had been an early admirer of Hitler's.) Although Horthy forced Gömbös into dropping plans for anti-Semitic legislation, the Hungarian government lurched to the right in the mid-1930s in what amounted to an experiment in homegrown fascism.

Like Germany, Hungary increasingly asserted central government control of agriculture in a calculated attempt to put Jewish merchants out of business. In Hungary, the chief instrument of this campaign was the agency known as Hangya, which aspired to nothing short of establishing a government-administered monopoly in fresh produce throughout the country. From the outset, Hangya laid special emphasis on putting the egg trade on what its leaders termed "a national and Christian foundation." Hangya built a nationwide chain of hundreds of warehouses and stores and relied increasingly on anti-Semitic propaganda to attract customers.

The Reichmanns found the playing fields of commerce increasingly tilted to their disadvantage, especially at the borders, where Hungarian customs officials frequently would stamp "Quality B" on a shipment of top-quality eggs bound from Beled for Vienna. Samuel went to Budapest and filed a complaint with the Department of Trade and Commerce but came away with nothing more than a letter entitling him to request arbitration the next time he disputed the verdict of a government quality inspector.

By the late 1930s, Hangya's failure to rid the egg trade of Jews had brought it under heavy political attack from the radical right, which called for sterner measures against the Samuel Reichmanns of the world. This, in addition to the brazenly anti-Semitic propaganda pumped out by fascist and other ultranationalist groups in Hungary, made Beled a less tolerant place. In 1936 or 1937, Samuel took the precaution of moving his parents out of the house he had built for them into the big house, which was more secure. In Vienna, meanwhile, Eva and her brothers were not too young to feel the chill. "It was not unusual to hear on the streets or in the parks the expression 'zau Jude'—'dirty Jew,' " Louis recalled. During his annual year-end exams at the Schwarzinger Schule, Edward struggled to maintain his concentration as Gentile boys pulled his payos and whispered insults. Once Edward and a friend were rowing in a lake in the Prater when they were rammed by four boys in another boat. "We defended ourselves as best we could," Edward said. "Later, one of them came to me and apologized. He asked for my address and we corresponded for a while. But not for long."

———

In early 1938, Samuel and Renée Reichmann began planning for what loomed as a major milestone in the family's history: Edward's bar mitzvah. Edward not only was the first-born of five brothers but the eldest grandchild of his branch of the Gestetner family. His proud parents invited hundreds of their friends and relatives to the ceremony, which was to be held on March 12 at the Schiffschul and followed by a reception in one of Vienna's grandest hotels. About two weeks before the bar mitzvah, David Reichmann, now seventy-five, was felled by a stroke from which he would never fully recover. Samuel decided to relocate the ceremony to Beled to accommodate his ailing father. Edward was dispatched at once to Hungary to begin working with the local rabbi to adapt the ceremony to the humbler yet no less exacting requirements of the village setting.

The Reichmanns were expecting a very special guest: Rabbi Jacob Grunwald, the Pápa Rebbe. Although Rabbi Grunwald was a cousin of Mrs. Reichmann's, he had bestowed a great honor upon the family in accepting the bar mitzvah invitation that Edward himself had precociously extended. On his frequent visits to Vienna for medical care, the Pápa Rebbe usually stayed with the Reichmanns. One morning in 1937, Edward had accompanied Rabbi Grunwald to the Schiffschul for morning prayers. On the way back to the apartment on Hafnergasse, the rabbi stopped to buy candy for Louis, Albert, Paul, and Ralph. "You already are a big boy," the Pápa Rebbe said to Edward. "What do you want instead?"

"Only that the rebbe should come to my bar mitzvah next year," Edward replied.

Rabbi Grunwald gave his assent, delighting Mr. and Mrs. Reichmann, who would not have presumed to invite so eminent a rabbi, relative or no. Although Beled was not far from Pápa, he had never set foot in the village. His visit was eagerly anticipated in Beled even among those community members who were not invited to the bar mitzvah.

Mrs. Reichmann left Vienna for Beled a week before the ceremony, accompanied by Eva, who was now fifteen years old. On Friday, March 11, the day before the bar mitzvah, Samuel arrived in Beled, with Louis, who was nearly eleven, in tow. Albert, nine, Paul, seven, and Ralph, four, remained behind in Vienna with Aunt Dadi and Trudy, their au pair.

That evening, on orders from Berlin, thousands of brown-shirted Nazis and their sympathizers poured into the streets of Vienna, chanting "One people, one Reich, one Führer!" and "Judah perish!" The mob rampaged through the city's Jewish neighborhoods, vandalizing stores and pulling Jews from taxicabs in their eagerness to assault them. Radio news reports from Vienna triggered sympathetic violence throughout Austria and western Hungary. In Beled, a roving gang of youths disturbed the Shabbat hush by hurling fusillades of stones and anti-Semitic epithets at Jewish houses.

Behind the stoutly shuttered windows of the family home on Beled's main street, the Reichmanns continued with their preparations, ignoring the racket outside as best they could. Finally, Mrs. Reichmann took the bar mitzvah boy aside and explained that the Pápa Rebbe would not be able to attend after all because travel had become too dangerous. Edward complained with such vehemence that his mother grabbed him by the hand and marched him next door to use the telephone in Simon's house. Maintaining her grip on Edward with one hand, she cradled the receiver against her shoulder and curled the bell with her free hand, asking the operator to put her through to Pápa. Mrs. Reichmann explained the situation to Rabbi Grunwald, who replied that only Edward could release him from his promise to attend. Renée handed Edward the receiver while keeping hold of his left hand, which she squeezed until he fairly shouted, "Ich bin moichel"—"I forgive you."

At daybreak, the German Eighth Army crossed unopposed into Austria. About 10:00 A.M. some two hundred of the Reichmanns' friends and relatives gathered at the little synagogue in Beled and watched as Edward donned his tefillin—his phylacteries—and delivered his droshe in a clear, strong voice. He gave what would have qualified as a manfully defiant performance had he given the larger events of the day so much as a second thought. But "to me, the big thing was that the Rebbe didn't come from Pápa," the eldest Reichmann brother would recall more than fifty years later. "That seemed a lot more important than the Germans taking Vienna."

While the Reichmanns and their guests were at sueda, the bar mitzvah reception that follows the reading of the Torah, Adolf Hitler returned to the Austrian city of Linz, his hometown, savoring what he later called the proudest hour of his life. On Saturday evening, the chancellor of Austria traveled to Linz and presented Hitler with a copy of a law enacted that afternoon in a special cabinet meeting. Article 1 was succinct: "Austria is a province of the German Reich." Less than twenty-four hours after the first Nazi troops crossed the border, Germany had annexed Austria, realizing a goal that Hitler had set forth as early as 1924 on page 1 of *Mein Kampf.*

Back in Vienna, meanwhile, a pogrom raged. "The underworld had opened its gates and let loose its lowest, most revolting, most impure spirits. The city was transformed into a nightmare painting by Hieronymus Bosch, the air filled with an incessant savage, hysterical screeching from male and female throats . . . in wild, hate-filled triumph," observed the German playwright Carl Zuckmayer, an eyewitness. Crowds gathered in the Leopoldstadt to jeer as even the most infirm and elderly Jews were forced to use their bare hands or toothbrushes to rub off anti-Nazi graffiti from sidewalks and buildings. Special delight was taken in tormenting the Orthodox, as men were shorn of their beards and payos—with swords if scissors were lacking. On the Taborstrasse, Leopoldstadt's main street, Orthodox women were forced to remove their wigs and dance around them as they burned.

While Austrian Brownshirts roamed Vienna inflicting their improvised harassments, the large SS "Death's Head" force that had followed the German Army into Austria began planning the systematic persecution of the country's 300,000 Jews. On Saturday evening, just as the Sabbath was ending, the Gestapo began rounding up Vienna's most prominent Jews.

On Sunday morning, Samuel dialed his own phone number in Vienna. Trudy answered. "Was ist neues?—What's new?" he asked her.

"Oh, nothing," she replied. "Only some men from the Gestapo were here."

Trudy was not being droll. Young and Gentile, she did not perceive the menace in a knock on the door and a simple inquiry as to her employer's whereabouts.

Samuel Reichmann would never again set foot in Vienna and was loath even to remain in Hungary for long. Reichmann was more convinced than ever that a horrible, apocalyptic war was coming and that his homeland would line up on the wrong side. All through the 1930s, Nazi Germany had maneuvered Hungary into its diplomatic and economic orbit. Faced now with an unbroken phalanx of fascism—Germany, Austria, Italy—that extended straight through the heart of Europe from the Baltic to the Mediterranean, Hungary had no alternative but to ally itself with Hitler, Reichmann believed. Why wait until the alliance was sealed in blood? The time to leave was now.

Both the acuity of Samuel Reichmann's pessimism and his decisiveness in acting on it put him in select company. Even after the Anschluss, the great majority of Jews in Austria and Hungary—Renée Reichmann included—continued to dismiss Nazi Germany as a manageable, passing threat to the established order. Although Mrs. Reichmann shared her husband's aversion to returning to Vienna, she argued in favor of remaining in Hungary. "My mother was not that keen to run away from Hungary," Louis recalled. "Her family was there and a lot was said about our schooling being interrupted." It was a brief debate, this being one instance in which Samuel put his patriarch's foot down hard. "My father was adamant," Louis added. "You could not talk to him about it."

On Monday, March 14, the day after his conversation with his uncomprehending au pair, Reichmann hired a car and crossed into Czechoslovakia. In Bratislava, he caught a train to Prague and from there flew to London in search of refuge for himself and his family. And so Edward's bar mitzvah marked not only his symbolic entry into manhood but the beginning of the Reichmann family's long years of exile.

Embellished in the retelling at countless Reichmann bar mitzvahs and wedding receptions over the years, the story of Edward's bar mitzvah—like the tale of how Samuel got his start in business—would become one of the girders of family identity. Not until 1990 would Edward finally set down his own account on paper in a long commemorative letter that he wrote after his mother died and sent to her ninety-nine grandchildren and great-grandchildren. In his written version, Edward ended with a flash forward to Montreal, 1962, and the bar mitzvah of his son, Joseph, the eldest of Samuel and Renée's grandchildren. Many distinguished guests had gathered from all over the world, but the most honored was Rabbi Josef Grunwald, who was the only surviving son of the late Rabbi Jacob Grunwald and, like his father, was known as the Pápa Rebbe. At the sueda, the Pápa Rebbe took Edward by the hand. "Ich bezohl mein tates," he said. "I pay you the debt of my father."

In appending this postscript, Edward tilted the emphasis of the tale toward the theme of respect—respect for tradition, the respect shown the Reichmann family by a preeminent rabbinical dynasty, the respect shown Edward by his mother, who took him aside and congratulated him: "This is all due to you." Edward could just as logically have concluded with the founding of Olympia & York, for the bar mitzvah in Beled was only superficially about bar mitzvahs and rebbes named Grunwald. Its real subject was the Reichmanns' sense of themselves as a family of exalted destiny—as the chosen of the Chosen.

If David Reichmann had not suffered his stroke when he did and if Samuel Reichmann had not placed such priority on his father's attendance at Edward's bar mitzvah, the Gestapo would have arrested Samuel on the evening of March 12, 1938. Had he been imprisoned, he likely would have emerged alive from the local SS jail, Rossauer Lande, or even from the concentration camp at Dachau, where many rich Viennese Jews were sent. Even so, to be spared the ordeal of Nazi imprisonment through the instrument of religious ceremony was a deliverance from evil that, from an Orthodox perspective, was literally a miracle, an act of God. To the devout Orthodox Jew, "luck" is a meaningless concept. One of Orthodoxy's fundamental tenets is that God is a constant, active presence in worldly affairs. "He did not merely create it and then leave it to run itself by rules of Nature which He had previously ordained. Nor does He let it turn itself while intervening supernaturally from time to time. He is constantly and directly involved—both in the affairs of Man and in the operation of nature."

———

While Samuel was in London, Renée returned to Vienna to fetch her three young sons and salvage what she could of the family's Austrian assets. Like many of Vienna's 33,000 Jewish-owned businesses, the Reichmanns' egg warehouse and poultry shop would be looted by freelance fascist goons before the Germans got around to officially "Aryanizing" it. Armed with her Hungarian passport, Mrs. Reichmann was able to spirit the family's household goods— the silver, the Persian carpets, and assorted other "honey"—out of the Hafnergasse apartment to Beled, where most of the belongings were locked away in a Reichmann Brothers warehouse, only to eventually be expropriated by the Hungarian government, along with the warehouse itself.

Mrs. Reichmann did what she could to comfort Rufka Klein, whose husband, Martin, and his brother Saul had been arrested by the Gestapo and locked up in Rossauer Lande. Mrs. Klein sought out a Viennese lawyer with close connections to the Gestapo. "He was a Jew-hater that lawyer," she recalled. "But I was desperate to find my husband." Through the lawyer, a bribe of $5,000 eventually was passed to an SS officer and both Martin and Saul Klein were freed. Rukfa and her husband immediately fled to Bratislava, traveling on her Czech passport, but Saul was stuck in Vienna. "He had no passport," Mrs. Klein recalled. "I used to tell Saul, 'You're a schmo. A young man should have a passport.' He was just too lazy to bother." To the rescue came Henrik Gestetner, Rufka's brother-in-law. Like his father and two of his brothers, Henrik was an engraver by trade. He risked a long prison term by forging a Czech passport for Saul Klein, who used it to escape to Belgium. "As far as I know, [Henrik] never did this for anyone else," Mrs. Klein said. "But for your own, you'll do anything."

Meanwhile, Renée flew off to London to join her husband in what proved a futile effort to gain English sanctuary. Ever since Hitler became chancellor in 1933, the nations of western Europe had—reluctantly—absorbed a steadily increasing outflow of Germans. Britain opened its gates a crack to Jews only after a group of distinguished English Jews headed by Otto Schiff, an investment banker of German origin, pledged that the Jewish community would bear the expense of supporting German refugees admitted to England until permanent homes could be found elsewhere. Schiff, who was not religious, "developed 'a close working relationship' with the Aliens Department of the Home Office, so that, in practical terms, German Jews were allowed into Britain on his authority."

The strict terms of the guarantee were used by Schiff and his government sponsors to limit not merely the number of Jewish refugees but also the type. The underlying principle of British policy toward Jewish refugees throughout the 1930s was that Jews by their presence and behavior created anti-Semitism. Thus, the most undesirable immigrants were the Orthodox—the most obviously Jewish—and middle-class Jews, who were more likely than their "betters" to insinuate themselves into British economic life by starting businesses or seeking employment. Moreover, the Schiff guarantee covered only Jews of German or Austrian nationality. Hungarian Jews of whatever type or class were, virtually by definition, also classed as undesirables.

This bias was succinctly expressed by the British passport control officer in Budapest in a memorandum he sent to his superior in London about six weeks after the Anschluss:

> I have refused to grant visas unless applicants can show they've been in the habit of visiting the U.K. or are required to do so on several occasions in the immediate future. In my experience, the type of Jew found in Central Europe, no matter what his status or position, is notoriously untruthful. . . . Every kind of pretext and artifice is employed by applicants to attain their ends.

As a frequent business traveler to London, Samuel Reichmann already had a visitor's visa stamped into his passport and was spared the ordeal of visiting the British Embassy amid the post-Anschluss crush. Mrs. Reichmann, too, already had a British visa, for she quite enjoyed traveling and occasionally would accompany her husband on his trips.

When in London, Renée often called on her mogul cousin, David Gestetner, who turned eighty-four in 1938. Although Gestetner never really retired, his only son, Sigmund, had succeeded him as managing director in 1922, despite having been severely gassed as an infantryman in World War I. In 1929, just before the great American stock market crash, D. Gestetner Limited became a public company, with a capital of £675,000. The great majority of shares remained in Gestetner hands, putting the family in the top rank of Britain's capitalist elite. The Reichmanns were much closer to the elder Gestetner, who remained strictly observant his entire life, than to Sigmund, who was "traditional but not religious," according to the eldest of his two sons, David. "My mother mainly visited David," Edward Reichmann said. "She wouldn't let herself be invited to Sigmund's house because she couldn't eat his food."

David Gestetner, or DG as he was known, maintained an ambivalent relationship with his extended family. Although he never returned to the Oberland after he struck it rich, he did send a steady supply of cash to scores of his less fortunate relatives in Hungary. "There was an endless flow of correspondence into Tottenham [site of Gestetner's corporate offices and main manufacturing plant], counter-balanced by a flow of cash in the opposite direction," observed Charles David, Gestetner's personal secretary. The Reichmanns' self-sufficiency no doubt elevated them in DG's estimation. When Gestetner made a trip to Vienna in the mid-1930s, he did the Reichmanns the honor of calling at the Hafnergasse apartment and accompanying the family to the Schiffschul. The elder Reichmann children were excited by the visit of this forbidding-looking patriarch, who figured so prominently in their mother's telling of Gestetner family history.

In a 1983 interview, Eva Reichmann said that in 1938 her parents "wanted to get a certificate for Palestine" and that her mother "went to see the David

Gestetner who was a big Zionist and gave a lot of money to Israel to try to help us to get it. He tried but he didn't achieve it."

Eva not only confused David, who was not a Zionist, with Sigmund, an ardent Zionist, but she seems to have forgotten that the state of Israel was not created until 1948; Palestine was still under the rule of Britain, which had imposed tight controls on Jewish immigration. It is also unlikely that good ultra-Orthodox Jews like the Reichmanns would have wanted to join the Zionist colony in Palestine except as a last resort—and in 1938 they were hardly desperate. If they had coveted Palestine certificates, there was no better string to pull than Sigmund Gestetner, who was a friend and benefactor of Chaim Weizmann, the great British Zionist. "My father got lots of relatives into Palestine in the prewar period," said his son, David. "He didn't succeed with every one. But if he tried on behalf of the Reichmanns, I'm sure he would have succeeded."

In any event, Mr. and Mrs. Reichmann left England empty-handed and flew on to Paris. After a few days spent scouting arrondissement IX, home to one of the French capital's few established ultra-Orthodox communities, the Reichmanns returned to Beled and prepared to move to Paris.

From the end of World War I though the early 1930s, France had the most liberal immigration policies of any major European nation. Between the world wars, France admitted a total of 120,000 Jews, of whom 70,000 settled in Paris. However, in France, as everywhere during the Great Depression, resentment of Jewish refugees mounted in tandem with unemployment. In addition, a sizable segment of the French population blamed immigrant Jews for the growing threat of war with Germany, arguing that Hitler's belligerence was not a function of imperial ambition but of hatred of the Jews. While the French government was not so naive to think that war could be averted by bowing to right-wing demands to expel Jewish refugees, it did begin restricting new immigration in 1934.

In 1936, a native French Jew, Léon Blum, was named prime minister of France. Defying the gathering forces of backlash, Blum's Popular Front government lavished large sums on refugee welfare and restored the open-door policy of the past. Within a few months, Blum was ousted from power, but on March 13, 1938—the day after the Anschluss—he capped a valiant comeback with a month-long return as prime minister. The second Popular Front government rescinded curbs on immigration enacted by its predecessor. During the waning days of the Blum restoration, Samuel Reichmann visited the French Embassy in Budapest and applied for a visa to France. The visa was issued on April 11, three days after Blum was again ousted but before his liberal visa policy could again be rescinded by his successor, Édouard Daladier.

The Daladier government was bent mainly on excluding poor Jews. Given the Reichmanns' Swiss bank account balance, they likely would have been admitted to France no matter whose policies were in force at the time. At a minimum, Samuel's exquisite timing smoothed matters and perhaps spared him a protracted bureaucratic ordeal.

Samuel and Renée decided it was best to leave their children in Hungary, at least until they got settled in Paris. They deposited Eva and Ralph with one of Renée's sisters in Győr. Louis, Albert, and Paul moved into the big house in Beled and were put under the care of Uncle Simon and his wife. The day after Passover in 1938, Samuel hired a car and drove Edward south to Pápa to begin his yeshiva training under Rabbi Grunwald. Samuel rented a small apartment near the yeshiva and paid in advance at a nearby restaurant for a whole academic season of lunches and suppers. Edward was grateful but ate at the yeshiva with the other boys just the same, not wishing to be thought a snob. By the time that Edward would next see his father, Europe would be at war.

Chapter 5

In Paris, as in Vienna, the Reichmanns' lives revolved around a synagogue, though there was no Parisian equivalent of the Schiffschul. The "Pletzl," the teeming Jewish immigrant quarter in the Marais, did contain a number of Hungarian shuls, but these were both too Hasidic and too homespun for Samuel's and Renée's liking. Among the native Jewish population of Paris, there were no more than five hundred Orthodox families, organized into two congregations. The Reichmanns joined the larger and less affluent of them, the Adas Yereim, which was led by Rabbi Elie Munk.

In his approach to theology as in his genealogy, Rabbi Munk was a seamless composite of French and German rabbinical traditions. A descendant of an eminent rabbinical dynasty that originated in Berlin, Munk himself was born and raised in Paris. In the early 1920s, he moved to Berlin to attend rabbinical seminary and took his first postings in Germany. In 1936, Rabbi Munk returned to his native Paris as an esteemed scholar and Talmudic authority. By arrangement of the chief rabbi of France, all questions of halakah that arose in Paris were referred to Rabbi Munk, who, in all matters, was a staunch traditionalist. If Rabbi Munk was a Frenchman and proud of it, he "tended to be Germanic in outlook, in his studiousness and the rigor of his religious observance."

Rabbi Munk's magisterial presence was not reflected in his synagogue, a "charmless little edifice" tucked away in the interior courtyard of an apartment building in the centrally located arrondissement IX. The Reichmanns would live in three different hotels during their stay in Paris, but none was more than a few blocks from Rabbi Munk's synagogue on Rue Cadet. "The Reichmanns were very close to my father," said Lady Amelie Jakobovits, the youngest of Rabbi Munk's seven children, who was ten years old in 1938. "Whenever they needed help or advice, they came to see him."

The 250 families of Rabbi Munk's community were the residue of a much larger contingent of Orthodox immigrants from Alsace-Lorraine that settled in the central arrondissements of Paris after the Franco-Prussian War of 1870–71. The Alsatians put down roots in a city in which traditional Judaism was virtually extinct. France had been the first country to fully emancipate Jews, and in its compulsion to assimilate Parisian Jewry was fully the equal of Austria. Within a generation or two, a great majority of the Alsatian families had gone native, abandoning Orthodoxy and fanning out from arrondissements IX–XII into more affluent districts on the western fringe of Paris.

The Reichmanns took up residence in a solid working-class district that was distinctly but not predominantly Jewish. This part of arrondissement IX was best known as the home of the Folies Bergère, the risqué burlesque troupe. On the neighborhood's narrow streets, kosher charcuteries and pâtisseries incongruously adjoined cafés and bars catering to the cabaret demimonde. For a change of pace from the Rue Cadet synagogue, Samuel prayed at a storefront shul just a few doors down from the rear entrance to the Folies Bergère on Rue Saulnier. Although the neighborhood was not fancy, it was a world of comfort removed from the refugee squalor of the Pletzl, which lay a half mile and five Métro stops to the southeast. "For us," Edward Reichmann recalled, "the Pletzl was where you went to buy a salami."

Samuel and Renée Reichmann entered their long period of exile with one crucial advantage over the typical refugee, Orthodox or otherwise: cash. "Many poor people—strangers—would come up to my parents' suite and ask for food or money," Edward remembered. "My parents helped them to the extent they could." In Paris, money bought a measure of physical comfort, though the Reichmanns certainly did not lavish their savings on plush accommodations. (At the first small residence hotel in which they lived, they paid a modest 720 francs a month.) More important, money bought freedom. The Reichmanns were free to practice their exacting brand of Judaism because they could afford to live in close proximity to the synagogue of their choice and to buy kosher food, which cost considerably more than regular fare. They also were free to remain in France because they were able to meet the major criterion for converting a short-term visa into a foreign residence permit: financial self-sufficiency. Refugees who entered illegally or who worked surreptitiously could be thrown into jail and left there indefinitely—as were hundreds of Jews in 1938 and 1939. To the satisfaction of the architects of French immigration policy, a large majority of the Austrian Jews admitted after the Anschluss quickly passed through on their way elsewhere.

In filing for his foreign residence permit, Samuel listed two separate cash holdings of £400 and 300,000 French francs. On her application, Mrs. Reichmann revealed additional assets of £90 and $5,000 in accounts at two discreet private banks in Paris—Banque Perls and Banque Saul Amar—that Samuel had not mentioned in his own application. This suggests that Mrs. Reichmann had her own bank accounts, which certainly would have been in keeping with her character but unusual for an Orthodox wife. There is no way of knowing how much additional wealth the Reichmanns had squirreled away in Switzerland and England, but chances are that it was substantial. In any event, the assets they disclosed were sufficient to satisfy the French authorities. Samuel was able to finance his family's two-year stay without benefit of a single paycheck.

On his residence permit application, Samuel stated that as an exporter of eggs to England, he found living in Paris advantageous to his business. In reality, he could do nothing from Paris to assist Simon, who, with the help of his two sons, had managed to keep Reichmann Brothers afloat by replacing the trade lost in Vienna with new accounts in Budapest. With the Daladier government's clampdown on immigrants, Samuel saw no point in applying for a job or starting a business of his own. His typical weekday began with an early visit to the Rue Cadet synagogue, followed by breakfast at the hotel. At midmorning, he liked to stroll over to Les Halles, the market district, and roam the stalls and warehouses, watching the local produce men work. After lunch, Samuel studied the Torah. He bought many books in Paris, not just religious texts but current affairs volumes, and read all the German-language dailies, hoping to keep abreast of the latest political developments. As for Mrs. Reichmann, duplicating the medical program she had created in Vienna was out of the question. Indigent patients abounded, but Orthodox physicians were scarce and her French nonexistent (as was Samuel's). For the first time in their lives, Samuel and Renée really did not have much to do—except wait and worry as the war clouds gathered.

Things picked up a bit when Eva and Ralph arrived from Hungary. Eva had missed her parents terribly. "I stayed with an aunt," she recalled, "but I cried so much she couldn't take it any longer so she sent me to my grandparents"—her Gestetner grandparents in Győr. "The crying didn't stop. So my grandmother decided that the first person who is going to Paris, she would send me along. And she sent me and my youngest brother, for whom I was responsible." Initially, Eva was unable to attend school because she spoke no French. However, she proved such an eager and adept pupil that her parents sent her first to a private tutor and then to Berlitz school. Within six months, Eva spoke passable French and served both her father and mother as translator.

According to Edward, second thoughts nagged at his parents during their first months in Paris. As the street violence unleashed by the Anschluss ebbed and Jewish life in Vienna regained a semblance of normalcy, even Samuel could not help but wonder whether he had overreacted. Swift flight had ensured their safety—temporarily anyway—but at what price? They had split the family in two and exchanged a busy, productive regimen of work and philanthropy for a limbo of enforced idleness in a city where, as Jews and foreigners, they were doubly outcast. "Paris before the war was not an easy life," recalled Abraham Schreiber, a fellow Orthodox refugee from Vienna who lived near the Reichmanns in arrondissement IX and saw them often. "The French in general didn't like 'étrangers' and tended to treat us like second-class citizens."

The Reichmanns did find a measure of solace and protection within Rabbi Munk's extraordinarily tight-knit congregation, which, being Orthodox, was no stranger itself to the contempt of ordinary Parisians. "The Rue Cadet community was very French, absolutely French, but that didn't mean the Reichmanns and the others who came in weren't made to feel welcome," said Lady Jakobovits, who is married to the former chief rabbi of England. "It was a wonderful community, with a great warmth that I've not encountered anywhere else since."

For the most part, the Reichmanns associated with a dozen other Austro-Hungarian refugee families, many of whom they had known in Vienna or the Oberland. The Reichmanns and their friends usually gathered at a restaurant called Ringer's, which was on Rue Buffaut just around the corner from the Rue Cadet synagogue. As the biggest and most rigorously kosher restaurant in Paris—and the only one under the supervision of Rabbi Munk—Ringer's was a landmark that drew Jews from all over the city, as well as tourists. For the Reichmanns, Ringer's appeal was strongly personal. The restaurant was owned by Abraham Schreiber, who allowed Samuel to cite him as a personal reference in his application for a carte d'identité. "I didn't let many people use my name like that," Schreiber said, "but I knew that the families of Gestetner and Reichmann were very fine, honest people who gave a lot of charity."

Schreiber had been a diamond merchant in Vienna but had family connections in the restaurant trade. He had left Vienna in the late 1920s and moved to Antwerp, the diamond hub of Europe and the home of the original Ringer's; the restaurant in Paris was started by Mr. Ringer's son. After the diamond business crashed in 1931, Schreiber moved to Paris and bought the local Ringer's, which thrived under his management. Eventually Schreiber knocked out the restaurant's back wall, doubling its seating capacity to two hundred, and began a lucrative sideline as a kosher caterer to big transatlantic cruise ships such as the Ile de France and the Normandie. In Ringer's basement, Schreiber even built a small assembly line for tinning meat conserves—kosher, of course.

Ringer's Shabitat, or Sabbath meal, was especially popular, but the restaurant bustled all the time and was beloved by central European refugees and American tourists alike for its "haimesh" style: informal, intimate, and homey. With about a hundred others, the Reichmanns were regulars at Ringer's. "They came to my restaurant almost every day," Schreiber recalled. "All the

Hungarians used to sit together at a big table and talk for hours. I was busy so I didn't have a lot of time to sit and listen. But I do know that a lot of decisions were reached at Ringer's."

In July 1938, just three months into their Parisian exile, Mr. and Mrs. Reichmann returned to Győr for a few weeks to see their children and wrap up loose ends. (Under the terms of their visa, the Reichmanns were allowed an unlimited number of trips to and from Hungary.) Among other chores, Samuel and Renée went down to city hall and obtained a notarized copy of their marriage license, which they would submit to French authorities some months later in applying for their residence permits. Such forethought was typical of the Reichmanns, whose meticulous attention to documentation served them well at every stop on their refugee's road.

Meanwhile, Samuel belatedly complied with a Nazi edict requiring all Jewish residents to submit a list of assets to the newly established Allgemeines Verweltungsarchiv Vermögensverkchsstelle, or Property Transfer Office, in Vienna. Wisely, Reichmann did not risk returning to Austria, instead filing through his lawyer in Vienna. In valuing his business at 11,158 reichsmarks, he employed an artless method of valuation: he simply totaled his accounts payable. To a list of the twenty-six customers who owed him money, Samuel appended this comment (in German): "The outstanding claims are mostly not realizable, but were nevertheless listed in their full amount." In addition, Reichmann listed personal assets including $5,000 worth of Hungarian County Central Credit Cooperative bonds paying 5 percent interest and a life insurance policy worth 668 reichsmarks. His filing made no mention of the small fortune in furnishings left in the Hafnergasse apartment. All in all, Samuel offered surprisingly slim pickings for someone afforded the perverse distinction of inclusion on the infamous "rich list" the SS had brought with it into Vienna.

Why Samuel bothered to comply with this offensive edict at all is not clear. It is possible that he might have been protecting himself against the possibility of a German conquest of France, or that in his cautious way he was keeping alive the option of returning to Vienna one day. The likeliest explanation is that he was thumbing his nose at the Nazis. With Samuel and his capital safely beyond Nazi reach, his filing was only nominally an act of compliance. Indeed, his depleted asset register carried an implicit message of defiance: "Sorry, suckers, the money's gone."

Nor is it clear why Samuel left his Hungarian bonds behind in Austria. Perhaps they were worthless. Or perhaps he had actually removed them to safety, too, and was baiting the Nazi asset-strippers. In any event, they did indeed bite. A few weeks after Samuel had filed, the Property Transfer Office sent a notice to the old Hafnergasse address "requesting" that the bonds be submitted to the

Vienna branch of the Federal Bank of Germany within a week. Apparently, Samuel ignored the order, if indeed he ever received it; by this time he and his wife had returned to Paris. In early September, well after its deadline had passed, the Property Transfer Office belatedly informed the Federal Bank that Reichmann had "left for an indefinite time for Hungary . . . Heil Hitler!"

Not long after this letter was posted, leaders of France, Britain, and Italy gathered at Munich to negotiate with Hitler, who had dominated European diplomacy throughout the summer of 1938 by demanding that Sudetenland, a German-speaking region of Czechoslovakia, be ceded to Germany. As the so-called Munich Conference proceeded, immigrant and native French Jews alike flocked to synagogues in Paris. Rumors of war spread during Rosh Hashanah services, sending hundreds of panicky immigrants fleeing into the streets. On September 30, the European powers opted for appeasement at Munich: the Sudetenland would be incorporated into Greater Germany, stripping Czechoslovakia of its mountain defenses and virtually inviting further German aggression. Even so, the predominant reaction in Paris was relief that war had been averted.

If the Reichmanns still harbored doubts about having fled Vienna in haste, they vanished after Munich. Samuel now began urging his brother to close down the egg business and bring his own family to Paris—along with Edward, Louis, Paul, and Albert. An optimist by nature, Simon still thought that Hitler's aggression somehow could be contained short of all-out war. In deference to his more pessimistic older brother, however, Simon agreed to at least visit Paris. Underwhelmed by his wanderings through the refugee ghetto, he cut short his visit and returned to Beled. On the very next Shabbat, Simon summoned Edward up from the Pápa yeshiva for a debriefing. "Uncle Simon felt that Paris was a horrible place," Edward recalled. "He did not see the Champs Elysées, the Louvre, or the Eiffel Tower, but knew all about Rue de Rosiers, Rue Pavé and the herring from Klapisch."

On November 6, a Polish youth angered at his family's expulsion from Germany entered the German embassy in Paris and gunned down a diplomat. Using the assassination as a pretext, Hitler unleashed a ferocious assault against the 300,000 Jews remaining in Germany. On November 9, which the Nazis dubbed "Kristallnacht," or "night of the broken glass," stormtroopers destroyed 191 synagogues in Germany. As the violence spilled over into Austria the next morning, the Nazi legions in Vienna made the Anschluss seem a mere rehearsal. Motorized SS squads leveled 42 synagogues. Only the Schiffschul was left standing, though its interior was obliterated by axe blows. Virtually every Jewish house was ransacked and four thousand shops looted. Some eight thousand Jews were arrested and packed into makeshift local jails or packed into cattle cars and shipped off to Dachau, the first of the Nazi concentration camps.

After Kristallnacht, the French government tightened the screws another turn, enacting new decrees that further restricted immigration and abridged the rights of foreigners already in France. Now, even naturalized French citizens could be stripped of their citizenship if deemed "unworthy of the title of French citizen" and interned in special detention camps along with other "undesirables." Caught in a roundup of Jews of no declared nationality—so-called stateless Jews—Abraham Schreiber spent a few weeks in one such camp, which the government euphemistically called reception centers or supervised lodging centers. The authorities released Schreiber only after he was able to prove that one of his children was French-born. Mrs. Schreiber kept Ringer's open throughout her husband's internment.

Samuel waited until the post-Kristallnacht uproar subsided before applying in February 1939 for permanent residence. In a sense, he was forcing the issue; his visa did not expire until July 1940. But who could be certain that Prime Minister Daladier would not next decide to summarily cancel all visas issued to Jews? In any event, there was added security in being able to respond to a gendarme's demand for papers with a carte d'identité instead of a visitor's visa.

In March, Germany dismembered Czechoslovakia with alarming ease. Czech forces offered no resistance as Nazi troops marched into Bohemia and Moravia. Czechoslovakia's other half, Slovakia, simultaneously declared its independence under a homegrown fascist government headed by Josef Tiso, who had sworn fealty to Hitler and Germany. The virulently anti-Semitic Tiso regime installed itself in Bratislava, the spiritual capital of Oberlander Orthodoxy. Mrs. Reichmann had a brother and a sister living in Bratislava, which lay just across the Danube from Hungary.

The beast now was perched atop the neighbor's fence, but the danger to Hungarian Jews, though proximate, did not appear imminent. While Nazi propaganda long had insisted that Bohemia and Moravia properly belonged within a "Greater Germany," Hitler had advanced no such claim against Hungary. To the contrary, Germany lately had been cultivating Hungary at Czechoslovakia's expense. In late 1938, German and Italian arbitrators had resolved a long-standing border dispute by restoring to Hungary a section of Slovakia inhabited by one million ethnic Hungarians. In occupying Czechoslovakia, Germany permitted Hungary to reclaim another chunk of territory lost through Trianon—Ruthenia—from Slovakia.

For the moment at least, Samuel perceived greater threat to his funds than to his sons. If war did break out and Hungary sided with Germany, as seemed certain, the French authorities could be expected to freeze the bank accounts of all Hungarian nationals in France. Furthermore, in the case of Reichmann's Swiss deposits, what was to stop Germany from invading Switzerland and looting every bank vault in Zurich and Geneva?

Ever since the Anschluss, vast sums of capital had begun pouring out of Europe into the United States. However, many Europeans thought twice about the United States as a financial haven when Washington, following London's lead, responded to the Nazi occupation of Bohemia and Moravia by freezing the American bank accounts of Czech nationals. To safeguard against future freezes, many Europeans of diverse nationality began masking their ownership of American funds—wisely, as it turned out, for in 1940 Washington would freeze the U.S. assets held by all citizens of the western European countries invaded and occupied by Germany: Denmark, Norway, the Netherlands, Belgium, and France. One popular technique of disguise was to use a bank outside the United States as a fiduciary agent to place funds in New York; in 1939 many London banks were doing an active business in such fiduciary dollar deposits. Other Europeans preferred to circumvent the banking system altogether and entrust their funds to the safekeeping of a private American citizen. Aficionados of the latter method ran a high risk of theft since they did not have any way of establishing legal ownership of deposits.

The Orthodox Jews of Europe were uniquely accustomed to doing business with one another on the basis of implicit trust. For hundreds of years, religious Jews had been sealing transactions with handshakes instead of legal contracts. Because the halakah subjects business dealings to a highly exacting code, observant Jews did not need to rely on the safeguards provided under secular law in dealing with one another across national borders. This tradition of financial insularity, which was powerfully reinforced by the bonds of family, was not merely a matter of convenience but an essential component of survival for an oft-persecuted race. With Hitler's rise, vast sums began flowing out of Europe through what amounted to an extragovernmental Orthodox banking system.

Within this system, Samuel Reichmann would function both as depositor and depositee, with an early emphasis on the former role. In Paris, Reichmann appears to have relied mainly on Charles Shimon Ullman as a financial conduit. Born in Antwerp in 1890, Ullman was a Belgian Jew of Hungarian descent who had gone to work for D. Gestetner Limited and married Marie Gestetner, one of the founder's six daughters. That Ullman was the most religious of David Gestetner's sons-in-law certainly did not hurt his career. At the end of World War I, he was appointed managing director of the Gestetner company's important Paris office. The Ullmans belonged to a small community of affluent Parisians that had coalesced around a synagogue on Rue Montevideo—a lonely outpost of traditional Orthodoxy in the chic arrondissement XVI. Although the Ullmans lived quite a distance from Ringer's, they patronized the place regularly and often dined there with Samuel and Renée, who had always been fond of her pretty older English cousin and her proper, stern husband with the big black mustache. Charles Ullman and Samuel Reichmann were both intensely serious, religious men of affairs who got on quite well together in a taciturn way and came to trust one another implicitly.

As a Gestetner by marriage and employment, Charles Ullman was widely and importantly connected on both sides of the Atlantic. Among his closest acquaintances was Siegfried Bendheim, a German Jew who had emigrated to New York during World War I and established a business office for his cousins, the brothers Oscar and Julius Philipp. Founded in Hamburg in the 1890s, Philipp Brothers was a small but strategically positioned commodities trading house. Working in conjunction with the Office of Strategic Services (OSS), the Washington-based forerunner of the Central Intelligence Agency, Philipp Brothers would make a vast fortune during World War II, in part by outbidding the German Reich for strategic metals all over the world. Widely known as a man of unimpeachable integrity as well as financial sophistication, Siegfried Bendheim was a pillar of the private Orthodox banking network. According to his son, Charles Bendheim, Siegfried held nearly $1 billion during the war for thousands of European Jews.

In the spring of 1939, Samuel Reichmann decided that the time had come to transfer much of his wealth to the United States but was loath to do so through the usual banking channels. As a Hungarian national, it was conceivable that his funds might one day be not only frozen by the U.S. government but also confiscated. Ullman naturally suggested his friend Siegfried Bendheim, who, as it turned out, was distantly related to the Reichmanns, a member of his wife's family having married a Gestetner. But in Reichmann's view, Bendheim's impeccable credentials were overshadowed by the fact that he was an immigrant to America—and a German at that. In his typically fastidious way, Reichmann wanted the added security that only a U.S. birth certificate could provide. Ullman suggested Charles, Siegfried's American-born, college-student son. "Reichmann was looking for a Yankee Doodle and Ullman recommended me," Charles Bendheim recalled a half-century later. "The thing was, though, no one told me."

Bendheim, who was attending Lafayette University in Easton, Pennsylvania, got a call one day from American Express informing him that it was holding a check for him at its office in Philadelphia. Bendheim went to fetch it and, to his amazement, was handed a cashier's check for $75,000 drawn on the Geneva office of the Swiss Bank Corporation. "That was a hell of a lot of money then and I had no idea who it was from—there were no instructions, no name, nothing," Bendheim said. "When they handed me the check, I looked at it and said something like, 'I told them not to send my allowance all at once,' and they looked at me funny. Actually, though, I was scared to death that something might happen to me on the way home and no one would ever know whose money it was." Bendheim immediately telephoned his father, who told him that he had no idea who had sent the money either. Siegfried

Bendheim instructed his son to make a written record of when he had received the check and to deposit it at his bank in Easton in a new account. "I asked to see the president of the bank to make sure the check was deposited correctly," Bendheim said.

The paper trail created by the American Express wire transfer came to a dead end in Switzerland. Swiss Bank Corporation was under no legal obligation to disclose the identity of its client to the U.S. Treasury Department or anyone else. For his part, Bendheim was aware that he was supposed to report a foreign funds transfer of such magnitude to the U.S. government. But who would believe that this fat, $75,000 check had descended anonymously upon him from afar, manna from Switzerland? Envisioning a red-tape tangle, Bendheim opted not to make the required filing. Samuel Reichmann had evaded the spirit of U.S. law certainly, but Bendheim was the one who broke it.

The $75,000 that Charles Bendheim held apparently represented only a fraction of the funds Samuel deposited anonymously in the United States. After the war, Bendheim met Eva Reichmann at a wedding in London. "As soon as she found out who I was she came right over and said that she'd really wanted to meet me because I was the only one out of all of them who had returned in full her father's money," Bendheim said. "Apparently, the others had taken out a certain percentage before giving Mr. Reichmann his money back."

In 1939 or 1940, Charles Ullman also smuggled a small fortune in gold bars from Paris to London on the Reichmanns' behalf. "I remember my Aunt Marie telling me how her husband came to England with a suitcase full of Reichmann gold," said David Gestetner, Sigmund's oldest son and a grandson of the founder of the duplicating firm. "The chauffeur picked him up at Victoria Station. But when he got back to his flat, Charles said, 'My God, the Reichmann gold.' He'd left the suitcase in Victoria Station. So they rushed back and found the suitcase just where Charles had put it down."

What Ullman did with the gold is not certain. Ullman's father-in-law, DG, had steadfastly refused to let his Hungarian relatives use the Gestetner company safe as a repository for their valuables. Charles David noted in his memoirs that DG had a way of "keeping friends and relatives at arm's length and refusing to get involved closely with any arrangements which might spell future headaches." In this case, the headache Gestetner was avoiding was that of serving as custodian of assets that had been smuggled into England. Charles David went to the Bank of England, made full disclosure and, no doubt after the requisite duties and fines had been paid, arranged for their safekeeping with the central bank. "At the end of the war," David wrote, "the deposits were intact and were reclaimed"—at least those that belonged to the few who had survived the Holocaust.

DG died in March 1939, while vacationing in Nice, and it appears that Sigmund, his successor, did not adhere as strictly to the Gestetner policy of familial nonentanglement. According to Edward Reichmann, a sizable portion of his father's gold and his mother's jewelry survived the war in the Gestetner safe. When D. Gestetner Limited moved its offices in 1991, a soiled manila envelope bearing the handwritten inscription, "Renée Reichmann," was found wedged into the back of the company safe. Inside was a diamond brooch (valued at about $3,000), which was turned over to Paul Reichmann, his mother having died in 1990. "Obviously, Mrs. Reichmann knew the brooch had not been returned," observed David Gestetner, who by then was running his grandfather's company. "But she never said anything and I would guess it was because she did not want to appear to accuse her relatives of wrongdoing."

———

In June 1939, France ordered all stateless aliens and foreign nationals enjoying the right of asylum to register for military service if between the ages of twenty and forty-eight. Once registered, foreigners were subject to call-up on twenty days' notice. This measure was enacted even though foreign Jews had been enlisting in the Foreign Legion in wildly disproportionate numbers. Of the 100,000 foreigners who enlisted or were drafted into the French armed forces by 1940, no less than 30,000 were Jews. For many Jewish refugees, military service was preferable to the chronic threat of expulsion from France. In addition, foreign Jews "were eager to show their devotion to France, their adopted country that had given them opportunities undreamed of in Central and Eastern Europe. Their own private struggles against Hitler had often begun long before, with personal experience of Nazi militarism, totalitarianism, and anti-Semitism."

Samuel Reichmann felt no great devotion to France, which had given him the opportunity only to sit on his hands, and had no intention of enlisting in any man's army. At forty-one, Reichmann still fell well within the age range of the military draft. However, he could plausibly claim that he had applied only for residence in France, not asylum, since his homeland, Hungary, remained a free, if not completely independent, nation.

Just before dawn on September 1, 1939, a massive German force crossed into Poland. Two days later, France declared war on Germany; World War II had begun.

No one in the Hungarian kaffee klatsch at Ringer's took the news harder than Blanca Stern. She was from Sárvár, an Oberland town not far from Beled, but had not met the Reichmanns until she moved to Vienna with her husband, Zsigmond, who owned a hardware store in Leopoldstadt. In the mid-1930s, Ziggy Stern had written a vehemently anti-Hitler article for an ultra-Orthodox newspaper in Vienna. When the Germans occupied Vienna, Stern did not wait around to debate his views with the SS. He immediately collected his wife and three children and fled to Hungary. "My father left Vienna without money, without anything," recalled Martha Stern Margulies. "He just walked out of his store. He didn't even tell my mother where we were going. She thought we were taking a vacation." The Sterns left their two youngest children with relatives in Hungary and took Martha with them to Paris. In August 1939, Mr. Stern returned alone to Hungary to fetch his son and daughter and was stuck there when war broke out. "They closed the borders down and my mother was crying all the time, wondering whether she'd ever see my father and her children again," Mrs. Margulies said. "I remember Mrs. Reichmann coming over to her [and telling her] that she must have hope and that she must stop crying because crying didn't do any good at all."

About the same time Ziggy Stern had returned to Hungary, the Reichmanns had arranged for Renée's sister, Olga, to bring Louis, Albert, and Paul to Paris. Leaving Győr on September 3, they had gotten no farther than the Austrian border. As Louis recalled, the Austrian border control officer took one look at Aunt Dadi's passport and said, "We have enough bloody Jews in Austria already and besides you won't get out the other side. Germany and France are at war."

The three younger brothers were eager to leave Hungary, which was becoming increasingly uncomfortable for all Jews. In 1938, not long after the boys' parents had left for Paris, the Hungarian Parliament passed the first of three major anti-Jewish bills. This First Jewish Law mandated large cutbacks in the number of Jews who could legally practice the "free professions" (law, medicine, engineering, architecture, and so on) and also sharply curtailed Jewish employment and ownership in business. In 1939 came the Second Jewish Law, which further restricted the economic and political rights of Jews and imposed a racial (as opposed to religious) definition of Jewishness for legal purposes. As a result of these two laws, some 250,000 Hungarian Jews lost their livelihoods.

The Reichmann brothers were too young to work, of course, but were directly affected by these measures just the same. The enactment of anti-Semitic legislation emboldened the hooligan element in Beled, forcing Louis, Albert, and Paul to run a gauntlet of taunting, stone-throwing, and worse in walking to and from school. "There were a lot of students who went to the college at Kapuvár," a larger town not far from Beled, Paul recalled. "On their way to the train in the morning they'd go through the village and take the opportunity to beat up a few Jewish kids, including the youngest ones." On the first seder night of Passover in 1938, a mob had rampaged through the Jewish quarter, smashing windows. The brothers were in Uncle Simon's house, which was equipped with sturdy shutters. "If he hadn't had shutters," Paul said, "he wouldn't have had windows."

France's declaration of war had the immediate effect of transforming every German and Austrian refugee within its borders into an enemy alien. Posters appeared throughout France ordering all German and Austrian men from seventeen to sixty-five years of age to assemble at certain places bearing a blanket and two days of provisions. Those who did not comply were rounded up by the police. In interning some fifteen thousand enemy aliens in some sixty crudely equipped detention camps, the French authorities did not bother distinguishing between supporters and foes of Hitler. That many of the internees possessed all the proper documents did not seem to matter. "Their official French certificates, testifying to the fact that they were loyal, recognized refugees, were mere scraps of paper, the butt of jokes by the very officials who had issued them."

Although Samuel Reichmann was a Hungarian citizen and had the papers to prove it, he had lived in Austria for ten years and was as disinclined as ever to take chances with his freedom. On September 2, the day after Germany bombed Danzig, Reichmann left Paris by train for Le Mont-Dore, a spa in the Massif Central that was well regarded among the Orthodox for its high-quality kosher hotels. Samuel spent five weeks in Le Mont-Dore, returning to Paris in mid-October for a few days. On October 18 he returned to Le Mont-Dore by train, accompanied this time by Renée, Eva, and Ralph. Capitalizing again on the advantage of money, the Reichmanns remained isolated in Le Mont-Dore for a full two months.

By the time the Reichmanns returned to their Paris hotel in mid-December, the war fever of September had given way to the ennui of what the French called the "drôle de guerre," the odd or funny war. (In English, the preferred translation was the harsher "phony war.") After advancing briefly toward the German front in the Saar basin, French troops drew back to a more secure position behind the Maginot Line. As Germany ran roughshod over Poland, the French, like the British, hunkered down and waited for the Nazis to make the first move, in what amounted to a virtual replay of World War I. In Paris, the citizenry "settled into their phony war as if in a state of peace. That signified relative comfort, few restrictions. The best opinion was that time was on France's side, that the war would be won without the shedding of blood."

In January 1940, Edward Reichmann's impetuosity put him square in harm's way. By this time, the Hungarian government required that all boys twelve and older undergo part-time military training. The Jewish community of Pápa was allowed to form its own regiment, which Edward and his fellow yeshiva students grudgingly joined. During training one Sunday, they stood at formation while a Hungarian Army officer made a speech in which he declared that every Jew in Hungary must be considered a potential spy. Edward stepped forward, saluted, and was granted permission to speak. "You are addressing a group of twenty-five boys who are all Jewish," he said, "and not one of us is a spy." The officer slapped him across the face and fourteen-year-old Edward retaliated in kind. He and the Gestetner cousin who broke ranks to come to his aid were arrested and thrown into jail, where they languished for two weeks.

Edward had a wealthy Gestetner uncle who lived in Papa and finally bribed the wife of the army officer into releasing the boys. "When we came back to school we expected a hero's welcome, but we didn't get it," Reichmann recalled. "They called us idiots. The community was very frightened of what might happen."

Edward managed to get through to his parents by telephone in Paris and told them he wanted to leave Pápa. Samuel and Renée decided that the time had come to bring all four sons to Paris. Mrs. Reichmann made the trip alone, leaving Paris by train in mid-February 1940. She made it no farther than the Italian border. Mussolini's fascist government was whipping up anti-Semitic sentiment as Italy prepared to enter the war as Hitler's ally. Denied admittance by Italian border guards, Renée returned to Paris. "She was sent back from Italy because she had 'Jew' on her passport," Eva Reichmann later recalled. Back in Paris, Eva continued, Mrs. Reichmann "went to the Hungarian Consul in Paris and he said he would fix it. The fixing was that he did not put in 'Jew.' So she tried again, and this time she got through."

Mrs. Reichmann arrived in Győr on February 20. Time was short. On March 1, Edward would turn fifteen and no longer would be entitled to travel on his parents' exit visa. Given Edward's recent clash with authority, who knew what fate might befall his application for travel papers? On the other hand, Samuel's and Renée's Hungarian passports were due to expire in July. If she failed to renew them now, she might never get another chance. At the passport office in Budapest they had told her it could take a month to process the paperwork. Edward granted himself a month's leeway with a stroke of a pen, altering the date of birth written into his passport from "III/1/25" to "III/31/25," but it still was not much time.

As the departure date approached, Edward had second thoughts. His spiritual mentor, the Papa Rebbe, had reacted frostily to his plans to leave yeshiva. "My Rebbe asked me bluntly, 'What will you do in Paris?' and refused to wish me good luck or even to say, 'Have a good trip,' " Edward recalled. "This was sufficient for me to tell mother categorically that I would not go to Paris." On March 11, following a stormy visit to Pápa, Mrs. Reichmann wrote Samuel a letter that would become one of Edward's most treasured possessions. It is quoted here in part:

Eli made such scenes. It was terrible. Every day he gets a little more mature. He has become smart. He says he will not be homesick in Papa, that he wants only to learn. I do not know how I will finish with him. He is more stubborn than ever. . . .

You asked [she'd just received a letter from her husband] whether I'm not ready yet to leave. I never tire of being home. Any time at home is too short. But when I am away from you, any time is too long. Even one minute is too much. So now you are laughing? I am writing of my most sincere and deep feelings and you are laughing? I will stop here because I don't want anyone to laugh at me. Perhaps I am old, but my heart is still young.

The Pápa Rebbe soon relented and on March 25, Mrs. Reichmann and her four sons left Győr and made their way around Austria by train, crossing through Croatia, Italy, and Switzerland without incident to reach France. "It was a nice trip," Louis recalled. "Personally, I enjoyed it and the others did, too. There were no signs of war." They reached Paris in early April, just in time for Passover—the first Passover in three years that the entire family had celebrated as one.

Chapter 6

On May 11, 1940, the Reichmanns and a few dozen of their friends gathered in the family's suite at the Hotel Montholon to observe the bar mitzvah of their second son, Louis. Rabbi Munk and his family attended, as did the leader of Paris's other strictly Orthodox congregation. Like Edward's bar mitzvah in Beled two years earlier, this was a celebration darkened by storm clouds of red, black, and white. The air raid sirens sounded in the midst of the proceedings, which were completed in the bunker under the hotel.

The phony war had ended abruptly the day before as Germany invaded Belgium, the Netherlands, and Luxembourg, and the armed forces of France and Britain advanced at last to engage the enemy. Paris had a serious scare toward the end of the first week of battle, when the Nazis broke through in northern France. The French high command informed Premier Paul Reynaud that there was nothing to stop enemy armored columns from reaching Paris in twenty-four hours. Officials at the French Foreign Office began dumping secret documents from their windows onto huge bonfires in the yard outside. The drifting smoke spread rumor and panic through the city, prompting many Parisians to take to the highways. The exodus continued even as German panzer columns bypassed the city and sped westward to the English Channel, stranding much of the French Army in Flanders.

Proportionately fewer Jews than non-Jews joined the exodus, and the tendency toward immobility was strongest among the most recent immigrants. "Even Jewish refugees from Germany and Eastern Europe seemed afflicted by what today must be seen as irrational behavior. If asked, they would say, 'But it can't happen in France.' " Even after the Belgian Army surrendered unconditionally and Paris filled with dazed refugees from the north, many of the city's residents—Samuel Reichmann included—continued to believe that the

French Army would regroup and combine with British forces to stop the German advance safely short of the French capital.

On June 3, some two hundred Luftwaffe planes leveled parts of arrondissements XV and XVI in the first bombing attack on Paris. The Germans hit schools and hospitals as well as military targets, killing 254 people, including 20 children. The Reichmanns were relieved to hear that Charles and Marie Ullman and their two children were unhurt. Ten-year-old Paul horrified his parents by venturing out of a bomb shelter during an air raid to sneak a look at the sky. "I guess I was curious to see how it worked," Paul recalled. "In the child's mind, the adventure stands out, not the fear."

After driving the British into the sea at Dunkirk, the Wehrmacht resumed its offensive against French forces on June 5. Outnumbered two to one, the French defenders quickly gave way. As many as 150,000 people a day were now fleeing Paris, but the Reichmanns stayed put, immobilized in large part by the imminence of the festival of Shavouth, which commemorates the giving of the Torah to Moses on Mount Sinai.

On June 8, four days before Shavouth, Samuel and Edward were having lunch at Ringer's when a distraught elderly man burst in and implored Abraham Schreiber to place an emergency call to the Chevra Kadisha, the Jewish burial society. (Jewish law and custom require a speedy burial.) The Reichmanns left their meal and walked outside. In the back of an open truck parked in front of Ringer's, something small lay covered by a blanket. "Under this blanket is my grandson," explained the old man, who had fled Antwerp in the truck. The boy had died just north of Paris in a strafing attack by a German plane. The Reichmanns waited until the corpse was loaded into a van sent by the Chevra Kadisha and then rushed back to the hotel. "We have to pack and get out of Paris," Samuel told Renée, who required convincing. After a short argument, Renée abandoned all hope of observing Shavouth in Paris, gathered her children together, and began packing most of the family's possessions into large boxes and suitcases.

They decided to ship their belongings to Biarritz, an Atlantic port city not far from the Spanish border. That very afternoon Samuel and his sons loaded the luggage into two taxicabs and went to the Gare d'Austerlitz, where they took their place in a huge line outside the freight office. They were still far from the window at 6:30, when it was announced that the freight office was closing and would reopen at 7:00 the next morning. Edward and Louis arranged the family's luggage into a makeshift bed and spent the night in the street outside the railway station. By morning they had worked their way almost to the front of the line and were able to arrange the shipment and still make it to the Rue Cadet synagogue by 8:30.

On June 9, as the French government itself began preparing to pull out of Paris, Samuel and Renée went to the Préfecture de police and, in conformance with the regulations governing foreign residents, obtained a "sauf conduit" authorizing them to travel to Biarritz by train or auto any time after June 10. The Reichmanns did not own a car and were unable to buy a ticket on a southbound passenger train at any price. Just in case they had to leave on foot, Renée bought a baby carriage. "We were afraid that Ralph, who was only six, might not be able to keep up as we walked out of Paris," Paul recalled.

At dawn on June 11, a thick layer of black smoke veiled the Paris sun, turning day into a freakish night that struck many as an augury of doom. The sky, one inhabitant noted in his dairy, "announced without question, some Apocalypse." Not until midday would the authorities confirm that German planes had hit gasoline storage tanks on the city's outskirts.

In his suite at the Hotel Montholon, Samuel Reichmann awoke early, slipped two gold ingots into his pocket, and took Edward with him out into a panicked city. As always, they began their day at the Rue Cadet synagogue. Soot was falling from the sky as speckled rain when father and son emerged from their morning prayers. Unable to find a taxicab, they began walking the familiar mile-long route south to the produce markets of Les Halles, where Samuel hoped to find a truck driver to transport him and his family to Orléans, seventy miles south of Paris. Samuel figured that they could make it to Orléans by nightfall, observe Shavouth there with some semblance of decorum, and then catch a train to Biarritz the following day. It took some doing, but Reichmann finally found a driver willing to accept the assignment in exchange for one of the gold bars.

It was nearly two o'clock by the time the truck pulled up in front of the Hotel Montholon. While Edward and his brothers began loading the truck, Samuel telephoned Ziggy Stern, who was living in a nearby hotel, and offered to take him and his family along. "Pack what you can," Samuel advised, "and we'll pick you up in half an hour." The Sterns made a party of six: Ziggy, Blanca, and their children, as well as Mrs. Stern's seventeen-year-old sister, Shari Levin, who had left Hungary to visit Paris in mid-1939 and had been stranded there when the war broke out.

Long before they reached the Porte d'Orléans, the Reichmanns were caught in what must be history's worst traffic jam: "Between June 9 and June 13, when the Germans arrived at the gates of the city, two million Parisians, men, women, and children, took off in utter panic toward the south, packing a few belongings on the roofs of their small cars or on the racks of motorcycles or bicycles or in baby carts, peddler's carts, wheelbarrows, or in any wheeled contrivance they could lay a hasty hand on." Food and drink was scarce at any price. Most of the towns south of the city had emptied in a chain reaction of fear, with only the occasional shopkeeper staying behind to profiteer. German and Italian planes were continually passing overhead and every now and then would swoop down to strafe the sluggish columns of civilians. The Reichmanns' flatbed truck was open to the sky and afforded no protection whatsoever. "The planes flew so low that you could see soldiers on the planes holding the machine guns," Louis recalled. "It was terrifying."

As the Reichmanns were passing Orly Airport, air raid sirens sounded. The driver stopped the truck and everyone ran for cover except Ralph, who stood immobilized with fright in the back of the truck. Eva soon returned to fetch her little brother, who as an adult would recall this incident as his earliest memory of childhood. The Reichmanns and Sterns found a small hut crowded with people and pushed their way in, only to discover, to their horror, that they had taken shelter over an underground gasoline tank.

When night fell, French police halted traffic and ordered all lights extinguished. Renée took Eva and the youngest boys and found shelter in a farmhouse, sleeping on straw spread on the floor. Samuel, Edward, and Louis spent the night in the open air and were drenched by a heavy rain. Edward arose just before dawn and saw some lights burning in a farmhouse nearby. He knocked on the door and in broken French asked the old woman who answered if she would sell him some hard-boiled eggs. She boiled about two dozen eggs in a huge tea can and put them in a bag along with a big loaf of bread. "Combien?" Edward asked. She touched his payos and said, "Rien de tout, petit Juif" (Nothing at all, little Jew).

At dawn, the motorized crawl resumed. About three o'clock in the afternoon—twenty-four hours after they had left Paris—the truck deposited the Reichmanns and the Sterns at the railroad station in Orléans. Eva accompanied her father to the local police station as translator. "The police said, 'Why did you come here? You're scared of the Germans? They'll be here sooner than in Paris,'" Eva recalled. With a struggle, the two families boarded the next train to Bordeaux, where they slept on the street and then caught another coach south toward Biarritz. While many foreign Jews would complain of rough treatment along the back roads of France, Paul, who was then ten years old, had pleasant memories. "I still recall that the French peasants received us with enormous hospitality, and shared food and shelter with us without hesitation."

While the Reichmanns—and most of the cabinet ministers of the French government—were en route to Bordeaux, the German Army entered Paris unopposed on June 14. By the time the Reichmanns finally reached Biarritz on June 18, Premier Reynaud had abandoned hope of persuading the French high command to fight on and resigned. Although Biarritz was a resort town equipped to handle visitors, every room was taken, and the family had no choice but to sleep under the stars with hundreds of other refugees, as they had done in Bordeaux. Each of the brothers walked barefoot whenever possible so as not to wear out his one pair of shoes. After three nights alfresco, Mrs. Reichmann noticed a van being loaded with furniture. "She thought maybe these people were moving to another place," Eva said. "She went and spoke to the representative of the agency and told her we would like to rent the house. She said, 'All right, come to my office.' My mother quickly took off her brooch and gave it to her. It wasn't important but it was a piece of jewelry. She got the house. We were so happy."

The day after the Reichmanns found shelter in Biarritz, France formally capitulated, as Marshall Philippe Pétain, the new head of state, signed an armistice with Germany. For Jews in particular, a fateful decision had arrived: whether to stay or go. The word from Paris was that the Germans were behaving with surprising civility. To a Jewish historian who had remained in Paris throughout its fall, "life in Paris seemed normal. One was not even alarmed for the Jews. The Germans were 'correct'; there were no massacres and no pogroms." (Those would come later.) Cheered by reports of the Nazis' deceptively mild behavior, a few million native Frenchmen and thousands of refugee Jews began straggling back to Paris and other northern cities. Remaining in France would prove a fatal error for seventy-seven thousand Jews, most of them refugees.

For the refugees in Biarritz, the flight path of least resistance lay through Spain, which was pro-German but officially neutral. Although unwilling to offer permanent sanctuary to refugees of any sort, the government of Francisco Franco was willing to issue a ninety-day transit visa to anyone holding an immigration visa to another country. This schizoid Spanish policy gave rise to a booming black market throughout southern France as the consulates of various Latin American republics turned a quick profit by selling visas with the tacit understanding that they would not actually admit the bearer to the issuing country. In mid-June 1940, an official of the American Jewish Joint Distribution Committee noted that in Bordeaux prices for Latin American visas of this nature were "very reasonable. . . . So are visas for Haiti, and, yes, for [Santo] Domingo and for any country willing to do business."

Samuel and Eva joined the line at the Haitian consulate in Bayonne, a city not far from Biarritz and, hours later, came away with an entry visa. In their accounts of the family's flight, both Eva and Edward discreetly avoided mentioning how their father obtained the Haitian visa. Undoubtedly, he returned to Biarritz that evening lighter in purse than when he had left. Armed with what he believed to be a valid Haitian document, Samuel went to the Spanish consulate and obtained a transit visa.

By the time Samuel returned to Biarritz, an alternative escape route had miraculously emerged. On the quay in Biarritz, Ziggy Stern had bumped into a Czech whom he had known in Vienna. This man was the captain of a coal boat that had stopped in Bayonne en route to England. He offered to take Stern along if he could get an English entry visa. At the British consulate in Bayonne, Stern joined a huge throng restrained by a cordon of police. During the long wait, a hailstorm broke out and even the police ran for cover. Stern slipped into the consulate and found a vice consul. Taking pity on the interloper, who broke down in tears as he explained his plight, the official agreed to stamp his passport. But when Stern reached into his jacket, he found an empty pocket and fainted dead away. After reviving him, the consul drew up a special visa, leaving blank the number of people authorized to enter England.

Several dozen fellow refugees joined the Sterns on the coal boat to England, but not the Reichmanns. "My father said, 'No, this is not for me,' " Eva recalled. " 'I am not going to risk U-boat attack.' " The captain refused to allow Mrs. Stern's sister, Shari Levin, on board because her Hungarian passport had expired. The Sterns sent the seventeen-year-old to the Reichmanns, knowing they would take care of her, papers or no.

Early the next morning, June 22, Samuel headed south to the border town of Hendaye on a scouting expedition. "My father left and we were just having lunch [when] he was already back," Eva said. "He had asked the Spaniards if they would let us through with the transit visas which we had and they said yes." Mrs. Reichmann dressed Shari in one of Edward's suits in the hope that she might somehow get six boys through the border on the passports for five.

At Hendaye, the Reichmanns hired three porters. "We had a lot of luggage," Edward recalled, "and also father and mother wanted to create as much confusion as possible." As the family waited to present its papers, Levin ambled off a short distance and then turned and walked into Spain. "No one paid any attention to me," recalled Levin, now Mrs. Shari Holzer. "I was standing about fifty meters into Spain and I got tired of waiting so I walked back right between the guards and Mrs. Reichmann started to scream, 'Shari, what are you doing! Go back! We are coming soon.' It was a long line."

The Reichmanns went to the train station at Irún, where a surreal pandemonium reigned. Thousands of people crowded the platform, waiting for trains that were running many hours late. As the train to Madrid pulled in, a voice over the loudspeaker announced that this was not today's train but yesterday's train. The crowd groaned and continued waiting while the Reichmanns, who hadn't understood the announcement, boarded using today's tickets and made themselves comfortable in the uncrowded cars of yesterday's train. During the trip, an inspector boarded and began checking passports. He nabbed Levin, whom he was duty-bound to turn over to the police in Madrid. For all its liberality in allowing refugees an escape route through Spain, the Franco government often dealt harshly with foreigners who entered illegally or overstayed their welcome, shutting them away in prisons or special refugee camps for a year or more. Instead of promptly turning Levin over to the police, though, the inspector took her home to his wife for a meal and a shower and then rendezvoused with Mrs. Reichmann and Eva at the Hungarian Embassy in Madrid. "He was just a very kind person," Mrs. Holzer remembered.

Officially, there was not much he could do, the Hungarian consul told Mrs. Reichmann. Unofficially, he suggested that she contact his daughter, who worked for a Hungarian industrialist who had lived in Madrid for years and was connected to Franco himself. The daughter came down to the embassy and took Mrs. Reichmann and Eva to meet this businessman, who lived in a small palace in one of Madrid's finest districts. Although he was not a religious man, he was happy to help a fellow Jew. That very night Levin was issued a new Hungarian passport and a Spanish transit visa. Levin stayed in a Madrid hotel with the Reichmanns for nearly two weeks before returning home to Hungary. "All I can tell you about the Reichmanns is that you never saw people so kind, so generous, so fine, so understanding," she said five decades later. "They treated me like a daughter—they gave me money if I needed it, anything. I joined the family. Especially when you're on the run, when you're in need, you know people best, and they always gave a helping hand. Always."

———

As recounted in the occasional interviews given over the years by Eva, Edward, and Albert, the family's passage to Tangier was made to seem wholly and desperately improvised. As the Reichmann siblings told it, their parents did not decide on Tangier until after they had arrived in Madrid. "In Madrid we looked around to see if there were many Jews and if it was possible to practice kashrut, and we found out that there were Jews but there was no kashrut," Edward has said. "We found out that in Morocco we could live a full Jewish life." In a 1983 interview, Eva, too, framed her parents' decision to go to Tangier in terms of religion. In Madrid, she said, we "inquired where there is a place with a minyan and kashrut. We were told to go to Tangier."

This making-a-virtue-of-necessity version of events has the slippery feel of spin control. It was well known throughout European Jewry that Madrid had been a Jewish ghost town ever since the Jews of Spain had been famously expelled in 1492. In any event, the nature of Jewish life in Madrid was irrelevant since the Reichmanns did not have the option of remaining. The Spanish government was emphatic and unyielding in its refusal even to consider granting residency to refugees. The ideal, as Spain's foreign minister put it, was to have foreigners "passing through our country as light passes through a glass, leaving no trace."

Moreover, the image of Tangier as a kosher oasis luring the Reichmanns to Morocco is simply a fantasy. Tangier was indeed home to a sizable minority of Jews, but most were Sephardim whose customs and practices differed from those of the Ashkenazim of central and eastern Europe. In fact, once there, the Reichmanns were so disheartened by local standards of observance that they started their own synagogue in a leased apartment and imported kosher meat from a city forty miles away. And there were so few other strictly observant

Ashkenazim in Tangier that to assemble a minyan (the minimum quorum of ten adult males required to conduct a public prayer service) Samuel often had to hire a Sephardic Jew or two to fill out the group.

Eva's and Edward's testimony notwithstanding, the evidence suggests that the Reichmanns did not land in Tangier by accident but by design—that they chose Tangier, as earlier they had chosen Vienna and Paris, albeit from among a set of options narrowed by the calamities of war. Eva herself implied as much in a letter submitted to the editor of the *Jewish Chronicle* in 1960, some twenty-three years before the interview cited earlier. In the letter, Eva stated that her family left Biarritz with an entry visa to Tangier already in hand:

> You might be interested to know with what genuine efforts the Spanish Government strove to help Jewish refugees during the last war. I was one of those refugees, and will never forget how very kind they were to us. My parents and their six children, the eldest of them being myself, then sixteen, fled from France the day after the Armistice, not knowing whether they would let us through, as we only had the Spanish 'transit by air' visas to Tangier. They made us welcome and helped us in every way.

Certainly the most affecting evidence that the Reichmanns left France bound for Tangier was imprinted in the memories of Abraham Schreiber and his family. In Biarritz, the Reichmanns had run into many members of their Parisian circle, including Mrs. Fenna Schreiber, Abraham's wife, and their two daughters. (The restaurateur himself had been arrested a second time by the French authorities and again interned in a detention center in central France.) Mrs. Schreiber and her daughters had fled Paris with no particular plan in mind, managing to stay a few days ahead of the Nazi legions as they raced south along the coast. Because Mrs. Schreiber had no passport, her options in Biarritz were limited and unappealing: she could cross illegally into Spain or reverse course and head back north to Limoges, where she had relatives. In presenting Mrs. Schreiber with a third option, Mrs. Reichmann made the refugee's penultimate sacrifice. "Mrs. Reichmann offered my wife her passport so she could go to Tangier in her place with the rest of the Reichmann family," Abraham Schreiber recalled. "They were going to paste my wife's photo in the passport and she was going to wear Mrs. Reichmann's blonde wig. When they got to Tangier, the passport then was to be sent back to Mrs. Reichmann, who would be waiting in Biarritz."

Although Mrs. Schreiber opted instead to flee to Limoges, where she soon was reunited with her husband, she was deeply grateful to Mrs. Reichmann. "I can't tell you how many times my parents told my sister and me the story of what Mrs. Reichmann had done," said Netti Schreiber Morgenstern. "They would tell us, 'You must never forget this.' "

Besides the Reichmanns, a half-dozen other habitués of Schreiber's restaurant landed in Tangier. "In Ringer's, I used to hear them talking about Tangier," Schreiber said of the Reichmanns and their Hungarian friends. "Everyone was figuring out what to do next, making plans just in case. I don't know who had the idea first to go to Tangier, but the Hungarians, they stuck together."

Like Shanghai and precious few other places, Tangier was an open city. In 1923, the ancient metropolis had been carved out of Morocco by treaty and ceded to a consortium of eight European nations. Although France, Italy, and other World War II belligerents belonged to the Tangier consortium, the city's unusual status was not immediately compromised by the outbreak of hostilities. The International Zone of Tangier not only remained neutral but extraordinarily hospitable. It imposed no immigration quotas or formal visa requirements and to enter—indeed to qualify for citizenship—all one needed was a passport (any country would do).

The Tangier option casts in a different light the Reichmanns' composure as the Germans were closing in on Paris. For Samuel in particular, contingency planning was virtually an avocation. And yet, unlike the great majority of the Jewish refugees in Paris, the Reichmanns had made no attempt to secure immigration visas to the United States or any other safe and distant place. Samuel and Renée apparently had decided that their best bet was to take shelter behind the shield of the French military for as long as possible. Perhaps the Germans would be repulsed. If not, they could pull out their ace in the hole: Tangier.

If this was indeed the plan, it went seriously awry while the family was en route to Bordeaux. As the German Army was marching into Paris on June 14, Spanish troops seized control of Tangier under the pretext of ensuring its continued neutrality. Spain, which had coveted Tangier for decades, made no effort to expel the two thousand war refugees—mostly Jews—who had gathered already in Tangier, but it did slam shut the city's open door. As a result, no foreigners were allowed to enter unless they had been "granted a special authorization from the Ministry for Foreign Affairs in Madrid. Although this authorization [was] granted with much difficulty in very few instances, in most cases no consideration seems to have been given."

But there was at least one Jewish refugee family allowed into Tangier after June 14. How the Reichmanns obtained Spanish Foreign Ministry authorization to enter occupied Tangier is not clear. Perhaps the obliging Madrid industrialist paved the way as he was helping Shari Levin return to Hungary. Another clue can be found in a document filed as part of a libel suit brought by the family in the late 1980s. In it, Albert Reichmann is quoted as saying that his parents had "strong connections" to the Spanish power structure even before the family arrived in Tangier "through people in Madrid, Jews or half Jews . . . a family named Salama, who were connected to Franco." The Salamas, the most powerful business family in Tangier and Spanish Morocco, were among the earliest and most generous financiers of the armed uprising in 1936 that had brought the Generalissimo to power.

If, as Eva suggested, her father obtained a special "transit-by-air" visa at the Spanish consulate in Bayonne, why did the Reichmanns not fly to Tangier as authorized? The most likely scenario involves Shari Levin, whose invalid Hungarian passport most likely would have landed her in jail the moment she tried to board an outbound flight anywhere in France. The Spanish border may have been porous in mid-1940, but French airports most assuredly were not.

After a brief rest in Madrid, the Reichmanns continued by train to the port of Algeciras, where they took a ferry across the Straits of Gibraltar, landing in Ceuta. The family then took a train to Tetuán, the capital of Spanish Morocco. "At the railway station there was an Arab peddler," Edward recalled. "Eva asked if there were Jews in town. He said with his hands, 'Muchos, muchos.' So Eva asked him to take us to the community leaders. He took father to a Mr. Hassan, a prominent family, an industrialist. Mr. Hassan immediately alerted a Mr. Bendahan, the president of the Jewish community. They came with cars to the railway station and put us in and took us home to Mr. Hassan's big house—because Mr. Hassan had a house big enough to accommodate parents and six children."

From Tetuán, the Reichmanns hired two cars to take them to Tangier, arriving there in mid-July. "There would be no more going farther," Edward remembered. "After all, there was no realistic possibility of going anywhere."

In fact, what Edward dismissed as unrealistic proved feasible even for many less affluent refugees. Half of the three thousand Jewish refugees who had gathered in Tangier in 1940 managed to leave by mid-1943, most of them heading for North America or Palestine. Meanwhile, refugees in greater numbers were disembarking in sporadic bursts from Casablanca as well as Lisbon, Marseille, Oran, Istanbul, and other Mediterranean ports. Between April 1939 and the end of 1942, nearly forty thousand European Jews reached Palestine alone. The Reichmanns remained in Tangier not for complete lack of alternatives but because it was everything they expected it to be—and more.

———

If, in fact, the Reichmanns had left Paris bound for Tangier, why did Eva and her brothers not simply acknowledge it instead of creating the impression of a chance arrival and reluctant residence? What was so bad about Tangier? In a word, plenty.

Had Mr. and Mrs. Reichmann valued religious traditionalism above all else, they would have either returned to the Oberland or, more sensibly, gravitated toward one of the communities of ultra-Orthodox refugees sprouting up throughout the Americas. Tangier's inadequacy as "a place of Torah" was not merely its lack of Ashkenazic infrastructure. Even by secular standards, Tangier was a moral sinkhole, and notorious as such throughout Europe. "Tangier in 1940 was not yet entirely the international elysium for crooks, outlaws, escapists, drunks, aberrant sexual eccentrics and sedulous voluptuaries of both sexes that since the war it has been," recalled Michael Davidson, a British memoirist and avowed pederast who arrived in the city about the same time as did the Reichmanns. "But even then almost any curious thirst could be assuaged; boys or pubescent girls of half-a-dozen races were two-a-penny, guilty manipulators of foreign currencies and the procurers of curious pleasures or illegal commodities lurked at every café-table; and the somberly sinful streets behind the Socco Chico were full of caravanserai with evocative names like Hotel Satan or Pension Delirium."

Nor would the Reichmanns have settled in Tangier had safety been their top priority. The British fortress at nearby Gibraltar was a strategic plum of the highest value rendered suddenly vulnerable by Germany's cakewalk through France. Hitler intended to take it and deny Britain the Mediterranean. By late June, ten Nazi divisions had massed on the French-Spanish border as Hitler's minions discussed terms of alliance with Spain. Although Franco was outwardly pro-Nazi and owed Germany a debt of honor for aid received during the Spanish Civil War, he was leery of Hitler and loath to take up arms again in any cause but his own. On the other hand, Spain was in no position to resist Nazi force; its army was overmatched by the Wehrmacht and much of the country verged on starvation. After France had fallen, "many observers assumed [German forces] would immediately push on through Spain to capture Gibraltar and perhaps spill over into North Africa. . . . Nothing seemed to stand in the way of such an operation, for Gibraltar at that time was practically an empty shell."

When the Reichmanns arrived in Tangier in July, the city's fate remained very much in doubt. It was not until October 1940 that Hitler and Franco met for the first time, in a rail car at the train station in Hendaye, the very spot at which the Reichmanns had crossed into Spain. By this time, the Germans had perfected plans for the assault against Gibraltar. After explaining "Operation Felix" in detail (Gibraltar, the Führer predicted, would fall on January 10, 1941), Hitler called on Franco to join the Axis right then and there. Over the next four hours, Franco worked a dozen variations of "I'd love to but. . . ." Hitler left in a foul mood. "I would rather have three or four teeth out than meet that man again," he supposedly said. Nonetheless, Germany applied increasing pressure on Spain until mid-1941, when Hitler gave up on sealing the western Mediterranean and, in what generally is seen as his greatest strategic error, shifted his focus back to the eastern front by invading the Soviet Union. It was not until an Allied expeditionary force landed in Morocco in late 1942 and pushed Axis forces out of northwest Africa that Tangier could at last feel that the threat of a Nazi incursion into Morocco had been laid to rest.

But if Tangier was perilous and profane, it also was one of the few places in the world in 1940 where a Jewish refugee could hope to rapidly rebuild his net worth. When asked why it was that so many of Ringer's Hungarian patrons went to Tangier, Abraham Schreiber replied: "To make business there, of course. Tangier was a free port. Everybody knew that." Added Alexander Heiden, who had spent several months as a habitué of Ringer's and the Rue Cadet synagogue and had also arrived in Tangier in mid-1940: "I think the Reichmanns and the rest of them decided in Paris to go to Tangier. Yes, of course, they did," he continued, with more certainty.

Well known to globe-trotting tourists as an oasis of exotic decadence, the city was no less renowned among wealthy Europeans as an outpost of anything-goes capitalism. In Tangier, merchants were free to export or import whatever they liked, and customs duties were among the lowest in the world. Gold and foreign currencies were exchangeable on the street at rates determined by the free market, the very free market. The government's role was not to regulate commerce but to liberate it. The International Administration taxed no incomes (corporate or personal) and asked no questions. To open a bank account, or, for that matter, to open a bank, all that was required was an address (a post office box would do).

If Samuel was shrewd in spotting Tangier's commercial potential from the distance of Paris, he was lucky that the Spanish government chose not to extend to it the same autarkic economic regime it had imposed in Spain. The Franco regime was intent not on reforming Tangier but on exploiting it as one of the last bastions of untrammeled capitalism in a world economy battening down for all-out war. Under Spanish control, Tangier would prove as free-wheeling as ever.

Even so, Samuel and Renée Reichmann's attraction to Tangier should not be misconstrued as greed. For Orthodox Jews, there were no truly friendly shores in 1940, no inviolable, accommodating refuge. If Nazi Germany's malevolence was unequaled, it was not without echoes around the globe; the whole world was a simmering pot of jingoism and anti-Semitism. Under such circumstances, the distinction between physical and financial security was blurry. Without money, the Reichmanns might well have tumbled into incarceration at any point along the path from Vienna to Paris to Tangier. With money, a Jew had at least a fighting chance, even, as it turned out, in a place such as Auschwitz.

PART II

EXILE
IN TANGIER

Chapter 7

As evoked in the memoirs of several generations of expatriate artists, itinerant aristocrats, and travel writers, Tangier seems less a city than a kind of municipal hologram—enticing but maddeningly elusive. Neither wholly African nor fully European, Tangier was an ancient crossroads settlement that for most of its three thousand years had been dominated and exploited by foreigners. If the night in Tunis had a thousand eyes, Tangier had at least as many faces, and most of those shown the newcomer were false. "Tangier is an oddity," complained the writer John Gunther, with "an atmosphere of fastidious duplicity."

On one thing at least visitors seemed to agree: Tangier was an entrancing sight from the deck of a ship. "From a distance it sparkles in the lively air of the Strait. . . . A white tooth, perhaps, gleaming in the dark head of Africa. The snowy whiteness of the city walls, the high, crenelated Casbah, the minarets tiled with old faience." The elation commonly produced by the first, shimmering glimpse of "Tanger la Blanche" tended to turn to disappointment and even disgust after the visitor had landed and encountered the teeming, squalid Arab quarter, the Medina. "On the outside," wrote an American who traveled to Tangier in 1893, "it is one of the most beautiful of cities: within it is the vilest; and the transition from one to the other gives me such a shock that I am almost tempted to say that the shining walls which glitter in the sun are but a whited sepulchre, full of dead men's bones and all uncleanness." Mark Twain, who alighted in Tangier in 1867 on what was billed as the world's first pleasure cruise, hardly noticed the offal-clogged streets for the city's sheer strangeness—"a foreign land if ever there was one."

The basic lesson of Tangier's history was this: geography is destiny. The city was founded about 1450 B.C. not by the cave-dwelling Caucasian tribes indigenous to the area—the Berbers—but by the seafaring Phoenicians. The first Jews had settled in Tangier by 700 B.C., if not earlier, and more appeared after the destruction of the Great Temple in Jerusalem in A.D. 70. Strategically located at the crossroads not only of Africa and Europe but of the Mediterranean and the Atlantic, Tangier over the centuries was batted from one great power to another like a great shuttlecock of stone. While the city often was the object of battle, at times it was simply abandoned by one master and claimed by another. In 1471 came the Portuguese, who were the first to name the city "Tanger" or "Tangere," a name adopted even by its Arabic inhabitants. Tangier's Jewish population swelled after 1492, when Spain expelled seventy-five thousand Jews, most of whom settled in Morocco.

By the turn of the twentieth century, Morocco had descended to a state approaching anarchy under a series of rapacious and unpopular Islamic sultans ruling from Fez. Having already added Algeria and Tunisia to its colonial empire, France in 1909 compelled the faltering sultan to grant it a protectorate over all of Morocco. Under the terms of a secret treaty, France ceded to Spain control over a sizable part of northwesternmost Morocco. In deference to Great Britain, which feared that Spain might fortify Tangier to rival Gibraltar, the city and its environs were carved out of the Spanish protectorate and neutralized. Taking the International Settlement of Shanghai as a model, France, Britain, and Spain worked out a multilateral system of government, which was imposed on Tangier after World War I. By 1928, Italy, Sweden, Belgium, Holland, and Portugal had ratified the arrangement and joined in administering the International Zone of Tangier.

Aside from minimal expenditures for public utilities, the eight-nation consortium accepted no responsibility for the welfare of the native population, the great majority of whom remained crushingly poor throughout the coming boom. The Committee of Control, Tangier's new supreme governmental authority, assumed a narrow, self-serving role: to secure for the nationals of the city's eight masters equal access to commercial opportunity. In reinventing Tangier as Inter-Zone, the powers in effect hung a giant sign on the city: "Tangier is open for business—any business."

In the years between World Wars I and II, foreigners by the thousands poured in as Tangier was transformed into what one writer called "a honeypot for the sticky fingered." Although tourism flourished throughout the 1920s and 1930s, it could not keep pace with the city's prime growth industry: money. Scores of new currency dealers and banks sprang up to service and place the capital that flowed into Tangier from the highly regulated economies of Europe. Even the look of Tangier changed radically as private developers made fortunes transforming an arid tract at the edge of the old Medina into a European-style quartier of office and apartment buildings. Known as "new town," the district "floated airily on a plateau above the old, like a wedding cake, stuccoed white, artificial and mondaine."

The Great Depression barely put a dent in Tangier's expansion. Indeed, its growth accelerated, as the influx of arrivistes was augmented by European refugees of all sorts and by Berber tribesmen fleeing famine in the Rif Mountains to the south. From 1932 to 1940, the population of the city nearly doubled, to about 100,000. The filthy streets and open sewers of the overcrowded Medina scandalized the travel writers of the 1930s no less than those of the 1830s. Living conditions were even worse in the shantytown newly sprung up on the outskirts of town. In hovels made of tin cans and driftwood lived hundreds of Berbers, who earned slave wages as construction laborers.

By the time the Reichmanns arrived, Tangier may well have been the most ethnically diverse city of its size anywhere in the world. All the variety of native folk that Twain had described in *Innocents Abroad* were still present—and as colorfully garbed, though many better-educated Arabs now wore business suits with their turbans and fezzes. The city's native Jewish population had tripled, to about fifteen thousand, in the interim. In Tangier, unlike other major Moroccan cities, Jews had never been sequestered in a ghetto, or mellah, but lived closely intermingled with Arabs in the old city. The Rue des Synagogues, which, as the name implied, was lined with tiny synagogues, twisted its way right through the heart of the Medina.

Since Twain's 1867 visit, the natives had been joined by a much-enlarged contingent of foreigners representing more than forty nations, among them 1,600 Frenchmen, 1,400 Englishmen, 1,000 Italians, 350 Portuguese, 300 Turks, 250 Poles, 200 Hungarians, 120 Germans, 90 Argentineans, 85 Swiss, 70 Belgians, and 60 Russians. But the most populous foreign group by far were the Spanish, at 13,000 strong. "Tangier must have been the most cosmopolitan place on earth," wrote one British expatriate. "After Shanghai closed up even the White Russians arrived! But whoever a person was, wherever he came from, he shared the attitude, usually only supposed to prevail amongst the British living abroad, of thinking that he had a perfect right to be there. This was what impressed me immediately as being most remarkable. . . . No one I ever met regarded himself as a foreigner."

———

At first, the Reichmanns took temporary shelter along with other new arrivals in a school of the Alliance Israélite Universelle (AIU), a Paris-based Jewish philanthropy active throughout North Africa. Messod Bendayan, a twelve-year-old Sephardic native of Tangier, stopped by the AIU school one day with some friends to take a peek at the Ashkenazi newcomers. "We went there out of curiosity," Bendayan recalled. "We didn't understand a word of their prayers; it all seemed very eastern. We thought it was curious that they were Jewish and we couldn't understand them. I remember Mr. Reichmann with his beautiful beard. He looked very patriarchal."

Within a few days, the Reichmanns had moved out of the school and into a modern apartment building at 25 Rue Molière, on the outer edge of new town. Completed in 1936, the four-story building stood a lone sentinel on the crest of a steep hill overlooking the bay. It had been designed by a concrete engineer moonlighting as an architect and resembled a blockhouse with balconies. The building's six apartments were solidly constructed and generously sized but devoid of ornamental frill. At first, the Reichmanns occupied both apartments on the third floor, which gave them the run of eight rooms plus two kitchens and two bathrooms—and an ocean view. In May 1941, they sublet one of the apartments to a refugee family named Schwartz and made do with half the space, paying rent of 650 Moroccan francs a month. The five Reichmann brothers split two bedrooms, allowing Eva her privacy. The apartment was sparingly furnished, containing little more than seven beds, a few divans, a half-dozen chairs and one giant dining room table. Throughout the dozen years the Reichmanns would live at 25 Rue Molière, the building was owned by a French family, the Saint-Auberts, who ran a pharmaceutical supply business on the ground floor. The Saint-Auberts were Catholic but during the war rented mostly to Jewish tenants and quickly became accustomed to the sight of Mrs. Reichmann's wig drying on a clothesline in the interior courtyard.

Not quite half of the fifteen hundred Jewish refugees living in Tangier in 1940 were Ashkenazim, most of them Poles who had arrived via Italy. However, the Sephardic natives referred disdainfully to all Ashkenazim, no matter their country of origin, as "los Pollakos." The chilly reception given los Pollakos was due not only to the dissimilarities in religious practice that so intrigued young Bendayan but also to a lack of communal feeling. Tangier's wealthy merchant families made only token efforts to help their impoverished fellow Jews. Under the leadership of Abraham Laredo, a notable exception to the rule of indifference, the Jewish community did organize a refugee relief committee, but it never raised much money. Albert Reinhard, a nephew of Laredo's active on the committee, struggled to persuade rich Sephardim to help even their own relatives. "If it's a goy, you can understand it," said Reinhard, his anger still fresh after fifty years. "But a Jew refusing to help his own like that? I was so disgusted."

In Tangier, the discord between the natives and the newcomers cut deeper than the division between observant and nonobservant Ashkenazim. Not long after they arrived, the Reichmanns called on Samuel Abramovici, a well-to-do local businessman who, though an atheist, was the Ashkenazi Jew of longest residence in Tangier, having arrived in 1912. The Reichmanns and Abramovici conversed in German. "A lot of refugees came to see my parents in getting started here," said Robert Abramovici, Samuel's son, who would remain in Tangier long after all the Jewish refugees had gone. "When I was young, the Jews here had a funny mentality. To them, Ashkenazim were nobodies. I remember an Ashkenazi doctor who did good work in Tangier and even he was badly treated."

The strictly observant Ashkenazim in Tangier brought an added measure of resentment down on themselves by declining to eat the local kosher food and instead importing supplies from Tetuán, a city forty miles distant. While Ashkenazic and Sephardic practices differ in many ways, those involving kashrut are particularly divisive because they tend to invert the most common forms of hospitality into occasions of hostility. For the most part, the Reichmanns did not accept dinner invitations from or extend invitations to Sephardim. While this policy gave offense, it was worse to show up and then refuse to eat. One festival day, Mr. and Mrs. Reichmann departed from their usual practice and visited the home of Joseph Muyal, who was a Sephardic mohel, or circumciser—a religious post inferior in status only to that of rabbi. Even so, Samuel and Renée politely declined all offers of food. After the Reichmanns departed, Muyal turned to his wife and hissed: "Those Pollakos, they think they are better Jews than us." For better or worse, the Reichmanns were considered the most rigorously observant family—native or refugee—that Tangier had seen in some time.

A wealthy jeweler offered the observant refugees the use of the lobby in his house as a Shabbat prayerhouse while Samuel scouted the city for permanent quarters. With a few other Orthodox families, the Reichmanns rented an old house in the Medina from an obliging Sephardi landlord. Edward and a few other boys knocked down some interior walls, did some hammering and sawing, and made a synagogue of the place. The congregation, such as it was, numbered only about twenty adults, not all of whom were convinced that the "Reichmann synagogue," as it was known, was needed. "It really was not so different," said Alexander Heiden, a fellow Hungarian, who attended regularly nonetheless. "Do you know the old story about the Jew who was shipwrecked alone on an island? When he was found, the island had two synagogues."

Samuel also decided the Ashkenazim needed a ritual bath, or mikveh, of their own. He and Edward explored the mellah in search of old mikvehs no longer in use. They found several. Edward took about thirty photographs of the least decrepit one, documenting its poor condition, the roof where the rainwater entered, the pipes that carried the water, and so on. The photos were sent to Rabbi Josef Grunwald, who by now had fled Deutschkreutz and emigrated to New York City. Rabbi Grunwald replied with a long, illustrated letter setting forth in detail what needed to be done to bring the mikveh up to strictly kosher standards. Within a month, the job had been completed and the Arab quarter of Tangier was home to a mikveh that would have done any Oberland village proud.

The Reichmanns enrolled Albert, eleven, Paul, nine, and Ralph, seven, in the grade school run by the Alliance Israélite. Disappointed by the overall quality of instruction, Renée did what in Beled or Vienna would have been unthinkable: she pulled her boys from the Jewish school and entrusted their education to Gentiles. All three were enrolled in what was then considered the best private school in the city—the Lycée Regnault, a French-run institution attended by the children of many of Tangier's diplomats. The Reichmann boys were refused permission to wear a yarmulke in school but were grudgingly allowed to skip Saturday classes. (Thursday was the free day in the lycée system.) "It was not a terribly alienating environment," Paul recalled. "I remember some teachers as very friendly. I was an eager student in certain subjects—mathematics always held first place with me—but there were others I couldn't care less about. One advantage I had was the seating arrangement. It was arranged by height with the shortest boys in the front. I was tall for my age so I always sat in the back row and got less supervision."

At thirteen, Louis Reichmann was too old for the lycée. That he spoke neither Spanish nor French would have handicapped him severely in attending public high school. At Mrs. Reichmann's request, the administrators of a local Catholic girls' school agreed to offer special instruction to a small group of refugee children, including Louis and Eva, who was seventeen. Louis might have been the only Orthodox boy who spent four years in a convent school. "At least I had my sister with me all the time," he recalled ruefully years later.

Edward, as always, was a special case. A self-confident, headstrong boy of fifteen, the eldest Reichmann brother believed he had had all the secular education he required to begin a career in business. He introduced himself to Jewish and Arab import-export merchants and began acting in a small way as a broker among them. By December, when the rainy season started, Edward had profits enough to go to a tailor and order two business suits and a gaberdine raincoat. "I was very proud of these clothes," Edward recalled, "but my parents became a little worried." Their concern only mounted as Edward began riding the rails between Tangier and Tetuán, the capital of Spanish Morocco, in the hope of drumming up more business. Early in 1941, "father and mother sat down with me for a serious talk," Edward said. "I was told that it was very nice that I was doing some business and earning some money but that at my age I should be studying more."

Along with Louis, Edward was taking daily Talmudic instruction with an accomplished Ashkenazi rabbi who had come to Tangier from Trieste. Meanwhile, the three younger brothers were tutored by another refugee rabbi after school every day and also on Thursdays and Saturdays, leaving little time for play beyond the occasional trip to the splendid white-sand beach that lined Tangier's harbor. Away from school, the younger brothers had little contact with other children, aside from a handful of refugee boys whose parents kept strictly kosher homes. Even the gregarious Edward had no real friends among the Sephardim. "Boys my age from the wealthy or upper middle-class families were generally not religious enough for me," he explained. During the family's first few years in Tangier especially, the brothers were one another's constant companions at home, in school, and on the street. "I have an image of the Reichmanns fixed in my mind from long ago," said Rachel Muyal, the niece of Joseph Muyal. "A whole troupe of brothers in their little hats coming down the Rue d'Italie in single file, the oldest in front clearing the way and the youngest bringing up the rear. They are walking fast, determined to get where they were going."

Meanwhile, Samuel got to work, too. According to Edward, his father arrived in Tangier bearing U.S. dollars and pounds sterling totaling $10,000 to $20,000. This capital, modest as it was, gave Samuel Reichmann a crucial advantage over other refugees, most of whom never would manage to make a living in Tangier and had to depend on handouts. The astronomical unemployment rate among refugees was not a product of anti-Semitic policy; in sharp contrast to the government of French Morocco, the Spanish administration did not enact a single anti-Jewish measure during its five-year tenure in Tangier and even refrained from informal harassment. The problem was that conventional job skills counted for little in Tangier, where the economy was wholly geared to the brokering of foreign currency and other commodities. To make a living in the trader's paradise that was wartime Tangier, one had to have capital and put it at risk.

Samuel could not easily have returned to the business of egg wholesaling for the lack of connections in French Morocco, which supplied Tangier with most of its produce. Moreover, with the threat of German invasion looming continuously in the early years of the war, Reichmann was loath to tie up his capital in bulky, perishable inventory. "My parents were looking for a business that would not tie them down—something that would let them go on—[so as] to be able to run the next night," Paul once explained. As an experienced export-import man, Swiss bank depositor, and monied refugee, Samuel had acquired all the expertise needed to qualify him for the quintessential Jewish vocation in Tangier: money changing.

In Tangier, as throughout the Diaspora, money changing had been a predominantly Jewish trade for centuries. During his visit to Tangier in 1867, Mark Twain had encountered numerous "Jewish money changers" in his tour of the Grand Socco, the bustling central marketplace of the old Medina. In 1940, Tangier's currency dealers, or cambios, dealt mainly in Moroccan francs and Spanish pesetas—both of which were legal tender in Tangier—for dollars, pounds, escudos, lire, guilders, and scores of more obscure foreign currencies. As in Twain's day, the cambios were penny-ante businesses lining the Rue es Siaghines, which was one of the main commercial thoroughfares of the Medina. While a few more substantial dealers operated from roofed-over cubicles optimistically advertised as "banks," most sat curbside at folding tables before blackboards bearing scribbled rates of exchange. The money changers were often mistaken for bookies by many first-time American visitors just off the tour boat.

The curbside cambio operators occupied the bottom rung of a financial pecking order topped by a dozen and a half genuine banks, most of which were branches of major Spanish or French banks. The most prestigious of them all were two indigenous houses—Moses Pariente and Banco Salvador Hassan e Hijos—each of which was owned by an aristocratic Sephardic family with long-standing ties to the British crown. The founder of the former, Moses Pariente, was awarded British citizenship in recognition of the loans he generously provided Admiral Horatio Nelson on the eve of his victory at the Battle of Trafalgar. By 1940, ownership of Pariente's bank had passed matrilineally to Aaron and Moses Abensur, who looked and acted like the British crown bankers they were. On a narrow street in the Medina was a commonplace door bearing a dull copper sign no bigger than a calling card. Inside, behind a grill stood a clerk, who admitted authorized visitors to the Abensur brothers' inner sanctum, a huge room sumptuously furnished with antique oak fittings taken from the wardroom of Admiral Nelson's *Victory*.

The Abensurs and Hassans were bound by marriage and overlapping commercial interests to perhaps a dozen other wealthy Sephardic families who collectively dominated the import-export trade of Tangier: the Toledanos, the Pintos, the Cohens, the Laredos, and so on. The men of the merchanting elite gathered every weekday at an elegant private club just off the Boulevard Pasteur, the new town's main thoroughfare, to eat lunch, play cards, and transact business. In time, a few of the wealthiest Ashkenazim would be admitted to the Casino de Tangier, but in 1940 this was out of the question. Instead, an ambitious Ashkenazi refugee hoping to make a few connections would have done exactly what Samuel Reichmann, Nicholas Rosenbaum, and a dozen other Hungarians and Poles did: haunt the Café Central, a freewheeling establishment popular with businessmen of all sorts. "I'd see Reichmann there all the time," recalled Heiden, who was busy reestablishing himself as a diamond dealer. "All the local bankers used to sit around Café Central making deals."

Reichmann got his start in foreign currency as a private speculator working out of his apartment. If, for example, Reichmann believed the value of the pound was likely to rise, he would go to a bank or a curbside cambio and purchase pounds, preferably with a currency he believed likely to decline in price. If the pound did in fact appreciate, he would eventually take his profit by swapping into Swiss francs, U.S. dollars, pounds sterling, or some other currency he deemed likely to rise. "Reichmann's business was different from Rosenbaum's, in that he . . . took more speculative risk," recalled Heiden, who was friendly with both men. By all accounts, Reichmann prospered in his new vocation right from the start, multiplying his trading capital at close if irregular intervals all during the war.

———

While Samuel set about reestablishing himself in business, Renée bought a portable Hermes typewriter and learned how to use it. She hunted and pecked hundreds of letters to relatives and friends, alerting them to the family's whereabouts and offering her services as a mail forwarder, for Tangier was ideally positioned to serve as an information conduit between occupied Europe and the rest of the world. In wresting control of Tangier, the Spanish government officially assured Great Britain that the highly efficient British Post Office and the British Eastern Telegraph Company could continue to operate without interference. The Spanish were as good as their word: mail was sent freely from Tangier without Spanish, Axis, or, for that matter, Allied censorship. Within a few months, according to Edward, Renée's mail was arriving—and departing—in sacks of thirty to forty pounds.

In her career as a postal intermediary, Mrs. Reichmann reconnected close relatives who had lost contact with one another and even acted as a financial transfer agent for the Klein family and others. By early 1941 Mrs. Reichmann had also begun sending small food parcels into Poland, Belgium, and France. The 500-gram parcels contained sardines, chocolate, almonds, and other concentrated foodstuffs, and were packed by Renée and her children with the help of a few other Orthodox families. This effort was a natural extension of the mail transfer service she provided to friends and relatives, though an increasing portion of the recipients were strangers, albeit Orthodox ones. Mrs. Reichmann obtained the names of a few dozen Jews hiding in Belgium and France through a contact in the French Jewish underground, which helped deliver the parcels. She also sent food to internees at Miranda de Ebro, the largest and grimmest of Spain's refugee internment camps. "When something was in the oven that might take an hour or two to bake, she would open her portable typewriter and start some correspondence," Edward recalled. "If she had only fifteen or twenty minutes free, she would sit down and start knitting."

Many friends and relatives of the Reichmanns who had remained in the Oberland began transferring their funds to Samuel for safekeeping through one of Mrs. Reichmann's wealthy Gestetner relatives living in Csorna. Through regular banking channels, this Gestetner deposited the funds in his own numbered account in Zurich before transferring them to Samuel's account. From Zurich, the funds were wired to Tangier, where several Swiss banks operated branch offices.

Renée's early relief efforts, combined with Samuel's role as synagogue organizer, made 25 Rue Molière the social hub of an exceptionally tight-knit circle of a dozen Orthodox Hungarian refugee families and bachelors, many of whom the Reichmanns had known in Paris, if not before: the Grussgotts, the Rosenbaums, the Rosenfelds, the Gabors, the Hollanders, the Schwarzes. Many of the same men who prayed at the house on Rue Cook in the mornings reconvened at the Reichmanns' flat in the evenings, accompanied by their wives and children. While the females assembled food parcels in the kitchen, the males talked business and studied Talmud in the next room. The Reichmanns' closest friends were the Grussgotts, fellow Hungarians (Mr. Grussgott had studied at the Beled yeshiva in his youth) who moved into a second-floor apartment at 25 Rue Molière in the spring of 1941. Zsigmond and Berta Grussgott were quite a bit younger than Samuel and Renée (the oldest of their five children was Ralph's age), but the Reichmanns and Grussgotts were in and out of one another's apartments so often that their downstairs neighbor was surprised that they did not leave Tangier together after the war.

In mid-1941 the Reichmann family ranks were bolstered by the arrival of the beloved Aunt Dadi. She had moved out of the Vienna apartment in 1936, after marrying Isidor Ehrenfeld, a wealthy businessman from the Croatian city of Zenta. Olga had given birth to a son, who was stricken with leukemia. Luckily, Olga happened to be with her son at a clinic in Zurich when Germany invaded and conquered Yugoslavia in April 1941. Renée wangled a pair of Tangier visas out of the Spanish authorities, and Olga and her son flew from Switzerland to Tangier, where they moved into an apartment of their own not far from the Reichmanns' flat. The family's joy at Aunt Dadi's escape from the Nazis was tempered by the uncertain fate of her husband back in Zenta and the hopeless condition of her son, who was not yet five when he died in 1942.

The war preoccupied even the youngest members of the Reichmanns and their refugee circle. The first thing every morning, Paul, who was not yet ten when the family arrived in Tangier, used to buy his own copy of *España*, Tangier's Spanish daily, and *La Dépêche Morocaine*, the city's leading French newspaper. (Tangier also had a British weekly, the *Tangier Gazette*.) Before going off to school, Paul would scan the two papers and clip out articles about the war, taking care to carve them into shapes that fit inside his school books. During class, he would prop up a textbook and study the news from the front. "I was very interested in the war," Paul recalled, "but this also put me in a position to come home and discuss it with my father, who spent the war years always eager for news."

Life in the city was no picnic, especially during the first few years of the war, when food, gasoline, and other basic commodities often were in short supply. But Tangier was spared real crisis by the resourcefulness of its merchants and by the Spanish government's ability to wheedle sugar, flour, butter, corn, beef, and other staples out of the American government, which was perhaps too anxious to buy Franco's neutrality.

If, in putting the Spanish merchant fleet at Tangier's disposal, Franco hoped to placate a city that he had antagonized through military occupation, there were limits to the generalissimo's desire to ingratiate himself with Tangierinos. The local Spanish authorities suppressed all forms of political dissent with a brutality characteristic of the Falange, reserving a special vindictiveness for Communists, real or imagined. The dictator had not forgotten that both the Spanish and Jewish populations of Tangier had strongly favored the opposition—that is, the Republican forces—in the civil war that had brought him to power in the late 1930s. (The city's Muslims, on the other hand, were predominantly sympathetic to Franco and the Nationalist side.) Furthermore, while Spain took pains to remain nonbelligerent in high affairs of state, in Tangier its pro-Axis tilt was plain to all. Some American and British sympathizers were booted out of the city, and Spanish troops watched impassively as Italian hooligans raided the British Post Office and sacked a British department store during the Christmas season of 1940. In early 1941, the Spanish evicted the mendoub, the local representative of the sultan of Morocco, and turned over his magnificent palace to the German government, ostensibly for use as a consulate. A huge swastika shield was installed over the entryway to the mendoubia, which soon was transformed into the main Nazi espionage base in North Africa.

The German chargé d'affaires in Tangier, Keith Reith, had plotted the assassination of Austrian chancellor Engelbert Dollfuss in Vienna in 1934. Reith's staff included a half-dozen hit men known as torpedoes. Italy, too, staffed its legation mainly with intelligence operatives, and by 1941 at least a hundred Axis secret agents were based in Tangier. The British were no less dependent on Tangier as a center of intelligence. After the fall of France in mid-1940, the British Royal Navy bombarded the French fleet at Oran and Dakar, inflicting heavy casualties. Outraged, the French government ordered all British diplomats out of French North Africa: Morocco, Algeria, and Tunisia. This left the international enclave of Tangier as Britain's sole diplomatic post in the region. The British Legation provided cover for agents of the Secret Intelligence Service (SIS), the "cloak" of Britain's covert operations, as well as of the Special Operations Executive (SOE). The SOE was the "dagger" of British intelligence, handling sabotage, assassination, and other "wet works."

The United States had no spies in Northwest Africa until 1941. Early in the year, the United States and French Morocco signed an accord under which the Americans agreed to ship food and other essentials to North Africa on the condition that they not be reshipped into Europe. Ostensibly to monitor these shipments, the United States dispatched twelve vice consuls to Casablanca, Rabat, Algiers, and Tunis. Their real mission was to collect political and military intelligence and aid Free French forces. This was the first major undertaking of the Office of Strategic Services. After the Japanese attack on Pearl Harbor in late

1941 brought America into the war as a full-fledged belligerent, the OSS strengthened its North African spy network and stationed a senior agent in the legation in Tangier to run the entire regional operation under the cover of the naval attaché. J. Rives Childs, who as the U.S. chargé d'affaires was closely involved in intelligence matters, contended in his memoirs that "from 1940 to 1944 there were probably few spots on the globe where more intense espionage and counter-espionage activities were concentrated than in Tangier."

With its genius for free-form commerce, Tangier turned intelligence into a virtual cottage industry. Known or reputed agents of every nationality, along with important businessmen and diplomats, were dogged by a ragged army of freelance amateurs who hawked their wares amid the bustle of the Socco Chico like so many tourist trinkets. "It would be 10 cents for 'Alster going to Gibraltar' or 'Pariente going to Tetuán,' " recalled Alphonso Rodriguez, an OSS agent stationed in Tangier during the war. At least one informant would make his way every Friday among the British, German, French, and Italian consulates, collecting his wages from each.

The machinations of Tangier's populous spy fraternity made the city a dangerous place. One night early in the war a huge explosion obliterated a cliffside villa in a lonely section of Tangier, sending what remained of the edifice crashing in a pile of flames down to the sea. Eight people—Nazi agents all—were killed. Spaniards in the employ of the SOE had dynamited the villa, which contained an infrared station that the Germans used to monitor Allied ships passing through the Straits of Gibraltar and to signal U-boats. As an encore, British intelligence planned to attach an underwater mine to a German dredger anchored in the Bay of Tangier. The explosives for this job, as for the previous one, were sent by ferry from Gibraltar in the British diplomatic pouch. Suspecting that the British were using their pouch to smuggle dynamite, a German agent placed a detonator next to it while the ferry was unloading at the quay in Tangier. The resulting explosion obliterated most of the quay, killing thirty-five. The violence alarmed the Reichmanns, but not half as much as did Renée's decision to leave Tangier in early 1942 and travel through the battlefields of Europe to Hungary.

Chapter 8

S purning the pleas of her husband and friends in Tangier, Renée Reichmann risked her freedom, and perhaps her life, in returning to Hungary in
February 1942. Mrs. Reichmann desperately missed her parents, who were
frail and fading, and apparently feared—prophetically—that she might never
see them again if she waited until the end of the war to visit Hungary. (Róza
Gestetner would die in 1943 and Adolf in 1944.) At the same time, the activist
in Mrs. Reichmann had been roused by vague but ominous reports out of Slovakia, Hungary's neighbor to the north, that Jews were being forced from their
homes and confined en masse in rural camps. All the same, Renée's departure
mystified her children. "Even looking at all this in retrospect," Edward mused
in an unpublished memoir, "I still cannot fully explain mother's strength and
motivation. From Tangier, it was certainly not yet at all clear in what way or
manner she could help anyone in Europe. . . . I can only come to the conclusion that many great achievements and deeds in history were accomplished by
will and not necessarily by logic and rationality."

To reach Győr, Mrs. Reichmann had to run a gauntlet of fascist, Nazi-
affiliated states: Spain, Vichy France, Italy, Croatia, and Hungary itself. Newly
independent Croatia then was knee-deep in genocide. After conquering
Yugoslavia, the Germans had carved it up and distributed the pieces among
their local confederates, including the Ustaše, the right-wing Croat nationalist
movement. Ustaše zealots murdered tens of thousands of Serbs and at least
twenty thousand Jews, including, the Reichmanns would learn later, Olga
Ehrenfeld's husband.

Mrs. Reichmann traveled on her Hungarian passport, which, thanks to that
obliging consul back in Paris, did not identify her as Jewish. She also was able
to gain a measure of institutional protection by obtaining a letter of introduc-

tion from the Spanish Red Cross. Traveling by train, she apparently made it back to Győr without incident in about two weeks. She had returned to a nation at war. The Hungarian army had first seen action in the German invasion of Yugoslavia and in mid-1941 had joined the Wehrmacht in its massive, misguided assault against the Soviet Union. In her hometown, many familiar faces were missing, including several of her brothers and brothers-in-law who had been drafted into labor battalions. Along with Gypsies, Jews were deemed unfit to bear arms by the Hungarian government but were pressed into national service as laborers in units attached to the military. Many of the fifty-two thousand Jews who served in the labor battalions perished under horrendous conditions on the Russian front.

Hungary's alliance with Nazi Germany was a sword of Damocles suspended over its Jews, but in Slovakia the blade already was falling fast. Germany had dismembered Czechoslovakia in 1939, occupying its eastern half, Bohemia and Moravia, which was incorporated into the Third Reich as a "protectorate." Nominally independent, Slovakia in reality was a German satellite run by an obeisant regime of homegrown fascists, the Hlinka Guard. In late 1941, the Slovakian government rounded up two-thirds of the country's eighty thousand Jews and imprisoned them in makeshift camps scattered throughout Slovakia. As they languished in detention, the fear grew that they would be deported again, this time to Poland, to work as laborers in Nazi-run factories. In fact, the great majority of these prisoners soon would be shipped to Poland—but to camps designed not for labor but for death. Unwittingly, Mrs. Reichmann had revisited the Oberland at the very juncture at which Hitler's war metamorphosed into the Final Solution.

Ever since Hitler's ascent to chancellor, the Nazi regime had tried to persecute the Jews into fleeing German territory. This strategy had failed, largely because none of the Western democracies was willing to open wide its gates to Jewish immigration. In the fall of 1941, Germany abruptly reversed course and prohibited further Jewish emigration. Hitler had decided to solve his "Jewish problem" by annihilating European Jewry, though he had not yet decided exactly how to go about it. On January 20, 1942, the senior administrators of Nazidom gathered at Wansee, near Berlin, to organize the logistics of mass extermination. The Jews were to be confined first to dozens of concentration camps and then funneled into six death camps in Poland: Chelmno, Belzec, Majdanek, Treblinka, Sobibor, and Auschwitz. In their eagerness to please their masters in Berlin, the Slovakian authorities provided the Nazis with the first transport to Auschwitz—a trainload of 999 girls sent from Poprad in late March, 1942.

In Slovakia, as throughout Eastern Europe, the Holocaust proved disproportionately fatal to the Orthodox. "In short," observed one writer, surveying the carnage in 1945, "whoever was more pious was utterly destroyed." The dis-

parity was not the deliberate product of Nazi policy. To the Nazis, Jewish identity was a matter of genetics, not religious belief or practice. Under the expansive definition incorporated into German law by the Hitler regime, a Jew in
essence was anyone with at least one Jewish grandparent.

The Orthodox death rate in the Holocaust exceeded the average among Jews
for one deceptively simple reason: the devout were much less likely to have left
while the leaving was good. The United States and Palestine—the most popular
prewar Jewish havens—were unacceptable to many Orthodox Jews on religious grounds. America was a trefe medina, a godless melting pot where Jews
were transformed into non-Jews in a generation or less, while Palestine was a
bastion of secular Zionism. Most important, there was no place even remotely
like home for strictly observant Jews, whose daily lives were a meticulously
woven tapestry of mutual interdependence. As the Nazis and their helpmates
dismantled the institutions of communal life, the natural inclination of the
Orthodox was not to flee and begin rebuilding their communities from scratch
in some distant, hostile land, but to stay put and pray for deliverance.

For the Jews of Europe in general, the alternatives to passive resistance were
four: armed self-defense, flight to the forest, refuge in a hiding place or false
identity, or slave labor (the option most famously exemplified by the Schindler-
juden). In practice, none of these tactics worked for long, if at all. The simple
fact was that once the Nazis pulled up the drawbridges, few Jews were in a position to save themselves. But for the great majority of concentration camp
inmates, the outside help they needed not only never arrived, it never was sent.
"The concept of rescue, like that of genocide, did not fully come into its own—
nor was it grasped by the world at large—until after the war."

Rescuing a major portion of the six million inmates would have required
large-scale military intervention. Early in the war, of course, all that Allied
forces could manage to do was stave off defeat. But even when victory against
the Axis appeared assured, the governments of Great Britain and the United
States would not be diverted from military goals by even the simplest of Jewish
rescue schemes. Allied bomber planes inflicted heavy damage on manufacturing plants a few miles from Auschwitz but made no effort to take out the rail
lines carrying Jews to the camp. "To kill the Jews, the Nazis were willing to
weaken their capacity to fight the war," concluded American historian David
Wyman. "The United States and its allies, however, were willing to attempt
almost nothing to save them."

Allied government policy reflected public indifference to the plight of European Jewry. For the most part, even such avowedly humanitarian institutions
as the Christian churches and the International Red Cross assumed the role of
silent bystanders. While the major Jewish organizations of the world raised a
righteous racket, they were by and large ineffective in championing rescue.
Riven by ideological conflict, American Jewish groups clashed bitterly over pri-

orities and tactics, leaching urgency from the cause of rescue and subordinating it to various political goals, notably the founding of an independent Jewish state in Palestine.

In the face of pervasive institutional stasis, it was left to individual Jews to help their own as best they could. For Mrs. Reichmann, European rescue and relief were ends in themselves, not pieces to be fitted into the puzzle of a larger political agenda. The single-minded intensity that she brought to this pursuit was a product of religious belief as much as the particularities of personality, for in the Torah the obligation to save an endangered life—the ancient doctrine of pikkuah nefesh—takes precedence over all other mitzvot, even that of keeping the Sabbath. "To save a life," says the Talmud, "is to save a world."

In returning to Hungary in early 1942, Mrs. Reichmann was effectively present at the creation of the Pracovna Skupina, or Working Group, an underground rescue group based in Bratislava. Although the leadership of the Working Group included Jews of diverse affiliation, its dominant figure was a fiery ultra-Orthodox educator and scholar named Rabbi Michael Ber Weissmandel. While Rabbi Weissmandel was an important rabbi in his own right, he was the son-in-law and protégé of one of the great eminences of Oberlander Orthodoxy: Rabbi Samuel David Ungar of Nitra, an ancient Slovakian mountain town. Even some Nazi officials acknowledged Rabbi Ungar's stature by referring to the Nitra yeshiva as the "Little Vatican" or the "Jewish Vatican." As a pious Oberlander, Renée Reichmann revered Rabbi Ungar without ever having met him. After the war, she went to great lengths to secure Tangier visas for the late rabbi's surviving relatives and students—ninety-nine people all told.

While the Zionist resistance in Slovakia was inclined toward the use of armed force, the Working Group relied on more classical means of rescue: ransom and bribery. Ancient and medieval Jewish history is replete with accounts of captive individuals and entire communities rescued through payoffs of one kind or another—a practice known as pidyon shevuyim. However, as European Jews were emancipated and assimilated, the tradition of pidyon shevuyim fell into general disrepute and was maintained into the twentieth century only within eastern Europe's ultra-Orthodox communities, which continued to adhere to the Torah imperative of rescue by any means necessary short of murder or idolatry. As the deportations began in Slovakia, the Working Group dangled bribes before SS and Hlinka officers from the top to the bottom of the chain of command. (Dieter Wislicny, the SS chief in Slovakia, took $50,000.) As a result, thousands of Jews were able to evade the dragnet, at least for a time.

Renée's brother in Bratislava, Henrik Gestetner, was at least peripherally involved with the Working Group. Gestetner had lost his printing and engraving plant as part of the "Aryanization" of Slovakian commerce and industry but had been exempted from deportation so that he could continue running the business for the government. He also held a Hungarian passport, which afforded him an extra measure of protection and allowed him to travel freely between Slovakia and Hungary. Among those whom Henrik helped escape through the Working Group's underground network was Isaac Klein, his brother-in-law, who had fled from Austria to Poland and then surreptitiously crossed into Slovakia. The day after Klein went into hiding in the northern Slovakian town of Liptovský Mikuláš, Gestetner arrived on the train from Bratislava (a twelve-hour ride) bearing money and travel instructions. When Klein reached Prešov, Gestetner popped up again. "Exactly what Henrik's role was with [the Working Group] I never knew," Klein recalled. "But he was definitely part of the team."

Jews hid in the thick forests along Slovakia's southern border and then crossed into Hungary in groups of a half-dozen or so in the company of a paid guide, usually a local Gentile capable of navigating tricky terrain in the dead of night. Often, guards were bribed on both sides of the border to look the other way. However, many of the ten thousand Jews who entered Hungary in this manner during 1942 failed to find refuge and soon were apprehended by the Hungarian police. "The local Jews, afraid of being punished by the authorities, hesitated to take them in," wrote Slovakian historian Lidia Rothkirchen. "Only a relatively small group came to the refugees' assistance and gave money to help them—most of these were Zionists or members of the Orthodox Community."

Among the latter were Renée Reichmann and her youngest sister, Gabriella, nicknamed "Reska," who still lived at home with her parents in Győr. Working with Henrik and other Orthodox Jews on both sides of the border, Renée and Reska met Jews after they had been smuggled across the border and guided them to hiding places in Győr, where newcomers were better able to blend in than in smaller towns and villages. Rescue efforts during this early phase of the Working Group's activities have not been well documented so there is no way of telling how many refugees the Gestetners helped save in 1942. In principle, it did not matter: as the Talmud said, to save a life was to save a world. This was dangerous work, done mostly after sundown, for Hungarian Jews caught helping illegal aliens risked arrest and internment. Reska was indeed arrested and jailed for more than a year. According to Edward, his mother barely escaped a similar fate. "One week after she left Győr [to return to Tangier] there was a search warrant out," he has said. "They were looking for her."

Renée, who remained in Hungary for nearly three months, did have a close call on her return trip. After crossing into Italy from Croatia, she was arrested by an Italian border guard who insisted that her Italian transit visa was invalid. As she examined her papers, Mrs. Reichmann realized to her horror that the border guard was correct: the visa only authorized east to west travel across Italy, making no provision for a return trip. She was taken off the train and locked in a cell for the better part of a day. According to Paul Reichmann, who did not learn of this incident until his mother informed him of it in 1988, Mrs.

Reichmann finally talked her way out of this tight spot, persuading the guard not only to let her go but to help her obtain a proper transit visa.

After passing through Italy without further incident, she stopped in Marseille to visit the Rosenfelds, Wetzlers, Koppels, and two other Orthodox refugee families she had met in Paris. Like the Reichmanns, these families had fled Paris at the approach of the German Army but had been unable to arrange sanctuary in the United States, Great Britain, or anywhere else and so were stuck in Marseille. Although the Mediterranean port was located in unoccupied France, their position was tenuous, for the Vichy government had enacted a series of discriminatory measures aimed at foreigners and Jews. And who could say when Hitler might decide to extend the zone of German occupation to encompass all of France? Mrs. Reichmann offered to help her friends get out of Marseille, cabling instructions to Eva to apply for Tangier immigration visas for the entire group.

Renée finally secured these visas a few months after she returned to Tangier, enabling all five families to leave Marseille in July 1942, which was just in the nick of time. The next month, the Vichy government began expelling foreign Jews by the thousands to the German-occupied zone, to be fed into the Nazi concentration camp system. In November, the Germans extended their zone of occupation to encompass all of France and finished the roundup of the Jews themselves.

Mrs. Reichmann returned to Tangier from the front lines of Holocaust rescue with newfound determination to help Hitler's captives in any way that she could, though she realized that from the distance of Morocco there was not much that she could do without the cooperation of Spanish officials. In accounts of Mrs. Reichmann's rescue work written by Orthodox partisans, Spanish officialdom is portrayed as bowing before the sheer righteousness of her cause. Her sons certainly have done nothing to discourage this notion. The reality is more intriguing—and, if anything, more impressive as a testament to Mrs. Reichmann's drive and resourcefulness. If the SS and Hlinka officers in Slovakia were susceptible to bribes, Spanish officials fairly demanded them, even for the routine functions of government. Renée Reichmann did not presume to attempt to alter the workings of power in Tangier. Instead, like Rabbi Weissmandel, she learned how to play a corrupt game by the house rules for selfless, noble ends.

———

Mrs. Reichmann brought back to Tangier a list of about a thousand names of Slovakian Jews, the great majority of whom were Orthodox and who had been deported to Nazi camps in Bohemia, Germany, and Poland. Her goal of expanding her food parcel program to make regular shipments to these camps seemed an exercise in futility even to some of the volunteers she recruited to help assemble the parcels. One day during a lull in the packing, a Sephardic youth named Abraham Pinto blurted out, "What's the use? Do you really think the Germans will allow the Jews to eat?" Mrs. Reichmann was unruffled. "If just one Jew eats the chocolate, I am satisfied."

The available evidence suggests, in fact, that most of the huge volume of food parcels mailed to concentration and labor camps by Jews from around the world never did reach their addresses. While many were stamped "undeliverable" and returned to their senders, pilfering incoming mail was virtually a perquisite of employment for Nazi camp guards. In some camps, the mails were looted systematically by the commandant himself. When Bergen-Belsen finally was liberated, British troops found warehouses crammed high with food parcels sent from Sweden by the World Jewish Congress. Yet it appears that in some camps food parcels were now and then delivered to a fortunate minority of inmates.

In the final, apocalyptic months of the war, Isaac Klein was starving in the Nazi slave labor camp at Kaupfering when, to his amazement, an SS guard handed him a food parcel. Nearly fifty years later, Klein still vividly recalled its contents: "144 pieces of lump sugar—about 2 pounds altogether—a can of tuna fish, and 20 cigarettes. The women prisoners got condensed milk instead of cigarettes. It was a miracle because our Nazi guards were starving, too." The parcel had been sent by Hilfssverein für Judische Flüchtlinge in Shanghai, better known as HIJEFS, a small but dauntless Orthodox aid group based in Montreux, Switzerland. (Mrs. Reichmann apparently established contact with HIJEFS during her trip to Hungary and worked closely with the group from 1943 until 1946. It is possible that some of the food in Klein's parcel originated in Tangier.)

Why would Hitler and his henchmen have allowed extra calories to prolong the lives of people they were bent on annihilating? The architects of Nazi genocide designed two types of prison camps that, in their own minds anyway, were distinctively different: the concentration camp, where deported Jews were collected, and the extermination camp, where they were gassed. For camp inmates, this was a cruelly capricious distinction: uniformly barbaric conditions made each camp a death camp in fact, if not in name. Although concentration camp deaths could hardly be considered accidental, neither were they planned in the strictest sense. Murder may have been the hobby of concentration camp commandants but it was not their job. If some prisoners put on a few pounds before they were shipped to Auschwitz, what did it matter? In the end, the Zyklon B would get them just the same.

There are indications that the German government itself made a business out of the sale of food parcels for shipment to the camps. After the fall of France, food dealers in Switzerland began advertising gift parcels at high prices for shipment anywhere in Germany and most of occupied Europe. At the request of the U.S. government, Swiss authorities investigated these mail-order purveyors and found that orders received by Swiss firms were being routed to German firms. The parcels were assembled from the stocks of port warehouses throughout western Europe looted by the Nazis as well as from cargoes captured on the high seas by German warships and submarines. "It is the opinion of this office," the U.S. consulate in Zurich concluded in early 1942, "that the entire organization is sponsored by the German Government to acquire foreign exchange at no great cost to Germany."

To mount her own large-scale parcel program, Mrs. Reichmann had to secure food in bulk, recruit volunteer labor, and arrange for transport. But the most daunting task she confronted was persuading the Spanish Moroccan government to grant her licenses to export food by the ton at a time when Spanish Morocco and Spain itself were desperately hungry. Spanish agriculture had not fully recovered from the civil war, which had brought starvation to many parts of the country. In emulation of fascist Germany and Italy, Franco's Nationalist regime in 1939 had responded to the economic crisis by imposing a policy of extreme autarky that would remain in effect, with minor adjustments, for two decades. With the avowed aim of making Spain self-sufficient, the authorities in Madrid clamped strict controls on every aspect of economic activity, creating horrendous bureaucratic inefficiencies as well as abundant opportunity for official corruption.

Oppressed at every turn by rampant, self-serving officialdom, producers and consumers joined in massive conspiracy against their masters in Madrid, creating an underground economy of a size and scope unparalleled in the rest of Europe. The term "estraperlo" came into wide use throughout Spain to connote not only the black market per se but the lifestyle of sharp, furtive practices adopted even by many privileged Spaniards. "Ladies of good society would boast: 'I bought some potatoes estraperlo,' with the same pride that they said: 'I bought this hat at Hélène's' when they returned from shopping excursions to Biarritz." Although everything worth having was offered estraperlo at one time or another, food was the enduring foundation of the black market. By some estimates, about one-third of all grain produced in the country in the 1940s was sold estraperlo, providing domestic growers with 60 percent of their income.

In the fall of 1940, Franco instituted a draconian set of legal penalties for black-marketeering. Although in the first year of the sanctions 88,000 estraperlistas were prosecuted and 1,300 sentenced to labor battalions, the black market continued to flourish. In the fall of 1941, Franco gave military courts jurisdiction over black-marketeering cases, with power to impose the death penalty. The immediate reaction was panic; mountains of discarded chickpeas were found in the Guadalquivir River. In the long run, though, even the imposition of capital punishment "had very little effect, because of the extreme shortages and the maladministration and growing corruption of the system." The lower levels of the enforcement system were staffed by a vast contingent of miserably paid civil servants and policemen, who, like the meanest manual laborers, had to work two jobs to make ends meet. Bribes were a commonplace temptation made irresistible by the pervasiveness of graft and patronage in the upper ranks of the army and the Falange Party, which Franco adopted as his own. "Without a powerful friend somewhere, it was difficult to live in Spain and certainly impossible to carry on business," concluded a U.S. journalist stationed in Madrid during World War II.

In Spanish Morocco, the tendency toward corruption was exaggerated by Spain's colonialist posture and its long-standing use of the protectorate as a garrison for elite military units. Bribe-taking was not the half of it: high government officials owned interests in black market enterprises and routinely manipulated the official rationing system to enrich themselves and their partners. Spain certainly did not introduce malfeasance to Tangier: the international administration it supplanted had basically acted as a tribunal of institutionalized patronage, and the slang word by which most Tangierinos referred to the grease applied to the official palm was Arabic—"baksheesh." But in fusing estraperlo with the ancient Islamic tradition of baksheesh, the Spanish brought favoritism-as-government to new heights.

The black market boss of bosses in the Spanish zone was, astoundingly, its highest-ranking economic official. A secret report filed by the U.S. naval attaché in Tangier in 1944 described Tomás García Figueras, then forty-three, as "an intelligent, well-educated man of no scruples" and "a born plotter and complete hypocrite." Figueras is still well known in Spain as the author of a dozen books on Moroccan history and culture. Although he may have been a scholar, Figueras was never a gentleman. As a youth, he joined the army and the Falange Party and rose through the ranks of each to become the chief administrator of Larache, a coastal smuggler's haven an hour's drive south of Tangier. As head of the Delegation of Economy, Industry, and Trade from 1942 to 1946, Figueras's reach expanded to encompass all of Spanish Morocco. Nothing could be exported from or imported into Tangier without a license bearing the signature of Tomás García Figueras.

In none of the dozen of Mrs. Reichmann's wartime letters that have found their way into public archives does she relate how she obtained his blessing, though it is evident that she encountered early resistance and had to make frequent trips to Tetuán, the Spanish Moroccan capital. As a rule, high officials like García Figueras held sway not through brute intimidation but through subtle, even ceremonial cooptation. In Franco's Spain, even the lowliest conniving clerk demanded respect from the person to whom he so decorously extended his palm for greasing. To excel at the stylized ritual of extracting special consideration from Spanish authority, it helped enormously to be Spanish oneself, of course, and to come introduced by the right people. For the newly arrived foreigner especially, personal connections to power were mandatory. And when that foreigner's ambitions were as grand as Renée Reichmann's, only the choicest ones would do.

Mrs. Reichmann's cause was aided immeasurably by the Allied invasion of Morocco in November 1942. In Tangier, Allied sympathizers were said to be "wild with jubilation" after American and British troops made surprise landings at three points to the south of the city along the largely unguarded coast of Morocco. "Operation Torch" was a smashing success. Allied troops routed Vichy French forces in a few days and pressed eastward, bypassing Tangier in pursuit of German and Italian armies in Algeria and points east. Although the Spanish would maintain control of Tangier until the end of the war, they were constrained in their pro-Axis sympathies by the knowledge that the Allies could have retaken the city at any time. "Before the Allied landing, the Jews in Tangier felt quite isolated and concerned for the future," Edward Reichmann recalled. Afterward, "we relaxed because the general feeling in our part of the world was that the Allies would end up victorious and that Spain would be smart enough not to join Germany." Indeed, the Franco government not only maintained a scrupulous neutrality but increasingly hedged its bets by looking for ways to ingratiate itself with the British and Americans.

———

In her networking, Mrs. Reichmann relied heavily on the extraordinary drive and precocity of her two eldest children. Seventeen going on twenty-five by the time she arrived in Tangier, Eva had matured into a beautiful, raven-haired extrovert who, on the outside anyway, resembled Renée's sister Olga more than her own mother, sharing not only her aunt's good looks but her vivacity. Eva picked up Spanish as easily as she had French and by 1941 was conversant in five languages, all but one of which (Hebrew) were of daily use in the international madhouse of Tangier. Eva's girlish charm was deceiving, though, for she had inherited her mother's spunk and sharp-tongued tenacity. "Maidie was so pretty but she could speak like a lawyer," said Messody Hadida, a Sephardi who, as secretary to the local refugee relief committee in Tangier, worked closely with both Reichmann women. Added Albert Reinhard, a refugee from Luxembourg who ran the same committee: "Of all the Reichmanns, I knew Eva best. She had great energy. It seemed to me that she often was the one who was really pushing things ahead."

Although Eva modestly described herself as her mother's secretary and translator, in truth she filled the role of junior alter ego. Renée not only brought her daughter along on her official audiences but frequently sent her on solo missions—especially when the task at hand required charming some Spanish gallant or another. If an important matter needed attention while

Renée was traveling, it was almost always Eva who filled in. Together, mother and daughter made a most dynamic duo. "They were a bit intimidating, actually," recalled A. David Fritzlan, who was a vice consul at the U.S. Legation in Tangier during the war. "In would come this tall, handsome woman with dark hair and pale skin and with this very beautiful daughter in tow—fashionably attired but never flashy. Mrs. Reichmann's manner was one of authority and confidence. She would speak in French and then her daughter would add something in English."

Through Eva, with an unwitting assist from young Albert, the Reichmanns succeeded in establishing a connection to the highest circle of Spanish power: the military. In the winter of 1941–42, Albert came down with a chronic fever and congested lungs. Before leaving on her trip to Hungary, Mrs. Reichmann took her son to Dr. Emil Manney, one of Tangier's finest physicians, who prescribed a change of climate for the twelve-year-old. With Eva and Aunt Dadi, the boy spent six weeks at El Parador, a plush ski resort near Ketama, a Rif Mountain town about halfway between Tangier and Melilla. Ketama was something of a Nationalist landmark, for it was in a nearby wooded glen that crack units of the Spanish Foreign Legion slipped into hiding in 1936, awaiting Franco's return from his Canary Islands exile.

While staying at El Parador, Eva befriended a local dignitary, Ros Angelos de Beneyto Ronda, or "Bebe" for short. Bebe, who was not much older than Eva, had recently married Captain José Jaime Beneyto Ronda, who was the military governor of the Ketama region of Morocco. Bebe had been born into an elite Spanish military family. Her father, General Enrique Arias, was a Nationalist stalwart who emerged from the Civil War as one of the highest-ranking military officers in Spanish Morocco. Bebe's brother, also named Enrique Arias, was a career officer in the Spanish Army and, like her husband, well on his way to the rank of general.

Not long after Albert and his guardians checked into El Parador, a huge storm dropped several feet of snow on Ketama, closing all roads out for a few weeks. "Our house was near the ski lodge," recalled Mrs. Beneyto Ronda. "When we were snowbound, I used to love to ride my horse over there and spend time with the people from Tangier. That's how I met Maidie. We were snowbound together. She was such a charming girl, so very genuine." The blizzard was uniquely discomfiting to Albert, Eva, and Olga, who, as El Parador's only Orthodox guests, had arranged to have kosher food shipped to Ketama by bus from Tangier. When the buses stopped running, Bebe came to the rescue. "I offered them whatever was in my house and they took potatoes, nuts, figs," Mrs. Beneyto Ronda recalled. "I saw Maidie morning, noon, and night for a month."

A few weeks after Ketama dug out from the snowstorm, Eva and her aunt took the much-improved Albert back to Tangier, arriving a week before

Passover. Before Eva had left El Parador, Edward had said, she "mentioned to Bebe that Passover was coming and the customary meals required a lot of boiled potatoes and that her family was worried about where they would get them with strict rationing in Tangier. . . . The family was at the seder when there was a loud knock at the door. Two Spanish soldiers stood outside with sacks of potatoes and sugar sent six hundred kilometers by Eva's friend." Mrs. Beneyto Ronda, Edward added, "turned out to be a very valuable contact for the rescue work."

While Eva was charming her way into the affections of the Spanish elite, Edward was rampaging across the landscape in furtherance of his budding career as an import-export merchant. Like his sister, Edward seemed a good deal older than he was because of his physical maturity, ambitiousness, and exuberant self-confidence. His parents decided to apprentice him and Louis to José Benaim Hachuel, who was one of the leading industrialists in Tetuán. An ancient Sephardic family of distinguished lineage, the Benaim Hachuels owned a complex of factories and employed a thousand workers in the manufacture of chocolate, candy, carpets, glass, soaps, paints, and other products. The Reichmanns had arranged an introduction to Mr. Hachuel through his brother, who owned the pharmacy they patronized in Tangier. Accompanied by Eva as translator, Mr. and Mrs. Reichmann met Hachuel in his palatial home in Tetuán. "Mr. Reichmann said he wanted his two oldest sons to learn the business of candy, cookies, and chocolate making," Hachuel recalled some fifty years later. "As a guarantee that they would not compete against me one day, he said he would put in the Pariente bank in my name the sum of $10,000. I said I trusted his word more than I trusted the $10,000, and he could send his sons any time."

Edward and Louis spent a year and a half working as unpaid assistants to Hachuel, who rotated them through a series of jobs that wholly encompassed not only the candy-making process but other aspects of his operation. Edward even designed his own Moroccan carpet, which Hachuel set aside and later gave to him as a wedding present. The brothers spent the entire workweek in Tetuán, commuting by bus and returning home Friday afternoon in time for Shabbat. In Tetuán, they shared a room in a little pensione and for a time were houseguests of the Benchimols, a well-fixed Sephardic family known for their charity. In every sense, the brothers led a spartan existence. "I always invited them to come to my house but they never wanted to come," recalled Hachuel, who was only mildly observant himself. "Once they did come, but ate nothing. They were very strict in that respect."

Like most educated Moroccan Jews, Hachuel was fluent in French. Edward was not, but his French was not as bad as his Spanish. After completing their tour of duty in the factories, Edward and Louis moved into Hachuel's head office and were instructed in procurement, marketing, and bookkeeping. "I had utter confidence in them both," said Hachuel, who had no sons or sons-in-law in the business. At one point, Hachuel went off on a month-long vacation and left his keys with the Reichmann brothers, trusting them to open all the factories in the morning and lock them at the end of the day. "After a year or so we felt we knew enough," Louis recalled. "Edward, especially, was very able. He was already running some departments."

True to their father's promise, Edward and Louis did not go into competition with Hachuel. Instead, Louis joined his father as his bookkeeper, while Edward returned to the import-export business in Tangier in partnership with Ernest Rosenfeld, a refugee boy about his own age recently arrived from Marseille on one of the visas supplied by the Reichmanns. José Benaim Hachuel helped the boys off to a rousing start by agreeing to buy raw materials through them. On Hachuel's behalf, Edward and his partner imported large quantities of animal fats, turpentine, resins, gum arabic, and other commodities, mostly from Argentina, Australia, and Portuguese Angola. "We quickly made a lot of money from Hachuel," Reichmann recalled. "He didn't seem to mind." To the contrary, Hachuel appreciated the neophytes' ingenuity and tenacity. "In those days, it was hard to get many raw materials, but they had a way of finding them," Hachuel said.

With the capital and credibility accumulated in serving so prominent an industrialist, Reichmann & Rosenfeld stood on its own as a full-fledged, albeit miniature, export-import house, with its own lines of credit at the Banque Commercial du Maroc and other banks and an industrial clientele scattered throughout the Spanish enclaves of Morocco—Ceuta, Melilla, and Larache, as well as Tetuán. While Reichmann & Rosenfeld generally prospered, the firm took losses in heating pads (the 110-volt models it imported would not run on Tangier's 220-volt wiring) and, as some tell it, an opportunistic foray into sugar cubes. At an auction in Tangier, the story goes, the partners bought a ton or two of sugar cubes that had become contaminated in a leaky warehouse, intending to resell them to a rum distillery. When the sugar was deemed unsuitable for distilling, the boys unloaded it on Arab coffeehouses, specifying on their invoices that the cubes were not to be used for human consumption but expecting full well that they would be. As tactfully as possible, Edward and Ernest warned their fellow refugees away from the cafés of their customers.

One of Reichmann & Rosenfeld's most ambitious early undertakings was sabotaged by Mrs. Reichmann in the name of the starving Jews of Europe. Edward and Ernest bought several hefty consignments of almonds from growers in Spanish Morocco and then hired forty or fifty Berber tribeswomen to crack the nuts and pack them for export to the United States. Three months into the venture, Mrs. Reichmann was delighted to learn from her own sources that her son had amassed a sizable inventory of almonds. Citing the maternal equivalent of eminent domain, Mrs. Reichmann ordered Edward to sell her the almonds at cost, refusing her son even a penny of middleman's profit.

In partnership with Rosenfeld, Edward paid a few thousands dollars at auction for a metal hangar on the Tangier waterfront formerly used as a depot by the Spanish Army. Reichmann bought the hangar because it seemed like a good value; he had no idea what to do with the structure or how to remove it from its present site. He bought a lot on the Rue de Fez and hired a crew of workmen. Using an elaborate color-coding system, Edward and his helpers disassembled the hangar, carted it to the Rue de Fez site, and put it back together again. With a little remodeling it made a decent parking garage where Prince Moullay Josef, the heir to the Moroccan throne, used to have his car washed when he came to Tangier from Rabat. "Whenever he arrived, the garage manager phoned me and I would come over quickly and we would have Arab tea or Arab coffee together," Reichmann recalled.

Using the makeshift garage as his showroom, Edward began dealing in used cars. For most of the war, new cars were extremely hard to come by in Tangier, the U.S. government having banned auto exports. "One day Edward came to see me and said, 'Voilà, you're a Ford agent and you can't get any cars. I can get you some cars,' " recalled Salomon Bendahan, the proprietor of Garage Universal, which was the official Ford dealer for the whole of Morocco. To Bendahan's surprise, Reichmann did indeed obtain a number of cars. Bendahan wrote down their serial numbers and cabled the list to his contacts in Detroit. "They told me it was quite possible that [Reichmann] had bought them from an American agent on the black market and had them smuggled over from New York," Bendahan recalled. "I never found out for sure where they came from. Reichmann was extremely shrewd. He was still very young but you could already see he had a business mind." Edward denied that the cars he had obtained had been smuggled, but he did not specify their origins.

Edward's relentless commercial prospecting added a number of strands to the web of valuable relationships woven by the Reichmann family. "I met a lot of prominent people on my travels, Jews and Spaniards, and when they came to Tangier I introduced them to father," said Edward, who also regularly briefed his mother on his adventures. "She listened carefully as her mind was always at work considering how to establish useful connections for rescue work."

———

Among the Jews of Spanish Morocco, all roads led to the Salama family. The Salamas were Sephardic Jews who first came to prominence in the late 1800s as import-export merchants in Melilla, which technically was part of Spain though it sat on the southern side of the Straits of Gibraltar. By the turn of the century, Jacob de J. Salama & Cia had branch offices in Tangier, Tetuán, Villa Sanjurjo, and Larache—García Figueras's original stomping grounds. The Salamas also diversified into manufacturing, accumulating industrial interests on both sides of the Straits. When the Spanish Civil War erupted in 1936, Isaac

Salama, the dominant brother of four, moved the headquarters of the family business to neutral Tangier and kept it there after Franco's victory.

Like other elite Sephardic families, the Salamas enjoyed commercial advantages because of their close personal ties to Francisco Franco. Spanish Morocco was the cradle not only of Spanish Nationalism but also of Franco's military career, which began when he was eighteen in one of the many Spanish wars against the Berber tribesmen. By the age of twenty-nine, Franco was the commander of the Spanish Foreign Legion, which was based in Morocco. The Salamas made a handsome profit as a supplier to Franco's units and later returned the favor by helping bankroll the rebellion in its crucial fledgling phase. Indeed, it was Salama money that paid for the private plane that secretly retrieved Franco from quasi exile in the Canary Islands on the eve of the uprising. The family was rewarded immediately with a contract to supply Nationalist forces with uniforms and perpetually thereafter with official authorization to import, export, manufacture, mine, or grow almost whatever it wanted.

Casual students of the Spanish Civil War might be surprised to learn that the Salamas' cozily symbiotic relationship with Franco did not diminish their stature within the Jewish community of Spain. Certainly the world community interpreted the war as a vicious assault on liberalism by fascism and sided overwhelmingly with the established Republican government. However, many Spanish Jews, especially wealthy ones, saw things differently. Although the Republican side was more democratic than the Nationalists, it also was militantly atheistic and quite socialistic. Furthermore, during the 1920s Franco had shown concern for the plight of Sephardim endangered in the endless dustups with the Berbers. While the generalissimo allied himself with many outspoken anti-Semites during the Civil War, he often took pains to distance himself from their views. After one particularly virulent radio broadcast from Seville by a Nationalist general, Franco sent an open letter to the Jews of Tetuán urging them to disregard anti-Jewish rhetoric.

One school of thought holds that Franco was descended from Marranos—crypto-Jews who converted to Christianity to escape persecution. Or perhaps he simply saw political advantage in cultivating the Sephardic business class. In any event, the Salamas were quick to recognize in Franco a receptive leader who could be cultivated for their own personal benefit and for the benefit of Spanish Jews in general. The Salamas were not a particularly religious family but were active in communal matters in Tangier and throughout the Spanish Zone.

Mrs. Reichmann had many allies in soliciting the support of Isaac Salama for her rescue and relief activities. The brother of Eva's friend, Bebe Beneyto Ronda, was a close friend of Enrique Salama, Isaac's brother. José Benaim Hachuel, whose family was allied with the Salamas in many spheres, had introduced Edward to one of the Salamas, who sent a bit of business Reichmann & Rosenfeld's way—somewhat prematurely as it turned out. "Mr. Salama hadn't realized that I was still a minor," Edward recalled. "I couldn't sign any more contracts with the Salama firm until my parents took me down to the courthouse and declared me of majority status."

However it was accomplished, Mrs. Reichmann gained an audience with Isaac Salama and made the most of it. As Edward recalled, "Salama not only agreed to contribute money but was really helpful in making the right contacts in Madrid and elsewhere." Salama introduced Mrs. Reichmann to the bishop of Madrid. Through the bishop, she was introduced to high officials of the Spanish Red Cross, which gave her a special pass that enabled her to travel freely throughout Spain and Spanish Morocco—a rare privilege at the time even for Spanish citizens. Salama also introduced Mrs. Reichmann to Ignacio Figueroa y Bermejillo, a scion of an old noble family and better known as the Duke of Tovar. After the Nationalist victory in the civil war, the Duke of Tovar had left his ancestral lands near Burgos in northern Spain and installed himself in Tangier, where he bought a magnificent house on "the Mountain," a wooded hill on the outskirts where the most privileged inhabitants lived.

Mention the late Duke of Tovar today to a resident of Tangier and the first reaction is likely to be a matter-of-fact reference to his homosexuality. The repressions of the Franco years accentuated Tangier's popularity as a haven of homosexuality, which, in the ultra-Orthodox view, was (and remains) an abomination. To the Reichmanns, though, the Duke's salient characteristic was that he was honorary chairman of the Spanish Red Cross in Tangier and thus, in Renée's discerning analysis, empowered to bestow upon the food-parcel program an enhancement of critical importance.

Late in the war, the Spanish Red Cross agreed to sponsor bulk food shipments from Tangier to Paris by the local arm of the American Jewish Joint Distribution Committee, which was the old refugee relief committee reconstituted. "It was the Reichmanns who established the original relationship with the Spanish Red Cross," said Albert Reinhard, who remained in Tangier until 1956, when he emigrated to the United States. Asked how the Reichmanns had managed this feat, Reinhard responded: "Through personal connections, I assume. That's the way things worked in Tangier."

Messody Hadida, who for seventeen years worked as Reinhard's secretary and assistant, was more forthcoming. Mrs. Reichmann, she said, bought the help of the Spanish Red Cross through the Duke of Tovar. "Every time there was a shipment of parcels a donation was made to the Duke of Tovar," she recalled. The payments were not made as bribes but as contributions to the Spanish Red Cross, and usually in the amount of 5,000 pesetas and came from the Joint Committee's pockets, not the Reichmanns', Mrs. Hadida said. "It was our money, but she was the one who had the contact with the Duke." Whether these "contributions" were in fact forwarded to the Red Cross was never clear.

The Duke "did what he liked," Mrs. Hadida said. "It wasn't our business." Asked why a wealthy nobleman would have required payment to help in a good cause, Mrs. Hadida guffawed. "To receive favors," she replied. "Would anyone [in Tangier] have acted differently? No. Everyone worked this way. Everyone!"

Reinhard concurred with this account except in one respect: "The money did not come from the Joint [Committee]," he said emphatically. "Any money paid the Duke of Tovar would have come from the Reichmanns' own sources." Asked why Mrs. Hadida would have claimed otherwise, Reinhard hesitated before replying: "I'd guess that she didn't want to embarrass the Reichmanns."

In any event, the Duke delivered. Because La Cruz Roja was entitled to ship through the Spanish Post Office without charge, Mrs. Reichmann paid no postage at all on most of her food parcel shipments. The Red Cross connection also speeded delivery. "We used to go to the office with the packages, tell them that we had, say, 1,500 of them—and they would usually give us the official stamp and papers allowing us to complete the transaction," Eva recalled. "They rarely even counted the packages; they took our word for it."

Spanish Red Cross sponsorship provided another, essential advantage. As the only fascist, avowedly pro-German regime among the nominally neutral nations, Spain was accorded deferential treatment in Berlin. Thus, shipments to concentration camps under the Spanish Red Cross label were least likely to be confiscated by the SS, especially when they came labeled: "Envio para Prisioneros de Guerra" (For prisoners of war). This designation was Mrs. Reichmann's bluff. Neither Spain nor the International Red Cross, for that matter, ever went so far as to designate concentration camp inmates POWs. Apparently Spanish Red Cross officials had no objection to a Hungarian refugee woman daring to do, in the name of fascist Spain, what Spain itself would not do.

Chapter 9

In any strictly Orthodox apportioning of moral credit for the Reichmanns' food parcel program, Samuel's share as titular head of the household would have loomed large. The Torah states that tzedoka, or charity from one's pocket, cannot be performed by a wife alone because she must ask her husband's permission to give money. Until mid-1944, the largest source of funding for the family's concentration camp shipments was Samuel's income from money changing. But besides tzedoka, there is hesed, the contribution of effort. While Samuel unquestionably was a generous man financially, his hesed was no match for his wife's or his daughter's. That is, he gave of himself much more sparingly than did Renée, for whom charity in either form was an extension of an intensely personal interest in the welfare of others.

Despite the prominence thrust upon him by his wife's activism and his own commercial success, Samuel never held official position in the Tangier community (or, for that matter, in Paris, Vienna, or Beled). Nor, of course, did Mrs. Reichmann, since Talmudic law excludes women from administrative and judicial responsibility. However, Renée's communal activism in Tangier was at once so grand in conception and yet so intimate in execution that it rendered the formalities of communal structure irrelevant. "Mrs. Reichmann was *the* leader of the Ashkenazi community," said Sol Koppel, a Sephardic native of Tangier who married a Hungarian refugee.

To be sure, Samuel's role as his family's chief provider consumed much of his time. However, the same could be said of almost any Jewish man in Tangier who did accept communal position. Fundamentally, Samuel's insularity was the product of personality rather than the constraints of familial duty. "You know, Mr. Reichmann would never even look at me," said Mrs. Leonie Kalman, a dress designer who was the most bohemian of the Hungarian refugees in Tangier. "He'd sort of look away, off in the distance somewhere." Added Alexander Heiden, the Orthodox diamond dealer who was a frequent guest at 25 Rue Molière: "He was a man with a closed-in character," noting, too, that Reichmann's reserved and gentle manner should not be confused with timidity. "Reichmann was very tough in business, even tougher than Rosenbaum."

Heiden was referring to Nicholas Rosenbaum, Samuel's friend and fellow Hungarian money changer. Reichmann and Rosenbaum defined opposite ends of the refugee social spectrum in Tangier. Although Rosenbaum was a member of the Reichmanns' circle of Orthodox émigrés, he was not its captive. A sportive, even dashing figure with movie star looks and a self-assured swagger, Rosenbaum moved with ease across all the boundaries of socially segregated Tangier. He was one of the few refugees admitted to the Jewish Casino de Tangier and also joined a country club on the mountain, where he chummed around with the French consul general and rode to the hounds with the local British gentry. His best friend was an Arab prince.

The idea of Samuel Reichmann on horseback or raking in a poker pot in the Casino de Paris boggles the mind. A bon vivant he was not. Reichmann's Sephardic acquaintances in Tangier remembered him as "sérieux," which means "serious-minded," or even "solemn." His piety mystified the locals. "He would come at seven A.M. from one part of the city to the other part to say the morning prayers," said one native Jew close to the family. "Then he'd leave and come back in the afternoon and say the other prayers. Then he goes home and what does he do? Pray. . . . When we went to make those famous packages he was in the other room, praying, praying, praying, praying. What would he pray for all the day?"

The short answer was that frequent prayer was a requirement of religious observance. In almost every sense, Samuel's life in Tangier was narrowly cast. And yet in moral terms, he covered an enormous amount of ground, moving with one bounding leap from the sacred to the profane every time he shifted his attentions from prayer to money changing.

That Samuel Reichmann had a talent for currency dealing should not have been surprising, for it was an integral part of his past success. As an exporter of eggs from Hungary and Poland to Austria, Germany, and England, Reichmann Brothers had routinely done business in five currencies. In shifting his personal savings out of Vienna into accounts in Zurich, Paris, London, and New York during the latter half of the 1930s, Reichmann had added to his expertise. In making a profession of currency speculation, Samuel also was able to cash in on his long-standing efforts to keep abreast of the latest political developments. The fluctuations of the Tangier currency market were a product of many factors, but none was more important than war news. Reichmann spent more time than ever working the telephone and studying the tea leaves of newspaper articles and radio broadcasts. As a multinational center of trade, diplomacy, and espionage, Tangier was awash in vital information, though it was not easily disentangled from the rumor and propaganda that also deluged the city.

No matter how hot or wet the day, Reichmann always wore his homburg and a dark wool suit as he made his rounds amid the riot of sound and color that was the Arab Medina. Win or lose, he was polite and pleasant in demeanor but spoke barely a word of Spanish or French and kept his speculator's cards close to the vest. Moroccan Jews in general were a superstitious lot, and as Reichmann's successes mounted, the Sephardi currency dealers invested the most trivial aspects of his daily routine with symbolic significance. Tangier was built into a steep hill that rose right from the harbor up through the old Arab quarter to the crenelated fortress of the Casbah. The newer European quarter was separated from the old city by a long ravine. In walking from his apartment to the Rue es Siaghines, Samuel had a choice of two, roughly equidistant routes. Either he could walk down to the base of the hill and make his way up through the Medina or he could turn the other direction when he left his door, take the Boulevard Pasteur over to the Arab quarter, and walk downhill to the Rue es Siaghines. When Reichmann, who generally favored the currencies of the Allied nations, was seen climbing uphill through the Medina, it was said that the price of the dollar and pound would rise that day. But if he took the downhill route, it was taken as a harbinger of a falling dollar and pound. "Father would smile at these stories but never commented on them," Edward recalled. "Naturally, they were of great help for his business."

Reichmann soon diversified from speculation into currency brokering, acting mainly as an intermediary between the curbside dealers of the Rue es Siaghines and the commercial banks through which they cleared. That is, Samuel bought up the surplus inventories of small cambios and resold them at a markup to the banks, which were willing to surrender a bit of profit for the convenience of not having to deal with each money changer individually. Although acting as a broker's broker in foreign exchange was modestly profitable at best, it was much less risky than speculating on the market and also positioned Reichmann to move into banking himself one day. By 1942, Reichmann had taken the next logical step in his evolution away from pure speculation and began developing his own foreign exchange clientele among the city's export-import merchants, most of whom were Sephardim. Although this put him into competition with the cambios and banks for which he cleared, he managed to maintain the wholesale aspect of his business even as he moved into retail. Reichmann also branched into the buying and selling of gold ingots and coins.

Reichmann and his fellow Hungarian money changers gave every appearance of prospering, though there is really no way now of quantifying their profits. Currency dealers in Tangier were under no obligation to report their earnings to the government, and the Hungarians were not the sort for loose talk. Even among themselves, the Hungarians wore poker faces. "Reichmann never talked about his business," said Alexander Heiden. "His business always was confidential, and Rosenbaum was the same way."

According to Louis Reichmann, who worked for his father later, Samuel added significantly to his winnings by holding his profits in U.S. dollars—correctly wagering, in effect, that America would win the war and the peace that followed. Although the Reichmanns lived much more modestly on Rue Molière than they had on Hafnergasse in Vienna, Samuel's earnings supported a series of unusual outlays: the kosher meat imports from Tetuán, the private school tuition and after-school religious instruction for his sons, the creation of the Rue Cook synagogue, the food parcel shipments, and so on. Taken together, these expenditures greatly exceeded the means of the average refugee.

———

Among refugee and native Jewish businessmen alike, Reichmann developed a reputation for strict honesty in his dealings. "Never once did we have the tiniest problem with Mr. Reichmann," recalled Messod Bendayan, who, like his father before him, was a senior officer of the Banque Commerciale du Maroc, which was the largest factor in the Tangier currency market during and after the war. "He was an ideal correspondent." Added Salomon Bendahan, who owned much real estate in the city and once held the Ford dealership for all of Morocco: "Reichmann carried out a lot of transactions on the phone and no one ever had cause to find fault with him. He did things very properly."

And yet the business in which Samuel Reichmann made his living in Tangier was ethically dubious by the standards that prevailed in the world outside. The avaricious, unprincipled money dealer is one of the hoariest anti-Semitic stereotypes: call him Shylock. There is nothing inherently disreputable about money changing, whether practiced by Jew or Gentile, native or refugee, man or woman. The fact was, though, that during and after World War II, the Rue es Siaghines was rife with suspect dealings. "For a true comprehension of the activities on this (currency) market the fact must be borne in mind that almost all transactions are based on contraband," reported Rives Childs in an official dispatch in 1943. As a money changer of note, Reichmann was by definition an important cog in Tangier's contraband economy, like it or not.

When the Spanish seized Tangier, they slapped new controls on the city's freewheeling commercial life. Foreign currencies of all nations still were allowed to trade freely, but the import or export of pesetas was banned. And while the city's merchants were free to import goods as they desired from abroad, nothing was to be exported without a permit from the Directory of

Economy, Industry, and Commerce—Tomás García Figueras's bailiwick. Meanwhile, the Vichy authorities in French Morocco also tried to clamp down hard on trade with Tangier. There was a war on, after all. In their attempts to impose their will on Tangier commerce, Spanish and French officialdom failed miserably. During daylight hours a trickle of merchandise flowed out from Tangier through the proper channels. But at night the city became a sieve, leaking goods by boat, bicycle, donkey, camel, car, and truck into the Spanish zone. From Spanish Morocco, much booty was re-smuggled into French Morocco along a long, sparsely populated border.

While contraband of every sort flowed through Tangier, many professional smugglers preferred to handle compact consumer goods such as cigarettes, lighters, nail polish, or wristwatches. By midwar, Tangier, a city of 100,000 inhabitants, was importing Swiss watches at an annual rate of 200,000 to 300,000. However, the contraband commodity of top choice throughout northwest Africa did not adorn the wrist. The Arabs of the region put little faith in either the Spanish peseta or the French Moroccan franc, preferring to put their savings into gold. Consignments of gold coins were shipped to Tangier from Switzerland via Portugal or Spain and then smuggled out in all directions, the price rising with the distance from Tangier. In mid-1942, for example, a British sovereign fetched about 1,400 francs in Tangier, 1,800 in Casablanca, 2,400 in Algiers, 2,800 in Marseille, and as much as 4,000 in Paris.

The free money market of Tangier was the hub uniting the disparate spokes of the region's contraband economy, since legitimate and black market buyers alike had to pay for imported merchandise not in the local tender but in the currency of the country where the shipment had originated: U.S. dollars for Parker pens, pounds sterling for Dunhill lighters, Swiss francs for Shaffhausen watches, and so on. These foreign currencies and a dozen more were legally obtainable from the banks of Tangier and the money changers of the Rue es Siaghines, which bustled throughout the war despite the almost complete demise of the local tourist trade.

The exchange dealers were under no legal obligation to interrogate their customers about the sources of the funds they wanted changed and would not have remained in business long had they indulged their curiosity by asking questions. "Ask me no questions," was the prevailing ethos of Tangier's contraband economy, "and I'll tell you no lies." To deal in foreign exchange in the International Zone during World War II was to function to a large degree as an appendage of the smuggling industry. Every money changer—Samuel Reichmann included—understood this fact, even if he remained blissfully ignorant of the nature of his clients' business.

Currency smuggling was a large, lucrative racket in its own right, only partly dependent on the traffic in merchandise. Invariably, the peseta and the various forms of colonial francs (Moroccan, Algerian, Tunisian) were worth more on the free Tangier currency market than outside, where exchange rates were fixed by the Spanish and French governments at artificially low levels. Pesetas or francs could be smuggled into Tangier, changed at a hefty premium into a stronger currency such as the U.S. dollar or Swiss franc, and then deposited in a local bank that was not required to report the account to the government— any government. Ironically, those best positioned to capitalize on the regional disparity in currency values were government officials, particularly the diplomats. "The temptation to take advantage was enormous—especially for anyone who had diplomatic privileges," said U.S. Vice Consul A. David Fritzlan. To the chagrin of Fritzlan's boss, Rives Childs, the legation's own chauffeur was caught smuggling currency in from Casablanca while driving the chargé d'affaires on official business.

For the Tangier money changers, the risk of trafficking in smuggled currency lay in not being able to resell the local currency they took in. The Moroccan franc was especially problematic. The city's administration required payment of taxes and custom duties in pesetas and took other steps to bolster the Spanish currency at the expense of its French rival, the franc, which also was weakened by a steep drop in the volume of goods imported from French Morocco. As a result, a horrendous glut of Moroccan francs accumulated on the Tangier market, which buckled in September 1941. Within a few weeks, the franc lost 35 percent of its value. The money changers could have alleviated the problem by shipping surplus francs to customers outside Tangier, except that buyers were scarce everywhere, even in French Morocco itself.

Tangier also had a surfeit of pesetas. Unlike the Moroccan franc, though, the peseta was in demand, notably in Lisbon, which was home to an unregulated currency market much like Tangier's. And so Spanish officialdom did not need to be bribed (not heavily anyway) into turning a blind eye as the Aero-Portuguese flight from Tangier to Lisbon left every week stuffed to the floorboards with peseta notes. In payment for the pesetas smuggled out of Tangier, escudos, dollars, Swiss francs, and so on flowed back from Lisbon through conventional channels. This not only had the effect of buoying the price of the peseta in Tangier but also augmented the city's supply of foreign currencies needed to pay for all those imported goods in the first place. In short, as Childs noted in one of the legation's frequent reports on the subject of foreign exchange, "The economic and financial life of Tangier depends largely on the export of pesetas."

Samuel's money-changing business and Renée's charitable enterprise were symbiotically linked in a variety of ways. For example, the Tangier import-export house Aaron & Jacob S. Cohen was at once Samuel's best foreign exchange client and the largest supplier of food for Renée's parcels. With branch offices in a half-dozen Moroccan cities, and long-standing strong ties to major suppliers throughout North and South America, the Cohen firm (founded 1914) was one of Morocco's biggest importers of food, especially flour, sugar, coffee, green tea, and vegetable oil. The Cohen brothers were such good customers of the Pillsbury Company that they were able to dispense with the usual letters of credit and buy from the American milling giant by paying cash on delivery. In late 1940, Jacob relocated to New York for the duration of the war to tend to the firm's relationships with Pillsbury and numerous other suppliers. The Cohens were a populous family—Aaron alone had seventeen children—and closely intertwined with the Pintos, another prominent merchant family of eminent standing in Tangier.

Eva was the linchpin of the Reichmanns' lucrative, multifaceted relationship with the Cohens. One afternoon in 1941 Abraham Pinto had been minding the counter for his uncles when in walked Eva, accompanied by her father, who said not a word. "She explained what it was she wanted," Pinto recalled. "Could I sell them merchandise they needed? She was so sympathique, so concerned. I sold her what she asked for. She started coming regularly, mostly to wait for her brothers to come from the teacher's." (The younger boys took Talmudic instruction in a house nearby.) Pinto was exactly Eva's age and so smitten with her that he offered to drop by the Reichmanns' apartment to help assemble food parcels. Soon, Eva also befriended many other Pintos and Cohens, including Jacob's wife. (When Mrs. Cohen died in 1948, her two daughters were still in their teens. Eva would marry later that same year and leave Tangier, bringing both Cohen girls along to London as her protégées.)

There is no question that relationships established through the family's relief work were useful to Samuel in prospecting for money-changing business. Government and business were more tightly bound in Spain than in many countries, not only because of Franco's relentlessly intrusive economic policies but because high officeholders were allowed to simultaneously function as private businessmen on a large scale. But was the reverse true? Was Samuel's money-changing franchise of use to Mrs. Reichmann and her daughter as they made the rounds of Spanish officialdom seeking permits and indulgences? More specifically, were favors done Mrs. Reichmann repaid by Mr. Reichmann's form of financial assistance provided politically well-connected smugglers?

In the archives of the Vaad Hahatzalah Relief Society, a long defunct New York–based Orthodox group, is a brief letter addressed to Mrs. Rebecca Reichmann (Renée's Hebrew name) and signed by Rafael Alvarez Claro, who, in the best Spanish tradition, was both mayor of Melilla and that port city's wealthiest merchant. Evidently, Mrs. Reichmann had written asking Alvarez Claro's help in the eleventh hour of her campaign to persuade the Spanish Foreign Ministry to issue protective visas to Jews in Hungary. Dated July 11, 1944,

Alvarez Claro's response was sent to Mrs. Reichmann at the Hotel Asturias in Madrid.

> It gives me great pleasure to respond to your letter and to thank you for those words of praise that I hardly deserve. I will rejoice only when you have achieved tangible success in your humanitarian work, which you do with such enthusiasm. I hope that my modest contribution will help obtain the best results.
>
> I do not have the honor of knowing the Spanish Ambassador to Budapest but I am sending him a letter of introduction for you and I'm sure that he will receive you and help you as best he can.
>
> I will do all I can to help you in your humanitarian work. Please know that I am at your service. Regards to your charming daughter.

Despite his gracious words, Alvarez Claro, through Allied eyes anyway, was a man of decidedly ill repute. In a 1942 report on the city's "leading personalities," the British vice consul in Melilla had this to say about him:

> Lord Mayor of Melilla. He is a vast, coarse man who was humping sacks of potatoes on Melilla quay, or something of the sort, years ago. During the Rif campaign and the Spanish Civil War he did very well out of the contraband business and was later credited with sabotaging his own ship. . . . Alvarez Claro is the head of the Falange here and hates the sight of us. . . . A nasty bit of work. He and Valino (Melilla's top-ranking military officer) seem to work hand in glove and are managing to "skin" the Melilla public well and truly.

Alvarez Claro was a known confederate of Hadj Ahmed Amor Zrak, the kingpin of Moroccan currency smuggling. In 1944, not long after Alvarez Claro's exchange of letters with Mrs. Reichmann, an OSS informant reported that the mayor had "arrived in Tangier clandestinely, bringing 2,000,000 francs for the account of a group of natives dealing in this contraband. He has received 500 pesetas commission on every 100,000 francs brought into Tangier. The present transaction was carried out through the intermediary of Hadj Driss Amor, the youngest son of Hadj Ahmed Amor. . . . Alvarez Claro is known to be bandit No. 1 in Melilla and Amor is bandit 1A."

Even allowing for the tendency of British diplomats in Morocco to demonize the Spanish and for the general unreliability of OSS reporting out of Tangier, it is evident that Alvarez Claro was not the sort of man one asked a favor of casually. It is not clear what quid pro quo Melilla's number one bandit required of the Reichmanns. If Samuel did in fact help Alvarez Claro launder his black market bankrolls, however, his actions would have been justifiable under the doctrine of pikkuah nefesh. More broadly speaking, the fact that the costs of

Mrs. Reichmann's early relief efforts were covered almost entirely out of Samuel's earnings from money changing ennobled his participation in what, in Tangier anyway, was essentially a sleazy sort of enterprise.

———

Allied intelligence agents in Tangier spent considerable time prying into local commerce, for the city was as much a battleground of "economic warfare" as of conventional military espionage. In the first few years of the war, the British naval blockade of Axis-occupied Europe was considered by many observers to be the most effective weapon in its arsenal. But even the mighty Royal Navy could not effectively police the entire Atlantic Ocean or Mediterranean Sea, and so Britain's economic warfare campaign turned largely around Allied political efforts to impede the flow of goods into Axis territory from the neutral nations of the world.

To this end, Britain in 1939 began compiling its so-called Statutory List, better known as the blacklist. Included on it were business firms in neutral countries that were owned by Axis interests, trafficked with the enemy, or both. Under the Trading with the Enemy Act, it was illegal for firms in England and throughout the British Commonwealth to trade with a blacklisted firm. Even before the United States entered the war, the State Department began collaborating with Britain in its attempts to police international trade and in mid-1941 unveiled its own blacklist—the Proclaimed List of Certain Foreign Nationals—which began as a virtual duplicate of the British list. Together, American and British authorities applied an ever-widening panoply of sanctions against the firms they blacklisted, attempting to rein them in through immediate penalties (such as cancellation of shipping insurance or curbing of oil supplies) and the threat of much more onerous postwar retaliation.

As a rule, the Allied techniques of economic warfare did not work well in Tangier, where smuggling was an ancient way of life. Or, as one discouraged official of Britain's Ministry of Economic Warfare put it, the city's inhabitants were "much addicted to, and well organized for, blockade evasion." In addition, the local authorities in Tangier resented the Allied measures as a meddlesome interference in Spanish governance of Tangier and did their best to sabotage them. The Spanish Chamber of Commerce, which was controlled by the government of Spanish Morocco, took out newspaper advertisements offering to advise Spanish-owned firms on how best to circumvent the economic controls imposed by the Allies.

Luckily for the Allies, Tangier and Spanish Morocco never figured importantly as a source of supply for the Axis war machine. The region had few natural resources of military value and no large-scale manufacturing aside from a mining company and a few fish canneries and flour processors. "The enemy is receiving no great benefit from this area," Childs concluded in a report to

Washington, "although the Germans are active in the free money market of Tangier."

In conquering France, the Germans also gained hegemony over French Morocco and began smuggling franc notes by the bale out of Casablanca into Tangier for conversion into pesetas (which were used to pay for imports of wolfram and other strategic materials from Spain) and various Allied currencies needed to fund German espionage operations and diplomatic missions throughout the world. The Germans traded mostly through the Banque Commerciale du Maroc, the largest French Moroccan bank, but also had agents working the Rue es Siaghines and even purchased control of one money-changing firm.

The Banque Commerciale du Maroc was jointly blacklisted by the British and Americans in 1942 and was not delisted until late 1943. In addition, at least three of the Sephardic money changers in Tangier were blacklisted by one or both of the Allied powers. Among them was Isais Chocron, who was considered the single most important operator in the city. Even so, Childs was not convinced that this handful of blacklistings made much of an impact on the remaining exchange dealers. "Considering their informal business methods," the chargé d'affaires concluded, "it must be realized that this is a very difficult situation to control strictly."

Childs's efforts to police the Rue es Siaghines also were frustrated by Edward Wharton-Tigar, the Special Operations Executive's man in Tangier. Unbeknownst to his American allies, Wharton-Tigar in 1942 set up a large black market operation through which gold, diamonds, postage stamps, and other valuables were brought into Tangier, converted into the currencies of Axis and Axis-controlled nations, and then smuggled to SOE headquarters in London in the British diplomatic pouch.

By Wharton-Tigar's own account, he did not deal with the curbside operators of the Rue es Siaghines but worked exclusively through various Jewish banks in Tangier, mainly one that had been founded before the war by a Polish émigré named Jakob Alster, who ranked among the largest currency dealers in the city. Even so, to fill Wharton-Tigar's orders for exotic enemy currencies, Alster had to work every nook and cranny of the Tangier market. Although Wharton-Tigar's machinations benefited all the Tangier money changers by substantially boosting demand, Samuel Reichmann does not appear to have had any direct dealings with Wharton-Tigar. "Mr. Reichmann was not an SOE agent or informant, that I can tell you with absolute certainty," Wharton-Tigar recalled a half century later. "However, he could have been involved in the secondary trading, the cutouts, from my operation." This was almost certainly the case, for Reichmann was on good terms with Alster and dealt with him routinely.

The British did not inform the U.S. Legation of Wharton-Tigar's operation until it threatened to blacklist Alster for trading with the enemy in late 1943.

The Americans concluded that the infractions for which Alster was cited had nothing to do with his work on behalf of the SOE but spared him a blacklisting at the request of their allies.

As for Samuel Reichmann, his name did not appear on the U.S. blacklist at any time during the war, and an exhaustive search of the archives of the American Legation in Tangier turned up no evidence that his activities were ever considered suspicious enough to warrant investigation for possible inclusion on the blacklist. This suggests that Reichmann stopped dealing with the Banque Commerciale du Maroc, which was one of his most important clients, for the duration of the French Moroccan bank's blacklisting. Otherwise, he would have been blacklisted, too. Because the initial American Proclaimed List in Tangier was simply lifted from the British list, it can also be stated with a high degree of certainty that Reichmann had not been blacklisted by the British either as of late 1942. But because the British government still has not declassified its statutory list, it cannot be determined definitively whether he was listed subsequent to 1942.

One member of the Reichmanns' inner circle was blacklisted by both the British and Americans. Emmanuel Hollander and his wife, Lily, were Oberlanders who had met the Reichmanns for the first time in Paris and were regular guests at their apartment in Tangier. A slight, bespectacled man who took great pride in his improbably powerful singing voice, Hollander and Zsigmond Grussgott took turns serving as cantor in the Reichmann synagogue on Rue Cook. Hollander was the only other refugee in Tangier who rivaled the Reichmanns' standards of observance. Hollander, who dabbled in money changing, was an opportunistic doer of export-import deals of all sorts, mainly involving Switzerland. He was placed on the blacklist in October 1941, after British intelligence intercepted a cable indicating that Hollander was negotiating a transaction with Hungary, which by this time had joined the Axis. After posting a £1,000 bond, Hollander was delisted—but briefly. He was restored to both blacklists after he was caught expediting a shipment of wool and hides to Germany via Marseille.

The blacklists were confidential but their contents had a tendency to seep into public circulation nonetheless. While many refugees shrugged off the news of Hollander's transgressions, the Reichmanns ostracized him. "The split was made by Edward Reichmann," recalled Heiden, with a hint of mockery. "You know, Edward was young and idealistic." When Hollander showed his face at the Rue Cook synagogue one morning, young Reichmann ordered the older man to leave and warned him that if he set foot in the synagogue again he would "break his neck." Although barely eighteen, Edward was a barrel-chested 180-pounder. Hollander left but returned at the start of the High Holidays, expecting to sing. With a friend of his, Reichmann dragged Hollander out behind the synagogue and beat him up.

Chapter 10

Once Mrs. Reichmann had secured the cooperation of the Spanish Red Cross, her food parcel ambitions were constrained mainly by the lack of funds. Until 1944, when Renée finally succeeded in raising financing outside Tangier, the shipments were financed by the Reichmanns and a half-dozen other Hungarian refugee families, with an occasional contribution from a wealthy Tangier merchant. Labor, though, was never in short supply. A revolving cast of two dozen volunteers, mostly Orthodox refugee mothers and their children, dropped by 25 Rue Molière to lend a hand. When a shipping deadline neared, Mrs. Reichmann often pulled her children out of school to help. "I remember the excitement of staying home from school certain days to help packing or packing through the night and being able to sleep in late," Paul has said.

In the archives of the American Jewish Joint Distribution Committee is a scrapbook containing a series of black-and-white snapshots showing the Reichmann brothers and their fellow volunteers at their labors. What these photographs convey is not the excitement that Paul recalled feeling but an almost ceremonial solemnity. While some of the middle-aged women can be seen cracking the occasional shy smile, each of the brothers invariably appears attentive to his task and oblivious to the camera. With their angular frames draped identically in white dress shirts, skinny black ties, sharply creased dark pants and snap-brim fedoras, the brothers project a European formality eerily at odds with their rough-hewn, vaguely Arabian surroundings. They look like a group of teenaged pallbearers moonlighting as factory workers.

Mrs. Reichmann and her helpers did their part to fill a huge void. Before the United States entered the war in late 1941, American organizations had been free to ship food and other supplies to Jews in occupied Europe and did so in large quantities. In Poland alone, the Joint Distribution Committee dispensed aid to 630,000 Jews in four hundred towns during 1940 and 1941. After Pearl Harbor, American relief agencies not only were expelled by Germany but were prohibited by their own government from shipping food into Axis territory. Restricting the enemy's food supplies was a basic goal of the Allied blockade of occupied Europe. Until very late in the war, the British high command in particular was adamantly opposed to allowing relief shipments for starving civilians—whether Jew or Gentile—through the blockade, arguing that food sent into Axis territory would benefit the enemy one way or another. At a minimum, provisioning captive Jews would enable Germany to reduce its own shipments of food to the concentration camps. In early 1941, this view was bluntly articulated by the British Embassy in Washington: "No form of relief can be devised which would not directly or indirectly assist the enemy's war effort."

Many Americans agreed with the British position. Even Jewish opinion was sharply divided on the issue at the time. As for the U.S. government, it was content to defer to the British in the area of economic warfare policy, though in late 1942 it did open a minuscule breach in the blockade by permitting U.S. relief agencies to send a paltry $12,000 worth of food parcels a month to specific addresses in Axis Europe. The blockade authorities did permit the International Red Cross to ship massive quantities of food through the blockade to feed Allied soldiers in Axis prisoner-of-war camps. Throughout the war, Jewish groups urged the Allied governments to pressure Germany into conferring prisoner-of-war status on Jews in the concentration camps. A precedent of sorts existed. The United States, Britain, and the Axis powers had an informal agreement under which their citizens interned in enemy countries were treated practically the same as POWs under the Geneva Convention; the arrangement included the right to receive food parcels. However, neither Britain nor the United States ever made a concerted effort to gain POW status for Jewish internees, and the International Red Cross itself tiptoed around the issue until the war was nearly over.

By Mrs. Reichmann's own reckoning, she shipped hundreds of parcels a week into occupied Europe in 1943. At one time or another during the war, her group sent food to Buchenwald, Oranienburg, Joshowitz, and Sohlfelds but in 1943 and 1944 by far the greater part was sent to two destinations: Birkenau-Auschwitz and Theresienstadt, an old Hapsburg garrison town in Moravia that had been converted in late 1941 into a Jewish ghetto. The Germans concentrated in Theresienstadt most of the Jews of Bohemia and Moravia, along with prominent elderly Jews from Germany and several countries in Western Europe, all for eventual transport to Auschwitz. At the same time, the ghetto functioned as the centerpiece of a brazen but effective propaganda campaign designed to disguise the true purpose of the concentration camp system. Promoting Theresienstadt to the world as a "model Jewish settlement," the Nazis gave it the façade of a prosperous, prewar village and permitted visits by Red Cross inspectors, who were led

> through spotless streets, houses bright in pastel shades, an adorable Maria Theresa village. On cue, a squad of singing Jewish girls, shouldering rakes, marched off to their gardening. White-gloved bakers unloaded fresh bread into a fake store. At another shop, fresh vegetables were displayed—for the first and last time. In the community center, Terezin's orchestra played Mozart. As the inspectors approached a soccer field, a goal was scored according to script.

The reality was that many elderly deportees did not last a month in Theresienstadt. In 1942, the death toll amounted to 15,891, more than half of Theresienstadt's average population of 31,510. No one could survive for long on camp rations alone. The typical meal was watery soup made from a rotted potato. Bread was rationed at a slice a day. "If once in a blue moon we were given meat scraps," one survivor recalled, "it was horse flesh, and there was more bad smell from it in the room than meat in the gravy." The SS soon realized that it could not very well keep up the fiction that Theresienstadt was the "model Jewish settlement" while denying its inhabitants the simple right to receive food parcels from home. And so the food parcel policy here was the most liberal in all of Nazidom. In this limited way, the Nazi-created myth of Theresienstadt was self-fulfilling. As one historian observed: "The difference for many between starvation and a modest level of survival was the food parcel from home. . . . Food parcels not only provided much needed protein and vitamins but assured inmates that their loved ones were still alive."

Mrs. Reichmann was one of the first mailers to exploit the uniquely advantageous circumstances of Theresienstadt, getting a jump of at least a year on the Joint Distribution Committee, which was not authorized by the U.S. government to begin shipping to the ghetto until May 1943 and did not send its first parcels until October. By August 1944 the group had sent 140,000 parcels containing seventy tons of sardines, dried fruit, and biscuits, all of it purchased in Lisbon. The 450 members of a contingent of Danish Jews who arrived in mid-1943 received regular food parcels from the King of Denmark himself. The International Red Cross did not make its own, timid entry into parcel mailings until the fall of 1943, sending parcels to 100 internees in various camps, mainly Theresienstadt.

Many prisoners at Theresienstadt were on someone's mailing list and were required by the camp commandant to acknowledge each parcel by signing a postcard that was mailed back to the senders via Prague. In and of themselves, these postcard receipts proved nothing. However, the postwar testimony of survivors demonstrated that a large if unquantifiable number of the parcels sent to Theresienstadt were in fact delivered. The Reichmanns saved hundreds of the postcards returned to them from Theresienstadt, as well as letters received after the war from grateful survivors, at least two of whom had the temerity to ask that parcels be sent to their homes.

Determining the fate of the parcels sent to Birkenau, also known as Auschwitz II, is much more problematic. The Nazis never intended the Auschwitz complex as a model of anything other than assembly-line murder. Food parcels sent to Birkenau were routinely confiscated from the mail room by the SS and often "turned over to Kapos and block supervisors as a prize of sorts." Guards stole even the prisoners' paltry camp-issued rations of bread and other items, rerouting entire shipments of food to their own kitchen. And yet Mrs. Reichmann insisted in an interview with officials at the U.S. Legation in Tangier in 1944 that even though SS commandants at Birkenau did not permit prisoners to acknowledge the receipt of food parcels, she "had definite knowledge that the Birkenau packages . . . are being received safely."

Mrs. Reichmann had a well-placed source within Auschwitz itself: Ida Ungar, a young ultra-Orthodox woman from Bratislava. Ungar, a young mother of three, was one of about one hundred women selected from among the mass of arriving prisoners to work as secretaries to the camp's SS administrators. These office workers nicknamed themselves the "Himmelfahrtskommando," or squad destined for heaven, because they were certain that they knew too much about Auschwitz's gruesome inner workings to be allowed to survive. In fact, quite a number did survive, as documented in the book *Secretaries of Death*. Throughout the war, the secretaries not only could receive mail but could send it out of Auschwitz. In October 1943, Ida Ungar sent a postcard to her husband in Bratislava in which she confirmed that since August alone she had received eleven letters plus nine parcels from Bratislava and two more from Portugal. Mrs. Ungar underlined the words "from Portugal" but nothing else in the letter. This was during the period that Mrs. Reichmann was unable to obtain export licenses from Spanish Morocco and so arranged to ship from Lisbon. Mr. Ungar no doubt passed on this information to Henrik Gestetner back in Bratislava, who relayed the good news to Tangier.

Ida Ungar would survive Auschwitz and in March of 1946, in commemoration of the first Passover since the end of the war, she sent a long letter to Mrs. Reichmann from her home in Bratislava, here quoted in part:

> It was two years ago that we were in Auschwitz, our souls burdened and our hearts sorrowful, and we had decided under no circumstances to eat [unkosher camp rations]. How great was our surprise and joy when we received the packages of matzoh you sent. Dearest Mrs. Reichmann, I cannot

describe our joy, not only that we had something to eat, but also that in those miserable and hopeless circumstances we had a sign, sent perhaps even from heaven, that there was a chance we might once again be free. God helped us so that we could be free and live as Jews. As I have already said to your brother Mr. Gestetner, there are no words to say how often, when we were already weary, your packages inspired us with courage and the knowledge that there were people who cared for us. How often that gave us the strength to hold out. The payment of this debt we can only entrust to the Almighty.

Ida Ungar, widowed now, moved to Tangier not long after writing this letter and in 1947 married Henrik Gestetner, whose first wife, Margit, had died in Auschwitz.

———

By 1944, 650 of the 1,000 refugees who remained in Tangier were completely dependent on handouts from the local Jewish refugee relief committee, which, in turn, relied heavily on the American Jewish Joint Distribution Committee. There was far from enough money to go around, and in their anguish the refugees turned on one another. "There are continuous quarrels, and we often hear very disagreeable remarks, threats and sometimes even suffer physical attacks," warned Abraham Laredo, the president of the local refugee relief committee. Conflict between Sephardic and Ashkenazi refugees had escalated to the point that the relief committee first was forced to post a policeman in its offices on payment day and then had the groups come in on different days to pick up their relief checks. While food was plentiful, political manipulation of the rationing system had inflated prices to exorbitant levels. Since housing was scarce, families, including many large ones, were forced to live in one-room apartments amid unsanitary conditions.

The seesawing peseta-franc exchange rate victimized the refugees and working-class Tangierinos alike. The city's merchants tended to switch from the sinking to the rising currency, repricing their inventories to capitalize on every major swing. "The two currencies in Tangier are like two parallel stairways for the elevation of prices; now one is used and then, when it is convenient, the other is used, always a step up, never a step down." The abusive practices of local retailers and black marketeers, when coupled with manipulation of the rationing system, caused horrendous inflation in the price of life's rudest necessities. During the six-week period of the franc's collapse in September 1941, the price of eggs rose by 100 percent, vegetables by 100 to 500 percent, sardines by 500 percent, and mackerel by 800 percent.

For the most part, the wealthy local Sephardim remained unmoved by the refugees' worsening plight. "People from the Joint came into Tangier and told us that we had to solicit money from the local merchants. I told them that we wouldn't get a penny," recalled Albert Reinhard. "We had a cocktail party at the Minzah Hotel and a big shot from the Joint came in and made a speech. This was not long before the war ended. We got nothing. These people were just not interested in charity."

The Reichmanns were not much interested in local charity, either. According to Reinhard, the Reichmanns gave neither to the refugee committee nor to the Jewish community in general during the war. To the contrary, by 1944 the Reichmanns were importuning communal officials for donations to their food parcel program, which seems to have been in danger of petering out. Early in the year, Samuel, in his wife's absence, wrote to Regina Klein in New York, pleading for her help in raising funds. "Everything is very expensive here, including the postage," he commented. "Now, you must understand that there are only six refugees here who are in a position to give. There are refugees here who have to be supported. They cannot be asked to do anything. There are more destitute people here than I have ever seen at any place before."

Even in the context of fund-raising, Samuel looked upon the local refugee community in terms of its capacity to give rather than its need to receive. That the Reichmanns attached higher priority to feeding their distant Orthodox brethren in Europe than to aiding the mixed bag of strangers with whom they happened to share Tangier was only natural and, according to Reinhard, occasioned only minor grumbling among the relief committee's wards, most of whom were only vaguely aware of the Reichmanns' parcel program. Fellow Jews who learned of the shipments were more likely to try to get a relative on the mailing list than to cast aspersions on the Reichmanns, for by 1944 the horrors of the Holocaust were widely known and even the hungriest Tangier refugees realized that their suffering was nothing compared with the plight of concentration camp inmates.

Mrs. Klein took the Reichmanns' appeal for funding to the Vaad Hahatzalah Relief Society. The Vaad, as it was known, had been founded in 1939 by the Union of Orthodox Rabbis of the United States and Canada for the purpose of rescuing Polish rabbis and yeshiva students who had fled into Lithuania. As the Nazi threat intensified, it broadened its scope and toughened its tactics. By 1943, the Vaad had emerged as the most forceful American champion of the Torah rescue imperative, as here articulated by Rabbi Eliezer Silver, its principal founder:

We are ready to pay ransom for Jews and deliver them from concentration camps with the help of forged passports. For this purpose we do not hesitate to deal with counterfeiters and passport thieves. We are ready to smuggle Jewish children over the borders, and to engage expert smugglers, rogues whose profession this is. We are ready to smuggle money illegally into enemy territory to bribe those dregs of humanity, the killers of the Jewish people.

The Vaad Hahatzalah backed up its words with secret deeds, though its rescue work was constrained by a chronic lack of funds. The Orthodox group's focus on strictly observant Jews and its strident radicalism repelled the much better heeled organizations of the American Jewish mainstream, especially the Joint Distribution Committee, which not only was loath to finance the Vaad's activities but used its influence to sabotage its fund-raising efforts. Appalled by what they saw as the Jewish establishment's complacency, the Vaad's leaders in mid-1943 broadened the group's rescue mission to include all European Jews, not just the "Torah-true." This change in policy enhanced the Vaad's fund-raising appeal, and the money came rolling in as never before, enabling the group to boost its budget from $160,000 in 1942 to more than $1 million in 1944.

Rufka Klein was eminently qualified to solicit the Vaad Hahatzalah's backing. Her husband, Martin, and his brother, Stephen, both were major donors to the relief group, contributing a share of the profits from Barton's Bonbonnière, a kosher candy firm the Klein family had founded in Brooklyn; Stephen even sat on the Vaad's governing board. By March 10, 1944, the Vaad had decided to back the Reichmanns, who were informed by cable: "Payment up to $3,000 guaranteed by us. Parcels should be sent at once to all possible ghettos in Lithuania, Poland, Slovakia and wherever else possible."

On this same day, Adolf Eichmann and his subordinates met at Mauthausen concentration camp to plan the deportation of the 750,000 Jews of Hungary. Hitler had reached the end of his patience with Hungary, the only one of his allies that had refused to deliver Jewish inhabitants into Nazi hands. By the spring of 1944, 63,000 Hungarian Jews had perished under forced servitude in labor battalions, but the Hungarian authorities had kept radical anti-Semitic groups such as the Arrow Cross under check and refused repeated demands to deport Jews into German custody. On balance, Jews had been better off in Hungary than anywhere else in Europe. But on March 18, Hitler summoned Admiral Miklós Horthy, the Hungarian head of state, to Klessheim Castle, near Salzburg. In response to Hitler's threats, Horthy agreed to deliver 100,000 Jewish "workers" to aid the German war effort but drew the line at a general deportation. At 9:30 that same evening, Admiral Horthy's train left for Budapest. About forty-five minutes later, German troops crossed from Slovakia into Hungary. Meeting no armed resistance, they soon occupied the entire country.

By the time that Germany invaded Hungary, the tide of battle had shifted decisively in favor of the Allies. Tragically, the likelihood of impending defeat gave added urgency to the Nazi effort to exterminate the remainder of European Jewry. Wasting no time, Eichmann flew into Budapest on March 19 to begin implementing the final solution in Hungary. As a warm-up, two hundred Jewish doctors and lawyers, chosen at random from the Budapest phone book, were arrested and deported to Mauthausen. Eichmann had arrived with an extermination plan that was at once highly detailed and brutally simple in its basic outline. It divided Hungary into six zones, each of which was to be emptied of Jews one by one, saving Budapest for last. In each zone, Jews were to be forced from their homes and interned in makeshift concentration camps. And then, as fast as logistically possible, they would be loaded onto freight trains and taken to the death camp at Auschwitz.

As usual, Eichmann shrouded his intentions in layers of deceit. "After the war," he assured a delegation from the Jewish Council of Budapest, "the Jews [will] be free to do whatever they want." In the meantime, Jews would have to wear the yellow star but would not suffer for it. Attacks by Hungarians against Jews would not be tolerated, Eichmann assured the Jewish leaders, many of whom took the Nazi at his word. "I do not believe that we shall suffer the same fate that befell Polish Jews," fantasized Budapest's preeminent Orthodox leader a few days after the German invasion. "We must be prepared for many struggles and deprivations but I am not worried for our lives."

For her part, Renée Reichmann was incapable of such blithe optimism. Ever since she had arrived in Tangier, her brother Henrik had been her most reliable correspondent, sending letters and postcards mixing family gossip with veiled accounts of political developments. (His missives, sent from Bratislava, had to pass through both Slovakian and German censors.) As early as January, Renée had grown so alarmed at the course of events back home that Henrik felt obliged to urge her to calm herself. "Don't exaggerate your fears," he wrote. But by February, Renée's requests for news from home had become so hectoring that Henrik reproached her, gently to be sure. "I can only conclude that you would like to have a long letter every day and that you miss our old home terribly," he wrote a few weeks before the German invasion. "I am sorry to tell you that it no longer exists. I will try to write more often but I cannot take the place of what you used to have, not even partially."

After the Nazi occupation, Renée unrepentantly barraged her brother with pleas for news of the family. He finally responded at length on March 27, after tearing up the letter he had written but failed to send the week before. "So much has come to nothing overnight that my report is totally superfluous today," Henrik wrote. "It no longer makes any difference whether Reska has received the mattress or not, for our brothers and sisters have more important problems now." As the Germans were marching into Hungary, Klára, one of the younger Gestetner sisters, had given birth to a stillborn child, Henrik continued, reporting what in hindsight reads like an augury of doom. "Things got very bloody as the placenta came out first and the child could not live. It weighed only 4.4 kilograms. Klára was in great danger for awhile but has improved and is calming down. Interestingly, she is always dreaming about mother. This time mother said that she should not complain because it is still meant to be that she will have three sons, but after a time."

Even from the distance of Tangier, Mrs. Reichmann seemed to realize that in reality, time was running out on the Jews of Hungary. Soon, she and her helpers had boosted their monthly food parcel output from 250 to more than 4,000—a sixteenfold increase. But almost from the moment that German troops first set foot in Hungary, Mrs. Reichmann shifted the focus of her efforts from relief to rescue.

Chapter 11

As Mrs. Reichmann herself told it, the notion of rescuing Jewish children in Hungary occurred to her not long after Germany invaded her homeland. "In March 1944, when the Germans practically occupied the whole of Hungary I saw the only possibility to save something, to take out children under fifteen years of age," she explained in a postwar letter summarizing her wartime activities. "My idea was that those children were incapable of work and therefore the Germans would be willing to let them go. That the beast aimed at the annihilation of the Jewish people was inconceivable." Mrs. Reichmann understood that she was in no position to approach the Germans directly. But having made scores of trips to Tetuán to secure export licenses for food parcel shipments, she was as well attuned to the nuances of Spanish Moroccan policy as any professional diplomat. She had an inkling that the high commissioner, General Luis Orgaz, might be willing to do more to help Jews. But would he go so far as to allow hundreds of young Hungarian Jews to emigrate to Tangier?

Mrs. Reichmann was just beginning to plot strategy when her prospects seemed to diminish from iffy to impossible. On April 8, General Orgaz peremptorily summoned to Tetuán fourteen of Tangier's most prominent Jewish leaders, among them the Reichmann allies Isaac Salama and Aaron Cohen, who were forced to listen in silence as the high commissioner launched a broadside against the Jews of Tangier. General Orgaz had recently honored an obligation incurred by his predecessor to pay off a 128,000-peseta debt owed to the Jewish community of Seville and was incensed that the Jews under his jurisdiction had contributed only 3,000 pesetas to help defray this extraordinary expense. For Purim, the general railed on, the High Commissariat had granted the Casino de Tangier a special gambling license for a charity fund-raiser, and what thanks did he get? Some 5 million francs were wagered and yet the community contributed only 50,000 francs to Spanish charities, saving the rest of the take for itself. "The incident itself hardly merits a report of this nature," C. Burke Albrick, the acting U.S. chargé d'affaires in Tangier, noted in a dispatch to Washington, "except for the fact that it demonstrates the extraordinarily childish behavior in which the highest officer in Spanish North Africa is wont to indulge."

In mid-April, right on Eichmann's schedule, the SS and its Hungarian help-mates began driving the Jews of northeastern Hungary from their homes into makeshift concentration camps. Eichmann made this, Hungary's most intensely Hasidic region, Zone I because the Yiddish-speaking, "alien" Hasidic masses were held in lower regard by the local Gentile population than were the more assimilated Jews elsewhere in Hungary. About fifteen thousand Jews were interned at Sátoraljaújhely, the site of one of nine concentration camps in Zone I, and another ten thousand at Huzst, which was Mrs. Reichmann's birthplace and home still to many relatives on her mother's side of the family. Even before the roundup was completed in Zone I, the deportations started in Zone II. Zone III included Győr; Beled and Csorna were part of Zone V. Eichmann planned to save Budapest for last.

Although the Nazis tried to camouflage their massive deportations with disinformation, the basic facts leaked to the outside world almost immediately. By late April, the United Press was reporting that 300,000 Jews had been interned in Hungary. At this advanced stage of the Holocaust, it was well understood that in the Nazi modus operandi, concentration was soon followed by deportation, annihilation, cremation. Although Washington loosed a fusillade of threats at German and Hungarian leaders alike, the Allies never seriously considered using military force to rescue Hungarian Jews. The U.S. War Department had bluntly, if confidentially, declared its priorities in an internal report a few months before the Germans invaded Hungary: "It is not contemplated that units of the armed forces will be employed for the purpose of rescuing victims of enemy oppression unless such rescues are the direct result of military operations conducted with the objective of defeating the armed forces of the enemy."

Meanwhile, Renée and Eva were rallying their supporters in the Spanish Red Cross and making the rounds of Tangier's preeminent Sephardim to drum up support for a rescue plan shrewdly crafted to take into account Spanish ambivalence. While on balance Spain had been willing to open its borders to Jews menaced by Nazi Germany, it was adamantly opposed to letting them remain in the country for long. The Franco government was reluctant even to welcome home expatriate Spanish Jews. In early 1943, Germany did Spain the favor of allowing it three months to repatriate all Spanish nationals—Jews included—living in occupied Europe. Presented with an opportunity to save four thousand lives, Franco and his ministers vacillated for weeks, insisting finally that the U.S. government guarantee that it would resettle any Jews who returned to Spain. Although the United States agreed, Spain in the end admitted only eight hundred of the four thousand.

In late 1943, ten Jewish refugee families had departed Tangier on a transport to Palestine sponsored by the Joint Distribution Committee. By early 1944, an additional four hundred Tangier refugees—including the Grussgott family—had signed a waiting list for the next boat to Palestine, and the Joint Distribution Committee was working through the fine points of a plan to resettle two hundred refugees in Canada. In the expectation that at least five hundred Jews would leave Tangier, Mrs. Reichmann reasoned, perhaps the Spanish government would be willing to allow into the city an equal number of Hungarian children. Tangier would suffer no net increase in its refugee population, and yet the Franco regime would be able to score humanitarian points that could redound to its advantage in dealing with the Allies.

Now that the defeat of the Axis appeared inevitable, Franco was eager to curry favor with the United States. "The war was coming to an end," recalled A. David Fritzlan, the U.S. vice consul for political affairs in Tangier. "By this time the Spanish could see the writing on the wall, and they knew they had to do everything they could to earn credit with us." Fritzlan, who met frequently with Mrs. Reichmann throughout 1944 and 1945, said that she did not need to be briefed on the new realities of Spanish-American relations. "She knew what was going on," Fritzlan said.

However, no one in Tangier—or Washington, for that matter—knew exactly what was transpiring in Hungary, where events were unfolding with a rapidity that defied outside comprehension. The fate of Beled was typical. Shortly after the German occupation, a Nazi army unit moved into the village, bolstering the Hungarian national police unit already stationed there. On May 10 and 11, the property of each Jewish family was meticulously catalogued and then expropriated, right down to the last spoon and sock. At the same time, all the Jewish-owned stores, including three belonging to members of the Reichmann family, were shut down. A few Beled Jews managed to escape to Budapest on forged papers or were exempted from deportation on the basis of medals awarded for military service in World War I, but the rest of the village's 330 Jewish residents were herded en masse down to the train station, forced onto cattle trucks, and transported either to Szombathely or Sopron for incarceration. The camp at Sopron was filled not only with Reichmanns but with Gestetners, for the Csorna Jews were concentrated there, as well.

In Győr, meanwhile, scores of Gestetners were among the 5,600 Jews sardined into a fenced-off section of Győrsziget, the island in the Danube that was the site of the original Jewish ghetto. Most people had to sleep in the open. In their search for hidden Jewish wealth, the local fascists interrogated and horse-whipped many prominent Jews, including a half-dozen rabbis. A barber removed half of each rabbi's beard and mustache while the ghetto commander, a draftsman by profession, used an indelible marker to draw human skulls and various pagan and fascist symbols on their foreheads.

Three of Renée's brothers—Henrik in Bratislava, Dezsö in Győr, and Antal in Ujpest, a suburb of Budapest—were able to remain at liberty for a time and made use of their training as engravers to forge Christian identity papers for many friends and relatives. Their sister, Reska, and her husband were among scores of Orthodox Oberlanders who made use of the forged documents to flee to Budapest, where they went into hiding. Masquerading as a Gentile, Reska went to work as a nurse for the International Red Cross (IRC). Able to circulate freely in Budapest in Red Cross uniform, Reska somehow obtained supplies of food, which by this time was in short supply in Budapest, and at great risk managed to deliver it to Jews in hiding.

On May 22, Isaac Salama, Aaron Cohen, and seven other Sephardic worthies laid the Reichmann rescue proposal before the high commissioner in an almost abjectly courteous letter. "Shortly will leave our city about 500 Jewish refugees from Central Europe and Turkey and this circumstance stimulates our request," it stated. The signatories asked that General Orgaz authorize the emigration of five hundred Hungarian children ranging in age from two to fifteen and promised to assume financial responsibility for the newcomers: "We guarantee that their stay in this city will not cause the least trouble or inconvenience to our beloved authorities or to anyone else in Tangier."

General Orgaz responded promptly to the Hungarian rescue proposal. In a May 23 letter to the head of the Jewish community of Tetuán, the high commissioner agreed to forward the request to Madrid and hinted that he endorsed it—but on one condition. "I hope," he wrote, "that you will not fail to send me, as soon as possible, detailed information" about the expected departure from Tangier of the five hundred refugees, "which will have to precede the arrival of the Hungarian children." The high commissioner underlined the phrase, "which will have to precede."

General Orgaz had called Mrs. Reichmann's bluff. In truth, both the Palestinian and Canadian emigration projects were fraught with complications, and there was no way of telling how many refugees would leave Tangier or when, though chances were that it would be later rather than sooner. (As it turned out, the Canadian and Palestinian émigrés—some five hundred all told—would not depart until September 1944.) Fearful that General Orgaz's contingency amounted to a death sentence for her project, Mrs. Reichmann began rallying broader support with the help of Isaac Salama, who had underscored his support by signing the letter to Orgaz twice, once as an individual and again as head of the family firm, Jacob de J. Salama. Salama may well have raised the matter with Franco himself.

In Tangier, the most valuable of all potential allies was Rives Childs, who, like his friend Orgaz, was himself rather difficult and sphinxlike. Blessed with phenomenal mental powers, Childs distinguished himself during World War I as a codebreaker for the U.S. Army in France. After the war he worked as White House correspondent for the Associated Press and then shipped out to the Soviet Union to work for a U.S. government relief program. In Leningrad, he married a young Russian woman of beauty and aristocratic lineage. He entered the U.S. foreign service in 1923 and was sent to Jerusalem. After postings in Egypt and Romania and on the Palestine desk in the State Department, Childs arrived in Tangier as a committed Arabist and budding literary scholar. During his lifetime, Childs wrote fifteen books, including three on Casanova (one written in German), one on the Restif de la Bretonne (in French), and another on Henry Miller, with whom he corresponded voluminously.

Although Childs's intelligence and sophistication—impressively displayed in his erudite and often elegantly worded dispatches from Tangier—were beyond question, his State Department career was less than sterling. During his four and a half years in Tangier, the State Department never saw fit to promote him from chargé d'affaires ad interim to a full-fledged consul general. Childs was a proud and prickly character, suspicious of his colleagues, peremptory in manner, and altogether incapable of the collegiality that counted so heavily in diplomatic service. Childs's Russian mother-in-law, who lived in the legation and often quarreled with her son-in-law at great volume, called him the Little Pasha. His fellow diplomats were no fonder of him. A year after David Fritzlan had joined his staff as a vice consul, Childs eyed him quizzically. "Fritzlan," he said, "I hardly know you. Meet me Sunday morning and we'll take a walk on the beach." Fritzlan did as he was told. "We walked for an hour," he recalled, "and Childs hardly said a word."

In Mrs. Reichmann's initial approach to Childs, she hit a stone wall, even though the legation had signed off on the food parcel program not six weeks earlier. "The Americans were not interested in Hungarian Jews at that point and not eager to let anyone talk them into any rescue idea involving Spain," recalled Albert Reinhard, the chief administrator of the local refugee relief committee, which by this time was functioning as the local arm of the Joint Distribution Committee in all but name. "To them, dealing with the Spanish was no different from dealing with the enemy. Especially when the request for help came from a family like the Reichmanns, who were foreigners and had nothing really to do with America, the American attitude was, 'Why should we do anything for that woman?' "

In his memoirs, Childs recalled his first, rather officious reaction to Mrs. Reichmann's request for U.S. intervention:

> I concluded by stating that, however sympathetic I might be to her objective, I
> was unable to perceive how I might justify my intervention with General

Orgaz in behalf of nationals of presumably Middle European origin, not of American nationality.

"I am sorry, madam, I can see no American interest involved to warrant action on my part. What am I to respond if General Orgaz raises such a question and asks: 'What is the American interest, Mr. Charge d'Affaires?'"

From the depth of her emotional concern I detected a film of moisture forming over the retinas of Mme. Reichmann's eyes. "And the humanitarian interest?" she softly inquired.

From the American point of view, the politics of Spanish rescue were even trickier than Reinhard realized or Childs acknowledged. In January 1944, the Roosevelt administration finally had bowed to mounting political pressure for Jewish rescue by forming the War Refugee Board (WRB). Spain figured importantly in the board's initial plans; the agency hoped that the application of diplomatic pressure would induce Franco to permit the use of Spain as a major channel of escape for Jews and other imperiled occupants of Axis Europe. The War Refugee Board even envisioned setting up three large "reception centers" along Spain's border with France. At American expense, thousands of refugees would be promptly moved through these centers to permanent homes overseas.

The WRB got nowhere in Spain because Carlton J. H. Hayes, the U.S. ambassador to Spain, flatly and repeatedly refused to present its proposals to the Spanish government. Hayes also impeded the flow of WRB funds into Spain and even succeeded in blocking the agency from installing its own representative in Madrid. Although Hayes was not entirely unsympathetic to the plight of Jewish refugees, he had gone to Madrid fixated on one goal: halting Spanish sales of strategic materials to Germany. By the time that the WRB got rolling in early 1944, Hayes had largely achieved his objective and was on the verge of wrapping up negotiations to stop the small remaining flow of Spanish tungsten to Germany. According to historian David Wyman, Hayes "concluded that diplomatic pressure for the WRB's programs might interfere with the final steps of his wolfram negotiations. He apparently considered the board's work of too little significance to justify any risk." Not until mid-July 1944 would Hayes privately concede, during a trip to Washington, that he had erred in not using his office to promote rescue via Spain.

Mrs. Reichmann's plan appealed to Childs in that it offered the disenchanted diplomat his first opportunity to involve himself in the au courant issue of Jewish rescue. But to champion from Tangier a proposal that ultimately required approval at the highest levels of the Franco government was to run the risk of appearing to be conspiring in an end run around Ambassador Hayes. Although Childs certainly was no toady, he could only lose from antagonizing Hayes, whose standing within the State Department vastly exceeded his own.

Whether Mrs. Reichmann was aware of the peculiar internal dynamics of the State Department's Spanish desk is not clear. In any event, she made the right tactical move in soliciting the support of Reinhard and Mordecai Kessler, the Joint Distribution Committee delegate on assignment in Tangier. Kessler relayed Mrs. Reichmann's plea for help to the Joint Distribution Committee's headquarters in New York at a most opportune time. For the committee, the Hungarian proposal offered the dually enticing prospect of saving Jewish lives while skirting the obstinate Hayes. The Joint Distribution Committee not only intervened on Mrs. Reichmann's behalf at the highest levels of the State Department but offered to assume the costs of maintaining the five hundred children in Tangier.

Apparently, it was Kessler and Reinhard who clued Childs into the sudden groundswell of support in Washington for the Tangier rescue plan. On June 1 Childs suddenly cast aside his formalist scruples and drove to Tetuán for an unofficial meeting with General Orgaz, during which he put the weight of the U.S. State Department behind the Reichmann plan. The high commissioner told the American that he had already forwarded the proposal to Madrid with his recommendation for approval, and he also backed away from the condition that he had set in his initial response. According to Childs, Orgaz said that "finding necessary supplies in Tangier for the children was the important question, rather than finances. For this reason, if departure of refugees now in Tangier . . . could be facilitated before [the] arrival of 500 children, he said it would facilitate matters; however, he had not made the one contingent upon the other necessarily."

Upon his return to Tangier, Childs immediately cabled the Madrid Embassy. "The embassy replied that the matter would be pushed," he recalled, "and it was." It fell to Fritzlan to deliver the good news to Mrs. Reichmann, who must have been more relieved than exultant. Without the high commissioner's support and the intervention of the U.S. Legation, her project would have expired stillborn. But Madrid's approval still was required, and time was running short.

———

On June 11, the first train to Auschwitz pulled out of Győr. Other transports followed until June 14, when, miraculously, deliverance seemed to be at hand. On this day, Adolf Eichmann announced that he was going to divert thirty thousand Hungarian Jews bound for Auschwitz to labor camps in Austria as a good faith gesture in his infamous negotiations with the leaders of Budapest Jewry to trade one million Jews for ten thousand trucks. Some fifteen thousand of the reprieved Jews were to come from Budapest and the balance from the provinces, including three thousand from Győr. In fact, the Győr contingent was to be the first "put on ice," as Eichmann unsettlingly put it, in Austria. However, the train carrying the lucky three thousand was accidentally misrouted and ended up in Kassa, the customary last stop in Hungary on the route to Auschwitz. At the Slovakian border the routing error finally was discovered. The train was halted and a cable sent to Eichmann in Budapest. Rezsö Kasztner, who headed the ransom negotiations with Eichmann, related the tragedy of the Győr train in high style at Eichmann's famous trial in Jerusalem in 1961.

> Nobody knows exactly what this is all about. And yet everybody knows this: They have come to the great crossroads. Which road will the train take? They cannot go to a telephone, not listen in, not tremble. And never are they going to learn what decision Eichmann made: "Well, if you are already at the Slovakian border, why don't you just continue! To Auschwitz! Alright?!"
>
> It was only a matter of the numbers of two trains being exchanged. The train from Győr went to Auschwitz, and with it went one of the great personalities of Judaism, Rabbi Dr. Emil Roth . . . going to his death with the 3,000 Jews fate had selected. Another train, one from Debrecen destined for Auschwitz, went to Austria instead. Fate is making its own decisions.

As the ill-fated Győr transport was making its way to Auschwitz, Renée and Eva Reichmann, unaware of the ghastly turn of events back home, called on Fritzlan to request a letter of introduction to the American Embassy in Madrid. On June 20, the Reichmann women returned to the U.S. Legation to pick up the letter of introduction, which was signed by Childs, and caught the train for Madrid. They arrived about June 25 and checked into the Hotel Asturias, a large, low-budget tourist establishment just off the Puerta del Sol. Although the Reichmann women encountered no great resistance as they made the diplomatic rounds, they had to remain in the Spanish capital for an entire month before the Foreign Ministry finally rendered formal judgment. It was during this excruciating month at the Hotel Asturias that Mrs. Reichmann wrote to Rafael Alvarez Claro, the mayor of Melilla, as part of a last-ditch attempt to develop the political critical mass needed to put her rescue plan over the top at the Ministry of Foreign Affairs.

While Renée and Eva waited in Madrid with mounting exasperation, the Jews imprisoned at Sopron were taken to the train station and locked in cattle cars bound for Auschwitz. One of the cars contained sixty-seven members of the extended Reichmann family drawn from four generations. The eldest was seventy-nine-year old Lidi Reichmann, Samuel's mother. (His father, mercifully, had died of natural causes in 1940.) The youngest, Simon's daughter Margit, had just turned one. Edith Reichmann, who at eighteen was the eldest daughter of one of Samuel's brothers, was one of only three Reichmann relatives on this transport who would survive Auschwitz. Years later, Edith, whose Hebrew name was Esther, or "Eszti" for short, recounted her ordeal to her sister-in-law, who wrote a privately published memoir, *Eszti's Story*, which is excerpted here. At the train station in Sopron, family members

> were squeezed mercilessly into these dark, dank wagons, without food, drink, or any possessions except the small individual bundles they had been permitted to take along. Men, women and children were pressed together in these horrific cages for three straight days, with no sanitary facilities other than a small bucket that had been placed in the corner for human waste. They suffocated in the crowded, airless cars, surrounded by the stench of human waste, stripped of all human dignity. They had no idea where they were being taken, or why.

The transport arrived at Auschwitz-Birkenau on a Shabbat morning. As soon as the car doors opened, the dazed and disoriented passengers were assaulted by Jewish kapos and herded into lines for "selection." With a flick of his hand or a wave of his stick, Dr. Josef Mengele, the infamous SS captain known as Dr. Death, indicated who was "unfit for work" and thus immediately destined for the gas chamber.

> An aunt and uncle of hers were clubbed on the head by a kapo who tried to separate them, and Eszti, who was caught between them, was beaten as well. When it was her family's turn to face Mengele, one of her small siblings was standing next to her. She was asked if the child was hers. Before she could answer, an uncle spoke up, 'No, no, the child belongs to Malke' (Eszti's mother). Eszti's life was saved with this sentence, and Eszti alone was sent to the right, as she looked relatively healthy and capable of work. . . . The rest of her family, including her mother and grandmother, aunts and uncles, and all of her seven brothers and sisters, were sent to the left. . . .
> After being ushered to the right, Eszti realized that she was holding a coat that belonged to one of her siblings. Her first thought was that her sibling should stay warm. She turned to the left to go after the family and return the coat, but everything had happened with such blinding speed that they were already far away. Eszti tried in vain to somehow communicate with her mother, willing her to turn around, to catch her eye, to send some silent message. She waited for a sign of acknowledgement that they still belonged together. She could only see her mother's back; her head was bowed, and she was holding the hands of the younger children. She was already far across the compound, getting smaller and smaller as the distance grew. Her mother never turned back.

When Mrs. Reichmann had arrived in Madrid, the ministry was distracted by the famous Kasztner train incident. After extracting ransom of $1.6 million, Eichmann authorized 1,684 prominent Jews to leave Hungary on a special transport to Lisbon. To reach Portugal, the so-called Kasztner train had to pass through Spain. Ever the punctilious bureaucrat, Eichmann insisted that the passengers obtain Spanish transit visas before departure. Spain's Foreign Ministry obliged and on June 30 the Kasztner train rolled west out of Budapest. Eichmann waited until the train passed through Vienna before he executed the double cross that he had apparently planned from the beginning and rerouted it to Germany.

For fear of offending the Germans, Spain and the other neutral powers were still resisting behind-the-scenes pressure from the United States to intervene with the Hungarian government and formally denounce the deportations. In late June, the conspiracy of silence was gingerly broken by Pope Pius XII, then by Gustav V, the king of Sweden, and finally by the International Red Cross and others. Steeled by the rising chorus of protests as well as by Germany's declining military strength, Admiral Miklós Horthy, the Hungarian head of state, finally stood up to the Nazis and ordered a halt to the deportations on July 6. By this time, 440,000 Jews had been cleared from the provinces, but most of Budapest's 230,000 Jews remained. Horthy's action enraged Eichmann, who, without Hungarian help, lacked the manpower to deport Budapest Jewry.

On July 9, Sweden sent a special envoy, Raoul Wallenberg, to Budapest to step up Swedish diplomatic efforts on behalf of the remaining Jews. About the same time, Switzerland and Spain also clambered onto the rescue bandwagon.

Four days later, the Spanish Foreign Ministry finally informed Mrs. Reichmann that it was preparing to cable instructions to its embassy in Budapest to issue the five hundred visas. (However, the cable was not actually transmitted until July 20.) Renée immediately relayed the good news to her husband in Tangier. Although the Reichmanns already enjoyed the backing of the Joint Distribution Committee, they decided to also involve their Orthodox confrères at the Vaad Hahatzalah. On July 14, Samuel sent a cable, in broken English, to New York: "We received visas for 500 Hungarian Jewish children to enter Spanish Morocco. Renée is actually at Madrid with intention to organize this. Doing everything possible. Has chances will ask your help. Cable if we can count with it." That very evening the Vaad responded enthusiastically: "Our organization ready support any project rescue children from Hungary."

The Joint Distribution Committee was miffed at the prospect of sharing responsibility—and credit—with its Orthodox gadfly. Joseph Schwartz, the committee's European chief, wrote the president of Tangier's Jewish Community, asking him to lobby the Reichmanns on his behalf. But Schwartz's pressure proved ineffectual: the Reichmanns were not about to freeze out the one organization that had been willing to finance its food parcel shipments.

———

Mrs. Reichmann and her daughter returned at last from Madrid to find a cable containing new and yet tragically belated instructions from the Vaad Hahatzalah: "Send maximum possible number of food parcels to camp Sátoraljaújhely Hungary. . . . Our funds in Mrs. Reichmann's hands to be used for this purpose. Will send additional sums soon. Send maximum number parcels permitted to this and other camps."

As usual, Renée got right to it. Aaron Cohen offered such a good price on chocolate that she decided not to include any other foodstuffs in the parcels destined for Hungary. ("[Cohen] contributes every month a fortune for the people of Tangier," Mrs. Reichmann wrote enthusiastically in a letter to the Vaad Hahatzalah. "Always give him the money.") Cohen also provided a warehouse free of charge for use in assembling the parcels. School was not in session, so even the younger Reichmann boys and their friends were allowed to stay up as late as four o'clock in the morning packing the chocolate. From New York, the Vaad Hahatzalah sent the names of 120 Jews who had been deported to Sátoraljaújhely mostly from the town of Szerencs. On her own, Mrs. Reichmann also decided to send parcels to the ghettos in Győr and Szombathely.

When the Vaad Hahatzalah applied to send another $3,000 to pay for the shipments to Sátoraljaújhely, the State Department cabled the legation in Tangier asking for its recommendation. Childs again called in Mrs. Reichmann, who explained that she hoped to ship to Hungary as she had to Czechoslovakia and Poland—that is, through the Spanish Post Office by arrangement with the Spanish Red Cross. Reichmann acknowledged her concern that the usual methods might not ensure delivery in Hungary. "With the exception of Budapest almost all the cities in Hungary are isolated," she wrote. "If we had more money we could hire a little ship to sail up the Danube. . . . The smallest ship which could leave would be seven tons. That I naturally would work out with the largest importer."

By mid-August, when Mrs. Reichmann wrote Martin and Rufka Klein in New York, she understood why she had not received replies to the cables she sent Jewish officials in Győr and Szombathely, though she still had not yet grasped the enormity of what had occurred in Hungary. It is impossible to send packages to Hungary, she wrote:

> We cannot locate the people as they have all disappeared. Those people who were at Sátoraljaújhely were deported and those who are still there cannot be located. All the cities except Budapest are Jew free, and even in Budapest the few Jews in the ghetto were scheduled to leave but at the last moment the Hungarian government allowed them to remain. It is impossible to find out who and where these people are. In fact, my brother David [Dezsö] who is now in a slave camp cannot even find his brother with whom he lived. He does not know where his wife and children are. He is the only one of his many friends who was sent to various places and finally returned to Győr. . . .

The days go by but it is hard to eat and sleep knowing that our brothers and sisters are sleeping in the open without warm blankets and have no food.

If Mrs. Reichmann suspected that rescue was no longer possible for the vast majority of the deportees, she did not commit her fears to print. To the contrary, from mid-1944 virtually until the end of the war, month after month, she prodded HIJEFS—the Vaad Hahatzalah's affiliate in Switzerland—the International Red Cross, and other relief organizations with requests for information about the whereabouts of the deported Hungarians. She got nowhere, of course. As late as September, six months after the deportations to Auschwitz had begun, HIJEFS admitted that it, too, hadn't a clue: "We have no details of various alleged camps for Hungarian Jews in Germany and Austria despite our greatest efforts." By mid-October, the people at HIJEFS thought they had finally puzzled it out, informing Mrs. Reichmann, who relayed the information to the Vaad in New York: "Hungarian Jews are in Waldsee. . . . [T]his information has been given to me by the HIJEFS."

Like HIJEFS, Mrs. Reichmann had fallen for a Nazi mirage. Have no fear, the Germans had told Jewish leaders, as the first transports to Auschwitz rolled out of Hungary; they are bound for Waldsee, a labor camp. Within a week or two, friends and relatives back in Hungary began receiving cards postmarked "Waldsee," all of which carried a variant of the simple message: "Arrived safely. I am working. I am well." For some Jews, signing a postcard from Waldsee was their last act before entering the gas chambers. As the Nazis hoped, the cards tranquilized Jews still awaiting deportation. "It is impossible to describe the effect these cards had on the Jews," recalled a young man who received a Waldsee postcard from his father. "One heard the exclamations, 'See! They're at work! Nothing has happened to them, and now nothing will happen to them for the war will soon be over!' "

⸻

Even as Mrs. Reichmann was shifting focus back to the doomed effort to feed Hungarian Jews, she kept nudging the Budapest rescue project along as best she could. She had no intention of sitting back and relying on the politicians. "In the afternoon [Rives Childs] called me again that he had received a cable from the War Refugee Board in Washington about the 500 children," she informed the Vaad Hahatzalah in late July. "They said they would do their best. However," she added, "you people will have to push it from your side."

Once Spain had approved the visas (the total authorized eventually was raised to 570, ostensibly to accommodate 70 adults to care for the children on the trip to Tangier), the next step was finding children to use them. There was no shortage of deserving candidates; Budapest's orphanages were jammed and on the outskirts of the city many children still languished in SS detention camps that would quickly empty if the deportations resumed. But not just any youths would do. As the plan's principal sponsor, the Jewish Community of Tangier reserved the right to select 200 recipients. Apparently, its list included relatives of the refugees already in Tangier as well as names supplied by HIJEFS and by the Orthodox community of Budapest. The Jewish Council of Budapest (of which the Orthodox were a part) was to fill the remaining 300 slots.

Through various intermediaries, Mrs. Reichmann solicited the involvement of the International Red Cross, which agreed to help arrange the children's passage to Tangier. The International Red Cross's involvement in the Tangier project proved a matter of considerable historic import. Throughout the war, the IRC had repeatedly refused pleas to broaden its scope beyond prisoners of war to include Jewish civilians interned by Germany. As the situation in Budapest deteriorated, the IRC's traditionalist resolve softened. In early July, the president of the Geneva-based International Red Cross requested Admiral Horthy's permission to allow an IRC mission into Hungary to provide humanitarian aid to deported Jews. On July 18, Horthy replied to this modest proposal by loosing a diplomatic thunderbolt: he not only invited the Red Cross into Hungary but offered to let about forty thousand Jews leave the country. Specifically, he proposed the emigration of Jewish children holding foreign visas and Jews of any age with a Palestine certificate.

Suddenly, mass evacuation from Budapest seemed a real possibility. Switzerland offered to admit 13,000 Jews on a temporary basis. Sweden stood ready to accept 10,000 more. The U.S. agreed to take 5,000 children, and prevailed upon Spain to issue another 1,500 visas over and beyond the 570 set aside for the Tangier group. Raoul Wallenberg and Charles Lutz, Switzerland's ambassador in Budapest, immediately took into protective custody a few thousand prospective émigrés, who were issued special passes—"Schutzpasse"—and placed in buildings under the extraterritorial jurisdiction of their respective embassies.

Although the Tangier proposal was temporarily lost in the furious shuffle of international diplomacy that followed the Horthy offer, Mrs. Reichmann was inspired by the sudden turn of events in the Hungarian capital to ask the Spanish government for another 700 visas. Why 700? Apparently, that was the number of additional names received from Montreux and the Orthodox leaders in Budapest after the first batch of 500 recipients were selected. "What was interesting about the second group," Eva Reichmann recalled, "is that when we got their names, I told my brother [Edward] to ask the Spanish . . . for permission to provide papers for another hundred. My mother, always one to think big, suggested otherwise. 'Let's ask for 700 and let him cut it down to 100.' "

Mrs. Reichmann again called on Childs, whose written recollection of the meeting was patronizing, to say the least.

She put me in mind somehow of Old Faithful geyser in Yellowstone Park which erupts, subsides and reappears after a fixed interval.

She herself was bubbling over. "You have been so successful," she murmured, "that I have come to ask you to approach General Orgaz once again, this time with a request for 700 visas for Jewish adults in Budapest."

I threw up my hands. "Dear Mme. Reichmann, you Jews are all the same. Gain an inch and you want an ell." She looked dismayed and I began to smile. "Never mind, I couldn't say 'no' to you once before and I can't say 'no' this time."

This time, it was Mrs. Reichmann and her daughter who made the trek to Tetuán to appeal to General Orgaz, who immediately agreed in principle, providing that adequate accommodations could be arranged for the additional children. Upon returning to Tangier, the Reichmann women stopped into the French Consulate General to promote an idea: Why not disassemble a vacant military barracks in Casablanca, transport the lumber to Tangier, and build a temporary shelter for 1,200 people?

Distracted by ripple effects of the Horthy offer, Red Cross representatives in Budapest made little progress in searching for the children on the Tangier list. In mid-August, Mrs. Reichmann received a bewildering cable from HIJEFS: "The Red Cross has opportunities for the departure of children under 10 years of age if they possess a visa for a neutral country. Send entry visas immediately to the International Red Cross in Geneva and to the representation of your country in Budapest." Was this meant to include the five hundred visas? Had Mrs. Reichmann's plan been subsumed into the larger rescue effort? The HIJEFS telegram offered no clue, omitting any mention of the Tangier project.

There is no record of a reply from Mrs. Reichmann. Nor was one necessary. On the very day that the HIJEFS cable reached Tangier, the Germans popped Horthy's trial balloon by refusing to supply exit visas to a group of Palestine-bound Jews that had been cleared for departure by Hungarian authorities. The extravagant hopes raised by the Horthy offer faded as it became apparent that Hungary and Germany were at an impasse. Without Hungarian cooperation, the Nazis had no hope of completing the annihilation of its Jews. On the other hand, German forces controlled Hungary's borders and Hitler had no intention of permitting a mass Jewish exodus. But might the Nazis permit small groups of Jews to leave under Spanish sponsorship? Given the stakes, it was worth a try. The Tangier project again was infused with urgency.

The International Red Cross soon decided to force the issue and, though the Tangier group still had not been fully assembled, applied for exit visas. When the Germans refused the request on or about August 31, the IRC leadership faced a moment of truth. For some time, the Jewish leaders of Budapest had been urging the IRC to assume responsibility for Jewish children, who were menaced not only by the malingering threat of deportation but by dwindling stocks of food and medical supplies and by the approaching Soviet Army. Soon, Budapest would be a city under siege. The IRC was sympathetic but required a legal pretext of some sort to intervene in Hungarian affairs, and the Tangier project provided it. To intervene on behalf of Hungarians in Hungary was to usurp the function of the national government. But since the Tangier five hundred held emigration visas, were they not, in a sense, already Spanish citizens under detention by a foreign power?

Just outside the Spanish Legation, the Red Cross set up a makeshift camp posted with signs in Hungarian, German, French, and Russian reading: "Under the Protection of the International Committee of the Red Cross." To extend its protection as broadly as possible, the Red Cross created a special office, known as Section A, which was staffed by the Jewish Council and financed largely by the Joint Distribution Committee. The Tangier visa holders were transferred from the camp into large houses and, following Sweden's lead, Spain issued its Tangier charges the Spanish equivalent of the Schutzpasse, the "pasaporte provisional."

Among Section A's most pressing priorities was finding children to use the three hundred Tangier visas that had been delegated to the Jewish Council. The selection process was slowed by communal politics, chiefly by the question of how many visas should go to Jewish children who had converted to Christianity. In a sense, the issue was cosmetic, since most "Christian Jews" had abandoned Judaism not out of conviction but desperation as the Nazi dragnet closed. However, the suffering of the orphaned offspring of converts was especially acute. Most Christian relief groups wanted nothing to do with them, while Jewish organizations were required by Hungarian law to disenfranchise converts. To fill the void, a group of Protestant priests founded the Good Shepherd's Committee, which was reconstituted as Section B of the Red Cross.

In Tangier, meanwhile, Mrs. Reichmann was unable to make any progress until it was manifestly evident that the Germans would not let any Jews out of Hungary. Not until September 21, five weeks after Mrs. Reichmann first approached General Orgaz, did Childs finally write to the high commissioner in support of her appeal. "Extending protection to 700 additional persons will not involve, as I understand it, any actual removal of these persons from Hungary, but will mean merely that they will enjoy protection from the Spanish Government," Childs noted in a letter to the high commissioner. "Any expenses incident to the further protection of these 700 persons will be borne by the agencies now occupying themselves with the 500 children and 70 adults."

Childs had uttered the magic words. Orgaz stopped stalling and conveyed Mrs. Reichmann's request to Madrid. With a nudge from the American Embassy, the Spanish Foreign Ministry again obliged, wiring instructions to Budapest to provide another seven hundred visas to Jews. With good news, though, came bad, as the Reichmanns were informed by an IRC telegram from Budapest that the organization had failed to locate the two hundred children on the list submitted by Tangier. Among the missing were a large number of Gestetner nieces and nephews. "I could not even save the children of my own brothers and sisters," Mrs. Reichmann lamented. "My heart is bleeding, but I must comfort myself that in their place other souls have been saved. We must pray to God that in his mercy he might save all our unfortunate brethren."

Apparently, Mrs. Reichmann was unaware that a score or more of her relatives in fact were among the group of 570 Tangier visa holders that was assembled under the joint protective custody of Spain and the International Red Cross by early October. This, as it turned out, was just in the nick of time. On October 15, with the Russian Army only one hundred miles east of Budapest, the Germans forced Admiral Horthy to step aside by threatening to kill his son. The Germans ushered the fanatically anti-Semitic Arrow Cross into power, and Budapest became hell on earth. As the Red Army besieged Budapest with heavy artillery from afar, Hungarian fascist Arrow Cross gangs roamed the city murdering Jews with clubs and pistols. To conserve ammunition, these sadists developed a technique for killing three Jews with one bullet. The three were bound together with rope. A bullet through the head transformed the lucky one into a human anchor as the trio was shoved into the freezing waters of the Danube. In the two months before the Russians liberated the city, the Hungarian fascists killed perhaps ten thousand Jews.

Just then, Eichmann returned to Budapest determined to close the Hungarian chapter of the Final Solution. By this time, Auschwitz was being dismantled, and the German rail system had all but collapsed. Eichmann improvised. His minions rounded up thirty-five thousand Jews, who were driven out of the city in long columns through bone-chilling rains, ostensibly to dig antitank trenches 120 miles to the west, in Austria. On the way to Austria, 15 to 20 percent of the deportees died of exposure or starvation or else collapsed and were shot by SS guards. Those who reached the work site but were judged unfit for hard labor were driven off into the woods to die.

The twin threats of deportation and Arrow Cross thuggery inspired herculean efforts on the part of the self-appointed protectors of Budapest Jewry. Sweden, Switzerland, the International Red Cross, and the Vatican issued thousands of new safe-conduct passes while the Zionist underground churned out at least 120,000 forged versions. New protected houses were established as fast as they could be purchased, rented, or borrowed. Between them, Red Cross Sections A and B sheltered 8,000 children in sixty houses, eight of which were under the joint protection of Spain. The protected houses were subjected to continual harassment and occasional invasion by SS squads and freelance gangs of Arrow Cross thugs. Wallenberg was especially daring in defying the Gestapo and fascists alike, intervening continually to protect his charges.

At first, the Arrow Cross authorities tolerated the rescue work of the neutral powers in the hope of winning their diplomatic recognition. On October 30, the Szalasi regime acknowledged the validity of many of the protective documents distributed by the neutral countries—including the first 570 Tangier visas—and granted extraterritorial status to all buildings posted with International Red Cross insignia. At the same time, the Hungarians set limits on the number of safe passes each power could issue and refused to recognize the second component of 700 Tangier visas, which had been approved in principle by Madrid but not yet issued in Budapest. The Spanish government made no protest, not wishing to antagonize the new Hungarian government.

Informed of this development through U.S. diplomatic channels, Mrs. Reichmann suggested an alternative use for the disputed visas so that they would not go to waste. By this time the IRC had shed the last remnants of timidity, demanding that Germany confer prisoner-of-war status on all foreign Jews in its concentration camps. Although the futile search for Waldsee continued, actual contingents of Hungarians had been identified at Bergen-Belsen and other German camps. Mrs. Reichmann contacted the Red Cross in Geneva and said that if it would help free Hungarians from the German camps, she would ask the Spanish government to authorize the issuance of seven hundred Tangier visas in Switzerland rather than Hungary. The IRC accepted, and on November 14 the American Embassy in Madrid conveyed Mrs. Reichmann's visa-transfer request to the Spanish government.

Not two weeks later, the IRC informed Mrs. Reichmann that it had run into a Nazi stone wall and did not need the Tangier visas after all. Refusing to simply let the authorization lapse, Mrs. Reichmann again changed tack. In her continuing efforts to locate Hungarian survivors, she assembled a long list of Jews in hiding in the countryside or detained in Hungarian army labor camps. List in hand, she flew to Madrid with Eva to try to persuade the Ministry of Foreign Affairs to revert to the original plan and make the seven hundred visas available in Hungary. Again, she won the backing of the U.S. Embassy. With Russian forces nearing the outskirts of Budapest, the Spaniards decided that the time for diplomatic niceties had passed. On December 4, the Foreign Minister wired instructions to Budapest to issue the additional visas at once.

From Madrid, Mrs. Reichmann immediately alerted HIJEFS in Montreux: "700 entry visas sent Friday to the Spanish Legation in Budapest. Sent a list of names via telegraph to the International Red Cross in Budapest. Intervene via Geneva so that we can find the people and deal with the special camps as quickly as possible like the 500 children."

Neither Mrs. Reichmann nor U.S. diplomats yet knew that Spain no longer had a chargé d'affaires in Budapest. On November 30, Angel Sanz Brinz secretly fled to Switzerland under orders from his government, which, given its militant anti-Communism, had good reason to fear the advancing Russian

Army. Naturally, Madrid did not name a successor. However, Giorgio Perlasca, an Italian citizen whom Sanz Brinz had hired to run the Spanish safe houses, changed his first name to Jorge and began acting the part of chargé d'affaires. As the Jews on Mrs. Reichmann's second list were located and brought to Budapest, Perlasca provided each with a visa and a spot in a protected house. Among the newcomers were Samuel's brother and business partner, Simon, and two of his sons, Ernö and Bennö, who in 1942 had been conscripted into a labor battalion that had spent most of the war in Hungary.

Despite his lack of diplomatic credentials, Perlasca, later dubbed "the Italian Wallenberg," proved a vigilant, courageous defender of the Spanish charges. At least twice, he faced down armed Arrow Cross squads. In one such incident, gunmen had lined up all the adults in the foyer of a protected house and were about to march them down to the Danube when Perlasca arrived. Walking up to the officer in charge, he shouted in broken German, "How dare you behave like this on the property of a friendly country?" Perlasca continued berating the commander with threats of diplomatic recrimination until finally he apologized and left.

During the Soviet siege, which began on Christmas Eve, fascist violence built to a horrifying crescendo. Szalasi and his government decamped to the Oberland city of Sopron, and gangs of heavily armed malcontents roamed the streets in search of Jewish victims. A fifty-man gang used grenades to blast through the locked doors of the largest of the Swiss-protected houses but were driven off by a Hungarian Army unit. A few days later, Arrow Cross thugs murdered 42 Jews at one of the diplomatically protected houses and dragged another 90 victims from an Orthodox almshouse to their deaths. In the most vicious single incident, a goon squad broke into a Jewish hospital and killed 154 patients, doctors, and nurses. Three days later, the Russians liberated Pest. For the Jews of Budapest, the long, bloody ordeal at last was over.

———

About 120,000 Jews were saved in Budapest, a sum roughly equal to the number that died under the German occupation. The vast majority of victims—tens of thousands all told—perished after the Arrow Cross putsch of October 15. The Swedes are credited with directly saving about 20,000 Jews with their papers and protected houses, and estimates of the number rescued by the International Red Cross, the Vatican, and the Swiss, Spanish, and Portuguese legations range from 11,000 to 30,000. The chaos of the time has frustrated attempts to arrive at a more precise accounting. Asked in 1989 how many Jews he helped save, Perlasca replied, "I don't know how many protective passes I handed out and how many people were helped by them."

Although the Spanish houses were subject to the occasional raid, their occupants suffered remarkably little harm. Spain, after all, was the only fascist state among the neutral powers, and feelings of right-wing solidarity probably inhibited all but the worst of the fascist thugs. Sanz Brinz's subtle bribery—and Perlasca's courage—certainly helped. By most estimates, Spain saved 3,000 Hungarian Jews, roughly one-third of whom held Tangier visas. No records have been found that would confirm that all 700 of the second install-ment of visas actually were issued. On the other hand, the number of Jews protected under the first batch may have exceeded the authorized 570 since the Spanish consulate issued pasaportes provisional to more than 70 parents of the 500 children.

Mrs. Reichmann herself put the total number she saved at 1,200 in the heartfelt letter of thanks that she wrote, in French, to Childs as he was prepar-ing to leave Tangier in mid-1945. In it, she said:

> Permit me, before your departure from Tangier, to express to Your Excellency from the bottom of my heart my most profound and everlasting gratitude for your extremely noble and generous assistance in the affair of the entry visas for Tangier for 500 children and 700 adults, for the most part of large families of Hungarian Jews. It is without a doubt, due to the intervention of Your Excellency that the requests for entry visas were accorded. . . . Thus, 1,200 innocent souls owe their survival to Your Excellency.
>
> I pray to God that blessings and success accompany you all your life, every step of the way.

Childs responded immediately and with uncharacteristic informality and feeling: "I was deeply touched by your letter. . . . I do not know of any work which I have done in my whole career which has given me greater personal satisfaction than the efforts made on behalf of these friendless persons. I think you give me too much credit to attribute their saving to my efforts, because I would never have known about them if it had not been for you."

Actually, scores of people in a half-dozen cities across the globe from Wash-ington to Montreux deserved a share of the credit, but the unlikely essence of the Tangier rescue project was this: what Renée Reichmann proposed, Gener-alissimo Francisco Franco disposed. Although apparently they never met, this ultra-Orthodox refugee and brutal fascist dictator made one of history's oddest couples. Over the years, the drama of the great Budapest rescue of 1944 has become the story of Raoul Wallenberg, who mysteriously disappeared after the Russians entered the city and was never seen again. There is no question that Wallenberg was the most daring and effective champion of Budapest Jewry and "one of the main heroes in the entire struggle to counter the Holocaust." However, the Swede's celebrity has tended to eclipse lesser luminaries, among them Renée Reichmann, whose star was further dimmed by the deep-seated suspicion aroused among Israeli Jews of the Franco government's postwar claims that it had nobly assumed an important role in Jewish rescue during the Holocaust. To this day, Mrs. Reichmann's achievements have been little noted outside Orthodox circles.

To be sure, unlike Wallenberg and others, Mrs. Reichmann did not risk her life on behalf of Budapest Jewry. She got no closer to the beleaguered Hungarian capital than Madrid. In a sense, her accomplishments were all the more remarkable given her distance from the center of the action. In an undertaking dominated by diplomats and statesmen, Mrs. Reichmann lacked official standing. She was not even a citizen of the country in which she lived. To be sure, her layman's status was not without its advantages, among them purity of motive and simplicity of purpose.

For Mrs. Reichmann, rescue was an end in itself—a moral imperative—not a piece to be fitted into the puzzle of a political agenda. She sprang immediately into action, submitting her first request to General Orgaz before it had even occurred to Budapest's Jewish leaders to ask for Spanish visas—and a good six weeks before Wallenberg first set foot in Budapest. And she and Eva were tenacious beyond the limits of tact. "They [were] in my office almost every week," recalled Fritzlan, the American consul. "I was not always glad to see them. But what could I do?"

The impact of Mrs. Reichmann's efforts cannot be measured solely by Tangier visas issued. Without doubt, the Spanish government would have responded to some extent to Allied diplomatic pressure to help Hungarian Jews even if she had never left the safe confines of 25 Rue Molière. The fact is, however, that it was the Reichmann plan that prompted Spain to depart from its generally unsympathetic policy toward foreign Jews and smoothed the way for all subsequent departures from that policy. Thus, Mrs. Reichmann deserves a bit of credit for all 3,000 Jews saved through Spanish intervention in Hungary. Similarly, it was her plan that prompted the International Red Cross to finally overcome its traditionalist scruples and succor Jewish civilians, first in Hungary and then throughout Europe—a historic breakthrough that helped ease the suffering of thousands of Jewish survivors. Just after the war, a portion of the 1,200 Tangier visas were recycled by communal leaders in Budapest to prevent the city's Russian liberators from sending four hundred Orthodox orphans to the Soviet Union. Instead, the children were placed into a brand new orphanage in Budapest, where they got, as Mrs. Reichmann approvingly noted in 1946, "a strict Jewish education."

While saving lives in Europe, Mrs. Reichmann was shaping lives at home. It would be difficult to overstate the force of her (and Eva's) example on her five teenaged sons, who served daily witness to her struggles while doing their small part to help. The Reichmann brothers would go on to amass wealth vast beyond their father's ambitions and to practice philanthropy on a scale as grand as the skyscrapers they built. But never would they equal the valor that their mother showed when it mattered most. For all Hungarian Jews, 1944 was a year of irreparable, apocalyptic loss. But for the Reichmanns, to paraphrase Winston Churchill's famous tribute to his countrymen, it also was their finest hour.

Chapter 12

For the Jewish refugees of Tangier, the climactic stage of the war was excruciatingly bittersweet. Hitler's defeat was increasingly assured, as Allied troops—the Americans, British, and French from the East, the Soviet contingent from the West—drove Nazi forces back toward the German heartland. But every Allied advance, it seemed, brought to light horrifying new evidence of Nazi persecution of the Jews. As anticipation of peace waxed, hopes for the inmates of concentration camps waned. In Jewish hearts, ambivalence reigned. Had military victory ever come at greater human cost?

In April 1945, British troops entered Bergen-Belsen and uncovered evidence of Nazi barbarism on a scale that shocked the world. In Tangier, the British paper, the *Gazette*, reported the horrors of Belsen and week after week ran a series of photos under the heading "Lest We Forget" and above captions that blended disgust and outrage in equal measure: "Mounds of unburied dead"; "Women guards whose bestiality and brutality equalled that of their masculine criminals"; "An oven of the crematorium where the bodies of thousands of victims of German bestiality were incinerated"; "The Butcher of Belsen, Joseph Kramer—Shining SS Light." If anything, the *Gazette*'s coverage was understated. "Evidence of cannibalism was found," stated the official report of the British Army. "The inmates had lost all self-respect, were degraded morally to the level of beasts. Their clothes were in rags, teeming with lice, and both inside and outside the huts was an almost continuous carpet of dead bodies, human excreta, rags and filth."

Even confronted by this vision of hell on earth, Mrs. Reichmann found ways to respond constructively—albeit from a distance, since there was no possibility of her going to Germany or Poland, which were strictly off limits to civilians. The British authorities did permit English religious organizations to send chaplains into Belsen to minister to the dying, and the Rabbi's Emergency Council, the English counterpart of the Vaad Hahatzalah, received authorization to send a handful of Orthodox rabbis to Germany, along with five mobile synagogue ambulances—blue trucks with a Star of David on both sides. One such rabbi, Solomon Baumgarten, was Viennese and well known to the Reichmann family. Mrs. Reichmann cabled Rabbi Baumgarten before he departed for Belsen, which the Nazis had used mainly as a dumping ground for female prisoners evacuated from Auschwitz, and asked him to search for her many nieces, any number of whom might have landed in Bergen-Belsen. With the Nazi empire shrinking by the hour, the Orthodox rescue network reverberated with the desperate pleas of relatives searching for survivors amid the chaos that had descended on Europe. The Vaad Hahatzalah barraged Mrs. Reichmann and its other European representatives with requests to find various relatives of board member Stephen Klein—putting special emphasis on his brother Isaac Klein and brother-in-law Franz Fischof. Meanwhile, Renée added her own petitions to the clamor, sending HIJEFS a three-page telegram listing dozens of her own missing relatives.

After the Red Army entered Budapest, Simon, Ernö, and Bennö Reichmann had fled to Romania and were spotted on the street in Bucharest by the former head of the Orthodox community of Budapest. He notified HIJEFS, which immediately alerted the Reichmanns: "Simon, Benoe, Ernoe well in Bukarest. Need help urgently." Samuel transferred 1,000 Swiss francs through a Tangier bank to HIJEFS, which, with difficulty, forwarded the funds to Bucharest. But the Reichmanns' continuing agony of uncertainty is evident in a letter Mrs. Reichmann wrote a week after Simon and his sons had been located. "My own affairs are also very wrong." she wrote. "I could not learn where are my nine brothers and sisters, the 82-year-old mother of my husband and his eight brothers and sisters. One of my sisters has nine little children, all under fourteen years, the other had eight, and the third has five. All have been deported and there is no news about them. In spite of my greatest effort I could not learn where they are, to send them a piece of bread and warm clothes."

On May 8, 1945, the Allies accepted Germany's unconditional surrender. In Tangier, the *Gazette* published a twelve-page extra with a front page that carried nothing but a flaming red "V" and the headline: "V-E Day" (Victory in Europe). In the city's Jewish quarter, the victory celebration was constrained by fear of the police force, which remained pro-German. A few weeks before V-E Day, the city's largest synagogue had not dared display the American flag during services held to commemorate the death of Franklin Roosevelt. In Casablanca, the Allied victory did indeed bring violence down on the local Jews. In celebration of Germany's defeat, a Palestinian flag was flown from the synagogue in the city's old quarter. A crowd of Arabs gathered, stoned the synagogue, and then stormed through the streets randomly beating Jews. The French police stood and watched.

A month after V-E Day, Mrs. Reichmann sent an anguished letter pleading with the War Refugee Board in Washington, D.C., to help locate her still-missing relatives. The Vaad Hahatzalah carried some clout in Washington, but Mrs. Reichmann did not pull this string. Instead she wrote to the WRB. Her letter was posted in an envelope that read simply, "War Refugee Board, Washington." She enclosed a list of her siblings, as well as Samuel's, annotated with a few tidbits of information—all of it badly outdated. In February, she noted, her brother Henrik had been sent from Auschwitz to a slave labor camp in Germany; Sándor Gestetner and wife had been "deported on their legs" from Budapest; Albert Gestetner had been sent to the Russian front with a labor battalion. "Our desperation is so great," Mrs. Reichmann added, "especially at present when we and the whole world know about the infinitely dreadful destiny passed by millions of deported people."

Florence Hodel, an assistant executive director of the WRB, replied promptly in what amounted to a form-letter rejection. There would be no special treatment for the Reichmanns, though Hodel did offer, with unwitting irony, to forward a copy of Mrs. Reichmann's list to the Vaad Hahatzalah.

In June 1945, there arrived at 25 Rue Molière an International Red Cross "Displaced Persons Field Post Card" bearing Isaac "Bubi" Klein's signature and a checkmark in three boxes denoting the messages, "I am well and safe," "Will write as soon as possible," and "Expect to be home soon. Do not write"—an unnecessary admonition since the card provided no indication of Klein's whereabouts. About the same time, from Franz Fischof the Reichmanns received another Red Cross form-postcard, with an even more truncated message—"I am well"—but a return address, a POW camp in Munich. And, by private mail, Rabbi Baumgarten reported that in Bergen-Belsen he had come across four Reichmann nieces: Edith Reichmann, Sari and Bella Grunwald, and Emma Stern. Later, Rabbi Baumgarten happily found two Gestetner nieces—Rosa and Sari—in a displaced persons camp in Frankfurt. About this time, too, Henrik Gestetner was found alive in a displaced persons camp in Germany. The Reichmanns tried to wire Henrik money through Switzerland and London but failed at both attempts. At the Reichmanns' request, HIJEFS advanced 1,000 francs to Rabbi Baumgarten, who passed through Montreux on his way to Bratislava.

Every instance of survival in the Reichmann family would be completely overwhelmed by countervailing catastrophe. If during 1944 Renée was slow to grasp the full dimensions of the tragedy that had befallen Hungarian Jewry, she did not shrink now from seeking confirmation of the most personal sort. As soon as Henrik had resurfaced, Renée cabled HIJEFS in Montreux: "Ask Henrik where Margit and Klára were deported to." The answer, inevitably, was Auschwitz. Henrik's wife, Margit, as well as his younger sister, Klára Duschinsky, and her five children, had been gassed upon arrival.

———

Despite Germany's defeat, the great majority of the 1.3 million Jewish survivors in Europe remained in mortal danger, imperiled now not by Nazi executioners but by enemies against which Allied firepower was useless: starvation and disease. Throughout Eastern Europe—and especially in Hungary and Romania—food, medicine, and shelter were in acute short supply. By the end of 1945, eight million Europeans were without homes and either wandering aimlessly through the Continent or living in the displaced persons camps run by Allied military authorities and the United Nations Relief Agency.

Orthodox survivors who returned to their hometowns typically found that every trace of their prewar lives had vanished except for the anti-Semitism of their neighbors. Anti-Jewish riots broke out in Poland, where 350 returning Jews were murdered in 1945 alone. Although the Allied occupation authorities were sympathetic to the plight of Jewish survivors, they were overwhelmed by the sheer scale of their mission and hamstrung by their own administrative bungling. The British, for example, decided that displaced persons in their zone of Germany should be classified by nationality rather than segregated by religion, as the Nazis had done. While the policy was well intentioned, its effect was cruel, as Hungarian Jews were forced to toil alongside Arrow Cross thugs in labor battalions organized by the British.

Despite horrendous transport problems, Mrs. Reichmann and her helpers managed to send more food to the Jews of Europe in 1945–46, when it did even more good than before. In 1945 alone, the Tangier group shipped to Switzerland some 15,600 kilos (more than 17 tons) of supplies, including 6 tons of tuna, 4.4 tons of matzoh, 4 tons of sardines, nearly a ton of rolled oats, and smaller amounts of biscuits, butter, and chocolate bars. For the first time, the Tangier group also sent bulk shipments of clothing to the Continent. Eva and her Aunt Olga ranged throughout Spanish Morocco and into Spain collecting used clothes, woolens, linens, and shoes. Eva recalled that her mother "told everybody that [it] had to be good clothing, not 'shmattes.' " In Barcelona, they collected new clothes from an apparel manufacturing firm owned by an Ashkenazi refugee who was a foreign exchange customer of Samuel's.

Getting these provisions to Switzerland was no minor feat, for the logistics of freight transport within Europe were a hopeless tangle. In Barcelona warehouses, food parcels packed with urgency in Tangier languished for months on end, awaiting the arrival of an International Red Cross transport. On at least one occasion, Mrs. Reichmann hired a truck to haul goods from Barcelona to a French border town, where a Red Cross truck waited, unwilling or unable to cross into Spain. By the time the IRC finally got a ship into Barcelona, 19 tons of cargo from Tangier lay waiting, including 5 tons of one-kilo food parcels that had been in storage for seven months.

———

An exhaustive search of the Office of Strategic Services archives strongly suggests that Samuel Reichmann's name did not begin popping up in OSS reports out of Tangier until the war was almost over. Ten such reports mention Samuel Reichmann, though never more than peripherally: five concern currency smuggling and five purport to implicate him in trafficking with the Nazis. These reports span a seven-month period, from November 1944 to June 1945, and consist of seven field reports and three Washington analyses based on them.

After Operation Torch, which culminated in the Allied conquest of North Africa in the spring of 1943, the highest-ranking OSS men were reassigned, leaving behind a skeleton crew of inexperienced, junior station chiefs: Richard Bownass (codename: CORAL) in Tangier and E. Willys Andrews (PANCHO) in Casablanca and Walter Cline (QUITO) in Fez. This trio of full-time operatives acted as the hub of a raggedy network of paid informants, or "subsources," in OSS lingo. The thousands of field reports generated by Moroccan subsources and carefully filed away in the National Archives in Washington, D.C., typify OSS intelligence in its rawest, most unreliable form. The great majority of them are poorly typed, one-page sheets based on secondhand information anonymously supplied.

As Morocco became a military intelligence backwater, its OSS remnant refocused attention on politics and commerce. Several of the most active OSS informants in Tangier seemed to take keen interest in activities of the money changers, motivated largely by an anti-Semitism that runs like a leaky sewer line through their reporting. (To this day, the identities of OSS subsources remain classified.) In late 1944, for example, "DAME" blamed the money changers for "the ruination of the whole of the working and laboring classes of the Tangier Zone." In another report written after Spain had blocked the accounts of Axis nationals, DAME assigned blame more particularly: "Those who are really worried are the 'Hassidum' [*sic*] Hungarian refugees, who had done nothing but deal in foreign exchange. They are the ones who have manipulated the rates of exchange to the detriment of Tangier."

DAME was the first subsource to point a finger at Samuel Reichmann, in a two-page report on a currency smuggling ring allegedly headed by General Mohammed Ben Mizzian Bel-Kaser, who was one of Franco's favorite generals and a political force in his own right. General Mizzian, who was one of the great Nationalist heroes of the civil war, lived in the Spanish port of Melilla, as did his father-in-law, a businessman named Hadj Ahmed Amor Zrak (the same

Zrak alleged to be a smuggling confederate of Rafael Alvarez Claros). Under General Mizzian's sponsorship, DAME reported, Zrak was smuggling francs into Tangier from French Morocco and Algeria "on a very large scale," taking a commission as high as 20 percent. In detailing the workings of this operation at some length, DAME implied that Reichmann acted in concert with the Mizzian-Zrak cabal but stopped short of stating it.

> This movement of currency has greatly favored the speculations made by the band of Hungarian Jews, chief of which is a certain Reichman [*sic*] who has the reputation of being past master in these kinds of deals. This band had monopolized the purchase of Algerian notes which they bought with a discount of 15% in relation to the value of the Moroccan francs. It was only much later that the reason why these people were buying up this currency was discovered. The money was exported clandestinely to Portugal. From there it was forwarded to Brazil and it seems that it was sold there to the Government at the rate of Frs. 50 to the dollar, and was used for the Brazilian troops who were to disembark in Africa.

DAME's reports carried a postscript: "It was reported at the time to this office that in June 1943 Reichmann's wife, a Jewess, was permitted to pass across the German frontier and three months later to return with nearly $200,000 in currency from Hungary."

Under the fledgling OSS protocols in force in 1944, the reliability of reports that were not based on firsthand observation was to be evaluated according to two benchmarks. The reliability of the source providing the information was graded by letter, ranging from "A" for "completely reliable" down to "F" for "untried." The reliability of the information itself was ranked on a numerical scale, with "1" standing for "report confirmed by others" and "6," the lowest category, for "truth cannot be judged." By latter-day intelligence standards, this was a crude, obviously flawed system. How could a station chief act as an objective evaluator when it was in his self-interest that his subsources be perceived in Washington as credible and productive?

In the fall of 1943, the OSS headquarters officer who ran the North Africa desk complained that the field reports from Morocco were "without exception" graded A-1. The Moroccan station chiefs responded by knocking their standard evaluation down one notch to B-2, which was still implausible as an average. CORAL assigned DAME's report a B-2. By the book, this meant that DAME, in CORAL's judgment, was "usually reliable" and that her, or his, report was "probably true."

Yet the report was demonstrably false in several respects. While DAME displayed a basic ignorance of the workings of currency markets throughout the memo, his (or her) theory about Brazil as the final destination of the smuggled

Algerian banknotes was particularly nonsensical. As for the postscript, the American Legation's own records establish that Mrs. Reichmann traveled to Hungary in 1942, not 1943, as DAME claimed. Furthermore, the allegation that she returned to Tangier carrying $200,000 is patently absurd. As $20 bills, such a cache would have weighed more than twenty pounds and could not easily have been hidden during a two-week train trip that carried Mrs. Reichmann across seven Axis frontiers and landed her in a jail cell in Italy.

OSS field reports were sent to Washington, where the Secret Intelligence Reporting Board affixed its own reliability rating and determined whether the information should be disseminated. In these early years, the Reporting Board rarely altered a field evaluation and so DAME's report, changed only slightly by its Washington editors, was again stamped B-2 and distributed through the middle ranks of the agency. The fact that William Donovan, the director of the OSS, was not on the routing list only affirmed the insignificance of Tangier's money changers in the global scheme of things. The most telling indication of a field report's quality was whether it was referred to the Research and Analysis (R & A) Branch for conversion into "finished" intelligence. An exhaustive search of the R & A archives suggests that DAME's report, like the vast bulk of raw field intelligence, did not make the cut.

In early 1945, two more field reports were filed referring to Reichmann in the context of currency smuggling by Spanish diplomats, most notably the Count of Churruca, who was the great-grandson of a famous Spanish admiral and a vice consul in the Spanish Embassy in Algiers. On March 21, the count was observed arriving in Tangier in a car containing "a large quantity of dollars." After checking into the Minzah Hotel: "Churucca [*sic*] contacted all the important exchange dealers in Tangier; finally, Rosenbaum bought the dollars. Source stated that in large transactions the risk is not taken by one single dealer, and therefore it seemed reasonable that Reichmann, Rosenberg and probably Emilio Sanz of the Banco de España were involved in the transaction."

Reichmann's friend and fellow Hungarian, Nicholas Rosenbaum, was more broadly implicated in a second report a few weeks later. Like the first, it was given a double C-2 rating, meaning the source was "fairly reliable" and the information was "probably true." Churruca, it stated, "maintains contact with Rosenbaum, an exchange broker of Tangier. Churucca makes a regular monthly trip to Tangier, bringing with him United States currency ranging in amount from 2,000 to 10,000 dollars. . . . Rosenbaum seems to be the principal buyer and seller of smuggled dollars in Tangier."

Another report connected Samuel to smuggling by Martinez de Orense, the Spanish consul of Rabat. Orense had driven into Tangier in a car said to contain "100,000 paper dollar bills" and was "seen talking with local exchange brokers, among them being Jacob Benchimol of 'El Globo,' Polish Jews Reichmann and Rosenberg and Nicholas Rosenbaum. It has not yet been ascertained if the 100,000 has changed hands." This report, too, was graded C-2 in Tangier, even though someone, most likely CORAL himself, underlined the phrase "100,000 paper dollar bills" and scrawled in the margin: "This is absurd." He also might have noted that Reichmann, Rosenberg, and Rosenbaum were Hungarians, not Poles.

Smuggling was of little practical import either to the U.S. Legation in Tangier or OSS headquarters in Washington unless American interests were directly threatened, which was obviously the case only when illicit transactions involved trafficking with the enemy. In the spring of 1944, finally bowing to pressure from the United States and Great Britain, Spain forced Germany to shut its oversized consulate. Although Tangier's refugees were gratified by the removal of the swastika shield from the door of the Mendoubia, the Nazi expulsion was largely symbolic. The Germans were allowed to relocate to Tetuán, and most of the Nazi agents recently expelled from Tangier now commuted to the city.

The first and most elaborate of the four field reports that purported to implicate Samuel Reichmann in Nazi currency trafficking and that purported to list all currency dealers known to deal with the Germans, whether directly or through intermediaries, was dated December 28, 1944. Last among the eight names listed was "Reichmann & Kahn," thus annotated: "Reichmann and his associate, Kahn, lived at 23 Rue des Synagogues; they sold dollars and Swiss francs to Hubert and a Military Attache of the German Consulate. Mr. Reichmann had the audacity to pass some federal dollars at the same rate as the others." (Hans Hubert was a blacklisted German national who worked for a Nazi front firm.) This last comment mystified the report's Washington editors, who added this footnote: "Source's meaning is not clear. Possibly the reference is to yellow seal dollars as opposed to blue seal ones." (The United States issued yellow-seal currency to its military personnel in North Africa. It carried a yellow mark to distinguish it from regular U.S. currency, which bore a blue seal.)

Although graded C-2 in Tangier and Washington, the report was manifestly inaccurate in two respects: Samuel never lived on the Rue des Synagogues nor had an associate named Kahn. Most likely, the reference was to Jacob Kahane, the Reichmanns' neighbor and fellow Orthodox Hungarian. As part of a libel suit that Renée Reichmann and three of her sons brought against *Toronto Life* magazine in 1987, investigators hired by the family interviewed Kahane, who confirmed that he and Samuel never were business associates and never lived on the Rue des Synagogues. In addition, "Kahane emphatically denied that Samuel did or would have traded with the Germans, or otherwise assisted them. Both Samuel Reichmann and Jacob Kahane dealt only with people they knew, the various moneychangers in the Socco Chico."

The three additional reports (all given a dual C-2 rating) containing a mention of Reichmann are principally concerned with Friedrich "Fritz" Eory. An Austrian national born in Vienna, Eory was a particularly repellent individual—a Jew who not only passed himself off as a Gentile but became an ardent Nazi. He emigrated to Spanish Morocco in 1939 and in Tangier set up an optician's shop that was used as a meeting place by enemy agents, including the local Gestapo chief. The U.S. Legation investigated Eory and concluded that his "connection with German intelligence was not important but . . . there is little doubt that he was sympathetic and assisted in whatever ways he could." Eory was blacklisted and expelled in May 1944, along with other Nazi agents. From Tetuán, Eory regularly returned to Tangier until he was expelled in August 1945, to Madrid.

Throughout his last months in Tangier, Eory appears to have been tailed devotedly by an OSS subsource named "NOMIS." The name Reichmann does not pop up in NOMIS's surveillance reports until January 12, 1945, and then only briefly: "Fritz Eory who was in Tangier this week had several meetings with Reichman's [*sic*] accomplices." The very next week, he was mentioned again: "As usual Eory went to see the Hungarians of the Reichmann gang in Rue des Siagnhins [*sic*]." Not until June did NOMIS again mention Reichmann: "Fritz Eory was in Tangier again on May 23rd. During each of his visits he sees refugee residents of the city of doubtful sympathies and through intermediaries has business transactions with Reichmann's exchange business."

In anticipation of military victory, the U.S. and British governments jointly launched the "Safehaven Project," the object of which was to block attempts by Germany and its allies to transfer assets to hiding places in neutral or pro-Axis countries. As a traditional haven of flight capital, Tangier figured importantly in Safehaven and the American Legation appears to have assigned the project high priority, reworking its blacklist files into a lengthy compendium of suspect Axis nationals. This document made no mention of the Reichmanns or any of their Hungarian friends, nor did any of the Safehaven reports cranked out in more desultory fashion by the Tangier station of the OSS. Rather, it was British intelligence that made the family a Safehaven target.

In July 1945, a Special Operations Executive agent in Tangier handed a report to a newly arrived American intelligence agent named Alphonso Rodriguez, codenamed "EA1." X2, the counterespionage branch of the OSS, sent Rodriguez to Tangier to placate the British, who were increasingly dissatisfied with CORAL's Safehaven reporting. EA1 passed on the British report to "Saint," code for X2 headquarters in Washington. Under the heading—"Subject: REICHMANN family, 25 Rue Moliere, Tangier"—the following appeared:

This Hungarian Jewish refugee family has always aroused a certain amount of suspicion, partly owing to the fact that Samuel, the father, has been reported as trafficking with the Germans, and partly on account of the frequent journeys throughout Spain and Spanish Morocco made by Samuel, Renée, his wife, and Eva, their daughter. It is now revealed that Eva, assisted by her mother, began sending food parcels to relatives in Hungary and because she was so successful in getting them through she became eventually representative in Tangier for the Vaad Hahatzala . . . and sent a large quantity of parcels to occupied countries on its behalf.

The comment about Samuel traveling frequently was mistaken, and the food parcel information was no revelation to the Tangier Legation. However, the report went on to level a charge that had not appeared in any OSS field report:

It has frequently been suggested that Reichmann smuggled goods into occupied countries in Red Cross food parcels and he has also been reported as trafficking in gold, forged notes and forged stamps. . . . If there is any truth in the assertion that smuggling was done via the Red Cross parcels, it is obvious that the whole Reichmann family is implicated. Although it seems probable that the family are engaged only in money making by crooked means . . . it would be interesting for us if some check could be made regarding the Vaad Hahatzala Relief Society and its connection with the Reichmanns.

On the copy of the report found in the OSS archives someone wrote "NT unfavorable" next to the subject heading, "Reichmann family," and "NT" next to Vaad Hahatzalah. According to Rodriguez, this meant that the OSS files in Washington had been checked and revealed no useful information—"NT unfavorable" standing for "no unfavorable trace."

This report did not find its way into Allied diplomatic channels until November 1945, when it was sent by the British Foreign Office to the American Embassy in London. The embassy, too, asked Washington to investigate the Vaad Hahatzalah. The Federal Bureau of Investigation (FBI) responded six weeks later. After reaffirming the legitimacy of the Vaad Hahatzalah, the FBI noted: "Regarding Eva Reichmann, she has received funds for purchase of food packages. No derogatory information on her is available. There is nothing in FBI files to prove or disprove that smuggling was done via the Red Cross parcels." A month later, the U.S. Treasury Department weighed in, affirming that the Vaad Hahatzalah's "standing is unquestioned." As for the Reichmanns, the department reserved judgment:

Treasury was advised by the [Vaad] that all dealings with the Reichmanns, who serve on the distribution committee in Tangier, had been satisfactory and that on the basis of work done they would not hesitate to recommend them. However, little information was available on the individuals themselves since the Tangier representatives were appointed by a committee in Switzerland. It is suggested that further investigation might be made on the activities of the family.

A few months later, the U.S. Embassy in London cabled the State Department, stating that the British Foreign Office "has now reported that their 'secret sources' in Tangier have no information on the Reichmann family beyond that given in [the initial report]. Embassy suggests that the American Legation, Tangier, comment on possibility obtaining further information locally." The original Safehaven report had boomeranged back from whence it came—Tangier. And in Tangier, the investigation into the Reichmanns, such as it was, expired—a casualty, it seems, of inertia as much as anything.

———

What, in the end, is one to make of all these declassified documents that bandied the Reichmann name back and forth across the Atlantic for more than a year? First, none of them contains anything remotely resembling conclusive evidence of wrongdoing. Nor is there any indication in government archives that either the American or British authorities ever took punitive action against any member of the Reichmann family. To the contrary, the United States and Britain each issued several travel visas to Samuel and Renée in the immediate aftermath of the war, and after Eva married in 1948, she moved to London and became a naturalized British citizen.

In its libel action brought in Canada in the late 1980s, the Reichmann family hired as an expert witness Ray S. Cline, a former deputy director of the Central Intelligence Agency who began his career with the OSS. "In the early days of the OSS the reporting system was often flooded or clogged with worthless material which an innocent observer might be inclined to take for gospel truth," observed Cline, then a professor at Georgetown University, in a thirteen-page analysis of the OSS files on the Reichmanns. "The pipeline quickly filled with all kinds of sensational allegations, many of them dubious and frequently erroneous. This data needs to be recognized for what it is and not treated as 'finished intelligence.'" No reports purporting to implicate Samuel were refined into finished form.

To believe that Samuel knowingly trafficked with Nazis in Tangier, even as Renée and Eva were exerting themselves mightily to frustrate Eichmann's murderous designs in Budapest, is to believe that within the Reichmann family the vilest sort of greed coexisted with the highest form of virtue. This is more than improbable: it is ludicrous, as is the notion that the Reichmanns' food parcel program was an illicit black market enterprise disguised as charity. On the other hand, given Samuel's close association with a smuggler and reprobate-for-all-seasons named Albert Grebler, the family's mysterious link to Rafael Alvarez Claro, and the element of fact wedged into OSS field reports along with rumor and supposition, it is conceivable that the family was directly involved in smuggling.

Toward the end of 1944, HIJEFS asked Mrs. Reichmann to go to Madrid on an urgent rescue matter. Renée asked the American Legation to endorse her application for a Spanish travel visa as it had in the past but this time was turned down flat by John Goodyear, Childs's second in command. Stung, Mrs. Reichmann retreated to her typewriter. "I withdraw [my] request," she wrote in a letter to Goodyear, "given that I was made to understand that some think that I wish to take advantage of the American authorities to smuggle goods into Spain. I will try to obtain a visa on my own." Mrs. Reichmann also wrote in protest to Childs, who responded with a letter that, though tactful to a flowery fault, backed Goodyear unequivocally. What prompted the Americans' change of heart is not clear, but their message was: we no longer trust you enough to sponsor your travel. The rebuke was all the more telling for its timing, the Spanish government having just issued the second batch of 700 Budapest visas the week before. Coming at the end of nearly eight months of successful collaborative effort to save Budapest Jews, the smuggling accusation—however implicitly it had been made—fouled the air with doubt like a cheap cigar after a fine meal.

In one sense, the OSS reports out of Tangier were utterly reliable: as reflections of suspicion at street level. Because informants tended to influence the rumor mill as much as they were influenced by it, objects of OSS surveillance in the city found that their reputations suffered, and the Reichmanns were no exception. By 1945, "rumors about the Reichmanns were in general circulation, though the family still was held in high regard," Albert Reinhard said. "I know the talk got back to the Reichmanns. My guess is that it bothered them, though I never heard any of them complain about it."

In the court of public opinion in a place as corrupt in every sense as wartime Tangier, the American standard of jurisprudence inevitably was reversed: the newly successful and the suddenly prominent were presumed guilty (of something) until proven innocent. Once implicated by OSS informants, the Reichmanns' best hope would have been a thorough investigation by higher, civilian authority. Instead, the inconclusivity of the inquiries made by the FBI, the Departments of State and Treasury, and the British Foreign Office in effect condemned the Reichmanns to a bureaucratic limbo of eternal suspicion. In effect, the family would leave Tangier with little barnacles of dubiety attached to the underside of its reputation for doing good. When, more than forty years after World War II ended, the Canadian press finally put the Reichmann family history up in dry dock, those suspicions that had attached themselves to Samuel and Renée in Tangier were, to the horror of their sons, exposed to public view. Although Paul, Albert, and Ralph would prevail in a major libel suit brought against chroniclers of the family's distant past, no number of legal victories could ever scrape the taint of Tangier from the Reichmann reputation.

Chapter 13

About two o'clock one morning in September 1945, Samuel Reichmann was awakened by his front-door buzzer. He got out of bed, walked down two flights of stairs to the front door. Standing on the front step was a skinny dark-haired little man holding a battered suitcase. He looked vaguely familiar. "Shmaya, it's me," he said softly. "Bubi Klein."

As Klein recalled the scene, Reichmann was flabbergasted. They had not seen one another since 1938, in Vienna—a lifetime ago at least. The last the Reichmanns had heard of Isaac Klein was that he was in a United Nations relief camp somewhere in Italy. But now, suddenly, here he was, the first of a hundred survivors who would land on their doorstep. The two men embraced and then hurried upstairs. Samuel awakened Renée, who greeted Klein like a son, and soon the whole Reichmann family was marveling at this smiling, weeping apparition from their past. Paul and Ralph soon returned to bed but the older children—Maidie, Edward, Louis, and Albert—would stay up with their parents until dawn, listening to Klein's odyssey and reminiscing about life before Hitler.

First, though, Mrs. Reichmann asked Klein what he wanted to eat. "Six eggs," he said. "Scrambled." This worked out to one for each year since Klein last had an egg. He ate in silence and then began his tale.

He told of how he had returned his parents to Poland and of the day in Tarnow when drunken, doped-up German soldiers had gone from house to house shooting every Jew they could find, and how he had lit the holy candles and said his final prayers, and how he felt when, inexplicably, the Nazis skipped the house he was in. He told of how he had stolen across the border into Slovakia and, with the help of Renée's brother, Henrik, and various Fischof relatives, he had passed through the Working Group's underground railroad into Hungary, where he picked up forged identity papers in Budapest and then lived for six months under an assumed Gentile identity in Győr, staying first with Dezső Gestetner and then renting his own room with funds supplied by Henrik.

After Germany occupied Hungary, Klein had sneaked back across the border into Slovakia and lived with Henrik until the few remaining Jews of Bratislava were rounded up by the SS and shipped to Auschwitz. Like Henrik and Dezső Gestetner, Klein was selected for labor. At Kaupfering, Klein lived on a few ounces of bread a day and the occasional mouthful of grass. He weighed less than ninety pounds when the Nazis closed the camp and marched the survivors to Dachau. By the time the Americans liberated Dachau, Klein lay delirious with typhus in a barracks filled with corpses. Despite the best efforts of HIJEFS and the Vaad Hahatzalah, it was Klein who got himself out of Dachau, hitching a ride with soldiers of the Jewish Brigade, a Palestinian unit attached to the British Army. Disregarding orders to remain in Italy, Jewish Brigade units crossed into Germany and brought Jews from Dachau and other camps to southern Italy, a staging area for covert immigration transports to Palestine. Klein wanted to go to America, not Palestine, and managed to get a message to his brothers in New York, who, in turn, alerted Mrs. Reichmann.

In July 1945, while Klein recuperated in a United Nations camp near Bari, Mrs. Reichmann had made another trip to Madrid, carrying a list of about one hundred names, most of them missing relatives. She persuaded the Ministry of Foreign Affairs to preapprove the issuance of Spanish visas for everyone on the list, which Madrid distributed to its consulates in France, Sweden, and Italy. When Klein, as instructed by cable from Tangier, presented himself at the Spanish consulate in Rome, he was, to his amazement, given preference even over a group of Spanish troops returning home from the Russian front and promptly issued a visa, with no questions asked. Klein went to Allied headquarters and swapped a carton of cigarettes for an exit visa. In hopes of catching a Brazilian ocean liner bound for Lisbon, Klein headed to Naples, only to find that he needed a Portuguese transit visa and would have to wait a month to get one. He located American military headquarters and talked his way onto a cargo plane bound for Casablanca. In Casablanca, he caught a train to Tangier. And in Tangier he took a taxi to 25 Rue Molière, where, for the first time since 1938, he felt truly safe.

Klein lived as a member of the Reichmann family during the three months he spent in Tangier waiting for his U.S. immigration visa to come through. "They wouldn't let me go anywhere else," he recalled. "Mrs. Reichmann even darned my socks. Such a loving, pious woman." He slept in Maidie's room during her frequent absences from home on one relief mission or another, and otherwise shared a king-size bed with Edward, who was just a year younger than Klein and had been a class behind him at the Talmud Torah in Vienna. First thing every morning, Klein prayed with Samuel and his sons at the synagogue on Rue Cook and in the evenings joined the food parcel work brigade. He also took English lessons from a private tutor (the Reichmanns advanced him all the expense money he needed against the promise of reimbursement by Klein's brothers) but still found himself with more leisure time than he knew what to do with. He went on hikes into the hills surrounding Tangier with the older Reichmann brothers and also joined them in marathon Ping-Pong sessions at a beachside amusement park.

Midway through Klein's stay in Tangier, Eva traveled to Madrid and returned with eight concentration camp survivors—Eszti Reichmann and the five other cousins whom Rabbi Baumgarten had found, plus two of their friends, both Orthodox orphans from the Oberland. The eight girls, all in their late teens or early twenties, were a pathetic sight upon arrival: human stick figures wearing clothes made from blankets. Mrs. Reichmann outfitted the newcomers from her stores of used clothing and, after moving her sons into a nearby hotel, put them up temporarily in the Reichmanns' own flat. In honor of the new arrivals, the family invited its closest friends to a big dinner at 25 Rue Molière. Shortly thereafter, at Mrs. Reichmann's request, Louis Kahane vacated the apartment across the hall, which was remodeled into a dormitory to house the girls.

As the Belsen survivors were settling into their new quarters, Tangier was unnerved by the latest turning of the screw of power politics. At the insistence of the Allies, the Franco government ended its five-year occupation of Tangier in October 1945, relinquishing control to a reconstituted International Administration. Sweden dropped out of the prewar group of nine governing nations and was replaced by the United States. The Soviet Union was entitled to join the consortium but declined to participate unless Spain, its bitter ideological enemy, was denied its traditional place in the governing group. When the United States and Great Britain refused to exclude Spain, the Soviet Union proved true to its word and refused to have anything to do with Tangier.

The practical effect of all the postwar maneuvering was to restore France to the driver's seat in Tangier. French nationals moved into most of the top positions in the new International Administration, replacing their Spanish predecessors as unceremoniously as Spaniards had supplanted Frenchmen five years before. All Spanish-authorized export licenses were suspended, stranding at the Spanish Post Office 580 food parcels, including some that Mrs. Reichmann was shipping to the International Red Cross in Geneva. Le Fur, the new chief administrator, soon released these parcels for export but dragged his feet in considering subsequent requests by Mrs. Reichmann and the refugee relief committee to send to Europe large quantities of butter, tapioca, and matzoh. In response to increasingly irate protests by Jewish leaders, Le Fur in effect declared bureaucratic war on the relief committee, threatening to shut it down entirely. By most accounts, the reformed International Administration's obstructionism was rooted not so much in anti-Semitism as in the sheer officiousness of its ranking bureaucrats. Reinhard and his supporters finally prevailed in this tussle with the chief administrator by rallying American support, but not without the loss of more precious weeks.

With the reestablishment of the International Zone, the citizens of Tangier's governing nations were automatically entitled to enter Tangier. Everyone else needed an entry visa. A few days after Le Fur took office, Mrs. Reichmann submitted a formal request for forty-five entry visas in the name of Hungarian and Slovakian survivors, almost all of whom were relatives of Orthodox refugees in Tangier. The International Administration approved her request, but only after the Joint Distribution Committee guaranteed that it would support as many as a hundred individuals financially. Two months later, Eva, in her parents' absence (they had gone to London to attend an Agudath Israel conference, during which Renée persuaded Sigmund Gestetner to provide financial assistance for the Gestetner refugees in Tangier), applied for another fifty-five entry visas and was summoned before Le Fur's successor, a Spaniard, who refused to commit himself one way or the other and hinted that the Jewish community's guarantee might not be enough this time—that a deposit of, say, 25 francs per refugee seemed reasonable.

Eva informed Reinhard, who complained to the American Legation, which again intervened. The International Administration then authorized the fifty-five visas without requiring a deposit. It did, however, attach some new conditions: the refugees were to arrive in groups of no more than fifteen and could remain only as long as it took to arrange emigration elsewhere—and no longer than six months in any event. The next time Mrs. Reichmann needed visas she bypassed the International Administration altogether and instead approached the Spanish Moroccan government. The Spanish proved as accommodating as during the war, immediately providing her with three hundred entry permits to Spanish Morocco, no strings attached. Later, the Tetuán government provided another one hundred visas, bringing the total number of entry visas obtained by the Reichmanns to more than five hundred.

The Reichmanns sent many visas to survivors who had no intention of coming to Morocco but who needed help in traveling to some other destination. With a Tangier visa in hand, a Jew languishing in a German displaced persons camp could obtain a transit visa to enter Belgium, say, or France, on his way to permanent refuge in North or South America. In what appears to have been a gesture of desperate optimism, Mrs. Reichmann also included in her applications the names of many close relatives—indeed, entire families of Gestetners—without knowing whether they were still alive. The great majority of the visas granted in their names were never claimed.

Mrs. Reichmann was particularly devastated to learn of the death of her brother Lajos. Conscripted into a labor battalion in 1942, Lajos Gestetner survived the worst of the fighting only to perish on the eve of Hungary's liberation by the Red Army. By this time, Gestetner's unit was stationed near his hometown of Győr, where a ragtag Arrow Cross militia held some 350 Jews prisoner. Taking pity on these prisoners, who were given no food at all by their captors, the Jewish labor servicemen began secretly delivering a portion of their own rations to the barracks. Apparently, a fascist patrol caught Gestetner carrying food into the camp and executed him on the spot. According to Isaac Klein, who was present when Mrs. Reichmann was belatedly informed of Lajos's death, she let loose an anguished cry, fell heavily to the floor and began "writhing like a snake. Then she went into her room and one by one her children went in to try to console her."

Of the hundred or so refugees who had straggled into Tangier by late 1946, some two dozen were relatives of the Reichmanns and virtually all of them were Orthodox Oberlanders. Paul, who was sixteen at the time, later remembered the newcomers as a plaintive lot: "A lot of people that came to Tangier were totally broken, without any spirit left, and they were so desolate. They were not interested in life—period. And those that were interested in life had no trust."

The Reichmanns helped their relatives secure their own apartments and, in some cases, to find employment. Edward hired one Gestetner cousin to run his parking lot and put a few others to work in his commodities trading operation while his father helped finance his Gestetner brother-in-law Henrik, who with a cousin, Oscar Gestetner, started a kosher food store specializing in European imports. Dezsö Gestetner started a kosher milk business, spending much of his time traveling in the countryside outside Tangier to oversee his suppliers' milking. Mor Schildkraut, Reska's husband, began producing woolen Orthodox prayer shawls, or tallith, for export to the United States. Meanwhile, Samuel's brother Simon set up his own money-changing firm using capital he had managed to save from the egg business in Beled.

Simon Reichmann and his two sons, Renée's four siblings—Henrik, Olga, Dezsö, and Reska—and their new spouses (each of them remarried) and assorted nieces, nephews, and cousins gathered every day in the apartment on Rue Molière. "In 1946 and 1947 there were never less than twenty to twenty-five people at my mother's table," Edward recalled.

There were not enough jobs to go around for the survivors in Tangier, most of whom had no alternative to life on the dole. Honoring its guarantee, the Joint Distribution Committee covered the costs of providing the newcomers with food, shelter, and medicine. The committee's "behavior to us is very noble," Mrs. Reichmann acknowledged in a letter to the Vaad Hahatzalah, having already assured her sponsors that she used its money sparingly: "I only touch it where absolutely necessary." Mrs. Reichmann spent about $4,000 in Vaad money equipping newcomers with beds, footlockers, tables, chairs, cooking utensils, bedsheets, and so on. She also gave out $220 in Vaad funds to buy wigs for a half dozen married women and a like amount to provide trousseaus for three brides.

There were many marriages among survivors young, middle-aged, and elderly, and Mrs. Reichmann had a hand in most of them. "She considered it her duty to create families, to rebuild a lost generation," Paul Reichmann observed. To this end, she took a special interest in the welfare of the dozen Orthodox orphans who had washed up in Tangier, whether relatives or strangers. To augment the funds contributed by the Joint Distribution Committee and the Vaad Hahatzalah, Mrs. Reichmann joined forces with her son Edward to organize a "Grand Concert de Musique Hébraïque" performed by survivors of Bergen-Belsen and Buchenwald. The concert, which was a calculated attempt to boost the morale of the performers as much as it was to raise funds to cover their living costs, was held at the Cinema "Le Paris," as was a benefit screening of the film *La Dernière Chance*. Edward had obtained the rights to it gratis from a relative of a business associate who was a film distributor in Switzerland.

Edward also took it upon himself to build a new synagogue to accommodate Tangier's expanded ultra-Orthodox community. On a trip to Paris in 1946, the eldest Reichmann brother recruited Rabbi Israel Lebowitz, a young Oberlander rabbi at loose ends. Although Rabbi Lebowitz was only in his thirties, he was a spellbinding speaker who after his stay in Tangier would attain prominence as the leader of New York City's large community of transplanted Viennese Jews. Edward bought a small apartment building and made over the bottom floor into a synagogue with about one hundred seats and an adjoining mikveh, or ritual bath. Over the synagogue, Edward built an apartment for Rabbi Lebowitz. When the new synagogue was completed, the family let its lease lapse on the Rue Cook synagogue.

———

As always, Tangier remained a place of monstrous, surreal contrasts. For most Holocaust survivors, the city was a limbo to be endured until permanent refuge could be arranged in America, Palestine, or some other distant land. But for the foreign diplomats, self-exiled aristocrats, and monied rakes of Tangier's social elite, Tangier was an exotic backdrop to a nonstop party that scaled new peaks of excess after Barbara Hutton, the Woolworth heiress, outbid General Franco for a great stone palace in the Medina in 1946. Soon, camel drivers, belly dancers, and tribesmen from the Rif were being summoned like movie extras for Hutton's lavish, theatrical fêtes. While the likes of Charlie Chaplin, Greta Garbo, and Claudette Colbert wandered through gilded rooms, Hutton perched atop a throne wearing an emerald and diamond tiara. At about the same time, the American novelist Paul Bowles and his wife, Jane, established themselves as the fixed star of a chic expatriate literary demi-monde steeped in alcohol, narcotics, homosexuality, and Islamic mysticism, and which at one time or another included Truman Capote, Tennessee Williams, William Burroughs, Allen Ginsberg, and Jack Kerouac.

Preoccupied not only with salvaging the human wreckage that had washed up on their doorstep but with exploiting the abundant commercial opportunities of postwar Tangier, Mr. and Mrs. Reichmann had neither the time nor the inclination to sip the fizzy punch of the city's sybaritic social scene. "As far as I know, the Reichmanns never even once appeared at a cocktail party," said the Ashkenazi customs broker Robert Abramovici, who was a very sociable man himself. "If Madame Reichmann had not married that man, maybe she would have gone to a party. She seemed more open-minded than her husband."

Even so, there was at least one overlapping link between the Reichmanns and their insular ultra-Orthodox circle and the Tangier jet set, and her name was Leonie Kalman. (Having since married a third time, she is now Mrs. Leonie Faludy.) Leonie had left Hungary with her mother and two sisters before the war and moved to Paris, where she attended pattern-making school and began making dresses for herself and her siblings. In 1937, the family moved to Tangier. "It was a tragic-comic life," Mrs. Faludy recalled. "The city was beautiful but we came with nothing. We celebrated when we bought our first armchair." Faludy set herself up in business as a dressmaker and soon diversified into carpet weaving. In 1941, she moved her looms into a run-down Moorish palace in the Casbah. "It was so cheap I had to buy it," said Faludy, who employed seventy-five Tanjawis as her business boomed after the war. Even Barbara Hutton became a customer, commissioning a vast snow-white carpet with gold trim. "It was a great life after the war," Mrs. Faludy recalled. "Every night it was another cocktail party, and with such interesting people—artists and intellectuals from all over the world."

Paul Bowles was a neighbor and a friend. "He was a very quiet somebody who was smoking what everyone was smoking in Tangier: marijuana," she recalled. "When he came to my dinner parties, he did not eat or drink but was always very witty." She also befriended Auberon Waugh, the aristocratic son of the British novelist Evelyn Waugh, and Claudio Bravo, the Chilean painter. By way of documenting her own bygone appeal, Mrs. Faludy pulled a snapshot from the drawer of a desk in the little apartment in Marbella in which she now lives. In it, a trim, modishly attired woman who resembles the actress Debra Winger is striding down a crowded Madrid street wearing dark glasses and a confident, almost sassy expression.

Although her memory is hazy on the point, Mrs. Faludy suspected that she first met Mrs. Reichmann across the counter of her dressmaking salon on Boulevard Pasteur. "It's possible she bought dresses from me, though she was always soberly dressed," Faludy said. "Never could you say she was wearing something expensive. We became friendly, though I could never be a real friend because I wasn't Orthodox." At Mrs. Reichmann's urging, in 1944 Mrs. Faludy began dropping by the flat on Rue Molière to help put together the food parcels for concentration camp prisoners. After the war, she agreed to take on as apprentice dressmakers four of the young Orthodox women who had survived Bergen-Belsen. As Mrs. Reichmann married off each of these girls, she sent replacements.

"I always felt a certain respect for Mrs. Reichmann," Mrs. Faludy said. "She was older than me, of course, and wiser. We used to talk. One day I asked her, 'You have a good-looking husband and such nice children. Do you ever get depressed?' She looked at me for awhile and said, 'Yes, sometimes I am depressed.' So I said, 'Well, what do you do when you're depressed?' She said, 'I take a good strong coffee, I put on my hat, and I go for a walk.' "

Reprising a long-standing Oberland tradition, Edward Reichmann married his first cousin, Edith Reichmann, on September 20, 1946. Both were twenty-one and had been born in Beled. Despite its echoes of prewar Hungary, this was not an arranged marriage in the usual sense. Isaac Klein had left just a few days after Eszti had arrived in Tangier as part of the Bergen-Belsen contingent, but it had been apparent to him that Edward was smitten with his cousin, who, for all her survivor's grit, was a petite, fragile-looking woman of striking good looks. "I think that Edward first fell in love with her beauty," Klein said.

Eszti was the lone survivor in her family. Her father, Joseph (the uncle whom Edward had followed to the mikveh back in Beled), had been conscripted into a Hungarian labor battalion. In 1943, the family had been notified of his disappearance in the Battle of the Ukraine; his remains were never recovered. Eszti's mother and six younger siblings had been sent straight to the gas chamber at Auschwitz. After three weeks in Auschwitz, Eszti had been shipped to Bremen, where the battalion worked sixteen-hour days clearing the rubble created by nightly Allied bombing runs. Next, she had been sent to a building materials factory in a nearby village to make cement blocks and bamboo partitions for prefabricated housing. With her fellow prisoners, Eszti was given just enough food to keep her alive and developed a severe case of boils. A few weeks before the war's end, Eszti had been marched on foot with the other surviving laborers to Bergen-Belsen, where she was assigned to a barracks filled with moldering corpses. She chose to sleep outside in the rain, contracted typhoid fever, and nearly died. By the time Rabbi Baumgarten arrived from England, Eszti was a walking skeleton.

Like many survivors of the camps, Eszti did not want to talk about her ordeal. Over the years, she would tell Edward her story in bits and pieces but kept to herself until 1994 what had been the most humiliating experience of her captivity. It occurred just before she was shipped out of Auschwitz and is here recounted in the family memoir, "Eszti's Story":

> It was Shabbos, a day the Germans chose because they wanted to further desecrate the Jews and their beliefs. . . . Eszti was among five hundred girls who were suddenly told to strip naked. Then they were shepherded to an outdoor square in front of a podium filled with German officers. Behind the officers, a band of Jewish prisoners played music, and the SS officers amused themselves at the sight of their helpless victims scurrying about like frightened animals. The women tried unsuccessfully to shield themselves with their hands and to hide behind their neighbors. They clung to one another, trying futilely to protect themselves. . . . While the music played, the Germans casually conducted another selection process, choosing those girls who appeared healthy in order to send them to work in other cities.

The union of Edward and Edith was an occasion of great, bittersweet joy for the Reichmann family. And yet in a letter to the Vaad Hahatzalah after the ceremony, Mrs. Reichmann wrote of it in an oddly detached, impersonal way: "The first transport of former camp inmates consisted of 8 young girls from Bergen-Belsen, whose parents, brothers and sisters perished in the gas chambers. From these 8 girls, 5 have already married, two to well-to-do men, the others also to very good young men, ex-prisoners, too, who found a living here." Of course, one of those "well-to-do men" happened to be her eldest son. Similarly, in none of her official correspondence did Mrs. Reichmann acknowledge that four of the Belsen girls were her nieces.

Many years later, Edward was equally circumspect in the occasional interviews he gave. As Edward told the story, his mother had asked Rabbi Baumgarten to "look for Orthodox girls from the Oberland who had lost everybody and to write her so she could 'adopt' them." To put it mildly, this would have been impractical, since there were hundreds of Oberland girls in the camps in Germany. And for the rabbi to have searched generally for Oberland girls and found only the four Reichmann nieces and a few friends would have been a statistical miracle. Edward's explanation of how he happened to marry a first cousin he had known since birth was even more transparently implausible: "One day, after a Shabbat stroll, Maidie said, 'I am not married, there is no one suitable here for me, but I know these girls [from Belsen] and some are suitable for you and for the family.' I told my father and he said, 'I agree, ask her who she recommends.' That woman is my wife. . . . She was also named Reichmann. She was a cousin."

These verbal contortions betray the Reichmann family's acute sensitivity to the paroxysms of accusation and recrimination that convulsed the Orthodox rescue network in the years after World War II, ripping apart the Vaad Hahatzalah. As the maneuvering over the creation of a Jewish state in Palestine intensified, the Orthodox groups that had joined together to form the Vaad Hahatzalah increasingly sacrificed the shared mission of rescue to their own separate political agendas. The acrimony was exacerbated by allegations of financial abuse and nepotism that reverberated from Montreux to New York.

Mrs. Reichmann had reason to expect that she, too, would feel the sting of backlash as this postwar inquisition gathered force. She was closely allied with two of the principal lightning rods of controversy and also was, in a perverse sense, conspicuous by reason of geography. Who could doubt the Vaad's rationale for pouring funds into such cities as London, Paris, Zurich, and Istanbul? But Tangier was an important outpost only because the Reichmanns had made it so. Moreover, there was no question that the Reichmanns exerted themselves mightily on behalf of their extended family; among the recipients of the food parcels and entry visas they sent to Europe were a great many relatives.

However, the Reichmann family's reworking of the story of Edward and Edith is best characterized not as an attempt to cover up impropriety but rather to avoid even the appearance of impropriety—of favoritism, to be specific. Until Mrs. Reichmann began receiving outside funding in 1944, she acted purely as a private individual and indeed would have been remiss in not first coming to the aid of her own. Once the Vaad Hahatzalah money started rolling in, most of the individual food parcels and all of the bulk shipments went to nonrelatives. The Budapest rescue project was equally expansive, as the overwhelming majority of the 1,200 Spanish visas distributed went to strangers. After the war, Mrs. Reichmann was able to obtain far more Tangier and Spanish Moroccan visas than her relatives required; she was constrained not by supply but demand. In the end, most of the survivors who came to Tangier were not Reichmann relatives; "Auntie Renée" just treated them as if they were.

Clearly, a portion of the $4,000 in Vaad funds that Mrs. Reichmann spent outfitting survivors went to her nieces, at least two of whom received support from the Joint Distribution Committee as well. Since these girls arrived with nothing, not even clothes, what they received was standard, not special, treatment. Even so, it would seem that at a time when Edward was tooling around in a new Chrysler, the Reichmanns could have covered the cost of a few tables and chairs from their own private funds.

But such was hardly the stuff of scandal. An exhaustive search of the Vaad's archives shows that the Reichmanns emerged unscathed from the organization's postwar inquisition; their name surfaced in none of the broadsides that flew back and forth across the Atlantic. Mrs. Reichmann was entrusted with far more relief money in 1946 than ever before—a grand total of $31,000, $10,000 of which was transmitted directly from New York and the balance via HIJEFS in Switzerland. The meticulous financial statement that she submitted for the year 1946 was accepted with one minor cavil, which, ironically, had to do with the Klein family. At New York's instruction, Mrs. Reichmann had advanced Isaac Klein and assorted Fischofs as much money as they needed while in Tangier from her Vaad funds, with the understanding that the Klein family would reimburse the organization. But when Mrs. Reichmann sent the Kleins a bill, the Vaad reprimanded her.

By the time this dispute was resolved in Mrs. Reichmann's favor, the Vaad Hahatzalah was coming unraveled. Ever the optimist, Mrs. Reichmann mailed in one last fund-raising pitch. "I receive again day by day petitions for entry permits from Romania, Hungary, and Czechoslovakia, besides pleas from the still existing camps in Italy for food parcels," she explained. But not even Mrs. Reichmann could muster the old verve. Instead of making the case for aid anew, she enclosed a copy of a long, impassioned letter that she had written two years earlier and suggested matter-of-factly that the board "study the contents of it again."

Chapter 14

Throughout the war, Mr. and Mrs. Reichmann had nourished hopes of returning to Hungary when the fighting ended. However, the horror stories that their relatives and other survivors brought with them to Tangier convinced them that the distinctive Orthodoxy of their native land had been extinguished beyond all proximate hope of revival. In Beled, for example, the forty-four survivors who straggled back found only a single, charred wall where the synagogue once stood and a gauntlet of unrepentant and resentful townsfolk who refused to return Jewish property that had been confiscated. Although more than half of the 473 Jewish communities of Hungary were officially reestablished soon after the fighting ceased, the great majority relapsed into oblivion as most survivors decided that emigration was the better part of valor. Conditions for Jews would only worsen as the Iron Curtain fell with a clang, and Hungary was transformed into a Soviet satellite.

Hungary's outcast status as a vanquished Axis power and Tangier's peculiar status as an international city combined to reduce the Reichmann family to statelessness. In 1946, Mr. Reichmann swapped his useless Hungarian passport for a carte d'identité issued by the Swedish consulate general in Tangier. By the time his Swedish identity card expired in mid-1948 every inch would be covered with border control stamps, most commonly those of Spain, Portugal, France, Belgium, Switzerland, and England. Although Reichmann occasionally traveled for pleasure, he spent most of the time tending to his financial affairs. For one thing, he consolidated the assets he had left for safekeeping in Great Britain and the United States with the profits that he had made in Tangier during the war. A portion of this wealth—perhaps the lion's share—was deposited in Switzerland. At the same time, Reichmann began settling accounts with the scores of Hungarian families who had entrusted their capital to him during the war. This task was sadly complicated by the high death toll in the Oberland and the difficulty of locating next of kin in the postwar chaos.

After the war, the Reichmanns also began considering new places to live. In February 1946, Samuel Reichmann wrote to Charles Ullman, the Gestetner in-law who had helped him transfer funds to the United States just before the fall of Paris in 1940. The Ullmans had fled from France to the United States that same year, settling in New York City. "I would very much like to have your opinion and advice on the following," Reichmann wrote. "We intended to get back to Hungary. Now that we have given up this idea completely, we do not know how to decide. You have an idea about my [financial] means. Here I always earn what I need to support my family, but nevertheless I would not like to stay here forever. At the moment I could get a visa for the United States right away. But for the time being it seems impossible to get a visa for Palestine. In your opinion what are our possibilities in America?"

In the fall of 1946, Samuel and Renée, accompanied by Eva, were able to scout New York City for themselves. At the time, U.S. officials were stingy even with visitor's visas, suspecting that many "tourists" had no intention of leaving. The Reichmann family, however, had connections in America, thanks to its continuing exertions on behalf of Orthodox relief and rescue.

After attending the World Agudist Conference in London at the end of 1945, Mrs. Reichmann had received a series of requests for help from the Agudath Israel World Organization, which was the chief political arm of non-Zionist Orthodoxy. As resolutely apolitical after as before the Holocaust, the Reichmanns had no interest in becoming dues-paying members of Agudath Israel. On the other hand, the American branch of Agudath Israel was among the staunchest sponsors of the Vaad Hahatzalah's relief work in the early years of the war, and Renée had corresponded with Jacob Rosenheim, the New York–based president of Agudath Israel, who was an outspoken critic of the International Red Cross's refusal to classify concentration camp inmates as prisoners of war. In March 1946, Rosenheim reinitiated contact with Mrs. Reichmann, asking her help in bringing to Tangier an Orthodox family stranded in Italy. Mrs. Reichmann happily obliged.

It was about this time that the Agudath leadership in America hit upon a novel way of rescuing homeless Orthodox dignitaries in Eastern Europe: it invited hundreds of rabbis and communal officials to a convention in New York to discuss Orthodoxy's postwar agenda. Once in the United States, the typical invitee could attend a few meetings and spend the next few months besieging the U.S. government at close range for permission to remain permanently. Either the Truman administration fell for the ruse, or wittingly succumbed to Orthodox political pressure, for the path that Agudath's guests followed to America was smoothed by the State Department. On paper at any rate, this was a huge convocation. Some three hundred "delegates" arrived from Prague alone, under the sponsorship of the Vaad Hahatzalah. State Department officials demanded to know why so many were coming from a single city. "They're not really from one city," said Irving Bunim, the Vaad's executive director. "They just happened to be in Prague." Lame as it was, this explanation carried the day. The entire group received tourist visas and eventually succeeded in gaining immigrant status, though most of them had to leave the United States and reenter through Canada.

The Reichmanns, who had been late additions to Agudath Israel's guest list, stayed with Martin and Rufka Klein in the Borough Park section of Brooklyn. One morning, Samuel took the subway into the Wall Street district and found 70 Pine Street, which held the offices of Philipp Brothers, the commodities trading firm cofounded by the Bendheim family. When Samuel arrived, Charles Bendheim was in a meeting. Bendheim's secretary interrupted her boss by telephone. "There's a Mr. Reichmann to see you." Puzzled, Bendheim replied: "I don't know any Reichmann." The secretary conferred with Samuel. "He says that you do and he can prove it," she said. Bendheim emerged from his meeting and brought Samuel back to his office. "There was nothing particularly distinctive about his appearance," Bendheim recalled. "To me, he looked like just another European; we saw a lot of them at the office." Reichmann introduced himself, cited the exact date and the amount of the cashier's check that Bendheim had received in 1940, and asked for his money back. "I sat down and wrote out a check for the full $75,000," Bendheim said. "He looked over the check, said 'thank you' and left. That was it."

Unlike many Agudath Israel "delegates," the Reichmanns left the United States even before their visitor's visa expired. Apparently, they did not find New York to their liking. Samuel and Renée's U.S. Immigration and Naturalization Service file contains no evidence that they bothered to apply for an immigrant's visa during their stay in New York. Not until the late 1950s would the Reichmanns tear themselves away from a Tangier roiled by the Moroccan independence movement and cross the Atlantic. What kept the Reichmanns in Tangier until colonialism's ignominious end was what had brought them to this outpost of untrammeled capitalism in the first place: the prospect of accumulating outsized wealth.

———

For all its complexity, postwar Tangier's appeal was aptly reduced to two sentences in an advertisement that appeared frequently in the Paris edition of the *Herald Tribune* after the war: "Tangier is waiting for you. Tangier knows NO restrictions of any kind!" For the most part (its petty harassment of Jewish relief agencies conspicuously excepted), the reconstituted International Administration lived up to its billing and, like its predecessor, practiced the unfashionable art of government by utter self-effacement. "Tangier knows no currency controls, trade barriers, immigration quotas, loyalty checks, red tape, or draft registration," observed a *New Yorker* magazine correspondent who profiled the city in the spring of 1952. "Its prosperity grows in direct ratio to the agonies and restrictions of the outside world. It is one of the few places on earth where anything goes."

An all-purpose refuge from regimentation, Tangier from 1946 into the mid-1950s was the oldest boom town in the world. During this period, the city's European population doubled, to 35,000, as the total number of inhabitants rose to 150,000. From sunup to sundown, seven days a week, year after year, the city was enveloped in a cacophony of wrecking ball, jackhammer, and cement-mixer. Gleaming new hotels and amusement palaces sprouted above the semicircle of white sand beach that lined the Bay of Tangier while apartment and office towers proliferated throughout the European quarter and especially along the Boulevard Pasteur, with its chic luxury shops and chrome cocktail bars. Even in the labyrinthine recesses of the Medina, the city's ancient Arab quarter, evidence of hammer and saw was omnipresent. The flood tide of development spilled over onto the sandy wastelands to the south and east of the city, giving rise to whole new neighborhoods of luxury flats ringed by a sprawling native shantytown named the "bidonville," after the word for the canteens worn by French soldiers. Discarded bidons were pounded flat and used by inhabitants of the slum for roofing.

In addition to Holocaust survivors, legions of non-Jewish refugees, political outcasts, and military deserters accumulated in postwar Tangier. "Every continental eruption sweeps a wave of refugees into Tangier, where, as in a geological formation, one layer on top of the other tells a story of successive catastrophes: Central European Jews, who fled Nazism, mingle in the cafés of the Little Socco (market) with Nazis who escaped postwar retribution, Spanish foes of Franco with compromised friends of Pétain, victims of Hungarian Communism with quislings from Belgium." Tangier was no less a haven for renegade capitalists. Large quantities of cigarettes, nylon stockings, automobiles, refrigerators, penicillin and other consumer goods—not to mention arms and narcotics—continued to pass through Tangier en route to European black markets, especially those in Spain, which was periodically subjected to embargo by the United States and other nations that disapproved of Franco's politics.

For the most part, however, postwar Tangier boomed as a repository for capital fleeing any number of threats at home: taxation, inflation, detection, confiscation, conflagration. "Tangier has in one respect begun to take over Switzerland's traditional role in the world—to provide safe refuge for nervous capital," *Fortune* magazine observed in 1950. In cooperating with the U.S. government's search for the ill-gotten gains of Axis nationals, Switzerland in 1945 had compromised its tradition of banking secrecy by revealing the identities of the owners of blocked accounts. As a result, the *Fortune* article continued, "sensitive international money began to search for a haven where even the U.S. would be treading with discretion and found Tangier." Going with the financial flow, two Swiss banks opened branches in Tangier.

In addition to inviolate secrecy, Tangier's incomparably free facilities for currency exchange gave it an advantage over rival flight-capital sanctuaries. In Tangier and Tangier alone, cash could be easily transformed at market rates into any one of a dozen currencies. At a time when exchange rates continued to be fixed by government fiat almost everywhere else in the world, Tangier's freewheeling money market was no less attractive to the speculator than to the furtive conservator. "The place is flooded with people whose main occupation is the financial game," observed the disapproving author of the *Moroccan Journal*, published in 1952. "One day I met two Frenchmen who told me, after five minutes' conversation, that they had come to Tangier with £3,000 which at the end of a month they were certain to double. When I showed some surprise, they assured me that they were doing nothing illegal but merely 'speculating in foreign exchange.' "

Given the virtual fetish that Tangier made of financial discretion, there's no direct way of quantifying the capital that flowed into the city during its postwar greening. The *Fortune* article noted that local "insiders" ranked the city's banking volume between that of Amsterdam and Brussels and remarked, "Quite a career for a drab Moroccan port." Since much of the capital that flowed into Tangier found its way into real estate, one can get a rough feel for the magnitude of the inflow by charting land costs. By the early 1950s, the value of prime properties had risen 5,000 percent from their wartime lows, and Tangier was said to feature the most expensive real estate in the world, outpacing even midtown Manhattan. Choice lots along the Boulevard (there was only one that mattered) fetched £130 to £150 per square meter while on the city outskirts good sites went for £50 per square meter.

Another telling, if equally indirect, measure of Tangier's capital-flight bonanza was the proliferation of the "Tangier corporation," which was a shell company registered in the name of a local resident who was paid a nominal fee to act as a front for its foreign owners. From 1945 through 1950, an average of five hundred new corporations a year were registered in Tangier. The Tangier corporation's chief attributes were three: it could transact any sort of business, it incurred no income tax liability, and it operated under cover of absolute secrecy. In effect, money credited to the account of a Tangier corporation vanished from the radar screens of government. Most such corporations were conduits that existed no more than the few weeks it took to arrange the transfer of funds from abroad into a numbered account at a Tangier bank.

In Tangier it was nearly as easy to start one's own bank as to open a bank account. A would-be banker only had to pony up about $400 in capital, select

a name, and incorporate. Thereafter, bank proprietors had to pay a sum aver-
aging $28 a year for "renewal of patent," and that was it, unless a bank held
gold bullion in bond, in which case it was required to obtain a license (for $60)
and file a brief annual statement with the International Administration. Along
the Boulevard Pasteur and adjoining avenues, banks proliferated relentlessly,
quadrupling in number from sixteen in 1945 to eighty-five by the early 1950s.
The city's banks "vary considerably in their scale and style," observed the
author of a primer on Tangier banking in the *Atlantic Monthly* in 1950.

> You take your choice—anything from a solid establishment (probably one of
> the pre-war ten) with impressive offices and plenty of capital-in-being, to a
> one-man operator sitting in a nine-by-five room on the fifth floor back of a
> walk-up. . . . "You too can be a banker" is Tangier's slogan. The smaller banks
> don't greatly resemble U.S. banks, even the ones in small American towns.
> Although they often handle vast sums of transient capital, you rarely see any-
> one actually inside them. Quite a few of them don't bother with checking
> accounts—or checks. One man enterprisingly installed what looked like a
> conventional front office, with grills, a line of tellers' windows, and the usual
> notices—"Deposit Accounts," "Government Bonds," "Foreign Exchange,"
> and so on. But it was all a dummy made of pâpier-maché. There were no
> tellers. In a back room he, his wife, and a cousin transacted the real busi-
> ness—helping Belgians, Swiss, Swedes, Danes, Austrians, Spaniards and any-
> one else, to ease their capital out of the country in which it lay locked.

Among the most substantial of Tangier's fledgling banks was the Banque
Samuel Reichmann. "Toda clase de operaciones bancarias con el Extranjero,"
proclaimed the advertisements Mr. Reichmann ran in a local business magazine. Translated literally, this meant: "Complete banking services abroad."
Translated from the local idiom into the language of conventional banking, it
meant: "We specialize in foreign exchange and the transfer of flight capital."

Samuel Reichmann's postwar evolution from money changer to banquier
was an incremental step driven as much by the preferences of his foreign
exchange clientele as by his own ambitions. Samuel had many foreign customers, and it was logical that a good number of them would turn to him when
they wanted to shift wealth to Tangier—all the more so because certain types
of foreign exchange transactions were a convenient conduit for flight-capital
transfer. "I'm sure he had clients who entrusted their fortune to him," said
Messod Bendayan, who dealt with the Reichmann bank virtually every day in
his capacity as a foreign exchange broker for the Banque Commerciale du
Maroc, which was the pivotal force in the Tangier currency market in the postwar period. "It wasn't his Tangier clientele who asked him to do this; it was his
foreign clients. The Spanish. The Spanish were not allowed to have deposits

overseas so, if someone like Mr. Reichmann, someone who could be trusted to be discreet, could say, 'You've got X amount of pesetas. What do you want? Dollars? Swiss francs? No problem. And if you want, I'll keep them for you.' " Et, voilà! The money changer was also now a banquier.

While the banking and money-changing facets of the business of Banque Samuel Reichmann were as inseparable as the two sides of a coin, they were unequally profitable, Bendayan continued. "It wasn't Reichmann's exchange operations per se that brought in the money. It was the commissions that he took in getting pesetas out of Spain. If a Spanish industrialist wanted to keep his money in Tangier, the dealer might take a commission of 10% or more." To compete with those eighty-four other local banks, Reichmann in effect had to return a portion of his profits to his depositors in the form of interest paid. On the other hand, he also enjoyed the banker's prerogative of using funds left on deposit to generate additional income. Downplaying commercial lending, the investment staple of conventional banking, Reichmann used the larger portion of his working capital to trade in and out of the Tangier currency market, in which, by this time, he was as expert as anyone.

———

Two of Banque Samuel Reichmann's most important clients in the postwar period were Albert and Henry Grebler, scions of a Hungarian Jewish family that had founded a watch manufacturing company in the Swiss valley town of La Chaux-de-Fonds. Leaving the watch business in the care of their sister Mienke, the Grebler brothers had left Switzerland in the 1930s in search of greener commercial frontiers. While Henry entered the textile manufacturing business in Barcelona, Albert moved to Tangier and soon became a local legend for all the wrong reasons. By all accounts, Albert Grebler was an odious character in every sense of the word—a short, rotund figure of such disheveled countenance that it took a while for the Jews of Tangier to realize that he was not a tramp but a miser. "He was a dirty, totally disgusting man who looked like he never washed or changed his clothes," said Rachel Muyal, who was one of the few Tangierinos to accept an invitation to Grebler's beachside wedding after the war. "He was the most impossible person. L'avarice!" she shouted, clenching both fists for emphasis. "It was just unbelievable. Even for his wedding, I don't think he went out and bought a new suit."

Robert Abramovici refused to do business with Grebler. "I worked with him two or three times and that was enough," Abramovici said. "He was a very mean man. There were always long delays when you gave him a bill. He liked to argue every cent. He was a rich man, you understand, but he walked around in espadrilles and wore the same suit for fifteen years. I had a friend who was a painter and I put on an exhibition for him in space that I leased from Grebler. Grebler came to me mad and said that he'd rented that space to

me for an office, not a gallery, and demanded a 10 percent cut of every painting sold."

Mention of the name Grebler elicited a shriek from eighty-year-old Leonie
Faludy. "Mama mia!" she exclaimed. "Grebler wanted to marry me." When
told of Mrs. Faludy's response, Rachel Muyal scoffed amiably. "He wanted to
marry the whole town," Muyal said. "At one point after the war I was bored and
wanted to leave Tangier," Mrs. Faludy continued. "Grebler had a fortune
already—in Mexico, I heard. I was interested in going to Mexico and so someone introduced me to Grebler. I went to see him. I told him my story and he just
stared at me. Finally, he said, 'Why go to Mexico? You could marry me right
here.' "

"Everyone in Tangier knew Grebler," she continued. "By the next day word
had gotten around and everyone called to congratulate me. 'Do you know how
rich Grebler is?' they said. One woman I knew came over to my flat to convince
me to marry him. I thought to myself, 'Well, he's very ugly and I don't care
about his money but maybe he has some hidden virtues.' I was wrong. One
night he took me to a very cheap restaurant and bought a terrible bottle of
wine. When we left he drew a line on the bottle and told the waiter to keep the
rest for him. I couldn't believe it! It was rather an illness in him, this extreme
greediness. It was not normal at all."

Grebler, who set himself up in Tangier as a freelance export-import man,
was blacklisted by both the U.S. and British governments in 1942 for sending
ten-kilo packages of wool to Germany through Switzerland. By 1943, he was
holed up in Portugal with a huge cache of industrial diamonds, some of which
he sold to Alex Heiden, the Reichmanns' friend. Dangling the diamonds before
officials at both the British Consulate and the American Legation, Heiden said
that he had access to additional supplies but refused to reveal their whereabouts unless assured of a commission. After futilely attempting to locate the
diamonds themselves, the Americans called Heiden in and threatened to blacklist him. Heiden talked. "According to his latest story, which seems to approach
the truth," wrote the vice consul who debriefed Heiden, "over 400,000 carats
of stolen industrial diamonds are in the village of Caldas da Rainha, Portugal,
in the possession of Albert Grebler . . . a thoroughly unsavoury character."

What became of Grebler's cache of industrial diamonds is a mystery. However, after the war Grebler returned to Tangier and added to his legend by erecting the tallest and most luxurious apartment building in the city. Located just
off the Boulevard Pasteur at the edge of the European quarter farthest from the
Medina, Grebler's building was the preferred address for the fastest of Tangier's
fast-money crowd. Among Grebler's tenants was the kingpin of the cigarette-
smuggling racket, an Italian whose quarters were entirely decked out in red
velvet. Grebler himself lived with his wife (a Casablanca woman three decades
his junior) and his elderly mother in a penthouse duplex that was sumptuously

outfitted—Mrs. Faludy described it as "a marble palace"—but left unfinished and virtually unlit. "He took out the lightbulbs to save on electricity," Faludy said. "So his poor old mother had to find her way in the dark from her bedroom down a long hallway to the bathroom."

Using Tangier as his base, Albert Grebler traveled widely through South America, carrying two suitcases stuffed with gold pieces. "There was a big difference in the price of gold coins in the international market and in South America," explained Messod Bendayan, who moonlighted on weekends as Grebler's assistant. "You couldn't send coins as merchandise but you could take them with you in your luggage. I'd guess he made $2,000 a suitcase."

Exactly when Albert Grebler became a client of Samuel Reichmann's is unclear. It is unlikely that Reichmann would have risked doing business with the Swiss émigré until after he was removed from the Allied blacklists, for otherwise Reichmann would have risked blacklisting himself. When Messod Bendayan went to work for Grebler in 1947, he found that both Albert and his brother Henry already were doing business with Reichmann. Bendayan himself had traded foreign exchange with Reichmann since 1945, when he left school at age seventeen to join the Banque Commerciale du Maroc, where his father was a senior executive. "Grebler took a liking to me, so I started working on the operations between him and Reichmann," Bendayan said in a 1993 interview. "Reichmann had other people in Spain, so he wasn't just working with the Greblers. But Grebler was a very important client of Reichmann's. This is what would happen:

> Albert might be in Barcelona, with his brother. He would phone me and say, "Young Messod, you'll be getting a call from me. When I ring, you are to go to Reichmann and he'll give you 10 or 20 million pesetas." (At the time that was about $700,000.) "Put them in my account at the Banque Commerciale and convert them into dollars or Swiss francs." Then I would go to Reichmann's office, just down the block. Reichmann's correspondents would be in Barcelona with Grebler. Grebler would ring and ask me if I had received the packet. Then Reichmann would give me a case with the dollars or pesetas. I didn't count them. I trusted Mr. Reichmann. So I would say, "Yes, I have just been given the package. Thank you. Goodbye." Then I would go to the bank, where they counted it, and it was changed, usually into dollars.

According to Bendayan, this sort of transaction, known as "parallel foreign exchange," was a staple not only of Reichmann's but of all the important Ashkenazi money changers in Tangier, who, unlike most of the native dealers, were well connected abroad. Parallel foreign exchange enabled industrialists like the Greblers to secretly convert their Spanish textile profits from pesetas to other currencies in quantities much larger and at rates far more advantageous than permitted by the Franco government without taking the risk of actually smuggling currency out of the country. While the Greblers broke the laws of Spain in the process, Reichmann as broker was subject only to Tangier law, which permitted parallel foreign exchange transactions—and a whole lot more.

The Greblers may have been averse to currency smuggling but not to smuggling per se. According to Bendayan and others, the Greblers routinely smuggled shipments of the Cauny brand wristwatches made in Switzerland into Spain via Tangier, thus avoiding the payment of import duties altogether. "The pesetas to pay for the watches would come back from Spain to Tangier, where they were converted into Swiss francs," Bendayan said. "Mr. Reichmann didn't know anything about the watches. He was not involved with merchandise. But when Grebler needed Swiss francs, he went to Reichmann." Bendayan said that although he dealt with other exchange dealers on behalf of the Greblers, "Reichmann was our most important counterpart. He was an ideal correspondent. Whatever you needed—dollars, pesetas, and so on—you could always find it at Reichmann's. Because of his [other] correspondents abroad, he always had what we needed and he was both a buyer and seller."

Bendayan thought that Samuel Reichmann and Albert Grebler made a decidedly odd couple. "They were totally different!" he exclaimed. "You can't compare potatoes and tomatoes. Samuel Reichmann was always very diplomatic, very respectful. The Greblers were more—well, tougher and more down to earth. From an abstract point of view, I think that Mr. Reichmann was a very respectable person. He was a real patriarch who brought his children up in a very honorable fashion."

But if, by the idiosyncratic standards of Tangier, Samuel Reichmann could be lionized for his integrity despite his association with the likes of Albert Grebler, he fell far short of respectability when judged according to more universal ethical codes, notably those of the Torah.

Even a cursory reading of the American and British journalism about postwar Tangier makes it clear that a reputation for honesty made within the International Zone counted for nothing outside it, given the city's overarching identity as a hub of dubious commerce. Indeed, business success in Tangier was considered prima facie evidence of immorality. "To make your mark in Tangier, you'd better be unblushingly avaricious and more than a little unscrupulous, otherwise the competition is too tough. And you must never trust your neighbor—he's probably up to no good, and he may be after your hide," scoffed the *American Mercury* in a 1952 article entitled "The Phony Gold Rush." In his novel *Let It All Come Down*, Paul Bowles likened postwar Tangier to New York City:

You must see how alike the two places are. The life revolves wholly about the making of money. Practically everyone is dishonest. In New York you have

Wall Street, here you have the Bourse. Not like the bourses in other places, but the soul of the city, its raison d'etre. In New York you have the slick financiers, here the money-changers. In New York you have your racketeers. Here you have your smugglers. And each man's waiting to suck the blood of the next.

All rhetoric aside, the business of Banque Samuel Reichmann and its peers consisted largely of helping well-heeled foreigners violate the laws of their homelands. In defense of Tangier's flight-capital-bloated banks, one could argue that many such laws were both misguided and unjust and even cast aspersions on the legitimacy of some of the governments that imposed them. On the other hand, the banks of Tangier collectively were no less welcoming to war criminals, crooked politicians, and gangsters of all sorts than to legitimately aggrieved citizens of a quasi–police state such as Spain. In facilitating illicit flows of goods and capital, the bankers of Tangier unquestionably enriched themselves and a black-marketeering elite at the expense of average folk—especially within the International Zone itself. Most dramatically, the runup in real estate values induced by massive inflows of flight capital priced much of the native population out of the central housing market and into the bidonville.

From the standpoint of Torah fundamentalism, the socioeconomics of Tangier banking were marginally relevant. By the prevailing halakic standards of the 1940s, no less than those of the 1990s, a businessman who aided and abetted the breaking of secular law was no less culpable morally than one who breaks the law—unless that law conflicted with an overriding religious imperative. Needless to say, changing a smuggler's bankroll and arranging surreptitious capital transfers at 10 percent per transaction hardly qualified as a higher calling.

On Samuel Reichmann's behalf, it could be argued that in accumulating wealth by disreputable, though not illegal, means, he was only doing what he could to ensure his own family's long-term survival in a chronically uncertain, menacing world. Given their own experience as refugees and rescue activists, the Reichmanns probably understood as well as anyone how closely net worth and survival had correlated during the Holocaust—how every Jew in Nazi captivity literally had a price on his head. However, such an argument seems altogether too forgiving. Reichmann's unholy association with Albert Grebler continued well into the 1950s, long after his family's financial security had been assured. Moreover, there were any number of Jewish businessmen in circumstances far more tenuous than those Reichmann faced in Tangier who would have drawn the line at doing business with a fellow Jew who had been blacklisted for trafficking with Nazi Germany.

Outside the office, Samuel shunned Grebler, whose irreligiousness deprived Edward of the opportunity to eject him from the Rue Cook synagogue as he had tossed out the Orthodox blacklistee Emmanuel Hollander. The notion of Grebler so much as sharing the Reichmann family's dinner table was almost blasphemous. But try as he might, Samuel could not compartmentalize Grebler into oblivion. In aligning himself commercially with a man who, by the standards of his own religious beliefs, was beneath contempt, Samuel debased himself.

Reichmann was regarded as a rich man long before he left Tangier, and this perception extended far beyond the family's little circle of Orthodox émigrés. As early as 1946, Reichmann's name was one of twenty-five that appeared on a list of the richest Jewish businessmen in Tangier, as compiled by local representatives of the World Jewish Congress. However, the size of his fortune remained a well-kept secret. Lips do not come any tighter than those of the Reichmanns, and the family owned nothing that was subject either to government-mandated disclosure or valuation by public markets. Messod Bendayan, for one, is convinced that Reichmann "made enormous profits," mainly by extricating pesetas from Spain and recycling them in Tangier, but conceded that he had no way of quantifying his fortune. "He had a sizable fortune, that was obvious to me from doing business with him, but no one could actually see it. He could have had $20 million stashed away and no one would have known."

Despite Reichmann's secretiveness, other businessmen in Tangier occasionally caught a glimpse of the formidable financial muscle he could muster. According to Robert Abramovici, the shipping agent, in 1954 the Banque Samuel Reichmann guaranteed the full amount of a $450,000 bank loan to a local Arab looking to expand his brick factory. For a banker of Samuel's innate conservatism to assume a liability of such size in a single transaction, suggests that his total capital was a large multiple of $450,000; $20 million—or more—was not out of the question. Abramovici has firsthand knowledge of the guarantee because the Reichmanns asked his advice when their client defaulted. Samuel honored his guarantee and took possession of the loan collateral—100 tons of heavy machinery stored in a warehouse on the Tangier docks. "One day Louis came to see me and said, 'What should we do?' " Abramovici recalled. "We figured out that they were paying as much in storage as the equipment and so forth was worth, which wasn't much because it was rusting badly. I think finally they just gave it up. It was a total loss."

In the mid-1950s, as well, Samuel approached José Benaim Hachuel, the Tetuán candyman who had employed Edward and Louis, with a proposal that startled the Sephardic industrialist. "I went to see him in his office and he pulled an enormous dossier from his desk and said, 'I have made studies to build a candy factory in New York,' " Hachuel recalled. "He had it all planned out in great detail, from buying the land to installing the machinery. He said he would invest $500,000 of his own money and that he needed another

$500,000 from me and my brother. It was an astronomical sum to me. Reichmann said, 'Why don't you have a family reunion and see how much you can raise?' I told him it would be difficult for us to live in an English-speaking country." Instead, Hachuel emigrated to Argentina, where he lost everything, and Samuel aborted the candy factory project. Again, if Reichmann was prepared to sink $500,000 into a single and quite risky business venture abroad, it stood to reason that this sum represented only a fraction of his net worth.

Chapter 15

If the inculcation of one's own values is the proper measure of a parent, then Samuel and Renée Reichmann stood seven feet tall. All six members of the next generation of Reichmanns—Eva, Edward, Louis, Albert, Paul, and Ralph—inherited the distinctive, rigorous identity of the Oberlander Orthodox as surely as if it were a tract of land, a sheaf of stock certificates, or some other equally tangible legacy. Although Edward and his brothers would diverge from one another in some aspects of religious practice over the coming decades, not one would dilute his or her Orthodoxy, which was the durable faith not only of their parents but of their grandparents' parents. For better or worse, Eva's generation of Reichmanns had been decisively stamped in the mold of a lost world, a world in which they had only briefly resided and yet in a spiritual sense would never leave.

Remarkably, this uniformity of religious identity was not achieved at the expense of individuality. In terms of basic personality, the six Reichmann siblings were extraordinarily diverse, covering the full spectrum from extreme extroversion to extreme introversion in three matched sets corresponding to birth order: Eva and Edward were assertive, emotionally volatile and outgoing to a fault, commanding attention wherever they went; Louis and Albert were as amiable as their elders but more easygoing and less demonstrative, content to remain at the spotlight's edge; Paul and Ralph were gangly, studious, and shy. If, as was generally agreed among friends of the family, Eva and Edward had been cast in their mother's mold and Louis, Albert, and Ralph essentially were variations of their father, Paul was a melding of parental personality. He inherited Samuel's retiring and gentle manner but his mother's drive and dauntless self-confidence. Paul was, in short, a most aggressive introvert.

In their approach to child rearing, Samuel and Renée Reichmann had been much less doctrinaire than one might have expected of Orthodox traditionalists. As Edward had begun traveling more widely throughout Morocco and Spain on business, he had let his hair grow and combed it in a way that made his payos less and less apparent. Once Edward's barber took the next step and snipped off his payos. "When I came home mother noticed it right away but didn't say a word," Edward recalled. The next Sunday, after Shabbat, Renée called Edward into her bedroom. On the table was a small mirror and some photographs of his father and his grandfathers.

"Look, Edward," she said quietly, "I understand that it's not easy for you to be in Tangier with no yeshiva and not even friends who are former yeshiva boys. But you should know that you have a big responsibility. You are the oldest of five brothers and the others will follow your example."

She handed Edward the photographs, pointing out the untrimmed beards and long payos of his grandfathers. However, Samuel appeared sans payos and with beard neatly trimmed. Renée passed her son the mirror. "Look in the mirror," she commanded. "If this goes any further, how will your son look?"

"Mother, I promise you," Edward replied, "my son will look better than your son." ("It sounded like a joke," Edward said later, "but I meant it and Mother believed me.")

Samuel made no mention of Edward's changed appearance until a few days after Renée had taken him in hand. While walking down the street with his son, Samuel mentioned that his mother had apprised him of their conversation. "I'm very pleased with your answer," Samuel said.

In its unwavering religiosity, the Reichmann family was typical of the small remnant of ultra-Orthodox families that came through the Holocaust. In a study of 708 Holocaust survivors living in Israel, Reeve Robert Bronner found that 61 percent of Jews who were ultra-Orthodox before the war remained so after, whereas only 9 percent of the moderately Orthodox maintained their religious identities. "The more intensely observant, the more likely to remain observant; the less intensely observant, the greater the likelihood of becoming non-observant . . . ," Bronner concluded. "Our study conveys the case for the retentive strength of the assiduously observant, and the holding power of religious upbringing."

Unlike the majority of their ultra-Orthodox peers, the Reichmann brothers were not constrained by poverty in the pursuit of their postwar ambitions. Whatever the size of the fortune that Samuel Reichmann accumulated in Tangier, his affluence made a crucial difference in launching his sons in their own careers. "The mistake a lot of people make with the Reichmann brothers is to think of them as first-generation wealthy," said Israel Singer, the executive director of the World Jewish Congress and a longtime friend of the family. "They are second generation."

Nor, strictly speaking, were the Reichmanns Holocaust survivors, having been spared the deprivations of the ghetto and the agonies of the concentration camp. In the view of many survivors who, like the Reichmanns, sought their postwar fortune in North American real estate, this distinction would be decisive in the rise—and fall—of Olympia & York. "The Reichmann boys never had that feeling inside, that inner fear holding them back," said an Auschwitz survivor who got his start in Toronto real estate about the same time as the Reichmanns did and achieved more modest but more enduring success. "As long as twenty years ago, I kept telling them to slow down, take their time. But their outlook is different. They never experienced the really bad times. They see only opportunity. Me, I'm always looking on the downside. I cannot forget when I did not have a piece of bread."

On the other hand, the younger generation of Reichmanns had even less in common with the average North American Jew or even the typical European refugee. In settling in perpetually vulnerable Tangier instead of seeking refuge in some safely distant land, and in mounting their own large-scale relief and rescue drive, the Reichmann family in effect passed the Holocaust era in the very shadow of the fortress walls of Theresienstadt and just down the street from Auschwitz-Birkenau. For Eva and her brothers, the Nazi menace was a fact of daily life that left a deep imprint in the soft clay of their adolescent consciousness yet did not cause them to suffer in a way that warped mind, body, or soul. To the contrary, the young Reichmanns' experience of the war years was on balance constructive, even uplifting.

For one thing, they were clasped throughout to the bosom of an exceptionally tight-knit and happy family; the Reichmann household was not nearly as austere as the rigor of the family's religious beliefs might suggest. "I was especially impressed with the very pleasant family relationship," said Arieh Handler, an Israeli emissary who spent a week in the Rue Molière apartment as the Reichmanns' guest after the war. "You could tell the boys all had great respect for their parents." Although Handler's business partner, Tibor Rosenbaum, was a close relative of Nicholas Rosenbaum, he preferred to stay with the Reichmanns, whom he knew only by reputation. "Their place was pretty widely known as a place where one could stay," Handler said. "Nicholas Rosenbaum was just a different type altogether. He was much more formal and not inclined to sacrifice to help others. The Reichmanns, though, were warm people, and a warm heart makes a warm house."

This was, moreover, a family that had overachieved in their people's hour of greatest need. In exerting themselves so tirelessly in the cause of Holocaust rescue, the Reichmanns—especially Renée—earned a place among the minuscule minority of people, whether Jew or Gentile, who proved equal to what was the greatest moral challenge of the era, if not the century. If the Reichmanns' wartime achievements warranted at most a footnote in the epic tale of World

War II, by the late 1940s, if not earlier, the family had attained wide renown within the haredi world. "When I went to Jerusalem or Paris or Antwerp, wherever, I was known," recalled Edward. "The name Reichmann sounded well."

The degree to which the family's wartime exertions molded the younger Reichmann generation was evident in the heartfelt testimonials that Paul, normally impassive in public, delivered via press interviews in the late 1980s at the peak of his own renown. "Renée and Samuel Reichmann were giants of a sort that only a handful emerge, usually during times of crisis," he once said, giving his father a greater share of the credit than perhaps he was properly due.

> They refused to become victims. They rejected the finality of Hitler's final solution and dared to do something about it. This was at a time when most of the world, including western civilization, had lost its claim to human dignity by encouraging genocide with their silence. With very little means, Samuel and Renée Reichmann struggled and sacrificed—knocked on doors, broke down doors, begged, cajoled—and actually achieved miracles. In the latter stages of the war, after their own families had already perished, they saved scores and scores of lives and fed thousands of starving people. After the war they rebuilt hundreds of families.

After his mother died in 1990, Edward could not discuss her accomplishments without getting teary-eyed. A few weeks after Renée's passing, Edward wrote two lengthy letters of reminiscence about his mother (and himself) and sent copies of each to all of her descendants. "I received many, many letters of condolences from people who knew her," wrote the eldest Reichmann brother, "but somehow I feel uncomfortable with it, because to describe her correctly, titles are not necessary. There is only a simple and short word for it: she was GREAT."

But if their parents' achievements inspired the Reichmann brothers, they also imposed the burden of great expectations. The legacy they shouldered had the heft of dynasty, for in their own minds as well as in genealogical fact they were as much Gestetners as they were Reichmanns. Indeed, to the extent that the family's wartime achievements were mainly Renée's doing, they can be seen as the culmination of a century or two of Gestetner noblesse oblige. Renée herself seems to have been acutely conscious of acting in the distinguished tradition of her father's family. In corresponding with unfamiliar institutions or by way of adding emphasis to a telegram she would sign her name, "Renée Gestetner Reichmann," or on occasion even "Renée Reichmann Gestetner." Late in 1945, she added this cryptic but clearly indignant postscript to a cable sent to HIJEFS in Switzerland: "Finally, know that I am honest, like the Gestetners and the rest."

Although Eva and her brothers shared a respect bordering on reverence for their parents, they differed greatly in the way they responded to their shared legacy of opportunity and obligation, as was to be expected of such various personalities. In business, these differences in character and aptitude among the brothers in time would cause friction, conflict, and resentment. Even so, the ties of familial affection and the shared experience of flight and extended exile that bound each to the other would hold tight through all the triumphs and calamities ahead.

———

As the press of postwar relief work subsided, the impetus within the Reichmann family began shifting to the next generation, especially to Edward, who, for all his willfulness, was in many ways mature beyond his years. As the eldest son, it was only (chrono)logical that Edward would be the first of the brothers to start a business, to marry, to father a child. But Edward raced through adolescence as if it were a steeplechase course and he a champion mount, leaping one hurdle after another with such alacrity that he left his brothers in his dust. Although Edward was only two years older than Louis, he preceded him in marriage by six years and in fatherhood by eight. Edward never worked for his father in Tangier, whereas Albert never worked for anyone but his father. Edward was five years older than Paul but entered business a good thirteen years earlier than the future Master Builder.

Although he would forever remain the dutiful eldest son, Edward had already eclipsed his father in some ways by the late 1940s. To begin with, he was, at least by his own reckoning, "a richer man than my father and the rest of the family put together." It was Edward, not his father, who had provided many of the family's relatives with their first jobs in Tangier, and Edward who built the new Orthodox synagogue—larger by half than the one that Samuel had organized earlier. At the same time, Edward moved beyond the narrow confines of ultra-Orthodoxy to raise funds for the larger Jewish community of Tangier and, as the only avowed Zionist in the family, even undertook assignments for the Haganah, the underground arm of Jewish resistance in British-controlled Palestine, in the last few turbulent years before the birth of Israel in 1948.

As the eldest son of parents who were exceptionally but narrowly accomplished, Edward's mentality was that of an ultra-Orthodox princeling compelled to enlarge his family's little empire of renown on all sides. His somewhat grand self-image was clearly rooted in childhood. It is telling that Edward and his equally self-confident older sister were the only Reichmann children who spent their formative years in Beled, where, for the first and last time in her adult life, Renée was undistracted by involvements outside the home: no poultry shop, no charity to lead, no lives to save. Bored with the one-dimensional provinciality of village life and enthralled still with the novelty of motherhood, Mrs. Reichmann turned the full force of her high-powered personality on her daughter and first-born son.

Precociously self-possessed, Eva and Edward entered adulthood with strapping egos unfettered by fear of failure, no matter how daunting the task at hand. In this regard, they were their mother's children, though they both lacked Renée's sardonic wit. To some extent, Mrs. Reichmann's humor was armor; she might not have been intimidated by the world outside but she was ever mindful of its dangers. Although as refugees, Eva's and Edward's experience was unusually broad and occasionally hazardous, their unshakable self-assurance made them naïfs of a sort. Late in the war, they were riding the train somewhere in Spain when an older couple boarded, took the seat ahead of them, and began speaking Hungarian. Delighted, Eva asked in Hungarian, "Oh, are you refugees, too?" The man warily answered in the affirmative. "Well, then, you must be Jewish," Eva said sunnily. "God forbid!" the man hissed angrily. "We are gypsies." Edward was deeply upset by the comment and all that it implied. "I just couldn't believe what I'd heard," he recalled.

Fortunately, Eva's and Edward's youthful egotism was tempered with altruism. By any standard, both were precociously philanthropic and, unlike some of their younger siblings, would remain as generous with their time as with their money as they settled into middle age. Eva and Edward gave with sincerity but never humility; unlike every other Reichmann, they not only were disinclined toward self-effacement but incapable of it. Eva especially was a domineering conversationalist. "In any group of people, Maidie was the center always," said Mrs. Naomi Heller, who was perhaps Eva's closest friend from 1958 to her death in 1985. "You had to hear her. You had to have her opinion. She insisted on dominating every room she walked into. She really talked nonstop, though she would tone it down some when her mother was around."

Edward was a great talker, too, but his compulsiveness also took more ambitious and masculine form. As the twenty-one-year-old surveyed the postwar landscape, he made the classic mistake of concluding that where he happened to have landed was the very best place to be. By 1946 his parents were at least thinking of moving on, but to Edward the future looked brightest through his own front window. In his view, which badly underestimated the growing militancy of the Moroccan independence movement, the International Zone of Tangier was destined to become "the Switzerland of North Africa," and he had every intention of becoming the richest man in Tangier (if not Switzerland itself). "Eli was always a very big dreamer," said Alexander Heiden. "He was never satisfied. He always wanted something bigger."

At twenty-one, young Reichmann cut a rather dashing figure in his tailor-made suits, his head shiny with the best hair oil, the requisite fedora pulled down low over the eyes at a jaunty angle, a cigarette dangling from his lips. He never did grow a beard, though he did not shave either; good Orthodox boy that he was, he used a depilatory powder. Edward was more virile than handsome, with a great square-jawed face and the broad shoulders and barrel chest that in the United States would have marked him as a former football player but in his case were a pure triumph of genes since he had never taken up any sport more strenuous than Ping-Pong. (Good eyes somehow were left out of his genetic endowment. He was the only brother who wore glasses; he also inherited his mother's painful stomach ulcer condition.) Edward looked a good ten years older than he was and thus was only a mildly incongruous presence at the Café de Paris, where, dressed for success, he breakfasted most mornings with the middle-aged movers and shakers of Tangier commerce.

When Isaac Klein arrived in Tangier in the fall of 1945, Edward already was luxuriating in the role of budding big shot, Reichmann & Rosenfeld having piled up profits in commodities trading in the war's final stages. "I remember Edward bragging about how he'd just made $5,000 on a single shipment of flour," Klein recalled. Reichmann tooled around Tangier in a maroon-colored Chrysler with an automatic transmission, a great novelty at the time. He bought the car from Édouard Michelin, a cofounder of the French tire-making company, who lived in a mansion on the mountain. Edward met Michelin after answering the retired mogul's classified ad offering a used motorcycle for sale and gradually coaxed him into parting with the car. One day Klein was riding with Edward when the Chrysler skidded into a ditch. Upon his return home, he sheepishly endured a tongue-lashing from his mother. "Renée was very cross because he'd gotten his shoes muddy," Klein said.

As a promoter, Edward was fearless: he would make a sales pitch to anyone, anywhere. But he was altogether too eager and hyperbolic in his entrepreneurial enthusiasms to qualify as slick. Even allowing for the proverbial grain of salt, there was no mistaking his intelligence and drive. "He tended to see things in a big way," recalled Arieh Handler, who traveled with Edward to Madrid. "You took him seriously, [despite] his obvious tendency to exaggerate. When I got back to England I said to a few of my friends, 'There's a man from a good family in Tangier who will go far.' "

After the war, Reichmann & Rosenfeld carved out a niche for itself as an impresario of elaborate barter transactions with Spanish customers. While the Franco regime continued its campaign to bolster the peseta by restricting Spanish importers' use of foreign currencies, it did allow firms to pay for imported raw materials by exporting manufactured goods of equal value. Not many exporters of, say, American flour or Belgian Congolese copper actually wanted to take delivery of Spanish truck parts or olive oil: they wanted cash. And so middlemen such as Reichmann & Rosenfeld searched the world for buyers of truck parts or olive oil, creating an elaborate grid of a half dozen or more interlocking transactions—some for cash, some for goods in kind. If just one component trade fell through, the whole credit-supported superstructure could come tumbling down. On the other hand, a smoothly executed multisided transaction could set a clever middleman's cash register to ring like an alarm bell.

Reichmann developed a specialty in worsted fabrics and leased office space in Barcelona, the center of the Spanish textile trade. When Eugene Zimmerman, an old childhood friend from Győr, arrived in Barcelona on a buying trip for his textile wholesaling business in Vienna, Reichmann volunteered his services as agent. "I was the one who found the manufacturer, but then Edward stepped in and financed the purchase," Zimmerman recalled. "I paid him and he paid the supplier, which saved me from having to get a line of credit myself. Edward already had one. He was well known in Spain."

One of Edward's best customers in Barcelona was La Preparación Textiles, the same Grebler-owned firm that was an important client of Banque Samuel Reichmann. Although Edward had had a nodding acquaintance with Albert Grebler for years, he did not meet Henry, the Barcelona brother, until 1947, in the course of helping to raise funds to build a new synagogue and mikveh in Barcelona. Although Grebler was masquerading as a Gentile, Edward decided that he was just too rich to ignore. After several angry confrontations and lengthy late-night dialogues about the meaning of Jewishness, Edward finally persuaded Grebler, who was twice his age, to make a large donation. As Grebler came out of the closet and began joining in Jewish communal affairs, he and Edward became fast friends for a time, making two trips to Israel together.

Back in Tangier, meanwhile, Edward simultaneously jumped aboard the postwar bandwagons in real estate and in banking by forming the Real Estate and Commercial Bank (RECB). By Tangier standards, the bank was solidly capitalized. Between them, Reichmann and Rosenfeld sank $150,000 into the RECB and, with the help of a prominent Madrid lawyer whom Edward had gotten to know over breakfasts at the Café de Paris, raised another $150,000 from a handful of Spanish and Italian businessmen with interests in Tangier. More than just another receptacle for European flight capital, RECB made commercial loans and acted as both principal and agent in local land deals. The bank also took the lead in organizing Tangier's first stock exchange, La Bolsa International Libre de Tanger.

To house the exchange, Edward and his partners in the bank, joined by outside investors, put up a six-story office building, the Reichmann family's first construction venture. Located a block off Boulevard Pasteur on the Rue de la Croix and designed by a leading Tangier architect, the building—dubbed "La Bolsa" after its major tenant—was lavish by contemporary standards. The stock exchange, along with a private dining club for its members, occupied the first and second floors, in quarters handsomely appointed in marble and leather. The Banque Samuel Reichmann moved into a spacious office on the second floor, while Edward worked out of the RECB office on the third.

Without really intending to, Edward found himself in the awkward position of competing, however tacitly, with his father for banking clients in Spain. Although the tradition of commercial primogeniture was at least as potent within Orthodoxy as without, Edward was the only Reichmann brother who would never work with his father. "The pattern was that my father had his business and my business was my own business," Edward said. "But we were close, me and my father—almost like brothers. Many times during the day he would come up to my office to have a coffee, or I would go down to his office. Had the family stayed in Vienna it's very likely that I would have gone to work for my father." This last statement is best characterized as wishful thinking. For an eldest son to be commercially isolated within a family as close as the Reichmanns was a remarkable, if rarely noted, state of affairs that brought Edward considerable anguish over the years.

———

Even as Edward was ranging throughout Western Europe in pursuit of his commercial dreams, he never considered moving away from Tangier. With what by the mid-1950s would be exposed as gross self-delusion, the eldest Reichmann brother saw Tangier emerging as a regional capital of Ashkenazi Jewry. "I believed in Tangier as a Jewish center," he recalled. "It was my dream to make a community of 1,000 Ashkenazim." To Edward's siblings, his grandiose vision of Tangier was not so much wrongheaded as irrelevant. They had their own dreams, and in pursuit of them Eva, Paul, Louis, and Ralph each would leave Tangier in the late 1940s and settle in England.

The first to leave the nest was Paul, who, in 1947, just before his seventeenth birthday, flew off to Antwerp, to attend yeshiva. Paul always had been the most studious of the brothers, excelling both at Torah learning and at mathematics and history. "Even as a child, Paul was always the most brilliant," said Alex Heiden. "He was always inside himself, thinking. He worked his brain at all times." Had circumstances allowed, Paul would have begun yeshiva when he turned thirteen in 1943. But the war and the inadequacy of Morocco's Sephardic yeshivoth (by Reichmann standards anyway) left him with no practical alternative to the Lycée Regnault, which he attended with growing impatience as the war ended and the scattered seeds of ultra-Orthodoxy's rebirth took root.

In 1946, while his parents were off on an extended swing through Western Europe, Paul dropped out of the Lycée Regnault and moved in with a recently arrived older cousin, Kalman Reichmann, who was living in a cheap tourist hotel on the beach. Kalman, the sole surviving child of Samuel Reichmann's oldest brother, had attended yeshiva in Hungary and was an accomplished Talmudist. "We worked day and night on one of the tractates," Paul recalled. "I didn't care what the school administrators thought, but I was worried that my mother would be upset. My hope was to impress her with all the knowledge that I had acquired in her absence." The strategy seemed to work. In any event, even after his parents returned Paul was allowed to continue studying with

Kalman, his secular education having come to an unceremonious end just short of the lycée equivalent of a high school diploma.

Paul yearned to go away to yeshiva but was chained to Tangier for a time by his lack of a passport. While Mr. and Mrs. Reichmann were able to travel freely on the Swedish carte d'identité they had obtained to replace their worthless Hungarian passport, establishing residence outside of Tangier was another matter altogether. After months of effort, the best the Reichmanns could do was get Paul a student visa to England and a transit visa allowing him to enter Belgium, his ultimate destination. In Antwerp, Rabbi Josef Grunwald, the son of Edward's late mentor, had reestablished the Pápa yeshiva in makeshift form after the war. Paul enrolled at Rabbi Grunwald's yeshiva in mid-1947 but was unable to remain more than a few months for lack of Belgian residency papers. Just before his transit visa expired, Paul returned to London and joined some sixty other boys in a small but well-established yeshiva, the first of four Lithuanian-style yeshivoth that he would attend over the next five years.

For the better part of two centuries, the great yeshivoth of Lithuania had maintained Torah scholarship in its purest, most rigorous form—that is, impervious to the influence of Hasidism and other innovations. Quite a number of Lithuanian rosh yeshiva and lesser rabbis managed to flee before the Germans arrived and after the war re-created their lost institutions as best they could mainly in Israel, the new postwar hub of the yeshiva world, and the United States. Like the colleges of the Ivy League, the various Lithuanian yeshivoth stressed their marginal differences while remaining essentially identical. First and foremost, they were bastions of Torah lishma—of Talmudic study for its own sake, as opposed to vocational purpose. In other words, the Lithuanian yeshiva was neither a rabbinical academy nor a teacher's college, though many of its graduates did in fact go on to join the rabbinate or teach professionally. This did not mean that the yeshiva existed merely or even mainly to indulge the intellectual curiosity of its students, or bachurim. These were institutions of high religious purpose, Torah study being both an obligation and an aspect of worship, and they were as devoted to building moral character as to increasing knowledge. Bachurim were expected to lead chaste, ascetic lives—the rigors of their schedule left little time in any event even for innocent diversion—and they were closely monitored by a rabbi-disciplinarian, the mashgiach.

In practical terms, the aim of the yeshiva was to produce a graduate capable of helping others in the Orthodox community with their learning and to assist in the religious development of his own children. At the same time, yeshivoth of the sort that Paul Reichmann attended were imbued with a grander sense of mission. "There is the almost mystical notion that in studying Talmud one is somehow enhancing the survival of the Jewish community as a whole." As Israel Salanter, a great Lithuanian rabbi of the nineteenth century, put it:

when a Jew in Vilna is diverted from studying Torah, a Jew in Paris converts to Christianity. The overriding social function of the yeshiva was to create "a cadre of people who will be the contemporary link in the long chain of tradition that began with the giving of the Torah to Moses on Mount Sinai."

In the residence hall of the typical yeshiva, the day began about 7:15 A.M. with the cry, often in Yiddish: "Wake up! Wake up to do the work of the Creator!" After reciting a morning prayer, the bachur went to the beis medrash, the main study hall, for the morning prayer service. From 9:30 to noon, the students studied together in pairs in preparation for that day's shiur, or lecture. Study in pairs—chavrusa—was an ancient tradition that emphasized learning through dialogue and debate. To enter the beis medrash of a large yeshiva was to immerse oneself in purposeful pandemonium: a cacophony of voices arising from a continuous swirl of movement. Students arranged in serried rows would be waving their arms or jabbing the air with their fingers by way of emphasis. While some bachurim preferred to stand, others would sit and sway rhythmically to and fro as if in a trance. The method behind this seeming madness was explained in a tractate of the Mishna that carefully lists "the forty-eight means by which Torah is acquired: by study, by the hearing of the ear, by the recitation of the lips . . . by consorting with fellow-students, by intense arguments among students."

At the appointed hour, the students trooped out of the big room and filed into several classrooms where they went over the day's assigned text with a rebbe, or teacher, in an hour-and-a-half session that alternated between lecture and freewheeling discussion. After a lunch break, students would devote half an hour or so to mussar, a study program of ethical and philosophical works. About 3:00 P.M., the focus shifted back to the Talmud, as the students returned to the big room and either reviewed the material covered in class or tackled a new passage. At 6:00 P.M. there was an hour-long supper break, and then the group returned to the study hall for a second study session. A 10:00 P.M. prayer service marked the formal conclusion of the day, though at most yeshivas the lights burned into the wee hours. Friday afternoon was left open for Sabbath preparations, but first thing Sunday morning it was back to work. "Looking at the program of study, it is difficult to imagine how people tolerate it without great hardship," observed one widely recognized authority on yeshiva life. "Surely a comparable program of college study would be judged very demanding, to say the least."

In content and methodology, the closest secular equivalent to the yeshiva was the law school, since what the Talmud contained was not a systematic code of law but a series of independent rulings. Elucidating the general principles relevant to a problem therefore required the marshaling of evidence from a large number of cases. Like his secular counterpart, the bachur measured his progress both by the breadth of the references he was able to cite in constructing his argument and the originality of that argument. However, mastering the Talmud was a far more challenging task, and not just because it comprised sixty-three volumes of 5,800 folio pages, plus thousands of pages of commentary. The Talmud "is a collection of paradoxes: its framework is orderly and logical, every word and term subjected to meticulous editing. . . . Yet it is still based on free association, on a harnessing together of diverse ideas reminiscent of the modern stream-of-consciousness novel. Although its main objective is to interpret and comment on a book of law, it is, simultaneously, a work of art that goes beyond legislation and its practical application."

By all indications, including his own account, Paul Reichmann thrived at yeshiva, maintaining throughout his years of study the intensity of commitment he had precociously demonstrated in affixing himself to cousin Kalman. In yeshiva life there were three orders of merit: brilliance, diligence, and piety. Everywhere he went, Reichmann earned top rank in the latter two categories and was just a cut below the pinnacle in the former. Every yeshiva had a handful of exceptionally brilliant students—called iluyim—who reigned as the stars of the beis medrash and who in time were expected to join the faculty. By his own admission, Reichmann was no iluy: "I became knowledgeable but I was not especially great in scholarship. That was never my goal. My ambition was just to acquire as much knowledge as I could." Edmund Tennenhaus, a Polish orphan, spent many days and nights studying with Reichmann in the yeshiva. "Paul came from a wealthier family than most of us, but it didn't seem to affect his attitude. To the contrary, I think he felt he had to do for others because of his own fortunate circumstances."

After nearly two years at Torat Emeth (The Law of Truth), Reichmann left London and headed north to Gateshead, which occupied the south bank of the Tyne River across from Newcastle. Here, in the heart of English coal-mining country, there had evolved a group of strictly Orthodox schools that emerged after the war as the Jewish educational capital of Europe. Reichmann attended the most renowned of Gateshead's schools, the Yeshiva Ben Joseph, for the better part of three years. But the institution that drew him to Gateshead in the first place was one he never did enter: the Kollel HaRabbonim. A kollel is an institute of higher rabbinical studies akin to a Ph.D. program. In the postwar era, Gateshead had the only well-established kollel in all of Europe.

In terms of its natural setting, Gateshead, a town of fifty thousand, was as ghastly as Tangier was idyllic. The winters were brutal, and in every season a pall of coal dust hung over the town like a shroud. "The clouds, like the shtenders [lecterns] of the Yeshiva, are carbon-coated and the odor of coal-dust permeates the town," reported one eyewitness as late as 1964. Gateshead's 150 Jewish families—all of which were strictly observant—lived clustered together in a half-dozen blocks of terrace housing, blocks that virtually enfolded the buildings of the educational complex. The town's Jewish quarter was said to resemble "a shtetl in the old tradition, lifted out of the history books and transplanted in northeast England." Gateshead inspired "an almost unparalleled, unswerving intensity of purpose, which seems to dissipate more easily . . . in the less harsh light of other settings."

Reichmann lived in a dormitory with about one hundred other boys, half of whom came from England and the rest from all over Europe, including Italy, Sweden, Switzerland, Denmark, France, and Belgium. While Gateshead was firmly cast in the classical Lithuanian mold in terms of curriculum, it departed from type in admitting Hasidic students, further adding to the remarkable diversity of its bachurim. At Gateshead, Reichmann was exposed to a half-dozen prominent Talmudic scholars on the faculty, including Rabbi Leib Gurwitz, a product of the great Lithuanian yeshiva at Mir. Reichmann was a fixture at Rabbi Gurwitz's shiurs, which, according to an account contemporaneous with Reichmann's stay at Gateshead, "excel in brilliance and sparkling Talmudic wit and are extremely popular with students." It would be a source of deep satisfaction to Paul Reichmann that the younger and more scholarly of his two sons, Henry, not only would go to Gateshead but also be taught by the son of Rabbi Gurwitz.

———

In April 1948, Paul left yeshiva and returned to Tangier to attend the wedding of his sister. The reception was a large and lavish affair held in the Moorishly elegant central courtyard of Hotel Valentina, one of Tangier's poshest hostelries. Virtually everyone who had ever aided Maidie and her mother in their charitable work was invited, whether devout or irreligious, Ashkenazi or Sephardi, refugee or native, Jew or Gentile. Despite the heterogeneity of the crowd, the banquet tables were segregated by sex, as was customary among the ultra-Orthodox, and the men danced only with men and women with women. "It was my first Orthodox wedding and to me the whole thing was very funny, with all the dancing and the mania of picture taking," recalled Leonie Faludy.

In his wedding photos, the twenty-five-year-old groom, Lipmann Heller, appeared as a chubby, cheerful-looking man wearing round-framed tortoise-shell glasses. Eva and "Lippa" Heller had first become vaguely acquainted in Vienna in the early 1930s. They had attended the Talmud Torah on Malzgasse at the same time but were not classmates since girls and boys were segregated in conformance with Orthodox custom. However, Lipmann's younger brother, Izzy, was a classmate and pal of Louis Reichmann's and the two boys frequently played together after school. Lipmann walked Louis home from his parents' house on many an evening and Eva occasionally answered his knock.

Before World War II, the odds would have been against the marital union of the Reichmann and Heller families. Although the Hellers, like the Gestetners, were a family of impeccable Orthodox credentials (Lippa's namesake and great-great-grandfather, Rabbi Yomtov Lipmann Heller, was the most renowned spiritual leader of seventeenth-century Vienna), their roots were sunk not in the Oberland but in the Hasidic stronghold of Galicia. In prewar Vienna, Lipmann's father, Fievish Heller, had been a follower of the transplanted Galician eminence, the Tschortkow Rebbe, while the Reichmanns associated with fellow Oberlanders in the Schiffschul community. Such differences in background receded in importance after the Holocaust, which drastically shrank the pool of marriageable haredim of both sexes. The consensus among both sets of relatives was that Lippa Heller and Maidie Reichmann were well matched in that each was the personable product of pious, strictly observant families with a flair for commerce. It did not hurt that Lipmann's wartime experiences as a refugee in England had inclined him away from the Hasidism of his father and toward the Reichmanns' brand of Oberlander Orthodoxy.

Lipmann had been only fifteen when he arrived in England in late 1938. After the Kristallnacht pogrom, the Hellers managed to secure a place for the two youngest of their three sons on a transport of 320 Orthodox youths to London organized by Rabbi Solomon Schoenfeld, who, as the leading haredi rescue activist in England, would later play an integral role in the same Vaad Hahatzalah network that included Renée Reichmann. The entire group of Viennese youths was first housed in a Jewish high school in North London and then dispersed among a dozen Orthodox hostels set up by Rabbi Schoenfeld. With the rabbi's help, Lipmann was able to line up a job for his father in Leeds, an industrial city in northern England, thus enabling his parents and older brother to qualify for English entry visas in the nick of time. Just a few days before Germany invaded Poland in 1939, the Hellers left Austria on the last prewar transport out of Vienna.

In Leeds, Fievish Heller founded a zipper manufacturing business that helped pay Lipmann's way through Gateshead yeshiva. He completed his studies a few years before Paul Reichmann enrolled, and returned to Leeds to join the family business. After his father died, Lipmann moved with his mother to London, where he devoted his days to selling zippers and his nights to correspondence classes in banking. He hoped to use the profits from the zipper business to start a small merchant bank of his own some day.

Edward and Eva had bumped into Lippa Heller while vacationing in the French resort town of Vichy in early 1948. A week after Eva had returned home, Heller showed up unannounced and remained in Tangier for a few weeks. While Lippa was quick to propose marriage, Eva was slow to accept. She confided her doubts to longtime family friend Regina Klein. "Lippa told Maidie that if they got married, his mother would have to live with them. So she said to him, 'Not me,' " Mrs. Klein recalled. "Maidie came home and told Renée that she wouldn't marry him because his mother had to live with them. 'I don't want that,' Maidie said. So Renée said to her, 'Look, don't be so fast judging people. If he is a good enough person to want his mother to live with him, then he will be even better to you as a wife.' So Renée finally talked her into it and you know she was right: Lippa turned out to be such a good husband."

Heller's mother, who was too ill to travel to Tangier for the wedding, died in London a year after the ceremony, having been attended to during her last months by her chastened daughter-in-law. Back in Tangier, the departure of the beloved Maidie left a void at 25 Rue Molière and in the Jewish community as a whole. She was not only her parents' sole daughter but her mother's right hand in all of her undertakings. With her younger brothers, Eva had filled the dual role of big sister and deputy mother. To Edward, who was closer to Eva than to any of his brothers, she was, irreplaceably, his best friend.

Chapter 16

As the only avowed Zionist in his immediate family, Edward Reichmann took great inspiration in a slim volume written by his father's uncle, Rabbi Zvi Reichmann, and published in 1926. In the book, written in Hebrew under the title *The Mountain of a Deer*, Rabbi Reichmann expressed a poetic, quasi-mystical yearning for Eretz Yisrael (the land of Israel) and recounted his several failed attempts to emigrate from Hungary to Palestine. "It was his lifetime's ambition to go to Jerusalem and live there," Edward observed. "But it was Heaven's will that he never did. A couple of times he was ready to go, with money in hand, and he got sick."

Zvi Reichmann's longing for the Holy Land was a common expression of religious zeal among Orthodox European Jews of his and earlier generations. Religious Zionism, in fact, had been the only Zionism until the notion of creating a Jewish state in Palestine coalesced into a political movement around the turn of the twentieth century. Many, but not all, Orthodox rabbis objected to political Zionism on theological grounds, it being a fundamental tenet of Judaism that the Messiah one day would restore the Holy Land to the Jewish people in a messianic second coming. As the Yishuv, the burgeoning Jewish settlement in Palestine, assumed a secular character, a segment of European Orthodoxy grew so vehement in its disapproval that anti-Zionism came to define them, just as opposition to Hasidism had defined an earlier generation of haredi ideologues.

Being pragmatic and resolutely apolitical folk, Samuel and Renée Reichmann's inclination had been to simply ignore Zionism and the ruckus it raised. They were neither Zionists nor anti-Zionists, and so Edward had begun his schooling in Vienna, a great hotbed of political Zionism, uninhibited by partisan parental allegiance. A precociously social and inquisitive lad, Edward befriended many boys who belonged to the city's bewildering array of Zionist youth groups (though he stopped short of joining one himself) and gained respect for the concept of militant self-reliance intrinsic to Zionism. After completing his grammar school education, Edward got a potent dose of old-fashioned religious Zionism at the Pápa yeshiva. The ties that Edward formed in these years would hold a lifetime. "For someone who is really religious, attachment to Israel comes naturally," he said. "But for me, Zionism was also nationalism."

Compared with Vienna, Tangier—indeed all of Morocco—was a Zionist backwater. During the early years of World War II, the anti-Semitic policies of the Vichy government of French Morocco suppressed what little Zionist activism there had been in Casablanca and the major cities of the Moroccan interior. But in Tangier, the Spanish imposed no such restrictions, and Edward Reichmann did his small part to fill the Zionist void in Morocco, writing to various youth groups and political parties to offer his services. Aside from shepherding the occasional visitor around the European quarter, however, there was not much for Reichmann to do to further the Zionist cause during the war years—or at least little more he would do, since he was no less offended than was his mother by the doctrinaire insistence of hardcore Zionists that their crusade for Jewish statehood should take precedence even over efforts to rescue concentration camp prisoners.

The liberation of Morocco by Allied forces in 1942–43 brought a surge in Zionist sympathies among native Jews radicalized by the persecutions of the Vichy regime. For the first time, the Zionist leaders of the Yishuv dispatched special emissaries to Morocco and the other countries of North Africa. Operating illegally for the most part, these emissaries organized emigration to Palestine while training selected youths in self-defense techniques. By 1946, branches of the Haganah, the Jewish military force in Palestine, had been organized in Morocco, Tunisia, and Algeria and placed under the command of the Haganah's European headquarters in Paris.

Edward Reichmann first made contact with the Haganah while in Paris on his honeymoon in September 1946. "It wasn't hard to do," he recalled. "I was well known in a number of synagogues and kosher restaurants in Paris." Reichmann's initial tie to the Haganah was through the Ligue Aéronautique Nesher, which operated out of an office in a basement apartment at 56 Rue de Chateaudun, not far from the tourist hotels in which the Reichmanns had lived from 1938 to 1940. Ostensibly an aviation club, Ligue Aéronautique Nesher in reality was a Haganah front (one of a number operating from the same address) created to raise funds and recruit pilots for the nascent Israeli Air Force. Shortly after this first encounter, Reichmann, who found himself frequently in Paris on his own business affairs and now Haganah matters, decided to lease a flat in the tony arrondissement XVI.

In Tangier, where Reichmann continued to spend most of his time, he helped to fashion a group of thirty to thirty-five young recruits, mostly native Jews, into a local Haganah cell. Initially, the group was headed by an operative sent down from Paris by Haganah headquarters. Reichmann soon succeeded in dislodging this outsider as Tangier chief, striking the decisive blow with a four-page, single-spaced letter to "Monsieur Paul," the head of the Haganah in Paris, in which he argued that his rival's past exploits as a forger and con man were hindering the organization in Tangier. Reichmann also laid out his ideas for improving matters in considerable detail. In reply, Monsieur Paul sent a terse cable: "Okay, do what you must."

During this period, the Paris office of the Haganah had two priorities: to procure arms for its guerrilla fighters in Palestine and to organize the evasion of the British-imposed restrictions on Jewish immigration into Palestine—a massive, complex undertaking known as Aliyah Bet. Concentrating initially on survivors stranded in the displaced persons camps of Western Europe, the organizers of Aliyah Bet in 1947 expanded their operations to include North African Jews. By this time, the desire to "make aliyah" (the literal translation from the Hebrew is "ascent") had become widespread among Moroccan Jews, the great mass of whom had been persuaded to look upon Palestine as a refuge both from their terrible, ageless poverty and the new threat of Islamic nationalism. However, French Morocco banned Jewish emigration, ostensibly to placate the sultan, who had complained insistently that departing Jews would join the Israeli army and take up arms against the Muslims of the Middle East.

The Zionist underground in Morocco organized clandestine escape routes through Casablanca, Tangier, and Oujda (an Algerian border town), then across the Mediterranean to the French port of Marseille, the major European embarkation point for Palestine. As the Tangier commander of the Haganah, Reichmann was deeply involved in Aliyah Bet in a number of ways. Among his operatives was a former American military officer who had been sent to Tangier after the war to run the local Voice of America station. Reichmann was able to use the station after hours to broadcast coded messages to colleagues on both sides of the Straits of Gibraltar. On occasion, Reichmann found himself out on the high seas at night facilitating the illegal transports in one way or another. He once sent his right-hand man, whom he had known as a boy in Beled, all the way to Marseille to pick up five hundred passports contributed by French Jews. In Tangier, the passports were doctored for use by fleeing Moroccans. "The forgeries weren't so good," Reichmann recalled. "In my mind there was no doubt that we would have been arrested the first time we tried to use them."

Trading on his mother's connections in Tetuán, Edward arranged a private audience with General José Enrique Valera, who had replaced General Luis Orgaz as high commissioner in 1945. Although Reichmann arrived in a black tie and formal smocking purchased especially for the occasion, General Valera struck a note of informality. "I know your sister," he said, and then inquired with mock incredulity as to why so beautiful a woman had to go all the way to London to find a husband. Getting down to business, Reichmann informed the general of the Haganah's plans to use the doctored French passports. "I told him that I didn't want to take people out through Tangier because I didn't want trouble with the Arabs and asked if he could embark from Ceuta." According to Reichmann, General Valera replied, "Do what you want." A few weeks later the group left for Marseille via Ceuta without incident using the shoddily forged French passports.

Reichmann did not inform his parents of his meeting with General Valera or, for that matter, of any other aspect of his covert work. "I was the only one in the family active in the Haganah," he explained. "For their own safety, I wanted my parents to ignore what I was doing. I think they were half aware of what was going on but they never mentioned it, which suggested to me that they approved to some degree. I know that they knew I was gone all night sometimes but they never said a word. If my mother thought I was with other women, she definitely would not have kept quiet."

In late 1947, the United Nations approved a plan to end the British mandate over Palestine and partition it into separate Arab and Jewish states. On May 14, 1948, the leaders of Jewish Palestine proclaimed the formation of the sovereign state of Israel, which was immediately attacked by the armed forces of Egypt, Syria, Lebanon, Jordan, and Iraq. The moment of truth had arrived for true-blue Zionists everywhere. Outmanned and underequipped on all fronts, Israel began its War of Independence a heavy underdog. Thousands of foreign Jews, predominantly Americans, answered the Jewish state's urgent call to arms. Edward Reichmann was not among them, though he did make a trip to Israel—his first—during a cease-fire. According to Reichmann's own account, which seems plausible, he had to choose between conflicting allegiances. "I was ready to go to Israel," he recalled, "but my parents were strongly against it. They wanted, above all, to keep the family together."

His Zionist zeal presumably now enflamed by Zionist guilt, the eldest Reichmann brother did what he could for the cause from the distance of Tangier. In the fall of 1948, he organized Tangier's first fund-raising appeal for the embattled Jewish state, inviting the wife of Israel's ambassador to France down from Paris for a gala reception at La Bolsa. Amid much Zionist hoopla, including a performance of Hatikva by the cadets of B'nai Akiva, the Mizrachi youth movement, Reichmann collected contributions from a hundred guests, including the estimable Isaac Salama.

Meanwhile, he continued in his capacity as an undercover operative to raise funds for the Haganah and to assist in the emigration of Moroccan Jews. With the creation of a Jewish state in Palestine, Jews were free to enter in much greater numbers. While many Europeans still required the Haganah's assistance to reach Palestine, for the most part it no longer had to be provided secretly. In Morocco, though, the French colonial authorities maintained their emigration ban even as the exodus took on added urgency with the massacre of forty-seven Jews by rioting Muslims in a pogrom in Oujda and a neighboring hamlet in June 1948.

During this same period, Reichmann created a network of Jewish informants within Tangier's banks to alert him to business transactions inimical to Israeli interests. In mid-1948, he learned that his archenemy of the blacklisting era, Emmanuel Hollander, was shipping tuna conserve to Egypt. In the name of the Haganah, Reichmann warned Hollander to desist or suffer the consequences. As had been the case in 1942, Hollander refused to defer to Reichmann, who then subjected the former blacklistee to an interview "Irgunstyle," meaning he had him roughed up. As Reichmann put it, "I caught him with a few boys." Suitably intimidated, Hollander flew to Paris to try to square himself with the Haganah and offered to surrender his profits from the tuna sales to the Haganah. The offer was accepted. From Paris, he was instructed to remit the funds directly to Reichmann, who gladly took Hollander's money but never did forgive him his transgressions. "Just before he died [in the late 1980s], the chief rabbi from Belgium came to see me and asked that I give him a letter of forgiveness for Hollander because he had never been allowed to travel to Israel. I refused to do it, even though he offered to donate to Israel a substantial amount of money."

———

In March 1949, Israel completed a resounding military victory over the Arab League forces. Jewish troops stood on the shores of the Red Sea to the south and at the foot of the Golan Heights in the north. Edward, of course, was ecstatic, but the entire Reichmann family found ample cause to celebrate Israel's triumph. Even for most strictly religious Jews, the theologically problematic aspects of a secular Jewish state faded into insignificance in light of the essential, miraculous fact of Israel's existence.

Every member of the Reichmann family would spend considerable time in Israel during its first few turbulent years. Eva and her husband grew so attached to it that they bought side-by-side burial plots in Jerusalem, both of which, tragically, would be prematurely utilized. With their parents' permission, Paul and Louis opted to visit Israel for the first time in 1950 instead of returning to Tangier from England for the high Holy Days. Paul decided to stay and attended two of the best of Israel's transplanted Lithuanian yeshivoth: Mir and Ponovezh, the latter of which today is widely considered "the Oxbridge of yeshivas." Ralph, too, would take instruction in Israel and in the mid-1950s Albert and Paul both would marry into a prominent Israeli Orthodox family of Hungarian descent, the Feldmans.

All the same, Edward remained the family's only avowed Zionist. By mid-1949, the French Moroccan authorities had legalized Jewish emigration and the Haganah faded away as many of its key members themselves made aliyah. Edward was tempted anew to join the exodus and made frequent trips to Israel with his wife, combining vacations with Zionist activities of one sort or another. He went so far as to apply for a bank charter in partnership with the ultra-Orthodox religious group Agudath Israel, which in Israel also functioned as a political party. The charter was granted but Reichmann withdrew before the bank opened its doors. "The government made a provision in the charter that said 51 percent of the shares had to belong to the party," Reichmann said. "I wanted to find a way to be in effective control of it. But it didn't work out."

While Reichmann's commercial frustrations inevitably dampened his Zionist ardor ("Israel under Ben-Gurion was a leftist country," he said; "that was not an attractive climate for Reichmanns"), he and his wife most likely still would have made aliyah if it had not been for his father's emphatic disfavor. "We both wanted to move to Israel very much," Reichmann recalled. "But my father practically begged us not to go."

Although Renée was no less desirous than Samuel of keeping her eldest son and her only two grandchildren close at hand, she was more sympathetic to Edward's longings, for as an activist by nature, she, too, felt the gravitational pull of the new Jewish state even though she never seriously considered converting, as it were, to Zionism. In the spring of 1949, Mrs. Reichmann accompanied Edward to a high-powered gathering in Paris convened to celebrate Israel's birth. A myriad of high-ranking Israeli and French officials attended, and Léon Blum, the former French prime minister, was the keynote speaker. "I was sitting with my mother in the back of the hall and we pushed our way up into the first row to hear Blum," Edward recalled. "My mother was definitely interested to meet these sort of people."

Later that year, Mr. and Mrs. Reichmann made their first trip to Israel to visit friends and tour religious sites. Their arrival was noted in the Orthodox press, for many of the surviving beneficiaries of the family's wartime relief efforts had settled in Israel and were not shy about expressing their gratitude. Indeed, by this time the Reichmanns' reputation for good works and business prowess had overflowed the narrow banks of ultra-Orthodoxy and spilled into the mainstream of Israeli society. "Somehow, the Reichmanns were considered a leading family," recalled Edward, striking a tone of modesty soon abandoned. "I personally had free access to all the prominent politicians and rabbis as early as 1949. When my parents came, they got the red-carpet treatment everywhere they went, as did many important visitors in those years."

While Samuel balked at entering the doors opened by the family's prominence, Renée happily hobnobbed with the Zionist elite. In 1952, she attended the bar mitzvah of the grandson of David Ben-Gurion, the greatest of Israel's founding fathers and its first prime minister. The following year, Yitzhak Ben-Zvi, Israel's first president, invited her to his office for a private chat. Accompanied by Albert and Paul (Samuel, as usual, declined), Mrs. Reichmann spent an hour with Ben-Zvi, who had his photographer commemorate the meeting with a group portrait. In it, Ben-Zvi is seated behind a large desk flanked on either side by the Reichmanns. In the background, a poster of the Zionist emblem and a portrait of Theodor Herzl, the father of political Zionism, loom large on the presidential wall. (Apparently, the Zionist imagery was a bit much for Paul and Albert, who, after all, did not share their older brother's Zionist allegiances. In 1957, Edward allowed a Yiddish newspaper in Montreal to publish the photograph but only after Paul and Albert were carefully cropped out.)

The Reichmanns figured tangentially in one of the major diplomatic controversies of Israel's formative years. In the spring of 1949, various Latin American nations urged the United Nations to rescind the diplomatic boycott its member nations imposed on Spain at the end of World War II. The motion fell well short of the required two-thirds vote. "What hurt Franco personally," noted one of his major biographers, "was that Israel, which had just been admitted into the United Nations, voted against the resolution," opposing it "not because the Spanish regime was undemocratic but because it had been the ally of the Nazis." Franco had hoped that his government's efforts to protect Jews menaced by the Germans would incline Israel in Spain's favor.

After its defeat in the United Nations, the Franco government loosed a propaganda barrage in which it grossly overstated its claim on Jewish gratitude, asserting that Spain had protected "all the Spanish Jews." In rallying political support, Spanish officials lobbied Tangier's Jewish community leaders, who obliged with several telegraphic testimonials. Unable to cable directly to Israel from Tangier, Joe Hassan, the community president, sent a telegram to World Jewish Congress headquarters in New York for relay to Israel. Later, in a second cable urging the World Jewish Congress to intervene on Spain's behalf in the U.N. controversy, Hassan recounted Mrs. Reichmann's achievements, without mentioning her by name.

On Halloween Day in 1950, the United Nations reconsidered the issue of Spain's diplomatic status. Israel again voted against a resolution to revoke the U.N.'s recommendation of boycott, but this time was joined by only nine other countries. The United States and thirty-six other nations voted in favor and ten abstained. Thus, the motion carried—barely—and within months, the United States and Great Britain had reopened their embassies in Madrid. Israel, however, refused to follow suit. Not until 1986—eleven years after Franco's death—would Israel establish diplomatic relations with Spain.

In 1960, the *Jewish Chronicle*, a daily newspaper widely circulated from London, published an impassioned apologia for Spain by Eva Reichmann Heller under the heading "Spanish Aid to Refugees" in its letters column. "I have witnessed many more events [other than the issuance of protective passes in Budapest in 1944] where the Spanish helped victims of Nazism, at a time when they still believed the Germans would win the war," she concluded. "Now that the Spanish Foreign Minister is visiting this country, maybe it would be possible to find a way to thank him for the sympathy, compassion, and pity his Government and fellow-countrymen felt for the innocent victims of Nazism."

This letter stirred a hornet's nest. As was its custom, the *Jewish Chronicle* published Eva's address with her letter and over the next few weeks she was deluged with dissenting opinion, not all of it politely expressed. "She took an awful lot of heat," recalled Rachel Brenick, Eva's youngest daughter. In Spain, the letter was reprinted in dozens of newspapers, prompting a flood tide of favorable mail, including a letter from the Spanish ambassador in London. "I got dozens and dozens of letters from people who said that at long last somebody thanked the Spanish," recalled Eva, who, according to her daughter, never tired of reminiscing about her wartime adventures in the politics of philanthropy.

The Reichmanns' willingness, publicly and privately, to acknowledge the vital role the Franco government played in its own rescue efforts did not win them any friends in Israeli government circles and may well have contributed to the tendency of the Zionist establishment to ignore the family's accomplishments in compiling Israel's official honor roll of Holocaust overachievers. Certainly Edward received nothing but discouragement in suggesting that Yad Vashem include J. Rives Childs, the chargé d'affaires in Tangier, among its "Righteous Gentile" honorees. (That Childs was a committed Arabist did not help.) In their own minds, the Reichmanns certainly were not apologists for a fascist dictator but witnesses to history. If their testimony did not square with Zionism's geopolitical agenda, then so be it. What had happened, happened.

Chapter 17

Through Arab eyes, postwar Tangier's chief distinction lay in being the home of Allal el Fassi, the founder of Istiqlal, the preeminent Moroccan nationalist party. Released in 1946 after nine years of imprisonment in Gabon, el Fassi returned to Morocco and established Istiqlal's new headquarters in Tangier, where, somewhat incongruously, he lived in the European quarter, not far from the Reichmanns' apartment on Rue Molière. From Tangier, Istiqlal published a weekly newspaper fiercely critical of French colonial policy and increasingly insistent on complete independence for Morocco. Although the French succeeded in pressuring the International Administration into suppressing the paper, Tangier remained "the de facto focus for Istiqlal conspiracy, and officials of the movement were regarded with some suspicion by the authorities," who occasionally arrested them.

In Morocco, in contrast to other Arab countries, the nationalist agenda was not explicitly anti-Semitic. In fact, Moroccan nationalist groups in general and Istiqlal in particular took pains to avoid antagonizing the Jewish population, which they considered a potential ally in their struggle against the French. However, the nationalist movement was too volatile and multifaceted to be controlled from an office in Tangier or anywhere else. Every city and village had its rabble-rousing fringe willing to exploit traditional Muslim contempt for the Jews, occasionally to catastrophic effect—notably the Oujda bloodbath of 1948. "In Oujda, at least," concluded a recent reexamination of the incident by an American historian, "diverse nationalist forces, Istiqlali sympathizers included, either provoked the pogroms and even helped organize them, or they escalated tensions among the Muslims."

What is more, Moroccan nationalism was hostile to foreigners virtually by definition. It was Samuel Reichmann's considered opinion that Tangier eventually would be absorbed into an independent Morocco and forcibly—perhaps violently—Islamicized. As long as his bank was prospering—and he was making more money in the early 1950s than ever before—Reichmann was disinclined to leave Tangier and its uniquely permissive financial climate. On the other hand, he wanted to ensure that whenever push finally did come to shove in Morocco, he and the rest of the family would be able to leave in a hurry for a place of prearranged, assured refuge.

In late 1950, his early-warning antennae aquiver, Samuel Reichmann visited the American Legation and applied for an immigration visa. His application was an exercise in subterfuge in that he declared an intent to reside permanently in the United States and to work as a merchant in the import-export trade. On Valentine's Day, 1951, Samuel and Renée Reichmann flew from Tangier to New York and were met at Idlewild Airport by Martin and Rufka Klein. Just two days into their supposedly permanent residency, the Reichmanns applied for permission to leave the United States for as long as six months. Mr. Reichmann's avowed purpose in returning to Tangier: "To liquidate my business." Granted a reentry permit, they returned promptly to Tangier, where they would continue to reside until 1958, though they were able to maintain their status as resident U.S. immigrants for nearly seven years by periodically renewing their reentry permit. The excuses Samuel made ranged from "business and familial" to "operation of one leg" and "attend son's wedding."

The groom in question was Louis, who in 1949 had moved to London. After five years working as his father's assistant, Louis, now twenty-seven, wanted to strike out on his own. Uninterested in a banking career and unable to see a way to make use of his candy-making training, Louis decided to learn a second trade. At his new brother-in-law's urging, and with his father's support, Louis joined his boyhood friend, Izidor Heller, as an apprentice to a well-known diamond dealer in the Hatton Garden district of London. The boys commuted by subway to Hatton Garden from the north London suburb of Golders Green, where they shared a bedroom in Lipmann and Eva Heller's apartment. Louis quite liked life in postwar London, especially after he met Marianne Fonfeder, a seventeen-year-old Hungarian survivor who had come to London to study in a Bais Yaakov girls' seminary. On the night of the festival of Purim in 1950, Marianne and several of her classmates were dispatched by the school to solicit donations from religious families in the Orthodox enclaves of north London. When the girls knocked on the Hellers' door, Eva invited them in as guests. Louis was immediately smitten with Marianne, known to her friends as "Marika." Within a few months of their first meeting, Louis and Marika Fonfeder were engaged to be married.

Fonfeder was from Békéscsaba, a sizable city in southeast Hungary near the Romanian border. Before the war, her father and uncle had owned a large textile wholesaling firm. Considered the wealthiest Jewish family in Békéscsaba, the Fonfeders occupied a vast house that spanned three corners of a city block in the very center of town. In 1943 the Hungarian fascist militia, the Nyilas, commandeered the house for its own use, forcing the family into an adjacent apartment. When the Russians liberated the city, they, too, established their headquarters in the Fonfeder residence, surrendering it grudgingly to surviving family members in late 1945. The Holocaust took an especially horrific toll on Békéscsaba, which was unusual in that the SS did not bother establishing ghettos but shipped the Jews straight to Auschwitz. After the war, only three Jewish children returned to the city: Marika, her sister, and one nonrelative.

Nathan Fonfeder, Marianne's father, had packed his three children off by train to Budapest at first word of the Nazi invasion of Hungary. Later, Mrs. Fonfeder was saved by the family doctor, who told the SS she was dying and had her sent off to Budapest in an ambulance. Mr. Fonfeder was sent to Auschwitz but was selected for labor. Marianne was hidden for six months by a Gentile family just outside Budapest and then was reunited with her mother, who gained entry to the famous Glass House, a former department store that was the largest of the many buildings under Swiss diplomatic protection. During the final weeks of the Red Army's siege of Budapest, a Nyilas patrol broke into the Glass House and marched its inhabitants—the Fonfeders included—to the Danube, where they were lined up before a firing squad. A massacre was averted at the last minute through the intervention of Swiss diplomats. "Everyone who stayed alive had a miracle story," Fonfeder recalled. "Because we were all doomed."

After the war, the Fonfeder family reassembled in Békéscsaba minus Marianne's older brother, who had been apprehended while in hiding in Budapest and murdered in Auschwitz. Nathan Fonfeder succeeded in reclaiming what remained of his property and reopened the family business. Then in 1948, the textile operation was expropriated by the local Communist authorities. At their insistence, Nathan Fonfeder continued to manage the business until 1949, when he and his family emigrated to Austria. In Vienna, he opened a new firm, Fonfeder Textiles, which did quite well. Marianne was sent off to London to continue her education, so rudely interrupted five years earlier.

Louis Reichmann and Marianne Fonfeder were married in Montreux, Switzerland, in 1951, to the delight of both sets of parents. The newlyweds would have preferred to remain in London but were unable to obtain permanent residency in England. Reluctantly, Louis returned to Tangier with his bride, who endured the ride into town from the airport in mostly silent amazement. "I remember seeing all these donkeys and the Arab women walking behind their men," Marianne recalled. "After London and Vienna, Tangier was quite a shock." Starting with a bit of capital provided by his father, Louis set himself up as a diamond vendor in association with Alex Heiden, who by now was living mainly in Antwerp, though he maintained a legal domicile in Tangier until 1958. "We weren't partners in the same firm, but we often bought together for the purpose of selling together, and we split the proceeds 50-50," said Reichmann, who estimated that his dealings with Heiden accounted for about half his business.

Although Louis was not nearly as visible in Tangier as Edward, he was more consistently held in high regard by those who did know him than was his flamboyant older brother. "Louis was the Reichmann brother I knew best," said Robert Abramovici. "He seemed more open to the non-Orthodox world than his father. He listened better than Edward and you could talk to Louis easier than you could to Paul." Operating out of his apartment on Rue Foucald, Louis was an instant success in the diamond business. "No one ever knew my size and vice versa, but I'd say that I was probably the largest dealer in Tangier, not counting Heiden, who really wasn't living in Tangier," Louis recalled. "The most vital part of the business was to know enough about the merchandise to be able to give someone exactly what he wants," Reichmann said. "I left myself ten percent profit, which in that trade is high. I was," he concluded cheerily, "very good at selling."

In 1952, Samuel and Renée finally moved out of 25 Rue Molière and into a new luxury apartment building at 71 Rue Foucalt, just a few doors down from Louis and his wife. The building was owned by Samuel Toledano, a Sorbonne-educated architect and a scion of a fabulously wealthy Sephardic family that had produced scores of great rabbis and had once owned most of the land under Boulevard Pasteur. Edward, who had hired Toledano to design the Bolsa, leased a half-floor in 71 Rue Foucalt and urged his parents to join him there. Toledano had fashioned the entire fourth floor into a vast flat that he had intended to occupy himself but rented to the Reichmanns after a foot injury left him unable to use the stairs. Samuel and Renée spent quite a bit of money furnishing their new place, which, at nine thousand square feet, was six times the size of the Rue Molière flat and even more sumptuously outfitted than the late, lamented apartment on Hafnergasse in prewar Vienna. Here, the Reichmanns would pass the mid-1950s as they had the mid-1930s: perched in an elegant aerie overlooking a bubbling volcano of political discontent.

In Tangier, the struggle for independence did not take a violent turn until March 30, 1952, when a pro-nationalist demonstration in the Medina erupted into a full-scale riot. As an Arab mob beat a Dutch tourist to death in the Socco Grande, the International Zone police opened fire, killing nine and injuring eighty. The angry mob spilled out of the Medina and rampaged through the city's European quarter, burning, looting, and stoning all foreigners in its path. The riot marked the beginning of the end of the International Zone's three decades as a playground of colonial capitalism. The flow of capital into Tangier would slow and then reverse, as secret wealth sought more politically stable havens, including that old standby, Switzerland. Although the writing was now unmistakably on the wall, the translation of nationalist slogans into government policy would be surprisingly protracted. Not until late 1959, a good three years after Morocco had gained its independence, would Tangier finally be stripped of its peculiar economic advantages.

While Samuel and his three eldest sons essentially spent their last years in Tangier making hay under a slowly dimming sun, Paul Reichmann moved to Casablanca and devoted himself to bringing religious education to the great impoverished mass of native Moroccan Jews. From 1953 to 1956, he worked without salary as the educational director of Ozar Hatorah (the Wealth of the Torah), an American-sponsored Orthodox group that administered some fifty schools throughout Morocco. From the salons of the Sorbonne-educated sons and daughters of the Sephardi elite to the mud-hut villages of rural Morocco and the miserable mellahs (Jewish quarters) of the cities, Reichmann traversed in its entirety the alien milieu of one of the Diaspora's oldest and most beleaguered communities. The work was exhausting and increasingly dangerous, but, in Paul's opinion, profoundly uplifting. "Even forty years later," he would recall in 1994, "if you ask what was my greatest achievement, I would say it wasn't anything to do with business: it was the work I did in Casablanca. Those were the most interesting years of my life."

Paul's transformation from yeshiva student to educator and social worker was no more improbable than his mother's evolution from housewife to Holocaust rescuer. Paul may have been the scholar in the family, but his Torah intellectualism was never of the ivory-tower sort. The moral weight of the example set by his mother's (and Eva's) wartime activism simply would not permit him to indulge his introversion to the point of self-absorption.

Many, if not most, Gateshead bachurim who departed from the path of scholarship became working rabbis. In the Orthodox tradition, the rabbinic title is conferred by an existing rabbi, who submits the student to an examination typically designed to test both Torah knowledge and human judgment. Those who pass receive a "semikah," which in essence is a to-whom-it-may-concern letter of endorsement. In late 1949, Reichmann decided to join a small group of Gateshead students undergoing examination by one of the leading rabbinic authorities of postwar England. After three days of sporadic testing, beginning in Gateshead and ending in London, Reichmann got his semikah, which he regarded not as a means to employment but as a trophy. He was Rabbi Reichmann now, but never would use the title and kept his semikah hidden away in a drawer. "I didn't want the complications of the title," he explained. "I never wanted to become a rabbi anyway. It was more just for fun that I took the test. The studies required for the exam were not part of the curriculum and passing the exam was irrelevant in a place like Gateshead."

By the time that Reichmann had earned his semikah, he had already enlisted in the cause of educating Moroccan Jewry. Like the Orthodox Jews of prewar Eastern Europe, albeit in their own distinctively superstitious way, the Jews of Morocco had long been marked by an intense religiosity. Although its Jewish masses were desperately poor and largely unlettered, Morocco also had produced a great many distinguished scholars and rabbinical dynasties. Maimonides, the most illustrious figure of Judaism's post-Talmudic era, even lived for a time in Fez. But as World War II ended and the flight to Palestine began, it seemed to Orthodox leaders both within Morocco and abroad that Moroccan Jewry's fate turned on a terrible irony: it had been spared the Holocaust only to face spiritual extinction in the postwar world. The overriding threat that they saw was not militant Islamicism, worrisome though it was, but rampant secularism.

Historically, the leading agent of the secularization of Moroccan Jewry was the Alliance Israélite Universelle. A Paris-based organization devoted to combating illiteracy among the Jews of North Africa, the AIU founded its first schools in Morocco in the 1860s. Over the opposition of many local rabbis, the Alliance built an efficiently run system that boosted literacy and undermined Jewish traditionalism in roughly equal measure, as an education expert with the American Jewish Joint Distribution Committee noted in the mid-1950s: "For a long time the Jews of Morocco saw in the Alliance school the only door towards progress and emancipation from the misery of the Ghetto, the solution to their problems. The discarding of religious practices as known in the Mellah was considered an integral part of the process of emancipation."

Although its schools functioned in effect as a privately funded—and intensively French—substitute for government-sponsored education, the Alliance Israélite fell far short of its implicit goal of universality. Morocco's Jewish population was dispersed among scores of remote villages, some of which contained no more than a dozen Jewish families. In 1939, for example, only 15,800 of Morocco's 56,000 school-age Jewish children were enrolled in the Alliance's forty-five schools, which in many locations had to turn additional applicants away for lack of space. In some communities, the Jewish elite took it upon themselves to organize Talmud Torah schools to provide a religious alternative to an AIU education. But the majority of children either went uneducated or attended traditional kuttahs—overcrowded, underfurnished facilities where the curriculum consisted solely of Hebrew and rote memorization of the Bible and the prayer book.

After World War II, the AIU began working with emissaries sent from Israel by the Jewish Agency to expand the traditionally minimalist Jewish component of its program, mainly by improving Hebrew instruction and by adding classes in Judaism and Jewish history. To train its own Judaic studies teachers of the future, the AIU founded a special school, the Ecole Normal Hébraïque, in a suburb of Casablanca. However, the implementation of even these modestly incremental reforms was impeded by heavy internal opposition. There were a large number of AIU teachers, "some of whom were francophiles and communists, who were determined to sabotage all efforts for increasing Hebrew education."

The ultra-Orthodox founders of Ozar Hatorah looked upon the collaboration of the AIU and the emerging state of Israel as a fearsomely unholy alliance. By bringing Torah-intensive education to Middle Eastern and North African Jews, whom they correctly identified as "the potential principal reservoir for immigration into Palestine for generations to come," Ozar Hatorah's leaders hoped to serve the cause of Judaic traditionalism in two ways: to save the Sephardim from creeping secularism while injecting godless Israel with a dose of old-fashioned piety. "In short," their manifesto proclaimed, "the problem is: Shall we succeed in providing education for these Jews with the idea that one day they will come to Palestine as a positive factor and a spiritual asset, or shall we leave them to their lot so that this Jewry will eventually come to Palestine broken in spirit and mind and dependent on the charity of others?"

———

Renée Reichmann had played a catalytic role in Ozar Hatorah's formation. In the spring of 1945, just as the war was ending, the Agudath Israel Youth Council in New York had informed her of its plans to send religious articles and food parcels to Jewish children in liberated Europe and North Africa. Asked only to forward a list of needy children under her supervision, Mrs. Reichmann responded with a remarkably trenchant six-page analysis of the spiritual state of Moroccan Jewry in which she argued that what was really needed was not prayer books, tefillin, and other religious items, but Orthodox schools of the sort that Agudas Israel had sponsored throughout Europe before the war.

Mrs. Reichmann's letter was widely circulated among ultra-Orthodox leaders in New York and helped build support for the cause of Moroccan education. In mid-1947, Rabbi Abraham Kalmanowitz, a great Torah authority who had been prominent in the leadership of Vaad Hahatzalah, spent a month touring Morocco and was at once appalled by the frightful poverty and encouraged by the stubborn religiosity of Moroccan Jewry. Upon his return, the rabbi assembled a group of wealthy Sephardic benefactors headed by Isaac Shalom, a Jew of Syrian origin who had made a fortune in New York as a manufacturer of handkerchiefs. In Casablanca, a committee of well-to-do patrons was organized and a small staff assembled. Within a few years, Ozar Hatorah had founded or assumed control of more than thirty schools in Morocco with an enrollment of nearly 5,000. Although decidedly inferior in terms of quality, Ozar Hatorah's schools resembled the Talmud Torahs the Reichmann boys had attended in Vienna in that they offered intensive Talmudic instruction coupled with a program of secular studies.

Inspired in part by the founding of Ozar Hatorah and acting in loose association with the organization, Paul Reichmann had begun tutoring young Moroccan boys in Talmud during his periodic trips back to Tangier in the late 1940s. (The Gateshead program was five months of study followed by a month's vacation.) Soon after transferring from Gateshead to Ponovezh yeshiva in B'nai Brak in 1950, Reichmann was asked to help in recruiting a group of young Moroccans to the school. In the role of Talmudic talent scout, Reichmann traveled through the bled, the vast Moroccan hinterland, for the first time.

After six months in Israel, Reichmann returned to Gateshead. "I was happy at Ponovezh. There were boys there whose knowledge was vast, and with hindsight I should have stayed," he recalled. "I just felt more at home at Gateshead. The student body there was more my kind." By this Reichmann apparently meant that Gateshead students both led less cloistered lives and were more ethnically diverse, including a large sampling of French-speaking Sephardim from North Africa and France itself. As one of the few French-speaking Ashkenazim at Gateshead, Reichmann fell in with a predominantly Sephardic crowd both at yeshiva and back home in Tangier. He was the lone Ashkenazi member of an informal salon of two dozen young, mostly Sorbonne-educated Sephardi intellectuals who met periodically in homes in Casablanca to debate religious topics. "These were people of advanced secular education just out of university who had just become interested in Jewish issues and did not have a real base of knowledge of the texts," Reichmann said. "Basically, they were trying to reconcile science with the Bible. I was there to provide the Talmudic view."

One of the central figures of this group, Moses Lasry, almost instantly became Reichmann's Sephardic soulmate and would remain his lifelong friend. The scion of an old, distinguished Sephardic family (his great-great-grandfather had been chief rabbi in Casablanca), Lasry was a brainy but confused young man struggling to reconcile the disparate aspects of his upbringing. As a boy, he had attended elite French-run private schools in Casablanca while taking instruction at home in the Talmud and Hebrew from a tutor hired by his father, who was a wealthy and deeply religious man. "I never lacked religious background," Lasry recalled. "But there was a disarray within me because of the pull of French culture." Lasry left Morocco in 1946 to complete his education in Paris, earning a degree in engineering and studying law at the Sorbonne.

In 1950, Lasry returned to Casablanca to work on his doctoral thesis and was introduced to Paul Reichmann by a mutual friend after a Shabbat service. Not quite twenty-one, Reichmann was a rail-thin six-footer with a dark, untrimmed beard who instantly captivated Lasry with his improbable blend of cheerful wit and religious and intellectual intensity. "I'd never met anyone like him," said Lasry, who, though he was a few years older than Reichmann, called him "Reb," an honorific usually afforded much older Orthodox men. "He was quite sharp in his views and his jokes but had a lot of personal charm. There was between us some kind of chemistry that had a lot to do with shared ideas and ideals. Paul was a tremendous idealist; a great fire burned within him. To me, he seemed like the prototype twentieth-century Jew—someone who was comfortable in business and society and at the same time did not give away an iota of his convictions. To some extent I modeled myself after him." Lasry paused and reflected briefly. "It's probably better to say that I valued everything he represented. Coming back from France I found myself a bit in the desert. Paul, for me, was a thing I could cling to."

By 1952, five years after he had first left home, Reichmann's own education had progressed to the point where he was ready for kollel. He passed the entrance exam for the Gateshead kollel but was told that he would not be admitted unless he promised to remain for a certain number of years. This stipulation was unusual—and offensive. "The administrators saw that I was involved with the Moroccan children and they didn't want me to come for a year and then leave," Reichmann explained. "But I didn't want to restrict myself so I refused the condition."

Reichmann again left England—for good this time—and returned to Israel, where he was admitted to the Jerusalem branch of the Mir yeshiva, the most peripatetic of the great Lithuanian academies. Mir had been Rabbi Kalmanowitz's yeshiva, and he was instrumental in moving the school to Vilna in 1940 and then to Kobe (Japan) and finally to Shanghai. After the war, the uprooted yeshiva was replanted in two locations: Brooklyn and Jerusalem. As was customary among talmidim, Reichmann chose Mir because of his admiration for its rosh yeshiva, Rabbi Chaim Leib Smulevitz, a Lithuanian famed for the brilliance of his mind.

While studying at the Mir yeshiva, Paul was introduced to Lea Feldman, the eldest daughter of a wealthy and religious family of diamond merchants that had lived in Jerusalem since fleeing Hungary in 1943. Born in the Hasidic stronghold of Satu Mare, Lea was only five when she reached Palestine and a strikingly precocious fifteen when she met her future husband. Physically mature beyond her years, Lea was exuberantly self-confident and, like her father, Moses Feldman, an accomplished lay Talmudicist, blessed with a photographic memory. "She was quite tall for her age and so knowledgeable in discussing intellectual issues that I was surprised to learn later that she was only fifteen," recalled Reichmann, who now was twenty-three himself. They saw each other frequently, accompanied always by a chaperon in the traditional way, waiting until Lea turned sixteen to announce their engagement.

In his tenth month of study at Mir, Reichmann received what he described as a "missionary" telegram from Rabbi Kalmanowitz, who fairly pleaded with him to leave yeshiva and move to Casablanca as educational director of Ozar Hatorah. "He told me that I was needed, that I must come," recalled Reichmann, who surveyed his teachers at yeshiva and found a majority in favor of answering the rabbi's call. His decision also was influenced by his friend Moses Lasry, who had become active in the leadership of Ozar Hatorah while working as an engineer for the U.S. Army Corps of Engineers, which was building a plant just outside Casablanca. Reichmann accepted the appointment by return telegram, even though he sensed a certain ambivalence on the home front. "It was expected in those days that sons would join their father in business," he said. "Later, I found a letter from my sister to my parents in which she confides her fears about my taking a job with no pay and no future: How would I ever get married and make a life for myself like this?" Although neither of his parents ever directly criticized his decision to join Ozar Hatorah, Paul knew from overhearing snatches of their conversation that they shared Eva's concerns.

In the late 1980s, Reichmann would be quoted as saying that he had "refused to go into business" because he "wanted to do something for the world." In a 1994 interview, Reichmann disavowed this statement: "Refused is not the right word. I was not antibusiness." Perhaps not, but a yeshiva student fresh from five years of musar (Jewish ethics) lectures would not have to be against business to be repulsed by the famously sleazy brand of business that was Tangier's raison d'être. In any event, Reichmann returned to Morocco determined to begin earning a living despite his lack of salary. He formed a partnership with Lasry and went into textile wholesaling, working out of a warehouse in the heart of Casablanca's commercial district owned by Lasry's father, who dabbled in textiles himself. Reichmann and Lasry dealt mainly in fibrane, a vibrantly colored, patterned cotton cloth commonly used to make apparel for Arab women. Edward Reichmann was one of Paul's principal suppliers, shipping bolts of fibrane and other fabrics from Barcelona.

When Reichmann first arrived in Casablanca the fate of Moroccan Jewry still hung precariously in the balance. Over the preceding five years, some 30,000 Jews had emigrated, mostly to Israel, but nearly 250,000 remained—75,000 in Casablanca, the largest Jewish community by a wide margin. The bled had been gradually depopulated of all but 40,000 Jews by a mass exodus to the cities, where the newcomers packed into mellahs that had been overcrowded for a century. In Marrakesh, the density per hectare reached 1,300 in the mellah, compared with 35 in the European quarter and 450 in the Medina. Conditions were even worse in Casablanca, which had seen a quintupling of its Jewish population from 1940 to 1950 alone. About four-fifths of all Moroccan Jews were totally destitute, and the "three T's"—trachoma, tuberculosis, and teigne (scurvy)—pervaded the mellahs and the bled alike.

The misery of Moroccan Jewry came as no surprise to Reichmann, but he had not realized until he reported for work in the summer of 1953 that Ozar

Hatorah had been virtually paralyzed by sectarian division. The central committee in Casablanca was polarized between nouveau riche socialites and serious patrons of educational reform, while both local camps were often at cross purposes with Ozar Hatorah headquarters in New York. The large conflict that enveloped the organization was the same one that had afflicted the Jewish rescue effort of the Holocaust era: strict Orthodox traditionalists versus nonobservant Jewish secularists.

Although Ozar Hatorah had been founded on the rock of Torah, its ideological solidity had soon fissured under its financial burdens. In 1949, the group agreed to shut down its fund-raising arm in the United States when the American Jewish Joint Distribution Committee agreed to finance a major expansion in Morocco. The money came with multiple strings attached, as the Joint Distribution Committee's director of European education bluntly noted in a confidential report: "The Office of JDC will supervise the work of Ozar Hatorah on every level including cleanliness, feeding, and education. AJDC funds will be paid out only after the standards are met."

The Joint Distribution Committee had not had to browbeat Ozar Hatorah into expanding its curriculum to include secular subjects, for Moroccan Jews themselves had emphasized their preference for balanced education. The issue was how best to meet this demand. The committee refused to provide the Orthodox group with funds to assemble its own lay staff and instead forced an accommodation with the equally reluctant Alliance Israélite, which assumed responsibility for secular instruction in most Ozar Hatorah schools. Like many marriages of convenience, this one was stormy from the start. "The AIU looks on all these [Ozar Hatorah] institutions as very temporary, of no value, and in competition with their own schools," observed Stanley Abramovitch, the Joint Distribution Committee official cast in the unhappy role of arbiter. By the spring of 1953, the flagship of the system, the Talmud Torah in Casablanca, had sunk into such disorder that the local community would have ousted Ozar Hatorah from the school had not Rabbi Kalmanowitz himself come to Morocco to negotiate a new modus operandi for the organization.

To implement the new regime, Rabbi Kalmanowitz forced a reshuffling of Ozar Hatorah's Moroccan leadership. The Joint Distribution Committee favored the choice of a professional educator for the director's job, but Kalmanowitz would not be moved: Paul Reichmann was his man. Reichmann, Lasry, and a young Sephardic rabbi named Aaron Monsoniego locked hands to form a triumvirate of Torah idealists who dominated Ozar Hatorah's daily workings through the sheer intensity of their commitment. "We were willing to take the heat," Lasry recalled. With Rabbi Monsoniego, the principal of the 1,000-student Talmud Torah in Casablanca, Reichmann overhauled the organization's religious curriculum and upgraded its teaching staff. At the same time, he traveled frequently to implement improvements in the satellite schools of Marrakesh, Meknès, Fez, and scores of smaller towns and villages. "Technically, the task was overwhelming, just getting all this done," Lasry said. "Paul's joining us made a real difference."

Ozar Hatorah added yeshiva-level classes at a number of its best schools, and Reichmann personally accompanied a group of advanced Moroccan students to England under special arrangement with the British Overseas Air Corporation. "These students had never been on a plane before and they refused to go unless they could sit on the floor," he recalled. With financial help from his parents and Isaac Shalom, Reichmann invested most of what little money he had saved to found in Tangier the first girls' seminary in Morocco. All twenty-five members of its inaugural class were graduates of French Moroccan lycées. "This school was important symbolically because the education of Jewish girls in Morocco had been so neglected," recalled Reichmann, who recruited the school's principal and its three teachers from Gateshead. He also persuaded a well-known rabbi from another English yeshiva to come to Tangier to run a new yeshiva founded by Samuel Toledano in conjunction with Ozar Hatorah.

It was not all Paul Reichmann's doing by any means, but his years with Ozar Hatorah brought a marked improvement in its performance. The tone of the Joint Distribution Committee's reports out of Morocco gradually metamorphosed from blunt skepticism about Ozar Hatorah's competence to growing exasperation with the Alliance Israélite's obstructionism. "Ozar Hatorah is now at the stage where it can begin to build better and new institutions," Abramovitch reported in late 1955. In reality, Ozar Hatorah already had reached its high-water mark in Morocco and could only watch as the institutions it helped build eroded and were swept away by the advent of an independent Islamic state and the mass exodus of the remaining Jewish population. Even so, Reichmann's certainty that his missionary efforts in Morocco were not in vain would only grow with the passing years as many of the students he sponsored ascended to positions of influence as scholars and rabbis. "Of the group that left Morocco to study in Israel and England in those years, almost all have become leaders and teachers in carrying on the Jewish tradition," he said in 1994, with evident pride.

———

The beginning of the end for Moroccan Jewry came in August 1954, as the nationalist movement marked the one-year anniversary of Sultan Muhammad V's forced exile to Madagascar by unleashing its first widespread terrorist campaign against the French. Jews were caught in the cross fire in many places, including some where Ozar Hatorah operated: Safi, Ouezzane, Ourika, Tiznit. In the worst outbreak of anti-Semitic violence since the pogrom at Oujda in 1948, seven Jews were massacred in the little town of Petitjean. There were repeated attacks on Jews in the mellah of Casablanca, causing many injuries but no fatalities. "It was generally believed that a mass attack on the Jewish quarter of Casablanca would have taken place had it not been for the protection given by the French authorities." At the same time, the frequently brutal methods that the French used against the Arab populace in suppressing guerrilla violence only broadened popular support for unconditional independence.

Among the Jews of the mellahs (though not the bled), the urge to flee Morocco had diminished steadily ever since the French Moroccan government had grudgingly re-legalized Jewish emigration in 1949. But the sudden escalation of violence in 1954 prompted a panicky stampede for the exits. Although Paul would stick it out in Casablanca until 1956, the year of independence, his oldest brother had had his fill of Morocco. Less fearful than disgusted at the turn of events, his grandiose vision of Tangier as a Moroccan New Jerusalem now in ruins, Edward was transformed from one of the city's most extravagant boosters to a prophet of doom. "There was no future for Tangier in an independent Morocco," he recalled. "I decided that it was time to sell everything I had in Tangier and I warned everyone I knew to sell, too."

Edward's exit was not a graceful one, though he did take care to arrange an orderly transition in the handling of Paul's gaberdine account, transferring it to another Jewish merchant in Barcelona. In Tangier, Reichmann & Rosenfeld hastily unloaded the parking garage on Rue de Fez and took heavy losses in liquidating its trading positions at a time of plunging commodities prices. The Real Estate and Commercial Bank was similarly afflicted, as it unloaded its major property, the office building at 16 Rue de la Croix, at a ruinous discount to cost. The building's value was undermined not only by the generally depressed market for real estate in Tangier but by the failure of its major tenant, La Bolsa Libre International, which foundered long before the riot of 1952 in its attempt to introduce public stock trading to Tangier. As early as 1950, *Fortune* magazine had described the Bolsa as "one of the quietest places in town. Boycotted by Tangier's bankers (who contend that they themselves can take care of any volume of stock trading) and cold-shouldered by the International Administration, the newly opened bourse has lived so far on a meager diet of accidental currency transactions."

By most accounts, though not his own, Edward would leave Tangier without paying all of his debts. "He is not remembered here with fondness," said Rachel Muyal, who, as proprietress of La Colonie book store on Boulevard Pasteur, functions today as the unofficial mayor of Tangier's shrunken Jewish community. When investigators hired by Edward's younger brothers arrived in Tangier in 1988 to gather information for the family's libel suit, Muyal introduced them to Harry Benchimol, an elderly relative of hers who had known the Reichmanns well. Benchimol arrived for his interview clutching a forty-year-old rubber check bearing Edward's signature. "It wasn't much, about 7,000 pesetas," Muyal said. "But Harry was so angry that he kept the check."

Again Edward considered making aliyah and again he was dissuaded, this time by his own doubts about Israel's "socialist" business climate as well as his father's unyielding opposition. Instead, Samuel gave his eldest son an assignment calculated to appeal to his sense of self-importance, which was undented by his financial troubles, while making constructive use of his daring and boundless energy. Leaving his wife and two young children in the care of his parents, Edward in late 1954 set off in search of the Reichmann family's future. "My father said, 'You are my eldest son . . . Go look in the world for another place because we may all have to leave.' So I went," Edward said, "on a world tour."

Chapter 18

H ad Edward Reichmann failed in his mission, the expedition he made to North America in late 1954 would have warranted no more than a footnote in the family history. As it was, Edward's success as pathfinder made him the pivot not only of the Reichmann family's move from the Old World to the New World but also of a shift in impetus from the older to the younger generation. Once in Canada, their life's great exertions behind them, Samuel and Renée happily left the striving to Edward and his brothers. During the Reichmanns' eventful first decade in Canada, it was the eldest brother's sheer dynamism that dominated the family agenda and powered its rise. Things would end badly for Edward in Montreal—far worse than in Tangier—doing deep, lasting damage to his psyche and opening a subtle rift in the Reichmann brotherhood that would never close. Well into the mid-1960s, though, Edward seemed the brother most likely to fulfill the exalted sense of destiny that the Reichmanns had brought with them from Tangier.

Before embarking on his transatlantic voyage in 1954, Reichmann stopped in Paris, where he picked up tourist visas for a dozen countries, including Mexico, Venezuela, Brazil, and several other Latin American nations in which European Jews had found refuge. Landing in New York City in early December, Edward checked into a hotel near Times Square and began his explorations. He visited the Klein family, of course, and was impressed by his tour of their chocolate-making factory in Brooklyn. In a generally futile attempt to drum up business, he made the rounds of the commodities traders and the export-import houses that he had dealt with from Tangier. On his first Shabbat, Edward crossed the Manhattan Bridge into Williamsburg, which was the new base of Satmar, the most Hungarian of the major Hasidic dynasties. Wedged in among some two thousand devotees in a hall in Williamsburg, Reichmann attended the Satmar Rebbe's tish, or ceremonial Shabbat meal. Elsewhere in Brooklyn, the ultra-Orthodox capital of America, he shared more intimate meals with his distant relatives, Rabbi Josef Grunwald (the Pápa Rebbe) and Rabbi Levi Grunwald (the Zelemer Rebbe), as well as with various Gestetner aunts and uncles who had resettled in Williamsburg after their sojourn in Tangier.

Although life in Brooklyn certainly met the Reichmanns' religious standards, in other ways the city—the whole country, for that matter—disconcerted the family scout. "I didn't like America," Edward said. "It was simple as that." Despite his limited English, he found the political environment unnerving, what with Senator Joseph McCarthy's anti-Communist smear campaign whipping America's Cold War paranoia into a lather. Although Reichmann was no less anti-Communist than his father, he knew from Hungarian history that leftists and Jews tend to be witch-hunted in tandem. Then, too, the simplistic us-versus-them polarity of 1950s America offended the cosmopolitanism that by this time was as much a part of the Reichmann makeup as religious parochialism. This only seemed paradoxical: after World War II, ultra-Orthodoxy by necessity was reinvented as a form of internationalism, as survivors fanned out around the world in search of safe haven. The typical extended haredi family was scattered over several continents and yet remained as close-knit as if they all still lived within a few blocks of the same little shul in der heim.

Many refugees who passed through Tangier had settled in Venezuela, and Edward knew that his father was partial to the notion of emigrating to Brazil. But the news out of South America was of strikes, riots, coups d'état. "I didn't have English, but I read the foreign papers and I could follow the headlines," Reichmann said. "I could get a feel for what was going on and I felt that South America was boiling."

So he looked north, to Canada, a country that, from a distance anyway, seemed to share the most attractive traits of its domineering neighbor to the south—notably a vibrant, largely unfettered economy and democratic governance—without the disability of Americanism. Montreal in particular appealed to him as the largest city in Quebec, Canada's only predominantly French-speaking province. "I knew least about Canada," Reichmann said, "but I was at ease in French." (Indeed, Edward soon would conclude that his French was superior—that is, closer to that spoken in France—to that of the average Quebecer.) The Reichmanns also had family in Montreal; Simon Reichmann, Samuel's brother, had moved there from Tangier a few months earlier, and both Louis and Albert had brothers-in-law who had emigrated to the city. After ten days in New York, interrupted by a long, unsatisfying weekend in Los Angeles, Edward flew north and checked into the Sheraton Hotel in downtown Montreal.

In the public library, he pored over economic statistics. Viewed from almost any angle, Canada's postwar economy offered the prospective entrepreneur vistas as inspiring as those from the peaks of the Canadian Rockies. Canada was in the midst of a truly momentous surge that would boost the value of its gross national product from $6 million in 1939 to more than $62 billion by 1967, transforming this lightly populated, geographically vast nation into the world's fourth largest industrial power. Coinciding with rapid economic growth, a sharp shift in population from country to city was under way, concentrating Canada's massive gains in wealth and in population in its two biggest cities: Montreal and Toronto.

Reichmann was no less impressed as he carried his investigation out of the stacks and into the streets of this most European of North American cities. Edward found that Montreal's blend of Old World charm and New World dynamism suited him, as did the unusual circumstances of the city's Jewish life. As a rule, newcomers to Canada felt less pressure to assimilate than did U. S. immigrants. Canadians "liked to think of their country as a mosaic rather than a melting pot," observed a leading historian of Canada's postwar era, adding that "Canadians did not press hard for immediate assimilation of immigrants and indeed seemed to welcome the infusion of European color." Toleration of ethnic diversity was especially pronounced in Quebec, where the French Canadian majority had struggled ever since Great Britain's conquest in 1759 to preserve its own distinctive culture in the face not only of English domination of Canada but the hegemony of the United States over its neighbor to the north. Especially in Montreal, Quebec's largest city, Jews were an integral part of the mosaic. At 100,000 strong, the local Jewish community was Canada's largest and most affluent.

After a week in Montreal, Reichmann decided to stay. He was so enamored of the city that he did not bother crossing into Ontario to explore Toronto. Assuming that his application for an immigration visa would be granted and that his wife and two children soon would arrive, Reichmann rented a little apartment, bought a car, and focused his energies on the problem of making a living. If anything, he progressed too rapidly: he hooked up with a couple of business partners, formed a company, and named it Olympia Trading Company—all before he had even decided what business to enter.

His new partners, Frederick and Eugene "Jack" Zimmerman, had grown up in Győr in the house directly across the street from Adolf Gestetner, Renée's father, and had chummed around with Edward and his brothers during their extended summertime stays with their maternal grandparents. The Zimmerman brothers had escaped deportation in 1944 by making their way under assumed Gentile identities to Budapest, where they hid in an underground bunker during the last months before the city's liberation by the Red Army and were kept alive in part by food delivered by Reska Gestetner, Renée's youngest sister. After the war, Jack had settled uneasily in Vienna and opened a wholesale textile business supplied in large part by Edward Reichmann from Barcelona. Fred Zimmerman had emigrated to Montreal in 1953 and Jack followed about a year later.

Olympia Trading was to be a 50-50 partnership between the two Zimmermans and Edward and Louis Reichmann, who was to join his brother at the earliest opportunity. The Zimmermans put up $75,000 and Edward matched, using funds loaned him by his father. "I know that at least some of the money came from his father because old Mr. Reichmann took us aside when he came to Montreal for a visit and said, 'Keep an eye on my money, will you?' " Jack Zimmerman recalled. "After what happened to Edward in Tangier, I guess he was a little nervous."

Deciding to set themselves up as importers, Edward and his partners obtained lists of foreign manufacturers from foreign embassies and consulates and began mailing queries overseas. Most of the first batch of letters went to Spain, the one country where Reichmann could offer local references. As he recalled, "This was a standard letter that said, 'I am in the import-export business here and if you don't have a representative in Canada, I would be glad to help. Please send samples.' " An initial decision to import plumbing fixtures from Spain foundered on the belated realization that Canadian and Spanish tastes in bathroom furnishings differed wildly. Then, mirabile dictu, ceramic tiles started arriving in the mail. That Montreal was in the midst of a suburban homebuilding boom was obvious even to the casual tourist. Yet a quick check of the yellow pages indicated that the city had but one established dealer in imported decorative tile. Olympia Trading, the first Reichmann business venture in Canada, opened its doors early in 1955 as an importer of Onda 5, Azuvi, and other brands of Spanish-made tile.

Years later the issue of who thought up the name Olympia would surface as one of the few matters of open, if indirect, disagreement among the Reichmann brothers. On the surface, the issue could not have been pettier. The name "Olympia" had no intrinsic value and what credit there was in its selection belonged to Edward, as Albert, Paul, and Ralph well knew but failed to acknowledge when Olympia & York first came to the notice of the press as a Toronto-based company. "The origin of the name 'Olympia' is in dispute even in the family," noted a *Wall Street Journal* article in 1978. "Ralph says it was meant to lend an aura of antiquity to the tile-importing business. Paul says it stems from the 1956 Olympic Games." (Why a Toronto company would have been named after an athletic event held in Melbourne, Australia, was left unexplained.) By 1982, when *Fortune* profiled the three younger Reichmann brothers at some length, the story of Olympia's genesis had taken more refined but equally preposterous form: Albert, Paul, and Ralph—the Toronto Reich-manns—supposedly "named their ventures Olympia because of Ralph's love of ancient Greek history."

As a product of the yeshiva, Ralph was steeped in ancient history but certainly not that of Greece. The fact was that Edward, by purest happenstance, had settled on the name Olympia within a few weeks of arriving in Canada while Paul and Ralph were still in Tangier. "I wanted to call the company Canadian Import Export, or North American, or something, but all the names I wanted were already taken," Edward recalled. "I was in the room at the Sheraton on Peel when the lawyer called to say all the names have been rejected." In idly examining the contents of his suitcase while conferring with his lawyer, Edward came across two new pairs of socks, still packaged. One pair carried the brand name Panther, the other Olympia. "How about Olympia?" he said impulsively, and so Olympia Trading Company was born.

The bogus explanations of Olympia's naming circulated by the Toronto brothers were smoke screens that obscured the seminal role played by Edward and Louis in the establishment of the family in Canadian business. Most reporters seemed to have assumed that there were three Reichmann brothers and were never told otherwise. Over the next two decades, Edward and Louis rarely would rate more than a mention in press coverage of Olympia & York and, in effect, were excluded from the New World chapters of the Reichmann family saga. Although Ralph would guide Olympia Floor & Wall Tile through its period of greatest growth and was primarily responsible for building it into one of the largest tile distributors in North America, the fact was that he did not found the business and did not dominate it until Edward and Louis left Canada in 1968. Over the years, though, Ralph grew quite attached to the myth of his founding of Olympia Floor and was seen as such not only by outsiders but by the company's own managers.

———

Edward's Canadian pioneering nearly ended before it had begun. Olympia Trading had just opened its doors when, in mid-February 1955, Reichmann was summoned to the local office of the Canadian Ministry of Immigration and issued an order of expulsion giving him thirty days to leave the country. There is no question that Edward had acted precipitously—even presumptuously—in renting an apartment, buying a car, and registering a corporation before obtaining official permission to stay past the time allotted under his tourist visa. Even so, the underlying fault lay not with Reichmann but with the discriminatory politics of Canadian immigration.

The live-and-let-live ambiance of Montreal was deceiving in the sense that anti-Semitism was no less prevalent in Canada than most places. While the laws of Canada did not discriminate against the country's Jewish inhabitants,

Canadian immigration policy long had been another matter altogether. With the onset of the Great Depression, Canada's door to immigrants of all kinds had closed, but it was shut most tightly to Jews. From 1933 to 1945, Canada received fewer than 5,000 Jewish immigrants. In comparison, during this period, 200,000 Jews were admitted to the United States, 175,000 to Palestine, and 75,000 to Great Britain. "Of all the western democracies, Canada had by far the worst record in providing sanctuary to Jewish refugees fleeing the scourge of Naziism." Nationwide public opinion polls taken in 1946 found that even Germans—the vanquished, hated enemy—were considered more desirable as immigrants than were Jews.

In 1948, however, with its booming economy now imperiled by labor shortages, Canada flung open the gates. By 1956, one million immigrants had entered—one-third from England and another third from Italy. While the miscellaneous remainder included thousands of Jews, the Ministry of Immigration rejected far more Jewish applicants than it accepted.

By the time that Edward Reichmann came knocking in 1955, Canada's discriminatory policies had been retooled for the Cold War. Now, no applicants were accepted from behind the Iron Curtain or Yugoslavia. In addition, all persons of "Asiatic race" were explicitly disqualified. Jews were excluded by more subtle means through the secret process known as "security screening." Although the avowed aim of security clearance was to bar Communists and Axis war criminals, Canadian authorities could use it to exclude anyone deemed undesirable without explanation. Starting in 1949, full security screening was imposed on all prospective immigrants from Israel, as well as visa applicants in Belgrade, Shanghai, and Stockholm "who are of Hebrew race." The Canadian authorities reinforced these barriers to Jewish immigration by refusing to accept visa applications in Israel and by requiring that all prospective immigrants live for two years in a country with a visa office to establish eligibility. In the mid-1950s, this so-called two-year rule was extended to the Jews of North Africa, effectively excluding them as well. Doubts that these policies were rooted in anti-Semitism "are dispelled by the language contained in immigration records," concluded *Double Standard*, a study of postwar Canadian immigration policy.

Although Edward's impulsiveness made him the Reichmann brother most prone to bureaucratic mishap, he was, like his mother and sister, a fearless improviser in dealing with government. With his expulsion order in hand, Edward jumped in his car and drove the 130 miles westward to Ottawa, the capital of Canada. On Parliament Hill he asked a uniformed guard, "Do you have a Jewish member of Parliament?" Two, came the reply: David Croll and Leon Crestohl. Edward wisely chose Crestohl, who not only represented Montreal but ever since his election in 1950 had made liberalized Jewish immigration his trademark cause. Reichmann talked his way into Crestohl's office. "I told him the situation, and showed him that I had put up $100 bail and my expulsion order. He tells me, 'Mr. Reichmann, let's go get some lunch.' I said, 'I am kosher.' He said, 'I am not, but here I am because I represent the community.' We were eating when all of a sudden he stands up and says, 'Here is the Minister of Immigration, Mr. Jack Pickersgill.' "

Pickersgill, who, like Crestohl, was a member of the Liberal Party, was a new broom in Immigration, having taken office in mid-1954. With the blessing of Prime Minister Lester Pearson, Pickersgill in 1956 would open the first major breach in the barriers against Jews by exempting a large number of North African Jews from the usual requirements. From the moment he took office, though, Pickersgill had the authority to overturn deportation orders on appeal. Indeed, ruling on such appeals was "the most exacting of all [my] duties," Pickersgill recalled in his memoirs. "I spent hours every month reading appeals and not infrequently quashed the orders."

Edward continued, "[Crestohl] said to Pickersgill, 'Here's a man with money, he has four brothers, this type of immigrant is what we need and he's here on $100 bail.' Pickersgill said, 'As you're here as a tourist it will take time to settle it, but your family can come now.' " Over the next few years, Crestohl would shepherd Samuel and Renée Reichmann and each of their remaining sons through the Ministry of Immigration's obstacle course.

Louis was the first to join Edward in Montreal, entering Canada with his wife and two-year-old son in November 1955, after a brief look around New York City. "I was happy to leave Tangier," Louis recalled. "Life there was pleasant but it was this light type of life; the atmosphere wasn't serious. I enjoyed it until I left but I didn't miss it."

To Edward's chagrin, Louis declined to fill the vacancy awaiting him at what shortly would become Olympia Floor & Wall Tile (Quebec) Limited. In his own much quieter way, Louis was nearly as resolute an individualist as Edward when it came to business. He had established himself as his own boss in Tangier and now was disinclined to tether himself to his domineering older brother. After aborting a half-hearted attempt at entering the homebuilding trade (he sold the one lot he had purchased, at a profit, without ever hammering a nail), Louis decided that importing ceramic tiles was the business for him after all. But instead of joining Edward, he decided in the fall of 1956 to leave for Toronto, where he invested $50,000—virtually his entire savings—to found a tile firm of his own. "I was discussing all the time with Edward what I was doing," said Louis, who insisted that his brother was not offended by his refusal of partnership. "He was always helpful, as I was helpful to him."

To encourage lenders and suppliers to look upon his fledgling operation as part of a larger enterprise, Louis named it Olympia Floor & Wall Tile (Ontario). Strictly speaking, though, Olympia-Ontario was wholly independent of Olympia-Quebec and 100 percent owned by Louis and his wife. Jack Zimmerman briefly considered joining Louis in the new venture but after visiting Toronto decided to stay in Montreal. "Even if Jack would have come with me," Louis said, "it would still have been an independent company."

At the same time, a third Olympia Tile was organized in New York City by Moses Lasry, Paul Reichmann's friend and former Ozar Hatorah colleague, who had immigrated from Morocco in 1955. Not long after he arrived, Lasry traveled to Montreal at Edward's invitation and took a crash course in the business of tile importing. "His generosity was remarkable," Lasry recalled. "If anything, I'm a friend of his brother's, not him, and he's not totally established himself in business and he's thinking about my future. The Zimmermans didn't want to expand into New York so Edward thought I should try it. He gave me all the information he had, including prices and the names of all his suppliers." Lasry started a tile business in 1956 and called it Olympia based on the same strength-in-numbers rationale that had prompted Louis to appropriate the name of the Montreal business. The image of solidarity was not entirely an illusion: although separately owned, the three Olympias often collaborated in purchasing. (Lasry would run Olympia–New York for twenty years, leaving the business only when all nine of his children had come of age and he could afford to devote himself fully to Torah study.)

———

Back in Morocco, France finally had conceded defeat in its long campaign to preserve its colonial privileges. In late 1955, Muhammad V triumphantly returned from exile to direct the organizing of a new government, which assumed control of French Morocco in March 1956 and then absorbed Spanish Morocco and the International Zone of Tangier at three-month intervals. Although Tangier's international administration was replaced on schedule in the fall of 1956, Morocco's new Royal Charter preserved the city's distinctive free-trade regime. Despite this surprise concession, the great majority of Tangier's European residents soon joined the mass exodus of foreigners from Morocco. The native Jewish population was equally unnerved by the advent of independence, even though Jews were granted full freedom and equality under the law for the first time in Moroccan history. The aliyah movement again went underground when the new government, which was anti-Zionist if not necessarily anti-Semitic, promptly banned emigration to Israel.

After completing a two-year term of study at a yeshiva in Israel, Ralph returned to Tangier in mid-1955 and soon decided to join his older brothers in Canada. Retracing Edward's and Louis's migratory route, he traveled to Montreal via New York. Edward offered to make room in the Quebec tile company for Ralph but as employee rather than partner—a not unreasonable offer considering his younger brother's lack of business experience. After several months in the employ of the Montreal firm, Ralph moved on to Toronto to join

Louis at the Ontario version of Olympia Floor & Wall. Still unmarried at twenty-three, Ralph moved in with Louis and his wife, who had rented a modern but exceedingly plain two-bedroom apartment on Palmerston Avenue just off Bloor Street.

Ralph soon wrote to Paul in Casablanca, urging him to come to Toronto and join him in the building materials business. Since marrying Lea Feldman in Montreux in 1955, Paul had settled down only in the metaphorical sense. He continued to spend most of his time traveling on behalf of Ozar Hatorah, accompanied now by his wife. The newlyweds had no fixed abode but lived out of a rather posh tourist hotel in Casablanca and floated from town to town as the work required. "My wife loved it and she made quite an impression everywhere we went," Paul recalled. "A woman at her level of knowledge was unheard of in Morocco." Life as an itinerant educator held its charms but was as financially as it was physically exhausting. If the newlyweds were going to start a family—and having children was virtually a requirement of religious observance among the haredim—Reichmann was going to have to get serious about making a living. A frightening outbreak of anti-French violence in Casablanca helped decide the issue. In mid-1956, Reichmann resigned from Ozar Hatorah and embarked with his wife for New York by way of London.

In London, per Ralph's suggestion, Paul called on the Expanded Metal Company, which manufactured a metal lathing used as a plaster backing, and made inquiries about North American representation at other companies that exported building materials. Unlike the brothers who preceded him, Paul also spent an extended period in New York City. "I looked at all sorts of businesses to buy," he said. He even considered partnering with Moses Lasry, who invited Paul to join him in his fledgling tile business, and then conferred with Lasry's uncle Eli, who had emigrated to New York years earlier and thrived as a manufacturer of auto parts. "I received some advice from Eli Lasry that had I followed it the problems of Olympia & York never would have happened," Reichmann ruefully recalled. "He told me that in America you shouldn't do business the way it was done in Casablanca, where the more successful a merchant was the more lines of merchandise he went into. He said that in America, the important thing is to be the best in one product and only one product."

While opportunity abounded in New York, neither Paul nor Lea took to the city itself. "Both of us were from small towns, really—Jerusalem was still a small town then and Tangier certainly was—and we found the environment rather bewildering," Reichmann said. "Today, I love it but at the time it seemed like a madhouse." Paul continued his commercial prospecting in Canada, using Montreal as a base. Edward urged his younger brother to seek his fortune in Toronto. As Jack Zimmerman recalled, "Edward always used to tell Paul, 'Toronto is the future, not Montreal, go to Toronto.'" Edward might have headed to Toronto himself had he been less of a Francophile and spoken better

English. Edward's advice was prescient: by the early 1970s, Toronto would supplant Montreal as Canada's business capital, in large part because the growing militancy of the French-Canadian nationalist movement frightened away investors.

Widely disdained as a kind of overgrown hick town, Toronto appealed to Paul because of its very dullness. It reminded him of "a quiet little English town, not unlike Birmingham." In the spring of 1957 he and his wife joined Louis and Ralph in the apartment on Palmerston Avenue, taking family togetherness to a claustrophobic extreme. Paul incorporated as a salesman of imported metal lathing, representing Expanded Metal Company among other vendors. He, too, used the name Olympia—Olympia Steel Products—though his operation was not formally affiliated with either tile company.

Within a few months of Paul's arrival, Louis Reichmann decided to return to Montreal. He sold Olympia Floor & Wall Tile at cost to Ralph and Paul, who merged Olympia Steel into the tile business. "The sale was more for family considerations than anything else—to give Paul and Ralph a base of their own," Louis recalled. To be sure, Louis's magnanimity was mixed with self-interest; after a year spent scrambling to gain his entrepreneurial footing, he was ready to concede that the Montreal tile business was a better business than his own. In belatedly accepting Edward's offer to join him as an equal partner in Olympia-Quebec, Louis in effect opted to invest in the Montreal-dominated present rather than the prospect of a Toronto-ascendant future.

From the distance of Tangier, Samuel Reichmann blessed this reshuffling of fraternal interests with cash, lending Paul and Ralph $20,000. The brothers each put in another $10,000, boosting their initial equity capital to $40,000. "In my father's mind that $20,000 was probably a gift," Paul said. "But we always intended to pay it back, and we did." In addition, Samuel bought a vacant lot and financed the construction of a new warehouse for Olympia Floor at a cost of about $86,000, all but $4,000 of it covered under mortgage.

By the time the new Toronto warehouse was completed in mid-1958, Samuel and Renée had finally pulled out of Tangier and settled in Brooklyn, where they lived with Renée's sister, Olga, and her husband. Olga had remarried in Tangier. But the elder Reichmanns liked New York no better than had their sons and in February 1959 entered Canada as landed immigrants. They settled first in Montreal, renting a flat within a few blocks of both Edward and Louis in Outremont. By mid-1959, Samuel and Renée had decided to join their younger sons in Toronto.

Samuel put off all business decisions until his commercial alter ego, Albert, could close down the Banque Samuel Reichmann and join him in Toronto, completing the family tableau. In October 1959, King Muhammad abruptly gave notice of his intention to revoke the royal charter under which Tangier's free foreign exchange market had been maintained since independence in

1956. A final panic ensued. Hundreds of Tangier corporations were dissolved and most of the city's remaining banks pulled out, taking their deposits with them. Tangier's two premier merchant banks, both Jewish-owned—Pariente and Hassan—relocated to Geneva. Transferring the Banque Samuel Reichmann to Canada was impossible, given Canada's restrictive banking laws. So Albert simply liquidated his father's bank and transferred its assets to Switzerland. Within a few weeks, Tangier had been financially denuded. "One motive for the abrogation of the charter had been to stop the leaking of capital out of Tangier: but now there was none to leak. The free money market drain had been plugged after the bath water had run out." Albert and his wife, Egosah, were among the last foreign-born Jews to leave Tangier.

PART III

A CANADIAN TALE OF TWO CITIES

Chapter 19

For more than a decade, from the mid-1950s until the late 1960s, the Reichmann saga would be a Canadian version of *A Tale of Two Cities*, with Montreal and Toronto taking the place of Paris and London. Although geographically divided, the family remained tight-knit by any standard. Rare was the month that a family member or two did not make the trip between Montreal and Toronto, usually by train. Although the Toronto contingent of the family was more numerous, it did most of the traveling. On Pesach, Rosh Hashanah, Yom Kippur, Hanukkah, and the other major festivals, the entire family gathered at Edward and Edith's home. "For holidays," Edward proudly recalled, "Montreal was the address."

Although Edward's fraternal preeminence reflected his status as eldest son, it was equally a function of his superior standing within the Jewish community of Canada. By 1963, Edward would be honored by Agudath Israel as "central lay figure in orthodox Jewish life in Montreal," and two years later he was the only family member (other than his wife) included in a one-time edition of *Who's Who in Canadian Jewry*. In the expansiveness of his public involvements in Montreal—though not their import certainly—Edward surpassed even his mother's activism in Tangier. Ranging far beyond the narrow confines of Orthodoxy, he involved himself broadly in communal affairs as well as in electoral politics at every level—municipal, provincial, and federal. "If I'd stayed in Canada," Reichmann said, "I probably would have run for office myself."

Such a pronouncement would be unthinkable coming from any other member of the family. The sheer scale of their wealth and commercial ambition eventually would force Albert and Paul into public prominence, but the Toronto Reichmanns' innate insularity was plainly evident during their first years in Canada. As Mr. and Mrs. Samuel Reichmann and their three youngest sons were taking their place as inconspicuously as possible within the ultra-Orthodox fringe of Toronto's Jewish community, the eldest Reichmann brother was descending on Montreal with all the subtlety of a boulder dropped into a pond from twenty thousand feet. Later, Edward would affect nonchalance about his prominence in Montreal. "Somehow from the first day I was known and liked," he said in 1994. "It wasn't that I was a name-dropper because I didn't have names to drop. People say the community was so open. But perhaps it was me that was open. Wherever I went in the world, I always found my place. It wasn't a big deal; it was easy."

Although Reichmann did indeed possess an innate charisma that smoothed his ascent, he worked Montreal the way a politician works a banquet hall. During his dozen years there, he attended countless fund-raisers, committee meetings, hearings, planning sessions, and receptions, as well as breakfasts, lunches, and dinners (at which, in observance of the requirements of kashrut, he usually went hungry). "Edward had this insatiable need to be thought of as a nice guy and an important person," recalled Sheldon Merling, a Montreal notary who assisted him in dozens of business transactions. "If he had his choice of receiving a complimentary letter from the prime minister of Canada or the mayor of Montreal or making $100,000 on a business deal, he'd take the letter every time."

In effect, the eldest Reichmann brother launched his campaign for public recognition on his third day in Montreal in dropping by the local Young Israel synagogue, which, as a Modern Orthodox congregation, offended the Reichmanns' standards of observance in ways too numerous to mention. After the Sunday morning services, Edward introduced himself to the rabbi, who invited him to stay for the weekly breakfast and then asked him to address the gathering. By his own admission, Reichmann was a plodding public speaker, and this was a predominantly English-speaking crowd. But he got up anyway and told tales of exotic Tangier in Yiddish mixed with French to a largely uncomprehending audience of several hundred. Although he knew he did not go over particularly well, Reichmann left with a feeling of accomplishment. "They might not have been able to understand me," he recalled, "but already hundreds of people in Montreal knew who I was."

The very next morning Reichmann impulsively decided to introduce himself to the richest and most influential Jew in Canada, if not North America: Samuel Bronfman, the crotchety lord and absolute ruler of the distilling giant Seagram Company, which had its head office in a mock granite castle directly across the street from Reichmann's hotel. With no aim other than to shake the hand of "Mr. Sam," Reichmann charmed and blustered his way onto Seagram's executive floor and into the presence of Edgar Bronfman, one of Mr. Sam's two sons and heirs, who fobbed the interloper off on the marketing manager responsible for Morocco. Reichmann's impromptu visit to Seagram's was astoundingly presumptuous and yet prescient in a way, for by the early 1980s the Reichmann family would generally be considered to have surpassed the Bronfmans as Canada's preeminent Jewish dynasty, snatching away its title as "the Rothschilds of the New World."

———

At the time that the Reichmanns were regrouping in Canada, the prevailing view among North American Jews was that the family's traditionalist brand of strict Orthodoxy was anachronistic and had no future on the most modern of continents. In writing about the ascendancy of Conservatism in 1955, the scholar Marshall Sklare pronounced Orthodoxy in America as nothing more than "a case study of institutional decay." On the surface, certainly, Orthodoxy's opponents had every reason to gloat. Ever since the turn of the century, second- and third-generation North American Jews had almost reflexively left the Orthodox shuls of their parents for Conservative and Reform congregations. The mass suburban exodus that followed World War II added a powerful new impetus to acculturation: for the first time, Jews en masse were leaving the old immigrant enclaves and starting anew in mixed neighborhoods. "From then on," noted historian Howard Sachar, "Jewish religious and cultural relations no longer were a matter simply of environmental osmosis. To maintain even the most casual Jewish identity, the new suburbanites were obliged much more actively to seek out institutional associations." The overwhelming majority of the new synagogues and other institutions organized in the 1950s and 1960s to meet burgeoning suburban demand throughout North America were non-haredi.

As it turned out, the forecasters had got it exactly wrong: instead of expiring on cue, strict Orthodoxy quietly but inexorably gained strength to emerge in the 1970s and 1980s as the new eight-hundred-pound gorilla of North American Judaism. By 1972, even Marshall Sklare was prepared to eat his errant words of prophecy. "Unaccountably, Orthodoxy has refused to assume the role of invalid," he observed in an "augmented" edition of his *Conservative Judaism.* "Rather, it has transformed itself into a growing force in American Jewish life."

In retrospect, it was apparent that Conservative Judaism's rapid postwar gains in popularity had obscured the less dramatic beginnings of a more enduring countertrend. In the middle decades of this century, at least 300,000 European Jews emigrated to the United States and Canada. Although only a minority of these newcomers, perhaps 10 percent, were strictly observant, their religious identities had been tempered into steel by the ordeals of the Holocaust era. It was not so much that they landed on these shores determined to hold on to their traditional ways as that they were incapable even of considering the alternatives. After all that they had been through, to compromise the strict Orthodoxy that had sustained them would have been the basest form of self-betrayal. And so, in contradistinction to all the preceding waves of Orthodox immigrants, this latest group wanted nothing more than to be left alone.

By the time the Reichmanns left Tangier, the reseeding of strict Orthodoxy was well under way in North America, though its first flowerings were still too modest to have attracted the notice of the Jewish community at large. Montreal, the separatist capital of Canada, was exceptional among North American cities in that traditional Orthodoxy never ceded much ground to the Conservative movement. But in Toronto, Orthodoxy not only had faded according to form but its reemergence had been retarded by the federal policies that prevented large-scale Jewish immigration until the 1950s. The Reichmanns arrived to find a multidenominational landscape lightly dusted with recently founded, makeshift Orthodox prayerhouses and day schools. Over time, the family's money and initiative would prove a crucial catalyst in the coalescence of these isolated and impoverished pockets of immigrant settlement into one of North America's most vibrant haredi communities.

———

The apartment that Ralph and Paul inherited from Louis on Palmerston Avenue was just a few blocks from the intersection of Spadina Avenue and College Street, which marked the heart of Toronto's Jewish quarter. Although Spadina Avenue's golden age was long over by the time the Reichmanns arrived, the district was still home to a half-dozen Orthodox prayerhouses. The one the brothers preferred was Schlome Emune Israel, which had been founded in the early 1950s by Rabbi Meyer Grunwald, a grandson of the rabbi who'd taught Renée Reichmann's father in Huzst. Schlome Emune's congregation was Hungarian and passionately Hasidic. Known as the Teytsher Rebbe, Rabbi Grunwald commanded a small but fervent following; many of his Hasidim had moved to Toronto only to be with him.

Samuel and Renée settled two miles due north of the Palmerston apartment in the more affluent district of Cedarvale, paying $31,000—all cash—to buy a modest, two-story brick house near a pleasant creek. In effect, the elder Reichmanns had leapfrogged their sons into Toronto Jewry's area of third settlement—the so-called Bathurst Street corridor. By the mid-1970s, the great majority of Toronto's 135,000 Jews would live within a twelve-block strip of territory bisected by Bathurst Street and extending northward from St. Clair Avenue for a half-dozen miles into the distant reaches of suburbia. Samuel and Renée Reichmann's new place (37 Heathdale Road) lay at the beginning of the corridor, as did the house that Albert bought (for $38,500) at 29 Glen Cedar Road. Samuel and Albert davened at the most staunchly traditional synagogue in the Cedarvale area, Talmud Torah Ets Chaim, even though it was predominantly Polish and not completely to their liking. By 1961, both Paul and Ralph had left Palmerston Avenue behind and rented flats within walking distance of Albert and their parents. Paul and his wife lived in a third-floor walk-up right on busy Bathurst.

In classic haredi fashion, in these early years in Toronto family members had virtually no contact with nonbelievers away from business. The Reichmanns were unusual in also keeping a certain distance from other haredim; they were a family apart within a people apart. This always was a matter of choice, not necessity. Among the two hundred or so ultra-Orthodox families that had settled in Toronto by the late 1950s were dozens of people the Reichmanns knew from Hungary or from the various stops along their exiles' path. And the Reichmanns were even more widely known than they were well connected, for their reputation for good works had preceded them to Canada. Although the Toronto Reichmanns were active in the religious life of their new community, they were disinclined to mix socially, except on their own terms.

The Reichmanns were too considerate to qualify as snobs in any conventional sense. The fact was that aside from the basic bonds of ethnicity and religious belief they had little in common with the mass of their fellow Orthodox immigrants, being neither impoverished nor Hasidic. Although their fundamentalist beliefs and spotty secular education marked the Reichmanns as parochials in the eyes of society at large, in some ways they were sophisticates. A man of considerable means since his youth, Samuel arrived in Canada as a full-fledged master of foreign currency markets and the discreet arts of international banking. And how many Canadian housewives had mastered the diplomatic subtleties of maneuvering a fascist government to noble ends?

But what definitively set the Reichmanns apart from their coreligionists was their abiding sense of being a family of elect destiny and of the requirements of dynasty that flowed from it. No matter how busy the brothers were at the office—and they adhered to a grueling schedule right from the start—Albert, Paul, and Ralph each were expected to drop by their parents' house every evening for a few hours of discussion of family and business matters. This custom would be strictly enforced until Mrs. Reichmann's death in 1990. Attendance at weddings, bar mitzvahs, and other family events was no less mandatory. "If there was a bar mitzvah or something in Israel and I didn't feel like going, my mother would call up and say, 'What do you mean you won't go?' " Paul recalled. "I simply could not afford not to be at a family affair, no matter what else I was doing. If my mother told me, 'Be there,' I'd be there. I had no choice."

The demands of dynasty would expand exponentially as the three Reichmann brothers began producing children of their own. Paul's first child, Vivian, was born in 1957 and would be followed over the next fifteen years by two girls—Rachel and Libby—and two boys—Barry and Henry. Albert also would father five children on roughly the same schedule, as would Ralph at a few years' remove. In Montreal, meanwhile, Louis would fall one short of the unofficial quota of five, fathering two sons and a daughter in addition to the son born in Tangier. Eva alone would equal her parents' output, giving birth in London to six children. Edward turned out to be the least prolific Reichmann of his generation; the two children that he had fathered in Tangier were his last.

Amid the placidity of Canada, Renée Reichmann, the matriarch of dynasty, was free to focus more narrowly on family affairs than at any time since the years preceding World War II. Despite the distance that separated Toronto from London, home of Lipmann and Eva Heller, and Montreal, Mrs. Reichmann would oversee the raising of all twenty-seven grandchildren with a relentless and opinionated attentiveness that was not always appreciated by her daughters-in-law, who were strong women in their own right, especially Paul's wife. ("At first, Lea and my mother did not get along so well," Paul conceded in a 1994 interview. "Because of her experience with my mother, Lea now does not tell any of our married children what to do.") Resistance was futile on the part of daughters-in-law and sons alike, given Mrs. Reichmann's overarching authority as enforcer of family unity.

Every Saturday at noon for three decades, the Toronto brothers and their wives and children, as well as numerous Hellers and Gestetners, would convene at Samuel and Renée's home to commemorate the final hours of Shabbat. These gatherings were informal and even tended toward raucousness as grandchildren begat great-grandchildren and the house was filled to overflowing. Nor was there an air of exclusivity to these affairs; invariably, a smattering of nonrelatives attended as guests. The more the merrier. On the other hand, the Reichmanns recognized no social obligation of reciprocity. The dictates of Reichmann family togetherness meant that they were almost always hosts on Shabbat, rarely guests.

———

When Edward Reichmann arrived in Montreal, the city's Jewish community consisted of a large mass of impoverished downtowners—mainly Orthodox immigrants, who were scattered along the length of St. Lawrence Boulevard, which was known as "the Main"—and an uptown elite that dwelled amid the wooded splendor of Mount Royal. Near its summit, in the town of Westmount, lived a Jewish patricianate of some fifty wealthy, long-established families. Sam Bronfman had moved to Westmount in 1928, occupying a huge mansion stuffed with servants, but, as a self-made multimillionaire, was regarded by the crème de la crème as a parvenu. Like the Bronfmans, the bulk of the old families had for nearly a century belonged to Shaar Hashomyin Congregation, which, though nominally Orthodox, was in fact a bastion of acculturation. Even so, a majority of the city's Jews had remained Orthodox in practice as well as name. In Montreal even the secular Jews "cultivated a rich folk culture and a powerful communal sense, based upon language, ideology and a memory of the past."

In choosing to settle in Outremont, a mostly middle-class enclave a few miles north of the downtown core, Edward staked out the middle ground between Westmount and the Main, both geographically and socioeconomically. (Louis and his wife also settled in Outremont, renting an apartment just two blocks from Edward and Edith's.) In terms of its Judaism, though, there was nothing middling about Outremont, whose few square miles were studded with a dozen small, intensely observant Orthodox congregations. After making the rounds, Edward decided to affiliate with the congregation with the deepest Hungarian roots: First Mesifta of Canada. Louis, too, joined First Mesifta, as did Fred and Jack Zimmerman.

First Mesifta had been founded in 1948 to minister to a few dozen Orthodox Hungarian orphans who had been admitted to Canada under a special government program. The boys attracted the sponsorship of Rabbi Jekutiel Judah Halberstam, the Klausenberg Rebbe. Before the war, Rabbi Halberstam led the Hasidic community of Cluj ("Klausenberg" in German), a major city in Romania, not far from the present-day border with Hungary. The bulk of the Klausenberg community—including the rabbi's wife and ten of his eleven children—were killed in Auschwitz, but Rabbi Halberstam survived to earn the nickname "the Wonder Rabbi" in honor of his herculean efforts to minister to Orthodox survivors in the displaced persons camps of Germany. Such was his renown that General Dwight Eisenhower asked to meet him during an inspection of Friedenwald and put an airplane at his disposal to fetch special items from Italy needed for proper observance of Sukkoth.

In 1947, the Klausenberg Rebbe had settled in Brooklyn, where he reestablished his Hasidic court and founded both a large synagogue and a yeshiva. First Mesifta began as the Montreal branch of the yeshiva. Rabbi Halberstam himself came to Montreal in 1948 to raise the funds needed to launch First Mesifta and to install one of his most promising disciples, Alexander Unsdorfer, as rabbi of the new congregation. Rabbi Unsdorfer, who was still in his thirties, was a pure product of the Oberland, born in Bratislava and trained in the famed yeshivas of his hometown and of Nitra.

By the time that Edward Reichmann joined the fold, First Mesifta had grown to two hundred members but remained financially precarious. "Edward revolutionized First Mesifta with his money and his energy," recalled Emile Rooz, one of those young orphans whose arrival in Montreal had prompted the formation of the congregation. Edward immediately became First Mesifta's biggest donor, single-handedly financing a remodeling of its synagogue. When the president of the congregation died in 1956, Reichmann was chosen to replace him. As president, "Reichmann was involved with First Mesifta almost as if it were his own business," said Rabbi Josef Unsdorfer, Rabbi Alex's son and successor at First

Mesifta. "He would sit in the office with my father hour after hour. There was no time day or night when my father couldn't get in touch with him."

Louis was named treasurer of First Mesifta and every member of the family was involved with the congregation to some extent. Each year, Mr. and Mrs. Reichmann and a son or two would come from Toronto for the First Mesifta annual dinner, at which Edward, as president, customarily held forth at great length on the state of the congregation and whatever else was on his mind. "Edward is not such a great speaker, you know, but after he finished his mother would be beaming from ear to ear," recalled Pearl Zimmerman, Jack's wife. "He was always her favorite. She adored Edward—just adored him!"

On his periodic visits to Montreal, the Klausenberg Rebbe invariably did Edward the honor of staying with him in his home, enhancing his status beyond that inherent in the office of president. At the same time, Reichmann's bond to the Klausenberg Rebbe had the effect of intensifying his own affinity for Israel. The Rebbe constantly spoke of the miracle of Israel's birth and urged his followers to settle there, predicting that "an influx of Orthodox Jews would transform the state into a veritable wall of fire which would render it indestructible." On his first visit to Israel in 1954, Rabbi Halberstam bought a large tract of land on the outskirts of Netayanah with the aim of founding an Orthodox community. Construction of Kiryat Sanz began in 1957. The Rebbe arrived a year later with the first fifty settlers.

Edward never did travel to Kiryat Sanz as part of the Klausenberg Rebbe's entourage, but he did meet him there several times on his own travels. As much as Reichmann admired the Rebbe, he never considered moving to Kiryat Sanz. "I didn't think of him as 'The Wonder Rabbi' or any of that," Reichmann said. "To me, the Klausenberg Rebbe was an enormous-caliber person and one of the most powerful speakers I ever heard."

Although First Mesifta commanded Edward's principal loyalties, he covered all the ultra-Orthodox bases in Montreal, binding himself by contributions of money and effort to numerous Torah institutions, including the Hasidic yeshivas of the Satmar, Lubavitch, and Belz sects, as well as the main Lithuanian-style yeshiva, Merkaz Hatorah. "There were a dozen congregations like First Mesifta and Edward was in the middle of everything," said Rooz, who quickly became one of his closest friends. "The whole Orthodox community looked to him." It came as no surprise when Agudath Israel, the most important ultra-Orthodox umbrella group in North America, named Reichmann president of its Montreal chapter.

As a prominent Orthodox lay leader, Reichmann established a close if occasionally contentious relationship with Rabbi Pinhas Hirschprung, who was regarded by acclamation as the chief Orthodox rabbi of Montreal. Blessed with a photographic memory, the Polish-born Rabbi Hirschprung had been one of the great Talmudic prodigies of prewar Europe. It was said that he could identify the page number and content of any tractate of the Talmud from its last few lines. Reichmann often accompanied Rabbi Hirschprung to the airport to meet the Klausenberg Rebbe, the Satmar Rebbe, and other visiting Orthodox dignitaries. By his own description, Reichmann's role as rabbinical greeter was a reflection not of his stature in the community but of his usefulness as a string-puller. Through Leon Crestohl, the member of Parliament (MP) who had intervened with the immigration authorities on the Reichmann family's behalf, Reichmann arranged it so that the rabbis were whisked through customs without having to wait in line.

Reichmann's sharpest clash with Rabbi Hirschprung came over the issue of segregation in the Bais Yaakov elementary school that his daughter Malkie attended in Outremont. Reichmann belonged to the board of the school, which, though classically Orthodox in its orientation, attracted students from many segments of the community and thus inevitably was a battleground for factional politics. At one point, the board's Zionist leaders advocated renaming the school, since the Bais Yaakov network had been closely associated with Agudath Israel in prewar Europe. Reichmann vehemently opposed any name change and also objected to a proposal that would have diluted the use of Hebrew by adding classes in English. And he was outraged when Hasidic leaders proposed that the Hasidic girls be sent off in the afternoons for separate religious instruction. When Reichmann discovered one night that Rabbi Hirschprung had thrown his support to the proponents of this plan, he drove to the rabbi's house, arriving after midnight. Rabbi Hirschprung appeared at an upstairs window in his pajamas and asked that Reichmann return in the morning. Reichmann refused and was granted an audience. "I told him that as a board member I would not tolerate this and that there would be a revolt among the leadership when they found out." The next day Rabbi Hirschprung retracted his support for the plan.

Despite his many institutional affiliations, Edward's brand of philanthropy was highly personal in the classic manner. During his years in Montreal, he supplied funds to hundreds of people, mostly fellow haredim. "Almost every night people were coming by the house to ask for money or for advice in business," Rooz said. "Edward had to be the boss in everything but he was always the most approachable [of the Reichmanns]. You didn't have to swallow your pride to ask his help." Indeed, in some cases they did not even have to ask. Not long after he had moved to Montreal, Reichmann happened to ride in the same dilapidated taxicab twice within a few weeks. He recognized the driver, Jacob Gross, from First Mesifta and asked him about how he was faring in the taxi business. Not so good, responded Gross, an immigrant and Holocaust survivor. The next time he rode with Gross, Reichmann loaned him $4,000 (interest free, as the Talmud requires) to buy a new cab. Gross repaid the loan in full from his expanded income.

Nor did Reichmann limit his largesse to the needy or, for that matter, to his ultra-Orthodox brethren. When his favorite notary, Sheldon Merling, built a new house, he made a gift of several thousand dollars' worth of decorative tile from Olympia Floor's warehouse. Merling, who is Jewish but not observant, was stunned. "He didn't do it to win me over because he knew that I already thought he was a nice guy," he recalled. "To him, this was how you treated your friends."

While the eldest Reichmann brother's overriding commitment was to ultra-Orthodoxy, he also established ties to other segments of the Jewish community of Montreal. His lifelong dalliance with Zionism continued, though, as before, he stopped short of actually joining any organization. However, when *Der Kanader Adler* (the Canadian Eagle), Montreal's main Yiddish newspaper and a bastion of Zionism, celebrated its fiftieth anniversary in 1957, Edward paid homage to the local Zionist leadership and tooted his own horn by buying a fat strip of space in the Golden Jubilee Edition. In a "letter to the publisher," he congratulated the publisher of *Der Kanader Adler* on behalf of the entire Reichmann family and illustrated his testimonial with three photographs: one of himself in suit, tie and gigantic smile; a second of Samuel looking grim in a passport photo; and finally Renée standing next to a seated Yitzhak Ben-Zvi, the president of Israel, and in front of a framed portrait of Theodor Herzl and an artist's rendering of the Zionist emblem. Beneath Edward's testimonial ran a laudatory article on the Reichmanns written by an anonymous contributor:

> The Jewish Community of Montreal has gained a new star in the last two years, Mr. Edward Reichmann. He has become very popular in the circles in which he is active. He is a son of a famous Jewish family that already filled a glorious chapter in Jewish history in pre-war Hungary and Vienna. . . . In the Reichmanns, Montreal has acquired a very positive addition, which will contribute greatly to the religious and cultural life of our community. We have few such families.

In buying space in *Der Kanader Adler,* Reichmann also was repaying his debt of gratitude to the Jewish member of Parliament who had helped him and other family members enter Canada, for Leon Crestohl was the son-in-law of the newspaper's founder. (Edward also directed the lion's share of his legal business to Crestohl's law practice.) Crestohl represented a contorted slice of the Main that had been gerrymandered into existence to ensure Canada's Jews at least one seat in Parliament. However, by the time that Crestohl first won election in 1950, Jewish predominance in the district had been eroded by Italians, Greeks, and other newcomers, and by 1956 its Jewish population had fallen to about 50 percent and was on its way to 30 percent. Crestohl endeavored to multinationalize his appeal; his campaign flyers came in eight languages: English, French, Hebrew, Italian, Greek, Polish, Hungarian, and Hebrew.

Like most Canadian Jews, Crestohl was a Liberal, which made him a bit leftist for a Reichmann's taste. In Edward's view, though, this drawback was overwhelmed by the advantage of having his own lawyer in Parliament and by the MP's stout championing of such nominally Jewish causes as liberalized immigration. That Crestohl, the quasi-observant son of an Orthodox rabbi, seemed well attuned to the needs of religious Jews only enhanced his appeal to Reichmann, who gladly contributed his money and his name to the MP's 1957 reelection campaign. In his capacity as president of First Mesifta, Edward was one of a half-dozen Orthodox leaders whose support was cited in a Crestohl flyer aimed at religious Jews. When Crestohl ran again in 1958, Reichmann's role expanded to include making stump speeches in French and Yiddish. In a subsequent campaign, Crestohl included a photo of himself and a smiling, bushy-bearded Samuel Reichmann in a flyer that also included shots of the MP posing with various Liberal Party dignitaries and with Eleanor Roosevelt, who was described as "the world's most beloved humanitarian."

"I became a great friend of Leon Crestohl," Reichmann has said, though Sophie Crestohl, the MP's widow, insisted in a 1992 interview that her late husband saw Reichmann as his law client and political supporter and not much more. "So Edward Reichmann was supposed to be Leon's good friend?" Mrs. Crestohl scoffed. "I can tell you this: I never met the man and he never once came to our house."

Mrs. Crestohl recalled speaking to Reichmann only once in a routine phone call that was indelibly stamped into her memory by a bizarre chance encounter that soon followed. Mrs. Crestohl was vacationing in Barcelona with a friend from Montreal when she decided to make contact with the local Jewish community. She looked up a Cohen and a Levy in the phone book but both men hung up on her. She then approached the porter at her hotel and asked, "Is there a Jewish church here?" The porter gave her a stricken look and whispered, "We have a Jewish night clerk. Ask him." That evening Mrs. Crestohl discomfited the night clerk with the same question. "Finally, he gave me a name—Grebler," Mrs. Crestohl recalled. "First the wife came on the phone, then the son, finally the father. [This was Henry Grebler, the brother of Albert.] We made an appointment to see him and the next day he showed the two of us around. Finally, he says to me, 'Since you are from Montreal, would you know a family named Reichmann?' I told him that two weeks earlier a Mr. Edward Reichmann had called my husband. He smiled and said, 'I'm glad to hear it because he owes me some money.' "

A few weeks after Mrs. Crestohl returned home from her vacation, Henry Grebler telephoned the Crestohl home from his room at the Windsor Hotel in downtown Montreal. "I went with my son to pick him up," Mrs. Crestohl continued. "This man gave me a gift, which I refused, of course. He came all the way to Montreal to get his money. My husband drew up a contract with him on Reichmann's behalf and settled the matter. The whole thing was very embarrassing."

In 1963, as Crestohl's latest reelection bid neared culmination, the MP would suffer a fatal heart attack at his home in Mount Royal. With the election only ten days off, the Liberal Party turned in desperation to Crestohl's widow and then to his son, neither of whom wanted to run. By this time, Reichmann had begun toying with the idea of running for office but wisely resisted the temptation to put his name forward. Eventually, the party bosses emerged from their back room to announce the surprising selection of Milton Klein as Crestohl's replacement. Klein, the son of a wealthy merchant, was a self-employed Montreal lawyer and Orthodox activist of no great prominence or political experience. He won by a narrow margin. "It was chaos," Klein recalled thirty years later. "The fact that I was elected was unbelievable."

Interviewed in 1992, Klein, who had left Parliament but was still working as a lawyer at age eighty-four, said he could not recall Reichmann playing a role either in his selection as a candidate or in the frenetic campaign that followed. "I think I only met him after the election," he hazarded.

When informed of Klein's comment, Reichmann did a slow burn and finally said, "I never said this to anyone before but the fact is that I made Milton Klein. I was one of the people who was asked to investigate who should run. Klein was a guy from a wealthy family who was mostly just running its business interests as a lawyer. But he also was president of Canadian ORT. [The Organization for Rehabilitation for Training is a major Jewish philanthropy active in technical and vocational training worldwide.] I knew ORT," Reichmann continued, "and I knew that Klein was Orthodox. So I approached him. I was the one who recommended Klein, and I convinced him that it would be a great mitzvah to go to Ottawa."

Virtually everybody else involved in Klein's selection as a candidate has died. However, Reichmann was able to produce a letter from Klein that cast into doubt the MP's memory, if not necessarily his credibility. Written in June 1963, just after his first-term election, on House of Commons letterhead, it is quoted here in its entirety:

I want to tell you how much I appreciated your monumental help in the last election. Working shoulder to shoulder with men like you makes any cause worthwhile. Your warmth and sincerity was a source of great strength for me and was something which I will never forget. There must have been many Reichmans [sic] in the long history of our people, because without them, there would have been no survival. Many many thanks.

Klein would hardly be the first politician to develop selective amnesia. Or perhaps his memory of Reichmann's role in his ascent to public office truly had faded. In any event, Reichmann's interest in federal politics died with Leon Crestohl. While pleased that the tradition of the Jewish MP continued, Reichmann would take no personal interest in Klein's career and would not be active in his future reelection campaigns.

Chapter 20

For Paul Reichmann, the most accomplished property man of his generation, real estate was an accidental calling. By 1958, the Toronto tile company had outgrown the warehouse Louis had rented in founding the business and, with the transatlantic encouragement of their father, Paul and Ralph decided to build their own warehouse rather than lease expanded quarters. They had a part-time architect work up a design and put the job out for bids but were astonished at the response: even the low bid of $125,000 seemed exorbitant. Convinced that he could do the job himself at significantly lower cost, Paul decided, again with his father's blessing, to act as his own contractor. On Colville Road, not far from Olympia Floor's rented warehouse, Paul found a lot and negotiated its purchase on his father's behalf. Samuel put down $4,000 cash and took out a mortgage to cover the $12,000 balance. Some eight months later, 56–58 Colville Road was completed at a cost of about $70,000, fully vindicating Paul's skepticism.

Olympia Floor & Wall Tile leased the building from Samuel Reichmann, its sole owner, for $1,133 a month and then turned around and sublet a quarter of the space for $767 a month. The resultant net rent of $366 was little more than half what Olympia had been paying for its old space. In 1959, the Reichmanns sold the building for $104,000. This modest but remunerative foray into real estate excited Paul's ambitions in a way that metallic lathing never had. He shifted his responsibilities at the tile company to Ralph and concentrated on making a go of it in the nascent industry of real estate development.

North America had been overrun with land speculators, builders, and landlords since earliest colonial times, but property development did not assume the character of a bona fide industry until large corporations specializing in the trade emerged after World War II. In transforming the continent's urban landscape with such basic innovations as the tract home, the high-rise apartment building, the shopping center, the industrial park, and the office-tower complex, the North American property industry would assume a monumental scale. Although the U.S. real estate market was ten times larger than Canada's, most of the largest developers of the 1960s, 1970s, and 1980s would be Canadian. Their superior size was largely a function of the Canadian government's aggressive use of subsidies and incentives to relieve the country's chronic shortage of housing. The policy makers in Ottawa had recognized "a need to create a building industry almost from scratch. [Ottawa] decided that it wanted more than just house-builders and houses; it wanted to see a new kind of building industry, with large corporations each capable of producing a sizable quantity of urban accommodation."

Paul Reichmann began with the incalculable advantage of operating in North York, a sprawling, sparsely populated township six miles northeast of downtown Toronto. From 1951 through 1960, North York's population nearly tripled, to about 228,000, ranking it first among metropolitan Toronto's thirteen municipalities. The value of building permits issued in North York would rise at an even faster rate, increasing twelvefold over this same period and making North York, in the infelicitous but accurate phrase of its mayor, the "buildingest" community in Canada. By the late 1960s, if not earlier, the township was thought to be generating more construction per capita than any other community in North America. There was, in short, no better place to get started, North York being to property development about what the Klondike had been to gold mining.

Ignoring the larger market for housing, Paul Reichmann decided to specialize as a developer of the sort of small warehouse-showroom he had built for the family tile company. He set up Olympia Industrial Association as an affiliate of Olympia Floor & Wall Tile and through it began developing one small site at a time in the vicinity of the intersection of Lawrence and Keele avenues on the western edge of North York. Years later he cheerfully confessed to making his fair share of mistakes. "I've heard people say that there is grass growing through the concrete at 56 Colville Road because I didn't know to take off the topsoil," he said in 1994. "I don't know if that's true because I've never gone back to look at it, but it is true that I did not know yet how to build."

When Albert arrived from Tangier in 1959, he followed in Louis's steps—that is, instead of entering into partnership with the brother who had preceded him to Canada—in this case, Paul—he set up a virtually identical company of his own. York Factory Developments Limited was founded with $40,000, most of it supplied by Samuel Reichmann. While Paul shared office quarters with Ralph, Albert ran York out of his apartment. One of his first building sites was the lot right next to the new Olympia tile warehouse on Colville Road.

It was telling that Samuel waited for Albert before making his own first equity investment in the real estate business. In Tangier, Albert had worked for his father for a dozen years, becoming not only his trusted right hand but his commercial alter ego: shrewd, steady, and tenacious. At thirty-two, Albert was a proven if narrowly experienced businessman. Paul, thirty, may have been a neophyte but he was a quick study and by mid-1961 had passed muster with his father. At Samuel's urging—which amounted to a command—Paul and Albert joined forces as partners in S. Reichmann & Sons and Reichmann Family Enterprises. The brothers set up a new office at 15 Benton Road, which was one of Paul's buildings. For Paul, the effect was like being presented with the combination to a safe, in that it multiplied his access to capital severalfold. No longer would he have to measure his progress a building at a time. Technically speaking, Paul's and Albert's existing companies would remain separate until 1964 when Olympia Industrial and York Factory were merged to create a small corporation of immense destiny: Olympia & York Industrial Development.

———

A property developer is to a building what a producer is to a feature film: conceptualizer, initiator, organizer, overseer. The developer acquires a site, selects an architect, obtains necessary permits and approvals, arranges financing, hires a contractor, lines up tenants or a buyer, and in general coaxes forth bricks and mortar—and, if all goes as envisioned, profit—from the void. Developing is a white-collar calling if not quite a profession; very few top executives of the major North American development companies ever wore T-shirts and tool belts to work. From the outset, the Reichmanns were unusual among developers in preferring to do their own general contracting. That is, Olympia & York assumed responsibility for selecting and supervising the subcontractors who employed the tradesmen who actually built buildings: carpenters, electricians, and so on. Although construction is labor-intensive, the work of development per se is not. With no more than a dozen employees, Olympia & York would erect one hundred buildings in its first decade.

A few weeks after their father had forced their commercial union, Paul and Albert hired their first engineer. William Minuk had met Paul over the counter at the North York building department, where he had taken a job as a plan examiner after graduating from college. "I was an engineer but I'd never actually built anything," Minuk recalled. "I took the job thinking they knew a lot more about construction than they did and they thought I knew a lot more than I really did."

In short order, though, Olympia & York became a paragon of cost-efficiency. Although the Reichmanns were not unusual in relying on freelance architects and consulting engineers to design their buildings, they and the handful of full-time staffers in their employ monitored the work done by outsiders with relentless intensity. Both brothers took blueprints home from the office every night in hopes of carving a few more leasable square feet from the gross square footage. Meanwhile, Minuk drove such a hard bargain in negotiating labor and supply contracts that subcontractors routinely went over his head to complain to the brothers, who were polite but unyielding. "They might tell me to give a job to so and so, but they never told me to ease up on price," Minuk recalled. In dealing with tenants, the Reichmanns were much more pliable but no less decisive. "They were very fast on the trigger in working out deals with people; they didn't fumble around and were exceptionally clear-minded in their thinking," said Kurt Rothschild, who owned an electrical contracting firm that worked on most of Olympia & York's early jobs. "And they did not quibble with the client. If a client wanted something, they gave it to him. No one could match the oomph of these fellows."

When the Reichmann brothers started out, the commercially fertile fields of north Toronto had already given rise to a trio of outsized industrial developers, the largest of which was Toronto Industrial Leaseholds. Founded in 1951 by the brothers Alex and Harry Rubin, who had immigrated from Poland before the war, Toronto Industrial Leaseholds (TIL) had cranked out one hundred buildings by 1957. Alex, the dominant Rubin brother, pioneered in applying the techniques of the assembly line to the production of industrial buildings—the "Rubin package," he called it. Soon TIL had topped the two hundred–building mark while expanding beyond Toronto to Montreal, Winnipeg, Calgary, and other cities. And yet once the Reichmann brothers had gained their footing, TIL dreaded bidding against them for a job. "It got so we just couldn't compete," lamented Stewart "Bud" Andrews, who was a senior manager of TIL in the late 1950s and early 1960s. "When it came to pricing a bid, there was no one in the same league as the Reichmanns."

During construction, the Reichmanns cut subcontractors as little slack as they had given the architects and engineers. With rare exceptions, Reichmann projects were completed in three to six months—on time, in any event—and on budget, even though their budgets left scant room for error and their buildings were a cut above the competition aesthetically. The bare-boned, utilitarian look of the warehouses mass-produced by TIL and its imitators grated against the Reichmanns' sensibilities. As Paul once put it, "We felt it looked horrible. . . . Typically, industrial buildings then consisted of a brick wall in front and concrete block. We made it brick all around and did some landscaping in front. This made quite a difference in appearance but did not cost us a lot. The extra cost was more than worth it because people would pay more in rent to be in a better environment."

Instead of merely devising a more pleasing alternative to TIL's standard design, the Reichmann brothers styled themselves as custom builders to industry. Each Olympia & York building was designed from scratch, though a certain sameness was inevitable, given not only the constraints of budget and function but the fact that the same young architect, Morley Sirlin, designed three-fourths of them. Sirlin had briefly toiled for TIL before starting his own practice in 1960. Olympia & York was among his first clients. "Paul and Albert were always very design conscious, always very progressive that way," Sirlin recalled. An early Olympia & York promotional brochure featured a photo spread of nothing but entryways.

Although Albert and Paul were interchangeable in terms of their authority within the company, their talents were more complementary than overlapping. Albert essentially functioned as general manager, administering the staff and overseeing the construction work. As Minuk put it, "Albert was the one who pushed the job along." Sirlin recalled Albert having "a memory like a trap. If he said, 'We want drawings Monday at two P.M.,' that's when you'd better have them or know the reason why. He was like a computer that way." Despite his penchant for precision, Albert was no high-strung taskmaster. Missed deadlines always brought a request for an explanation but never prompted a tirade. Albert spent far more time reassuring battle-weary subordinates than cracking the whip over them. He was, in fact, something of a soft touch. When Frank Wos, the company's first construction supervisor, mentioned one day that he needed a few thousand dollars to buy a car, Reichmann wrote out a check for $2,000 on the spot. "There was no palaver about repayment or anything," Wos recalled. "He just handed it to me."

While Paul inspired admiration from afar, Albert won his employees' affection. By all accounts, Albert was looser and more easygoing than his younger brothers, if no less reserved. Company staffers even saw, or thought they saw, the occasional flash of regular-guy devilment beneath the straitlaced ultra-Orthodox exterior. Albert did not seem to mind at all when he would leave the office during the lunch hour and find a group of pretty girls from the Elite Blouse factory next door slumped up against his white Continental sedan. "If his father hadn't been around, I think Albert could have had a little fun," Sirlin said. "Who knows, maybe he did. I do know that he got a big kick out of the girls leaning on his car."

Paul, on the other hand, drove a funereal-looking, black Chrysler sedan, and if the Elite Blouse lunch bunch had been gathered around his car, he might not even have noticed it. Superficially, at any rate, the Yiddish term "luftmensch" (literally, a man who lives on air—meaning a visionary, a dreamer) seemed to suit Paul Reichmann perfectly. He was Olympia & York's resident egghead, a deep thinker who scouted building sites, envisioning profit-producing brick and drywall in place of meadows and maple trees. Unlike many real estate visionaries, Paul also became adept at converting his ideas into a pro forma—a set of documents detailing the economics of a project. Although he routinely descended from the clouds of his own cerebration to consult his brother or, less frequently, his father, this nonpracticing rabbi seemed a remote, otherworldly figure to his employees. "The word for him was lofty," Wos said. "He was never involved with the lower echelons."

While Paul happily left employee relations to his brother, Olympia & York's designated dreamer was also its deal man. When it came to purchasing land or arranging financing terms with lenders, the luftmensch in Reichmann vanished. "Paul Reichmann is an indefatigable negotiator with the patience of Mount Rushmore," said William Mulholland, who as chairman of the Bank of Montreal would have extensive dealings with Olympia & York throughout the 1970s. Perhaps more surprising, given his basic introversion, Reichmann was a persuasive, charismatic salesman. "We'd never even heard of the Reichmanns before Paul approached me and my brother but we decided to go with them mainly because Paul was such a wonderful person to do business with— polite, calm, to the point," said Edward Starr, who in 1961 decided to relocate his apparel manufacturing business from downtown Toronto to North York. "He instilled total confidence. We just knew that he was the right person. We had no doubt about it."

Beneath Paul's understated and formal exterior lay a fiercely competitive businessman. One night Reichmann dropped by Morley Sirlin's tiny office and was outraged to see a rough sketch of a design that he had commissioned for a prospective client tacked up on the wall in full view. Reichmann's worry was that a rival developer might see the drawing and steal away his client before he could clinch the final lease agreement. "Oh, was he mad," said Sirlin, who removed the drawing at once.

One of the Reichmanns' first clients was a fledgling electronics retail firm run by Peter Munk, who was the scion of one of the premier Jewish banking families of Hungary's prewar era. Munk, who is Albert Reichmann's age, escaped Hungary a few months after the Germans invaded. As the chief executive officer of Horsham Corporation, Munk today is one of Canada's preeminent corporate moguls. Another of the company's most important early clients was the Stone family, strictly observant Jews who owned American Greeting Cards, which was active in Toronto but based in Cleveland. As much as the Reichmanns valued these relationships, they realized that to trade on the shared bonds of their ethnicity and religion was to marginalize their business. The net of Paul's salesmanship was broadly cast on the commercial waters and brought in a diverse catch, including such substantial Canadian concerns as Aikenhead Hardware, Simpson-Sears, Berkel Products, and Longman's Publishing and such large American and British corporations as Pet Milk, Mattel, and Ronson.

Like Edward and Louis in Montreal, the Toronto Reichmanns succeeded in building a company with a predominantly non-Orthodox staff and a heavily non-Orthodox clientele without diluting their identities as Orthodox Jews or discarding inconvenient aspects of their religious practice. "I respect the Reichmanns because they are not crypto-Jews, not closet Jews. They are the same on the street as in the home," said Israel Singer, who was a developer in Toronto before becoming executive director of the World Jewish Congress. "When all is said and done, this fact about them will remain: they did not compromise at all with regard to Judaism."

In business, strict observance set the brothers apart in a hundred ways, some as simple as the yarmulkes on their heads or the mezuzahs on their door-jambs and others tending to complication—notably, keeping kosher and keeping Shabbat. In 1962, Albert and Paul attended the gala opening of a large facility they had built for Ronson Corporation, a large consumer products company. The building's steel superstructure already had been erected when Louis Aronson, the chief executive of Ronson, flew over in his private plane and decided that he did not like the look of it. The Reichmanns dismantled a part of the structure and had a concrete false front installed. As a gesture of gratitude, the Ronson people had taken the trouble of serving the brothers a special assortment of kosher food at their grand-opening party, not realizing that the platter fell short of Reichmann standards. The brothers stalled until their hosts vanished and then Albert pushed the food toward two employees who had accompanied them and hissed, "Here, eat this—or at least make it look like we ate some of it."

Olympia & York shut down its construction sites during the Sabbath and the Jewish religious festivals—a total of 64 or 65 days a year. From the time of their earliest projects, the Toronto Reichmanns incorporated these mandatory job-site shutdowns into their agreements with subcontractors. The effect was to roughly double work time lost to about 120 days all told, since the brothers were unable to compel non-Orthodox laborers to toil on Sundays or Christian holidays. What with Rosh Hashanah, Yom Kippur, Sukkoth, and Simchat Torah (not to mention Labor Day), Olympia & York crews were idle for most of September, which in Canada was crunch time, construction being far more expensive in winter. Olympia & York's truncated work schedule added cost to many jobs and in open bidding occasionally meant the difference between winning and losing a contract in the first place.

While the typical construction worker did not mind resting on Saturdays and Jewish holidays, the prolongation of building schedules strained the Reichmanns' relations with their own employees, who, after all, were under intense pressure to complete buildings quickly and cost-effectively. Reichmann job sites were informally policed by the ultra-Orthodox community of north Toronto, though their surveillance efforts were impaired by the Shabbat prohibition against driving. One Saturday afternoon Sirlin was driving through Etobicoke, a township several miles east of North York, when he spied Wos,

Olympia & York's construction super, poking around a warehouse-in-progress. "Oh, relax," scoffed Wos when Sirlin upbraided him. "Even Aaron Gestetner can't walk all the way out here." Gestetner, who worked for Olympia & York as a bookkeeper, was the family's most vigilant enforcer of the Shabbat work ban.

A few months later, though, Wos was spotted at another site on a Saturday. The following Monday morning, Albert Reichmann summoned his Catholic super to his office and said that he had been seen working on Shabbat. "He told me that someone had reported it to his father," Wos recalled. "I said it was true but I had to get this job done. Then he says to me, 'Do you want me to be excommunicated?' I never forgot that. He understood me and he made me understand his position." Wos also clashed with Paul Reichmann over the issue of Sabbath observance, to opposite effect. One Sunday morning, Paul told Wos to meet him at a building site. Wos grudgingly complied. "We were walking around the site," he recalled, "and I said to him, 'Paul, I respect your religion. I want you to respect mine.' He never spoke to me again, not one word." Aside from the silent treatment, Wos suffered no other recrimination and remained in Olympia & York's employ for another three years.

According to Paul Reichmann, the Sabbath work ban was even more problematic in the tile business than in property development. Contractors generally liked to be able to drop by a warehouse every day but Sunday to pick up tile as needed and take Sunday off. Olympia Floor & Wall Tile's customers thus were faced with the choice of double-ordering on Friday or taking their business elsewhere on the weekend.

During one particularly exasperating stretch of enforced idleness, Minuk dropped a complaint into a conversation with Aaron Gestetner. "We're closed half the time," Minuk said. "I can't make a profit this way." Gestetner's reply brought Minuk up short. "No, no, you don't understand," Gestetner said. "We will succeed not in spite of our religion, but because of it." When his cousin's comment was repeated to him years later, Paul Reichmann bridled at the seeming implication that the family's rigorous observance was a business strategy. "If you have something that is prohibited to you for whatever reason, you react to it differently than if it's a matter of choice," Reichmann said. "For us, working on the Sabbath did not enter the realm of choice. It was simply not possible."

In Reichmann's view, the regimen of strict observance need not be an impediment to business. "The conflict is more within the person than with the world he would go into," Reichmann argued. "Often you find a Jewish businessman who eats kosher at home but is embarrassed when he's eating with the prime minister or whomever and comes up with a story that he's a vegetarian or he has stomach cramps. I have never had a problem either as a youngster or later with my Jewishness. I think it actually helped to be very clear about who I was, both in appearance and in behavior." The brothers' emphatic Jewishness undoubtedly put off some unquantifiable number of prospective clients. On balance, though, "the market was receptive to the newcomer and to fresh ideas no matter where they came from," Reichmann said. "There seemed to be no preference given to the old, established builders."

———

Just the same, Olympia & York's earliest years continue to be shrouded in a haze of illegitimacy as a result of persistent and often far-fetched speculation about the company's original sources of financing. Edward Starr remembered someone telling him in all seriousness in the early 1960s that the Reichmann brothers were secretly backed by the King of Morocco. The personage most often cast by the rumor mill in the role of Deep Pocket was Samuel Reichmann himself. In a chapter on the Reichmanns in *The Acquisitors* (published in 1981), Peter Newman observed that the Reichmann family had entered property development "with a heavily financed rush" only after Samuel relocated to Toronto and added:

> A bank manager who worked at Yonge and Eglinton at the time recalls Samuel and Paul coming in to deposit a cheque that he later described as "big enough to choke a horse," even though he was in charge of a branch that customarily dealt with large sums of money. Rumors persist that the elder Reichmann arrived with at least $30 million plus much valuable jewelry. Other stories claim that the seed money really came from the English branch of the Rothschild family through Samuel's wife, Renée, a cousin of David Gestetner. . . . The mystery has never really been explained, but until he died at the age of seventy-seven in 1975, Samuel had ready access to large amounts of cash, with bankers from several continents only too pleased to extend credit for his family's expanding ventures.

The belittling of Jewish commercial success as a product not of meritorious enterprise but of financial conspiracy is a classic canard of anti-Semitism. In the Reichmanns' case, though, the issue of secret wealth cannot be dismissed out of hand. For one thing, speculation about the financial underpinnings of Olympia & York was as prevalent within the Reichmanns' own ultra-Orthodox circle as it was among the company's vanquished commercial rivals. And why not? Upon his arrival in Canada, Samuel had had a Swiss bank account for thirty years and had functioned for the past fifteen years as an important cog in the underground economy of Tangier. All in all, he probably knew as much about the hiding and covert transfer of capital as any Toronto banker, the vast majority of whom never had to outwit Hitler and his minions.

"When Samuel and Renée Reichmann emigrated to Canada in 1959 their 'fortune' was $410,000," the family would later declare. Although no documentation was offered in support of this figure, it was in fact taken from the official immigration card that Mr. Reichmann filled out at Malton Airport in early 1959 upon entering Canada. On it, he disclosed that he was carrying $10,000, already had transferred $200,000 to Canada, and planned to transfer an additional $200,000. "Although with comfortable means, he was not rich—certainly not by present-day standards," asserted the Reichmanns. "The fact is that Samuel Reichmann did not have a fortune."

Actually, no such conclusion can be supported on the skimpy basis of an immigration card. The immigration authorities did not require Samuel to disclose his net worth, only how much money he intended to bring into the country. The $410,000 was best understood as traveling money. For a man who had been scattering capital in strategically placed locations ever since the early 1930s to have arrived in Canada carrying his entire fortune in his immigrant's knapsack, as it were, would have been strikingly out of character.

When the Reichmann patriarch died in 1975, he left an estate in Canada with a value of $2.2 million, mostly in the form of securities issued by Olympia & York. However, Samuel Reichmann's Canadian will ultimately is no more useful than his immigration card in determining the size of the fortune he had amassed in Tangier. If, as seems likely, the largest portion of Reichmann's wealth remained on deposit in Switzerland, he could have simply shifted the funds to his heirs by intrabank transfer and Canadian authorities would never have been the wiser. But if the question of Samuel Reichmann's wealth seems destined to remain forever swaddled in murk, his financial role in Olympia & York was revealed in some detail by selected references to the company's private financial statements made in the family's late-1980s libel suit. (The statements themselves were not disclosed to the court.) As of the end of 1963, the combined balance sheet of all Reichmann-owned companies in Toronto showed total paid-in capital of $142,639. In addition, various members of the family had advanced another $534,720, mostly reinvested dividends. Of this total of $677,358, Samuel Reichmann had provided $107,183.

But equity investment is not everything. After all, Paul's very first project, the Olympia Tile warehouse on Colville Road, was wholly financed with money that Samuel borrowed in his own name. The court papers do not address the issue of the extent to which Samuel assisted his sons indirectly, either by borrowing on their behalf or by guaranteeing loans made to Olympia & York. However, there does exist anecdotal evidence to suggest that the Toronto brothers were buoyed in their early real estate maneuverings by a safety net of cash that never showed up on any corporate balance sheet.

"I was never the nosy sort, but it was evident that the Reichmanns were financially strong right from the start," said Nick Karababas, who was deputy building commissioner for North York at the time the brothers got their start. At city hall one day in 1960, Karababas bumped into Gordon Baker, who headed the township's industrial commission. To attract new industry, North

York was issuing tax breaks to real estate developers but insisted that unproven builders post a letter of credit or some other sort of financial guarantee. Baker told Karababas that he had recently met with Paul Reichmann for the first time and asked for such a guarantee. Reichmann reached in the pocket of his jacket and pulled out a sheaf of Canadian Treasury bill receipts totaling $300,000—which was at least three times Olympia's paid-in capital at the time. "Will this do?" Reichmann supposedly responded. "Baker told me he almost fell off his chair," Karababas recalled.

But if the Reichmann brothers had access to funds of such magnitude, they were held in reserve. A close examination of the public records pertaining to a dozen and a half of the Reichmanns' earliest buildings revealed no trace of any lush subterranean flow of secret funds. While Olympia & York as a rule was not required to specify its sources of interim construction financing in public records, at an average cost of $150,000 to $250,000 per building the sums involved were modest in any event. What is more, each of the buildings without exception was refinanced upon completion in conventional fashion—through long-term mortgages issued by established local lending institutions. More than anything else, it would be Paul Reichmann's ingenuity at devising novel methods of borrowing from the obvious sources that would lift Olympia & York into the first rank of developers.

Nor was there anything suspiciously meteoric about Olympia & York's rise. The land registry records in Toronto show a gradual, incremental increase in the size of the brothers' projects. By the end of 1963, Olympia & York had accumulated assets of about $4 million. By contrast, the assets of Revenue Properties Incorporated, the Rubin brothers' holding company, amounted to nearly $20 million and included about sixty buildings. Alex Rubin, the original master builder of North York, recalled being only vaguely aware of Olympia & York until mid-1965, when the Reichmann brothers formed a partnership with the Oelbaum family of Toronto to acquire a moribund development project in North York for $17.8 million. But even in making this large transaction, the Reichmanns displayed no financial muscle; every penny of that $17.8 million was supplied by the Oelbaums or borrowed from banks and insurance companies.

Unless the Reichmanns open Olympia & York's books to outside scrutiny—a remote possibility at best—invidious speculation about the company's early sources of financing will continue. However, the available evidence strongly suggests that the issue is a red herring. If anything, Olympia & York's early growth was constrained by limited access to capital. While the Rubin brothers and many other Canadian developers raised large sums during the 1960s by selling stock to the public, the Reichmanns never even considered this alternative, for "going public" would have compromised both the family's control over the company and its privacy. Paul's creativity and inspired salesmanship,

Albert's exacting administration, the brothers' melding of aesthetics and cost-efficiency, their exalted reputation for integrity—all these qualities set the Reichmanns apart from run-of-the-mill developers and were more than adequate to explain their initial success.

———

Frank Wos, Olympia & York's first construction supervisor, was and remains an affable, rough-hewn man of unvarnished opinions. "I'm a construction man. I got a job to do, I go for the throat," he said, demonstrating the point with hands the size of frying pans. When asked in 1994 the secret of the Reichmanns' early success, Wos did not hesitate. "Their edge was their integrity," he said. "They put themselves on the line and they lived on the line." In his own fashion, Bill Minuk, who left Olympia & York in the late 1960s to form his own development company, expressed the same view. "The Reichmanns very early on developed a high degree of respect as being very honest," Minuk said. "We developed a lot of business just on that basis. If they shook on a deal, that was it. Their word was their bond."

During Olympia & York's heyday, this deceptively simple phrase, "their word is their bond," would be so often intoned in praise of Albert, Paul, and Ralph Reichmann that the brothers should have copyrighted it for use as a corporate motto. As it was, the phrase became so embedded in the iconolatry of the Reichmanns that it would continue to be repeated, like a mantra, by the family's underinformed admirers long after it had ceased being literally true.

By law, a deal was not a deal in the Canadian property business until both dotted lines were signed; in other words, the developer's signature was his bond—his only bond. However, as Orthodox Jews and as former inhabitants of Tangier, the Reichmanns were a product of cultures where the written contract was seen as an irrelevance or even an impediment to commerce. When possible, they preferred to deal on the basis of a verbal agreement sealed with a handshake. "In all the years we worked together, Paul and I never had a piece of paper between us," Sirlin said. But like every other Toronto developer, the Reichmann brothers hired lawyers who drew up deeds and leases that were registered at the courthouse, as the law required.

Although under-the-table payments were not unknown in the Toronto construction trades of the day (Wos left one of his previous employers for fear of becoming inveigled into a kickback scheme), the milieu in which the Reichmanns got their start was not so much corrupt as rife with petty chiseling by builders and landlords for whom commercial real estate was a sideline to dressmaking, auto repair, loan-sharking, or some other business. Meanwhile, many professional developers made a living out of low-balling project bids and then billing clients for construction cost overruns and supposedly unforeseen operating expenses. According to Paul Reichmann, Olympia & York never billed a tenant for extras. On those rare occasions when the company's costs did exceed expectation, it simply swallowed the difference. "I'm a tough negotiator," Reichmann said, "but once a negotiation is finished the client is king."

What was most striking about the Reichmanns' dealings in Olympia & York's embryonic stage was not that they invariably lived up to their end of a bargain but that they did not always hold their clients to the same standard. Often, their word was not only their bond but an all-purpose warranty. Once Sirlin was reviewing a plan for Delta Electronics, a local retail chain, with its president, who insisted that he had been quoted a price that included a fieldstone lobby. Sirlin, who had designed a conventional lobby, telephoned Paul Reichmann. "I don't remember it that way," Reichmann replied, "but if he says I said he could have stone, then give him stone." Similarly, Wos once was dispatched to make repairs to a long-completed building that had been flooded through no fault of Olympia & York's. "I didn't like it because I knew it was caused by the tenant's bad maintenance," Wos recalled. "I told Albert it was not our responsibility. He said, 'No, it's not, but it is my money. So go back and fix it.'"

According to Paul Reichmann, such practices had nothing to do with his family's morality. "It wasn't a question of having more honorability or integrity than other people," he insisted. "That's rubbish. It was just good business." But if the Reichmanns insisted that they were merely ringing variations on the old saw, "The customer is always right," their grateful clients and baffled competitors read a deeper, moral meaning into what by the standards of the real estate trade were extraordinarily enlightened practices. This inclination was as much a reaction to the intensely spiritual aura that the brothers projected as to their conduct. "I don't think of them as Jewish," a rival developer once told a reporter. "I think of them as Mennonites, with the black beards and soulful eyes. You always have a feeling you are being examined, and found sadly lacking."

Compared with the typical suburban developer, the Reichmanns seemed as if they had descended from another planet. Even Albert, the most worldly of the brothers, often did not think to carry cash with him during the workday. Minuk usually had to pick up the check when he and the boss stopped for lunch while out inspecting construction sites. "I didn't mind," Minuk recalled. "He always paid me back." Paul, meanwhile, was notorious for borrowing $10 for cab fare from an employee at the last minute before heading to the airport on a business trip. At the same time, the brothers were abstemious beyond the requirements of their faith. "The food they ate was totally nondescript and not appetizing at all," said Oskar Lustig, an ultra-Orthodox Hungarian immigrant who joined Olympia & York as an accountant in the early 1960s. While Albert was rather dapper, Paul and Ralph often looked as if they dressed themselves out of Salvation Army bins. "I think Paul's wife was watching how he dressed in those days so his clothes were all right but his shoes!" Lustig exclaimed. "His shoes looked horrible, very old-fashioned and scuffed. And Ralph wore shirts to work that I wouldn't have worn in the dark."

Extreme piety of any denomination is not in and of itself a guarantee of integrity in business; a fair-sized prison wing could be filled with fundamentalist Christian ministers and Orthodox rabbis convicted of financial fraud in recent decades in the United States alone. And yet Paul Reichmann's protests notwithstanding, the Reichmanns' founding approach to real estate development exemplified the code of the Lifnin Mishuras Hadin—or the Extra-Righteous Jew—as articulated by Maimonides in the Mishneh Torah:

> The commerce of the talmid chacham [the Jewish role model] has to be in truth and in faith. His yes is to be yes and his no, no; he forces himself to be exact in calculations when he is paying, but is willing to be lenient where others are his debtors. . . . He should keep his obligations in commerce, even where the law allows him to withdraw or retract, so that his word is his bond. But if others have obligations to him he should deal mercifully, forgiving and extending credit.

Since most of the Reichmanns' early enthusiasts did not know Maimonides from Hippocrates, it was to be expected that they would frame their appreciation in secular, even non-Jewish terms. "To all sorts of people," observed Oskar Lustig, "the Reichmanns seemed to represent the nostalgic past of Europe— and not just the Jewish past." In Toronto, bastion of Britishness, it was not Lifnin Mishuras Hadin that provided the context for understanding the Reichmanns but the Protestant equivalent: the Code of the English Gentleman. Even some of the Reichmanns' more knowledgeable admirers succumbed to this transliterative fallacy. "The Reichmanns were not only following [Jewish] law but had a super-duper, gentlemanly code that any WASP could recognize," said Joe Lebovic, a yeshiva-trained Toronto developer who had fallen away from the strict Orthodoxy of his youth. "They were WASPier than WASPS."

Chapter 21

A few months before Paul Reichmann had begun his experiment in do-it-yourself building in north Toronto, Edward and Louis Reichmann had bought the north Montreal warehouse leased by their tile company. Acting in partnership with the Zimmerman brothers, they paid $35,000 and turned around a year later and sold the building for $80,000 while simultaneously leasing it back from the new owners for Olympia's continued use. Inspired by this quick profit and bored with the drudgery of wholesaling ceramic tiles, Edward turned his managerial responsibilities at Olympia Floor over to Louis and devoted himself fully to the property development business as the chief proprietor of Three Star Construction Limited.

Like Paul and Albert in Toronto, Edward hitched his star to the industrial segment of the property market and did his own general contracting. In other crucial respects, the eldest brother, as usual, steered his own idiosyncratic course. As an entrepreneur, his defining traits were prodigious energy and audacity. While Paul and Albert (under their father's watchful eye) kept their ambitions on a tight leash, Edward built to the limits of his capacity to obtain financing—and then some. At a time when the Toronto brothers were still turning out 60,000-square-foot warehouses at $150,000 to $250,000 a pop, Edward graduated to the development of a $15 million office complex that altered the skyline of north Montreal. In the ceramic tile business, too, the Montreal brothers set the pace, making two acquisitions that elevated Olympia Floor & Wall to dominance throughout Quebec while putting the family into manufacturing for the first time.

Edward not only outpaced his younger brothers in laying the foundations of empire but did so in a way that compelled attention and publicized the Reichmann name. Paul and Albert, if given the choice, would have shunned the limelight forever, but their eldest brother luxuriated in it, making political speeches, holding press conferences, giving interviews and appearing on television at every opportunity. "Edward's reputation here just galloped," said Nahum Gelber, a prominent Montreal lawyer. "In a business sense, he quickly became a household name."

Although Edward Reichmann's headlong expansionism was ideally suited to the sunny business climate of the late 1950s and early 1960s, he would prove ruinously incapable of adjusting to changed circumstance. Even when Edward was at the top of his game, his success was a turbulent mix of triumph and miscalculation. If Edward was more prolific than his younger brothers, he was never as proficient a deal maker as Paul nor as efficient an administrator as Albert. Actually, he was no good at either; his talents were fatefully imbalanced in favor of promotion over execution, enthusiasm over calculation, growth over profit. There was a certain untethered, careening aspect to Edward's advancement that was evident long before he hit the wall in Montreal, a tendency first manifested as high turnover among his business partners.

That those partners never included Samuel Reichmann was unfortunate, for Edward, perhaps even more than his younger brothers, would have benefited from the restraining influence of his father's conservatism. Naturally, Samuel gave both of his Montreal sons a word of advice every now and then but was never an officer of Olympia Floor (Quebec) or Three Star Construction. By contrast, the Reichmann patriarch served as chairman of the board of Olympia & York from its formation in 1961 until his death in 1975.

Both Edward and Louis Reichmann insist that they were not disappointed by the one-sidedness of their father's involvement. Edward, especially, had never lacked for self-confidence, and the Montreal brothers owned by far the bigger business at the time that Samuel aligned himself with his Toronto sons. What is more, Edward had always been ambivalent about commercial affiliation with his father. While he longed for the paternal endorsement implicit in partnership, he was leery about any infringement on his entrepreneurial freedoms. For his part, Samuel had been loath to invest in his volatile, headstrong eldest son's ventures in Tangier and apparently saw nothing during his brief stay in Montreal to change his mind. No doubt he considered Louis's involvement inconsequential as a mitigating factor since Edward effortlessly dominated his brother in business and out. From a purely financial point of view, Samuel Reichmann's decision to back his Toronto sons and not their Montreal brothers was the most consequential investment decision he ever made.

Edward Reichmann began his transformation from merchant to developer by persuading the Zimmerman brothers to stretch their existing partnership beyond ceramic tiles to accommodate his ambitions. At the same time, Edward recruited two new partners: Viliam Frankel and his brother-in-law, Mauric Treitel. A dozen years older than Reichmann, Frankel and Treitel were

Slovakian-born Holocaust survivors who had prospered in Montreal as importers of laces and embroideries. Both men belonged to First Mesifta. "In Mesifta, everyone was good with Edward," Frankel recalled. "He had a lot of friends." Three Star Construction was incorporated in January 1958 with $150,000 in capital. Between them, the brothers Reichmann and Zimmerman owned a 50 percent stake and the Slovaks held the remaining 50 percent. Like Louis Reichmann, the Zimmermans were silent partners, leaving three active partners, the "Three Stars," as it were: Edward Reichmann, Frankel, and Treitel. Only Reichmann had experience in property development. "I'd already built the Bolsa in Tangier and, anyway, building wasn't such a complicated industry," he recalled with characteristic bravado. "It was nothing I was afraid of."

Three Star Construction got off to a quick, modestly profitable start as a developer of small apartment buildings and industrial warehouses. But by the fall of 1958, the partnership that underlay the company already was coming unraveled. "By nature I am a very independent person," Reichmann said. "I wanted to be Reichmann, not Three Star Construction." In his entrepreneurial fearlessness, Reichmann was, to all his partners, a bit frightening. "Edward always was a very fast goer, a very big jumper," Frankel said. Three Star's assets—empty lots and buildings in various stages of completion—were divided in half, and Frankel and Treitel immediately entered into competition with Reichmann as proprietors of a new company, Three Star Properties.

Even so, by all accounts, this was an amicable parting. North Montreal was booming, and there was business enough to keep even two Three Stars busy. In fact, Reichmann later would facilitate one of his ex-partners' largest projects by selling them a vast tract of undeveloped land—at a profit, naturally. (The $400,000 sales price was more than double what Reichmann had paid for the property not six months earlier.) But if Reichmann did not begrudge Frankel and Treitel their ambitions, he did bemoan the gaping hole their departure opened in Three Star's balance sheet. Unlike the Toronto branch of the family, the Montreal Reichmanns certainly never inspired whisperings about hidden fortunes. "Edward was always saying, 'Jack, I need money. I gotta have more money,' " Zimmerman recalled. "But Fred and I felt he was taking big chances as it was." Not six months after Frankel and Treitel departed, the Zimmermans decided to strike out on their own, too. "Finally," Zimmerman continued, "I said, 'Edward, you know what? This isn't working. Why don't you just take Three Star?' "

Edward, with Louis's acquiescence, responded to this suggestion by making a preemptive bid to buy the Zimmerman brothers' half-interest not only in Three Star but in Olympia Floor & Wall Tile as well. The Reichmanns offered $150,000 cash plus a year's wages apiece, which, at $200 a week, amounted to another $20,000 or so. Having quite sensibly assumed that the partnership would be unwound by a swap of their piece of Three Star for the Reichmanns' stake in Olympia, the Zimmermans saw Edward's offer as an opening gambit. "I still think Edward was 100 percent sure that we'd turn him down and come back to him with our own bid," Jack Zimmerman explained. "But what he offered sounded like a lot of money, so we took it before he could change his mind." In actuality, had the Zimmermans balked, Reichmann would have raised his bid, not withdrawn it. To let Olympia Floor go would have halved the size of his empire-in-chrysalis while jeopardizing his only business association with a family member. Given Louis's preference for tiles over real estate, he no doubt would have remained with Olympia even if the Zimmermans had purchased control.

The money to buy out the Zimmermans came from an improbable source: Venezuela. In his climactic dealings with the Zimmermans—and unbeknownst to them—Reichmann had been emboldened by the success of parallel negotiations with a new set of partners led by Tibor Pivko. An affable, broad-shouldered high school dropout who spoke seven languages, Pivko was a Slovakian Jew who had fought in the Czechoslovakian army during World War II and fled to Venezuela on the eve of the Communist takeover of his native land in 1948. An electrician by trade, Pivko made a small fortune in Caracas as a manufacturer of electrical fixtures, furniture, plastics, and steel pipes and also established himself as a builder of commercial warehouses. Fearful by 1959 that Venezuela was going the way of Castro's Cuba, Pivko traveled to Montreal to scout business opportunities and was introduced to Edward Reichmann by a mutual friend. "We liked each other right away," recalled Pivko, who is four years older than Reichmann. "We met in the afternoon, ate something together, and talked into the morning. By one or two o'clock we had a deal."

Pivko persuaded several business associates in Venezuela—Slovakian refugees all—to join with him in backing the Reichmanns. The most important of them, Bertalan "Bondi" Steiner, moved to Montreal, as did Pivko. For an initial cash investment of $800,000, the Venezuelan group bought a half-interest both in Three Star Construction and Olympia Floor, which Louis now ran in tandem with an older cousin, Salomon Gestetner, who had passed through Tangier and settled in Montreal. Pivko personally held half of the Venezuelans' share, giving him a 25 percent interest—the same percentage owned by Edward and by Louis. For the first time since he had arrived in Montreal five years before, Edward's wherewithal was, temporarily, synchronous with his ambitions.

From the start, Reichmann's relationship with Bondi Steiner was tempestuous. In Tibor Pivko, on the other hand, Edward had finally found a commercial soul mate, if not a counterweight—a Canadian equivalent of his Tangier partner, Ernest Rosenfeld. "Whenever something needed to be done, we did it together," Pivko recalled. "I went with Edward everywhere."

Although Pivko, like Reichmann, was physically imposing, outgoing and largely self-taught, the two men fundamentally were more complementary than similar. Pivko was a down-to-earth, blue-collar sort who preferred the logistical challenges of the construction site to the airy abstractions of finance. In this limited sense, he played Albert to Edward's Paul. Although the Slovakian émigré routinely joined his new partner in conferences with Three Star's lenders, he attended as the silent sidekick. "Edward did the talking," Pivko conceded, "and that was fine with me." A strong personality in his own right, Pivko decided that his own interests were best served by deferring to his partner, whose drive and capacity for financial elaboration exceeded his own. "Edward was very difficult to hold back," Pivko recalled. "His head was going all the time. I'm more conservative, and so is Louis."

"If any partner of Edward didn't agree with him," Jack Zimmerman observed, with no apparent rancor, "he'd go find one who did." In affirmation of his fealty, Pivko made large contributions to First Mesifta and even enlisted as one of the congregation's four vice presidents, though he was not Orthodox. Even Steiner, who was no more religious than Pivko, took a seat on First Mesifta's executive committee.

Together, Reichmann and Pivko decided to forgo apartment construction and focus Three Star exclusively on the industrial market. On St. Lawrence Boulevard, the main north-south thoroughfare connecting the working-class precincts of north Montreal to the city center, Three Star built a four-story industrial building generic in every respect save one: a thirty-two-lane bowling alley in the basement. At 130,000 square feet, 8400 St. Lawrence was about twice as large as the Toronto brothers' typical early project and daringly located on the outer reaches of the city's established industrial district. And yet, in defiance of the norm in stodgy Montreal, Three Star had begun construction before it had signed a single tenant to a lease. "Before Reichmann came along, industrial buildings in Montreal were all built to order," recalled Emile Rooz, who as a commercial real estate broker specialized in Reichmann properties. "He was the first developer to make a business out of speculative building."

To Reichmann's and Pivko's delight, the building was almost fully leased even before it was completed, mainly to dressmakers, furriers, and other needle-trade manufacturers eager, at a price, to forsake their slummy sweatshops downtown for modern quarters in the suburbs. Recognizing that the suburban exodus of the needle trades had only begun, Reichmann and Pivko snapped up big chunks of land in the vicinity of 8400 St. Lawrence at low cost and began erecting industrial buildings of varying size as fast as they could, transforming what had been an economically marginal area of delapidated rental houses and weed-strewn empty lots into a thriving modern industrial district known as "the Chabanel." Several competitors—notably Frankel and Treitel—followed suit, but Reichmann and Pivko were the Chabanel's most prolific developers, putting up two dozen warehouses and light manufacturing plants over a three-year span. Three Star made good money in the Chabanel, though Reichmann's preference for selling buildings rather than managing them for lease income prevented the company from fully exploiting the dramatic rise in land values brought about by its pioneering efforts.

———

The infusion of Venezuelan capital also reactivated the Montreal brothers' ambitions in ceramic tiles. Until the Reichmanns entered the business, Montreal Floor & Wall Tile Limited had all but monopolized the Montreal market. John Capra, the founder and owner of Montreal Floor, did not take kindly to Olympia Floor's aggressive sales tactics. "Capra was our sworn enemy," Zimmerman recalled. "He once told me that he was going to push us out of the business." Louis Reichmann took it upon himself to mollify Capra, applying the balm of his low-key charm on frequent expeditions to Montreal Floor's offices. Edward, too, occasionally took time away from his real estate maneuvering to stop by on his way to work in the morning and share a coffee with Capra. When Capra decided in 1960 to retire, he asked Louis if he was interested in buying his firm. "I came right back to the office and told Edward and he immediately began negotiations," Louis said.

The parties reached agreement on a price of about $710,000. Capra was such an eager seller that he accepted $285,000 cash and took back a note for the $425,000 balance; as collateral, the Reichmanns and their partners put up the building at 8400 St. Lawrence. Samuel, Albert, and Ralph came in from Toronto to attend the ceremony at which the final papers were signed and posed with Edward, Louis, and others for a formal photograph taken in Montreal Floor's capacious warehouse to commemorate the transaction. Louis spent the better part of a year gradually merging Montreal Floor and Olympia, with an eye to fully exploiting in terms of pricing and product line the combined firms' total dominance of the Montreal market. He also oversaw the opening of branches in Quebec City and Ottawa, establishing Olympia Floor & Wall as the predominant dealer in all Quebec.

In acquiring Montreal Floor, the Reichmanns inherited Capra's longstanding relationship with the Provincial Bank of Canada, one of the two French banks among Canada's nine chartered banks. But it was the Bank of Montreal, the oldest and largest of Canadian banks, that emerged as lead banker to both the tile and property development companies. "At one point, the Bank of Montreal was chasing Edward," Nahum Gelber recalled. "Not only was he invited down to the head office for lunch but they served him a kosher meal, which," the lawyer added, only half-facetiously, "was a milestone event" in the Jewish history of Montreal. The Bank of Montreal extended the Reichmann businesses a credit line that by the mid-1960s fluctuated between $3 million and $5 million.

Like Paul and Albert but without his father's help, Edward passed muster at the mortgage departments of some of the oldest and stodgiest institutions in the land: North American Life, Standard Life, Montreal Trust, Dominion Life, Imperial Life. However, institutions of this ilk were willing to issue mortgages only after a building had been completed and the many pitfalls inherent in the construction process surmounted. As a rule, construction loans were provided by wealthy investors and were more expensive and harder to come by than first mortgages. For a developer as hyperactive as Edward Reichmann, who at any given time might have a half-dozen building projects under way, the availability of construction financing acted like the regulator on an automobile engine: it governed the pace of advancement.

Enter Nahum Gelber, who had first met the Reichmanns while representing John Capra in the sale of Montreal Floor. Gelber came away from the deal impressed by the way Edward in particular had handled himself. For his part, the elder Reichmann brother recognized in the shrewd, amiable downtown lawyer someone worth cultivating. Like many Jewish law firms of the day, Chait, Aronovitch, Salomon and Gelber acted in ad hoc fashion as an investment bank, matching up clients in need of capital with other clients seeking such high-return investments as construction loans. Gelber and his partners created their own investment vehicle, the Principal Fund, to facilitate their matchmaking—and turn a profit. "A lot of lenders developed a certain confidence in our judgment," Gelber recalled. "They'd say, 'If the Principal Fund is going in, then we're going in, too.' "

Through Gelber and the equally well-connected notary, Sheldon Merling, Reichmann established ties to a dozen secondary market lenders, most of whom were wealthy Jewish merchants of his father's generation, and emerged as one of the biggest private borrowers in Montreal. Three Star's single most important source of financing was an obese retired lumber baron from Sault St. Marie named Saul Friedman. Friedman, who suffered from diabetes, liked to sit in Reichmann's office quietly puffing a pipe while Edward attended to business. "I didn't mind," Reichmann said. "He was a man of caliber, if odd." Friedman, an avid stock-market investor, kept carefully ordered piles of stock certificates on his dining room table. Upon returning home at the close of the business day, he stopped by the table and talked to his stocks, according to Reichmann, who witnessed the ritual many times: "He'd say, 'Oh, there you are GM. You did well today! But GE, you did badly, I'm going to get rid of you, GE.' "

In mid-1961, the Reichmann brothers tapped their Bank of Montreal credit line to finance a second tile acquisition. Again, John Capra was the catalyst. Capra had sold his tile dealership but still owned a minority interest in the local manufacturer that had supplied Montreal Floor with much of its product:

Pilkington's Tiles Canada Limited, which was controlled by the venerable British firm of Pilkington's Glass PLC. In attempting to sell his minority stake back to the British, Capra learned that Lord Pilkington, too, was eager to cash out his investment in the Canadian tile-making subsidiary, which was floundering badly.

In offering, through Capra, to sell the company to the Reichmanns, Lord Pilkington essentially waved the white flag of surrender. Although in the last analysis Pilkington's Tiles' wounds were self-inflicted, the proximate cause of its decline was Olympia Floor & Wall Tile's rise. By 1961, the Quebec and Ontario divisions of Olympia Floor between them had captured half the Canadian market for ceramic tiles. Because the two Olympias imported the bulk of their product from overseas—Japan gradually supplanting Spain as the main source—its rapid growth had come at the expense of Canadian producers, who were not particularly efficient to start with. When the Reichmanns acquired Montreal Floor, Pilkington's in effect lost its biggest customer. "We continued to buy from Pilkington's but much less than Capra had," Louis Reichmann recalled. "It was far more profitable for us to bring in tiles from Japan. In fact, we could sell Japanese imports at retail for 75 percent of Pilkington's manufacturing cost."

This astounding price differential between Japanese and Canadian-produced tile was not the product of superior technology but of the severely depressed value of the yen relative to the dollar. By 1961, however, the yen had begun a sharp rise. "Until Pilkington's came along we hadn't really thought of moving into manufacturing," Louis said. "But with Japanese tiles starting to rise in price, we felt we needed our own domestic source of supply." Louis, who had made frequent buying trips to Japan with Ralph, telephoned his brother with a question: If Olympia-Montreal were to acquire Pilkington's, how much of its annual production would Olympia-Toronto commit to purchase? "It was a very substantial percentage," Louis recalled. "Any other manufacturer would have fainted from pure excitement over such an order."

The Reichmanns and Pilkington's representatives quickly reached agreement on a price, leaving the brothers' religious beliefs as the sole remaining obstacle. As strictly observant Jews, the Reichmann brothers could not in good conscience profit by ownership of a manufacturing plant that operated on Saturdays. However, it took a minimum of seven days of continuous operation to bring Pilkington's huge kiln up to the temperature required to bake tiles. In other words, if the kiln was shut down every Saturday as required under strict Sabbath observance, it would never be functional. The Reichmanns reached a preliminary agreement to acquire Pilkington's but made it conditional on receiving a rabbinical dispensation that would permit continuous operation of the kiln. Edward flew to Brooklyn seeking the imprimatur of Rabbi Levi Grunwald, an esteemed halakic authority.

Various Rabbis Grunwald had been reconciling conflicts between faith and commerce for generations. Rabbi Moses Grunwald, the great sage of late nineteenth-century Hungary, issued responsa, or rabbinical rulings, on the issue of Sabbath operation of a barrel factory, a shoe workshop, steam-operated millstones, a machine for the manufacture of butter, and another for the sawing of wood. Although the latter-day Rabbi Grunwald would not authorize the Reichmanns to manufacture tiles on the Sabbath, he saw no halakic reason why the kiln had to be shut down. However, to simply let a red-hot kiln stand empty through the Sabbath would severely damage it. The Reichmanns' solution was to operate the kiln as usual, except that the wagons moving through it were filled not with "raw" tiles but already baked ones that were defective in some way. No damage, no production, no violation, no problem—except for the waste of energy.

Having brought Pilkington's Tiles to its knees, the Reichmanns scooped up the old-line manufacturer for about $300,000, a price primarily determined by the value of its inventories and the land under the company's manufacturing plant. "We paid no premium at all over book value," Louis said. "Why would we, for a company that was living off of England?" In mid-1961, Lord Pilkington himself came to Montreal to sign the papers ridding his company of its Canadian albatross. Attuned to the growing militancy of the French Canadian nationalist movement in Quebec, the Reichmanns immediately changed the company's name from the overtly Anglophone Pilkington's to the patriotic but ethnically neuter Maple Leaf Ceramics of Canada.

———

Buoyed by the growth of Olympia Floor and Three Star Construction, Edward Reichmann cut an increasingly wide swath through Montreal Jewry. He gave generously to all the major institutions of the community at large—the Combined Jewish Appeal (CJA), the Jewish General Hospital, Mount Sinai Hospital, and so on—and became a fixture at Jewish fund-raising events of all sorts. In the breadth of his community involvement, Edward boldly departed from the rest of the family. In Toronto, Albert, Paul, and Ralph would incur considerable ill will in annually rebuffing delegations sent by the United Jewish Appeal in tacit protest of its support of institutions that, in their view, were antithetical to Orthodoxy and thus debasing of Judaism.

Although Edward Reichmann craved the respect of the Bronfmans and the other dynastic business families who dominated Montreal Jewry, he did not aspire to joining their ranks; he was no more a social climber than were his younger brothers, though he was in fact far more sociable. He went out almost every night, whether to a card game, a movie, a nightclub or, most commonly, to a fund-raising banquet. By all accounts, Reichmann's social hyperactivity was less a function of ambition than aversion to solitude. "Edward always had to have company," Rooz said. "Even when he was working, he hated to be alone." By the mid-1960s, the eldest Reichmann brother would have made hundreds of new acquaintances in Montreal but his inner circle of friends remained compact and homogeneous, consisting of his brother Louis and a half-dozen fellow Eastern European immigrants and First Mesifta congregants. His idea of big fun was to knock off work early on Friday, go home, invite his closest friends over for a sauna, wrap himself in a towel and spend the last few hours before the onset of Shabbat playing gin rummy.

Nor was Edward Reichmann any less committed than the Toronto branch of the family to strengthening the fledgling institutions of ultra-Orthodoxy. However, his approach was at once less ideological and more ambitious. Whereas the Toronto Reichmanns initially limited themselves to acting as donors, Edward cast himself in the role of fund-raiser as well as contributor. Like most people, he believed that to receive you must give. Edward thought of the checks he wrote less as donations than strategic investments, and was confident that he could make them pay for First Mesifta and the ultra-Orthodox community in general.

Among the potentates that Edward met on the Jewish banquet circuit was Hyman Grover, who was one of Montreal's wealthiest and most philanthropic businessmen. That Grover also was president of the city's largest Reform congregation made him, in the conventional ultra-Orthodox view, an enemy. Like many Reform and Conservative Jews, though, Grover believed that a vibrant Orthodoxy was essential to Judaism's survival. It took some doing, but Edward persuaded Rabbi Unsdorfer to allow him to invite Grover to the dinner that marked the opening of First Mesifta's annual campaign drive. Grover accepted the invitation and, without altering his own practice of Judaism one whit, soon emerged as an indispensable supporter of First Mesifta and particularly its yeshiva. In time, Grover even was named "honorary president" of the yeshiva and served as chairman of the fund-raising dinner to which Reichmann had first invited him.

Reichmann pursued members of the first family of Canadian Jewish philanthropy, the Bronfmans, with surpassing intensity. One of six siblings raised in an Orthodox household by Russian immigrant parents, Sam Bronfman harbored a lifelong ambivalency toward his religious heritage but was a traditionalist in many ways and was possessed of a fierce quasi-tribal loyalty that encompassed all segments of the Jewish community. Through Rabbi Hirschprung, the de facto chief Orthodox rabbi of Montreal, Bronfman funneled considerable sums annually to yeshivas and other traditionalist institutions. "Rabbi Hirschprung had a good relationship with Sam Bronfman," Edward said. "My contribution was to push him not to be shy in asking for money."

At the same time, Reichmann availed himself of every opportunity to shake a Bronfman hand himself. As early as 1956, he in effect bought his way into the Combined Jewish Appeal's annual "Samuel Bronfman Dinner" with a $10,000 contribution and worked the black-tie crowd with unabashed ardor, as he did in succeeding years. He got nowhere with Mr. Sam, himself, but did strike up a relationship with Abe, the oldest and most religious of the Bronfman brothers. "Abe Bronfman once told me that he put on the fringe every day," Reichmann recalled. (The Torah attaches great importance to the wearing of fringes, or tsitsith, as a visible reminder of the obligation to keep the mitzvot.) Through his role as local host to the Klausenberg Rebbe, Reichmann also got to know Abe's brother-in-law, Barney Aaron, the only Orthodox member of the Bronfman clan. Aaron had attended yeshiva and served as Hebrew teacher to the Bronfman family before marrying Mr. Sam's eldest sister. Drawn to the Klausenberg Rebbe, Aaron frequently visited Reichmann's home to pay homage to the Hasidic eminence. Aaron, a wealthy man in his own right, contributed generously to Rabbi Halberstam's causes, including First Mesifta.

The big pay-off from Reichmann's cultivation of the Bronfmans came when the Orthodox leadership of Outremont began raising funds to build a new Bais Yaakov elementary school. Appointed chairman of the building committee, Reichmann not only secured a contribution of $250,000 from Abe Bronfman but persuaded him to attend a turning-of-the-sod ceremony as guest of honor. The invitations that Reichmann printed up for the occasion sent a little temblor of outrage through Orthodox Outremont. Although scores of people had made important contributions to the campaign, none were mentioned in the invitations—much less accorded the honorific of "sponsor." Only three names appeared: Rabbi Hirschprung, A. Bronfman, and E. Reichmann.

A delegation of aggrieved philanthropists went to the chief rabbi and accused Reichmann of aggrandizing himself at their expense. In his defense, Reichmann told Rabbi Hirschprung that if he had filled the invitation with the names of all those who deserved a share of the credit, Abe Bronfman might assume that he would not be missed and skip the ceremony. Whether Rabbi Hirschprung accepted this explanation is not certain, but Reichmann did attempt to mollify his critics by distributing a name-heavy program that featured an "introduction," "opening remarks," an "address," and no less than four "greetings" before Rabbi Hirschprung took the podium and Abe Bronfman demonstrated his way with a shovel.

Reichmann's unusually expansive approach to philanthropy also paid commercial dividends. If, in later years, Reichmann was reticent about this aspect of his philanthropy, he was emphatic about it at the time, going so far as to engage the minister of national revenue—the Canadian equivalent of the Internal Revenue Service—in protracted legal battle. On its income tax returns for 1961 and 1962, Olympia Floor & Wall Tile (Quebec) deducted the full amount of its contributions to Jewish charities as a "promotional expense." For 1961, the $8,376 contributions so claimed amounted to 28.4 percent of the company's income and in 1962 rose to $10,188 for a still-hefty 23.1 percent.

However, the minister of national revenue soon intervened, disallowing any deduction of charitable donations amounting to more than 10 percent of total income. Edward and Louis Reichmann appealed the ruling to the supreme taxing authority in Canada, the Tax Appeal Board. With what the judicial arbitrator in the case described as "unmistakable frankness," Olympia argued in its appeal that

These expenses take the form of donations to institutions, the principals of whom are to a great degree in business for themselves running independent businesses divorced from their roles as executives of the institutions involved; that all these donations were made for the purposes of goodwill and in the hope and expectation of acquiring contracts from these executives of the institutions for their private businesses.

What's more, the notice of appeal continued, the tactic of mutual back-scratching worked: "In actual fact, many of these executives of the institutions so benefited, did give contracts and business to Appellant." Indeed, Olympia's sales manager later testified that the donations generated as much as 25 to 30 percent of the company's total sales, which were described vaguely as "over one million dollars."

The Tax Appeal Board was unmoved by the Reichmanns' arguments. In rendering his decision, the board's arbitrator first delivered a homily on the meaning of charity, citing the *Shorter Oxford English Dictionary,* Corinthians, Henry Drummond, and the *Encyclopaedia Britannica,* but ignoring entirely the Jewish concept of tzedoka, before ending on an oddly confessional note: "My notion of the human attribute of Charity or Love has hitherto been far too restricted," J. O. Weldon admitted, adding that he was now convinced "that 'The Greatest Thing in the World' is love." His soliloquy completed, Mr. Weldon then flatly rejected Olympia's appeal: "A charitable donation can not, by any stretch of the imagination, be regarded as a promotional expense."

The Reichmanns appealed this decision, too, taking the matter over the heads of the Tax Appeal Board to the highest civil authority in the land, the Exchequer Court of Canada. In 1970, seven years after the filing of the Reichmanns' first appeal, the Exchequer Court would finally decide in Olympia Floor's favor, finding that a payment made to a charity was not in fact a "gift" under the law when it was made to generate sales and therefore was fully deductible as a business expense. "Such contributions," the court held, "could not be distinguished from advertising expenses."

For the Reichmanns, though, the joy of victory no doubt was tempered by embarrassment. In Jewish thinking, charity—tzedoka—is so fundamental to righteousness that it is considered an act of justice, not sentiment.[8] In real life, which is to say life away from tax court, the Reichmann brothers espoused the highest ideals of charity and lived up to them: they gave munificently, ungrudgingly, and often anonymously, to boot. There was no shame in taking the tax deductions allowed under secular law. But in their eagerness to maximize those write-offs, Edward and Louis constructed a legal argument by which they characterized their own tzedoka in the crassest possible terms. In other words, from the jaws of legal victory they snatched a kind of spiritual defeat.

Chapter 22

No business in North America is more susceptible to the vagaries of local politics than property development. No matter how many billions of dollars of muscle a developer can muster, it is impossible to break ground in the humblest hamlet without first running a gauntlet of planning commissions, zoning boards, councils, and so on. And no matter how grandiose a project, in the end it is reduced to a series of lots and plots on a local property tax roll and an address in a local telephone directory. It is no wonder that real estate interests tend to be the largest contributors to local political campaigns in any municipality large enough to stage them. Nor is it surprising that many developers operate like local politicians, schmoozing and glad-handing their way from banquet hall to golf course to city hall to construction site and back again in an ordeal of contrived bonhomie.

When it came to the politics of development, the Toronto Reichmanns were like ballplayers who skipped the minor leagues and headed right to the majors. At the height of Olympia & York's power, Paul and Albert Reichmann enjoyed considerable access to the heads of state of Canada, the United States, Great Britain, the Soviet Union, Israel, Mexico, and other nations. And yet during their formative years in North York, the Reichmanns followed the rules (as specified in planning ordinances and building codes) without ever really playing The Game. They were no more likely to be seen working the room at a mayoral fund-raiser than cracking jokes over a beer on the nineteenth hole at the country club. "They've always had a good name but North York people don't really know the Reichmanns," said Mel Lastman, the longtime mayor of North York. "They never asked me for a single thing." Even in dealing with the officials who wielded direct decision-making power over their projects, the Reichmanns were as impersonal as possible. "Our dealings were always very correct, but I never had much contact with them," recalled Sam Beckett, the local building commissioner. "They preferred to work through emissaries."

The studied distance the Reichmanns kept from city hall in North York should not be interpreted as contempt; over the years, the brothers would repeatedly recruit government officials for top executive positions at Olympia & York. And as recent immigrants speaking heavily accented English, Albert, Paul, and Ralph would have been hard-pressed to backslap their way to preeminence even if so inclined. But even as their accents diminished, the Toronto brothers would resist the entanglements of politics at the local, provincial, and national levels for as long as they could. "The fact is, the Reichmanns really are rather apolitical," said Ron Soskolne, who in the mid-1970s would leave his post as a senior planner for the city of Toronto to join Olympia & York.

By contrast, Edward was impelled to involve himself in the fractious municipal politics of Montreal not only by an expansive ego that yearned for public approbation as organically as a houseplant seeks a sunlit window but by the highly politicized nature of business in Montreal. The fact that a pair of immigrant brothers were able to thrive as developers in North York without having to play politics was testament to the basic integrity of government in North York and Toronto in general. Montreal, on the other hand, at the time of Edward and Louis Reichmann's arrival, was one of the most dysfunctional metropolises in North America.

———

Ever since Great Britain conquered Quebec in 1759, Montreal has been the principal political battleground pitting Canada's French minority against its English majority. The English forcibly Anglicized Montreal, reinventing it as their garrison in Quebec. The belated industrialization of Quebec's farm economy after World War I and a surge in the French Canadian birth rate in the 1940s reestablished French numerical superiority in Montreal and bolstered the dormant cause of Quebecois nationalism. However, the grassroots impetus to reform was thwarted by Maurice Duplessis, the iron-fisted premier of Quebec. Although nominally a nationalist, Duplessis cemented himself into office through alliance with Quebec's most reactionary elements: organized crime, the English business establishment, and the Catholic Church. By the mid-1950s, three out of four Montrealers were Quebecois and yet "the center of the great city, dominated by English cultural and business institutions, remained essentially English-Canadian."

In late 1954, several weeks before Edward Reichmann landed in Montreal, voters had struck the first great blow against the Duplessis machine by electing Jean Drapeau mayor. The bespectacled, owlish Drapeau, who had grown up in the traditional working-class French Canadian milieu "furious at the hoity toity English," was both a committed Quebecois nationalist and a crusading lawyer determined to free his stagnant, demoralized native city from the stranglehold of corrupt politicians and their gangster cronies. "Réalisons!" was Drapeau's rallying cry. "Let's get it done!"

The property development business, though relatively free of mob influence, was the linchpin of political corruption. Under Montreal's peculiar system of government, the mayor was subordinate to a six-person executive committee, which, in turn, was elected by a ninety-nine-member city council. To gain a seat on the executive committee, an aspirant traditionally had to buy a half-dozen votes at about $10,000 apiece. Once elected to the ruling committee, a member could recoup this investment many times over by taking bribes from land speculators looking to get suburban tracts rezoned from commercial to residential. "To get the zoning change, the land speculator spreads the money around. Some would go to the chief of the permits department to draft a favourable recommendation. Then key executive committee members would get a healthy cut. After passing the executive committee, the land speculator's motion would then go to council where it would cost about $5,000 a vote to get the measure through."

In his first term as mayor, Drapeau made considerable progress in fighting prostitution, gambling, and other criminal specialties but was unable to clean up government itself. In his frustration, Drapeau overreached, fueling a voter backlash that Duplessis and his machine exploited. In 1957, just as Edward Reichmann was organizing Three Star Construction, Drapeau was narrowly defeated at the polls by a Duplessis stand-in, and the bad old days were back again. In his early real estate dealings, Reichmann was retarded nearly as much by his distaste for bribery as by a chronic insufficiency of capital. In 1960, after Duplessis's death, Drapeau again ran for mayor as the leader of a new party, the Montreal Civic Party. "We are," he warned, "past the hour for ordinary reforms." Although Drapeau's oratory was as uncompromising as ever, defeat had leavened his reformism with pragmatism. When it came to financing his comeback campaign, for example, he emulated the machine; Drapeau's campaign manager brazenly put the arm on contractors and suppliers.

No arm-twisting was required to induce Edward Reichmann to contribute to Drapeau's 1960 campaign or to volunteer his services to the Montreal Civic Party as fund-raiser and speechmaker in Orthodox neighborhoods, just as he had been doing for Leon Crestohl since 1956. To an essentially straitlaced developer like Reichmann, Drapeau's sixteen-page platform was doubly appealing: he not only promised reforms that would sweep away the corrupt vested interests that impeded an honest man's advance in the property business but proposed some $700 million worth of big public construction projects to revitalize the city. In backing Drapeau in 1960, Reichmann grasped what proved to be a fleeting opportunity to ingratiate himself with a man destined to become virtually mayor for life. After winning reelection, Drapeau would remain in office interminably, unassailable in his popularity. In the election of 1966, for example, he took nearly 95 percent of the vote.

Drapeau's return to power coincided with the election of Jean Lesage, a reform-minded Liberal, as the new premier of Quebec. Lesage's ascent marked the start of La Révolution Tranquille—the Quiet Revolution—which began as little more than a push to raise the quality of government services delivered to the Quebecois masses to the same level that prevailed in English Canada. Over time, the Quiet Revolution would take on an increasingly confrontational tone, paving the separatist movement's path into the political mainstream. Right from the beginning, though, Lesage and his fellow "new nationalists"—Jean Drapeau included—met with tenacious resistance as they set about dismantling the two-hundred-year-old structure of English privilege in Quebec. In Montreal especially, the well-fortified English elite dug in, slowing the pace of Quebecois progress to a crawl.

Montreal's ethnic warring made for a treacherous business environment. William Zeckendorf, an American developer active throughout Canada from the mid-1950s to the mid-1960s, complained in his memoirs of "the complex and ever-present business of things French versus things English waiting to trap the unwary" in Montreal. He cited the example of an allied developer who had offended the entire Quebecois nation by naming a new hotel after Queen Elizabeth. "To the French this was just one more bitterly resented, politically exploitable instance of arrogance on the part of the English. To many of the English . . . this was just one more instance of the overexcitable French seeking out and finding trouble where none existed. . . . To us, this was a lesson and a warning that whatever name we chose for our project, it had better be French—or there would be no project."

For Montreal Jewry, the polarization of political life along ethnic lines was disconcerting. Although the Quiet Revolution did not make an issue one way or the other of the Jewish role in the "New Quebec," Jews could not help but fear a recrudescence of the nasty anti-Semitism of the Old Quebec; Henri Bourassa, the father of French Canadian nationalism, had once declared that "the experience of every civilized country is that the Jews are the most undesirable class of people any country can have." On the other hand, the Jews of Montreal shared with French Canadians the indignities of second-class citizenship and tended to support their aspirations—albeit as unobtrusively as possible.

By nature and circumstance, Edward Reichmann was far more emphatically pro-Quebecois than the average Montreal Jew. "To me, it was simple," he recalled. "In every real sense, Montreal was a French city." Luckily for Reichmann, who went by Edouard in Montreal, his natural sympathies were in sync with his economic self-interest as a developer; that is, land-use planning and construction permitting were exclusively the purview of local and provincial government—of French Canadian officialdom. Like Zeckendorf, Reichmann understood that any project that ruffled French Canadian feathers was doomed. But Reichmann went far beyond Zeckendorf, who, after all, was not a resident of Quebec, in casting himself in the role of partisan. Even before he became a naturalized citizen of Canada in 1962, Reichmann began making public demonstrations of his support for the Quebecois cause.

As a practical matter, Reichmann was forced to take a stand on the especially inflammatory issue of bilingualism by Olympia Floor's 1961 acquisition of Pilkington's Tiles, which had been maintained as an unyielding Anglophone bastion for decades. Not long after the deal closed, Reichmann telephoned the factory and inquired, in French naturally, about the availability of a certain hue of tile. "I'm sorry, sir," he was told in English. "We can't speak French."

"Do you mean you do not know how to speak French?" Reichmann responded, in English.

"No," came the reply. "We are not allowed."

Reichmann immediately drove out to the plant and located the general manager, an Englishman, who assured the new owner that he had been correctly informed: Pilkington's Tile was proudly monolingual.

"I'm not telling you to fire anyone," Reichmann replied. "But until a certain balance is reached, every person you hire has got to be French."

Outraged, the man threatened to resign on the spot. In accepting his resignation, Reichmann took a calculated risk. On one hand, he and Louis were neophytes in ceramic manufacturing and had counted on retaining Pilkington's management group. If the general manager's colleagues followed him out the door, who would keep the plant running? On the other hand, Pilkington's existing customer base, to say nothing of its prospective clientele, was heavily French Canadian. Furthermore, how would it look to his contacts in the Drapeau administration if he ran Pilkington's as an Anglophone preserve? As it turned out, in de-Anglicizing Pilkington's, Reichmann won all the way around. He voided a policy that he found personally offensive, curried favor at city hall, and was able to replace the general manager with his assistant, who proved no less competent and far more adaptable to political reality.

———

Jean Drapeau was a lawyer by training but a builder at heart and, for a time, by profession, as well. From 1950 until 1954, he had been vice president of a real estate company owned by Joseph Henri Brien, who was his wife's uncle as well as the future mayor's bagman-in-waiting. After Drapeau's defeat in 1957, Brien named him a director of two development companies active in north Montreal. Having scrutinized the property business from the inside, Drapeau was ready upon his restoration to the mayoralty to purge the land-use planning bureaucracy of corrupt civil servants. He approached this task with alacrity, for he was eager to get on with the job of remodeling dowdy, decrepit Montreal into a modernist beacon of French Canadian culture and commerce.

Actually, the Drapeau building boom had gotten off to a spasmodic start during the mayor's first term with Bill Zeckendorf's announcement of plans for a huge office-and-retailing complex—"a sort of Rockefeller Center–cum–Grand Central Station," as he put it—in the moldering heart of Montreal. The project's centerpiece was to be a forty-two-story office building that would rank as the tallest building in the entire British Commonwealth. The prevalent local reaction was shock, even disbelief; after all, no major building had been completed in Montreal in half a century. Edward Reichmann, though, took inspiration from the news: If a Zeckendorf could do this, why not—someday—a Reichmann?

Zeckendorf's progress was slow. By the time the American decided to name his oversized undertaking Place Ville Marie (patriotically echoing the name of the original French settlement on the site of Montreal), Drapeau had regained the Hôtel de Ville, and by the time the complex was formally dedicated in the fall of 1962, scores of lesser skyscrapers had begun sprouting in its shadow. Although the great majority of downtown projects were undertaken by private enterprise, the Drapeau administration obligingly greased the skids. In gratitude, Zeckendorf lauded the mayor as "a political Hercules" while the developer of another downtown project credited city hall with doing everything but manning the bulldozers. Drapeau's vision of La Nouvelle Montréal extended far beyond "centre ville" to encompass the entire metropolitan area. To spur suburban development and slice the Gordian knot of downtown traffic, the Drapeau government gradually reworked the city's entire transportation system, overlaying it with a complex new grid of bridges, expressways, a boulevard, and a subway system that politicians had been promising voters for fifty years.

Three Star Construction's development of the Chabanel was perfectly in sync with the Drapeau administration's larger efforts to decongest the city center. As one of north Montreal's most prolific developers, Edward Reichmann would have wielded a certain clout at city hall even if he had supported Drapeau's opponent in the 1960 election. As it was, Reichmann enjoyed exceptional access to the highest echelons of the city government. His relationship with Drapeau was cordial enough but formal and ceremonial—like the mayor himself. In between election campaigns, Reichmann generally only saw Drapeau when bringing visiting Orthodox dignitaries down to the mayor's office for photo opportunities. Having strayed into the anti-Semitic fringe of the nationalist movement as a youth, Drapeau as mayor was ever alert to opportunities to demonstrate his lack of animus toward Jews. Reichmann established a much more intimate connection to city hall through Lucien Saulnier, who, as chairman of the executive committee of the city council, was chief administrator to Drapeau's chief executive officer. "Edward was very friendly with

Saulnier," said Emile Rooz, the real estate broker. "It was more than just business with them."

Born and raised in north Montreal, Saulnier had gone to work at age seven after the death of his father, a milkman. "I can't ever remember playing hockey or baseball as a boy," he would recall. After graduating from high school, he got a job as an office boy for a Jesuit-owned printing company while taking night classes at the University of Montreal. Saulnier worked his way up to advertising manager of a parish monthly and acquired a haberdashery as a sideline. In 1954 he got caught up in the maelstrom of municipal politics and won election to the city council as a blunt-spoken Mr. Clean. Saulnier helped found the reformist vehicle of Drapeau's return to power, the Civic Party, which in 1960 wrested control of the city council by a two-to-one margin. Elected chairman of the executive committee virtually by acclamation, Saulnier went about his business "with toe-tromping efficiency, unencumbered by old political debts."

Reichmann's befriending of Drapeau's only political equal was quite an achievement, considering not only the loftiness of Saulnier's position but the man's difficult, enigmatic personality. Saulnier was a devout, melancholic Catholic who once conceded that his greatest fault was "pride, hidden under airs of modesty." On weekends, he liked to retreat to an estate on the Ile Bizard where "he would spend time with his six children, relax with prize roses and the *Requiem* of Berlioz and dabble in Lewis Mumford's *The Culture of Cities*, Plato, Thurber, Montesquieu and the detective exploits of Chesterton's Father Brown."

Although Saulnier and Drapeau were allies in reform and close collaborators in running the city, theirs was a prickly relationship, shadowed by rivalry. A man of stern, lantern-jawed countenance, Saulnier appointed himself the moral conscience of the Drapeau administration—its "Archangel Gabriel," in the words of one biographer. "My sole ambition," he once said, "is to prove that honest men can assure an intelligent government. For too long it has been assumed that honesty is a synonym for insignificance." As attentive to the appearance of propriety as to propriety itself, Saulnier had almost a visceral aversion to accepting campaign contributions on behalf of his party, legal or otherwise.

To Edward Reichmann, Saulnier's ethical fastidiousness in office was admirable. If Saulnier had been born Jewish instead of Catholic, no doubt he would have been as Torah-true as they come. On the other hand, there was nothing self-denying about this self-made man's attitude toward commerce. He was, after all, a businessman-cum-politician and no more a priest than Edward was a rabbi. Like Drapeau, Saulnier saw the crane and wrecking ball as agents of municipal redemption. More narrowly, he ascended to citywide office as an unabashed booster of the North End.

Although Reichmann and Saulnier occasionally visited one another's homes, their social interaction was minimal and secondary to what might be termed their working relationship. Despite their demographic dissimilarities— one a Catholic native, the other an immigrant Jew—Saulnier and Reichmann were kindred spirits in that both were stubbornly independent, Francophile businessmen of high principle and great ambition. On a more mundane but perhaps more important level, the two were joined by a shared passion for the minutiae of the politics of North End development. Wherever and whenever they encountered one another, Saulnier and Reichmann talked zoning bylaws the way diehard baseball fans talk statistics.

In building Place Crémazie, the pièce de résistance of his career as a developer, Edward Reichmann and his partners placed a large and nakedly public wager on the Drapeau administration's ability to realize its vision of La Nouvelle Montréal. Having already transplanted much of the needle trade from its warrens downtown into light-manufacturing plants in the North End, Reichmann now set out to create a "prestige address" just a few blocks from the Chabanel. As originally conceived, the project consisted of two attached fourteen-story office buildings, two light-commercial buildings of equal height, and a thirty-five-store shopping center. But if Reichmann saw Place Crémazie as the logical progression of his Chabanel pioneering, the $13 million complex was generally viewed as a quantum leap into the unknown. Place Crémazie was "believed to mark the beginning of a new era in the commercial layout of the city" in that it was "a radical departure from the concentration of business downtown," observed the *Montreal Star* in one of the least skeptical of the news articles prompted by the project's mid-1962 groundbreaking. "The project is the first of its kind in the north end of the city and will duplicate on a lesser scale the function of Place Ville Marie and Place Victoria in downtown Montreal."

Place Crémazie was strategically located near the intersection of three of the mightiest arteries of Montreal's updated transit system: St. Lawrence Boulevard, Metropolitan Boulevard, and Le Métro, the new subway, which, though named after Paris's famous system, resembled it not in the least. Reichmann liked to describe Place Crémazie as "the first building complex conceived in connection with Montreal's subway system." He and Tibor Pivko had begun buying up property along Metropolitan Boulevard, the main east-west thoroughfare in northeast Montreal, even before Drapeau reclaimed the mayoralty in 1960 and added to their holdings as the transportation planks in the administration's campaign platform coalesced into projects. Three Star snapped into place the final 31,000-square-foot piece in its 250,000-square-foot property jigsaw puzzle in October 1961, just a few weeks before Saulnier appeared before the North End Businessman's Association and repudiated the building of elevated expressways.

For Reichmann and Pivko, the city's decision to widen without elevating Metropolitan Boulevard was highly advantageous, indeed crucial.

But by this time, so many new skyscrapers were under way downtown that excitement over the novelty of large-scale construction had given way to predictions of a rent-crushing glut. If premium office space was likely to be available at a discount in the city center, why would any first-rate company isolate itself in the déclassé North End? Defying the odds, Reichmann did indeed fill his complex with tenants. When Place Crémazie was first announced, "some people shook their heads in disbelief," Three Star Construction gloated in an advertisement placed in local newspapers in the spring of 1964. "They considered the project daring but little short of foolhardy. Well, now all of this is history. Place Crémazie completed two of its four towers in record time and left the decision to the business and organization leaders of Canada. Their response was immediate and definite: just eight months after completion of the first two towers, 91 percent of the available space is gone!"

From the distance of three decades, it is difficult to gauge the extent to which Reichmann might have benefited from his ties to Saulnier in assembling the four-block site for Place Crémazie. Saulnier died in 1989 and Reichmann is uncharacteristically reticent on the subject of their relationship. Subway routing and other transportation planning issues of vital interest to property developers were thrashed out by the city council and its committees in forums open to anyone with the patience to endure them. Saulnier may well have confided his private opinion about the likely outcome of these debates to Reichmann, but such handicapping of the public processes of policy making, however well informed, hardly amounts to inside information.

Yet there is no question that Saulnier went out of his way to boost the project once construction had begun. Not six weeks after the first shovelful of sod had been turned, the chairman toured the site with the city's director of public works and the city hall press corps in tow. In the spring of 1963, a few weeks before the scheduled completion of the first building (and a few weeks after Three Star had begun running newspaper advertisements soliciting tenants), Saulnier generated another round of press notices by announcing that the City Assessors Department had received executive committee authorization to lease 29,000 square feet in Place Crémazie. That fall, Saulnier moved his haberdashery off rue Crémazie into the Place Crémazie shopping center, signing what appeared to be a standard five-year lease at $33,000 per year. Unassumingly described as a "tailleur et chemisier," Saulnier was one of two dozen shopping center tenants whose names were featured in the Christmas card that Place Crémazie distributed in 1963.

In private, meanwhile, Reichmann repeatedly sought Saulnier's help in overcoming hurdles placed in his path by one municipal department or another. "I was with Edward a few times when he had appointments with city construction inspectors who were objecting to something," recalled Rooz, who as a self-employed broker was involved with Place Crémazie from assembling the site to leasing space. "So we went down to see Lucien Saulnier and he helped out." Added Pivko, who also recalled accompanying Reichmann on the occasional visit to city hall: "It definitely helped that Saulnier liked us—no question about it. We had an inside position."

In recollecting his dealings with Saulnier thirty years later, Reichmann was oddly evasive and contradictory. On one hand, he seemed proud at having gained preferred access to so powerful an official. "Saulnier was the top man," he said, "so I used to go to see him." On the other hand, he seemed loath to leave the impression that he used that access to his benefit as a developer: "I never took unfair advantage of my personal relationship with Saulnier." By this, Reichmann seemed to mean that whenever Saulnier came to his aid he did so on the merits of the project and not as a favor for a friend and political supporter. Whether even "the Black Pope" of Montreal, as some of Saulnier's less ethically scrupulous political rivals sneeringly called him, was capable of such fine-tuned purity of motive is doubtful. The very act of his inserting himself in matters that did not routinely cross his desk was, by any reasonable definition, a form of favoritism. But so what? Uncovering evidence of a pattern of favoritism in the workings of the municipal government of a major North American metropolis is like finding a wad of used gum under the counter of a truckstop diner. Mildly unpleasant perhaps but neither surprising nor particularly significant.

In the end, the issue is most noteworthy for Reichmann's discomfort at being seen as having conformed to type. For Edward and his brothers, it was not enough to exemplify the highest standards of a profession when that profession—real estate development—was notoriously sleazy, no more than it had been enough for their father to hold himself out as the most respectable of Tangier bankers when, in the lexicon of conventional banking, respectable and Tangier were antonyms. To achieve success on their own terms, the Reichmann brothers somehow had to master the world of commerce and yet transcend commercial morality—to immerse themselves in the shark-tank of real estate and yet emerge not only unscarred but dry as a bone. This was impossible, though the Toronto brothers were able to prolong the suspense in part by keeping their distance from the politicians during their North York years. That a developer had no such luxury in Montreal suited Edward Reichmann just fine. And so it was that the eldest Reichmann brother came to excel at a game that he could not bring himself to acknowledge playing.

———

On October 29, 1963, nearly nine years after he had emigrated to Canada, Edward Reichmann reached the apogee of his career in Montreal as he hosted a stageful of prominent government officials—including Mayor Drapeau and Eric Kierans, the revenue minister of Quebec—at Place Crémazie's dedication, which marked the completion of the first of its four minitowers. Drapeau's attendance was a real coup, given his well-established aversion to ribbon-cutting, and apparently was the result of Saulnier's importuning. Edward and Louis were no less honored by the presence of their father, who had made the trip from Toronto with Paul expressly for the occasion, which included a gala but strictly kosher reception for several hundred people. After unveiling a plaque, Mayor Drapeau praised his hosts' courage and initiative and observed that with the opening of Place Crémazie, the North End should no longer be considered the far end of the city but rather "an extended part of downtown Montreal."

For the oldest Reichmann brother, the day was a carefully calculated exercise in political positioning. Mindful of the mounting backlash against the influx of foreigners and their capital into Canada, Edward wrapped himself in maple leaf bunting in noting in his comments to the press that Place Crémazie was entirely Canadian-made. In his prepared remarks, delivered alternately in English and French, Reichmann mined the same self-servingly patriotic vein, praising Canada as a country that "still offers great opportunities to those willing to face the challenge of innovation."

At the same time, Reichmann left no doubt about where his sympathies lay in the great Anglo-French struggle over Quebec's future. It is unlikely that anyone left Place Crémazie that day without knowing that it was one of the first buildings in Montreal equipped with bilingual signs. And at Reichmann's insistence, the policemen's chorus on hand for the opening followed the obligatory "O Canada" with a ringing version of "O Carillon," a Quebecois anthem by Octave Crémazie, the nineteenth-century French Canadian writer after whom the building was named. Finally, Reichmann delivered a speech so overtly political that some listeners half expected him to announce his candidacy for electoral office:

We new Canadians understand the hopes and fears of this province, its desire to survive, the legitimate aspirations of the majority. And we find ourselves in full sympathy with the Quiet Revolution sweeping the Province of Quebec on the economic, cultural and spiritual levels. One feels it in every area of life in Quebec today and the achievement of such understandable objectives will be all to the good of Canada.

Thirty years after the Place Crémazie gala, the notary Sheldon Merling would retain only a single vivid memory of the event: the oddly touching sight of his friend and client, Edward Reichmann, guiding Lucien Saulnier, the Black Pope of Montreal, along the kosher hors d'oeuvre table. "He was patiently explaining to Saulnier, 'See, this is chopped liver, this is whatever.' My first thought," added Merling, who is only casually observant, "was I couldn't believe Saulnier didn't know what chopped liver was. But I also remember being proud to see Edward sticking to his principles in the midst of this big success. As a Jew, it made me feel good."

Long before Place Crémazie was finished—and just two months after its triumphant opening—Reichmann attracted even greater attention in unveiling plans for a more glamorous if less daring new project: La Tour Laurier. Named for Wilfrid Laurier, Canada's first French Canadian prime minister (1896–1911), La Tour Laurier was the Reichmann family's first attempt at a downtown office tower. Announced at the end of 1963, the proposed $15 million skyscraper excited wide interest in Montreal not only because of its impressive height—at thirty-nine stories it would be just three floors shy of the Place Ville Marie tower—but also because of the novelty of its design. La Tour Laurier was to be a round skyscraper, the first in Canada.

The notion of a circular tower originated with William Strong, a Toronto architect whom Edward had hired on the recommendation of Paul and Albert. Strong later insisted that there was nothing gimmicky about his design. "[I] had the idea of the circular form costed out against the conventional rectangular shape," Strong said. "The circular building turned out to be less costly. Where we lost on the grapefruit we made up in the bananas. It was a very functional building, and the round ground floor plan gave you more offices on the periphery. You could lay out more offices in less space than you could in a rectangular form."

Reichmann and Pivko paid $1.2 million for a prime site on Sherbrooke Street, today Montreal's busiest downtown thoroughfare, and astounded other aspirant developers by reaching preliminary agreement with a most prestigious lead tenant: the Montreal Amateur Athletic Association (MAAA), which in essence was an exclusive private men's club and a bulwark of the city's old Anglophone establishment. The athletic association was to occupy the base of the building, which was to connect to a new luxury hotel. Three Star hoped to complete La Tour Laurier by the fall of 1965, in plenty of time to cash in on the anticipated commercial bonanza brought by Expo '67.

Although La Tour Laurier never would make it even to the hole-in-the-ground stage, the publicity generated by its announcement had the immediate effect of adding to Edward Reichmann's stature as a man of consequence in Montreal business circles and within the Jewish community. By the mid-1960s, according to Pivko, the value of Three Star Construction's assets exceeded its debts by about $5 million and Olympia Floor and Maple Leaf Ceramics between them had a net worth of another $3 million. Edward's one-third share of these fast-growing, profitable enterprises (by this time Pivko and the Reichmanns had bought out the other Venezuelan investors) easily made him a millionaire on paper.

Yet when the La Tour Laurier project was unveiled, Edward and his family were still living in one half of a small duplex on Durocher Street that he and Louis had jointly acquired in 1958. Louis and his family lived in the other half of the duplex, which was only a few blocks from First Mesifta. In early 1964, Edward asked his realtor friend Rooz to scout the section of Outremont around Parc Pratt, which was a dozen blocks from Durocher on the way up to Mont Royal. Despite Rooz's best efforts, Reichmann fixated on a house that was not even on the market. The young doctor who owned 1826 Lajoie Avenue had just finished remodeling and had no thought of selling. But Reichmann sent Rooz back repeatedly until the doctor named a price, which was instantly accepted. About two weeks after his thirty-ninth birthday, Reichmann bought the house for $82,000, which in Rooz's estimation was at least twice its market value. "For the same money," Rooz said, "he could have bought a bigger place in a more prestigious neighborhood but he didn't want to be far from First Mesifta."

A year later, Rooz would represent Louis Reichmann in purchasing for $48,000 a four-bedroom house at 6145 de Vimy, just a block from Edward's new place. In their dozen years in Montreal, Edward and Louis would never settle more than a few blocks apart for long. For six of those years, they even shared a common wall in the duplex on Durocher. Edward valued the proximity to his brother, but for the most part it was Louis, in bringing up the rear, who ensured that it was maintained. These household logistics were revealing of the essence of their relationship: in subordinating himself to his older brother in every facet of their lives, Louis conspired in his own eclipse.

True to form, Edward's new place was bigger and more prominently located than his brother's. It was a blocky, two-story brick affair that sat incongruously among a few dozen older houses—some of which deserved to be called mansions—of rock and stone. The neighborhood blended the nouveau and the haute bourgeoisie, and was considerably if not predominantly Jewish. Jack and Pearl Zimmerman lived there, as did another of Reichmann's ex-partners, Viliam Frankel. Edward sank a tidy sum into remodeling his new property, which, like the homes of many affluent Orthodox Jews, was far bigger and fancier on the inside than it looked from the street. In the backyard, Edward installed a permanent sukkah, a kind of booth used in the observance of Sukkoth. In the basement, he put in a large sauna and a well-equipped game room.

Aside from improving his living quarters and putting a little more swagger in his step, success did not alter Reichmann as much as it slipped his turbocharged personality into even higher gear. He chain-smoked his way through fourteen-hour workdays, shifting frequently from real estate matters to his duties as an

Orthodox communal leader. Whoever he was with and wherever he went, Reichmann vied to establish himself as the center of attention. On his occasional forays to the horse track with his closest friends, Edward usually insisted on taking all bets. "Why go to the window?" he'd say. "I'll give you the same odds right here." At dinner parties and banquets, he liked to hold forth not only on current events (including his latest business deal) but on selected topics from the history of the Reichmann family. His wife, Edith, was a refined and stoic sort who nonetheless acquired a long-suffering air when out in company with her husband, wincing slightly as he launched into the umpteenth recitation of a favorite tale, occasionally even disputing his recollections.

In mid-1964, a few months after Edward and Edith acquired the house on Lajoie, their seventeen-year-old daughter, Margaret, married and moved away to Monsey, New York, where her new husband was attending yeshiva. The wedding of "Malky" Reichmann attracted some five hundred guests from around the world, the ceremony's scale inflated by its dual purpose of commemorating the first wedding of a Reichmann grandchild as well as her father's ascension to Montreal macherhood. Like Eva Reichmann's wedding twenty-six years earlier in Tangier, the event was held outdoors in the courtyard of a posh hotel and was strictly kosher in every aspect but its guest list, which included many prominent Montrealers who were either nonobservant or Gentile. In photographs taken during the wedding reception, ancient rabbis in full Hasidic garb can be seen mingling, after a fashion, with nattily dressed politicians and businessmen, illustrating the duality of Edward Reichmann's ambition with the vivid surreality of a dream.

Chapter 23

W illiam Zeckendorf figured peripherally in the saga of the Montreal Reichmanns, but his porcine presence loomed in the foreground of Olympia & York's story. In 1965, Paul and Albert Reichmann eclipsed their rivals in the industrial building trade by gaining control of a Zeckendorf development called Flemingdon Park. For Olympia & York, this was the first in a string of five extraordinary deals that would define the Reichmann brothers' distinctive approach to real estate over a twenty-five-year period. If at the time the Flemingdon Park transaction seemed an exercise in minnow-swallows-whale improbability, in retrospect it would seem foreordained, like the conveyance of a legacy from father to son. For if Bill Zeckendorf was the prototype of the developer as high-rolling visionary, then Paul Reichmann would be the breed apotheosized.

Born in 1905 in a small town in Illinois, Zeckendorf moved to New York as a boy and dropped out of college to go to work for his uncle's Manhattan real estate office. After gaining control of Webb & Knapp, he transformed the stodgy brokerage into the biggest and most daring dealer in real property in American history—at least until Olympia & York came along. Zeckendorf could have grown rich merely by banking the income from the properties he snapped up at bargain prices in New York City during the World War II years. Instead, he leveraged himself to the teeth to finance La Place Ville Marie in Montreal, Zeckendorf City in New York, Century City in Los Angeles, the Mile High Center in Denver, L'Enfant Plaza in Washington, D.C., and other gargantuan developments.

A fast-talking, cigar-chomping, fun-loving, self-promoting bear of a man, Zeckendorf was as flamboyant as Reichmann was reticent. He could not have better embodied Hollywood's stereotypical image of the wheeler-dealer had he been sent from central casting. Zeckendorf worked from a circular, windowless office that sat atop a Madison Avenue skyscraper like a mutant hatbox and liked to hold court at lunch and after hours at a swank midtown nightclub that leased space in a Webb & Knapp building. His most prized possessions included a 100-acre estate in Greenwich, Connecticut, a lavishly appointed DC-3, a fifteen-foot phone cord, and a toy Doberman pinscher, which he and his wife brought to Park Avenue parties in a silk bow tie and leather wing collar.

Although Zeckendorf was "as much of a hedonist as any man who works twelve hours a day can be," a *Fortune* writer once observed, "otherwise he behaves as if mere money were a little beneath him." For him, as for Reichmann, wealth ultimately was but the means to the end of creating heroically original and difficult real estate ventures. Zeckendorf considered himself something of a creative genius. "I make bananas out of peanuts," he once boasted. "I make grapefruit out of lemons. What I like to do is recognize a great piece of land and conceive a suitable edifice for it." Even when Webb & Knapp began to stagger under the weight of the high-cost loans that buttressed Zeckendorf's grandiosity, the developer was unrepentant. "I'd rather be alive at 18 percent," he quipped, "than dead at the prime rate."

In 1955, Zeckendorf discovered Canada. Montreal's Place Ville Marie was but the grandest of a dozen major Webb & Knapp projects north of the border. In Canada, as in the United States, Webb & Knapp did it all—apartment buildings, houses, shopping centers, industrial parks, urban redevelopment projects, skyscrapers—and quickly established itself as the country's largest and most daring developer.

In late 1957, just as Paul Reichmann was putting that first Colville Road job out to bid, Zeckendorf entered into partnership with the Reichmanns' future archrivals: the brothers Rubin of Toronto Industrial Leaseholds. In selling a two-thirds interest in TIL to Zeckendorf for $3 million, the Rubin brothers gained access to Webb & Knapp's corporate treasury and yet were able to keep operating control of their company. "For me, it was a very easy deal to do," Alex Rubin recalled. "The whole thing was really Zeckendorf's idea." The one-sidedness of the arrangement was predicated on the American real estate impresario's appreciation of the young Canadian's promise as a developer. In introducing Alex Rubin to the board of directors of Webb & Knapp (Canada), Zeckendorf bestowed what he no doubt considered the ultimate compliment, hailing his new protégé as "the young Bill Zeckendorf of Canada."

Even before Zeckendorf provided him with the combination to Webb & Knapp's safe, Rubin had begun negotiating to buy a 400-acre tract of North York farmland known as the Flemingdon estate. The site was owned by a housing developer who was getting cold feet in what would prove a momentarily soft market. Rubin's own feet were fine; his problem was keeping a poker face as he considered the site's potential. The Flemingdon estate lay squarely in the path of the Don Valley Parkway, a proposed north-south expressway that would link the Trans-Canada Highway to downtown Toronto. Scheduled for completion in the mid-1960s, the Don Valley Parkway would slice the driving time between North York and the city center to about twelve minutes. As Rubin walked the estate, he imagined its transformation into a de novo suburban community mixing apartments, stores, and office buildings according to the highest contemporary standards of planning and design.

Acting on Webb & Knapp's behalf, Rubin paid a few million dollars for the Flemingdon estate and later snapped up 100 acres of adjacent land. Zeckendorf quickly blessed Rubin's ambitious plans for Flemingdon Park and ground was broken in 1960. Within a matter of months, Rubin had fallen out with his mentor over Toronto Industrial Leasehold's costly attempts to diversify into shopping center development and resigned to start a new company of his own. Webb & Knapp liquidated the shopping centers and poured the money into Flemingdon Park. Focusing its own efforts on building apartment towers, the company sold off much of the project's industrial acreage to other developers or to business corporations, including the Gestetner Company. When David Gestetner transferred to the copier-maker's Toronto office from the London headquarters in 1962, he was abashed to discover that the local manager had overlooked his cousins, the Reichmann brothers, in selecting a general contractor for the new sales office. "I would have liked to have used them but the matter had been decided by the time I arrived," Gestetner recalled. "I always had the impression Paul and Albert felt slighted, but I'm not sure because they never said anything to me about it."

———

As it turned out, Flemingdon Park was one of Webb & Knapp's last great undertakings. In 1962, the company started to unravel under the tremendous burden of the debt Zeckendorf had taken on to finance his multiple megaprojects. Webb & Knapp lost $20 million in 1962 and a ruinous $32 million in 1963. An inveterate optimist, Zeckendorf was slow to grasp the gravity of the situation. "Exactly when we moved from a hopeful position into a desperate situation, I cannot say," he admitted in his memoirs. "I was doing what I had always done." Both in the United States and Canada, Zeckendorf did begin selling off assets to raise cash but with a prideful reluctance that belied Webb & Knapp's increasingly dire predicament and prefigured Paul Reichmann's self-destructive intransigence three decades later. "That a beleaguered Webb & Knapp owned a property was a signal to some potential buyers to hold back or bid low, in the expectation that, in our eagerness for cash, we would hold a fire sale," Zeckendorf complained. "I resisted this downgrading in every way possible."

In mid-1963, Zeckendorf bowed to pressure from the outside directors of Webb & Knapp (Canada) and resigned his posts as its chairman and chief executive. Under James Soden, the Canadian company's president, the subsidiary devised its own survival strategy—one that hinged on Flemingdon Park, the largest and most attractive of its remaining assets. The millstone around Webb & Knapp Canada's corporate neck was a $23 million bond issue that had been floated to finance Place Ville Marie. Soden's sales pitch to his nervous bond-holders went something like this: We don't have the cash to continue making payments to you. If we default and you choose to force us to liquidate right now, you'll recoup only a fraction of your investment. But if you agree to swap your bonds for stock in a reorganized Flemingdon Park, eventually you could get all your money back—and more.

There was just one catch, but it was huge. Having run out of cash to pay con-tractors, Webb & Knapp had had to shut down Flemingdon Park at an awkward stage of incompletion and let most of its employees go. The company did not have a prayer of realizing sufficient value to cover the bonds unless the project was completed. Soden needed a partner, another developer capable of reviving Flemingdon Park and yet willing to surrender a large chunk of future profits to Webb & Knapp and its bondholders. In mid-1963, Soden began dangling the project before scores of developers throughout Canada and the United States—to no avail. "The real estate community saw us reaching the bottom of the bar-rel and thought that whatever was left must not be very good apples," Soden recalled. "In reality, there was nothing wrong with Flemingdon Park that cash couldn't cure. But when you're down, you're down, and people just don't want to deal with a loser." In addition to the stigma of impending corporate collapse, it had yet to be proven that major tenants would forsake downtown Toronto for office towers in Flemingdon Park or anywhere else in suburban North York.

Soden did not know Olympia & York to approach it, and the company was still too small to bother with in any event. For their part, the Reichmanns knew that Flemingdon Park was on the block but did not give it a second thought. "It just seemed out of our league," Paul Reichmann said. Nevertheless, in their own small way, the Reichmanns capitalized on the market void left by the mothballing of Flemingdon Park. Olympia & York bought two tracts of land on the project's periphery and on each put up a strip of a half-dozen warehouses and light-manufacturing plants. At the same time, the Reichmanns reaped greater long-term advantage by hiring Flemingdon Park's construction man-ager: Keith Roberts. "I was aware of the Reichmanns because they were doing a lot of one- and two-story industrial buildings," Roberts recalled years later. "I called on Albert unannounced to see what the job prospects might be. They had less than ten people and were reluctant to hire anybody else. I lowered my sights a bit, offering to start at $10,000. I talked for a while with Albert and Paul in their office kitchen."

The Reichmanns would never make a more important hire. At forty-one, Roberts was a gifted, broadly experienced builder who would remain with

Olympia & York for thirty years, becoming in fact what Paul Reichmann would be metaphorically: Olympia & York's master builder. "Roberts had been a real high-profile guy for us," recalled Bud Andrews, his boss at Webb & Knapp. "When the Reichmanns got him, they got the best."

Roberts cut nearly as novel a figure in the rough-and-tumble world of the construction trades as did the Reichmann brothers. He was an Englishman of considerable polish and rugged good looks—a pipe-smoking, public school–educated engineer who resembled the actor Christopher Plummer. Born in Sheffield, where his father was the town engineer, Roberts attended Eltham College in Kent but left after the outbreak of World War II to join a general contractor, which assigned him, as site engineer, to the building of a munitions factory and an aerodrome. Later, he saw combat in Europe in an engineering unit of the British Airborne Division. After the war, Roberts built army camps throughout the Middle East and was wounded in Palestine when a terrorist bomb that he was dismantling exploded in his face. Demobilized in 1947 with the rank of major, he joined a large British general contractor and worked as a site engineer in England until 1953, when he and his wife emigrated to Canada. Roberts built breweries and worked as general manager of a small Toronto construction firm before joining Webb & Knapp in 1962.

With the addition of Roberts, the Reichmann brothers began moving up in the world—literally. Having mastered the craft of building one-story warehouses and light-manufacturing plants, the Reichmanns naturally aspired to verticality and that meant office buildings. Branching into the construction of multistory structures was a logical but daunting move, for it required special design and engineering expertise. Although Roberts was not an office-tower specialist per se, he had made a career out of building whatever needed building.

In late 1964, Mony Life Insurance Company of Canada bought a corner lot in Flemingdon Park and asked the Reichmanns to put up a four-story office building. Olympia & York would own the structure and as landlord lease out the story-and-a-half that the insurer did not occupy. As Paul Reichmann pondered the project's economics, he came to the conclusion that its very ordinariness made it risky. "With a conventional four-story building, we knew that we couldn't do any better than anybody else in the area," he recalled. "So we said that we wanted to build to sixteen stories and make it the outstanding office building in north Toronto." The management of Mony took some convincing but went along. Completed in 1967 at a cost of $15 million, North American Tower was the Toronto equivalent of Place Crémazie: the first top-quality office building outside downtown.

The Mony project nearly ended before it started. To build to sixteen stories rather than four, Olympia & York required more land. When the Reichmanns approached Webb & Knapp in May 1965, seeking an additional half acre, they were rebuffed, albeit in a most enticing way. The property in question was encumbered by mortgages and could not be detached from the rest of the acreage for separate sale, a Webb & Knapp executive explained. "We can't sell you a half acre," he said in effect, "but we'd love to sell you three hundred."

By this time, Jim Soden was nearing desperation in his efforts to save Webb & Knapp Canada. A few weeks earlier, Webb & Knapp Inc., the U.S. company that was Zeckendorf's flagship, finally filed for bankruptcy protection. "To be frank about it, we were on the ropes," Soden conceded. "If Olympia & York hadn't come along when they did, I think we would have been bankrupt ourselves within weeks." Soden had no time for games. In response to a tentative expression of interest from the Reichmann brothers, he laid out his terms: Webb & Knapp would sell a 50 percent interest in Flemingdon Park for $18 million, at least $3 million in cash. "For Webb & Knapp," Paul Reichmann recalled, "it was not a matter of getting the right price but the right deal."

For all the progress that Olympia & York had made during the two years that Soden had been shopping Flemingdon Park around North America, the deal that he now proposed represented a quantum leap for the Reichmanns. In most ways, Olympia & York had always been a conservatively run company, at least in the context of the high-risk industry in which it operated. For one thing, the Reichmanns shied away from speculating on land prices by holding large tracts of property in inventory. Nor, in deference mainly to Samuel Reichmann's wishes, had the brothers undertaken many building projects "on spec," that is, without having signed up tenants before breaking ground.

At the same time, the Reichmanns' aversion to adding to corporate overhead was so extreme that they added staff only under duress. Oskar Lustig, who joined Olympia & York in mid-1963 as its first professional accountant, was so overworked initially that he considered quitting. "I was unhappy at first because it was a tremendous amount of work," Lustig recalled. "By this time they were really popping, building all over the place, but they still had less than a dozen employees, and the back office was way behind the front office. Their philosophy was that if you can do a job with one person, do it with one. And if eventually you need three people to do the same job, then try it with two. You watch the dollar."

Flemingdon Park was larger and more complex by several orders of magnitude than any of the brothers' previous undertakings. Even with the addition of Roberts, who knew the project inside and out, would the firm's small staff be equal to the task? Then there was the problem of money: Olympia & York did not have it. To raise the cash minimum of $3 million, the Reichmanns would have to borrow against every property they owned, imperiling the fruits of a decade's hard slogging on a single deal. If the Flemingdon Park revival failed, Albert and Paul would have to start over from scratch.

The Toronto Reichmanns had arrived at the proverbial fork in the road. Had the decision been left to Albert, Ralph, and Samuel Reichmann, who was active in Olympia & York as its chairman, the family likely would have passed on Flemingdon Park and consigned the company to a fate of relative ordinariness. They were not so much opposed to making a deal as stunned into passivity by the sheer scale of the opportunity and the risks implicit in it. Paul, on the other hand, was enraptured by Flemingdon Park's possibilities and with the family's uneasy assent began negotiations with Webb & Knapp. "There's gold on the table and no one wants to pick it up," he confided to Gilbert Newman, Olympia & York's auditor. "Are we making a mistake somewhere? Am I missing something?"

As Flemingdon Park would be the springboard of Olympia & York's vault into the first rank of property developers in Toronto, so, too, was it the vehicle of Paul Reichmann's emergence as the company's dominant, propulsive force. Like all the destiny-defining transactions to follow, Flemingdon Park was his deal from start to finish. At thirty-five, the fourth-born brother had had a decade of self-schooling in the fundamentals of development and was eager for the Ph.D.-level challenge that Flemingdon Park represented. His grasping of the opportunity afforded by Webb & Knapp's collapse was the first indication that he, like Zeckendorf, was a developer of towering ambition. However, unlike Big Bill, who luxuriated in his outsizedness in every sense, Reichmann preferred to portray himself as an accidental overachiever. As he told it, his ambition was a by-product of Olympia & York's success, not its fuel. "I never set out to build a giant company," Reichmann would recall in the mid-1990s. "The fact that the company happened to grow so fast right from the start made us want to sustain that rate of growth."

For the observant Jew, commercial ambition is an intrinsically touchy subject. As Reichmann conceded, "personal drive is supposed to be devoted more to matters of the mind than to business." Within haredi society, the study of Torah is regarded not merely as the highest form of achievement but as every adult male's solemn religious duty. As a product of some of the world's finest yeshivas, Paul Reichmann was steeped in the culture of the Book and would remain unswervingly loyal to it. During Olympia & York's life, he would distribute hundreds of millions of dollars among yeshivoth and other schools around the world, ranking him the greatest patron that Orthodox education has seen or is likely to see. And yet Reichmann rarely would be found at the kollel that he founded in 1970 a few blocks from his house in North York. By all accounts but his own, Reichmann devoted himself so obsessively to business after he had discovered his calling as a developer that he had little time left for study.

Like overachievers of all denominations, Reichmann was hard-pressed even to make time for his wife and children. One Purim in the early 1960s, Reichmann told the architect Morley Sirlin to drop by his apartment that evening to discuss a business matter. Sirlin arrived at the scheduled time and found three men in line in the vestibule. The Reichmann children already were in their costumes and their father's increasingly hurried consultations were punctuated by a ringing telephone, as people kept calling from Yesodei Hatorah to see what was keeping the family. Finally, Mrs. Reichmann put the children in a taxicab and sent them on ahead alone. By the time the architect finally sat down with his client, "Lea was stomping back and forth," Sirlin recalled. "She was furious. Finally she said, 'I'm not married to a man. I'm married to a business machine.' " Reichmann look abashed but remained silent, waiting for the storm to pass.

Especially around fellow haredim, Reichmann tried to mask the ferocity of his drive with nonchalance even as he chain-smoked his way through every business day for thirty years. (He finally managed to kick the habit in the mid-1980s.) But whatever inner anguish Reichmann suffered in neglecting the mitzvah of study would remain a private matter until the mid-1980s when, at the very peak of his corporate empire building, Reichmann began pining in press interviews for the lost Talmudicism of youth. "If someone asked me what my greatest achievement in life was, I would not point to Canary Wharf," he volunteered in 1988. "I feel that study is more important than what I'm doing here." At the same time, Reichmann held out the work that he'd done for Ozar Hatorah in the 1950s as his finest hour: "Building schools in Morocco was a type of work which gave me enthusiasm. I wasn't at all interested in business. . . . I think that what I did in those years was a greater achievement than what I've done since."

But if the fact of Reichmann's commercial ambition was as incontrovertible as the office complexes in which he came to specialize were colossal, its psychological underpinnings remained obscure and elusive. Reichmann was of little help to those who would understand what made him run. Questions about his makeup and motives visibly discomfited the man and tended to be shrugged off with a tight half-smile, a polite pause, and a change of subject.

When pressed, Reichmann implied that he was compelled to fill empty lots by the same sort of impulse that drives a painter to fill empty canvases. "There is the purely mathematical approach and there is the creative part of building," he said. "One can get carried away with the creative part. It became exciting to me to do different kinds of developments. My ambitions grew in terms of the size and scope and the creativity of the projects." In his heyday, Reichmann would come to loathe the formulaic at least as much as he feared failure, and he would go to audacious lengths to keep from repeating himself. "There is an enjoyment in being able to do something that others consider difficult if not impossible," he once said with deceptive mildness. What Reichmann found utterly irresistible was the showcase project that had been tainted by another developer's failure and thus became stigmatized by an aura of once and future doom. For him, ultimate triumph lay not just in proving himself but in proving the world wrong.

If any developer deserved to be called an artist, then Paul Reichmann was that man. Make no mistake, though, the essence of the art of development is financial, not architectural. Reichmann was unusual in that he would simultaneously excel at corporate finance and project finance. That is, he elaborated Olympia & York into a corporation of great structural ingenuity even as he was creating some of the most elaborate office complexes in the world. However artfully contrived, the structural complexities of Olympia & York served the pragmatic ends of minimizing the company's tax liabilities while maximizing its use of financial leverage of all sorts. In other words, the Reichmann billions hardly piled up by accident; Paul was no less compelled to build a great fortune than to build great buildings.

Aside from a taste for deluxe home furnishings inherited from his mother, the material trappings of wealth held no great appeal for Paul, whose only extravagance as a billionaire would be collecting rare Talmudic manuscripts. It is often said of moguls who do not consume as extravagantly as they achieve that for them money is just a way of keeping score. But for any son of Samuel and Renée Reichmann, money could never be merely the currency of ego. Samuel Reichmann's business career had been devoted to the construction of a series of ever steeper firewalls of wealth designed to shelter his family from the malevolent forces arrayed against the religious Jew in Hitler's Europe. Through the rescue and relief campaign funded by Samuel and directed by Renée, the family even managed to extend a lifeline deep into occupied Europe. One of the fundamental lessons of the Reichmanns' Holocaust odyssey was that at the margins of the Orthodox experience money could easily mean the difference between self-reliance and self-betrayal, freedom and captivity, and ultimately between life and death.

In postwar North America, the threat that the Reichmanns perceived to their survival was symbolized by the Reform temple, the public school, and the television set. The Reichmann brothers founded Olympia & York with the goal not merely of making a living but of generating sufficient surplus to finance a local infrastructure of schools, synagogues, and the other institutions required to maintain a high standard of religious observance and safeguard the next generation against the rampant secularism of North America. At the same time, Paul continued to honor the transatlantic pull of his commitment to Sephardic education as the Jews of Morocco and other Arab lands resettled in Israel, France, and elsewhere. The cause of Orthodox education generally could use as much money as Reichmann could supply, and he began his business career eager to compensate financially for what he no longer contributed as a frontline activist. For the Reichmanns, philanthrophy was not an out-growth of Olympia & York's success but a facet of its raison d'être.

Paul's extraordinary commitment to the welfare of his people coexisted with less selfless motives. Endre "Andy" Sarlos, a Hungarian-born money manager who would work closely with the Reichmann brothers throughout the 1970s and 1980s, has theorized that Paul was driven "by an insatiable need for recognition." Reichmann's egotism, if egotism it was, did not take the usual form of preening in every available spotlight. Unlike Donald Trump, who epitomized the vaingloriousness of the 1980s, Reichmann would name nothing after himself and kept a determinedly low profile until the last few years of Olympia & York's ascendancy. Increasingly, he would come to measure success by the degree to which his buildings imposed a "permanent imprint" on the skylines of great cities. Even so, Reichmann winced slightly when Sarlos's comment was repeated to him. "There may have been an insatiable drive but not for recognition," he replied. "I've had recognition from my childhood on through my adult life. If I hadn't been accepted into certain milieus the way that I have been, perhaps this would be correct. But I not only was accepted, I had more recognition than I really deserved both in the Jewish community and in the business community."

If Reichmann's rebuttal was perhaps more revealing than intended in con-firming how important it was to him to be held in high regard, it was mislead-ing in its implication of effortlessness. The recognition that he had received as a youth was mainly the reflected glow of his parents' reputation in ultra-Orthodox circles, increasingly augmented by his own prowess at yeshiva and his zeal as a Torah activist. But like credits from an obscure junior college, his haredi credentials did not transfer to the corporate world. Olympia & York's exalted reputation was painstakingly built from scratch, though the com-pany's unofficial corporate motto—"Their Word Is Their Bond"—in a sense represented the fulfillment of an ambition of Paul's that predated his emigra-tion to Canada. From the moment that he began moonlighting as a textile mer-chant in Casablanca, "Paul's priority was always building a reputation of the highest quality," said Moses Lasry, his partner in the venture. "For him, it was a mission with a capital 'M.' "

As the scion of a family greatly admired by its peers, it was only natural that Paul, like his eldest brother, should want to prove himself a worthy heir to both the Reichmann and Gestetner names. But it seems likely that his precocious stress on reputation was also a reaction against his legacy—that the fuel of his pride in family was laced with the additive of shame. To put it mildly, Samuel Reichmann's lucrative Tangier career as a conduit for smuggling profits and flight capital did not measure up to the standards of irreproachable respectabil-ity to which his sons aspired and came to epitomize in Canada. Samuel was no robber baron, but had he placed as high a value on reputation as did Paul he would not have serviced the likes of Albert Grebler nor remained in Tangier for a full thirteen years after Hitler's defeat.

———

Had Paul Reichmann not been as gifted as he was driven, the anatomy of his ambition would have been a moot concern. Throughout Olympia & York's heyday and, more tellingly, even after its collapse, Reichmann would be publicly lauded for the brilliance of his mind. Lewis Ranieri, a Salomon Brothers investment banker widely regarded as the greatest real estate intellect on Wall Street during the 1980s, once told a reporter, "Paul Reichmann plays the game in three dimensions while everyone else plays it in one." Gerald Rothman, a well-regarded English property executive who worked for Olympia & York for years, would be equally overwhelmed by the brilliance of his boss: "Paul has one of the fastest working brains I've ever seen. . . . He is an Einstein of building and Einsteins don't usually do buildings."

Many who crossed his path in business would come right out and say it: Paul Reichmann is a genius. The man himself would advance no such claim, shrugging off the compliment whenever it was made in his presence. The word "genius" is at once bombastic and imprecise, and thus offended Reichmann's sense of decorum and his verbal exactitude in equal measure. The term seems most aptly applied to Reichmann in the sense of someone "ahead of his time," for a developer's basic talent is to envision in detail the evolution of an urban area—a city, a suburb, a neighborhood, a street, a block—and to build accordingly. This is an ability easily underestimated, for the highest examples of the developer's art are so seamlessly integrated into their surroundings, both economically and aesthetically, as to make their existence seem necessary, their success inevitable. Conversely, there is no commercial demise swifter and more public than that suffered by the misconceived real estate project.

Every commercial building sits on two foundations: one made of concrete and the other of numbers. From the developer's perspective, a physical building is the three-dimensional projection of a set of documents known as the pro forma, which is the real estate equivalent of the business plan. As it happens, the forecasting both of costs and of revenues is more problematic in real estate development than in most businesses. For better or worse, most industries employ their own salaried labor force, but the labor-cost component of a building is the product of negotiation with scores of independent subcontractors. On the revenue side, market demand for office and commercial space tends to fluctuate much more precipitously and idiosyncratically than for many commodities. In short, real estate development is full of traps for the unwary or analytically impaired.

By Reichmann's own description, his commercial decision making was rooted in Talmudic method, the essence of which is neither memorization nor the exercise of pure reason but rather the production of a fresh, original interpretation of ancient wisdom (a "chidush"). From time to time in interviews, Reichmann would extol the superiority of the yeshiva over the university and business school as a training ground for business. "With the Talmud you have texts written two, three thousand years ago, with each generation adding its own commentaries," he observed. "In general studies, law, or engineering, for example, a student usually ends up specializing. The Talmudic student doesn't have that luxury. We must deal with a multitude of subjects; none is ever exhausted." The Reichmann brothers, a reporter once noted, "consider the rigors of ancient Hebrew law better business training than a Harvard MBA." Declared Paul: "My nine-year-old son can discuss civil and real estate law with me as a result of his Talmudic studies." Even Albert Reichmann, who had never attended yeshiva, got into the act. "When you learn the Talmud," he proclaimed, "you learn everything."

As Olympia & York left rival developers in the dust, Paul's Torah-trained brain would be mythologized into a kind of invincible covert weapon. Brokers on Bay Street spent their lunch hours leafing through the Talmud in hopes of discovering Reichmann's secrets. They searched in vain. After all, the Forbes 400 is hardly dominated by former bachurim. From the perspective of the average haredi businessman, Paul Reichmann was as miraculously exceptional a figure as an Einstein or Picasso was to the average scientist or painter. But if Reichmann's unusualness buttressed the claims of genius made on his behalf, it also was true that the traits he had in common with other brilliant people—whatever their ethnicity or educational background—were more germane than the experiences he had shared with the typical yeshiva student.

Whatever the influence of the yeshiva on his mental development, it did not take Reichmann long to master the art of the pro forma. Once while riding in the backseat of a car with Reichmann, Moses Lasry, the Moroccan-born engineer, began explaining a business proposition he was entertaining. "I got out two sentences before Paul held up his hand for me to stop and said, 'Do you have any papers with you?'" Lasry handed over ten pages of financial analysis and resumed speaking. Reichmann again silenced him with an upraised hand and Lasry simply watched as his friend "read through those papers like a chapter from a novel." As they neared the end of the ride, Reichmann turned to Lasry and offered a terse summation: "There are easier ways to make money."

The economics of Flemingdon Park were considerably more complex than Lasry's hastily aborted venture. Webb & Knapp already had completed eight apartment buildings, a shopping center, a golf course, and a handful of industrial and office buildings, and had prepared sites for a dozen more buildings of various types. The project's value, both current and prospective, was a function of the interplay of four distinct real estate markets: residential, commercial, industrial, corporate. Although the difficulties of rethinking the tangled mess that was Flemingdon Park had scared away other developers, to Reichmann they were a snap. "It was not a complex analysis," he observed years later. "It was very, very simple."

There was, however, the little matter of $3 million in cash. Through Gil Newman, their outside auditor, the Reichmanns were able to raise the entire sum without putting a single building in hock. Newman's other clients included the Oelbaum family, which had made a fortune in the paper business and then diversified into construction lending to property developers. Newman introduced Paul and Albert to the Oelbaum family members who ran its real estate investment portfolio: Ronald Oelbaum and his two brothers-in-law, Barrie Rose and Marshall "Mickey" Cohen.

Paul Reichmann hit it off especially well with Cohen, who at thirty-three was the dominant member of the Oelbaum contingent. The son of a men's clothing designer, Cohen was a lower-middle-class Toronto boy who had pulled himself up by the bootstraps of his own academic excellence before marrying an Oelbaum. As a philosophy major at the University of Toronto, he had received a grade of A + + + + + + + + + for an essay on Immanuel Kant. Cohen went on to law school and in 1960 set up his own tax and securities practice, which was largely devoted to furthering Oelbaum interests. "Although he was smart, he wasn't pretentious or arrogant," wrote one chronicler of Cohen's career. "He smiled and joked and laughed a lot. People liked him. Somehow, the friendly name 'Mickey' seemed to suit him perfectly." (For his part, Paul Reichmann was so impressed with Cohen that in 1985 he would hire him as president of his own family's holding company, Olympia & York Enterprises. Cohen joined the firm after a stint as deputy finance minister of Canada, the highest tax policy position in the land.)

Like Paul Reichmann, Mickey Cohen recognized gold when he saw it lying around. The Oelbaums agreed to kick in all $3 million in equity needed plus another $3 million in debt financing to become the Reichmanns' equal but silent partners. Each family would own a 25 percent interest (to Webb & Knapp's 50 percent) but the Reichmanns would make all the real estate decisions. As for the balance of the purchase price, the partners had no trouble lining up $12 million in credits from Great West Life Assurance and other lenders. After everything was in place, Cohen and the Reichmann brothers held one last all-night marathon meeting to rethink in its every particular a deal that still seemed too good to be true.

On June 28, 1965, Webb & Knapp announced the sale of most of Flemingdon Park—306 acres all told—to Central Park Estates, a newly formed joint venture company controlled by the Reichmanns. Reversing their titles at Olympia & York, Paul was president and Albert the sole vice president of Central Park Estates. Rather than scale back the project, as prudence would have seemed to dictate, the new owners increased its budget to $157 million, from

the original $100 million, and set an accelerated five-year completion sched-
ule. Reporters did not so much give the Reichmanns the benefit of the doubt as
ignore entirely the question of their credentials. Happily, this would prove one
instance in which journalistic oversight impersonated foresight. Exceeding
their ambitious original plan in almost every respect, the brothers would transform Zeckendorf's white elephant into the largest suburban office park in
Canada. Completed ahead of schedule, Flemingdon Park would prove every bit
the bonanza that Paul Reichmann had envisioned.

Chapter 24

As the Toronto brothers' star ascended with Flemingdon Park, Edward and Louis Reichmann descended into financial crisis. By the fall of 1966—not quite three years after the auspicious opening of Place Crémazie—catastrophe loomed in Montreal. Three Star Construction had fallen a few months behind on Place Crémazie's $11 million mortgage, and another $600,000 in loans secured by the La Tour Laurier site was about to come due. The Bank of Montreal, the Reichmanns' lead bank, was demanding $2 million in additional collateral. Worse, Edward and Tibor Pivko had had to shut down several large industrial building sites near Dorval airport for lack of funds, leaving $1 million in unpaid construction bills.

The Montreal Reichmanns needed cash, lots of it, but Three Star already had tapped out the bravest of its lenders and sucked dry the treasuries of its sister companies, Olympia Floor and Maple Leaf Ceramics. "Any time there was extra cash, it went to the real estate business," recalled Louis Reichmann, the tile overseer. To raise cash for Three Star, Edward and his partners had sold Maple Leaf's factory and Olympia's main showroom-warehouse (leasing back the premises as tenants) and used the tile companies' credit to collateralize large construction loans. These loans now were a noose cinched tight. If Three Star went bankrupt, Olympia and Maple Leaf would swing from the same gallows. Nor had Edward and Louis any hope of averting personal bankruptcy if their corporations went down. To obtain financing, the Reichmanns and Pivko had had to personally guarantee the repayment of many millions of dollars in corporate borrowings.

Things could have been worse. On a consolidated basis, the value of the assets of the tile and real estate businesses still exceeded their liabilities, though not by much. Reichmann's immediate problem was liquidity—that is, his companies' cash flow was inadequate to meet their fixed obligations. The conventional solution would have been to sell off a few choice properties and apply the proceeds to debt repayment. But the Montreal Reichmanns had bolted shut this escape hatch in having relied so heavily on cross-collateralized borrowing, which had the effect of binding together all their various assets into one indivisible whole. For example, the La Tour Laurier site did multiple duty in serving as collateral for a $750,000 first mortgage on the property itself and $600,000 in additional borrowings made in the name of Three Star, Olympia Floor, and Maple Leaf.

That the Montreal Reichmanns now balanced on the edge of ruin was not entirely their own fault. In the mid-1960s the Canadian economy had gradually degenerated into recession, which in mid-1966 induced one of those periodic paroxysms of banker paranoia known as a "credit crunch." Throughout Canada, construction shut down as lenders shifted emphasis from making new loans to calling in old ones. Only the most creditworthy developers could add to their indebtedness, and Three Star Construction certainly did not qualify.

In Quebec, the economic slump was exacerbated by the scent of gunpowder. Beginning in 1963, the Front de Libération du Québec had waged a terrorist campaign of bank robberies (to collect "voluntary taxes"), armory raids, and bombings. The injection of terror into the political struggle over Quebec's place in the Canadian federation spooked big business. Many of Montreal's largest companies began redirecting their expansion and some pulled out altogether. In time, the corporate exodus would accelerate, exacting a punishing toll on the Quebec economy. However, the mere spread of indecision in the corporate ranks immediately jolted the city's property developers, many of whom had exacerbated their vulnerability by overestimating the beneficial effects of Expo '67. As he tracked the Montreal market's decline, Edward was reduced to rueful contemplation of the advice he had given his brother Paul in 1956: Toronto was indeed the future and the future had arrived ahead of schedule.

Three Star's La Tour Laurier project was afflicted not only by the gathering glut of downtown office space but by the Montreal Amateur Athletic Association's withdrawal as lead tenant. At the eleventh hour, the leadership of the MAAA bowed to internal pressure to submit the issue of Tour Laurier to a vote of the membership. "I didn't much care because the directors had been supporting me," Reichmann recalled. "The vote was supposed to be just a formality." According to Ronald Wilson, then MAAA president, the vote was evenly split. "Personally, I was in favor of La Tour Laurier but we decided that with so much opposition it was better not to proceed," Wilson said. "We still had a lot of old-timers who remembered moving to Peel Street and didn't want to go through it again." Reichmann's interpretation was not as benign. "In my opinion, this was the only clear incident of anti-Semitism I experienced in Montreal," Reichmann recalled. "There was a point of view among the members that why should they have a Jew as a landlord when there were plenty of good Englishmen available? I was blackballed but I chose not to fight it. What good would it have done? I wasn't going to change their minds."

Three Star Construction's wounds were mainly self-inflicted even so. Unlike Olympia & York, the company was never a particularly efficient developer; Edward lacked his brothers' rigor in controlling costs. More important, he knew no posture other than headlong. Although both Pivko and Louis Reichmann favored a more deliberate pace, they could not muster sufficient force to restrain their gung-ho partner. However grim the macroeconomic outlook, there always arose a special opportunity that, strictly on its own merits, made irresistible sense to Edward, who, for example, interpreted Webb & Knapp's collapse not as a warning to put his own house in order but as fate's invitation to bargain hunt. Reichmann went so far as to put himself forward as a bidder for Place Ville Marie and even spent a week in desultory talks with Webb & Knapp, which soon found better-heeled buyers.

As early as mid-1964, the centerpiece of Reichmann's own little empire, Place Crémazie, had begun falling short of his extravagant expectations. That vacancies in the end were minimal was a testament both to the tenacity of Reichmann's salesmanship and his use of a dubious tactic that Paul later would employ to ultimately disastrous effect in New York City and London: the bought lease. To entice prime clients into Place Crémazie as the market softened, Reichmann agreed to take over their existing leases in what almost by definition were older, less appealing buildings. At the same time, Three Star's construction budget for the last two of the complex's four office buildings ballooned as a result of customized improvements promised certain tenants. Originally budgeted at $13 million and supported with a long-term mortgage of $9 million, Place Crémazie in the end cost nearly $16 million.

To generate the cash needed to pay subcontractors and complete the last of Place Crémazie's four office buildings, Reichmann approached Majer Goldstein, a prosperous merchant who had earlier bought one of Three Star's Chabanel buildings as an investment. Goldstein was a Polish-born survivor whose postwar route to Canada had led through Chile and Bolivia. Along the way, he had established close business ties to a group of fellow Polish refugees who had made a fortune in Mexico City. In November 1964, Reichmann flew to Mexico and returned with an agreement to sell a two-thirds interest in the project to the Goldstein-led group for $4 million. However, Three Star retained management control of Place Crémazie and also had the right to buy back the equity stake it had sold to the Mexicans at any time over the next five years. (This option would be taken over and exercised by Olympia & York.)

Place Crémazie's struggles were a harbinger that Edward Reichmann chose to ignore as he plowed ahead at warp speed with the last of Three Star's major undertakings: the Côte des Lieses Industrial Park. In 1962, as Three Star's work in the Chabanel district was drawing to a close, Reichmann and Tibor Pivko had bought a large tract of undeveloped land along the Côte des Lieses near Dorval International Airport. Here, Three Star built some two dozen warehouses and light-manufacturing plants—as a rule, single-occupant premises built for sale rather than lease—gradually augmenting its original landholding with additional purchases. Three Star made good money along the Côte des Lieses only to badly overreach in the end. In July 1964, even as crisis loomed at Place Crémazie, Reichmann and his partners made the last of their land purchases, for $1.4 million, putting down $100,000 in cash and borrowing the rest. On a portion of the new site, Three Star began work on a large warehouse at 4895 Fisher Street.

The Fisher project was one of two Côte des Lieses buildings left incomplete when Three Star's financing ran dry in the fall of 1966. A third building, 6210 Côte des Lieses, had been completed but was largely vacant—disastrously so, for at 160,000 square feet it was the largest building in the park. A local paper wholesaling company had tentatively agreed to lease the entire building but had backed out when its owner and Edward Reichmann became embroiled in a dispute over design and construction methods. Three Star had no hope of recouping the $2 million it had invested in this ill-fated trio of buildings—or, more urgently, of placating the trade creditors and lenders that besieged it on all sides—unless all three were completed, occupied, and refinanced. That would take time and money, and Three Star had nearly run out of both.

By all accounts except Edward Reichmann's own, the final months of Three Star's struggle to regain solvency was the most excruciating period of his life. Throughout, Reichmann put on a brave if not exactly happy face, confiding in no one but his partners. Not even Jack Zimmerman, his close friend and neighbor, sensed the depth of Reichmann's anxiety. "Edward would never show his real feelings in the company of other people," Pivko recalled. "But when he talked to me or to Louis about the business, he was very nervous."

The suspense was protracted by a conspicuous absence of the ill will that financial collapse usually engenders. "Don't forget that these people had made money with Edward in the past," observed Nahum Gelber, the Chait Amyot lawyer, who took charge of creditor negotiations. "But there also was a personal sadness insofar as Edward was concerned because everybody liked and respected him." A number of major creditors cut Reichmann slack by extending repayment schedules for a second or third time. Haim Siegel agreed to give Olympia Floor two more years to repay a $100,000 loan that came due September 16, 1966, but set a stiff condition: both Edward and Louis would have to put up their homes as collateral. The Reichmann brothers swallowed deeply and signed the papers.

Edward Reichmann got forbearance and more from Majer Goldstein. When Reichmann and Pivko failed to make several payments on Place Crémazie's mortgage, imperiling the value of the Mexican group's investment, Goldstein seized the rent roll and paid the mortgage himself rather than attempting to seize the complex itself. "We didn't want to make a court case so we worked something out," Goldstein recalled. Acting on his own, Goldstein also extended Reichmann a large personal loan. "I'm certain that Majer made that loan knowing that Edward was going to go bust," said Sheldon Merling, who acted as the notary for both men. "He just liked him that much."

Sure enough, Goldstein's loan served only to prolong the inevitable. Sometime in early October, Edward must have realized that his increasingly frenzied efforts to halt Three Star's slide into bankruptcy were all for naught. Virtually overnight, his sense of urgency vanished, leaving an almost eerie acquiescence. He stopped going into the office regularly and made plans to leave the country. "Basically, he just turned the whole thing over to me and walked away," Gelber said. Reichmann wore his sudden passivity like armor. He was not indifferent—far from it—but emotionally incapacitated. There was in fact an emergency exit; Three Star, Olympia Floor, and Maple Leaf would not go bankrupt after all. But for Edward Reichmann the means of his rescue were so humiliating that he had dropped the lifeline extended him almost as soon as he had grabbed it, like a rope of fire.

———

The tricky intrafamily dynamics of the rescue of the Montreal Reichmanns were rooted in this seminal reality: each of the five brothers had arrived in Canada intent on founding a business of his own. While the bipolar partnership structure that evolved—Edward paired with Louis in Montreal; Albert, Paul, and Ralph united in Toronto—tempered their individualism with family considerations, each brother maximized his managerial leeway. Even the brothers who were subordinate in terms of personality—Louis and Ralph—acted as their own bosses in running the two tile companies and relished their entrepreneurial prerogatives no less than did their more freewheeling property-developer brothers.

From the outset, the two sets of Reichmann brothers disavowed fraternal competition. In real estate, Edward and his Toronto counterparts—Paul and Albert—occasionally referred corporate clients to one another rather than cross the provincial border and build in one another's backyards. Although this arrangement was informal, the two tile businesses were legally bound by a remarkably one-sided noncompete agreement negotiated when Louis sold the Toronto firm to Ralph and Paul in 1956. Under the sales contract, the brothers divided Canada: the Montreal brothers took Quebec and the national capital of Ottawa, which lay just inside Ontario; the Toronto brothers got the rest of Canada. The effect was to make Olympia-Quebec a prisoner of its own success. Having rapidly established its complete dominance of Montreal and the province, the company was unable to grow any faster than the Quebec economy as a whole. "We reflected our market," Louis observed. "We were a mature business."

The two sets of Reichmann brothers cooperated to varying degrees. In real estate, the only attempt at joint venturing was slight: a promotional pamphlet that Three Star and York Factory Development coproduced in 1961 (and that left the distinct impression that York was the Toronto arm of Three Star). Informally, Edward's younger brothers—Paul especially—sought his advice and counsel. During a trip to Toronto in 1960, Edward and Tibor Pivko had gone with Paul to inspect one of his earliest building sites. "We were standing there talking and finally Paul asked Edward, 'What do you think I should do?' " Pivko recalled. "I remember it like today, Paul asking his brother what he would suggest for the future. Edward said, 'The best thing is for you to join Albert and father and do industrial buildings.' In the early years, the other brothers looked up to Edward like anything. He was the number one guy."

In the tile business, meanwhile, Louis and Ralph collaborated extensively. They traveled together on buying trips to Japan and Spain and routinely placed joint orders that squeezed a better price out of tile manufacturers than either company could have obtained on its own. In addition, Olympia-Ontario's assurances of support were crucial to the Montreal brothers' decision to acquire Pilkington's Tile in 1961. In short, the two branches of Olympia Floor reaped the advantages of superior economies of scale without actually combining to form a single firm. Had the Montreal and Toronto tile operations been merged, certain overhead costs could have been eliminated but at a price unacceptable to both Louis and Ralph: co-presidency. According to Louis, "the subject of merger never came up for discussion."

As Three Star began faltering in 1964 and 1965, Edward insinuated into the family agenda the notion of closer ties between Three Star and Olympia & York. According to Pivko, what Edward was angling for was not so much joint participation in real estate development projects—though this held some appeal—as it was selling his father and younger brothers a minority stake in Three Star. Not that it mattered. Whatever Edward was selling, the Toronto Reichmanns were not buying. The message implicit in their polite but resolute rebuff of Edward's tentative advances was plain enough: "You're on your own, big brother."

Albert, Paul, and Ralph could read the separatist writing on the wall in Montreal, and they also knew an ominously distorted balance sheet when they saw one. To bind Olympia & York to debt-bloated Three Star and its heavy investment in Montreal's increasingly dubious future would have been like chaining a yacht to a capsizing speedboat. A little eddy of annoyance and resentment now whirled within the Montreal-Toronto relationship. "When they started to succeed in Toronto, it went to their heads a little," Pivko said. "No question about it, there was a problem, especially with Edward and Paul. Not that they were yelling and screaming. It wasn't like that. But there was a distance that wasn't there before."

When Three Star hit the skids in 1966, Edward was loath to approach his younger brothers for financial help. As always, Louis deferred to Edward, wielding his managerial duties at the tile company like a set of blinders. In the end, it was Three Star's exasperated creditors who forced the eldest Reichmann brother to swallow his pride and send an SOS to Toronto. "We agreed to give him some months to bring his brothers in," said Goldstein.

By this time, Paul and Albert were preoccupied with Flemingdon Park. The last thing they wanted to do was immerse themselves in their older brothers' commercial misadventures. On the other hand, the Toronto Reichmanns must have understood that they could not ignore Edward's and Louis's plight except at their own peril. A multimillion-dollar bankruptcy in Montreal was certain to tarnish the family name not just in Quebec but nationwide. What is more, if the family were to lose control of the Montreal tile operation, Olympia-Ontario's operations could be severely disrupted. Even so, "the brothers in Toronto were not really willing buyers," said Gelber, who represented both branches of the family in the matter.

In the end, the impasse was broken from on high, by the enforcer of family solidarity and matriarch of dynasty: Renée Reichmann. "Mrs. Reichmann held the family together through this," Pivko said. "All the boys would listen to the mother; she had a say in every major decision. When the Montreal group needed help, she made sure the help was given. She really pushed the Toronto brothers to come in."

As the oldest of the Toronto brothers (and as the less important officer of Central Park Estates), Albert led the rescue party into Montreal. His entry, though belated, was peremptory. "I woke up one day," Gelber said, "and I found myself dealing with Albert Reichmann instead of Edward Reichmann." Working closely not only with Gelber but Pivko and Sheldon Merling, Albert got off to a rocky start. "Albert was a little aggravated because Edward had understated the amount of money needed by a factor of three," Merling recalled. Albert stabilized the situation by pumping at least $2.5 million into Three Star during the first few months of what proved to be protracted negotiations with the company's creditors. While the threat of involuntary bankruptcy soon receded, the task of clearing away the legal and financial debris and of conveying ownership of the Montreal assets to Olympia & York would drag on into 1969.

Edward's and Louis's equity in Three Star Construction was wiped out. That is, their interest in Place Crémazie, the La Tour Laurier site, and all other properties was transferred to Albert for the nominal sum of $1 along with responsibility for the debts they carried. However, the Montreal brothers were not reduced to penury; Olympia & York put about $290,000 cash into their pockets in repurchasing Olympia's Montreal warehouse and Maple Leaf's factory. More important, the two oldest Reichmann brothers would still have their good name, in the sense that the awful mess of their affairs was successfully untangled and all the claims against them settled, usually in full. Even so, Edward would never fully recover emotionally from the ordeal of his Montreal denouement. "He was always a very proud man," Gelber said. "The biggest setback for him was not the collapse of his enterprise but the loss of face within the family that came from being bailed out by his younger brothers. In this respect, I think he suffered terribly."

Camouflaging his hurt as best he could, Reichmann told everyone, even close friends, that he had done his brothers the favor of selling them his businesses because he had decided at long last to make aliyah—to move to Israel. While this cover story eliminated the possibility of staying in Canada, Edward would have had it no other way. Having been thoroughly eclipsed by Paul and Albert, he had no intention of remaining in their shadow, which, at the time, did not extend all the way to Israel. Then, too, his Zionist longings were genuinely aroused in June 1967 by Israel's victory in the Six-Day War. Israel's subsequent absorption of the West Bank, the Sinai, the Gaza Strip, and the Golan Heights marked a dynamic new phase of Jewish nation-building and Reichmann wanted to do his bit. In the fall of 1967, Edward and Edith left Montreal bound for Tel Aviv by way of Miami Beach.

Louis was left more frustrated than traumatized. The tile business that he had built and ably managed had collapsed through no fault of his own but because it was yoked to Three Star Construction. His younger brothers asked Louis to join Olympia & York as manager of its newly acquired tile operations in Quebec—not as an employee but as an owner, albeit not an equal owner. Louis, with his wife's firm support, demurred; he, too, preferred to strike out on his own. "Hashi is more laid back than his brothers," explained a close friend. "He likes to wear short sleeves year round. It sounds trivial but it's important to him. Paul doesn't like it because he thinks short sleeves look quaint, inappropriate. Hashi has a high regard for his brothers, but just didn't want to be part of the empire building. He'd been through that once with Edward. Hashi likes to sleep nights."

In his own explanation, Louis preferred to accentuate the positive. "I am an independent type by nature," he said. "My attitude is that of a small businessman. Whatever I establish and it grows, that's my satisfaction." At age forty, he had time to start again from scratch—a new business in a new country. "We wouldn't go anywhere without a set Orthodox community," Louis recalled, "and there is no place in the world where there is a bigger choice than New York City." By the time that Louis and his wife moved to the borough of Queens in 1968, he had already spent considerable time scouting business opportunities in New York and had decided to try to reestablish himself as an importer of ceramic tiles. To this end, he founded Louis Reichmann America Corporation, the ownership of which was evenly divided between Louis and his wife.

Although the bailout of the Montreal businesses was effected without serious mishap, it did put a temporary strain on Olympia & York's balance sheet. In the spring of 1967 the Toronto brothers took the risk of allowing Olympia-Quebec to default on that $100,000 loan from Haim Siegel and waited six months before coughing up the $27,000 needed to bring the loan current again. And not until 1969 did Albert, Paul, and Ralph exercise Edward's option to repurchase the two-thirds interest in Place Crémazie held by Goldstein and his Mexican partners. Under the terms of the option, which expired in 1969, the Reichmanns were entitled to buy back the stake at the original sales price—$4 million. All told, Olympia & York shelled out at least $8 million in cash and assumed responsibility for $13 million in real estate–related debt.

In the end, the rescue proved profitable. "You could argue that Edward's brothers bailed him out because it was in their financial self-interest to do so," said Gelber—who evidently had not reckoned with Renée Reichmann's maternal clout. The prize was Louis's tile operation, which was acquired at little more than book value. The consolidation of the Toronto and Montreal tile companies put substantial additional cash flow and earnings at Olympia & York's disposal; according to Pivko, Maple Leaf Ceramics alone netted about $200,000 in the year after its acquisition. The Toronto Reichmanns also turned a modest profit in selling off the Montreal real estate, though cashing out the largest properties took several years. Place Crémazie fetched $17 million, for a $1 million profit, while the La Tour Laurier site was sold for $2.2 million, leaving a surplus of $850,000 over the mortgages. Purchased for $790,000 (all of which went to pay off Three Star's trade creditors), 4895 Fisher was sold for $1.1 million. Olympia & York decided to hang on to 6210 Côte des Lieses, which was refinanced and fully leased.

Finally, the bailout benefited the Toronto Reichmanns by strengthening their reputation for integrity in Canadian banking circles. For an outside party, even a close relative, to voluntarily assume responsibility for a corporation's bad debts was rare, indeed. "By and large," Gelber observed, "the creditors were motivated by two considerations: a desire to salvage as much as they could, and of course they also wanted to maintain a relationship with the Reichmann family."

Within the Jewish community of Montreal, however, Albert Reichmann's handling of a minor aspect of the reorganization of Edward's businesses put a small blemish on the Toronto brothers' still-pristine reputation. Working through Sheldon Merling, Majer Goldstein reached an agreement with Albert whereby Goldstein assumed ownership of a building in the Côte des Lieses Industrial Park in repayment of the last-minute loan he had made to Edward. In computing a certain tax aspect of the transaction, Merling made a mathematical error of about $2,000 in Reichmann's favor, which the notary did not catch until after the property and some cash had changed hands. "When I brought the error to Albert's attention, he refused to adjust the price," Merling said. "Basically, his attitude was he just didn't want to bother with it." In Goldstein's mind, though not in actual fact, Reichmann's behavior was tantamount to theft.

While Merling took the rebuff in stride, Goldstein was infuriated by what he thought was Reichmann's cavalier treatment of the notary, who legally was liable for any errors he had made. Goldstein refused to take the $2,000 that Merling dutifully offered him. When Albert telephoned a few years later on an unrelated business matter, Goldstein refused to take the call. "A man who could steal $2,000 from a notary—a multimillionaire who could steal from a notary, I should talk to him?" said Goldstein, unable to contain his anger some twenty-five years after Merling had erred.

———

Although the Reichmann brothers would remain close-knit by any reasonable standard, some of the old stitching had unraveled, leaving little gaps of embarrassment and indignation where before there had been seamless connection. This, too, pained Mrs. Reichmann, who for years had done what she could to defuse the competitive rivalries building among her five sons. The key to maintaining fraternal solidarity, Renée once advised a younger mother of six sons, was to write each son every week and tell him what his brothers are doing. The spectacular success of Olympia & York in the coming decades obviated any hope of repairing the tear in the family fabric; the more the Toronto brothers—especially Paul—were hailed as commercial geniuses, the more fallible Edward and Louis seemed by comparison. No amount of letters from Mom could paper over the schism. Over the years, Edward stubbornly stuck to his cover story—that he had sold out to make aliyah. In a 1994 interview, he took issue even with the mild observation that "all businessmen have their ups and downs." "I didn't," he insisted. "I had only ups, never downs."

Whereas Louis, content in the anonymity of his self-exile to Queens, wanted no part of Paul's and Albert's empire building, Edward never completely adjusted to having been shunted from center stage to the wings. Even with people who had every reason to know better, he promoted the misimpression that he was importantly involved in Olympia & York behind the scenes. "Whenever Edward spoke to us about Olympia & York after he left, it was always, 'We decided to this' or 'We're going to do that,' " Jack Zimmerman said.

Edward's illusionism was not only a form of self-aggrandizement but his contribution to preserving the myth of the family's superhuman solidarity. To his credit, he refrained from criticizing his Toronto brothers in public or private. Even so, to those who knew Edward best, his submerged feelings had a way of seeping to the surface, like ink through layered blotting paper. When Olympia & York finally collapsed into insolvency, Edward could not quite mask his ambivalence. On one hand, the family's business reputation had been besmirched and its fortune massively diminished. On the other, Paul's nose-dive finally lifted from Edward the burdensome role of misfit in a family of charmed destiny.

In 1989, at the height of Olympia & York's renown, Tibor Pivko visited Edward in Jerusalem. In some ways, Pivko had borne the brunt of Three Star's collapse. Not only was the fortune he had brought with him to Canada from Venezuela wiped out, but his marriage ended and the Canadian tax authorities pursued him relentlessly for five years. In 1971, the minister of revenue brought action against Pivko and Edward and Louis Reichmann, seeking nearly $900,000 in back taxes for 1961 through 1965 on a series of technicalities. As the only partner remaining in Canada, the burden of defense fell solely on Pivko. In 1976, the case finally was settled as the three partners agreed to pay the government $65,000 among them. In the meantime, the taxman had garnisheed Pivko's pay (he had gone to work for a mortgage broker) and slapped a lien on his house. Despite it all, Pivko retained a high opinion of all five Reichmann brothers. "The Reichmanns are gentlemen," he said. "I cannot tell you anything bad about them."

By the time that Pivko visited his ex-partner in Israel, Edward Reichmann had again reinvented himself, this time as a debt-averse developer of luxury properties, and was thriving. "When Edward left Montreal we were still friends, but I had the feeling that even with me he could not admit his defeat," Pivko said. "When I got to Jerusalem, the first thing he had to show me was all his success there, all the buildings he'd done. I had the feeling all the time that he was really saying, 'We had a bad time there in Montreal, but we never went bankrupt, and now look!' In his own mind," Pivko concluded, "Edward had never stopped being the 'Big Reichmann.' "

PART IV

EMPIRE
OF THE SONS

Chapter 25

In the saga of Olympia & York, as opposed to that of the Reichmann family, the rescue of the Montreal companies was a sideshow to the main event of the era, Flemingdon Park. The Toronto brothers accelerated their payout from the landmark project by shrewdly investing another $75,000 in the site. The beneficial effects of the construction of the Don Valley Parkway had been diminished by an intragovernmental dispute that had blocked construction of a strategically located highway underpass at Flemingdon Park's north end. The problem was money; the Province of Ontario, Metropolitan Toronto, and the Township of North York had squabbled incessantly over how to share the $300,000 cost of the underpass. The Reichmanns broke the impasse by offering to contribute $75,000 if the three governments split the balance. "It was a simple thing but by unblocking our lands it freed up millions of dollars in value," Paul Reichmann recalled.

Within two years, Central Park Estates had converted soaring land values to cash by selling off all the apartment buildings that Webb & Knapp had completed (containing 880 units), as well as the acreage for the additional 6,000 apartments called for in the project's revised plan. These and other asset sales generated proceeds slightly in excess of the $17.8 million that the Reichmanns and the Oelbaums had paid for the entire site. The Oelbaums got their $3 million back, and the partners went on to realize a profit of at least $25 million in putting up nearly a dozen buildings on the remaining acreage and adjoining sites. When completed in the early 1970s, Flemingdon Park would rank as the largest suburban office park in all of Canada.

In building out Flemingdon Park, Olympia & York added a dozen employees to the construction department run by Keith Roberts. The most important newcomers were Otto Blau, a wiry, self-effacing Romanian immigrant, and

John Norris, a jut-jawed bulldog of an Englishman who had spent several years in the silver helmet and red tunic of the Royal Guards to the Queen of England. At the same time, many of the Reichmanns' first contingent of employees resigned, having been effectively displaced by Olympia & York's growing emphasis on high-rise construction. While the transition caused a certain amount of resentment, little of it was directed at the Reichmanns, who did not fire anyone but let attrition take its course. Even Frank Wos, the construction supervisor who had felt the lash of Paul Reichmann's silence for three years, left praising both brothers. "As far as I was concerned," he said years later, "I could not have been associated with a better class of people."

At the same time, Morley Sirlin was gradually superseded as Olympia & York's architect-of-choice. "Paul felt bad about pushing me aside," Sirlin said. "But he told me that they had to start selling the architect to the tenant and that the big companies wanted bigger-name architects. I understood." For one office tower project at Flemingdon Park, the Reichmanns interviewed John C. Parkin, a devotee of the international style of modernism and perhaps Canada's best-known architect. The brothers had begun evolving toward a greater appreciation of architecture as an element of property value, but they were not prepared to give the famously temperamental Parkin the artistic license to which he had become accustomed. The interview was short and not particularly sweet.

This job—and many to follow—went instead to Bregman & Hamman, a local firm founded in the 1950s and well on its way to establishing itself as the architect of choice for the major Toronto developers. Sidney Bregman and George Hamman put their emphasis not on perfecting and promoting a trade-mark style of architecture, but on doing a quality job on time and within budget. They were, a rival once acknowledged in double-edged homage, the "perfect developers' architects." Olympia & York's relationship with Bregman and Hamman would persist through occasional rough patches for more than thirty years.

With Bregman and Hamman's help, the Reichmanns experimented on a small scale at Flemingdon Park with what would become Olympia & York's forte: the multiuse office complex. Olympia & York created Olympia Square by constructing a two-acre plaza next to the sixteen-story office building it had built for Mony Life. The building, which was designed by Bregman & Hamman, was one of seven office buildings singled out by *Canadian Architect* magazine in 1966 for exemplifying fresh thinking in the office field. At the far end of the plaza, which was fitted out with retail shops, bank branches, a sunken garden, and reflecting pools, the Reichmanns built a companion tower of twenty-four stories named Forester House after its anchor tenant, the Independent Order of Foresters. "Gently sweeping flights of steps and changing levels create visual interest and spatial excitement," an early Olympia & York promotional brochure enthusiastically described Olympia Square.

Sales rhetoric aside, Olympia Square proved as big a disappointment aesthetically as it was a success commercially. For one thing, as Paul Reichmann later deadpanned, the head Forester "liked every color as long as it was green." Worse, Olympia & York clad the precast concrete spandrels of both towers with what it hailed as "self-cleaning, white-glazed ceramic tile" in hopes of enhancing their appearance while developing a new market for the family tile business. But before Ralph's operation could be renamed Olympia Floor & Wall & Spandrel Tile, the experiment backfired disastrously. As the weather turned from hot to cold and back again in the cycle of the seasons, the tiles began cracking and falling off, pockmarking the towers and saddling the Reichmanns with costly repair bills. "It was a serious problem," Paul recalled with a touch of annoyance. "We'd tested the adhesive very carefully." After Olympia Square and its fiasco of falling tiles, the Reichmann brothers would think twice before again bestowing the corporate name on any of their creations.

───

In the spring of 1966, as the wealth generated by Flemingdon Park was just beginning to flow into Olympia & York's coffers, Paul and Lea Reichmann bought a house, their first in a dozen years of marriage. Mrs. Reichmann had just given birth to Barry, her fourth child, and was overjoyed to leave the third-floor walkup on Bathurst Street. The Reichmanns paid $90,000 ($67,500 in cash) for a five-bedroom home in Glenwood, a tastefully rendered section of vintage suburbia that lay just inside the southeastern border of North York. First subdivided in the late 1930s, Glenwood was a quiet, affluent neighborhood of gently curving, curbless streets, custom-built homes, and wooded lots complicated by the occasional ravine. It was populated by professional and business people of all ethnic backgrounds, one-fifth of whom were Jewish.

Glenwood had much to recommend it, but its principal attraction to Paul Reichmann was its proximity to Yesodei Hatorah. Although this combination school and synagogue had been closely identified with the family since its founding, the Reichmann men had davened there infrequently and never on Shabbat because it was not within easy walking distance of their homes. In the late 1960s, Yesodei Hatorah came fully into its own as a Reichmann institution as the family migrated, couple by couple, up the Bathurst Street corridor to Glenwood. Samuel, who continued to put in a daily appearance at Olympia & York's offices, and Renée were the first to follow Paul and Lea's lead, paying $75,000 cash for a home a few blocks away. Then came Ralph and Ada, who bought a house a few doors down from Paul and Lea's place on Strathallan

Wood. Albert and Egosah brought up the rear, opting to buy a vacant lot on Forest Wood, which was one block over from Strathallan Wood, and build a new house.

The purchase of these four properties amounted to a stake of claim driven deep; after decades of wandering in exile, the Reichmanns at last had found a home. Thirty years later, all three brothers would still live in extensively remodeled and expanded versions of the houses into which they had moved in the 1960s. All eight sons born to the Toronto brothers attended Yeshiva Yesodei Hatorah, receiving a fundamentalist education much like that given their fathers in Vienna. (In prewar Europe, this sort of elementary school would have been called a Talmud Torah or cheder rather than a yeshiva, which was a more advanced place of learning for youths thirteen and older, but in North America the term "yeshiva" was indiscriminately bestowed on Orthodox religious schools for boys of all ages.) After graduating from Yesodei Hatorah, each of the Reichmann boys would be sent off to a bona fide, topflight yeshiva in New York, New Jersey, England, or Israel. This was the Orthodox equivalent of going off to prep school, in that it was predicated both on a certain level of parental affluence and dissatisfaction with the local alternatives.

Not until the mid-1980s would the family found its own yeshiva gedolah, or advanced yeshiva, which was called Mesivta Yesodei Hatorah to distinguish it from the grade school. The yeshiva evolved from a course of instruction that Paul Reichmann organized for his younger son, Henry, who had gone off to yeshiva in Lakewood, New Jersey, but lasted only a month. "He needed more challenge than the school provided," his father recalled with evident pride. Paul put two teachers on the family payroll and invited a half-dozen other overachieving local youths to join his son for daily instruction at a neighborhood synagogue. When Henry left Toronto two years later to attend Gateshead, Paul's English alma mater, his place was taken by another boy, and what had started as a private study group soon evolved into a full-fledged yeshiva with a building of its own—all paid for by the Reichmanns.

The Reichmanns were unusual among patrons of Torah institutions in laying equal emphasis on educating girls and boys. In 1967, the brothers organized the building of a handsome new girls' grade school at 85 Stormont Avenue in Glenwood. Here, the distaff branch of Yesodei Hatorah was consolidated with the local Bais Yaakov school, which had occupied a dilapidated rental house nearby. The Reichmanns covered half of the cost of the project from their own pocket and obtained the balance of the funds needed from two local developers (both of whom were Orthodox), who had bought some of Flemingdon Park's choicest apartment buildings from Central Park Estates in partnership with the Reichmanns. All seven of the brothers' daughters would graduate from the new school, Bais Yaakov Elementary, which opened with an enrollment of two hundred.

The Reichmanns also were instrumental in upgrading Bais Yaakov High School for Girls and Teachers College for Women. The Reichmanns were one of fifteen founding patrons of the high school, which had opened in 1960, and both Samuel and Renée were especially active on its behalf. Samuel was the guest of honor at the school's tenth anniversary banquet, and a campus of the seminary would be posthumously named after Renée. At the urging of Paul and Albert, the high school building committee hired as general contractor Bill Minuk, who had left Olympia & York to start his own company. "I think the reason the Reichmanns brought me instead of just doing it themselves was because they thought it might be cheaper in the end," Minuk said. "I think they were worried that if they'd built it themselves, they would have gotten stuck for the whole bill." As it was, the Reichmanns, as usual, were the single largest contributor.

Today, Bais Yaakov has attained such predominance among the ultra-Orthodox in North America that it is virtually a generic term for girls' education. But in the 1960s, it was still a distinct movement in competition mainly with various Hasidic alternatives. Founded in 1917 in Poland, Bais Yaakov had universalized formal religious education for girls throughout Eastern Europe, including Hungary, and had been transplanted to North America by the Orthodox influx at midcentury. While the Yesodei Hatorah boys' schools exemplified the tradition of Torah study for study's sake, a Bais Yaakov education had a distinctly vocational flavor in the sense that it was geared to preparing girls for the responsibilities of marriage, motherhood, and running a household.

The depth of the Reichmanns' pockets enabled the Yesodei Hatorah and Bais Yaakov schools to maintain an unusual degree of independence from the larger Jewish community. Virtually all of Toronto's other Jewish schools—including those of more centrist Orthodox bent—received subsidies from the Board of Jewish Education, an arm of the central community organization, now known as the Jewish Federation of Greater Toronto. The federation's money came with strings attached in the form of "affiliation requirements" governing teacher certification, class size, curriculum, and so on. In the view of the Reichmanns and their fellow haredim, the board's requirements had a pronounced secular tilt. Even more objectionable was the notion of subjecting Torah institutions to requirements imposed by outsiders who were not themselves strictly observant. "I remember at one Board of Education meeting where the criteria were discussed, I was in disagreement with everything that was said by the director," recalled Paul Reichmann, who resigned soon afterward from the Board of Education committee on which he briefly served as Rabbi Grunwald's representative.

The ideologically and sexually segregated classroom lay at the center of the multichambered cocoon of strict observance in which the Reichmann brothers sought to enclose their children. As a rule, the Reichmann children were allowed to play only with other young haredim, as later they would date only other strictly Orthodox boys and girls. Their exposure to television and to secular newspapers, magazines, and books was carefully regulated, and they were not allowed to attend nonreligious movies or rock concerts. For the most part, this regimen produced the desired result. "In my son's generation, there is definitely no revolt," Edward Reichmann, who raised his children in the same manner, observed in 1995.

———

It was typical of Paul Reichmann that he would lose interest in Flemingdon Park once its success seemed assured, which, as it happened, was long before it was completed. Even as development of Olympia & York's first showcase undertaking continued apace, Reichmann shifted his attention to a large adjoining tract that the company had purchased in 1964 at a cost of nearly $1 million to build a cigarette-making plant for Rothmans of Pall Mall of Canada Limited. In 1964, the U.S. surgeon general issued its landmark report linking cigarette smoking to cancer, and Rothmans pulled out of the project, leaving Olympia & York with the land.

Improvising his way from mishap to milestone, Paul approached Shell Canada, the Canadian subsidiary of the Anglo-Dutch oil giant Royal Dutch Shell Group, which was one of the largest and wealthiest corporations in the world. Shell Canada was planning to build a new data processing center in suburban Toronto but had not yet selected a location. The oil company's initial response to Reichmann's query was that it was indeed interested in buying part of the Rothmans site but intended to act as its own general contractor. Reichmann countered by offering to give Shell Canada an option on the land on the condition that the company at least take a look at a building proposal. Olympia & York offered a development plan so authoritatively detailed and aggressively priced that Shell management was quickly persuaded to go with the Reichmanns. "It wasn't a tough sell," Paul recalled. "That was one of the things that was so exciting and surprising to us as emigrants to Canada: the field was totally open for anyone who had what it took to do the job."

The value of the Shell Canada transaction to Olympia & York was immeasurably enhanced by the innovative way in which the building was refinanced upon its completion. Shortly after Shell had announced the letting of the data center contract to Olympia & York in 1966, Paul Reichmann received a letter from Robert Canning, who was a vice president of Bell Gouinlock, a Toronto investment dealer specializing in bond financings. Bell Gouinlock was a small but innovative firm then in the early stages of revolutionizing commercial real estate finance in Canada. Canning had not heard of Olympia & York until he learned of its Shell Canada coup in the fine print of the *Daily Commercial News.*

Like every other developer, Olympia & York had refinanced its completed buildings by obtaining a mortgage from an insurance company. As a rule, developers had to pay a full two percentage points above the interest rate at which a AAA-rated corporation borrowed. In 1960, Canning had pioneered a technique that enabled developers to cut their financing costs by accessing a bond market that long had been the exclusive preserve of top-rated government and corporate credits. The linchpin of Canning's method was the "net net lease," which obligated a tenant not only to pay rent but to cover all operating costs, including repairs. Under the net net lease, the only financial exposure the landlord bore was the risk that a tenant would go broke and be unable to live up to its lease obligations. But if that tenant was an agency of government or a AAA corporation, the risk of default was slim indeed. Canning was able to convince an increasing number of institutional investors that there was no real difference between buying bonds floated by a Shell Canada or buying so-called first-mortgage bonds issued by a developer and backed by a net net lease with a Shell Canada. Developers who availed themselves of Bell Gouinlock's services found that they not only could borrow at a substantially lower rate of interest but could obtain loans for as much as 100 percent of the appraised value of the building instead of the maximum of 75 percent to which insurance company mortgages were limited by law.

Despite the advantages offered by first-mortgage financing, developers had been slow to adopt Canning's innovation. For one thing, the big insurers were determined to hang on to their mortgage business and were in a position to exact a measure of revenge on defectors to Bell Gouinlock. Not that the great majority of developers required much encouragement to hew to the path of least resistance. "Most developers didn't even know what a bond dealer was," Canning recalled.

In Paul Reichmann, Canning found a client whose ambition and savvy exceeded his own. Bell Gouinlock helped finance the Shell Canada data center and every other major building that Olympia & York would build in Canada over the next two decades—a dozen all told. In the process, Reichmann and Canning refined the net net lease and the first-mortgage bond to a fearsome perfection. "What Paul was excellent at was his ability to listen and ask questions of all sorts of people and then go off by himself and use his own brain finesse to improve on something," Canning said. "My God, he was brilliant at it! He was better than his lawyer, better than his accountant and, yes, better than his financier. He was better than everybody at everything. For twenty-five years, I said he was the most brilliant man I ever met."

Under the terms of the lease that Reichmann negotiated with Shell Canada, the oil company agreed to pay rent of $355,000 a year for twenty-five years, for a total of $8.8 million. One of Reichmann's most ingenious variations on the net net lease was that he was able to persuade his tenants to pay above-market rents by granting them an option to buy its building at an attractive price that declined steadily to zero over the twenty-five-year duration of the lease. In effect, Olympia & York credited each lease payment against the cost of purchase, enabling its tenants to buy the buildings they occupied on the installment plan. The present value of the Shell Canada lease worked out to $3.3 million, which was considerably more than the $2.5 million it had cost to construct the building. By issuing $3.3 million in first-mortgage bonds through Bell Gouinlock, Reichmann was able not only to pay off high-cost construction loans with cheaper debt but to come out $800,000 ahead. "Paul always used to tell me that I allowed him to capitalize his profit up front," said Canning, who said that Olympia & York usually was able to obtain a loan equal to about 120 percent of a building's cost.

Reichmann used the remainder of the Rothmans site to build larger back office facilities for two other AAA-rated stalwarts of the Canadian corporate establishment: Texaco Canada and Bell Telephone Company of Canada. All told, Olympia & York was able to borrow $22 million against the three buildings by issuing first-mortgage bonds. Conventionally financed, these three buildings would have yielded no more than $8 million among them. The extraordinary capital windfall produced by this trio of transactions, coupled with the profits generated in building out Flemingdon Park, propelled Olympia & York into the first rank of commercial developers in the Toronto area. Even Alex Rubin, who was still the most active of Olympia & York's rivals in industrial development, felt uncomfortably like a spectator at the corporate equivalent of a Cape Kennedy launch. "We were doing a huge amount of development but not anything as sophisticated," Rubin conceded. "The fact was none of us in the business were of the Reichmanns' caliber financially. We were country bumpkins by comparison."

Soon Canning was deluged by calls from developers eager to learn Olympia & York's secrets. "They thought maybe it was the financing but that was just part of the equation," Canning said. "Paul was brilliant at convincing the best names in Canada to use Olympia & York when they needed a building built, and that was because Olympia & York delivered in spades." What had most impressed Robert Scrivener, the president of Bell Canada, was that Olympia & York had not deviated one iota from its original proposal in building the Bell data center at Flemingdon Park. Scrivener was so impressed, in fact, that he hired the Reichmanns to put up a huge office building in Ottawa—Place Bell Canada—and offered to provide glowing references on Olympia & York's behalf to all comers, even journalists. "They are a first-class, top-notch developer," he told a *Wall Street Journal* reporter. "They finish projects on time and they do what they say they will do." In proving their mettle to corporations of such caliber as Bell Canada, the Reichmann brothers acquired a cachet that no amount of advertising could buy. As one observer put it, "They were still known only within a narrow circle, but it was the circle with the cheque-books."

While putting the finishing touches on Flemingdon Park, the Reichmanns began developing a new 250-acre industrial park a few miles north and a second, 100-acre park near the Toronto International Airport, as well as numerous single-building projects throughout the Toronto area. None of these suburban undertakings held Paul Reichmann's interest for long. As his next defining challenge, as his true encore to Flemingdon Park, he would breach the highest rampart of the Canadian property business: Toronto's financial district.

The Reichmanns had made a first, tentative foray downtown not long after they acquired Flemingdon Park, building an eighteen-story office tower at University Avenue on the fringes of the financial district. Completed in 1967, the building was named "Global House" after its anchor tenant, Global General Insurance Company. Six blocks away, Olympia & York soon built a second, mid-sized tower without bothering to sign a lead tenant in advance. This building, like Global House before it, was fully and profitably leased in short order, for Olympia & York had caught the crest of a lucrative wave of office construction that was transforming the downtown business district of every major city in Canada.

Not until about 1960 had downtown office projects emerged as an important source of revenue for Canadian developers. Annual spending on new office construction rose steadily into the mid-1960s and then exploded, more than doubling between 1967 and 1974 alone, to $1.2 billion. The office-tower boom was firmly rooted in two fundamental postwar economic trends: huge increases in the number of white-collar jobs and the increasing commercial dominance of the large corporation. Although industry en masse sought expanded space in the suburbs, major white-collar organizations—corporate and governmental alike—generally were willing to pay a premium for the prestige and convenience of a downtown address. To accommodate the demand for office space while wringing maximum profit from increasingly expensive sites, commercial developers built to unprecedentedly massive scale. The skyscraper-ing of Canada reached its zenith in Toronto, which by the mid-1970s had supplanted Montreal as the national business capital.

The Toronto equivalent of Montreal's Place Ville Marie was the Toronto-Dominion Center, on King Street in the heart of the financial district. The intersection of King and Bay streets was known as "the MINT" after the four banks whose fortresslike buildings had long dominated its corners: the Bank of Montreal ("M"), the Canadian Imperial Bank ("I"), the Bank of Nova Scotia ("N"), and the Toronto-Dominion ("T"). In the early 1960s, the Toronto-Dominion got the jump on its archrivals by joining with Fairview Corporation, the real estate arm of the Samuel Bronfman interests, to quietly buy up property along King Street. In 1967, ground was broken on a new fifty-five-story bank headquarters designed by Mies van der Rohe. A forty-three-story tower soon followed, and the addition of a thirty-story building brought the Toronto-Dominion Center's square footage to 3.3 million, slightly surpassing Place Ville Marie.

The launching of the Toronto-Dominion Center brought the downtown property market to full speculative boil. Land prices soared and real estate brokers swarmed, confronting longtime property owners in the central business district with a difficult but welcome question: sell or hold? Like many developers, Paul Reichmann was convinced that land prices would continue spiraling generally upward for years. Unlike most of his rivals, he held this conviction so emphatically that he was willing to wager his company on it.

In 1967, Olympia & York acquired the old Metropole Hotel and some adjoining properties at the intersection of York and King streets, just a few blocks from the MINT, which inevitably emerged as the focal point of the downtown land rush of the 1960s. To finance these land purchases on top of everything else they were doing, the Reichmanns had to take out a second mortgage against Global House and seven of its prime suburban properties. On this site, Olympia & York would erect its tallest and most distinctive-looking building to date—the twenty-seven-story, 900,000-square-foot, granite-clad York Center. Long before excavation of the site began, Reichmann had resumed shopping. By early 1969, he had cut a $16 million deal to acquire a plum of a property in the heart of one of the MINT blocks.

Since 1929, the Toronto Star Limited had published the *Toronto Daily Star*, the largest newspaper in Canada, out of a twenty-story building at 80 King Street West. In the mid-1960s, the old-line company had decided that it needed a larger and more modern plant and discreetly began accumulating property adjacent to its building, which was just down the block from the emergent Toronto-Dominion Center, while keeping open the option of building on an eight-acre tract it owned on the Toronto waterfront. Careful not to tip their hand, Star executives refused all public comment. Clued to the opportunity by a well-placed real estate broker in early 1969, Paul Reichmann talked his way into a meeting with Beland Honderich, the *Star*'s president and publisher, right about the time he decided to sell the old plant and build anew on the waterfront.

As it turned out, Reichmann was not the only bidder for 80 King Street, but he was the only one who did not bother haggling with Honderich. The publisher named his price—$16 million—and Reichmann accepted on one condition: that the Star entertain no other offers while Olympia & York lined up financing. At the same time, Reichmann was the only developer who offered to build the *Star* a new building at a guaranteed price. That this little-known, soft-spoken, thirty-eight-year-old immigrant advanced his unconventional proposals with such earnest understatement only piqued the publisher's interest. "I had Olympia & York checked out with the banks we knew and our auditors," Honderich said. "One thing I always had to smile at was that their free cash flow at the time was only something like $50,000. But the banks thought highly of them and so did Bell Canada."

Honderich even was willing to take back a mortgage from Olympia & York but only if Reichmann found a major financial institution to guarantee its payments. When the Canadian Imperial Bank of Commerce, Olympia & York's lead bank, balked at providing such a guarantee, Reichmann called on Tom Engel, the treasurer of North American Life Insurance. Engel had met Reichmann in the early 1960s, when North American began branching out from mortgage lending into investing in real estate for its own account. As the first head of the new real estate department, Engel had taken a keen interest in Flemingdon Park, and seriously considered buying the half-dozen apartment buildings that the Reichmanns had acquired from Webb & Knapp.

Engel had known for months that something was afoot with 80 King Street. North American Life had its offices adjacent to the *Star* property at 112 King and 105 Adelaide. As it happened, Engel first learned of the *Star*'s decision to sell from Paul Reichmann, who had beaten him to the punch without even knowing they shared the same boxing ring. Engel told Reichmann that he would gladly provide the guarantee he sought on one condition: that Olympia & York take North American as its partner in developing the site. Reichmann and Engel negotiated the terms of an alliance and formed a joint venture company—NALOY—of which Olympia & York held 70 percent and the insurer 30 percent.

When the *Star* announced the sale of its King Street and adjoining properties in March 1969, every developer and property speculator in Toronto took envious note. "People were flabbergasted," recalled Paul Braun, who was then treasurer of Toronto's largest developer, Cadillac Fairview Corporation (formed by the recent merger of Cadillac, the suburban developer, with the Bronfmans' Fairview). "The *Star* site was a great location. A lot of people had been negotiating for it. But the Reichmanns were willing to roll the dice. They just walked in and said, 'What's your price? Fine.' Handshake. Deal." When the terms of the sale were registered at the courthouse, Olympia & York's rivals were flabbergasted all over again. Because the *Star* would not be vacating its old building until the new one was completed, Honderich had agreed to a remarkably protracted payment plan. NALOY had not put so much as a penny down, and it had a full year to make its first payment—a mere $1.4 million of the $16 million purchase price. A second payment of $8.6 million was scheduled for the fall of 1973, and the $6 million balance did not come due until 1978.

North American transferred its MINT block properties to the joint venture company at the same price per square foot that the Reichmanns had paid for the *Star* building. The Reichmanns added to NALOY's holdings by narrowly outbidding a rival developer for a building recently vacated by Royal Trust Company. "Each of us could submit a single bid in a sealed envelope," Albert Reichmann recalled. "How much to bid was a crucial decision, because the Royal Trust property was in the middle of our assemblage. We could have built without it, but the project would be much smaller and less interesting. The envelopes were opened, and Royal Trust announced the other developer bid $1.5 million. We got the property with a bid of $1.537 million. As far as we could figure, both parties arrived at the same bid per square foot and multiplied this amount by the number of square feet involved. But they rounded down to arrive at an even amount, and we were content to bid an odd number." Paul Reichmann told Engel that he had decided on a hunch to tack the $37,000 onto NALOY's bid at the last minute while driving downtown to submit it to Royal Trust.

In mid-June, the Reichmanns delivered the second blow of a one-two punch to their competitors' ribs as the *Toronto Star* announced that it had selected Olympia & York to build a $19 million, twenty-six-story tower on the newspaper's waterfront property. In the press anyway, the odds-on favorite had been Campeau Corporation, an Ottawa-based company that in the mid-1960s had begun an ambitious redevelopment of the Toronto waterfront. "The thing that really appealed to me about Olympia & York was that I'd get a firm price," Honderich recalled. "I thought that we could probably save money going with the Reichmanns. It was also crucial that it be finished on time. We'd ordered new presses and the building had to be ready to receive them."

In devoting all of page 2 of its June 17 edition to the news of its planned move to 1 Yonge Street, the *Toronto Daily Star* brought the Reichmanns to the attention of the general public for the first time. The *Star* ran no less than five stories, one of which was wholly devoted to Olympia & York. Although to this point the Toronto Reichmanns had studiously kept a low profile, Paul hardly seemed a reluctant participant. He posed for a photo, in which he looked almost chipper, and exuded a rather self-important enthusiasm in the interview he gave, predicting that the *Star* project would mark the beginning of a new era of waterfront development. "There's the challenge of starting to create a new area," he said. "We recognized from the start of negotiations that this presented a great challenge to all those involved—The Star, the architects, and ourselves, because what the first development does will have a tremendous impact on the total environment and future development of the waterfront."

Over the next few months, the *Star* published two more photos of Paul, each extraordinary in its way. In the first, he was seen sharing a laugh with Honderich as they signed the final development agreement. In the context of Reichmann iconography, the photo was historic for two reasons: it depicted Paul Reichmann smiling, and, more shocking still, it showed him bareheaded, which, on the face of it, was an egregious violation of haredi decorum. In the second photo, taken during the groundbreaking ceremonies, an appropriately behatted Reichmann was captured taking a drag from a cigarette while staring straight into the camera with a coolly appraising gaze faintly tinged with defiance. He looked like a haredi version of a film-noir detective. Standing alongside him at an odd, oblique angle was seventy-two-year-old Samuel Reichmann, who appeared tiny, disoriented, and altogether inconsequential next to the ultra-Orthodox Sam Spade.

Never had the Reichmann brothers had greater incentive to build efficiently than with the 1 Yonge Street project, and the price guarantee that Paul had given Honderich was not the half of it. Olympia & York could not demolish the old Star building and begin developing its prize MINT-block site until the newspaper was installed in its new quarters. Completing the new facility was expected to take two years, which was time enough for the supply of downtown office space to leap ahead of demand and render infeasible, at least temporarily, a new development of the colossal scale that the Reichmanns envisioned at King and Bay. The brothers made constructive use of this period of involuntary delay by holding an architectural "beauty contest"—their first—for the project that would become First Canadian Place. Instead of simply choosing an architect on spec, as it were, Olympia & York solicited proposals from a number of architects.

To Honderich's great relief, 1 Yonge Street was completed on schedule in early 1971. "Olympia & York did everything it promised to do. They met all the targets exactly," recalled Honderich, who, like Scrivener, was transformed into a well-connected cheerleader for the Reichmanns. But before the brothers could begin demolishing the old Star building—a formidable task in its own right—and select an architect for the project that would mark the next quantum leap in their evolution, they again were distracted by a family crisis. This time the alarm bell sounded in London.

———

William Stern had just finished Havdalah, the evening benediction that marks the end of Shabbat, at his home in London on March 13, 1971, when a friend telephoned with news that took his breath away: Lipmann Heller, Eva Reichmann's husband of twenty-three years, was dead. "I remember it like yesterday," Stern recalled two decades later. "It may have had to do with the fact that his place in synagogue was right next to me and that he was so young but the shock of his death was great." Word of Heller's passing sped through the Orthodox community of north London on that cold March night. "His death shocked everyone to the core," said Lady Amelie Jakobovits, one of Eva's closest friends. "What has it been?—twenty-three years now—and it still disturbs me."

For the Reichmanns, Heller's death at age forty-eight was the first great family tragedy since the Holocaust. By all accounts, Eva never recovered emotionally from her grief; a measure of her flair and vivacity was permanently extinguished. In Canada, meanwhile, Renée Reichmann was no less devastated by her son-in-law's demise. "Her only daughter suddenly was a widow with six kids to take care of," explained Mrs. Pearl Zimmerman, the wife of Edward and Louis Reichmann's erstwhile business partner in Montreal and a frequent guest in the homes of all the Reichmanns. "It seemed to weigh on her constantly. Whenever a good time was being had, you could see that at some point Mrs. Reichmann would remember what had happened—'Oh, but my son-in-law'—and she'd become subdued again. She never got over Lipmann Heller's death—never, ever."

Like Edward Reichmann in his Montreal heyday, Lipmann Heller had been an Askan, a community benefactor whose advice and counsel were sought as eagerly as his money. Rachel Heller Brenick, the youngest of his children, was only six years old when her father died but retained vivid memories of the nightly ritual of supplicants lining up in the foyer of the family home in Golders Green in anticipation of her father's return from London's financial district, where he ran his own small merchant bank, between eight and nine o'clock. "Some nights there was a queue until two in the morning," Mrs. Brenick recalled. "The only day we [children] saw him was the Sabbath. As soon as it ended he began receiving people again. Even on the night that he died people came to see him, not knowing."

Eva Heller was as well known as her husband and even more beloved within the populous haredi community of Hendon–Golders Green. Often acting in tandem with Lady Jakobovits, Eva was a ubiquitous presence in Orthodox philanthropy, becoming so ardent a champion of the Hasmonean Grammar School for Girls that even some of her closest friends later would unwittingly describe her and Lipmann as its founders.

About 3:00 A.M. on the night of her husband's death, Eva came down from her bedroom to the living room and instructed her eldest son, Philip, to fetch a packet of pound notes from the safe. She handed the cash and a long list of names to Rabbi Abraham Gubbay, who, along with Eva's brother-in-law, Ralph Halpern, spent the entire night at the Heller home. (All three Heller boys attended Rabbi Gubbay's yeshiva; in fact, Anthony Heller had been studying at the rabbi's home at the moment of his father's death.) Purim was just a few days off, and Lipmann Heller, as usual, had promised money to quite a few people. At Eva's request, Rabbi Gubbay distributed the cash in her husband's stead. "Each person that received money was astounded that Mrs. Heller had thought of them in her great distress," Rabbi Gubbay recalled.

The impact of Lipmann Heller's death was exacerbated by unnatural circumstance. There was, to be sure, nothing particularly gruesome about the way he died. He simply collapsed and tumbled down the stairs. Eva, who was home alone with her husband at the time, immediately summoned an ambulance but Lipmann died without regaining consciousness. Nor was there any mystery, medically speaking, about the cause of death. The death certificate listed two, in descending order of importance: "1. a. Ventricular Asystole; b. Myocardial Infarction; c. Myocardial Ischaemia [translation: massive heart attack]. 2. Diabetes. Hypertension." Although even some of Heller's friends had not known of his diabetes, it could not have come as much of a surprise to them that a man five feet ten inches tall who had gradually ballooned to nearly three hundred pounds should have been so afflicted. The problematic diagnosis, for his surviving relatives at any rate, was the hypertension. To this day, the events that preceded—and seemingly precipitated—Lipmann Heller's death remain an awkward and painful subject within both the Heller and Reichmann families.

On the very day of his heart attack, Heller had quarreled bitterly with Rabbi Solomon Schoenfeld, his spiritual adviser and mentor. According to Jonathan Schoenfeld, Rabbi Schoenfeld's son, Heller was one of the most loyal of the three hundred boys that his father had brought out of Vienna in the early stages of World War II. "A surprising number of them disassociated themselves from my father out of embarrassment and feelings of inadequacy at their youthful circumstances," said Schoenfeld, who added that his father's sheer irascibility also tended to drive away his protégés. "Especially in his later years," Schoenfeld said, "he was forever arguing with everyone." The subject of Heller's final dispute with Rabbi Schoenfeld is unclear and, in any event, of secondary importance. What mattered was that death removed the possibility of reconciliation. "That Lippa, who had been so close to Rabbi Schoenfeld, died not at peace with him was terrible for Eva and the whole family," said one well-placed source. "There were people who considered it a bad omen."

Worse, the eponymous London merchant bank that Lipmann Heller had owned and managed for two decades had fallen into a financial hole so deep that it threatened his widow and children with penury. (Aside from the home and its contents, Eva's husband—once a multimillionaire—left an estate with a gross value of only £8,862.) Led initially by Edward and then Paul, Eva's brothers came to her aid, covering a portion of the Heller firm's deficit out of their own pockets and negotiating the sale of the remnants of Heller's merchant bank to his friend and shulmate, Willie Stern. "Paul, who struck me as the leader of the family, was a very unemotional person," recalled David Freeman, a well-known London solicitor who had often acted for Lipmann Heller in the past and represented Stern in his purchase of Heller & Company. "But even with Paul there was emotion as far as Maidie was concerned. The impression that stands out most from the whole experience was that among all of Maidie's brothers, there was colossal, overwhelming admiration for their sister."

The collapse of Heller & Company was a catastrophe in its own right, quite apart from its founder's death. While still a relatively young man, Lipmann Heller seemingly had scaled the pinnacle of ultra-Orthodox commercial aspiration, climbing out of the déclassé needle trades into the tonier reaches of merchant banking. Heller's achievement was akin to what Samuel Reichmann had done in graduating from money changing to commercial banking, though Tangier's Pasteur Boulevard brooked no comparison to London's starchy financial district—"the City"—which in the 1950s remained as definitive a preserve of Britain's upper crust as Eton, the clubs of Saint James, or the House of Lords. Heller & Company was a small firm, with no more than two dozen employees at its peak, and never did quite grasp the top rung of London merchant banking. Even so, in its heyday the firm was well regarded both in the City and within the ultra-Orthodox precincts of north London alike and made its owners a potful of money. "At one point, Lipmann was more than well-to-do: he was rich," said Morris Joseph, a banker who joined the Heller bank shortly after its formation and would remain until its dissolution.

In 1970, not quite a year before his death, Heller had greatly enhanced his standing in the City by selling an 18 percent interest in his firm to First Bank of Maryland, a venerable old-line Baltimore bank. With First Maryland's backing, Heller laid plans to open offices in New York City, Tokyo, Mexico City, and Rio de Janeiro to complement the branch he already operated in Zurich. "If the Heller bank had survived the early 1970s," Morris Joseph lamented, "today it would be a very large and profitable institution."

It was not incompetence that killed First National Maryland & Heller Limited—at least not on Lipmann Heller's part—but rather the entanglements of family. In 1965, his brothers, Asrael and Izidor, had bought Amalgamated Food, which manufactured ice cream in Israel under the well-known brand names Artic and Kartiv. When the ice cream company began floundering, Lipmann's eldest brother, Asrael, prevailed upon him to come to its rescue. Through the London merchant bank, Heller advanced Amalgamated Food millions of dollars and also guaranteed multimillion-dollar loans to the company by Barclays Bank, Bank Hapoalim, Bank Leumi, and other major Israeli banks. The Heller brothers' desperate effort to salvage their investment in Amalgamated Food ended in catastrophe on March 7, 1971, when a judge in Tel Aviv forced the company into receivership. Five days later, Lipmann dropped dead.

Apparently, Heller had been distraught over the impending ruination not only of his bank but of his personal reputation. In the immediate aftermath of Heller's death, executives of First Bank of Maryland lodged accusations of deceit tantamount to fraud against their late partner. In documents filed with the Securities and Exchange Commission, First Maryland claimed in effect that Lipmann Heller had cooked the books of Heller & Company to hide its exposure to the family-owned ice cream company and that it had had to pump nearly $4 million into the merchant bank to cover "certain questionable loans which were discovered on Mr. Heller's death." First Maryland served notice of its intent to sue Peat Marwick Mitchell, which had audited Heller & Company's financial statements for 1969 and 1970, but changed its mind at the eleventh hour. Ironically, First Maryland was itself sued by a court-appointed liquidator looking to salvage some value from the bad loans that Heller had made to his brothers' company.

This suit was settled out of court. In the end, the various accusations of misconduct made against Heller were neither validated nor refuted by judicial verdict, consigning his once-sterling reputation to an eternal limbo of rumor and suspicion. And while Heller's death had the effect of drawing the Reichmann family even closer together, it opened an irreparable rift between Eva and the Hellers. Eva's sorrow was laced with anger at her brother-in-law Asrael, whom she blamed for luring Lipmann into the ice cream morass. "My sister never forgave him," Paul Reichmann recalled.

Chapter 26

As the Reichmanns' first tour de force office complex, First Canadian Place elevated Olympia & York from the status of suburban aspirant to world-class developer in one vaulting leap. For all the ingenuity and daring the brothers had shown at Flemingdon Park, as a suburban development it was peripheral by definition and failed to attract much notice outside the trade. What is more, Olympia & York had inherited both the basic concept of Flemingdon Park and a ready-made site; the Reichmanns had realized someone else's vision. First Canadian Place, on the other hand, was a monumental undertaking that transformed Toronto at its core and bore the brothers' imprimatur from start to finish. Upon completion, the complex's seventy-two-story main tower ranked as the tallest building in the British Commonwealth and the eighth tallest in the world. More important to the Reichmanns, First Canadian Place was a commercial triumph of the first order made all the sweeter by the protracted ordeal of its creation.

Using First Canadian Place as a working laboratory for the reinvention of the technology of skyscraper construction, Olympia & York built the massive main tower with startling speed and cost-efficiency; the company began leasing out the lower one-third of the building only sixteen months after ground was broken and completed construction six months later. And yet the project as a whole consumed more than a decade, during which the Toronto office market cycled alarmingly from boom to bust to recovery to incipient boom. The volatility of the local real estate economy tested the Reichmanns' nerve and slowed progress to a crawl in its latter stages. Worse, the brothers found themselves mired in partisan municipal politics for the first time. In opting for collaboration over confrontation, Olympia & York established a precedent that would figure importantly in every major undertaking to come. Although the

Reichmanns had to drastically redesign their pet project to placate the politicians, they succeeded in their goal of creating the foremost corporate address in all of Canada.

Assembling and clearing the site for First Canadian Place alone took four years, or more than twice as long as required to build the main tower. Midway through this process, the project was elevated from just-another-outsized-downtown-redevelopment into a landmark undertaking by the Reichmanns' recruitment of the Bank of Montreal as a partner. The Bank of Montreal was the oldest and snootiest of Canada's Big Five chartered banks, the chairmen of which then immodestly regarded themselves as nothing less than the "custodians of the free enterprise ethic" in Canada. In aligning itself with the Reichmanns, the Bank of Montreal conferred upon the family the commercial equivalent of knighthood while bolstering the project itself in more tangible ways. The bank contributed a choice property right on the MINT corner, put its financial muscle at Olympia & York's disposal, and filled the role of anchor tenant. The complex was called First Canadian Place because the Bank of Montreal was Canada's first bank and advertised the fact incessantly.

Paul Reichmann did not so much woo the Bank of Montreal as back the bank into its own, very special corner. Even before Olympia & York established its toehold on King Street with the purchase of the Toronto Star properties, the Bank of Montreal had acknowledged internally the need to replace its old building at the corner of King and Bay streets. Built in the early 1940s, the ornate, low-rise edifice at 50 King had been perfectly adequate as the bank's main Toronto branch and center of its Ontario operations during Montreal's long ascendancy as Canada's business capital. But as Toronto surged to the fore, 50 King was too small to accommodate the Bank of Montreal's growing staff and too short and old-fashioned to symbolically represent the grand seigneur of Canadian banking at what had become the nation's banking crossroads.

Rising to the challenge thrown down by the Toronto-Dominion Center in the mid-1960s, the Canadian Imperial Bank of Commerce had hired its own world-famous architect—I. M. Pei—and replaced its old quarters on the MINT with the striking Commerce Court. The complex's fifty-seven-story main tower surpassed Toronto-Dominion's fifty-five-story headquarters as the tallest building in Canada. Architecturally speaking, at any rate, by 1972 the Bank of Montreal had become the dwarf of the MINT, and that just would not do. That much was obvious. The question that increasingly bedeviled Toronto developers was when the bank would do something about it.

Ever since 1968, the Bank of Montreal had been deluged with proposals. "Everybody and his dog was interested in getting the Bank of Montreal to go in with them on a new building," recalled Malcolm Spankey, who was the bank's national real estate development manager at the time. A series of downtown landmarks were dangled before the bank as redevelopment sites, each more unlikely than the last—the old City Hall, the Royal York Hotel, Union Station— and each completely off-base. "In terms of address we figured that we already had the best site in Canada bar none," Spankey said. "Why move when you already have the best? Plus, we were interested in preserving our identity with that corner."

Olympia & York's rivals were well aware that the Bank of Montreal preferred to stay put. But in cutting the deal to acquire the *Toronto Star* building, Paul Reichmann had established a blocking position on the Bank of Montreal's flank that left other developers with no practical alternative but to try to entice the bank into leaving the MINT. The bank itself could have seized the initiative by acquiring the properties between 60 King (the bank owned it as well as 50 King) and the *Star* building at 80 King but instead watched as the Reichmanns snapped them up. By the time that Paul Reichmann finally approached the Bank of Montreal, he had gained a decided tactical advantage: Olympia & York had assembled a site suitable for a major tower but the bank had not. "Our site was really not that big," Spankey conceded. "It could not have supported a building of major height unless you made it a needle." Even so, Reichmann did not come on strong. "Olympia & York could have done a very interesting building without us, but Paul never pushed that in our talks," Spankey said.

Spankey did his homework and concluded both that the economics of the sort of massive redevelopment project that the Reichmanns envisioned were superior to the bank's other options and that Olympia & York was a suitable partner. On the latter point, he encountered skepticism at the highest levels of the bank. "The question came up whether Olympia & York had the experience to do a development of such size," Spankey recalled. "I said that I knew of no other builder in Canada that had done a building as big so the question really had to be asked of every developer. Also, in view of the fact that Olympia & York had built Place Bell Canada in Ottawa [which, though only twenty-six stories, was a capacious 1.5 million square feet] and their track record generally, I argued that they were as capable as anyone else." The fact that Olympia & York was going to build next door to the bank with or without the bank's participation also was "a crucial factor," Spankey noted.

The contractual agreements binding Olympia & York and the Bank of Montreal were highly complex and would not be fully worked out until the tower was nearly completed. But the essence of the partnership was straightforward: the bank would pool 50 and 60 King Street with the properties already assembled and in return would get a 25 percent undivided interest in the project, as well as a set amount of space in First Bank Tower at a fixed, long-term rental rate. (Olympia & York would own a 50 percent interest in the complex and North American Life 25 percent.)

By 1972, Paul Reichmann had assembled 90 percent of the city block bound by King, Bay, Adelaide, and York streets—a site larger than that of Commerce Court or the Toronto-Dominion Center. "When I did Global House, I did want to make a better-looking building than the ones around it, but my concern was really just the economics of the project," Reichmann recalled. "But with First Canadian Place we went a step beyond this approach to try to create a project that was not only commercially viable but fulfilled a need of the area itself." To design the complex, Olympia & York paired local favorite Bregman & Hamman with Edward Durell Stone Associates, a New York City firm whose lushly decorative, unabashedly old-fashioned style had won it an avid following among the sort of giant corporations to which Olympia & York would increasingly cater. The Reichmanns had hired the Stone firm for the recently completed Place Bell Canada and were well pleased with its work.

As usual, both Paul and Albert worked closely with their architects. "They were at all the design meetings, and they made all the design and cost decisions," recalled Tonu Altosaar, a junior Bregman & Hamman architect assigned to the project. At times, Altosaar found himself badly out of sync with his clients. "I was an enthusiastic young architect and I was sometimes taken to task by the Reichmanns for being a little too rash in thinking of the building as pure architecture," he recalled. For example, Altosaar opposed the idea of filling the lobby with chandeliers. "I would have preferred something leaner, less showy." he recalled. Later, the architect would concede the error of his ways when he saw how much the chandeliers and the plush carpets in the lobby appealed to civilians. "You learn that you don't design a monument for yourself but a building for people to use."

Although the architecture of First Canadian Place was stylistically unadventurous, the business strategy that underlay the project was daring. The Reichmanns effectively decided to compete not only with the shiny new office complexes across the street but with the suburban malls that were draining the life out of downtown Toronto. As Olympia & York noted in the plan it submitted to the Toronto City Council, "the concept of large office towers with marginal public activities relegated to the basement was clearly understood and rejected." Instead, Olympia & York's architects produced a design featuring two office towers clad with white marble and set atop a mammoth three-story podium filled with retail stores and topped with small parks and landscaped plazas. The great height of the towers was mainly a function of economics: more floors means more leasable space. But ego also played a part. The Bank of Montreal would again command the MINT and its logo—a big blue *M*—would be affixed to the top of a tower, which, at 935 feet, would be enthroned in the *Guinness Book of World Records* as the tallest bank building in the world.

In the summer of 1972, Olympia & York submitted its plans for the project's first phase to the Toronto City Council. Despite the massiveness of the undertaking and the necessity of closing off several small public thoroughfares threading through Olympia & York's "superblock," the Reichmanns had every expectation of a prompt rubber-stamping. In Toronto, as in Drapeau's Montreal, the city government for years had smiled upon the property industry as its indispensable partner in urban redevelopment. As expected, the "King-Bay project," as First Canadian Place was dubbed at first, sailed through the City Council, though John Sewell, the leader of the council's small antideveloper faction, sarcastically proposed the imposition of a two-thousand-foot height limit. As president of NALOY, Paul Reichmann signed a development agreement with the city of Toronto on October 26, 1972—which, as it turned out, was just in the nick of time.

———

If the political equivalent of lightning struck the city government of Toronto in the municipal election of December 4, 1972, then the twin lightning rods of popular discontent were the skyscraper and the high-rise apartment building. Many of the city's less affluent residents had been unsettled—literally so in many cases—by the great building boom that had begun in the early 1960s and had radically altered the look and feel of what had been an almost willfully provincial city. Oblivious to the force of the gathering backlash, the city hall establishment had repeatedly and often callously disregarded the wishes of average citizens in its eagerness to keep the wrecking ball swinging. In the 1972 campaign, a long-germinating grassroots reform movement unexpectedly burst into full flower as a loose coalition of antiestablishment candidates captured eleven of the City Council's twenty-two seats. Toronto voters also elected as their new mayor a social science professor named David Crombie.

After taking office in January 1973, the new regime formally requested the guidance of the city planning, development, and legal departments on how to restrain downtown development. In June, the department chiefs urged the would-be reformers to go back to basics and draft a new zoning law and a new downtown plan. Because this would likely take at least two years, they suggested a temporary measure to hold the lid on development in the interim. In September, Mayor Crombie and the reformist wing of the new council unveiled a new bylaw seemingly so radical that it was widely reported in the press as the leading edge of a populist antidevelopment backlash in North America. The measure banned new buildings higher than forty-five feet—or four to five stories—unless the City Council voted an exemption. (A series of complicated further restrictions were added later.) Leading lights of the property industry howled with outrage, variously denouncing the new bylaw as "unnecessary," "arbitrary," "extreme," "immoral," and "an attempt to rule by individuals rather than law."

Although Paul and Albert Reichmann agreed with their fellow developers, they wisely held their tongues. It was hard to imagine that the City Council would order the demolition of a partly completed new skyscraper. But First Bank Tower still was little more than a massive hole (the first steel column was not erected until January 1974), and the antidevelopment forces had homed in on Olympia & York ever since it had bought the old Toronto Star building. One of Olympia & York's most vociferous critics was Dan Heap, a neighborhood activist and future alderman. "Who made downtown land so valuable?" Heap had thundered in a newspaper column at the time. "Who made the land around Pearl Street worth $150 a foot? Not Mayor [William] Dennison or the other politicians who brag about it. Not the Toronto Star and the ad men who make money off it. Not the real estate speculators and financiers like Olympia York [*sic*] who juggle it back and forth. They don't make people willing to go there and spend money for that land; they only take advantage of them. Who did make that land so valuable? The working people of Toronto, that's who."

Luckily for the Reichmanns, the City Council did not go so far as to impose its new height limit retroactively; projects that had been issued building permits before the bylaw was enacted were automatically exempt. But if First Bank Tower could not be stopped, First Canadian Place still could be crippled. The project's Achilles heel was its second phase, which amounted to about 30 percent of the complex and was not covered under the existing building permit. Anticipating drastic action by the City Council, Olympia & York had rushed its Phase II plans to the mayor and the City Council during the summer of 1972 and had taken the precaution of hiring a politically high-powered downtown law firm. But the reformists would not be stampeded, and in the end the Reichmanns did the politic thing and did not force the issue by formally applying for a second phase building permit. Olympia & York had no practical alternative but to wait until the new bylaw had been imposed and then apply for an exemption to build its second tower. And then, inevitably, all hell broke loose.

Political opposition to First Canadian Place coalesced around the planned demolition of three old and arguably historic buildings that NALOY had acquired: 50 King (the Bank of Montreal), 112 King (the Provincial Bank), and 140 King (the *Globe & Mail* newspaper). The fate of the newspaper building in particular emerged as a cause célèbre of antidevelopment forces. The newspaper, which was scheduled to move into new quarters along Front Street at the end of 1973, had reserved the contractual right to tear down its old building before conveying the site to Olympia & York, thus saving itself about $2 million in taxes. In late 1973, the City Council intervened. By a 12–8 margin the council "requested" that Olympia & York work up a comprehensive study of the economic and planning implications of the First Canadian Place project and that the *Globe & Mail* building be left untouched for the time being.

With an application for exemption pending before the City Council, it was Olympia & York—not the newspaper—that found its neck on the political chopping block. The axe would certainly fall if the *Globe & Mail* defied the council and dynamited 140 King Street. Paul Reichmann entreated James L. Cooper, the newspaper's publisher, to postpone demolition. Cooper refused. Reichmann tried to entice the council into authorizing demolition by offering to add a public park to First Canadian Place; Olympia & York would pick up the $2 million tab for the park but let the city spend the money as it saw fit. Again, no dice. Finally, a month before demolition of the newspaper building was to begin, Reichmann sent a letter to Cooper offering to indemnify the newspaper for any additional tax it incurred in conveying the site with the building intact. "We desperately need your help," the developer pleaded. ". . . I am worried that if your building is demolished, although we couldn't help it, it will be taken out against us. This is why I have offered to indemnify you against the possible loss of $2,000,000 because even that premium is less of a loss to us than stopping the job only two-thirds done."

When Cooper rejected the offer, Olympia & York's lawyers delivered a copy of Reichmann's letter to the City Council as evidence of the developer's goodwill. The ploy succeeded in isolating the *Globe & Mail*, which postponed demolition, but it also backfired on the Reichmanns. Instead of letting Olympia & York off the hook, the City Council raised the preservationist ante by voting to request the developer "to begin negotiations with the consortium" that owned the Provincial Bank building—112 King—to preserve it as well as 140 King. As the reformists well knew, they effectively had directed Paul Reichmann to begin negotiations with himself, since the Provincial Bank was one of two properties that North American Life had contributed to the project at its outset. (Indeed, the only reason it was still standing was that Olympia & York was using it as a construction office.) As such, it was an integral underpinning not just of Phase II but of the entire project. If the City Council were to rule 112 King off limits, the whole superstructure of agreements binding Olympia & York to its partners would collapse like multimillion-dollar Tinkertoys.

———

The Sturm und Drang of municipal politics was only the Reichmanns' most immediate concern. By the beginning of 1973, 10 percent of the office space in Toronto stood vacant, twice the normal rate, and yet developers were continuing to erect downtown skyscrapers at a furious pace. The value of new construction permits issued in 1973 would top $1.9 billion, more than double the previous high registered just two years earlier. By some accounts, Toronto was now the per capita construction capital of North America. As the developers of the largest single project on the boards, the Reichmanns were particularly vulnerable. If the forces of supply and demand did not come more favorably into alignment by the time First Bank Tower was scheduled to open in 1975, the financial consequences could be horrendous. On the other hand, Paul Reichmann had assembled his dream site. To do nothing with it, to sit and wait for a cloudless sky, would have been an anticlimax crueler perhaps than bankruptcy. He also took comfort in the fact that his partner, the Bank of Montreal, had a pair of the deepest pockets in Canada. With the support of both the Bank of Montreal and North American Life, the brothers decided in the spring of 1973 to begin excavation.

Olympia & York work crews had not yet finished preparing the site in the fall of 1973 when the Organization of Petroleum Exporting Countries (OPEC) jolted the industrialized West by imposing an oil embargo. Before it ended, the average price of OPEC crude had quadrupled to $12 a barrel. This, the first of the two great OPEC oil shocks of the 1970s, wreaked global economic havoc and tipped the economies of the United States and Canada into the longest and deepest recession since World War II. As corporations curtailed spending on new plant and equipment, the outlook for office leasing was wreathed in gloom. The Reichmanns and their partners had cause anew to back away from the First Bank Tower project but again chose to keep to schedule. In January 1974, the first steel column was erected in a pit five stories below street level. A mere sixteen months later, the first tenants began moving in.

Phase I of First Canadian Place was completed with a speed and efficiency that fundamentally altered the economics of this and all future Olympia & York undertakings. In his decade in the Reichmanns' employ, Keith Roberts, Olympia & York's vice president of operations, had supervised the building of half a dozen office towers before tackling First Bank Tower. While all these past projects had been successfully completed, the prevailing methods of high-rise construction increasingly had offended the creased-pants perfectionism of this former British Army officer. "You can't imagine the chaos that existed," Roberts recalled. "You had stick-in-the-mud people who had been doing the same things for years and were reasonably successful and so the system had no impetus for change, even though a tremendous amount of time and money was lost in high-rise construction—especially of office buildings." The prospect of building First Bank Tower, which was more than twice as tall as anything Olympia & York had erected, was all the challenge Roberts had required to rethink the methodology of skyscraper construction from the ground up, as it were.

In tacit acknowledgment of their own limitations and their confidence in Roberts, the Reichmann brothers had always allowed their construction chief great latitude. "They left me alone, basically," said Roberts, who in 1972 had begun touring building sites all over North America in search of fresh solutions to familiar problems. "I was particularly interested in establishing how much time a man actually worked out of an eight-hour working day; to analyze lost time and actual productivity," Roberts said. After a full year of research, Roberts and his small staff had drawn up a detailed operating plan that promised to save a small fortune by foreshortening construction of First Bank Tower. Paul and Albert Reichmann were delighted. "Both of them understood the approach very quickly," Roberts recalled, "and were willing to take the risk of experimentation, which was considerable."

To facilitate Roberts's ideas, the brothers even instructed its architects to modify their basic design. In addition, the company had to make multimillion-dollar investments in new cranes, elevators, and the like. Buying new equipment was one thing, persuading subcontractors to adjust their own approach to accommodate it quite another. Olympia & York had to "convince every subcontract bidder to totally reassess his estimates of cost and construction time," Roberts observed. Even one of Roberts's assistants predicted that the plan would fail because construction laborers would not be able to master its logistical intricacies. To induce subcontractor cooperation, Olympia & York took the unusual and risky step of guaranteeing its own performance as general contractor. "If the job had gone awry," Roberts recalled, "the subcontractors would have brought enormous financial claims against us."

Mechanically speaking, Roberts's plan relied on six innovations: a giant truck turntable surrounded by eleven unloading bays; a bank of nine oversized elevators; two giant cranes able to climb up the building's steel frame as it rose; a high-speed system for transporting wet concrete; a special double scaffolding for installing the marble cladding; and a computerized central control room. This array of equipment enabled Olympia & York to greatly reduce the time wasted in transporting workmen up and down the building. Equally dramatic efficiencies were realized in moving matériel from delivery truck to point of use. At First Canadian Place, installing a trailer load of marble required only five man-hours of labor instead of the twenty-six that would have been required using conventional methods. For drywall, insulation, glass, sheet metal ductwork, ceiling tiles, lighting fixtures—whatever the job—the savings achieved were of comparable magnitude.

By Olympia & York's own calculations, labor time was reduced 1.3 million man-hours all told. At an average of $20 an hour, this amounted to $26 million, or about 15 percent of the total cost of the project. Of such efficiencies are great fortunes made. And yet, by all accounts, the quality of the workmanship met the most demanding standards. The Reichmanns, in effect, gave back a portion of their labor cost savings by purchasing materials of exceptionally high quality, including 700,000 tons of marble, 800,000 tons of granite, carpets imported from Britain, and lighting fixtures from Germany.

Roberts's system gave Olympia & York a big cost advantage in competitive bidding against most other developers—and the bigger the project, the bigger

Olympia & York's margin of superiority. While other developers adapted the company's innovations to their own use, Roberts and his staff continued to refine and elaborate their system, which Olympia & York would employ to hugely beneficial effect on every future high-rise project. "Keith Roberts," Paul Reichmann would say after the company's long, lucrative run had come to its sorry end, "was an extraordinary construction genius."

In building First Bank Tower, Roberts and crew encountered only one serious hitch, and it had nothing to do with the new methods. In midproject, the slabs of Carrara marble arriving from Quebec began subtly lightening in hue. Appalled at the prospect of a two-tone skyscraper, the Reichmanns terminated their Quebec supply contract and dispatched Otto Blau, their Romanian-born purchasing manager, to Italy on an emergency mission to secure an alternate source of supply. Blau succeeded, buying a good piece of the mountain that had provided the stone for Michelangelo's *Pietà*. Once the Italian stone began arriving, Olympia & York's crews began working virtually around the clock. Despite a five-month interruption, the exterior cladding was finished only about a month behind schedule. In commemoration of Blau's resourcefulness, Albert Reichmann had a small plaque installed on the thirty-fourth floor. It read: "These stones were brought over by Otto, Patricia's father, with sweat and tears, Anno 1975."

To finance construction, Olympia & York floated $70 million in first-mortgage bonds and borrowed $30 million from a consortium of a dozen Canadian banks led by the Canadian Imperial Bank of Commerce. The Bank of Montreal was not part of the group but agreed—for a fee—to guarantee the bank borrowings for the project. In other words, if Olympia & York defaulted, the Bank of Montreal would make good on the payments. To win this extraordinary concession from its partner, the Reichmanns had to offer as collateral virtually everything they owned. Like Flemingdon Park, First Canadian Place was all or nothing at all. "The Reichmanns had a lot of property at Flemingdon Park, but that only went so far as security," said Malcolm Spankey, who remained the bank's principal liaison with the brothers from the beginning to the end of the project. "They took enormous risks—corporate and personal—but they came through."

———

In the end, the great Toronto skyscraper crackdown of the mid-1970s proved much ado about not very much, though the drama was a long time playing out. While many downtown projects were delayed, few were denied exemption from the forty-five-foot height limit. The antidevelopment faction of the City Council was gradually outmaneuvered and finally neutralized by Mayor Crombie, a moderate initially mistaken for a reformer. In urging adoption of the holding bylaw, the mayor had seemed to side with the opponents of the property industry. But in seeing to it that the law provided ample grounds for exemption, Crombie effectively blocked the radical solutions the reformists sought. "Crombie's style was one which allowed him to come down to a position very close to where the old guard had always been, without getting tarred with the old-guard brush," observed one of his biographers. "He supported big downtown developments . . . just like any old-guard politician would have. But he did it all with the protective colouration of a holding bylaw which, in fact, was thin and unsubstantial."

First Canadian Place was a case in point. Although Crombie basically favored the project, he refrained from public demonstrations of his support and was slow to assert himself in support of Olympia & York's application for exemption even behind the scenes. "The mayor was a friend but not an ally," Paul Reichmann recalled. "He thought the project was the right thing to do but he didn't want to come out and take a stand politically."

Crombie did depart from previous mayors in taking a stand on the aesthetics of urban redevelopment. In fairness, the holding bylaw was not merely a smokescreen for his pro-development stance but a mechanism for pressuring skyscraper builders into making design changes. "When I look at the skyline of Toronto," Crombie said in defending the idea of a height limit, "all I seem to see are these great boxes. No variety. Just boxes." Crombie wanted to beautify redevelopment, not stop it, and he attracted to his administration a cadre of young, self-styled progressive architects and urban planners. Among them was Ron Soskolne, a young South African who had come to Canada in 1969 to study architecture at the University of Toronto and was soon caught up in the anti-development movement. After the election, Soskolne joined the city planning department in a senior position. First Canadian Place had been the first project to cross his desk.

The Reichmann brothers did not want Crombie and his praetorian guard fiddling with an architectural plan three years in the making. But it was less risky to appease city hall than to fight it. Soskolne met Paul Reichmann for the first time across a table in the offices of the *Globe & Mail*, to which he had been peremptorily summoned during the battle over preserving 140 King. The publisher of the newspaper "lectured at me for twenty minutes in his office in the most strident way, while Paul Reichmann sat silently at the table," Soskolne recalled. "After this guy had shot his bolt at me, Paul explained very gently that he'd started assembling the land about four years before, had agreements with the *Globe & Mail* to demolish its building and that if this wasn't done the paper would suffer a heavy tax loss. Paul indicated that he'd be pleased to negotiate design changes but had no choice but to demolish the building. I sort of said, 'Oh,' and saw the light—that this wasn't a case of a big, bad developer capriciously disregarding the wishes of the city."

In essence, Olympia & York wholly reworked the design of the second phase of First Canadian Place in exchange for authorization to demolish all three of the

purportedly historic buildings in the project's path. The details of this rapprochement were worked out gradually in a lengthy series of meetings between
Paul Reichmann and his lawyers and Crombie and his assistants, mainly
Soskolne and Michael Dennis, the mayor's senior policy man. "I'd meet with
Paul on a regular basis to discuss the next step, whatever it was," recalled Crombie, who estimated that he met with Reichmann at least a dozen times. "He was
careful about the process and never pushed beyond what was reasonable."

In deference to the Crombie administration's preference for a less monolithic
complex, Olympia & York abandoned plans for a second outsized tower and
instead proposed adding a thirty-six-story building with a separate four-story
pavilion. Because Soskolne felt strongly that parks "in the air" were not used,
Olympia & York dropped its planned park from atop the three-story podium to
street level. While these and numerous other changes boosted Olympia &
York's expenses by a few million dollars, returning to the drawing board was,
in the Reichmanns' estimation, a small price to pay to preserve the project's
financial and territorial integrity. Paul Reichmann's negotiations with city officials were generally harmonious, smoothed by an initially grudging but genuine mutual respect; in fact, Olympia & York eventually would employ in senior
positions Michael Dennis, Ron Soskolne, and a third Crombie praetorian,
Anthony Coombes.

Even so, the bargaining was protracted by political theater. As Mayor Crombie shadow-danced his way toward the middle of the stage, his City Council
foes strewed his path—and the Reichmanns'—with every procedural obstacle
they knew how to devise. "We knew when crunch time came we wouldn't have
the votes," recalled John Sewell (who in 1978 would become mayor of Toronto
himself). "But we never backed down from a fight. Our basic problem was we
just didn't have many ways to protect historic buildings in those days."

As the politics of Phase II played out in slow motion, the building of Phase I
was speeding along Keith Roberts's artfully greased skids. On February 4,
1975, the Toronto Construction Association held its annual meeting on the
fifth floor even as construction crews toiled away above. A month later, the
tower was topped off. On May 18, right on schedule, the first tenants began
moving into the completed lower twenty-two floors. In August, the City Council at last voted Olympia & York its second-phase exemption by a 13–6 margin.
By year's end, all seventy-two floors had been completed at a total cost of not
quite $200 million.

———

The completion of Phase I would not end the Reichmanns' struggles along
King and Bay. When First Bank Tower was topped off, the Canadian economy
was still mired in a deep trough and the office market in Toronto had not
regained its equilibrium. Although the volume of new construction permits

issued had fallen steeply during the mid-1970s recession, the market remained burdened by a stubborn backlog of unleased space. Not until 1977 would the vacancy rate finally dip below 10 percent. Wisely, the Reichmanns delayed the construction of the second phase, which would add one million square feet to First Canadian Place when finally completed in 1982.

In a departure from standard industry practice, Olympia & York handled the leasing of First Bank Tower itself. "Olympia & York was not out shopping for deals with agents and they got a good deal of respect for it," said Malcolm Spankey, the Bank of Montreal's property man. "I went with Albert to some presentations. But the best agent we had was Paul. He was low-key. He didn't pressure. He knew the project down to the smallest detail and he just laid out the deal with authority." Olympia & York was willing to cut special deals to attract large and prestigious tenants to First Bank Tower, in some cases going so far as to buy them out of their existing leases. Unlike many downtown landlords, though, the Reichmanns drew the line at cutting rents to fill space. From their earliest days, the brothers had preferred to take the calculated risk of waiting out a soft market to writing twenty- or thirty-year leases at rates likely to prove ruinous in the long run.

In the end, it would take the Reichmanns about four years to fully lease their new seventy-two-story flagship. While the deficit of $20 million that accumulated in the interim strained Olympia & York's finances, the company's solvency was never in jeopardy. Virtually simultaneously with the completion of the tower, Paul Reichmann was able to arrange long-term financing at much lower interest rates than the construction loans that Olympia & York promptly paid off. Moreover, Paul had always assumed that filling First Bank Tower might take as long as five years, or a bit longer than actually proved the case, so Olympia & York already had borrowed sufficient funds to cover its operating deficit. The financial burden was further eased by a clause in its agreement with the Bank of Montreal by which the bank was obligated to cover half the cost of debt service during the lease-up of First Bank Tower.

By 1979 the surfeit of office space in Toronto had given way to what would prove a lasting shortage. Under John Sewell, the city enacted a tough new downtown plan that drastically curtailed the size of future office towers. According to Paul Reichmann, the first tenants to move into First Bank Tower paid gross rents of $12.50 a square foot on average while the late arrivals shelled out $45 a square foot. Rents would continue to escalate into the mid-1980s, and the value of the land on which First Canadian Place rested would reach a peak of nearly $100 a square foot—eight times what Paul Reichmann had paid for the Toronto Star site in 1967.

If, in the end, First Canadian Place was not exactly what the Reichmann brothers had envisioned, it was everything they could have hoped for: their first, fully realized masterpiece of the commercial art of development. Olympia

& York moved its own offices into First Bank Tower, with both Paul and Albert installing themselves on the thirty-second floor. "Middle is more comfortable," Paul quipped, facetiously inverting his actual business philosophy in deflecting a reporter's query about his and Albert's comparative lack of altitude. Make no mistake, the Reichmann brothers in their own understated way were utterly enamored of First Canadian Place, which they would show off in the years to come in lobbying municipal officials and prospective partners from distant cities. "Half the money in Ontario is within a few blocks of this building," Albert proudly told a reporter. Although Olympia & York would undertake even grander projects, First Canadian Place would forever remain special to the brothers. As their first landmark achievement in North America, First Canadian Place was both an emphatic reaffirmation of the Reichmanns' vision of themselves as a family of select destiny and a seventy-two-story haredi explorer's flag planted, proudly and immovably, in the soil of the assimilationist continent.

Chapter 27

E ven as it grew into a multibillion-dollar enterprise, Olympia & York would remain extraordinarily tightly held in every sense. The Reichmanns never seriously considered selling common stock to the public, and no amount of talent, loyalty, or seniority entitled a nonfamily employee to the merest sliver of equity ownership. The issue was not control per se; the family could have ensured its dominance of the company without owning even a simple majority of its shares. Nor were the Reichmanns compelled by greed in the conventional sense; family members would give away a much larger proportion of their wealth than they ever spent on themselves. The fact was that the Reichmanns looked on Olympia & York as an extension of family in the most literal sense. "To us, O & Y wasn't just a company," said Philip Reichmann, Albert's oldest son and heir apparent. "It was more that the company was a member of the family." And, of course, you don't sell a son or daughter, no matter how great your need for growth capital.

Even within the family, Olympia & York stock was concentrated in few hands. To be sure, trusts were set up through which ownership of the family enterprise eventually was to have been distributed among all twenty-seven of Samuel and Renée Reichmann's grandchildren. But from Olympia & York's founding to its untimely demise—a span of more than thirty years—its common stock was never held by more than eight family members: Albert, Paul, and Ralph, each of whom owned 25 percent of the company jointly with their wives; and their parents, who owned the remaining 25 percent stake. Olympia & York was as narrowly cast in terms of executive authority as ownership. No outsider—indeed, no nonrelative—would ever sit on the board of the ultimate holding company. The original directors included the three brothers, their wives (Egosah, Lea, and Ada), and their father. Each of the wives also held the corporate title of vice president.

As chairman of the board, Samuel Reichmann presided over its formal meetings, which were convened roughly once a quarter. But because these sessions were mainly devoted to the routine rubber-stamping of corporate documents offered up by Albert and Paul, the most powerful position on the board was secretary. As secretary, Paul drew up the board's agenda and recorded the official minutes; he wielded the rubber stamp, in other words. In deference to Samuel, who never really learned English, meetings were conducted in Hungarian. For the most part, the important family discussions of Olympia & York's affairs took place not in the boardroom at First Bank Tower but in the living room of 160 Dalemount Avenue during the brothers' mandatory nightly visits to their parents.

It is doubtful that any company as large as Olympia & York became ever revealed so little about its finances, and what began as a benign insistence on privacy would devolve into purposeful, even Machiavellian secrecy as the company's fortunes soured. But even as the Reichmanns' corporate dealings increasingly assumed an abusive aspect, the family continued to exemplify an extraordinarily high standard of public spiritedness. Their philanthropy was as distinctive for its constancy as its volume, for, in contrast to the usual pattern, it was not a by-product of outsized wealth. Long before they entered the ranks of the super rich, the Reichmann brothers routinely set aside a heaping portion of their income for charity. Indeed, one reason the family attached such importance to maintaining 100 percent ownership of Olympia & York was to ensure that it remained as much an instrument of philanthropy as of commerce.

In the judgment of the brothers and their parents, the traditional obligation to give away 10 percent of their income seemed inadequate in light not only of the family's long tradition of tzedoka but of the nature of the real estate business. "The standard of giving a percentage of earnings is not easy to apply in a business like property development where the gain is in value creation, rather than regular earnings," Paul explained. "So we gave based on our sense of the value of Olympia & York's assets, which tended to increase more rapidly than profits." In effect, the annual percentage of profits donated ran closer to 30 percent than 10 percent.

The Reichmanns would not vault into the ranks of the world's richest families until the end of the 1970s. But even before the annual volume of the brothers' giving soared above the $40 million mark, the impact of their philanthropy was concentrated by the narrowness of its scope: their largesse exclusively benefited strictly Orthodox institutions and individuals. And within the compact and generally impoverished haredi world, the $3 million to $5 million a year that the brothers handed out during most of the 1970s went a long way indeed. Within the parameters fixed by their religious identity, their giving was largely improvised and loosely organized at best. "It was us responding to requests more than anything else," Paul said. The brothers left the paperwork to a handful of employees but insisted on making every funding decision of any consequence themselves, usually after consultation with one another. "The Reichmanns' giving came out of their left pocket in that it was ad hoc and personal," said Kurt Rothschild, a Toronto communal leader who was closely involved in certain aspects of the family's philanthropy.

In Toronto, the Reichmanns' support of the Yesodei Hatorah, Bais Yaakov, and other religious schools was only the most visible aspect of their giving. With great tact and discretion, the brothers quietly provided small sums to hundreds of needy haredim, as well as dozens of the Jewish immigrants from Morocco who had settled in Toronto in large numbers. (One unexpected effect of Olympia & York's collapse would be a burgeoning of the welfare rolls in North York.) Besides cash, the brothers dispensed business advice, countersigned for mortgages and business loans, and mediated the occasional family or estate dispute. Even after insolvency would render Olympia & York unable to repay billions of dollars in corporate loans, the brothers would continue to pay monthly on personal guarantees of loans made to equally unfortunate local haredi businessmen.

Even at this early stage, however, the bulk of the family's philanthropy flowed overseas, mainly to yeshivoth and other religious schools in Israel and France. As a matter of principle, the brothers made at least a small donation to every ultra-Orthodox school that solicited their support. Although the Reichmanns were not yet the largest patron of haredi education, they already loomed large in the yeshiva world as one of the few Ashkenazi families to champion the underdog cause of Sephardic religious education.

The Sephardic Jews of the Arab lands of North Africa and the Levant had continued to flee their homelands in massive numbers throughout the 1950s and 1960s. Many of the most impoverished and least educated of them settled in Israel, where they were afforded second-class treatment in every respect by the Ashkenazim who had founded the Jewish state and dominated its institutions. While many immigrants reacted to their hardships by redoubling their efforts to assimilate, a minority of religious Sephardim defiantly clung to their traditions. The vast majority of religious schools were Ashkenazi-run institutions that could not have accommodated the vast immigrant influx even if they had cared to. The Sephardim needed their own schools but were frustrated in their organizational efforts by the indifference of the Israeli government and a paucity of financial support from Sephardim abroad. By 1969, Sephardim slightly outnumbered Ashkenazim in Israel, and yet only 7,126, or 38 percent, of the 18,760 boys attending yeshivoth were Sephardi. Enrollment at Sephardi yeshivas was only 1,652, or 8.8 percent of the total for Israel.

For Paul Reichmann, the campaign to provide religious instruction for dislocated Sephardim was an extension both logical and personal of the work he had done in Morocco. Many of the rabbis and administrators at the forefront of the Sephardi religious education movement in Israel and in France (the European locus of Jewish immigration from North Africa) were boys whom he had taken under his wing at Gateshead or former colleagues from Ozar Hatorah in Casablanca. Reichmann gave generously of both his time and his money, keeping closely informed of the inner workings of dozens of schools. "The time that Paul devoted to institutions and charity then was unbelievable," recalled his chum, Moses Lasry, who was instrumental in organizing a French offshoot of Ozar Hatorah. Reichmann was one of a half-dozen contributors who gave $25,000 apiece to found Ozar Hatorah France in 1971 and over the years would send millions more. Although Lasry usually went to Toronto to see his old friend—often with an eminent Sephardic rabbi in tow—Reichmann would fly to France for important meetings. "I used to object when people called Paul a philanthropist," Lasry said. "He's a leader, not a philanthropist. He knows the problems from firsthand."

In both France and Israel, the Reichmanns backed members of the Toledano family, the great Moroccan rabbinical dynasty, in the founding of yeshivoth and other schools. Paul also worked in close support of the legendary activist Moishe Pardo, a Syrian Jew who had given up his business in the late 1940s to devote himself to the religious education of Sephardic girls in Israel. Operating from his base in B'nai Brak, Pardo set up dozens of girls' schools throughout the country. Reichmann had first met Pardo in 1948, when he had passed through Tangier on an early expedition.

At the same time, Paul and his brothers were contributing to Ashkenazi yeshivoth in Israel and elsewhere; indeed, the lion's share of the Reichmanns' philanthropy went to Ashkenazi institutions, which, after all, were far more numerous. However, Paul leveraged his family's contributions to Sephardic institutions by fund-raising on their behalf. "Because it was unusual for Ashkenazim to be that involved with Sephardic schools, our participation was a stamp of approval that encouraged many others to do the same," said Reichmann, who put the arm not only on fellow Ashkenazim but on wealthy Sephardim, including Edmond Safra, the reclusive banking billionaire of Lebanese origin. "Edmond Safra came to my office and wrote a check for $1 million at a time when $1 million was a lot of money for us to give to a single institution," Reichmann recalled in 1995, when $1 million was again a prohibitive sum. "If someone was to come looking for money for an Ashkenazi yeshiva today, I'd make a contribution. But if he was from a Sephardic institution, I'd help him get money from twenty other people, too."

———

For all their generosity, Paul and his brothers were rigorously discriminating in their philanthropy; their governing precept was not "Ask and ye shall receive" but "If a brother shows no mercy to a brother, who will?"

Rabbi Irwin Witty, the director of the Toronto Board of Jewish Education, was asked in the mid-1970s to approach the Reichmanns for financing on behalf of Adin Steinsaltz, an Israeli scholar acclaimed throughout the Jewish world as the author of the twenty-six-volume *Punctuated, Explained and Translated Talmud*. One Sunday, Rabbi Witty telephoned Paul Reichmann, who listened politely and finally asked, "From whom does he have haskamah?" *Haskamah* is a Hebrew word meaning a rabbinical endorsement attesting to an author's piety.

"I'm sure he has haskamah but I don't know from whom," Rabbi Witty replied.

"If you find out," Reichmann said guardedly, "I'll think about it."

In essence a populizer of Talmud, Steinsaltz had always been disinclined to seek the official imprimatur of the ultra-Orthodox rabbinate. Rabbi Witty did not bother returning to Reichmann, who no doubt heaved a sigh of relief years later when Rabbi Eliezer Schach, the powerful chief Ashkenazi rabbi of Israel and a greatly esteemed halakic authority, leveled a broadside attack on Steinsaltz's work as rank heresy. "People say that these new-style Gemaras increase the number of learners," thundered Rabbi Schach. "But God doesn't need this learning. God wants the 'old' learning."

Rabbi Witty also approached Reichmann on behalf of a modern Orthodox rabbi who headed a school in Jerusalem. The two were invited to stop by Reichmann's after Havdalah one Saturday. "He welcomed us very nicely to his home," Rabbi Witty recalled. The conversation progressed smoothly until the rabbi mentioned his affiliation with B'nai Akiva High School, which, as a Modern Orthodox institution, offended the Reichmann notions of observance. In B'nai Akiva, to cite a superficial example, boys could wear kippahs instead of fedoras.

"I do not hold with B'nai Akiva," said Reichmann, while writing out a check for $1,000.

"But, Mr. Reichmann," the rabbi hastily replied, scrambling into the life raft of secondhand haskamah, "Rabbi Schach says that our girls are something special."

Without comment, Reichmann ripped up the check and wrote out a new one—for $2,000 this time.

But if the Reichmanns had little trouble picking out their haredi brethren from among the supplicants crowding their doorstep, Olympia & York would suffer repeatedly for the Reichmanns' inability to differentiate between business and philanthropy with equal clarity. In theory at least, the brothers drew a sharp line of demarcation. "In business we have to look at the bottom line," Albert once told a reporter. "If it's not profitable, we can't do business." But in practice, the Reichmanns' deep-seated sense of communal obligation occasionally caused them to mingle charity and business to calamitous effect.

Olympia & York's first American venture was a disastrous suburban development in New Jersey that began in 1973 with the rescue of ultra-Orthodox investors in a land scheme gone awry. Within the Reichmann family, the costly episode was ruefully known as the "Siedenfeld affair."

Isiah Siedenfeld was a pious, learned man who taught at a rabbinical seminary in Spring Valley, an ultra-Orthodox enclave in Rockland County, an hour's drive north of New York City. Siedenfeld was not a rich man by any means, but in the mid-1960s he was able to scrape some extra money together to buy a little piece of property, which he sold at a nice profit. He bought a bigger piece of land, again turned a nice profit and again reinvested the proceeds. Soon, he was approached by friends and neighbors wanting to invest along with him in his next deal. Siedenfeld not only obliged but promised his silent partners that they could withdraw their funds any time they wanted. As his winning streak continued, his renown spread from Spring Valley through the other ultra-Orthodox communities of the Catskills into the haredi precincts of Brooklyn and across the Hudson River to the yeshiva town of Lakewood, New Jersey. Millions of dollars—many of them hard-earned indeed—were entrusted to Siedenfeld by a few hundred investors from all walks of haredi life.

Siedenfeld lost his magic when local land values slumped in the early 1970s. Distressed at learning that land prices go down as well as up, his investors began pulling their money out. By early 1973, he was unable to cover the withdrawals and panic spread through the ultra-Orthodox precincts of the New York City area. In meeting halls from Spring Valley to Borough Park, widowed Holocaust survivors and suddenly penniless yeshiva prodigies told their tales of Siedenfeld woe. Siedenfeld signed over his real estate business to an ad hoc committee of communal leaders and went into hiding—not in Brazil, as widely rumored at the time, but in California. Paul Reichmann's help was solicited by Avraham Fruchthandler, a young haredi businessman and community activist with close family ties to one of Brooklyn's best yeshivas, Chaim Berlin. In December 1973, the Reichmanns made Siedenfeld's investors whole by purchasing a 2,000-acre tract of undeveloped property in Old Bridge, New Jersey, for $9.3 million. The brothers paid $1,650,000 in cash and borrowed the remainder.

As Paul Reichmann told it years later, he only got involved because he thought Olympia & York would be able to salvage full value and more from the site. "I made the mistake of thinking it could be a profitable venture," he said. Moses Lasry, who lived in Spring Valley and whose brother-in-law had invested with Siedenfeld, begged to differ: "I would say that Paul acted impulsively and I doubt whether he really thought of it as a business venture. There was justification to help Siedenfeld from a human point of view, and it was not only Siedenfeld but dozens of families that saw their savings disappear. Despite his keen mind, Paul is a man of heart. I've seen tears in his eyes on more than one occasion."

Olympia & York's efforts to develop the Old Bridge site served only to multiply the final tab on the Siedenfeld bailout. Olympia & York gradually bought another 600 acres adjacent to the site and in the late 1970s laid plans to build from scratch what amounted to a new town: 10,500 housing units, 2 million square feet of office space, a shopping center measuring 1.3 million square feet, and an eighteen-hole golf course. Despite years of effort and many millions sunk into planning and architectural studies, Olympia & York never even broke ground on the $1.2 billion Old Bridge project. Right from the start, local residents and officials feared that the huge development would spoil the semi-rural nature of the area and did all they could to obstruct Olympia & York's efforts. However, the coup de grace was struck by the Army Corps of Engineers, which in 1986 recommended that about 60 percent of the site be set aside as federally protected wetlands. "What we lost in the end was three or four times what we'd paid Siedenfeld for the land in the first place," Reichmann said.

Over the years, the Reichmann brothers would lose many millions more in providing backing to haredi businessmen whom they had come to know and admire through their philanthropic endeavors. In perhaps the most costly of these episodes, Paul Reichmann would have to cover a $25 million loan guarantee he had provided to Joe Neumann, a New Yorker who had done well in the strong markets of the 1980s as an operator of nondescript office buildings in Manhattan. When Neumann ran into severe financial trouble in 1989, Reichmann agreed to back him. "It was more to help him than anything else, though there was some thinking that by helping him I might be helping strengthen the market." Instead, the market weakened and Neumann defaulted on numerous loans. His was not the only guarantee on which Reichmann had to pay off. "It was a personal fault of mine to be too willing over the years to make loans and sign guarantees for people," Reichmann said in 1995. "I believe it was a mistake, and it's one I'm still paying for monthly."

———

One of the 613 commandments, or mitzvoth, in the Bible is that every man should write a sefer Torah—that is, copy by hand the Five Books of Moses onto a parchment scroll. Given the difficulty of this task, it became customary for haredi men of mature years and a certain affluence (the going rate for a sefer Torah of average quality these days is about $20,000) to commission a sofer or professional scribe to do the job for them, leaving the last few lines blank. The recipient then completed the scroll himself.

In 1969, Samuel Reichmann had commissioned a sefer Torah from a preeminent and apparently overworked scribe in Bnei Brak, Israel. The production of Reichmann's scroll dragged on long past the year or so typically required for such an assignment. "My father always used to ask me how it was coming," recalled Edward Reichmann, who was then living near Tel Aviv, about twenty miles from B'nai Brak. "I used to go see the sofer and I was always angry because never was it coming." Finally completed in early 1975, the sefer Torah was shipped to Toronto in time for Shavouth, the festival commemorating the giving of the Torah to Moses at Mount Sinai. In consultation with Rabbi Levi Grunwald, the family planned to commemorate the completion of Samuel's sefer Torah with a public ceremony on the second day of the two-day Shavouth festival, which in 1975 fell on a Sunday.

On the Thursday preceding the ceremony, Samuel completed the scroll at his home. On Sunday morning, May 16, 1975, Albert, Paul, Ralph, and their families gathered at Samuel and Renée's house on Dalemount Avenue. Later, it would occur to Lea Reichmann, Paul's wife, that her father-in-law's color had been unusually high, though he seemed his usual cheery self. Paul and Lea's eldest daughter, eighteen-year-old Vivian, arrived late. As was his custom, Samuel fetched his granddaughter a chair.

"Apu," Lea Reichmann gently admonished, using an old Hungarian endearment for "grandfather." "What are you doing? You get up to bring a granddaughter a chair? Educationally, it's unacceptable."

Samuel shrugged off the comment. "She's coming to my home to respect me," he replied. "I don't think it's beneath me to do this for my granddaughter."

The family had obtained police approval to close off Dalemount Avenue, which was only a few blocks long anyway. At the intersection of Dalemount and Fairholme Avenue a large canopy, or huppah, was set up in the street. About 10:50 A.M. a delegation of one hundred congregants left the Yesodei Hatorah synagogue a few blocks away and advanced along Fairholme led by a haredi color guard of five men, each bearing a sefer Torah. At 10:55 Samuel Reichmann left his house, scroll in hand, and walked slowly down Dalemount accompanied by his family. The two contingents hit their marks exactly, converging at the huppah right at 11:00. Samuel immediately handed the scroll to Paul, who stood at his side. "I don't feel well," he gasped, and collapsed heavily to the street. Reichmann died where he fell, never having regained consciousness. He was seventy-seven.

On the afternoon of May 18, a crowd of one thousand mourners gathered in Bathurst Lawn Cemetery in North York to pay their last respects. It was a somber and an increasingly tense occasion. Eva Heller and her six children had arrived from London, but Edward and his wife were still in transit from Tel Aviv. Renée insisted that the ceremonies be delayed, even though, according to haredi custom, burial rites had to begin before sundown on the first day after death. By the time Edward finally arrived, there was little time to spare. In his funeral oration, Rabbi Grunwald, who had flown in from Brooklyn, drew a pointed contrast between Jewish immigrants to North America whose religious faith succumbed to their excitement over the secular opportunities of their new homeland and Samuel Reichmann, who had literally died of his excitement at fulfilling an important mitzvah.

Medically speaking, whether Samuel Reichmann perished of a massive stroke or a massive heart attack was an issue of muted debate among his survivors. His death certificate listed no cause of death, and an autopsy was both pointless and religiously forbidden. Whatever its cause, Samuel's death came as a terrible shock to his family, for he had been in good spirits and, despite his advanced years, had seemed in good health. What is more, his passing altered the inner workings of the extended family in ways that were profound yet imperceptible from the outside in the same way that changes in blood chemistry cannot be glimpsed through the skin. "When my father-in-law died, all of our lives changed," Lea lamented two decades later. "It still isn't the same. It's something we talk about all the time."

If Renée was the enforcer of Reichmann solidarity, Samuel had been the family's ameliorator. "My father-in-law was a great man—strong and quiet," said Marika Reichmann, Louis's wife. "He had tremendous wisdom and gave valuable counsel to many, many people. The greatest compliment I can give my husband is to say that he resembles his father." This was said in the presence of an obviously gratified Louis, who said: "As a child I always wanted to be like him. For as long as I have a memory of my father—for more than sixty years—I remember him as the most soft and genuine person."

As witnesses to the family's years of flight and early exile, and as fathers and businessmen now themselves, the brothers were more cognizant than their wives of Samuel's hard side: the acuity of his pessimism, his decisiveness in evading mortal danger, the intensity of his desire to amass wealth, his trader's shrewdness. If the brothers were dubious of the opportunism their father had shown in the smuggler's paradise that was Tangier, they kept it wholly to themselves and in every visible way accorded their father the respect due a deceased patriarch. On the first anniversary of Samuel's death, as on every succeeding year, Louis, Albert, Paul, and Ralph gathered at his grave and recited the Kaddish, a traditional prayer of remembrance that "is regarded as a proof of the ethical life of the deceased, as remembered by affectionate survivors." In their father's honor, the Toronto brothers founded a yeshiva in his name in B'nai Brak. Beit Shmaya, as it was known, was the first eponymous Reichmann institution, though the brothers' modesty limited them to using only their father's given name—the Hebrew one, naturally. In restricting Beit Shmaya's enrollment to Moroccan immigrants, the Reichmanns made the new yeshiva do double duty symbolically. "Our whole family felt strongly," Paul said, "that the Moroccan association the family had through its many years in Tangier should be acknowledged in this way."

Over the years, Beit Shmaya would evolve into a campus of a half-dozen buildings, including what is probably the finest dining hall in any Israeli yeshiva. Thanks to the shrewdness of Reichmann's original land purchase, the yeshiva's expansion was largely self-financed. The unused acreage Beit Shmaya owned appreciated rapidly, enabling it to raise millions for additional construction by selling off raw land to developers piece by piece. By the time the final two lots were sold in 1995, Beit Shmaya would rank among the largest Sephardic yeshivas in Israel.

In his final act as family conciliator, Samuel Reichmann left a will in which he tried to strike a balance between safeguarding Olympia & York's stability and more broadly redistributing the fruits of the family's good fortune. Samuel instructed that his 12.5 percent interest in the company was to be held undivided in trust. Any dividend income was to go solely to Renée. Upon her death, the stock was to be distributed among all six of his children in uneven ratio. Four-fifths of his shares were to be equally divided among Eva, Edward, and Louis and the remaining one-fifth among Albert, Paul, and Ralph. In the meantime, all the shares were to be controlled by four trustees: Renée and her Toronto sons. In other words, as long as Renée survived, Eva, Edward, and Louis could not cut off a slice of what soon would balloon into one of the world's great fortunes without the permission of their mother and younger siblings.

While Eva and Louis could only consider themselves fortunate, Edward was torn between gratitude and indignation. Although seven years had passed since Olympia & York had bailed out Three Star Construction, the eldest Reichmann brother remained mortified not so much by failure per se—he had failed in business before—as by the circumstances of his rescue. For Edward, the conditions attached to his inheritance underscored yet again his subordinate status within the family. Even after the passage of twenty years, the question of his ownership interest in Olympia & York would be one subject the normally loquacious Edward categorically refused to discuss. Even so, Samuel Reichmann's legacy inevitably tightened the bonds of family by giving all six of his children and their heirs a vested interest in Olympia & York's success.

Samuel's death brought the family closer together literally as well as figuratively. Concern for her bereaved seventy-seven-year-old mother prompted Eva to finally agree in principle to leave London and take up full-time residence in Toronto. Renée, in turn, reluctantly agreed to move out of the two-bedroom home on Dalemount Avenue that she had shared with Samuel since 1967. Through Olympia & York, the Toronto brothers paid $155,000 in cash to buy a much larger house just a few doors down from Albert's. A large additional sum was invested to transform two floors of 1 Forest Wood into separate quarters for Renée and Eva and a third floor into shared space.

Although Eva would indeed spend more time in Toronto than ever before, she never did move to Canada. The remodeling of 1 Forest Wood dragged on for more than two years, prolonged by the ambivalence of all concerned. In the end, Renée decided that she could not leave her Dalemount residence after all, and Eva was unable to pull herself away from her London home until she had succeeded in marrying off the remaining three of her six children. Her brothers secretly rejoiced for if truth be told they had not been keen on their sister and mother cohabiting in the first place. "We were hoping Eva would remarry and we thought living with my mother would not help her prospects," Edward recalled. "None of us ever said anything to her, because she didn't want to hear about remarrying."

Meanwhile, Edward and Edith moved from Israel to Florida to be closer to Renée, who had begun wintering in Miami Beach in the 1960s. (No doubt a desire to avoid Israel's stiff inheritance tax also contributed to Edward's decision to make reverse aliyah.) On Chase Avenue, Edward bought two houses, one for himself and one for his mother, who gladly abandoned the apartment she rented under a long-term lease. Edward put in a swimming pool and built a covered walkway connecting the two houses. Ensconced in her new house in Miami Beach, the Reichmann matriarch held court all winter long, summoning each of her daughters-in-law and their broods down from the frozen north one by one for extended visits.

Nominally, at least, Renée's influence had never been greater. In addition to gaining sole control over 25 percent of Olympia & York stock, she succeeded Samuel as chairman of the company. Asked a few years after his mother's death in 1990 what role she had played in the company as chairman, Paul replied, "She was not much involved," but then smiled cryptically and told an anecdote about Prince Charles, who had once stopped by Olympia & York's office in London to inspect the scale models of Canary Wharf. The tightly scripted Royal Visit left no time for chitchat until Reichmann was escorting the Prince of Wales to his car. "I understand that your mother is the chairman of your company," said Prince Charles, with what Reichmann interpreted not only as genuine interest but sympathy. "How does that work for you?" In lieu of disclosing his reply, Reichmann offered a wry observation: "You could say we had the same problem."

Although the prospect of maternal intervention would hang over her sons like a storm cloud on the far horizon, Renée did not concern herself with Olympia & York except as its workings impinged on her overriding priority: family. By contrast, Samuel had taken a keen businessman's interest in all of its undertakings. He had maintained an office at the company and used it frequently until the end; indeed, he'd put in a few hours two days before he died. "My late father came to the office on a Friday and died over the weekend," Paul once boasted to a journalist. "We're made that way."

The elder Reichmann's influence gradually had diminished, as Olympia & York ascended to a level of entrepreneurial risk-taking that exceeded its chairman's predisposition and perhaps, at times, his understanding. Even so, Samuel had been well suited to the role of eminence grise in that he was inclined to speak his mind but not stamp his foot. Until the end, the brothers had continued to consult their father on every important decision. To a degree, Samuel's Old World sensibilities had combined with Albert's innate cautiousness to rein in Paul's high-powered ambition. Thus, the effect of the patriarch's death was to weaken Albert in his essential role as foil to his brilliant younger brother and tilt the balance of power within the company a bit further toward Paul—and toward risk.

Chapter 28

A s they rose swiftly and secretively into the commercial stratosphere, the Reichmanns would trail great billowing clouds of mystery behind. But there was one question that the brothers would repeatedly answer before it could even be asked: What will you do for an encore, boys?

By the spring of 1976, just six months after First Bank Tower was completed, the focus of Paul Reichmann's ambitions had shifted south of the border. The postwar skyscrapering of Canada had reached the stage where the big development firms—Cadillac Fairview, Olympia & York, Trizec, Daon, Oxford, Campeau—had begun tromping on one another's toes in every major city from Halifax to Vancouver. There was more room to maneuver in the American property market, which was ten times the size of Canada's, less strictly regulated, and less competitive to boot. In the United States, property was still a fragmented, regional industry. Canadian developers not only tended to be larger and stronger financially than their American competitors but benefited from an image of chic progressivity in the still-emergent field of urban redevelopment. "Being Canadian opens doors," boasted the head of a Toronto architectural design house that built a large U.S. clientele in the 1960s and 1970s. "Americans realize our cities are better; the standard of design in our shops, our shopping centres, parks and public buildings is far superior. They love Canada's ambience and they want to buy it."

In the late 1970s, all of the big Canadian developers were busily conquering America, but Olympia & York was easily the most ambitious of the lot, launching downtown building projects in no less than ten cities over a five-year span. The market that first tickled Paul Reichmann's fancy was the one that had suffered the worst in the great North American real estate slump of the mid-

1970s. As Reichmann put it, "New York, because it was in [a] time of depression, was the obvious city in the search for buys."

The bargain that Olympia & York found in Manhattan in 1976 and secured in 1977 proved one of the most lucrative purchases in the modern history of real estate, as measured both by the magnitude of the capital gain and the swiftness with which it was realized. In a single transaction, the Reichmanns acquired eight skyscrapers from Uris Building Corporation for a mere $46 million down just as the New York property market began to pivot from bust to a boom of epic proportions. "As soon as I heard about the Uris deal," recalled William Mulholland, the chairman of the Bank of Montreal and a former Big Apple resident, "I told Paul that he'd make a billion dollars—and he did." In fact, the market value of the eight Uris properties would triple within a few years and within a decade would rise tenfold, to about $3 billion.

Even so, as Exhibit A in the case for Paul Reichmann as genius—a case that was imposed on the man by his admirers—the Uris deal was overblown. Reichmann himself never claimed to have spotted value in the Uris buildings that others could not see. Over the three years before the Reichmanns entered the picture, three other investors had been poised to snap up the Uris package only to see their deals founder at the last minute. Two of them—John Ritblat of British Land and Donald Knab of Prudential Insurance Company—were victimized by circumstances beyond their control. The third—the New York developer Sam Lefrak—got greedy. But all saw what Reichmann saw: that the Uris properties were available for a fraction of what they would have cost to build anew. "You needed very little imagination to see it [the New York office market] would turn," Paul later conceded. "Our luck was that it turned much more quickly than we had thought. We expected it to turn within five years and it turned in 24 months."

While Paul Reichmann did demonstrate an extraordinary clarity of thought and great tenacity at the negotiating table, the critical element of the Uris deal was sheer daring. Reichmann was, as one New York official would memorably put it a few years later, "the biggest crapshooter this town has ever seen." In essence, he believed with such conviction that the New York City office market would strongly rebound that he bet his company on it. The $46 million cash payment required of Olympia & York may have been modest relative to the book value of the Uris buildings, but it was an awful lot of money for the Reichmanns at the time. In fact, they had to borrow half the sum from a bank. The brothers also had to assume $288 million in mortgages outstanding against the Uris properties and $25 million in ground leases at a time when the struggle to lease First Bank Tower already was crimping their finances. If the Uris buildings had generated operating losses instead of profits, could the company have covered the payments on that $313 million in additional liabilities? No one, not even Reichmann, could know for sure. But if not, Olympia & York would have been history.

In Reichmann's analysis—which, as usual, was painstaking—the potential rewards of the deal outweighed the risks. In this, he was proven right beyond his most extravagant expectations: the Uris transaction was a wager brilliantly calculated. But if truth be told, what attracted Reichmann to the Uris deal was not just the probability of success but the thrilling possibility of failure. "Paul knew perfectly well the risks he took and liked taking them," said Robert Canning, perhaps Reichmann's closest financial confidant throughout the 1970s. "He was a gambler."

Through Canning's firm, Bell Gouinlock, Reichmann not only raised financing for building projects but also speculated in the bond market. In early 1976, shortly after Olympia & York had floated its first public bond issue to help finance First Canadian Place, Canning called his client with the news that the bonds had traded up to a price of 102 from the initial 100. Intrigued, Reichmann asked Canning what he knew about the next corporate bond issue coming to market. Canning supplied a few essential facts and Reichmann placed a $500,000 order on the spot. Within a few weeks, the bonds had risen smartly and Reichmann was up by $100,000 or so. At a meeting at Olympia & York one afternoon, Canning found himself sitting between Albert and Paul. "I asked Albert what he wanted to do with the bonds. He said, 'Don't ask me. That's Paul's area,'" Canning recalled. "I told Paul he may want to take his profit, but he decided to stay in and eventually he lost money. It didn't seem to bother him. He told me, 'My religion won't let me go to Las Vegas. This is my Las Vegas.'"

Andy Sarlos, the Toronto stock market speculator who attached himself to the Reichmanns, considered Paul "a shrewd player but a true gambler, always convinced that he will win. He lives to make deals and enjoys taking the risks and raising the stakes. . . . I would compare him to a guy who sits in a casino and is able to count the number of cards in a Black Jack game—three or four decks at a time. Casino managers are deathly afraid of people like that—people who know how many kings, sevens or nines have been dealt. Dealers know that, if you can do that, you can figure out the probabilities of winning or losing bets. Very few people have that capability in business. Paul used that same talent to comprehend very complex real estate deals. He had the nerve of a poker player (and) the mental ability of a card shark [sic]." In interviews, Paul Reichmann always disavowed the gambler label, though not with the vehemence one might have expected of a man of such manifest piety. "I don't think I am [a gambler], but it is difficult for a person himself to decide about his character," he said a few years after Olympia & York's collapse. "For me there is an enjoyment or a challenge in being able to do something others consider difficult. The foundation was having an opinion and after analysis of that opinion coming to the conclusion that it is in fact the right opinion before acting on it. What some might call gambling was that I was willing to risk my fortune on what were not yet proven facts."

———

For most of the twentieth century, commercial real estate in New York City had been the private preserve of a dozen family dynasties established in the late 1800s by working-class Jewish immigrants, mainly Russians. "The great names were Tishman, Uris, Rudin, Durst. It was understood that what was passed down from father to son was not just portfolios but reputations, contacts, and savvy: the password that got you inside the doors of the Chase Manhattan, the secret handshake to win the confidence of the union bosses, the right dialect of Yiddish to do business with the city government." (With rare exceptions, the first families of New York real estate conformed to the standard American pattern in vaulting from Orthodoxy to nonobservance in a generation or two.)

Decade after decade, the ruling dynasties of the Skyscraper Club got first look at the best properties that came on the market and absorbed most of the money that the major banks were willing to commit to building projects in Manhattan. Gradually, the entrepreneurism of the developer elite ossified into conservatism. In the 1960s, as in the 1920s, Manhattan was booming, but the output of the leading families had declined to a new office tower every two or three years. "The position of these families astride the industry was so strong, and their inventory of buildings so large, that if care was taken, the third and fourth generations could now be assured of having thriving empires. . . . Steady accumulation was best, these sons seemed to agree."

Percy and Harold Uris, the American-born sons of a Latvian immigrant ironworker, departed from pattern in being at least as willing as their father to take risks. Disdaining aesthetic nicety ("The only beautiful building," Percy once proclaimed, "is the one that's fully rented"), the brothers Uris were prolific and proficient developers who in the 1950s and 1960s amassed Manhattan's largest portfolio of office towers—13 million square feet all told. In 1971 their Uris Building Corporation opened 55 Water Street, which, at 3.3 million square feet, was then the largest office center in the world. A new midtown skyscraper had nearly been completed a few months later when Percy died of a heart attack. Burdened by his grief and the difficulties of leasing the new properties into a softening market, Harold decided to sell the family's controlling interest in Uris Building, which was traded on the New York Stock Exchange, and retire.

Harold Uris found no takers until 1973, when one of the premier English property companies, British Land, commenced negotiations. Its chief, John Ritblat, was a highly regarded property merchant thought to have a fine eye for value. Ritblat, who would continue to run British Land well into the 1990s, negotiated a transaction that artfully extracted full benefits from the tax and financing advantages peculiar to British property companies, only to be blindsided by a higher offer from a last-minute American contender. "We went home one Friday, our contract signed and expected the deal to take place Monday, only to find that over the weekend Uris had sold out to National Kinney," Ritblat lamented. "The Kinney people were incredibly naive, totally amateur. They thought we had somehow found oil under the floor. What we had actually found, of course, was the key to the financing."

National Kinney Corporation was less a business than the corporate detritus of Steve Ross's ambition. The humbly born Ross had started out in the funeral home business in Brooklyn, branched into parking lots, and in the 1960s acquired companies by the dozen. Any sort of company would do, for all he was concerned about was erecting a ladder of assets tall enough to reach the stars—the stars of Hollywood, that is. In 1969, Ross acquired the film studio Warner Brothers, around which he would build the entertainment conglomerate Warner Communications Incorporated. Once Ross had gained entrée to Hollywood, the funeral homes and parking lots lost their magic. He did not want the old déclassé businesses tarnishing the stock market sheen of his glamorous Hollywood operation, so in 1971 he bundled together the unwanted assets to form National Kinney and appointed Andrew "Pete" Frankel its chairman and president. Although National Kinney was spun off in the stock market as a separate company, Frankel continued to take his orders from Ross because Warner Communications owned a majority of Kinney's shares.

Steve Ross's love for Hollywood was not monogamous. As a corporate deal maker, he remained a man very much on the make. For Ross, the Uris package essentially was an impulse purchase. What Brooklyn boy would not have thrilled to own a Manhattan skyscraper or two? Ross just happened to buy ten of them, paying $113 million on the eve of the worst real estate collapse in New York since the Great Depression. The Uris buildings were evenly divided between midtown and the Wall Street district at the very tip of Manhattan. The heavy losses sustained by Kinney's new Uris Building Corporation subsidiary depressed its stock price and that of Warner Communications as well. In Ross's charmed career, he would make only one deal worse than buying the Uris buildings—selling these same buildings to Olympia & York. "Some close to Ross," his biographer observed, "would later say that he would feel publicly humiliated as the value of the Uris properties skyrocketed, since it meant that this deal became emblazoned as the single megadeal where he had not won."

It has been said that when the U.S. economy catches a cold, the real estate industry comes down with pneumonia. No mere cold, the recession of 1973 to 1976 proved financially fatal for many American developers. As usual, the property industry had invited its own ruin. In most major U.S. cities and many minor ones, developers had been running amok ever since the mid-1960s. Manhattan, as ever, was the definition of excess. From 1969 through 1972 alone, sixty-one new office towers had opened, adding 51 million square feet, or 40 percent of all new office space developed since World War II.

City hall had been as blithely bullish as any high-rolling builder, resorting to financial gimmickry to mask its profligacy. As municipal services deteriorated and crime and taxes rose, big corporations began fleeing Manhattan for the suburbs. When recession finally hit, the local real estate boom turned abruptly to bust. Thirty million square feet of office space stood empty and tenant corporations were trying to sublease fifteen million more. Hundreds of brownstones and small apartment houses in marginal areas of the city were abandoned by their owners. By the spring of 1975, New York City balanced on the ragged edge of insolvency, and nightmare visions of race riots and crime waves haunted the city that never sleeps.

Not long after Pete Frankel lauded the Uris deal as "a giant step toward evolution of National Kinney as a complete real estate company," Steve Ross began looking for the exit. How could Warner Communications soar when it was tethered to the second-class mishmash that was National Kinney? But if Warner was to unload its stake in National Kinney, the Uris buildings would have to go. Ross and his minions rattled every doorknob they could find in their search for a buyer. National Kinney surrendered ownership of a money-losing suburban development to its mortgagors and lost the newly completed and largely empty office tower at 1633 Broadway to bank foreclosure. Ross enlisted the help of the experienced New York developers the Milstein brothers, who sold off interests in three hotels and a Philadelphia office tower. Try as he might, though, Ross could not get out from under the burden of his ten remaining skyscrapers. It was driving him to distraction.

New York's first families of property were having problems of their own, of course, though most were buoyed by the uninterrupted flow of income from vast apartment holdings. (There was one prominent casualty among the elite: the most visible and respected of the old builder firms, Tishman Realty and Construction Corporation, was dismantled. Various Tishmans set about organizing a new company and would eventually reclaim the family's place in the skyscraper club.) All the developer families were so heavily invested in New York City that they had no alternative but to believe in its survival; if the Big Apple was out of business, so were they. Conversely, if the city did have a future, a better buying opportunity was hard to imagine. From time to time, members of the old elite would display a stiff upper lip in an interview or speech, but their words betokened hope, not conviction, and in general they were sellers, not buyers.

A crowd of out-of-town developers also looked over the Uris package. Among them were the Reichmanns' Canadian archrivals: Trizec Corporation and Cadillac Fairview. Trizec was in the throes of its own financial crisis and its quality-conscious managers were unimpressed, in any event, by the Uris brothers' handiwork. "They were crappy buildings," snapped a former senior executive of Trizec, who made no secret of begrudging the Reichmanns their good fortune. Quality was not an issue with Cadillac Fairview, according to Bernard Ghert, then its executive vice president: "They weren't trophies, but on the whole they were decent, functional buildings in good locations." However, Ghert added, he and his colleagues concluded that waiting for a rebound in the New York market likely would tax the patience of their public shareholders. "If you are too conscious of the pressure to show quarterly increases on your income statement," he said, "you don't take a chance on assets that may be lucrative in the long term but are problematic today."

The Uris package attracted keener attention from several big insurance companies, which were loaded with cash and eager to add to their real estate investment portfolios at a time of depressed prices. In late 1975, the Prudential Insurance Company of America, the largest life insurance company in the country, entered into negotiations with National Kinney and quickly reached agreement to buy all ten of the Uris office towers at what Donald Knab, the Pru's senior real estate officer, later termed an "exceedingly fair price." Knab was flabbergasted when the deal he had negotiated was rejected by Prudential's directors. "It was the only time in my career that the board did not take one of my recommendations," Knab recalled, his disappointment still evident twenty years later. "Our board had serious concern that New York would go into bankruptcy and rejected the agreement on that basis alone."

Knab's defeat left the field open for Sam Lefrak, whose family company owned fifty thousand apartments in Queens and Brooklyn. Although Lefrak nominally was a member of New York's dynastic elite, being a wealthy second-generation builder with a third-generation heir waiting in the wings, he was just not the establishment type. A shrewd but excitable man prone to yelling and arm-waving, Lefrak (he preferred to go by Le Frak on ceremonial occasions) was a highly competitive publicity hound who seemed to relish the public squabbles in which he was constantly embroiled. Lefrak qua Le Frak eventually would campaign for a seat on the board of the Metropolitan Museum of Art, one of the toniest redoubts of Manhattan high society, but at first he styled himself as an outsider, denying any desire to join the skyscraper-building families on what he derided as the "Isle of Capri." Even so, the outer boroughs were not big enough to contain Lefrak, who began venturing into Manhattan in the mid-1960s, building a couple of apartment towers. In 1972, he put up an office tower in midtown, which quickly became his single most valuable property.

Lefrak's motor-mouthed flamboyance masked a deep, intuitive conservatism. About six months before the New York real estate market went into its mid-1970s tailspin, Lefrak had begun battening down his hatches. "I called in my treasurer and said anything we can't make a profit on by the end of the year sell at the market value," he recalled. Lefrak husbanded his cash and emerged in 1975 in a buying mood. He began dickering with National Kinney before Prudential Insurance came along and resumed negotiations after the insurer withdrew. "All the parties have shown enthusiasm," Lefrak told a reporter in the spring of 1976 and added that there was "a good chance" that the deal would be consummated.

By this time, a few rays of sunlight had poked through the black skies over Manhattan. "Office Renting Here Called Good Omen," read the headline of a *New York Times* article in March that noted a decline in the vast backlog of vacant midtown office space. Although building anew in Manhattan remained inconceivable, the notion of buying an existing skyscraper or two had become au courant all across the country. Sam Zell, a Chicago investor who later would join forces with the Reichmanns to build an office tower in his hometown, published a long article in a real estate trade publication in which he concluded that "the opportunity of acquiring real estate in its current distress offers the greatest single economic opportunity for investors in our time." In a May 1976 cover story featuring Lefrak, *Business Week* noted the rising speculative fever in real estate. "Competition is fierce, both from quick-turnaround speculators after a fast buck (known unflatteringly as 'junk men') and staid institutions, such as insurance companies and pension funds. . . . The demand for quality properties, in fact, is so keen that some observers wonder if it has not exhausted the supply."

Enter Paul Reichmann, in a bargain-hunting mode. To advise him on the Manhattan scene, he hired Edward Minskoff, a third-generation member of one of the dynasties. A restless and independent sort, Minskoff had recently formed his own little real estate brokerage after leaving the storied Wall Street investment bank of Lehman Brothers. In most ways, Minskoff was the anti-Reichmann: a glib self-promoter in $1,000 suits and designer suspenders. On the other hand, he had energy to burn and knew the Manhattan market inside and out. Eddie Minskoff had first called on the Reichmanns in 1970, long before most Wall Street investment bankers had discovered Olympia & York. "I found both Reichmann brothers easy to speak to," Minskoff recalled. "They asked questions, and as long as I gave intelligent answers, I got respect." Minskoff inspected Flemingdon Park, and brought Paul down to New York for a lunch with senior managers of Lehman Brothers. Minskoff stayed in touch, calling every few months with one idea or another. Reichmann had little use for brokers as a rule but thought Minskoff creative.

In the summer of 1976, Minskoff represented Olympia & York in a failed effort to buy the forty-eight-story tower at 1633 Broadway, near Times Square. Completed in 1971, this was the last office tower that the Uris brothers erected.

National Kinney had acquired it along with the rest of Uris Building Corporation but was unable to fill it with tenants. The building was only about 40 percent occupied when Steve Ross decided not to repay the bank loans that had financed its construction. Morgan Guaranty was one of four banks that seized the property in 1974 and put it up for sale. By 1976, the banks were desperate to unload 1633 Broadway, but when Paul Reichmann met with Morgan's vice chairman, he unexpectedly found himself on the defensive. "He was really pressing me to find out if I had an ulterior motive," Reichmann recalled. "He just couldn't believe that someone healthy and normal would buy into New York. That's how depressed New Yorkers were about their city."

Olympia & York offered to assume the $63 million in outstanding loans against 1633 Broadway and throw in $7 million in cash. This $70 million bid was pending when Morgan and its fellow banks sold the building to a German developer for $82 million. The Werner Otto Group at first had ruled out New York City in its search for American property investments but had decided on the basis of "recent studies" that "midtown Manhattan was very viable" after all. Reichmann had every reason to fear that he had missed the party. Luckily for him, Sam Lefrak was too tight by half in his own bargain-shopping.

By this time, Lefrak had spent nearly a year haggling not only with National Kinney but with the banks that held the mortgages on the Uris buildings. Lefrak, who was once described by a fellow developer as "a vicious negotiator," insisted that the banks rework their mortgages to stretch out payments far into the future and adamantly refused to put up as much cash as Steve Ross required. "I don't buy anticipation," Lefrak later said. "If you want to sell me anticipation, I'll give you anticipation money. When I get it, you get it." By September 21, when Ross met for the first time with Reichmann in his offices in Rockfeller Center, National Kinney had despaired of ever coming to terms with Sam Lefrak.

Steve Ross and his minions had never heard of Olympia & York. Harold Grabino, the Kinney executive assigned the task of selling the Uris buildings, was dubious. "You look at a pair of Orthodox guys from Toronto, with their dark suits and skull-caps, and you have to wonder if they're in a league to make this deal," Grabino said. A shrewder man might have questioned his own credentials. Grabino was a deal maker all right, as was Ross, but they knew next to nothing about real estate. When it came to skyscrapers certainly, no one at Kinney or Warner was in Paul Reichmann's league as a deal maker.

The Uris package was reduced by one when Citibank decided to buy 111 Wall Street, which it occupied as sole tenant. That left nine buildings containing about 10 million square feet of leasable space: 55 Water Street (53 floors, 3.6 million square feet); 1290 Avenue of the Americas (43 floors, 1.9 million square feet; 245 Park Avenue (46 floors, 1.6 million square feet); 2 Broadway (32 floors, 1.6 million square feet); 1301 Avenue of the Americas (46 floors, 1.4 million square feet); 320 Park Avenue (34 floors, 673,000 square feet); 850

Third Avenue (21 floors, 550,000 square feet); 10 East 53rd Street (38 floors, 350,000 square feet); and 60 Broad Street (39 floors, 1 million square feet).

National Kinney's terms were essentially the same as those presented Lefrak: $55 million in cash and assumption of all $300 million in outstanding mortgages, most of which were held by major New York banks. Unlike Lefrak, Reichmann considered these loans an inducement, not an obstacle, since they sported interest rates that were well below current market rates of 12 percent—as low as 5 percent in some cases. Moreover, by Reichmann's calculations, the total transaction cost worked out to about $30 a square foot, or one-third of what was known in the trade as replacement cost. "I asked Paul why he wanted to buy the Uris buildings," Bob Canning recalled. "He said, 'Well, Bob, I went and looked at every one of them. I knew we couldn't build them for anything like the price being asked, so I bought them.' "

The buildings did have their drawbacks, though. Most had been poorly maintained under National Kinney's stewardship, and some needed extensive remodeling and retrofitting. The cost of bringing the Uris towers close to the quality standard that Olympia & York had established with First Canadian Place could easily exceed Kinney's $55 million cash price. Earning a return on investment would thus require hefty increases in rental rates. As it was, the cash flow generated by the package of buildings was barely enough to cover the mortgage payments. The problem was not so much vacancies—the midtown buildings were close to full and things were looking up even at 55 Water—but that in their eagerness to attract such major corporate tenants as J. C. Penney, Sperry Rand, and ITT Corporation, the Uris brothers had written a number of long-term leases at low fixed rents. To cite a particularly egregious example, American Brands, which occupied most of 245 Park, was paying only $6 a square foot—one-third of the current open-market rate—under a lease that still had thirteen years left to run.

In essence, Olympia & York's Uris acquisition was conceived as a gamble on the market itself, the purest such gamble of the Reichmanns' career to date. In a rebounding market, the company would be able to offset the drag of Uris's under-market leases by filling vacancies and renegotiating expired leases at higher rates. Although the city's fiscal crisis remained a gun pointed at the heads of developers, the threat of bankruptcy receded in October 1976, when President Gerald Ford moderated his opposition to a bailout (a rebuff immortalized by the tabloid headline, "FORD TO CITY: DROP DEAD") and consented to a federal loan. That President Ford reluctantly bowed to political reality came as no surprise to Paul Reichmann. "We felt that New York is the most vital city in the world," he said. "And we knew that, sooner or later, it would reassert that vitality." By Reichmann's reckoning, it could take as long as five years for the office market to work off the large backlog of vacant space. But when the market finally did turn, he believed that it would turn with a vengeance, as surplus gave way to shortage. "A boom in New York rents wasn't a hope," he later recalled, "it was a conviction."

On November 11, National Kinney announced that it had reached "a preliminary understanding" to sell the nine Uris buildings to a buyer that it declined to identify. The premature announcement irked Paul Reichmann, who had not finished methodically working through a mountain of paperwork with a legion of lawyers, accountants, and engineers, most of whom were not Olympia & York employees. Every lease and service contract for every building—hundreds of legal agreements all told, many quite complex—had to be analyzed, and every mortgage loan had to be redocumented and rolled over.

Finally, on March 12, 1977, National Kinney announced the sale of the Uris buildings to Olympia & York, subject to certain conditions. The most problematic of these conditions concerned National Kinney's negotiations to buy the land under 245 Park Avenue, the so-called American Brands building. This valuable site was owned by Penn Central Railroad, which was eager to sell but at a price—about $25 million—that Kinney had been hesitant to pay. National Kinney had put in a bid of $19.6 million, which Penn Central flatly rejected in early 1977. For fear of queering the sale to Olympia & York, the Kinney people told Reichmann that they had reached agreement with Penn Central over price and just needed time to wrap up the formalities. When Reichmann learned in mid-June that in fact Kinney had never had an understanding with Penn Central, he was livid. "I cannot understand why we have been kept completely in the dark until about ten days ago," he complained in a letter to Andrew Frankel. "I find this so shocking that I hope some of my information is erroneous."

Despite Reichmann's insistent prodding, Kinney's negotiations with Penn Central dragged on and on through the summer. The Uris package was whittled to eight when J. C. Penney Company exercised its option to acquire National Kinney's 51 percent interest in its headquarters building at 1301 Avenue of the Americas. Olympia & York negotiated a reduction in its cash outlay for the remaining buildings to $46 million, but Frankel seemed in no hurry to bring matters to a conclusion. Reichmann's anger modulated into suspicion. By late summer of 1977, the Manhattan office market was showing signs of recovery, even hints of vigor. "I think there was a period when Frankel had second thoughts about selling," he recalled. "I had doubts about our agreement so I went to see Steve Ross," to whom Frankel reported. To Reichmann's surprise, Ross not only reaffirmed his commitment to sell but said that he didn't much care how much Olympia & York paid. "He said that from his point of view his company would be better irrespective of the price because owning the buildings was depressing its stock price."

Reassured, Reichmann pressed on. On Friday, September 19, 1977—a year almost to the day from when Reichmann first sat down with Steve Ross—a cast of dozens gathered in the swank midtown Manhattan offices of National Kinney's law firm, Paul, Weiss, Rifkin, Wharton & Garrison. By late afternoon, all the papers had been signed and Olympia & York had wired the $46 million to Kinney's bank account. Paul Reichmann hurried back to his suite at the Waldorf Towers to prepare for the Sabbath.

Over the next year and a half, Olympia & York would invest $80 million to upgrade the Uris buildings and their management. The thirty-four-story tower at 320 Park Avenue, best known as the headquarters of ITT Corporation, was virtually gutted and rebuilt. Olympia & York quickly recouped its investment as the average rent paid by its New York tenants rose from $7 to $10 a square foot to more than $30 in a few years' time. Meanwhile, the Uris vacancy rate—13 percent at the time of the purchase—receded virtually to zero as even mammoth 55 Water Street filled with new tenants. As the old, money-losing Uris leases expired, they would be renewed at rates unimaginable when Reichmann first shook hands with Ross. Just before the sale to Olympia & York closed, Harold Grabino had concluded that Kinney might have been able to sign new leases in the American Brands building at $18 a square foot by 1981. "That would have put us in fat city," Grabino ruefully recalled. But come 1981, Olympia & York would be filling vacancies in 245 Park at $60 a square foot.

Over the years, press coverage of Olympia & York would abound with varying estimates of the magnitude of the Uris bonanza as reporters added or subtracted a billion here, a billion there. Because Olympia & York never resold the buildings as a package, their rise in market value could only be approximated. In Paul Reichmann's mind, the basic math was simple. Olympia & York paid $30 a square foot for about 10 million square feet of office space. When the Manhattan office market reached its peak of prosperity in the late 1980s, the Uris buildings were worth $300 a square foot on average.

By the mid-1980s, Olympia & York's Uris purchase would be hailed in print as "the deal of the century," and no one seemed inclined to argue the point, though the century remained a decade and a half shy of completion. "There have been two great deals in the history of New York," Meyer S. Frucher, a top appointee of Governor Mario Cuomo, proclaimed in 1987, upping the rhetorical ante by two centuries. "The first was when the Dutch bought the island of Manhattan. The second was when the Canadians bought the island again." In reality, as in legend, Uris was an extraordinary coup—a once-in-a-lifetime deal that lifted the Reichmanns into the ranks of the richest families in the world. But in thrusting the brothers into the limelight in North America's business capital, the Uris transaction also accelerated the process of media alchemy by which their talent, reticence, and idiosyncrasy were apotheosized into myth.

Chapter 29

I n some ways, Paul Reichmann had been a precociously mature business-man right from the start. Even as an adolescent, he had had no time for fri-volity, and he brought to business the same focused, probing intellect that had distinguished him as a student of Talmud and Mishnah. Even so, his transition from the sequestered spiritualism of yeshiva to the hurly-burly of property development was protracted. Intellectually, Reichmann may have taken to real estate with the avidity of a prodigy, but he held tight to the cultural values of the yeshiva. For years, he continued to look as if he had just stepped out of the beis medrash at Gateshead or Ponovesh, where unworldliness in all things was both a badge of honor and a suit of armor. Well into the 1970s, Oskar Lustig, Olympia & York's ultra-Orthodox accountant, still was laughing—discreetly, to be sure—at Paul Reichmann's shoes.

But by the time of the Uris deal, Reichmann had discovered quality footwear. In fact, he had become a bit dapper in his own, strictly monochromatic way. "We could never tell how many suits Paul had," said one top Olympia & York executive, "because they all looked the same." His suits were as dark as ever but now were custom-tailored of the finest gaberdine and set off with costly, if demure, silk ties. Reichmann retained a full beard but kept it neatly trimmed and well short of the rabbinical lengths of his youth.

By Reichmann's own description, these outer changes were emblematic of his gradual acculturation. "In my twenties, belief in God and the divine nature of the Torah was absolute," Reichmann observed in 1995. "Intellectu-ally, that hasn't changed for me. With some people it does change. They say, 'Yes, I still believe but. . . .' I don't have a but. But that doesn't mean my behavior is as governed as it would have been had I not moved out into the world. I have not compromised in certain things but the mind is definitely affected by the world. My adherence is less ironclad than it was when I was a student." Although the relaxation of Reichmann's attitude of separateness was so slight as to be imperceptible to the nonreligious Jew, he had agonized over every little departure from tradition. "Hegel said that the smallest revolutions are the revolutions of dress, but these things mattered a great deal to Paul," said a source close to the family. "I remember him being very uneasy about trimming his beard."

While refining his appearance, Reichmann also had polished his manner. Particularly in contrast to the boorishness of many real estate dealers, Reichmann always had come across in his business dealings as an Old World gentleman: soft-spoken, attentive, courteous, wise. Reichmann was a tall man, about six-foot-one, yet there was something almost elaborately self-effacing about his very presence. It was not merely his shy smile or stoop-shouldered posture but the all-encompassing attitude of fastidious reserve that he projected. He seemed folded up within himself like one of those collapsible metal cups that come in handy on camping trips. When interviewed, Reichmann at times was quite forthcoming, even animated in recounting his business thinking, but would become reticent and at times visibly flustered when asked how he had felt about something. Lea Reichmann, who was as extroverted as her husband was introverted, seemed to be able to make him blush at will with her confrontational teasing.

The contrast between the timorousness of Reichmann's manner and the reality of his standing as one of North America's most driven and accomplished entrepreneurs had its comical aspects. The manner in which he answered the telephone at home was particularly incongruous. "Helleeeeeww," he would say with such hushed, pursed-lip unctuousness that he seemed to be impersonating Peter Sellers playing an overeager undertaker or a fawning maître d'.

If, in large measure, Reichmann's celebrated politesse was a product of his character, it also had its theatrical aspect. Like any gifted salesman, he learned over the years how to fashion the raw materials of his personality into a promotional persona. By the time of the Uris deal, he had been courting tenants, lenders, and assorted public officials for two full decades and was a most practiced persuader. "Paul has a hell of a way with him," said Stanley J. Honeyman, a proper British gentleman who in 1979 chose Olympia & York over several other suitors angling to acquire the development company he ran, English Property Corporation. "He's quite a charmer, you know." When operating in his salesman's mode, Reichmann was as amenable as he was charming. At one point during the construction of Place Bell Canada in Ottawa, the project had gone $250,000 over budget, prompting an anxious phone call from Robert Scrivener, the chief executive of Bell Canada. "Don't worry," Reichmann replied. "It's our obligation." Yes, Their Word Was (Still) Their Bond.

As the accommodating aspect of Reichmann's persona was being apotheosized into legend, reporters overlooked or ignored his other side, his hard side. From his earliest days in the business, Reichmann had exhibited backbone, but as Olympia & York amassed clout, its chief matured into a businessman of truly obdurate will. "It wasn't easy in Paul's heyday to disagree with him," said John Zuccotti, who became Olympia & York's principal real estate lawyer in New York shortly after the Uris deal and would remain in the Reichmanns' service for nearly fifteen years. "He'd say he liked to hear conflicting points of view but it really wasn't true." Zuccotti once had to talk Reichmann out of firing an accountant whose calculation of the market value of an Olympia & York property was far below the boss's own intuitive estimate. "Paul was just outraged that it was so low," Zuccotti continued. "I thought Paul's own valuation impractical myself, but he had such a forceful, optimistic way of looking at a property that he convinced himself he was right. I wouldn't call him an arrogant man, but he has great faith in his own intellectual abilities, especially in real estate."

When at an impasse in a negotiation with an outsider, Reichmann was capable of sitting and staring silently for five minutes, fifteen minutes, half an hour, or however long it took to unnerve his counterpart into concession. "The standing of Olympia & York became such that in many situations we were able to dictate terms," Reichmann recalled. "The question was always, Who is the client? If I'm the client, I'm more apt to dictate terms than if I'm selling."

Olympia & York's final collapse into the sheltering arms of the bankruptcy court would be forced in large part by Reichmann's failure to recognize that he was no longer the client but a supplicant to his bankers. Along the way, Reichmann and the minions who emulated him would needlessly alienate numerous financial and business corporations by their increasingly ruthless efforts to extract every last advantage in negotiating a transaction. "Paul worked very, very hard at getting the next sixteenth of a point, the next 10 basis points," said a longtime Olympia & York executive. "He always wanted to do the perfect deal at the perfect moment, and that caused transactions to become convoluted and protracted to the point where everyone would be exhausted and fed up." The first major institution so antagonized was Olympia & York's partner in First Canadian Place, the Bank of Montreal. Reichmann's increasingly contentious relationship with William Mulholland, the bank's formidable chairman and chief executive, was a telling precursor of the catastrophe to come.

A graduate of Catholic boarding school, the U.S. Army, and Harvard, Mulholland had spent seventeen years as an investment banker at the blue-blood Wall Street house of Morgan Stanley. When the senior management of one of his major clients, Brinco, was wiped out in a plane crash in 1969, Mulholland stepped in as chief executive. About the same time he joined Brinco, a Canadian company in the midst of a massive hydroelectric project in Labrador, Mulholland was named to the board of the Bank of Montreal, an honor that was not what it once was. The Bank of Montreal, the oldest of Canada's Big Five banks, was a grand old oceanliner grounded on the shoals of inertia. The bank that insiders still proudly called The First was now mocked on Bay Street as The Worst. In 1974, the Bank of Montreal's overburdened chairman offered to step down if Mulholland would leave Brinco and run the bank. Over the objections of certain board members, who were appalled by the prospect of an American commanding "The First," Mulholland was installed as president.

By the time Mulholland took charge in early 1975, First Bank Tower was hurtling toward completion. The new president was in favor of the building project he had inherited but paid it little heed at first. A husky outdoorsman type, Mulholland set about bullying the Bank of Montreal out of its complacency. His way of getting acquainted with the staff was to drop into an underling's office unannounced, fix its occupant with a cold eye, and inquire, "And what do you do?" To induce managers to think for themselves, Mulholland did not so much issue commands as make ominously cryptic observations. As staffers by the hundreds were sent packing from all levels, Mulholland also recast the bank's balance sheet, shifting billions of dollars from no-brainer investments in the money markets into higher-margin commercial loans. By 1977, the ocean liner had swung about sharply. Profits rose and so did the bank's stock price; by 1979 the Bank of Montreal ranked as the most prolific lead manager of syndicated commercial loans in the world. Awarded the additional title of chief executive, Mulholland was hailed as a miracle worker and gloried in his acclaim.

Mulholland's relationship with Paul Reichmann was a mix of friendly consultation and elaborate dispute. Every now and then, Reichmann, who was an avid self-taught student of the financial markets, would take the elevator from his thirty-second-floor office in First Bank Tower to the sixty-eighth floor and spend an hour talking interest rates or housing starts with Mulholland. "Paul Reichmann had an easy, charming way," the banker said. "An hour with Paul always stood out as more interesting than an hour with other people. He's a very smart and talented guy, even if he is exasperating at times."

Under its partnership agreement with Olympia & York, the Bank of Montreal was entitled to participate in Phase II of First Canadian Place on the same basis as it had in Phase I—that is, as a 25 percent partner with various preferential rights as the complex's name tenant. Olympia & York's arduous search for an anchor tenant for the second tower eventually led to Sun Life Assurance Company of Canada. Sun Life liked the site and was willing to lease about 400,000 square feet but did not want to be part of First Canadian Place. "They wanted their own design and identity—something totally separate," Reichmann recalled. While Olympia & York was willing to accommodate the insurer, the Bank of Montreal refused to accede to the recasting of Phase II into a separate project from which it would be excluded. Reichmann and Mulholland continued to go round and round on this issue long after Sun Life had lost interest and gone off in search of a less problematic development site.

"After two and a half years of impasse, we finally settled it in forty-five minutes," Mulholland recalled. "The first thing I'd learned about dealing with Olympia & York was that a negotiation wouldn't end until they got what they wanted. Nothing gets settled until Paul is ready to talk turkey, so all I did was rope-a-dope it for a while, a long while. With Paul, the real trick was to wait him out. After many, many unproductive meetings, our negotiations would always end in the same way. I'd get a call from Paul and he'd say, 'I wonder if you have a few minutes. I'd like to drop by.' We'd talk platitudes for a while and then we'd saw off a compromise." In this case, the Bank of Montreal agreed to let Olympia & York make the second building a separate project in exchange for an option to acquire an interest in the building at a later date. Sun Life's withdrawal actually helped Olympia & York, which was able to replace it with an even more prestigious name tenant—the Toronto Stock Exchange—and at higher rents.

The second-tower battle overlapped with an even more intractable wrangle over the distribution of the operating profits from First Canadian Place. This was a highly technical dispute that turned around the practical interpretation of dozens of vague clauses in the contract binding Olympia & York and the Bank of Montreal, which argued that it was being substantially shortchanged by its partner. After several attempts at arranging arbitration failed, the bank sued Olympia & York in the Supreme Court of Ontario in 1987. An out-of-court settlement was reached, the terms of which were not disclosed. However, Mulholland said that Olympia & York paid the bank "a good many millions of dollars." Asked for comment, Reichmann at first said that he had no recollection of a suit ever being filed, but he later accused Mulholland of negotiating in bad faith. Reichmann said he had been willing to let the bank's outside legal counsel arbitrate the dispute: "I said, 'He has an excellent reputation. I'll take his word.' But Mr. Mulholland told me, 'You are naïve. If my lawyer disagrees with me, I will fire him and get a new lawyer.'" Mulholland's only response to Reichmann's allegation was a laugh.

The altercations over accounting methodology and profit participation may have been convoluted and legalistic, but at least large sums of money were at issue. By contrast, the fight Olympia & York picked over 302 Bay Street was at once straightforward and petty. First Canadian Place occupied nine-tenths of a city block. The agreement among Olympia & York, the Bank of Montreal, and North American Life stipulated that if the opportunity arose to buy any of the remaining properties on the block, the partners would buy them together, in proportion to their interest in First Canadian Place—that is 50, 25, and 25 percent, respectively. In early 1979, Crown Trust Company, Toronto's quintessential silk-stocking trust company, decided to move out of its old headquarters at 302 Bay Street and into leased space in First Canadian Place. Together,

Olympia & York and the Bank of Montreal bought 302 Bay as equal partners (North American Life passed). Under the terms of the bank's agreement with Olympia & York, if one partner decided it wanted to sell its interest in 302 Bay, the other partner would be given right of first refusal. Olympia & York managed the eight-story building, which was profitably leased.

All went smoothly until John McCool, the head of the Bank of Montreal's real estate division, found a letter in his in-box requesting his signature on a contract providing for the sale of 302 Bay to the Bank of Nova Scotia. The transaction was set to close in a week or so. McCool lost his cool. Olympia & York not only had arranged to sell its interest in the building, but the Bank of Montreal's, too—and to one of its archrivals at that. Mulholland was outraged: "I sure as hell didn't want the Bank of Nova Scotia opening a branch right next door to us." McCool called Reichmann to complain and notify him of the bank's desire to exercise its option to buy Olympia & York's half-interest in 302 Bay. Under the threat of a lawsuit, Olympia & York canceled the sale and sold its interest in 302 Bay to the Bank of Montreal. Mulholland never did discuss the incident with Reichmann but was convinced that Olympia & York's attempt to sell 302 Bay was no innocent misstep. "You had to be on your toes at all times with Paul," Mulholland said. "If you weren't, he was not above trying to stampede you." Reichmann denied that he had done anything of the sort: "That is rubbish. There can be no conceivable reason for us to try to sell a building without the bank's knowledge."

Admire Bill Mulholland or loathe him, by the late 1970s he was the most powerful figure in Canadian banking and arguably in all of Canadian business. The Bank of Montreal not only was an indispensable source of credit but was the name tenant of Olympia & York's flagship development. The value of Mulholland's goodwill was at least equal to that of the chief executives of Bell Telephone of Canada, Shell Canada, and the other corporate tenants that Paul Reichmann had gone to such lengths to accommodate and impress. Whether Reichmann acted precipitously in trying to sell 302 Bay, he clearly antagonized Mulholland over a piddling sum—revenue of some $5 million. Perhaps the most plausible explanation was that he had a deep-seated aversion to the constraints and forced intimacies of partnership—to the accommodation of coequals. Even with his brothers, Paul would be able to sustain only the form of partnership, not the spirit. But whereas Paul was able to finesse his fraternal relationships, in Bill Mulholland he encountered a will as indomitable as his own.

Finally completed in 1982, the second tower of First Canadian Place—Exchange Tower—was Olympia & York's last major office project in its home city. The company would build out West—mainly in Calgary and Edmonton—but in the aftermath of the Uris transaction, the focus of the company's property development activities swung from Toronto to New York City. Its World Financial Center project, which spanned the years 1980 through 1987, would rank as the largest office development in the history of Manhattan. In New York, as well, the Reichmanns established the headquarters of a new U.S. operating subsidiary of Olympia & York. By the mid-1980s, Olympia & York would employ some 350 people in New York, or nearly as many as worked in the corporate headquarters in Toronto.

From 1977 until Canary Wharf was launched in London in 1987, Paul Reichmann would split his time evenly between the Toronto and New York offices. Many of his stays in New York would end with a late afternoon dash to LaGuardia Airport to make it home to Toronto before the Sabbath began. As legend had it, at any rate, Reichmann once arrived after sundown and walked all the way to his house from the Toronto airport—a distance of four miles— rather than violate the Sabbath prohibition against automotive transport. On occasion, his wife would join him in New York for a weekend spent in the company of his brother Louis in Queens. When Reichmann had first explored New York in the late 1950s, the city had put him off. Now that the Reichmanns were on a par with the Rockefellers as the largest private property owners in Manhattan, he found the place much more to his liking.

Initially, Reichmann had returned with trepidation. During the protracted negotiations to acquire the Uris package, he recalled, "many people I knew told me scare stories about doing business in wild New York." It was not just the pervasiveness of mob influence in the construction trades or the city's often rancorous labor relations or the nastiness of its municipal politics. The Big Apple, Reichmann was told, was the capital of the side deal; everybody was working a private angle in hopes of diverting into his own pocket a rivulet of the gargantuan sums of cash flowing through the city's economy. The Reichmanns were not completely inexperienced at out-of-town investment, having by this time built three large office buildings in Ottawa, but the brothers found that the management of these properties could be rigorously controlled from Toronto and did not bother with opening an office in Ottawa. New York, on the other hand, was a foreign city, and responsibility for many aspects of managing the Uris properties—including the collection and disbursement of cash— had to be locally vested.

Reenter Avraham Fruchthandler, the young ultra-Orthodox businessman and communal leader from Brooklyn who had approached the Reichmanns in 1973 on behalf of Isiah Siedenfeld's hard-pressed investors. Paul Reichmann had stayed in touch with Fruchthandler ever since the Siedenfeld affair and had come to believe he was a man of piety and unimpeachable integrity. That Fruchthandler, who ran a family real estate company in Borough Park, was a small-timer by Olympia & York's standards mattered less to Reichmann than did his impeccable haredi credentials. In hopes of reinforcing the bonds of shared ultra-Orthodoxy with the golden bar of joint investment, Reichmann approached Fruchthandler during the Uris negotiations and made him an offer he could not refuse: join us as a senior administrator and you will be able to invest as an equity partner not only in the Uris deal but in all future U.S. projects. Never before had the Reichmanns been willing to surrender equity to an employee in even a single project. If the offer extended to Fruchthandler betokened the brothers' respect, it was more tellingly a measure of their apprehension. Fruchthandler put up about $750,000, entitling him to 3 percent ownership of the Uris building.

Fruchthandler was given the title of senior vice president and put in charge of most of the forty Uris Building Corporation corporate managers who came with the properties. The Reichmanns augmented their ranks with specialists hired away from other New York property firms as needed. Fruchthandler was outranked at first only by William Hay, whom the Reichmanns brought down from Toronto and installed as executive vice president. A former senior executive of Webb & Knapp (Canada), Hay had negotiated the sale of Flemingdon Park to the Reichmanns and gone on to become president of Trizec. Ousted in the housecleaning that followed the acquisition of Trizec by Peter and Edgar Bronfman in 1976, Hay had just begun looking for a job when Paul Reichmann called to offer one. Like Fruchthandler, Reichmann valued Hay mainly for his rectitude. A stiff-backed, taciturn Scots lawyer, Hay functioned as the Reichmanns' "Shabbas goy" in New York. Every Friday afternoon, title to the New York buildings was temporarily signed over to Hay so that the maintenance and other operational chores that tenants required on Saturdays would not put the Reichmanns in violation of the Sabbath work prohibition.

Hay's contribution to the evolution of the Reichmanns' American empire would pale in comparison with those made by two former Toronto city officials who joined Olympia & York in 1978 after putting the finishing touches on the city's hugely ambitious downtown plan. The first hired was Ron Soskolne, the city planner who had taken the lead for the city in forcing the redesign of First Canadian Place. Passed over for the post of city planning commissioner, the thirty-five-year-old Soskolne had paid a call on Paul Reichmann. "I went to get advice on how to break into the development business and he offered me a job on the spot," Soskolne recalled. Although Soskolne was attached to the Toronto office as vice president of planning and development, at Paul Reichmann's request he would devote most of his time to projects south of the border. "Ron Soskolne is an extraordinary professional as far as planning and maintaining relationships with government," Reichmann said later. "He is the best I've ever seen at going to a new city and understanding it rapidly."

When Michael Dennis heard that Soskolne had joined Olympia & York, he called and asked if the Reichmanns might have a spot for him, too. Dennis came from a family of developers in Toronto and his rebellion against that aspect of his legacy had taken very public form. A lawyer by training, he had first made his mark as a long-haired, radical-populist critic of the property industry. It was Dennis who, as an adviser to Mayor Crombie, had authored the 1973 bylaw that had incensed Toronto developers by imposing a forty-five-foot height limit on new downtown buildings. Dennis then moved into city hall as founding director of a new housing department that did its best to goad private sector developers into improving the city's housing stock by competing with them. In his own opinion, Dennis's overriding achievement as a residential developer was the massive, three-thousand-unit St. Lawrence Market housing project.

By the time he had joined Olympia & York, Dennis was thirty-five years old. He had cut his hair and toned down the leftist rhetoric but rejected the suggestion that he had somehow switched sides in a battle of right versus wrong. "The city was our training ground," he said. "Development, starting things up, untying knots, helping—that's what I'm good at. The trick in every major task is not to comprehend how difficult it's going to be—if you did, you'd never undertake it." As Dennis grew older, he never would disavow his 1970s crusading but, to the contrary, was increasingly inclined to lionize the achievements of the cadre of progressive planners and architects that had coalesced around Mayor Crombie. He insisted, for example, that the St. Lawrence Market was a greater feat of development than the World Financial Center. "It started with less momentum," he argued. "We had to create it from scratch."

For his part, Paul Reichmann did not hold Dennis's youthful politics against him. Like his fellow developers, Reichmann had been put off by the young firebrand's savaging of private sector interests. But both Paul and Albert took a utilitarian—that is, apolitical—approach to personnel matters and, what is more, had used city hall as a recruiting ground since their earliest days in North York. "I think anyone who does the job well at city hall, working for the public interest, must be able to do a good job for a developer," Paul once said. "The more he incorporates the public interest, the more successful the project will be." Self-serving as these words looked in print, Reichmann would live up to them in practice. His largest projects all would be predicated on the contrarian notion that catering to the public interest was not merely a means to an end but a critical component of a property's enduring value. In addition, Reichmann, to a much greater extent than most developers, recognized the overwhelming importance of land costs in the equation of urban redevelopment, and virtually by definition there was only one source of cut-rate land downtown: the government.

Dennis joined Olympia & York as executive vice president in charge of development for the American company. His hiring would prove the most fruitful the Reichmanns had made since the addition of Keith Roberts some fifteen years earlier. In essence, Dennis had left government not because he had tired of the good fight, but because it no longer provided him a ready outlet for his energy. Throughout his long tenure with Olympia & York, the fire within Dennis would continue to burn hot and very close to the surface. He was a supremely self-confident, excitable man who ran on only one speed—flat out—and shared with his boss an all-consuming passion for the herculean undertaking. Michael Dennis—not Albert Reichmann—would fill the role of alter ego to Paul Reichmann on the definitive projects of his career: World Financial Center and Canary Wharf. "If I want a replacement for myself," Reichmann told a reporter as early as 1984, "Michael would be an ideal candidate."

Olympia & York U.S.A. was further enlivened by the addition of a third executive vice president: Edward Minskoff. After acting as a broker-consultant on the Uris deal, Minskoff had continued to lob investment opportunities Reichmann's way. Unlike Fruchthandler (or Dennis, or Hay, or the Reichmanns themselves, for that matter), Minskoff was widely connected in real estate circles not only in New York but across the country. What is more, Reichmann was impressed with him as an idea man. "There are certain talents which are in the creative field, development of new ideas, new concepts," Reichmann testified in a lawsuit that Minskoff brought against his partner in Ficor, the real estate brokerage he had cofounded. "Mr. Minskoff had these particular talents, so I was very much interested for him to join [Olympia & York]. . . . As an executive he was wanted for his creative talents, not for his expertise in the field, because that you can hire easily."

Reichmann offered Minskoff a full-time position with Olympia & York as early as 1978. Unlike Dennis, Minskoff drove a hard bargain, insisting on the same sort of sweet deal given Fruchthandler. Reichmann initially refused to give equity to Minskoff, who continued to figure importantly in the evolution of the U.S. company as an outside broker. By the fall of 1980, Fruchthandler's stake in the Uris properties alone was worth many millions. He told Paul Reichmann that he was loath "to keep all his eggs in one basket" and offered to sell a portion of his investment to the Reichmann family. With Fruchthandler's assent, Reichmann instead offered Minskoff the opportunity to purchase half of Fruchthandler's 3 percent carried interest. After protracted negotiations, the parties settled on a price of $10 million. Minskoff put up no cash, borrowing the full sum from the Reichmanns, and finally joined Olympia & York in 1981 as an executive vice president. "I wanted to be president," Minskoff recalled, "but Paul was already."

Minskoff's own employment contract was by far the best real estate deal he ever would make. When he left Olympia & York five years later, the Reichmanns would buy him out for $40 million. Minskoff paid back the $10 million he had borrowed plus $4 million in interest and walked away with $26 million in cash. Needless to say, this would do nothing for the morale of Michael Dennis, Ron Soskolne, and the dozen other senior Olympia & York officers who were at least as deserving as Minskoff but had never been similarly favored with a piece of the action.

———

If the dynastic families of Manhattan real estate did not hail the Reichmanns as conquering heroes, neither did they give them the proverbial cold shoulder. "I didn't detect any backlash against the Reichmanns," recalled Richard Roth Jr., the second-generation chief of Emery Roth & Sons, which long had reigned as the developer elite's preferred architect. "What was bothering people at the time was that the Port Authority had built the World Trade Center and was still trying to fill it. The Reichmanns' purchase of the Uris buildings was different in that it did not add capacity; it just changed ownership. Plus, soon afterward the market in the city became really terrific. Olympia & York's competition was making so much money, too, that no one was jealous."

Local sentiment gradually would turn against the Reichmanns, soured in equal measure by resentment of the increasing magnitude of their success and their aloofness. The old families did business in a highly personal way that belied the size of their empires and the city itself. Whether friend or foe, the developer dynasties were bound together by a century-long shared history and were intimately acquainted with one another and with the coterie of architects and lawyers who serviced them and the city officials who regulated them and accepted their campaign contributions. In a word, Manhattan real estate was a club—one of the wealthiest and most inbred clubs American business has ever seen.

In Toronto, the Reichmanns had always kept their distance from the establishment, and in entering Manhattan saw no need to alter their preferences to accommodate the local taste for chumminess. In New York as in North York, both Paul and Albert (who visited much less frequently) led sharply compartmentalized lives, socializing rarely and only within ultra-Orthodox circles. The brothers rarely ventured outside their hotel suites or Park Avenue offices even for meals, preferring to avail themselves of Olympia & York's own kosher kitchen. When they did submit to the ritual of the business meal, they dined at Lou G. Siegel's glatt kosher restaurant on 38th Street, where they were the reluctant celebrities du jour. "Going into Lou Siegel's with Paul was like walking into Grand Central Station with Madonna," joked one top Olympia & York executive (who conceded that he had never actually accompanied Madonna anywhere).

Paul Reichmann's contact with established New York developers would be infrequent and episodic: he tried unsuccessfully to buy a midtown site from the Fisher brothers, discussed a joint undertaking with Mortimer Zuckerman, and bumped into Lew Rudin here and there (and came to consider him "a very fine gentleman"). To the bafflement of the local real estate fraternity, the Reichmanns did not bother with campaign contributions and steered clear of political banquets and real estate industry gatherings of all descriptions. "The Reichmanns in New York was the story of the dog that didn't bark," said Peter J. Solomon, an investment banker who served as deputy mayor for economic development in the late 1970s. "You knew they were out there, but you didn't see them around like the other builders. Perhaps they'd learned over the years that it wasn't worth their time to get to know a deputy mayor. But it's one thing to try to ingratiate yourself and another merely to be on speaking terms. Most people weren't shmucks about it. They'd at least call occasionally to talk."

Paul Reichmann's first foray into Manhattan development followed, however circuitously, from the Uris transaction. As it turned out, National Kinney failed to live up to its promise to purchase the land under 245 and 320 Park Avenue before selling them and the other six Uris buildings to Olympia & York. After Olympia & York took possession of the Uris package, Reichmann was able to negotiate directly with Penn Central, the bankrupt railroad that owned the two parcels. Reichmann figured that he held the upper hand. The judge in charge of the Penn Central case had ordered the company's trustees to liquidate its assets as expeditiously as possible, and no other bidder was likely to surface since the terms of leases Olympia & York had inherited along with 245 and 320 Park strongly favored lessee over lessor. However, Victor Palmieri & Company, the court-appointed liquidator of the railroad's real estate portfolio, drove a hard bargain. Rejecting Olympia & York's lowball offer, the Palmieri firm bundled the two Park Avenue leaseholds together with a decrepit fifteen-story office building that Penn Central owned—466 Lexington, near Grand Central Station—and put all three properties up for auction as a package.

The tactic annoyed Reichmann. What did he want with a musty pre–World War I relic seemingly fit only for the wrecking ball? But if 466 Lex was virtually worthless, quite a number of local New York developers coveted the land on which it sat, as the Palmieri people well knew. In the end, Reichmann was one of a dozen developers that submitted bids. At $40.3 million, Olympia & York topped the field. Sam Lefrak was perhaps the least gracious loser. "When I called Sam to tell him we'd gone with another bidder, he started screaming and yelling that the auction had been rigged. He wanted to submit another bid," recalled Larry Shafran, the Palmieri officer in charge of the auction. "An hour later an envelope was delivered to my office. Sam upped his bid by a lot but it was still lower than what O & Y bid." Lefrak was beginning to dislike these interlopers from Canada.

The intensity of developer interest in 466 Lexington was a sign of a market rapidly regaining vibrancy. By the time the auction was completed in mid-1978, the threat of municipal bankruptcy had passed, New York City's economy was expanding again, the corporate exodus from Manhattan was starting to reverse itself, and a new mayor, Edward Koch, had enacted new subsidies to stimulate development. By year's end, the backlog of vacant office space that had burdened developers throughout most of the 1970s had vanished and more than thirty new office towers were under construction to meet the pent-up demand for premium quality space. Eager to demonstrate that Olympia & York built as cleverly as it bought, Paul Reichmann decided to get into the act by transforming 466 Lex, the dowdiest of Olympia & York's Manhattan properties, into its local showpiece.

Reichmann again hired the architect Edward Durell Stone along with Emery Roth & Sons, which had designed most of the Uris towers. The basic architectural plan had nearly been completed when the seventy-six-year-old Stone died in August 1978, after a brief illness. Shortly thereafter, Reichmann stopped by Stone's offices to inspect the preliminary drawings, which had been tacked up in panels along the walls of a conference room. Richard Roth and Peter Capone, the Stone firm's managing partner, literally walked Reichmann through the plans. "He walked slowly around the room with his hands behind his back in a very rabbinical pose, grunting occasionally," recalled Roth, who had never before met Reichmann. "When we got to the last panel, he thanked us and left. He never said a word." In this case, as Roth soon learned, Reichmann's silence betokened approval.

The conventional approach would have been to demolish 466 Lex and build a much larger, modern skyscraper, but Reichmann decided instead to create a new building atop the skeleton of the old. The structure was stripped down to its steel girders and extended upward to add six stories. A small central courtyard was expanded into a cavernous glass-and-stainless-steel atrium rising the full height of the building's twenty-one stories. Lined on two sides by balconied offices (which fetched the same premium rents as offices with outer windows), the atrium featured Manhattan's first glass-enclosed elevators. The ground floor was wholly given over to a shopping plaza. At a total cost of $90 million, this was said to be the most costly remodeling project in the history of New York City.

During construction, Roth spent long hours with Keith Roberts, John Norris, and Otto Blau but never again saw Paul nor once met Albert Reichmann. "Working with the Reichmanns was completely different from working with the old families," Roth recalled. "With them, it's a very personal, intensive exposure. I met with Harry Helmsley two or three times a week for years. Resnick, Kaufman, Rudin—you'd meet with them all the time." Nor were Roth and his firm accustomed to meeting strictly kosher planning standards. "We had to write all our job specifications to Olympia & York's policy of no work on Saturdays or Jewish holidays," Roth added. "Later, Burt Resnick called needing a drywall spec in a hurry, so I pulled out one we did for 466 Lex and sent it over. On Monday he called and said, 'What do you mean we can't work on Saturdays?' "

Although the reinvention of 466 Lexington would be accomplished with Olympia & York's usual smooth dispatch, the economics of the project were jeopardized by political discord. In undertaking the remodeling, the Reichmanns had counted on obtaining a tax abatement from the Koch administration, which spent its first year in office tossing sugared subsidies to every developer that came trick-or-treating. By early 1979, city hall had decided that enough was enough. Peter Solomon, Koch's deputy mayor, decided to dramatize the new selectivity of the abatement program by taking a stick to the dog that never barked. "We wanted 466 Lex renovated, no question," Solomon recalled. "But this was not IBM or Philip Morris building a new home office, which brings a lot of peripheral development to an area. If the effect of a project was just to shift tenants from one building to another at higher rents, which ended up in the developer's pocket, the intrinsic case for abatement was not all that strong."

When the Industrial and Commercial Incentive Board duly rejected Olympia & York's abatement application (while approving six others), the news made the front page of *The New York Times*. Deputy Mayor Solomon was quoted criticizing Olympia & York for refusing to accede to the city's requests that it impose a rent ceiling on the remodeled building: "We do not wish to allow the use of tax incentives to result in unwarranted profits for developers, and we don't want rental levels to become so burdensome that businesses will be induced to leave the city." In a politic response, Reichmann expressed sympathy for the city's concern about windfall profits but pointed out that converting an old building into prime office space was far riskier than building anew.

Paul Reichmann wiped the egg off his face and did what any self-respecting member of the old Manhattan developer elite would have done from the start: he hired a well-connected lawyer to fix things. It was revealing of the clubby nature of Manhattan real estate that Reichmann essentially had only two choices. Samuel "Sandy" Lindenbaum was a second-generation specialist in land-use and zoning law who had been the Skyscraper Club lawyer-lobbyist of choice for years. His archrival, John Zuccotti, had just returned to his law practice after winning plaudits as deputy mayor during the city's recent financial crisis. Both men were technically proficient lawyers who knew their way around city hall. But whereas Lindenbaum was a notoriously combative infighter who worked on a contingency basis, Zuccotti was an affable master of conciliation who charged by the hour. Reichmann chose Zuccotti.

Zuccotti quickly brokered a compromise with Peter Solomon's office. The city agreed to award a $16 million abatement applicable to about half the office space. Rents on the abated portion of the building would be controlled but Olympia & York would be free to let out the remaining half at whatever the traffic would bear. Olympia & York moved its own offices into the building, which was renamed the Park Avenue Atrium, and persuaded the powers-that-be to change its official address to 237 Park Avenue, even though it was not actually on Park Avenue. According to Larry Shafran, who had initiated the protracted process of changing the building's address on behalf of Penn Central, the address change was worth an additional $2 to $3 a square foot in rent. Although the building took a bit longer to fill than expected (as usual, Olympia & York refused to haggle), in the end the reinvention of 466 Lex as 237 Park proved successful in every respect, and yet it would be dwarfed into insignificance by Paul Reichmann's New York encore—the World Financial Center.

Chapter 30

As the spotlight swung his way in the aftermath of the Uris deal, Paul Reichmann ducked and dodged his way through a series of press interviews. Reichmann insisted, appearances notwithstanding, that he, Albert, and Ralph formed a triumvirate of coequals at the helm of Olympia & York. "We have not had one disagreement in 25 years," he told the *Toronto Globe & Mail*. "We trust each other implicitly and, if something comes up, whichever one of us has time takes charge. It saves time." In *The New York Times*, Paul was quoted as saying that he and Albert functioned interchangeably as co-presidents: "In major negotiations, it depends on who is available at the time." Albert concurred, describing himself and Paul as "more or less interchangeable." In a separate interview, Albert said, "We work well together because we think alike. We always come satisfactorily to the same unanimous conclusion."

The Reichmann brothers' relations had always been remarkably harmonious, but their interchangeability was a myth fostered by Paul with the acquiescence of the rest of the family. In 1978, Paul and Albert testified separately in support of a lawsuit brought in New York City against National Kinney by Eddie Minskoff, who had not received the commission promised him by the seller as the main broker on the Uris deal. The Reichmanns' depositions were sealed at the brothers' request but summarized by Minskoff's lawyer as follows: "Paul Reichmann testified . . . that in accordance with the standard practice of the Reichmann brothers, if Paul is handling a deal then Albert is not involved and vice versa. Indeed, Albert Reichmann testified on his deposition that he was 'a third party in [the Uris deal].' " To be sure, Paul and Albert did function interchangeably in minor ways—in signing documents, say, or returning unsolicited phone calls. But the essence of the family approach to corporate management was not the sort of free-form fungibility implied by the brothers' public comments, but its opposite: division of labor.

Of the three Reichmann brothers, Ralph had always had the most clearly and narrowly defined role. From Olympia & York's founding through its collapse, the youngest Reichmann brother ran the tile business as his own fiefdom. Ralph, prince of tiles, had no involvement in real estate development and ceased even sharing office space with his brothers as early as 1965. When Olympia & York moved its headquarters to downtown Toronto in 1969, Ralph remained behind in North York, running Olympia Floor & Wall Tiles from an office adjoining its showroom-warehouse. For their part, Paul and Albert had little interest in the tile company, which was a subsidiary of Olympia & York Development, except as a source of cash and credit to support their building projects.

On the development side of the business, Paul from the beginning had functioned as Olympia & York's idea man and deal doer and Albert as its administrator and construction overseer. These roles had not been imposed arbitrarily but were the organic product of the brothers' own inclinations and the company's needs. Happily, their innate abilities diverged so markedly that each had been able to do what he did best within the context of their shared responsibility for the company as a whole. Paul and Albert were not interchangeable but complementary parts, the finely meshed rack and pinion of Olympia & York's driving wheel.

But compatibility was not parity, and therein lay the rub. Albert's steady competence simply was no match for Paul's impassioned, compulsive brilliance. Inside Olympia & York, the imbalance in fraternal talents had been apparent from the start. "Albert is a good man but there are a lot of Alberts in the world," observed Bill Minuk, Olympia & York's first staff engineer. "Paul was the one who made the company special." While an equal owner in fact and an equal partner in theory, Albert in practice had found himself increasingly in thrall to Paul as Olympia & York's projects grew in size and complexity. Albert had the grace and good sense not to fight his gradual diminution from coequal to human sounding board, but that did not mean that he was happy about it.

For his part, Paul carefully subordinated his will to the dictates of family etiquette. Although he was unquestionably Olympia & York's captain, his hand rested furtively on the tiller. Within the highest councils of family and company—which amounted to the same thing—Paul tended to participate rather than preside, suggest rather than command. Over the years, Paul's corporate title would become encrusted in euphemistic curlicue as he was "promoted" from vice president to senior vice president to executive senior vice president. But never was he president. In deference to his status as the eldest of the Olympia & York brothers, Albert had been named president upon the formation of the company and would hold tight to his title for three decades, even as his influence over the company's affairs inexorably declined.

Paul's promoting of the myth of interchangeability helped his brothers, especially Albert, save face. Although Paul in part acted out of affection for his brothers, the myth also had its self-serving aspect. With 50 percent of Olympia & York's shares between them, Albert and Ralph had the votes to stymie Paul's every initiative if they had so chosen. Ralph already had what he wanted: management control of Olympia Floor & Wall Tile. But it behooved Paul to placate his older brother as best he could, and so the rhetoric of his self-effacement came laced with flattery. "There's no genius required for Olympia & York's success," Paul proclaimed in 1988, at the peak of that success. "The strongest tools in any company are sound judgment and common sense. In that regard, Albert is the stronger. He's the one who was in business with my father."

Of course, words alone could not satisfy Albert, who was only forty-six when Samuel Reichmann died and unwilling to content himself with succeeding his father as eminence grise. In his own unassuming way, Albert yearned to do his own development deals, as he had before Samuel had prevailed upon him and Paul to join forces. It was not the approbation of outsiders that Albert craved— he had it already and would have preferred anonymity in any event—but a proprietor's self-respect. He wanted to prove to himself and to his family that Paul's dominance of Olympia & York was a function of happenstance rather than necessity. But how? Ever since Flemingdon Park, the scale of Paul's pet projects had monopolized the company's resources. Yet starting a company of his own was unthinkable, if only because withdrawing his capital from Olympia & York would have caused its collapse.

Albert's dilemma was solved by the Uris transaction, which generated wealth vast beyond even Paul's immediate ambitions. Beginning in the late 1970s, Olympia & York launched a continent-wide building blitz of a magnitude that had not been seen since the heyday of William Zeckendorf. Within a span of four or five years, the company would launch projects in Boston, Calgary, Chicago, Dallas, Denver, Edmonton, Fort Lauderdale, Hartford, Miami, Orlando, Portland (Oregon), San Francisco, and Seattle, among other cities. These were boom times in the business generally—especially for Canadian developers—and Olympia & York no doubt would have entered some of these cities even if Paul had been an only child. As it was, the company now was developing for two. There were "Paul's deals" and "Albert's deals," explained a former senior executive of the company. "The quid pro quo between the brothers seemed to be that Paul could do the megastuff in New York and Albert would do the ministuff in other places, and they wouldn't try to rein each other in." This arrangement remained a private matter between brothers, never officially acknowledged inside the company or out.

Olympia & York's two-track approach to development was effected without the trauma of power struggle or corporate reorganization. Albert wanted to build his own buildings, not an empire within an empire. Although the brothers may not have functioned interchangeably, their employees did, shuttling back and forth as needed between Paul's and Albert's projects. The brothers themselves got along better than ever, as the tension born of Albert's mounting frustration dissipated. Paul continued to seek Albert's counsel in matters large and small, and Albert now relied on Paul for advice on his deals. From the outside, the new modus operandi was evident only in the projects themselves. For one thing, the brothers' taste in architecture was quite different. Paul was a neoclassicist who liked his skyscrapers majestic but simple, with clean lines fashioned in marble—like First Canadian Place. Albert was more of a modernist and preferred towers of jagged, asymmetrical design in which tinted glass, steel, and masonry were combined to novel effect.

The brothers' approach to the business of development was equally disparate. Paul was an independent sort, disinclined to bring partners into a project unless they contributed something he desperately lacked, whether cash or a strategic site. And under no circumstances would Paul surrender control; he would rather walk away from a project than take a backseat. By contrast— and ironically so—Albert relied heavily on a series of outside partners in his bid to establish himself as a force in his own right. Albert was not as creative or well rounded a developer as his younger brother, nor as self-contained a personality; he both needed help and enjoyed the give and take of collaboration. Albert's method was advantageous for Olympia & York to the extent that it obviated the need for the company to make large additions to staff and overhead—something that both brothers were keen to avoid.

Almost without exception, Albert's partners sought out and found him, for the Uris bonanza brought a buzzing swarm of do-I-have-a-deal-for-you promoters and brokers from all over North America. For the most part, these pitchmen were given a cordial hearing. "Accustomed as I was to flashy real estate developers with stainless steel teeth, I was surprised and charmed by Albert and Paul Reichmann," recalled Michael Young, a Dallas broker who first made the trip to Toronto in 1978. A few months later, Young got a call from Albert, who asked him to investigate a site in downtown Dallas that had been offered to Olympia & York and on which the company soon built a thirty-six-story tower of polished pearl-gray granite.

The dozens of partnerships that Albert created involved a disparate cast of characters but were all variations on the same basic deal. While the partner contributed a site and a development concept, Albert put up all the money needed to finance construction and assumed sole responsibility for arranging a mortgage upon completion. Olympia & York typically took a controlling interest of 75 percent or 80 percent, though a few of Albert's projects were 50–50 joint ventures. Almost without exception, Albert allowed his partners to fully

David Reichmann, Hungary,
mid-1930s (courtesy Louis and
Marika Reichmann)

Adolf Gestetner, Győr, 1927
(courtesy Edward Reichmann)

Róza Gestetner, Győr,
circa 1930
(courtesy Edward
Reichmann)

Renée Gestetner, Győr, 1919
(courtesy Edward
Reichmann)

25 Rue Molière, Tangier
(the Reichmann apartment
was on the third floor)
(courtesy Louis Saint-Aubert)

Eva and Renée Reichmann, Tangier, 1946
(courtesy Louis and Marika Reichmann)

Ralph Reichmann, Paul Reichmann, Isaac Klein, unidentified woman, and Albert Reichmann, Tangier, 1945 (American Jewish Joint Distribution Committee)

Food parcel assembly at the Reichmann apartment, Tangier, 1945 (American Jewish Joint Distribution Committee)

**Louis and Albert Reichmann,
Tangier, 1945**
(American Jewish Joint
Distribution Committee)

Louis Reichmann (left) and Isaac Klein (on truck), Tangier, 1945
(American Jewish Joint Distribution Committee)

Spanish Red Cross sponsorship, a crucial advantage in getting food parcels into concentration camps (courtesy Yeshiva University Archives)

✚ CRUZ ROJA ESPAÑOLA
TANGER

ENVIO PARA PRISIONEROS DE GUERRA

EXPEDIDOR — EXPEDITEUR

FRANCO DE PORTE
FRANC DE PORT

Nombre y dirección
Nom et adresse

Dirección del prisionero:
Adresse du prisonnier:

Renée
REICHMANN
TANGER

CROIX-ROUGE FRANÇAISE
à destination de
American Joint Distribution Committee
19, RUE DE TEHERAN
(FRANCE) PARIS

Survivors gather at the engagement party of Simon Reichmann and Rose Ungar: (from left to right) Simon Reichmann, Henrik Gestetner, Deszö Gestetner, Kornell Gestetner, Eva Reichmann, Samuel Reichmann, Renée Reichmann, Rose Ungar, Ilona Gestetner, Olga Ehrenfeld, Tangier, 1946 (courtesy Louis and Marika Reichmann)

Eva Reichmann, Tangier, 1946, (courtesy Edward Reichmann)

The wedding of Edward
and Edith Reichmann,
Tangier, 1946 (Samuel is at left,
Renée is at right)
(courtesy Edward Reichmann)

Edith Reichmann, Tangier, 1948
(courtesy Edward Reichmann)

Albert, Paul, and Renée Reichmann with Israeli president Yitzhak Ben-Zvi in his office, Jerusalem, 1956 (courtesy Edward Reichmann)

Commemorating the Reichmann acquisition of Montreal Floor & Wall Tile: (from left to right) Ralph Reichmann, Edward Reichmann, Albert Reichmann, Samuel Reichmann, Oubald Boyer of the Provincial Bank of Canada, John Capra (front), and Louis Reichmann, Montreal, 1960 (courtesy Edward Reichmann)

Edward Reichmann, at microphone, addressing Agudath Israel dinner, New York, 1962 (Rabbi Moshe Feinstein is seated immediately to his left) (courtesy Edward Reichmann)

Albert, Paul, and Ralph Reichmann in the Olympia & York boardroom, Toronto, 1965
(*Globe & Mail*, Toronto)

Paul and Samuel Reichmann at the
groundbreaking for the Toronto Star
Building, Toronto, 1969
(*Toronto Star*)

First Canadian Place, Toronto
(courtesy Olympia & York)

Gilbert Newman and Ralph
Reichmann, early 1980s
(*Toronto Star*)

World Financial Center, New York (Steve Moore)

**Albert, Paul, Renée, Louis, Edward, and Ralph Reichmann,
Waldorf-Astoria Hotel, New York, 1987**
(courtesy Edward Reichmann)

John Griffiths, Margaret Thatcher, and Paul Reichmann, London, 1988
(courtesy Olympia & York)

Vladislav Malkevich, the Soviet head of the Canada-Soviet Business Council, shakes hands with Albert Reichmann as Soviet prime minister Nikolai Ryzhkov and Canadian prime minister Brian Mulroney look on, Moscow, 1989 (Ron Poling/Canapress)

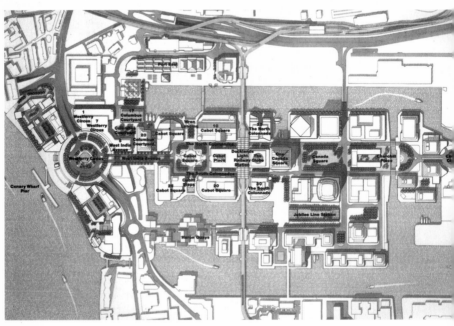

Canary Wharf, London
(courtesy Olympia & York)

20 Cabot Square, Canary Wharf, London
(courtesy Olympia & York)

The Docklands Light Railway leaving Canary Wharf
(courtesy Olympia & York)

David Reichmann
(Reuven Castro)

**Albert and Paul Reichmann leaving a meeting with
their creditors, Toronto, April 13, 1992**
(Jeff Wasserman, *Toronto Sun*)

**Edward (second from left) and Edith Reichmann with Teddy Kollek, the mayor
of Jerusalem (center), at the opening of the Bell Center, Jerusalem, 1993** (Vera Etzion)

recoup their investment when the property was mortgaged, leaving Olympia & York with 100 percent of the risk going forward. Although Keith Roberts, Ron Soskolne, and other Olympia & York staffers often figured importantly in design and construction, Albert entrusted the day-to-day management of the finished building to his partner, who pulled down a salary or a management fee. The net effect was to put Olympia & York in the unfamiliar position of entrusting its interests to a motley crew of strangers and acquaintances.

Although Albert's projects spanned the entire United States, he developed a special affinity for California and Florida both as real estate markets and as places to do business. While Paul took naturally to the pace and rigor of New York City, easygoing Albert preferred the comparatively casual style and sunny weather of Los Angeles and Miami. In downtown Los Angeles, Olympia & York joined forces with O'Melveny & Myers to develop a twenty-six-story, 640,000-square-foot office building on a site that the law firm had optioned. On Wilshire Boulevard in West Los Angeles, Olympia & York put up a slightly smaller, bronzed-glass tower known as the World Savings Center in conjunction with a Cleveland developer and a savings and loan association. Eddie Minskoff was instrumental in finding and negotiating both of the Los Angeles projects.

In Florida, Olympia & York generally invested alongside the Shapiro family. A pre–World War II immigrant to Canada, William Shapiro had made a bundle turning his Toronto-based Electrolite Products Limited into the largest lighting manufacturer in the British Commonwealth. Shapiro had a plant in North York, not far from the original Olympia Tile warehouse, and had known the Reichmann brothers from their earliest days in property development. In the early 1970s, Shapiro sold his lighting company and moved into the property trade himself, understudied by his son, David, who had got his start working on Olympia & York job sites during his summers away from school. In 1979, the Shapiros decided to move to Florida and prospect for deals in what was then one of the hottest real estate markets in the world and persuaded Albert Reichmann to back them. Olympia & York put up $2 million and Bill Shapiro kicked in $500,000 to create Olympia & York Florida Corporation, of which the Reichmanns owned 80 percent and the elder Shapiro 20 percent.

Operating out of an office in Fort Lauderdale and another in Miami, the Shapiros began buying up undeveloped land throughout southern Florida. Once that $2.5 million in founding capital had been exhausted—and it did not last long—the Reichmanns alone would supply all the additional funds needed. In 1982, Albert agreed to facilitate the elder Shapiro's estate planning by buying out his 20 percent interest in Olympia & York Florida. Although the company's land portfolio already had dropped significantly in value, Shapiro got his original $500,000 back and then some while retaining a residual 20 percent interest in the properties. "In my view," said an Olympia & York executive involved in the transaction, "Albert decided to give Shapiro a gift." A new joint venture company was created, Olympia & York Southeast Equity Corporation, with David Shapiro as the Reichmanns' 20 percent partner. The younger Shapiro put no cash into the new company.

Although Albert would sink more money into the venture with the Shapiros than any of his other partnerships, he fashioned three other development alliances of nearly equivalent significance in terms of the magnitude and number of investments made. Of these, the association of longest duration, predating even the Uris deal, was with Zeev Vered, the only Orthodox Jew among Albert's main partners. Born in Germany, Vered had emigrated to Palestine with his parents in 1935. He left school at thirteen to go to work and later fought in the Israeli army during the War of Independence. In 1950, he emigrated to Canada and picked up a degree in civil engineering at McGill University. In 1956, he moved to Ottawa and set up a construction business, Ron Engineering Construction Eastern Limited. Unlike Olympia & York, Vered's company mainly acted as a contract builder, as opposed to an owner-developer, and grew large and prosperous on government contracts.

The Reichmanns had first crossed paths with Vered in the early 1970s, when Olympia & York branched into Ottawa. Olympia & York did well for itself in Canada's capital, developing Place Bell Canada and two large, high-quality office complexes (L'Esplanade Laurier and 240 Sparks Street) under exclusive lease to two federal government agencies. The speed with which the Reichmann brothers established themselves as a force in Ottawa impressed Vered, who aspired to recast Ron Engineering in the Olympia & York mold—that is, to do less contract building of schools and the like and more development of office towers as a principal. Vered's Israeli-style abrasiveness rubbed many Canadians the wrong way, but Albert admired the toughness and tenacity he displayed in dealing with subcontractors. Beginning in the early 1970s, Olympia & York and Ron Engineering Construction jointly developed two small office buildings in downtown Ottawa and a third on a twelve-acre site on the outskirts of the city. All three properties were managed by Arnon Development, Vered's property management company, as were several other existing properties that they jointly purchased.

As the Uris money began cascading in, Reichmann and Vered raised their sights and broadened their scope. They submitted unsuccessful joint bids on large government building projects in Ottawa, Edmonton, and elsewhere. In Denver, Colorado, they laid ambitious plans for a mixed-use development on 625 acres, only to sell the site they had assembled for $20 million, producing a $7 million profit. In Seattle, they took an option on a site in conjunction with Marshall Field & Company but let it go when plans to build a huge new store came to naught. Reichmann and Vered would bring to completion office-tower developments in Seattle and Portland, Oregon. These properties, as well as an apartment complex in Portland that the partners also built, were managed by

Zeev's son, Arnie, who was one of three Vered brothers (two were trained as engineers, one as a lawyer) to join Ron Engineering.

Albert also put Olympia & York into the notoriously volatile "condo conversion" business in partnership with Oskar Brecher, a senior executive of Cadillac Fairview who had quit the company in 1980 after finding himself on the wrong side of a power struggle at the top. A postwar immigrant to Canada from the Hungarian-speaking region of Transylvania, Brecher was an erudite, cosmopolitan sort with a degree in architecture and an MBA from Harvard Business School. Brecher, who had run Cadillac Fairview's residential development arm from Manhattan, decided to strike out on his own in the fast-money specialty of converting rental apartments to condominiums and co-ops in the New York area. As his tenure with Cadillac Fairview was drawing to a close, Brecher called on Albert and made the case for condo conversion, Hungarian to Hungarian.

Brecher set up a company, American Landmark, in which he owned a 25 percent stake and bought a 300-unit apartment building in Edgewater, New Jersey, which was converted at a cost of $45 million—all of which was supplied by Olympia & York. By the time it became apparent that this project was a money-loser, Brecher had bought an abandoned Alcoa plant in Edgewater and put American Landmark into a partnership with a trio of developers who were Washington, D.C.'s most prolific condo converters. Soon, Olympia & York had nearly $250 million tied up in residential properties in the New York and Washington areas.

Albert also backed a Connecticut developer named David Chase. Born David Cielsa, Chase was a Polish Jew who had emigrated to the United States in 1946 as a seventeen-year-old survivor of Auschwitz and other concentration camps. Settling in Hartford, he attended high school, took engineering classes in college, and got his start in business as a door-to-door salesman. He soon founded a discount department store and had made his first million by age twenty-seven. In the late 1950s, Chase moved into property development in Hartford and then gradually diversified his company, Chase Enterprises, into broadcasting and insurance. By 1986, Chase would appear on *Forbes* magazine's list of the four hundred richest Americans, with a net worth estimated at $185 million.

At the time Chase was first introduced to Reichmann by a mutual acquaintance in 1979, his ambitions still exceeded his net worth by a considerable margin. Downtown Hartford was booming with new construction, and Chase, a beefy man of considerable if gruff charm, persuaded Reichmann to back him in two local office towers—one of sixteen stories and another of twenty-seven—and a seventeen-story tower in Springfield, Massachusetts. Although the ownership of each property was split 50–50, Olympia & York provided 100 percent of the financing, which amounted to about $80 million. With Chase,

Olympia & York also bought an undeveloped twenty-seven-acre tract of land in south Boston and a piece of land in Deerfield Beach, Florida.

———

To John Zuccotti's surprise, Paul Reichmann had insisted on accompanying him to New York City Hall for the final negotiating session over the tax abatement for 466 Lexington. The meeting broke up in the late afternoon of a cool, invigorating spring day in 1980. Zuccotti felt like taking a victory stroll. "Let me show you an interesting development opportunity," the lawyer said to his client. They walked the few blocks to the World Trade Center and through its mezzanine windows gazed upon what Zuccotti jovially described as "the BPCA sandbox"—a desolate ninety-two-acre strip of sand along the western tip of Manhattan Island. This was the first Paul Reichmann had heard of Battery Park City Authority (BPCA) and its tortuous campaign to create a city-within-a-city on landfill from the excavation of the World Trade Center foundation.

The BPCA was a state agency that had been formed by the New York legislature in 1968 to direct the $1 billion mixed-use project. A development master plan had been completed and a $200 million bond issue floated to finance preparation of the site's complicated infrastructure. But the momentum thus generated gave way to inertia as the project became a political shuttlecock batted between state and city and between champions of subsidized housing for the middle class and the poor and advocates of luxury apartment construction. Then came New York City's fiscal crisis and the real estate market's descent into horror. Conditions were especially bad in the Wall Street district, which for years had been losing prime corporate tenants to midtown landlords. Nor was anyone—politicians, builders, or civilians alike—able to muster much enthusiasm for the project's dust-laden plan, which was based on the voguish, 1960s concept of new towns. Battery Park City's apartment and office towers were to be built at opposite ends of the site on multilevel concrete platforms, or "pods," between which, as one critic put it, "pedestrians would be shunted back and forth as strictly as cattle in a stockyard." Then, too, the plan came spooled in red tape, imposing unduly complicated controls over every detail of development. Had not the BPCA already spent most of its bond-sale proceeds, the project no doubt would have been left to die as quiet a death as possible.

But in 1979 Battery Park City was revitalized by a shrewd bureaucratic maneuver that had the effect of putting Richard Kahan in charge of the BPCA. A thirty-two-year-old lawyer with a degree in urban planning, Kahan had worked briefly for Sam Lefrak before his appointment as chief executive of the state's Urban Development Corporation. Inspired by a vision of Battery Park City as "the last great urban laboratory," Kahan commissioned a new master plan on a ninety-day deadline. His urgency was as much a product of dread as enthusiasm, for in November of 1980 that $200 million bond issue started coming due. The state of New York stood behind the bonds and was unlikely to sully itself by letting BPCA default, but Kahan knew that a bailout would be less politically unpalatable if he could get the project moving. Fortunately, the new master plan he received from Cooper-Ekstut Associates was at once more practical and aesthetically appealing. Now, Battery Park City was to be integrated into the city's street grid and harmonized with its existing architecture. The pods, enclosed walkways, and other monolithic elements of the original design were jettisoned in favor of more general urban design guidelines that left developers greater latitude.

In July 1980, a few months after Paul Reichmann had first peeked into its sandbox, Battery Park City Authority invited thirty developers to make proposals for the six million square feet of commercial space envisioned under the new master plan (along with some fourteen thousand apartments in a dozen towers). The members of the Skyscraper Club had always been one-building-at-a-time developers. "They didn't know from master plans," gibed the architect Richard Roth. "To them, a master plan was a building and the sea." To accommodate the local aversion to the risks of megadevelopment, the BPCA had broken up the six million square feet into six separate parcels, each of which was liberally baited with tax abatements. The abatement for the largest plot, which was two million square feet, was 50 percent higher than for the other five. "This was because we believed the hardest parcel to lease was the first," Kahan explained. "Once somebody stepped forward to take it, the other four million square feet would be more desirable."

Reichmann sent Ron Soskolne down from Toronto to make a closer inspection of the sandbox than had been possible from the World Trade Center mezzanine. He was appalled. "From a developer's point of view, it was just awful," Soskolne recalled. "It was a barren wasteland which was pushed up against the side of lower Manhattan. Rumor had it in fact that the mafia used to dump bodies there." On the other hand, the site only looked as if it were in the middle of nowhere. In fact, it was separated from the Wall Street financial district by nothing more than a four-lane road. And it came cheap. According to Reichmann's calculations, the effect of the ten-year tax abatement was to virtually eliminate land as a cost of development and enable Olympia & York to undercut rival downtown landlords by as much as $5 to $8 a square foot.

As Reichmann pondered the economics of building on the Battery, the question that preoccupied him was whether the office market would be able to absorb six million additional square feet in the mid-1980s. The outlook was problematic but encouraging. Since the real estate collapse of the mid-1970s, the downtown market had come back strong. Office rents had nearly doubled since 1978, only about 4 percent of the sixty-five million square feet of prime office space stood vacant, and predictions abounded of a zero vacancy rate by

1982. On the other hand, another economic recession was virtually certain to strike the city (and country) before the Battery Park City office complex could be completed. If the slump was severe, the real estate brokers' carefully honed projections of supply and demand would not be worth the paper they were printed on.

To some imponderable extent, lower Manhattan's vulnerability to recession was offset by the burgeoning of Wall Street employment. The financial services industry, the district's main employer, was expanding at an explosive rate that gave every indication of continuing through the 1980s as old Wall Street was recast in vastly expanded, modern form. In the Uris tower at 55 Water Street, Olympia & York already owned the largest office building in lower Manhattan. It housed several major investment banks, which had begun bidding against one another when space became available internally. Quite a number of rival developers were looking to capitalize on the financial industry's obvious appetite for new space. In fact, Olympia & York's own market research strongly suggested that there already were more than enough office projects in the works to meet Wall Street's demand for additional space. "We concluded," Reichmann said, "that there was no real need for the Battery Park City project."

But the Reichmann brothers and their brain trust of former Toronto city planners also concluded that they could make a success of Battery Park City just the same. "We were confident that we could create a vehicle that would be competitive with the other space available, even allowing for the disadvantage of the location," Reichmann said. In other words, Olympia & York envisioned filling the complex with tenants lured away from rival landlords. "In urban areas the cost of land is generally a more important component of the economics of a project than the cost of building," Reichmann continued. "On this project, we knew that essentially we'd be paying nothing for the land and that therefore we could afford to fill the buildings by offering special deals."

Olympia & York was one of twelve developers to submit proposals to the BPCA in October 1980. Aside from Cadillac Fairview and a lone Chicagoan, all of the other contenders were New Yorkers—among them Sam Lefrak, Harry Helmsley, Robert Tishman, Paul Milstein, and George Klein. Olympia & York alone committed to building all six million feet at once and completing it by 1987, or twice as fast as anyone else. "We are only interested in developing the commercial component of Battery Park if we can develop the entire project as an integrated whole," Reichmann declared in the formal commitment letter he submitted to Richard Kahan. "The whole project must be completed contemporaneously if it is to have the critical mass to overcome its separation from the central business district."

Although Reichmann had radically departed from the Battery Park City Authority's script, he had done so in a way that delighted Kahan, who had simply assumed that the commercial complex would be developed New York–style—one building at a time. The faster the center was built, the sooner BPCA would reap its own rewards and solidify its finances. By the agency's own estimate, the present value of the various payments due it through 1997 under Olympia & York's proposal was $189 million. The comparable figure for the plans submitted by other developers ranged from $145 million to $181 million.

Before the BPCA made its selection, many of the bidders met with Kahan and his assistants and modified their proposals in various technical ways. Paul Reichmann went alone to his meeting with Kahan armed with nothing but a single sheet of blue paper, which he extracted from his jacket pocket after the requisite pleasantries. He unfolded the sheet and gazed briefly at its neat rows of figures. "You have quite a lot of debt here to be paid off," he said. Kahan, who was all too familiar with the BPCA's bond repayments schedule, wearily agreed. Reichmann set the piece of paper on Kahan's desk and pointed. "If I were to guarantee the repayments in that column," he continued, "would I be on the right track to getting the job to develop Battery Park City?"

The column that Reichmann had indicated totaled $50 million. Kahan struggled to keep his composure. "What I really wanted to do at that moment," BPCA's president recalled, "was to jump up from my desk and kiss the man on both cheeks. . . . What Reichmann alone understood was that I had only one urgent concern—paying off those bonds."

But Kahan was silent, as were his minions. "We sat in the room absolutely stunned that someone would put this on the table and we weren't really sure how to respond," said Barry Light, a BPCA vice president. Finally, the agency's general counsel asked a politely skeptical question: How could the BPCA be certain that Olympia & York actually would offer such a guarantee? "Well," Reichmann said, "I just did."

No other bidder was willing to do the same. "I reached essentially the same conclusions as the Reichmanns," conceded Kenneth Laub, a Manhattan broker who advised Cadillac Fairview on Battery Park City. "But I would never have put $50 million on the line like they did. Nor could I, in good conscience, have recommended that my client do it. We just didn't have the experience, composure and confidence of the Reichmanns." In mid-November, the BPCA announced its choice of Olympia & York. The selection was conditional on the signing of a development contract so complex that it would take the agency and Olympia & York a full year to negotiate.

Despite the clear superiority of Olympia & York's proposal, the selection of a Canadian firm generated a fair amount of grousing and political maneuvering. Sheldon Solow, a second-tier New York developer, publicly complained that the selection of an "out of the country" developer was "outrageous" because New York taxpayers' money had carried the project over the years. Sam Lefrak, having been aced out a third time by Olympia & York, was equally incensed. Lefrak had begun working on the Battery Park site in 1973, helping the authority complete the landfill and fashion the site's infrastructure, which included a waterfront esplanade, and building the first apartment complex. The fact was that at $154 million the value of Lefrak's bid fell short of Olympia & York's by nearly $40 million. Nonetheless, he preferred to blame his latest humiliation at Reichmann hands on politics. BPCA "started dealing from the bottom of the deck," Lefrak said, "and we said arrivederci."

The Battery Park project was speculative building of breathtaking audacity. The Reichmanns committed to a project on an unproven and rather déclassé site fully expecting a recession and without the security of having locked in a single construction loan or a single tenant. Olympia & York would have to pay the BPCA $50 million even if it never broke ground but would lose an incomparably greater amount if it built the complex and failed to fill it.

On November 20, 1980—just one week after the Battery Park City contract was awarded—Albert Reichmann scored a coup of equal magnitude as Olympia & York beat out Cadillac Fairview, Campeau Corporation, and a score of other rivals to win selection as lead developer of the Yerba Buena Garden project in San Francisco. Like Battery Park City, Yerba Buena was a hugely ambitious downtown redevelopment project that had languished in political limbo ever since it had been proposed in the 1960s. Not until 1980 did the city get around to soliciting bids for the three-block commercial core of the project. As a West Coast deal, Yerba Buena fell into Albert's purview, and he supervised the preparation of Olympia & York's winning bid with minimal input from his brother. However, his would prove a maddeningly Pyrrhic victory. Over the coming decade Olympia & York would invest about $40 million and come away with nothing to show for it as, for reasons beyond the company's control, Yerba Buena never got off the ground. This was not all bad for Olympia & York: to simultaneously finance both Yerba Buena and World Financial Center might have been a stretch. But for Albert personally the stillbirth of his last best hope at a megasuccess would prove a bitter blow.

Within days of winning the Battery Park City contract, Olympia & York began soliciting proposals from a dozen major architects, seven of whom agreed to submit an initial plan despite the abbreviated three-week deadline set by the company. From the start, one of the leading contenders was Argentine-born Cesar Pelli, who headed Yale University's graduate school of architecture and ran his own private practice on the side. On Christmas Eve, 1980, two of Pelli's designers drove through a snowstorm from New Haven to deliver the plans and models to a lone receptionist standing sentinel in Olympia & York's deserted offices on Park Avenue. With an enthusiasm only slightly diminished by disappointment, the travelers unpacked their boxes and made their sales pitch to the uncomprehending secretary. Cesar Pelli & Associates made the first cut, along with Mitchell/Giurgola and Gunzel Frasca.

At four o'clock one afternoon a few weeks later, Pelli presented a modified version of his initial proposal to a group of senior Olympia & York executives that included Albert Reichmann. That Pelli arrived for this semiformal presentation at Olympia & York's Park Avenue office attired in a tuxedo was a case of gilding the lily if ever there was one. As one Pelli biographer wrote: "One is immediately struck by his politesse and seemingly effortless charm. . . . [He] has an accent, carriage, and courtly manner that would fit nicely into a 1930s film about life on the Riviera." Pelli explained to a nonplussed Albert Reichmann, who was similarly if less formally attired, that he was attending a black-tie affair that evening and would not have time to change.

The Reichmanns entrusted their latest architectural beauty contest to an in-house committee of four: Keith Roberts, Ron Soskolne, Michael Dennis, and Anthony Coombes, a former chief city planner of Toronto who was the last member of the old Crombie contingent to join Olympia & York. The committee made a quick decision. "Cesar Pelli's design stood out head and shoulders above the rest from the very beginning," recalled Soskolne, an architect himself. "What was special about it was that it managed to strike a balance on the one hand being quite simple and easily constructable and on the other hand having a lot of flair, capturing in a sense the essence of what the New York skyscraper had been about historically."

One Sunday morning at eight o'clock, Soskolne got a call at home in Toronto from Paul Reichmann, who was in New York. Reichmann said he and his brother had the day free and wanted to run through Pelli's designs for Battery Park. By noon, all four members of the committee had gathered in Olympia & York's New York office. At first, Paul and Albert reacted coolly. To their eyes, the Argentine's design seemed monumental enough to hold its own against the twin towers of the World Trade Center but a bit quaint-looking to appeal to the high-powered financial services corporations that were their likeliest tenants. Why, in short, didn't it look as austere and imposing as First Canadian Place? Soskolne explained that Pelli's approach was something new in architecture, an attempt to fuse the interior design principles of the minimalist international style that prevailed in the 1950s and 1960s with the more expressive exteriors of the classic skyscrapers of the 1920s and early 1930s, as epitomized by the Chrysler Building. By the time the meeting broke up at 6:00 P.M. the Reichmann brothers had been won over: Cesar Pelli it was.

Five months later, Olympia & York unveiled its design for the complex soon to be known as World Financial Center to universal acclaim. Pelli's design featured four towers with immense bases, ranging in height from thirty-three to fifty-one stories. The towers were set back at the third, ninth, and twenty-fourth floors, evoking the profiles of Wall Street structures of earlier vintage. Each was sheathed in a subtle combination of granite and reflective glass, with the stone slipping away in stages leaving glittering top sections surfaced in glass. Rejecting the flat-top look of modernism, Pelli topped his towers with crowns sculpted from copper, each with a slightly different pyramidal or conical shape. The crowns, noted one critic, suggested "the classical or Art Deco towers of the 1920s and 1930s without nostalgia or whimsy." In addition to the four main towers, two nine-story, octagonal "gate houses" marked the entrance to the complex. The centerpiece of the complex was a glass-vaulted galleria, or "winter garden," nearly as large as the concourse of Grand Central Station. The various buildings were joined by a three-acre plaza, with a formal terrace stepped down to the river's edge and a mile-long waterfront esplanade.

Paul Goldberger, *The New York Times*'s influential architecture critic, praised Pelli's complex as "the finest group of skyscrapers since Rockefeller Center. . . . The four towers are probably the most successful attempt to give life to the skyscraper form in the last generation." Ada Louise Huxtable, the semiretired doyenne of American architecture criticism, followed with a paean of her own in the *Times*, lauding the grouping as "a coordinated and architecturally first-rate urban complex of the standard, significance and size of Rockefeller Center. . . . There has been no large-scale development of comparable quality since the 1930s." Huxtable even had a kind word for the developer: "To everyone's considerable surprise the large Canadian company wanted to do the whole project at once. This is a scale of real estate investment unfamiliar to New York, where developers have traditionally preferred monumental penny-ante operations."

To Paul Reichmann, the comparisons with Rockefeller Center were deeply gratifying, for in deciding to undertake the Battery Park City project he had found inspiration in the history of the twelve-building, Art Deco architectural masterpiece in midtown. Begun in the late 1920s and not fully completed until the start of World War II, Rockefeller Center had been erected during the worst depression in American history. John D. Rockefeller Jr. persisted through public controversies over every aspect of the six-million-square-foot project, including its famous bas-relief sculptures and murals, and in the face of skepticism so universal that it made him the butt of Broadway humor, as immortalized in the Gershwin lyric: "They all laughed at Rockefeller Center." The architecture critics of the day had been equally cruel in reviewing the original plans. "The whole effect," Lewis Mumford had sneered in *The New Yorker*, "is mediocrity—seen through a magnifying glass." Undeterred by the brickbats, Rockefeller not only sold Standard Oil stock to keep the project going through its darkest days but insisted throughout on what he called "the last five percent"—that is, spending one-twentieth extra to ensure premium quality.

In November 1939, "Junior" Rockefeller drove a two-pound, solid silver rivet to complete the steel skeleton of the final building. During the day's ceremonies, which were carried nationwide on the RCA radio network, Mayor Fiorello La Guardia turned to Rockefeller and said: "Look around you and see if you could put up a few more centers in the city." Exhausted, Rockefeller could only smile wanly. Who could have imagined that the person who would finally accept La Guardia's challenge was not a Rockefeller, a Morgan, or a Mellon—or, for that matter, not a Uris, a Tishman, or a Ross—but an ultra-Orthodox emigrant to Canada who, on the day that last rivet was pounded, was a nine-year-old boy counting the weeks when he could leave the Hungarian village of Beled and join his parents in their Paris exile?

Chapter 31

In adding voluminously to Canada's supply of quality office and industrial
space throughout the 1960s and 1970s the Reichmann brothers filled an
economically productive role with élan. To believe that the family deserved to
prosper, one did not have to believe in a just and righteous God—capitalism
alone would do. Fundamentally, what elevated the Reichmann family from
rich to super-rich was not merit but massive economic dysfunction: Paul and
Albert Reichmann were quintessential creatures of inflation.

Inflation had begun agitating the intertwined economies of the United States
and Canada in 1966, just as the Reichmanns were making their transition to
big-time development with Flemingdon Park. In 1973, coincident with the
launching of First Canadian Place, the Organization of Petroleum Exporting
Countries (OPEC) imposed the first of its infamous embargoes, and the rate of
inflation leaped above the double-digit threshold, where it would remain
through most of the remainder of the decade. In 1979, in the rosy afterglow of
the Uris deal, OPEC struck again, bringing about a doubling of oil prices that fed
cost hikes into almost every product and marketplace. From 1966 to 1980 the
average price of goods and services in North America increased by 250 percent
all told—a surge without precedent in the modern history of the continent.

The impact of the chronic inflation of the late 1960s and 1970s was hugely
disparate, making winners of some and losers of others. Whereas investors in
the stock and bond markets saw the real value of their holdings fall sharply,
owners of "hard" assets such as oil, precious metals, and real estate profited
hugely. In most markets, real estate prices did not merely rise with inflation but
outpaced it. The fact that many property owners borrowed heavily to buy added
greatly to their winnings, for in addition to reaping multiple tax breaks, mort-
gagees were able to repay their loans in inflated dollars worth less than those

they had borrowed. A rising tide lifts all boats, but chronic inflation and the high interest rates it engendered also swamped quite a few. The U.S. and Canadian economies were highly unstable in the 1970s, veering confoundingly between boom and bust. Numerous developers large and small were unable to navigate these choppy seas and went under, but by virtue of its cost-effectiveness as a builder and financier Olympia & York fashioned for itself an exceptionally wide margin of error. By the end of the decade, the Reichmanns had amassed a portfolio of about one hundred buildings containing 30 million square feet and generating an annual cash flow of $230 million. By almost any measure, the family ranked among the biggest winners of the Age of Inflation.

The Federal Reserve Board did not begin to make a serious effort to wring inflation out of the U.S. economy until late 1979. As the Fed adhered with newfound tenacity to its tight-money policies, interest rates soared to the highest levels of the twentieth century. The prime rate, the rate banks charged their most creditworthy borrowers, briefly tickled 21 percent. Burdened by the high cost of money, the economy staggered, and in late 1981 fell into a brief but nasty recession that marked the vanquishing of inflation and the beginning of an equally protracted era of disinflation. In terms of investment, the 1980s would be the 1970s turned inside out; stocks, bonds, and other things financial soared in value while the tangible things of the economy lagged and in some cases were sharply discounted. At the same time, the wheel of fortune turned full circle from rewarding debtors to penalizing them heavily. The real cost of money—interest rates adjusted for inflation—would remain exorbitant throughout the 1980s.

That the Reichmanns would utterly fail to adapt to the overriding new reality of disinflation was not for lack of attention to the fundamentals. For years, Paul had tracked macroeconomic trends and their financial implications much more closely than had the typical developer or corporate mogul. As Olympia & York had ascended into the ranks of North America's best-heeled companies, he took full advantage of his ready access to the most astute economic thinkers on Bay Street and Wall Street, including the two most celebrated financial market economists of the day: Henry Kaufmann of Salomon Brothers and Albert Wojnilower of First Boston, the "Dr. Doom" and "Dr. Death" of interest-rate forecasting. Reichmann even added a full-time economist to Olympia & York's New York staff, hiring Michael Astrachan away from Merrill Lynch.

Paul brought to his intellectual analysis of inflation a double-barreled bias born of experience that stretched back to the Old World, before Olympia & York's founding. Tales of the ruinous inflationary spiral of post–World War I Hungary—the Hungary in which Samuel Reichmann had begun his rise to wealth—were embedded in Reichmann family lore. And while an abiding mistrust of the value of paper currencies was virtually a birthright of the Reichmann brothers' generation of European Jews, a generation whose hopes for the future depended on diamonds sewn into coat linings and gold coins stuffed into toothpaste tubes, Paul, Albert, and Ralph were unusual in having come of age in Tangier, where financial volatility was an industry, as sons of a foreign exchange dealer who had put his faith in gold, the dollar, the Swiss franc, and God, though not necessarily in that order.

The efforts of the Fed notwithstanding, Paul and his brothers believed that inflation was ineradicable. As Jack Cockwell observed of the Reichmanns: "They believe that inflation will go on forever and are willing to buy at 20% interest, with a 3% return, figuring that it will work out in the end because inflation will drive up rents and property values." In failing to recognize the Fed's clampdown as an epochal turning point, Paul Reichmann had plenty of company. A decade and a half of constant inflation had produced "a new common wisdom, now shared by the rich and poor and middle class alike," noted one historian. "Steadily rising prices were considered a permanent fixture." In Paul Reichmann's case, conviction would harden into obstinacy even as overwhelming contrary evidence mounted.

Nonetheless, the advent of the Age of Disinflation in itself did not doom Olympia & York. Even without the stimulus of systemic inflation, property values and rents would keep rising in most markets until the end of the 1980s, and Paul would continue to display a singular talent for creating wealth from vacant lots. In time, Paul would overreach his talent and good fortune with the ruinously ambitious Canary Wharf. Ironically, the Reichmann brothers first went wrong in trying to cushion the risks of property development by putting Olympia & York into other businesses. Most large corporations, especially those dependent on an industry as volatile as real estate, seek added stability by branching into other fields. However, the brothers sabotaged their prudent intentions by persistently buying the wrong businesses at the wrong time. The golden touch they had shown from the moment they entered real estate turned leaden outside it.

The Reichmanns' fundamental error lay in concentrating their investment in the energy and natural resources industries. As property developers, the brothers felt a natural affinity for oil, timber, minerals, and the like. "In real estate," Paul once explained, "you must take a long-term approach to the value of investments and the same is true of natural resources." What is more, the value of assets in the ground tended, like the ground itself, to rise with inflation. The Reichmanns' taste for inflation-hedge assets dovetailed nicely with their preference for buying Canadian, since energy and natural resources were by far Canada's two largest industries. "The fact that the base of the company's business remain Canadian was important to Paul," said John Zuccotti, Olympia & York's New York lawyer. "He was very conscious of Olympia & York's place in the Canadian economy."

On the other hand, the fortunes of natural resource producers pendulated in tandem with the general economy, just as real estate did. Thus, the overriding effect of diversifying into natural resources was to reinforce rather than diminish the volatility of Olympia & York's operations while doubling up the Reichmanns' bet on inflation—a bet they began to lose even before they had finished placing it.

The Reichmanns exacerbated their strategic errors by allowing themselves to be sucked into the "takeover game." Adjusted for inflation, the Dow Jones industrial average had declined by half from 1969 to 1979 as North American stock markets in general were reduced to the great discount bin of capitalism. In many cases, companies were trading at big discounts to book value. Why this should have been so was not well understood then nor easily explained in retrospect. But what it boiled down to was this: virulent inflation had leached value from paper money in all forms, including stock certificates. By any historic measure, stocks were cheap as the Reichmanns began diversifying Olympia & York—so cheap in fact that an increasing number of old-line corporations were falling prey to corporate raiders. By the late 1970s, the takeover battle had taken hold as the new blood sport of capitalism, enlivening the lingo of Wall Street with new metaphors of war and mayhem: black knight, dawn raid, freeze-out, greenmail, lock-up, midnight raid, poison pill, shark repellant, and so on.

If Paul and Albert Reichmann were leery of joining the hostilities, it was not because they identified with the beleaguered managerial class or bought into its self-serving rhetoric. As immigrants and as haredim, the brothers had begun at much further remove from the centers of economic power than had the typical self-styled takeover maverick. But the Reichmanns felt no real kinship with the swashbuckling new breed of acquisitor either. Most important, as unassimilated Jews, the Reichmanns were sensitive to the anti-Semitic undertones of takeover warring, which frequently pitted Jewish aggressors against Gentile defenders. Eschewing the hostile takeover, the brothers publicly avowed their intent to make long-term minority investments in well-run establishment corporations. "We want to become important shareholders in many companies with 20 percent to 30 percent positions," Paul told a reporter.

This statement was best characterized as sincere but wishful. In practice, the Reichmanns' stock market investing would prove as much an exercise in improvisation as strategy. In their major investments, the brothers typically would barrel past that self-imposed 20 to 30 percent limit in pursuit of majority ownership and the prerogatives of corporate control.

———

The Reichmanns actually got off to a good start in their stock market adventuring in acquiring English Property Corporation in 1979 for about $140 million. Based in London, English Property owned ten million square feet of office space in England, Ireland, France, and Belgium, but what really attracted the

Reichmanns to the company was its stockholding in the Canadian developer Trizec. The third largest Canadian developer, Trizec was especially strong in its home city of Calgary, a booming oil center that the Reichmanns were eager to enter. English Property held 21 percent of Trizec's shares directly and another 58 percent in partnership with Edper Investments, the holding company of Edward and Peter Bronfman. Although English Property overall owned a larger stake in Trizec than did the Bronfmans, it had ceded control to Edper.

By the late 1970s, the oft-told tale of the corporate disinheritance of Edward and Peter Bronfman had acquired something of the resonance of Greek tragedy. They were the sons of Allan Bronfman, youngest brother to the tyrannical Mr. Sam, who could not forgive his better-educated sibling his successes as a Seagram's executive and finally banished him to the corporate equivalent of Siberia. When Edward and Peter came of age, Sam banned his nephews from the Seagram payroll and eventually forced them to sell him half the stock they had inherited from Allan. Later, the brothers sold the rest of their Seagram shares on their own terms and washed their hands of their hated uncle. Peter, the most withdrawn and driven of the pair, matured into a reclusive multimillionaire of such deep insecurity that he is said to have darned his own socks and worn galoshes on sunny days to save on shoe leather.

By the time that Mr. Sam's sons, Charles and Edgar, assumed control of Seagram, their cousins Edward and Peter had begun building their own company, in which real estate development figured prominently right from the start. In 1971, the Bronfmans merged their real estate development company into Trizec in exchange for 10 percent of its stock and a pair of seats on its board. By the mid-1970s, Trizec was floundering so badly that English Property offered to sell a controlling position to the Bronfmans. Edper Investments sank more money into Trizec, fired many of its senior executives, and reorganized the company, which thrived anew in the booming property markets of the late 1970s.

The Bronfman brothers did not want the Reichmanns or anyone else snatching their crown jewel, and put out a press release stating that "it would regard [O & Y] as an uninvited and unfriendly partner in Trizec." But Edper had no right to dictate to English Property, which had invited the Reichmanns' investment in hopes of warding off the unwanted attentions of a Dutch raider. For their part, Paul and Albert had never met the Bronfman brothers (though they knew them by reputation, of course) and made no effort to establish contact with them, except for Paul's placatory noises in the newspapers. "There has been a very mistaken notion in the press that we are unfriendly bidders," Paul told a reporter. "It is not Trizec we are bidding for but English Property. . . . Trizec is a very well run company and if our offer is accepted for English Property we anticipate doing nothing to change its management structure."

After several weeks of long-distance skirmishing, a six-man Edper team flew to London and prepared to take the fight directly to the Reichmanns by topping their offer for English Property. Late one night, the Edper contingent was relaxing in the lobby of their hotel when in walked Paul Reichmann, suitcase in hand. Reichmann checked in and disappeared into the elevator. A few minutes later, he reappeared, suitcase still in hand, and headed out the door. "I guess he got to his room and found he was in the wrong hotel," recalled Trevor Eyton, Edper's lawyer. "It's the Canadian way at the very least to be courteous, so we went over to shake his hand. He obviously liked that and he obviously didn't want a public fuss, so he said, 'Why don't we go inside and talk?' "

In the lobby of the Churchill Hotel, Reichmann sat down with Eyton and Jack Cockwell, Edper's managing director, and in ten minutes' time hashed out the general terms of a cease-fire. Back in Canada, Olympia & York and Edper refined the understanding reached in London into a formal agreement. "Whenever we reached a difficult point," Eyton recalled, "Paul and Albert would step outside the door for thirty seconds and then come back saying they'd just had a board meeting." Under the terms of disengagement, Edper agreed not to make a bid for English Property. In return, the Reichmanns acceded to Bronfman control of Trizec, contenting themselves with four of the eighteen seats on its board. Olympia & York duly completed its acquisition of English Property and the Bronfmans and the Reichmanns each came away owning about 40 percent of Trizec.

But if the Bronfmans had maintained control of Trizec, the Reichmanns had stolen the headlines ("Joining the Towers That Be," hailed *Maclean's*). And why not? Whereas the Bronfmans merely had held on to what they already had, the Reichmanns had gained an equal share of the profits generated by Trizec's twenty-four million square feet of apartment buildings, shopping centers, and office towers. "I always thought those Bronfmans were smart," quipped Ira Gluskin, Bay Street's leading analyst of real estate stocks, "but it turns out the Reichmanns were smarter." This snap judgment would be validated over the next decade, as Olympia & York's investment in Trizec rose some twentyfold in value, making it easily the most lucrative of all the Reichmanns' stock market gambits.

———

In a movie version of the fight for English Property, the principals would have held their climactic meeting at the airport in Casablanca and afterward Jack Cockwell, as played by Claude Rains, would have turned to Paul Reichmann, played by a bearded Humphrey Bogart in a yarmulke, and said: "Paul, this could be the start of a beautiful friendship."

The pairing of Olympia & York and Edper marked the beginning of an enduring alliance that greatly accelerated the Reichmanns' evolution from stock market neophytes to savvy, hardened takeover players. Without question, the bond between the Reichmann and Bronfman camps was cemented by the mutual respect and admiration of its principals. Even so, the term "friendship" was altogether too sentimental in its connotations to characterize a relationship that began as a shotgun marriage and would remain definitively an arrangement in mutually beneficial expediency.

The strongest of the ties that bound Olympia & York and Edper ran not between the two sets of owner-brothers, who in fact rarely conversed with one another, but between Paul Reichmann and Jack Cockwell, whom even Peter Bronfman conceded was "the heart of Edper." Nine years younger than Reichmann, Cockwell was a Protestant South African who had grown up on a family farm in the Boer country outside Capetown. Despite a runtish physique, Cockwell had boxed and excelled at rugby. "South Africa is a country where you are taught very early to think about survival," he once said. In 1966, Cockwell left his homeland for a job in Montreal. In the employ of the accounting firm Touche Ross, Cockwell distinguished himself as the rare numbers jockey who was as imaginative as he was technically adept. He was, in fact, a prodigy who reinvented accounting technique as he mastered it, much as Paul Reichmann would alter real estate finance to suit his purposes. Among the Touche Ross clients whom Cockwell impressed was Peter Bronfman, who lured him to Edper in 1968.

Cockwell rapidly rose through the ranks at Edper Investments, bringing tenacity and definition to what had been a meandering redeployment of the Seagram's patrimony of Edward and Peter Bronfman. Recasting Edper in the mold of a European merchant bank, Cockwell adopted a highly systematized approach to managing a diverse array of corporations. Instead of buying into underperforming companies and passively awaiting improvement, Cockwell and his patrons preferred to take control—forcibly if need be—and then parachute in a commando team of managers to retool the acquisition to conform to Edper's system. The companies acquired were piled one atop the other in an ingeniously convoluted structure of interlocking ownership designed to maximize Bronfman control while minimizing equity investment. Cockwell built to the sky. By the mid-1980s, Edper would be virtually an economic nation-state unto itself, consisting of 152 companies with assets of $120 billion. "The Bronfmans entrusted Jack Cockwell with their family legacy, and he created a corporate empire larger than that of their cousins Charles and Edgar, and one that rivalled Sam's," observed Patricia Best and Ann Shortell, chroniclers of Edper's rise.

Like Paul Reichmann, Cockwell was a ferociously driven man to whom money and the things it bought meant little per se. Even the famously miserly Peter Bronfman once described Cockwell as "tighter than the bark on a tree." To be fair, he was not merely one to drive a hard bargain, but a corporate monk who wore his three-piece suit like a hair shirt and inculcated Edper with "a Jesuitical approach to business, a disciplined, ascetic, no-nonsense, suffer-in-this-life philosophy." An autocrat who treated public companies like private fiefdoms, Cockwell had such faith in the superiority of his intellect and managerial methods that he tended to react to opposition as a personal affront. His everyday speech was peppered with profanity and his raging assaults on file cabinets and other inanimate objects became the stuff of legend on Bay Street. Fortunately for Edper, Cockwell shrank from contact with the outside world. Even within the empire, he was elusive. "He preferred to be the invisible hand, more than adviser but less than chief executive," noted Best and Shortell.

Although Paul Reichmann did not much care for the South African's bully-boy style, he quickly developed an overriding admiration for his intellect and drive. If truth be told, Cockwell was one of the few businessmen whom Reichmann would come to consider his equal in sheer brainpower—and vice versa. In the final analysis, though, Paul's appreciation of Cockwell was utilitarian: almost invariably, the "Edperizing" of an acquired company boosted its earnings and its stock price.

If Cockwell was Edper's mercurial high priest, Trevor Eyton was its affable minister of state. A college jock turned tweedy corporate lawyer, Eyton was as consummate an outside man as Cockwell was an inside operator. Indeed, until the mid-1980s the business world assumed that Eyton was not just the front man but *the* man at Edper. Unlike Cockwell, Eyton was not all business all the time. He knew how to tell a story, slap a back, and smoke a cigar—whether conspiratorially or celebratory—with the boys. Although the rumpled Eyton looked unassuming, he was in truth a shrewd and secretive deal maker of vaulting ambition. For him, Edperizing corporate Canada was not a holy war but a career move. At heart, Eyton was a nouveau establishmentarian who yearned for appointment to the Canadian Senate, where he envisioned himself holding forth as the business voice of his generation.

Although the Reichmanns would adopt some of Edper's methods in managing their own portfolio of stockholdings, Olympia & York would never give rise to a Cockwell or an Eyton. Paul Reichmann was both owner and operator, a Peter Bronfman and a Jack Cockwell rolled into one. There was no room within Olympia & York for a second mastermind or even a front man. On the other hand, the Reichmanns' hurtling post-Uris expansion left them no choice but to rely increasingly on other people to help run the show, if not share the power. Paul Reichmann had spoken the truth during the English Property battle in disavowing any desire to remake Trizec; he much preferred to invest in well-managed companies that would fatten the family fortune while distracting him as little as possible from the grand real estate projects that so obsessed him. In allying themselves with Edper, the Reichmann brothers gained access to a capacity for corporate management that exceeded their own and thus enabled them to adopt a much more adventurous approach to diversifying Olympia & York.

What Olympia & York provided in return was no less essential to Edper. First and foremost, the money that the Reichmanns invested in tandem with Edper was money that Edper did not have to shell out itself to gain control over a company. In this sense, collaborating with Olympia & York was one of the least financially hazardous of the many ways in which Cockwell leveraged the Bronfmans' equity capital. In addition, the Reichmanns' exalted public image was useful to Edper. Even as they were bonding with the Reichmanns over Trizec, Cockwell and Eyton captured the establishment fortress Brascan Limited in a battle so viciously prosecuted that the government of Ontario promptly enacted legislation to prevent a recurrence. The siege of Brascan irrevocably branded Edper as the piratical bad boys of Canadian business. By contrast, the Reichmanns were seen as gentlemen—"Not Quite Our Sort," as they would say in the clubs, but estimable in their mystifyingly Jewish way and, above all, noncarnivorous.

The corporate establishment was slow to recognize the existence of the new Reichmann-Bronfman alliance and to understand its ominous implications. And so it was that stodgy Royal Trust Company, a venerable Toronto institution that was Canadian old money incarnate, unwittingly turned to Olympia & York in 1980 for help in fending off a rival developer, Robert Campeau, in what was one of the most celebrated contests of the entire takeover era in Canada.

Campeau's bid for Royal Trust was both the latest in a series of misguided attempts to buy respectability and a sound business notion. Pension funds were becoming an important source of financing for real estate development, and the Royal presided over the largest repository of investment funds in Canada. But when Campeau offered $21 a share for a stock stuck in a $12 to $16 trading range, Royal Trust Chairman Kenneth White was incensed. "I don't see why you don't go and take over something else! Really, this is my company," White supposedly railed. At White's behest, a dozen big banks and other establishment heavyweights bought up Royal Trust shares on the stock market and stoutly refused to tender them to Campeau, who tested their resolve by raising his bid to $23 a share. Would White's phalanx of pinstriped bodyguards hold?

White, for one, could not be sure. The Royal's chairman already had exhausted the ready supply of allies, but his investment banking advisers suggested a new name: Reichmann. The idea of breaking open the Royal Trust piggy bank appealed no less to the Reichmanns than to Campeau. Responding to White's cautiously extended invitation to invest in the Royal with an avidity that put the banker's back up, Paul Reichmann said he would gladly buy 50 percent. When White balked, the brothers said that they would settle for 10 percent with the aim of eventually boosting their stake to 20 percent. White decided, in the words of one adviser, that "there was no reason not to be reasonable" and made a fateful misjudgment in admitting the Reichmanns to his coterie of protectors. As Trevor Eyton later put it, White's advisers "went running around and said, 'OK, we've protected you from the big bad wolf,' but Ken White probably never thought to ask, 'What about the big bad bear?' "

Big Bad Paul spent $33 million to buy 9 percent of Royal's shares on the open market. After Campeau conceded defeat, Olympia & York purchased the 5.4 percent holding he had amassed and kept right on buying. Even as Olympia & York's position rose to 23 percent, White maintained a celebratory attitude. (Paul Reichmann explained that Olympia & York inadvertently ended up with 23 percent because of a block purchase and would dispose of the extra 3 percent.) "The Reichmanns said they wanted 20 percent of Royal Trustco and I have no reason to think they want more," White told a reporter. "They're honorable people." White was downright chipper when asked about the Reichmanns at Royal Trust's annual meeting. "We like them," he said. "They're all right." A few weeks later, White's brave face fell as Edper announced that it had acquired 10 percent of Royal Trust. Edper kept on buying, eventually amassing a stake of 17.4 percent to go with the Reichmanns' 23 percent. White was pressured into resigning, and Royal Trust was promptly Edperized.

In the battle's aftermath, the Reichmanns maintained their usual silence. But at a few years' safe remove, Eyton would offer a fishy account of how Brascan had come to invest in Royal Trust. As Eyton told it, Olympia & York had amassed 18 percent of the company before Reichmann showed up at his office one day with a proposition. "He came to us and said, 'I would like you to be a partner in the Royal Trustco investment and I'd be happy for you to manage the investment. We're a separate investor but we'd be happy for you to take the initiative and speak to management,' because basically he knew us and trusted us. We took it as a great compliment. We always knew they liked us so our immediate reaction was to try to do what he asked." Then, too, Eyton acknowledged, Edper already had a stake in the financial services industry and thought that Royal Trust would make an excellent addition to its London Life Insurance Company.

By this time, the Reichmanns and Edper had jointly owned Trizec for more than a year and had recently collaborated on the acquisition of Ernest W. Hahn Incorporated, one of the largest U.S. shopping center developers. If the Reichmanns had been loath to shoulder the additional burden of managing a company in their own industry, it strained credulity to think they would have leaped at acquiring control of a bank trust company without advance assurances of aid from their Edper allies, with whom they were in frequent contact.

The matter was touchy for several reasons. First, it was emphatically not in the Reichmann brothers' best interests to be seen as a stalking horse for Edper and the Bronfmans. Second, under federal and provincial law, stock purchases amounting to more than 10 percent, if made simultaneously by buyers acting in concert, constituted an illegal takeover bid. The awkward, lawyerly phrasing of Eyton's recollection of Reichmann's invitation—"We're a separate investor but . . ."—betrayed a sensitivity to the issue of collusion.

In investigating the Royal Trust affair, the Ontario Securities Commission (OSC) focused on the opposite issue: Had White failed his fiduciary duty to his shareholders in organizing the Royal's incestuous defense? A visibly uncomfortable Paul Reichmann was summoned to testify, as were a dozen establishment worthies, in four days of hearings. In slapping White's wrist with a brief ban against trading his personal accounts, the OSC overlooked the hugely pregnant questions of when Olympia & York and Edper had teamed up in pursuit of Royal Trust and what terms of agreement bound them to one another. To put it mildly, Paul Reichmann had never been one to trust implicitly anyone outside his family or religious community. Nor were the Edper boys, whose stock in trade was domination and control, the sort to casually rely on partners whose wealth and willpower equaled their own.

The Trojan Horse conquest of Royal Trust cemented an alliance between the Reichmanns and Edper Bronfmans that would have far-reaching consequences not only for the parties themselves but for Canada. By the middle of the 1980s—the takeover decade—just nine families would control half the shares of the three hundred companies that comprised the main Toronto Stock Exchange index. The Reichmanns and the Edper Bronfmans arguably were the two richest of the lot and unquestionably the most acquisitive. But even as their money power would combine to dramatic, public effect, the inner mechanisms of their partnership would remain willfully obscured from view.

———

The English Property deal was the first of several lucrative investments that Olympia & York would make in other developers. But when the Reichmanns ventured away from the familiar terrain of property, they tended to overpay in acquiring corporate assets. No matter how intensively Paul studied other industries, he never would master them the way he had real estate. Fundamentally, his missteps were less a product of ignorance than of the arrogance of certitude. Given the inevitability of continued inflation, what would it matter in twenty or thirty years if he had had to pay a premium of 10 percent or even 50 percent over present value to acquire a well-endowed oil or timber producer? The important thing was to buy the company and tuck it away before somebody else did. And so in 1980 and 1981 the Reichmanns plunged headlong into natural resource stocks, laying out nearly $1 billion to make a half-dozen investments at the very top of a horribly inflated market.

The OPEC-engineered price hikes of the 1970s had sent the profits of North American oil companies through the roof. Although subtle signs of disinflation's impact were evident as the 1980s began, the majority view was that the bonanza would continue indefinitely—or at least as long as supplies held out, for the industry's delight in its gusher of good fortune masked an undercurrent of rising concern about the declining rate at which major new oil fields were being discovered. When fear and greed come into synchronous alignment in the stock market, look out. In 1981, the billion-dollar takeover—a historical rarity—became commonplace as a dozen major energy and resource companies became the object of frenzied bidding contests.

Canadian corporations were disproportionately involved in the mania, for reasons that had as much to do with politics as geography. Foreign domination of Canadian industry had been a burr under the saddle of Canadian national pride for a century or more. During the 1970s, nationalist resentment had risen in tandem with the soaring price of oil and other commodities. In October 1980, the long-standing protectionist drift of Canadian economic policy culminated in the enactment of a radical set of measures known as the National Energy Program (NEP). Its aim was to force the return of Canadian resources to Canadian ownership by subsidizing domestic producers and penalizing foreign ones in ways both subtle and brazen. The NEP went so far as to authorize the expropriation of much of the acreage that foreign-owned oil companies held in the rich Hibernia and Beaufort Sea fields within the Arctic Circle.

For acquisition-minded Canadian companies like Olympia & York, the nationalist backlash was a godsend. Even before the NEP was enacted, the Reichmanns entered negotiations to acquire a controlling stake in Brinco Limited, the natural resources company that—coincidentally—once had been run by Bill Mulholland of the Bank of Montreal. As a foreign-owned company, Brinco increasingly found itself hamstrung by restrictions imposed by the Foreign Investment Review Agency, an arm of the federal government. Enter the Reichmanns, who negotiated the purchase of 50.1 percent of Brinco for about $95 million. The investment bankers that Olympia & York hired to help with the transaction had argued that Brinco's asking price was too steep. Paul Reichmann "thanked them and told them he was not seeking such advice." Olympia & York's investment enabled Brinco to close on a pending $88 million acquisition of Cassiar Resources Limited, a British Columbia asbestos producer predominantly owned by foreign interests, thus enabling the Reichmanns to "Canadianize" two companies at once.

With Brinco in hand, Paul Reichmann made a play for a much larger Canadian oil producer—Hudson's Bay Oil & Gas, which was controlled by Conoco, the ninth largest U.S. oil company. Dome Petroleum, Canada's largest home-owned oil producer, wanted to acquire Hudson's Bay and refused to take no for an answer. After it had been rebuffed by Conoco, Dome retaliated by making a tender offer for 20 percent of Conoco's own shares. To raise the cash it needed to defend itself, Conoco decided to sell its stake in Hudson's Bay after all—but not to Dome. Morgan Stanley & Company, Conoco's investment banking adviser, knocked on Olympia & York's door in its search for an alternative buyer. The Reichmanns submitted a bid of close to $1 billion for Hudson's Bay, but it was lost in the tumult of larger events. The liquor giant Seagram Company Limited stepped in and threatened a takeover of Conoco, which found a white knight in E. I. du Pont de Nemours & Company. Du Pont came away with a controlling interest in Conoco, Seagram with a minority stake, and Dome Petroleum got Hudson's Bay after all.

Next, Paul Reichmann drew a bead on Hiram Walker Resources, an old-line Canadian distillery company that had diversified into oil and gas. Reichmann thought Walker a good investment in its own right but also hoped to persuade its chief executive, Bill Wilder, to join with him in making an acquisition. Wilder had been a senior officer of Gulf Canada, the second largest Canadian oil producer. Gulf Oil, the American multinational giant, owned 60 percent of Gulf Canada, and Reichmann hoped to do to it what Dome Petroleum had just done to Conoco: use the club of heavy stock purchases to persuade an American company into parting with its Canadian subsidiary. Reichmann quietly accumulated a block of Hiram Walker shares in the open market and then telephoned Wilder to invite himself over for a "brief chat." Reichmann did not have far to go since Hiram Walker had its headquarters in First Canadian Place.

As Reichmann walked into his office, Wilder quipped, "Have you come to collect the rent, Mr. Reichmann?" As Wilder later explained it, he was only trying to put his visitor at ease. To Reichmann, though, Wilder's comment seemed more gibe than joke. "No," he replied coolly. "I checked before I came and it's fully paid." It was all downhill from there. Wilder was not interested in taking a run at Gulf Oil, and the Hatch family, Hiram Walker's upper-crusty founding family, was disinclined to welcome the Reichmanns as minority partners in their company. Reichmann believed that his 10 percent stake (assembled at a cost of $200 million) warranted a seat or two on Walker's board at the least, but his hints to this effect were pointedly ignored. He would neither forgive nor forget.

Although they failed to land a major oil company, the Reichmanns did not come away empty-handed from the megadeal frenzy of 1981: they acquired the Canadian pulp and paper manufacturer Abitibi-Price for $536 million. The brothers had been content to own 10 percent of Abitibi-Price, the largest newsprint producer in the world, until the wealthy Pathys shipbuilding family of Montreal offered to buy a large block of stock at $27.50 a share. The Reichmanns countered with a bid of $28, and then Kenneth Thompson, a billionaire publisher who was one of Abitibi's biggest customers, stepped in with a $31 offer. The Reichmanns raised to $32, and the bidding war came to an abrupt end as Thompson and the Pathyses sold their shares to Olympia & York, which ended up owning 94 percent of Abitibi. Paul conceded that he had not invested in Abitibi with the goal of acquiring the company but had just "reacted to the bidding."

A few months later, Reichmann acted even more impulsively in acquiring a stake in Macmillan Bloedel, Canada's largest producer of lumber and plywood. Macmillan Bloedel had become a pawn in an epic attempt by Edper to take over Noranda Mining, the grand old man of Canadian mining, with vast holdings of copper, zinc, gold, and other minerals. In desperation, Noranda Mining retaliated by offering to buy a big chunk of Macmillan Bloedel. A Bay Street broker got a line on a 20 percent block of Macmillan and offered it to Paul Reichmann, who reacted as a trader might, buying it on the spot for $280 million. Reichmann kept half the shares and sold the rest to Noranda, which thereby gained control of the lumber company. In the end, though, Edper just opened its jaws wider and swallowed both Noranda and Macmillan Bloedel. The Reichmanns held on to their shares in both companies and thus maintained a partnership with Edper that encompassed four corporations: Trizec, Royal Trust, Noranda, and Macmillan Bloedel.

The Reichmanns' stock market spree was mercifully cut short in the fall of 1981 by the advent of a severe recession belatedly induced by the tight-money policies the Fed had adopted two years earlier. The natural resource stocks deflated like an overcooked soufflé as panic buying was supplanted by panic selling. By mid-1982, the market value of Abitibi-Price, the Reichmanns' largest investment outside real estate, had fallen by $200 million. All told, the Reichmanns' hastily assembled stock portfolio had lost about one-third of its $1 billion value, saddling the brothers with the first public financial debacle of their careers. Unlike many investors, the Reichmanns held tight to their natural resource shares as Paul publicly reaffirmed his faith in an inflationary future. In mid-1982, the Federal Reserve Board relaxed its stranglehold on the U.S. economy after thirty-three months of pain inflicted in the name of long-term gain. The economy soon regained its footing, triggering a sharp decline in interest rates and an explosive autumn rally in the stock and bond markets. Natural resources and other inflation-hedge stocks rebounded from their lows but lagged behind the market averages and would continue to do so throughout most of the coming decade. Reichmann had got it exactly wrong: the Age of Disinflation was at hand.

Chapter 32

In entering the stock market—the floodlit center stage of capitalism—the Reichmanns unavoidably attracted more attention to themselves than ever before. Business reporters from throughout Canada followed the English Property–Trizec, Royal Trust, and Abitibi-Price dramas as closely as their sportswriting colleagues tracked the annual struggle for the Stanley Cup. In the United States, Olympia & York's maneuverings became a staple of *Wall Street Journal* coverage for the first time. The barrage of breaking news begat the usual explosion of feature articles, and the Reichmanns found themselves profiled in national business magazines and splashed across the front pages of newspapers. The effect of this journalistic outpouring—much of which was adulatory in tone—was to enhance the legend of the Reichmann brothers and retail it to a much larger audience.

In a page-one profile of the brothers entitled "Billion-Dollar Men" published in the summer of 1981, the *Globe & Mail* noted the "sense of awe they have inspired in people who watched them build their empire bloodlessly, calmly, systematically" and then delineated The Legend of the Reichmanns:

It is said that in an industry the public generally considers ruthless and disruptive, the Reichmanns offer stability and reliability.

It is said that they consummate deals worth millions with a handshake and then keep their word even when, in time, the deal becomes less advantageous for them.

It is said that their business acumen is second to none.

It is said that they are the smartest real estate people in the world.

So much has been said so often that Paul Reichmann, the 50-year-old vice-president of Olympia and York, can only look terribly tired and shake his head at hearing the laudatory allegations yet again.

"The usual exaggeration," he says of whatever plaudit is handed him for comment.

As the article implied, whatever role the brothers had played in mythologizing themselves had been unwitting and involuntary. The Reichmann qualities of reserve and humility were genuine—even if these traits did indeed redound to Garboesque effect as Olympia & York's rise to prominence brought the spotlight swinging the brothers' way.

During the company's fledgling years, the Reichmanns had gritted their teeth and granted the occasional interview to an enterprising reporter. Like most proprietors of privately held companies, the brothers had drawn the line at opening their books to the press but understood that a certain amount of publicity was useful in establishing their commercial credibility. In 1965, a *Globe & Mail* photographer even persuaded Albert, Paul, and Ralph to pose together informally in their offices. While building a new office tower for the *Toronto Star* a few years later, Paul and Albert had done their bit to help their client publicize the project. But as Olympia & York came into its own in the 1970s, the Reichmanns indulged their innate reclusivity and spurned reporters and photographers alike. When Albert unexpectedly encountered a clutch of press photographers at a reception for an Israeli official at the Oakdale Golf and Country Club in Toronto, he hid behind a column for nearly two hours and then dashed the lensmen's last hope by walking backward from the room. A second group photo of the Reichmanns did not enter the public domain until 1981, when the brothers were snapped paparazzi-style while attending their first annual meeting of Abitibi-Price.

Although Paul was no less averse to self-exposure than were his brothers, he developed a more sophisticated view of the uses of corporate publicity in directing Olympia & York's stock market maneuvering. The fact was that contests for control of public corporations often were determined by the manipulation of public opinion, and to simply refuse to deal with the press was to tie one's hands. However, to offer for-the-record comment was to risk locking oneself into an untenable position, and so, like many other takeover warriors, Reichmann added the not-for-attribution interview to his deal maker's arsenal. As circumstances required, at times he was willing to go on the record and even on occasion to cooperate in the researching of a profile of Olympia & York that ranged beyond the topical confines of its latest acquisition move.

At the same time, Paul posted the boundaries of his life outside business with "no trespassing" signs. Publicity "can't be avoided," he admitted, "but I would like personal things to remain private." The author of the *Globe & Mail* piece cited above described Paul as displaying "thinly veiled revulsion" at her suggestion that he and his brothers were newsworthy personally. "I have never believed that anyone reads, remembers or cares about all that silliness that is published about where we come from or who we are," Reichmann snapped. "Your readers are not interested in that. As people we are no different from any other of the three million people around this city."

This was the single most outlandish thing Reichmann would ever say for quotation. The notion of the Reichmanns as regular Toronto Joes was simply ludicrous, as Paul himself no doubt realized. What is more, the press had not yet given him call to complain about invasion of privacy; the sum total of biographical information published about the family to this point amounted to a few innocuous—albeit error-marred—stock paragraphs slipped into articles focused on Olympia & York itself. And yet Paul's uncharacteristic churlishness was understandable as a symptom of the psychic strain brought on by the family's mounting wealth and prominence, for his and his brothers' object was not merely to minimize personal publicity but to continue to segregate themselves socially in hopes of preserving a distinct, ultra-Orthodox identity.

It was easy enough for the brothers and their wives to politely refuse the increasing number of invitations extended them and to restrict their socializing to the same tight ultra-Orthodox circle as before. Even in business, Albert and Paul mixed as little as possible, taking the risk of offending Bill Mulholland of the Bank of Montreal by routinely spurning his invitations to attend the dinners the bank held on the sixty-eighth floor of First Bank Tower to expose its corporate clients to such barnstorming eminences as Henry Kissinger. "Paul had a completely compartmentalized life," said the investment banker Robert Canning, who continued to speak with Paul three or four times a week well into the 1980s. "I never even knew if he had children or didn't have children." Nor were the Reichmanns tempted to indulge themselves in the usual material trappings of nouveau billionairehood. Paul was able to add to his collection of rare Judaic religious texts and Albert to buy the occasional canvas by Chagall, but there were no palatial new homes, no chauffeured Rolls-Royces, no yachts, no Learjets, no stables of pedigreed mounts, and so on. Outwardly, the private lives of which the Reichmanns were so protective changed not at all even as Olympia & York's spectacular growth added zeros to the family's net worth.

For the Reichmann brothers and their wives, the overriding challenge of their commercial success lay in preparing their children to assume responsibility for the family empire while at the same time insulating them from the corrupting effects of the wealth and celebrity they had amassed. If this was the generic dilemma of the parent as billionaire, it was exacerbated in the Reichmanns' case by the exacting requirements of their faith; their mission was to raise offspring who were not merely competent and well adjusted but devoutly observant. "I used to ask Paul all the time, 'How can you raise your children in conditions like this and expect a normal generation?' " recalled an ultra-Orthodox neighbor of Reichmann's. "He would just smile and say nothing. Paul very much believed in God and I think he felt that a religious upbringing would balance out the problems, that it would influence his children in the right direction against this evil, the money."

Reichmann himself did not consider money evil per se, but he did indeed adopt a spare-the-Torah-and-spoil-the-child approach to child rearing, as did all four of his brothers. Paul took the added precaution of limiting his children's exposure to Olympia & York, going so far as to avoid all mention of the company in their presence. "Basically, I did whatever I could to keep Olympia & York out of the daily lives of my children," he said. "I wanted that they should grow up no different from their classmates. There are too many rich homes where the children grow up to be bums or develop all kinds of negative traits." Albert took the opposite tack, bringing home the scale models of every one of Olympia & York's buildings for his kids to play with. "The business wasn't highlighted for me. It was just always there, like electricity," recalled Albert's eldest son, Philip, who greatly enjoyed accompanying his father on his Sunday inspections of construction sites.

To a far greater degree than the heirs of most moguls, the next generation of Reichmanns bore the burden of living up to not only their forebears' outsized accomplishment but their impossibly exalted reputation. The awed regard of the business community was not the half of it. Within the teeming global village that was ultra-Orthodoxy, Olympia & York was considered the pinnacle of haredi commercial achievement—a quasi-miraculous exception to the rule of low-wage servitude and penny-ante entrepreneurship that predominated among the observant. But what elevated haredi admiration for the Reichmanns to near reverence was the constancy of their religiosity in the face of their secular success. "The Reichmanns are the only super-rich people I know of who stayed Orthodox," observed Joe Lebovic, a developer who himself fell away from the strict Orthodoxy of his Hungarian youth as he amassed millions of his own in Toronto. "They gave a big boost to the Orthodox community because for the first time people could say, 'Well, we have our rich people, too—in fact, the richest of them all.' "

Philip Reichmann recalled being "startled" when a few hundred guests showed up at his bar mitzvah in Toronto in 1972. "That was probably when the family's special standing first dawned on me." By the early 1980s, the Reichmanns had no rival as the first family of global ultra-Orthodoxy. Their "honesty, modesty and philanthropy were all spoken of in haredi communities as a 'kiddush hashem' [divine blessing]," noted the Israeli journalist David

Landau in a book chronicling the worldwide haredi renaissance of the 1970s and 1980s. "Rabbis and writers apostrophized them in reverent hyperbole, reminiscent of eighteenth-century Jewish religious leaders' worshipful rejoicing over Nathaniel Mayer Rothschild, the devout founder of the famous banking house."

As was only to be expected, the Reichmanns' children would turn out to be considerably more acculturated than they were themselves. The younger generation spoke English without an accent, for a start, and tended to be a bit less rigid in matters of observance, less sedate in appearance, and more inclined toward displaying if not luxuriating in their wealth. Edward's daughter Malky offended tradition by divorcing as a young woman, while one of Albert's daughters, Libby, went so far as to marry outside the fold. But what was most remarkable about the next generation of Reichmanns and Hellers—the generation composed of Samuel and Renée's twenty-seven grandchildren—was their essential homogeneity in terms of religious belief and practice. In embracing the strict, traditionalist Orthodoxy of their parents, the first post-Holocaust generation of Reichmanns maintained a continuity that spanned three centuries and as many continents.

In fact, the Reichmann sons typified their generation of North American haredim in being much more thoroughly steeped in the Torah than their fathers had been. Even Philip, who had been fixated on Olympia & York from boyhood, spent eight years in yeshiva before embarking on a business career at twenty-one. (His father had never gone to yeshiva.) In his own estimation, Paul, the best-educated member of his generation, could not hold a candle to his two sons, Barry and Henry, both of whom would remain full-time students into their late twenties. "My sons outwardly are much more modern than I am, but their commitment to study is much stronger," Paul said with evident satisfaction. "Today, the average young person in his twenties has a much, much broader knowledge than his parents had. There may be a greater gap between knowledge and practice than in the past, but immersion in the book does set certain parameters of behavior."

If anything, one could argue that the Reichmanns and their wives were too effective as parents, for their success in inculcating Orthodoxy seemed to have been achieved at a loss of individuality in their charges. Even to some friends of the family, the next generation on balance seemed blandly ordinary, excessively normal. One close observer went so far as to dismiss the lot as "ciphers and nonentities." This seems a harsh judgment in several respects. To begin with, it fails to recognize the family's own emphasis on Torah learning, at which quite a number of the boys excelled. Second, it makes no allowance for youth; the majority of the Reichmann heirs were still in their twenties or early thirties when Olympia & York collapsed in 1992 and could not be expected to have yet come into their own, precocity not being a typical third-generation trait. Most important, perhaps, it underestimates the sheer difficulty of growing up Reichmann, of coping simultaneously with the pressures of outsized expectations and an exacting regimen of religious instruction.

———

This third generation of Reichmanns covered such a broad expanse of years that it constituted virtually a generation and a half. Its eldest member, the Tangier-born Malky, was only fourteen years younger than her Uncle Ralph but twenty-five years older than her youngest cousins, who were born in the early 1970s. Even so, the Reichmann cousins—like their parents—formed an exceptionally tight-knit group. Albert's, Paul's, and Ralph's children had grown up together as neighbors in North York, as had Edward's and Louis's in Outremont. And the Canadian cousins had overlapped with one another and with their London relatives at yeshiva and at countless family and religious gatherings. "My children's generation of the family is very close," said Marika Reichmann, Louis's wife. "They get together on every occasion they can."

The various branches of the Reichmann cousinhood differed importantly from one another only in the way they related to the overwhelming, mushrooming presence of Olympia & York. Albert's, Paul's, and Ralph's sons had come of age in the company's shadow, subtly but firmly encouraged by their fathers to assume that they would inherit not only the largest portion of one of the world's great fortunes but collective responsibility for running the family company, as well. Most of the older sons and sons-in-law of the Toronto brothers eventually made an effort to accept this intimidating destiny and joined Olympia & York, however briefly and unhappily. (The notion of a daughter working at Olympia & York or anywhere else lay beyond the pale of haredi respectability.) Thanks to the redistributive effect of Samuel Reichmann's will, all twenty-seven cousins stood to inherit Olympia & York stock, albeit in unequal amounts. Yet not a single descendant of the three eldest Reichmann siblings—Eva, Edward, and Louis—ever worked for the company.

Resisting the pull of Toronto, the extended family's center of financial gravity, had required no effort whatsoever on the part of Joseph, Edward's only son. The eldest male of his generation, "Yossi" Reichmann, as he was known, was acknowledged within the family as its outstanding Talmudist. As a young boy in Outremont, Yossi had made a habit of leaving for school so early in the morning that passing police patrols used to pick him up and bring him home, assuming he was out on the street without permission. At thirteen, the boy had gone away to Monsey and at sixteen moved onto Ponovezh, bearing an armful of letters of introduction, which his father had solicited from prominent rabbis. Yossi Reichmann excelled at Ponovezh and maintained a close association with its head, the venerable Rabbi Eliezer Schach, long after he had left yeshiva.

Yossi married at age twenty-one, and two years later, in 1972, reluctantly entered business. "My son was never interested in business," Edward Reichmann confessed. "I pushed him into it."

Edward assigned his son a supporting role in his comeback business venture. After emigrating to Israel in 1968, Edward had bought land in Kiryat Ono and built a factory for custom-printing textiles by means of a heat transfer technique newly developed by the Swiss company Ciba (now Ciba-Geigy). The business was an immediate success. At commercial fairs throughout Europe, Reichmann struck up relationships with textile manufacturers and formed 50–50 joint ventures to replicate the Kiryat Ono plant in New York, Paris, London, Capetown, and Melbourne. In each case, an Israeli work crew built the factory and trained the workers with capital supplied by the local partners. Edward sent his son to New York to represent him and learn the business as his eventual successor.

Succession soon proved a moot issue as Edward Reichmann's dreams of corporate empire again foundered. The Ciba-Geigy technology he had licensed only worked with synthetic fabrics. As the fashion in yard goods began shifting back to natural fibers in the mid-1970s, Reichmann at least managed an expeditious exit from a collapsing market. He sold the Kiryat Ono plant for $1 million and salvaged a comparable sum by selling all of his interests overseas, except for New York, which proved temporarily unsalable. It finally was unloaded at a loss in 1978. Luckily, Yossi Reichmann had dabbled in real estate during his apprenticeship. With his father's backing, he had acquired and renovated a half-dozen tenement buildings in the East Village section of Manhattan. These apartments provided an income sufficient to permit Yossi to return to full-time study in Israel and support a family that eventually numbered seven children.

Turning down teaching positions offered by various yeshivas, Yossi Reichmann founded a tiny kollel. On a side street in Jerusalem, he cultivated obscurity and knowledge with equal avidity in a school that he did not even bother naming. He wrote but did not publish and taught but did not fund-raise, preferring to finance the kollel out of his own pocket with help from his father. The school's $50,000 annual budget covered room and board for fifteen to twenty students. "When my son is learning with his boys, he seems more like one of the students than a teacher," Edward said. "He's exactly like his mother: he likes to go unnoticed." But if, in his modesty, Yossi was his mother's son, he long ago earned the admiration of his father, the businessman.

Louis Reichmann, meanwhile, had succeeded where brother Edward had failed a second time, founding a business in New York that he was able to pass on to his two sons. Louis had devoted his first year in Queens to a futile effort to reenter the business of importing ceramic tiles but in 1969 unloaded his tile inventories and began importing stationery and school supplies, mostly from

Japan, which he knew from his years with Olympia Floor. Reichmann soon integrated wholesaling into the manufacture of pens in Japan under the brand name "Buffalo." In 1970 Louis Reichmann America Corporation acquired another midsized importer of school supplies, DriMark Products, which operated out of a large warehouse on Long Island. All of this was accomplished without fraternal assistance. "None of my brothers were involved," Louis recalled, with evident satisfaction.

Increasingly worried about DriMark's dependence on Japan as a source of supply, Reichmann scouted Italy but was unimpressed by the quality of the pens and other school supplies available for export. Adopting the same basic strategy that Olympia Floor & Wall Tile had employed in acquiring a Canadian tile producer in the early 1960s, Reichmann in 1981 built a state-of-the-art factory of his own in Port Washington, Long Island, to manufacture a full line of pens and markers. When the plant was completed, Louis's older son, Charles, left yeshiva at age twenty-two and went to work for DriMark as understudy to his father. Louis's other son, Andre, who had supplemented his own yeshiva training with an engineering degree, joined the company a few years later. DriMark's push into the domestic manufacture of writing instruments proved a resounding success. By the mid-1990s, the company's annual turnover had more than quadrupled even as the percentage of its sales derived from imports had declined from 100 percent to 10 percent. "It became an American company," said Louis, who had turned over daily management of the company to his sons and settled into a contented semiretirement, a multimillionaire in his own right.

That none of Edward's and Louis's children chose to return to Canada, site of their fathers' humiliating business failure, was not surprising. But the combination of proximity and detachment maintained by their Heller cousins was curious indeed. With Eva's encouragement, two of her three sons and all three of her daughters and their husbands would eventually settle in Toronto. That each of the Heller sons and sons-in-law entered property development in Canada and yet never worked for Olympia & York said as much about the Hellers' pride in their late father's distinguished rabbinical lineage (his namesake, the original Yomtov Lipmann Heller, known as Tosafoth Yomtov, is still widely studied to this day) as it did about Reichmann exclusiveness. "I didn't grow up thinking of myself as a Reichmann," recalled Philip Heller, the eldest of Eva's sons, with a smiling hint of diffidence. "We were a bit off by ourselves in London and at the time my mother's family was just my mother's family. My uncles weren't yet the heroes they became."

Evelyn, the eldest of Lipmann and Eva Heller's six children, was the first to move to Toronto. In 1972, she had married Paul Jacobs, a New Yorker whose wealthy industrialist father, Harold Jacobs, was one of the most prominent Orthodox lay leaders in the United States. The couple settled in New York City, where young Jacobs worked as a real estate lawyer. Quickly disheartened by life in the least civil of American cities, Evelyn Jacobs lobbied for a change of venue. The Jacobses scouted Los Angeles, Baltimore, and other cities before moving to Toronto in the spring of 1974. "We looked around but I had family in Toronto," explained Mrs. Jacobs, who had inherited her mother's vivacity and good looks.

A few months later, Evelyn's brothers, Philip and Anthony, arrived from London in search of greener entrepreneurial pastures. After four years at Gateshead, Philip had joined Heller & Company in late 1970. A few months later, the footsteps in which he had just begun to follow were obliterated with his father's death and the ruination of the family firm. Philip worked for a time at a zipper factory that his father had owned in partnership with another man until it was sold and then kicked around in a series of dead-end jobs. After Philip married and Anthony finished yeshiva, Eva urged her sons to go to Toronto and learn the real estate business at their uncles' knee. "I'm sure if we had wanted to, we could have gone to work at Olympia & York," Philip recalled, "but it was always envisioned that Anthony and I would run our own business. We have entrepreneurial blood in our veins."

The Heller brothers did take an office in newly completed First Bank Tower and cut their teeth on a small industrial development in North York that had been brought to Olympia & York by a third party looking for a joint venture partner. The Reichmanns financed the project and took a 30 percent equity interest, leaving 20 percent for their nephews. The Hellers parlayed this first effort into other industrial construction projects of their own and also branched into small apartment buildings and shopping plazas. Often they acted in concert with their brother-in-law, Paul Jacobs, who had also hung out his shingle as a developer. Although the Hellers now found and financed their own projects, they continued to rely on their uncles' counsel. "We were able to get their time when we needed it, pretty much equally," said Philip Heller, who, after a few years' hard slogging through the ditches of the property business, began to second-guess the virtues of self-reliance. But when he spoke with his Uncle Paul about joining Olympia & York, he was gently dissuaded. "He said Olympia & York had become so big that we would end up learning the company, not the development business," Heller recalled. It is likely that Paul also was leery of allowing his nephews a decade's head start over his own two sons, who had yet to complete grade school.

In 1979, yet another Heller—Vivian—moved to Toronto with her husband, Joseph Solomon, who also went into real estate, setting up yet another small firm. Although each of the Hellers and Hellers-in-law prospered in real estate, in the astronomy of Toronto business they were like well-formed balls of dust orbiting Jupiter. This was unfair in the sense that the Hellers proved themselves skilled, respectable operators who sank their own money into projects of their own devising. On the other hand, the Reichmann aura was so powerful during Olympia & York's heyday that important doors had a way of opening at the mere whisper of family connection.

In March 1981, the extended Reichmann family gathered in Antwerp to celebrate the engagement of Rachel Heller, Eva's youngest, to Morris Brenick, the son of a local wealthy diamond dealer. Among the guests was a diamond merchant named Natan Gutwirth, a widower five years older than Eva. Edward Reichmann had known and admired Gutwirth's brother in Paris after the war. Taking the role of matchmaker upon himself, Reichmann invited Gutwirth and his sister to his hotel suite for coffee and cake. "Of the six of us Reichmanns, my sister was the biggest personality," Edward said. "By that, I mean that she was the sort of person who could walk into the White House and see the president and would not have to prepare for it. It would have just come naturally to her. Natan Gutwirth is also a personality."

When the conversation turned to one of Eva's favorite subjects—her family's Holocaust rescue efforts—Gutwirth held his own. Gutwirth was a Dutch Jew who had been studying in the famous yeshiva in Telshe, Lithuania, when Germany invaded Poland in 1939. With the Nazis closing in from one side and the Red Army from the other, Gutwirth helped persuade the honorary Dutch consul in Kaunas, Lithuania, to provide a thousand visas to the Dutch colonies of Curaçao and Dutch Guiana, now known as Suriname. With these visas, the Orthodox community in Telshe was able to obtain transit visas to Shanghai, which was then under Japanese occupation, from the Japanese consul, Chiune Sugihara, who was later dubbed the "Japanese Schindler." With hundreds of fellow Lithuanian bachurim and fifteen thousand other Jewish refugees all told, Gutwirth waited out the war amid the relative safety of Shanghai, which was to East Asia what Tangier was to Europe. Gutwirth's tale impressed Eva, who spent a few more days in Antwerp than she had planned.

Not long after her daughter's engagement party, Eva herself was engaged (sans party). Just two weeks after Rachel wed Morris Brenick in Toronto in July 1981, Eva married Natan Gutwirth in New York City. Although, in keeping with Orthodox custom, none of Eva's children attended her wedding, her remarriage was enthusiastically endorsed by the whole Reichmann family. Eva settled in Antwerp, where, by all accounts, she thrived. "She was quite happy with her second husband," said Alex Heiden, the Antwerp diamond dealer who had had a crush on Eva as a young man in Tangier. "She made a beautiful apartment in Antwerp." She offered to give her home in Golders Green to any one of her six children willing to return to London and live in it, but there were no takers. Eva sold the place to Ralph Halpern, the brother of Ralph Reichmann's wife, Ada.

In mid-1982, Rachel Brenick gave birth to twins in Jerusalem, where her husband was studying at kollel. As she had done after the birth of every preceding grandchild, Eva flew to Jerusalem to take over her daughter's household for a few weeks. During her stay in Jerusalem, Eva took the family for a weekend in the resort town of Tiberias. On a Sunday afternoon Eva went down to the Sea of Galilee and wrote a farewell letter to her children on the letterhead of the Plaza Hotel. She assured her daughter that she had never felt better but that at the age of sixty-two she wanted to make certain that she was prepared for death, whenever it might come.

After spending a year in Jerusalem, Morris and Rachel Brenick moved to Toronto, completing the Heller family tableau. (David Heller, the family Torah scholar, was the only one of Eva's children who did not move to Toronto, remaining in Israel.) Brenick spent his first year and a half in Toronto studying in the Reichmann-funded kollel on Coldstream Avenue and then entered business as a wholesaler of pearls. After six months in the pearl trade, Brenick surrendered to destiny and entered property development. Like his Heller in-laws, Brenick spurned the offer of employment at Olympia & York. In partnership with Anthony Heller, he renovated a little shopping plaza in the "Beaches" section of East Toronto and went on to do a series of similar projects on his own.

The Hellers constituted a family circle within a circle, in that they generally preferred one another's company to that of their Reichmann cousins. Even so, they, too, settled in the same area of North York and took their place within the Orthodox community that coalesced around their rich relations. Among them, the Hellers had two dozen children, all of whom attended Yesodei Hatorah or the Bais Yaakov schools along with their Reichmann cousins. Every Saturday at noon without fail, the Hellers showed up at Renée Reichmann's house on Dalemount Avenue to join in the family's Shabbat Kiddush and pay obeisance to the matriarch of the dynasty. "Eva's kids may be the smartest of their generation," said a source privy to the family's inner workings. "Ultimately, though, their lives aren't quite their own."

———

Philip Reichmann was the first member of his generation to join Olympia & York. Born in Tangier in 1957, Philip gravitated to business as naturally as his cousin Yossi had taken to Talmud, working summer jobs at Olympia & York throughout his years at yeshiva. During the building of First Bank Tower, Philip was given the job of prying open crates of marble cladding and comparing the serial numbers on the back of the panels to the numbers on the building plans. "It was very frustrating," he said. "There wasn't a single one missing." After a final year of schooling in Jerusalem, Philip returned to Toronto in 1978 and joined the company full-time. He was promised nothing. "I was made to understand that it was whatever I made of it," he said. "There was no plan laid out for me. It was, 'Let's see where this goes.'" For the first year or so, he struggled to find his bearings. "It's not easy for any young person to get in step in an organization that's already up and running fast, and it's certainly not a simple matter when you're the boss's son," he said. "I might have fantasized about leaving, but I never seriously considered it."

At his own request, Philip began in the retail leasing department as assistant to the man responsible for renting out the many shops in First Canadian Place. When his boss left the company six months later, he was promoted to fill the vacancy. After another year in retail leasing, young Reichmann was shifted into a position closer to the heart of the company as understudy to the vice president in charge of office leasing for Canada. In 1980 his new boss was transferred to the New York office, and Philip replaced him. Not yet twenty-four, he now was director of leasing for the biggest developer in North America. Philip displayed none of his Uncle Paul's precocity of talent but he was hardworking, sensible, and likable—much like his father.

Although the entire family took comfort in knowing that there was at least one member of the next generation willing and perhaps able to take responsibility for the corporate legacy, the rapidity of Philip's rise seemed to stir ambivalence in his Uncle Paul, who had succeeded perhaps too well in insulating his children from the distractions and temptations of Olympia & York. Both of his sons were devotees of Talmud who showed no inclination toward business and, in any event, were eight and fifteen years younger, respectively, than their cousin Philip. Vivian, Paul's eldest child, had married Israel Muller, a Brooklyn boy in the Yossi Reichmann mold—a talmid hacham. In the ultra-Orthodox marriage market, a scholarly youth like Israel Muller was considered a catch, and Paul was proud to support his son-in-law in his regimen of full-time study. As the yeshiva world's leading patron, he could hardly have done otherwise. Still, he had the politics of succession to consider, too.

Enter Frank Hauer, the scion of a well-to-do Orthodox family in the nursing home business in Los Angeles. Born in 1958, a year after Philip Reichmann, Hauer was a well-mannered, studious sort who had spent ten and a half years at a yeshiva in Cleveland. In 1980, he was introduced to Rachel "Goldy" Reichmann, Paul's second-born daughter, by mutual friends of the two families. Frank Hauer and Goldy Reichmann was a match very nearly not made. "Our first meeting didn't go so well," Hauer said with a delicacy that suggested it would be his last word on the subject. "A year later it was suggested that we meet again." They were married in Toronto in 1982 and moved to Israel, where Frank continued his studies at a kollel. A year later, the impending birth of their first child prompted a move to Toronto. The new father became a full-time student at the Institute for Advanced Talmudic Training, the Reichmann-sponsored kollel on Coldstream Avenue.

Hauer had always planned to go into business one day but was in no hurry to leave the life of the Book. One Saturday evening about a year after Hauer had moved to Toronto, his father-in-law took him aside at a Shabbat gathering and said, "It would be my last wish to push you to leave the kollel, but. . . ." Reichmann explained that Jack Gringorten, Olympia & York's longtime head of property administration, wanted to retire but was willing to remain another year to groom a successor. Paul told his son-in-law that this was an ideal opportunity to enter the company, that property administration was one of the foundations of the real estate business and complementary to but distinct from leasing, his nephew Philip's bailiwick. Hauer said he would have an answer the next day. That night he talked it over with his wife and decided to accept his father-in-law's offer. The very next morning, Gringorten dropped dead of a heart attack. Paul Reichmann asked Malcolm Spankey, the Bank of Montreal's recently retired property manager, to fill in for Gringorten long enough to groom his son-in-law for the job. Spankey was honored to accept.

Hauer was allowed to wean himself from Talmud. For the first year, he basically shadowed Spankey from 9:00 A.M. to 2:30 P.M. in Olympia & York's offices downtown and then drove out to the kollel and studied until 6:30. Hauer's only problem on the job was remaining alert. "You get a little bored just observing," he said. "Where it really got interesting for me was when we had to rework a very badly written management contract for a building in Ottawa. We spent a lot of time clarifying many words and phrases in the contract and I felt very much at home in this." Spankey gradually shifted his operating authority to Hauer, who was awarded the title of vice president well before his two-year apprenticeship officially ended. Ironically, he established a closer working relationship with Albert than with his own father-in-law; Gringorten had reported to Albert, and his successor continued the tradition. Meanwhile, Hauer and Philip Reichmann proved highly simpatico, recapitulating in their own way the early relationship of "Mr. Paul and Mr. Albert," as Hauer respectfully called them. "Philip and I confided in each other right from the start," Hauer recalled. "He was the best sounding board I had."

As Hauer completed his corporate training, Ralph Reichmann's burly, blue-eyed son David was beginning his. Born in 1960, David would prove the most driven and entrepreneurial of all the Olympia & York cousins. In addition to the burdens of dynasty that he shared with Albert's and Paul's children, the gregarious David was freighted with the frustrations of his father, the forgotten, ultra-introverted Reichmann brother. Although the marginality of Ralph's role was largely of his own making, by some accounts he could not forgive Paul his dominance and looked to his three sons and especially to David, his eldest, to redress the talent imbalance in his own generation. Ralph "expected David to get everything he didn't and couldn't," a friend of David's recalled. "There was a lot of pressure to 'best' Paul. [His parents felt] the only one who could rival Paul, in terms of intelligence and charm, was David."

David followed directly in the footsteps of his Uncle Paul in attending Gateshead and Ponovezh, excelling in his studies at both yeshivas. Not long after his twenty-first birthday, he decided that the time had come to return to Toronto and join the family business. "I went to my father and my uncles and I said I want to learn business properly," David recalled. "I don't want to be the head of a department because I'm my father's son. I want to understand the guts of the business—for the responsibilities I had to take on in the future. My father and uncles, they started at the bottom. They went through every department. They had many advisers and have many advisers, but they know the guts of the business."

The family hired a business school professor from York University to instruct David and his younger brother Steven in the fundamentals of business. They were joined by Albert's second son, also named David, who was six years younger than Philip. For six months, these three immersed themselves in secular learning in an office on the thirty-first floor of First Bank Tower. "It was good for them," said Philip, who was a bit envious. "If I had it to do over again, I would have done the same thing." After their tutorial, the Reichmann boys fanned out through the company: David I moved to New York to work on World Financial Center; Steven joined Trizec, the development company the Reichmanns controlled in tandem with the Edper Bronfmans; and David II took a job at Abitibi-Price and then was rotated to Bramalea, a development company acquired by Trizec. Both David I and Steven ended up working under their father at Olympia Floor & Wall Tile, as did their younger brother, Abraham.

Over the years, the Reichmann tile operation had grown enormously, as Ralph broadened its product line to encompass the universe of flooring materials and expanded its tile manufacturing capacity. The largest wholesaler of tiles in Canada by a wide margin, Olympia Floor and its affiliates would sustain a rapid pace of growth through the building boom of the 1980s. At its peak in 1988–89, the tile company would employ 3,200 workers and was netting $130 to $140 million a year after taxes on sales of $300 to $325 million—a profit margin of about 45 percent. Olympia Floor's extraordinary profitability was entirely Ralph's doing. Right from the start, his most salient trait as a businessman had been exceptional tenacity in controlling costs. "Albert and even Paul were a lot more easy-going than Ralph," recalled Bill Minuk, the engineer who ran Olympia & York's general contracting operations in the early years. "As a contractor I was used to thousands of dollars washing in and out, but here was Ralph worrying about fractions of a penny."

Olympia Floor & Wall Tile was big but not big enough to accommodate Ralph and his three sons. "Ralph is not an easy man to work for, and he was a lot tougher on his sons than any of us," said a longtime Olympia Floor manager who worked closely with all three Reichmann boys at one time or another. "He gave them areas in the company to run but still they always had to go back to daddy to check A, B, and C. They are smart boys, with a real business mentality, and they had some great ideas but Ralph did not want to change." David and his brothers were captives of a cruel irony indeed, thwarted by the father who had pushed them to excel to compensate for the blighting of his own ambitions. All three would leave Olympia eventually and go into business for themselves (Steven invested in a computer technology venture with the eldest son of one of the Edper Bronfmans), prompting a dismayed Ralph to anoint one of their Gestetner cousins as his heir apparent.

—

In mid-1984, Edward and Edith Reichmann stopped by Antwerp to visit Eva on their way home to Israel from a trip to North America. Eva had recently completed an extensive remodeling of the house in which her new husband long had lived and wanted to show off her handiwork. It seemed to Edward that his sister was not quite her usual exuberant self. Eva made no complaint but fed herself a steady diet of aspirin. From Antwerp, Edward and his wife flew on to Zurich, intending to spend the weekend. On Saturday evening, just after Havdalah, Natan Gutwirth called from Antwerp with bad news. Eva had fainted and had been rushed to the hospital. She had regained consciousness but was completely disoriented.

The next morning Edward and his wife caught a six o'clock flight back to Antwerp. By the time they arrived at the hospital at 8:30, Eva was undergoing exploratory surgery. At noon, a young doctor called Mr. and Mrs. Reichmann into her office. (Gutwirth had left the hospital briefly to tend to some urgent matter.) The doctor said that Eva had a brain tumor and that it was probably malignant, though further tests were needed. "I didn't want to believe her," Edward recalled. Even so, he immediately placed transatlantic calls to each of his brothers, leaving it to them to convey the bad news to their mother. He could not bring himself to call her.

Early the next day, a conscious but still deracinated Eva was wheeled onto an airplane, accompanied by her relatives and a physician. Upon landing, she was taken by ambulance to New York University (NYU) Hospital, where she was examined by Dr. Joseph Ransohoff of NYU and another specialist. In testing Eva, the doctors had drained the fluid that had built up around the tumor. When the anesthetic wore off, Eva had regained coherency. Dr. Ransohoff gave it to her straight: tests had confirmed that she had a malignant and inoperable brain tumor. "He was so direct and matter of fact with her that both Natan and I wanted to kill him," Edward recalled. "By a week later, though, I realized that he'd taken the right approach." Because Dr. Ransohoff had been so blunt, Eva found a measure of solace in his statement that he had had patients with similar tumors who had undergone chemotherapy and survived a few years. "She accepted that she was dying," Edward said, "but she thought she had longer than she did."

The only Reichmann sister spent most of the last eleven months of her life in New York undergoing treatment. Besides the chemotherapy, her skull was opened periodically to drain the fluid that had accumulated. When not in the hospital, Eva stayed with her brother Louis and his wife in their home in Kew Gardens, Queens, where she received a continuous stream of visitors, including her children, her brothers, and her eighty-six-year-old mother. Occasionally, she traveled to Toronto, where she stayed with her son Philip and his family. By all accounts, she was stoic in her suffering. "My sister remained a believer—religiously," Edward said.

In the midst of Eva's treatment, Morris Brenick's father, Joseph, died suddenly in Antwerp. On his way to Belgium, young Brenick switched planes in New York City and was astounded to find his mother-in-law and her brother Louis waiting for him at John F. Kennedy Airport. "All she had to do was look in the mirror to know she was dying, but she never complained once," Brenick said. A few weeks later, on December 25, Rachel Heller Brenick gave birth to her fourth child and first son. By Orthodox custom, the first-born son is to be named after one of his two grandfathers. It is customary as well for husband and wife to take turns naming their children. It was Morris's turn, which meant that the new arrival would be named after Joseph Brenick rather than Lipmann Heller. "The first thing my mother-in-law said when our son was born was, 'Oh, your mother is going to be so happy,' " Brenick said. "That a person so close to dying would put someone else's happiness ahead of her own to me was extraordinary."

Eva Reichmann Heller Gutwirth died on January 14, 1985, in Toronto. A few months before, Edward Reichmann had sought to defuse what he termed "a very delicate situation" by posing a question to one of Israel's preeminent halakic authorities: Should a widow who remarried be buried next to her first husband or in a place of her second husband's choosing? Rabbi Shlomo Auerbach ruled in favor of the first husband and, at Edward's insistence, put it in writing. With Natan Gutwirth's assent, Eva was laid to rest next to Lipmann Heller in a cemetery plot she had bought herself on the Mount of Olives.

Chapter 33

I n most people, success induces a creeping conservatism, as the lust for more is increasingly counterbalanced by a fear of losing hard-won gains. More than anything else, it is the compulsion to persist in taking outsized risk in pursuit of outsized reward ad infinitum that separates the empire builder from the corporate custodian, however growth-minded he may fancy himself. The Reichmann brothers illustrated this principle in continuum, with Ralph occupying the conservative end of the spectrum, Albert the great middle, and Paul the pole of continuous, compulsive hazard. In essence, Paul doubled his developer's bet at every step of Olympia & York's grand progress from Flemingdon Park to First Canadian Place to World Financial Center to Canary Wharf.

The World Financial Center was much more daring in concept than First Canadian Place, being three times as large and located on the fringes of settlement rather than in a prime downtown block. In implementing the Battery Park scheme, Reichmann compounded his risk by adopting a dubious marketing tactic to which William Zeckendorf had famously resorted in the 1950s to get Place Ville Marie off the ground in Montreal. In his initial prospecting for tenants, Zeckendorf had run into a wall of antipathy toward himself as a foreigner and toward his project, which, in the view of the Montreal establishment, was impossibly ambitious. The New Yorker did not break through until he induced the Royal Bank of Canada to move into his tower by buying its headquarters building. To attract tenants to First Canadian Place, Paul Reichmann had bought out the occasional lease but never an entire building. In Manhattan, he found himself in the same position that had bedeviled Zeckendorf in Montreal: he was an outsider promoting a radical notion in the face of universal skepticism and scattered hostility. When the U.S. economy nosedived into recession in late 1981—not quite a year after Olympia & York had won the Battery Park contract—Reichmann's vision of a showplace office complex sprouting from a sandbar along the Hudson River appeared more of a chimera than ever.

The buying of an old building to fill a new one is essentially a short-term financing strategy. With a major lease or two in hand, a developer can go to a bank or insurance company and borrow the money needed to finance construction of the new building. (Meanwhile, the purchase of the old building is mostly self-financing, as the developer typically is allowed to simply take over the existing mortgage.) Eventually, the developer is left with a large vacancy in the old property when the tenant occupies its new quarters. If he fails to fill it, and if the new project proves uneconomic, the developer suffers a double disaster: two money-losing investments supporting two mortgages.

The first office tower that Olympia & York agreed to buy in hopes of solidifying the World Financial Center concept was 59 Maiden Lane, a 932,000-square-foot building in the heart of the Wall Street district. It was owned by City Investing Company, a conglomerate best known for its Home Insurance subsidiary. In 1979, City Investing had put its fifteen-year-old headquarters up for sale, but its broker, Cushman & Wakefield, had found no takers, Olympia & York being one of a dozen prospective buyers who thought the $175 million asking price too steep. After Olympia & York had landed the Battery Park contract, John Cushman III returned to Paul Reichmann to pitch a new idea: buy 59 Maiden Lane, and City Investing will lease space in the first of the Battery Park towers. After much hard negotiating, City Investing leased 700,000 square feet for thirty-five years at rents a bit above the going rate and Reichmann took 59 Maiden Lane off its hands for the full $175 million. "I credit the Reichmanns with keeping things on an even keel," Cushman said after the deal was done. "They are warm people who don't lose their sense of humor just because a billion dollars or so is at stake. You can't appreciate those qualities unless you've been in this world of upper-end real estate. It is filled with very strange, very nasty creatures."

For Olympia & York, the transaction amounted to little more than a promising start. Some 89 percent of the planned space remained unleased. Although City Investing was a blue-chip tenant, it was not the sort of company that compelled emulation, being neither a household name nor a pacesetter in the emergent financial services industry.

Then, once again, opportunity knocked as if on cue. As the City Investing negotiations were coming down to short strokes, Paul Reichmann got a call from Peter Cohen, the chief executive of Shearson Loeb Rhodes, one of Wall Street's biggest brokerage houses. American Express, the venerable charge card and traveler's checks giant, had just acquired Shearson in a billion-dollar transaction hailed as a landmark in the emergence of the new Wall Street. As part of a postacquisition housecleaning, American Express had decided to sell its headquarters at 125 Broad Street. To this end, Cohen and a few other senior executives gathered in the office of James Robinson, the chief executive of American Express, to consider likely buyers. "The only one we could think of was Olympia & York," Cohen recalled. Having once shaken Paul Reichmann's hand (though he could not quite remember where or when), Cohen volunteered to make the phone call. "The conversation went like this: 'Paul, do I have a deal for you. Here's what we want to accomplish,' " Cohen recalled. "Within 48 hours he'd come down from Toronto to see us."

Sanford Weill, American Express's newly installed president, shouldered aside Cohen, his former protégé, and took charge of the negotiations. When the rubble of write-offs and bankruptcies was cleared from the new Wall Street in the early 1990s, Weill would stand unchallenged as the shrewdest deal maker of the whole misbegotten era of financial services empire building. This Brooklyn-born son of Polish immigrants had built Shearson by absorbing scores of failing brokerages and then sold his creation at a premium price to a premium company. As president of American Express, Weill would hasten its transformation into a financial supermarket. Long before the American Express experiment went awry, costing first Cohen then Robinson their jobs, Weill would switch corporate horses. As chief executive of Primerica, he would build yet another financial services combine, which by the mid-1990s ranked among the twenty largest corporations in America. In a field surfeited with grand theorists and airy conceptualizers, Sandy Weill was a shirt-sleeved pragmatist who excelled at fitting together complex corporate machinery.

American Express's initial preference was to sell 125 Broad and lease back the space it occupied in the 1.2-million-square-foot structure, which was not far from the 59 Maiden Lane building and of roughly the same vintage. As it turned out, though, AmEx could not take full financial advantage of selling unless it vacated the premises. Moving into a new building would have the added advantage of enabling American Express to cohabit with Shearson, which had its head office in the World Trade Center. Reichmann suggested the City Investing deal as a prototype: Olympia & York would buy 125 Broad if American Express moved into one of Battery Park's four towers. Begun in September 1981, the Reichmann-Weill negotiations soon foundered on mutual exasperation. "Paul doesn't do anything precipitously," said Cohen, who acted as Weill's second. "You could say something to him and he might not respond for ten minutes or more. He was impossible to negotiate with in this deal, just torture. But it wasn't all Paul. Sandy was always afraid that Paul was getting the best of him, since he didn't know real estate. Sandy likes to revisit issues, too, and this time he was extra careful."

By February 1982, Reichmann and Weill were ready to resume their struggle with renewed urgency. Reichmann made a critical concession in agreeing to give AmEx an option to buy half of Tower A when its lease expired. He even promised to build a fireplace for Weill, who had had to move heaven and the New York City Building Department to get a fireplace in his 106th-floor office in the World Trade Center. Meanwhile, James Robinson, a courtly Southerner born and bred to the corporate elite, applied the balm of due regard. One evening the American Express chairman put in a call to Reichmann at his suite in the Waldorf Towers, which was just a few blocks from Robinson's own midtown residence. "I'd like to come and meet you," Robinson said, "because I'd like to know my landlord."

Robinson's deference flustered Reichmann. "No, no," he responded. "I'll come and see you."

Robinson persisted. "Really, Paul," he said. "I think I should come and see you."

The courtesy call that Robinson did in fact pay would not have been noteworthy had not Reichmann himself recounted its circumstances so frequently. "The point is that Reichmann told the story with great admiration and sentimentality," said an investment banker who heard the anecdote several times while helping Reichmann raise funds for Canary Wharf in the late 1980s. "It was the courtesy of it that got to Paul. He seemed quite touched by the fact that the chairman of this establishment giant would make a point of coming to see him. Why else attach such importance to a ten-minute car ride?"

On March 22, 1982, Olympia & York dropped its latest bombshell on the Skyscraper Club: a preliminary agreement with American Express on what that company proclaimed in a press release as "the largest real estate transaction in history." Olympia & York would buy 125 Broad for $240 million and lease two million square feet in the largest of the four Battery Park towers to American Express for $2.2 billion in rent over thirty-five years. An exultant Paul Reichmann posed for a press photograph in which he, Robinson, and Weill peeked out playfully from between the oversized scale-model towers of the office complex. With nearly half of the six million square feet in office space now spoken for, Olympia & York was emboldened to bestow a new name, World Financial Center, on what basically was still a fourteen-acre hole in the ground.

The reaction of the real estate trade was polarized between public hosanna and private fulmination. "This is monopoly of the highest level," waxed Edward S. Gordon, who ran an eponymous real estate brokerage that ranked among the city's largest. If the Reichmanns held on to the AmEx and City Investing buildings, they would upon completion of the World Financial Center own twenty million square feet, which amounted to about 8 percent of the city's total office stock and was more than twice the inventory boasted by their nearest rival, the Rockefellers. "They have made the project real," Gordon continued, "and they have closed off other new construction downtown for the next three or four years. . . . Why should anyone go head to head with them, builder or lender?"

As a rule, New York developers, as opposed to brokers, were appalled at the Reichmanns' willingness to buy and empty existing office buildings to fill new ones—especially at such rich prices. Olympia & York had agreed to pay $240 million for an undistinguished building that American Express had bought in 1974 for $32 million; in terms of price, this was the Uris deal reversed. "All they did," sneered one anonymous skeptic in the *Times*, "was buy a tenant." John Zuccotti found himself besieged as he made his rounds of the real estate establishment. "A very successful developer told me in all seriousness that he thought Paul was stark, raving mad," Zuccotti recalled. Sam Lefrak, who had taken to privately calling Paul and Albert by the derisive nickname "the rabbis," predicted that even if Olympia & York succeeded in filling World Financial Center the company would collapse from the effort.

As it turned out, Reichmann and Weill would spend another year negotiating one another to death. Before the transaction they had tentatively agreed to and so publicly celebrated in March could close in June, office rents in Manhattan began declining steeply as the recession took its toll. Meanwhile, Congress enacted attractive new tax breaks for office-building owners. After confessing to having second thoughts, Weill told Reichmann that American Express now preferred to buy rather than lease a tower in the World Financial Center. While Reichmann's own preference had always been to maximize Olympia & York's ownership, he was only momentarily disheartened. American Express's eagerness to become an equity partner in World Financial Center reflected even more favorably on the project and also would reduce the burden of financial risk that Olympia & York bore. Weill's change of heart also gave Reichmann an opening to negotiate a lower price for 125 Broad.

The two again quickly reached agreement in concept only to spend months hashing out the details. Instead of leasing 80 percent of Tower A, American Express committed to buying and occupying the entire building, which Olympia & York would build and sell to AmEx for $478 million. In exchange, AmEx reduced the price of its old headquarters by $80 million, to $160 million. In revealing the new terms of arrangement, Weill sounded exasperated: "We agreed on a basic deal in March, and that deal, I would guess, has changed fifty times. And what you're seeing is the fifty-first version." Even so, Weill would walk away from the marathon negotiations professing admiration for his adversary across the table, admitting that he had been impressed and perhaps even a bit intimidated by Reichmann's ability to negotiate without resorting to notes. "He is very tough," Weill said, "and very, very smart."

———

Paul Reichmann was as relentlessly innovative a financier as he was a property developer. These two facets of his singular talent were intertwined, for the rapidly mounting scale and complexity of Olympia & York's undertakings put a premium on financial creativity. Increasingly, though, high finance became a second outlet for Reichmann's commercial perfectionism, if not quite an end in itself. In the hothouse environment of the 1980s—an era of rampant financial experimentation—this alternate aspect of Paul Reichmann's risk-taking compulsion came into full flower. "There really is no one like him in the world of finance," Stephen Karpf, a Wall Street banker specializing in real estate, said in 1989 as the anything-goes era drew to a close.

In 1983, with the U.S. and Canadian economies having rotated from severe recession to robust expansion, Reichmann set a goal of borrowing $3 billion over the next two years, using the Uris properties as collateral. His plan was to use half of this staggering sum to pay for the construction of World Financial Center and a half dozen other office projects—Albert's deals—in Portland, Dallas, Boston, and other U.S. cities; to finance another round of stock market investments; and to pay down high interest debts that Olympia & York had taken on in 1980–81. Reichmann began his borrowing program in conventional fashion, refinancing one of the Uris buildings (245 Park Avenue) with a $220 million mortgage from Aetna Life & Casualty Company. This was one of the largest mortgages ever written and yet it left him far short of $3 billion. To Reichmann, the implication was clear: to sustain its rapid growth, Olympia & York would have to tap novel sources of financing.

In Canada, Olympia & York had raised part of the long-term financing for First Canadian Place and other buildings by floating the occasional public bond issue, but these were of modest size and did not trade widely. In the United States, the Wall Street investment banking house Salomon Brothers had over the preceding decade pioneered a new genre of finance by pooling together thousands of home mortgages to create mortgage-backed securities. Having already "securitized" more than one-quarter of the $1 trillion of the home mortgages in the United States by the early 1980s, Salomon Brothers was keen to apply the same basic methodology to office buildings and shopping centers but needed a developer with the stature and daring to put the concept over with investors. "Olympia & York was obviously the preeminent group in North America," recalled Lewis Ranieri, Salomon's resident genius of real estate finance. "I knew it would make a great bell cow."

That Paul Reichmann and Lew Ranieri one day would do business together was a foregone conclusion, given that both were intellectually avid, grandly ambitious men obsessed with the intricacies of real estate finance. While their interaction would prove invaluable to both Olympia & York and Salomon Brothers, the two forged a bond that transcended corporate affiliation. After Ranieri was ousted from Salomon in a 1987 power struggle, Reichmann would pony up $50 million to help Ranieri set up his own investment bank. "Paul was one of three people who helped me when I needed it most," Ranieri recalled. And when Olympia & York came crashing down five years later, unleashing a flood tide of anti-Reichmann revisionism, Ranieri stood by him in private and in public.

Their relationship had begun in 1980, when Ranieri dropped by Olympia & York's headquarters to introduce himself. He returned frequently to Toronto as he made his endless circuit around North America as a traveling preacher of the gospel of securitization. "It took me a while to get to Paul; he was much more secretive then even than he is now," recalled Ranieri, an ebullient, unvarnished Brooklynite who had gotten his start at Salomon in the mailroom. "I tried to give him all the free advice I could. I tried to make myself valued and not behave like some rug merchant showing up just when he has something to sell." But sell he did, though it took a while for Reichmann to warm to Ranieri's vision of a securitized future. "Paul didn't know what I was talking about at first," he continued. "Unlike some people at the time, though, he listened and caught on quickly. He's a powerful intellect."

Much as he liked Ranieri, Reichmann was no one's pet guinea pig. In the fall of 1983, he interviewed a half-dozen Wall Street investment banks before finally hiring Salomon Brothers to help craft a landmark $1 billion financing. Eventually, it was decided to jointly securitize two of the Uris buildings—1290 Avenue of the Americas and 2 Broadway—and the Park Avenue Atrium. All three buildings were fully leased and had risen greatly in value since Olympia & York had acquired them. As part of the "due diligence" required of it as manager of the offering, Salomon Brothers had to analyze all 250 tenant leases, hire a structural engineer to inspect the buildings, retain real estate appraisers to establish their current market value, and do their own projections of the rents these properties would generate over the next ten to fifteen years. The object was to demonstrate to investors a high degree of probability that Olympia & York would be able to repay the $1 billion it was borrowing, with interest. To make the case, Salomon Brothers had to put in its sales prospectus detailed financial information of a sort that Olympia & York had never before disclosed, even to many of its bankers. "I had a real tug of war with Paul over this," Ranieri recalled. "Ultimately we got what we needed, but it was like pulling teeth with pliers."

Technically speaking, what Olympia & York did was to pool the financing on the three buildings into a new first mortgage and then sell fifteen-year notes backed by the liens against the buildings. On Salomon's advice, the interest rate on the notes was to be adjusted monthly, floating not quite two percentage points above the Treasury bill rate. This was done to make the notes more appealing to savings and loan associations, which were loath to be locked into fixed-rate mortgages now that regulation had forced them to begin paying variable rates of interest to depositors. Even so, Salomon Brothers' salesmanship was sorely tested. Half of the institutions that had tentatively committed to invest pulled out after further pondering the risks of New York real estate. In the end, Olympia & York fell a bit short of its goal as some forty investors—predominantly S&L's—bought $970 million worth of notes. Even $30 million shy of $1 billion, the financing still ranked as history's largest commercial mortgage transaction by far.

Over the next few years, Olympia & York would become the first developer to raise large sums in the U.S. commercial paper market, where the most credit-worthy corporations did their short-term borrowing, and would also make pioneering forays into the corporate bond market in London—the Eurobond market. In diversifying his sources of financing, Reichmann managed not only to borrow more cheaply but to increasingly insulate Olympia & York from the financial risks of its empire building. In entering the securities markets, Reichmann found that he did not have to offer the sweeping guarantees of repayment with which he had had to placate his Canadian bankers. If, for example, Olympia & York failed to make a payment on that $970 million issue, those forty investors would have no recourse to Olympia & York itself but could lay claim only to the three buildings that secured the notes. By the time Olympia & York completed its $3 billion mid-1980s borrowing program, Reichmann had managed to replace almost all of the recourse debt on the books of Olympia & York's American subsidiary with the nonrecourse variety—a technical distinction that later would prove of great import.

———

In building out the World Financial Center, Olympia & York again put to profitable use the management methods pioneered in building First Bank Tower and refined on the dozen lesser skyscrapers that followed. Not that all went according to plan. Subsurface soil conditions varied greatly within the ninety-three-acre landfill site, which was also criss-crossed by train tunnels and cooling and utility lines. John Norris, Olympia & York's construction manager for the project, struggled to put together a labor force adequate to the task of building so massive and elaborate a project at a time when construction in general was booming throughout the New York area. At the project's peak, Olympia & York employed 120 subcontractors and 4,000 workers, including a cadre of skilled metal workers brought in to craft the pyramidal crowns Cesar Pelli had designed for each of the four main towers.

Commercial developers often depart from an architect's plans both to cut costs and to solve technical problems. Such changes often are opposed by the architect, and the result is endless squabbling in which art, or at least design craft, bumps heads with commerce, leaving all concerned with a migraine. All things considered, Pelli's group and Olympia & York's project staff proved unusually compatible. The cause of harmony was served by the Battery Park City Authority's insistence that the design that Olympia & York had submitted in winning the contract be appended to its ground lease, legally binding both architect and developer. More important, in Pelli, Paul and Albert had found their architectural alter ego. Supplanting the late Edward Durell Stone as the Reichmann brothers' favorite architect, Pelli would win two additional major Olympia & York commissions: the central towers for the stillborn Yerba Buena project in San Francisco and Canary Wharf in London.

Pelli was unusual in not bemoaning the practical limitations of site, budget, and function under which he toiled. To the contrary, he insisted that these constraints encouraged rather than frustrated creativity—indeed, that the art of architecture was the resolution of conflicting demands. For their part, the Reichmanns never considered architecture an art form nor mistook themselves for Medicis. But from the outset of their careers, the brothers had set themselves apart from rival builders by emphasizing aesthetics in the belief that quality pays. As they built a blue-chip corporate clientele, the brothers became more attuned to the nuances of design and more prolific in using deluxe building materials. These tendencies came to fruition with the World Financial Center, which featured twenty-seven varieties of marble in its lobbies alone, and was unabashed in what Brendan Gill of *The New Yorker* described as its "gilt-and-marble opulence," its "imperial Roman grandeur." Although both brothers remained closely involved in design matters throughout the building of the complex, they advanced their pet ideas with a politesse that charmed Pelli, a famously courtly man himself. "They're extraordinarily polite," Pelli recalled. "They treat you with more respect than developers usually treat architects. They listen carefully and say little. They understand everything the first time around."

Pelli and his minions did clash repeatedly with Anthony Coombes, Olympia & York's design manager, over the most art-intensive aspect of the complex: an elaborate, four-acre plaza on which Olympia & York and Battery Park City Authority together would spend nearly $15 million. Periodically Coombes proposed spending cuts, which the architect opposed in gentlemanly but firm fashion. "You could tell Pelli was getting upset because his eye would start to twitch," recalled Thomas Koslowski, the BPCA's director of architecture and design. "Finally, he'd say he was going to quit and take his name off the project but that first he was going to call Albert." In the end, the architect saw the project through without Reichmann's intervention. Coombes typically placated Pelli by reducing the sum to be cut from the budget and leaving it to the architect to decide the particularities of implementing cost-saving measures.

At the same time, Olympia & York and the Pelli group collaborated to solve technical difficulties that arose. For the exterior cladding, Pelli had specified Polychrome, a warm gray granite quarried near Bagotville, Quebec. After one-third of the Polychrome needed had been supplied, the orange crystal that imparted warmth to the stone disappeared. No matter where the quarrymen dug they were unable to relocate the crystal. Tom Morton, Pelli's project manager, chartered a plane and made the rounds of other Quebec quarries, to no avail. Reprising the journey he had made when the marble for First Bank Tower's facings had lightened in hue, Otto Blau, Olympia & York's purchasing whiz, flew to Italy with Morton to scout some thirty alternative kinds of granite. Upon their return, it was decided that it was best to stick with Polychrome, as Morton explained, "because the change in grain would be more evident than the changing tone."

Olympia & York did look to Italy in solving another troublesome aspect of granite supply, which was that the panels arriving from Bagotville varied erratically from the prescribed thickness of one and a quarter inches. The problem was mainly mechanical; North American equipment was incapable of cutting granite to a quarter-inch tolerance. The stonecutters in Quebec also were plagued by fractures, especially when working with large two-by-ten-foot panels needed for the upper walls. Olympia & York began shipping rough blocks of granite from Canada to Italy, where stonecutters had achieved a tolerance of one-sixteenth of an inch by adapting marble-cutting equipment to granite. From Italy panels that were reliably an inch and a quarter thick were shipped to Ireland, where a subcontractor mounted them on steel frames. Then it was on to New York for installation. Despite the added expense incurred in shipping a small mountain of granite halfway around the world and back, the superior labor cost-efficiency achieved cut Olympia & York's total cost to $4 per square foot, compared with $4.50 for panels quarried, cut, and mounted in Quebec.

The Olympia & York–Pelli team faced its greatest construction challenge in customizing the interiors of each of the four towers to suit its major tenant (or owner, in American Express's case). A year and a half after persuading American Express to relocate to the World Financial Center, Olympia & York signed up publisher Dow Jones & Company, which leased 400,000 square feet in Tower A as a combination corporate headquarters and newsroom. Although this time the Reichmanns did not have to buy an old building to fill a new one, they did agree to adapt Tower A to accommodate the production of one of America's largest daily newspapers, *The Wall Street Journal.*

In the summer of 1984 came the blockbuster lease that put the World Financial Center over the top. Merrill Lynch & Company, the largest brokerage on Wall Street, committed itself to leasing 3.9 million square feet, or two full towers. Merrill Lynch's managers had driven a hard bargain, making no secret of the fact that they were negotiating simultaneously with the Port Authority of New York and New Jersey, the government entity that owned the World Trade Center. Terms were not disclosed, but Merrill executives said that it would cost the company 25 percent less to move into the World Financial Center than it would have to stay put and lease overflow space in dribs and drabs. Paul Reichmann also surrendered to Merrill an option to buy 49 percent of one of the towers and agreed to buy the brokerage giant's existing headquarters building, which, at 1.8 million square feet, was larger by far than either the City Investing or American Express buildings recently added to Olympia & York's bulging portfolio of Manhattan property.

Like Dow Jones, Merrill Lynch and American Express insisted that the interiors of their buildings be redesigned to their specifications, forcing Olympia & York to reconfigure heating, plumbing, elevator, and other basic systems. Indeed, the alterations that Merrill ordered for Tower B added so much weight that Olympia & York had to install additional structural steel to strengthen the building's frame. Meanwhile, American Express insisted that eighteen completed floors in its building be torn up and redone to accommodate its latest acquisition, the investment bank Lehman Brothers Kuhn Loeb. If it had not been for Olympia & York's capabilities as a general contractor, last-minute changes of such magnitude would have wrecked the budget.

Olympia & York's work crews put in epic overtime to customize the towers and still finish them on time. That Olympia & York would in fact meet the ambitious schedule that Paul Reichmann had laid out at the start was a tribute not only to the ingenuity and dedication of the company's site managers but also to its exceptionally harmonious relationship with New York City's troublesome construction unions. To be sure, John Norris, Olympia & York's English bulldog of a construction boss, and the union chiefs did a fair amount of snarling at one another. Yet during the project's six-year duration, it was not hit by a single significant strike or work stoppage.

In New York City, labor peace was a commodity that had to be purchased, just like steel or marble. Long before Olympia & York won the contract for Battery Park City, it had been well established that many key unions in the local construction trades were controlled by organized crime. One reason that building costs in New York were the highest in the country is that the mob has long wielded union-negotiated construction contracts as instruments of extortion. The basic demand—"Pay us off or we'll shut you down"—was backed by the threat—usually implicit—of physical retribution.

As the first two World Financial Center towers were nearing completion, tales of the seamy side of New York construction received their latest public airing in a way that proved particularly embarrassing to Olympia & York. To publicize a sixteen-month investigation into racketeering in the construction trades, the New York Commission of Investigation held a one-day hearing in which Olympia & York construction boss Norris reluctantly filled the role of star witness, along with George Morrison, a particularly well-compensated member of the World Financial Center's unionized building crew. Olympia & York's records showed that the company had paid Morrison for working more than twenty-four hours a day for 221 days in 1984 alone—or a princely $385,631, all told—even though he had not bothered to show up much of the time, preferring to make the rounds of vacation spots in Mexico, the Caribbean, and Europe.

Because Local 15 of the International Union of Operating Engineers had designated Morrison master mechanic/operating engineer, under the union's contract with Olympia & York he was entitled to his hourly wage whenever a crane was operated, whether he himself was on the job or at the beach. According to the Commission of Investigation, Morrison was one of eleven workers on Olympia & York's payroll who held no-show or featherbed positions at Battery Park. All belonged either to the International Union of Operating Engineers or the International Brotherhood of Teamsters. "I didn't write the rules," Norris testified before the commission. "I inherited them." He said that in no other American city had Olympia & York been forced by unions to hire unneeded workers. "We regarded it as a cost of building" in New York. After its one-day hearing, the commission folded its tent without taking action against Olympia & York or the unions or making any real attempt at reform.

In his testimony, the hard-bitten Norris had walked a fine line between cooperation and truculence. He certainly saw no need to apologize. From where he sat, Olympia & York was a victim, not a co-conspirator. Norris had not discussed the sordid details of the union contract negotiations with his ultimate superiors, Paul and Albert Reichmann. The sums involved were minuscule compared with the project's overall cost, and Norris could only assume that the Reichmanns would not want to jeopardize their grandest project for the sake of a few million in payoffs. Morally speaking, though, the hearing put the brothers in an untenable position. The Torah sanctioned the paying of bribes to save lives, but placating mob-controlled labor unions was another matter. The fact that neither Paul nor Albert had dealt personally with the unions was immaterial. If, as proprietors, they could not allow any of their employees to work on the Sabbath, they could not countenance the paying of bribes either. It is possible, though unlikely, that the Reichmanns had not realized in launching the project that the World Financial Center would rise from a foundation of crooked labor contracts. In any event, after the hearing, the brothers no longer had the option of what politicians call "plausible deniability." Even so, construction work on the Battery would continue for another two years under the same arrangement that had governed the project from the beginning.

Even by the standards of the real estate industry, which is far less bureaucratic than most, Olympia & York was always sparingly staffed. By the mid-1980s, the Reichmanns employed about seven hundred people in their Toronto headquarters and another six hundred in the United States, mostly in New York City, to which the company shifted its development staff with the advent of the World Financial Center project. (These figures exclude Olympia Floor & Wall Tile.) Although Olympia & York now was twice as big as Cadillac Fairview and Trizec in terms of asset values, it employed only half as many people as did these rival developers. This employment disparity was all the more remarkable considering that neither Cadillac Fairview nor Trizec did its own general contracting work.

The consensus among Olympia & York's rivals—and indeed many of its own executives—was that the company was not just lean but undermanaged. "I always had the feeling that the Reichmanns never had a high enough regard for management," said Bernard Ghert of Cadillac Fairview. "They thought the valuable people in the world were the people who made the deals, the entrepreneurs." At issue was the balance struck between entrepreneurism and administration, between enlarging the empire and running it. When Oskar Lustig joined Olympia & York in 1963 as head accountant, the company's bookkeeping had lagged so far behind its deal making that he nearly quit almost before he had begun. Although Olympia & York absorbed an entire accounting firm through piecemeal hirings during the 1970s, its grasp never did quite equal the Reichmanns' reach.

In its entrepreneurial bias, Olympia & York mirrored the predilections of Paul Reichmann, who tended to lose interest the instant a project became fait accompli. Refusing to submit to the confines of routine or administrative structure, Reichmann ranged across the full breadth and depth of the company, immersing himself in whatever it was that compelled his immediate attention. Reichmann was not one of those corporate strongmen incapable of delegating. Like it or not, he had to rely on others to keep the machinery running while he was absorbed in the nuances of structuring Olympia & York's latest bond issue or choosing the proper shade of marble for a skyscraper's cladding. Given the boss's unpredictability, his underlings spent a lot of time looking back over their shoulder. This frustrated Reichmann, who recognized the symptoms of dysfunction but not its cause. "This was something that plagued me for years," he later confided. "I would make a decision and leave it to people to put it into effect. But then I would keep getting calls from people in New York or London asking me about what they should do. I'd tell them to handle it themselves, but the calls kept coming. It's hard to find executives who will operate on their own."

At the same time, Olympia & York suffered from the opposite problem: a tendency for executives to exploit the looseness of the company's administrative structure to establish their own managerial fiefdoms and otherwise aggrandize themselves at the company's expense. This was particularly the case in New York, which was once removed from the seat of family power in Toronto. By the early 1980s, the Reichmanns had ceded daily management of the U.S. subsidiary to a half-dozen mutually mistrustful feudal chiefs. The most problematic was Eddie Minskoff, who later outlandishly insisted that the $40 million profit he made investing alongside the Reichmanns did not begin to reflect his value. "I built that company into the largest developer in America. I did it. Me. The Reichmanns weren't around much," Minskoff claimed in 1992. "Paul had the wherewithal and foresight and trust to back me," he conceded. "But the genius behind what Olympia & York did in the U.S. was me, not Paul Reichmann."

Olympia & York's management deficiencies did not hamper performance in the most entrepreneurial aspects of its business. To the contrary, the company's improvisatory flair gave it an edge in megadeveloping, which is wildly unpredictable by nature. At the same time, the routine aspects of the business tended to get short shrift. During the construction of the World Financial Center, BPCA administrators often had trouble getting answers to questions as basic as "How tall is Tower A?" or "How many square feet in Tower B?" "With all the other developers we dealt with [mainly involving the construction of apartment buildings] there was a real definite structure of authority. Even with the more family-oriented firms you knew exactly who you had to talk to to get something," Tom Koslowski recalled. "With Olympia & York, it was never like that. You'd ask for something and the person who got back to you might be in leasing, and the next time it was someone from construction or finance. It might be a lawyer. And the numbers that came back had a way of changing, which didn't give you a lot of confidence that you ever got the right answer."

According to Koslowski, Olympia & York never did submit a full set of properly certified documents attesting to the floor size of each building in the complex, as required under its contract with Battery Park City Authority. (Koslowski was convinced that Olympia & York had in fact completed the documents, or otherwise the company would not have been able to obtain certificates of occupancy from the New York City Department of Buildings.) So elemental a failing by a developer typically would have prompted a lawsuit. In this case, litigation was never considered, given that the World Financial Center provided BPCA with 80 percent of its annual revenues. "Olympia & York basically saved the authority," Koslowski said, "so we chose not to make an issue out of it." As a result, the actual size of the complex remained something of a mystery around the BPCA. "We always used to throw out the number 6 million square feet, but my guess is that's net [leasable space only]," Koslowski said. "The gross is probably more like 8 million."

Olympia & York's dealings with tenants were similarly afflicted by sloppiness. Olympia & York was slow to bill out common-area charges in its buildings and often let tenants occupy space before they had signed on the dotted line. Bell Gouinlock, the investment bank with close ties to the company, occupied an office in First Canadian Place for five years before its president was presented with a lease. Olympia & York was equally lax in collecting past due rent and yet for years refused to discount its posted rates to hold on to a tenant. One of the least noticed but most telling precursors of Olympia & York's collapse would be the wholesale loss of tenants from First Canadian Place in the late 1980s.

"Nobody else in the industry would have allowed their flagship to just sink like that," argued James Soden, the former head of Trizec. "You can say the Reichmanns at the end weren't sticking to their knitting but my point is that it never was their knitting. Olympia & York was just about the best there ever was at building buildings. But they were not good at the more sophisticated aspects of the real estate business, such as continuous marketing to tenants. They did not relate well to tenants in general. Tenants have to be catered to as people. You have to hold their hand and keep them happy."

As devout haredim, of course, the Reichmanns made every effort to keep their hands to themselves. Quite apart from their religious identity, the brothers were just not the gregarious, customer-service type. To some extent, they could compensate by hiring proxy handholders, and did. But Olympia & York was as understaffed in property management as in every other aspect of its business. This inadequacy in part was the product of a calculated effort to suppress overhead costs. But at some deeper level, perhaps even subconsciously, the Reichmanns were simply uncomfortable at directing a large group of strangers, the great majority of whom were nonharedim. Both Paul and Albert moved through the company—*their* company—like downed pilots behind enemy lines. "Half the time you wouldn't even know they were around," recalled a senior manager in the New York office. "When they were in town, they liked to come into the office very early, before anyone else got there. At some point in the day, you'd turn around and there would be Paul or Albert." As for Ralph, he added, "had I not met him once, I wouldn't believe that he exists."

At the suggestion of Gil Newman, Olympia & York's chief administrator, all managers in Olympia & York's regional real estate offices once were invited to the Toronto headquarters for what was billed as a morale-boosting orientation session. The employee multitudes had already assembled in the capacious thirty-fourth-floor boardroom of First Bank Tower when Paul and Albert slipped in unannounced and took their places at the head of the table, next to Newman. There followed a long silence, which Paul finally broke. "Thank you for coming," he said sheepishly. Another awkward silence grew until Newman took it upon himself to ask one of the visitors to identify himself and explain what he did. As Newman worked his way around the table, the Reichmanns listened without comment. When the last of their employees had spoken, Paul again expressed his thanks, got up, and left the room. There would be no more attempts at forced corporate togetherness in this least paternalistic of family-owned companies.

The Reichmanns' management aversion also was apparent in the way they went about diversifying Olympia & York. Oil, timber, metals, and other so-called hard assets appealed to them not merely because they tended to rise in price with inflation but because their value was not dependent on corporate management and the expert orchestration of capital, technology, and labor required to create wealth in most industries. In other words, Abitibi-Price could collapse tomorrow and the timberlands it owned would retain an intrinsic value. In this sense, Abitibi's hoard of timber resembled gold locked away in a bank vault in Zurich or Geneva. Put another way, the human element was less important in natural resources than in the service industries, in which, as the cliché has it, the assets go down the elevator every night.

While the Reichmanns had an eye for entrepreneurial talent in property development, they were singularly unqualified to gauge the abilities of the men who ran the big public corporations of North America. The brothers had not grown up on these shores, gone to college or business school, or worked their way up a corporate ladder. In short, they did not know the members of the managerial class and made no effort to get to know them even as Olympia & York took its place among the most powerful corporations in Canada. To the contrary, the Reichmanns shunned all contact with the corporate elite, outside of the occasional business negotiation, of course.

As it would turn out, Abitibi-Price and most of the other companies in which the Reichmanns invested in diversifying Olympia & York were not nearly as well run as advertised. The Reichmanns proved hesitant to revise their originally favorable judgment and seemingly incapable of bringing about improvement once they did. In tacit acknowledgment of this managerial deficiency, the Reichmanns created a new executive position in 1984 and filled it with another of their Bay Street advisers, David Brown of Burns Fry. Brown's assignment was to manage Olympia & York's burgeoning portfolio of investments in other companies. He would last a year. "Paul makes all the decisions but sometimes forgets to tell other people what he's doing," Brown complained after resigning to return to Bay Street. "The idea of going to work for [the Reichmann brothers] was fascinating. I thought I'd become part of the family, taking part in all the decisions. That just didn't happen. Paul said I wasn't aggressive enough. I said, 'You never opened the door.' "

Chapter 34

In 1984 the Reichmanns resumed their drive to diversify Olympia & York. About the middle of the year, the company shelled out $232 million (Canadian) to buy a big block of stock in the second largest developer in North America, Cadillac Fairview. With 22 percent of Cadillac Fairview to go along with their 40 percent of Trizec and 100 percent of Olympia & York, the Reichmanns sent the pulses of conspiracy theorists racing. Was Paul Reichmann bent on becoming the John D. Rockefeller of real estate?

In reality, Reichmann was a stock market opportunist, not a budding monopolist. In his informed view, Cadillac Fairview's out-of-favor stock was a bargain relative to the intrinsic value of its assets. Cadillac's top brass evidently agreed, for in the spring of 1984 the company registered with securities regulators a plan to buy a block of its own shares on the public market for $13.50 a share. Once this tender offer had begun, Cadillac was prohibited by law from altering its terms, and so the company's management and its largest shareholder—the Seagram Bronfmans—could only watch helplessly as Jimmy "the Piranha" Connacher of Gordon Capital stepped in and picked the market clean at $13.75 a share. Whether Connacher acted on his own or at the behest of Paul Reichmann, who had frequently acted through Gordon Capital in the past, was unclear but of academic interest only. The Reichmanns ended up with the stock and thus did to the Seagram branch of the Bronfman family what they had done to the Edper Bronfmans in buying into Trizec five years earlier.

This time, there would be no alchemy of enmity into comity. Neither the Seagram Bronfmans nor Cadillac Fairview's executives ever looked upon the Reichmanns as anything but interlopers. "We didn't like the idea of another big real estate company owning shares in the company," said Bernard Ghert, who had succeeded John Daniels as chief executive in 1982 and would maintain a correct if testy relationship with the Reichmanns until it came time to sell Cadillac Fairview. "Even though their investment was passive, it sort of tied your hands because you'd have to always try to gauge their reaction to things before you did something." Although Olympia & York owned twice as much stock as the Bronfmans, neither Paul nor Albert was invited to join the board or to participate in the company's lesser decision-making councils. The brothers did not much care. All they wanted from Cadillac Fairview was what in fact they got: a smartly rising stock price.

For Paul Reichmann, Cadillac Fairview was a momentary diversion from his stalking of Gulf Canada, which he had been pursuing with varying degrees of intensity since 1981. When its parent company, Gulf Oil, had come under attack from the Texas raider T. Boone Pickens in the fall of 1983, Reichmann had flown to Pittsburgh to try to persuade Gulf's management to part with its 60 percent–owned Canadian subsidiary, which was a huge company in its own right with annual revenues of $5 billion. Olympia & York's $1.7 billion offer was given short shrift by Gulf's management, which was smugly confident of victory. Not six months later, though, Gulf sold itself to Chevron in the most costly corporate acquisition ever. Paul Reichmann gave it another shot, flying to San Francisco to meet Chevron's leaders, who were willing to sell at $25 a share. Reichmann offered $17 and was shown the door. "It wasn't even considered for five minutes," recalled Reichmann, who nonetheless returned to Toronto confident of holding the upper hand.

As Reichmann well knew, Chevron's acquisition of Gulf Canada had to be approved by Ottawa, which continued to favor the Canadianization of the oil industry. In early 1985 Ottawa announced that it would allow control of Gulf Canada to shift to Chevron but only if the subsidiary was promptly offered "for sale to Canadian-controlled purchasers." As it happened, by this time Olympia & York was the only Canadian company willing to risk a major oil acquisition. In a tour de force of deal-making technique, Paul Reichmann used the leverage inherent in his position as sole bidder to extract concessions not only from Chevron but from the Canadian government. Most important, Reichmann made his purchase of Gulf Canada conditional on Olympia & York receiving a gargantuan $500 million tax break. Behind a veil of secrecy, the Mulroney government granted an advance ruling allowing Olympia & York's novel use of an arcane maneuver known on Bay Street as the "Little Egypt Bump." Named after a famous Chicago stripper, this loophole enabled an acquirer to redepreciate for tax purposes assets that already had been fully depreciated. No other corporation had ever made such aggressive use of the Bump and none ever would. After the Gulf Canada transaction, the government amended the law to prohibit the technique as specifically adapted by Olympia & York.

Confident that the ruling he sought would be forthcoming, Reichmann went ahead and signed a preliminary agreement with Chevron in March 1985, to buy Gulf Canada in two stages for $3 billion. He then returned to Ottawa and extracted another major concession, as the federal government in effect agreed to buy the refineries and other Gulf Canada assets that Olympia & York did not want to keep. That is, Reichmann negotiated the sale of Gulf Canada's so-called downstream assets at a rich price to Petro Canada, the state-owned oil giant. To swing this transaction, Reichmann had to make a concession himself, tossing Gulf's prize exploration acreage in the Beaufort Sea into the $1.8 billion grab bag of assets to be spun off to Petro Canada.

When word of the sweet deal Olympia & York had cut with Petro Canada leaked, even many members of Prime Minister Brian Mulroney's own Tory caucus were outraged. Rattled by the uproar, Mulroney instructed Petro Canada to back out. According to author Peter Foster, Reichmann advisers operating in deep-throat mode "cleverly worked the press to paint Mulroney's behavior in its worst light." Although the prime minister's about-face had angered him, Reichmann was not altogether displeased at the turn of events. He had had second thoughts himself about surrendering the Beaufort Sea acreage and also saw an opportunity to renegotiate his understanding with Chevron. After Reichmann threatened to walk, Chevron shaved $200 million off its asking price for Gulf Canada. Meanwhile, Olympia & York negotiated a scaled-down sale of assets to Petro Canada that allowed it to hang on to Gulf's Arctic exploration rights.

Adding another artful layer of complication, Reichmann took pains to arrange things so that the acquisition was effected not by Olympia & York buying Gulf but by Gulf buying Abitibi-Price. In the process, Reichmann had to overcome the skepticism of many directors and executives from both Abitibi and Gulf. It was worth it, for the Reichmanns thus were able to finance the transaction in part from Gulf Canada's own treasury, as in a leveraged buyout. In a final virtuoso flourish, Reichmann had Gulf Canada buy out its minority shareholders for cash and stock, saving Olympia & York the considerable expense of doing so. "The Gulf deal was straightforward, without any complications," Reichmann deadpanned in its aftermath. Edper's Trevor Eyton, himself a master of Byzantine deal making, offered an aficionado's praise. "I am dazzled by its complexity," Eyton told *Business Week*.

———

October 17, 1985, was a red-letter day in the history of the Reichmann family as Paul and Albert hosted a reception for fifteen hundred people to commemorate the official opening of the World Financial Center. The gatehouse of Tower A was thick with television cameras and politicians eager to bask in the glow of a complex that had sprouted as if by magic from a sandbar and gave every indication of living up to its advance billing as the second coming of Rockefeller Center. Just three years after the first spadeful of landfill had been turned,

Tower A and Tower C had been finished and occupied and the rest of the center was hurtling toward completion. Ronald Reagan had been returned to the White House for a second term, Wall Street was reveling in the biggest bull market in a generation or two, and with the uncanny timing for which it had become famous, Olympia & York was unveiling a magnificently realized architectural symbol of the resurgent American fantasy of boundless wealth. For all his frustrations, Tom Koslowski could only look around him that day and marvel at what had been so swiftly accomplished. "All of us at my table were sitting there just in awe of Olympia & York's ability to get things done," he recalled.

The Reichmanns would have preferred to celebrate the opening of the World Financial Center as they had First Canadian Place's completion: in private. However, Paul and Albert well understood that this latest success was not the family's alone. The realization of the World Financial Center had brought the entire Battery Park City project to critical mass, transforming a twenty-five-year political ordeal into a triumph of government that simply could not be allowed to pass unheralded. Meyer "Sandy" Frucher, who was Governor Mario Cuomo's appointee as the latest president of the Battery Park City Authority, joined forces with Michael Dennis, a former government official, and the politically connected Howard Rubenstein & Company, Olympia & York's New York public relations counsel, to persuade the Reichmann brothers to make the opening of the complex a gala event.

Some four thousand gilt-edged invitations were mailed in the names of Paul and Albert Reichmann. No mention was made of Ralph, who, seemingly content in the role of forgotten brother, did not attend the ceremonies or the luncheon that followed. But Ralph's son, David, was there, as were Philip Reichmann and Frank Hauer. Louis and Marianne Reichmann came in from Queens with a son and daughter in tow. Frucher introduced himself to Renée Reichmann, who, though confined to a wheelchair, was abeam with maternal pride. "You should be very proud of Paul and Albert," Frucher said. "This is really quite a wonderful thing they did." Mrs. Reichmann's reply surprised Frucher. "I have other children, too," she said and talked at some length about Edward, Louis, Ralph, and the recently deceased Eva. "Finally," Frucher recalled, "she allowed that she was in fact proud of Paul and Albert."

At one point during the ceremonies, Governor Cuomo turned to Albert and said, "Your mother seems very pleased with how it's turned out." Albert nodded in agreement. "I hope now we'll get a raise," he quipped.

Top officials of American Express, Merrill Lynch, Dow Jones, and the other major tenants sounded a chorus of praise and gratitude. Governor Cuomo waxed as eloquent as usual in lionizing the daring and skill of the brothers Reichmann, hailing the complex as "a soaring triumph for them, the state and for the city. It makes a point: it was done conjunctively." New York City mayor Edward Koch credited the new complex with affirming New York's status as the financial capital of the world. "This is that part of the city," Mayor Koch proclaimed, "that will be recognized as the new Wall Street—Wall Street II." In their comments, Sinclair Stevens, Canada's minister of industry, and Alan Gottlieb, the Canadian ambassador to the United States, put an internationalist gloss of a different sort on the event, emphasizing the complex as an auspicious symbol of the special economic relationship that Canada and the United States long had enjoyed.

Albert Reichmann mounted the dais wearing a genial, mildly bemused expression that suggested he was not quite sure why he had ever agreed to such an immersion in limelight. "Ah, ladies and gentlemen," ventured the president of the largest developer in the world. "I just would like to thank you for attending this assembly and say that we are very pleased to open the complex to the public." Then he sat back down.

Paul's speech was much more expansive, as befitted a figure who now was arguably the most powerful businessman in Canada and was unquestionably riding high. In recent weeks, Olympia & York had cinched the acquisition of Gulf Canada, and the Canadian Imperial Bank of Commerce had done Paul the honor of electing him to its board of directors. (Many Canadian businessmen, though not Reichmann, viewed appointment to the board of one of the Big Five banks as a career-crowning achievement.) In New York, meanwhile, David Rockefeller had in effect acknowledged Reichmann as the new king of Manhattan real estate by inviting him to join the board of directors of Rockefeller Center Properties Incorporated, a newly created company through which the Rockefeller family had sold a minority stake in the crown jewel of its property empire to the investing public. Reichmann was one of only five directors, one of whom was Rockefeller himself. In his own sober, gracious way, Reichmann was luxuriating in the newfound role of corporate potentate as he took the podium at the World Financial Center. "First and foremost," he said, "I'd like to thank the American spirit, which is one of total freedom. . . . As Canadians, we were accepted with open arms and received the utmost cooperation from everyone involved from beginning to end."

Like his brother Edward at the Place Cremazie opening two decades earlier, Paul went on to construct an edifice of political ideas atop a foundation of bricks and mortar. "I know I shouldn't make a political speech," Reichmann continued, "but it's that I feel strongly about this project, some form of agreement where people of both countries can benefit from cross-border activities." He endorsed the Mulroney and Reagan administrations' efforts to dismantle barriers to trade between Canada and the United States, suggesting that expanded trade held out the best hope of ameliorating what he termed "the tragedy of government deficits." An optimist to the core, Reichmann predicted that Canada was capable of doubling its gross national product over the next ten to fifteen years under a free-trade regime and he invited the business executives in the audience to "come and invest in Canada, on the same basis as we have come here."

Frucher asked Governor Cuomo and Mayor Koch to jointly ring a gong of the sort long used to signal the opening of trading on the floor of the New York Stock Exchange. When Cuomo's hand slipped from the rope in midpull, Koch did the honors his favorite way—solo—prompting a laugh and a sotto voce comment from the governor, as Paul and Albert looked on with indulgent smiles. From a second-floor balcony reams of old-fashioned ticker tape cascaded down on the assembled multitude. (This was a costly touch, the advent of computerized trading having made ticker tape scarce.) If the traders on the floor of the New York Stock Exchange had trafficked in reputation instead of stock, surely the Reichmann family that day would have hit an all-time high.

To be sure, the World Financial Center was not yet a paying proposition, its construction being only about 70 percent complete. But there was every indication of an impending bonanza. For a start, the complex rested on a solid foundation of a bargain-priced ground lease and cost-effective construction. During his protracted courtship of Merrill Lynch & Company, Paul Reichmann had taken William Schreyer, its chief executive, on a tour of the nearly completed Tower C, which American Express would own and occupy in its entirety. "He was in awe," Reichmann recalled. "He turned to me and said, 'It's so beautiful. But who is going to pay for it all?' Of course, he was talking about his own building. I said, 'You are.' " What Reichmann meant was that Olympia & York's construction methods would enable it to cover its costs without charging above-market rents (which Schreyer would not pay in any event).

James Robinson III, the chief executive of American Express, was delighted with Tower C. "It came in right on budget," he recalled. "Paul builds a high-quality product." Olympia & York made a profit of about $50 million as general contractor to American Express.

By the time the first two towers were completed, an impressive 93 percent of the World Financial Center's 6 million square feet of office space had been leased at an average rent a bit below the going rate in the intensely competitive lower Manhattan market, or about $40 per square foot. Michael Dennis and crew had had to scramble to replace City Investing, the first tenant Olympia & York had signed, after the conglomerate decided in early 1985 to liquidate itself. About 70 percent of the space City Investing was to have occupied was re-rented (at higher rates) to the investment bank Oppenheimer & Company. The 500,000 square feet still remaining empty in Tower A would be filled well before Towers C and D were completed in 1987.

As a shopping center, the complex would prove a costly bust. About 70,000 of the 250,000 square feet designated as retail space in the building plan was so poorly located or awkwardly configured as to be unusable. While this was partly the fault of design specifications imposed by the BPCA, the company had no one to blame but itself for its misadventures in trying to fill the remaining 180,000 square feet. The struggle did nothing to improve the professional standing of Philip Reichmann, who served as the project's retail leasing director, commuting regularly between Toronto and New York. Olympia & York misread the market initially in conceiving of the World Financial Center as a venue for top-of-the-line luxury goods: fine wines, imported chocolates, jewelry, Cuban cigars, champagne, and so on. By the time the company scaled down its misguided up-market pretensions to conform to downtown realities, it had dropped more than $30 million. "Philip perceived himself as a real force, but he surrounded himself with incompetent courtiers who essentially bled the operation," said a senior Olympia & York executive in New York. "Paul recognized what was going on, but he would not interfere with Albert's son. Albert just shrugged it off."

Despite the retail fiasco, World Financial Center still generated large net operating profits right from the start, and even after Wall Street ceased booming and began contracting in the late 1980s, all four of the center's office towers would remain leased almost to capacity. "Each tower was a major financial success in its own right," said Joel Simon, the chief operating officer of Olympia & York's U.S. subsidiary. "Altogether, they produced several hundred million dollars in cash profits." Meanwhile, the market value of the buildings appreciated rapidly. By some outside estimates, the complex, which cost about $1.5 billion to construct, had risen in value to $3 billion by 1989. (This figure included Tower C, which was wholly owned by American Express.)

The economics of the venture were complicated by Olympia & York's ownership of the three used skyscrapers it had taken in trade to lure City Investing, American Express, and Merrill Lynch across the West Side Highway to the World Financial Center. Paul Reichmann had agreed to pay top dollar for each of these buildings, none of which measured up to the World Financial Center in terms of quality but, at a collective 4.5 million square feet, came uncomfortably close to rivaling it in size. Michael Dennis liked to say that Olympia & York had taken Cadillacs as trade-ins on Rolls Royces, but Chevy Blazers seemed a more apt description of this trio of large but, by Manhattan standards, ordinary office towers. Even so, in the robust leasing market of the late 1980s, Olympia & York was able to replace departing tenants with new tenants paying higher rents and operate all three buildings at a substantial profit. As late as mid-1991, the vacancy rates at 59 Maiden Lane, 125 Broad Street, and 1 Liberty Plaza would remain less than half of the average for Manhattan as a whole.

To Paul Reichmann, the commercial fate of his trio of trade-in towers was a minor distraction at most. If they had operated at a loss—that is, if in purchasing them, Olympia & York had provided the World Financial Center with what amounted to an intracompany subsidy—then so be it. At age fifty-five, Reichmann had evolved to the point where profit mattered less to him than his legacy as a developer—and a Reichmann. What pleased him most about the new complex along the Battery, he told a reporter a few days after its opening, was that it would leave a "prominent imprint on New York City." As Reichmann hoped, the World Financial Center would become a new photographic metaphor of Manhattan, displayed to gorgeous effect in countless advertising campaigns, television programs, and Hollywood films and featured on numerous magazine covers. To be sure, it remained important to Reichmann that Olympia & York's developments be economic; financing the next megaproject depended on it. But the notion of property development as an exercise in profit maximization had ceased to compel him. The success of the World Financial Center marked Reichmann's graduation to a new and ultra-ambitious phase of his career in which his priority—indeed, his compulsion—became creating privately owned developments with the impact of large-scale public works.

From the outset, Reichmann had intended the World Financial Center to stand as a monument to something more than Olympia & York's ability to make money. This was perhaps most evident in the large amount of space—some two million square feet, or 25 percent of the total—Olympia & York ceded to non-revenue-producing use. By any standard, the building lobbies were huge and the four-acre outdoor plaza that ran between the complex and the Hudson River was accurately, if immodestly, described by Sandy Frucher as "the most important to be built in New York within this generation." Certainly no existing commercial complex, not even Rockefeller Center, boasted anything remotely as grand as the Winter Garden, the 130-foot-high, glass-vaulted pavilion that was the complex's centerpiece, prompting architecture critics to resort to comparisons to the grand concourse of Grand Central Station.

It was important to Paul Reichmann that Olympia & York and by extension the Reichmann family be seen not merely as the most proficient developers in the world but as the classiest, so as to turn inside out the prevalent stereotype of the ultra-Orthodox as money-grubbing sharpies. Even in the complex's less visible amenities, Reichmann insisted on the highest quality. "Go take a close look at the handicapped elevators some time," Lew Ranieri said. "They are the most elaborate ones I've ever seen. I used to tease the hell out of Paul about them. Paul put all sorts of money—at least $40 or $50 million—into improvements he knew would not be recoverable through the leases just to make the place special." Reichmann displayed such perfectionism in building the World Financial Center that Ranieri could only assume that he intended it to be his swan song in property development. If only it had been so.

—

By 1985, the Reichmann brothers had no rival for the appellation bestowed upon them by the *Economist* magazine: "Kings of Officeland." Even so, their actual accomplishments had continued to lag behind their mythological ones. In the idealized version of the saga that had unfolded in the press and seeped into popular consciousness, the Reichmanns' success had been expunged of all discordant, contradictory elements. The occasional blunders the brothers had made (notably Paul's flurry of ill-conceived stock market investments in 1981 and Albert's solo misadventures in the hinterlands of American development) and the intractibility Paul had displayed in his dealings with the Bank of Montreal and others either had been underplayed or overlooked. The Reichmanns instead were portrayed as infallibly astute—as Midas crossed with Solomon— and celebrated as ecumenical icons of old-fashioned virtue in business. This had the effect of sanding to a deceptively smooth benignity Paul Reichmann's complex, contrary, and eccentric personality.

The turning point in both the iconology and the business fortunes of the Reichmanns came with the Gulf Canada acquisition, which closed in early 1986, not long after the World Financial Center opened. In landing Gulf Canada, Paul Reichmann had proved himself a masterful deal maker. But all that his tactical brilliance would accomplish in the end was to make this misbegotten megadeal a bit less of a financial disaster. Reichmann's decision to pay $2.8 billion for Gulf Canada was predicated on projections of a modest increase in crude oil prices, to $33.75 per barrel in 1985 and to $35 in 1986. Blinded by his faith in a favorable long-term outlook for natural resources, Reichmann persisted in his pursuit of Canada's second largest producer even as the wellhead price of petroleum declined by half during the year it took him to pull together the various strands of this complex deal. Not long after Gulf Canada was in hand, the global oil market buckled under the weight of massive surpluses. Crude plummeted to $13 a barrel, or one-third of the price Reichmann and his advisers had projected. "Can you imagine what price they would get for Gulf now?" a top Chevron executive gloated. Having overpaid for Gulf Canada by at least $1 billion, the Reichmanns never would come close to climbing back to the breakeven point on this, the largest of all their stock market investments.

The Gulf Canada deal proved nearly as costly in terms of public relations. In August 1985, when disgruntled public officials leaked word of the massive tax write-off permitted Olympia & York through the dubious mechanism of the Little Egypt Bump, a furor erupted in Parliament. John Turner, the leader of the Liberal opposition, blasted the granting of a $1 billion tax break to one of the richest families in Canada. The vehemence of the backlash startled Paul Reichmann, who in his own mind was only doing what he had always done: maximizing Olympia & York's advantages under the law. Reichmann reacted with muted indignation, issuing a press release pointing out that Olympia & York's tax savings would amount not to $1 billion but to $500 million over five years, "with another $50 million to $90 million savings after that time." Furthermore, Reichmann added, the notion that Olympia & York had received a concession from Ottawa "is a totally wrong understanding." The advance tax ruling the Mulroney government had obligingly provided "is simply an interpretation of law," he said. "It is nothing given."

Needless to say, Reichmann's semantic hairsplitting and his casual dismissal of the additional $50 million to $90 million to be extracted from the public purse as so much spare change only exacerbated the damage done to the family's image. Just two months later, Paul plunged the family back into the ice bath of bad publicity as Olympia & York announced the hiring of Mulroney's deputy minister of finance, Marshall "Mickey" Cohen. John Turner again raised a ruckus in Parliament. Was Cohen's new job a payoff for the favorable tax ruling? The Liberals' suspicions were further excited when it was revealed that Reichmann had first approached Cohen in February 1985, as the Department of National Revenue was just beginning to consider the Gulf Canada deal. Midlevel officials in the department's tax policy branch had been strongly opposed to Olympia & York's novel use of the Little Egypt Bump. When a memo to this effect crossed Cohen's desk, he sent it back to be redrafted along more "balanced" lines and then recused himself from further consideration of the matter. By the time the tax ruling was brought down in mid-July, Cohen had accepted Reichmann's job offer. Yet he did not resign his government post and join Olympia & York for another three months.

Paul and Albert Reichmann had known Mickey Cohen for twenty years. As a young tax lawyer, Cohen had negotiated the terms of the investment partnership that his in-laws, the Oelbaums, had formed with the Reichmanns to acquire Flemingdon Park. Not long afterward, Cohen had separated from Annette Oelbaum and abandoned his law practice in Toronto for a job in Ottawa, where he had remarried and found his métier as a smoothly persuasive, apolitical federal bureaucrat. He served in succession as deputy minister of three of the most important cabinet ministries: Industry, Energy, and Finance. In the process, Cohen developed a reputation as a "Teflon man." As one former colleague put it, "Criticism hits things, not him."

True to form, there would be no official investigation of the coincidence of Cohen's hiring and the favorable tax ruling given Gulf Canada. After a few days of headlines, the Liberal opposition went in search of other targets of political opportunity. Whether the timing of Paul's approach to Cohen was an example of naïveté or Machiavellian calculation remained open to debate. For his part, Cohen denied any wrongdoing: "The department was involved in the deal both above me and below me, but not me." At a minimum, Cohen and Reichmann had flouted proscriptions against the appearance of conflict of interest.

In concept at any rate, Mickey Cohen's hiring represented a bold leap forward in the Reichmanns' succession planning. The fifty-year-old Cohen became president and chief executive of a newly created holding company, Olympia & York Enterprises, which took title to Gulf Canada and the family's other stock market investments. The Reichmanns laid plans to pay off much of the debt incurred in acquiring their 60 percent stake in Gulf Canada by floating a $1 billion issue of preferred stock through Olympia & York Enterprises. The option of selling common shares in the new holding company was briefly considered and rejected; the brothers were not prepared to share control with outsiders. However, Paul noted, "if ever the next generation wants to go public, [the structure] will be in place."

As it turned out, the rout in the oil market forced Olympia & York to cancel the preferred stock issue. Even so, Paul Reichmann refused all invitations to second-guess his acquisition of Gulf Canada and reiterated his faith in the long-term prospects of Canadian oil. This was not mere bravado. Even as the Canadian oil industry shut down more than half its drilling rigs, the Reichmanns pushed ahead with a $90 million investment inaugurating a $3.3 billion program to develop Gulf's massive Amauligak field in the Beaufort Sea. "The question in this business," declared Paul, implying that in his own estimation, anyway, he had graduated from oil industry neophyte to expert, "is not what the stock market will do but what the [oil] market will be five or six years from now." Indeed, he hailed the ruinous decline in crude prices as an ideal opportunity to add to the family's oil patch holdings. "When everybody tries to run out," he vowed, "that's when we will be the most active."

———

True to Paul's contrarian word, in March 1986, the Reichmanns used their newly acquired oil company to launch a takeover bid for Hiram Walker Resources, the old-line distiller and oil producer that had rebuffed Paul's advances five years earlier. The Reichmanns' strategic aim was twofold: to add to their oil and gas holdings while diversifying Gulf Canada beyond energy. Hiram Walker's prime asset remained its highly profitable liquor operation, which owned the Canadian Club brand among others and was second in size only to Seagram among Canadian distillers. If Gulf were to absorb the whole of Hiram Walker, the resulting combine would be the fifth largest industrial company in Canada.

In finally making their play for Hiram Walker, the Reichmanns staged what amounted to an ambush of Bud Downing, Hiram Walker's chief executive. The brothers did Downing the dubious courtesy of rousing him from a hotel bed in California with a 5:00 A.M. conference call informing him that Gulf Canada would announce an offer to pay $32 a share for 38 percent of Hiram Walker when stock market trading began in an hour. Albert told Downing that he hoped they could work out a "friendly" deal. The executive replied that the last-minute offer put a lot of pressure on him and his company. Paul gave a nervous snort and said: "That's why we're doing it."

Thus began the Reichmann brothers' first overtly predatory takeover bid. Within days of the predawn phone call, the die was cast. Armed with investment banking analyses that estimated Hiram Walker's breakup value at $40 a share, the Hiram Walker board rejected Olympia & York's $32 a share bid on the grounds that it "significantly understates the value and does not reflect the prospects of Hiram Walker Resources" and criticized the Reichmanns for making "a coercive attempt to pressure shareholders into a hasty decision." For his part, Paul Reichmann was annoyed by Hiram Walker's refusal to play along. He had not expected resistance. He telephoned several of the company's board members "to find out why Walker was not rolling over and accepting its fate. Reichmann told them he had thought the whole thing would be more friendly."

Other bidders surfaced and there ensued a protracted, multisided takeover battle, replete with the fashionable bare-knuckle legal tactics, convoluted financial maneuvering, and barefaced public relations posturing of the takeover game. Early on, the Reichmanns were dealt a damaging blow when Hiram Walker contracted to sell its liquor business to the British food and beverage giant Allied-Lyons PLC. When Olympia & York went to court seeking to block the sale, the judge not only denied the Reichmanns' request for an injunction but defended Hiram Walker's management from the harsh criticisms leveled at them by Olympia & York's lawyers. "When under attack the target does not have to sit idly by without defending itself," Mr. Justice Robert Montgomery of the Supreme Court of Ontario scornfully observed. "An earlier Goliath was dispatched with a slingshot." (The role reversal implicit in Judge Montgomery's metaphor stung perhaps more than he realized; in the Bible, of course, Goliath was the Philistine strongman slain by the cunning David, the archetypal King of the Israelites.)

Olympia & York appealed the ruling and then simply blew away rival bidders in boosting its offer to $2.2 billion—or $38 a share for all the outstanding stock of Hiram Walker. The company's board accepted the sweetened bid but refused to rescind the pending sale of the liquor division to Allied-Lyons, which promptly sued to ensure that Hiram Walker's new owners honored the company's contract to sell Hiram Walker–Gooderham & Warts. The Reichmanns' costly victory would be hollow unless they somehow found a way to hang on to the distillery operation. Their hopes hung by two threads: the Ontario Supreme Court might reverse Judge Montgomery's ruling on appeal and disallow the sale, or the federal foreign investment review agency, Investment Canada, might withhold approval on the grounds that the nation's economic interests would be better served if Canadian ownership were maintained.

Paul Reichmann and his aides played the card of Canadianization with ham-handed insistence, twisting arms behind the scenes in Ottawa and casting aspersions on Allied-Lyons at every turn, privately and publicly. Olympia & York's clout—and Mickey Cohen's contacts—assured that the company's importunings were heard at the highest levels of government. The Reichmanns got a hearing, but it did them no good. The feeling within the Mulroney administration was that they had used all their chits in their relentless lobbying in the Gulf Canada deal.

Sir Derrick Holden-Brown, Allied-Lyons's chief executive, was unwavering in his assurances that the British company would maintain the status quo not only in Windsor, Ontario—the site of Hiram Walker's major distillery—but throughout Canada. He obliged union officials by putting it in writing: no asset sales, no plant closings, no layoffs. When Sir Derrick, sporting a Canadian Maple Leaf tie, visited Windsor, he seemed embarrassed at the warmth of his reception. Meanwhile, Paul Reichmann tangled himself in a web of prevarication and contradiction as he tried to finesse the question of his plans for Hiram Walker–Gooderham & Warts. He assured one and all that the liquor business would be better off under his stewardship than Holden-Brown's but was loath to foreclose any postacquisition options. The suspicion grew in Windsor that Olympia & York intended to sell all or part of the liquor operation to Seagram, which had long coveted it. If Walker were to be absorbed into Seagram, layoffs were sure to follow. Reichmann, too, made the rounds in Windsor but his presence only hardened the opposition of politicians and union leaders.

Ron Dickson, who headed the United Auto Workers local that represented many Hiram Walker employees, was so put off by Reichmann's fence-sitting that he fired off a mocking letter to the editor of the *Windsor Star:*

> Despite Mr. Reichmann's many attributes as a successful businessman and decent human being, and his devotion to duty, family and religion, he still has something to learn even from a Scottish working man of the old school. That is, to be a part of humankind, one must be a participant in the affairs of humankind and not an aloof observer. Additionally, in the real world of less celebrated men, that part of the planet where most of us dwell, a man's word is not enough unfortunately. That is why, being the unredemptive realists that we are, we at local 2027 prefer Allied-Lyons as our new employer. Anything they say, they sign. We invite Mr. Reichmann to do the same.

Early one morning a week or two before Investment Canada was expected to render judgment, Ron Dickson and his lawyer met with Reichmann in his suite at an Ottawa hotel. After listening to Reichmann's pitch, the union leader reiterated his support for Allied-Lyons and underscored the point by handing his host a copy of his letter to the editor. Dickson watched transfixed as Paul Reichmann, perhaps for the first time in his life, simply blew his top. Reichmann rose from his chair and strode angrily around the room. He dismissed Judge Montgomery as a "traffic court judge" who knew nothing of corporate law and denounced executives of Hiram Walker, Allied, and virtually everyone else who was opposing him, including Dickson. "The Englishmen are laughing at you behind your back," he told Dickson. Around noon, Reichmann suddenly snapped back into character, interrupting his tirade to say that he was late for a meeting with the minister of energy and apologize for having to leave. He shook hands with both his visitors. "Well," he said, "whoever becomes the new owners of Hiram Walker, I hope we can still be friends."

The union leader was speechless with astonishment. In the elevator, Dickson's lawyer turned to him and said: "That man is incapable of listening to anyone."

On July 9, 1987, the Ontario Supreme Court rejected Olympia & York's appeal of Judge Montgomery's ruling. Two days later, Investment Canada cleared the sale of Hiram Walker–Gooderham & Warts to Allied-Lyons. The battle was lost but Reichmann fought on. When the Canadian Broadcasting Corporation's radio news program, *As It Happens*, telephoned Olympia & York for reaction to Investment Canada's decision, the head man himself returned the call. "Why are you fighting so hard over this?" Reichmann was asked. "Why do you want the distiller so badly?" These straightforward questions drew a response so convoluted that Reichmann got lost within his own argument.

> It's very important for Gulf Canada in its present circumstances of the world prices of oil to have a diversification in a stable product and assure its ability in the future to continue its exploration and development of oil reserves. But that is not the principal question at this point in time. Sometimes one might look at this as if it were a soccer game, let's say, where scoring is what counts. That is not the situation. There are five important legal issues before the court. In the first one, the court of appeals this week when they dismissed our appeal stated that part of the agreement had a contravention to the Canada Corporation Act and that the er . . . I do not have the document in front of me.

Various lawsuits that Allied-Lyons and the Reichmanns had brought against one another were still pending in Toronto. About a month after the Investment Canada decision, Paul and Albert traveled to London with Mickey Cohen to petition for a truce. Luckily for the Reichmanns, Sir Derrick Holden-Brown was amenable. Paul and Sir Derrick quickly shook hands on the basics of an agreement: the lawsuits would be dropped and Olympia & York (through Gulf) would join Allied-Lyons as a minority partner in Hiram Walker's liquor business. To be specific, the Reichmanns would sell Allied a 51 percent stake in Hiram Walker–Gooderham & Warts and hang on to the remaining 49 percent, at least temporarily, for the English retained the right to buy out the Reichmanns eventually.

In translating this agreement-in-principle to contract form, Paul Reichmann and his minions not only looked their English gift horse in the mouth but tried to extract a few teeth. "They have a different style of negotiating and they tried it on Sir Derrick [but] he just didn't buy it," recalled an Allied-Lyons lawyer, echoing the earlier complaints of the Bank of Montreal's Bill Mulholland. "They don't start at one issue and go to issue twenty. They deliberately obfuscate the issues. . . . You can never get an issue settled. They keep chopping away at you, and you find that at the end of the day you have more issues than those with which you started." Holden-Brown, who had flown to Toronto to close the deal, finally said that enough was enough. Reichmann apologized, blaming a series of "misunderstandings." It was a Friday. Reichmann asked Sir Derrick to remain in Toronto until Shabbat ended. On Sunday morning he went down to the Englishman's hotel and in an hour's time resurrected the original agreement, which was promptly finalized without further incident.

───

As a business proposition, this was a not unhappy outcome for the Reichmanns. The brothers not only saved face after an embarrassing defeat but retained half ownership of Hiram Walker's liquor business in partnership with a company much better qualified to run it than was Olympia & York. But like Olympia & York's relentless politicking in the Gulf Canada deal, the Hiram Walker contretemps was not easily reconciled with the Reichmanns' image as the sage and gentlemanly philosopher kings of Canadian business. Long before the drama had played out, Paul Reichmann had begun trying to limit the damage with a spin control campaign camouflaged as apologia. "My brother and I goofed somewhere along the line," he told a hometown reporter in midbattle. "A misunderstanding developed. . . . Had we known it would be unfriendly, we would not have gone near it. It's not our style."

In reality, the unfriendliness was present right from the start as a result of the brothers' calculated use of the element of surprise in launching their bid for Hiram Walker. Reichmann's mea culpas were disingenuous but effective. In the press anyway, there would be no rush to rejudgment. Reporters closely documented Paul Reichmann's actions but shrank from drawing the logical conclusion: that he was as relentless and predatory an acquisitor as any. Instead, it was suggested that Reichmann had somehow acted "out of character." He had not—but neither had he acted reprehensibly in deciding to pursue Hiram Walker. The hostile takeover was not a violation of the law, whether civil or halakic, but an affront to the self-serving etiquette of the corporate elite.

The dubious aspect of Reichmann's conduct in the Hiram Walker affair lay in his elaborate dissembling. Why not just come right out and call a raid a raid? After all, Reichmann disdained the typical old-school corporate boss as much as did his allies at Edper and took a certain satisfaction in bending such men to his will. At a critical point in Olympia & York's climactic negotiations with Gulf Canada's top executives, many of whom would shortly be out of a job, both Paul and Albert pushed away from the table and departed, leaving it to their aides to explain that the brothers would not be back for a few days because they had decided to get a head start on the weekend. "In part, this was deal theater," recalled a key member of the Olympia & York team. "The Reichmanns wanted to show these people that their precious deal only mattered so much to them, that they were above it all." At the same time, it was of inestimable advantage to the Reichmanns to be perceived as gentlemanly iconoclasts rather than anti-establishment raiders. After all, they had taken great pains to position Olympia & York as the landlord of choice among the corporate elite of North America. Their benignly exalted image also had served to disarm takeover targets and bank lending officers alike.

All in all, the Hiram Walker and Gulf deals marked a turning point in the Reichmann saga much more easily recognized in retrospect than contemporaneously. If Paul Reichmann's tuxedo image was a little frayed at the cuffs, he still headed the list of North America's best-dressed businessmen. Even a blunder as colossal as their mistimed purchase of Gulf Canada barely put a dent in the Reichmanns' smart-money aura. After having acquired a controlling 60 percent interest in Gulf Canada, the brothers offered the company's minority shareholders a chance to swap their stock for cash or new shares. Gulf Canada's own directors were convinced that an overwhelming majority of stockholders would take the money and run. They were wrong. "We were amazed at how many people stayed in," recalled Alf Powis, a mining executive who was arguably Gulf's most influential board member. "Why didn't people tender? I don't know. Inertia? Capital gains? There were also a bunch of people out there saying, 'Well, we'll stay with the Reichmanns. They know how to make money.' "

For his part, Paul Reichmann saw no reason to alter course after the financial debacle of winning Gulf Canada and the embarrassment of losing Hiram Walker. Although Reichmann continued to invoke diversification as his aim, what had begun as a strategy would end as mere rationale. "When I say that Paul is a deal maker," observed Andy Sarlos, the Bay Street money manager, "what I really mean is he's a deal addict. . . . The goal of making a new deal was not to become rich, it was to make bigger and bigger deals, simply for their own sake—and with the hope of topping his previous best."

Actually, Reichmann was twice addicted: to the thrill of the chase and to the postcapture opportunities for financial elaboration. Just as he never stopped pursuing new acquisitions, he never ceased reshuffling the assets he had already acquired. With the addition of the many subsidiaries of Hiram Walker and Gulf Canada to Abitibi-Price, Reichmann had a great many new pieces to play with. For the rest of Olympia & York's existence, he would keep a legion of MBAs busy continuously redeploying the many component parts of the family's industrial empire to maximum immediate advantage in the financial markets. But even Reichmann's skill at the opportunistic arts of corporate finance would not, in the end, be enough to offset the disastrous consequences of his flawed investment judgment.

Chapter 35

By the mid-1980s, the ultra-Orthodox community of North York was bursting at the seams, swollen by the high birthrate characteristic of haredim everywhere and by a continuous influx of new immigrants to Toronto—not from Europe this time but the overburdened Hasidic settlements of New York City and its environs. In their open-ended willingness to underwrite schools, synagogues, and the other infrastructural undergirdings of the strictly observant life, the Reichmanns had played the leading part in the Orthodoxification of Toronto ever since the late 1960s. "There is a vibrant ultra-Orthodox pocket here that did not exist before the Reichmanns," observed Rabbi Irwin Witty, the longtime director of the Board of Jewish Education in Toronto. "It wasn't the Reichmanns alone who brought it into being but they had great impact."

Paul and his brothers had always welcomed—and occasionally solicited—contributions to the many institutions under their sponsorship. But as the Reichmanns' wealth had burgeoned, other donors had fallen by the wayside in Toronto, happily leaving it to the billionaires in their midst to pick up the tab. The community of some four hundred haredi families that coalesced around the Reichmanns had continued to observe the forms of shared decision making; each school and synagogue was run by a board, on which non-Reichmanns greatly outnumbered Reichmanns. But in the end, only one opinion truly mattered. The family was treated with such deference by its coreligionists, most of whom were financially beholden in one way or another, that its authority rarely required assertion. In effect, if not intent, the Reichmanns' overwhelming generosity had transformed the ultra-Orthodox fringe of Toronto's Jewish community into a banana republic. Even so, Reichmann domination occasioned only minor grumbling until 1986, when the brothers imported a zealous young haredi rabbi named Jacob Hezekiah Sofer from Israel.

In their North York neighborhood, the Reichmanns over the years had assembled all the components of a self-sufficient ultra-Orthodox community in the Old World mode with the exception of a chief rabbi. Rabbi Meyer Grunwald, the Tsaitcher Rebbe, had filled the role until his death but had been succeeded by rabbis of decidedly inferior stature. Despite its explosive growth in the 1970s and the 1980s, Toronto's ultra-Orthodox community had suffered no loss of cohesiveness, as Reichmann money and prestige effectively substituted for the glue of spiritual authority. In a sense, the cause of congregational unity was served by the lack of rabbinical counterweight to the Reichmanns' influence. However, no one came to feel the absence of rabbinical leadership more keenly than did the brothers' own yeshiva-steeped sons.

Enter Rabbi Sofer, who was still in his thirties and at that awkward stage of being acclaimed more for his lineage than his accomplishments. Directly, if distantly, descended from the great Hatam Sofer, the founding father of Oberlander Orthodoxy, Rabbi Sofer also was the son-in-law of one of the most powerful contemporary figures in Israeli ultra-Orthodoxy: Rabbi Israel Moshe Dushinsky, the head of Jerusalem's Beth Din, or Orthodox communal court. Rabbi Sofer's appeal to the Reichmann brothers was threefold: he was Hungarian, his religious pedigree was impeccable, and he was available. (Rare was the Israeli rabbi willing to make reverse aliyah.)

The Reichmanns installed Rabbi Sofer at Minyan Avrecheim. Better known as the Boat Shul (the humble quarters it occupied had formerly housed a boat dealership), Minyan Avrecheim was one of three North York synagogues most closely associated with the family. Although the Reichmann men davened at all three shuls on occasion, there were marked familial preferences based on subtle differences in approach. Most members of Albert's branch of the family, along with two of Ralph's sons, preferred the Boat Shul, which was a bit less Old World in its forms of worship than the old family flagship, Yesodei Hatorah, which Ralph himself preferred. Paul and his sons usually could be found at Zichron Schneur, which was just a few blocks down Bathurst Street from the Boat Shul and was the most intellectually arduous of the trio.

Rabbi Sofer did not prove a popular choice with the Boat Shul congregation. "Rabbi Sofer tried with mixed results to continue along the old Hungarian Hasidic path he followed in Israel but most members here are not Hasidic but at best Hasidically influenced—like the Reichmanns themselves," said Joseph Lebovic, a Boat Shul regular (and no relation to the local developer of the same name.) Worse, the Israeli proved personally ambitious far beyond the family's expectations as he lost no time trying to parlay his status as "the Reichmanns' rabbi" into community-wide preeminence in Toronto. "Rabbi Sofer was not brought here with the intent of making him chief [Orthodox] rabbi," said

Philip Reichmann, one of the mainstays of the Boat Shul. "But he felt that his position should be larger than just the rabbi of one shul."

While Toronto had its share of eminent Orthodox rabbis over the decades, none had been able to bridge the community's many ethnic and theological divisions and establish universal authority. Few had even tried. By the mid-1980s, Toronto was home to more than forty Orthodox congregations, ranging in size from Ahavas Achim-Nachlat Israel with twenty member families to Shaarei Shomayim, the leading modern Orthodox congregation, with fourteen hundred families. Although admiration of the Reichmanns cut across all the lines of sectarian division within Orthodoxy—indeed within the Jewish community at large—the family's stature did not translate into a general willingness to submit to the fundamentalist dictates of a newly arrived immigrant haredi rabbi.

Rabbi Sofer launched his campaign for supremacy by attacking the local rabbinical establishment's approach to a particularly troublesome aspect of Shabbat observance. It is clearly forbidden to carry anything, even a prayer book, in the public domain on the Sabbath. However, the Talmud explained in great detail how by means of poles and pieces of string one can symbolically close off a public domain and nominally render it a private domain in which carrying is permitted. This theoretical private domain is called an eruv, which in Hebrew means mixing or combining. In a sense, the eruv treats all the inhabitants of an area as if they were members of a single household. Eruvs have long been in place in most communities around the world with a significant Orthodox population. In major cities, eruvs tend to be highly complex rabbinical concoctions that incorporate sea walls, power lines, telephone lines, and so on, as well as the more prosaic poles and string. Careful monitoring is required because if the continuous perimeter is breached, the eruv is invalidated. Indeed, many haredim choose not to carry within an eruv for fear that a part of it may collapse during Shabbat.

After World War II, Toronto's eruv came under the supervision of Rabbi Abraham Price, a Pole who had emigrated to Canada in 1939 from Germany and was appointed director of a major Toronto yeshiva. Rabbi Price was a former Talmudic prodigy whom many considered the most accomplished Torah scholar of the postwar era in Toronto. Beginning in the 1950s, Rabbi Price pushed the boundaries of the eruv northward to accommodate Jewish flight to the suburbs. He took great pride in his eruv, which was said to be the largest in the world, and in his worldwide reputation as an eruv expert. Rabbi Price was so learned, in fact, that he might well have been acclaimed as Toronto's unofficial chief rabbi had he not been such an autocratic, curmudgeonly sort.

By the time Rabbi Sofer burst upon the scene, Rabbi Price was eighty-six years old and long past his heyday. Although he had maintained his scholarly reputation, his yeshiva was defunct and his congregation largely dissipated. During his first year in Toronto, Rabbi Sofer several times had called on Rabbi Price, who was not particularly impressed with the newcomer's erudition. As the newcomer was leaving after his first visit, Rabbi Price was heard to say, "This man has to sit down and learn some things." For his part, Rabbi Sofer apparently concluded that Rabbi Price was faltering and vulnerable. He was aware, as well, that his patrons never carried on Shabbat. Or, as Philip Reichmann put it, "Paul and my father always felt there was a problem with the eruv."

One Saturday, the members of Toronto's Orthodox congregations arrived for Shabbat services to find posters tacked to a wall of their synagogues. Written in Hebrew, the posters harshly attacked the validity of Rabbi Price's eruv. While the technical basis of the challenge was vague and incomplete, its central contention was absolutely clear: to carry within the eruv was to violate the sanctity of the Sabbath. The document was signed by Rabbi Sofer and four rabbis who taught at Reichmann-sponsored schools, including the head of the kollel, Rabbi Jacob Hirschfield. The effect of its posting was galvanic; no one in the Reichmanns' religious circle talked of anything else for weeks. In making a brief rejoinder before his own congregation, Rabbi Price cried bitterly and then retreated to his study to write a formal defense of his eruv.

Whether Rabbi Price's eruv was sound was an issue of paramount concern to the many Orthodox Torontonians who did carry on the Sabbath; nothing less than their religious integrity suddenly was at stake. The issue was so complex technically that most lay persons were not even qualified to hold an opinion on it. At the same time, a great majority of the Orthodox rabbinate and laity were united in their outrage over the inflammatory tactics of Rabbi Sofer, who had made no attempt to raise his concerns through proper channels. Although few people suspected that the Reichmanns had explicitly authorized the attack Rabbi Sofer led on Rabbi Price and his eruv, many community leaders held the brothers responsible nonetheless for not publicly disassociating themselves from his campaign of intimidation—his failed campaign.

By most estimates, only about 10 percent of the Orthodox population of Toronto stopped carrying per Rabbi Sofer's instructions while awaiting a ruling on the eruv from a special rabbinical tribunal, the Vaad HaRabbonim. They waited in vain, for after protracted consideration the panel neither affirmed nor invalidated Rabbi Price's eruv but ducked the issue by authorizing the Reichmann rabbis to create their own eruv. They did not bother. Like an equally bitter battle over kosher butchering standards that took place in the 1920s, the great eruv battle of the 1980s produced no winners, only losers.

———

In Toronto—as in almost every other place in the world—relations between the haredim and the rest of the Jewish community had been mutually antagonistic long before the great eruv controversy erupted. It is a basic tenet of faith among the ultra-Orthodox that they alone are fully and authentically following the word of the Creator, but with some exceptions (most notably the Lubavitcher Hasidim) they are disinclined to proselytize, preferring to withdraw from the contagion of nonbelief into self-imposed quarantine. For its part, the Jewish majority generally concedes the importance of a vibrant Orthodoxy to Judaism's survival but tends to resent the rebuke implicit in haredi separatism and to look down on the ultra-Orthodox as intolerant, antiquarian cultists.

The Reichmanns were a special case. "The Reichmanns were held in the greatest respect in the Jewish community from A to Z," said Rabbi Gunther Plaut, the longtime rabbi of Holy Blossom Temple, Toronto's (and Canada's) largest Reform congregation. "People were impressed that they were strict about their observance and so public about their observance yet so private in the way they led their lives." The brothers' good manners also recommended them to outsiders. In contrast to many rank-and-file haredim, family members were unfailingly civil in their chance encounters with the less observant. Stephen Speisman, a Ph.D. historian employed by the Jewish Federation of Greater Toronto, often crossed paths with Paul Reichmann on Saturday afternoons in the mid-1980s on his way to attend Shabbat services at Shaarei Shomayin, Toronto's great bastion of modern Orthodoxy. "My custom is to wear a beret and my suit is not necessarily black," Speisman said. "Most people from the [ultra-Orthodox] community would turn the other way rather than greet me. But with Paul Reichmann, he would always say 'Good Shabbos' to me first, even if I was wearing my checked coat."

Make no mistake—however conciliatory their style, the Reichmanns were as categorical in their religious beliefs as their less politic coreligionists. "The Reichmanns will accept non-Orthodox people as fine human beings but just do not see them as religiously authentic," said Kurt Rothschild, the Toronto communal activist who acted as the Reichmanns' unofficial liaison with the larger Jewish community in Toronto. Inevitably, the family felt the sting of backlash as the ultra-Orthodox community not only grew rapidly in numbers during the 1970s and 1980s but increasingly asserted itself on basic issues of belief and practice, resulting in the battle over the eruv.

———

The mounting friction between the ultra- and non-Orthodox in Toronto was as much a matter of money as religious practice for, to the great annoyance of the Canadian Jewish establishment, the Reichmanns refused to cut the larger community in on what was a philanthropic bonanza. As the value of Olympia & York's assets soared in the aftermath of the Uris purchase, the Reichmann family's philanthropy was freed from financial constraint. "Olympia & York's strength was in our minds so large by the late 1970s," Paul said, "that we believed we could afford to give whatever we thought was right." The family's giving was so extemporaneous as well as so vast that not even its members knew exactly how much was handed out over the years, but Paul's best estimate was that the annual giving climbed from $10 million to $20 million in the mid-1970s to $50 million to $60 million by the mid-1980s. Whatever the exact tally, the Reichmann brothers probably ranked as the most munificent Jewish donors in the world during Olympia & York's heyday.

Despite the rapid growth of the local ultra-Orthodox community, the great bulk of the Reichmanns' millions continued to flow overseas, to some one thousand haredi institutions scattered throughout the United States, South America, Europe, and the Middle East. Two-thirds of them were in Israel, where the strictly observant population was both more numerous and impoverished than in North America. While yeshivoth—both Sephardi and Ashkenazi—continued to claim the lion's share of the family's largesse, huge sums also flowed into hospitals and welfare organizations tending to the ultra-Orthodox. In Israel, for example, a Reichmann fund assisted all haredi newlyweds—provided that the groom was registered in a kollel—with home mortgages of as much as $12,000 and a supplementary, interest-free loan of $3,000 to cover basic furnishings.

Meanwhile, the Reichmanns gradually expanded the purview of their giving in Toronto to encompass a wide range of clinics and hospitals of diverse religious affiliation—Jewish, Catholic, Protestant. "Medical care is something we all need and in which religion makes no difference," said Paul in explaining the ecumenicism of the family's medical philanthropy. Unlike some fundamentalist religious groups, the ultra-Orthodox tend to be progressive medically, taking to heart the Talmudic instruction to the sick, "One may not rely on miracles." In fact, many haredi rabbis "maintain their own worldwide network of contracts with the top men in every branch of medicine, and are able to refer their followers to the best hospitals and the most advanced treatments."

In addition to their gifts to such Jewish hospitals, the Reichmanns made sizable, regular contributions to Jewish Family and Child Services and to a variety of Jewish old age homes. However, the brothers routinely rebuffed fund-raising appeals from the United Jewish Appeal (UJA) and the other central organs of the Toronto community. "The impact of the Reichmanns' refusal to give to our general campaign went far beyond the family itself because it sent a powerful message to others in the Orthodox community to follow suit," lamented Mark Gryfe, the UJA director in Toronto.

The brothers found it harder to hold their purist stance after 1977, when Bais Yaakov High School became the first of the schools in the Reichmann orbit to accept funding from the community at large. After long negotiation, the Board of Jewish Education obligingly categorized its modest payment (which amounted to only 5 percent of Bais Yaakov's annual budget) as a grant rather than a subvention, thereby exempting the high school from the affiliation requirements that the haredim found objectionable. The inauguration of community funding of Bais Yaakov High (the board's grant was provided annually and rose both in absolute and relative terms to account for more than 20 percent of the high school's budget) created an expectation of reciprocity of which the Reichmanns were well aware. After 1977, Paul Reichmann recalled, "it became a bit of a game of chicken between us and the UJA."

The brothers were not about to begin pumping money into programs that strengthened Reform and Conservative Judaism. But Albert Reichmann extended an olive branch when a UJA delegation headed by Albert "Tubby" Cole came calling on behalf of the 1977–78 general campaign. The Reichmanns had just decided to contribute $7 million over five years toward the building of a new yeshiva complex in Israel. Albert agreed to route the entire contribution through the UJA, thus allowing the organization to inflate its campaign totals and attract matching funds. "It was not a formal pledge," conceded Irwin Gold, UJA director at the time. "Albert wrote some numbers down on a napkin." Albert made the first of the promised payments, delivering a satchel containing $750,000 in cash to the UJA's offices. But then the yeshiva project was canceled as the Israeli government backed out of an agreement to help fund it, and the Reichmanns refused the UJA's requests to funnel other of the family's charitable contributions through the organization. "The Reichmanns kept their faith with us," Gold said, "but it was a dead end anyway."

Every year a high-powered new chairman accepted the honor of heading the UJA's annual fund-raising drive hoping that he would be the one to finally overcome the Reichmanns' refusal of the community's embrace. In 1986, during the battle over the eruv, the Jewish establishment's resentment ratcheted up another notch as the family—at Albert's behest—decided to make its first gift to the United Way of Greater Toronto. After Gordon Cressy, the latest in a long line of United Way presidents to call on the Reichmanns, finished his pitch, Albert stared at him impassively for a full minute and a half. Wholly unnerved, Cressy nonetheless resisted the temptation to elaborate and struggled to return Reichmann's gaze without seeming defiant. "That is a good presentation," Reichmann finally told Cressy and pledged $100,000, which was not a great deal of money relative to Olympia & York's size but not exactly spare change either. UJA fund-raisers would have to wait another four years before logging a similar breakthrough.

———

The influx of ultra-Orthodox families to Glenwood over the years created an insular minority community within a generally tolerant but uncomprehending larger community. Aside from the chance sidewalk encounter, the Reichmanns and their coreligionists had no social intercourse whatsoever with their nonobservant neighbors. For all practical purposes, the family's dealings with Glenwood's non-Orthodox majority were restricted to what was for many suburbanites a secular equivalent of religion: residential real estate.

The extended Reichmann family was an overwhelmingly dominant force in the Glenwood property market. Within an area of about a dozen square blocks, the Reichmanns owned at least forty houses, purchased at a total cost of about $20 million but worth many times that in market value even after the Toronto real estate market collapsed in the early 1990s. A dozen of these served as residences for teachers and students at the Reichmann schools, especially Yesodei Hatorah and the Institute of Advanced Talmudic Study. The remainder were family homes, the great majority of which were purchased during the 1980s, as Paul, Albert, and Ralph expanded their own holdings and also began buying properties in trust for their sons and daughters. As the next generation moved out on its own, some of its members rivaled their elders as neighborhood property accumulators. By the late 1980s, Steven Reichmann, Ralph's second-born son, and his wife, Shirley, owned houses at 29 Forest Wood (just two doors down from Uncle Albert and Aunt Egosah), 31 Forest Wood, 33 Forest Wood, and 460 Glencairn.

The Reichmanns almost always paid in cash—$340,000 here, $935,000 there—and rarely sold. The family's heavy net buying undoubtedly provided a boost to property values in Glenwood Park, which, in any event, rose precipitously virtually without pause. (In 1965, Paul and Lea Reichmann had paid $90,000 for a house at 241 Strathallan Wood in establishing the family beachhead in Glenwood. In 1989, it cost Paul $2.2 million for a marginally larger house just a block away for his younger son, seventeen-year-old Henry, who was still in yeshiva in New Jersey.) Then, too, the Reichmanns met most of the usual criteria of neighborly good conduct, being quiet, well-mannered folk who maintained their properties beautifully and minded their own business. And yet their prolific real estate maneuverings engendered much fear and consternation among the neighbors, many of whom were inconvenienced by never-ending construction and remodeling projects and came to feel, moreover, as if Glenwood Park were being transformed, deed by deed, zoning variance by zoning variance, into a Reichmann family compound.

One afternoon in the early 1980s, a longtime Glenwood Park resident who lived around the corner from a Reichmann noticed a suspicious-looking man sitting in a car parked on the street near his house. After an hour, he went out and confronted the stranger. "Sorry, sir," the stranger mumbled in response, "Reichmann security." By such ad hoc means did the neighbors learn that the Reichmanns had assembled a private security force of a dozen off-duty police officers to watch over their many properties day and night. The prevalent reaction was one of ambivalence. The entire neighborhood was afforded an added measure of protection against crime. But who could relax living next to a family with its own police force?

Although the Reichmann brothers continued to live far below their means, the mid-1980s brought a substantial upgrading in lifestyle nonetheless. Ralph was the first brother to create a more luxurious dwelling for himself. In the late 1970s, he enlarged 214 Strathallan Wood and added an indoor swimming pool and mikveh in the backyard. A half-dozen years later, Carl and Bonnie Lindros, parents of future National Hockey League superstar Eric Lindros, moved into the house directly behind the Reichmanns, 411 Glencairn, and soon began lobbing complaints about the mikveh's height and proximity to the lot line. Undeterred, Ralph bought the house next door to his new neighbors and a second residence two doors down in the other direction. The effect was to isolate the Lindroses and their next-door neighbor, Andrew Common, within a band of Reichmann-held territory extending from Strathallan all the way through the block to Glencairn. Ralph razed the newly purchased houses and filed an application with North York officials to sever the rear one-third of both lots and add the land to his own lot at 214 Strathallan Wood.

Ralph's severance application was a lighted match tossed into the bubbling swamp of Lindros resentment. They hired a lawyer and not only fought the severance application but challenged the legality of the mikveh, which was connected to the rear of the Reichmanns' house by a long covered walkway. The Lindroses contended that the walkway violated the applicable zoning bylaw, which specified that any accessory building on the property had to be detached from the main dwelling. Ralph took a chain saw and satisfied the legal standard of detachment by making a five-centimeter cut in the walkway. The Lindroses then complained that the bathhouse exceeded the maximum fifteen-foot height limit and gathered twenty-six signatures on a petition demanding that the township of North York take action against the Reichmanns. After much skirmishing, it was determined that the building had never been measured using the exact methods prescribed under the bylaw. "Unquestionably, the building is close to the maximum height," George Dixon, the city solicitor of North York, neutrally observed after inspecting the premises, "it might be a few inches more, it might be a few inches less."

Before a measurement could be taken, the Lindroses and their supporters prevailed upon Milton Berger, the longtime councilman for the neighborhood, to intervene on their behalf. At Berger's urging, the North York City Council took the extraordinary step of voting unanimously to hire a private lawyer selected by Mrs. Lindros to haul Ralph Reichmann into the Provincial Offense Court, which had authority to levy fines of as much as $25,000 for zoning infractions. The council's action caught Ralph unaware and also surprised the neighborhood, which had grown accustomed to watching the Reichmanns get pretty much whatever they wanted out of the North York building department and committee of adjustment.

The Reichmanns rallied with some belated politicking of their own. The family, especially Albert, had a friend in Mel Lastman, who was a local institution as the longtime mayor of North York. "Albert never said no to me," recalled Lastman, who was a tireless fund-raiser for community causes. Reichmann had made a $1 million donation to a local hospital through Lastman and contributed $3 million to the State of Israel bond drive the year that the mayor was its main honoree. Once Mayor Lastman had asked Albert to sponsor him in a swimathon and received what he considered an astounding offer. "Albert said, 'If you jump in without your trunks, I'll give $1,000.' That really threw me," Lastman said. "That didn't seem like a Reichmann." The mayor wore an old-fashioned, full-body suit and thus swam without trunks. Albert paid up.

Just two weeks after the City Council had decided to intervene on behalf of the Lindroses, it voted—again unanimously—to rescind its action. The *Globe & Mail* quoted an "exasperated" Mel Lastman. "It's going to go behind closed doors," the mayor said. "I think we can work things out." Things were indeed worked out—to the satisfaction of Ralph and Ada Reichmann. Not long after the Reichmanns' severance application was approved, the Lindroses decided to sell their house and leave the neighborhood. The mikveh, which never was formally measured, stood as tall on the day the Lindroses departed as on the day they had moved in.

It was not just Ralph's mikveh that annoyed the Reichmanns' neighbors. Behind his ultramodern house at 25 Forest Wood, Albert installed an indoor swimming pool enclosed within a glass-walled structure so large and so brightly lit that some irritated neighbors took to calling it "the subway station." Meanwhile, Paul paid $885,000 to buy the adjoining houses on either side of his home at 241 Strathallan Wood. Both were demolished to make way for a remodeling project so extensive that it amounted to a reinvention of 241 Strathallan. Most of the newly acquired land was used to create a meticulously realized, arboreal refuge of a yard that enveloped the house on three sides. "Landscaping," an admiring neighbor observed, "is the family specialty."

The result was elegant rather than ostentatious and by billionaire standards rather modest. That the remodeling of 241 Strathallan would take five full years and several million dollars to accomplish was a function of the perfectionism of Lea Reichmann, who directed the project as authoritatively as her husband ran Olympia & York. Paul was not allowed so much as a peek at his new study—a capacious, rectangular room lined from floor to ceiling on every side with oak book shelves—until its every nuance had been completed to Lea's satisfaction. (These shelves would be entirely filled with Talmudic and other religious texts; like his mother, Reichmann read secular books avidly but did not display them in his library.) Lea Reichmann was so displeased with the $1 million handiwork of the first landscaper hired that she brought in a second firm to rip it out and start over.

The Reichmanns moved out for the duration of the project and took up residence a block over at 1 Forest Wood, the house that Olympia & York had built for Renée Reichmann, who had taken title to the place but never actually lived there. But their neighbors on Strathallan and Alexandra Wood did not have the luxury of temporarily relocating and thus had to suffer the annoyances of living next to a construction zone for five years. Since many of them lived downgrade, this meant enduring a continuous flow of watery sludge. By all accounts, Paul and Lea were duly apologetic and prompt in offering reimbursement for damages, and their reinvented residence in the end was welcomed as a tastefully rendered prop to local property values. But there was no mistaking the exasperation and bewilderment in the voices of the Reichmanns' neighbors a decade later as they pondered the mystery of the project's duration. If Olympia & York could put up the tallest office tower in Canada in eighteen months, why had it taken Paul and Lea Reichmann five years to remodel 241 Strathallan Wood?

The next generation of Reichmanns as a rule aspired while still in their twenties to the same standards of domestic luxury to which their parents had graduated in their fifties. That is, as the Reichmann sons and daughters married and moved out on their own, they tended to live not below but a bit beyond their present means, in anticipation of one day coming into their Olympia & York inheritance. The Reichmann brothers and their wives seemed to frown upon and indulge their children's material longings in roughly equal measure, cautioning them against self-indulgence, on one hand, and furnishing them with ample cash, on the other. From the neighbors' vantage point, though, the pertinent issue was not financial but aesthetic. While the Reichmann brothers' own houses were larger and fancier than the average Glenwood Park dwelling, their scale and sumptuousness were not evident from the street and not visually disruptive. By contrast, some of the younger Reichmanns did not mind advertising a bit. As a rule, they built houses that were much larger (relative both to their own grounds and the surrounding dwellings) and much showier than the ones in which they had been reared, and they often did not bother with the camouflage of artful landscaping.

The younger generation's tendency to bombast was manifested most controversially in the misadventures of the ill-starred David, Ralph's eldest son, who completed his yeshiva training in Israel and England and returned to Toronto in 1983. Two years earlier, at age twenty-one, David had married Rachele Friedman, the daughter of a wealthy haredi businessman who had grown up amid the spectacular natural beauty of Lugano, which forms part of a finger of Swiss territory that juts down into the lake country of northern Italy. David and Rachele were well paired in terms of pedigree but not personality. Where he was exuberant and impulsive, she was reserved and calculating. "She was very Swiss is the best way to put it," said Mira Dishel, who later worked as David's secretary. "She was the opposite of him in every way."

In mid-1987, David and Rachele Reichmann paid $900,000 in cash for a house at 413 Lytton Boulevard. Late one night a few weeks later, Joan Foy opened her front door to find a pretty young stranger who implored in heavily accented English, "I'd like to buy your house. Please can I buy your house. Please." Mrs. Foy, who had lived with her family at 415 Lytton for seventeen years, knew that a Reichmann had just bought the house next door, but decided to play dumb. "Oh," she replied, "and who might you be?" Rachele Reichmann smilingly declined to answer and promptly departed.

The next day, Mrs. Foy got a telephone call from a polite young man who said it had been his wife who had knocked on her door last night and that they really did want to buy her house. "I see," she replied noncommittally. "By the way, what is your name?"

"David," he replied hesitantly. "David Turner." (At the time, John Turner was much in the news as leader of the Labour Party in Canada.)

"I had to laugh," Mrs. Foy recalled, "because I knew it was a Reichmann. Later, David apologized for not telling me who he was right away."

The Reichmanns were known in the neighborhood as shrewd, patient buyers who rarely used real estate brokers and who routinely disabused sellers of the notion that billionaires do not mind paying a big premium above market value. "Don't try to hold up a Reichmann," counseled Mrs. Foy. "Let's say your house is worth $800,000 and you ask $1 million, they'll laugh you right out the door. David walked through my house and he knew exactly what it was worth." To Mrs. Foy money was not an issue. She and her husband still had three children at home and just were not ready to leave the neighborhood. David Reichmann persisted for nearly a year, even telephoning the Foys several times from Lugano while visiting his in-laws. The couple who owned the house on the other side of the Reichmanns' lot were not interested in selling either.

Had David Reichmann succeeded in buying an adjoining property, he could have had a yard as well as a house. As it was he applied to the North York committee of adjustment for permission to build a house that would cover 44 percent of his lot, far above the allowable maximum of 33 percent. A waiver to the pertinent bylaw was duly granted, setting off alarm bells up and down Lytton Boulevard. The neighbors' concern hardened into opposition when they got a peek at the blueprints filed with the building department. The plans showed a 5,900-square-foot structure of three stories, each 10 to 12 feet high, built atop a massive foundation raised 5 feet above grade. "It's going to tower over everything on the street," complained Mary Boeckh, who had lived directly across the street for forty years. To some, the building looked more like a "gaudy hotel" than a home. "David told me, 'Don't worry, it will be just like my father's house," Mrs. Foy recalled. "In my opinion, Ralph Reichmann has one of the finest homes in Toronto. I told David it wouldn't be anything like his father's house. Poor David. I think he really did want a house like he grew up in. But his wife wanted a big, big house, so what could he do?"

David hired Sean-Thomas Limited, an Orthodox-owned general contractor favored by the family. The existing house was leveled and all eleven trees in the yard removed. The oldest of the trees was so large that its root system extended deep into the Foys' property. When it was felled, the roots ripped up through the surface, lifting the deck of the Foys' pool skyward. In the spring of 1988, workmen began excavating the cleared lot to a depth of forty feet in places. All the tiles promptly fell off the Foys' swimming pool. "Whenever there were problems, one of the Reichmanns would scurry over and say they'd make it right," Mrs. Foy said. "I said to David, 'To add insult to injury, they're your tiles, Mr. Reichmann.' We both had to laugh at that." Olympia Floor & Wall Tile provided a better brand of replacement tile. "The Reichmanns were more than generous in compensating us for damages."

A concrete foundation with walls two feet thick was poured and then construction stopped suddenly in the summer of 1988, never to resume. The workmen cleared off, leaving a gargantuan, concrete-lined pit protected on all sides by a rickety snow fence. The local children did their best to turn the semi-abandoned site into a playground, swinging from the steel reinforcing rods protruding from the concrete and generally risking their necks. Boeckh, the Foys, and twenty other neighbors collaborated on a letter of protest to David Reichmann and his general contractor. Reichmann, who had been transferred to New York by Olympia & York, did not respond. Tom Schonberger of Sean-Thomas wrote back, promising that construction would resume "within the next few weeks." It did not. A year passed. In the fall of 1989, the exasperated neighbors persuaded the *Toronto Star* to publish an article highlighting their complaints. A dozen of them posed for the accompanying photo, standing grim-faced before David Reichmann's "monster hole" and giving the thumbs-down sign.

The hole would remain even after the property was sold (for a lucrative $1.675 million) in late 1989. But immediately after the article appeared, a watchman was posted at the site and a security fence installed. "The Reichmanns really tried to appease everyone, which was difficult under the circumstances," said Mrs. Foy, adding that she was not surprised that the family reacted as it did to the publicity. What did catch her off guard was the reaction of her neighbors. "You wouldn't believe the number of calls I got from people just frightened to death of having a Reichmann next door," she recalled. "They all wanted my advice. 'What should we do? The Reichmanns are going to build next to us.' There was this image that they were going to take over the neighborhood house by house."

To a degree, the mid-1980s surge of anti-Reichmann sentiment on the home front was an outgrowth of the family's success. Subtle changes in the family's social demeanor also played a part, as the next generation of Reichmanns began asserting themselves. Fundamentally, though, the problem was one of proportion. Most families that amass enormous wealth vault up the social ladder two or three rungs at a time and enter the rarefied realm where the super-rich associate only with one another and the super-famous. But the Reichmanns stayed put, literally and figuratively, and the sheer magnitude of their presence increasingly unnerved and intimidated the regular folk with whom they came in contact. Rubbing shoulders with giants will make even a tall man feel like a midget.

Chapter 36

Over the years, each of the Toronto brothers had formed deep personal and religious attachments to Israel, which had served as Edward's home base since 1968. Paul and Ralph had attended yeshiva in Israel, as had many members of the next generation of Reichmanns and Hellers, and both Paul and Albert had married women from Israel. The family had chosen B'nai Brak as the site of their memorial to their late father—the Beit Shmaya yeshiva—and sister Eva had been buried in Jerusalem. Paul especially was widely connected within Israeli rabbinical circles, with dozens of friends and acquaintances throughout the country. For one reason or another, each of the Toronto Reichmanns had made at least one trip to Israel every year during their three decades of residence in Canada. In the early 1980s, Albert and Ralph each bought an apartment in Jerusalem and began spending the Sukkoth and Pesach holidays in Israel. During the Canary Wharf years, Paul, too, would become a more frequent visitor than before, often flying in from London to spend the weekend in B'nai Brak or Jerusalem.

And yet Albert, Paul, and Ralph never came to share Edward's Zionist ardor. Like most strict traditionalists, the Toronto brothers were disquieted by the very notion of a secular Jewish homeland. In the ultra-Orthodox view, the founders of Israel had presumed to do what the Messiah was destined to do: restore Jewish dominion over the Holy Land. On the other hand, the Reichmanns were not ideologues but pragmatists who recognized that even a secular Jewish state served a useful purpose as a refuge from persecution and, furthermore, that it was in the self-interest of the family and of ultra-Orthodoxy generally to cultivate good relations with the government in Israel, no matter how godless its leaders might be. As businessmen, though, the Toronto brothers gave Israel wide berth during Olympia & York's first two decades for, by North American standards certainly, the Israeli economy was both puny and perilously narrow-gauged. Worse, in the Reichmann view, Israel was essentially an experiment in state socialism, with its high tax rates, militant labor unions, and heavy regulation of the private sector.

In the late 1970s, the Toronto brothers had reconsidered their aversion to Israel as the Uris bonanza began to roll in, pushing Olympia & York to take its first steps beyond real estate and North America. Then, too, Menachem Begin's election in 1977 as prime minister had ended the Labor Party's unbroken twenty-nine-year rule in Israel and marked the beginning of a swing to the right under the Likud. Finally and perhaps most important, Sar-Shalom Shiran had stepped down as Israeli budget director with the change of government and accepted a job offer from Olympia & York. Paul Reichmann had first met Shiran while securing government approvals for the Beit Shmaya project and had come away thinking him "an extremely fine gentleman"—even if he did work for a leftist regime. During a state visit to Washington in early 1977, Shiran accepted Paul's invitation to visit Toronto and returned to Israel agog with admiration for his host. "There are no superlatives too big to describe his imagination and skill," he said later.

After joining Olympia & York in 1978, Shiran put the Reichmanns onto a half-dozen investment opportunities in Israel, the most significant of which involved the development of a new government quarter, or kirya, in Tel Aviv, Israel's capital. For many years, the national government had been quartered in an unwieldy collection of houses converted to office use. Adapting a concept that had been kicking around for a few years, Olympia & York submitted a proposal to develop a modern, cost-efficient government office complex and to finance its construction by selling off the old houses, which sat on highly valuable land. Paul Reichmann met with Simha Ehrlich, Begin's finance minister, who was enthusiastic. However, the plan itself antagonized the public employee unions, which feared that the consolidation of government offices would bring a net loss of jobs, while the involvement of the Reichmanns—rich, mysterious, Orthodox foreigners—affronted vested interests galore. After one brief but tempestuous discussion in the Knesset, the Begin government tabled the proposal. "The whole thing was highly politicized," Paul recalled. "We were not trying to do a Canary Wharf. To us, it was more of a service to the government than a business opportunity."

With Shiran's help, the Reichmanns also pursued an acquisition of Bank Tefahot, Israel's leading mortgage bank and among the most profitable of several state-controlled banks that the Begin government wanted to privatize. Clal, a consortium of three of the largest Israeli banks, owned a minority stake in Bank Tefahot and desperately wanted to buy the rest. However, members of the Knesset finance committee balked at approving a sale to Clal and instead dangled the bank before the Reichmanns at a bargain price of $17 million. A majority of the committee favored selling Tefahot to the Reichmanns on the cheap, in hopes that the purchase would encourage the brothers to make additional investments in Israel. However, Clal rallied, putting pressure on Finance Minister Ehrlich, who announced that the government would sell its controlling interest to the Canadians only if they bought out the other shareholders— namely Clal—at the same time. The effect was to quadruple the cost of the acquisition to Olympia & York.

Talks continued for many months as the deal was continually adjusted to conform to changing political and economic conditions and the Reichmanns' mounting ambivalence. After nearly two years of fitful negotiations, the brothers finally pulled their bid for Bank Tefahot, which went to Clal. At about the same time, Olympia & York also backed away from negotiations to acquire a controlling stake in Ararat Insurance, a company traded on the Tel Aviv stock exchange. "There was an intent and a will to do something in Israel," Paul recalled, "but there was always some gap that we couldn't bridge." By 1980, the brothers were convinced anew that trying to do business in Israel was simply not worth the aggravation and stopped trying, parting with Sar-Shalom Shiran on friendly terms.

The retreat of the Toronto brothers restored Edward to primacy as the family's Israeli entrepreneur. When Begin was elected, Edward and his wife had ended their self-imposed, two-year exile in Miami Beach and hurried back to Jerusalem. "When Begin came in, I felt I could start doing big business in Israel," Reichmann recalled. Although the business he ended up doing in fact was not big—certainly not by Olympia & York's standards—Edward's accomplishments as a developer were impressive nonetheless. Each of Reichmann's four building projects were modest in scale but distinctive in character. "His projects are really something," observed Shahar Elan, a journalist with *Ha'aretz*, Israel's leading daily newspaper. "Nobody builds to such a high class in Israel."

Reichmann began his real estate comeback by buying the uncompleted part of Kiryat Wolfson, a luxury residential development on the outskirts of Jerusalem. He turned a tidy profit in building its remaining eighteen villas, one of which he sold to brother Albert and another to Ralph. Edward also kept a villa for himself but soon sold it for a proverbial offer he could not refuse—$1.7 million. Reichmann's second and more renowned residential project was the Academy House, a seven-story apartment building adjacent to the prime minister's residence in one of Jerusalem's priciest neighborhoods. By all accounts, Academy House set new standards of luxury and security for Jerusalem apartment dwellers. Many of its thirty-two apartments came equipped with a four-meter-square Sukkoth balcony and even the light fixtures were made of gold. Reichmann kept one of Academy House's thirty-two apartments for himself and sold the rest at prices ranging upward to $3.3 million apiece for the two penthouses.

Reichmann's remaining two projects were stylish urban shopping malls in Jerusalem. "I'm basically a city center man, a believer in the downtown. My projects are all aimed at revitalizing city centers," Reichmann told a reporter in the mid-1980s, in what amounted to a declaration of contrarian belief, the central districts of Jerusalem and other Israeli cities having deteriorated over the preceding decade as a result of rampant suburbanization. Reichmann's pioneering was applauded by officials in Jerusalem—including Mayor Teddy Kollek—and attracted an amount of public attention disproportionate to the size of his projects.

In the city's Rehavia district, Reichmann built a small upscale shopping plaza around a historic windmill. Despite rents that were among the highest in Jerusalem at about $50 a square meter, "the Mill," as Reichmann called his complex, was fully rented virtually from the moment it opened. Shortly after the Mill opened, Reichmann paid $2 million for a plot on King George Street, just off Jaffa Road. This inner-city site had been excavated in the 1950s by the Valero family for a cinema that was never built. The "Valero hole" had been sold in 1980 to Israel Discount Bank, which secured construction permits for a new headquarters but never got around to building it. Reichmann finally filled the void, persisting through endless hassles over city zoning and design regulations that delayed construction by two years, and built an enclosed mall with three floors of shops and three floors of offices. He called the complex the Bell Center, after the handsome set of bronzed bells displayed in the lobby.

Reichmann succeeded in his second go-around as a developer by being as patient and cautious as he had been heedlessly daring during his years in Montreal. While his newfound conservatism to a degree had been forced on him by the intrinsic difficulties of doing business in Israel, Reichmann also had learned from the errors of his youth. Focusing on one carefully chosen project at a time, he now financed construction wholly on a cash basis, eschewing bank financing. He kept overhead costs to a minimum by employing only a secretary, an accountant, and a driver and contracting out for everything else, taking pains to limit his vulnerability to the chronic absenteeism of Palestinian construction workers. "His solution—which has taken on the proportions of a cause—has been to hire Jewish workers and Arabs from inside the Green Line, an idea that has been much talked about in the building industry, but has rarely been pursued so vigorously as by Reichmann," the *Jerusalem Post* noted approvingly. "The bait used to lure Jews, who have long disdained construction work, is competitive wages and better working conditions, using modern and well-maintained equipment."

By Reichmann's own rough estimate, he invested a total of $25 million into his four projects, all from his own pockets. Where this money came from remained something of a mystery—one on which Reichmann himself shed little light, beyond saying that property development was not his only business in

Israel and that he had done well for himself over the years trading in U.S. and European stock markets. According to Paul Reichmann, Edward also shared in Olympia & York's profits after 1975. The Olympia & York brothers periodically voted special cash distributions to the company's shareholders, including Edward, Eva, and Louis, each of whom had inherited one-third of their father's original 12.5 percent stockholding.

In any event, Edward's pockets must have been deep indeed, for even as he was sinking $25 million into property he and his wife led a discreetly luxurious life, furnishing a succession of million-dollar apartments with costly antiques and spending a few months every year vacationing in Zurich, Saint-Moritz, and Miami Beach. At the same time, Reichmann upheld the family tradition for munificent philanthropy. Through the Edward and Esther Reichmann Foundation, he and his wife founded their own yeshiva—Maalot Hatorah—in dual tribute to Samuel Reichmann and to Edith's parents and eight siblings, and became major benefactors of Sharei Chesed, the main Orthodox hospital in Jerusalem, and numerous other medical institutions, synagogues, and schools throughout Israel. The man who had moved into the Reichmanns' old Wolfson Towers apartment found an eight-inch-thick bundle of charitable receipts wedged into the back of a desk drawer. He turned them over to a friend, Michael Hausman, who worked as a broker at a company Reichmann set up to sell the Academy House apartments. Before returning the receipts, Hausman riffled through them and was amazed to find that each was made out to cash in amounts ranging upward from $5,000. "The pack amounted to at least a quarter of a million dollars and these were his small donations—not the kind you give with a check and take off your taxes," Hausman said. "People knew that they could come to Reichmann's door and he would give charity to anyone who needs it."

Although Edward's good works and success in business made him again a man of achievement in his own right, his stature in the ultra-Orthodox community and in Israel still was mainly derived from his famous last name. As the only Reichmann of his generation living in Israel, Edward often acted in ad hoc fashion as the family's representative but held no official position in Olympia & York. A large portion of the Toronto brothers' funding of Israeli hospitals and clinics was funneled through Edward, who took a particularly active interest in medical philanthropy.

Edward saw all four of his brothers regularly, what with the vacations they took together in various combinations and the many bar mitzvahs, matriculations, weddings, and other family events that they still were compelled to attend by their aged but ever-vigilant mother. Edward was especially close with easygoing Albert, whose tolerance of his eldest brother's foibles seemed inexhaustible. Before Edward's reincarnation as a Jerusalem developer had taken hold, Albert had backed him in several new ventures in Canada, at least two of which ended as disastrously as had Three Star Construction, though on a smaller scale. The collapse of a discount wholesaling business in Montreal resulted in the Bank of Montreal suing to collect a debt of $634,000. Albert had personally guaranteed Edward's indebtedness up to $100,000 and honored the obligation. However, Olympia & York balked at paying off on a second guarantee in the same amount, no doubt because Paul objected. The matter was not resolved until 1986, when the Reichmanns and the Bank of Montreal arrived at an out-of-court settlement. Meanwhile, the failure of Edward and Albert's joint attempt to develop an apartment building in Montreal had prompted the Canadian Imperial Bank of Commerce to file a suit demanding repayment of a $171,000 loan. The Reichmanns countersued but lost and again Albert had to reach into his pocket.

Although these episodes put barely a dent in Albert's burgeoning net worth, they were ordeals of déjà vu for the whole Reichmann family, especially Edward. Even when confronted with the court papers, Reichmann would simply refuse to acknowledge this second round of business failures in Canada as he continued to deny that Three Star Construction had been saved from ruin in the late 1960s by his younger brothers' intervention. Although Edward never badmouthed Paul and in fact seemed to take a certain fraternal pride in Olympia & York's triumphs, at some deep level he had not adjusted to his own eclipse as "the Big Reichmann." As he aged, Edward increasingly exuded a lion-in-winter aura of bruised majesty. Michael Hausman, who left Reichmann's employ in 1990, recalled, "He'll sit in the back of the synagogue but everyone has to stand up when he passes by. You cannot interrupt him when he talks. He's elegant, forgetful."

In the early 1980s, the Agudath Israel newspaper in Jerusalem floated Edward Reichmann's name as a worthy candidate for mayor. A few other ultra-Orthodox papers echoed Agudath's call, but Reichmann reluctantly declined to answer it, citing both his friendly relations with Mayor Kollek and his latter-day aversion to the spotlight. "As far as the religious vote, I probably could have got all the factions together," Reichmann recalled, "but in Israel I was always behind the scenes politically and I wanted to stay there."

———

It was telling that the word "God" is nowhere to be found in Israel's declaration of independence. Like most of his generation of Zionist leaders, founding father David Ben-Gurion was an agnostic who assumed that religion would never play an important role in the affairs of the Jewish state. Even so, to soften opposition to Israel's formation, in 1947 Ben-Gurion formally pledged to the small but vociferous haredi community, as represented by Agudath Israel, that the state would cede control of marriage, divorce, and some other social matters to the Orthodox rabbinate and sanction the creation of an independent religious school system. In return, Agudath afforded de facto recognition to a government whose very existence it opposed in principle. The Ben Gurion–Agudath Israel pact marked the beginning of a marriage of convenience between Israel's secular majority and haredi minority that was uneasy from the start and only grew stormier over the years.

Agudath Israel objected to the enactment of a "secular" constitution, to the celebration of Independence Day, to the use of a national flag, and to mandatory military service, among other things. Despite the unpopularity of its positions, the Agudath was able to muster growing political influence, thanks to a national electoral system based on proportional representation that made it virtually impossible for either of the main parties—Labor and Likud—to form a coalition government without the support of smaller, special-interest parties. After Begin's election in 1977, the Likud proved willing to pay a higher price than had previous Labor governments to placate Agudath and other religious parties, boosting public appropriations to ultra-Orthodox education and housing and exempting all yeshiva students from the military draft.

Far from placating the haredim, Begin's concessions only seemed to sharpen their social militancy. Most notoriously, the ultra-Orthodox tried relentlessly but unsuccessfully to amend the Law of Return to deny Israeli citizenship to non-Orthodox converts. Although its practical effects would have been modest, this "Who-is-a-Jew" law stirred angry debate all around the world, for its underlying purpose was to strip the Conservative and Reform denominations of their legitimacy. At the same time, there emerged an ultra-ultra-Orthodox fringe that often resorted to vigilantism, descending en masse on vendors who failed to close by a certain hour on Friday afternoons, stoning cars that passed by haredi neighborhoods during Shabbat, and firebombing bus shelters festooned with advertising of scantily clad women. Mayor Kollek had to be hospitalized during an election campaign after he was knocked down and beaten by an ultra-Orthodox mob in Mea Shearim, Jerusalem's densely populated main haredi district.

At times the violence turned inward, for the ultra-Orthodox were no less bitterly divided among themselves. Agudath Israel was composed of three basic factions: Hasidic, Lithuanian, and Sephardic. The Lubavitcher Rebbe dominated the Hasidic wing of Agudath from New York while his implacable archenemy, Rabbi Eliezer Schach, was Israel's leading Lithuanian rabbi and commanded the allegiance of ultra-Orthodox Sephardim as well. In 1984, the ninety-year-old Rabbi Schach took Agudath Israel down a notch by organizing a Sephardic splinter party named the Shomrei Torah Guardians, or Shas. Four years later, Rabbi Schach led the Lithuanians out of Agudath Israel by forming yet another party, Degel Ha-Torah (Torah Flag). Adding an extra element of internecine intrigue, the Sephardic sage Rabbi Ovadia Yosef began vying bitterly with Rabbi Schach for control of Shas in the name of Sephardic self-determination.

Although the Reichmann family had personal ties to all the haredi factions, its deepest allegiance was to Rabbi Schach, the head of Ponovezh yeshiva. Paul, of course, had studied at Ponovezh—as had many members of the next generation of Reichmanns—and he and all his brothers regarded Rabbi Schach as ultra-Orthodoxy's preeminent living sage. "We are Rav Schach's men," Edward said bluntly.

Even so, the increasing politicization of ultra-Orthodoxy distressed and appalled the Reichmann brothers, whose interests had always transcended the factional boundaries that obsessed so many of their coreligionists. "It so happens that the family—my parents and grandparents as well—never accepted the constraint of belonging to any partisan group," Paul said. "We refused to get involved in these rivalries in Israel, which was easy because no one really made an effort to involve us." The brothers made no contributions to any of the political parties, and when Paul visited B'nai Brak he underscored the family's studied neutrality by visiting Rabbi Schach and then making his way by chauffeured limousine to Rabbi Yosef's residence as measuredly and ostentatiously as possible. Such subtleties were lost on the press, which generally looked upon the Reichmanns' essential role in Israel as that of carte-blanche bankers to Rabbi Schach. Or, as one unnamed Israeli source told the *Globe & Mail:* "Whenever Rabbi Schach needed funds for a yeshiva or a hospital, or whatever, the Reichmanns came up with the cash."

This widely held view was largely the product of Paul's leadership of a highly—and inaccurately—publicized 1987 campaign to raise a $100 million "rescue fund" for Israeli yeshivoth. Enrollments had grown at an astronomic rate throughout the 1970s and 1980s, outpacing even the growth of the Reichmann fortune and forcing many institutions deep into debt to survive. During one of Paul's visits, Rabbi Schach mentioned that yeshiva indebtedness was the most pressing problem facing the ultra-Orthodox community. "His idea was not to pay off the debt—it was too big for him to think of that—but to create new financing sources to relieve the pressure," recalled Paul, who promptly offered his services.

Aided by a young activist rabbi in B'nai Brak and a small band of volunteers in Toronto and New York, Reichmann organized a program with the dual aim of imposing fiscal discipline on the yeshivas while saving them from ruin. Paul put up $35 million in Reichmann family funds and helped raise another $65 million from hundreds of contributors large and small. Whipped into a frenzy by overstated reports in religious newspapers, ultra-Orthodox rabbis by the dozen descended on two hotels—one in B'nai Brak and the other in Jerusalem—where Reichmann and his helpers were said to be receiving applicants. (They were not.) One paper reported that Reichmann was in Toronto but had to move out of his house to escape the throng of applicants. (He did not.) In the end, the money was divided among one thousand yeshivas, all of which had to promise to reduce their reliance on debt financing in the future. Press reports to the contrary, Rabbi Schach did not direct the distribution of the emergency aid exclusively to his loyalists. "Rav Schach wasn't involved at all in distributing funds; I doubt that he even knew what we were doing," said Reichmann, who saw to it that the $100 million was fairly distributed among Ashkenazi and Sephardi institutions.

But if the Reichmanns remained above the partisan fray personally, their philanthropy unavoidably had political consequences. For a start, the massive sums the family poured into haredi education, health care, and welfare enabled the factional leaders of ultra-Orthodoxy to free up other funds for overtly political uses. The haredi parties could now press with greater force their claims against one another, as well as their demands on the government. The Reichmanns' generosity thus had the wholly inadvertent effect of exacerbating the stridency of haredi politics.

At the same time, the brothers unwittingly injected themselves into the increasingly fractious political struggle over national security. "Toward Palestinians, all the religious parties share roughly the same cast of mind," an Israeli commentator noted in 1989. "They see Arabs in general, and the Palestinians in particular, as wholly alien—goys who are particularly menacing because of their proximity." On the other hand, Rabbi Schach and the leadership of both Degel Ha-Torah and Shas saw in Zionism a commitment to territorial expansion and military adventurism that they believed would only harm the Jewish people and so were willing to trade land for peace. The Reichmanns shared this moderate view, and yet in making religious merit the definitive criterion of their giving occasionally put themselves in the awkward position of backing ultra-Orthodox fringe groups that made an armed crusade of Jewish resettlement of the occupied territories. For example, the family made a hefty contribution toward the building of an Orthodox synagogue in Ariel, a West Bank settlement with a particularly well-equipped civilian militia. During the intifada, groups of settlers from Ariel repeatedly retaliated for acts of Palestinian terrorism by rampaging en masse through the nearby Arab town of Bidya, beating villagers indiscriminately and burning their olive trees.

Worse, a great many of the zealots who staked a claim to the Holy Land with a sefer Torah in one hand and a rifle in the other were products of the Israeli yeshivoth system and thus beneficiaries of Reichmann funding. While the family could not fairly be held responsible for the warping of its own religious ideals in the perfervid political climate of Israel, Paul and his brothers must have felt a certain moral queasiness just the same—especially after a yeshiva-trained fanatic gunned down Prime Minister Yitzhak Rabin in 1995. Asked in the wake of Rabin's assassination to assess the impact of the Reichmanns' philanthropy on religious education in Israel over the past three decades, Paul seemed as ambivalent as he was modest. "We did help greatly in many situations and no doubt there were some institutions that might not have survived without specific help," he replied. "But if you take it overall, I do not believe that our influence was so great. It's difficult to assess the effect of our investment in a cause that has so many adherents. But our motivation was fulfilling a [religious] duty rather than anything else."

———

To Edward Reichmann's delight, the *Jerusalem Post* certified his business comeback in mid-1987 by publishing a long, complimentary profile accompanied by a photo of the developer with Mayor Kollek at the opening of the Mill. In the interview Reichmann gave the *Post,* he gladly discussed his own projects but declined comment on his famous brothers or on family matters. "I was never interested in publicity," he insisted. "More recently things have gotten out of my personal control. . . . It wasn't a change of strategy." Reichmann refused to elaborate on his cryptic complaint, which in fact was a reference to the advent of the City Hall project in late 1986. While Edward had indeed kept a relatively low public profile during his years in Jerusalem, no doubt he would not have minded the publicity the City Hall project generated had he been invited to participate. Aside from the occasional courtesy briefing, Edward would play no part in a development so ambitious that it made his own adventures in urban renewal seem trifling by comparison.

Virtually from the moment that Jerusalem had been partitioned between Israel and Jordan in 1948, the ancient city had been enlivened every few years by a controversial new scheme to build a proper City Hall. "It used to be that the only people who made money in Jerusalem were architects and carpenters," joked Uzi Wexler, chief executive of the Jerusalem Development Authority during much of the 1980s. "The architects, because they drew up all the plans, and the carpenters because they built the shelves on which the plans were put." Over a thirty-five-year period, no less than nine City Hall schemes died aborning, both for lack of funds and a surfeit of intransigent opinion on issues of design, location, cost, and historic preservation. As the city government grew, it made do with space in three dozen locations. The mayor's office and the council chambers were located downtown in the old Barclays Bank building, which was built in 1932 and pockmarked with bullet holes during the Six-Day War of 1967.

In 1986, Ron Soskolne of Olympia & York traveled to Israel with a Toronto architect named A. J. "Jack" Diamond to consider a city-sponsored hotel project in Tel Aviv on behalf of a group of wealthy Canadian investors that included Albert Reichmann. The group had been assembled by Jack Daniels, the former chief executive of Cadillac Fairview, which was Diamond's best client. When the Canadians found themselves at an impasse in their negotiations in Tel Aviv, they drove up to Jerusalem and asked the city engineer, Amnon Niv, to intervene on their behalf. Niv quickly agreed to do what he could to help and then changed the subject. "He told us he had this fabulous project that we should see and pulled out the drawings," Diamond recalled. "He was right." Niv had devised a new City Hall development scheme that shifted emphasis from costly and disruptive new construction to the remodeling and reconfiguration of the Barclays Bank and adjoining buildings to create a municipal campus. The Tel Aviv hotel project all but forgotten, Diamond and Soskolne soon returned to Toronto and briefed Albert and Paul Reichmann on City Hall Square.

The project was intriguing architecturally and manifestly of great civic import but problematic as a business venture. For one thing, the Reichmanns would not be able to indulge their strong preference for owning what they built; you not only cannot fight City Hall, you cannot buy it either. As a developer, Olympia & York would be entitled to fees but these would be so modest relative to costs that the company easily could end up in the hole if the project was afflicted by the delays and cost overruns for which Israel was notorious. Like the aborted Tel Aviv Kirya, the Jerusalem City Hall project was a venture more philanthropic than commercial and as such appealed far more to Albert than to Paul, who was struggling as it was to find time to meet his obligations as Israel's preeminent patron of Orthodox education.

With Paul's blessing, Albert entered into negotiations with Jerusalem city officials on Olympia & York's behalf and soon reached an understanding. The Reichmanns would assume responsibility for managing construction of City Hall Square and lend the city the first $30 million for what was expected to be a $65 million project. In return, the city would pay Olympia & York an annual fee equal to 2.25 percent of the sum borrowed and would assume full responsibility for any cost overruns.

In keeping with Albert's usual modus operandi, he brought in an outside partner as construction manager. He tapped Zeev Vered, the Ottawan who had acted as Olympia & York's partner in a half-dozen North American ventures, including the development of office towers in Portland and Seattle. Vered had emigrated to Canada from Israel and welcomed the City Hall project as a stepping stone to prominence in his native land. Even so, Vered drove a hard bargain with Reichmann, who was characteristically conciliatory, ceding his partner a 40 percent stake in the project instead of the customary 20 percent. That is, Vered was entitled to 40 percent of the fees but was not required to supply any portion of the $30 million in financing. This arrangement was effected through the formation of a new company, Ron Engineering and Construction (International) Limited, of which Olympia & York owned 60 percent and Vered 40 percent.

The Reichmann-Vered joint venture company commissioned proposals from I. M. Pei, Cesar Pelli, Moshe Safde, and Jack Diamond. At Soskolne's urging, Reichmann chose Diamond, who, in turn, hired three Israeli architects to help. Diamond's team refined Amnon Niv's basic plan into a design that silenced even many of the most outspoken critics of previous proposals with its sophisticated blending of old and new, of Western and Middle Eastern. Two new buildings were to be added to eleven existing buildings (which had been erected over 130 years and spanned a wide variety of architectural styles) and were to be integrated into a whole through the use of such devices as an ancient aqueduct, a series of courts and gardens, and a network of ramps and stairways that led upward to a vast central plaza surmounting the site. Easily accessible from all points of the compass, including the Arab precincts of East Jerusalem, the plaza would afford scenic views of many of the city's most famous landmarks, and with room for as many as twenty thousand people, it also would fill a practical function in this hyperpoliticized capital. "We needed a place for demonstrations," Uzi Wexler explained. "People used to have to go to Tel Aviv to hold protests."

Shortly before the cornerstone was to be laid, Rabbi Schach and three other of Israel's most illustrious haredi rabbis wrote a letter to the Reichmanns urging them to withdraw from the City Hall development unless the city killed plans to build a new soccer stadium adjoining an ultra-Orthodox neighborhood. The rabbis opposed the Manahat stadium project on the grounds that it would bring traffic jams and other disturbances that would infringe on the Shabbat observances of the haredim. The letter arrived in Toronto a few days before Albert was to fly to Jerusalem. As soon as he arrived in Israel, Reichmann met with the rabbis and told them he did not think it likely he could get the stadium project canceled but might be able to persuade city officials to attach conditions that would minimize its disruptions—say, by requiring that Saturday night games start well after Shabbat had ended. According to Reichmann, the rabbis agreed to let him negotiate a compromise arrangement. However, the very next morning, just hours before the ceremonies were to begin, one of the rabbis telephoned Reichmann to say that he had changed his mind and again urged Olympia & York to pull out of the City Hall project unless the city killed Manahat or relocated it.

Albert immediately telephoned Paul in Toronto and brought him up to date. "I indicated to him that I had a personal involvement for a long time, both to the city, to the mayor, and Zeev Vered, so I just can't walk away," Albert recalled. "He said, 'You can do it on your own, but I am not interested to have Olympia & York involved.' " Albert, who'd always been the least religiously doctrinaire of the Toronto brothers, conferred with Kollek and decided, to the mayor's great relief, to risk the wrath of the ultra-Orthodox rabbinate by personally sponsoring the project. At the cornerstone-laying, which went off without a hitch, no mention was made of the rabbis' objections or of Paul's precipitous withdrawal. Indeed, Kollek made a point of thanking both Reichmann brothers, lauding them as "the best [developers] in the world."

In practice, the substitution of Albert Reichmann for Olympia & York would prove largely cosmetic in its impact. Soskolne and other company staffers continued to work on City Hall Square and the money that Albert loaned the city came out of Olympia & York's coffers rather than his own pocket. In almost every other respect, the project would vex all concerned. The original $65 million estimate would prove too low by half as the project was bedeviled not only by municipal red tape but by fierce infighting between members of the Vered family and most of the other participants. "The Vereds drove everyone crazy with their paranoid style," recalled one key actor in the drama. By most accounts, Albert Reichmann did yeoman's work in soothing tempers and holding the project together. In the end, he, too, would turn against Zeev Vered, filing a lawsuit accusing his longtime associate of embezzling $1.8 million in fees from their Israel partnership. Vered filed a counterclaim, accusing Reichmann of altering the development contract behind his back. Vered asked the court for $8.7 million in damages. As of November 1996, the case is still pending.

Widely hailed upon its completion in 1993 as a magnificent addition to the Jerusalem cityscape, City Hall Square would rank as Albert's proudest achievement as a developer. Outside of Israel, though, the project was overshadowed virtually to the vanishing point by Paul's simultaneous mounting of a project of such grandeur, such monumental audacity, that it seemed more akin to the undertakings of pharaohs and kings than to those of rival property developers: Canary Wharf.

PART V

BABEL ON THE RIVER THAMES

Chapter 37

U ntil Paul Reichmann became infatuated with Maggie Thatcher's England, he had never much cared for the place. During his years at yeshiva in London and in Gateshead-on-Tyne, young Reichmann had discovered firsthand the intolerance and elitism embedded in the British class system. "One reason I was surprised at how quickly we [Reichmanns] were accepted in Canada," he recalled elliptically years later, "was because I'd gone to school in England." Over the years, he had returned occasionally to England to see his sister and in 1971 had spent an exhausting two weeks helping to salvage the wreckage of Lipmann Heller's merchant bank. He had traveled to London with much greater frequency once Olympia & York had begun its pursuit of English Property Corporation in 1979 but found England no more to his liking during his first go-around as a developer than he had as a yeshiva boy.

Reichmann had returned to England with modest expectations. His and Albert's overriding interest in English Property was its stockholding in Trizec Corporation, the Canadian development company controlled by the Edper Bronfmans. But once the brothers had parlayed control of English Property into a partnership with the Bronfmans, they decided to do what they could with the rest of their newly acquired foreign assets. English Property owned a nice-sized portfolio of commercial properties throughout England, Ireland, Belgium, and France but did not have a single development project in the works. To Paul Reichmann, especially, English Property's quiescence was unnatural. "Paul is not interested in managing buildings. He wants to build and build to a big scale," said Stanley Honeyman, English Property's longtime chief executive officer.

Like New York City, London had suffered a devastating collapse in property values during the recession of the mid-1970s. Many a developer was ruined, none more spectacularly than Willie Stern, the would-be savior of Heller & Partners. But London, unlike New York, had not seen a boom follow the bust when the economy returned to health. One problem was that local government in England had the power to throttle commercial development and used it. London's innate predisposition against development was reinforced in the 1970s by studies that concluded that less and less office space would be needed in the city center as advances in technology allowed employers to spread out geographically. Office projects that did succeed in running the gauntlet of strict planning controls tended to exhibit a cookie-cutter sameness, not in appearance so much as in their internal architecture. The typical postwar British office building was configured as a series of wings protruding from a circular core containing central services such as elevators and plumbing. As a rule, each wing was only forty-five feet deep and configured as two rows of long, narrow offices running along a corridor. Everyone got a window but this awkward configuration wasted space and energy galore.

All in all, London was an uncongenial setting for the kind of massive, pathbreaking schemes that had become Olympia & York's forte. Taking Honeyman's advice, Paul Reichmann had started small. In 1980 English Property began developing a three-story office building in the chic Knightsbridge district of London. In Canada or the United States, Olympia & York would have made a few months' work of such a project. But the Knightsbridge building took English Property nearly two years to complete, or about as long as it had taken to put up the seventy-two-story First Bank Tower. Reichmann also met with officials from the Department of the Environment to discuss the novel (for England) notion of building office buildings over railway stations, of which London has an abundance. A few years later, one of the more imaginative British developers would build successfully atop Victoria Station, but at the time Whitehall was dismissive of Reichmann's suggestion, labeling it impractical. "Things would take five or six times longer to achieve [in England] than they would in North America," Reichmann later recalled. "If a project had a certain cost in dollars, we would find it was double that in pounds. The work habits were poor; the level of interest was low."

Thoroughly disillusioned, the brothers decided in 1983 to sell English Property, leaving it to Honeyman to find a buyer. It was not an easy sale. Finally, in 1985 another of the old-line U.K. developers, Metropolitan Estates & Property Corporation, acquired English Property for £112.5 million. Neither Paul nor Albert bothered to fly over to London for the closing of the transaction.

Only in retrospect would Paul Reichmann realize the extent to which his view of the London scene had been colored by the musty, yellowed pane that was English Property Corporation. It somehow had escaped his notice that the struggles of a new generation of English planners, architects, and developers had begun to loosen the straitjacket of tradition. Stuart Lipton, arguably the most successful of the new breed, was an unabashed admirer of North American design and fast-track construction methods. In 1983, just as the Reichmanns were washing their hands of London, Lipton joined with another astute young developer, Godfrey Bradman, to win a contract to redevelop British Rail lands within the old medieval heart of London, formally known as the City of London. In a dozen separate phases, Lipton and Bradman would assemble Broadgate, a £2 billion, fourteen-building complex containing 2.7 million square feet of offices and shops. In its scale and sophistication, Broadgate was a project in the Olympia & York mold, though Paul Reichmann no doubt would have attempted to build in a few years what took Lipton and Bradman a decade to complete.

With Broadgate, Lipton and Bradman caught a wave. In the mid-1980s a long-gathering trend toward globalization of securities trading accelerated into a mania in London, thoroughly discrediting those 1970s forecasts of declining demand for office space. In the City, the financial capital of Europe, the major investment banking and brokerage firms expanded even faster than the rapid growth of the markets warranted in anticipation of the "Big Bang." In 1983, the British government worked out an agreement with the London Stock Exchange to discard many of the practices that long had throttled competition in English markets. It was decided that these reforms would not be phased in but implemented with a bang, as it were, at the opening of trading on October 19, 1986. Persuaded that the Big Bang would bring big profits, American, Japanese, and European investment houses acquired British firms and pumped them full of growth capital.

The securities industry's growth also was a boon to the City Corporation of London. The City Corporation was a stout bulwark of the old establishment—an utterly British hybrid of municipal government, freemason's lodge, medieval guild, and profit-making corporation, presided over with great pomp and circumstance by the lord mayor of London. The City Corporation was the planning authority for the City and also its largest landlord, owning one-sixth of the choicest property within its dominion—the so-called Square Mile. Since the early 1960s, the City Corporation had used its powers to keep the supply of office space within the Square Mile stable at about 56 million square feet. The desired effect was achieved: as demand for space rose, rents soared. By the mid-1980s, office rents in the City were the second highest in the world, trailing only Tokyo. What is more, very few of the City's office buildings could accommodate the capacious, high-tech trading floors—known in plannerese as large open area floors, or LOAFs—that had become de rigueur in the securities business.

Unconstrained by British traditionalism, the American and other foreign-owned investment banks that increasingly dominated the financial scene in London barraged the City Corporation with complaints and began scouting outlying areas for office sites. First Chicago Corporation built a new London headquarters within earshot of Covent Garden; Salomon Brothers leased space in a new building of exceptional width built over the tracks of Victoria Station; Citicorp enrolled in a riverfront project in Billingsgate, where fish-mongers once plied their wares. Credit Suisse First Boston (CSFB), a Swiss-American combine that was arguably London's mightiest investment bank, scandalized its British peers by announcing plans not only to abandon the Square Mile but to leave the West End altogether and build a new headquarters on a tract of decrepit East End waterfront known as the Isle of Dogs.

The Isle of Dogs was not an island at all but a sizable peninsula that dangled like a tonsil into the Thames about two and a half miles upriver from the old port. In the mid-1800s, the Isle of Dogs had been the shipbuilding capital of Europe. As the British merchant fleet continued its vast expansion, additional docks were built farther downriver. Constructed during World War I, the Royal Victoria and Albert and King George V Docks—collectively known as "the Royals"—were capable of handling the largest ocean-going vessels.

Dockbuilding effectively created the East End, a term that only came into use in the 1860s. What had been pleasant riverside hamlets populated mainly by sailors were engulfed by shoddily built housing for the low-wage laborers who worked the docks and toiled in the manufacturing plants that the expanding port attracted. In 1890, a social historian of the day memorably derided the East End as "an evil plexus of slums [that] hides human creeping things, where filthy men and women live on penn'orths of gin, where collars and clean shirts are decencies unknown, where every citizen wears a black eye, and none ever combs his hair." Most of Jack the Ripper's infamous 1888 murders occurred within screaming distance of the docks, and the opium dens that so intrigued Charles Dickens were nearby in Limehouse. The East End remained a bleak, forbidding place even as the emergence of the British welfare state after World War II alleviated the worst of its poverty and life on the dole supplanted life as a wage slave. To generations of Etonians, Oxonians, and Cantabrigians who went to work in the City (or kept an office there at least), the East End existed only as a geographic metaphor for all that was déclassé in England's capital.

Even so, the docks continued to hum with activity until the mid-1960s. With the advent of container freight transport (the tidal Thames was too shallow to permit the deep-draft container ships to advance any farther than Tilbury, twenty-six miles from London), the old docks were abandoned one after another, like dominoes toppling in slow motion seaward along the River Thames. A municipal catastrophe of the first order, the demise of the Port of London wiped out 150,000 jobs and transformed five thousand riverside acres into a wasteland of derelict warehouses and graffiti-covered council estates collectively known as Docklands. While the inner harbor, which lay between London Bridge and Tower Bridge, was rehabilitated to new uses, the downstream docks were left to rot. More than an eyesore or poverty belt, Docklands affronted the national pride as a gravely literal symbol of the ruin of Empire.

Margaret Thatcher believed stridently in reducing the role of government in British life. However, her approach to urban renewal was derived from the paradoxical proposition that only Whitehall's intervention could bring the solution of free-market forces to bear on this quintessentially local problem. Michael Heseltine, Thatcher's secretary of state for the environment, returned from a fact-finding tour of the United States advocating adaptation of two American innovations: the urban development corporation and the enterprise zone. Heseltine took the lead in pushing through Parliament legislation that wrested planning authority over most of Docklands from local government and vested it in a new entity, London Docklands Development Corporation (LDDC), which was answerable only to the secretary of the environment. At the same time, the Port of London and other public agencies were ordered to sell their vast derelict acreage in the Docklands to the LDDC, which began functioning in mid-1981. These draconian measures were opposed by local activists and the officials of the various municipalities in Docklands—long a Labour stronghold—in fifty days of rancorous hearings in Parliament.

Heseltine stocked the board of LDDC with big-time property men. Sir Nigel Broakes, the LDDC's first chairman, was an archetypal city mogul who preferred to inspect the devastation of Docklands while puffing a cigar in the back seat of his chauffeured Rolls-Royce. By contrast, Reg Ward, the LDDC's chief executive, was a coal miner's son and former tax inspector who improbably but accurately described himself as a "romantic dreamer with both feet firmly in midair." Smitten with the herculean task of "creating a new economy in what was a void," as he liked to say, Ward literally lived on the premises, sleeping on a camp bed in the LDDC's offices.

Ward's and Broakes's brief was to attract maximal private investment with minimal use of public funds. The LDDC used the lion's share of its initial allocation to buy and clear derelict lands, to build roads, and to mount a marketing campaign aimed at the businessman. Large, development-ready sites were offered at cost. And in place of the usual welter of stringent planning controls, the LDDC offered building permits on request. In terms of land use and design, the corporation's pitch was blunt: "Have it your way."

Docklands proved a tough sell even so. The stigma of the East End ran deep. Transport proved an equally intractable impediment. Although the Isle of Dogs was only two and a half miles from the Bank of England in the heart of the city, proximity was not the same as accessibility, not by any means. To discourage theft and smuggling, the warehouses of the Millwall and the West India Docks had been isolated behind extensive water basins and high security walls. Since narrow roads designed for horse-drawn carriages were built only around the circumference of the Isle of Dogs and across the "island's" neck, the area became a commercial cul de sac. Other than the river itself, the Isle of Dogs was connected to the rest of London only by a meandering two-lane road. Neither British Rail nor the London Underground operated a single station within Docklands proper. In the view of businessmen contemplating capital investment, there remained a disquieting air of unreality about the Docklands experiment.

At first, only a few homebuilders were willing to take a chance on Docklands. In 1982, Parliament enhanced the area's appeal by adopting a program to implement Heseltine's other pet idea, the enterprise zone, throughout England. Some 480 acres in the center of the Isle of Dogs was designated as one of the first and the largest of such zones. Commercial developers who built within it would be granted a ten-year exemption from property taxes and allowed to write off 100 percent of the cost of capital expenditures against income. According to the LDDC, the net result was that a developer could put up an office building for half what it would cost in the City. At the same time, Whitehall approved plans to build a low-budget, light-rail transit system to connect the Isle of Dogs and other parts of Docklands with the rest of London.

These pump-primers, coupled with Mrs. Thatcher's reelection in 1983, finally did the trick. Up-and-coming commercial developers began buying low-cost sites on the Isle of Dogs and putting up warehouses and light assembly plants. Land prices rose in steep trajectory, attracting bigger developers, who in turn brought more substantial buildings and tenants. Before long, two hundred companies employing 5,700 workers had let space; the LDDC's expenditure of £140 million had drawn private investment of £800 million. The union-busting newspaper industry put the Isle of Dogs over the top as an industrial site. In 1984, the *Daily Telegraph* decided to abandon its cramped quarters on Fleet Street and construct a new high-tech printing plant on the Isle of Dogs. The *Financial Times* and other newspapers would soon follow suit.

In 1985, Michael von Clemm, a free-thinking American who ran the Eurobond powerhouse Credit Suisse First Boston, went down to Docklands to have a look around. Jointly owned by a leading Swiss bank and a top Wall Street investment bank, CSFB was considered the very prototype of the global investment bank. It had outgrown its quarters in the City and von Clemm had become frustrated by his attempts to secure additional space at reasonable cost. While having lunch on a barge with officers of the LDDC, von Clemm spied an abandoned banana warehouse on Canary Wharf, the Isle of Dogs' most central pier. "The loading bays, through which all the fruit was brought in, were all wide open," he recalled. "It was clearly just a purpose-built shell for a modern trading room. And so that became my kind of first idea. . . . Why couldn't we convert that building into a state-of-the-art dealing room?"

Von Clemm brought over an American developer named Gouch Ware Travelstead to advise him. G. ("Don't call me Gouch") Ware Travelstead was not well known outside New York and not remotely in the Reichmanns' league as a developer. But at a barrel-chested six-foot-two, the forty-eight-year-old made up in swagger what he lacked in achievement. Travelstead ran the real estate investment subsidiary of First Boston Corporation, which was the American parent firm of CSFB. Under his leadership, First Boston had become the first Wall Street investment bank to invest sizable sums of its own money in property development. His first take on Canary Wharf was typical: "I looked at Mike and said, basically, 'I think you're nuts.' " But the more Travelstead pondered the peculiar dynamics of the London office market and the Isle of Dogs' bounteous tax benefits, the more excited he grew. The trick, he believed, was to Think Big. Lifting a page from the Paul Reichmann playbook, Travelstead argued that von Clemm should forget about converting the banana warehouse and think instead about developing an entire office complex at Canary Wharf. "The only way you'll get your traders to come down here is if you get a whole lot of other traders to come down here at the same time," Travelstead told von Clemm. "It's called critical mass."

The LDDC had commissioned a consultant's study that advised against high-density development (that is, office towers) on the Isle of Dogs. But Reg Ward ignored it. His and Travelstead's ambitions interacted like jet fuel and a torch; they met somewhere in midair and zoomed off into what one LDDC staffer termed "cloud cuckooland." Buoyed by Ward's support, Travelstead persuaded CSFB, First Boston, and another preeminent American investment bank, Morgan Stanley, to join forces to set up Canary Wharf Development Company Limited. (First Boston held 40 percent, CSFB 30 percent, and Morgan Stanley 30 percent. Travelstead owned 40 percent of First Boston's equity stake and so had a personal interest of 16 percent in Canary Wharf.) Travelstead assembled a small cadre of helpmates, mostly Americans. Chicago-based Skidmore, Owings & Merrill drew up a master plan of breathtaking audacity: twenty-two buildings containing ten million square feet of leasable space and costing £2.5 billion to develop. "I think we all blinked four times when we actually had the drawings uncovered for us," recalled Christopher Benson, a soon-to-be-knighted developer who had replaced Nigel Broakes as LDDC chairman. "It was a shock because it was so huge, exciting because it was so new and it really could transform the whole of the East End."

A government-subsidized project of such import required the blessing of the prime minister herself. After the requisite high-level consultations, the LDDC agreed in principle to sell the Travelstead consortium seventy-one acres within the Isle of Dogs enterprise zone at a cut-rate price in exchange for a £68 million contribution toward the building of the Docklands Light Railway. Canary Wharf was publicly unveiled in the fall of 1985 to general amazement. "I wouldn't think twice" about building in Docklands, scoffed Sydney Mason, chairman of Hammerson Property Investment and Development, an old-line U.K. property company. Promptly nicknamed "Gee Whiz" by disbelieving

Britishers, G. Ware responded in kind. "The Brits are scared of scale," he told an American reporter. "Size is something they just don't deal with very well."

The City Corporation of London invited Travelstead to Guildhall to explain his project to about one hundred of its elected members and the lord mayor himself. The American accepted but checked his salesman's charm at the door. Asked what portion of its operation CSFB could be expected to leave behind in the City, Travelstead snapped, "Nothing," and glared at his interlocutor. "The effect on the room was electric," recalled Michael Cassidy, chairman of the City Corporation's planning committee. "We're not used to people speaking to us that way, especially in the presence of our ceremonial head. It was seen as throwing down the gauntlet."

Cassidy encouraged this interpretation, for he was trying to goad a recalcitrant majority of city councillors into acceding to his committee's plan to take the wraps off office development in the Square Mile. By early 1986, Cassidy had carried the day. The City Corporation adopted a new planning regime designed to allow the supply of office space within the Square Mile to rise by twenty million square feet, or 35 percent. "There's going to be a dramatic boom in good-quality modern building in the City of London," Cassidy predicted. The city's adoption of a pro-development stance was widely viewed as an epochal event. "After half a dozen centuries on the fence, you might say," tweaked the *Financial Times*, "the City of London finally came out for capitalism."

Travelstead was not intimidated. "We're going to change the marketplace," he crowed. "We're going to teach the Brits a lot." However, his bravado did not cut any ice with his investment bank partners. First Boston, CSFB, and Morgan Stanley were unwilling to formally commit to Canary Wharf by signing a master building agreement with the LDDC unless Travelstead proved that he could fill the two million square feet included in the project's first phase. To his dismay, Travelstead found prospective tenants equally reluctant to pre-let space in a project that had not yet secured official backing. Without a master building agreement there would be no tenants, but without tenants there would be no master building agreement. (There was a catch and it was Catch-22.) Try as he might, Travelstead was unable to induce the suspension of disbelief that is the essence of the promoter's art. "Travelstead was a hype merchant," sneered one well-placed political adviser to Mrs. Thatcher. "He'd sit next to a government minister and fib outrageously—'I've just signed up Barclays [Bank].' "

The American swallowed a bit of pride and tried to enlist the support of a British developer to help him get the Canary aloft. He approached Stuart Lipton and Godfrey Bradman, who, unlike most U.K. property men, did not suffer from Docklands-phobia. Their joint venture company, Stanhope Rosehaugh, already had completed a modest-sized building on the Isle of Dogs, and they were laying plans for a massive project farther downriver at the Royals. But neither Lipton nor Bradman cared much for Canary Wharf—or its headstrong promoter.

Travelstead also made hurried rounds in North America. In Toronto, he met with Cadillac Fairview but got nowhere. "There were just too many problems with it," recalled Bernie Ghert, Cadillac's chief executive. Travelstead got a warmer reception when he knocked on Olympia & York's door in the fall of 1986. Although the construction of the World Financial Center still was a year from completion, its success seemed assured and Reichmann was already casting about for a suitably magisterial encore. Canary Wharf's sheer scale and daring intrigued him right from the start, but there was no point in getting excited unless Travelstead was willing to relinquish control of the project. Reichmann deputized Michael Dennis to negotiate with Gee Whiz while he began analyzing the opportunity in his methodical way. Olympia & York made a proposal to Travelstead that would have had the effect of shouldering the American to the sidelines. Not yet sufficiently desperate to conspire in his own eclipse, Travelstead turned down Olympia & York's offer and carried on fruitlessly in his search for allies.

In March 1987, CSFB and Morgan Stanley pulled the rug out from under Travelstead, informing him that they still intended to occupy their own buildings in Canary Wharf but had changed their minds about helping finance the venture. They withdrew from the consortium, leaving Travelstead and First Boston alone together. In June 1987, Maggie Thatcher won a resounding victory in her third general election. Invigorated with renewed purpose, her government decided it had had its fill of Travelstead's dithering in Docklands. Sign the master building agreement by July 17, he was told, or call it a day.

In New York, Michael Dennis bumped into a First Boston executive who told him of the new deadline and suggested imploringly that only Olympia & York could save Canary Wharf now. Dennis relayed the message to Paul Reichmann, who telephoned Bill Davis, a former premier of Ontario with whom the Reichmanns had had friendly dealings over the years. Reichmann knew that Davis was a director of First Boston and asked him to sound out Peter Buchanan, the investment bank's chief executive. Davis returned with an invitation from Buchanan: let's have lunch, tomorrow. Reichmann flew down to New York and over lunch worked out the general terms of an agreement under which Olympia & York would substitute for Ware Travelstead. It was July 1, a national holiday in Canada. Reichmann immediately went to his office in the Park Avenue Atrium and began placing phone calls to cabins and cottages all over Canada in search of the lawyers, accountants, and appraisers he wanted with him. Fly to London, he told them—tonight.

———

Reichmann and his team descended from the clouds into the midst of a spirited debate over the city's growth prospects and its implications for real estate. The Canary Wharf project lay atop a conceptual foundation supplied by the Henley

Centre for Forecasting, a well-regarded London think tank. In 1986, at the height of Big Bang mania, the Henley Centre issued a study projecting that financial services employment in the city would rise by 200,000—to some 420,000 all told—over the coming decade. To accommodate this growth, it was suggested, an additional thirty million square feet of office space would be required. The City Corporation's own studies were not nearly as bullish. In fact, Michael Cassidy, its planning chief, publicly criticized the assumptions under-pinning Canary Wharf as "wildly optimistic." Stuart Lipton had recently com-missioned a study by Jones Lang Wooten that projected the demand for new office space over the coming five years at seven to nine million square feet. On the basis of these figures, Lipton concluded that there would be demand for space at Canary Wharf but not nearly as much as Travelstead was counting on.

By mid-1987, it appeared that Jones Lang Wooten was far closer to the mark than Henley Centre. In terms of employment and profitability, Big Bang was proving anticlimactic. Although the markets themselves remained strong, with the global bull market in stocks and bonds rampaging into its fifth consecutive year, many investment houses in the City found that they had added more high-priced talent than needed and began sloughing off staff as quietly as possible. The American firms were particularly disappointed, having made little head-way in selling a cornucopia of fancy new financial instruments developed state-side. "It's like selling shoes in Africa," said one crestfallen American investment merchant. "Lots of barefoot people, but they don't want shoes."

Paul Reichmann arrived at what would prove the single most important decision of his career as a developer in typical fashion: having done his home-work. Ever since Dennis had begun negotiating with Travelstead in the fall of 1986, Reichmann had been pondering the conflicting analyses of the future of commercial real estate in the English capital, as well as studies of the outlook for the U.K. economy as a whole and of London's likely place in the emerging new world order of high finance. He emerged from his self-taught tutorial aglow with optimism. "The British economy has been transformed, in fact, rev-olutionized, and is growing faster than any in the Western world," he declared in a speech in early 1988. "The importance of London as a worldwide center of financial services industry has been reaffirmed. . . . There is and will continue to be a demand for prime office space in London which, for various reasons, the traditional business districts cannot begin to satisfy. For the next decade, we expect London to be the strongest commercial real estate market—in both Europe and North America." (So much for New York City, which Reichmann had lauded just two years earlier as "the best, strongest single market in the world for office space. There is nowhere else where past growth—and in my opinion, future growth—can match that of New York.")

Maggie Thatcher would not have put it any differently herself. If Mrs. Thatcher did not deserve as much credit for the revival of enterprise in the

United Kingdom as she claimed—that is, 99.9 percent—her boldly conservative government had indeed done much to liberate the private sector since coming to power in 1979. Certainly Reichmann believed that the so-called Thatcher revolution had altered England at its very core. "Each time I go to London, the more enthusiastic I become as I meet the younger people," he declared. "Their attitude is quite different from that of their parents. In 1979, when we acquired English Property Corporation, the business environment was stale. The young people I interviewed for jobs were bureaucratic. They had goals, but their goals were just to live, to carry on. Today, that is totally changed. Young graduates want to be entrepreneurs, to go into a business where they can be creative."

Mrs. Thatcher's commitment to Canary Wharf was set in stone, but the question of the hour was whether, after having suffered the frustrations and embarrassments of alliance with a bumptious American, her government should now shift its support to another foreigner. Although no British developer ever publicly indicated an interest in taking over at Canary Wharf, Paul Reichmann had the feeling that one or two were lurking behind the scenes. Mrs. Thatcher worked her way through a thick dossier of news articles about Olympia & York and sent Lord David Young, her newly appointed secretary for trade and industry, to take the Canadian's measure in person. Lord Young had once been a developer himself but admitted that Reichmann had had to walk him through the project twice before he had grasped it. "I was staggered that he had both the confidence and the resources to do it," Lord Young recalled. "I can't recall anyone doing that sort of thing on such a scale." Lord Young reported back favorably to his boss: Paul Reichmann was for real—and no Ware Travelstead.

Olympia & York had to simultaneously come to terms with the London Docklands Development Corporation and hammer out revised partnership agreements with First Boston, Credit Suisse First Boston, and Morgan Stanley that were no less crucial to the project's survival. Paul Reichmann left most of the face-to-face negotiating to Michael Dennis but closely reviewed each day's progress. At one point, Olympia & York won what Reichmann privately considered a significant victory as the LDDC officials accepted the company's wording for a clause specifying Olympia & York's entitlement to damages should the government fail to honor its commitments to improve public transport to the Isle of Dogs. The day before the final agreement was to be signed, an LDDC official said the damage clause had been vetoed by No. 10 Downing Street. Reichmann learned later that the permanent secretary of the Department of Environment had spent two hours with Mrs. Thatcher going over the final version of the voluminous contract. "Out of all of it, she picked out something that I was surprised they'd ever agreed to in the first place," recalled Reichmann, who was both impressed and encouraged by Mrs. Thatcher's acumen.

"It showed the high level of interest she was taking in the project. I came away feeling we had a real supporter at No. 10."

The British government offered Olympia & York the same sweet deal given the Travelstead group: a two-hundred-year lease at £400,000 an acre. This was cheap even by Docklands standards; by mid-1987, land on the Isle of Dogs was going at £1 million an acre. Plus, Olympia & York would be entitled to the same lush enterprise zone tax breaks attached to the site. On the other hand, the company also would inherit its predecessor's obligation to fund the project's public open spaces and internal roads, to kick in £68 million toward the cost of improving the Docklands Light Railway, and contribute £2.5 million toward a job retraining program for local residents. But even when these extras were factored in, Olympia & York's land costs would be so low—some £50 a square foot compared with an average of £500 in the City—that Reichmann figured that Olympia & York would be able to build to a standard of high-tech quality and elegance never seen before in London and still offer office space at half the going rate in the Square Mile.

Even so, Reichmann knew it would not be easy to fill Canary Wharf's towers. Since the time of Olympia & York's initial talks with Ware Travelstead, Reichmann had done what amounted to his own informal market survey of major corporate tenants in London. Through Charles Young, a former president of Citibank Canada who had recently been transferred from Toronto to London, he had arranged meetings with dozens of top executives of major British corporations and financial institutions headquartered in the City. "I asked them all, 'Are you satisfied with your existing space?' The answer was a strong no. People were also unhappy at being spread out among many locations," Reichmann recalled. "But when I asked them, 'Would you move to Canary Wharf?' the answer also was no. They just didn't want to be outside the City." However, Paul Reichmann had never been a man to take "no" or even "perhaps" for an answer. He was confident that the combination of below-market rents and the sheer magnificence of Canary Wharf would prove irresistible.

Nor was Reichmann blind to the problem of transport. Unless Docklands could be made easily accessible to West London, Canary Wharf would glitter over Docklands like an Emerald City without a Yellow Brick Road. Although the Docklands Light Railway (DLR) had just been dedicated by Queen Elizabeth and would be operating in a few weeks, Reichmann knew that in the long run the DLR alone would be inadequate to serve a complex of Canary Wharf's size. As he saw it, a billion pounds or two of investment would be needed to build new roads and tunnels and to extend the London subway system to the Isle of Dogs. Reichmann was willing to pick up his share of the tab and was confident that Mrs. Thatcher's government would do its part.

Finally, the Canary Wharf project's timing was parlous. The U.K. economy could not boom forever. In fact, a recession already was overdue. But the threat of impending recession had not dissuaded the Reichmanns from launching First Canadian Place in 1973 or the World Financial Center in 1980. Olympia & York now owned some forty major office towers, almost all of which were filled to capacity and collectively generating cash flow of about $400 million a year. Even the Gulf Canada fiasco had only momentarily depleted Olympia & York's coffers. Meanwhile, four years of sharply rising stock prices on Wall and Bay streets had boosted the market value of the company's battered portfolio of natural resource stocks. Olympia & York's net worth now exceeded $10 billion, which placed the Reichmanns among the dozen richest families in the world.

For the first time, though, Olympia & York's mastermind faced a muted chorus of dissent from within. "I was dead against Canary Wharf," recalled Keith Roberts, who, as senior vice president for corporate operations, remained both the company's highest-ranking construction executive and its most senior Englishman. Roberts feared that Olympia & York would not be able to build Canary Wharf with its customary speed or cost-efficiency. "The English construction industry just didn't have the experience of the sort of megaprojects that we did," Roberts recalled. "They lacked a certain amount of the expertise required to do a Canary Wharf." Otto Blau, who as Olympia & York's purchasing chief had played a vital role in both the First Canadian Place and World Financial Center projects, couched his opposition in more personal terms, telling Reichmann in so many words that he would rather retire than have to move to London to work on Canary Wharf.

Within the family councils, meanwhile, Paul also ran into doubts. A few months before the climactic negotiations of July 1987 had commenced, Paul had asked Albert to go to London and make his own evaluation of Canary Wharf. "As I became more interested in the project, it was important for me to check on myself," Paul explained. "That's probably the reason Albert and I didn't go together to London." It was not the only reason. Albert did not like the idea of rushing into another massive undertaking even before Olympia & York had put the finishing touches on the World Financial Center. As for Canary Wharf itself, Albert concluded that the risks of the project were as outsized as the potential rewards. "Albert was a lot less enthusiastic than Paul," Roberts recalled wistfully. "If Albert had been in charge, perhaps I may have succeeded in talking him out of it." In the end, though, Albert did not oppose his brother; indeed, he would join Paul as a director of Olympia & York Canary Wharf Limited, the subsidiary created to direct the project. Ralph, too, grudgingly acquiesced.

Within the Reichmann family and the upper management ranks of Olympia & York, it would be said in retrospect that only Renée Reichmann could have dissuaded Paul and that she would indeed have taken a resolute stand against Canary Wharf on the grounds of common sense had she been her old self. But at eighty-nine, Mrs. Reichmann was fading fast.

The skepticism Paul encountered only hardened his contrarian convictions. After all, if he had listened to the naysayers, Olympia & York would never have built First Canadian Place or the World Financial Center. True, Canary Wharf posed a challenge several orders of magnitude greater than those the company had faced in Toronto and New York. But that, in the final analysis, was precisely what made it irresistible to the Master Builder. Canary Wharf held the potential not only of putting the Reichmann imprint on the skyline of the historic capital of the English-speaking world but of catalyzing a reversal of a westward shift in London's population dating from the Great Fire of 1666. First Canadian Place and the World Financial Center were grand vehicles of urban renewal that had won the plaudits of mayors, governors, and premiers, but Canary Wharf was a venture of national consequence. As the centerpiece of the Thatcher government's Docklands redevelopment scheme, Canary Wharf had become nothing less than an architectural referendum on Thatcherism. Whatever the outcome of the Docklands experiment, Canary Wharf was likely to stand for generations as the Iron Lady's principal architectural legacy to the nation.

On Friday, July 17, just a few hours before the midnight deadline set by the British government, Michael Dennis signed the master building agreement that Travelstead had been dodging for more than a year. (Paul Reichmann was in the midst of his Sabbath observances.) At the same time, Olympia & York formalized its agreements with the Travelstead consortium. Both CSFB and Morgan Stanley obligated themselves to proceed with plans to build new headquarters buildings at Canary Wharf. In return, Olympia & York agreed to pay £73 million to the two investment banks and First Boston, which collectively had sunk about £83 million into the project. In effect, the Reichmanns refused to reimburse the group for the £10 million in management fees it had paid out to First Boston as managing partner; £4 million of this sum went to Travelstead. Although Olympia & York allowed Travelstead to remain as a "consultant" to the project, as a practical matter, this Reichmann manqué's involvement ended the moment the genuine article took charge.

Olympia & York's entry conferred a credibility upon Canary Wharf that it had always lacked. Even the project's critics seemed stunned into reconsideration by the sudden materialization of the greatest property company on earth amid the dingy wastelands of the East End. In the press, Olympia & York was roundly hailed as Docklands' savior. To a greater extent than ever before in the company's history, the publicity focused on Paul Reichmann personally. "Reichmann Uncages Canary Wharf," read the headline in the *Sunday Telegraph*. "Quiet Man Will Make Canary Sing," trilled the *Sunday Times* in an article that began by observing that "Paul Reichmann is blessed with humility and humour in almost equal proportions" and concluded that "after the broken promises and the seemingly unending headaches and heartaches of the past year Reichmann is like an icepack on a throbbing head."

In his own soft-spoken way, Reichmann swaggered no less than Travelstead had. Olympia & York's chief publicly vowed that the company would complete in five to seven years a project that the Travelstead group had estimated would take as much as fifteen years. Reichmann added that Olympia & York would not bother to secure construction loans but would finance the first phase from its cash flow. "We will fund it ourselves," he said. "We can complete it on our own strength." Self-financing on such a scale was unheard of, but Reichmann urged the press to mark his words well. "We have never made a statement," he said, "that has not been kept exactly."

Chapter 38

On October 19, 1987, only two months after Olympia & York had taken over Canary Wharf, panic convulsed the global bourse. In chaotic trading in New York, the Dow Jones industrial average fell 508 points, and other stock market indices in North America, Europe, and Japan took a comparable pasting on a day that would live in infamy as "Black Monday." Taking into account its 235-point decline in the preceding few trading days, the Dow had dropped 30 percent in less than a week. For investors, the meaning of the stock market collapse could be all too precisely measured. But what exactly did it signal for the economy? Was Black Monday a harbinger of recession—or, like 1929's Black Tuesday, of depression—or a kind of colossal hiccup caused by technical factors peculiar to the increasingly self-referential financial markets of the 1980s?

Even as the Crash of 1987 knocked $1 billion off the market value of Olympia & York's $5 billion stock portfolio, Paul continued to go about his business with undiminished optimism. In November, as scheduled, Lord David Young, Mrs. Thatcher's trade and industry secretary, ventured out to the Isle of Dogs to drive the ceremonial first pile for Canary Wharf. (Unwittingly symbolizing Olympia & York's haste to get on with the project, Lord Young pulled the switch fifteen minutes early, before most of the Reichmanns' guests had arrived from upriver.) And whatever the message that the market was broadcasting, the one that Paul Reichmann was programmed to receive was this: it is time to bargain hunt. In the aftermath of Black Monday, Reichmann wheeled and dealed in the stock market with a fervor not seen since the oil stock mania of 1981.

As always, the Reichmanns were buyers by preference and sellers by necessity. A few weeks after Black Monday, Olympia & York cashed out its 22 percent stake in Cadillac Fairview at a handsome profit when the firm was sold to JMB Realty Corporation in partnership with some forty pension funds and other institutional investors. As Cadillac Fairview's largest shareholder, Olympia & York could have blocked its sale. Instead, the brothers acceded to the wishes of the company's management, but only after their financial gamesmanship added a final fillip of strain to their testy relationship with Bernie Ghert, the company's chief executive, and Leo Kolber, its chairman and all-around eminence grise of the Seagram Bronfmans' investment empire.

Having decided that the time had come to sell Cadillac Fairview, Ghert and Kolber first offered the company to Olympia & York, but the Reichmanns thought the asking price too high and passed. Kolber then negotiated an agreement with Paul Reichmann, who pledged that Olympia & York would participate in the sale of the company to a third party, as long as the price fell within certain parameters. The next day, the board of Cadillac Fairview was meeting when a letter arrived from Reichmann that altered the terms of agreement as Kolber had understood them. "Leo was pissed off and I was pissed off," Ghert recalled, "but in retrospect it was almost funny. By then, what else could we have expected from Paul?" Kolber made a few minor concessions and an agreement was formalized.

The field of potential acquirers was narrowed to two: JMB and Deutschebank, the giant German bank. "At one point when Paul was away in London, Albert called and said, 'Go with Deutschebank,' " Ghert recalled. "Then Paul came back and said, 'No, go with JMB.' After we decided to go with JMB, the Reichmanns went around telling the institutions [that had agreed to finance JMB's bid] that the deal with JMB wouldn't happen in the end. I think they wanted the deal that I worked out with JMB to fall apart and have the company fall into their laps at a cut-rate price." Instead, the Reichmanns sold their interest to JMB for $550 million and walked away with a $300 million profit on a three-year investment.

Shortly afterward, Olympia & York announced another equally lucrative transaction involving Allied-Lyons, its reluctant senior partner in Hiram Walker–Gooderham & Warts. Come the fall of 1988, Allied would have the right to buy Olympia & York's 49 percent interest in the liquor business and leave the Reichmanns with nothing but a heaping pile of cash to show for their latest attempt at diversification. Instead, Paul Reichmann worked out a deal to swap Olympia & York's stake in the liquor business for $370 million in cash and preferred shares convertible into 10 percent of Allied-Lyons's common stock. Olympia & York emerged as the largest shareholder in the London-based conglomerate, whose internationally known products included Baskin-Robbins ice cream, Tetley tea, and Teacher's scotch. At the same time, Reichmann was able to complete the transformation of Sir Derrick Holden-Brown, Allied's chairman, from antagonist to ally. This was strategically important because the politically well-connected Holden-Brown was in a position to offer invaluable help in promoting Canary Wharf to members of Britain's governmental and corporate elite.

Meanwhile, the Reichmanns spent a few hundred million dollars adding to holdings in Gulf Canada and Abitibi-Price and to a more recent addition to Olympia & York's portfolio—the Santa Fe Southern Pacific Corporation, which had been formed in 1983 in an attempt to merge two of the most storied railroads of the Old West: the Atchison, Topeka & Santa Fe and the Southern Pacific. The corporations that owned them were combined, but the two railroads continued to operate separately, pending approval by the Interstate Commerce Commission (ICC). In 1986, the ICC confounded expectations by ruling against the merger of the Santa Fe and the Southern Pacific and ordering Santa Fe Southern Pacific to sell one of the railroads. The ruling plunged the company into chaos: its chief executive officer resigned, its stock collapsed, and the takeover artists at Henley Group Incorporated began circling. Henley bought 5 percent of Santa Fe's stock and offered to help the company devise ways to "increase shareholder values." Leave us alone, Santa Fe's management responded, we'll do things our way.

Santa Fe, which was based in Chicago, was much more than a railroad. It owned vast grazing and farmlands in the West and considerable commercial real estate, including 9 million square feet of office space, mostly in California. The company's energy subsidiary was one of the largest independent producers of crude oil in the United States, and with total annual revenues in the $6 billion range, Santa Fe Southern Pacific was larger than either Gulf Canada or Abitibi-Price. On the basis of information publicly available, Paul Reichmann concluded that the company's parts were worth considerably more than the whole as priced in the stock market. Olympia & York had begun buying Santa Fe shares in May 1987, and by Black Monday had laid out $465 million to amass a 6.2 percent stake.

After the crash, Reichmann sent Mickey Cohen to Chicago with a proposal to restructure Santa Fe. Robert Krebs, Santa Fe's new chief executive, gave Cohen the same cold shoulder his predecessor had given Henley Group. However, Krebs did an about face after the stock market collapse knocked Santa Fe's share price down from $65 to $41 at Black Monday's close. Santa Fe invited both Henley Group and Olympia & York to submit formal acquisition offers. For $63 a share cash, Krebs said, it is yours. At this price, which worked out to almost $10 billion total, the acquisition of Santa Fe would rank as the biggest ever outside the oil industry. Both Olympia & York and Henley Group began separate talks with Santa Fe. However, on the basis of confidential information that Reichmann squeezed out of Santa Fe during the negotiations, he decided that $63 was too rich a price, as did Henley Group.

Olympia & York went back to buying Santa Fe stock on the open market, boosting its holding above 9 percent with purchases ranging from $38 to $48 a share. The rumor on Wall Street was that Olympia & York and Henley Group would join forces to launch a hostile tender offer. Reichmann and Mickey Cohen fanned such talk by meeting with Michael Dingman, Henley Group's chief, who did indeed want to ally himself with Olympia & York. Confident that Reichmann shared his determination to confront Santa Fe's management, Dingman publicly threatened a proxy fight. Now Reichmann had Dingman just where he wanted him. According to *The Wall Street Journal*, Reichmann met with Bob Krebs and "distance[d] himself from Mr. Dingman, even saying he had never met him." Reichmann and Krebs quickly set the terms of a separate peace: Olympia & York would get two seats on Santa Fe's board in return for a pledge to back management. Dingman's proxy fight was over before it started. Henley Group sold its Santa Fe shares and faded away.

With Krebs's blessing, Olympia & York spent another $245 million to boost its stake in Santa Fe to 19.9 percent. Had Krebs let the proverbial fox into the henhouse? "I trust them . . . I don't feel threatened at all," Krebs said, adding that Olympia & York, unlike Henley Group, had engaged in "constructive" dialogue. "When we brought them on board, we said we thought Olympia & York's expertise could help us with our real estate and energy businesses. We still feel exactly the same way." Krebs's faith proved well founded; the Reichmanns were content with one-fifth ownership and a few seats on the board. And why not? Olympia & York, as one Wall Street analyst put it, "is like a general partner at Santa Fe. . . . For all intents and purposes, everyone else is now a minority shareholder in an Olympia & York company."

If Santa Fe was the largest of Olympia & York's new investments, Campeau Corporation was the most fateful. Robert Campeau was the Ottawa-based developer whose attempt to acquire Royal Trust Company in 1979 had succeeded only in chasing the old-line Toronto institution into the unsheltering arms of the Reichmann and Bronfman brothers. Campeau had continued to play the takeover game with little success until 1986, when he pulled off one of the most improbable takeovers of the junk bond era. With the backing of First Boston, the same Wall Street investment bank that had followed Ware Travelstead all the way to Docklands, Campeau mounted a hostile takeover of a company with a stock market valuation ten times that of Campeau Corporation—Allied Stores, an American department store giant best known for its Brooks Brothers and Ann Taylor chains.

In the business press, Bob Campeau and Paul Reichmann generally would be portrayed as the great odd couple of Canadian business in the 1980s. Actually, Campeau was quite odd all by himself. Many of the same reporters who wrote admiringly of Reichmann's gentlemanly ways merrily recycled anecdotes about Campeau's club-footed social climbing, his facelifts and hair transplants, his sheep-brain injections (for longevity), his volcanic temper tantrums, his nervous breakdowns, and his years of commuting between a wife in Ottawa and a Montreal mistress by whom he had fathered two children that his first family did not know about. After Campeau had bested him in the takeover battle, the head of Allied Stores complained of being "blindsided by a trainload of clowns." Even the head of First Boston, Campeau's indispensable takeover ally, described him as "a living water torture."

And yet Reichmann not only admired Campeau but identified with him in some ways. Like Reichmann, Campeau was a born outsider, for a start. The son of a blacksmith from the outback of Ontario, Campeau could say that his first achievement was surviving to adulthood; he was one of fourteen siblings, seven of whom died young. Like the Reichmann brothers, Campeau had not attended college. (He had even skipped high school, dropping out after eighth grade.) As a humbly born, poorly educated French Canadian, Campeau began his career nearly as far removed from the Anglophone centers of power in Canada as had the Reichmanns. Like Olympia & York, Campeau Corporation rose into the first tier of North American property development powered by its founder's imaginative daring and prescient timing, on one hand, and his mastery of mundane fundamentals, on the other. Campeau Corporation was one of the few major developers other than Olympia & York to do its own general contracting. In fact, Campeau was even better schooled than the Reichmanns in the nitty gritty of building, having started out as a carpenter, and was such a stickler for quality workmanship that he fined his workmen for sloppiness.

Paul Reichmann had become well acquainted with Campeau long before he invested in his company. They had initially crossed paths in the late 1960s, when Olympia & York branched into Ottawa with the first of four office projects. As the Reichmanns were muscling onto his turf, Campeau was leading the redevelopment of the Toronto waterfront with a series of bold projects, including a luxury hotel. Olympia & York had outbid Campeau Corporation, the odds-on favorite, in winning the contract to construct a new lakeside office tower for the *Toronto Star*. When Royal Trust turned to Olympia & York to help ward off Campeau a decade later, Paul Reichmann called his fellow developer and told him that he had nothing against him personally. Campeau appreciated the gesture and later sold his block of shares in Royal Trustco to Olympia & York at a handsome profit. In 1985, Reichmann began buying Campeau Corporation stock in the open market, assuring its chief executive officer that his investment was not a prelude to a takeover attempt. Campeau, who owned more than half his company's shares in any event, was flattered. He offered the Reichmanns a seat on his board, which Albert dutifully filled.

While pursuing Allied Stores, Campeau approached Paul Reichmann looking for a portion of the $300 million in equity he needed to swing the deal. Kim Fennesbresque, a First Boston banker, accompanied Campeau to his meeting with Reichmann and observed that his client, whom "he knew could be gruff and short-tempered, acted solicitously, almost fawningly" toward Reichmann. By all accounts, Campeau's theatrical deference fed Reichmann's ego. "Paul Reichmann didn't aspire to be any role model for Robert Campeau, but I think he felt flattered by the attentions of a clearly talented and very successful man," one Olympia & York insider theorized.

As politely as possible, Reichmann told Campeau that he and his brothers did not want to invest directly in the Allied deal, since they knew nothing about department stores. Reichmann suggested instead that Olympia & York buy a 50 percent interest in Campeau's Scotia Plaza, a sixty-eight-story tower under construction just down the block from First Canadian Place on King Street. To Bob Campeau, Scotia Plaza represented more than the future headquarters of his company (and of its name tenant, the Bank of Nova Scotia, as well). The tower, richly clad in reddish-brown marble, was to be his crowning achievement as a builder and the centerpiece of his real estate empire. That Scotia Plaza, which was to open in a year and a half, was only 25 percent preleased, did not dampen Reichmann's acquisitive ardor in the least. He and Campeau quickly reached agreement: Olympia & York would pay $50 million cash and assume half of the $440 million in construction loans against the building.

As Campeau made what seemed to be impressive headway in his post-acquisition efforts to reorganize Allied Stores, Reichmann regularly added to Olympia & York's holdings of Campeau shares. After Black Monday cheapened the stock, he stepped up his buying, amassing nearly 11 percent by early 1988, when Campeau made a typically precipitous return to the takeover wars. His target this time was Federated Department Stores, which, as the owner of Bloomingdale's and 649 other stores scattered around America, was an order of magnitude larger than Allied Stores. Again, Campeau approached Reichmann and again Reichmann opted to invest in Campeau's company rather than his deal. Olympia & York shelled out $260 million for debentures convertible into Campeau common stock. Campeau used the proceeds to help finance a careening, apocalyptic bidding contest with venerable R. H. Macy & Company. The excitable Canadian again prevailed, paying $6.6 billion or $73.50 a share for a company that had traded at $33 just six months earlier.

The Reichmann family emerged from the chaos as the second largest shareholder in a company that in a year and a half had been transformed from a modest-sized property developer into the largest department-store company in the world by the explosive combination of its founder's overweening ambition and a borrowed $13 billion. History's verdict would not be kind. Soon, Robert Campeau's face would be appearing on the cover of *Fortune* under the headline, "The Biggest Looniest Deal Ever." But Paul Reichmann saw no cause for alarm. In the aftermath of the Federated acquisition, he broke his public silence on the subject of Bob Campeau long enough to predict that the merger of Allied and

Federated would create a "very extraordinary retail firm" with "a great future." In its own way, this would prove as revealingly catastrophic a misjudgment as those that underlay Canary Wharf.

———

Philip Heller, the late Eva Reichmann's eldest son, got the shock of his life when he picked up the latest copy of *Toronto Life* on October 19, 1987—a day that, to the Reichmann family, would forever be known as Black Monday in more ways than one. On the magazine's cover was a photograph of his mother, flanked by various Reichmann relatives, taken at her wedding in Tangier in 1948. Even as Heller was warily perusing the lengthy article inside, entitled "The Mysterious Reichmanns: The Untold Story," advertisements featuring the same family photo were being plastered onto billboards around Toronto. Evelyn Jacobs, Philip's sister, nearly drove off the road when she first saw her mother's face looming through her car windshield. "It's a bizarre feeling to see your mother in her wedding dress coming at you like that," Mrs. Jacobs recalled. "Bizarre and very unpleasant." The family's reaction to the article itself was even more pronounced. "I have read enough about anti-Semitism and the way it was propagated and the way it was advocated [to know] that a lot of what is in here corresponds with the prescriptions found in *Mein Kampf* from Hitler," fumed Paul. The readers of *Toronto Life*, he added, were encouraged to "view these people [the Reichmanns and their Orthodox associates] as usurpers, influence peddlers, crooks, and whatever else."

Elaine Dewar, a well-known Toronto freelance journalist, had devoted a full year to writing the voluminous article, which would win first place in two categories in the Canadian National Magazine Awards. Written in the first person, the article was perhaps best described as an investigational travelogue. Dewar began by positing the Reichmanns' European past as a mystery and then beguilingly recounted her attempts to unravel it along a reportorial path that led from Toronto and Montreal to Tangier, Vienna, Paris, Jerusalem, and other foreign capitals. In short, "The Mysterious Reichmanns" was a journalistic adventure story, and an absorbing one. But if Dewar's unconventional methods added drama to her quest, they also imparted a fuzziness to her argument. Questions raised but left unanswered accumulated along the way like overlapping rubber-stampings on a passport, stranding the reader somewhere between insinuation and assertion.

Rashomon-like, the article could support multiple, even contradictory interpretations. "Our view," said Marq de Villiers, the editor of *Toronto Life*, "is the family emerged from our piece with honor, particularly the mother, who emerged as a heroine." By contrast, Conrad Black, a Canadian newspaper mogul and industrialist friendly with Paul Reichmann, described Dewar's article as "a murderous piece . . . that suggested the entire Reichmann fortune was based on selling wartime contraband to the Nazis. As Paul explained to me, 'It is as if they called my mother a hooker.' Rather more defamatory even than that, I thought."

For the Reichmanns, the very existence of such an article came as a shock. During the Gulf Canada and Hiram Walker battles, a faint undertone of censure had crept into coverage of Olympia & York for the first time. The disagreeable aspects of Paul Reichmann's behavior in these two deals had been documented in great detail in *The Master Builders*, which was published in 1986 and was the first book-length look at Olympia & York. But even as the brothers' business affairs were subjected to increasingly rigorous scrutiny, the Reichmann family's European history remained a story untold in the press. *The Master Builders* had devoted only 4 of its 258 pages to the family's pre-Canadian history, a ratio roughly mirrored in newspaper and magazine coverage of the Reichmanns' doings. It was as if the first twenty-five or thirty floors of the seventy-two-story First Bank Tower had been wrapped in some thickly impenetrable covering. You knew those bottom floors existed, for otherwise this outsized monument could not stand. But what, exactly, did they look like? How sturdy was the foundation they provided? For how long would the richest, most powerful business family in Canada be permitted the luxury of having no past?

Sooner or later, those wraps would have to come off, for the Reichmanns were business-world celebrities now, and the gross inadequacy of the historical record increasingly affronted public curiosity. Had the brothers known what lay in store, they might well have offered their authorized reminiscences to the *Globe & Mail, Maclean's*, or another major Canadian publication that routinely covered Olympia & York and thus had a vested interest in maintaining civil relations with the family. As it was, the brothers continued to be ruled by reclusiveness, and so it was left to Elaine Dewar to tell the story her way, filling the historical void with what amounted to a small book—fifty-five thousand words unspooled across seventy pages and illustrated with a series of vintage family photos supplied by a Gestetner in-law whom Dewar had tracked down in Israel. Although none of the Toronto brothers had been quoted, Edward Reichmann had spoken with Dewar about aspects of the family history, conferring an aura of quasi officiality upon the piece. Albert, Paul, and Ralph were furious with their eldest brother, who in turn was mortified by the uses to which Dewar had put some of the information he had supplied. For the entire family—for the grandchildren of Samuel and Renée no less than their sons—the *Toronto Life* article was a crushing blow.

Just two months after Olympia & York had committed to Canary Wharf, the publication of the *Toronto Life* article confronted the Reichmann brothers with what for them was an equally momentous and even more difficult decision: to sue or not to sue. Libel litigation would expose the Reichmanns to a scrutiny of a sort the family had never before faced. Given the broad scope of Dewar's article, virtually every aspect of their private lives could be subjected to court-mandated discovery. At the same time, the publicity generated by a legal battle inevitably would attract even more attention to the offending article. Finally, even if the brothers were convinced that the article was libelous, how could they be certain that the lawyers and investigators who would begin rummaging around in the family's past might not uncover a bona fide skeleton or two? The Reichmann brothers had been boys at the start of World War II. Did they really want to make a legal case out of the proverbially loaded question, "What did you do during the war, Daddy?" forty years after the fact?

On the other hand, if allowed to stand unchallenged, the void-filling Dewar article was certain to be accepted by the rest of the press as authoritative and thus would serve as a foundation for all future coverage about the family. It was a matter of no small concern to the Reichmanns that Dewar had yet to finish fleshing out their story. By the time the *Toronto Life* article appeared, its author already was hard at work expanding her magazine piece into a four-hundred-page book scheduled to be published in the spring of 1988 in Canada by Random House and simultaneously in the United States by Viking Press. A British deal also was in the works. In the family's view, Dewar's book could only exacerbate the damage that *Toronto Life* had done to its reputation.

For legal counsel, the Reichmanns turned to Davies, Ward & Beck, a major Toronto firm whose ties to the family dated back nearly thirty years. David Ward tended personally to the Reichmanns' request for advice on the *Toronto Life* matter, bringing in a junior partner named Steven Sharpe to help. Libel law was not among Davies, Ward's specialties and so, with the Reichmanns' assent, Ward hired as co-counsel J. Lorne Murphy and John Laskin, two well-known Toronto libel lawyers. "The difficult thing at the outset was that the Reichmann brothers were too young to have had personal knowledge of many of the things raised in the article," Sharpe recalled. "No one was in a position to say, 'No, that's not right. I was there and it didn't happen that way.'" (Renée Reichmann's memory was no longer reliable.)

The most sensational of Dewar's insinuations hinged on a declassified report that she had found in the Washington, D.C., archives of the Office of Strategic Services, the principal U.S. intelligence agency during World War II. On the recommendation of their lawyers, the Reichmanns promptly hired Kroll Associates to find the report Dewar had cited and any other documents in the OSS files that mentioned the family. Based in New York, Kroll Associates generally was considered the foremost corporate private eyes in America.

Within days of the publication of "The Mysterious Reichmanns," the Reichmanns formally notified *Toronto Life* and Elaine Dewar of their intent to sue. A few weeks later, the brothers also issued libel notices to the *Toronto Sun* and Dianne Francis, who had written a column in the *Sun* praising the Dewar piece. The notices prompted the *Globe & Mail* to weigh in with an article of its own. "By suddenly slapping two publications with back-to-back libel notices," concluded reporter Jan Wong, "the Reichmanns are sending a signal: Stay out of our past or we will make it expensive." Paul and his brothers would strenuously object—in court—to this statement. Even so, Wong might well have escaped a libel notice had not she provided a platform for Leo Heaps, a Toronto writer who had assumed the role of the brothers' journalistic nemesis well before Elaine Dewar had begun researching her story and whose own history was nearly as colorful and tumultuous as that of the Reichmanns. Despite hiring two sets of private investigators, the brothers never did answer to their own satisfaction the question, "Who is Leo Heaps and why is he out to get us?"

Heaps had grown up in Winnipeg, Manitoba, the driven yet dilettantish son of a deeply committed, accomplished man. His father, Abraham A. Heaps, was one of the first Jews elected to Canada's House of Commons and a cofounder of the forerunner to today's national socialist party, the New Democratic Party of Canada. In 1943, Leo enlisted in the Canadian Army and was shipped out to England, where he yearned impatiently for combat. He first saw action as part of the massive Allied force that landed at Normandy on D-Day and later parachuted into Holland as part of the colossal blunder known as Operation Market Garden. The Allies' plan was to drop a massive airborne force behind German lines to seize five bridges across the Rhine, the last and most crucial of which was located in the Dutch town of Arnhem, sixty miles behind enemy lines. But the Allies had not counted on bad weather or the presence of a German panzer division and SS units at Arnhem. Some 1,130 of the 10,000 paratroops originally landed were killed and another 6,000 taken prisoner, but not before a fierce street fight immortalized in the book *A Bridge Too Far.*

In the deadly chaos of Arnhem, Leo Heaps found his métier. By the second day, Major General R. E. Urquhart, who, as commander of the First Airborne Division, was "the one man who might have brought cohesion to the British attack," was pinned down with three other high-ranking officers in a house near the bridge. General Urquhart and his colleagues were debating whether to make a dash for it when, to their amazement, a British Bren gun carrier emerged from the smoke of battle and clattered to a stop outside. "It was driven by a ubiquitous Canadian lieutenant called Heaps who was soon to develop a reputation for turning up in the most unlikely places at the most unexpected times with his Bren carrier," General Urquhart recalled in his memoir of Arnhem. "In fact, I never really discovered to which unit he belonged. In battle, some men have charmed existences: Heaps was such a man. He took unto himself the role of mobile freelance." Captured by the Germans, Heaps escaped from a prisoner train by removing a partition and jumping onto a grassy embankment. While hidden by the Dutch resistance, he helped rescue a few hundred troops stranded on the far bank of the Rhine. For his role in this mission, Heaps won the Military Cross.

Promoted to captain, Heaps remained on active duty until the eve of Germany's surrender. He entered Bergen-Belsen on the day of its liberation and conducted his own horrific inspection tour of the concentration camp. (It is conceivable that among the survivors he encountered was Edward Reichmann's cousin and future wife, Edith.) Heaps began composing his first book, *Escape from Arnhem*, on the ocean liner carrying him back to Canada from England. Written in a plain, understated style that credibly conveyed the confusion of battle and advanced no claim of heroism for himself, Heaps's memoir was well received back home. He dedicated the volume to the father he idolized. Two decades passed before Heaps undertook his second book, a biography of his father.

In a sense, it was all downhill for Heaps after *Escape from Arnhem*. He would continue in the role of mobile freelance for the rest of his life without again coming close to the glory of Arnhem, though he did return briefly to the field of battle in 1948 as a military adviser to the Israeli army with the rank of major. According to newspaper accounts, Heaps brought about a truce between feuding Haganah and Irgun factions at Tel Aviv. "After they'd laid down their guns, a doctor tended a bullet wound in Heaps' arm, both sides toasted him in lemonade and then a bomb ended the short-lived truce." Returning again to Canada, Heaps married, fathered four children, and made a modest living dealing in art in Ottawa and investing in real estate in Montreal.

In 1964, Heaps went to England with a film script and decided to settle in London with his family. He wrote four plays and four film scripts and also dabbled as a theatrical producer but had his greatest success in England as a sleuthing collector of Canadiana, especially Eskimo art and artifacts. In the early 1970s, Heaps returned to Canada, a middle-aged rebel without a cause. Leo made one attempt to follow directly in his father's footsteps, running for a Parliament seat under the National Democratic Party banner, but was soundly thrashed. "My father was someone who always wanted to right a wrong but he lived to a large degree in the shadow of his own father," said Adrian Heaps, Leo's only son.

In his later years, Heaps became an increasingly prolific if amateurish writer. Aside from the political thriller *Quebec Plot*, his only attempt at a novel, he generally wrote nonfiction derived from his own experiences or tangentially related to them. For the most part, Heaps's books attracted little attention and sold poorly. What notices he did receive tended to be sharply negative and his literary disappointments made him increasingly cantankerous. "Adversity was his fuel," recalled his son Adrian. "If there was no adversity, he'd invent it to keep himself going." He wrote blistering letters to the editor and flouted propriety as the enfant terrible of the Kew Gardens Tennis Club in Toronto. Not content to privately disdain the club's Saturday evening social night, he organized an "antisocial night" but nobody would come—an elegant if unintentional paradigm of futility.

In 1984, Heaps brought suit in New York City against Simon & Schuster and almost everyone else connected with *Vengeance*, a best-selling book that purported to tell the story of the hunt for the masterminds of the 1972 massacre of Israeli Olympic athletes at Munich. The Mossad agent who had led the covert venture had met Heaps through some mutual military acquaintances and hired him as ghostwriter for a book to be published in Canada by Lester & Orpen Dennys. Heaps and the Mossad agent soon had a falling out and a replacement writer was hired. Malcolm Lester of Lester & Orpen had no further contact with Heaps until *Vengeance* became a hit three years later. "He accused me of stealing 'his' idea and said he'd take us for a million bucks," recalled Lester, whose publishing house was among those Heaps sued. After protracted legal wrangling, Heaps came away empty-handed when a judge dismissed his suit short of trial. "In my opinion," added Lester, who'd considered several earlier book proposals by Heaps, "it was basically a shakedown. But at some level Heaps also convinced himself that he'd been wronged. It was like he was able to manufacture his own righteous indignation."

In early 1985, Heaps signed a deal with McClelland & Stewart, Canada's leading independent book publisher, to write a book on the Reichmanns. Heaps persisted even after his initial hope of writing an authorized biography was dashed by the brothers' refusal to participate. In the spring of 1986, a few months before Dewar began her reporting, Heaps submitted a manuscript that McClelland & Stewart rejected as unpublishable and possibly libelous. Infuriated, Heaps publicly accused his publisher of conspiring with the Reichmanns to suppress his book. In her article on the libel controversy engendered by the *Toronto Life* piece, Jan Wong quoted Heaps, who repeated his conspiracy allegation. "What they've done to *Toronto Life* is a warning," added Heaps, who claimed to be working on a new Reichmann book that was, as he himself put it, "too hot to handle."

———

In January 1988, the Reichmanns made good on their legal threats. Renée Reichmann joined Albert, Paul, Ralph, and Olympia & York Development in bringing suit for libel in the Supreme Court of Ontario against *Toronto Life* and Elaine Dewar. The suit included a damage claim of $102 million (Canadian), which was about $101.9 million larger than the largest libel award in Canadian history. In an interview later in 1988, Paul Reichmann described the decision to sue as the most agonizing he had ever made. "If the decision were monetary," he said, "the decision would have been the opposite. Going to court will kill any vestige of privacy left to our family. . . . Because of our position in world Jewry and in Canadian business, we had no choice. We will spare no cost, time or effort until every part of this story is proved false in a court of law. It is our duty to our families and our community."

Mrs. Reichmann was not a plaintiff in two additional libel suits that her sons brought for a few million dollars in damages apiece, one against the *Toronto Sun*, another against the *Globe & Mail*. As Paul's comments implied, the suit against *Toronto Life* was the most significant of the three by far. Like most Canadian libel cases, it would end short of trial in a negotiated settlement—but only after three years of costly legal maneuvering that would fill box after box in the court archives with documents. In a sense, though, the Reichmanns dealt themselves a public relations defeat the moment the legal battle was joined. Taking action against *Toronto Life* was one thing: given the scope and ambition of Dewar's work, the historical record was at stake. But in simultaneously going after the *Toronto Sun* and the *Globe & Mail* for what were wholly derivative, minor articles, the Reichmanns appeared to be doing exactly what Jan Wong had suggested they were doing: posting their distant past with "No Trespassing" signs. Soon, commentators all across the country were citing the Reichmanns' outburst of litigiousness in trend pieces on the rise of "libel chill" in Canada.

The implicit threat of retaliation by the Reichmanns wreaked havoc with Canada's leading business journalism awards program, which was sponsored by the Royal Bank of Canada and the Toronto Press Club. Fearing that the Reichmanns might sue the members of the judging panel of the National Business Writing Awards, the contest's chief judge unilaterally decided to scratch "The Mysterious Reichmanns" from the competition on the advice of Royal Bank's legal counsel. In protest, the editors of *Toronto Life*, the *Globe & Mail*, the *Toronto Star*, and many other publications pulled their entries, reducing the number of submissions by half.

There was equal irony in the spectacle of the Reichmann brothers stampeding the very profession that for years had portrayed them (inaccurately) as too much the gentlemen to wield the club of litigation. Although the Reichmanns were not amused, there was nothing to be gained in antagonizing the best and the brightest of the national business press by shattering one of their favorite punch bowls, however inadvertently. In lashing out at the *Sun* and the *Globe & Mail*, the Reichmanns had overreacted in their anguish—and would tacitly acknowledge as much by failing to aggressively pursue either.

The statement of claim the Reichmanns lodged against the *Globe & Mail* strongly suggested that the newspaper was the object of misdirected wrath. About two-thirds of it was devoted to a chronology of the Reichmanns' acrimonious dealings with Heaps, culminating with an allegation of attempted extortion. According to the Reichmanns' court filing, Heaps had told them that he had uncovered what he termed "disturbing information" about Samuel

Reichmann and threatened to publish it unless the family either paid him $250,000 to write a favorable history of Olympia & York or $1 million to destroy the biographical manuscript that he had already written. Heaps vehemently denied the charge, which never did receive a full airing in court. However, Avram Bennett, the owner of McClelland & Stewart, said later that Heaps had first broached the notion of a $1 million payoff in meeting with him and Jack McClelland, who had commissioned the Reichmann book in the first place. "He said that we should tell the Reichmanns that for $1 million he'd set aside the book he'd written and do another one," Bennett recalled. "What he was suggesting was out and out blackmail."

As a practical matter, the Reichmanns could not bring a libel suit against Heaps himself until his manuscript actually was published. But by shoehorning the extortion allegations into their complaint against the *Globe & Mail*, the Reichmanns in effect fired a warning shot across the bow of any editor who might be tempted to lend Heaps a hand.

Meanwhile, Kroll Associates had begun an investigation that would venture far beyond the contents of Dewar's article in probing the family history. "Rarely has the firm gotten an assignment as open-ended as this one," recalled Steve Rucker, a senior Kroll official who acted as case manager on the Reichmann investigation. "Our instruction from the Reichmann brothers was to find out everything we could about their parents' lives in Tangier and before. There were no limits, either in terms of expenses incurred or where we took the investigation." At any given time over the next two years, Kroll had as many as a dozen investigators on the case, at a cost to the Reichmanns of $1,500 per person per day. An invoice included in the court file showed that Kroll racked up $844,625 in charges in the first three months of 1988 alone for work performed in Canada, New York, Washington, the United Kingdom, France, Spain, Germany, Austria, Switzerland, Hungary, Israel, and Morocco. Kroll Associates' final tab never was disclosed but probably exceeded $5 million.

Kroll investigators made a special effort to develop relationships among the few hundred Jews remaining in Tangier. Jeffrey Heyman, the Kroll operative who spent the most time in Tangier, went far beyond the call of duty and ended up marrying a local woman. Great effort was expended to locate anyone who had known the Reichmann family in Tangier—no matter how tangentially—and scores upon scores of taped statements were taken all over the world. Kroll investigators tracked a former OSS agent stationed in Tangier all the way to an unmarked grave in the Philippines. In Paris, the firm unearthed Samuel and Renée Reichmann's police file, which in 1940 had been loaded onto a barge with the files of a few hundred thousand other foreign residents and accidentally sunk in the Seine during the French government's flight from the approaching German Army. Many years after the war, the barge was raised and the surviving documents were culled for the names of current French residents and figures of historical note. The remaining papers were destroyed except for a small sampling that happened to include the Reichmann file, which Kroll located in a warehouse in the Paris suburb of Créteil.

Legally speaking, an open-ended investigation made sense. In Canada, in contrast to the United States, a plaintiff in a libel case need not prove malicious intent but merely that what was published was defamatory. In other words, Canadian libel cases tend to turn around basic questions of fact. If the Reichmanns could outresearch Dewar, they would hold the tactical high ground and had a good chance of winning. In personal terms, however, the unleashing of Kroll Associates was hugely risky. In effect, Paul and his brothers had decided to investigate their parents far more thoroughly than Heaps or Dewar ever had. And if Kroll did uncover something scandalous, there was no guaranteeing that knowledge of it could be confined within the family. Under the discovery rules of Canadian courts, if the case against *Toronto Life* went to trial, the Reichmanns' lawyers would have to disclose to the other side all relevant information dug up by investigators in their employ, whether it supported or undermined their case. Although the defense was restricted in its use of such information, it could well find its way into the public record. It was entirely possible, in other words, that the Reichmanns could win their legal battle and lose the public relations war.

Chapter 39

In the fall of 1988, Olympia & York sponsored a five-day celebration of the opening of the public spaces at the World Financial Center. The first event was a glittering black-tie benefit for Nancy Reagan's favorite charity, "Stop Cancer," featuring a performance in the Winter Garden by the Philadelphia Orchestra with Isaac Stern and Mstislav Rostropovich. Some seven hundred celebrities, socialites, and tycoons basked in the glow of the Reichmanns' crowning achievement. "The center reminds me of Egypt and the pyramids," marveled telecommunications billionaire John Kluge, who, like most of Olympia & York's guests, had never before met a Reichmann. More than fifty thousand people would visit the World Financial Center during the gala, an event without precedent in the history of the Reichmanns, but the family's dominant member was not among them. Paul Reichmann was in London, unable to tear himself away from Canary Wharf.

From mid-1987 well into 1991, Canary Wharf would be not merely Reichmann's priority but his Xanadu. While the affairs of empire frequently required his presence in Toronto, New York, and other world capitals, he would spend fully a quarter of his time in London during these years. To speed the boss's transatlantic commuting, Olympia & York bought its first jet, a Gulfstream III, and paid a few million pounds for a grand but dilapidated house in the Hampstead Heath section of London, complete with three acres of grounds and a small lake. Reichmann planned eventually to tear the house down and build a new one. In the meantime, he would indulge his aficionado's taste in luxury-hotel suites, migrating among the Inn on the Park, the Savoy, and Claridge's as the mood struck him. His wife frequently joined him in London and together they spent many weekends as guests in the north London home of Ollick and Naomi Heller. Ollick was a first cousin of the late Lipmann Heller and Naomi had been Eva's close friend and business partner. The Hellers' place in Golders Green afforded Paul easy access to his preferred place of worship in London: the shul of Rabbi Simcha Rubin, the aged Sassover Rebbe, who was perhaps *the* most strictly Orthodox member of the London rabbinate.

Olympia & York opened a luxurious office in rented quarters on Great George Street, just off Parliament Square in the heart of the city. Against his better judgment, Michael Dennis agreed to fill the position of chief executive of the newly created Olympia & York UK on temporary reassignment from the New York office. Dennis had recommended to Reichmann that Olympia & York enter into a joint venture with Stanhope Properties, Stuart Lipton's Olympia & York–like company, rather than try to build a British subsidiary even as it was building Canary Wharf. Reichmann was not unaware of the advantages to be gained by allying with a technically adept, politically well-connected local developer, but sharing ownership would have diminished the degree of Olympia & York control to something less than complete, and to Reichmann that was anathema. Ironically, what convinced him that Olympia & York could go it alone in London was his absolute faith in the abilities (if not the strategic judgments) of his reluctant draftee and professional alter ego, Michael Dennis. "Michael's combination of skill, intelligence and experience was unique in the business," Reichmann said in 1995. "Even today, you won't find many people intellectually in his league."

To fill the post of president of Olympia & York UK, Reichmann recruited Charles Young, an American who had gotten to know the Reichmanns during his long years in Toronto as president of Citibank Canada. Young, whom Citicorp had transferred to London from Toronto in 1986, was a personable and well-connected banker who had been the first person to call Reichmann's attention to the Docklands.

Reichmann filled the rest of the upper management ranks of his new London company with Britishers. Robert John, a forty-year-old lawyer turned banker, was the youngest and most important of the lot. In fact, Reichmann would come to see John as Dennis's eventual successor. As the chief of the corporate lending division of County Bank, the merchant banking arm of giant National Westminster, John had worked closely with Ware Travelstead in a doomed effort to make Canary Wharf palatable to British banks. When Olympia & York took over the project, John set about trying to convince Reichmann to retain his bank as a financial adviser. Reichmann promptly offered John a job instead. "I asked him, 'What would you like me to do?' " recalled John, a talkative, impassioned Welshman. "His response was elliptical: 'What would you like to do?' I told him that although my background was in finance, I wanted to work on the development aspect of the project as Michael Dennis's deputy. He said, 'If that's what you want to do, fine.' I accepted in principle before we even talked about salary."

Reichmann also rehired the two senior executives of the former Olympia & York holding, English Property Corporation: Stanley Honeyman and his deputy, Gerald Rothman. When the Reichmanns sold English Property in 1983, Honeyman had gone into semiretirement, but Rothman had moved to California and joined Landmark Land, a recreational development company in which Olympia & York had recently purchased a minority interest. Bored with Carmel, Rothman left the Reichmanns' service after a few years and went to work in New York City as the chief of English Property's American subsidiary. The sheer audacity of Canary Wharf—"There's never been a project like it," he marveled, "at least not since England was countryside"—lured Rothman back to London, where he joined the Reichmanns' new U.K. company as chief administrator. "The regime for running the London office was like the wheels of a jumbo jet, which go from 0 to 300 mph the moment they touch ground," Rothman recalled. "Within nine months of starting we had a couple hundred corporate employees going flat out and you couldn't even see the site for all the work crews swarming over it."

Reichmann and his minions decided to retain Skidmore, Owings & Merrill, the distinguished American architectural firm that had drawn up the original master plan of Canary Wharf, but instructed it to redesign the project from the ground up. This painstaking effort would consume nearly five months—an eternity in Olympia & York time.

Early in the process, Reichmann concluded that the main problem with Canary Wharf was that it was not ambitious enough in concept. "We have realized that our success is not dependent on one area of the economy, financial services, but rather all of the U.K. economy because of the revolution taking place in British business and British businessmen," he declared. The European Community's epochal decision to dismantle many intracontinental trade barriers beginning in 1992 would redound to the benefit of London, which would emerge as "the business capital of Europe," Reichmann predicted. "In the long run, the confidence in the political stability and democratic tradition of England will cause international companies to choose the U.K. as the base and location of their expansion." As Reichmann saw it, fully two-thirds of London's existing supply of office space was technologically outmoded and no amount of building-code tinkering by the City Corporation could close the huge gap between supply and impending demand. Nor were the suburban office parks that had sprung up on London's periphery equal to the task. Only Docklands fit the bill. "The difference between East London and other areas," Reichmann said, "is that it is the only one of enough size for a full business district to develop."

Reichmann predicted that within two decades, Docklands would be to the City what midtown Manhattan had become to Wall Street, and that the "Canary Wharf District" would have established itself as London's Park

Avenue. Under Olympia & York's revised master plan, Canary Wharf would include twenty-four office buildings with more than twelve million square feet of space, as compared with Travelstead's twenty-two buildings and ten million square feet. On two separate sites to the north and south of this massive seventy-one-acre core, Olympia & York would add three million square feet of housing, retail, and hotel development on twenty-two additional acres. The company would begin at once on Phase I, which would consist of the eight largest and most centrally located office towers. "But for the restraints of site logistics and availability of men and materials, we would consider having all 24 parcels under construction simultaneously," Reichmann declared in unveiling his grandiose new plan at a crowded press conference in March 1988. As Reichmann saw it, the Canary Wharf District would be completed in seven to ten years.

The press interviews that Reichmann had begun granting with increasing frequency to promote Canary Wharf were studded with quotations so outlandishly bullish, so blithely triumphal, that they evoked the prefight hype of professional boxers. "This is not a risky project," he told a reporter from the *Globe & Mail*. "On a scale of one to ten—if the risk with Battery Park was nine—here it would be one." This claim was so ludicrous on its face that most of the commentators who later cited it did not bother with refutation but simply passed it off as bravado. It was nothing of the kind; Reichmann's every action over the next few years suggested that he truly believed that the odds at Docklands were indeed overwhelmingly stacked in his favor. At age fifty-seven, he was a man who had ceased believing in the possibility of his own failure. Or, as Reichmann himself would concede after Olympia & York's collapse, "The fact that I had never been wrong created character flaws that caused me to make mistakes."

As a devout Orthodox Jew, Paul Reichmann believed perforce in a God who was directly involved in man's daily affairs. When his nephew-in-law Morris Brenick had decided, while living in Toronto in the early 1980s, to go into real estate, Reichmann had taken him aside at a family gathering and hammered this lesson home. "Paul told me, 'If you are now going into business, I will tell you that what multiplied my initial success by a factor of a hundred had nothing to do with my own efforts. It was God's will that I was successful on such a scale,' " Brenick recalled. As Reichmann triumphed again and again over seemingly daunting odds, he could only have assumed that his increasingly grand works had found favor with God. By the time of Canary Wharf, he seemed to have come to believe in his project, if not himself, with the same absolute faith with which he had always believed in God. "The only question that enters our minds is: Will success happen immediately or later?" he had proclaimed at the Canary Wharf groundbreaking.

In secular terms, Reichmann's flaw was hubris in the classical mode. But for a devoutly religious Jew to assert his certain success was tantamount to blasphemy, since only God could have known the project's outcome. Indeed, in the view of some of Reichmann's coreligionists, Canary Wharf per se was ambitious beyond the bounds of Orthodox norms of modesty. "When I saw the size of Canary Wharf, I didn't believe any person would have the guts to build something like that," said one Orthodox leader who had been generally admiring of the Reichmanns. "I don't believe God wants anyone to be as big as the Reichmanns were becoming."

At the same time, Paul Reichmann's heightened personal visibility also stirred confusion and unease within the ultra-Orthodox community and beyond. Few suspected him of indulging a taste for the spotlight, though no doubt he took a certain satisfaction in seeing photos of himself with the prime minister in the paper. One could argue that Reichmann's frequent participation in interviews, press conferences, photo opportunities, and so on was necessary to the survival of a politically contentious project highly dependent on government sponsorship. The issue was not cause but effect, and the effect was to publicize the Reichmann name to new heights of renown, not only in London but throughout the world.

The curiosity of the public came mixed with baser motives. At a time of rising anti-Semitism in England, Paul Reichmann's high-profile championing of his luxury-tower Xanadu stirred apprehension within the Jewish community of London. For the most part, these concerns were privately articulated and were tempered by an admiration of the Reichmann family that ranged far beyond the bounds of ultra-Orthodoxy, just as it did in Toronto. No local Jewish leader would have presumed to advise a Reichmann on how to conduct himself in public. However, the underlying unease did explode to the surface after the *Financial Times* ran a caricature of Reichmann along with an article on Canary Wharf. The newspaper was bombarded with complaints, including a letter from the secretary-general of the Board of Deputies, the central organ of English Jewry, denouncing the unflattering (but recognizable) drawing as a "racial stereotype." The furor subsided after the editor of the *Financial Times* apologized, only to re-flare when a columnist for the *Jewish Chronicle* argued that the caricature lay within the bounds of journalistic propriety: "It is ludicrously thin-skinned to suggest key Jewish figures like Reichmann should be above robust caricature."

Over the years, Reichmann had—in his own mind, at any rate—succeeded in reconciling his edifice complex with his understanding of Jewish history and religious doctrine. There had been, for a start, the troubling precedent of the Tower of Babel. In Genesis, it was written that after the great flood the descendants of Noah had said to one another: "Let us build ourselves a city and a tower with its top in the heavens; let us make a name for ourselves lest we be scattered all over the earth. . . . So the Lord scattered them all over the earth, and they stopped building the city. For this reason it was called Babel, because there the Lord confused the speech of all the earth." The preponderance of Talmudic commentary on this biblical passage argued that it did not mean that the erection of the tower was the cause of diversity of languages per se but rather demonstrated the futility of all of man's attempts to maintain unity by material means alone. The commentary of Ibn Ezra, the great twelfth-century scholar and philosopher, included this interpretation of the motives of the builders of the tower: "It is probable that they were neither so foolish to believe that they could ascend to heaven, nor were they afraid of another flood. They merely wanted a central and conspicuous city which would ensure them fame."

In a memorable 1983 encounter, a reporter had flustered Paul Reichmann by suggesting during an interview that the coming of the Messiah—which is one of the most basic and joyful tenets of ultra-Orthodoxy—would confront the Reichmann family with its "ultimate problem" as property owners.

> "Why is that?" [Reichmann] asked, puffing his ever-present Lark cigarette.
>
> "Because it says in Talmud that when the Messiah comes, all property will cease to have value."
>
> "It says that in the Talmud?" Reichmann asked in disbelief.
>
> "What it says specifically," answered the reporter, "is that if a man offers you property for one dinar which you know to be worth a thousand dinars, don't buy it, because when the Messiah comes it will be worth nothing."
>
> Snuffing out his Lark, Reichmann pondered so hard that his dark eyes fairly danced with intensity. Perhaps he was thinking ahead to a deal that would, in the family's unique style, attend to the interests of both parties. A deal the Messiah himself could not refuse.

Actually, all the Reichmanns' real estate ventures balanced the secular and the divine, in that the family devoted such a huge share of its income to building Klal Yisrael, the global community of devout Jewry. If Reichmann's grand vision of Canary Wharf as the center of a third business district were realized, Torah fundamentalism stood to reap a bonanza vast beyond the imagining of its adherents.

At the same time, though, he intended Canary Wharf to be more than the sum of its cash flow. The project was an attempt not only to benefit from London's emergence as the business capital of the new Europe but to help it achieve such status over the more centrally located Berlin, the once and future capital of Greater Germany. Although the notion of building "Maggie's Monument" greatly appealed to Reichmann, the concept of Canary Wharf was bound to hold deeper, more personal meaning as well for an Austrian-born Jew who had twice been driven into exile by Hitler's army before reaching the age of eleven. What better symbol of the Reichmanns' survival as a family or of traditional Orthodoxy's rebirth in the wake of the Nazi Holocaust than to build a new city-within-a-city so "central and conspicuous" in its way that it would cast a shadow over all of Europe? Canary Wharf "is a challenge of creativity and will make a contribution for generations to come," Reichmann predicted. "It will be recognized as the best in Europe and . . . the world."

If Paul Reichmann harbored any doubts about the religious implications of his compulsion to build latter-day "towers with their tops in the heavens," he had worked through them by the advent of the Docklands megaproject. Indeed, like the accomplished bachur that he was once, he had synthesized a Talmudic rationale for his open-ended ambition as a developer. When asked in a 1988 interview with a business journalist to explain the roots of his commercial drive, Reichmann responded with an exegesis of Genesis 1:1–2:3. "A literal translation from the Hebrew reads that on the seventh day, God 'rested from all his work that God created to do,' " Reichmann noted. "Commentators struggle with the meaning of the last two words. Ibn Ezra says that in God's creation, the seeds were there for everything that will ever be. Thus God finished the world in six days and gave it to the people as the raw material 'to do,' to create with. In other words: 'Here is the material, now you people take it and develop it.' "

Like the World Financial Center, Canary Wharf was to contain enormous, finely detailed public spaces. Despite the complex's massive size, Paul Reichmann insisted that it be master-planned down to the smallest detail. Even the street furniture—lamp posts, litter bins, handrails, telephone boxes, signs, and so on—were custom-designed. "I can't tell you the agony of doing it," said Robert Turner, the Skidmore architect who did most of the redrafting. "It would be a hell of a lot easier just to get them out of a catalogue of existing designs but Olympia & York would never consider that."

To advise on the public spaces and gardens, Olympia & York hired Sir Roy Strong, a proper and accomplished British gent recently retired as director of the Victoria and Albert Museum. With Anthony Coombes, Sir Roy spent long hours soaking up the look and feel of the streets around Grosvenor and Berkeley squares and also Bloomsbury Estates, with its Bedford, Tavistock, and Woburn squares. The object, Coombes explained, was "to make places [at Canary Wharf] that were both memorable and comfortable." Olympia & York's method recapitulated the way in which eighteenth-century London had taken shape, with the public squares being constructed first, thus defining the character and quality of the estates that followed.

Despite Olympia & York's efforts to impart Englishness to Canary Wharf, its basic layout bore the Parisian stamp of the beaux arts revival—a style that had become a Skidmore, Owings trademark. A tree-lined avenue of Haussmannesque proportions ran down the center, linking together a turning circle or circus at river's edge with a single square featuring a fountain, a rectangular train station, and a double square that ended in a semicircle. Around the carefully placed geometries of these central elements office buildings of varying heights and sizes were organized in groups. The effect was monumental, formal, and decidedly un-English, at least as defined by Brian Edwards, a professor of urban planning and author of a book on Docklands. To Professor Edwards, Canary Wharf suggested "American heroic urbanism rather than the subtlety of the English picturesque movement."

Although Canary Wharf remained imposing by any standard, the new master plan greatly lowered its profile. In the version commissioned by Travelstead, the infrastructure—roads, parking lots, utility and mechanical systems, and so on—lay above ground, encased in what amounted to a colossal pedestal for the office towers. At Olympia & York's direction, Skidmore, Owings streamlined the infrastructure and put most of it underground. This had the effect of bringing the ground floor of the complex much closer to water level. In place of the trio of 850-foot buildings that was to have formed the colossal centerpiece of Travelstead's Canary Wharf, Reichmann envisioned a single, 800-foot skyscraper of fifty stories flanked by two towers of forty and thirty-nine stories, respectively.

Reichmann ruffled British feathers by relying heavily on North American architects, principally Cesar Pelli & Associates; Pei, Cobb, Freed & Partners; Skidmore, Owings & Merrill; and Kohn, Pedersen, Fox Associates. Although Reichmann thought highly of Richard Rogers, Norman Foster, Terry Farrell, and other preeminent British architects, he decided to go with North American firms because of their far more extensive experience with large floor-plate buildings, which were two-a-penny in Manhattan but very much a novelty in London—as were skyscrapers, for that matter. "Paul and Michael were suspicious of the capacity of the British to deliver the kind of buildings they wanted," said Robert John, who was part of a dissident contingent within Olympia & York that unsuccessfully argued for greater diversity in building type. "Not everyone here wants big, fat buildings."

Even at its reduced height, the central tower—dubbed One Canada Square—would surpass Britain's tallest existing building by a good 200 feet. Designed by Cesar Pelli, One Canada Square would be visible from all over London and as far as 20 miles distant in Kent. Pelli rather presumptuously described his tower as London's first genuine skyscraper, dismissing the existing tall buildings in London as lacking "the required flair or dignity." Clad in stainless steel and capped with an illuminated pyramid, Pelli's square-shaped tower had a sleek and sober postmodernist look. However, the other office buildings in the first phase were variations on a neoclassical theme. Using a disparate array of materials and colors, each of these buildings in its own way attempted to evoke the London architecture of the Edwardian Age.

Canary Wharf's sheer novelty—its size and daring—made it a cause célèbre in London in a way that the World Financial Center never had been in New York. "The scale and complexity of Canary Wharf are unprecedented in British urbanism," Professor Edwards observed. Indeed, as the largest commercial construction site in the world, Canary Wharf established itself as a tourist attraction long before it opened. "I can't think of anything that has given such a sense of spectacle for a very long time," said Sir Roy Strong, the Olympia & York consultant, putting a positive spin on Canary Wharf's giantism. "The whole Mall complex, from Admiralty Arch to the Victoria Memorial and the main facade of the Palace—which all went up before the First World War— was probably the last thing." Strong singled out the fountain planned for Cabot Square as "the most outstanding example since the Trafalgar Square fountains in the twenties—or the Victoria Memorial itself. People will flock there just to see that, because no one has done anything like it for decades. It's the sheer scale. I mean, jets of water 40 feet high."

But to Paul Reichmann's dismay, Strong's raptures proved atypical. Olympia & York's elaborate plans seemed to have something to offend everyone in England with a professional opinion. The most overt hostility emanated from aggrieved classicists. Francis Tibbalds, a leading architect and head of the Royal Town Planning Institute, which with 14,000 members was the ultimate arbiter of Englishness in its field, was scathingly critical of Olympia & York's design: "The layout is simplistic and banal, the architecture lumpy and medi-ocre. The whole looks like a chunk of some aging, tired and dreary U.S. down-town dropped from a great height onto the Isle of Dogs." (Tibbalds would continue to direct withering fire Olympia & York's way throughout the build-ing of Canary Wharf. As phase one neared completion, he offered this critique: "It's every bit as bad as I feared it would be. Future generations will wonder how we allowed it to happen.")

Canary Wharf also offended the Prince of Wales, whose layman's crusade against modernist architecture had raised a great hue and cry in London ever since 1984, when Charles gave a speech in which he criticized a planned exten-sion to the National Gallery as "a monstrous carbuncle on the face of a much-loved and elegant friend." The Prince's utterances culminated in a widely watched and hugely controversial 1988 television program, "HRH the Prince of Wales: A Vision of Britain." The prince wrote his own script, which attacked much of postwar architecture essentially as an affront to Olde Englishness. At one point he was shown examining the scale models of Canary Wharf, which was among the half-dozen projects that bore the brunt of the prince's attack. "Thinking big is very American," intoned the prince in voice-over mode, "but sheer bigness has never looked all that right in London." Charles then zeroed in on Pelli's fifty-story tower: "I personally would go mad if I had to work in a place like that." Sir Roy was delegated to issue a polite but pointed response.

"Canary Wharf is being built the way it is to make the prince's future subjects prosperous," he told The Times, "and it has the particular favor of the prime minister."

Ironically, the predominantly neoclassical architecture of Canary Wharf was lambasted in some quarters as typifying the sort of old-fashioned, récherché approach that appealed to Prince Charles and other fuddy-duddies. "The architecture plays it so safe," lamented the critic Charles Jencks, "more Prince Charlesesque than Post-Modernism." Members of the so-called High-Tech school of architecture thought that the look of Canary Wharf should have made explicit its function as a state-of-the-art financial trading center, in the manner of the futuristic headquarters that Richard Rogers had designed for Lloyds of London in the city or his equally famous Pompidou Center in Paris. Such buildings were products of what some called the "bowellist" school of architecture, given its preference for the public exposure of a structure's vital inner organs—pipeworks, elevators, and so on.

Pelli's tower also was roundly criticized for being too tall relative to Saint Paul's Cathedral, even though, as Pelli pointed out in his defense, the city's great domed landmark was more than two miles from the Isle of Dogs. "We must remember that when St. Paul's was built all the buildings around it were tiny," Pelli retorted. "The important buildings are not in the scale of the body of man, but in the scale of his ideas. St. Paul's was like that, and, I hope in its own way, the tower will be as well." To many Londoners, Pelli's comment seemed the height of pretension. Even Margaret Thatcher, Canary Wharf's most ardent English admirer, stepped gingerly around the issues of scale and skyline. In the public remarks she made after driving the ceremonial first pile, the prime minister said only that the thing she liked most about the architecture of Canary Wharf—its "most thoughtful and wonderful touch"—was that the complex did not interfere with East London's view of Saint Paul's Cathedral. As it turned out, though, the tower did pop up in the views of Saint Paul's from most other points on the compass, including Hampstead Heath, Primrose Hill, Waterloo Bridge, and Greenwich Park.

The opprobrium heaped upon the new Canary Wharf was a great disappointment for Paul Reichmann, who had taken a keen personal interest in Olympia & York's redesign and had every hope that it would be greeted as warmly as had the company's entry into the troubled project. Reichmann took the criticism to heart only in the sense that he tried to foster greater architectural diversity among the sixteen office buildings in the project's secondary phases. Such British experimentalists as Allies & Morrison and Troughton McAslan and the more celebrated Norman Foster and Aldo Rossi were among the architects commissioned to design buildings on the complex's waterfront facing. But Reichmann saw no need to alter the new master plan or the first-phase architecture. Let the brickbats fly, for Canary Wharf would succeed, of that he had no doubt. With God and Michael Dennis on your side, what did a few critics matter?

———

No single project, not even the Docklands Gargantua, could monopolize the entrepreneurial energies of as compulsive an opportunist as Paul Reichmann, who would not turn sixty until 1990 and viewed Canary Wharf not as the capstone of his career but as the largest and latest stepping stone. "Given the way we believe in the future for London and for Europe, I would be very surprised if we stop at Canary Wharf," Dennis proclaimed in mid-1988. "Paul Reichmann would like me to take on another six projects. The problem is finding the human resources to carry them out." Through Olympia & York's New York office, meanwhile, the Master Builder pursued an additional half-dozen major development projects, the largest of which rivaled even Canary Wharf in scale and complexity. "My ambition was open-ended," Reichmann would concede after Olympia & York's collapse. "In hindsight, that was a great error."

To replace Dennis as U.S. development chief, the Reichmanns in 1988 hired Meyer "Sandy" Frucher, the latest in a long line of senior executives recruited from government. Like Dennis, Frucher was a 1960s campus activist who had cut his hair and donned suit and tie but remained much more politically liberal than his new bosses. Frucher's hiring testified even more dramatically to the Reichmanns' eclecticism as employers in that he was the sort of person the brothers shunned as a matter of course outside the office: a lapsed Orthodox Jew. The son of a Polish immigrant to New Jersey, Frucher had received a strict Orthodox upbringing only to turn skeptical and rebellious in his middle teens. Tossed out of several yeshivas, he went to public high school and never looked back. "Both Paul and Albert were intrigued by my family background," said Frucher, who discussed his apostasy over dinner with the brothers on several occasions. "I think they were genuinely interested to know why I had left the path."

At Columbia University, Frucher had gotten involved in the civil rights movement and cofounded a group known as Student Struggle for Soviet Jews. This led to volunteer jobs with Democratic political candidates in New York and the presidential campaigns of Robert Kennedy and Eugene McCarthy. After picking up a master's degree in public administration from the Kennedy School, Frucher embarked on a career in government while keeping a hand in as a political campaigner. Frucher rose through the ranks to become chief labor negotiator for the state of New York under Governor Hugh Carey, earning a dual reputation as a shrewd and knowledgeable official on one hand and, as *The New York Times* once put it, as "an abrasive political scuffler" on the other. When Governor Mario Cuomo appointed Frucher chief executive of the Battery Park City Authority in 1983, the outcome of the World Financial Center project still hung in the balance. Although a property development neophyte, Frucher endeared himself to the Reichmanns by taking a decidedly nonbureaucratic approach to problem solving. "I was laser-focused on getting the World Financial Center done because my great fear was that it would fail," said Frucher, who, not long after his forty-second birthday, decided that the time had come to make his fortune in the private sector and accepted the Reichmanns' offer of employment.

Frucher inherited two megaprojects: Yerba Buena Gardens, the government-sponsored redevelopment in downtown San Francisco that had progressed scarcely at all since Olympia & York's entry in 1980 through no fault of the company's own; and a project in midtown Manhattan that slightly predated Canary Wharf and was to have been Olympia & York's encore to the World Financial Center. The idea was to build a mixed-use complex on the West Side around a novel centerpiece: a new Madison Square Garden. John Zuccotti, Olympia & York's New York planning counsel, also represented Paramount Communications, which owned the existing Garden. Knowing that Paramount was thinking of relocating its famed sports arena, Zuccotti introduced its top executives to Paul Reichmann. Soon, Olympia & York and Paramount had announced plans to jointly redevelop a twelve-block strip of old rail yards and run-down industrial property about fifty blocks due north of the World Financial Center. Olympia & York would build the complex and hold title to all but the new Madison Square Garden. The project's cost was estimated at $2.5 billion, or $1 billion more than the World Financial Center.

It fell to Frucher to try to get the project over a critical political hurdle. Paramount's participation was premised on the New York transit agency, the MTA, donating a piece of land as the site of the new Madison Square Garden. The MTA demanded in return that the city rezone the entire area, in which the agency owned much land. The planning commission balked at granting sweeping zoning concessions for a project that would not come to fruition for years. Then, too, Mayor Ed Koch was heading into a fall election and facing complaints about overdevelopment on the West Side. Frucher eventually persuaded the MTA to back off its zoning demand by cutting them in as a full partner in the project only to have Paramount get cold feet and decide to remodel the existing sports arena rather than build a new one. The project died by degrees in the late 1980s, to the chagrin of Reichmann and his new American development chief. "This was one we really wanted," said Frucher, who kept a scale model of the project on display in his office years after the project had expired.

Meanwhile, Frucher guided Olympia & York's entry into a new megaproject in Tokyo. With office space in short supply, the Japanese government decided in 1988 to build what amounted to a new downtown on several man-made islands along the edge of Tokyo Bay. The goal was to create a state-of-the-art financial district that would solidify Tokyo's claim to parity with New York and

London as a world financial capital. Tokyo Teleport Town, or "Tokyo Bay" as the project was known within Olympia & York, was to be built in three stages, the first of which was predominantly housing. Mitsubishi Corporation, the Japanese trading colossus, invited Olympia & York to join it and two Japanese insurance companies in bidding on a portion of the second phase, which was to include thirty million square feet of office space. "I asked the Japanese exactly what they wanted," said Larry Graham, Olympia & York's project manager for Tokyo Bay. "They kept pulling out pictures of the World Financial Center and saying, 'Build this, build this.' "

What evolved was a plan for an office complex of 12 million square feet, a third again as big as the Battery Park colossus. For more than a year, Graham virtually commuted between New York and Tokyo as he studied the Tokyo market, negotiated with various officials, and supervised the work of the local architects and planners he had hired to assist Olympia & York. Michael Dennis flew over from London at one point, and Graham made four detailed presentations to Paul Reichmann in New York. "He thought of it as his next project after Canary Wharf, though he had his concerns," said Graham, who estimated that Olympia & York's part of Tokyo Bay would have cost between $6 billion and $7 billion.

On average, land prices in downtown Tokyo were four times those in Manhattan or the City and yet the Japanese government had no intention of luring developers to Teleport Town with the sort of tax breaks and subsidies that formed the economic foundation of the World Financial Center and Canary Wharf. This troubled Reichmann, as did the familiar issues of peripheral location and mass transit. In addition, neither Graham nor his boss was convinced that the Tokyo office market was as healthy as it appeared to be. All in all, Reichmann was in no hurry to commit to a formal bid but kept Graham working on Tokyo Bay just the same. If the project proved out, fine. In the meantime, he explained, the relationships that Graham was developing in Japan would prove useful whenever and however Olympia & York chose to expand into Asia.

Chapter 40

I n his late fifties, Albert Reichmann finally came out from under his brother Paul's shadow and emerged as a man to reckon with in his own right. Acting on his own, or in loose association with various Jewish groups, Reichmann conducted what amounted to a freelance campaign of shuttle philanthropy on behalf of the Jews of the USSR during the turbulent final years of the Soviet Empire and also established himself as the leading patron of the renascent Jewish communities of Hungary and Slovakia. In his own self-effacing way, Albert brought full circle Renée Reichmann's legacy of rescue and relief while becoming the first of the brothers to return to Hungary since their hasty departure for Paris in 1940.

As Renée and Eva Reichmann had developed relationships with Spanish officialdom from the local consul in Tangier to Generalissimo Francisco Franco himself, so four decades later Albert Reichmann, despite his lack of official standing, gained extraordinary entrée to Communist leaders throughout the Soviet Union and Eastern Europe. Although Mikhail Gorbachev as a rule made himself inaccessible to officials of the world's Jewish organizations, Reichmann met with the Supreme Soviet in the Kremlin a half-dozen times from 1988 to 1991. Wherever Reichmann traveled behind the fast-crumbling Iron Curtain—Moscow, Leningrad, Kiev, Budapest—he was afforded the sort of reception usually reserved for a head of state. The Communist chief of Lithuania had the airport in Vilnius repainted and was on hand to greet Reichmann, flanked by half of the local politburo, a military color guard, a brass band, and an ethnically costumed youth chorus. And why not? In lands reawakening to the profit motive and starved for capital and Western know-how, an emissary from the empire of Reichmann evoked the wealth-creating promise of capitalism far more vividly than could any American president.

Albert did business as he did good, negotiating a series of agreements that put Olympia & York into the vanguard of Western companies hoping to profit from perestroika. Gulf Canada formed a joint venture to explore for oil in Siberia, while Abitibi-Price studied the feasibility of constructing a big paper mill outside Leningrad. In Moscow, Olympia & York itself laid ambitious plans for two outsized real estate projects, including a $250 million office tower that, at sixty to eighty stories, was billed as the tallest building in the USSR. In Hungary, meanwhile, Reichmann invested in a major bank and department store and launched a $100 million office building project in the renascent heart of old Budapest.

That most of Olympia & York's commercial ventures in the USSR and Hungary came to naught in the end mattered little to Reichmann, whose overriding aims were charitable and philanthropic. "It seemed to me that Albert was trying to give some clout to the Jews living behind the Iron Curtain," said Joe Lebovic, the Hungarian-born Toronto developer who sank considerable sums of his own money into several of Reichmann's ventures in Hungary and traveled with him to Budapest. "I know it wasn't because he was looking to make an extra ruble in Russia. I can assure you that the money Albert spent in Russia and Hungary to preserve Judaism was a hell of a lot more than he made there or ever hoped to make there with Olympia & York."

Albert's new path traced a retreat as well as an advance, for by the mid-1980s it had become painfully evident that he was not remotely Paul's peer as a property developer. Albert's deal-making extravaganza of the late 1970s and early 1980s had added a number of trophy properties to the family's office-tower portfolio, among them Chicago's Olympia Center, a sixty-three-story tower of rose-colored Swedish granite built in partnership with the investor Sam Zell. In downtown Boston, Olympia & York had restored to its bygone grandeur a century-old building once occupied by the Boston Stock Exchange while pairing it with a new forty-story tower of blue mirrored glass. The result, Exchange Place, was as much a triumph of politics as architecture, since the local historical society initially had been adamantly opposed to Olympia & York's involvement. As business ventures, though, most of Albert's projects had proven disappointing at best, while his forays into residential development in Florida, California, and elsewhere qualified as absolute disasters, racking up losses that would in the end total at least $500 million and probably closer to $700 million, according to internal Olympia & York estimates. While the company would have been better off sticking to the office market, it suffered even more fundamentally for Albert's heavy reliance on outside partners, some of whom were marginally competent, marginally respectable, or both—and all of whom naturally put their own interests ahead of the Reichmann family's.

Olympia & York would lose $200 million to $250 million alone on the Florida land deals promoted by Bill and David Shapiro. The second costliest of

Albert's misadventures—at about $125 million—were the condo conversion projects in New York and Washington done in partnership with Oskar Brecher. Both of these ventures had suffered irredeemably from awful timing, having been launched when the property markets in which they operated were over-bought—that is, about to be purged of speculative excess by a collapse in prices.

In Florida, the Shapiros bought land galore with the Reichmanns' money but were unable to make productive use of it. Scores of ambitious schemes were floated by Olympia & York Southeast's dozen-person staff, but in the end the company did precious little building beyond a $55 million office tower in downtown Orlando, an industrial park in Fort Lauderdale, and a few scattered residential developments. In 1986, Olympia & York Southeast had announced plans to build an $800 million, mixed-used complex in downtown Miami in the World Financial Center mold, only larger. That Miami Center never got off the ground was not entirely Olympia & York Southeast's fault. Clearly, though, David Shapiro was completely out of his depth in attempting a project of such scale and complexity. Even in Orlando, site of Olympia & York Southeast's only office tower, Shapiro had fallen short of the mark. The building was to have been the nucleus of a three-tower, 1.5 million-square-foot complex. However, plans for further construction were canceled when Shapiro failed to lease out much of the first building, which never did turn an operating profit under his management.

As for Brecher, the land underneath the old Alcoa plant that he had purchased in New Jersey for remodeling into condominium apartments was so thoroughly polluted as to constitute a toxic waste dump unto itself. At Brecher's behest, Olympia & York poured millions into a futile attempt at cleaning up the site but eventually sold the plant back to Alcoa, which sealed it tight. The even costlier problem was that Brecher and his associates in Washington, D.C., allowed a huge inventory of unsold units to accumulate as they waited in vain for the condo market to recover to the point where they could price the apartments at a profit. At one time, Olympia & York had $240 million tied up in condos.

Like most of Albert's partners, Brecher and the Shapiros had every incentive to prolong their ventures with the Reichmanns for as long as possible. Neither had any capital at risk personally and yet were entitled to a healthy cut of the profits (25 percent in Brecher's case and 20 percent in the Shapiros'), if ever there were any. In the meantime, they pulled down hefty salaries or management fees and were entitled to pass along their costs to Olympia & York in full.

By all accounts, Albert Reichmann's critical failing as a deal man was not a lack of intelligence. "Albert is very smart," said an Olympia & York executive who worked closely with him for many years. "You could give him a description of a complicated, problematic transaction and he'd listen and he'd be able to tell you in words of one or two syllables what you'd just told him and what should be done." But Albert could have done with more of his brother's toughness, for he was inclined to indulge his partners as he would his friends. "Albert is a real softie in many ways," observed another Olympia & York executive. "He's just too nice a man for this business."

In 1984–85, the Reichmanns had strengthened the management of their American subsidiary by persuading the company's principal outside tax lawyer, Gerald Kelfer, and its main accountant, Joel Simon, to join the company as executive vice presidents. These two scrutinized Albert's grab bag of partnership investments with unprecedented rigor and concluded that most of them were not serving the Reichmanns' best interests and should be reworked or terminated. Although Albert rarely took issue with the numbers that Kelfer and Simon served up, he rejected their recommendations as overly "negative," preferring to give his partners and their stubbornly optimistic forecasts the benefit of the doubt. Paul Reichmann discreetly encouraged the senior staff's campaign to clean up the partnerships but refused all entreaties to intervene and do what Albert would not do himself: cut off the cash.

Not long after Kelfer and Simon had joined Olympia & York, the company's litanies of partnership woes lengthened when its 50–50 joint venture with the Connecticut developer David Chase went sour. The two office towers that Chase and Reichmann had jointly developed in Hartford were good, solid properties that had generated a few years of operating profits. By 1986, however, downtown Hartford was badly overbuilt and the usual pathology of soaring vacancies and declining rents had taken hold. Worse, Chase was embroiled in a bitter dispute with the city of Hartford. In exchange for tax abatements and other incentives provided before Reichmann had entered the picture, Chase had agreed to surrender to the city 20 percent of the cash flow from the two buildings. After auditing Chase's books, city officials accused him of shortchanging them and became so exasperated with his intransigence that they threatened to slap the Chase–Olympia & York partnership with a lawsuit under the federal racketeering statute known as RICO.

Although Olympia & York's executives were skeptical that the city could make RICO charges stick, they had their own doubts about Chase's accounting methods. Moreover, the Reichmann brothers—Albert no less than Paul—were loath to have their reputation sullied by racketeering charges, no matter how insupportable they might have been. Olympia & York stepped in and negotiated an out-of-court settlement that both placated the city of Hartford and let David Chase off the hook. Under their agreement with the city, Olympia & York and Chase each were supposed to contribute half of the $24 million settlement. As it turned out, Olympia & York paid the full amount, half of which was carried

on its books as a "loan" to Chase. Albert also protected his partner from journalistic scrutiny by insisting as a condition of settlement that the city permanently seal all public records pertaining to its dispute with Chase.

Albert's avuncular temperament was better suited to giving away money
than making it, though the world of big-ticket philanthropy was no less shark-
infested than real estate, especially where it overlapped with international politics and government. What is more, Albert always had been less religiously
rigid than were his yeshiva-trained younger brothers and less inclined to
restrict the family's largesse to the ultra-Orthodox. Even so, it was not until the
mid-1980s that Albert had begun to assert himself as a philanthropist. In part,
Albert filled a void left by Paul, who was increasingly preoccupied with the
affairs of commercial empire as Olympia & York expanded and diversified. At
the same time, Albert was troubled by the incongruity between the increasing
breadth of the family's business interests and the stubbornly narrow purview
of its giving. Like it or not, the acquisitions of Gulf Canada and Hiram Walker
had tipped the balance of Olympia & York's involvements from private to public. With billions of dollars now invested in heavily regulated businesses
employing many thousands of workers, Albert believed that it was in the family's own best interest to share its wealth more broadly. Although Paul appreciated the logic of Albert's argument, he would not have acted on it if left to his
own devices.

To some imponderable degree, Albert was additionally inspired to philanthropic activism by his dissatisfaction with Paul's increasingly obsessive and
self-important leadership of the family business. In devoting himself mainly to
philanthropy, Albert in effect opted out of the empire-building rat race, much
as his brother Louis had in leaving Canada in the late 1960s, and recast in
more constructive form his power-sharing arrangement with Paul. That is, in
exchange for Albert's continued subordination in corporate matters, Paul tolerated his brother's reordering of the family's philanthropic priorities, as earlier he had let him run amok in doing his own development deals within
Olympia & York.

———

The Communist government of the Soviet Union was antireligious by definition, of course, but the country's Jews had been singled out for special abuse
ever since 1945, when anti-Jewish discrimination became official policy in
education and employment. After Stalin's death, official encouragement for
anti-Semitism diminished considerably, though Nikita Khrushchev crippled
organized Judaism through his broadly based antireligious campaigns of 1958
to 1964. In a land where thousands of synagogues once had flourished, only
about sixty remained. Hebrew was a forbidden language, Yiddish virtually forgotten, and such religious practices as circumcision and kosher slaughtering

subjected to capricious restriction. Israel's victory in the Six-Day War of 1967 inflamed the Zionist longings of many Russian Jews, inspiring the boldest among them to organize to demand the right to emigrate to Israel. A few Jews were allowed out, but the great majority of the thousands of applicants were not only refused exit visas but fired from their jobs, harassed by the authorities in ways both petty and profound (the most outspoken were imprisoned), and generally reduced to the purgatorial status of nonpersons. Their plight quickly became a cause célèbre in the West, where they were known as the refuseniks.

As the era of détente arrived and the Soviets sought to develop international trade, the Kremlin cranked open the gates to Israel a bit further in concession to Western public opinion. Emigration increased sharply in 1971 and hit a new peak of 33,500 in 1973, but with at least 400,000 Jews looking to leave, the Kremlin was not moving fast enough to suit American Jewish groups or the U.S. government. In 1974, Congress enacted the Jackson-Vanik amendment, which formalized the political linkage between trade and emigration. U.S. officials also raised the Jewish issue with a variable degree of force in arms control talks with the Soviet government. The arm-twisting seemed to help; by 1979, refuseniks were being allowed their freedom at the rate of 50,000 a year. But then the USSR invaded Afghanistan, Ronald Reagan succeeded Jimmy Carter, and the Cold War returned with a vengeance. Annual emigration figures plunged below 1,000 as Soviet authorities resumed their harassments with renewed vigor. The U.S. State Department's annual human rights report for 1985 found that Jews were the worst treated of all the USSR's minorities and that refuseniks bore the brunt of official anti-Semitism.

Very few of the two million Jews remaining in the Soviet Union met the qualifications of religious Orthodoxy. Even in the worst of times there had been those who kept the Sabbath and ate only matzoh on Passover, but after sixty years under Soviet rule "the vast majority of Jews had little or no religious orientation or inclination." And yet on holy days, synagogues were thronged with young refuseniks, as had been the case ever since the late 1960s. For most, synagogue-going was a defiant expression of Jewish identity and solidarity with Israel. At the same time, a small but growing minority of the protesters developed an attachment to the religion of their grandfathers. Some even aspired to strict observance, though they lacked the means and the training. In the 1970s, a small underground of Hasidic communities emerged in Moscow, Leningrad, Riga, and other cities. Against all odds, a Jewish religious revival had taken uncertain root in the stony soil of Soviet atheism and Russian anti-Semitism.

World Agudath Israel, the same New York–based Orthodox organization that had helped fund the Reichmanns' food parcel shipments out of Tangier, decided in 1980 to do what it could to stimulate Orthodoxy's reemergence in the USSR. A special aid committee—Vaad Hatzalah Nichei Israel—was founded to send religious emissaries, or shluchim, into the Soviet Union. The shluchim, who paid their own way, smuggled in supplies—books, kosher food, tefillin, and so on—and offered covert religious instruction, moving from city to city over a period of no more than two weeks. Among Agudath Israel's earliest recruits was Rabbi Shlomo Noach Mandel, a dedicated young haredi educator from Toronto, who made his first trip in early 1984. Rabbi Mandel ran the Toronto branch of Or Someyach, an Orthodox educational group based in New York, and counted the Reichmanns among his major donors.

In 1986, Rabbi Mandel joined forces with Jeanette Goldman, one of Toronto's leading pro-refusenik activists, to try to recruit Albert Reichmann to the cause. Mrs. Goldman, the Toronto chairman of Canada's national Committee for Soviet Jewry, lived just a few blocks from Reichmann and had been a friend of the family for years. One evening in the fall of 1986, Goldman and Mandel lugged a television set and a VCR over to Albert's house and showed him *The Gates of Brass*, a stirring documentary about the West's championing of the refuseniks. "He seemed to know nothing about the movement but became very enthusiastic immediately," Goldman recalled. "From that time on, Albert really made it his mission. It was as if he became hooked right on the spot."

Reichmann began writing letters to high Canadian government officials in support of such famously beleaguered refuseniks as Ilya Essas, Ida Nudel, and Josef Begun and scored an early success when he persuaded Pat Carney, Canada's energy minister, to participate in the Committee for Soviet Jewry's adopt-a-refusenik program. At Rabbi Mandel's urging, Mordecai Neustadt, the head of Agudath Israel's Soviet aid committee, soon flew up from New York and made certain that Reichmann had been fully briefed on the Orthodox angle. "Yes, he'd done things to help particular refuseniks but I suggested to him that he should get involved more generally," recalled Neustadt, who had become known as the malach ha-goel, or "redeeming angel" among the widening circle of observant Jews in the USSR. "It was my dream to get him to go to Russia and see for himself the religious awakening going on."

Reichmann was a latecomer to the refusenik issue, but his timing proved opportune. Although Mikhail Gorbachev's ascent to power in early 1985 had raised hopes of reform, including more freedom for Soviet Jews, it was not until the summer and fall of 1986 that the new general secretary began to take his first tentative steps to open up and democratize the Soviet system. To be sure, these early initiatives brought no improvement in conditions for Jews. The KGB was as brutal as ever in suppressing Jewish dissent, and exit visas still were sparingly rationed. But hopes were rising.

Over the years, Canadian officials generally had been more emphatic than their U.S. counterparts in protesting the mistreatment of Soviet Jews. In 1985, not long after Gorbachev had taken charge, Joe Clark, Canada's secretary of state for external affairs, had met in Moscow with Foreign Minister Andrei Gromyko and broached the Jewish issue repeatedly but to no avail. Gorbachev replaced Gromyko, an old-line Communist, with Eduard Shevardnadze, who in September 1986 accepted Clark's invitation to come to Canada. As soon as Shevardnadze's visit was announced, Reichmann wrote to Clark and urged him to again take a firm stand on behalf of the refuseniks. Clark received hundreds of such missives, but Reichmann's was among the few to which he responded immediately, inviting Olympia & York's president to a luncheon he was organizing to introduce the Soviet minister to corporate leaders. Shevardnadze proved much friendlier than Gromyko, going so far as to smilingly accept a petition rolled up to resemble a Torah scroll from one of the hundreds of Jewish demonstrators who dogged his path in Ottawa. Even so, Clark was unable to extract anything more than vague, noncommittal human rights assurances from his Soviet counterpart in their talks.

After Shevardnadze had gone home, Clark offered Reichmann a bit of gentle instruction in the political realities of human rights diplomacy. Governments can only do so much to pressure one another into policy shifts, said Clark, who urged Reichmann to begin using the lever of Olympia & York's commercial might to benefit Russian Jews. In terms of its foreign trade, the USSR was essentially a Third World country in its tendency to export raw materials and import finished goods. (Soviet factories did turn out a wide range of manufactured goods at low cost for domestic consumption, but they were generally of inferior quality.) In hopes of gaining access to Western technology and managerial know-how, the Gorbachev government was already taking steps to authorize the formation of joint ventures with Western corporations. "Joe Clark mentioned to me that the Russians really don't like when government gets involved telling them what to do in their own country," Reichmann recalled. "I came to the idea that maybe it is not bad to do business with them. If you do business, then you supply butter instead of guns."

After the United States unilaterally lifted curbs on exports of oil and gas technology to the USSR in early 1987, Western leaders looked expectantly to Moscow for a reciprocal gesture and took heart in the release of more than one hundred political prisoners. During a trip to Moscow in April, Secretary of State George P. Shultz took time away from arms control talks to attend a highly publicized seder at the American ambassador's residence for fifty prominent refuseniks. Never before had so high-ranking a U.S. official risked antagonizing Soviet officialdom by conferring with dissidents.

In May, Reichmann made his first trip to Moscow, accompanied by his wife, his son Philip, several senior executives of Gulf Canada, Rabbi Mandel, and Neustadt. Reichmann did not meet with Gorbachev on this inaugural expedition but spent many hours in the Kremlin just the same. In a series of meetings at Energy and other ministries, Reichmann and the Gulf Canadians laid the basis of what would become a joint venture to develop an oil field in the Soviet Arctic. With his Orthodox confreres, meanwhile, Reichmann made the rounds of the officials in charge of cultural and religious matters, accompanied always by a Canadian Embassy official. The higher a Soviet official's rank, the more warmly the visitors were received. "Perestroika had taken hold at the most senior levels of government but five or six rungs down from the top you'd just get the blank stare," recalled Philip Reichmann, who sat in on many of his father's meetings. In keeping with his own inclinations as much as out of deference to diplomatic protocol, Albert Reichmann carefully segregated his business and human rights agendas. While he had every hope that the Soviets would infer a linkage and ease up on the Jews in anticipation of capital investment by Gulf or by Olympia & York itself, he did not want to put himself in the position of negotiating the purchase of religious freedoms.

Again working through the Canadian Embassy, Reichmann also met many of the better-known Moscow refuseniks. This aspect of his activities was intentionally high profile, even showy. One evening Reichmann and his entourage made their way to a group dinner with the refuseniks in a private apartment in a small fleet of limousines supplied by the embassy. "For the refuseniks," Neustadt explained, "visibility was safety. The more they were known to the world outside, the better they felt." Although continued KGB harassment kept the religious revival movement behind closed doors, Reichmann was able to confer with several of its leaders, including Ilya Essas, a Lithuanian refusenik and self-taught Talmudist who had begun to assemble an underground Torah network in the eastern USSR years before help arrived from the West.

Upon his return to Toronto, Reichmann made the first of a series of large donations to Neustadt's group and also hosted a fund-raiser at his home. Although Reichmann accepted Neustadt's invitation to join Vaad Hatzalah Nichei Israel's steering committee and was by far its largest contributor from 1987 through 1991, he rarely would attend its meetings, instead depending on Rabbi Mandel to represent him. In fact, Reichmann came to rely on the diligent if somewhat officious educator as his chief aide-de-camp in all aspects of his Soviet philanthropy. Although Mandel never was Reichmann's employee, he would work more closely with him during Olympia & York's final years than did anyone on the company payroll.

The missionary agency Vaad Hatzalah Nichei Israel was only the first of the many conduits of Reichmann's Soviet philanthropy. A few months after returning from the USSR, Albert took the lead in setting up a new organization, the Joint Committee for the Preservation of Jewish Heritage, dedicated to the restoration of Jewish cemeteries and synagogues in the Soviet Union. Based in New York, the Joint Committee was a loose coalition of Orthodox and ultra-Orthodox interests brought together and held in place by Reichmann's money and amiability. In conjunction with the World Jewish Congress, Reichmann surreptitiously funded a nascent underground Jewish radio network organized by Ilya Essas—a sort of Radio Free Soviet Jewry.

By the fall of 1987, the first flickerings of glasnost and perestroika had kicked up a fierce debate among Soviet Jews and their champions in the West. The KGB had eased up a bit in its bullying of Jewish dissidents and many of the most long-suffering refuseniks were being released from prison and granted exit visas; in October, Ida Nudel, a refusenik leader who had organized food parcel shipments to Jewish inmates of Soviet prisons, was flown to Israel on the private jet of the American industrialist Armand Hammer. On the other hand, the Kremlin had yet to deliver on promises to permit large-scale Jewish emigration and allow freedom of religious expression. "Don't be blinded by Gorbachev's dazzle," warned Natan Sharansky, the most celebrated of all the liberated refuseniks, during a whirlwind tour of Canada. "The gap between perception and reality has never been greater."

In the weeks before the first Reagan-Gorbachev summit, scheduled for Washington in early December, the Jewish establishment backed away from its campaign to engage the Soviets in substantive negotiations to concentrate on lobbying U.S. officials to place human rights high on the agenda of what was fundamentally an arms control meeting. Protest marches were planned in Washington, Tel Aviv, Moscow, and elsewhere to coincide with Gorbachev's arrival in America, but Reichmann saw no reason to curtail his own initiatives to suit the cautionary mood. In November, he made a second trip to Moscow, accompanied on the newly purchased Olympia & York jet by his brother Louis. The plane was loaded with food, books, and a wide variety of medicines supplied by Jeanette Goldman's committee but purchased largely with funds contributed by the Reichmanns. "Most of these things were for the Orthodox community but not exclusively," Goldman said. "Albert attached no strings."

Again Reichmann met with a variety of high Soviet officials (but not Gorbachev) on matters commercial and charitable and also convened a round-table discussion with some forty Jewish activists drawn from both the secular and religious segments of the Moscow community. "Most of those present advocated a two-tier approach: the release of the refuseniks and broader rights for Jewish religious and cultural activities," wrote a *Jerusalem Post* reporter who found out about Reichmann's unpublicized visit. "But some of the activists later criticized Reichmann for 'breaking ranks' . . . with the worldwide Jewish effort to demonstrate and protest against Soviet policies during the period of the Washington summit."

Reagan and Gorbachev, as expected, signed a treaty eliminating middle-range nuclear weapons but issued no formal statement on human rights. And yet, in a modest way, Reichmann's political incorrectness seemed validated when a month after the summit, the group he chaired, the Joint Committee for the Preservation of Jewish Heritage, reached agreement with Soviet authorities to open up even the remotest corners of the country to foreign Jewish visitors. This, assuredly, was a small step in the grand scheme of things but a concession of more than symbolic import to Reichmann, for it permitted observant Jews to visit the graves of their ancestors—for the first time, in many cases—and restore them to proper condition.

Reichmann was on hand in Moscow for the official signing of the Joint Committee's protocol in January 1988. It was on this trip, his third, that he first met with Mikhail Gorbachev. Accompanied by the Canadian ambassador and a half dozen functionaries, Reichmann spent twenty minutes with Gorbachev in the Kremlin discussing Soviet economic and social policy. No mention was made of Gulf Canada's continuing attempts to negotiate a joint venture. What Gorbachev thought of his visitor is not known. It is safe to say, though, that he had never shaken the hand of a richer man.

———

All things considered, Jews had fared better under Communism in Hungary than anywhere else in Eastern Europe or in the Soviet Union itself. Most of the 200,000 Hungarian Jews who had survived the Holocaust had fled immediately after World War II or during the failed anti-Soviet revolution of 1956, leaving a documented Jewish population of about 80,000, heavily concentrated in Budapest. János Kádár, whom Moscow installed as party chief in suppressing the 1956 uprising, was known as the inventor of "goulash Communism" because he introduced a measure of private enterprise that helped make Hungary the most prosperous and liberal state in the Soviet bloc. Unlike other Eastern European party bosses, Kádár was favorably disposed toward Jews (he had hidden in Budapest's Jewish quarter during World War II). Under his rule, Jews occupied key positions in the party and the economy and were allowed a full complement of communal institutions, and yet the practice of Judaism virtually disappeared by the 1970s as the state enforced its monopoly over educating the young.

In Kádár's later years, Budapest allowed Western Jewish groups to reestablish a tentative presence in Hungary. In the late 1970s, the World Jewish Congress gained a solid foothold by supporting Hungary's campaign to persuade the United States to grant it the most favored nation trade status long denied the USSR. In 1980 the American Jewish Joint Distribution Committee was allowed to reestablish a communal welfare service in Budapest, and in 1987 Hungary departed from the Soviet hard line by reestablishing limited diplomatic relations with Israel. Like every Warsaw Pact state but Romania, Hungary had severed links to Israel during the Six-Day War of 1967. While the refashioning of ties to foreign sponsors strengthened the Hungarian Jewish community, it also incited an internal power struggle for leadership. With only a few hundred members, most of them poor and elderly, the Orthodox were too weak to vie with latter-day Neologists and Zionists for their fair share of communal resources.

In the spring of 1987, Albert Reichmann stopped in Budapest for a few days on his way back to Toronto from his first trip to the Soviet Union. In the history of the Reichmanns, this was a momentous occasion—the first visit by a family member to the old country since Renée and Eva had returned in 1960 to visit the graves of relatives. And yet Reichmann's visit was so loosely organized that he did not bother making advance contact with Budapest's Orthodox community, whose president, Herman Fixler, happened to be out of the country when the billionaire stopped by to introduce himself. Fixler, a Holocaust survivor, was not a young man but he was so avid for a well-heeled patron and so excited to learn of his near brush with a scion of the famous Reichmann family that he immediately wangled an invitation to Toronto. Fixler returned from Canada with a pledge of $100,000 to begin restoring Budapest's sole remaining Orthodox synagogue, the roof of which had been badly damaged in a fire years earlier and had been in imminent danger of collapse ever since.

In February 1988, Albert returned to Hungary, accompanied by his wife, Egosah, and his brother Edward and sister-in-law Edith. The Reichmanns spent a long weekend in Budapest as the guests of R. Mark Palmer, the U.S. ambassador to Hungary, who had made quite a name for himself in Budapest as an activist diplomat who enjoyed the spotlight. At forty-six, Palmer was a Soviet specialist who had once served as a speechwriter for Henry Kissinger and had risen steadily through the State Department ranks. From the moment he had arrived in Budapest in 1986, Palmer had sided openly with the pro-democracy dissident movement and yet had managed to ingratiate himself with many high-ranking reform Communists as well, playing tennis with the prime minister and even persuading the Soviet ambassador to join him at the local McDonald's for lunch—an event the Hungarian press dubbed "the hamburger summit."

Palmer had a twofold interest in establishing connections to the Reichmann family. An outspoken believer in the democratizing influence of private enterprise, Palmer was hoping to promote direct foreign investment in Hungary. As Hungarian expatriates, the Reichmann brothers were more likely than the typical Western billionaire to consider doing business in Hungary. In addition, Palmer's years on the Soviet desk had instilled in him an appreciation of the Jewish factor in East-West relations. In the mid-1980s, a variety of Jewish groups had begun urging the Kádár government to memorialize the Hungarian victims of the Holocaust by erecting a statue to Raoul Wallenberg, the Swedish diplomat who had vanished into the Soviet gulag system after saving thousands of Jews. Loath to raise the issue of Hungarian complicity in the Holocaust and to risk offending Moscow, the Communist authorities capitulated only after Palmer threatened to install the statue on the grounds of the U.S. Embassy. From what he knew of the Reichmann brothers, Palmer suspected that their influence could be useful in helping win religious freedoms for

Hungarian Jews and in nurturing the still-tenuous relationship between Budapest and Tel Aviv.

At a glatt kosher dinner in their honor at the ambassador's residence, Edward and Albert met Hungary's deputy prime minister, top officials of the economic and cultural affairs ministries, the National Bank of Hungary, the Hungarian Credit Bank, and the Budapest Chamber of Commerce, as well as members of the Hungarian diplomatic corps and the chief rabbi of Hungary. "Mr. Palmer was very interested in what was going on in Israel so he spent more time talking with me than Albert," recalled Edward, who later was reproached by Israel's foreign office for critical comments he had made about Shimon Peres. Apparently, Palmer had mentioned Reichmann's critique in an official report to the State Department, which passed them on to the Israeli ambassador.

The next day the Reichmanns hired a limousine and driver and made a quick tour of the Oberland, driving through Győr and Csorna to Beled. In place of the bustling, prosperous village of their youth, the Reichmanns found a socialist ghost town. To be sure, a thousand people still lived in Beled (down from a peak of three thousand), but commerce had vanished along with the Jews, leaving a handful of run-down shops on a main street that had been lined with two dozen Jewish-owned establishments (three of which were owned by members of the Reichmann family). Even the creek that had run the length of the village had run dry, leaving a ditch filled with weeds and assorted refuse. The big house that Samuel Reichmann had bought in the 1920s was still standing but had been divided into six apartments. After knocking on a few doors, the Reichmanns wandered through the house and the remnants of their father's egg-processing plant, snapping photographs. Afterward, they had a cup of coffee in the restaurant-tavern across the street and were surprised to learn that their old home was still known as "the Reichmann house" and that many villagers even had a vague understanding of the magnitude of Olympia & York's success.

The Reichmanns then visited the Jewish cemetery, which was the only remnant of Beled's Jewish community, other than the one-room building that had housed the Talmud Torah. The cemetery, too, had been trashed during the war. The gravestones that were not destroyed by the Hungarian troops who used the cemetery for target practice had been used as paving stones in the village. The handful of Jews who had returned to Beled after the war had put the cemetery back together as best they could. Ever since the deportations of 1944, villagers had been digging holes in search of valuables the Jews were thought to have buried. Aside from a silver table found on the site of a former Jewish-owned restaurant, nothing much was found, and yet the mystery of the missing "Jewish treasure" had continued to inspire furtive, nocturnal explorations, usually in the cemetery. The Reichmanns were relieved to find that the graves of their grandfather and most of their other relatives were intact, if disordered, and later arranged to have the cemetery wholly restored and maintained by a full-time caretaker. The brothers and their wives said their prayers for the dead and returned posthaste to Budapest, emotionally spent by their journey through the past.

In March, a month after the Reichmanns' visit, ten thousand protesters carrying banners demanding "Press Freedom," "Real Reform," and "Freedom of Assembly" marched through Budapest in the biggest antigovernment demonstration since 1956. In May, a new generation of Communist leaders headed by Karoly Grosz wrested power away from the Kádár regime and began accelerating Hungary's slow-motion evolution away from centralized state control of the economy to a free-enterprise system. In hopes of stimulating business investment in Hungary, Grosz promptly visited the United States as the guest of George Soros, the billionaire Hungarian expatriate fund manager, and also made a swing through Canada at the invitation of Andy Sarlos, the Reichmanns' high-rolling Bay Street confidant, who had returned to Hungary in 1987 to scout deal-making opportunities in his native land.

In making his first investment in Hungary, Reichmann followed Sarlos's lead. In 1988, the owner of Skala, the largest department store chain in Hungary with 350 outlets, offered to sell Sarlos a 50 percent interest in the business, which had been losing money for several years and was on the verge of bankruptcy. Sarlos joined with Reichmann and Ervin Haub, a German supermarket mogul, to acquire half of Skala for $32 million. (Under its new owners, the chain was restructured and was approaching the breakeven point when Sarlos unloaded his shares at a $5 million profit. In time, Reichmann, too, sold his stake to Tengelman Group, Haub's company.) Meanwhile, Sarlos joined with Soros to try to raise a mutual fund of as much as $100 million to invest in Hungarian businesses. Reichmann helped promote their First Hungary Fund as a member of its board of directors but did not invest in the fund, telling Sarlos that his overriding interest in Hungary was philanthropic and that he did not want to muddy the waters by amassing a big investment portfolio on the side.

As Reichmann relied on Rabbi Mandel to handle the administration of his Russian philanthropy, so in Hungary he mainly worked through an Orthodox layman named David Moskovits. Born in 1946 in Transylvania, the province of Romania that borders on Hungary, Moskovits was the son of a Hasidic couple who had decided after the Holocaust to return to their hometown rather than emigrate to the West. In 1955, his father was arrested as an enemy of the people and sentenced to prison. After six years of hard labor, Moskovits was freed through the intervention of the Skulener Rebbe, a Hasidic leader who had also remained in Romania. In 1961, the Moskovits family was allowed to emigrate to Canada and settled in Toronto, where, like every other ultra-Orthodox family, they benefited from the largesse of the Reichmanns. After finishing yeshiva, David settled in New York, where he prospered in plastics manufacturing and was active in Hasidic charities. In 1987, Moskovits returned from a trip to Romania and Hungary determined to make his mark by championing the underdog cause of Orthodoxy in Eastern Europe. He had had little luck raising funds until he knocked on Albert Reichmann's door and hit the jackpot.

In effect, Reichmann decided to adopt Moskovits's cause as his own. In mid-1988, shortly after Kádár's ouster, Reichmann and Moskovitz launched the Endowment for Democracy in Eastern Europe, which issued a formal mission statement as misleadingly bombastic as its name: "To foster the ideals of freedom, democracy and individual rights through Eastern Europe by promoting cultural pluralism." In practice, the endowment's commitment to pluralism would extend no further than Orthodox Judaism. As the principal conduit of the Reichmann family's Hungarian philanthropy, the Endowment for Democracy would rank by a wide margin as the largest financial contributor to the religious revival of Hungarian Jewry. Working closely with Orthodox communal leaders in Budapest, the endowment in its first year of operation alone invested a few hundred thousand dollars to upgrade the quality and increase the supply of kosher food to the Budapest community, which, in turn, organized regular shipments to Orthodox kehillahs in outlying cities not only in Hungary but in Slovakia and Romania. A mikveh was rebuilt in Budapest at a cost of $135,000. Two Hungarian-speaking Orthodox rabbis were brought back from Israel to minister to the congregations in Budapest and Debrecen, Hungary's second largest city. An afternoon Hebrew school, the first in Hungary since World War II, was opened in the Orthodox Synagogue, which was refurbished at a total cost of $165,000.

Although almost all of the money that Albert laid out in Hungary and the Soviet Union flowed from family coffers, neither Paul nor Ralph participated in their brother's East European philanthropies. Paul was less optimistic than Albert about seeding an Orthodox revival in Hungary or the USSR and did not share his brother's feelings for the old homeland. "My sole attachment to Hungary is the books I have," Paul said in 1995. With his wife, Paul had visited Vienna, his birthplace, in the early 1970s but left in a hurry. "I wanted to walk along the streets and look at the old places," he recalled. "But ten minutes into our walk, I asked my wife to return to the hotel with me and leave the city. Once we were in the airplane I felt like an idiot. But it was just too much emotion going back. The whole environment reminded me of the Hitler days. My instinctive reaction was, 'What am I doing here?' "

During the final phase of Olympia & York's preeminence, Paul's and Albert's relationship thus would be increasingly attenuated by what amounted to a reversal of their youthful roles in the family. Whereas Albert had started out wholly dedicated to business as his father's apprentice in the Banque Samuel Reichmann, Paul had kept his distance from the fast-money whirl of Tangier. Inspired by his mother's example, Paul had dedicated himself to the missionary work of bringing the Torah to the illiterate Jews of Morocco. And yet in the end, it was Albert—an activist-tortoise to Paul's hare—who assumed Mrs. Reichmann's activist mantle.

Chapter 41

The mutual admiration society formed by Paul Reichmann and Margaret Thatcher was the rock on which the new and improved Canary Wharf was founded and, in time, would founder. The developer and the prime minister had met for the first time in the fall of 1987, some two months after Olympia & York had formally assumed control of the project, and got on so well that Mrs. Thatcher agreed to formally launch Canary Wharf a second time. Six months after her trade and industry minister had driven the ceremonial first piling, Mrs. Thatcher went down to the Isle of Dogs herself in May 1988, and, with Reichmann at her side and a hard hat on her head, sent a second piling into the riverbed for good measure. Afterward, at a champagne reception at Banqueting Hall for 250 of the United Kingdom's most important businessmen, Reichmann delivered a bluntly appreciative speech that delighted the prime minister. "Without the inspiration and wholehearted support of Mrs. Thatcher's government," he said, "Olympia & York would not be making a commitment of this magnitude."

In her lengthy, improvised remarks, Mrs. Thatcher returned the compliment—eventually. "When I learned about this project," she began, "it seemed to me one of the most exciting that we had ever known. Ten years ago it would not have been possible even to think in such bold, ambitious terms." After an extended paean to the foresight of her own policies, Mrs. Thatcher stooped to flatter. "I do have to thank and congratulate Mr. Reichmann and Olympia & York for their vision. We have to thank them for their faith in Britain." The compliments that Mrs. Thatcher and Paul Reichmann exchanged from the dais were the secular equivalent of marriage vows: public affirmations of a private understanding quickly reached and deeply grounded. On a state visit to Canada by the prime minister a week later, Reichmann was one of three business leaders whom she praised by name in an address to Parliament, noting Canada's growing involvement in Britain's national life. "Paul Reichmann . . ." read a caption in the *Economist*, "Mr. Big."

Gaining entrée to No. 10 Downing Street had been no great achievement in itself, given the importance of Docklands to the prime minister. G. Ware Travelstead had been in and out of No. 10 like an outsized jack-in-the-box, albeit for meetings with aides to Thatcher rather than the lady herself. Unlike Travelstead, Reichmann succeeded in parlaying access into alliance. In so doing, he relied heavily on the advice and contacts of two important behind-the-scenes agents of the Conservative Party's ascendancy: Tim Bell and Sir Alistair MacAlpine.

In 1978, the Conservative Party had hired Saatchi and Saatchi, the up-and-coming advertising agency where. Bell worked, to mastermind an image makeover that proved vital to Mrs. Thatcher's elevation the following year from leader of the opposition to prime minister. Bell, the televisual maestro of the Saatchi firm, would remain one of Mrs. Thatcher's most trusted advisers throughout her tenancy at No. 10. In 1986, Bell left Saatchi & Saatchi and with a partner set up a consulting firm of his own, Lowe Bell Communications Limited Incorporated, which Olympia & York hired as its London public relations counsel after taking over Canary Wharf.

Sir Alistair MacAlpine was a scion of a wealthy construction dynasty whom Mrs. Thatcher appointed treasurer of the Conservative Party in recognition of his large contributions to its coffers. Sir Alistair's father had founded an eponymous firm that had grown into one of Britain's largest construction firms and was one of four English firms that the Travelstead consortium had selected to serve as general contractors on Canary Wharf. Although Sir Alistair was a shareholder in Sir Robert MacAlpine Limited and sat on its board, he left its running to relatives and devoted himself principally to politics and antiques. Paul Reichmann had been introduced to MacAlpine on an early trip to London and found him to be "a most charming man, with time on his hands. You can go into his antique shop, inspect his wares, and spend a few hours with him without any trouble." It was Sir Alistair who had arranged the first meeting between Reichmann and Thatcher's emissary, Trade and Industry Minister David Young, during Olympia & York's negotiations with the London Docklands Development Corporation. In fact, their meeting had taken place at MacAlpine's townhouse in Whitehall.

Reichmann took the advice of Stanley Honeyman, the senior English executive in his employ, and went alone to his first meeting with Mrs. Thatcher. "I told him that otherwise he wouldn't get a word in edgewise," Honeyman recalled. "One to one, Margaret Thatcher is a listener, but in groups, she debates. Paul is just the opposite. In groups, he is more of a listener." It was good advice. Reichmann later told Honeyman that the prime minister not only had listened intently but was so intrigued by his explanation of his plans for Canary Wharf that she had even gotten down on one knee to take a closer look at scale models he had brought.

Despite her starchy manner, Mrs. Thatcher was a middle-class product, a grocer's daughter born over the shop. In her cosmology, it was the self-made entrepreneurs, rather than the stodgy captains of industry or city toffs to the manner born, who were the prime movers of the free-enterprise system that she held so dear. "I think Paul was especially intriguing to the prime minister because he's a very ambitious entrepreneur and yet he's also highly religious, shy, and almost academic in his demeanor," Tim Bell observed. "This seems like a contradiction and it makes him unlike any other property developer in the world, including other Jewish ones. And of course," Bell added, "Paul would tell everyone that he only came back to England because of Margaret Thatcher. That made him all the more appealing to her."

Although Mrs. Thatcher never did refer to Reichmann's religion in her public comments, her appreciation of him must be set in the context of her philo-Semitism. For three decades, she had served as the member of Parliament for Finchley, a middle-class north London community about 20 percent Jewish at the time she was first elected in 1959. The close association Mrs. Thatcher developed with her Jewish constituents was as much a product of ideological affinity as political calculation. "It was the Jewish belief in self-help that she found most telling," wrote Hugo Young in his biography of Thatcher. "Ambition and self-advancement are more explicitly blessed in Jewish teaching than they are by Christianity." As prime minister, she was fond of holding up British Jewry as an exemplar of entrepreneurial virtue and appointed far more Jews to ministerial and cabinet positions than had any of her predecessors. In early 1988, a few months before the Canary Wharf piledriving, the prime minister bestowed a peerage upon Rabbi Immanuel Jakobovits, England's chief rabbi and an outspoken supporter of Mrs. Thatcher's brand of social conservatism. Indeed, in Hugo Young's view, the rabbi's speeches had served as "a valuable source-book" for Mrs. Thatcher's own.

As part of its continuing campaign to ingratiate itself with the powers-that-be in London, Olympia & York in the spring of 1989 would lease a prominent place in the upper-crust social calendar of the season by sponsoring the first Royal Gala Preview of the Chelsea Flower Show. Paul and Albert Reichmann's guests that day included the Princess of Wales and a few hundred other august if nonroyal personages. Amid the passing parade of lords, ladies, ministers, and managing directors, Paul Reichmann noticed a vaguely familiar little man eyeing him with unabashed delight. Finally, this person came over and pumped Reichmann's hand. "I want to tell you," said Brian Griffiths, who was Mrs. Thatcher's chief of policy (and an evangelical Christian), "how nice it is to meet you and how absolutely marvelous it is to see you wearing that [he pointed to Reichmann's yarmulke] in the midst of this. It could only have happened under Margaret Thatcher."

The Reichmann-Thatcher affinity ran deeper than shared beliefs, to basic personality. As impresarios of the highest order, they combined great professional competence and vaulting ambition with a self-confidence so unassailable that it seemed like naïveté. In her remarks at Olympia & York's Banqueting Hall reception, the prime minister could not resist citing herself: "If I might add a quotation—it's not a very old one, it's really a Thatcher one. It is, 'The art of politics is the art of making the impossible happen.' And that, in fact, is what we have been doing." Substitute the words "property development" for "politics" and Thatcher's immodest dictum would have served as aptly as Reichmann's credo.

Even so, the relationship between Reichmann and Thatcher should not be misconstrued as friendship. They met no more than half a dozen times, though they spoke additionally over the telephone. In keeping with Orthodox notions of modesty, Reichmann would bow slightly instead of shaking Mrs. Thatcher's hand. He called her "Prime Minister," she called him "Mr. Reichmann." They were allies, not chums. "Mrs. Thatcher would not have thought to have him to a dinner party," Tim Bell said. For his part, of course, Reichmann did not have dinner parties.

After Canary Wharf collapsed, there would be those in the Olympia & York camp who implied that Reichmann had been strung along by Thatcher, even that he was "betrayed" or "double-crossed." That Reichmann himself never advanced such a claim, in private or in public, had nothing to do with tact or chivalry: it just had not happened that way.

Mrs. Thatcher was nothing if not a true believer, and her belief in Canary Wharf was amply reinforced by self-interest. If Reichmann's billions succeeded in bringing Docklands redevelopment to critical mass, the prime minister would be able to claim a great political and ideological victory in revitalizing a vast wasteland at little cost to the public purse. Political vanity also played its part. As one former senior British official put it, with acid tact: "There was great enthusiasm at the prime ministerial level to see a scheme that could become a symbol of Thatcher's Britain." In any event, the Iron Lady would remain a steadfast, hectoring champion of Canary Wharf until the day she was so abruptly turned from office in late 1990. Privately, Reichmann liked to tell the story of how Mrs. Thatcher had silenced a subcabinet meeting in which the project had come under sniper attack from bureaucrats. "How many of you—if you had made a great fortune—would be willing to wager it as Mr. Reichmann is doing?" she had demanded disdainfully.

If Reichmann erred, it was not in trusting Margaret Thatcher's motives but in aligning himself and his project so closely with this most inflammatory of political leaders. To be sure, Canary Wharf had been politicized long before Reichmann arrived on the scene. But in embracing Thatcherism and its namesake with such avidity, Reichmann reaped the same whirlwind of opposition that would sweep the Iron Lady from office only three years after Olympia & York had committed to the massive Docklands project. "Canary Wharf's close identification with Thatcher made popular opinion of the project more divisive," Bell said, "while giving it a higher profile, which in itself created controversy."

On the advice of Bell and others, Olympia & York spent a small fortune in attempting to remold public opinion in Canary Wharf's favor. The company conducted no less than twenty thousand tours of its Docklands site, bombarded real estate agents with mailings, and kept up a steady drumbeat of advertising in print and on radio and television. Deliberately blurring the line between advertising and journalism, Olympia & York put together a twenty-three-page, magazine-like pamphlet entitled "Canary Wharf: The Untold Story" and published it as an insert in London newspapers. In a similar vein, the company sponsored a lavishly illustrated, quasi-scholarly book—*London's River*—which conveyed the impression that Canary Wharf was the fortuitous culmination of nine hundred years of English history. *London's River* concluded with the prediction that when the redevelopment of Docklands was done, the district, "with Canary Wharf at its heart, will then be seen as an achievement as awe-inspiring in its way as any on the Thames since William the Conqueror began the White Tower"—in 1066.

Nowhere was Canary Wharf opposed more bitterly than in its own backyard, the Isle of Dogs. As working class Labour strongholds, the various communities of Docklands were strongly anti-Thatcher to begin with. Even many local advocates of redevelopment resented the way in which Whitehall had emasculated their municipal governments in setting up the London Docklands Development Corporation and disdained the agency as a lapdog of the property industry. Local opposition only intensified as the LDDC's blend of tax breaks and laissez-faire planning turned the Isle of Dogs into one big construction zone. The noise and traffic jams might have been tolerable had redevelopment also brought jobs, but the companies that relocated to Docklands generally brought their employees with them or recruited out for workers with specialized skills. Meanwhile, many existing jobs in Docklands were lost as redevelopment knocked down countless old buildings and uprooted scores of small businesses. In fact, as measured in terms of local employment throughout Docklands, the LDDC's efforts resulted in a net decrease of four thousand jobs from 1981 to 1990. Travelstead had not helped matters by rebuffing community activists with blunt contempt, saying "We're not here to pour money down black holes." The locals had exacted a measure of revenge during Canary Wharf's sod-turning, at which Travelstead had hosted a few hundred carefully culled dignitaries, including the governor of the Bank of England. Peter Wade, a tugboat operator turned community activist, smuggled about one hundred protesters through Travelstead's security perimeter and reduced his big day to chaos by releasing a herd of sheep and upending beehives. "The Japanese bankers were petrified," Wade recalled, "because when they have demonstrations back home, generally somebody ends up getting killed."

Paul Reichmann not only gave Peter Wade a hearing but ended up offering him a job as Canary Wharf's "community relations" director. Wade, who was born and raised on the Isle of Dogs, awakened on the morning after his appointment was announced to find obscenities daubed on the walls of his house. Anger transmuted the ambivalence Wade had felt in going over to the other side into determination. "This thing was going to go ahead," he recalled. "You can stand outside for the duration of the building, but you're getting sod-all from it. . . . I made no bones about it; I told Olympia & York, I'm here to get everything I can out of you for this community.' "

Wade set up a portable office on the job site from which he dispensed counsel to Docklands-based subcontracting firms, which eventually were awarded £50 million in business, and recruited construction workers. With the goal of providing five hundred jobs to local residents, Olympia & York cofounded a training center on the Isle of Dogs. At Wade's direction, the company also contributed cash and equipment to local schools, community centers, hospitals, and so on. All told, Olympia & York spent £2.6 million, or nearly $5 million, on Wade's community programs. This was a pittance compared with the $3.8 billion the Reichmanns would spend on the construction of Canary Wharf—or the amount of money they would donate to English ultra-Orthodoxy, for that matter—but it was more than nothing and, in Wade's estimation, earnest money in every sense. "The people from O & Y clearly demonstrated their long-term commitment," he said after construction had been terminated by Olympia & York's collapse. "The others come in and throw you a few scraps and then piss off somewhere else."

However, Olympia & York's community relations, advertising, and promotional programs were not nearly sufficient to tip the balance of public opinion in favor of Canary Wharf. The company was fortunate that it never faced a referendum in London and that English courts were unsympathetic to attempts by the borough of Greenwich and a coalition of Docklands community groups to shut down the project with environmental lawsuits. Over the long run, Canary Wharf's unpopularity would be a factor in Parliament's hesitance to approve the Thatcher government's requests for appropriations to fund desperately needed transit improvements tying Docklands more closely to the rest of London. But the politicization of the project proved most damaging initially in Olympia & York's dealings with the three executive branches critically involved with it: Environment, Transportation, and Treasury.

In the United States, the power civil servants wield is derived mainly from bureaucratic inertia. But in England the senior civil servants of a branch of the national government constitute a quasi-autonomous, professional elite not unlike the tenured teaching staff of an American university. Although civil servants must answer to the political appointee who heads their department as minister, their ultimate allegiance is not to the party but to the "permanent" government—that is, to their own ideals of professionalism and public service. In deference to this ethos, English property developers traditionally have kept a studied distance from politicians while guiding their projects through the shoals of government planning and licensing requirements.

With a project of Canary Wharf's size, however, the politicians hardly could have been avoided—especially since the LDDC was itself not only a creature of the national government but Conservative to the core. Still, in dropping Mrs. Thatcher's name frequently and in soliciting the assistance of such political power brokers as Sir Alistair MacAlpine, Paul Reichmann unwittingly antagonized the permanent government right from the start. Honeyman's fair complexion reddened at the very mention of MacAlpine. "I was appalled to hear of his involvement," he recalled. "I was personally indignant to hear that the bloody treasurer of the Conservative Party was sitting in where political bosses don't usually sit and aren't supposed to sit."

Even within the Department of Environment, the LDDC's parent, the project inspired deep skepticism. The essence of the art of property development is informed intuition; reasoned analysis only takes a developer so far and then he must take a leap of faith into a future uncertain by definition. The leap that Paul Reichmann made with Canary Wharf so outdistanced the prosaic fundamentals of supply and demand that it seemed launched in defiance of them. Unlike developers, civil servants are held to standards of accountability that leave little latitude for creative risk-taking. They need proof, or the nearest equivalent. From a civil servant's point of view, the problem with Canary Wharf was not merely that it did not make sense on paper but that Olympia & York had made no attempt to make sense of it on paper. "To people like me, it seemed too risky," said a former high-ranking civil servant in the Department of Environment. "Right from the start I felt it had enormous locational problems, and I personally could not make the arithmetic work to show a positive return on the level of capital expenditure contemplated, given current levels of rent in London. A Conservative government tends to assume that the private sector forecasts demand before it adds to supply, but I never saw a proper forecast either from Olympia & York or from Travelstead. It all became rather a matter of faith."

Despite such reservations, the Department of Environment would back Canary Wharf to the hilt—Michael Heseltine, the political godfather of the LDDC, was still environment minister, after all. At the same time, the skepticism of the ministry's senior civil servants flowed through the front and back channels of the permanent government to Transportation and Treasury, where the politicians had no vested interest in Docklands and the civil servants were disinclined to recalibrate their departments' spending priorities to fit Paul Reichmann's outsized ambitions. In 1989, Olympia & York and the permanent government squared off over the critical issue of extending the city subway system, the London Underground, to the Isle of Dogs. Reichmann and his minions reacted as they would have back in Toronto or New York—by going over the heads of the bureaucrats to the politicians, further antagonizing the minions of the permanent government. Reichmann would get what he wanted, but so belatedly that his victory was Pyrrhic. "Olympia & York consistently misjudged the English character, especially how politics and public administration interact," the former Department of Environment man continued. "I think they thought they could apply political pressure and that would make things happen. But they failed to appreciate the objectivity of the public sector here. They just got that bit very, very wrong."

———

Building Canary Wharf was easily the most herculean of Olympia & York's feats of construction. The project's difficulty was not simply a function of its overwhelming size. Phase I was roughly equivalent to the World Financial Center in that it required simultaneous construction of eight buildings—though at 4.5 million square feet, their total square footage was half that of the Manhattan complex. But the inaugural phase in London also included the infrastructure (roads, turning circles, parking garages, a railway station, and so on) for the entire project, which covered four times the area that the World Financial Center did. More important, the London site's odd configuration and inaccessibility created horrendous logistical problems of a sort more typically encountered in wilderness than in a great city.

The Manhattan location had been difficult in its own right, in that it consisted of landfill hemmed in to the west by the Hudson River and to the east by a heavily traveled highway. However, Battery Park City Authority had allowed Olympia & York to make free use of vacant land to the north and south to deliver and store building materials. On the Isle of Dogs the company was not able to use adjacent lands for the simple reason that there were none; the site was almost entirely surrounded by water. Indeed, six of the first eight buildings had to be built entirely over water on great concrete mats supported by steel pilings. What is more, when work began, the site was a veritable moonscape: no roads, water pipes, sewer, electricity, or telephone lines. "I have never worked on a site where we are doing everything, like this," recalled Richard Griffiths, an Olympia & York senior vice president who served as one of the project's two construction chiefs. "Normally you just put up a building in the city without even thinking of all the support structures that are needed."

Griffiths, an architect by training, was another of Olympia & York's alumni of the Toronto city planning office. He had joined the company as an assistant to John Norris, Olympia & York's construction boss in New York. (Norris, an Englishman, left Olympia & York for another company after the World Financial Center was completed rather than return to work in his native land.) Griffiths shared responsibility for the building of Canary Wharf with George Iacobescu, who had cut his teeth on World Financial Center as understudy to Otto Blau, Olympia & York's master procurer. Like Blau, Iacobescu was a Romanian emigrant to Canada. Dan Frank, a third member of Olympia & York's "Romanian Mafia," also graduated from World Financial Center to Canary Wharf. Frank was Olympia & York's resident expert in construction logistics.

To facilitate construction, Olympia & York had to encircle the entire site by two temporary roadways atop pilings sunk into the riverbed of the Thames. These so-called water roads were built in conjunction with a fabled British firm—Thomas Storey—that helped develop temporary bridges used by Allied troops in World War II. At the same time, a dozen barges had to be brought in and anchored to provide office and storage space on site. Although the River Thames caused problems, it also provided a ready-made solution to the bottlenecks created by the East End's hopelessly inadequate roadways. About 80 percent of all the construction materials that went into Canary Wharf would arrive by barge from Tilbury, a port city twenty-six miles and two and a half hours downriver.

For building materials suppliers, Canary Wharf was a gargantuan sugar plum parceled out in the form of more than one hundred major contracts. Although many were let to British firms, Iacobescu worked his international network of contacts and did not hesitate to offend the locals by selecting a foreigner with a superior bid. Aker, a Norwegian company, won the contract to provide the cement and built a floating cement plant that was towed over from Norway on two giant steel pontoons and anchored off the Isle of Dogs. In Germany, Iacobescu outbid Walt Disney Company, which was building its Euro Disney Park near Paris, for a prime crop of large nursery-grown trees. Olympia & York bought vast quantities of marble, slate, and stone from suppliers in Canada, Brazil, Finland, Bulgaria, Italy, India, and other foreign countries.

Even before construction had begun, Paul Reichmann had publicly committed himself to a hugely ambitious and exact schedule, promising that the first group of six midrise office buildings would be ready for occupancy in the second quarter of 1990 and One Canada Square—the fifty-story tower—six to eight months later.

Reichmann and his aides had acknowledged from the start that Olympia & York would not be able to exercise the degree of management control over construction to which it had become accustomed in North America and so the company had started out by sharing the general contractor's role with Lehrer McGovern International Limited (LMI). Although LMI was headquartered in

New York, it was 50 percent owned by the British construction giant Bovis International Limited and thus spanned the two worlds Olympia & York was trying to bridge. The company created another bureaucratic layer on the job site by appointing a separate management contractor for each of the eight buildings. With the exception of the main tower, which was managed by Ellis Don MacAlpine, an Anglo-Canadian joint venture company formed expressly for this purpose, all the management contractors chosen for Phase I were English firms. The great majority of subcontractors selected were British, as well, though many began as reluctant participants, overawed by the scale of Canary Wharf and put off as well by Olympia & York's insistence that they accept unlimited financial liability for cost overruns.

Agreement was quickly and fairly painlessly reached with the three main British trade unions representing construction workers on a thirty-nine-hour workweek ending one hour before sundown on Friday afternoon and resuming one hour after sunset on Saturday. Thirteen Jewish holidays were written into the contract, along with Christmas Day, Boxing Day, and New Year's Day. By mid-1988, some twelve hundred laborers were swarming over the site, which was festooned by three dozen bright-orange tower cranes. This maelstrom of construction activity generated a ferocious din. Visitors who flew to the site by helicopter described the jarring sensation of running into "a wall of noise" as they penetrated Canary Wharf's air space.

From time to time, the stoop-shouldered, black-clad figure of Paul Reichmann could be seen picking his way through the mighty clamor of the job site with Griffiths or Iacobescu at his side. As with the World Financial Center and First Canadian Place, Reichmann kept close tabs on every aspect of Canary Wharf but intervened sporadically, as one detail or another caught his attention. He was once spotted on the platform of the Docklands Light Railway, checking to see if the noise levels had been adequately reduced. He might decree a preference for a certain shade or a type of window design—and then change his mind a few weeks later. "I never mind doing a U-turn, if I can find something better," Reichmann once told Iacobescu, who endured the boss's Olympian perfectionism with tongue-in-cheek humor. "We propose," Iacobescu said, "Paul disposes."

———

In its London headquarters on Great George Street, just off Parliament Square, the company set up an elaborate "marketing suite" filled with beautifully rendered 100-to-1 scale models, each of which cost about as much as a house in a London suburb. The suite's anteroom featured models of First Canadian Place, World Financial Center, and lesser Olympia & York developments. In an inner room sat a huge tabletop model of London in which every major building in the city, whether completed or under construction, was represented but only

Canary Wharf was illuminated by a shaft of light that seemed to descend from the heavens. At the push of a button, colored lights lit in serpentine sequence, tracing the paths of key transportation routes, actual and proposed, to the Isle of Dogs. The room also featured separate scale models of the entire Canary Wharf complex and of One Canada Square as well as a mock-up of an office in the fifty-story tower offering computer-simulated views from each corner.

The purpose of all this showmanship-in-miniature was to induce corporations to prelease space that would not become available until the end of 1990 at the earliest. Between them Credit Suisse First Boston and Morgan Stanley were obligated, under the terms of the agreement that had transferred ownership of Canary Wharf to Olympia & York, to lease about 1 million square feet. That left three-quarters of the development's first phase still to let and the sooner the better, since nothing imparted credibility to a speculative project quicker than a fistful of gilt-edged, long-term leases. A confidential clause of Olympia & York's contract with the two investment banks conferred added urgency; if Olympia & York failed to let at least another 1 million square feet by July 1, 1990, a "critical mass" provision would kick in, giving Credit Suisse and Morgan Stanley the option of unilaterally canceling their leases and pulling out of Canary Wharf.

Paul Reichmann understood that superior quality alone would not be sufficient to lure the first tenants, that he would have to begin by offering space in Canary Wharf at a discount. On the other hand, he also knew that when the time came to arrange permanent mortgage financing for Canary Wharf, the amount that Olympia & York would be able to borrow would be determined mainly by the rental income due under lease agreements with tenants. In other words, the higher the rents charged, the more the company would be able to borrow against any given building, regardless of how much it had cost to construct. Ever since Flemingdon Park in the late 1960s, Reichmann's singular ability to mortgage new properties in excess of their intrinsic value had been an essential component of his success, generating many hundreds of millions of dollars in expansion capital. He had begun Canary Wharf with every intention of employing his trademark financing method on an unprecedented scale, factoring its use into his long-term planning not only for the London development but for Olympia & York itself.

With this financing strategy uppermost in mind, Reichmann used the same basic pricing approach with Canary Wharf that he had with World Financial Center, holding firm on rents while freely offering such one-time inducements as rebates, fitting-out allowances, and introductory rent-free periods. In addition, Reichmann again was prepared to take over an existing lease or even buy a building to induce a major prospect to move. All in all, Olympia & York was prepared to undercut City landlords by 50 percent or more in terms of net cost of occupancy while insisting on a base rent of £30 a square foot, or about 25 percent of the going rate in central London.

The company began its leasing campaign by working through a handful of London's most prestigious real estate brokerage firms. In England, commercial real estate brokering—otherwise known as chartered surveying—is a staid, gentlemanly profession in which the senior partners of one firm are disinclined to call on a rival firm's clients. After a brief, fruitless attempt to play by London rules, Reichmann decided that Olympia & York would do the job itself and installed a New Yorker named Peter Marano as his London leasing director. Marano, a former First Boston investment banker, was well acquainted with Canary Wharf, having been part of Ware Travelstead's team. "Marano was Olympia & York's bypass around the chartered surveyor industry," said Kean G. M. Hird, a director of the Imry Group of Companies, which owns a large portfolio of London property. "Basically, he was seen around town as an arrogant interloper. But he's tenacious—a big bloke with presence—and he had plenty of fees to pay."

Mindful of the limits of his own brand of New York hard sell, Marano frequently asked Paul Reichmann to accompany him on his sales expeditions. "I used to wheel Paul in to meet the top people," Marano recalled. "His frame of reference was so wide that there was almost always some angle, some mutual acquaintance he could use to get a conversation going. Then he'd say something like, 'The last time I saw Margaret Thatcher . . .' and off we'd go into economics or politics for a while. He used the chit-chat to see what people were like and then we'd get around to Canary Wharf. A lot of people in real estate will say, 'Here's what we're prepared to do for you.' But Paul's approach was more, 'Tell us what you need and we'll make it work for both of us.' He had a nice way of saying, 'How do you want us to shake up the money?' "

Even so, the leasing of Canary Wharf would prove a Sisyphean struggle from beginning to end. As usual, Reichmann shot the moon: his ambition was not merely to fill Canary Wharf at a profit but to cream the elite off the top of the London office market. He insisted that Olympia & York would rent only to companies looking for new executive quarters, that his towers would not be given over to banks of computer equipment, telemarketing cadres, or back office operations of any sort. And he was leery of marginalizing Canary Wharf by filling it with the London offices of American and other overseas companies. If Canary Wharf were in fact to form the nucleus of a third London business district to rival the city and the West End, Olympia & York would have to attract a host of major British companies.

Reichmann and his lieutenants pitched every major U.K. corporation that would receive them—and dozens did, including such establishment bellwethers as British Petroleum, British Gas, and British Telecom. But the fundamental, irreducible fact of the matter was that an overwhelming majority of British executives did not want to move to Docklands at any price. Although class snobbery figured in their reluctance, rank-and-file employees tended to be as unenthusiastic as their bosses. Reichmann "didn't realize that British people and businesses are tied by invisible threads to places: to the Bank of England, or just to a set of streets, some shops, a restaurant," observed one native-born London property man. Stuart Lipton of Stanhope, the most Americanized London developer, advanced a similar argument: "Londoners are used to living in villages. The City of London is a village as well as one of the biggest clubs in the world. It's all about walking—two centuries of walking, at a slow and measured pace."

Many of the British citizens on Olympia & York's London payroll harbored misgivings about their boss's vision of the Isle of Dogs as the City reincarnate but wisely kept them to themselves once the project got under way. As an outside adviser, Tim Bell was freer to speak his mind and did. "Paul never understood one thing about Canary Wharf: it's in the wrong place," Bell said not long after Olympia & York had surrendered control of the development to its creditors. "London people don't go to Docklands. You can offer massive subsidies and they still won't go." Bell said that during the project he had repeatedly expressed this view to his client, but to no avail. "Paul would tell me about the other projects he'd done that had been judged impossible but had succeeded, like World Financial Center. To be fair, I never said, 'It won't work, period.' I told him it would be very, very difficult. Paul would say, 'Yes, but we can make this work.' Dreamers don't like to be awakened."

By 1988, corporations in search of more office space in central London had an abundance of choice for the first time in a long time. As predicted, the City Corporation's liberalized planning regime had stimulated much remodeling and new construction within the Square Mile, and the West End, too, was crawling with cranes and bulldozers. In the hunt for tenants, Canary Wharf's location was only the most telling of Olympia & York's competitive disadvantages. As a newcomer to London's notoriously incestuous business circles, Olympia & York had no old-school ties to trade on and was excluded from the innermost chambers of gossip and market intelligence.

In its dealings with the City, Olympia & York picked up the gauntlet that Travelstead had petulantly thrown down. Michael Dennis maintained continuous contact with Michael Cassidy, the City Corporation's planning director, asking his advice from time to time and making certain that he was invited to every ceremonial event. As Reichmann had hoped Cassidy watched from the sidelines as Olympia & York did its damnedest to lure tenants away from the landlords of the City. According to Cassidy, the City Corporation only once deigned to join the fray, to help Stanhope Properties sign the European Bank for Reconstruction to a Broadgate lease. Although the European Bank was not a particularly large tenant, it was symbolically important as a harbinger of the new, supranational Europe that was to emerge after 1992.

Reichmann might have compromised the loyalties of the City establishment by inviting its huge pension funds and trust companies to join in developing Canary Wharf as silent partners. But instead of trying to co-opt the City, he chose to infiltrate it, acquiring a one-third interest in Stanhope Properties for £137 million in mid-1988. Reichmann was no less a foreigner than before, but no foreigner who owned a substantial piece of England's finest development company could continue to be classed an interloper. "Olympia & York certainly knew what was going on in the sharp end of the City," Cassidy observed, "because Stuart Lipton *is* the sharp end of the City."

When Reichmann had made his first exploratory rounds of London in early 1986, he had invited Stuart Lipton to his suite at Inn on the Park for a cup of tea. "My first impression of Paul was the same as my last, that he was obviously a great intellect," Lipton recalled. "What really fascinated me was that he knew every detail of his projects, right down to the planning of a floor. Usually, developers are either financiers or builders but he had both skills and to a high degree." For his part, Reichmann considered Lipton the best developer in England and was particularly impressed with Broadgate, which he described to the press as "the only development in central London up to North American standards." Begun in 1983 in partnership with Rosehaugh PLC, Broadgate was still very much a work in progress when Olympia & York barged into London. Only half of its fourteen buildings had been completed and one-third of its three million square feet spoken for. Like Bell, Lipton told Reichmann what he did not want to hear. "Paul thought he could move people out of the City," Lipton said. "I said to him that the City was the City and you'd never move it."

Over and over again, Lipton would underscore his words with actions, filling Broadgate to capacity while space in Canary Wharf went begging. Even many U.S. and Canadian multinationals with long-standing ties to Olympia & York turned Reichmann down this time. Shearson Lehman Brothers, the American Express subsidiary headquartered at World Financial Center, had consolidated its several London locations into a single building at Broadgate just as Olympia & York arrived on the London scene. As a courtesy to Paul Reichmann, Peter Cohen, Shearson's chief executive, toured the Canary Wharf site with Dennis and was, as he put it later, "staggered by the enormity of it." But when Dennis popped the question—"What would it take to get you down here"—Cohen begged off. "I'm sorry," he said, "but we just got settled in Broadgate."

Meanwhile, Olympia & York held protracted talks with four British banks, including two of the clearinghouse giants: Barclays Bank and Midland Bank, which required so much space for a new headquarters that it would have taken all of one Canary Wharf building and most of an adjoining one. To accommodate Midland, Reichmann sent his architects back to the drawing board to fuse the two buildings into one. A voluminous lease was drawn up and substantial agreement reached on many crucial points. At the last minute, though, the negotiations derailed when Reichmann refused to shave a few pounds off the base rent of £30 a square foot. "We thought at the time that we were making good progress and didn't need to do it," he recalled. "In retrospect, we should have done everything we could to make this deal. A major British bank was ready in principle to lead the way to Docklands. Even at half-price or quarter-price, it would have been worth it." But Reichmann would not budge and his stubbornness would turn out to be, in his own estimation, "a grave error."

Chapter 42

I n taking over Canary Wharf, Reichmann had seemed to relish the project as a test of Olympia & York's financial muscle as much as its development expertise. By the fall of 1989, Olympia & York had sunk about $2.2 billion into the Isle of Dogs, much of it in prepayment for construction work yet to be completed. Reichmann could have eased the enormous strain of financing Canary Wharf by inviting other U.K. developers or financial institutions to join with Olympia & York, but he never made any real effort to enlist minority partners, for fear that they would somehow circumscribe his control of the massive undertaking.

However, Paul did give protracted consideration to the idea of selling a minority ownership interest in Olympia & York's American subsidiary, in which the Reichmann family directly held a 25 percent stake. The U.S. company had been owned in its entirety by the Canadian parent company (which was, in turn, entirely owned by the family) until late 1986, when a change in the tax treaty between the United States and Canada made it advantageous to shift partial ownership directly to the family, which infused $622 million cash into the company in exchange for the 25 percent stake. Most of this minority interest was held by limited partnerships that Albert, Paul, and Ralph had set up for the benefit of their children. In the spring of 1989, the brothers, at Paul's urging, decided to mount a discreet effort to shop the family's quarter interest. Olympia & York hired Lazard Frères & Company, the Wall Street investment bank best known as Felix Rohatyn's firm, to approach well-heeled institutional investors in the United States and also retained the London office of the Swiss Bank Corporation to canvass the rest of the world.

In Paul Reichmann's view, such a sale was desirable for several reasons. For a start, it would placate the majority of family members who did not work at Olympia & York and were increasingly eager both to lay their hands on some ready cash and to diversify their patrimony beyond the family company. At the same time, Reichmann hoped that bringing in a big pension fund or insurance company as an active minority partner would force the "professionalization" of the U.S. company by the mere fact of its staid, unblinking presence—or, as Reichmann himself put it, through the "discipline of inquiry." As it was, the subsidiary was too loosely structured and too slapdash in its management methods to suit Reichmann, who was shrewd enough to realize that it was what he himself had made it. "Paul would be the first to tell you that he's not a hands-on, day-to-day manager," said John Zuccotti, Olympia & York's longtime counsel in New York.

Lazard Frères attracted preliminary offers from several institutional investors of the caliber that Reichmann sought. After negotiations that continued well into 1990, though, Reichmann would turn them all down. "The prices were not as high as he wanted," recalled Zuccotti, who at the start of 1990 joined Olympia & York full-time in the newly created position of president of the U.S. company. "I was not asked my opinion, but they seemed like reasonable offers to me."

Similarly, Reichmann had flirted all through the 1980s with the idea of selling stock in Olympia & York to the public but never could subject himself or this most private of family companies to the demands and expectations of total strangers. Unlike the sale of the family's 25 percent stake, a public stock offering would have had the virtue of reinforcing Olympia & York's debt-heavy capital foundation with new equity. Alternatively, Reichmann could have deleveraged Olympia & York by selling prime assets, instead of using them as loan collateral, thus sparing the company the burden of burgeoning interest payments. First Canadian Place or World Financial Center no doubt would have excited a frenzy among Japanese investors, who in the late 1980s paid huge premiums to acquire Rockefeller Center and other top-of-the line American office properties. As it was, Robert Canning, the Toronto investment banker, had a Japanese client willing to pay the extraordinary price of $250 million for a 50 percent interest in the twenty-eight-story Aetna Canada Center, one of Olympia & York's lesser properties in Toronto. Reichmann pondered the unsolicited offer briefly and informed Canning that the Aetna Center was not for sale.

Reichmann's aversion to selling, which in the end would be revealed as one of his greatest deficiencies as a businessman, ran so deep that it seemed encoded in his very genes. When it came to office towers, his ownership compulsion was rooted equally in sentiment and avarice—that is, in a craftsman's pride in his handiwork, on one hand, and a hatred of paying taxes, on the other. Reichmann was masterful at wringing maximum advantage from the abundant tax write-offs and deferrals that flowed from mortgage-financed property ownership. Eventually, the tax bill would come due, but the more buildings that Olympia & York owned and the more debt it carried, the longer it could put off tax day. At the same time, Reichmann was no less disinclined to weed out his stock market portfolio, whether by unloading subpar investments or by taking a profit in his relative handful of winners. By 1988, the value of Olympia & York's 40 percent holding in Trizec had risen about twenty-five-fold since 1979, and yet Reichmann could not bring himself to part with a single one of his millions of shares.

To pay for Canary Wharf, Reichmann organized a series of borrowings of breathtaking scale. Olympia & York's epic, late-1980s borrowing binge was typical of the penultimate phase of Reichmann's stewardship of Olympia & York in that it was at once masterfully executed—enabling the company to borrow maximal amounts at minimal cost and with minimal disclosure—and, at the same time, fundamentally misguided. Having completed his refinancings of the Uris properties in the mid-1980s, Reichmann now put many of Olympia & York's North American trophy buildings deep in hock as he added significantly to the company's indebtedness.

The most creative of these megafinancings was an $800 million Eurobond issue secured by the largest of the World Financial Center buildings, Tower B. In a novel twist, the company specified that it would make interest payments on these bonds in dollars and principal payments in yen, which at the time was at an all-time high against the dollar. In effect, Reichmann laid an $800 million wager that the disparity would be resolved in favor of the U.S. currency. He soon was proved right, and Olympia & York locked in a $100 million trading profit. "Most people would consider it a matter of luck," Reichmann bragged. "But luck is actually in the timing. If the fundamentals are sound, we do not worry about timing." Olympia & York borrowed another $530 million against One Liberty Plaza, the Manhattan skyscraper acquired to induce Merrill Lynch to lease space in World Financial Center. The entire sum was provided by a single Japanese lender, the Sanwa Bank.

In Canada, meanwhile, Olympia & York floated $300 million in bonds secured by the Exchange Tower in downtown Toronto, quickly followed by a $475 million offering—the largest corporate bond issue in Canadian history—backed by the adjacent First Canadian Place complex. The financial data included in the sales prospectus for the First Canadian Place issue underscored both the vastness of the wealth the Reichmanns had amassed and their continued willingness to put it at risk. Montreal Trust appraised Olympia & York's ownership interest in the complex at a colossal $905 million, or about a dozen times what Olympia & York had invested in building it. This market value estimate was mainly derived from operating profits, which amounted to a lush

$60 million in 1989. First Canadian Place was a gold mine, and yet Olympia & York's $47 million cut of the profits would not cover the $52 million in interest Olympia & York would have to pay annually on the $475 million of newly minted bonds. The shortfall would have to be covered from other sources.

The Reichmanns also borrowed heavily against their stock portfolio. They used most of their shares in Trizec to collateralize a $500 million loan from Citibank and a group of Japanese institutions that included Tokai Bank, Fuji Bank, and Daiwa Bank. But the pièce de résistance of Olympia & York's borrowing program was a $2.5 billion loan made by a consortium of eleven international banks headed by the Hongkong & Shanghai Banking Corporation, which itself advanced $750 million. To secure this so-called Jumbo Loan, Olympia & York mortgaged most of its stockholdings in Gulf Canada and Abitibi-Price and also provided a guarantee that obligated the company to repay the loan even if the Gulf and Abitibi stock alone would not suffice. By agreeing to this draconian requirement, Paul Reichmann persuaded the banks to advance what was by any standard an enormous sum without fully opening Olympia & York's books to their scrutiny.

By the time that Albert Reichmann made his first trip to the Soviet Republic of Lithuania in the spring of 1989, Mikhail Gorbachev's reforms had loosed the multiheaded monster of nationalism within the Soviet Empire. By the end of this epochal year, the Warsaw Pact would have crumbled along with the Berlin Wall as the vassal states of Eastern Europe declared their independence from Moscow one by one. Meanwhile, the USSR itself faced a growing threat of dismemberment as republics from the Baltic to the Black Sea asserted long-suppressed claims of national sovereignty with increasing force. In political terms, the nationalist independence movement assumed its most radical form in the Baltic republics of Latvia, Estonia, and Lithuania, all of which had been forcibly annexed under the Stalin-Hitler pact of 1940. In each of the Baltic states, People's Front movements cowed the local Communist parties into stunned acquiescence and in the fall of 1988 held founding congresses that amounted to defiant festivals of national rebirth. Gorbachev had never intended glasnost to go this far. But would he use military force to reassert Moscow's dominion over the Baltic republics?

Reichmann's attention was first drawn to Lithuania during the winter of 1988, when the local Soviet authorities in Vilnius, the Lithuanian capital, began removing gravestones from an ancient Jewish cemetery for use as building materials. Vilnius, which the Jews called Vilna, was a name that resonated deeply in the consciousness of religious Jews in particular, for it had been the European capital of Talmudic study throughout most of the eighteenth and nineteenth centuries, and its great rabbinical academies had served as the prototype of the ultra-Orthodox yeshiva of the twentieth century. Vilna had continued to flourish as a center of religious learning and Yiddish culture into the mid-1930s, when its Jewish population peaked at about fifty-five thousand. By the 1980s, though, only a thousand Jews remained. Of the 160 synagogues that existed before the war in the city, only one survived—a turn-of-the-century wreck that was as cold as a tomb during the long Lithuanian winter because the authorities would not permit the building to be hooked up to the city's central heating system.

And yet, against all odds, a small circle of observant Jews had formed in Vilnius around Vladimir and Carmella Raiz, longtime refuseniks who had found religion in the early 1980s. As soon as the desecration of the cemetery commenced, Mr. Raiz sent an SOS to Rabbi Shlomo Noach Mandel in Toronto. Rabbi Mandel went straight to Albert Reichmann, who had met the Raizes on one of his trips to Moscow and had been moved by their story. Reichmann, in turn, alerted his friends in Canada's Ministry of External Affairs, which lodged an informal protest through its consulate in Vilnius, and also established direct contact with Lithuania's Communist Party boss through Rabbi Ronald Greenwald, freelance Orthodox envoy extraordinaire.

Born in 1934 on New York's Lower East Side, Greenwald was the Jewish paradox incarnate. He was, for a start, a pious man with a flair for the machinations of Republican Party electioneering. While teaching at a yeshiva and running a summer camp in the Catskills, "Rabbi Ronnie" labored to deliver the ultra-Orthodox vote of Rockland and King counties to a succession of candidates, including Representative Ben Gilman, his main political ally. Then, too, Greenwald's easy amiability and disheveled appearance belied a talent for precise, secretive dealings. In his forties, he belatedly entered business, parlaying his bulging Rolodex into a gig as an international broker in aluminum ore, copper, phosphates, and other raw materials in partnership with a Lithuanian expatriate. Working out of modest offices in Manhattan, Greenwald brokered so many trades with the USSR, East Germany, and other enemy nations that he was required to register as a foreign agent. At the same time, Greenwald no less assiduously worked his global connections to help free political prisoners—only some of whom were Jewish—in Mozambique, Cuba, Argentina, El Salvador, and elsewhere, and was an important go-between in the East-West spy swap that resulted in the release of the famed refusenik Natan Sharansky in 1986.

The deeper that Albert Reichmann involved himself in the cause of Soviet Jewry, the more he heard about Rabbi Ronnie. In early 1988, Reichmann called Greenwald to ask his help in obtaining a Soviet visa for someone. The New Yorker, who had never met any of the Reichmann brothers but admired the family's philanthropy, attended to the matter and then flew to Toronto to compare notes with Albert. As Reichmann began considering property development projects in Moscow, Greenwald set up appointments for him with the mayor of Moscow and the president of Avto Export, the USSR's biggest auto company, which owned a choice building site in Moscow. Greenwald had never heard of Vladimir and Carmella Raiz but promised Reichmann that he would see what he could do for them when next he was in Lithuania. As it happened, Greenwald and his business partner left for Vilnius a few days after Raiz had alerted Reichmann to the desecration of the cemetery.

Greenwald arranged a late-night meeting with Raiz on a Vilnius street corner and came away determined to help him. "I thought him to be rather sad and alone, not like other refuseniks I've spoken with," Greenwald recalled. Raiz and his wife had spent most of their adult lives in refusenik limbo, having first applied for permission to emigrate to Israel in 1972. Vladimir, a Ph.D. molecular biologist, was initially refused on the grounds that he possessed state secrets and then fired from his government job. Although Carmella, a concert violinist, managed to hang on to her job for some years, the Raizes eventually were reduced to poverty and accused of "parasitism." Throughout the 1970s, they took part in demonstrations and hunger strikes, wrote letters of protest, and generally courted deportation. Like other refuseniks, they lived in fear of the KGB, which kept them under constant surveillance and frequently pulled Vladimir in for interrogation. The harassment intensified after the Raizes turned to Orthodoxy and Vladimir, who changed his name to Zev, began organizing clandestine seminars for other converts. Even within the larger refusenik community, the Raizes were isolated by the intensity of their religious beliefs.

In meetings with Algirdas Brazauskas, the president of the Supreme Soviet of Lithuania, Greenwald raised the cemetery issue and also did his best to humanize Raiz's plight. "I explained to him that I was kosher and so was Raiz and what a hardship it was for him to try to live this way in Vilna," Greenwald said. As the party boss listened, he tore a strip from a piece of paper, asked for the spelling of "Raiz," wrote the name down and tucked it in his pocket. Encouraged by the gesture, Greenwald said that if Brazauskas helped Raiz, he would see to it that Albert Reichmann included Lithuania in his search for business opportunities in the Soviet Union. Brazauskas had never heard this name either but grew visibly excited by his visitor's explanation. "You've heard of the Rockefellers," Greenwald said. "The Reichmanns are bigger, only they're kosher, too."

By the time that the New Yorker returned home, the ransacking of the Vilnius cemetery had ceased, though there was not much left to plunder. To Greenwald's relief, Reichmann not only agreed to go to Lithuania but volunteered to personally fly Zev and Carmella and their two young sons to Israel on the Olympia & York jet if a deal could be made for their release. Greenwald and his partner began cobbling together a three-way joint venture in which their own firm, Global Technology Group, would join with Olympia & York and

Lithuania's agricultural ministry to promote Lithuanian farm products in the West. Meanwhile, Brazauskas apparently kept his part of the bargain, importuning Gorbachev himself for the release of the Raiz family. Greenwald fretted over a back-channel warning from one of his KGB contacts, who said that Zev Raiz would not be allowed to emigrate until the year 2000. But the deputy director of OVIR, the Soviet emigration agency, and a high official of the religious affairs ministry personally assured Reichmann that Moscow would no longer block the Raizes' path to freedom.

The credibility of this promise was bolstered by dramatic recent changes in official Soviet policy toward the Jews. In February, Nobel Prize winner Elie Wiesel headed a delegation of one hundred foreign Jews who gathered in Moscow to commemorate the opening of the first officially sanctioned Jewish cultural center in the USSR. A week later, a new yeshiva, the first permitted to operate on Soviet soil in sixty years, opened on the outskirts of Moscow. (It was organized by Rabbi Adin Steinsaltz, the Israeli scholar whose work Paul Reichmann had declined to fund years earlier. Although the new yeshiva was too liberal even for Albert's taste, he supported its founding with a large donation nonetheless.) Meanwhile, OVIR had become much less niggardly in doling out exit visas. In 1988, 19,343 Jews had been allowed to emigrate, more than double the previous year's total, and in April 1989, the monthly exodus exceeded 4,000 Jews—a tally unmatched since 1979. None of the remaining refuseniks had waited as long as had the Raizes. What was to be gained by protracting their agony?

Reichmann scheduled an early May meeting in Vilnius with Brazauskas and Prime Minister Vytautas Sakaluaskas. As the big day neared, the Raizes struggled to maintain their composure. Over the years, the local office of OVIR had told them on three separate occasions that an exit visa had been approved, but each time the authorization had been revoked at the last minute by an unseen hand. Of course, never before had a Western billionaire interceded on their behalf.

On May 6, the Olympia & York Gulfstream touched down in Vilnius bearing a party of five: Albert and Egosah, Philip Reichmann and his wife, and Rabbi Shlomo Mandel. Albert and his son went right from the airport, which had been entirely repainted in anticipation of the Reichmann visit, into meetings with Brazauskas, Sakaluaskas, and other senior Lithuanian officials. The business negotiations went off without a hitch, ending with the signing of a protocol establishing the agricultural joint venture. But there would be no exit visa after all. Greenwald's informant had been right: the KGB had opposed the release of the Raizes and Gorbachev had decided not to press the issue, leaving Brazauskas twisting in the diplomatic wind.

Only later would the Raizes realize that they had sealed their fate early in their struggle by humiliating the overzealous KGB operative assigned to tail them.

Vladimir had written an open letter to the head of the KGB critiquing the agent's performance and had it distributed to the Western press through his contacts in Moscow. After the letter was published, the agent had shown up outside their apartment building with an eight-man goon squad. "I'll never forgive you," he shouted, purple with rage. "So long as I live, you'll never get out of here." This man soon was replaced and forgotten by the Raizes, who had no way of knowing that their self-appointed nemesis had gone on to rise within the KGB, putting him in a position to make good on his vow.

It was after midnight by the time that Reichmann and his entourage arrived at the Raizes' apartment, which was filled with fellow refuseniks primed for celebration. "We could tell by the look on Albert Reichmann's face that the hour of our freedom had not yet come," Carmella Raiz recalled. "He shook his head no as he offered some words of consolation." The party had ended before it began, but the Canadians tarried nonetheless. "We could tell that Mr. Reichmann felt too sorry for us just to breeze through our home and then leave us to ponder our fate," Mrs. Raiz added. By the time that Reichmann finally took his leave on that sorry day, it was four o'clock in the morning. He would return.

In the meantime, Reichmann continued to take a close personal interest in the Raizes' welfare. For years, Mrs. Raiz had had to commute monthly from Vilnius to Moscow to use its mikveh, a round-trip of twenty-eight hours. After three years of effort, the Raizes finally obtained permission to reconstruct the old mikveh in the synagogue in Vilnius but could not afford to equip it with a water heater, the lack of which was something more than an inconvenience during the winter. On Yom Kippur, Greenwald was working in his office when Reichmann called to ask him to arrange to have a boiler installed in the Vilnius mikveh. Greenwald was flabbergasted by the request. "Do you know how many people use that mikveh—one," he said. "But this is what's in his mind, this very busy man, this billionaire, on Yom Kippur. That someone so wealthy could be so simple and well-mannered is almost frightening to me."

———

Paul Reichmann and his English-born executives might not have agreed on whether British corporations could ever be persuaded to call Docklands home, but on one thing there was universal agreement within Olympia & York: the lack of mass transit links between central London and the Isle of Dogs was the single greatest impediment to Canary Wharf's success. When Peter Marano took a bigwig down from the city to look over the site, he preferred to go by the Riverbus, a Thames ferry that Olympia & York had purchased in partnership with another Docklands developer and subsidized as a kind of VIP taxi service. The Riverbus was scenic and reliable, but a money-loser and altogether ill suited to the task of transporting thousands of workers to and from the office. The alternatives to the ferry were two: private car or the Docklands Light Railway. As Marano saw it, this was akin to a choice between suicide by razor blade or overdose.

Driving to Canary Wharf from the city required navigating a tangle of hopelessly undersized two-lane roads. "I'd be at the stage of being ready to close [on a lease] and then—Kaboom!—the CEO would get stuck in traffic going down and the deal was off," Marano complained. The Docklands Light Railway (DLR), which local residents had sarcastically dubbed the "Dear Little Railway," was a semiautomated, high-tech tram able to carry no more than fifteen hundred passengers an hour and swarming with more technological bugs than a tropical swamp. The DLR was forever malfunctioning in minor ways, and when its computer system crashed altogether, service could cease for as long as twenty-four hours. To Olympia & York's annoyance, the DLR's travails were chronicled by certain London newspapers with sadistic thoroughness. "The press viewed the DLR as a real Achilles heel," said Robert John, the Olympia & York director most closely involved in transport issues. They were right.

Historically, development has followed a path blazed by transport: first came the river and then the river town; first the railroad and then the frontier settlement; first the highway, then the suburb. From the outset of the Docklands experiment, the LDDC's own planning staff considered the area's utter deficiency of modern transport infrastructure as the chief constraint on its redevelopment. "We knew that if we were really going to hit the jackpot, we needed to get the transport system up to the levels of the rest of London," said Peter Turlick, the LDDC's chief planner. However, heavy outlays for East End mass transit had not fit with Mrs. Thatcher's militant insistence in the inaugural years of her rule on cutting public spending. There were few aspects of the Thatcher Revolution as audacious as its assumption that Docklands could be transformed from an abandoned cul de sac of steamship commerce into a showpiece of renascent private enterprise without heavy public expenditures on transport.

Until Ware Travelstead's group had come along, the best the LDDC could do was a token light rail system connecting the Isle of Dogs to the central precincts of the East End. But with Canary Wharf projected to bring fifty to sixty thousand new jobs to the Isle of Dogs by the mid-1990s, the LDDC at last was able to secure large appropriations for roadworks, notably the Limehouse Link, a tortuously corkscrewed tunnel that would directly connect the Isle of Dogs to central London's major east-west thoroughfare. At a minimum cost of £220 million, or £2,000 an inch, this 1.8 kilometers of tunnel would prove to be the costliest stretch of road ever built in Britain. The LDDC also secured financing for a £90 million upgrading of the Docklands Light Railway, with the government and the Travelstead group contributing £45 million apiece. By the time that Olympia & York took over, this obligation had risen, in tandem with the project's costs, to £67 million. In addition, Olympia & York agreed to cover the £25 million cost of constructing the DLR station planned for Canary Wharf itself.

The speed with which Olympia & York set out to build Canary Wharf left scant room for error on the transit front. Robert John was confident that Olympia & York could meet its schedule, but he was not so sure about the LDDC and the Department of Transportation. As Paul Reichmann had elaborated his vision of Canary Wharf into an entire business district, John and his colleagues became convinced that even an efficient light rail system would not suffice, that what Canary Wharf really needed was a hookup to the city subway system. Olympia & York hired a team of expert consultants and submitted a detailed proposal to extend the Bakerloo line to the Isle of Dogs. Although the Bakerloo was one of the few subway lines with excess capacity, Olympia & York's plan was coolly received by London Transport, which was preoccupied with schemes to relieve rush-hour overcrowding in central London. However, John did take heart in back-channel reports that Paul Channos, the minister of transportation, thought the Bakerloo proposal had some merit.

One Thursday, John learned that Channos had scheduled a transit-planning summit meeting the following Tuesday. "I went to see Paul," John recalled, "and we agreed that if we were going to get our proposal to the top of Transport's project list, we had to change the nature of the debate." On Monday, John had delivered to Channos a letter in which Olympia & York offered to pick up part of the costs of extending the Bakerloo Line and the next morning hustled over to the Department of Transportation to confer with two senior civil servants, who were unable to fully mask their displeasure with Olympia & York's peremptory tactics. As John had hoped, Channos decided at the afternoon meeting that the Bakerloo concept deserved serious consideration and instructed London Transport to flesh it out in conjunction with Olympia & York. The transport arm of the permanent government complied with Channos's wishes but grudgingly. "They were questioning everything we put forward," John recalled. "They thought we were trying to steamroll them, that the whole planning process was overaffected by cash."

When the Bakerloo notion proved technically unfeasible after months of slow-motion study, Olympia & York rallied by working up a new plan to extend the Jubilee Line instead. At considerable expense, Olympia & York did preliminary design work, developed engineering specifications, and even surveyed subcontractors. However, in January 1989, the major British transport agencies published a strategic plan for central London in which Olympia & York's Jubilee Line proposal was relegated to low flame and a back burner. Reichmann took his objections right to the top. Olympia & York "had an entrée at No. 10 Downing Street that overruled everything else," complained David Bayliss, the director of planning for London Transport. "I find the whole thing a very curious arrangement."

Margaret Thatcher's intervention was lightly camouflaged with a weighty new document, the East London Rail Study, which superseded the earlier report. It was prepared not by the government's own transport experts but by a private consulting firm, which took as its a priori assumption that a subway line should be extended to the Isle of Dogs. The question was which one. The answer, unsurprisingly, was the Jubilee. "It is sometimes argued that the Jubilee Line extension will only serve Docklands and so is rather a luxury," conceded Cecil Parkinson, who by now had replaced Channos as transportation minister. "But in fact it takes a much-needed line south of the Thames, crossing over to Canary Wharf and then connecting the whole of that part of London to the underground system for the very first time. The line then carries on to the East End where the service is desperately needed." Parkinson's point was valid but academic; the fact was that the Jubilee Line extension would not even have been on the government's agenda in 1989 had not Paul Reichmann and crew put it there.

By the government's own estimate (which would prove too low by half) the Jubilee extension would cost £1 billion. After lengthy negotiations with Parkinson, Reichmann agreed to kick in £400 million. Because the bulk of Olympia & York's payments would be spread over twenty-five years, the present value of its contribution was £180 million—big money certainly but not nearly 40 percent of what was needed. Treasury Secretary Norman Lamont argued that Olympia & York should be required to make a larger contribution and so Parkinson reluctantly resumed his negotiations with Reichmann, to no avail. "We were able to improve the terms but not the sum," Parkinson recalled. "The Treasury was still unhappy and so I decided to settle the matter once and for all." On November 15, Parkinson again met with Reichmann, who was implacable, and then with Lamont, who would not budge either. "We agreed to settle the matter at No. 10," Parkinson said. The next morning Parkinson announced, in effect, that Mrs. Thatcher had cuffed her Treasury secretary into line and that the Jubilee project would proceed on the terms to which Reichmann had agreed: £400 million over twenty-five years.

Olympia & York had won what, for a foreign company especially, was a remarkable political victory, but in a battle, not a war. The Reichmann-Thatcher deal still had to be incorporated in legislation and enacted by Parliament, which was no Thatcher rubber stamp. And even if Parliament afforded swift passage of a Jubilee funding bill, subway service to Canary Wharf would not begin until 1996 at the earliest. Nonetheless, euphoria reigned in Olympia & York's offices on Great George Street in the wake of Parkinson's announcement. "The Jubilee Line was the last piece of a puzzle," Michael Dennis exulted. Assured now—at least in his own mind—of tube line access, Paul Reichmann promptly announced that Olympia & York had decided to proceed with Canary Wharf's second phase, which would add another sixteen buildings to the eight already under construction and would be timed so that its completion would coincide with the opening of the new and improved Jubilee Line.

———

A week after Paul Reichmann had completed his single-handed transformation of British transportation policy, brother Albert arrived in Moscow as part of a big Canadian delegation headed by Prime Minister Brian Mulroney. The Mulroney visit, the first by a Canadian head of state since 1971, capped months of working-level trade talks in which Reichmann had figured importantly as the Canadian chairman of the newly formed Canada-USSR Business Council. The group was the brainchild of Edward Balababa, a Toronto trade lawyer who had initially approached Reichmann in hopes that he might host a private lunch or two. As chairman, Reichmann did much more, helping persuade more than 150 companies to join up. At a lunch in Moscow on November 22, Reichmann signed the papers establishing the council and posed for the obligatory photos with his Soviet counterpart, as Mulroney and Soviet Prime Minister Nikolai Ryzhvov beamed in the background. Among the seven Canadian-Soviet joint venture deals unveiled at the lunch was a protocol signed by Abitibi-Price and the Ministry of Timber to explore the possibility of building a giant state-of-the-art newsprint recycling plant near Leningrad.

That evening a convoy of limousines flying the Maple Leaf flag slowly made its way through Moscow's snowbound western suburbs. Reichmann had persuaded Mulroney to make room in his schedule for an "unofficial" visit to Rabbi Steinsaltz's new yeshiva, which had just been issued an eviction notice by the city authorities in Moscow. After the prime minister gave an impromptu talk to a few dozen students crammed into a tiny room, Rabbi Mandel picked his way through the throng and led one of the older students back by the hand to meet Mulroney. It was Zev Raiz, who was studying at the yeshiva with his son. Mulroney listened attentively as Raiz delivered a fervent plea. "Your situation is quite extraordinary," the prime minister replied. "We will do everything we can to help." But it was Reichmann who received the loudest applause of the evening—in reporting that he had seen to it that the yeshiva would not be closed until new quarters were found.

During his stay in Moscow, Reichmann also held high-level discussions of a joint venture project that had been conspicuous by its absence on the list unveiled at the luncheon. In conjunction with the USSR Chamber of Commerce, Olympia & York had tentatively agreed to build an office tower on a one-thousand-acre site on the Moscow River about two miles from the Kremlin. The Russians were so enamored of the idea that they had jumped the gun and announced the deal two weeks before the Mulroney visit and had further annoyed Reichmann by specifying a height of sixty to eighty stories and a cost of $250 million, though the undertaking still was very much up in the air in every sense. Talks continued, though, and within a few months Olympia & York's headquarters staff had put the finishing touches on a plan for a forty-story office tower and adjoining hotel-apartment building. Even at forty stories, the office tower would easily eclipse Moscow's tallest existing building, but the Russians balked. "They're saying, 'Make it taller'; we're saying 'no,' " Ron Soskolne, Olympia & York's in-house planning guru, complained at one point. Soskolne finally got the Russians to go along by promising to include taller buildings in subsequent phases of what was envisioned as a decade-long project.

Reichmann's highly visible role in the Mulroney trade mission and his chairmanship of the Canadian-Russian Trade Council considerably enhanced his standing within the Canadian business community. For the first time, a Reichmann brother had donned the mantle of corporate statesman—and in a way that appeared to position him not in the mainstream but in the vanguard, for in business no less than in international relations Communism's sudden collapse seemed to be opening a whole new world of possibility. The three hundred business people who accompanied Mulroney and Reichmann to Moscow constituted the largest Canadian trade delegation ever to an emerging market. "The Berlin Wall fell just two weeks before we got to Moscow," Balababa recalled. "The euphoria was incredible."

Meanwhile, statesmanship of a different sort burnished Reichmann's reputation within the Jewish community of Toronto. In 1989, for the first time ever, Albert, on behalf of the family, made a pledge to the general campaign of the United Jewish Appeal (UJA). No one was more surprised than Mark Gryfe, the UJA's newly appointed director, who called on Reichmann with Julie Koshitsky, the 1989 campaign cochairperson. "Going in, the view on the Reichmanns was that if you asked for too much, they'd just say no," Gryfe recalled. "But you couldn't ask for too little without insulting them. So the usual approach was to open with a high figure and come down from there." This strategy went out the window when Reichmann immediately agreed to Koshitsky's opening bid. After a few moments of stunned silence, Gryfe managed to stammer out a request for a large supplemental contribution. Again, Reichmann agreed. "And on top of that," Gryfe continued, "we'd also like . . ." Reichmann cut him off. "Don't push your luck," he cautioned with a smile, and Gryfe and Koshitsky burst out laughing.

To placate Paul and Ralph, Albert restricted the uses of the family's ground-breaking gift to exclude non-Orthodox religious institutions. It was agreed that Reichmann would mail the UJA three separate checks every month. One would go to the Jewish Family and Child Services (JFCS), which helped support poor Jewish families in the Toronto area. (The Reichmanns had contributed to this agency in the past but always directly.) The second check would be made out to the Jewish Immigrant Aid Society (JIAS), to support it in its basic mission of assisting impoverished Jewish immigrants. The third check also would go to the JIAS to help support a few hundred Soviet Jews who had been stranded in Ladispoli, Italy, after the United States had rejected their applications for refugee status on the grounds that they could not demonstrate "a well-founded fear of persecution" if they had remained in the Soviet Union.

These arrangements were formalized through an exchange of letters and adhered to scrupulously by Gryfe. Even so, the distinction that Reichmann drew between religious and nonreligious institutions proved sharper in theory than in practice. The generosity of Reichmann's contributions enabled the United Jewish Appeal to shift a portion of its general-fund allocations from the JFCS and JIAS to other community institutions, including non-Orthodox schools. Albert understood this but did not seem to mind. In fact, not long after he had finalized his agreement with Gryfe, he made a personal contribution to the very sort of institution that the conditions attached to the family's UJA bequest were designed to exclude. At the request of Bernie Ghert, the former chief executive of Cadillac Fairview, he pledged $100,000 of his personal funds to Kehillat Shaarei Torah, a Modern Orthodox congregation in suburban Toronto that was trying to raise $400,000 to pay down a burdensome debt. Ghert, whose own affiliation was Conservative, told Reichmann that he believed it better that a Jew join a non-Orthodox congregation than none at all. "I know Paul wouldn't have agreed but Albert did," Ghert said.

———

Paul Reichmann's empire-building bent was never more nakedly displayed than in mid-1989, when, at a time when commercial real estate was changing hands at astronomic prices, he tried to add the world's tallest building to his trophy case. Humbled by the decline of its retailing empire and menaced by corporate raiders, Sears, Roebuck & Company had put its 110-story Chicago headquarters up for bid in late 1988. Built in the early 1970s, the Sears Tower was an economically marginal building, the priority of cost-effective design having been subjugated to the novelty of extreme height; that the windows on its upper floors were prone to popping out was only the most obvious of its structural defects. Olympia & York was familiar with the Chicago market, having completed its own 63-story skyscraper a few years earlier. Filling the 1.8 million square feet of space that Sears planned to vacate after selling its famous tower would have been daunting in the best of times, but the Chicago office market had begun to erode. All in all, no one within Olympia & York could muster much enthusiasm for buying the Sears Tower except Reichmann himself.

Like Rockefeller Center, which Mitsubishi was then in the process of acquiring, the Sears Tower would likely have gone to a Japanese buyer had not the Japanese Ministry of Finance intervened. Behind the scenes, Tokyo warned off

Japanese investors, arguing that the purchase of so conspicuous a monument would inflame anti-Japanese sentiment in the American heartland. Olympia & York was the only foreign company among the four finalists and, more important, the only bidder willing to offer at least $1 billion, which was of great symbolic significance to Sears management. By June 1989, Sears believed itself so close to finalizing a sale to Olympia & York for $1.1 billion that it ceased negotiating with other bidders. However, three exhausting months later, Reichmann abruptly pulled out, leaving Sears executives open-mouthed and empty-handed. Olympia & York covered its hasty retreat with a few rapid-fire bursts of complaint about an impending increase in Sears Tower's property tax assessment, but the overriding reason could be reduced to two words: Robert Campeau.

On September 12, the very day that Olympia & York terminated its talks with Sears, the board of Campeau Corporation voted to put the Reichmann brothers in charge of an emergency effort to restructure the company's huge U.S. department store operation. In acquiring Allied Stores and Federated Department Stores back to back in 1986 and 1988, Bob Campeau had piled so much debt atop both department store chains that they had had to set new sales records virtually every month just to break even. As soon as the U.S. economy began to cool just a bit in early 1989, Campeau's department stores started running short of cash. In April and again in August, Campeau turned to the Reichmanns, his largest shareholders, who grudgingly loaned the Man Who Would Be Department Store King $75 million, not nearly enough to halt the bleeding. Bankruptcy loomed. In hopes of salvaging what had become a $560 million investment, Paul and Albert grudgingly agreed to head Campeau Corporation's reorganization and to provide a loan guarantee that would enable the company to borrow additional funds.

Forced to try to reinvent the world's largest department store operation even as he was directing the world's largest property development, it dawned on Paul Reichmann that he had no business buying the world's tallest building. It was not just the demands on his time. For Reichmann, the Campeau crisis was a splash of ice water in the face, an intimation of Olympia & York's own financial mortality. He could take some comfort in knowing that the loans to Campeau were collateralized by real estate, including the 50 percent of Scotia Plaza that Olympia & York did not already own, but the larger portion of his $560 million investment was unsecured. If Campeau were to go under, Olympia & York would be left with a gaping hole in its own balance sheet at a time when Reichmann needed all the financial strength he could muster to complete Canary Wharf.

The plan that Olympia & York hastily devised in consultation with various Wall Street investment bankers recommended that Campeau Corporation sell the classiest of its department store lines, Bloomingdale's, to raise cash and further proposed that the company's bondholders accept a 30 percent reduction in the value of their bonds in exchange for new shares of stock, which would be worthless if Campeau went bankrupt but potentially lucrative if the company was revived. The response to the Reichmann rescue plan was underwhelming. Bob Campeau balked at selling Bloomingdale's, his most lustrous trophy, for anything less than a king's ransom while the bondholders held out for a better deal, suspecting that the Reichmanns were holding another few hundred million dollars in reserve. As one close student of Campeau observed: "The Reichmann reputation for infallibility had convinced some bondholders that the company's problems would soon be solved and that Campeau and the Reichmanns were using their well-publicized troubles as a convenient opportunity to steal back the bonds."

The bondholders were right in suspecting that Paul Reichmann was hoping to profit at their expense but wrong in considering Olympia & York's restructuring plan an opening gambit. Having failed to recapitalize the Allied and Federated chains on the backs of their fellow creditors, the Reichmanns had no intention of putting another penny into Campeau Corporation. Left with no practical alternative, Allied and Federated soon filed for Chapter 11 bankruptcy protection, saddling all concerned—the Reichmanns included—with heavy losses. Many of the same bankers who had prematurely hailed the Reichmanns as Campeau's saviors after that September board meeting now denounced them in the press, albeit from behind the screen of nonattribution. "Clearly the Reichmanns are doing everything they can to distance themselves from Campeau's troubles," one banker complained in the *Globe & Mail*. "We're still waiting to see if Paul Reichmann is going to come out of the hole he's hiding in and do something for Campeau."

These attacks were rooted in nothing more than pique. The Reichmanns had never promised to save Campeau at any cost and certainly were under no obligation, moral or legal, to bail out its banks, many of which also were lenders to Olympia & York. Even so, Campeau's lenders and bondholders had anticipated miraculous deliverance and could not forgive the Reichmanns their human fallibility. "Up until Campeau, the Reichmanns were Midas," one Olympia & York executive observed. "Paul, perhaps believing his own myth, got more involved with Campeau than he should have. I don't know why. I can imagine that he admired Campeau's audacity and through him saw a way to put Olympia & York into retailing with a real estate bailout. But Campeau put a big dent in the myth and had a painful effect with a lot of the banks, especially the Japanese."

For Paul Reichmann especially, the Campeau debacle was mortifying. But at least the furor raised distracted attention from Olympia & York's own increasingly parlous financial condition. On December 29, Reichmann sold a one-third equity interest in the crown jewel of his American empire, World Financial Center, for $309 million. The deal "was done in an extremely short time frame, particularly for a transaction of this magnitude," and the management of the U.S. company "did not participate in any price negotiations and, to it, there did not appear to have been much price or other substantive negotiations," testified Joel Simon, the U.S. company's chief operating officer, in an affidavit later filed in state court in New York. "The buyer," Simon added, "was described initially only as a 'friendly merchant bank.' . . . Either shortly before or after the transaction closed, I learned that the investor was a Bronfman-controlled entity—Carena."

Carena Developments Limited was the holding company for the Bronfmans' real estate interests, including its controlling stake in Trizec, which was 40 percent owned by Olympia & York. By all accounts, Carena's investment in World Financial Center was not meant to be long-term. Paul Reichmann "represented that the investment would be short-term if Carena chose to sell it," Manfred Walt, a Carena vice president, testified in his affidavit. That is, Reichmann said that "he was negotiating with another purchaser who would likely be amenable to buying that interest from Carena on favorable terms within three to six months." Indeed, shortly after the transaction closed Reichmann instructed his American executives to begin looking for a third party to buy out Carena by June of 1990.

The World Financial Center deal astonished Simon and his colleagues, who were acutely aware of their boss's aversion to selling assets. Why, then, at a time when Reichmann was methodically if unenthusiastically considering the sale of a 25 percent stake in the U.S. company, would he suddenly turn around and sell a big chunk of his proudest possession to Edper or anyone else? Well, for a start, Reichmann had no shortage of uses for the $309 million in cash he received. More important, the sale provided him with a seemingly objective validation of the current value of Olympia & York's investment in World Financial Center; if someone was willing to pay $300 million for a one-third equity stake, it stood to reason that the remaining two-thirds had a net worth of $600 million. Until 1989, the question of Olympia & York's net worth had been largely academic. But under the terms of the recent Jumbo Loan, the company now was required to maintain a net worth of at least $2.5 billion, as documented at year end by an independent auditor.

Olympia & York's U.S. executives did not like the look of the World Financial Center transaction and neither did its outside auditors. Was it truly a sale as advertised or merely a short-term loan extended to Reichmann by his friends and allies at Edper? That is, had Edper agreed to help Reichmann dress up his books to meet the year-end accounting deadline in repayment of a past favor or in expectation of a future one? "Assurances were given by Paul Reichmann that while this was a transaction with friends and the Reichmanns may some day do a favor for them, it was a real sale," Simon testified. After Price Waterhouse, the outside auditors to the Toronto-based parent company, offered similar assurances to the U.S. auditors, the World Financial Center deal was duly booked as a sale, enabling Olympia & York to write down its Campeau investment and still report a total net worth in excess of $2.5 billion for 1989.

Later events would reinflame the suspicions of Olympia & York's American executives and eventually lead to a bitter confrontation with Reichmann and a legal battle with Edper. Until then, though, Edper's partial ownership of World Financial Center would remain a closely held secret. Although Carena Developments, the Edper entity in question, was a publicly traded company, it did not disclose the transaction to its shareholders. Nor did Olympia & York notify World Financial Center's creditors or its operating partner in the venture, the Battery Park City Authority. Whether properly classified as a sale or a loan, the World Financial Center transaction suggested that Olympia & York was not nearly as strong financially as was presumed. Had the bankers who were infuriated over the Reichmanns' supposed "betrayal" of Campeau realized that the brothers could not have bailed out their fellow Canadian even if they had wanted to, their anger would have metamorphosed into horror, for the $20 billion in debt that Olympia & York had amassed made even Campeau's $13 billion seem modest.

Chapter 43

On February 13, 1990, Renée Reichmann died in her sleep at her home in Toronto. At ninety-one, she had outlived Samuel by fifteen years and her eldest child by five years. Although she had retained her mental faculties until the very end, her health had begun to deteriorate precipitously in her late eighties, forcing her to spend her last few years in a wheelchair. Mrs. Reichmann had suffered increasingly from the stomach ulcers that had plagued her ever since the 1920s and had nearly died in early 1989 after a severe gastrointestinal attack while at her winter home in Miami Beach. On the day of their mother's funeral, a Wednesday, her sons shut down Olympia & York entirely, giving all their employees the day off. After a crowded funeral at the Yesodei Hatorah Synagogue, Mrs. Reichmann was laid to rest next to her husband in Bathurst Lawn Cemetery.

The *Toronto Globe & Mail,* the *Canadian Jewish News,* and other newspapers across Canada ran brief obituaries of Mrs. Reichmann. But in the ultra-Orthodox world, her passing was an event of global import. All American Airlines and Air Canada flights into Toronto were fully booked for a week as prominent rabbis and rank-and-file haredim by the thousands flew in from all over the world to pay their respects during the seven-day shivah period. "Toronto International Airport," marveled one non-Orthodox eyewitness, "was black." To accommodate the massive influx, the Reichmanns installed rows and rows of chairs in the living room of their mother's home and hired a dozen taxis to ferry their guests to and from the airport.

Among the mourners was Carmella Raiz, who had left Lithuania in late 1989 on a temporary visa that Reichmann had helped secure. Mrs. Raiz had spent most of her time in Washington, lobbying U.S. officials to assert themselves more forcefully on her family's behalf. Rabbi Shlomo Mandel had flown down to

Washington to accompany her to her meeting with Richard Schifter, the assistant secretary for human rights. A few weeks after the meeting, which was cordial but inconclusive, Reichmann had invited Mrs. Raiz to spend the weekend in Toronto. She accepted, fearing the worst. "I was very worried, knowing how much depended on his willingness to continue on our behalf," she recalled. "Hasn't he tired of spending his time on a 'hardship case' like the Raiz family? But the meetings with this wonderful man dispelled my fears." Now, a month later, she had returned to pay her respects. "I searched for the right words to say to the inscrutable Albert Reichmann, but he preempted me," she recalled in her memoirs. "No sooner had I set foot in the crowded hall than he got up from his low shivah stool and hurried toward me. He was in the torn clothes of a mourner, his face drawn and his eyes sunken. Nevertheless, he immediately started asking me about my problems."

Renée was survived by her five sons and ninety-nine grandchildren and great-grandchildren. Shortly after the mourning period ended, Edward, now the eldest member of the family, returned to Jerusalem, wrote two long letters setting down his earliest memories of his mother and mailed a copy to each of her descendants. "When we were sitting shivah in Toronto, several of my nephews and nieces came with their children and sat down in front of me and asked me: 'Uncle Eli, tell us something abut Nagy-Mama,' but I was not in a shape to talk and tell," Edward wrote. "Lots of people who came to the shivah told stories, stories they heard from different sources. Many of them, even if basically true, had parts of it distorted, because Angyu became a legend in her lifetime, and it is a pity that stories of great persons have to be distorted. The greatness of Nagy-Mama," he concluded, "lies precisely in her simplicity and directness."

Mrs. Reichmann left an estate that was valued at $210 million, largely on the basis of an affidavit submitted by Albert, who, along with Paul and Ralph, served as executor. Mrs. Reichmann's wealth consisted almost entirely of shares in Olympia & York Development and Reichmann Holdings Limited. Like Samuel Reichmann, she bequeathed her stock, albeit unevenly, to all five sons and to Eva's heirs. (The value Albert attached to his mother's 12.5 percent stake implied a total family fortune of nearly $1.7 billion.) Renée also left $100,000 apiece to two of her many grandnieces, Daphne and Marcel Gestetner, both of whom lived in Toronto and suffered from congenital hearing disorders. Daphne, who was nineteen, used $66,000 of her gift as a down payment on Renée's residence, 160 Dalemount, which she acquired from the estate for $439,000.

Under the terms of Samuel Reichmann's will, his shares in Olympia & York were to be held in trust until his wife died, at which time they were to be released and divided among his six heirs. However, the three Toronto brothers, who served as executors of the estates of both parents, apparently did not make all the distributions required of them for reasons that remain unclear. "There was never any distribution of Olympia & York stock to the Hellers," said Philip Heller, Eva's eldest son. "I don't know why, because it was kept so close to the vest by those who knew what was happening. I suppose if we'd known then that Olympia & York was going to crash, we'd have jumped up and down and demanded our due. But it wasn't as if any of us really needed immediate cash." The stock would have been distributed had Olympia & York survived. "It became a moot issue," said Paul.

Despite the gradualness of Mrs. Reichmann's decline, her death was a devastating blow to the family. "One of the commandments is 'Honor your father and your mother,' but the amount of respect this family had for Mrs. Reichmann was beyond biblical," said Frank Hauer, Paul's son-in-law. In 1995, Frank and Rachel Hauer became the first of her descendants to saddle a newborn daughter with the burden of expectation implicit in the name "Renée."

Although the extended Reichmann clan remained close-knit by any reasonable standard, the matriarch's passing inevitably diminished its cohesion. None of her sons had the authority—or the desire, for that matter—to compel mandatory attendance at weddings, bar mitzvahs, and the like. The Toronto members of the family—Hellers included—continued to gather for the traditional Shabbat Kiddush, now at the home of Albert and Egosah instead of at 160 Dalemount, but attendance soon petered out. Given her husband's utter dominance of the family's business affairs as well as her own robust exuberance, Lea Reichmann would have been a more logical successor as Shabbat hostess. "I'm sure if Paul had asked Lea, she would have done it," said Evelyn Jacobs, Eva's daughter, a few years after Mrs. Reichmann's death. "But Paul's priorities were elsewhere."

Shortly after Mrs. Reichmann died, Rabbi Ronnie Greenwald flew off to Poland on one of his secret rescue missions. Greenwald was in his Warsaw hotel room when his best KGB contact called from Moscow on March 6 with stunning news about Zev Raiz. Now, some ten months after the KGB had prevented Reichmann from flying the Raizes to Israel, Greenwald's informant said that the word had come down that the Raizes finally would be set free. "Are you absolutely sure?" Greenwald demanded. Count on it, he was told.

Greenwald's skepticism was understandable. The last thing he had heard out of the KGB was that Zev Raiz would be let out by the year 2000 if he was lucky. What finally had caused the KGB to relent, eighteen years after the Raizes had first applied to emigrate to Israel? Greenwald could not be certain, but he was aware that in recent months Washington had exerted more pressure on the Raizes' behalf than ever before. When George Bush had met with Mikhail Gorbachev in Moscow in late 1989, he had presented him with the names of twenty Jews that the United States judged unfairly denied permission to emigrate, and the Raizes headed the list. In February, Secretary of State James Baker had met in Moscow with Soviet Foreign Minister Eduard Shevardnadze. At one point, Baker excused himself and ducked into an adjoining room to consult with Schifter. "Quick," Baker told Schifter, "give me the name of a single refusenik we should demand." Schifter later recalled that he "felt very uncomfortable because I was being called upon to play God. But I gave him the name of Vladimir Raiz."

Meanwhile, Lithuania's political showdown with the Soviet Union was approaching the flash point. In a daring bid to move with the times, Algirdas Brazauskas had led a faction that had broken from the central party and formed an independent Lithuanian Communist Party. Even so, on February 24 both versions of the Communist Party had been thrashed by Sajudis, the Lithuanian independence movement, in the first open parliamentary elections anywhere in the USSR in seventy years. In a few days, the new parliament would vote on a resolution proclaiming Lithuania an independent nation. Its outcome was a foregone conclusion; the question was whether Moscow would respond by sending in the tanks. Whether the nationalist ferment in Lithuania was working to the Raizes' advantage or disadvantage was unclear. Unquestionably, though, Lithuania's political volatility made any attempt at rescue more complicated and potentially more dangerous as well.

As soon as Greenwald's KGB informant had rung off, Greenwald telephoned Zeesy Schneur, the executive director of the New York Coalition to Save Soviet Jews. Mrs. Schneur in turned called David Dinkins, the newly elected mayor of New York City, who was riding through the streets of Washington, D.C., in a limousine bound for the Soviet Embassy, where he was to address a protest outside organized by Mrs. Raiz. Mayor Dinkins did not have a chance to speak with her before delivering his speech so she learned of Greenwald's breakthrough with everyone else. After Dinkins finished, Mrs. Raiz raced into a nearby office building and telephoned Greenwald, who was unable to convince her that deliverance was at hand. "Until I hear from Zev that he has the visa in his hand, I will not believe it," Mrs. Raiz told Greenwald. "No, until I hear that Zev is safely in the air I will not believe it."

Greenwald then telephoned the Vilnius apartment of Zev Raiz, who was grateful but no less skeptical than was his wife, pointing out that he had not heard a word from OVIR, the Soviet government agency that issued exit permits.

"It's true, believe me," Greenwald insisted, in Yiddish.

"I hope so," Raiz replied wearily. "I do."

"Listen carefully," Greenwald said. "Start packing all your baggage. Leave all your shmattes. Take only what's important. Reichmann is going to pick you up."

Greenwald then called Albert Reichmann, who was jubilant. "Baruch Hashem [Thank God]," Reichmann said. "That's wonderful, just wonderful." Greenwald listened for the sounds of hidden doubt but heard none. "Albert might have been skeptical, too," Greenwald recalled. "But if he was, he didn't show it to me. 'More power to you,' he told me."

Reichmann quickly consented to fly to Moscow and take Raiz to Tel Aviv himself. His one hesitation concerned the requirements of properly mourning his mother. Three times a day for the next eleven months Reichmann would have to say Kaddish, the traditional prayer for the departed. Its proper performance required a quorum of ten men—a minyan. Greenwald assured Reichmann that somehow he would arrange for a minyan at the Moscow airport.

The next day, March 7, Reichmann received a fax from Brazauskas, who remained the most powerful Communist official in Lithuania. When last they met, during the failed emigration attempt of May 1989, Brazauskas had assured Reichmann that he would continue to work to secure the Raizes' release, and he had been as good as his word. The Lithuanian had gone to Moscow and again made the case for freedom to Gorbachev, who gave his assent and refused this time around to back off when the KGB objected. Brazauskas's faxed message was badly garbled but welcome just the same: "I am glad to inform you that your request on the emigration of Mr. Raiz from the USSR I was eble to sold positiyvely. I look forward to you information on the time of your arrival."

Reichmann immediately telephoned Brazauskas and arranged to pick up Raiz and his son on March 19 in Vilnius. Greenwald, meanwhile, was working his political connections in Washington to publicize the Soviet concession before it could be withdrawn. New York Representative Ben Gilman posed with Carmella Raiz for a photographer and then read a statement into the *Congressional Record* on the floor of the House. New York Senator Daniel Patrick Moynihan put out a lengthy press release in which he noted that 357,000 other Soviet Jews had been allowed to emigrate since the Raizes had first applied for permission to exit in 1972 and offered congratulations to Brazauskas, Reichmann, Greenwald, Dinkins, and former Secretary of State George Shultz, in that order.

On March 11, relations between Vilnius and Moscow were strained to the breaking point as Lithuania proclaimed its independence, putting Gorbachev squarely on the spot. If he acceded to Lithuania's unilateral declaration of independence, Estonia, Latvia, and even many non-Baltic republics likely would follow suit. On the other hand, if he were to bring Lithuania to heel with brute force, he would damage his credibility as a reformer, as the godfather of glasnost and perestroika. On March 13, Gorbachev drew a line in the sand, branding Lithuania's declaration of independence "illegal and invalid" and refusing to negotiate unless it was rescinded. On this same day, as scheduled, Zev Raiz went down to the OVIR office in Vilnius and picked up exit visas for himself and his eldest son, Shaul, who was twelve. (Shaul's brother, seven-year-old Moshe, was with his mother in America.)

On March 14, Greenwald flew into Moscow from Warsaw. The next day a KGB source called with alarming news: that night the Soviet border with Lithuania would be sealed and the international airport in Vilnius closed. Greenwald called Raiz and urged him to leave Lithuania before midnight. Raiz said he could not go because his son was running a high fever. "Put him in a blanket and get out of there," Greenwald replied. Zev and Shaul Raiz caught the night train to Moscow and crossed into Russia an hour before the border was closed. Upon arriving in Moscow, the Raizes sought shelter at the Kuntsevo yeshiva in the outskirts of the city.

On Friday, March 16, the Kremlin sent an ultimatum by telegram to the Lithuanian government: rescind the declaration of independence by March 19 or else. March 19 was the very Monday that Reichmann was to have picked up the Raizes in Vilnius. There was no possibility now of flying into Vilnius but Greenwald was able to secure Soviet permission for the Raizes to leave from Moscow and a day earlier than planned. At about 7:30 A.M. New York time on Friday, Greenwald reached Reichmann at his brother Louis's house in Queens and recounted the latest, ominous developments. To reach Moscow by Sunday morning, as Greenwald now advised, Reichmann would have to travel on Shabbat. However, he understood that under the doctrine of pikkuah nefesh, he was not only permitted but required to violate the rules of Shabbat to save a life.

That same morning Reichmann caught a commercial flight to London, where the Olympia & York jet awaited him. Meanwhile, his wife, Egosah, flew to London from Toronto with one of Albert's Olympia & York aides in tow. In Washington, meanwhile, Carmella Raiz was suffering the final agonies of two decades of suspense. She had known a refusenik who had waited for years for an exit permit only to be run off the road by a truck on her way to the Moscow airport. "No one could anticipate what our unpredictable enemy, both vindictive and ruthless, would do next," Mrs. Raiz recalled. "I was truly afraid, for Moscow was no place to sit around waiting in those days."

On Saturday, as the Reichmanns were preparing to depart from London, the self-proclaimed Republic of Lithuania rejected the deadline imposed by the USSR and called on the "democratic nations" of the world to recognize its independence. Even as the Reichmann party headed for Moscow, Soviet troops stationed in Lithuania began "training" exercises while military jets swooped back and forth through the skies over Vilnius. While the Reichmanns were en route, Greenwald received phone calls from a friend in London and another in Tel Aviv. "Both of them said the same thing," he recalled, "that the Arab world was very upset that Russia was sending so many Jews to Israel again and that there were Arab elements that would like nothing more than to shoot us down on our way to Tel Aviv."

Greenwald borrowed a car and picked up Zev and Shaul Raiz at the yeshiva. Accompanied by a vanful of yeshiva students, Greenwald and his passengers arrived at the Sheremetyevo Airport without incident and rendezvoused with the Reichmanns in the main terminal. Surrounded by watchful but silent KGB operatives, Albert Reichmann assembled a minyan from the yeshiva contingent and led a Kaddish in a well-traveled airport corridor. After the service, Greenwald took Reichmann aside and informed him of the warnings he had received. "The biggest hit the Arabs could make would be to take down a Reichmann," Greenwald said. After discussing matters briefly with his wife, Reichmann replied that that was a risk they would just have to take.

Aside from the sadistic thoroughness with which customs officials inspected Raiz's luggage (resulting in the confiscation of his wife's violins, which required special clearance), all went well until the actual moment of departure, whereupon Greenwald was unable to locate his exit visa. He still had his passport but his visa was gone. A replacement would have been easily obtained had it not been Sunday and all government offices closed. Reichmann and Greenwald each found a telephone and began calling every Soviet official they knew, including the minister of religion, but to no avail. "Wait until Monday," they were uniformly told (with variable courtesy).

Luckily, the most influential of his Lithuanian contacts had agreed to come to the airport to see Raiz off. He was Leonas Jankauskas, who had recently retired as a high-ranking officer of the Soviet Army to manage the largest broadcasting company in Lithuania. Jankauskas took the five highest-ranking KGB men down into a basement room for a meeting, from which he emerged in twenty minutes, flashing a broad smile and a thumbs-up sign. "How did you do it?" Greenwald asked. Jankauskas held up an open hand, signifying the number five, and explained that he had promised to give each KGB inspector a television set. Greenwald now was free to go, exit visa or no.

It was late Sunday evening by the time the Olympia & York jet finally lifted off. Once airborne, Greenwald proposed a toast but the pilot urged him to wait until the plane had safely cleared Soviet air space. At Reichmann's instruction, the pilot did place a call to Carmella Raiz, who was nervously sitting by a telephone in New York City. "Despite the poor reception and the noise of the engines," she recalled, "I was able to hear the pilot's voice: Zev and Shaul were on the plane. 'Have you crossed the Soviet border?' I shouted into the phone, but they did not hear me." Mrs. Raiz resumed her vigil. "How far is it to Tel Aviv?" someone asked her. "Four hours and eighteen years," she replied.

Despite the late hour, a throng of reporters and well-wishers awaited at Ben-Gurion Airport in Tel Aviv. Raiz's emergence from Reichmann's plane touched off wild singing and dancing among the hundreds of Russian émigrés who had come to welcome one of their own. "I feel," Raiz said, "as if I came from Egypt on eagles' wings." Amid the tumult, Albert and Egosah Reichmann slipped away so surreptitiously that Greenwald did not even have a chance to say good-bye. "I assumed after I left your plane that you and your wife would be following shortly thereafter," wrote Greenwald in a fax he sent to Toronto that very day. "Please accept my most profound apologies for not extending a proper farewell."

On March 21, the day after Reichmann had dropped off the Raizes, Malev, the Hungarian national airline, suspended its charter flights from Budapest to Tel Aviv after a militant Arab group in Lebanon had threatened violence against any airline transporting Russian Jews to Israel. Malev also requested Aeroflot, the Russian airline, to stop ferrying Jews to Budapest from Moscow and Leningrad. By this time, Jews were fleeing the USSR in such numbers that the exit gate had been knocked off its hinges. Emigration now was constrained by the availability not of exit visas but of airplane seats. Bowing to diplomatic pressure applied by Arab nations, the Kremlin had repeatedly refused the U.S. government's appeals to allow direct flights from the USSR to Tel Aviv. By default, Budapest had emerged as a vital transfer point, accommodating about three-fourths of all Soviet Jews bound for Israel. Thus, Malev's sudden loss of nerve threatened to put a serious crimp in the outflow of emigrants from the USSR. "We are making every effort to open additional routes," announced Moshe Arens, Israel's foreign minister, "but pressure must be applied to the Hungarian government."

After leaving Tel Aviv, Albert and his wife had stopped off in Switzerland for a few days en route to Canada. A high Israeli official telephoned Reichmann in Zurich and asked him to intervene with the Hungarian government. Reichmann agreed to help, then called Andy Sarlos in Toronto. The next morning Sarlos flew to Zurich, where Reichmann and his Gulfstream waited on the tarmac. After Reichmann and Sarlos landed in Budapest, a phalanx of motorcycle policemen escorted them from the airport to a series of meetings with the prime minister, the minister of external affairs, the minister of transportation, the leader of the opposition, and lesser officials. "Everyone agreed to cooperate, so we then worked out security arrangements for Budapest airport, and Albert went to Israel to obtain some necessary assurances," Sarlos recalled.

Malev's general manager was fired and on March 28, the Hungarian government announced the resumption of a full schedule of flights from Budapest to Tel Aviv. The Islamic group did not carry through with its threats against Malev, and the emigration of Soviet Jews to Israel via Budapest continued unabated. Reichmann again slipped away unnoticed—no mention of him was made in any of the newspaper coverage of the Malev episode—and flew to London and then on to Toronto. The credit for Malev's reversal was by no means Reichmann's alone. Pressure had been exerted on the Hungarian regime by many parties, including the U.S. government. However, the fact was that for the second time in as many weeks, Albert Reichmann had fulfilled the moral imperative of rescue, of pikkuah nefesh, with the same sort of selfless élan that his mother had displayed during World War II. The Reichmann family would memorialize Renée in many ways, but there would be no tribute more felicitous than her third-born son's actions in the weeks immediately following her death.

———

After sitting shivah in Toronto, Paul Reichmann returned to London with a sense of renewed urgency verging on trepidation. He had promised that the first few Canary Wharf buildings would be fitted out and ready for tenants in the spring of 1990, but bad weather, the odd labor strike, and the bureaucratic perversities of British construction management methods had combined to push the project six months behind schedule. On March 27, Reichmann had reached the limits of his impatience. Ellis Don MacAlpine was sacked as construction manager for One Canada Square, which was both the tallest and the tardiest of the eight buildings under construction, and its employees given twenty-four hours to clear out their desks. Keith Roberts, Olympia & York's most prominent Canary Wharf skeptic, flew in from Toronto to implement at One Canada Square the same streamlined management approach used to such great effect in building World Financial Center and First Canadian Place. "Keith resisted but I insisted," Reichmann said. "With the smaller buildings I was content to keep the others, but for the tower I knew I had to have Keith."

With Roberts at his side in London at last, Reichmann could concentrate on meeting the critical mass deadline. Unless Olympia & York preleased another 800,000 square feet by June 30, Morgan Stanley International and Credit Suisse First Boston would be freed of the obligation to take one million square feet between them. Both investment banks were likely to pull out if given the chance, for each now required only about half of the new space for which they had contracted in the mid-1980s, when it seemed as if the good times would roll on forever. Morgan Stanley was particularly uneasy for it was obligated to purchase its building, whereas Credit Suisse was to be a tenant. By the fall of 1989, Morgan was insisting on reworking its contract with Olympia & York. Reichmann grudgingly complied. After months of grueling negotiations, the investment bank reaffirmed that it would in fact purchase 25 Cabot Square and occupy it as soon as it was finished. In return, Reichmann made a concession that would come back to bite him hard. Come December 12, 1991, Morgan Stanley would be entitled to relieve itself of the financial burden of real estate ownership by selling the building back to Olympia & York for the same price it had agreed to pay: $240 million.

In the two and a half years since Olympia & York had assumed control of Canary Wharf, the company had been able to sign only one tenant to a lease. By March 1989, Reichmann and his minions had been so desperate to show evidence of progress in their high-powered marketing campaign that they had persuaded Merrill Lynch & Company, World Financial Center's largest tenant, to sign a nonbinding letter of intent and then put out a press release implying that this agreement was a far more sanguinary event than it actually was. As hoped, the announcement generated much positive publicity; back in Toronto, the *Globe & Mail* went so far as to hail the signing of a "breakthrough lease." In reality, the agreement signified nothing more than Merrill Lynch's willingness to continue negotiating. In the end, those negotiations would go nowhere. It was not until the fall of 1989 that Olympia & York landed its first bona fide tenant—Texaco Incorporated, which preleased a 200,000-square-foot building in its entirety. To accommodate the American oil giant, which planned to relocate its London headquarters, then in the tony Knightsbridge section of West London, Reichmann decided to accelerate construction of two waterside buildings that were to have been part of the project's second phase.

Had Texaco been a U.K. corporation, its signing may well have loosened the logjam of indifference and skepticism that obstructed Olympia & York in London. As it was, the selling of Canary Wharf only grew more difficult as the deadline neared. Midlevel employees of Morgan Stanley and Credit Suisse not only became increasingly vociferous in their private bad-mouthing of the project but compromised the confidentiality of the critical mass clause of the firm's contract with Olympia & York. "It was supposed to be a secret, but every time I went to the City, guys would say, 'Well, we hear Morgan Stanley and First Boston aren't going to have to go to Canary Wharf after all so why should we?' " recalled Peter Marano, Olympia & York's leasing director.

In the higher corporate echelons of the United Kingdom, meanwhile, the onset of recession was lengthening the odds against the project. Having boomed for nearly a decade, the London property market staggered into 1990 like a hod carrier under a double load of brick. The British equivalent of the prime lending rate had risen to 15 percent from 8.5 percent in mid-1987, and as the sharply rising cost of money stifled economic activity, big corporations postponed or canceled plans to move into expanded office quarters and began economizing, often by laying off workers. The vacancy rate in central London had more than tripled, to 10 percent, over the preceding two years, and with a staggering thirty-five million square feet of additional space under construction, U.K. developers were bracing for a replay of the property collapse of the early 1970s. Paul Reichmann's pet project in Docklands, the *Economist* presciently quipped in late 1989, "is in danger of becoming a $7 billion White Elephant Wharf."

In their public statements, Reichmann and Michael Dennis ignored the fog bank of gloom that had enveloped London property and continued to proclaim their belief in the inevitability of Canary Wharf's success and of the brightness of London's future as the emergent capital of the new Europe. Reichmann backed up his defiant words with £30 million cash when an ill-conceived attempt by Rosehaugh PLC to shore up its balance sheet by selling new shares of stock stirred panic selling of property shares on the London Stock Exchange.

As Rosehaugh's joint venture partner in Broadgate and other developments, Stanhope Properties came in for especially rough treatment, knocking down the value of Olympia & York's 33 percent stake. Like John D. Rockefeller in the Crash of 1929, Reichmann stepped in and stanched the bloodletting by buying up big blocks of Rosehaugh. In accumulating a 10 percent stake in ailing Rosehaugh, Reichmann was said by the *Financial Times* to be "signalling a striking vote of confidence in London."

Meanwhile, in its pursuit of tenants, Olympia & York refused to match the hefty discounts offered by anxious landlords in central London, standing firm on a base rent of £27 to £30 per square foot. To be sure, the company baited its tenant trap with rent-free periods, fitting-out allowances, signing bonuses, and other increasingly liberal cash inducements that had the effect of reducing by as much as half the net cost of occupancy in the early years of a twenty-five-year lease.

Thanks to a flurry of June deals—all with American-based companies—Olympia & York squeaked under the deadline. After six months of wooing, the London office of the advertising agency Ogilvy & Mather consented to lease 100,000 square feet while Skidmore, Owings & Merrill did its bit for client relations by leasing 46,000 square feet in the project it had master-planned. Manufacturers Hanover Trust, the big New York City bank, took 200,000 square feet in One Canada Square, and American Express Company on June 25 signed up for its own 300,000-square-foot building. At nine o'clock on June 29, the day before the deadline, Olympia & York crossed the threshold, thanks to one additional small lease. To varying degrees, Reichmann involved himself personally in all these last-minute deals. "He was right there, hovering, while we were getting it done but he didn't seem as focused as usual," Marano recalled. "He looked like he was under a lot of stress."

Meeting the deadline alleviated Reichmann's burden only marginally. He had avoided disaster, for the moment, that is, but Canary Wharf's fate still hung in the balance. Tenants still had to be found for half of the 4.5 million square feet of space in the project's first phase. And where was Reichmann going to find the additional cash to make good on the extravagant concessions he had made to the new tenants? John Zuccotti and Sandy Frucher had taken the lead in negotiating the Manufacturers Hanover and American Express deals not only because these companies were based in New York but because Michael Dennis and other members of the London staff had balked at the generosity of the terms. "We in New York saved the day, but the deals we did were extremely costly to the company," Frucher admitted. "These were real, drop-your-pants deals." The fitting-out allowance granted American Express alone was more than £30 million, or £100 per square foot. All told, Olympia & York had assumed responsibility for more than a half-dozen leases, which could end up costing it as much as £25 million a year for the duration of the recession.

It was no wonder that the attainment of contractual critical mass brought not even the slightest pause in Reichmann's wheeling and dealing. In July, Olympia & York signed several more lease deals, including a small one with London Wall Holdings, which was Canary Wharf's first British tenant and the first Lloyd's of London member agency to forsake the City, and another with the *Daily Telegraph*, which took 125,000 square feet in One Canada Square. To cinch the deal, Reichmann reluctantly bought the *Telegraph*'s six-story building just 100 yards from Canary Wharf for £40 million, or £15 million more than the newspaper had paid five years earlier. The *Daily Telegraph* was controlled by Conrad Black, who certainly did not let his friendship with Reichmann stand in the way of extracting a deal hugely advantageous to himself and his company.

Reichmann had had to pay through the nose, but he had gotten what he needed: a fistful of long-term leases with base rents of between £27 and £30 per square foot. The sum total of payments to which Olympia & York was entitled over the next twenty-five years under these contracts was enormous— more than £400 million under the American Express agreement alone. Four buildings had been preleased in their entirety and, according to Olympia & York's reckoning, would operate at a profit from the day they were occupied. These were the sorts of numbers that Reichmann literally could take to the bank and the sooner the better, for Olympia & York had reached the limits of its ability to finance Canary Wharf, yet it still required about $1 billion to finish Phase I. At the time Olympia & York had inherited Canary Wharf, Reichmann had vowed that he would persist with its construction through two recessions, if need be. The Master Builder's sincerity was beyond question, but his judgment was something else again.

———

During 1990, the major Jewish organizations of the world abruptly shifted emphasis from raising their voices in protest of Moscow's treatment of Jews to raising funds to finance their mass emigration and resettlement. Nearly 187,000 Jews would leave the Soviet Union by year's end—more than double 1989's record total of 70,000—and predictions abounded that a majority of the 1.8 million Jews remaining would flee within a few years, even though the USSR had discarded all but the last vestiges of official anti-Semitism. The issue no longer was government oppression; it was fear. Gorbachev's political reforms had combined with the Soviet Union's continuing economic collapse to stir up a maelstrom of anger and ethnic chauvinism of such intensity that it seemed a portent of civil war. As Pamyat (meaning "Memory") and other street-level hate groups became increasingly brazen in their anti-Semitic agitation, Jewish circles were flooded with whispered rumors of impending pogroms.

The United Jewish Appeal set a goal of raising $400 million for a special campaign, "Operation Exodus," to speed Russian Jews to safety abroad. Albert Reichmann was approached but declined to contribute, citing other priorities. As a supporter of the refusenik cause, he took a measure of satisfaction in the winning of free emigration but continued to focus his philanthropic efforts abroad on rebuilding religious infrastructure. Right from the start, many U.S. and Canadian government officials had advised that any attempt to replant Judaism in Communism's stony soil was bound to fail. "They felt I was naive, and maybe I was," Reichmann said in mid-1989, "but I felt that most people are better off to stay than to leave." Even as the mass exodus from the USSR began, Reichmann continued to attach more weight to the opportunities opened by the restoration of religious and political liberties than to the threat of recrudescent anti-Semitism, disturbing as it was. In fact, in both the USSR and Hungary, Reichmann stepped up his giving in 1990 and 1991.

Reichmann gave directly to virtually every Orthodox rabbi, shaliach, mohel, shohet, sofer, and mashgiah operating in the Soviet Union. Reichmann money also was funneled into the restoration of dozens of cemeteries and Jewish monuments throughout the country and formed the financial foundation of a network of small yeshivas set up by Agudath Israel in Kishinev, Vilnius, Baku, Tbilisi, and other cities. Albert even provided financial assistance to Hasidic sects that organized group pilgrimages to their towns of origin in the Ukraine and Byelorussia. With heavy backing from Reichmann, the Union of Jewish Religious Communities in the USSR was set up in Moscow to weave together the various local strands of emergent Orthodoxy into a single national communal organization.

Meanwhile, Reichmann joined forces with the World Jewish Congress and its president, Edgar Bronfman, to simultaneously de-Sovietize and kosherize Moscow's Great Synagogue. Its head, Rabbi Adolf Shayevich, was a government appointee who had sat on the USSR's official anti-Zionist committee and was suspected by many of his congregants of being a KGB operative. Reichmann took the lead in getting Rabbi Shayevich to step aside and in persuading the Moscow community to accept in his stead Rabbi Pinchas Goldschmidt, an ultra-Orthodox firebrand from Israel. "In Moscow, the Jews were still very scared, even of other Jews who held official status," said Mordecai Neustadt, the Agudath Israel activist. "Mr. Reichmann, with all his status, helped a lot to make people feel more secure, more chutzapanik." Rabbi Goldschmidt also supplanted Rabbi Shayevich at the helm of the Union of Jewish Religious Communities, and thereby became chief rabbi of the USSR in all but name. With Reichmann's backing, Rabbi Goldschmidt founded Moscow's first strictly Orthodox yeshiva and a women's seminary, as well.

Reichmann continued to meet at irregular intervals with Mikhail Gorbachev, who seemed increasingly eager to publicize the possibility of major capital investment by the Olympia & York family of companies as his economic reforms ran into stiffening political opposition. Tass, the official Soviet news agency, reported in May 1990 that the Soviet president and the Canadian billionaire had again conferred in the Kremlin and noted that "Gorbachev supported Reichmann's activity and stressed its particular importance during this crucial moment in the transformation of the Soviet national economy" and that Reichmann "expressed understanding and readiness to help perestroika succeed in specific, mutually profitable forms of co-operation." As this carefully qualified statement implied, Reichmann's feet were getting cold. Gulf Canada's negotiations on the Arctic joint venture were progressing nicely but the Abitibi-Price recycling plant, the Moscow office tower, and various lesser projects were foundering on perestroika's dimming prospects.

In Hungary, it was a much different story. Ever since the ouster of the Kádár regime, foreign companies had poured money into Hungary, which many North American multinationals viewed as a port of entry into all of Eastern Europe. "If you stand in a lobby of the Forum Hotel, you are lucky not to get knocked down. A gold rush is on in Hungary," observed Mark Palmer in early 1990 just before he resigned as U.S. ambassador to Hungary to manage the Central European Development Corporation (CEDC), a private investment vehicle that began with $50 million supplied by a select group of North American investors of Hungarian descent, including Albert Reichmann and Andy Sarlos. Ronald Lauder, an heir to the Estée Lauder cosmetics fortune and a former ambassador to Austria, was the combine's chairman and dominant partner. CEDC got off to a quick start by spending $10 million to acquire a half interest in a venerable Budapest merchant bank and began scouting additional investments throughout Eastern Europe.

Olympia & York soon teamed with CEDC and the Sarlos-Soros investment vehicle, First Hungary Fund, to launch a $100 million construction project in Budapest. The twelve-story office building was to be the new headquarters of Magyar Hitel Bank, Hungary's largest bank, which contributed a choice piece of downtown property to the undertaking in exchange for a 50 percent ownership interest. Olympia & York was to manage the project for a fee and also invest $5 million for a 17 percent stake.

These were both substantial ventures, especially by Hungarian standards, but of less interest to Reichmann personally than the work of his Endowment for Democracy in Eastern Europe. On December 17, the seventh evening of Hanukkah, in 1990, some 2,500 people gathered in the Budapest Convention Center for the dedication of the American Endowment School—also known as Mesorat Avoth, but best known as the Reichmann school—the first private parochial school of any sort to open in Hungary since the advent of Communist rule in 1948. Albert Reichmann played host to numerous Jewish dignitaries from around the world as well as Hungary's foreign minister and the

U.S., Canadian, and Israeli ambassadors to Hungary. Of all of Reichmann's philanthropic projects, the Budapest school was dearest to his heart. "My father gets absolutely emotional at fund-raising dinners for the school when he hears young Hungarians discussing things Jewish," Philip Reichmann said. "He doesn't like to admit it, but the fact is the school in Budapest is especially important to him because the family came from Hungary."

For years, a state-run Jewish high school had operated in Budapest but it offered only two hours a week of Jewish studies, conformed to the official ban against the teaching of Hebrew, and by 1986 had an enrollment of nine. By contrast, the Reichmann school was a full-fledged Jewish day school in the North American mold, spanning kindergarten through twelfth grade and combining religious and secular instruction in roughly equal measure. The Hungarian government, which was still Communist after all, had been grudging in its support of the school, consigning the endowment's license application to bureaucratic limbo for about a year. "Finally, we told the government that Reichmann was coming to Budapest next week and he was expecting a document to sign," said David Gold, an American of Romanian descent whom David Moskovits recruited to serve as codirector of the school project. "The only reason we got the license was the power of the Reichmann name. That was more important even than the money."

The government granted the Endowment for Democracy a fifty-year lease on a century-old hulk of a building, one façade of which had marked the border of the Jewish ghetto established during the Nazi occupation and which served as a makeshift hospital. Before World War II, 44 Wesselenyi Street had housed one of the city's best Jewish schools. (Among its alumni was Joe Lebovic, the Toronto developer, who contributed $50,000 toward its restoration. "It would have cost me a hell of a lot more," Lebovic said, "if Albert had known I'd been a student there.") After the war, the Communist authorities used the building as a vocational school and allowed it to deteriorate badly. Reichmann laid out $1 million to modernize the structure and also guaranteed the Ministry of Education that he would cover any shortfall in the school's projected $1.5 million operating budget from his own pocket.

The school's birth was complicated not only by government foot-dragging but by partisan wrangling within the Jewish community itself. The local Zionists, bolstered by the restoration of diplomatic relations between Israel and Hungary, wanted a school primarily dedicated to transforming Hungarians into Israelis. While Moskovits faced heavy pressure from his fellow Hasidim back home in New York to create a school in their image, the Neologues in Budapest were adamantly opposed to a narrowly ultra-Orthodox curriculum. Ron Lauder entered into competition with Reichmann by organizing a nonreligious Jewish school of his own in Budapest. Finally, there was bad blood between Moskovits and the World Jewish Congress's Hungarian liaison, who was so active in support of the school that Moskovits came to suspect him of trying to usurp his share of the credit for its founding.

Reichmann's talent for conciliation was sorely tested but prevailed in the end, resulting in an institution that began by playing it right down the middle. The American Endowment School served three kosher meals a day and required male students to wear yarmulkes but was evenly balanced between the teaching of Jewish culture and of Judaism per se. The World Zionist Organization, Israel's educational arm, supported but did not dominate the school, supplying a dozen of its sixty-seven teachers. Designed for 350 children, the school opened with a student body of 498 and soon expanded to 550. The school's popularity was not a pure barometer of Jewish yearning, for it offered English language instruction in place of the Russian long imposed by the government, easily outclassed the typical public school in terms of quality, and yet charged no tuition. Even so, at a time when Hungarians by the thousands were stepping forward to assert the Jewish identity they had kept hidden, sending estimates of the country's Jewish population soaring from 80,000 to 200,000, the Reichmann school unquestionably helped awaken a long-suppressed appetite for the meat that had been missing in Goulash Judaism.

Chapter 44

Without anyone quite noticing, the commercial property business had taken leave of economic reality some time in the mid-1980s. From 1985 to 1989, the national office vacancy rate in the United States had risen by a double-digit figure every year, yet developers had continued to add to supply in record amounts, inspired by the optimism native to their species and by the profligate lending of banks large and small. Although the United States led the world in overbuilding brought on by overlending, the same basic phenomenon occurred in Australia, Canada, Japan, Great Britain, and the Scandinavian nations. Banks "have rarely overlent so extensively and for so long as they did against land and commercial buildings in the 1980s," the Wall Street credit expert James Grant later noted in testimony before Congress. When the advent of global recession in 1990 finally brought bankers to their senses, almost every city in North America and foreign capitals from Stockholm to Tokyo were left with canyons of unwanted, uneconomic office space.

New York City, the cornerstone of the Reichmanns' property empire, was especially hard hit. By the end of 1990, the vacancy rate on Wall Street was nearly 20 percent and in midtown a slightly less ruinous 17 percent. Rents already had dropped 10 to 15 percent from their 1987 peaks and showed no sign of bottoming out. The last time Manhattan property had been this depressed, Paul Reichmann had made the most inspired deal of his life. But a decade and a half after the Uris deal, the Reichmanns were more vulnerable than the Uris brothers had ever been. With twenty-three million square feet in fourteen skyscrapers, Olympia & York hadn't a prayer of dodging the debacle; it *was* the market in Manhattan. And as the Big Apple went, so went Olympia & York: Manhattan accounted for more than 70 percent of the company's total square footage in the United States.

Although the World Financial Center would hold up pretty well, the map of Olympia & York's lesser Manhattan holdings was immediately dotted by disaster. The company had the misfortune of owning 60 Broad Street, the headquarters of the investment bank Drexel Burnham Lambert. After coining outsized junk-bond profits all through the 1980s, Drexel declared bankruptcy in early 1990 and promptly vacated twenty-three of 60 Broad's thirty-one floors. Unwilling to pay the rent increases Olympia & York sought, ITT Corporation pulled its headquarters out of 320 Park Avenue when its lease expired at the end of the year, leaving the 640,000-square-foot structure completely empty and in desperate need of remodeling. Two Broadway, the oldest of the Uris buildings, was 40 percent vacant. Olympia & York's largest Manhattan tower, 55 Water Street, was 90 percent occupied, but nearly half of its existing leases were set to expire over the next two years and tenants were demanding large decreases in rents in line with the collapsing market.

In Toronto, which was second only to New York in importance to the Reichmanns' real estate fortunes, it was a less dire version of the same sorry tale. Olympia & York's four largest office towers were reporting a combined vacancy rate of nearly 17 percent, compared with 11 percent for the downtown market as a whole. The company's stubborn refusal to match lower rents and other incentives offered by rival landlords already had cost it several sizable tenants at First Bank Tower, where the vacancy rate had soared above 20 percent. Finally, Philip Reichmann, Olympia & York's senior vice president for office leasing, invited the city's commercial real estate brokers to lunch at First Canadian Place to make what the *Globe & Mail* later characterized as "a startling admission"—that is, the company "would willingly slash rents and offer the enticing deals that, in the past, it had dismissed."

Meanwhile, the recession exposed the critical structural defect in Olympia & York's foundation. During the 1980s the Reichmann brothers had attempted to hedge their colossal investment in real estate by spending some $10 billion to acquire major industrial corporations. But instead of giving Olympia & York the buoy to windward it needed in the turbulent property markets of the early 1990s, the acquired companies dropped into deficit faster than a two-ton anchor. Campeau Corporation was an unmitigated disaster. Meanwhile, Gulf Canada, which accounted for 35 percent of the Reichmanns' investment portfolio, and Abitibi-Price both posted sizable losses in 1990 and took a pounding in the stock markets. All told, the value of Olympia & York's stock portfolio dropped by about $1 billion in 1990 and would lose another $1 billion the following year.

By the fall of 1990, Olympia & York was in serious jeopardy. The market value of the company's assets still exceeded its $20 billion in liability by a substantial if shrinking margin, but Olympia & York's cash flow had diminished to the point where Reichmann could not continue to finance Canary Wharf from his own corporate coffers and have enough left over to meet the payments coming due on Olympia & York's massive debts. To halt work in Docklands until the recession had run its course would waste Olympia & York's hard-won marketing momentum in London (modest though it was), require a massive writedown of the company's multibillion-dollar investment, and, in Reichmann's judgment, run a high risk of damaging the project's credibility beyond hope of recovery. The prospect of his beloved Canary Wharf degenerating into White Elephant Wharf was simply unbearable to Reichmann. On the other hand, Canary Wharf was no less likely to fall to rack and ruin if Olympia & York began defaulting on its debts and thus invited the all-encompassing doom of forced bankruptcy.

In hindsight, the prudent thing would have been for Reichmann to gather his many creditors together, present them with a comprehensive restructuring plan, and ask their forbearance while he implemented it. The odds would have been in Reichmann's favor, for Olympia & York's creditors were not likely to want to wager $20 billion on the dubious proposition that the company was worth more dead than alive. But candor carried a mortal risk of its own. Even the bankers who knew Olympia & York best had no real appreciation of the severity of its cash-flow problems, and the shock of discovery might well have panicked the company's lenders into an every-man-for-himself stampede, thus precipitating the very bankruptcy Reichmann hoped to avoid. Perhaps more to the point, to throw himself on the mercy of his creditors ran counter to the Master Builder's every instinct, especially his predilections for privacy and control. He would have had to open his books to outside scrutiny and suffer committees of bankers breathing down his neck and second-guessing him at every turn. And, he would have had to undergo a public humiliation as the press retailored his legend to fit the reality of failure.

Even so, had Reichmann known that real estate values would plummet in 1991 and continue falling into 1993, and that commercial real estate would not begin to rebound until 1995, he no doubt would have taken his medicine with all due haste. As always, though, his economic outlook was biased toward optimism; he trusted to the future. More important, he believed in his own abilities to guide Olympia & York through whatever lay ahead as absolutely as he continued to believe in the inevitability of Canary Wharf's success. In other words, Reichmann decided to wing it, to keep his arms and legs churning like a broad-jumper in midleap until economic recovery took hold and restored the foundations of Olympia & York's prosperity.

———

In the waning months of 1990, Reichmann at last arranged a megaloan to finance the construction of Canary Wharf, thus buying himself some time. A syndicate of eleven international banks advanced £500 million, or about $980 million, while the European Investment Bank separately provided another £100 million, specifically for infrastructure work. Reichmann had to agree to a higher rate of interest than usual but breathed a sigh of relief, for he figured he now had in hand all the money he needed to complete the first phase of the project.

Meanwhile, Reichmann began his own piecemeal restructuring of Olympia & York, the most visible aspect of which involved the sale of large pieces of the empire. Olympia & York sold off much of what it had acquired through its 1986 raid on Hiram Walker: Consumers Gas, a utility company, brought in $900 million; the U.S. assets of Interprovincial Pipeline $580 million; and the 10 percent stake in Allied-Lyons, the British beverage giant, $800 million. Although the bulk of the proceeds of these sales went to retire the loans taken out to finance the Hiram Walker deal in the first place, a few hundred million dollars were left over for Reichmann to play with. Virtually the entire remaining contents of Olympia & York's tattered stock market portfolio also was put up for sale—Gulf Canada and Abitibi-Price included—but Reichmann continued to demand higher prices than anyone was willing to pay.

The real estate market was so depressed that the Reichmanns as a rule could not have sold their major office properties at prices that even covered the mortgages on them. Olympia & York did sell some real estate odds and ends, as well as the tile company, to members of the Reichmann family for a total price of about $460 million. Wealthy families have been known to strip companies of choice assets in anticipation of a bankruptcy filing, but the Reichmanns were trying to bolster Olympia & York at their own expense, paying full price for properties that were among the least attractive in the corporate portfolio. All told, the family sank some $620 million in cash into Olympia & York during the year-and-a-half preceding its bankruptcy. "From a family point of view, we compounded the mistakes we made at Olympia & York by adding to our investment in the company," Paul later admitted. "The simple explanation is that we just did not expect the company to collapse."

The Reichmanns laid off a few hundred Olympia & York employees and took other measures to both reduce the company's costs and squeeze more cash out of its operations. In the case of the condo conversion partnerships with Oskar Brecher, Olympia & York completely liquidated the assets—the inventory of unsold apartments—and took its loss. Although Brecher himself had no personal liability, Olympia & York's partners in the Washington projects—Myer Feldman and Scott and Gary Nordheimer—were obligated to reimburse Olympia & York for half the losses. When the trio refused to pay, Olympia & York sued and won. But by the time the case was completed, the Nordheimers had filed for bankruptcy.

Olympia & York shunted aside David Chase as manager of the two joint-venture buildings in Hartford, though the developer retained his 50 percent equity interest. Chase, who had pocketed millions of dollars in management fees during his association with the Reichmanns, put up a determined fight, flying off to Toronto to lobby Albert at every turn of the screw. To the amazement of Olympia & York executives, Albert in the end softened the blow of Chase's removal by lending the Connecticut multimillionaire $10 million for a completely unrelated venture. In Florida, David Shapiro proved himself more adept in clinging to the Reichmann gravy train than he had ever been at development. "I think the problem in Florida was that Albert didn't want to have a personal conflict with Bill Shapiro over his son's performance, awful as it was," said one Olympia & York executive. The Reichmanns' partnership with the Shapiros would not be dissolved until the spring of 1992.

The Reichmanns quietly withdrew from the office towers planned for Moscow and Budapest and also from the Jerusalem City Hall project, which was still about two years from completion. Albert had committed to supplying as much as $30 million of construction financing, which the city of Jerusalem would pay off gradually over a twenty-year period. However, in early 1991 Paul shut off the cash spigot and dispatched one of his most trusted lieutenants, Israeli native Michael Astrachan, to Jerusalem to try to get back the $17.6 million that Olympia & York already had advanced to the city. Teddy Kollek's administration graciously let the Reichmanns off the hook, taking out a bank loan to repay the brothers in full.

———

In February 1991, the Reichmanns reached an out-of-court settlement with Elaine Dewar and *Toronto Life* magazine, ending a legal battle of three years' duration shortly before Olympia & York's suit was to have gone to trial. Under the terms of her agreement with the family, Dewar withdrew the book she had written about the family. Meanwhile, *Toronto Life*, which had exhausted its $1 million libel insurance policy in the pretrial skirmishing, agreed to make hefty contributions to four local charities selected by the Reichmanns—the Hospital for Sick Children, Mount Sinai Research Institution, the Toronto Hospital, and the John P. Robarts Research Institute—and published an extraordinarily abject full-page apology, quoted here in part:

> Let us unequivocally and categorically say that any and all negative insinuations and allegations in the article about the Reichmann family and Olympia & York are totally false. The Reichmann family has earned an enviable reputation over the years, not only since coming to Canada but also prior to that in Tangier, Vienna and Hungary, as a family of great integrity and adhering to strict ethical principles in all of its activities. We sincerely regret having published an article which could have in any way undermined this reputation.

The Reichmanns clearly had triumphed, but in settling short of a trial had failed to fulfill Paul's pledge to press the lawsuit against *Toronto Life* "until every part of this story is proved false" in court. In a 1996 interview, Paul said he could not recall exactly why he and his brothers decided to settle the case but that it "had gone on long enough and that the terms of the settlement proved that the allegations were wrong." The *Toronto Life* article had indeed been discredited, but many of the questions raised had not been laid to rest with definitive answers, in part because Olympia & York's lawyers introduced in evidence only a fraction of the information gathered by the Jules Kroll investigative agency. Although Paul insisted that the Kroll firm turned up nothing untoward about his parents' activities in Tangier, he confessed to having second thoughts about the decision to sue *Toronto Life*. "I'm ambivalent about whether it was worth it," he said. "Perhaps in time the article would have just been discarded as rubbish anyway."

To the Reichmanns' dismay, their victory over *Toronto Life* did not deter Leo Heaps. In 1992, more than seven years after Heaps began working on his Reichmann book, the British edition of *Esquire* magazine would publish a Heaps-penned article, "Empire of the Sons," that purported to reveal "the true story of the Reichmanns and the family secret that they were so desperate to conceal." The piece, which was filled with basic errors of fact, depicted Samuel Reichmann as a craven opportunist and alleged that on at least one occasion he had trafficked with Nazi Germany during World War II. Albert, Paul, and Ralph immediately sued for libel in London, naming Heaps and *Esquire* as defendants. The suit was still pending when Heaps died of a heart attack in 1995. The Reichmann family and *Esquire* have yet to settle.

—

It is one of finance's cruelest truisms that creditworthiness is inversely correlated to need—that is, a lender is most likely to extend credit to the borrower who seems most capable of doing without it. Determining creditworthiness is as much art as science, for it is essentially an exercise in predicting the future: How likely is Company X to repay a loan of Y dollars over the next Z years? Typically, such judgments are based on an analysis of voluminous amounts of confidential financial data provided by the prospective borrower and updated quarterly once a loan has been made.

In the beginning, Olympia & York had been subject to the same disclosure rules as every other small, unproven developer. As the company grew, Paul Reichmann induced major banks to relax their requirements to accommodate his desire for privacy. The exemption he won was rooted in solid achievement, for Olympia & York was a superbly proficient developer with an unblemished if brief credit history. Ultimately, the star treatment Reichmann was afforded in banking circles was a function of his own understated brand of charisma.

"Paul's demeanor was just so different. He always seemed like more of a wise man than a developer," recalled one senior Canadian banker who approved a series of large loans to Olympia & York. "Soft-spoken, highly intelligent, seemingly open, he presented himself as a brilliant yet humble visionary, and bank presidents and chairmen just ate it up." After the Uris deal, his aura glowed with an intensity that bedazzled all but the most disciplined bankers. In short, Paul Reichmann was one of history's biggest beneficiaries of a practice known in banking parlance as "lending on C"—on character.

In negotiating the terms of loans, Reichmann mixed aggression and accommodation in disarming fashion. On one hand, he was utterly relentless in trying to borrow as cheaply as possible. On the other hand, he went to unusual lengths to assure bankers that they would get their money back. Typically, developers shield their companies from the risks of their building projects by financing each one as a freestanding venture. This way, if a project goes awry, the most the developer can lose is title to the building in question; the bank has no legal recourse to his corporate assets. Although Reichmann, too, financed each building separately for tax reasons, he typically backed his project loans with a corporate guarantee. In other words, if worse came to worst, Olympia & York itself would be legally obligated to make the lender whole. While Reichmann's willingness to put his whole company behind every project he did seemed in itself an affirmation of his moral superiority, his liberal use of corporate guarantees tended to paper over the underlying issue of Olympia & York's creditworthiness. Ultimately, the guarantees had value only insofar as the company was able as well as willing to pay off its debts.

For years, Reichmann provided his bankers with earnings statements and balance sheets that were rudimentary at best, and it was not until the late 1970s that he bothered to get an unqualified opinion from a Big Eight accounting firm. Bankers did know more about the company than did journalists but not by much, and, like everyone else, they tended to be overawed by the often exaggerated report that they read in the newspapers. The company began to open up a bit in the early 1980s, mainly as a consequence of Reichmann's drive to tap into the public credit markets. To issue bonds secured by 59 Maiden Lane, 55 Water Street, or any of the other half-dozen office towers refinanced in this manner, the company was required by law to issue a prospectus. While the Reichmanns ended up disclosing a great deal of financial data about their major properties, Olympia & York itself remained securely shrouded from view.

The essential problem Reichmann's bankers faced was not knowing what they did not know, beginning with Olympia & York's organizational structure, which was not set down on paper until after it collapsed. Consisting of more than fifty distinct entities interwoven with one another and with a network of family partnerships, Olympia & York was almost infernally complex. Only Paul

Reichmann understood exactly how all the parts fit together, and he guarded the knowledge closely. "The one thing that Paul never gave out was a consolidating audit—one that showed all the intracompany transactions and contingencies," said the same senior banker quoted above. "As it turned out, he did a lot of special deals with people that were never written down. I don't think he had his own private ledger or anything, but he'd do deals that had to be papered after the fact—handshake, I'll-take-care-of-you type of deals that even other Olympia & York people didn't know about."

There is nothing to suggest that Reichmann's dealings were illicit, though certainly quite a number of them proved to be misguided. Nor was Olympia & York's might a product of promotional smoke and mirrors; its cash flow and net worth may have been puffed up in the rumor mill but were genuinely enormous nonetheless. Paul Reichmann was not a con man but a dreamer whose penchant for secrecy was equally a product of a generalized mistrust of others and a desire to maximize his entrepreneurial prerogatives. The less that lenders, rival developers, regulators, and the public at large knew about Olympia & York's inner workings, the greater the leverage Reichmann gained over the potentially malevolent forces arrayed against him as an ultra-Orthodox immigrant Jew, and the freer he was to indulge his genius for improvisation and experiment.

Reichmann's increasingly desperate efforts to retain the confidence of Olympia & York's lenders led him to what amounted to a double life. In private, he was the Harry Houdini of real estate, scrambling continuously to extricate himself from the spike-lined coffins and padlocked straitjackets of Olympia & York's excessive indebtedness. In public, he carried on in the mode of magisterial invincibility he had adopted in taking over Canary Wharf. Although Reichmann did admit that his diversification drive had not panned out, he conceded nothing to critics of his Docklands project and seemed to welcome the recession as a fresh opportunity to display his contrarian brilliance. "Our future growth will be in real estate," he proclaimed in a *Time* magazine interview. "We will build when everyone else has stopped building." Rumors that he was running short of cash were "rubbish," Reichmann huffily informed *The Wall Street Journal,* and those who suggested otherwise, he told *The New York Times,* were "children who don't know what they are talking about."

Having failed to disclose Olympia & York's sale of a 35 percent interest in the World Financial Center to Edper in 1989, Reichmann compounded his offense in the fall of 1990 by secretly buying back a portion of the stake for the family's own account. When Edper's Carena Development unit had bought the stake, Reichmann had promised Jack Cockwell that he would find a third party to buy him out by June 1990. But with the Manhattan real estate market a shambles,

Reichmann was unable to attract an investor that was both suitably docile and willing to meet Carena's asking price. By August, Cockwell's patience had worn thin and he put Reichmann on formal notice with a letter. Unless Olympia & York itself bought back the World Financial Center stake within thirty days, Cockwell warned, Edper would find its own buyer, exposing Reichmann to the risk of having to share control of his prize complex with an unfriendly new partner. Over the next few months, Reichmann and Cockwell worked out a compromise. On October 31, an obscure Reichmann family company, 917024 Ontario Incorporated, bought 50 percent of Carena's stake for $140 million, borrowing the entire sum from a second Edper company. Ironically, the Reichmann family thus became a silent 17.5 percent partner in Paul's proudest creation.

Although Reichmann later would refuse categorically to comment on his dealings with Carena, the logic behind this transaction seemed plain enough. Edper was able to remove from its balance sheet an equity investment of dwindling value by converting it to a loan. Meanwhile, Reichmann consolidated his control of his flagship U.S. property without having to lay out any cash whatsoever. For Reichmann especially, this was one sweet deal—so sweet, in fact, that it cast doubt on the assurances he had given to the executives of his U.S. subsidiary at the end of 1989. What he had insisted was a genuine sale done at arm's length now had metamorphosed into a loan advanced on terms highly advantageous to him. Had they known of it, Olympia & York's outside auditors might well have insisted on revising the company's 1989 financial statements to reclassify the sale to Carena as a loan instead. That not only would have played havoc with Olympia & York's finances—turning an annual profit into a loss while reducing net worth and boosting indebtedness—but would have cast doubt upon the integrity of its accounting and caused lenders to wonder generally what was going on with Olympia & York.

Reichmann evaded the potentially lethal problem posed by his sweetheart deal by keeping it secret from his American executives, who would have been obligated to disclose it to their auditors and to Olympia & York's partners in the World Financial Center. Later, when the transaction came to light, Reichmann went so far as to deny that it had taken place on the grounds that the paperwork documenting it was not completed until after Olympia & York had declared bankruptcy. However, Carena Development's own actions put the lie to Reichmann's claim, for in January 1991, Edper reported the transaction as a completed sale to the Internal Revenue Service.

Even as he was negotiating his secret compromise with Cockwell, Reichmann had become embroiled in his first potentially ruinous showdown with a lender. In mid-1989, Sanwa Bank had loaned Olympia & York $530 million against One Liberty Plaza, the former Merrill Lynch headquarters in New York. With the Japanese economy running short of the essential lubricant of credit, the Ministry of Finance in 1990 had begun pressuring Japanese banks to reduce their foreign loan balances and repatriate their capital. To Reichmann's dismay, Sanwa Bank demanded that the One Liberty Plaza loan be paid off in full when it came due on October 22. Reichmann did not have $530 million in cash lying around but even if he had, complying with Sanwa's wishes would have set a dangerous precedent. While Sanwa's legal entitlement to demand its money back was clear, Olympia & York did have the option of extinguishing its debt by surrendering ownership of the building to Sanwa, for this was one loan that Reichmann had not backed with a corporate guarantee. This gave the Japanese pause, for One Liberty Plaza's market value now was well below $530 million.

The impasse persisted long past the due date as the Sanwa–Olympia & York loan agreement was amended on October 22, October 29, November 16, and November 21. On Christmas Day, Reichmann flew to Tokyo with John Zuccotti to take up the matter at the highest levels of Sanwa Bank and the Japanese government. Reichmann had become accustomed to triumphing through sheer force of will, but in Tokyo he met his match. A compromise agreement was effected through an additional series of amendments dated January 11, January 30, February 6, February 13, February 26, February 28, and March 21, 1991. Reichmann eventually managed to persuade Sanwa to defer repayment of the balance of the loan indefinitely but only by agreeing to make two $100 million payments, the first of which was due forthwith. Later, Reichmann would conclude that he had erred in settling with Sanwa, that Olympia & York would have been better off husbanding its cash and letting the bank seize One Liberty Plaza.

Olympia & York's other banks were aware of the confrontation with Sanwa but tended to interpret it as evidence not of the fragility of Reichmann's finances but of Japanese unreasonableness. Not many companies could be expected to willingly make a lump sum payment of $530 million, especially in the midst of a recession. However, Olympia & York was unable to muster even the first $100 million due Sanwa from its diminished cash flow. Reichmann made the payment from the proceeds of a new $160 million loan advanced in June 1991 by a group of North American and European banks led by J. P. Morgan & Company, which publicly reaffirmed its confidence in Olympia & York. The Morgan group drove a hard bargain just the same, requiring that Olympia & York mortgage its interests in the World Financial Center and other New York office towers. If the Morgan syndicate had realized that Reichmann intended to use the bulk of the funds to pay down the Sanwa loan, they probably would not have advanced the money in the first place.

———

The private foundations created by the Vanderbilts, Rockefellers, Mellons, Fords, and other leading families of American capitalism outlasted their creators and have remained a potent social force for many decades. Rather than distribute the interest earned on a conservatively invested capital endowment as did the great family foundations, the Reichmanns continuously gave away their principal by dipping directly into Olympia & York's massive cash flow to fund their philanthropies. Over the years, the brothers had talked sporadically of endowing a foundation or setting up an institute as a conduit for their outsized giving, but never got around to it. "It was always to do tomorrow," Paul said.

Given the vast sums at stake, Paul's casual admission of procrastination hardly suffices as an explanation of the Reichmanns' failure to utilize the common techniques of memorializing private fortunes by institutionalizing them. When prodded, Paul conceded that he and his brothers were loath to lop off a chunk of Olympia & York's asset base to endow a billion-dollar foundation because the resulting dent in the company's balance sheet would have curtailed its ability to borrow. But he neglected to mention what would seem to have been the overriding factor in the family's unconventional approach to philanthropy: an unwillingness to delegate authority. Whereas the brothers were perfectly willing to let Olympia & York's non-Orthodox executives act as their proxies in routine business matters, their philanthropic decision making turned on their most deeply held beliefs. On whom could the brothers rely to apply their religious standards in the daily disbursement of large cash donations? A close relative, perhaps, but who among them would have been capable of administering a major nonprofit foundation? To staff Olympia & York's upper management ranks, the Reichmanns recruited talent from other development companies. But who at the Ford or Rockefeller foundations knew haskamah from Omaha?

While the brothers' intensely personal commitment to philanthropy was as laudable as it was unusual, their aversion to institutional structure proved catastrophically self-defeating. As Olympia & York's coffers ran dry in 1991, the vast flow of the brothers' giving shriveled to a trickle and then stopped utterly. "The precipitous end of their charity was the greatest aspect of the Reichmann tragedy," a top executive of a major worldwide Jewish organization lamented a few years after Olympia & York's collapse. "Even with the failure of the business, they would still be the most important people in Jewish life today if they'd only set up a foundation."

The sudden cessation of Reichmann funding sent a jolt of panic throughout the ultra-Orthodox world. For many recipients, Reichmann money was both indispensable and irreplaceable. Albert's beneficiaries in the Soviet Union were left particularly vulnerable, for Olympia & York's crisis of survival coincided with the ouster of Mikhail Gorbachev and the emergence of a rebarbative ethnic nationalism in which anti-Semitism figured prominently. In Israel, the ultra-Orthodox rabbinate considered declaring a day of prayer to beg for divine mercy—a measure usually taken only in times of war or natural disaster.

Dozens of yeshivoth and charitable institutions were faced with a choice between curtailing and even closing their operations or borrowing at exorbitant interest rates to make up for lost Reichmann funding.

By most accounts, Albert took the family's financial ruination particularly hard. This seemed paradoxical, but if Paul had more reason to feel guilty, Albert, too, had ample cause for self-recrimination. Over the years, he occasionally had provided the countervailing judgment that Paul required, but rarely with sufficient force to rein him in. Then, too, while Paul was galvanized by his continuing efforts to prevent Olympia & York's collapse, Albert already had been deprived of his defining role within the family. Even if a corporate bankruptcy somehow were averted, it would be years, if ever, before the family fortune was replenished to the point where Albert could resume his shuttle philanthropy. Paul, too, deeply regretted the deterioration of the family's philanthropic legacy, but it was his nature to intellectualize its impact, while the empathetic Albert suffered rather more for his tendency to personalize things. He had gotten to know many of the people who depended on the family's largesse and now felt as if he had failed them. Like Paul, though, Albert was a stoic who suffered privately. "Even with me, my father didn't talk much about what was happening or confide his feelings but I could see it in him," said Philip, his eldest son.

Olympia & York's fate was a topic of intense speculation within Toronto's ultra-Orthodox community, which proportionally had as much riding on the outcome as the company's banks, and yet, out of respect and affection for the Reichmanns, the subject was rarely raised in the presence of family members, who, for their part, continued to go about their business as if nothing had changed. "The Reichmanns had always had a very simple social life so they didn't have far to fall socially," observed Kurt Rothschild, who took it upon himself to find alternate sources of financing for the Reichmann-sponsored schools in North York. "Someone else would have had to run away to Siberia to get away from it all, but they shook the same hands and said hello to the same people. If they were embarrassed, they didn't show it."

———

In the fall of 1991, revenue from Canary Wharf at last began trickling into Olympia & York's coffers as tenants began occupying the first of the ten buildings scheduled for completion by the spring. Morgan Stanley, the third tenant to move in, decided to operate its own fleet of minibuses to spare its employees the tribulations of commuting by the Dear Little Railway. Although by this time the British government had committed £4 billion to improving East End transport links, Canary Wharf still was not reliably accessible except by water. However, Olympia & York's tenants as a rule were delighted with the complex itself, which was hailed even before its completion as an outsized masterpiece of construction engineering, if not of architecture (professional opinion in England remained generally negative). "From the marbled caverns at the foot of its 50-storeys-high central tower to its glass-domed railway station and elegant public spaces, the Canary Wharf development is breathtaking . . . ," hailed the *Economist*. "It is already clear that the reclusive Reichmanns have honoured the commitment they made in 1987. They promised that Canary Wharf would be magnificent; and it is." And at a total cost of about $4 billion, the project would come in a mere 1 percent over budget.

For Paul Reichmann, Canary Wharf's opening was intensely bittersweet. On one hand, the complex as realized struck exactly the blend of colossality and elegance for which he had strived. Sparing no expense, Reichmann commissioned a series of photographs from which he assembled a folder of exquisite poster-sized prints that he carried with him as he made his corporate rounds, like a painter toting his portfolio. As a business venture, though, Canary Wharf now was certifiably a bust. In the year preceding the opening of the first building, Olympia & York had landed only one more tenant, leaving Reichmann's Xanadu only 55 percent leased. By the fall of 1991, the London office market had gone from bad to worse, with a vacancy rate of 20 percent in the city and double that in Docklands. As the competition for tenants degenerated into a bare-knuckled struggle for survival, Olympia & York had stopped holding the line on base rents of £27 to £30 per square foot and was practically giving space away. "The horrors of the recession are bad enough," the *Economist* reported. "But London's top estate agents agreed that the Reichmanns' company, Olympia & York, is rapidly becoming the biggest bogey of all."

Swallowing his free-enterpriser's pride, Reichmann asked the British government for a helping hand. In late 1990, the Conservative Party had ousted Margaret Thatcher as prime minister, replacing her with John Major, who had toured Canary Wharf and also met with Reichmann at No. 10. "Major's attitude toward the project was no different from Thatcher's," Reichmann said carefully. "Of course, he and Thatcher were further apart in terms of character." That is, Major was less passionate in his support of Canary Wharf and less inclined to use the power of his office to accommodate Reichmann. The new prime minister did please Reichmann by shifting management responsibility for the Docklands Light Railway to the London Docklands Development Corporation but essentially ignored the developer's pleas to accelerate the construction of the Limehouse Link and the Jubilee Line. And when Environment Minister Michael Heseltine, the political godfather of Docklands redevelopment, proposed that the government itself lease space in Canary Wharf to house several thousand civil servants, Major allowed the idea to languish in political limbo week after week before finally deciding against it. There would be no government bailout of Canary Wharf.

Worse, Reichmann got nowhere in his efforts to arrange separate long-term mortgages for each of the Canary Wharf buildings. Most banks had stopped making new real estate loans by this time and instead were pressing developers to put up additional collateral to secure existing loans. Under conditions this dire, even many of the banks to which Reichmann was closest were loath to continue giving him and his rosy forecasts the benefit of the doubt. "I think Paul could have financed at a price," said an investment banker involved in Olympia & York's fund-raising efforts, "but the terms were not what he was used to getting and he dragged his feet until it was too late." By the fall of 1991, Reichmann had spent more than a year trying to refinance Canary Wharf and had nothing to show for his efforts but a single £50 million mortgage for one of the smaller buildings. It was as if the fortune that Reichmann had invested in the Docklands and now desperately needed to keep Olympia & York intact had been locked away in a safe to which he did not have the combination.

On October 24, 1991, Morgan Stanley tripped the alarm bell at Olympia & York headquarters by formally exercising its option to sell its Canary Wharf building, 25 Cabot Square, back to the developer for £128 million ($240 million). Reichmann had until midnight December 12 to come up with the cash or risk a lawsuit from one of the founding partners of Canary Wharf.

After fruitlessly making the rounds of the usual lenders in Europe and North America, Reichmann got on his Gulfstream and made a last-ditch swing through Asia in November. Accompanied by his wife and various advisers, Reichmann touched down in Tokyo, Hong Kong, and Singapore. Time and again, he walked into a business meeting and, ignoring the agenda, began showing off his photographs of Canary Wharf, oblivious to the baffled looks exchanged all around him. "In a touching, almost naive way, he'd say, 'If I can just get people to see Canary Wharf, they'll see how beautiful it is, and everything will be all right,' " said one of the aides who accompanied Reichmann. Sandy Frucher, Olympia & York's American development chief, flew halfway around the world to rendezvous with the boss in Singapore only to be told upon arrival that Reichmann had decided to meet with the chief of the Singapore Investment Authority accompanied only by his wife. Frucher, an excitable sort, was annoyed but held his tongue. "In Singapore," Frucher recalled, "Paul was as dejected as I'd ever seen him."

When asked later whether the strain of keeping Olympia & York from collapsing caused him sleepless nights, Reichmann insisted that he never let the pressure get to him. "When I can't sleep, I take a pill," he snapped. "My frame of mind was good." However, Frucher was not the only close associate capable of reading the pain through the cracks in Reichmann's stoical façade. By the time he returned from his Asian trip, the bags under his eyes were bruised by fatigue, and he was uncharacteristically prone both to hot flashes of temper and to wistful reminiscences about the old days. "He was not the same Paul, in control of everything," observed a banker who had known Reichmann for years and spoke with him two or three times a week throughout Olympia & York's unraveling. "As masterful as Paul was, he couldn't stay on top of the empire when the markets turned. Days would go by while we waited for a decision on something that should have taken an hour."

Although Reichmann failed to raise the $240 million, he did persuade Li Ka-Shing, a billionaire reputed to be the largest property owner and richest man in Hong Kong, to shell out nearly $58 million for a 49 percent interest in one of Olympia & York's most troubled properties, 60 Broad Street. To keep up appearances with his banks, Reichmann had continued to make mortgage payments on the former Drexel Burnham headquarters even though it was a lost cause, being completely vacant and in dire need of a hugely expensive remodeling to remove asbestos. Although Olympia & York received no cash from Li Ka-Shing, his investment had the effect of reducing the $160 million mortgage against the building by nearly two-thirds.

Reichmann's financing woes jolted him into admitting to himself that it was possible, though not inevitable, that Olympia & York would go bankrupt. He confided his concerns to three strategically chosen employees: George Iacobescu, one of Canary Wharf's two project managers; Frank Hauer, his son-in-law, who had been temporarily posted to London as Iacobescu's assistant; and Vinay Kapor, the senior Olympia & York architect in London. Reichmann took them aside and told them that no matter what befell the company in the months ahead, they were to see to it that each of the Canary Wharf buildings was completed. "I wanted to make sure my work would outlast the company, if it came to that," said Reichmann, who said that he chose Iacobescu, Hauer, and Kapor because "they were high enough in the organization to do what I wanted done but not too high to create panic. If I'd told Michael Dennis or Robert John, there would have been panic within the company."

As the December 12 deadline neared, James Allwin, Morgan Stanley's real estate finance chief, tried to work out a compromise with Reichmann but could not pin him down to terms. Reichmann sent a personal letter to Robert Greenhill, Morgan Stanley's senior investment banker, appealing for more time to come up with the $240 million. Greenhill talked the matter over with Allwin and others and offered a measure of leniency as the deadline arrived. "What we kept getting back from Olympia & York was that they didn't have a fundamental problem but had run into some short-term difficulties," a senior Morgan official recalled. "We said, 'OK but the time has come for us to get at least some of the money.' "

After a week of intensive negotiations, Greenhill sent a brief letter to Reichmann outlining the basis of a compromise agreement under which Olympia & York would make an immediate payment of about £50 million. Reichmann marked up the letter and sent it back. Late in the afternoon of New Year's Eve day, Morgan Stanley faxed a contract proposal to Olympia & York headquarters. The parties worked through the night, communicating by fax and telephone, and by eight the next morning seemingly had come to terms. All that remained was for Olympia & York to draw up a contract documenting the oral agreement. A few days later, though, Reichmann called Allwin to urge a change in terms. Thoroughly exasperated, Allwin told Reichmann that unless Morgan received a signed agreement soon, it would sue. On January 9, the firm made good on Allwin's threat. Olympia & York promptly countersued, alleging that Morgan Stanley was itself to blame because it had failed to arrange the loan that Olympia & York had been counting on to purchase 25 Cabot Square. It really was not much of an argument, but it bought Reichmann a bit more time to maneuver.

Chapter 45

Olympia & York's collapse into bankruptcy in 1992 had many underlying causes. Or, as one London banker put it as the end neared: "This
thing is dying of a thousand cuts"—many of which were deep and self-
inflicted. However, the mortal wound might well have been Paul Reichmann's
use of short-term debt to finance long-term assets—a cardinal error that has
been the undoing of countless empire builders and fast-money speculators
down through the ages. In the mid-1980s, many property developers increasingly had resorted to short-term borrowing in hopes that long-term interest
rates eventually would descend from double-digit levels and allow them to
secure twenty- or thirty-year mortgages at affordable rates. But none had done
so with the panache of Reichmann, who exulted in entering markets that had
been inaccessible to developers until Olympia & York proved itself the exception
to the rule. Long after rates had come down, Reichmann continued to prowl
the short-term markets in his quest for the perfect financing. If his taste for
financing exotica carried with it certain risks, so be it; he was supremely confident of his ability to improvise. And so it was that Olympia & York's collapse
began as an object lesson in the perils of financial volatility in general and of
the commercial paper market in particular.

Olympia & York entered the fateful year of 1992 with about $1.1 billion in
commercial paper, which is a generic term for corporate promissory notes of
one to ninety days' duration. Corporations typically issue commercial paper as
a lower-cost alternative to drawing down bank credit lines. The notes are purchased mainly by investment dealers and institutional investors attracted by
rates of interest slightly higher than those offered by Treasury bills and other
government-issued securities. Commercial paper is graded by the same agencies that rate corporate bonds, on the basis of their assessment of the issuer's

general creditworthiness. Reichmann was able to win coveted investment-grade ranks from the rating agencies without opening Olympia & York's books by agreeing to the unusual practice of pledging specific assets as collateral. As 1992 began, Olympia & York had three separate issues trading in the commercial paper market: one of $416 million backed by some of the Reichmann family's privately held utility assets; a second—Olympia & York Commercial Paper II—of $400 million collateralized by shares from the Reichmann stock portfolio; and a $250 million program secured by the Exchange Tower, the lesser of First Canadian Place's two towers.

On February 13, Dominion Bond Rating Service (DBRS) downgraded a $475 million bond issue secured by First Canadian Place and Olympia & York Commercial Paper II. In so doing, the DBRS took Olympia & York to task for its secretiveness. "The lack of any financial information," chided DBRS, has "created doubts in the mind of the investor." If anything, the agency's action was both belated and timid, but it alarmed many of Olympia & York's noteholders just the same. The company's finances may have been shielded from scrutiny but the carnage in real estate was plain enough. "The question is if [the Reichmanns] are not in trouble, why aren't they in trouble," said Ira Gluskin, the widely followed Bay Street real estate analyst. Commercial paper typically is rolled over when it matures—that is, the issuer gives investors new paper to replace the old instead of cashing them out. Increasingly, though, Olympia & York's noteholders were unwilling to renew; they wanted their money back.

Luckily for Reichmann, Olympia & York was on the verge of securing a large loan with Olympia & York's four main banks in Canada: Canadian Imperial Bank of Commerce (CIBC), Royal Bank of Canada, Bank of Nova Scotia (informally known as Scotiabank), and National Bank of Canada. After his unsuccessful swing through Asia in late 1991, Reichmann had turned to his Canadian banks, the so-called Gang of Four, and requested a few hundred million dollars to tide Canary Wharf through what was expected to be a difficult 1992. Although Reichmann's immediate need for cash was much more acute than he let on, he had driven his usual hard bargain over the terms of what was to have been a $240 million credit. "He could have closed that sucker any time he liked," a Gang of Four banker complained later. "But he nickeled and dimed us on every aspect of the loan." To be fair, the talks also were complicated by the banks' demand that the company put up more collateral to back its existing loans. This became a sore point after Reichmann informed the Canadians that he had already granted additional collateral to Citibank, Olympia & York's lead bank in the United States.

After the DBRS downgrading, though, Reichmann stopped his dithering and agreed to terms. On February 28, a group of Olympia & York executives (not including Reichmann) and representatives of each of the four banks gathered in the forty-fourth floor boardroom of First Bank Tower to sign the loan agreement. However, the meeting ended almost before it began when Robert Hall, a senior officer of Royal Bank, asked his fellow bankers to adjourn to a private room down the corridor. Hall said that over the preceding few days, Olympia & York had exhausted an emergency $60 million Royal Bank credit line to pay off expiring commercial paper. Worse, Hall added, most of the company's remaining $1 billion in notes would be coming due throughout March. "It was awful," recalled one of the bankers briefed by Hall. "We had been talking about advancing $240 million to help Canary Wharf and all of a sudden we were looking at an additional 600- to 700-million-dollar problem."

The loan officers returned grim-faced to the boardroom. After an angry exchange with the Olympia & York contingent, the bankers gathered their things and left. Later that afternoon, a contingent of top Olympia & York executives led by Gil Newman, Paul Reichmann's right-hand man in Toronto, called at each of the four banks to plead the company's case. Later Reichmann himself worked the telephones but to no avail.

By March 2, when the Gang of Four formally withdrew its loan proposal, the money markets were buzzing with rumors that Olympia & York was about to collapse and might take a major bank or two with it. On March 3, another $40 million slug of commercial paper came due. In the morning, noteholders lined up at CIBC, the paying agent, only to be told that they would have to wait. After a mad scramble, Olympia & York managed to come up with the cash, which was distributed to noteholders just minutes before the close of that day's trading.

Inundated with calls, Dominion Bond Rating Service reaffirmed its investment-grade ratings of Olympia & York's commercial paper and suggested that "the rumours about the company have gotten out of hand." For his part, Paul Reichmann tried to calm investors by announcing that he had made a deal to sell Olympia & York's stock in Interprovincial Pipeline for $655 million and would use some of the proceeds to retire commercial paper. However, Reichmann's admission that he had to sell assets to pay off notes served only to deepen investors' alarm and accelerated their rush to the exits. Reichmann and his finance staff spent the week of March 9 rummaging through every corporate cubbyhole in search of spare cash, rushing the day's receipts over to the paying agent banks for distribution to noteholders every evening between 5:30 and 6:30.

Into the breach stepped Donald Fullerton, the chairman and chief executive of Canadian Imperial Bank of Commerce, better known as "the Commerce." Paul Reichmann went back farther with Fullerton than with any other banker. When Olympia & York had begun doing business with the Commerce in the early 1960s, shifting its checking and payroll accounts from Royal Bank to a CIBC branch in North York, Fullerton was a young loan officer on a fast track to the top. For many years Olympia & York had done business with no other bank and ascended steadily in the hierarchy of the Commerce's corporate clientele as Fullerton climbed the managerial ladder. In 1985, Reichmann accepted Fullerton's invitation to join the Commerce's board of directors, cementing their long-standing relationship of mutual trust and symbiotic dependence. Even as Olympia & York expanded its banking roster to include ninety-one institutions by the late 1980s, the Commerce retained its status as the company's lead bank. Forthright and outspoken without being autocratic, Fullerton was respected by colleagues and rivals alike. He was planning to retire in June 1992, at age sixty, and would be succeeded by A. L. Flood, who, as the Commerce's longtime head of corporate banking, had worked closely with Olympia & York for years.

With the eruption of crisis at Olympia & York, Fullerton's hopes of a graceful exit went by the boards. No banker was more justified in resenting Paul Reichmann than Fullerton, who had been kept in the dark like everyone else. On the other hand, no banker was more culpable than Fullerton, for, as Olympia & York's lead bank, CIBC had effectively sanctioned the company's exemption from standard disclosure requirements and done more than any other Canadian lender to put Reichmann over with the world banking community. But if Fullerton was angry and embarrassed, these emotions apparently were overridden by apprehension. An Olympia & York bankruptcy would blow a big hole in Fullerton's own balance sheet, for CIBC was easily the company's largest lender, with $1.2 billion in loans outstanding.

The critical question for Fullerton and Olympia & York's bankers generally was whether the company was suffering a temporary cash squeeze—a liquidity crisis—or was hopelessly insolvent. Reichmann argued that his company's problems were transitory but did nothing to restore his tarnished image by balking still at making full financial disclosure. Fullerton apparently decided to play for time, to do what he could to keep Olympia & York afloat until he could get a better sense of the company's condition. Under his prodding, the other Gang of Four lenders agreed to join the Commerce in advancing $126 million of the recently aborted $240 million loan. At the same time, CIBC separately advanced another $30 million to Olympia & York. Fullerton also took the lead in persuading Canary Wharf's construction lenders to advance another £53 million, or $89 million. Of the eleven banks in the original syndicate, only the Finnish bank, Kansallis-Osake-Pankki, refused to participate, but was replaced by the Bank of Hongkong & Shanghai.

These were considerable sums but not nearly sufficient to stem the tide. On March 15, Olympia & York failed to redeem the Exchange Tower notes, all $250 million of which had come due. Had Royal Trust, the trustee for the noteholders, exercised its right to issue a notice of default, Olympia & York would have had little choice but to file for bankruptcy protection right then. But Reichmann managed to wriggle out of a tight spot by dangling the prospect of a government bailout before his creditors. That is, Olympia & York advised Royal Trust "on an extremely confidential basis, that a proposed sale for refinancing of the Exchange Tower complex had been all but fully negotiated, involving certain banks, with support from the Ontario government and the federal government," reported the lawyer representing Royal Trust on the matter. If the bank Royal Trust were to declare Olympia & York in default, the lawyer added, no doubt echoing Reichmann's own warnings, "the government-sponsored financing would definitely disappear." Royal Trust postponed action against Olympia & York indefinitely.

In truth, there was no "government-sponsored financing" worthy of the name. Reichmann had indeed worked out a refinancing plan under which Olympia & York would raise the funds needed to retire the commercial paper by selling the Exchange Tower to the CIBC and other banks for $250 million. However, Olympia & York would be obligated to buy back the building at the same price within two years, making this more of a loan than a true sale. The banks wanted the repurchase guaranteed by the government, meaning in effect that if the Reichmanns failed to buy back the building as promised, Brian Mulroney and Ontario premier Bob Rae would. While both the federal and provincial governments were willing to consider aiding Olympia & York, neither had committed to doing so and indeed were vacillating wildly behind the scenes as they wrestled with the question of how much damage an Olympia & York bankruptcy might inflict on the Canadian economy and financial system. Reichmann thus was not entirely to blame for misleading Royal Trust but did nothing to clear up any potential misunderstanding.

———

From New York, John Zuccotti had kept tabs on the parent company's financial contortions with mounting alarm. Olympia & York's American subsidiary faced two heavy debt payments: a $65 million interest payment on a bond issue backed by one of the World Financial Center towers due March 25 and the next $100 million installment to Sanwa Bank on April 1. All $165 million would have to be supplied by the parent company, for the U.S. subsidiary's cash reserves had been exhausted. Reichmann had repeatedly assured Zuccotti that Toronto would provide the full sum right up until the mid-March day that he summoned him to a meeting at his home in Toronto and informed him that he could not spare the cash after all. "John didn't show his anger, given the circumstances. I mean, Paul was a man on the verge of his own financial ruin," recalled a Zuccotti confidant. "But he was furious; there's no question that he considered it a personal betrayal."

The parent company, too, faced an imminent deadline. On April 1, a $440 million mortgage would come due on Scotia Plaza, the Toronto skyscraper that Bob Campeau had built in partnership with the Bank of Nova Scotia, which kept its headquarters in the building and owned the land under it. The mortgage on Scotia Plaza, which exceeded its current market value by a wide margin, was held by a syndicate of banks co-headed by Scotiabank, the Commerce, and Royal Bank and including several Japanese banks. Olympia & York asked the Scotia Plaza lenders to defer repayment but met stiff resistance from Scotiabank, whose top executives were greatly put out with Paul Reichmann. (Dennis Belcher of Scotiabank would be one of the few bankers to publicly blast Reichmann when Olympia & York had finally come tumbling down, accusing him of having done "everything he could to disguise how bad things were. He is the architect of his own demise.")

Just a few weeks earlier, Don Fullerton and Allan Taylor, chairman of the Royal, had persuaded their Scotiabank counterpart, Cedric Ritchie, to join them and National Bank in advancing $126 million to Olympia & York. But now Fullerton agreed with Ritchie that Paul Reichmann's scrambling, piecemeal efforts to stave off collapse were futile, that the time had come for Olympia & York to sit down with all of its banks and devise a comprehensive restructuring plan. And that, in turn, meant that Reichmann would have to step aside as president of Olympia & York, for he had destroyed the last shreds of his credibility with his continuing reluctance to fully open the company's books. The bankers had an ally in Albert Reichmann, who had returned to Toronto in mid-March from a series of meetings with European bankers determined to assert himself, however belatedly, to save the family company.

Recognizing that he was outnumbered, Paul regained the initiative by offering to help choose his own successor. He called Zuccotti in New York to inquire about the availability of Thomas S. Johnson, a cerebral, by-the-book American banker who in 1988 had been named president of Manufacturers Hanover Trust Company at age forty-eight. After Chemical Bank had acquired Manny Hanny in 1991, Johnson resigned rather than accept the number-two job at the combined banks. At Zuccotti's suggestion, Reichmann then had interviewed Johnson for the newly created post of chief financial officer of the U.S. company but the banker was not interested. Now Reichmann checked with Fullerton and a few other key bankers and won their endorsement for Johnson as Olympia & York president. Who knew better than a banker how to placate other bankers? At Reichmann's request, Zuccotti called Johnson but was told that the banker was on a Caribbean cruise. Zuccotti left messages for Johnson all over Manhattan and then flew to Puerto Rico, where the unemployed banker's ship would dock next. When Johnson landed, he called Olympia & York's offices, which patched him through to Zuccotti's hotel room in San Juan. After explaining the situation, the Olympia & York emissary asked, "Are you interested in the job?"

"Yes," Johnson replied carefully. "But I'm in the middle of a vacation right now."

"I'm afraid it can't wait," Zuccotti said, "I think we should meet right away. How's half an hour?"

"But I'm in Puerto Rico," replied Johnson, nonplussed.

"So am I," Zuccotti said.

The next day Johnson flew straight to Toronto with Zuccotti and began negotiating the terms of his employment with Reichmann and Olympia & York's lead banks.

On March 22, Reichmann at last abandoned the forced smile of his insistent public optimism and, through a spokesman, conceded that Olympia & York could not continue in its current form and would have to restructure its balance sheet to survive. The admission made front pages throughout the world and shocked even the select company of businessmen who considered themselves Paul Reichmann's friends and confidants, for he had confided in no one outside the company, with the possible exception of his wife. Lew Ranieri, who had left Salomon Brothers and started his own investment bank in New York, learned of Olympia & York's troubles via *The Wall Street Journal* early March 23 and immediately called Reichmann. "I couldn't read anything into Paul's voice; he spoke in his usual low monotone," Ranieri recalled. "From what he said, though, I don't think he understood the severity of the situation. I think he believed that he still had a lot of goodwill with the banks and that he could work it out."

On March 24, Olympia & York announced Johnson's hiring as president of the company and his appointment as chairman of a new committee formed to direct negotiations with lenders. Its other members were Michael Dennis, Gil Newman, John Zuccotti, and Robert S. "Steve" Miller. A former vice chairman of Chrysler & Company, Miller had been a key member of the team that saved the auto giant from bankruptcy in the early 1980s. He had then joined James D. Wolfensohn Incorporated, a small but high-powered New York investment bank. In his pinstripes and thick-lensed glasses, Miller looked like the soul of corporate propriety but in fact was something of a wild man. In the spring of 1980, he had traumatized a roomful of nervous bankers by announcing Chrysler had just declared bankruptcy but then advised them to check their calendars. "April fool's," he said. On other occasions, he jokingly threatened suicide by holding a toy water pistol to his head and doffed his suit jacket and shirt to reveal a Superman costume. Miller now would be devoting his full energies to Olympia & York as vice chairman of the new committee. In addition to the Wolfensohn firm, the Reichmanns had hired two other premier investment bank advisers: J. P. Morgan & Company of New York and Burns Fry Limited of Toronto.

Olympia & York announced that neither Paul nor Albert Reichmann would participate directly in talks with the banks, leaving the day-to-day negotiations to the committee. However, Paul's public relations mouthpiece hastened to add, confusing the issue, "Nothing changes as far as the top executive leadership is concerned, which remains with Paul and Albert. Putting this group in place allows Paul to spend more time on Canary Wharf." This was news to Olympia & York's bankers, who had certainly intended to change the company's executive leadership. After all, Paul had ceded the presidency to Johnson and accepted a demotion to vice chairman. (Albert retained the title he had held since Olympia & York's founding—chairman.) Olympia & York had never bestowed the title of chief executive officer on anyone and did not now, but Paul had assured Johnson that he was to function as CEO in all but name. "Olympia & York needed someone to be senior and to have the authority and that was to be Johnson," Paul said later. "Albert and I would be there guiding him but whatever his title, Tom Johnson was to run the company."

On March 27, Johnson led Olympia & York's new committee into a meeting in Toronto with senior representatives of twenty of the company's largest lenders. Flanked by the brothers Reichmann, Johnson ran the meeting in no-nonsense fashion, vowing full cooperation. "You will soon receive every scrap of financial information you need," he said. "I am here to tell you that we want to work with you." Johnson admitted that Olympia & York was incapable of paying off the Scotia Plaza mortgage on April 1 and asked the bankers to refrain from declaring the company in default, promising to have an "interim" restructuring plan ready for review on April 6. Paul Reichmann, poker-faced as usual, said little. All in all, Johnson's debut was well received. Even Ced Ritchie, the angriest of Reichmann's banker critics, seemed mollified. "I read in the papers that everybody seems to think it's a controllable situation," Scotiabank's chairman told reporters. "I would tend to agreed with that." The consensus in banking and real estate circles—and in the press—was that Olympia & York was likely to survive, albeit in diminished form. "If, like some banks, a real estate company can be 'too big to fail,' " opined *The Wall Street Journal,* "Olympia & York appears to be that company."

The conventional wisdom might well have been proven correct had not Paul Reichmann departed decisively from the rescue script he had helped write, however grudgingly, and reasserted his control of Olympia & York. Either Reichmann had only pretended to collaborate in his own managerial eclipse or had balked at the last minute. In any event, he cut his hand-picked successor off at the knees after the March 27 meeting. Olympia & York's bankers had inadvertently sealed Johnson's fate by assuring Reichmann that they still valued his input. "Our view was that he should be involved," one key banker said at the time. "He's the owner and operator of the company. People lent him a lot of money, and we want him there." Although Reichmann had ceded his title, he alone understood Olympia & York's finances in all their byzantine complexity, and he still commanded the personal loyalties of many of its senior executives. So Reichmann stonewalled Johnson, just as he had been stonewalling his bankers for so many years, and began working up a plan of his own.

After years of mounting subterranean tension among the Reichmann brothers, a schism opened. Infuriated by Paul's recalcitrance, Albert and Ralph confronted their brother behind the closed doors of family, arguing that the time had come to take a conciliatory posture with the banks. Step aside, they demanded, and let Johnson do what he has to do. Like Olympia & York's other employees, Johnson never witnessed an argument among the brothers. But Paul would tell him one thing and Albert would tell him the opposite. Albert and Ralph together controlled a sizable majority of Olympia & York's shares and had the legal right to impose their joint will on the corporation. In the end, though, neither possessed the strength or determination required to bring Paul to heel.

On April 3, a thoroughly exasperated Johnson left Toronto and flew back home. He would not return. Olympia & York announced that it had rescheduled the follow-up session Johnson had promised bankers, pushing it back a week to April 13. From his home in New Jersey, meanwhile, Johnson demanded a large severance payment. When Paul offered a token sum, Johnson communicated a threat to stir up a ruckus by hiring the politically well-connected public relations firm of Hill and Knowlton, which on April 9 issued a terse press release noting that Johnson was "involved in discussions with Olympia & York Chairman and Chief Executive Officer Paul Reichmann regarding his relationship with the company." Whether this was sarcasm or an innocent mistake was not certain. In reality, Paul held neither title; he had only behaved as if he did. Reichmann grasped the implied threat in Johnson's announcement and offered $2 million, which is what he was to have received as a bonus if Olympia & York was successfully restructured. Johnson accepted, and Albert insisted that Paul cover the payment with a check drawn on his personal account.

Ironically, just days after Reichmann had run off Johnson and ended the most serious threat to his executive authority he had ever faced, he lost effective control of one of the principal kingdoms in his empire, as Zuccotti coolly informed him that the U.S. subsidiary no longer would transfer its temporary cash surpluses to corporate headquarters. Olympia & York's American subsidiary was on the verge of insolvency itself, Zuccotti explained, and needed every dollar it could muster to keep its own lenders at bay. In effect, Zuccotti argued that his fiduciary duty to the creditors of the U.S. company now outweighed his duty to his employer. "I rationalized my stand as follows," he recalled. "Since Paul, as owner of the company, was the beneficiary of what I was doing to prevent it from falling into Chapter 11, to some extent I was protecting him from himself."

Reichmann did not see it this way, of course. To him, Zuccotti's defiance was not a principled stand for the common good but an act of mutiny that harmed the parent company by constraining his own ability to improvise financially.

On the other hand, Zuccotti could not be removed from his position without putting the U.S. company at serious risk, for the relationships he had built with lenders had superseded Reichmann's own to some uncertain extent. Then, too, Zuccotti's credibility helped underpin the new restructuring committee set up to placate the parent company's banks. Reichmann could reasonably hope to blame his problems with Johnson on the banker's own hunger for executive power and his extravagant compensation demands (he had wanted Olympia & York's banks to back his employment contract with a $3 million letter of credit), but if a second member of the committee followed Johnson out the door, Reichmann's own conduct and motives would come under intensified suspicion.

Reichmann seethed over what amounted to Zuccotti's ultimatum but surrendered without a fight or even an angry word. "He wasn't happy about it but he said he understood," Zuccotti recalled. "From April on, he and I had a kind of modus vivendi that was never articulated. The understanding was that he would take care of Canada and I would hold the fort in the U.S. He would call and ask how it was going. But he did not give me instructions anymore. I don't think Paul understood when he hired me what kind of man I was in terms of character," Zuccotti continued. "I don't think he thought I was capable of drawing a line on him."

—

On April 13, four hundred bankers and lawyers representing ninety-one banks gathered in the ballroom of the Sheraton Centre Hotel in Toronto to get their first peek at Olympia & York's tentative restructuring plan. Rather than run the gauntlet of reporters and photographers at the main entrance, Paul and Albert ducked in through a fire exit and down a stairwell. With Tom Johnson conspicuous by his absence, Steve Miller did most of the talking, devoting the first hour and a half of the three-and-a-half-hour session to a discussion of Olympia & York's financial condition. As Miller finished running through the numbers, trolleys piled high with 270-page financial reports were wheeled into the ballroom and distributed to the bankers, few of whom could resist the temptation to thumb through the document as Miller presented the Reichmann plan, such as it was. Olympia & York "has very substantial equity and if allowed to operate and manage those assets there is every reason to expect the company to recover its footing," said Miller, conceding a need to rework only about $4 billion of the company's $20 billion in debts. Olympia & York in time would repay every penny it owed, Miller continued, if only lenders agreed to defer some interest and all principal payments in the coming months and loaned it another $260 million, mostly for Canary Wharf.

After the meeting, Miller, insouciant as always, fielded questions from reporters. If banks failed to go along with Olympia & York's proposal and forced the company to liquidate, the result "would be a disaster for all concerned," said Miller, making explicit the threat implicit in Reichmann's hard-line approach. Miller also introduced as Johnson's successor the man who had been his boss at Chrysler Corporation, Gerald Greenwald. Nicknamed "the Hoover" for his ability to suck up large quantities of information, Greenwald, like Miller, had made a career as a Wall Street investment banker after leaving Chrysler. Reichmann bestowed the additional title of deputy chief executive on Greenwald, begging the question of exactly whose deputy he was, since officially Olympia & York did not have a chief executive officer.

Meanwhile, the bankers were back in their hotel rooms, doing a collective slow burn as they studied Olympia & York's financial report. Although it contained information new to many lenders, it still was grossly incomplete. Olympia & York admitted to losing $302 million in 1990 but offered no figures at all for 1991 or 1992 and made only a token effort to justify the suspiciously large net worth it claimed—nearly $4.7 billion. As for Olympia & York's preliminary restructuring plan, it turned out to be little more than a demand for forbearance. In effect, Reichmann was insisting that his bankers continue to trust him blindly. "It's the same Olympia & York arrogance as always," one banker fumed. "They want concessions but they won't let us see what's behind the curtain."

The day after the Sheraton summit, representatives of Credit Lyonnais, Commerzbank, Hongkong & Shanghai Bank, Swiss Bank Corporation, Bank of Tokyo, and a score of other large foreign banks gathered for lunch in the private dining room of the Toronto law firm Osler, Hoskin & Harcourt. This was an exceptionally high-powered and unhappy crew, for they belonged to the twenty-two-bank syndicate that had the largest loan outstanding to Olympia & York—the $2.5 billion Jumbo Loan, now better known as the "Dumbo Loan." The value of the collateral—the bulk of Olympia & York's stockholdings in Gulf Canada and Abitibi-Price—had fallen almost since the day the loan had closed in 1989. Miller had publicly identified the Jumbo Loan as one of the three problem megaloans that would have to be reworked.

Someone in the Jumbo lender group had gotten hold of a confidential Olympia & York memo detailing the series of private deals cut with Citibank and the Gang of Four in the frantic last weeks before the company's March 23 announcement that it had run out of money. In exchange for a series of small additional loans, Olympia & York had pledged all sorts of assets to these five banks to beef up the collateral on preexisting loans—a practice known as cross-collateralization. The value of the new security Olympia & York had provided greatly exceeded the sums of cash it received, a clear indication of Reichmann's desperation. The net result was that Citibank, CIBC, Royal, Scotiabank, and National Bank had significantly improved their position at the expense of Olympia & York's other eighty-six banks. While such preferential treatment was an outgrowth of Reichmann's secretiveness, the wrath of the Jumbo lenders was directed mainly at their fellow bankers for what the *Globe & Mail* later characterized as "banking's moral equivalent of insider trading in stocks."

As the group discussed its options, Richard Ross of Hongkong & Shanghai passed a note to Charles Heidsieck of Credit Lyonnais. Amending Cato's historic pronouncement to the Roman Senate, "Carthago delend est" (Carthage must be destroyed), the note declared: "Cross delend est" (Cross-collateralization must be destroyed). The phrase quickly became a rallying cry for Olympia & York's foreign bankers.

On April 15, Olympia & York called a meeting to discuss what became known as the "lights-on loan"—$8 million to cover daily operating expenses while bankers pondered the company's larger request for new money. Greenwald and Miller ran the meeting; the Reichmann brothers were observing Passover and did not attend. As bankers were filing into the boardroom on the twenty-eighth floor of First Bank Tower, Heidsieck pointed at Paul Farrar, a senior vice president of CIBC, and said angrily: "The cross-collateralization must be destroyed." Farrar conceded nothing. This truculent exchange set the tone for an unproductive meeting, which was adjourned after a few hours.

On April 20, the meeting reconvened and again the Reichmanns were busy at their Passover observances. Speaking for the foreign lenders generally, Ross of the Hongkong & Shanghai said that international lenders would not loan any more money to Olympia & York unless two conditions were met: first, the cross-collateralization granted the Favored Five must be undone; second, all ninety-one banks must sign a so-called standstill agreement promising not to take unilateral action against Olympia & York to collect on bad loans. When Ross had finished, the Bank of Nova Scotia contingent left the room and huddled briefly in the hallway. Dennis Belcher, the ranking Scotiabanker, returned to announce that he could not agree to a standstill because five days earlier his bank had declared Olympia & York in default on a $200 million loan and already was moving to seize the collateral. It was as if Belcher had pulled a lighted stick of dynamite from his briefcase. Unless it was extinguished, Olympia & York would be ripped apart in a matter of days.

The other bankers turned as one on Belcher, demanding that the Bank of Nova Scotia reconsider its precipitous, selfish action. On this issue anyway, the other members of the Gang of Four stood with the foreign banks. The CIBC's Farrar warned that Scotiabank "could bring down the whole house of cards." Belcher was unbowed. "My job is to protect my bank," he snapped. "You can take it or leave it."

The other banks kept hammering away at Belcher, who finally left to consult with his superiors across the street at headquarters. He returned in a conciliatory mood, promising that the Bank of Nova Scotia would not seize Olympia & York assets after all but would continue to work with the other banks. The catastrophe of bankruptcy had been averted but there was no undoing the damage to interbank relations caused by Belcher's harsh initial position. Only one foreign bank, Hongkong & Shanghai, was willing to join the Gang of Four in granting Olympia & York the $8 million lights-on loan on April 22.

Meanwhile, Greenwald, Miller, and the rest of Olympia & York's management were making no progress in their efforts to intimidate and cajole the banks into seeing things Paul Reichmann's way. By the end of April, Reichmann had bowed to prevailing opinion and began readying a new survival plan as a handful of Olympia & York's largest lenders continued to keep the company alive on a drip-feed of expense money. Time was running out on Olympia & York, which now was in arrears on indebtedness secured by four major office towers: Exchange Tower, Scotia Plaza, One Liberty Plaza, and 2 World Financial Center. On May 1, another delinquency was added to the list as the company failed to make an interest payment on a $900 million bond issue secured by three Uris properties. In each case, Olympia & York had managed to persuade its creditors not to take legal action against it.

But on May 4, an ominously volatile new factor was introduced into the equation when Olympia & York failed to make a $17 million interest payment on debt secured by First Canadian Place. Unlike the other bond issues on which the company had fallen behind, this one was both publicly traded and widely held by institutional investors—pension funds and insurance companies rather than banks—who as a rule had no other loans to Olympia & York and thus no real incentive to show mercy or even patience. To the contrary, at the behest of bondholders, Royal Trust immediately sent a letter of default to Olympia & York, which had a grace period of seven working days to cover the interest payment or risk the seizure of its flagship property.

On May 7, Olympia & York unveiled its revised survival plan during a meeting in the thirtieth-floor boardroom of the main tower of Canary Wharf with some fifty bankers. Like its predecessor, plan two was audaciously anticlimactic and poorly received. The only significant change, which hardly qualified as a concession given the parlous state of Olympia & York's finances, was a proposal to issue shares of stock to bankers willing to forgo principal payments for five years. All told, the Reichmanns were prepared to surrender a 20 percent stake in Olympia & York itself and 30 percent of the equity in Canary Wharf. Greenwald wreathed the notion in grandiose rhetoric, hailing it as a milestone in Olympia & York's history. "After decades of total family ownership," he said, "the company is inviting lenders to join hands as partners in the business"—a business that happened to be hopelessly insolvent. But the only partners Reichmann wanted were the minority sort. Even at this desperate juncture, he held tight to his control of the company, specifying that the shares issued lenders would not carry voting rights.

———

Not even the ruination of Olympia & York could destroy Paul Reichmann's faith in the essential rightness of Canary Wharf. In hindsight, Reichmann would candidly admit to having made many strategic errors but bristled at the presumption—widely held among Olympia & York's obituarists—that Canary Wharf was the most grievous of them. In fact, Reichmann would go so far as to argue that Canary Wharf was a casualty of the company's collapse rather than a contributory cause. "Olympia & York brought Canary Wharf down, not the other way around," he insisted in 1995. "Olympia & York's problems were extremely deep; Canary Wharf's problems were not deep."

On its face, this was ludicrous. Canary Wharf drained enormous sums of cash from the corporate treasury while adding greatly to the company's fatally outsized debt burden. It is certainly possible that Olympia & York would have survived the real estate collapse of the early 1990s had not the Reichmanns frittered away so much money on failed corporate acquisitions in the 1980s. However, it is equally plausible to argue that Olympia & York could have survived even its misbegotten stock market adventuring had it not poured billions into refurbishing the Isle of Dogs. In the end, attempting to determine the causality of the disaster that befell Olympia & York is as futile as trying to resolve the chronology of the chicken and the egg, and is essentially irrelevant in any event.

To a remarkable degree, Reichmann succeeded in imbuing Olympia & York's senior executives in London with the same unremitting passion for the kamikaze mission that was Canary Wharf. "He is the smartest businessman I've ever come across," Peter Marano, the project's leasing director, said after the fall. "I don't think any of us finally gave up until we had the door slammed on us." When Olympia & York finally surrendered control of Canary Wharf to court-appointed trustees, "it felt to all of us like being hit in the face with a fist," added Gerald Rothman, Canary Wharf's chief administrative officer. "There was not a dry eye among all of us hardbitten fellows."

Even as the London property market slid deeper into the abyss of recession in 1991, Reichmann had convinced himself that Olympia & York was making crucial progress in marketing Canary Wharf to the corporate establishment. "By the end of 1991 we had broken down some psychological barriers," Reichmann said. The chairman of the London Stock Exchange called to say that his board had approved Canary Wharf as a possible new location for the exchange, which was cramped in the City. After four years of effort, Olympia & York was so close to signing Barclays Bank to a lease by March 1992 that Reichmann had Andrew Buxton, the bank's CEO-in-waiting, call Flood of CIBC to confirm that a final agreement was imminent. However, Barclays soon pulled back as the dimensions of Olympia & York's financial crisis became evident. At the end of March, Olympia & York had further brought a barrage of adverse publicity down on itself in London by failing to make the £40 million down payment on its £400 million contribution to the Jubilee Line extension.

After the mid-April Toronto summit session with the company's bankers, Steve Miller had flown to London to ask Canary Wharf's syndicate of eleven construction lenders for £110 million to keep the project going for another ninety days or so. He got £5 million. By the time that Olympia & York unveiled its revised restructuring proposal on May 7, Canary Wharf needed another £20 or £30 million just to make it through the end of the month. Immediately after presenting the new plan to its banks, Reichmann and his lieutenants convened a separate meeting to press the Group of Eleven for an emergency £50 million loan. Farrar, the Commerce's resident tough guy, was the first banker to speak. "We aren't going to put another penny into Canary Wharf," he said. "This turkey won't fly."

Farrar's was the voice of doom. As Olympia & York's lead bank, the Commerce was bound by banking tradition to help the company organize its restructuring efforts, however belated they may have been. Or, as one writer put it, "Like a senior officer on a sinking ship the CIBC was expected to oversee the bailout." The Commerce had seemed to accept this responsibility, putting up the lion's share of the new money advanced to cover Olympia & York's operating expenses both in Toronto and London, while Don Fullerton himself had been active in keeping the Bank of Nova Scotia and other malcontents from breaking out the lifeboats. Evidently, though, Fullerton had recently changed his mind, for the subtext of Farrar's blunt-spoken renunciation was that as far as the Commerce was concerned, the Reichmanns now were on their own.

Fullerton never did publicly explain what in particular had convinced him to pull the plug on Olympia & York. In early May, whatever hopes he harbored of a Canadian government bailout of the company had been dashed by unequivocal statements by high officials. As for Canary Wharf itself, Farrar claimed at the May 7 meeting that the CIBC had only recently realized the extent to which Olympia & York had offered costly inducements to lure tenants to the Docklands. Not everyone found this explanation convincing, least of all Paul Reichmann, who, according to one eyewitness, "kept glaring at [Farrar] like he was the devil." No less outraged at the Commerce's about-face, Farrar's fellow bankers ordered him from the room. By the next morning a compromise had been effected as the CIBC agreed to contribute to a token loan, but relations among Olympia & York's banks had been poisoned irreparably. A week later, an English court found against Olympia & York in the legal battle over 25 Cabot Square, ruling that it must pay Morgan Stanley the full $240 million it had promised. It was all over now but the filing.

On the evening of May 14, after one more miserable day spent racking his brain for miracles, Paul Reichmann dispatched his lawyers to apply for bankruptcy court protection for Olympia & York Development and its twenty-eight Canadian subsidiaries. The successful application included all of the Reichmanns' Canadian real estate holdings as well as their natural resource companies, ranking Olympia & York's as the largest corporate bankruptcy in Canadian history by almost any measure. Although Paul Reichmann remained nominally in charge of the company, he could not make a move without the approval of the court, which allowed him five months to work out a restructuring plan with his Canadian creditors that would enable some semblance of Olympia & York to eventually reemerge from bankruptcy as a going concern. In the meantime, the company would not have to make any loan repayments. This dispensation was purchased at a high cost, for the very act of filing for protection under the Companies' Creditors Arrangement Act erased the Reichmann family's equity in Olympia & York in one fell swoop, reducing the book value of its stockholding to something less than zero.

At least one of Reichmann's Canadian advisers had urged him to simultaneously seek protection for Olympia & York's American subsidiary under Chapter 11 of the federal bankruptcy code. Although the U.S. company was no less insolvent than its Canadian parent, Zuccotti and his top aide, Sandy Frucher, had been able to mollify its creditors with a combination of candor and artful bluster even as Reichmann was antagonizing the Canadian lenders, and the New Yorkers were loath now to stigmatize themselves by going back on their promises and implementing a bankruptcy filing. Push came to shove when Zuccotti was urged to conserve cash by refusing to pay a $75 million New York City property tax bill about to come due. Zuccotti, a former deputy mayor, threatened to resign. "I've spent too much of my life working with the city to do this," he told Reichmann, who backed off and let Zuccotti continue trying to restructure the U.S. company outside of bankruptcy.

In England, meanwhile, Reichmann and his loyal minions made a desperate last-ditch attempt to persuade John Major to bail out Canary Wharf by relocating a few thousand civil servants but succeeded only in giving the project's many critics a chance to get in their last licks. Even the sober-sided *Times* of London let fly, castigating Canary Wharf as "an ill-conceived act of Tory social engineering" and an "architectural folly" in an editorial vehemently opposing any government aid to Olympia & York in any form.

On May 27, Canary Wharf's construction lenders met and decided by a 7 to 4 vote not to extend any more expense money to Olympia & York, which was left with no choice but to seek the U.K. equivalent of bankruptcy court protection. As soon as Olympia & York filed, ownership of Canary Wharf immediately reverted to its bankers, wiping out Olympia & York's equity investment. English bankruptcy law is more onerous than Canada's in that it requires the petitioner to immediately surrender control to a court-appointed administrator, whose job it is to devise a plan in the best interests of the creditors. In other words, Reichmann was out on his ear, replaced by three partners of the accounting firm Ernst & Young, who had three months to decide whether Canary Wharf should be salvaged in its entirety or sold off in bits and pieces. Granted a mere £10 million to carry the project through to the end of the year, the administrators fired most of Olympia & York's four hundred London employees and shut down construction.

The net effect of the two transatlantic bankruptcy filings was to dismember the greatest property development empire the world had ever seen while making irreversible the dwindling of the Reichmann family's investment in Olympia & York. In five short years, the Reichmanns had squandered $10 billion, a reversal of fortune of a magnitude unequaled in modern history.

Chapter 46

―――――――

The ruination of Olympia & York had eviscerated Paul Reichmann's net worth and shredded his business reputation, but it seemed neither to dishearten nor to humble him, at least not initially. For a good six or seven months after the bankruptcy filings, he continued to fight the fight he had just lost, taking an unrepentantly grudging posture with his creditors while scouring the globe for investors willing to advance the funds he needed to reclaim and complete Canary Wharf. In fact, the very day that Olympia & York put the project into administration, Reichmann had telephoned two of his most trusted construction managers, George Iacobescu and Vinay Kapor, and asked them to remain on the job, offering to put them on his personal payroll if need be. "It was an instinctive thing on my part rather than a definite plan," Reichmann recalled. "I wanted the talent in place in case I was able to make a comeback."

Reichmann shrank from public view after Olympia & York's fall, skipping press conferences and refusing for-attribution interviews, but the party line as spouted in his stead by Michael Dennis, Gerald Greenwald, and Steve Miller was downright Panglossian. "Olympia & York is continuing in business," Miller insisted. "If I can make an analogy for you, it's as though you're walking down the street, you notice it's raining, you open your umbrella, and you keep going. The Companies Creditors Arrangement Act is the equivalent of opening the umbrella. We are still moving forward." Meanwhile, in his private comments to reporters, Reichmann portrayed himself as a victim of peculiar circumstances and short-sighted, disloyal bankers. A few days after Olympia & York had surrendered control of Canary Wharf, *The Wall Street Journal* ran a front-page article that opened with Reichmann bemoaning his rough treatment by the Canadian Imperial Bank of Commerce. "Why are they doing this to me?"

Reichmann had supposedly complained to an unnamed associate. "These people are my friends."

When Canary Wharf entered administration, 57 percent of its 4.5 million square feet had been leased but only 14 percent was actually occupied by tenants. Reichmann was devastated anew when the construction lenders—the new owners—refused to honor the lavish fit-out allowances and other financial concessions that Olympia & York had granted to lure tenants. Both American Express and Chemical Bank (which had merged with Manufacturers Hanover) promptly canceled their plans to move to Canary Wharf, adding 530,000 square feet to the project's ruinous backlog of unleased space. "It would have been relatively easy for the banks to carry Canary Wharf with a little added investment, and the value preserved would have been manyfold," Reichmann complained a few years later. "What they did was irrational. The cancellation of these lease deals was a whim of people who didn't understand what they were dealing with."

The $2 billion loss that Olympia & York belatedly disclosed for 1991 would have been much larger—well above $3 billion—had Reichmann been willing to recognize the financial consequences of Canary Wharf's failure, as his outside auditors had urged him to do. "The value of the development has been materially impaired," argued Price Waterhouse in officially qualifying its opinion of Olympia & York's 1991 figures. "Generally accepted accounting principles require that the amount of the impairment in value should have been estimated and provided for in these financial statements." Paul Reichmann's stubborn refusal to book a loss on his beloved Docklands development was the financial equivalent of storing a corpse in the freezer in hopes of an eventual cryogenic solution to the "problem" of death. But if the fortune he had poured into Canary Wharf was irretrievably lost, the complex itself was simply too big to be laid to rest. As the *Economist* observed, "It is set in eight square miles of concrete and its future affects London's future."

Throughout the summer of 1992, the trio of court-appointed administrators held preliminary talks with about a dozen parties—most of them British—interested in acquiring all or part of Canary Wharf. In the end, not a single bona fide offer was submitted, but the most serious of several near offers was advanced by a group of investors put together by Paul Reichmann, who had concentrated his fund-raising efforts in New York City. "I was amazed at Paul's frame of mind," said Peter Cohen, the former Shearson Lehman chief executive, whose advice Reichmann solicited while making the rounds in Manhattan. "I'd heard that he'd had a lot of sleepless nights, that all the demons had come out. But when I saw him he seemed amazingly relaxed, very philosophical about what had happened, and totally focused on how he might salvage Canary Wharf."

Three corporate heavyweights headed Reichmann's investor list: Lew Ranieri, formerly of Salomon Brothers and now head of his own investment bank; Sanford Weill, the chief executive of Primerica, who had met Reichmann over the negotiating table while president of American Express; and Lawrence Tisch, the penny-pinching billionaire chairman of Loews Corporation and CBS Incorporated. Reichmann had gathered commitments for £250 million and was still working at raising more when he submitted a letter to the Canary Wharf lenders, who were collectively owed £568 million, tentatively offering to buy a 50 percent interest in the completed part of the project for £350 million. Had Reichmann been able to work out a deal, he would have returned as Canary Wharf's overseer but not as its owner since he was not putting up much money himself. As it was, his feeler was rebuffed by a solid majority of the project's banks, which had not abandoned hope that they would be made whole and were loath to unload their loans at a discount to the very man who had defaulted on them in the first place. Paul persisted, cobbling together a second, equally provisional offer. But Weill dropped out of the investor group, and the banks again sent Reichmann packing.

Reichmann's precipitous attempts to settle up with Canary Wharf's lenders further undermined his standing with his Canadian creditors, who, after all, were owed a much larger sum and were no less restive. Olympia & York failed to meet a mid-June deadline for submitting a restructuring plan to the bankruptcy court in Toronto, got another month's grace and then let the revised deadline expire, too. Finally, in mid-August of 1992 the company filed a provisional plan with the court under which creditors would be offered shares of stock in return for five years' leeway in repaying $8.6 billion in debt. If Olympia & York succeeded in repaying the full sum during the five-year period, the Reichmanns would retain a controlling 51 percent interest in what was to become a publicly traded company, leaving creditors with the remaining 49 percent. But if the company came up short, the family's stake would fall to as little as 20 percent, and its creditors would walk away with 80 percent.

Paul Reichmann had made what he considered a major concession in agreeing to share ownership of Olympia & York with outsiders, but his creditors were underwhelmed. The plan was suspiciously sketchy in many respects, and even those lenders who accepted that it made sense to preserve Olympia & York's property portfolio intact had no intention of scaling back their own claims to enable the Reichmanns to maintain a controlling interest. "It's a crap shoot," sneered a lawyer representing a group of bondholders. "They are betting on the real estate market turning around in the next few years. If it does, they get lucky." Stillborn, the plan was soon abandoned. Granted an extension of a few months, Reichmann and his minions returned to the drawing board.

In the fall of 1992, the remnants of Paul's credibility were tattered anew as it was belatedly revealed that the Bronfmans and the Reichmanns together had secretly owned a 35 percent stake in the World Financial Center since 1989. Apparently a handful of Olympia & York's largest banks knew already but the great majority were infuriated that the information had been withheld from them. "A lot of bankers spent their morning consulting lawyers," an American banker said the morning after the revelation. "We were told time and again that the Reichmanns did not have a personal stake in the World Financial Center." Bay Street analysts who tracked Edper were no less stunned, for the company's top executives had repeatedly denied that any link existed between the Bronfman and Reichmann real estate empires outside of their well-known Trizec alliance. "I've told fifty people in the last year that we had no relationship with Olympia & York" outside of Trizec, said Gorden Arnell, a top Bronfman executive, adding lamely that he had done so "without a twitch of conscience" because the Reichmann family had promised to eventually buy back Edper's World Financial Center stake using Trizec shares instead of cash.

The World Financial Center disclosure did not emerge from the bankruptcy court in Toronto but was leaked to the press by someone at Olympia & York's American subsidiary. John Zuccotti and his New York team had known from the start that the Bronfmans had bought into the World Financial Center through Battery Park Holdings Incorporated but had never been informed that Edper had turned around and sold half of BPHI to the Reichmanns in 1990. By the spring of 1992, however, the U.S. executives suspected that the Reichmanns did in fact hold an undisclosed interest in World Financial Center and confronted Paul. "To the question 'Do you have a stake in BPHI?' as put by John and others, Paul gave no straight answer," said one American executive. Reichmann said later that his employees had no business putting such a question to him: "The sale of equity in the holding company was not relevant to the operations of the company." In July 1992, Zuccotti withheld a $5.8 million interest payment due lest some of it end up in the Reichmanns' pockets, for he had promised the U.S. company's lenders that no cash payments would be made to the family until it had worked through its financial problems.

There ensued a circuitous and increasingly testy series of negotiations between Edper and the U.S. company. In a letter written September 25, Gerald Kelfer, an Olympia & York executive vice president, agreed to pay all monies due BPHI on one condition: "that we shall be satisfied, in our sole discretion, as to the ownership of BPHI." On September 29, David Ferguson of Edper replied: "It is completely unacceptable to ourselves that all prior unmade distributions and future distributions be conditional on you being satisfied as to the ownership of BPHI. The ownership of BPHI is irrelevant to whether distributions are made . . . ," Ferguson argued. "Irrespective of this issue, you have the assurance from Mr. Paul Reichmann that no Reichmann family member has any direct or indirect benefit ownership interest in BPHI."

Ferguson was correct, but only because on September 27 the Reichmanns had cut a deal to sell their interest in BPHI for $35 million to a Toronto businessman with close ties to Edper. Unlike the transactions that had preceded it, though, this last sale was publicly acknowledged by Paul Reichmann, effectively discrediting his past disavowals of a secret stake in World Financial Center. Despite the sale, the dispute between Edper and the U.S. company persisted and landed in state court in New York. Joel Simon, the chief operating officer of Olympia & York U.S.A., submitted an affidavit in which he laid bare Reichmann's World Financial Center machinations. Although it was Reichmann who had been caught in a lie, he apparently considered himself the aggrieved party and flew down to New York for what became known within the company as the "Et Tu, Brute" meeting. For the last time, Reichmann sat at the head of the massive, custom-made table in the boardroom in the Park Avenue Atrium, flanked by Zuccotti and the other senior U.S. executives, and quietly reproved his employees for ingratitude and disloyalty. "Paul didn't raise his voice but he was very emotional," recalled one attendee. "Anger, sorrow, frustration—it was all there."

Reichmann was no less unyielding in dealing with his Canadian creditors. In late October, a week after he had secured yet another extension from the court, Reichmann submitted a second restructuring plan that went beyond its predecessor in offering to surrender 80 percent ownership of Olympia & York's three trophy properties in Toronto—First Canadian Place, Exchange Tower, and Scotia Plaza—to the Gang of Four banks. Once again, though, Reichmann insisted on a five-year moratorium on debt payments and on retaining majority ownership of Olympia & York itself. The response was swift and caustic. "Olympia & York's proposal is garbage," said the head of the committee representing the First Canadian Place bondholders. "We're not happy with them even keeping a small ownership position," a banker added. "But this, this is ridiculous." In six months of negotiation, Reichmann and his creditors had rung up many millions of dollars in legal fees among them and were no closer to a consensual agreement to reorganize Olympia & York than on the day the company filed under the CCAA.

Olympia & York's bankruptcy protection was set to expire at the end of 1992, and with the prospect of obtaining yet another extension virtually nil, Paul Reichmann in mid-November at last gave up the ghost of his ruined empire. After securing a general legal release—under which the Reichmanns' creditors renounced the right to sue any family member—Paul and his brothers surrendered managerial control of Olympia & York to their creditors and in effect walked away.

Olympia & York Development was dead, long live Olympia & York Properties! Under a reorganization plan approved by the Toronto court in early 1993, the Reichmanns' stock portfolio and majority ownership of five of their office towers were to be liquidated—that is, handed over to lenders who had claimed them as collateral. From the remaining assets, though, the creditors also fashioned a new company as a going concern. Christened Olympia & York Properties, it emerged from bankruptcy protection in March 1993, endowed with full ownership of three office buildings in Calgary, two in Ottawa, and one more in Edmonton—plus a 20 percent equity stake in each of the three Toronto trophy towers. (The remaining 80 percent was held by the Gang of Four banks.) The plan was to use the cash flow generated by these properties to gradually pay down the loans held against them. Thanks to two members of the next generation of the family, Olympia & York's surviving remnant became a vehicle of Reichmann ambition once again.

At the time of Olympia & York's collapse, Philip Reichmann and Frank Hauer had been running the parent company's property management and leasing arm, which accounted for about half of total headquarters employment. As the company's troubles worsened, it was left to Reichmann and Hauer to reduce operating costs by firing workers by the dozen. The pair remained on the job throughout the bankruptcy reorganization and were offered salaried positions with Olympia & York Properties, which was to be staffed mainly by seventy-five former Reichmann employees who had clung to their jobs. Reichmann and Hauer wanted to remain, but as owners, not employees. In mid-1993, a few months after the birth of Olympia & York Properties, Reichmann and Hauer paid a few million dollars to acquire the company's property management and leasing arm. In essence, they reacquired the services of their former employees, the furniture in their offices on the twenty-ninth floor of Exchange Tower, and contracts to manage nine office towers the family once owned for an average annual fee of 3 percent of gross rents, or about $10 million. "We needed to find the silver lining in the cloud," explained Philip, whose younger brother David joined him at Olympia & York Properties.

The new Olympia & York was at most a faint glimmer of the old, but it was turning a profit and offered its principals, neither of whom had yet turned forty, a foundation on which they could hope to build a major real estate company and to restore the family's business reputation in the process. Philip and Frank had thought long and hard before deciding to perpetuate the Olympia & York name. "We spent many hours debating it and sometimes we still do . . . ," Reichmann said a year later. "But one of our objectives is to return that nameplate to its original luster."

Paul Reichmann had not finally let go of Olympia & York until he had been able to glimpse the possibility of mounting a de novo comeback. In August 1992, about the time that the company finally submitted its first restructuring plan to its creditors, Ron Soskolne made a scouting expedition to Mexico City. Soskolne, who was one of a handful of longtime aides put on the Reichmann family payroll after Olympia & York's collapse, was surprised at how warmly he was received. Albert Reichmann had paved his way, visiting the Mexican capital in 1991 at the invitation of President Carlos Salinas de Gortari, who was eager to bring to bear American real estate expertise on his country's huge backlog of urban construction projects. "People were aware of Olympia & York's problems but that was overridden by a great admiration—almost a reverence—for the quality of the buildings we had produced," Soskolne said.

At Soskolne's recommendation, Paul Reichmann made his first trip to Mexico in December 1992. Like many North American businessmen, Reichmann came away impressed with the Salinas government and its program to right the infamously volatile Mexican economy by taming inflation, reducing government deficits, and privatizing industry—a regimen not unlike the one that Margaret Thatcher earlier had prescribed for England. "The Salinas administration was made up of really extraordinary people," Reichmann said. "They had the economy growing rapidly and there was a great upgrading of many things in Mexico, including the style and quality of urban development."

Speed, not quality, long had been the watchword of office development in Mexico, for with an inflation rate that periodically zoomed above 100 percent, costs had a way of ballooning out of control virtually overnight and wrecking the best-laid plans. The instability of the Mexican economy and the constant threat of earthquakes raised the ante on large building projects and retarded the evolution of a real estate development industry in the American mold. Historically, Mexico City's chronically insufficient supply of office space had kept rents three times as high as those in major U.S. and Canadian cities. However, in the early 1990s the expectation of a sweeping free-trade agreement with the United States had spurred a speculative office building boom in Mexico City, as wealthy families from all walks of commerce piled into real estate in pursuit of a quick peso. By 1993, the vacancy rate had climbed from 1 percent to about 13 percent, and rents had begun to fall. Even so, Reichmann was convinced that Mexico City remained grossly undersupplied with the sort of first-class office accommodations that had been Olympia & York's specialty.

The Mexican project that first excited Reichmann's interest was a massive government-sponsored undertaking known as Santa Fe. Begun in the late 1980s, Santa Fe was to be a model city built from scratch on a 3,600-acre suburban tract that adjoined some of the most affluent residential sections of Mexico City but had once been used as a garbage dump and gravel pit. In Soskolne's estimation, Santa Fe was to Mexico City what Century City had been to Los Angeles twenty years ago. The Salinas regime had located a major new university in Santa Fe and a dozen major corporations, both Mexican and foreign multinationals (including Daimler-Benz, Goodyear Tire and Rubber, and Hewlett-Packard), either had occupied new office buildings there or had announced plans to do so. It was estimated that sixty thousand people would work in Santa Fe by the end of 1993. A huge, marble-laden shopping center was nearing completion and the construction of a two-thousand-unit residential complex was about to begin. High government officials encouraged Reichmann to devise a way to remedy Santa Fe's greatest deficiency—the lack of a commercial nucleus, a town center.

Reichmann and Soskolne quickly concluded that such a project was feasible both architecturally and commercially, but there was the little matter of money. *The Wall Street Journal* had reported that the Reichmann family emerged from Olympia & York's collapse with a private fortune of $400 million but appeared to have confused the prices the family had paid for Olympia Floor & Wall Tile and the four mediocre real estate properties it had bought from Olympia & York in 1991 with the current market value of these assets minus debts. The family did own the tile company (for which it had paid $144 million) free and clear but it was not nearly as profitable as it had once been, and Queen's Quay, 5410 Yonge Street, the Charlottetown Mall, and the Place de Bourgeoise were all burdened with hefty mortgages and high vacancy rates. What is more, as part of their settlement with creditors, the brothers had agreed to repay $131 million owed Olympia & York by Reichmann family members. Andy Sarlos, the Toronto money manager, estimated that the collapse of Olympia & York left the family with $100 million at most.

Ralph continued to run the tile company but also was president of RF Real Estate Investments Incorporated, the family company that had purchased Queen's Quay and the other properties. Although the only other two officers listed in RF's incorporation papers were tile company employees, both Paul and Albert shared in its ownership, as implied by its name—"RF" standing for "Reichmann family." Albert's second son, David, had briefly worked for RF upon its founding in 1992, before joining his brother Philip at Olympia & York Properties. One of Paul's sons-in-law, Henry Brackfield, also joined RF Real Estate. Brackfield, who had recently married Paul's third daughter, Libby, had been apprenticed to Hauer during Olympia & York's last years.

Whatever RF Real Estate's and Olympia Tile's net worth, Paul was unable to use these companies to finance his return to development and apparently he had no other ready source of cash, for on February 16, 1993, he took the desperate measure of borrowing $15 million against his Toronto house from a private lender who was not identified in documents on file in the land registry office in Toronto. Whoever loaned Reichmann the money did him a big favor, for 241 Strathallan Wood was not worth anywhere near the $15 million he borrowed against it.

Reichmann invested the $15 million, or at least a portion of it, in a newly formed partnership with George Soros, who was generally regarded as Wall Street's, if not the world's, reigning financial speculator. From an office in midtown Manhattan, the Hungarian-born Soros ran the Quantum Fund, which not only had risen in value by an average of 35 percent a year since its founding but had suffered only one down year in its thirty-three-year existence. "No other investor has produced better results for such a long period—not Peter

Lynch, not Warren Buffett," observed *Business Week*. Soros ranged impulsively across all the financial markets, but he was perhaps most adept and unquestionably most audacious as a trader of currencies—Samuel Reichmann's old bailiwick. In the fall of 1992, Soros had attained new notoriety by turning a $1 billion profit in a few days' time by amassing a huge short position in the pound sterling. Basically, he bet the house on the proposition that the British government, despite its vehement denials, was about to give up its costly effort to prop up the pound and let it seek its natural level.

By the time that Paul Reichmann began casting around for a comeback vehicle, "the man who broke the Bank of England," as Soros had been dubbed by Fleet Street, controlled about $7 billion in net assets and was in search of new worlds to conquer. Albert Reichmann had gotten to know Soros while serving with him briefly on First Hungary Funds' board of directors, but Paul did not meet him until late 1992. After returning from Mexico, Reichmann put together a list of twenty investors in hopes of persuading ten of them to contribute to a $250 million real estate development fund. The first two agreed to kick in $25 million apiece, but Reichmann's plans changed abruptly after a long conversation with prospect number three, Soros, who offered to put up all $250 million and then some. Soros was a real estate neophyte but he sensed that commercial property values had been beaten down so low that they must soon rise, and as someone who had lost $800 million himself on an errant stock market bet in 1987 was willing to forgive Reichmann his costly Canary Wharf blunder. Reichmann had been "the most successful real estate developer in the world," Soros said later. "I am basically looking to invest my own money, and I want to go with the best."

In February 1993, Soros created a $525 million real estate fund under the Quantum banner. Most of the money was supplied by investors in Quantum's existing funds with Soros personally kicking in a quarter of the total. As manager of the Quantum Realty Fund, Reichmann would receive half of an annual fee equal to 1.5 percent of total assets (or $7.8 million in 1993) and 10 percent of any profits earned above a certain level. At the same time, Reichmann and Soros also formed Reichmann International L. P. to jointly pursue development projects in Mexico or wherever else opportunity might beckon around the world. Reichmann International was a 50-50 joint venture, with Reichmann and Soros each getting three seats on its board of directors. Ownership of the Reichmann half was divided among the three Toronto brothers but rested mainly with Paul.

About six months after Paul set up Reichmann International, Albert founded a separate entity called Reichmann Asia to do contract development work in China. This opportunity arose when Charoon Pokron CP Holding, a Thai agribusiness company with extensive land holdings throughout China, approached the Reichmanns looking for help in developing a large commercial complex in Shanghai. Reichmann Asia did not put up any financing itself but earned a fee for organizing and administering the project. By this time, Reichmann Asia was at work on another half dozen projects in China. "We're interested in becoming a vehicle for channeling third-party real estate investment from North America to China," explained Ron Soskolne, one of several former Olympia & York employees who split time between Reichmann Asia and Reichmann International.

Paul took no role in the Chinese venture, just as Albert had nothing to do with Reichmann International. Although Paul would have welcomed his brother's active involvement in his partnership with Soros, Albert had barely begun to recover emotionally from Olympia & York's ruination and was loath to again yoke himself to his domineering younger brother.

Paul was unable to muster much enthusiasm for his new vocation as vulture investor. For him, sifting the wreckage of the real estate collapse was a chore, a way to generate the capital needed to finance future Reichmann International projects and reestablish himself as a world-class developer. As always, though, Reichmann applied himself methodically to the task at hand. The Quantum Realty Fund made its first investment a large one, shelling out $634 million to buy thirty-five properties, mostly midsized office buildings, apartment complexes, and shopping centers located in the eastern half of the United States. The seller was the insurer Travelers Corporation, which, like most American real estate lenders, was staggering under the weight of all the second-class property it had seized to cover delinquent mortgages. Quantum put up $210 million to finance the purchase (Soros kicked in another $90 million from his own pocket), leaving Reichmann with ample cash for other deals. Over the next year, he would spend the balance of Quantum's remaining funds to purchase condominiums in New Jersey, undeveloped land in Florida, and an office tower in midtown Manhattan, as well as another six office buildings and two apartment buildings from Travelers.

Even as Reichmann was establishing himself as an important new player in the hyperactive market for distressed U.S. real estate, he devoted most of his energies to getting Reichmann International going in Mexico. Indeed, Reichmann's preoccupation with Mexican development strained his relationship with Soros, who was not as optimistic about the short-term economic outlook south of the border. Although Soros was willing to defer to Reichmann's judgment, his in-house real estate lieutenant, Evan Marks, objected vehemently. Marks ran G. Soros Realty Incorporated, a company that Soros set up in 1992 to manage his burgeoning real estate interests around the world. (About the same time that Soros had joined forces with Reichmann, he had also established joint real estate ventures in England and Argentina, among other countries.) Marks argued that Reichmann should stick to buying existing buildings at discount prices rather than assume the far greater risks of developing new properties in Mexico or anywhere else. With global real estate still in the dumper, Marks had a valid point, but his sniping infuriated Reichmann, who was accustomed to deference, if not reverence, from hired hands.

In late 1993, Soros agreed to a restructuring of Reichmann International that removed the Marks thorn from Reichmann's side. Soros gave up one of his seats on the board of Reichmann International Mexico, which left Reichmann with three of five votes. At the same time, the board of the New York–based Reichmann International was cut back to five seats, with Reichmann giving up a seat. As a result, Reichmann emerged with managerial control of the Mexican venture, and Marks was left in charge of running the Quantum Realty Fund. Within a few months, though, Soros had, to Reichmann's delight, replaced Marks as manager of Quantum Realty with Vernon Schwartz, a former Olympia & York executive and staunch Reichmann loyalist.

Meanwhile, in Mexico City in November 1993, Paul Reichmann made his first public appearance since Olympia & York's collapse. With Mayor Manuel Camacho Solis at his side at a press conference, he unveiled plans for three developments in Mexico City with a total estimated value of nearly $1.5 billion.

The largest and most advanced of them was the Santa Fe town center, or Centra Oeste at Santa Fe, as it was officially known. A master plan commissioned by Reichmann International envisioned a $600 million complex of thirty office, commercial, and apartment buildings connected by a series of dramatic public spaces and ascending a gradual incline to a hilltop by means of staircases, terraces, and walkways. Although most of the buildings were small, Centra Oeste's total space of 6 million square feet was comparable to World Financial Center. "With Santa Fe, we're not pioneering a whole new area like with Canary Wharf," Soskolne maintained. "It's like building in Chelsea instead of the East End"—although the inadequacy of the transport links between Santa Fe and the central city unhappily echoed the Docklands.

Reichmann International also planned to build a forty-two-story, stone-and-glass office tower on Paseo de la Reforma, overlooking Chapultepec Park in the city's central business district. At a cost of $250 million to $300 million, the Chapultepec tower was calculated to set a new standard of office luxury at the highest rents in the city. Reichmann was quite enamored of the design he had commissioned from the Toronto architect Eberhard Zeidler, predicting publicly that the building "will be a landmark that will rival any in the world."

Reichmann's third project was the most visionary of the lot and, naturally, the dearest to his heart. Before the massive 1985 earthquake that leveled much of Mexico City, historic Alameda Urban had been one of the city's busiest districts. Although the Salinas government had done much to restore public amenities, business had hung back. To restore the area to commercial critical mass, Reichmann proposed a massive $600 million mixed-use development covering two full city blocks. He considered the site ideal for tourist hotels and retailers but believed that if Alameda Urban was to be rehabilitated, the government would have to lead the way by preleasing large blocks of office space for its own use. Encouraged to proceed by lengthy consultations with high government officials, Reichmann hired Richard Legorreta, Mexico's leading architect, and nine other A-list architects of differing nationalities, commissioning each to design a building in the fourteen-building complex. "The idea was to create a world-class amalgam of design talent to provide office space of a North American magnitude within the context of a Mexican aesthetic," Reichmann explained. "If it isn't done right, it could be a flop. Or it could be an architectural marvel."

Reichmann began rehiring selected members of the old Olympia & York development team, including the Englishman John Norris, who had left the company after the World Financial Center to go to work for the Lefrak family in New York, and the master logistician Dan Frank, who had taken a job in Kuala Lumpur after Canary Wharf shut down. Vinay Kapor, an architect who had impressed Reichmann with his business acumen, was put in charge of Reichmann International's new branch office in Mexico City. At his father-in-law's request, Henry Brackfield (who had been born in Mexico City and was fluent in Spanish) left RF Real Estate in Toronto and moved to Mexico City.

Instead of attempting to gradually reestablish his bona fides as a developer, Reichmann in effect was proposing to take up where he had left off in London. Taken together, the Mexico projects were of a piece with Olympia & York's signature projects—or "Canary Wharf with enchiladas on the side," as the Canadian writer Walter Stewart put it. But while Reichmann's compulsion for the outsized undertaking was intact, it was tempered now by a hard-won pragmatism. Mindful of the building boom already under way in Mexico, as well as his own mishaps in London, Reichmann vowed that he would not break ground on any of the projects without having first preleased much of it and lined up construction financing in advance. "Building there on a spec basis would be suicide," he publicly conceded in discussing his pet Alameda Urban project. Reichmann International also departed from the Canary Wharf model in recruiting a local partner to help with Centra Oeste at Santa Fe. Empresas ICA Sociedad Controladora, Mexico's largest construction company, was to involve itself in all aspects of the development as a 49 percent owner and construction manager.

———

Although Paul and Albert had gone their separate ways in business, members of the next generation of the family were not averse to joining forces. Olympia & York Properties was the first entity to span the great fraternal divide, uniting

Paul's son-in-law Frank Hauer and Albert's sons Philip and David. Then, in 1994, Paul's son Barry joined Albert's son-in-law Laurence Koenig to invest in the acquisition of a nursing home chain in partnership with longtime Reichmann family friends, the Fruchthandlers of Brooklyn and the Kuhls of Toronto. George Kuhl was president of Meadowcroft Group, a privately held company that owned and operated two dozen nursing and retirement homes in Ontario. Kuhl joined with the Reichmann group and other investors to pay $220 million for Central Park Lodges, the nursing home subsidiary of Trizec Corporation, the developer once co-owned by the Reichmanns and Edper Bronfmans.

Ralph's sons were more inclined both to go it alone and to dabble in technology rather than real estate. Steven, Ralph's second son, teamed up with Bruce Bronfman, a son of Peter Bronfman, to buy a controlling interest in NHC Communications Incorporated, a small Toronto-based manufacturer of data processing equipment. Young Bronfman knew the founder of National Hav-Info and brought in Reichmann, with whom he had worked briefly at Trizec. National Hav-Info was the largest of a half-dozen venture capital investments made by Reichmann, who apparently financed his portfolio by taking out second mortgages on several houses he owned in Glenwood. Meanwhile, Steven's older brother, David, had eclipsed all other members of his generation of Reichmanns in entrepreneurial audacity in aspiring to build a company he had founded in Tel Aviv, Darcom Communications, into the dominant long-distance carrier not only in Israel but throughout the Middle East.

In 1989 David had made what proved to be the shrewdest move of his life, becoming the only member of the extended Reichmann family to convert the greater portion of his stock in Olympia & York to cash before the company's collapse. By all accounts, David's decision to sell was prompted by his own restlessness rather than any sense of foreboding about Olympia & York. According to Paul, David was bought out by his father, not by the company. Just thirty, David suddenly had at least $200 million cash to play with.

During the construction of the World Financial Center, David had worked with several companies installing state-of-the-art telecommunications facilities in the complex and had become fascinated with the technology. By the late 1980s, the Israeli government was readying plans to deregulate Bezeq, the state-run telephone monopoly and open up telecommunications to all comers. As David pondered Israel's telecom future, visions of mogulhood danced in his head, for he had the capital and the right connections to the Communications Ministry, which soon would carve up the telecom pie by issuing a series of licenses. The minister of communications was a member of Shas, the ultra-Orthodox party founded by Rabbi Eliezer Schach, the Israeli religious leader and venerable head of Ponovezh yeshiva, to which the Reichmann family had sworn its primary allegiance. David had attended Ponovezh and had established himself as a major benefactor of Rabbi Schach in his own right since coming into his inheritance.

For help in preparing his license applications, Reichmann looked up Gerald Lowe, a telecommunications consultant in New York who had done work for Olympia & York. "He didn't know anything, just nothing about the business. He only had his dreams," Lowe recalled. "I'm sitting here thinking, I don't think this guy has any idea of how much money we're talking about here. I said, 'David, do you really know what you're getting into?' He just looked at me and said something like, 'But I have a couple hundred million dollars.' I was like 'What!' All of a sudden I said, 'Holy smokes, I've got a client.' "

In 1991, David and his wife, Rachele, moved to B'nai Brak, the haredi sub-urb of Tel Aviv in which Ponovezh was located. He later told an Israeli reporter that his father and uncles were skeptical about his plans but gave him their blessing anyway. "They respected my ambition," he said, "but said that I always had a job back home if I wanted it." David also had less respectable rea-sons for leaving Toronto and the cloister of family, for he had secretly begun to abuse cocaine and also had taken a mistress. Rachele had learned of her hus-band's transgressions and pressured him to leave Toronto for Israel, before his parents and uncles found out. "She wanted him away from the family, the mis-tress, and the drug problems," a friend of David's recalled. "She felt they could make a whole new start in a new country."

In B'nai Brak, David and Rachele at last had realized their aspirations to lux-ury living, buying a three-story apartment building and converting it into a lavishly appointed villa complete with a butler, a maid, two nannies, and two drivers for their four cars. David reserved the basement and first floor for use by the company he had founded, Darcom Communications (Darcom was an acronym for David and Rachele's Company). In 1992, Reichmann outdid all other applicants in winning four of the most coveted licenses issued by the communications ministry. "It's like telecommunications was this pond frozen over by Bezeq," groused one industry veteran. "Finally—finally—we managed to break the ice, and then this stranger comes along with his fishing rod and starts pulling out all the fish."

The most important of its new licenses allowed Darcom into the business of providing companies with video-conferencing services and with private-line access to a low-cost dial tone for long-distance calls. But what Reichmann most coveted was a fifth license, which was to be issued in 1994, authorizing its recipient to compete with Bezeq as a long-distance carrier in its own right. To win this plum of plums, Reichmann decided he needed a partner and sold a one-third interest in Darcom for $10 million to IDB Communications, a Los Angeles company with an impressive collection of leased and owned satellites. In addition to bolstering Darcom's credibility as a bidder for the long-distance licenses, IDB provided Darcom with the phone lines and equipment needed to capitalize on the licenses it already had won. Reichmann hired a handful of experienced, well-connected senior executives, among them a former CEO of Bezeq, and also acquired a small Israeli company to help Darcom "go operational." When the *Jerusalem Post* profiled Reichmann at length in May of 1993, he seemed every inch the mogul-in-waiting. "I believe the telecommunications business is the business of the next twenty years," he proclaimed.

But in late 1993, *Globes,* a major Israeli financial paper, punctured Reichmann's balloon with a hard-hitting article that argued that Darcom was a monopoly-in-the-making and owed its good fortune in the license lottery to political arm-twisting by Rabbi Schach. The exposé had a devastating emotional effect on Reichmann, who vanished for several days during a business trip to New York and was drugged virtually to the point of catatonia when finally located. David's parents took him to Toronto and put him into a sanitorium, where he spent six weeks and then returned to Tel Aviv. In May 1994, Darcom took another body blow when it was revealed that a grand jury in Los Angeles was investigating IDB Communications' finances. The company's stock nosedived and its very survival suddenly was cast into doubt, as was Darcom's. Reichmann, who was a good forty pounds overweight, began complaining of chest pains. In late July, he took a vacation in Switzerland with his wife and children but left after several days for a business meeting in London. On August 1, he returned alone to Israel.

The only public account of David Reichmann's last hours is that of Ziva Buganim, a sometime prostitute, drug addict, smuggler, and petty thief who claimed to have been David's mistress for two years—a statement supported by a number of people, including the policemen who investigated Reichmann's death. After meeting Buganim on an airplane, Reichmann had put her up in a studio apartment in Tel Aviv's tourist district and visited her once or twice a week, indulging in both sex and drugs. "He was a good man. Nice," Buganim told *Vanity Fair* magazine, which in early 1996 published the definitive article on Reichmann's death. "But he didn't stand behind his words"—his avowed religious beliefs. "He didn't know who he was or what he was doing. He didn't like the ultra-Orthodox life at all. I think he wanted no part of it any more." Buganim said that Reichmann carried a little silver box filled with cocaine. "The drugs he used, it wasn't just a little. It was a lot. Cocaine. Heroin. A lot of it."

On the evening of August 1, Reichmann paid his last visit to Buganim, who had not seen him in four or five months. Reichmann snorted more cocaine than usual and fell asleep on the bed around 2:00 A.M., after asking to be awakened in a few hours. Around 6:30 Buganim tried to rouse him but found he was not breathing. At 6:47 she called an ambulance, which arrived eleven minutes later. The paramedics spent a futile half an hour trying to revive Reichmann, whose body was taken to the morgue for further examination. Apparently, Reichmann died of a heart attack induced by cocaine ingestion. (The family refused to permit an autopsy on religious grounds.)

Bowing to pressure applied by two leading haredi rabbis, the Tel Aviv police concocted a phony story for public dissemination, telling reporters that Reichmann had been found slumped over the wheel of his car on the side of a road between Tel Aviv and B'nai Brak. A few reporters ferreted out the true story but were unable to get their articles in print in what amounted to press self-censorship. "My editors, they said it was too yellow," recalled Yaariv Ben-Yehuda, the police reporter for IDF Radio. "We all decided to close it off at the news desks," Ben-Yehuda added. "The IDF, Ma'ariv, *Yediot Aharonot*—all the desks would close it off."

Thousands of haredi mourners joined Ralph and Ada Reichmann and other family members at David's funeral. As the ancient Rabbi Schach looked on from his limousine, several Ponovezh rabbis eulogized their student and benefactor. "God Almighty brought him to his death in a sudden manner in order to sanctify him, the way the Reichmann family, a very special family in our generation, has made holy the name of the Lord all these years," Rabbi David Povarsky said. Many newspapers ran memorials placed by the Israeli government.

For all practical purposes, Darcom died along with its founder, as scores of customers and employees departed in the months after Reichmann's death. The true story of his demise did not emerge until after Ziva Buganim was arrested on drug charges in mid-1995 and imprisoned. Buganim's estranged husband, Eli Buganim, who was in jail himself when Reichmann died, contacted the Tel Aviv police and threatened to expose their cover-up unless his wife was promptly released. Put off by the police, Buganim contacted a Tel Aviv television station, which broke the story. *Yediot Aharonot*, Israel's largest daily, followed by publishing the article it had earlier suppressed, though most newspapers in Israel and Canada maintained their silence, as did the Reichmann family itself. Rachele, David's widow, left Israel with her five children and moved to New York, where she had relatives.

David "had leadership qualities, but he had these inner doubts," recalled Akiva D. Mayer, an avuncular electronics executive who had come out of retirement to work at Darcom and who was one of the few people in whom Reichmann confided in the year before his death. "The question is, did the family put the pressure on him, or did he do it to himself to try to live up to the family name? I think it was the latter."

———

On December 1, 1994, Ernesto Zedillo took office as the president of Mexico, succeeding Carlos Salinas. Although Paul Reichmann was sorry to see Salinas go, he had every confidence that Zedillo would maintain the Mexican government's enthusiastic support of Reichmann International's Santa Fe, Chapultepec, and Alameda Urban development projects. Reichmann had met Zedillo, a Yale University–educated economist, once during his presidential campaign and was a guest at his inaugural banquet, sitting at the president's own table, where, to Reichmann's surprise (he had not been consulted in advance), he was served a glatt kosher meal. "It was clear to me that Zedillo saw his mission as completing the job that Salinas had started in the economy," Reichmann said.

Reichmann International had received building permits for both the Santa Fe and Chapultepec projects in November. A few days after Zedillo's inauguration, workers began preparing the Santa Fe site. Chapultepec was to get under way in a month or two. Reichmann had just about finished negotiating a construction loan for Santa Fe with Serafin and had persuaded his partner on the project, Empresas ICA Sociedad Controladora, to also make a large equity investment in the Chapultepec tower. The extension of the Reichmann-ICA partnership to include the downtown skyscraper was to be formalized on December 20. However, the documents never were signed, for the Mexican government chose the day of the scheduled closing to acknowledge that it could no longer afford to prop up the peso and to devalue the Mexican currency by 15 percent against the dollar. The move triggered panic selling of the peso that within twenty-four hours had forced the Zedillo government to cut the Mexican currency loose from its exchange-control moorings and let it find its own level in world markets. Within six weeks, the peso had lost 35 percent of its value and domestic interest rates had soared from 14 percent to 45 percent, wreaking havoc throughout the Mexican economy.

At Soros's urging, Reichmann put all three projects on hold until the markets stabilized and the extent of the damage to the economy could be gauged. "For the time being, I haven't made up my mind about Mexico," a manifestly crestfallen Reichmann said in an interview at his Toronto home in mid-February, 1996. "It's a great disappointment, of course, but we were to some extent lucky. It's a lot easier to slow down now than it would have been in ten months. If this had happened in the middle of the projects, it would have been catastrophic for me personally." All told, Reichmann International had invested about $50 million in Mexico, mostly in land purchases.

Not only had Reichmann International's development program stalled, but the other vehicle of Reichmann's partnership with Soros—the Quantum Realty Fund—had also gone off track. Although recovery had yet to really take hold in U.S. commercial real estate markets, the asset value of the fund had risen about 35 percent since its founding. Even so, the foreign investors who held the balance of its shares were unhappy with their after-tax returns, which had been deflated by the tax liabilities incurred by the fund. In the initial prospectus, Reichmann International had warned that an investment "may give rise to significant levels" of federal, state, and local tax but promised that the fund adviser would take "all appropriate measures to attempt to minimize such taxes." Reichmann had done what he could to shelter income, but Soros's offshore investors had grown accustomed both to tax-free investing and to bountiful short-term trading profits.

A few days after the February board meeting of the Quantum Realty Fund, Soros told Reichmann that he wanted to find a third party to buy out the foreign investors. Reichmann was taken aback, knowing that a mass exit of the original Quantum shareholders would be interpreted as a repudiation of the fund and thicken the patina of failure now accumulating on his comeback. Reichmann International remained a 50-50 joint venture, which meant that Soros could not make changes in the fund without Reichmann's consent. Reichmann deferred to Soros, for he saw nothing to gain from defying the man who had singlehandedly bankrolled his return to action. "I have a good relationship with Soros, in that this has been a profitable venture," Reichmann said a few days after Soros had broached the subject of restructuring the fund.

This carefully worded statement hardly constituted a ringing endorsement of the joys of partnership with the Man Who Moves Markets. Reichmann's relationship with Soros was cordial enough but had not blossomed into anything resembling friendship. Although Reichmann had prevailed in his battle with Marks, he was not so much grateful for Soros's backing as resentful of the indignity of having had to play politics after having ruled by fiat for so long at Olympia & York. "There is no reason not to want the relationship [with Soros] to continue," Reichmann added tepidly, "but at the same time, the relationship is in an area where I have the expertise and he does not, nor do his employees." For his part, Soros was going through a rough patch as his flagship Quantum fund trailed the stock market in 1994 and in 1995 had begun declining in absolute terms. For Soros, a trader no less by temperament than training, five to ten years suddenly seemed a very long time indeed to wait for his investment in Paul Reichmann to bear the fruit of capital gains. What becomes of a marriage of convenience that is no longer convenient?

Ever since he had joined forces with Soros, Reichmann had resisted the temptation to bid on Olympia & York properties, on the theory that it was better to start fresh than to attempt to cut a deal with the company's aggrieved creditors. But now that his partnership with Soros was inactive at best, Reichmann shifted tack. Acting out of desperation as much as desire, be began plotting a comeback of the most literal sort. "Over the last two weeks I've been updating myself on Canary Wharf and Olympia & York's U.S. properties," said Reichmann, a bit sheepishly, in the February interview. "I'll spend a few weeks studying the information and then, who knows?"

Reichmann's attention was drawn mainly to Canary Wharf, which had emerged from administration and reentered the commercial marketplace. In late 1993, the project's construction lenders had reached agreement among themselves to buy Canary Wharf by converting their £568 million in loans into equity and to contribute another £278 million to pay off the unsecured creditors, cover the £98 million down payment on the Jubilee Line, and resume construction and marketing of the first phase of the project. As soon as the London commercial real estate market rebounded from the depths in 1994 and 1995, major corporations reconsidered Docklands as an office site and Canary Wharf's new British-led management team scored a series of notable leasing successes, signing up Barclays de Zoete Wedd, one of the classier U.K. merchant banks, and the *Daily Mirror* newspaper. Morgan Stanley, which had sued Olympia & York and had been on the verge of pulling out of the project in 1992, took an additional 350,000 square feet on top of the 450,000 square feet it already occupied. By the spring of 1995, Canary Wharf was 75 percent leased, exceeding the previous high-water mark by a good twenty percentage points, although at £20 to £25 a square foot, rents were only about half the going rate in the City.

By this time, Lew Ranieri and Sandy Weill were otherwise preoccupied, but Reichmann succeeded in persuading another of his erstwhile backers, Larry Tisch, to join him in making another bid for Canary Wharf. The other investors Reichmann recruited included Michael Price, a well-known Wall Street fund manager, and Edmond Safra, the billionaire banker who shared Reichmann's interest in Sephardic education. Cargill, the Minneapolis-based grain-trading giant, decided against making an equity investment but did agree to provide debt financing. However, Soros declined to participate and his refusal marked the end of his partnership with Reichmann, who soon sold his 50 percent stake in Reichmann International to Soros for $27.5 million. (By year end, Soros would have sold his 28 percent stake in the Quantum Realty Fund to the Wall Street investment bank Goldman Sachs & Company.)

The Reichmann group did not have the field to itself. By mid-1995, a half-dozen potential acquirers were circling, including Prince Alaweed bin Talal bin Abdulazisi Alsaud of Saudi Arabia and the Hwangs, a wealthy Hong Kong family. Reichmann also had to contend with Jerry Speyer, an American developer, who was making a determined effort to woo away Larry Tisch. Speyer was a real threat, but the Saudi prince was a Reichmann ally masquerading as a rival. Only thirty-eight, Alaweed was the largest shareholder of Citicorp, which was one of the new owners of Canary Wharf. Working through Citicorp, the prince in mid-1994 had submitted a proposal to buy Canary Wharf but was turned down. Alaweed's offer was made in strictest confidence, but a friendly banker had tipped Reichmann, who pulled himself away from Mexico long enough to invite himself to the prince's yacht, which was anchored off Cannes.

The Saudi was impressed that his guest had learned of his bid. After much ceremonial circumlocution, Reichmann finally popped the question that had brought him halfway around the world. "If your proposal had been accepted, who would have managed Canary Wharf?" Reichmann inquired.

"I would have given you a call," Alaweed replied.

The next spring, as Reichmann was readying his own Canary Wharf bid, he again met with Alaweed, who also was approached by Jerry Speyer soon after. To the prince, the choice was clear, Reichmann's recent Mexican misadventures notwithstanding. "Reichmann knows how to manage real estate better than anyone else in the world," Alaweed later said. The Arab investor and the Jewish developer formed a covert tactical alliance. "We decided to bid separately and keep the door open," Reichmann explained. "His theory was that if one of us failed and the other succeeded, we could join together." Later, the prince disclosed that one of his aides had asked if Reichmann's Jewishness might not be an obstacle to effective partnership. "Reichmann's an Orthodox Jew, and I'm an orthodox Muslim," Alaweed responded. "We're both orthodox, so where's the problem?" For his part, Reichmann similarly acknowledged an odd kinship with the Arab: "He is traditional and religious, yet modern"— much like Reichmann himself.

Canary Wharf's new owners were receptive to offers but were in no particular hurry to sell now that the complex was making what seemed to be inexorable progress toward the breakeven point. For all practical purposes, the ranks of bidders was soon narrowed to two: Reichmann and Alaweed. In August, the prince withdrew his proposal and announced that he was investing $100 million to acquire 10 percent of International Property Corporation, the Reichmann consortium. Just before midnight on October 2, 1995, the bank owners announced an agreement to sell Canary Wharf to IPC for about £800 million—or about 95 percent of the sum total of money they had lent, including the additional £278 million in new credit they had extended in bringing the project out of administration in late 1993.

During a seven-hour visit to Reichmann's Toronto home in late October, the mood was palpably different from what it had been in February, when the partnership with Soros was unraveling. It was as if a siege had been lifted. For the first time in a long time, the phone in the library was ringing off the hook with congratulatory calls from around the world. Lea Reichmann's face was positively abeam with pride and relief as she discussed her preparations to venture forth from the cloistered confines of 241 Strathallan Wood and join her husband on an extended trip to London. For his part, Paul Reichmann, as always, skipped lightly over the emotions of the moment but spoke animatedly of his plans for Canary Wharf. "Regaining Canary Wharf means a lot to me for several reasons," Reichmann said, but was willing to expound on only one. "It's the largest project I've ever undertaken and the only one that I never finished. It was left half done, and it needs to be finished."

Although the business plan that Reichmann had presented to Tisch, Price, and his other backers was modest in scope, projecting a gradual attainment of profitability as the vacant space in the twelve completed buildings was leased or sold, clearly he still clung to his grand vision of Canary Wharf as London's third business district—a core of two dozen office buildings surrounded by vast retail and residential development. This time, however, he vouchsafed no predictions of Canary Wharf's inevitable success. "It will be a struggle," he conceded. "I'm not kidding myself." While Reichmann undoubtedly had learned from his failures, his ambition now was tethered as much by financial dependence as by hard-won wisdom. Between them, Tisch and Price own more than 50 percent of IPG, to Reichmann's 5 percent, and in effect assert control.

Epilogue

"What distinguishes the Reichmanns," Trevor Eyton said in 1988, at the height of Olympia & York's long and profitable run, "is their intelligence, their thoughtfulness. They are, in a sense, philosophers." Tempting as it would be to credit Paul Reichmann and his brothers with having alchemized anti-Semitism into philo-Semitism, the fact is that ignorance underlay their towering public image like a fault line under a skyscraper; the Reichmanns were venerated without ever having been understood as haredim or, for that matter, as businessmen.

In no sense philosophers for all their intelligence and seemliness, Edward, Louis, Albert, Paul, and Ralph Reichmann were pious men of action whose exceptional family background instilled in them high purpose and a degree of self-reliance that served them well in business in many ways but also bred an insularity that left large, fateful gaps in their knowledge, judgment, and capabilities. These shortcomings were exacerbated as Paul, the most driven and prodigiously gifted of the brothers, gained dominance over the family and the family company, transforming the highest councils of each into echo chambers for his own increasingly daring propositions. Rarely has extreme commercial ambition come as demurely packaged as in the person of Paul Reichmann, whose religiosity did not blunt his secular ambitions but rather seemed to feed a self-assurance that swelled into megalomania. With the possible exception of Michael Milken, no businessman in recent memory has wielded as much economic power as unilaterally as did Reichmann at Olympia & York's zenith.

While Milken tumbled from his perch into a prison cell, the legality of Paul Reichmann's conduct was never at issue. But if Reichmann was an honest man, in the end he fell well short of the standard of ethical irreproachability to which he had aspired as a young merchant in Casablanca. In his increasingly desperate efforts to save Olympia & York from bankruptcy while maintaining his domination of the company, Reichmann dissembled and connived in ways that left all sorts of people feeling ill-used, including many of Olympia & York's most valued employees. The most embittered was probably Michael Dennis, who submitted a claim for nearly $20 million in severence, back pay, and deferred compensation.

Even in his heyday, Paul Reichmann was so unrelenting in his financial perfectionism that at times, in fact, not even his signature was his bond. Almost lost amid the Sturm und Drang of Olympia & York's apocalyptic final months was a court ruling that cast into damning long relief the recent complaints of the company's creditors about Reichmann's slippery negotiating tactics. In mid-1992, after a lengthy nonjury trial, a New York judge ruled that in 1983 Olympia & York had unjustifiably reneged on a signed commitment to borrow $250 million from Teachers Insurance and Annuity Association of America to help finance the World Financial Center. (Olympia & York hadn't borrowed the money as agreed because Reichmann had arranged much more favorable terms with another lender.) In 1996, the New York State Supreme Court awarded Teachers $41 million in damages.

Outwardly, anyway, spectacular failure has changed the Reichmann brothers' way of life as little as had the spectacular success that preceded it. Albert, Paul, and Ralph and their wives continue to reside in the same houses in which they have lived since the 1960s and to practice their faith in the same synagogues as do humble rank-and-file members of the ultra-Orthodox community that once revolved around them. In most families, the loss of a $10 billion fortune might have been expected to raise an embarassing ruckus of accusation and recrimination, but the Reichmanns have all maintained a decorous silence, nursing their grievances privately while continuing to honor the requirements of family as conscientiously as they practice their religion. Their fortune has vanished, but the Reichmanns' familial bonds—like their religious identities—were forged in titanium.

Like Edward and Louis before them, Albert and Ralph have been yanked from history's stage, no doubt to their immense relief. However, the fourth-born brother gives every indication of continuing to command the spotlight. Now that he has been dethroned as the Philosopher King of business, Paul Reichmann in his mid-sixties is manifestly what he has long been: one of the most resilient and tenacious entrepreneurs of the twentieth century.

Just a few weeks before this book was to go to press, I got word that Paul Reichmann wanted to see me. On October 15, 1996, we had breakfast in the dining room of the St. Regis Hotel, which had supplanted the Waldorf-Astoria as Reichmann's favorite New York hotel. In the year since I'd last interviewed Reichmann, he had regained Canary Wharf and was once again virtually commuting between Toronto and London, with an occasional side trip to New

York. Although Reichmann, as always, was so soft-spoken as to verge on inaudibility, in his own low-key way he was again a man on a mission.

On the telephone, Reichmann had said that with Canary Wharf securely in hand he was prepared to speak more candidly about the circumstances that led to Olympia & York's collapse. For the most part, what this meant was that he was newly willing to point the finger at Olympia & York's bankers—particularly the Canadian contingent.

By 1996, Olympia & York's much-maligned stock market portfolio had doubled in value from its low-water mark in 1991 and 1992—or, rather, it *would* have had it remained intact. As it was, Olympia & York's secured creditors had liquidated most of the stock in 1993 and 1994 after forcing the company into bankruptcy. "Those assets were sold at the worst possible time," Reichmann said. "Had we been allowed to restructure the company, those assets could have been delayed until 1995 and 1996. The Reichmann family fortune still would have been pared down, but the banks need not have lost a single penny." It is virtually impossible to confirm this assertion independently, but bank losses would unquestionably have been greatly reduced if not eliminated by a better-timed stock sale. Of course, the banks had no way of knowing in 1992 that the stock market was poised to soar the way it has in the mid-1990s.

The catastrophe of liquidation could have been avoided, Reichmann continued, had Olympia & York's Canadian bankers only listened to Citibank, which favored restructuring the company and employed bankers with the skill and experience to make it work. "Had Citibank been given the cooperation of the Canadian banks, Olympia & York would have been saved," Reichmann said. "I'm not criticizing the Canadian banks," he added, not very convincingly. "Don Fullerton [of Canadian Imperial Bank of Commerce] was very supportive of restructuring at the beginning, but at some point he changed his mind. I do not know why he did and I never asked. It was a judgment call that he made, and it was fully within his prerogative to make it. It could have simply been a decision that it was better to take care of their shareholders than to salvage a client."

For his own part, Reichmann admitted to having made "quite a few mistakes for lack of experience in restructuring. I did have good advice," he added, preparing to deflect blame to Steve Miller, Gerald Greenwald, Michael Dennis, and others, "but it was not good enough. The people advising me were among the brightest people in the world, but not sufficiently experienced in restructuring."

As for Canary Wharf, Reichmann said, abruptly tacking from the past toward the future, 84 percent of the space in the twelve completed buildings had been leased, and the complex was generating a small monthly operating profit. Moreover, Citibank had agreed in principle to relocate its London headquarters to Canary Wharf and was on the verge of signing a long-term lease for 540,000 square feet. Under their original business plan, Reichmann and his backer had projected that no new construction would be undertaken until 1999 at the earliest. However, accommodating Citicorp will require putting up a new building, Reichmann said. "The exciting part of this transaction is that it jump-starts our plans to build Canary Wharf to its full dimensions"—meaning twenty-four office buildings surrounded by extensive retail and residential development. "There are still people who don't want to leave the City, but today any major space user in London will at least *look* at Canary Wharf," Reichmann said. "It is now a viable alternative to any site in the City or the West End."

Reichmann predicts that two of his three projects in Mexico City will be revived in 1997, and he pointedly notes that First Canadian Place bonds are currently trading at a price that implies a value of about $270 million for the complex—a quarter of its value at its late-1980s peak. "At some point," Reichmann says, "I'll make an offer for it." The odds are stacked against Reichmann building a second company the size of Olympia & York or of regaining billionaire status. But he appears now to have a decent chance of going down in history not as the Man Who Blew $10 Billion but the Man Who Blew $10 Billion and Changed the Face of London.

Paul's resilience might seem surprising, but then he is more than a businessman: He is a Reichmann. There is an old Yiddish folk saying that every cat likes fish but few will enter the water. The Reichmanns entered the water. Whether it was an audacious commercial gamble like Canary Wharf or a dauntless attempt to rescue fellow Jews from the Nazis, the Reichmanns have always acted, always dared, always engaged the world around them. Their activism—be it financial or philanthropic—was the product not only of religious faith but of their abiding belief in themselves as a family of elect destiny. And that, indeed, is what they are, for the Reichmann saga could easily have ended at any point on the family's improbable journey from Beled to Vienna to Paris to Tangier to Toronto to the wastelands of East London. The family may never be as rich or as revered as they were but recently, but history suggests that the final chapter of the Book of Reichmann has not yet been written.

Notes

I OBERLAND EXODUS

Chapter 1

3 The depopulation of Jewish Hungary. *Encyclopedia Judaica*, s.v. "Hungary."

4 The Seven Communities were Eisenstadt, Mattersburg, Deutschkreutz, Frauenkirchen, Kittee, Kobersdorf, and Lackenbach.

4 Leopold, or Leib, Gestetner also is mentioned in one of the responsa of the Hatam Sofer (Book "Even Haezer, Part II," 86).

4 The Jewish history of Csorna. *Pinkas Hakehillot: Encyclopedia of Jewish Communities, Hungary* (Jerusalem: Yad Vashem, 1976), s.v. "Csorna." For background on the Gestetners in Csorna, see Laszlo Horvath, *Sopron és Sopronvármegye Ismertetője, 1914–1934* (Sopron: Székely és Társa Kőnyvnyomdai Vállalat).

4 The wedding of Amram Grunwald and Esther Gestetner. Gestetner family tree, provided courtesy of David Gestetner.

4 Gestetner and Grunwald women gave birth to forty-two children. Register of Jewish births, marriages and deaths for Győr, 1846–95 (Salt Lake City: Genealogical Society of Utah, 1965).

5 The Jewish repopulation of Hungary. *Encyclopedia Judaica*, s.v. "Hungary."

5 Dates for Eliyahu Reichmann. Register of Jewish births, marriages and deaths for Nýirbátor, 1846–95 (Salt Lake City: Genealogical Society of Utah, 1965).

5 The derivation of Reichmann as a Jewish name. In Yiddish the Hebrew name Rachel became Reichel. The surname Reichelson denotes "the son of Reichel." Variations of the name include Reichmann, Reichstein, and Reichenheim. Benzion Kaganoff, *A Dictionary of Jewish Names and Their History* (New York: Shocken Books, 1977), 187.

7 "In the Talmudic Age, the Talmud was right. . . ." Rabbi Samuel Holdheim (1806–60), quoted by Paul Johnson, *A History of the Jews* (New York: Harper & Row, 1987), 334.

7 Orthodox Jews "accept as divinely inspired. . . ." *Encyclopedia Judaica*, s.v. "Orthodoxy."

7 "Directing its appeals to the feelings. . . ." Philip Birnbaum, *Encyclopedia of Jewish Concepts* (New York: Hebrew Publishing Company, 1993), s.v. "Hasidim."

8 Eli Reichmann "was middle-of-the-road Orthodox. . . ." Interview by author, Queens, N.Y., 8 August 1994.

9 "I have already replied. . . ." Jacob Katz, "Toward a Biography of the Hatam Sofer," in *From East and West: Jews in a Changing Europe,* ed. Frances Malino and David Sorkin (Oxford: Basil Blackwell, 1990), 241.

10 "If your liberal brethren. . . ." Solomon Poll, *The Hasidic Community of Williamsburg* (New York: Free Press of Glencoe, 1962), 13.

12 Budapest as the fastest growing city in Europe. William McCagg, *Jewish Nobles and Geniuses in Modern Hungary* (New York: Columbia University Press, 1972), 31.

12 The Jewish demographics of Budapest. Ibid., 30.

13 "The Jews played a singularly important role. . . ." Randolph Braham, *The Politics of Genocide,* vol. 1 (New York: Columbia University Press), 7–8.

13 "Even in imperial Germany and tsarist Russia," McCagg, *Jewish Nobles and Geniuses in Modern Hungary,* 37.

13 "In Vienna, Berlin, London. . . ." John Lukacs, *Budapest 1900* (New York: Weidenfeld & Nicolson), 94.

14 "Office duplicating for the first time. . . ." W. B. Proudfoot, *The Origin of Stencil Duplicating* (London: Hutchison), 67.

14 Arnold was one Gestetner who strayed far from the life of strict observance. An accomplished salesman and irrepressible bon vivant, Arnold antagonized his cousin and employer by amassing large unpaid debts while representing the company in Milan. "Whatever money he made was soon dissipated on women and the gaming tables. 'Larger than life' would, perhaps, be an adequate description," observed DG's grandson, also named David Gestetner, in an unpublished corporate history.

14 "There can be no doubting . . . as religious practice." Charles David, "The DG I Knew," an unpublished manuscript provided courtesy of David Gestetner.

15 "He was my master. . . ." Raphael Patai, *Apprentice in Budapest* (Salt Lake City: University of Utah Press, 1988,), 82–83.

15 Satu Mare is now part of Romania.

16 "They practically took the food from their own mouths. . . ." Zvi Reichmann, *The Mountain of a Deer* (Turña, Slovensko: Leopold Glanc, 1926).

16 "I spent a lot of time. . . ." From an untitled, unpublished memoir by Edward Reichmann, written in the mid-1980s and provided courtesy of the author.

16 The children of David and Lidi Reichmann. Register of Jewish births, marriages and deaths for Beled, 1836–95 (Salt Lake City: Genealogical Society of Utah, 1965).

Chapter 2

18 "They had three or four rooms. . . ." Elaine Dewar, "The Mysterious Reichmanns," *Toronto Life,* November 1987, 156.

18 Birthplaces of the Gestetner siblings. Győr municipal archives, registry of citizenship.

18 "When somebody came to the city. . . ." Dewar, "The Mysterious Reichmanns," 156.

18 "Totally absorbed in the study of Torah. . . ." Paul Reichmann, interview by author, Toronto, 20 November 1994.

18 "She was not what you would call an intellectual. . . ." Ibid.

19 "It happened during World War I. . . ." Edited version of unpublished memoir, 6–8. One of the most striking aspects of this account is its utter if offhanded disdain for "the worker," presumably a Gentile, who must be lured into overtime with a case of beer—watered-down beer no less—and who is accorded no share of the credit for the herculean feat accomplished or of the Portiz's tip. He must have been a very skilled worker, indeed, to have installed palatial-sized glass panes while drunk.

20 "Milk and butter were still unobtainable. . . ." Tudor Edwards, *The Blue Danube* (London: Hale, 1973), 130.

21 "People carried bags. . . ." Joseph Wechsberg, *The Vienna I Knew* (Garden City, N.Y.: Doubleday, 1979), 140.

21 "An egg cost . . . in exchange for butter and eggs." Edwards, *The Blue Danube*, 131.

23 The history of Beled. *Pinkas Hakehillot: Encyclopedia of Jewish Communities, Hungary*, s.v. "Beled."

24 In the early 1930s, Berger's business finally succumbed to years of neglect and closed, reducing its proprietor to penury. The yeshiva survived, supported by other patrons, including Samuel Reichmann. In 1933, one of the wealthier Gestetners took Berger under his wing, inviting him to the town of Neipest. With Amram Gestetner's backing, Berger started another yeshiva, which flourished until the Germans occupied Hungary. In 1944, Berger was deported to Auschwitz and died there.

25 "There were many jobless people. . . ." Gyula Sagi, interview by Mihaly Benkő for author, Beled, Hungary, 4 March 1996.

25 Simon also married a Gestetner. Simon's wife, Terez Grausz, was the daughter of Flora Gestetner of Beled.

26 Statistics on Austrian egg consumption. "The Present Position of Poultry Keeping in German Austria," *Monthly Bulletin of Agricultural Science and Practice* (Rome: International Institute of Agriculture, 1921), 887.

26 "To foster export . . ." Ignatius Daranyi, *The State and Agriculture in Hungary* (Budapest: Royal Hungarian Minister of Agriculture, 1905), 80. See also *Agricultural Hungary* (Budapest: Royal Hungarian Minister of Agriculture, 1908).

26 For background on the egg industry in Hungary and the Oberland before World War II, see Ottó Domonkos, *A nyugatmagyarországi tyukászatról* (Budapest: 1944); József Hary, *Magyarország baromfi, tojás, toll külkereskedelme* (Budapest: 1932).

27 "Perhaps the bleakest in Eastern Europe." E. Garrison Walters, *The Other Europe* (Syracuse, N.Y.: Syracuse University Press, 1988), 208.

27 The relative standing of European egg exporters. "On Poultry-Farming in Europe," *Monthly Bulletin of Agricultural Science and Practice,* 1911, 481.

29 Vienna's Jewish conversion rate as the highest in Europe. George Berkley, *Vienna and Its Jews* (Cambridge, Mass.: Abt Books, 1987), 54.

Chapter 3

30 "Nine-tenths of what the world celebrated. . . ." Stefan Zweig, quoted in Berkley, *Vienna and Its Jews,* 38.

31 "Yesterday grand soirée. . . ." Johnson, *A History of the Jews,* 391–2.

31 "Vienna appeared to me in a new light." Adolf Hitler, *Mein Kampf* (Munich: Franz Eher Nachfolger, 1930), 59–60.

31 Herminengasse 6. This and subsequent Reichmann addresses in Vienna are taken from a document on file at Wiener Stadt-U. Landesarchiv (City and National Archives of Vienna), Magistratsabteilung 8 (Municipal Council 8).

32 "A mighty fortress. . . ." Charles Richter, *The Vienna Kehileth: Adas Yereim 25 Years Journal* (New York: Adas Yereim, 1967), 3.

33 "Quite a number of youngsters. . . ." Teddy Kollek, *For Jerusalem* (New York: Random House), 6.

33 The Reichmann aversion to organizational entanglement. It probably was no coincidence that Edward was both the only avowed Zionist in the family and the only brother to complete his grade-school education in Vienna.

33 "A famous horror." Dewar, "The Mysterious Reichmanns," 138.

33 "Catastrophe for Hungarian agriculture. . . ." League of Nations, *European Conference on Rural Life,* vol. 27 (Geneva: League of Nations, 1939), 59.

34 Decline in index of agricultural prices. Ibid., 60.

34 Germany accounted for 47 percent of Hungarian egg exports in 1929. Antonin Basch, *The Danube Basin and the German Economic Sphere* (New York: Columbia University Press, 1943), 5.

35 The nanny. During the postwar haredi renaissance, a number of rabbis inveighed against the use of non-Jews as au pairs. But it was common practice in prewar Vienna—that is, among the Orthodox minority who could afford servants.

35 "Well, they wouldn't sell it any cheaper." Interview by author, New York, 24 March 1993.

35 "If she could have had more children. . . ." Interview by author, New York, 6 May 1993.

35 "The Vienna school was much more demanding. . . ." Interview by author.

35 "My father had certain expectations. . . ." Ibid.

36 "The children looked up to their parents. . . ." Interview by author, 6 May 1993.

36 "My mother was absolutely determined. . . ." Interview by author.

36 Schwarzinger Schule as bastion of anti-Semitism. Unpublished memoir, 39.

36 "We all looked forward. . . ." Interview by author.

36 "As a boy . . ." Ibid.

37 "Most people thought that the Wollsteins. . . ." Murray (formerly Mor) Stern, telephone interview by author, 16 November 1993.

37 "His visitor had to have a tea." Interview by author.

38 "He didn't want to use the money. . . ." Unpublished memoir, 13.

38 "Grandfather and grandmother had six married children. . . ." Edited version of letter of 25 February 1990.

38 Uncle Yossi's mysterious ritual. Edward's unpublished memoir, 14.

39 "I went up to their apartment . . . Lola got." Interview by author, 24 March 1993.

39 "Mr. Reichmann was very *frum*. . . ." Abraham Schreiber, interview by author, London, England, 29 September 1993.

39 "She never showed her emotions. . . ." Interview by author, 24 March 1993.

40 "Something almost unbelievable . . . religious fanaticism." Telephone interview by author, 22 January 1996.

40 Renée's reaction to her brother's death. Isaac Klein, interview by author, New York, 23 March 1993.

40 "A nation apart . . . the distinction between the sexes. . . ." Adin Steinsaltz, *The Essential Talmud* (London: Weidenfeld and Nicolson, 1976), 144.

40 "She never gave Shimi. . . ." Interview by author, 6 May 1993.

40 "She looked like a freak. . . ." Ibid.

41 "Communism might not be such a bad thing. " Alexander Heiden, interview by author, Antwerp, Belgium, 21 November 1993.

42 "Rarely did I sleep in my own room. . . ." Interview by author, Jerusalem, 25 April 1993.

42 "I did errands for them. . . ." Ibid.

43 "Very few people could help. . . ." Unpublished memoir, 28.

44 "I saw Renée and Olga almost every day. . . ." Interview by author, 6 May 1993.

Chapter 4

45 Anti-Semites with canes; destruction of the Café Produktenbourse. Ruth Beckerman, *Die Mazzesinsel* (Vienna: Locker, 1984), 20.

45 Bombing of Jewish shops. Bruce Pauley, *From Prejudice to Persecution* (Chapel Hill: University of North Carolina Press, 1992), 201.

46 "In our circles. . . ." Freud to Marie Bonaparte, cited by Berkley, *Vienna and Its Jews*, 213.

46 "The Austrian Jews . . . behaved like ostriches." Tamar Berman, quoted in Berkley, *Vienna and Its Jews*, 246.

46 The Orthodox "tended to be oblivious. . . ." Pauley, *From Prejudice to Persecution*, 226.

46 Rabbi Grunwald and the radio. Edward's unpublished memoir, 38.

47 Samuel's evolution from "pessimist" to "superpessimist." Interview by author, Jerusalem, 22 April 1993.

47 "My father was absolutely determined. . . ." Interview by author.

47 R. Walther Darre, *Das Bauerntum als Lebensquell der nordischen Rasse* (Munich: I. F. Lehman, 1929).

47 The visit to Smidel & Co. Unpublished memoir, 30.

48 "A national and Christian foundation." *Tájékoztató a baromfi és tojásforgalmi · kőzpont mükődéseről és orszagos szorvezetéről* (Budapest: 1944).

48 "It was not unusual to hear on the streets. . . ." Interview by author.

48 "We defended ourselves as best we could. . . ." Interview by author, 25 April 1993, Jerusalem.

49 "You already are a big boy . . . my bar mitzvah next year." Unpublished memoir, 39.

49 Edward's bar mitzvah. Edward Reichmann, interview by author, 25 April 1993; Louis Reichmann, interview by author. Also Edward's unpublished memoir, 40-1, and his letter to his mother's grandchildren and great-grandchildren, 5 March 1990, provided by Edward Reichmann.

50 "Austria is a province of the German Reich." Alan Bullock, *Hitler and Stalin* (New York: Alfred A. Knopf, 1992), 567.

50 "The underworld had opened its gates. . . ." Peter Gay, *Freud: A Life for Our Time* (New York: W. W. Norton, 1988), 619.

50 Samuel's conversation with Trudy. Interviews by author of Edward and Louis Reichmann.

51 "My mother was not that keen . . . could not talk to him about it." Interview by author.

52 "He did not merely create it. . . ." David Landau, *Piety and Power* (London, Martin Secker & Warburg, 1993), 44.

53 "He was a Jew-hater . . . for your own you'll do anything." Interview by author, 24 March, 1993.

53 Schiff's "close working relationship" with the Aliens Department. Geoffrey Alderman, *Modern British Jewry* (Oxford: Clarendon Press, 1992), 278.

54 "I have refused . . ." British Passport Control Officer, Budapest, to Director, Passport Control Department, 25 April 1938, Public Records Office, HO 213/94.

54 D. Gestetner Ltd.'s public stock offering. *Dictionary of Business Biography*, vol. 2., 523.

54 "Traditional but not religious." David Gestetner, interview by author, London, 9 September 1993.

54 "My mother mainly visited David." Interview by author, 25 April 1993.

54 "There was an endless flow. . . ." Charles David, "The DG I Knew," 18.

54 "Wanted to get a certificate for Palestine . . . he didn't achieve it." Transcript of an unpublished interview by David Kranzler, 1 May 1983, Reichmann family archives.

55 S. Gestetner as friend of Chaim Weizmann. In late 1940, one of Weizmann's grandsons was born at Sigmund Gestetner's country estate at Boshom, a safe distance north of London near Bognor Regis. The Gestetners had volunteered to shelter the Weizmanns' pregnant daughter-in-law during the Nazi bombing raids on London. Vera Weizmann, *The Impossible Takes Longer* (London: H. Hamilton, 1967), 183.

55 "My father got lots of relatives. . . ." Interview by author.

Chapter 5

57 "Tended to be Germanic . . . charmless little edifice." Chaim Bermant, *Lord Jakobovits* (London: Weidenfeld and Nicolson, 1990), 115.

57 "The Reichmanns were very close to my father." Interview by author, London, 8 September 1993.

58 "For us the Pletzl was. . . ." Interview by author, 22 April 1993.

58 "Many poor people . . ." Ibid.

58 Paying 720 francs for a hotel room. Prefecture de Police (Paris), archives of the Casier Central des Etrangers, Dossier 1633, 265.

58 The relatively high cost of kosher food. "Poorly paid," the typical Orthodox émigré in Paris "could not afford to buy the more expensive kosher meats required by Jewish law. Nor could they observe the Sabbath, since many businesses in the clothing and textile trades remained open on Saturday. Even home-laborers who ostensibly controlled their own work schedule were forced to work the entire week in order to earn a subsistence income." David Weinberg, *A Community on Trial* (Chicago: University of Chicago Press, 1977), 55.

58 Mr. and Mrs. Reichmann's cash holdings. Their applications for residence permits can be found at the Prefecture de Police (Paris), Casier Central des Etrangers, Dossier 1633, 265.

59 "I stayed with an aunt. . . ." Interview by Kranzler.

60 "Paris before the war. . . ." Interview by author.

60 "The Rue Cadet community was very French. . . ." Interview by author, London, 26 September 1993.

60 Samuel's application for a carte d'identité. Prefecture de Police (Paris), Casier Central des Etrangers, Dossier 1633, 265.

60 "I didn't let many people use my name. . . ." Interview by author. On his application, Samuel also cited as a reference Mr. A. David, who worked in London for the Zurich bank Banque Wohl et Landau.

60 "They came to my restaurant. . . ." Ibid.

61 Samuel's list of assets. Allgemeines Verweltungsarchiv (General Administrative Archive) Vienna, file 34103.

61 The notices from the Property Transfer Office. Ibid.

62 "Uncle Simon felt that Paris. . . ." Edward Reichmann, open letter to his mother's descendants, 5 March 1990.

63 "Unworthy of the title . . . undesirables." Richard Cohen, *The Burden of Conscience* (Bloomington: Indiana University Press, 1987), 8.

63 Details of A. Schreiber's arrest and detention. Abraham Schreiber, interview by author.

63 Samuel's application for permanent residence and expiration of visa. Prefecture de Police (Paris), Casier Central des Etrangers, Dossier 1633, 265.

64 Techniques of disguising ownership of U.S. bank deposits. Brendan Brown, *The Flight of International Capital* (London: Croom Helm, 1987), 122.

65 Siegfried Bendheim had an American business partner named Charles Ullman, but he was no relation to the man who married Marie Gestetner. However, Bendheim had a marital connection of his own to the Gestetner family. His wife had a French cousin, Marcel Weil, who married Alice Gestetner, Marie's sister. The Weils lived in Paris before the war and were well known to Charles Ullman.

65 Philipp Brothers' lucrative trading during World War II. A. Craig Copetas, *Metal Men* (New York: G. P. Putnam's Sons, 1985), 58–60.

65 Siegfried Bendheim holding $1 billion. Charles Bendheim, interview by author, New York City, 10 November 1993.

65 "Reichmann was looking for a Yankee Doodle . . . make sure the check was deposited correctly." Ibid.

66 "As soon as she found out. . . ." Ibid.

66 "I remember my Aunt Marie. . . ." Interview by author.

66 "Keeping friends and relatives at arm's length. . . ." David, "The DG I Knew," 19.

67 "Obviously, Mrs. Reichmann knew. . . ." Interview by author.

67 Foreign Jews "were eager to show their devotion. . . ." A. Honig, quoted in Susan Zuccotti, *The Holocaust, the French, and the Jews* (New York: Basic Books, 1993), 32.

67 "My father left Vienna without money . . . crying didn't do any good at all. " Martha Margulies, telephone interview by author, from London, 20 October 1993.

68 "We have enough bloody Jews in Austria. . . ." Interview by author.

68 "There were a lot of students . . . he wouldn't have had windows." Interview by author.

69 Details of the Reichmanns' departures from and returns to Paris. Prefecture de Police (Paris), Casier Central des Etrangers, Dossier 1633, 265.

69 "Settled into their phony war . . ." Herbert Lottman, *The Fall of Paris* (London: Sinclair-Stevenson, 1992), 4.

69 Edward's confrontation with Hungarian military officer. Interview by author, 1 June 1994, Miami Beach.

70 "She was sent back from Italy. . . ." Interview by Kranzler.

70 Edward's alteration of his passport. Edward Reichmann, interview by author, 28 December 1994, Miami Beach, during which the passport was examined by author.

70 "My Rebbe asked me bluntly. . . ." Unpublished memoir, 43.

70 "Eli made such scenes. . . ." Copy of the original letter in Hungarian supplied by Edward Reichmann, along with his translation into English.

71 March 25 departure from Italy. Interview by author of Louis Reichmann.

71 "It was a nice trip. . . ." Ibid.

Chapter 6

72 "Even Jewish refugees from Germany. . . ." Lottman, *The Fall of Paris*, 142.

73 "I guess I was curious. . . ." Keith Wheatley, "Men at Wharf," London *Times*, 2 October 1988, London insert, 13.

73 "Under this blanket. . . ." Unpublished memoir, 49.

73 The wait at the Gare d'Austerlitz. Interview by author of Edward Reichmann, 22 April 1993.

74 Details of the Reichmanns' "sauf conduit." Prefecture de Police (Paris), Casier Central des Etrangers, Dossier 1633, 265.

74 "We were afraid that Ralph. . . ." Interview by author.

74 "Announced without question, some Apocalypse." Museum curator Yvon Bizardel, quoted by Lottman, *The Fall of Paris*, 265.

74 Samuel's conversation with Stern. Interview by author of Edward Reichmann, 22 April 1993.

74 Speckled rain. Ibid., 266.

74 "Between June 9 and June 13. . . ." William Shirer, *The Collapse of the Third Republic* (New York: Simon & Schuster, 1969), 24–25.

75 "The planes flew so low. . . ." Interview by author.

75 "Combien? . . . petit Juif." Unpublished memoir, 52.

75 "The police said, 'Why did you come here?. . . .'" Interview by Kranzler.

75 "I still recall that the French. . . ." Zuccotti, *The Holocaust, The French, and the Jews*, 38.

75 "She thought maybe these people. . . ." Interview by Kranzler.

76 "Life in Paris seemed normal. . . ." Léon Poliakov, *L'auberge des musiciens* (Paris: Editions Mazarine), 1981, 18.

76 Latin American visas were "very reasonable. . . ." Morris C. Troper, quoted by Yehuda Bauer, *American Jewry and the Holocaust* (Detroit: Wayne State University Press, 1981), 46.

76 Details of Ziggy Stern's consulate visit. Martha Margulies, interview by author.

77 "My father said, 'No. . . .' " Interview by Kranzler.

77 "My father left. . . ." Ibid.

77 "We had a lot of luggage. . . ." Unpublished memoir, 53–54.

77 "No one paid any attention to me. . . ." Interview by author, Brooklyn, N.Y., 16 November 1993.

77 "He was just a very kind person." Ibid.

78 "All I can tell you about the Reichmanns. . . ." Ibid.

78 "In Madrid we looked around. . . ." Dewar, "The Mysterious Reichmanns," 146.

78 "Inquired where there is a place. . . ." Interview by Kranzler.

78 "Passing through our country. . . ." Jordana y Sousa, quoted by Michael Marrus, *The Unwanted* (New York: Oxford University Press, 1985), 260.

79 "You might be interested to know. . . ." *Jewish Chronicle,* 15 July 1960, 22.

79 "Mrs. Reichmann offered my wife. . . ." Interview by author.

79 With the approach of German troops, the French guards at the internment camp fled. As a result, Schreiber and the other prisoners got free. With a companion, Schreiber bought a car and headed south to Biarritz. "We just drove right through the German troops," he recalled. "They were hurrying to the coast and just ignored us." By the time he reached Biarritz, his wife and daughters were gone. He then headed east to Pau and then north to Limoges, where he and his family remained until mid-1941, when they emigrated to the United States.

79 "I can't tell you how many times. . . ." Netti Morgenstern, interview by author, London, 29 September 1993.

80 "In Ringer's, I used to hear them talking. . . ." Interview by author.

80 "Granted a special authorization. . . ." Memorandum submitted to the American Jewish Joint Distribution Committee (AJJDC) by the Jewish community of Tangier, 24 February 1944. Archives of the AJJDC, AR 3344, 1045.

80 "Strong connections. . . . to Franco." Albert Reichmann, from the text of an interview by Elaine Dewar, included in the Fresh Statement of Defence, *Reichmann et al. vs. Toronto Life Publishing et al.,* Supreme Court of Ontario, p. 22.

81 "At the railway station . . . no realistic possibility of going anywhere." Dewar, "The Mysterious Reichmanns," 143.

82 Palestine emigration figures. Marrus, *The Unwanted,* 206.

82 "Tangier in 1940 was not yet entirely. . . ." Michael Davidson, *The World, the Flesh and Myself* (London: David Bruce & Watson, 1973), 194.

82 "Many observers assumed . . ." Robert D. Murphy, *Diplomat Among Warriors* (Garden City, N.Y.: Doubleday, 1964), 47.

82 "I would rather have three or four teeth out. . . ." George Hills, *Franco: The Man and His Nation* (London: Hale, 1967), 337.

83 "To make business there. . . ." Interview by author.

83 "I think the Reichmanns. . . ." Interview by author, Antwerp, Belgium, 21 November 1993.

II   EXILE IN TANGIER

Chapter 7

87 "Tangier is an oddity. . . ." John Gunther, *Inside Africa* (New York: Harper, 1953), 106.

87 "From a distance it sparkles. . . ." Iain Finlayson, *Tangier: City of the Dream* (Hammersmith: HarperCollins, 1992), 20.

87 "On the outside. . . ." Henry M. Field, *The Barbary Coast* (New York: C. Scribner's Sons, 1893), 27–28.

87 "A foreign land if ever there was one." Mark Twain, *The Innocents Abroad* (Hartford, Conn.: American, 1869), 55.

88 "A honeypot for the sticky fingered." Finlayson, *Tangier: City of the Dream*, 70.

89 "Floated airily on a plateau. . . ." Ibid., 8.

89 Tangier's ethnic demographics. J. Rives Childs, "Foreign Population of Tangier," 20 July 1944, National Archives (U.S.), State Dept., 881.5011/7-2044.

89 "Tangier must have been. . . ." Gerald Richardson, *Crime Zone* (London: J. Long, 1959), 104.

89 "We went there out of curiosity. . . ." Interview by author and Gill O'Meara, Paris, 17 November 1993.

90 Mrs. Reichmann's wig drying. Louis Saint-Aubert, interview by author and O'Meara, Tangier, 7 December 1993.

90 "If it's a goy, you can understand. . . ." Interview by author, New York City, 16 December 1992.

90 "A lot of refugees came to see my parents. . . ." Interview by author and O'Meara, Tangier, 6 December 1993.

91 Joseph Muyal's anger at the Reichmanns. Rachel Muyal, interview by author and O'Meara, Tangier, 3 December 1993.

91 "It really was not so different. . . ." Interview by author.

92 "It was not a terribly alienating environment." Interview by author.

92 "At least I had my sister. . . ." Interview by author.

92 "I was very proud . . . should be studying more." Unpublished memoir, 61.

93 "Boys my age. . . ." Ibid., 81.

93 "I have an image. . . ." Interview by author.

93 Samuel arriving in Tangier with $10,000 to $200,000. Edward Reichmann, quoted in the examination of Albert Reichmann, 29 March 1989, 190, *Renée Reichmann et al. vs. Toronto Life Publishing et al.*, Ontario Supreme Court, Toronto, court file no. 25372/88.

93 "My parents were looking. . . ." Tom Fennell, "The Roots of Power," *Maclean's* magazine, 10 October 1988, 42.

94 "I'd see Reichmann there . . . took more speculative risk." Interview by author.

95 The volume of Mrs. Reichmann's mail. Dewar, "The Mysterious Reichmanns," 132.

95 "When something was in the oven. . . ." Unpublished memoir, addendum of 13 November 1994, 16.

96 "I was very interested in the war. . . ." Interview by author.

97 Tangier as Britain's sole intelligence post in North Africa. John Beevor, *SOE: Recollections and Reflections, 1940–1945* (London: Bodley Head, 1981), 130.

98 "From 1940 to 1944. . . ." J. Rives Childs, *Let the Credit Go* (New York: K. S. Giniger, 1983), 174.

Chapter 8

99 "Even looking at all this. . . ." Unpublished memoir, 64.

100 "In short whoever was more pious. . . ." Moshe Scheinfeld, quoted in Samuel Heilman, *Defenders of the Faith* (New York: Schocken Books, 1992), 33.

101 "The concept of rescue. . . ." Leni Yahil, *The Holocaust* (New York: Oxford University Press, 1990), 573.

101 "To kill the Jews. . . ." David Wyman, *The Abandonment of the Jews* (New York: Pantheon Books, 1984), 5.

102 Pikkuah nefesh as overriding priority. Birnbaum, *Encyclopedia of Jewish Concepts*, s.v. "Saving a Life."

103 "Exactly what Henrik's role. . . ." Interview by author, New York, 24 March 1993.

103 Livia Rothkirchen, "Hungary—An Asylum for the Refugees of Europe," in *Yad Vashem Studies on the European Jewish Catastrophe and Resistance* (Vol. 8), (Jerusalem: Jewish Agency, 1968), 134–35.

103 "One week after she left. . . ." Dewar, "The Mysterious Reichmanns," 132.

103 Mrs. Reichmann's detention in Italy. Examination of Paul Reichmann, 27 September 1989, 237–38, *Renée Reichmann et al. vs. Toronto Life Publishing et al.*

104 For Orthodox accounts of Mrs. Reichmann's rescue work, see David Kranzler, *Thy Brother's Blood* (Brooklyn: Mesorah, 1987); David Kranzler and Eliezer Gevirtz, *To Save a World*, vol. 1 (Lakewood, N.J.: C.I.S., 1991); Yossef Wertenschlag, "La Dette de Reconnaissance au Caudillo," *Kountrass* 32 (January–February 1992). *To Save a World* was dedicated to Mrs. Reichmann, "who left a magnificent legacy of mesiras nefesh on behalf of Klal Yisrael during the darkest days of the holocaust."

105 "What's the use?. . . ." Dewar, "The Mysterious Reichmanns," 165.

105 The contents of Klein's food parcel. Interview by author, 11 November 1992.

105 The Germans' food parcel dealings. One Swiss dealer offered a choice of seven parcels, ranging in price from the $2.25 "Ute" model, which consisted of 1 lb. of roasted coffee, to $12.75 for the "Weser," which included 2 lb. 3 oz. of roasted coffee, 2 lbs. 3 oz. of chocolate powder, and 1 lb. ½ oz. of Ceylon tea. Other dealers charged about $5.20 for 12 tins of boneless sardines in oil, $8.25 for 11 lb. of figs, $7 for 11 lb. of dried fruit, and $12.50 for a package containing 2 lb. 5 oz. of sausage and a like amount of bacon and cheese. See James B. Stewart, "Organization in Switzerland for the Purchase of Food Packages Going to Germany," 27 January 1942, State Department.

106 "It is the opinion of this office. . . ." Ibid.

106 "Ladies of good society would boast. . . ." Thomas J. Hamilton, *Appeasement's Child* (New York: A. A. Knopf, 1943), 172.

107 "Had very little effect. . . ." Stanley Payne, *The Franco Regime, 1936–1975* (Madison: University of Wisconsin Press, 1987), 387.

107 "Without a powerful friend. . . ." Hamilton, *Appeasement's Child*, 145–46.

107 "An intelligent, well-educated man. . . ." U.S. Naval Attache-Tangier, 20 October 1944, National Archives (U.S.), Intelligence Division, Office of the Chief of Naval Operations, XL-2207 and XL-2284. See also "Report on Confidential Biographic Data for First Quarter of 1945," 10 April 1945, State Dept., 844: "García Figueras's reputation as an expert in the extraction of graft has been a constant topic of conversation in Tangier's commercial circles."

108 "Before the Allied landing. . . ." Unpublished memoir, 68.

108 "Maidie was so pretty. . . ." Interview by author and O'Meara, Tangier, 6 December 1993.

108 "Of all the Reichmanns. . . ." Interview by author, 16 December 1992.

109 "They were a bit intimidating. . . ." Interview by author, Washington, D.C., 30 March 1993.

109 "Our house was near the ski lodge . . . for a month." Interview by author and Angelica de Diego, Madrid, 26 November 1993.

110 Eva "mentioned to Bebe . . . contact for the rescue work." Dewar, "The Mysterious Reichmanns," 132. Mrs. Beneyto Ronda insisted in a 1993 interview by the author that she could not recall having played any part in the Reichmanns' relief efforts and flatly denied that she ever sent potatoes or anything else to the apartment on Rue Molière. "Only to the hotel in Ketama," she said indignantly. "They have changed the story."

110 "Mr. Reichmann said he wanted. . . ." Interview by author and de Diego, Madrid, 26 November 1993.

110 "I always invited them . . . utter confidence in them both." Ibid.

111 "After a year or so. . . ." Interview by author.

111 "We quickly made a lot of money. . . ." Interview by author, 1 June 1994, Miami Beach.

111 "In those days, it was hard. . . ." Interview by author.

112 "Whenever he arrived. . . ." Unpublished memoir, 85.

112 "One day Edward came to see me . . . he had a business mind." Interview by O'Meara for author, Tangier, 9 December 1993.

112 "I met a lot of prominent people. . . ." Unpublished memoir, 78.

113 Franco's open letter to the Jews of Tetuán. *American Jewish Yearbook*, vol. 39 (1937–38), 324.

114 "Mr. Salama hadn't realized . . . contacts in Madrid and elsewhere." Interview by author, 31 May 1994, Miami Beach.

114 "It was the Reichmanns who. . . ." Interview by author, 19 January 1994, New York.

114 "Every time there was a shipment. . . . Everyone!" Interview by author and O'Meara.

115 "The money did not come. . . ." Interview by author, 19 January 1994.

115 "We used to go to the office. . . ." Kranzler, *Thy Brother's Blood*, 249.

Chapter 9

116 "Mrs. Reichmann was *the* leader. . . ." Interview by author and de Diego, Madrid, 27 November 1993.

116 "You know, Mr. Reichmann would never . . ." Interview by author, Marbella, Spain, 1 December 1993.

117 "He was a man. . . ." Interview by author.

118 "Father would smile. . . ." Unpublished memoir, 76.

119 "Reichmann never talked. . . ." Interview by author.

119 Samuel holding his profits in dollars. Louis Reichmann quoted in the examination of Albert Reichmann, 29 March 1989, 264, *Renée Reichmann et al. vs. Toronto Life Publishing et al.*

119 "Never once did we have the tiniest problem. . . ." Interview by author and O'Meara.

119 "Reichmann carried out a lot of transactions. . . ." Interview by O'Meara.

119 "For a true comprehension. . . ." Childs, "Rise of the Peseta and Fall of the Franc on the Tangier Free Exchange Market," 18 December 1943, State Dept., 881.5151/27.

120 Statistics on volume of smuggled Swiss watches. Ibid. The America Legation in Tangier frequently commented on the prevalence of black market dealings in its reports to the State Department. See especially "Proposed Reestablishment of the Peseta in the International Zone," 11 October 1940, 881.515/8; "The Black Market in Tangier and Spanish Morocco," 20 May 1942, 881.50/46; "Exchange Fluctuations in Tangier," 16 July 1942, 881.51/20; "The Rise of the Peseta and the Situation of the Moroccan Franc on the Tangier Exchange Market," 14 September 1943, 881.5151/24; and "Tangier Exchange Market," 23 June 1944, 881.5151/6-2344. See also the report by the American Consulate in Casablanca, "Developments in French Morocco regarding Movement of Capital," 12 September 1941, 881.51/85; and "Tangier as a Foreign Exchange Market and Center of Undesirable Transactions" by the Special Areas Branch of the Foreign Economic Administration, June 1944.

120 The price of smuggled gold coins. Childs, "Traffic in Gold in Morocco and French North Africa," 18 August 1942, State Dept., 881.515/21.

121 "The temptation to take advantage. . . ." Interview by author.

121 Smuggling by the U. S. Legation's chauffeur. State Dept., Tangier legation, general records (1944), 820.02. Childs apparently did not have a clue as to what was going on until mid-1944, when a State Department headquarters employee passed along a tip received from an anonymous source in Tangier. Childs had the local OSS station chief in Tangier investigate his chauffeur, a Russian national. It turned out that the chauffeur had a confederate in Casablanca who bought dollars from newly arrived American sailors at the rate fixed by the French Moroccan government—about 50 francs to the dollar in mid-1944. Meanwhile, in Tangier, a dollar was worth 90 to 92 francs—a premium of 80 percent over the Casablanca price. While driving

Childs to Casablanca, the chauffeur smuggled in francs, picked up dollars, and returned to Tangier with the chargé in the backseat none the wiser. The limousine's diplomatic plates made it immune to inspection by either French or Spanish border guards. It was typical of Tangier's Byzantine ways that the circumstances by which the Russian was implicated prevented his receiving so much as a reprimand from Childs. The OSS happened to have an informant who knew one of the chauffeur's co-conspirators, who worked as the night porter at the Minzah Hotel. The informant gave this porter a sealed bundle supposedly containing 100,000 francs and told him to deliver it to a phony address in Casablanca. Unable to locate the drop point, the Russian returned to Tangier and opened the package, finding newspaper strips cut to the size of 1,000-franc notes. The chauffeur concluded that he had come under suspicion and stopped his illicit activities. "The news of this would-be smuggling incident has spread among the other chauffeurs at the Legation . . . and I feel certain that at least for the time being their activities along smuggling lines have been stopped," the OSS chief reported to Childs, adding, "I do not think it necessary to mention this in any way to your chauffeur as it might tip off the hand of my contact."

121 The collapse of the Tangier currency market in 1941. Childs, "Depreciation of the Peseta on the Tangier Free Market," with attachments, 28 October 1941, State Dept., 881.5151/17.

121 "The economic and financial life. . . ." "Rise of the Peseta and Fall of the Franc on the Tangier Free Exchange Market," 18 December 1943.

122 "She explained what it was. . . ." Dewar, "The Mysterious Reichmanns," 161.

122 Rafel Alvarez Claro to Rebecca Reichmann, 11 July 1944, Yeshiva University Archives, Vaad Hahatzalah collection, box 42, folder 203.

123 "Lord Mayor of Melilla. . . ." Report of British Vice Consul in Melilla, 27 July 1942, attached to Childs, "Leading Personalities of Melilla," 22 September 1942, State Dept., 881.44/2.

123 Alvarez Claro "arrived in Tangier clandestinely. . . ." Source Z, "Currency Manipulation and Contraband," 14 December 1944, National Archives (U.S.), Office of Strategic Services, A 46163.

124 "Much addicted to. . . ." M. F. Cullis, "Report on Recent Visit Abroad," 29 October 1943, attached to Childs, "Analysis of Proclaimed List for Tangier and Spanish Morocco with Regard Particularly to Post-War Listing," 21 February 1944, State Dept., 711.3.

124 "The enemy is receiving no great benefit. . . ." Childs, 21 February 1944.

125 "Considering their informal business methods. . . ." Ibid.

125 The SOE's black market operation in Tangier. Edward Wharton-Tigar, *Burning Bright* (England: Metal Bulletin Books), 86–88.

125 "Mr. Reichmann was not an SOE agent. . . ." Interview by author, London, 22 September 1993.

125 Alster spared blacklisting. Childs, "Recommendation of £5000 Bond from Jacob Alster," 1 July 1943, State Dept. 840.51/10970.

126 Hollander's delisting. Childs, "Proposal for Deletion from the Proclaimed and Statutory Lists of Emannuel Hollander, Rue Goya 43, Tangier," 23 November 1942. State Dept., 740.00112A, European War, 1990/21530.

126 "The split was made. . . ." Interview by author.

126 Over the years, Edward's account of his ejection of Hollander from the synagogue assumed a featured place in his repertoire of reminiscences. Privately, the other Reichmanns often complained about their voluble eldest brother's tendency to exaggerate in recollecting the family history, but in this case they backed Edward emphatically. Indeed, in a deposition taken in 1989 in a court case in Canada, Paul, who was thirteen years old in 1942, testified under oath that he clearly recalled Edward's rough treatment of Hollander. At the same time, two surviving members of the Grussgott family—eyewitnesses both—stepped forward to corroborate the story as well. And Ernest Rosenfeld, Edward's first business partner, has said privately that he was among those who helped administer the beating to the blacklistee.

Chapter 10

127 "I remember the excitement. . . ." Examination of Paul Reichmann, *Reichmann et al. vs. Toronto Life Publishing*, Ontario Supreme Court, 3 August 1989, 133.

127 The photos of the food parcel assembly were taken by Albert Reinhard and donated to the Joint.

128 The Joint's Polish aid. Seymour Finger, ed., *American Jewry during the Holocaust* (New York: American Jewish Commission on the Holocaust, 1983), 24.

128 "No form of relief can be devised. . . ." Ibid.

129 "Through spotless streets, houses bright. . . ." Ruth Schwertfeger, *Women of Theresienstadt* (New York: St. Martin's Press), 1989.

129 "If once in a blue moon. . . ." Zdenka Morsel, quoted in *Women in the Resistance and the Holocaust*, ed. Vera Laska (Westport, Conn.: Greenwood Press, 1983), 236.

129 "The difference for many. . . ." Schwertfeger, *Women of Theresienstadt*, 42.

129 Food parcel shipments to Theresienstadt by the Joint Distribution Committee. Laura Margolis, "Memorandum to Professor Ehrenpreis Regarding Parcels to Theresienstadt and Bergen-Belsen," attached to a letter of 2 February 1945 to Moses Leavitt, archives of the American Jewish Joint Distribution Committee, cabinet 51, Sweden.

130 On 14 January 1946, Felix and Hermine Schap of Brno, Czechoslovakia, addressed a request for a shipment of Passover matzohs to the "Renée Reichmann Company, Tangier." The Schaps had spent three and a half years in Theresienstadt. From the Reichmann family archives.

130 "Turned over to Kapos. . . ." Yahil, *The Holocaust*, 371.

130 "Had definite knowledge. . . ." C. Burke Albrick, "Food Packages for Jews," 10 April 1944, State Dept., 840.1

130 Lore Shelley, *Secretaries of Death* (New York: Shengold, 1986).

130 "From Portugal." Ida Ungar to Desider Ungar, 15 October 1943, Reichmann family archives.

130 "It was two years ago that we were in Auschwitz. . . ." Ida Ungar to Renée Reichmann, 20 March 1946, Reichmann family archives.

131 "There are continuous quarrels. . . ." Letter by Abraham Laredo, 23 December 1943, archives of the AJJDC, AR 3344, 1045.

131 "The two currencies in Tangier. . . ." Letter to the editor of *España*, 23 June 1944, cited in Childs, "High Cost of Living in Tangier," 29 June 1944, State Dept., 881.5017/6-2944.

131 Food price inflation caused by the collapse of the franc. Childs, "Exchange and Monetary Situation in the Tangier Zone," 7 October 1941, State Dept., 881.51/86.

131 "People from the Joint. . . ." Interview by author.

132 "Everything is very expensive here. . . ." Undated letter, AJJDC archives.

133 Vaad Hahatzalah budgets. The Vaad's audited financial statements for 1943, 1944 and 1945, Yeshiva University Archives, Vaad Hahatzalah (VH) collection, box 5, folder 42.

133 "Payment up to $3,000 guaranteed. . . ." National Archives, State Dept., Special War Problems Division, F.W. 840.48 Refugees/5509A.

134 "I do not believe that we shall suffer. . . ." Fulop Freudiger, quoted by Martin Gilbert, *The Holocaust* (New York: Holt, Rinehart and Winston, 1985), 663.

134 "Don't exaggerate your fears. . . ." Henrik Gestetner to Renée Reichmann, 1 January 1944, Reichmann family archives.

134 "I can only conclude. . . ." Henrik to Renée, 18 February 1944, Reichmann family archives.

134 "So much has come to nothing overnight . . . will have three sons but after a time." Henrik to Renée, 27 March 1944, Reichmann family archives.

Chapter 11

136 "In March 1944, when the Germans. . . ." Renée Reichmann to Vaad Hahatzalah, 2 October 1946, Yeshiva University archives, VH collection, Box 41, Folder 197.

137 "The incident itself. . . ." Elbrick, "Convocation of Prominent Tangier Jews by Spanish High Commissioner," 18 April 1944, State Dept., 881.4016/60.

137 Eichmann's anti-Hasidic bias. Randolph Braham, *The Politics of Genocide*, 536.

137 "It is not contemplated. . . ." Quoted in Wyman, *The Abandonment of the Jews*, 291.

138 Spain's admitting only eight hundred Jews. *Encyclopedia Judaica*, s.v. "Spain."

138 "The war was coming to an end . . . knew what was going on." Interview by author.

138 Cataloging of the property of the Beled Jews. Among the dozens of individual inventories in the Hungarian State Archives at Sopron (V. 6/1, 106, 116) is that of Miksa Rapoport and Regina Reichmann, the childless elder sister of Samuel. Like his father-in-law, David Reichmann, Rapoport was a Talmudic scholar who dabbled in shopkeeping. The inventory of the Rapoports' property, cited below in its entirety, is striking both for its brevity and its meticulousness.

2 wooden wardrobes
1 glass bookcase
1 glass kitchen cupboard
1 dressing mirror, in three parts
2 night stands
1 couch, with worn gray cover
1 round table
3 chairs
1 round iron stove, in poor condition
1 Singer sewing machine, with cover
2 candlesticks, one with 5 branches
1 wooden cupboard, worn
1 bed
2 dough molding boards, with rolling pins
3 sisymbriums
1 winebasket
1 hammer
1 stool

Note: no extra dresses, shoes, or underwear were found.

138–39 Descriptions of atrocities committed in the ghetto of Győr can be found in oral testimonies taken by the Jewish Agency for Palestine and filed at Yad Vashem, including those of Marton Fuchs (015/2158), Akiba Lefkovits (A-14486), Olga Szekulisz (1521/140 C), and Sandor Schwartz (1221/115 C). Also see the entry for Győr in *Pinkas Hakehillot*, p. 240; Braham, *The Politics of Genocide*, 621–23; and Jeno Levai, *Black Book on the Martyrdom of Hungarian Jewry* (Zurich: Central European Times, 1945), 149–50.

139 "Shortly will leave our city . . . or to anyone else in Tangier." Copies in Spanish and English, 22 May 1994, State Dept., Tangier legation, general records (1944), 840.1. The ten signatories were Isaac Salama, P. P. Jacob de J. Salama (Isaac Salama), Aaron S. Cohen, Delmar, Simy Marques, Amram Benaim, J. Abitbol, M. Cohen (Mauritania), B. Lasry, and Jacob Benmaman.

139 "I hope that you will not fail. . . ." Letter to Jacob Benmaman, president of the Jewish Community of Tetuán, 23 May 1944, copy in English, State Dept., Tangier legation, general records (1944), 840.1.

140 Childs's exploits as a codebreaker are recounted in David Kahn, *The Codebreakers* (New York: Macmillan, 1967), 336–39,

140 "Fritzlan, I hardly know you. . . ." David Fritzlan, interview by author.

140 "The Americans were not interested. . . ." Interview by author.

140 "I concluded by stating. . . ." J. Rives Childs, *Vignettes: An Autobiographical Fragment* (New York: Vantage Press), 30.

141 Hayes "concluded that diplomatic pressure. . . ." Wyman, *The Abandonment of the Jews*, 226.

142 Kessler's intervention with Childs. Kessler sent Childs copies of the Jewish community's letter to General Orgaz and the High Commissioner's response to Benmaman. "May I add," Kessler wrote, "that this movement is being directed by Mrs. Reichman [*sic*], a Hungarian refugee, whose name does not appear [as a signatory] because she herself is enjoying the hospitality of the city." Kessler to Childs, 30 May 1944, State Dept., Tangier legation, general records (1944), 840.1.

142 "Finding necessary supplies in Tangier. . . ." Childs to Secretary of State, copy of telegram, 2 June 1944, Tangier legation, general records (1944), 840.1.

142 "The embassy replied that. . . ." Childs, *Let the Credit Go*, 160.

143 Kasztner's testimony. Ernest Landau, ed., *Der Kastner-Bericht über Eichmanns Menschenhandel in Ungarn* (Munich: 1961).

144 "Were squeezed mercilessly. . . . Her mother never turned back." Marika Reichmann, *Eszti's Story* (Brooklyn: Tova Press, 1995), 16–18.

145 "We received visas for 500. . . ." Samuel Reichmann to Moses (Martin) Klein, 14 July 1944, Yeshiva University archives, VH collection, box 41, folder 197.

145 "Our organization ready. . . ." Vaad Hahatzalah Emergency Committee to Samuel Reichmann, 14 July 1944, Franklin D. Roosevelt (FDR) Library, War Refugee Board (WRB) records, Vaad Hahatzalah–Licenses NY 617586.

146 "Send maximum possible number. . . ." Vaad Hahatzalah Emergency Committee to Renée Reichmann and Sigmund Grussgott, 7 July 1944, ibid.

146 "[Cohen] contributes a fortune. . . ." Unaddressed letter dated 27 July 1994, ibid.

146 "With the exception of Budapest. . . ." Renée Reichmann to Vaad Hahatzalah, 27 July 1944, ibid.

146 "We cannot locate the people. . . ." Renée Reichmann to "my dears," undated, Yeshiva University archives, VH collection, box 36, folder 129.

147 "We have no details of various alleged camps. . . ." HIJEFS to Renée Reichmann, 24 September 1944, Reichmann family archives.

147 "Hungarian Jews are in Waldsee. . . ." Renée Reichmann to the Vaad Hahatzalah Emergency Committee, 18 October 1944, Yeshiva University archives, VH collection, box 41, folder 197.

147 "It is impossible to describe. . . ." Moshe Sandberg of Kecskemet quoted in Gilbert, *The Holocaust*, 671.

147 "In the afternoon. . . ." Renée Reichmann to the Vaad Hahatzalah Emergency Committee, 27 July 1944, FDR Library, WRB records, VH–Licenses NY 617586.

148 "What was interesting about the second group. . . ." Kranzler, *Thy Brother's Blood*, 250–51.

149 "She put me in mind somehow of Old Faithful. . . ." Childs, *Vignettes,* 31.

149 "The Red Cross has opportunities. . . ." HIJEFS to Reichmann Gestetner, 15 August, 1944, Reichmann family archives.

150 "Extending protection to 700. . . ." Childs to General Orgaz, 21 September 1944, State Department, Tangier legation, general records (1944), 840.1.

151 "I could not even save the children. . . ." Renée Reichmann to the Vaad Hahatzalah Emergency Committee, 18 October 1944, Yeshiva University archives, VH collection, box 41, folder 197.

152 Conveyance of Mrs. Reichmann's proposal to transfer the 700 visas to Switzerland. American Embassy in Madrid to Spain's Ministry of Foreign Affairs, "Note Verbale," 14 November 1944, State Dept., Tangier legation, general records (1944).

152 IRC's refusal of the Tangier visas and revival of U.S. support for original rescue plan. Memorandum, 30 November 1944, American Embassy in Madrid, State Dept., Tangier legation, general records (1944).

152 The Foreign Ministry wiring Budapest. Carlton Hayes to State Dept., "Protection to Jews in Hungary by Spanish Legation at Budapest," 7 December 1944, Tangier legation, general records (1944).

152 "700 entry visas sent Friday. . . ." Reichmann to HIJEFS, 4 December 1944, Reichmann family archives.

153 "How dare you behave like this. . . ." Ernie Meyer, "The Second Wallenberg," *Jerusalem Post,* 29 September 1989.

153 "I don't know how many. . . ." Ibid.

154 "Permit me, before your departure. . . ." Reichmann to Childs, 13 June 1945, State Dept., Tangier legation, general records (1945), 840.1.

154 "I was deeply touched. . . ." Childs to Reichmann, 13 June 1945, Ibid.

154 "One of the main heroes. . . ." Wyman, *The Abandonment of the Jews,* 240–41.

155 "They [were] in my office. . . ." Interview by author.

155 "A strict Jewish education." Renée Reichmann to Vaad Hahatzalah, 2 October 1946, Yeshiva University archives, VH collection, box 41, folder 197.

Chapter 12

157 "Evidence of cannibalism was found. . . ." Quoted in Gilbert, *The Holocaust,* 795.

158 Mrs. Reichmann's list was cabled to HIJEFS on 9 February 1945 and included relatives on both hers and Samuel's side of the family.

158 "Simon, Benoe, Ernoe. . . ." HIJEFS to Reichmann, 17 March 1945, Reichmann family archives.

158 "My own affairs are also very wrong. . . ." Renée Reichmann to Mordecai Kessler, 21 March 1945, AJJDC archives. Had she survived, Lidi Reichmann would have been eighty, not eighty-two.

159 "Our desperation is so great. . . ." Renée Reichmann to the War Refugee Board, 7 June 1945, Reichmann family archives. Apparently for added emphasis, Mrs. Reichmann signed this letter "Renée Reichmann born Gestetner."

159 Hodel to Reichmann, 3 July 1945, Reichmann family archives. "I regret very much that the War Refugee Board is not in a position to undertake inquiries of this nature concerning specific individuals," Hodel wrote.

159 Bubi Klein's card, 11 June 1945, Reichmann family archives. The card was addressed to Samuel, but Klein's salutation on the flip side was "Liebe Renée."

159 Franz Fischof to Rufka Klein c/o Renée Reichmann, 7 June 1945, Reichmann family archives.

159 "Ask Henrik where Margit. . . ." Reichmann to HIJEFS, 1 July 1945, Reichmann family archives.

160 "Good clothing, not 'shmattes.' " Interview by Kranzler.

161–67 The ten OSS reports containing mention of Samuel Reichmann. National Archives, Record Group 226 (Office of Strategic Services), reports: VT-2082, 9 November 1944; A-46163, 14 December 1944; VT-2226, 28 December 1944; VT-2306, 17 January 1945; VT-2304, 19 January 1945; VT-2406, 7 February 1945; A-50153, 16 February 1945; VT-2635, 21 March 1945; A-54025, 19 April 1945; VT-3024, 2 June 1945.

161 "The ruination of the whole. . . ." VT-2082, 9 November 1944.

161 "Those who are really worried. . . ." VT-2963, May 17 1945. In Washington, an OSS editor attached this clumsy but not inaccurate comment: "The 'Hassidum' Jews form a special sect of orthodox Jews. In contrast to other orthodox Jews, who place emphasis on observance of Mosaic laws, they stress the expression of religious experience."

162 "This movement of currency . . . $200,000 in currency from Hungary." VT-2082, 9 November 1944.

163 "A large quantity of dollars . . . were involved in the transaction." A-54025, 19 April 1945, based on field report VT-2635, 26 March 1945.

163 "Maintains contact with Rosenbaum . . . smuggled dollars in Tangier." A-55750, 17 May 1945, based on field reports from 10 to 13 April.

163 "100,000 paper dollar bills. . . . This is absurd." VT-2406, 7 February 1945.

164 "Reichmann and his associate . . . blue seal ones." VT-2226, 28 December, 1944.

164 "Kahane emphatically denied. . . ." Plaintiff's brief entitled "SS and Other Government Reports," *Reichmann et al. vs. Toronto Life, et al.,* Ontario Supreme Court, 6 September 1988, p. 16.

165 Eory's "connection with German intelligence. . . ." U. S. Embassy Madrid, "Fritz Eory," 17 December 1945, State Dept., 881.00/12-1745.

165 "Fritz Eory who was in Tangier. . . ." VT-2306, 17 January 1945.

165 "Fritz Eory was in Tangier again. . . ." VT-3024, 2 June 1945.

166 "This Hungarian Jewish ..." VTX 10 (enclosure), 25 July 1945. OSS archives also contain an edited version of this report, C.I.D. XL 26959, dated 5 November 1945.

166 "Regarding Eva Reichmann. . . ." FBI report, 5 January 1946 quoted by Ray Cline in a report commissioned by Davies, Ward & Beck on behalf of the Reichmann family, 12–13. Provided by Cline.

166 "Treasury was advised. . . ." Byrnes to American Embassy, London, 19 February 1946, copy in Tangier legation, general records (1946).

167 The British Foreign Office "has now reported. . . ." American Embassy, London, to the Secretary of State, Washington, 1 May 1946, State Dept., copy in Tangier legation, general records (1946).

167 "In the early days . . ." Cline's report to Davies Ward, 2.

168 "I withdraw [my] request. . . ." As translated from French, Renée Reichmann to "Monsier le consul," 7 December 1944, State Dept., Tangier legation, general records (1944).

168 "Rumors about the Reichmanns. . . ." Interview by author.

Chapter 13

169–70 Klein's Holocaust ordeal. Isaac Klein, interviews by author, 11 November 1992 and 24 March 1993.

170 Spanish authorization of visas. Alfonso Garcia-Conde to Senorita Renée Reichmann, 30 July 1945, Yeshiva University archives, VH collection, box 41, file 197.

170 "They wouldn't let me go anywhere else. . . ." Interview by author, 11 November 1992.

171 Le Fur's conflict with the refugee group. Abraham Laredo to the Administrator of the International Zone, 26 November 1945 and 2 January 1946, AJJDC archives, AR 4564, 106.

172 The Joint Distribution Committee's guarantee of support. Reinhard to Le Fur, 22 October 1945, State Department, Tangier legation, general records (1945), 8401.

172 Approval of the Reichmann visa request. International Administration authorization, 22 October 1945, Yeshiva University, VH collection, box 41, folder 197. The first six names on the list were Albert, Henrik, and Kornel Gestetner; and Simon, Benö, and Ernö Reichmann.

172 Eva applying in her mother's absence. Eva Reichmann to the Administrator of the International Zone, 9 January 1946, State Dept., Tangier legation, general records (1946), 8401.

172 The Administrator's recalcitrance. Note, 9 January 1946, State Dept., Tangier legation general records (1946). The note is unsigned but appears to be by David Fritzlan to Paul Alling, who had replaced Rives Childs as chargé d'affaires. In any event, the author was plainly exasperated by the administrator's officiousness:

"There seems to be no reason why those who most require shelter and protection in view of their passed martyrdom should have to face drastic formalities from an Allied International Administration especially when a sound guarantee is given in their favour."

172 Approval granted with strings. International Administration authorization, 19 January 1946, Yeshiva University archives, VH collection, box 41, folder 197.

172 The Reichmanns obtaining more than five hundred visas. The Spanish Moroccan government apparently approved the five hundred visas in gross but issued authorizations only as needed in the name of the recipient. At least three such authorizations were made: 12 March 1946, 60 recipients; 5 May 1946, 9 recipients; 27 June 1946, 11 recipients. Yeshiva University archives, VH collection, box 41, folder 197.

172 Death of Lajos Gestetner. Testimony of Mrs. Desidrius Krausz, taken 15 May 1945 at Győr by the Jewish Agency of Palestine, YIVO Institute for Jewish Research, file 3635.

173 "Writhing like a snake. . . ." Interview by author, 11 November 1992.

173 "A lot of people that came to Tangier. . . ." Fennell, "The Roots of Power," 42.

173 "In 1946 and 1947. . . ." Interview by author, 1 June 1994.

173 The Joint Distribution Committee's "behavior to us is very noble." Renée Reichmann to the Vaad Hahatzalah, 2 October 1946, Yeshiva University archives, VH collection, box 41, file 197.

173 "I only touch it. . . ." Renée Reichmann to the Vaad Hahatzalah, 20 March 1946, Yeshiva University archives, VH collection, box 41, file 197.

174 "She considered it her duty. . . ." Fennell, "The Roots of Power," 43.

175 "As far as I know . . ." Interview by author and O'Meara.

175 "It was a tragic-comic life . . . always very witty." Interview by author.

175 "It's possible she bought dresses. . . . 'I go for a walk.' " Ibid.

176 "I think that Edward. . . ." Interview by author, 11 November 1992.

177 "It was Shabbos. . . ." Reichmann, *Ezsti's Story*, 21.

177 "The first transport. . . ." Renée Reichmann to the Vaad Hahatzalah, 2 October 1946, Yeshiva University archives, VH collection, box 41, file 197.

177 "Look for Orthodox girls. . . . She was a cousin." Dewar, "The Mysterious Reichmanns," 286.

177–78 Allegations of financial abuse within Vaad Hahatzalah. Yeshiva University archives, VH collection. See Isaac Sternbuch to the Vaad Hahatzalah, 18 December 1945 (box 35, folder 124); Solomon Schonfeld to Irving Bunim, 6 September 1946 (box 39, folder 181); Bunim to Stephen Klein, 9 December 1946 (box 13, folder 1); Julius Steinfeld to Bunim, 26 December 1946 (box 2, folder 12,), and Bunim to I. Sternbuch, 6 June 1947 (box 36, folder 130).

179 Renée's financial statement. Yeshiva University archives, VH collection, box 36, folder 130.

179 "I receive again day by day . . . study the contents of it again." Renée Reichmann to Vaad Hahatzalah, 16 January 1947, Yeshiva University archives, VH collection, box 41, file 197.

Chapter 14

180 Samuel's carte d'identité. Reichmann family archives.

181 "I would very much like. . . ." Samuel Reichmann to Charles Ullman (original in French), 19 February 1946, Reichmann family archives.

181 Jacob Rosenheim reinitiating contact. Rosenheim to Renée Reichmann (original in German), 20 March 1946, Reichmann family archives.

182 "They're not really from one city. . . ." Amos Bunin, *A Fire in His Soul* (Jerusalem: Feldheim, 1981), 179.

182 "There's a Mr. Reichmann to see you . . ." Interview by author.

182 "Tangier is waiting. . . ." Joseph Wechsberg, "Anything Goes," *New Yorker,* 12 April 1952, 70.

183 "Tangier knows no currency controls. . . ." Ibid.

183 "Every continental eruption. . . ." William Schlamm, "Tangier," *Fortune,* August 1950, 136.

183 "Tangier has in one respect . . . and found in Tangier." Ibid., 139.

184 "The place is flooded. . . ." Rom Landau, *Moroccan Journal* (London: Hale, 1952), 8.

184 "Quite a career . . ." Schlamm, "Tangier," 139.

184 Real estate inflation. Rom Landau, *Portrait of Tangier* (London: Hale, 1952), 104.

185 "You take your choice . . . country in which it lay locked." Raoul Simpkins, "Banking in Tangier," *Atlantic Monthly,* December 1950, 86.

185 "Toda clase de operaciones. . . ." *Gong,* August 1950 (exact date unknown), 4.

185 "I'm sure he had clients . . . commission of 10 percent or more." Interview by author and O'Meara.

186 "He was a dirty . . . bought a new suit." Interview by author and O'Meara.

186 "I worked with him. . . ." Interview by author and O'Meara.

187 "Mama mia! . . . not normal at all." Interview by author.

187 Grebler blacklisted. J. Rives Childs, "Firms and Individuals Proposed for Inclusion on the British Black and Statutory Lists," 11 June 1942, State Department, 740.001.

187 "According to his latest story. . . ." Harry Schwartz to Rives Childs, 16 February 1943, as cited in the plaintiff's brief "An Analysis of Eleven of the Defamatory Stories Contained in the Toronto Life Article," *Reichmann et. al vs. Toronto Life et al.,* Ontario Supreme Court, 14.

188 "A marble palace . . . long hallway to the bathroom." Interview by author.

188 "There was a big difference. . . ." Interview by author and O'Meara.

188 "Grebler took a liking . . . usually into dollars." Interview by author and O'Meara.

189 "The pesetas to pay for the watches . . . a very honorable fashion." Ibid.

189 "To make your mark in Tangier. . . ." John Taberner, "The Phony Gold Rush," *American Mercury,* December 1952, 82.

189 "You must see how alike. . . ." Paul Bowles, *Let It All Come Down* (London: John Lehmann, 1952), 126–27.

191 List of the richest Jewish businessmen in Tangier. Memo 30 December 1946, Hebrew Union College archives, World Jewish Congress collection. The list also included Reichmann's fellow Hungarian refugees Emmanuel Hollander, Nicholas Rosenbaum, M. Rosenfeld, and J. Grussgott.

191 "Made enormous profits . . . no one would have known." Interview by author and O'Meara.

191 "One day Louis came to see me. . . ." Interview by author and O'Meara.

191 "I went to see him. . . ." Interview by author and de Diego.

192 The question of Samuel Reichmann's wherewithal is further complicated by the delicate issue of what use, if any, he made of the large sums entrusted to him by European Jews who perished in the Holocaust. According to Jack Zimmerman, whose parents were among the scores of Oberlanders who deposited funds with the Reichmanns during the war, Samuel was still searching for heirs of deceased depositors when he came through Montreal in 1959.

Chapter 15

194 "When I came home . . . pleased with your answer." Unpublished memoir, 79–80.

194 "It sounded like a joke. . . ." Ibid.

194 "The more intensely observant. . . ." Reeve Robert Brenner, *The Faith and Doubt of Holocaust Survivors* (New York: Free Press, 1990), 46.

194 "The mistake a lot of people make. . . ." Interview by author, New York City, 2 November 1992.

195 "The Reichmann boys never had that feeling. . . ." Interview by author, Toronto, 26 April 1994.

195 "I was especially impressed . . . makes a warm house." Interview by author, London, 19 September 1993.

196 "When I went to Jerusalem. . . ." Interview by author, 2 June 1994, Miami Beach.

196 "Renée and Samuel Reichmann were giants . . . rebuilt hundreds of families." Dianne Maley, "The Philosopher King," *Report on Business,* December 1988, 63.

196 "I received many, many letters. . . ." Letter of 25 February 1990.

196 "Finally, know that I am honest. . . ." Renée Reichmann to HIJEFS, 6 October 1945, Reichmann family archives.

194 "I remember Edward bragging

197 "A richer man. . . ." Interview by author, 1 June 1994.

198 Eva and Edward's encounter on the train. Ibid.

198 "In any group of people. . . ." Interview by author, London, 13 September, 1993.

198 "Eli was always a very big dreamer. . . ." Interview by author.

199 "I remember Edward bragging . . . gotten his shoes muddy." Interview by author, 11 November 1992.

199 "He tended to see things. . . ." Interview by author, London, 19 September 1993.

200 "I was the one. . . ." Interview by author, Montreal, 18 May 1994.

201 "The pattern was that my father. . . ." Ibid.

201 "I believed in Tangier. . . ." Interview by author, 1 June 1994.

201 "Even as a child. . . ." Interview by author.

201 "We worked day and night. . . ." Interview by author.

202 "There is the almost mystical notion. . . ." William Helmreich, *The World of the Yeshiva* (New York: Free Press, 1982), 116.

203 "A cadre of people. . . ." Ibid., 95.

203 "The forty-eight means. . . ." Quoted in Landau, *Piety and Power,* 194.

203 "Looking at the program of study. . . ." Helmreich, *The World of the Yeshiva,* 98.

204 The Talmud "is a collection of paradoxes. . . ." Steinsaltz, *The Essential Talmud,* 4.

204 "I became very knowledgeable. . . ." Interview by author.

204 "Paul came from a wealthier family. . . ." Interview by author, Passaic, N.J., 15 May 1995.

204 "The clouds, like the shtenders. . . ." Hanoch Teller, quoted in Miriam Dansky, *Gateshead* (Southfield, Mich.: Targan Press, 1992), 20.

205 "A shtetl in the old tradition. . . ." Ibid., 27.

205 "An almost unparalleled. . . ." Ibid., 24.

205 "Excel in brilliance. . . ." Arnold Levy, *The Story of Gateshead Yeshiva* (Taunton-Somerset: Wessex Press, 1952), 27. This book contains a photograph, captioned "A 'Shiur' by Rabbi Gurwitz," that appears to include Paul Reichmann, the third boy from the left.

205 "It was my first Orthodox wedding. . . ." Interview by author.

206 Lippa Heller's background. Interviews by author of Ollick and Naomi Heller and Morris and Rachel Brenick, London, 13 September 1993.

206 "Lippa told Maidie. . . ." Interview by author.

Chapter 16

208 "It was his lifetime's ambition. . . ." Interview by author, 22 April 1993.

209 "For someone who is really religious. . . ." Telephone interview by author, 22 March 1994.

209 "It wasn't hard to do. . . ." Ibid.

210 The letter to "Monsieur Paul." Edward Reichmann to Monsieur Paul, 9 January 1949, copy provided by Reichmann.

210 "OK, do what you must." S.E.R. to Reichmann, undated, copy provided by Reichmann.

210 "The forgeries weren't so good. . . ." Interview by author, 22 March 1994.

210–11 Edward's audience with General Valera. Ibid.

211 "I was the only one in the family . . . would not have kept quiet." Ibid.

211 "I was ready to go. . . ." Ibid.

212 "Just before he died. . . ." Ibid.

212 "The Oxbridge of yeshivas." Landau, *Piety and Power,* 204.

213 "The government made a provision. . . ." Dewar, "The Mysterious Reichmanns," 150.

213 "Israel under Ben-Gurion . . . begged us not to go." Interview by author.

213 "I was sitting with my mother. . . ." Ibid.

213 "Somehow, the Reichmanns. . . ." Telephone interview by author, from Zurich, 22 March 1994.

214 "What hurt Franco personally. . . ." Hills, *Franco,* 407.

214 Hassan's cable. Cited by M. Mitchell Serels, *A History of the Jews of Tangier* (New York: Sepher-Hermon Press, 1991), 167–68.

214–15 "I have witnessed many more events. . . ." *Jewish Chronicle,* 15 July 1960, 22.

215 "She took an awful lot of heat." Interview by author.

215 "I got dozens and dozens. . . ." Interview by Kranzler, 18.

Chapter 17

216 "The de facto focus of Istiqlal conspiracy. . . ." Finlayson, *Tangier,* 69–70.

216 "In Oujda, at least. . . ." Michel Laskier, *North African Jewry in the Twentieth Century* (New York: New York University Press, 1994), 101.

217 The details of Samuel and Renée Reichmann's movements between Tangier and the United States are drawn from documents contained in a sixty-one-page file on Samuel Reichmann at the U.S. Immigration and Naturalization Service, fifty-seven pages of which were obtained by the author under the Freedom of Information Act.

218 "Everyone who stayed alive. . . ." Interview by author, New York City, 23 August 1994.

218 "I remember seeing all these donkeys. . . ." Ibid.

219 "We weren't partners. . . ." Interview by author.

219 "Louis was the Reichmann brother. . . ." Interview by author.

219 "No one ever knew my size . . . very good at selling." Interview by author.

220 "Even forty years later. . . ." Interview by author.

220 "I didn't want the complications. . . ." Ibid.

221 "For a long time the Jews of Morocco. . . ." Stanley Abramovitch to M. W. Beckleman and H. Katski, "Ozar Hatorah," 7 June 1955, AJJDC archives, AR 4564, 100.

221 Alliance Israélite enrollment in 1939. Raphael Patai, *The Vanished Worlds of Jewry* (New York: Macmillan, 1980), 105.

222 "Some of whom were francophiles. . . ." Laskier, *North African Jewry in the Twentieth Century*, 160.

222 "The potential principal reservoir . . . on the charity of others." "Report of Ozar Hatorah (1946/7)," October 1947, AJJDC archives, AR 4564, 102.

223 "I was happy at Ponovezh . . . to provide the Talmudic view." Interview by author.

223 "I never lacked . . . a thing I could cling to." Interview by author, Lakewood, N.J., 22 February, 1995.

224 "The administrators saw. . . ." Interview by author.

224 "She was quite tall. . . ." Ibid.

225 "He told me that I was needed . . . a life for myself like this?" Ibid.

225 "Refused to go into business . . . do something for the world." Maley, "The Philosopher King," 61.

225 "Refused is not the right word. . . ." Interview by author.

225–26 Sectarian division within Ozar Hatarah. See especially Abramovitch, "Postscript on Memo on Ozar Hatorah," 2 January 1953, AJJDC archives, AR 4564, 101.

226 "The Office of JDC. . . ." Judah Shapiro, "Report on Visit to Casablanca," 28 June 1950, AJJDC archives, AR 4564, 102.

226 "The AIU looks on all these. . . ." Abramovitch, "Memorandum on Visit of Rabbi Kalmanovitch [*sic*]," 8 June 1953, AR 4564, 101.

226 "We were willing . . . made a real difference." Interview by author.

226 Rabbi Kalmanowitz's championing of Reichmann. "We were also told by Rabbi Kalmanovitch that he is bringing a young man, Mr. Reichmann, from Tangier, now studying in Israel, to be in charge of the Ozar Hatorah and Eim-Habanim schools in Casablanca . . . ," an annoyed Stanley Abramovitch noted in a memo to his superiors in New York. The rabbi "preferred people who religiously are more in his line rather than qualified educators. We are faced therefore with an educational organization which has no educator qualified to direct it. I think that we should demand of Ozar Hatorah that they hire a first class qualified educator. One cannot thinking of expanding without such a qualified person." Abramovitch, "Memorandum on Visit of Rabbi Kalmanovitch." When Abramovitch's comments were read back to Reichmann for the first time forty years later, he bristled. "It's true that I did not have the educational qualifications," Reichmann conceded, "but I had the more important qualification. Rabbi Kalmanowitz created the Ozar Hatorah in Morocco, not the Joint, and he wanted idealists to run it."

227 "These students had never . . . ." Interview by author.

227 "Ozar Hatorah is now at the stage. . . ." Abramovitch, "Report on AJDC Educational Activities in Morocco," 1 December 1955, AJJDC archives, 45/64, 100.

227 "Of the group that left. . . ." Interview by author.

228 "It was generally believed. . . ." Laskier, *North African Jewry in the Twentieth Century*, 127.

228 "There was no future. . . ." Interview by author.

228 "One of the quietest places. . . ." Schlamm, "Tangier," 138.

228 "He is not remembered . . ." Interview by author.

229 "My father said. . . ." Dewar, "The Mysterious Reichmanns," 144.

Chapter 18

231 "I didn't like America. . . ." Interview by author, 25 April 1993.

231 "I didn't have English . . . at ease in French." Dewar, "The Mysterious Reichmanns," 144.

232 Canadians "liked to think of their country. . . ." Kenneth McNaught, *The Penguin History of Canada* (London: Penguin Books, 1988), 290.

233 "I know that at least some of the money. . . ." Interview by author.

233 "This was a standard letter. . . ." Interview by author.

233 "The origin of the name. . . ." Amanda Bennett, "Canadian Realty Firms Make Waves in U.S. with Major Projects," *Wall Street Journal*, 24 April 1978, 1.

234 "Named their ventures Olympia. . . ." Shawn Tully, "The Bashful Billionaires of Olympia & York," *Fortune*, 14 June 1982, 89.

234 "I wanted to call the company. . . . 'How about Olympia?' " Telephone interview by author, from Prague, 5 April 1994.

234 Edward and Louis's exclusion from the family's Canadian business history spared the Montreal brothers themselves the embarrassment of seeing their mishaps recounted in print and also benefited the Toronto brothers by keeping the family image in Canadian business circles free of the tarnish of calamity. The omission also had the effect of inflating Paul's and especially Ralph's early contributions to the family's success in Canada, as illustrated by the following remarks from the first book about the Reichmann family: "Neither of [the] elder brothers played a part in the development of the family's North American empire. For the future of the empire, the significant arrival was that in Toronto via New York in 1956 of young Ralph, and, a year later, of his brother Paul. On Densley Ave., not far from the present site of the tile business, Ralph set up an import business based on contacts the Reichmanns had with Spanish tile makers." Peter Foster, *The Master Builders* (Toronto: Key Porter Books, 1986), 10–11.

235 Immigration figures for 1933 to 1945. "Of all the Western democracies. . . ." Irving Abella, *None Is Too Many* (Toronto: L & O Dennys, 1982), ii.

235 The barriers to Jewish immigration. Reg Whitaker, *Double Standard* (Toronto: Lester & Orpen Dennys, 1987), 63–64.

235 "Are dispelled by the language. . . ." Ibid., 64.

235 "Do you have a Jewish member . . . Mr. Jack Pickersgill." Dewar, "The Mysterious Reichmanns," 144.

236 The postwar retooling of Canada's discriminatory immigration policies. Jack Pickersgill, *My Years With Louis St. Laurent* (Toronto: University of Toronto Press, 1975).

236 "The most exacting of all [my] duties. . . ." Ibid., 240.

236 "Here's a man. . . ." Dewar, "The Mysterious Reichmanns," 144.

236 "I was happy to leave. . . ." Interview by author.

236 "I was discussing all the time. . . ." Ibid.

237 "Even if Jack would have come. . . ." Ibid.

237 "His generosity was remarkable. . . ." Interview by author.

238 "My wife loved it. . . ." Interview by author.

238 "I looked at all sorts of businesses . . . and only one product." Interview by author.

238 "Both of us were from small towns. . . ." Ibid.

238 "Edward always used to tell Paul. . . ." Interview by author.

239 "A quiet little English town. . . ." Maley, "The Philosopher King," 61.

239 "The sale was more for family. . . ." Interview by author.

239 "In my father's mind. . . ." Interview by author.

240 "One motive for the abrogation. . . ." Finlayson, *Tangier,* 76.

III   A CANADIAN TALE OF TWO CITIES

Chapter 19

243 "For holidays, Montreal was the address." Interview by author, Miami Beach, 28 June 1994.

243 Edward honored as "central lay figure. . . ." Agudath Israel of America selected Edward Reichmann as one of two "Torah Ambassadors of Canada" honored at its annual dinner in 1963. (The other honoree was from Toronto.) In singling out Reichmann, who was described in the banquet program as a "prominent industrialist and Torah patron," Agudath Israel also recognized the Reichmann family's rescue and relief work during and after the war. Agudath Israel program notes courtesy of Edward Reichmann. See also "Huge Demonstration for Genuine Torah Judaism," *Jewish Press,* 29 March 1963.

243 *Who's Who in Canadian Jewry* (Montreal: Jewish Institute of Higher Research; General Rabbinical Seminary of Canada, 1965), 269. (Edith Reichmann, 499.)

243 "If I'd stayed in Canada. . . ." Interview by author, 22 April 1993.

244 "Somehow from the first day. . . ." Interview by author, 5 April 1994.

244 "Edward had this insatiable need. . . ." Interview by author, Montreal, 3 October 1994.

244 "They might not be able to understand. . . ." Interview by author, 31 May 1994.

245 "The Rothschilds of the New World." See Peter Newman, *The Bronfman Dynasty: The Rothschilds of the New World* (Toronto: McClelland and Stewart, 1978). On March, 14, 1988, *U.S. News & World Report* published a profile of the Reichmanns entitled "The 'New Rothschilds.' "

245 "A case study of institutional decay." Marshall Sklare, *Conservative Judaism* (Glencoe, Ill.: Free Press, 1955), 264.

245 "From then on. . . ." Howard Sachar, *A History of the Jews in America* (New York: Alfred A. Knopf, 1992), 680.

245 "Unaccountably, Orthodoxy has refused. . . ." Sklare, *Conservative Judaism*, augmented ed. (New York, Shocken Books, 1972), 264.

246 $31,000 cash for 37 Heathdale Road. Land Registry Office, Toronto, Transfer B37513 (West York), 26 August 1959.

246 $38,500 for 29 Glen Cedar Road. Land Registry Office, Toronto, Transfer B53219 (West York), 6 September 1960.

247 "If there was a bar mitzvah. . . ." Interview by author.

248 "At first, Lea and my mother. . . ." Ibid.

248 "Cultivated a rich folk culture. . . ." Michael Marrus, *Samuel Bronfman* (Hanover: Brandeis University Press, 1991), 111.

249 First Mesifta of Canada. The Hebrew word "mesifta" means synagogue, the implication being that this was the first Hasidic synagogue in Montreal. That distinction properly belonged to the Lubavitch Hasidic sect, which opened a synagogue in 1941, eight years before First Mesifta.

249 In Europe, the Unsdorfer and Gestetner families had been obscurely but poignantly connected. In 1944, S. B. Unsdorfer, Rabbi Alex's brother, ended up in the same barracks in Auschwitz as Henrik Gestetner, Renée's brother. Unsdorfer survived to document his experience in a book, *The Yellow Star* (Jerusalem: Feldheim, 1983).

249 "Edward revolutionized First Mesifta. . . ." Interview by author, Montreal, 19 May 1994.

249 "Reichmann was involved. . . ." Interview by author, Montreal, 19 May 1994.

250 "Edward is not such a great speaker. . . ." Interview by author, Montreal, 18 May 1994.

250 "An influx of Orthodox Jews. . . ." Harry Rabinowicz, *Hasidism and the State of Israel* (Rutherford, N.J.: Fairleigh Dickinson University Press, 1982), 149.

250 "I didn't think of him as 'The Wonder Rabbi'. . . ." Interview by author, Miami Beach, 28 June 1994.

250 "There were a dozen congregations. . . ." Interview by author.

250 Rabbi Hirschprung's photographic memory. Landau, *Piety and Power*, 217.

251 "I told him that as a board member. . . ." Interview by author, Miami Beach, 18 January 1995.

251 "Almost every night. . . ." Interview by author.

252 "He didn't do it to win me over. . . ." Interview by author.

252 "The Jewish community of Montreal has gained a new star. . . ." (translated from Hebrew) *Kanader Adler*, Golden Jubilee Edition, 22 November 1957, 79.

252 Crestohl's multilingual campaign flyer, featuring photos of Samuel Reichmann and Eleanor Roosevelt. Leon Crestohl general listing, archives of the Canadian Jewish Congress (Montreal).

253 "I became a great friend of Leon Crestohl." Interview by author, 22 April 1993.

253 "So Edward Reichmann was supposed to be. . . ." Interview by author, Montreal, 11 March 1992.

253 "Finally, he gave me a name. . . . The whole thing was very embarrassing." Ibid.

254 Crestohl's death. "Leon D. Crestohl Dies amid Election Campaign," *Montreal Star*, 25 March 1963.

254 "It was chaos . . . after the election." Interview by author, 19 November 1992.

254 "I never said this to anyone. . . ." Interview by author, 31 May 1994.

254 "I want to tell you. . . ." Klein to Reichmann, 14 June 1963, copy courtesy of Edward Reichmann.

Chapter 20

256 Details of the 56–58 Colville Road project. Land Registry Office, Toronto, 274713, 274714, 296180, 296575, 301694, 301697, 301807, 305808, 313675 (all North York).

257 "A need to create a building industry. . . ." James Lorimer, *The Developers* (Toronto: J. Lorimer, 1978), 16.

257 The value of building permits issued for North York rose from $9 million in 1946 to $129 million in 1958. *North York: Realizing the Dream* (Burlington, Ont.: Windsor Publications Canada), 50.

257 North York as "buildingest" community in Canada. "The Buildingest Now—The Biggest by 2000," *Willowdale Enterprise*, 8 January 1969, 9. See also Godfrey Scott, "Dormitory Community No More, North York Lures Industry," *Toronto Globe & Mail*, 11 March 1960, 4.

257 Paul's early real estate projects were financed by a variety of limited partnerships, including Colville & Sheffield, Rozray Investments and Bradwell Investments.

257 "I've heard people say. . . ." Interview by author.

257 York Factory's initial capitalization of $40,000. *Reichmann et al. vs. Toronto Life Publishing et al.,* Ontario Supreme Court, Plaintiff's brief entitled "An Analysis of the Defamatory Stories Contained in the Toronto Life Article," 3.

258 Details about the formation and combination of the various Reichmann companies were taken from filings made with the Companies Branch of the Ontario Ministry of Consumer and Commercial relations under the names Olympia Floor & Wall Tile, Olympia & York Investments (1964) Ltd., Olympia & York Developments Ltd., and York Factory Development Ltd. In 1967, S. Reichmann & Sons, Reichmann Family Enterprises and Olympia & York Industrial Development were amalgamated to form Olympia & York Developments Ltd., which would remain the principal vehicle of Paul and Albert's commercial ambition until its bankruptcy in 1992.

258 "I was an engineer . . . ease up on price." Interview by author, Toronto, 28 September 1994.

259 "They were very fast on the trigger. . . ." Interview by author, Toronto, 28 April 1994.

259 "It got so we just couldn't compete. . . ." Telephone interview by author, 2 August 1994.

259 "We felt it looked horrible. . . ." Jim Powell, *Risk, Ruin and Riches* (New York: Macmillan, 1986), 31.

260 "Paul and Albert were always very design conscious. . . ." Interview by author, Toronto, 30 September 1994.

260 "There was no palaver. . . ." Interview by author, Toronto, 6 October 1994.

260 "If his father. . . ." Interview by author.

261 "The word for him was lofty. . . ." Interview by author.

261 "Paul Reichmann is an indefatigable negotiator. . . ." Telephone interview by author, 2 September 1994.

261 "We'd never even heard of the Reichmanns. . . ." Interview by author, Toronto, 27 September 1994.

261 "Oh, was he mad." Interview by author.

262 "I respect the Reichmanns. . . ." Interview by author, New York, 2 November 1992.

262–63 The Ronson Corp. reception; Sirlin's upbraiding of Wos. Morley Sirlin, Frank Wos, interviews by author.

263 "He told me that someone had reported it. . . ." Interview by author.

263 Paul said later that he did not recall clashing with Wos over the issue of Sunday labor but insisted that he and his brothers "meticulouly respected the religion of all our employees."

263 "We're closed half the time . . . but because of it." William Minuk, interview by author.

263 "If you have something that is prohibited. . . ." Interview by author.

263 "The conflict is more within the person . . . the old, established builders." Interview by author, Toronto, 19 February 1995.

264 "With a heavily financed rush . . . credit for his family's expanding ventures." Peter Newman, *The Canadian Establishment*, vol. 2: *The Acquisitors* (Toronto: McClelland & Stewart, 1989), 277.

264 "When Samuel and Renée . . . did not have a fortune." *Reichmann et al. vs. Toronto Life Publishing et al.*, Ontario Supreme Court, Plaintiff's brief entitled "An Analysis of the Defamatory Stories Contained in the Toronto Life Article," 3–4.

265 The Reichmanns' immigration card was provided by the Toronto law firm Davies Ward Beck, by permission of the family.

265 Last will and testament of Samuel Reichmann, 17 February 1972, Office of the Registrar of the Surrogate Court, Judicial District of York, Toronto.

265 Financial data about the Reichmann companies. "An Analysis of the Defamatory Stories . . . ," 3.

265 "I was never the nosy sort . . . almost fell off his chair." Telephone interview by author, 5 May 1994.

266 A dozen and a half of the Reichmanns' earliest buildings. Properties researched at the Land Registry Office in Toronto included 16 Apex Rd., 30 Apex Road, 38 Apex Rd., 16 Benton Road, 22 Benton Road, 99 Carlingview Drive, 56 Colville Road, 35 Densley Ave., 760 Lawrence Ave. West, 1000 Lawrence Ave. West, 48 Prince Andrew Place, 52 Prince Andrew Place, 58 Prince Andrew Place, 14 Ronson Drive, 70 Ronson Drive, 73 Samor Road, 480 University Ave., 100 Wingold Ave., 75 Wynford Drive, 90 Wynford Drive and 100 Wynford Drive.

266 Revenue Properties' assets. Revenue Properties annual report for 1963, Metropolitan Toronto Reference Library.

266 Alex Rubin's vague awareness of the Reichmanns. Alex Rubin, interview by author, Toronto, 27 September 1994.

267 "I'm a construction man . . . lived on the line." Interview by author.

267 "Their word is their bond." Interview by author.

267 The ethics of property development in suburban Toronto. See Pierre Berton, "Some Questions about Land Profits in North York," *Toronto Star*, 13 March 1962; and Catherine Wismer, *Sweethearts* (Toronto: J. Lorimer, 1980).

268 "I'm a tough negotiator. . . ." Interview by author, 20 November 1994.

268 "I don't remember it that way. . . ." Ibid.

268 "I didn't like it. . . ." Interview by author.

268 "It wasn't a question . . ." Interview by author, 20 November 1994.

268 "I don't think of them as Jewish. . . ." Walter Stewart, "Good and Rich," *Weekend Magazine*, 13 October 1979, 29.

268 "I didn't mind. . . ." Interview by author.

268 "The food they ate. . . ." Telephone interview by author, 19 September 1994.

269 "The commerce of the talmid chacham. . . ." Rambam, Mishneh Torah, Hilkhot Deot, Chapter 5, halacha 13, as quoted by Meir Tamari, *In the Marketplace* (Southfield, Mich.: Targum Press, 1991), 15–16.

269 "WASPier than WASPs." Interview by author, Stouffville, Ontario, 28 September 1994.

Chapter 21

270 Purchase and sale of warehouse at 370 Beauharnois/8890 Verville St. Bureau de la Division d'Enregistrement de Montreal, deed 1282677 and deed 1379733.

271 "Edward's reputation here just galloped. . . ." Interview by author, Montreal, 20 May 1994.

272 "In Mesifta, everyone was good. . . ." Interview by author, Montreal, 18 May 1994.

272 Details of Three Star's incorporation. Département du Procureur-Général, Province de Québec, Ficher Central des Enterprises, Dossier 1285-1465.

272 "I'd already built the Bolsa . . . not Three Star Construction." Telephone interview by author, 5 April 1994.

272 "Edward always was . . ." Interview by author.

272 Sale of undeveloped land for $400,000. Bureau de la Division d'Enregistrement de Montreal, deed 1604065, 23 May 1962.

272 "Edward was always saying . . . just take Three Star?" Interview by author.

272 Reichmann offer to Zimmermans. Jack Zimmerman and Louis Reichmann, interview by author.

273 "I still think Edward. . . ." Interview by author.

273 "We liked each other right away. . . ." Interview by author, New York City, 15 July 1994.

273 Terms of the Venezuelans' purchase. Tibor Pivko and Edward Reichmann, interviews by author.

273 "Whenever something needed. . . ." Interview by author.

274 "Edward did the talking . . . so is Louis." Ibid.

273 "If any partner of Edward. . . ." Interview by author.

274 First Mesifta titles. First Mesifta annual reports and brochures, archives of the Canadian Jewish Congress.

274 "Before Reichmann came along. . . ." Interview by author.

274 Three Star's development of the Chabanal. Representative projects included 10 East Port Royal and 9691 to 9699 St. Lawrence Boulevard (see instruments 1441381, 1561484, 1579129, and 1794439); 5832 Decarie Boulevard (instruments 131735, 1347086, 1351911, 1361090, and 1367592); and 505 Rue de Louvain (see 1486514, 1521136, 1526368, and 1629822), Bureau de la Division d'Enregistrement de Montreal.

275 "Capra was our sworn enemy. . . ." Interview by author.

275 "I came right back to the office. . . ." Interview by author.

275 The sale of Montreal Floor. See instruments 1480524-5, Bureau de la Division d'Enregistrement de Montreal.

275 "At one point, the Bank . . ." Interview by author.

276 "A lot of lenders. . . ." Ibid.

276 Saul Friedman's eccentricities. Nahum Gelber and Edward Reichmann, interviews by author, 28 June 1994.

277 Olympia Floor's 50 percent market share by 1961. Louis Reichmann, interview by author.

277 "We continued to buy from Pilkington's . . . excitement over such an order." Ibid.

278 Moses Grunwald's responsa. Jacob Katz, The "Shabbas Goy" (Philadelphia: Jewish Publication Society, 1989), 212.

278 "We paid no premium. . . ." Interview by author.

278 "Edward always had to have . . . " Interview by author.

279 In addition to brother Louis, Edward's inner circle included Emile Rooz; Tibor Pivko; Fred and Jack Zimmerman; Leopold Braun, a plastics manufacturer; and Alex Rosenbaum, a relative of the Tangier Rosenbaums.

279 "Rabbi Hirschprung had a good relationship . . . put on the fringe every day." Interview by author, 18 January 1995.

280 Invitation to the Bais Yaakov groundbreaking and event program, copies provided by Edward Reichmann.

280 Olympia Floor's tax deductions. Olympia Floor & Wall Tile (Quebec) Ltd. vs. Minister of National Revenue, Tax Appeal Board, 30 May 1967, cited in 1967 Dominion Tax Cases, 359.

281 "These expenses take the form . . . contracts and business to Appellant." Ibid., 359–60.

281 "Over one million dollars." Olympia Floor & Wall Tile (Quebec) Ltd. vs. Minister of National Revenue, Exchequer Court of Canada, 11 February 1970, 1970 Dominion Tax Cases, 6086.

281 "My notion of the human attribute. . . ." Olympia Floor & Wall Tile (Quebec) Ltd. vs. Minister of National Revenue, Tax Appeal Board, 30 May 1967, 362 and 358.

281 "Such contributions could not be distinguished. . . ." Olympia Floor & Wall Tile (Quebec) Ltd. vs. Minister of National Revenue, Exchequer Court of Canada, 11 February 1970, cited in 1970 Dominion Tax Cases, 6085.

281 Tzedoka as an act of justice. Birnbaum, Encyclopedia of Jewish Concepts, s.v. "Charity."

Chapter 22

283 "They've always had a good name. . . ." Interview by author, Toronto, 28 April 1994.

283 "Our dealings were always. . . ." Telephone interview by author, 5 May 1994.

284 "The fact is, the Reichmanns . . ." Interview by author, Toronto, 29 April 1994.

284 "The center of the great city. . . ." John Conway, *Debts to Pay* (Toronto: James Lorimer, 1992), 54.

284 "Furious at the hoity toity English." *Current Biography,* 1967, s.v. "Jean Drapeau," 100.

285 " 'Réalisons! . . .' " Brian McKenna and Susan Purcell, *Drapeau* (Toronto: Clarke Irwin, 1980), 102.

285 "To get the zoning change. . . ." Drapeau aide Gerry Snyder quoted in ibid., 98.

285 The tactics of Drapeau's campaign manager, Joseph Henri Brien. Ibid., 129–31.

286 The developer that named the Queen Elizabeth Hotel was the Canadian National Railway, which was a partner of Zeckendorf's in Place Ville Marie.

286 "To the French. . . ." William Zeckendorf with Edward McCreary, *The Autobiography of William Zeckendorf* (New York: Holt, Rinehart and Winston, 1970), 185.

286 "The experience of every civilized country. . . ." Stuart Rosenberg, *The Jewish Community in Canada* (Toronto: McClelland & Stewart, 1970 and 1971), 145.

286 "To me, it was simple. . . ." Interview by author, 5 April 1994.

287 Edward's confrontation with Pilkington's manager. Edward Reichmann, interview by author, 5 April 1994.

288 "A sort of Rockefeller Center. . . ." Zeckendorf, *Autobiography of William Zeckendorf,* 170.

288 "Edward was very friendly. . . ." Interview by author.

289 "I can't ever remember. . . ." "Man at Work," *Time* magazine (Canadian edition), 6 January 1961.

289 "With toe-tromping efficiency. . . ." Ibid.

289 "Pride, hidden under airs . . . Chesterton's Father Brown." McKenna and Purcell, *Drapeau,* 176. See also Laure Hurteau, "La Famille Saulnier, Une Equipe Homogène," *Actualité,* January 1961.

289 "My sole ambition. . . ." "Man at Work."

290 "Believed to mark the beginning . . . in downtown Montreal." "Crémazie Project Under Way," *Montreal Star,* 10 July 1962.

290 "The first building complex . . ." Ibid. See also Marc Lechasseur, "Le nord de la ville de Montréal se développe," *Le Petit Journal* (Montreal), 15 July 1962.

290 Saulnier's appearance before the North End Businessmen's Association, "Zoning Regulations Will Be Stabilized," *Montreal Star,* 1 November 1961.

291 "Some people shook their heads. . . ." "Place Crémazie Called Success Story of '64, With 2 New Wings Scheduled to Open May 1," *Montreal Gazette,* 17 April 1964.

291 Saulnier's well-publicized tour of Place Crémazie. See "Technique remarquable employée au chantiers de Place Crémazie," *Le Devoir* (Montreal), 24 August 1962; and "Technique ingénieuse utilisée pour la première fois à Montréal," *La Presse* (Montreal), 25 August 1962.

291 City Assessors Dept. lease. "Municipal Assessors to Move," *Montreal Star,* 16 May 1963.

291 Saulnier's Place Crémazie lease. See lease 1712319, Bureau de la Division d'Enregistrement de Montreal.

291 Place Crémazie Christmas card, copy provided by Edward Reichmann.

291 "I was with Edward a few times. . . ." Interview by author.

291 "It definitely helped. . . ." Interview by author.

292 "Saulnier was the top man . . . relationship with Saulnier." Interview by author, 28 June 1994.

293 "An extended part of downtown Montreal." "Ceremony at Place Crémazie," *Montreal Star,* 30 October 1963.

293 "Still offers great opportunities. . . ." "New Office-Shopping Complex, Place Crémazie, Opened Here," *Montreal Gazette,* 30 October 1963.

293 "We new Canadians. . . ." Ibid. Edward's remarks also were given prominent and approving notice in Montreal's French newspapers. *Le Petit Journal* published a photo that included Samuel and Paul Reichmann with its lengthy article, "Les gratte-ciel à l'assaut du nord de Montréal," 3 November 1963.

293 "He was patiently. . . ." Interview by author.

294 "[I] had the idea of the circular form. . . ." "Reichmanns' Circular Tower Didn't Get Off Ground," *Montreal Gazette,* 24 December, 1988, D-4.

294 Purchase of Tour Laurier site. Deed of sale 1716492, Bureau de la Division d'Enregistrement de Montreal.

295 Purchase of 1826 Lajoie Ave. Deed of sale 1733941, Bureau de la Division d'Enregistrement de Montreal.

295 "For the same money. . . ." Interview by author.

295 Purchase of 6145 de Vimy. Deed of sale 1850114, Bureau de la Division d'Enregistrement de Montreal.

296 Edward's taking of bets. Interviews by author of Jack Zimmerman and Emile Rooz.

Chapter 23

298 "As much of a hedonist. . . ." Gilbert Burch, "Man in a $100-Million Jam," *Fortune,* July 1960, 104.

298 "I'd rather be alive at 18 percent. . . ." Jeffrey Robinson, *Minus Millionaires* (London: Boston: Unwin Hyman, 1987), 202.

298 "For me, it was a very easy deal. . . ." Interview by author.

299 "I would have liked to have used them. . . ." Interview by author. If the brothers were miffed, they didn't hold a grudge. Decades later, as Gestetner was nearing the end of his long tenure as head of the family company, he wrote to Paul asking his advice on what to do with the building in Flemingdon Park. "He did me the favor of going out personally to look at the building and wrote me a very nice letter back," Gestetner said.

299 "Exactly when we moved. . . ." Zeckendorf, *Autobiography of William Zeckendorf,* 294.

299 "That a beleaguered Webb & Knapp. . . ." Ibid., 297.

300 "The real estate community saw us. . . ." Telephone interview by author, 28 July 1994.

300 "It just seemed out of our league." Interview by author, 20 November 1994.

300 "I was aware of the Reichmanns. . . ." Powell, *Risk, Ruin and Riches,* 282.

301 "Roberts had been a real high-profile guy. . . ." Interview by author.

301 Details of Roberts's career. "His 'Swan Song' a Record-Breaker," *Real Estate Weekly,* 26 April 1982, 2.

301 "With a conventional four-story. . . ." Interview by author, 20 November 1994.

301 Enticing rebuff by Webb & Knapp. James Soden and Paul Reichmann, interviews by author, 20 November 1994.

302 "If Olympia & York hadn't . . ." Interview by author.

302 "For Webb & Knapp . . ." Interview by author, 20 November 1994.

302 "I was unhappy at first. . . ." Interview by author.

303 "There's gold on the table. . . ." Foster, *The Master Builders,* 19.

303 "I never set out to build. . . ." Interview by author, 19 February 1995.

303 "Personal drive is supposed. . . ." Ibid.

304 "Lea was stomping. . . ." Interview by author.

304 "If someone asked me. . . ." Fennell, "The Roots of Power," 25.

304 "Building schools in Morocco. . . ." Lawrence Lever, "Born-again Anglophile of Docklands," London *Times,* 9 May 1988, 23.

304 "There is the purely mathematical approach . . . difficult if not impossible." Interview by author, 19 February 1995.

306 "By an insatiable need for recognition." Interview by author, Toronto, 28 April 1994.

306 "There may have been . . ." Interview by author, 19 February 1995.

306 "Paul's priority. . . ." Interview by author.

307 "Paul Reichmann plays the game. . . ." Neil Barsky, "Paul Reichmann Scales Real Estate's Heights, Including Sears Tower," *Wall Street Journal,* 5 September 1989, 1.

307 "Paul has one of the . . ." Interview by author, London, 19 September 1993.

308 "With the Talmud. . . ." Maley, "The Philosopher King," 56.

308 "Consider the rigors . . . his Talmudic studies." Tully, "The Bashful Billionaires of Olympia & York," 96.

308 Paul's Torah-trained brain as secret weapon. By 1990, Paul Reichmann would have had his fill of talk of his Talmudic edge. "I have read about the accomplishments of my family being related to Talmudic studies," he told a journalist. "What is correct is that education and the way one absorbs and applies education affects all and everything in the world." In quoting the rabbinical sages, Reichmann then offered what amounted to a telling self-criticism on the verge of

Olympia & York's collapse: "Someone who does not increase his knowledge stands still. The one who does not study deserves to die." Barbara Amiel, "The Man Who Made the Canary Fly," London *Times*, 28 March 1990, 18.

308 Paul's backseat advice. Moses Lasry, interview by author.

309 "It was not a complex analysis. . . ." Interview by author, 20 November 1994.

309 In 1963, a few years before the Flemingdon Park opportunity emerged, the Reichmanns had borrowed $400,000 from the Oelbaums to finance construction of a light manufacturing plant at 54 Prince Andrew Place. This was a routine financing arranged lawyer to lawyer and did not involve any direct contact between members of the two families. Even so, the fact that the Reichmanns repaid this loan according to schedule went some small way toward establishing their bona fides with the Oelbaums.

309 "Although he was smart. . . ." Linda McQuaig, *Behind Closed Doors* (Toronto: Viking, 1987), 279.

309 The structure of the Reichmann-Oelbaum partnership. See *Amelia Rose vs. Minister of Revenue*, Federal Court of Canada, cited in Dominion Tax Cases 1971, 5481–86.

309 Financial details of the Flemingdon Park transaction. Land Registry Office, Toronto, instruments A-168699, A-168703, A-168705, A-168706, and A-168711.

310 Coverage of the Flemingdon Park purchase. "Webb-Knapp (Canada) Property in Toronto Sold for $17.8 Million," *Wall Street Journal*, 30 June 1968, 5; "Webb & Knapp Site in Canada Is Sold to Reichmann Unit," *New York Times*, 29 June 1965, 45; and "Here's the Thin Vein of Hope for Webb & Knapp Shareholders," *Financial Post*, 24 July 1965, 59.

Chapter 24

311 Three Star late on Place Crémazie mortgage. Majer Goldstein, interview by author, Montreal, 4 October 1994.

311 $600,000 due on La Tour Laurier loans. Instruments 11990811 and 2026768, Bureau de la Division d'Enregistrement de Montreal.

311 Demand for $2 million in additional collateral. Instrument 1938011, Bureau de la Division d'Enregistrement de Montreal.

311 $1 million in unpaid bills. Tibor Pivko, interview by author, New York City, 22 July 1994.

311 "Any time there was extra cash. . . ." Interview by author.

311 Personal guarantees of corporate borrowing. See, for example, instruments 1497417, 1798531, 1854554, 1898833, and 1936825, Bureau de la Division d'Enregistrement de Montreal.

312 Cross-collateralization of the La Tour Laurier loans. Instruments 1716493, 1751496, and 1794440, Bureau de la Division d'Enregistrement de Montreal.

312 "I didn't much care. . . ." Interview by author, 5 April 1994.

312 "Personally, I was in favor." Interview by author, Montreal, 4 October 1994.

312 "In my opinion . . ." Interview by author, 5 April 1994.

313 The ballooning of Place Crémazie's budget. Tibor Pivko and Majer Goldstein, interview by author. In addition to the $9 million first mortgage, Three Star took out a second mortgage of $5.2 million. See 1748757, Bureau de la Division d'Enregistrement de Montreal.

313 Sale of stake to the Goldstein group and option granted the sellers. Instruments 1792598 and 1792599, Bureau de la Division d'Enregistrement de Montreal. The investors included Goldstein (who owned a 27.5 percent interest in the partnership), Alfredo Berenstein (55 percent), Abraham Nickin (10.5 percent) and Irving Lask (7 percent).

314 Final Côte des Lieses land purchase. Instrument 1762863, Bureau de la Division d'Enregistrement de Montreal.

314 A paper wholesaler (Rosenbloom Paper) agreed to lease 6210 Côte de Lieses. Emile Rooz and Tibor Pivko, interviews by author, 22 July 1994.

314 "Edward would never show his real feelings. . . ." Interview by author, 22 July 1994.

314 "Don't forget that these people. . . ." Interview by author, Montreal, 3 October 1994.

314 Extension of the Siegel loan. Instrument 1762863, Bureau de la Division d'Enregistrement de Montreal.

315 "We didn't want to make a court case. . . ." Interview by author.

315 "I'm certain that Majer made . . ." Interview by author.

315 "Basically, he just turned . . ." Interview by author, 3 October 1994.

316 "We reflected our market. . . ." Interview by author.

316 "We were standing there talking. . . ." Interview by author, 15 July 1994.

316 "The subject of merger. . . ." Interview by author.

316 "When they started to succeed in Toronto. . . ." Interview by author, 22 July 1994.

317 "We agreed to give . . ." Interview by author.

317 "The brothers in Toronto . . ." Interview by author, 3 October 1994.

317 "Mrs. Reichmann held the family together. . . ." Interview by author, 22 July 1994.

317 "I woke up one day. . . ." Interview by author, 3 October 1994.

317 "Albert was a little aggravated. . . ." Interview by author.

317 $2.5 million in aid provided. Most of these emergency cash infusions were structured as loans in the name of Bruce Finkler, an Olympia & York lawyer. See, for example, instruments 1929150, 1949525, and 1976554, Bureau de la Division d'Enregistrement de Montreal.

318 The Montreal brothers pocketed $290,000. Deed 2059714, Bureau de la Division d'Enregistrement de Montreal.

318 "He was always a very proud man. . . ." Interview by author, 20 May 1994.

318 "Hashi is more laid back. . . ." Interview by author, 1994.

318 "I am an independent type . . . a bigger choice than New York City." Interview by author.

319 Belated payment of the Siegel loan. Instrument 2152603, Bureau de la Division d'Enregistrement de Montreal.

319 Exercise of the Place Crémazie option. Instrument 2127356, Bureau de la Division d'Enregistrement de Montreal.

319 "You could argue. . . ." Interview by author, 3 October 1994.

319 Sale of Place Crémazie and La Tour Laurier. Instruments 2215169 and 2485914, respectively. Bureau de la Division d'Enregistrement de Montreal. Both sales were arduously prolonged by the failure of the buyers to make promised payments on schedule. In the case of Place Crémazie, the buyer, a Massachusetts-based real estate investment trust, was in such shaky condition that at closing it failed put up the $1.2 million down payment. Instead of canceling the deal, the Toronto brothers took back a series of IOUs from the trust and eventually accepted $2.5 million worth of oil and gas leases in lieu of cash. This was Olympia & York's first investment in the oil business.

319 Purchase and sale of 4895 Fisher. Instruments 2654609 and 2654610, Bureau de la Division d'Enregistrement de Montreal.

319 "By and large, the creditors. . . ." Interview by author, 3 October 1994.

320 "When I brought the error. . . ." Interview by author.

320 "A man who could steal . . ." Interview by author.

320 "I didn't . . ." Interview by author, by telephone from Jerusalem, 6 August 1994.

320 "Whenever Edward spoke to us. . . ." Interview by author.

321 Tax action brought against the Reichmanns and Pivko. Tax Review Board cases 71-147 (*D & D Holdings Inc. vs. The Minister of National Revenue*) and 71-837, 71-836, and 71-838 (*Tibor Pivko, Edouard Reichmann and Louis Reichmann vs. The Minister of National Revenue*). Also Federal Court of Canada, Trial Division cases T-1103-73, T-1104-73, T-1104-74 (*Louis Reichmann, Edouard Reichmann and Tibor Pivko vs. Her Majesty the Queen*). Rulings for all three cases provided courtesy of Mitchell Klein.

321 "The Reichmanns are gentlemen. . . ." Interview by author, 22 July 1994.

321 "When Edward left Montreal. . . ." Ibid.

IV   EMPIRE OF THE SONS

Chapter 25

325 "It was a simple thing. . . ." Interview by author, 20 November 1994.

325 Sale of apartment buildings. For example, see instruments A-186031, A-195879 and A-199305, Land Registry Office, Toronto.

325 Profit of at least $25 million. Robert Canning, telephone interview by author, 6 September 1996.

326 "As far as I was . . ." Interview by author.

326 "Paul felt bad. . . ." Interview by author.

326 Interview with Parkin. Morley Sirlin and Paul Reichmann, interviews by author, Toronto, 29 October 1995.

326 The "perfect developers' architects." An unidentified "colleague" quoted by Marjorie Harris, "Sidney and George's Billion-Dollar Baby," *Quest* (Toronto Edition), February 1977, 10.

326 "Seven Office Buildings," *Canadian Architect*, June 1966, 47.

326 "Gently sweeping flights of steps. . . ." Olympia & York, "Olympia & York Projects 1970-1," Toronto Public Library, Metro Affairs branch.

327 "Liked every color. . . ." Interview by author, 11 November 1994.

327 "It was a serious problem. . . ." Ibid.

327 Paul and Lea's purchase of 214 Strathallan Wood. Grant 483131 (North York), Land Registry Office, Toronto.

327 Samuel and Renée's purchase of 160 Dalemount. Grant 550960 (North York), Land Registry Office, Toronto.

328 "He needed more challenge. . . ." Interview by author, 19 February 1995.

329 "I think the reason. . . ." Interview by author.

329 The Bais Yaakov movement. See Shoshana Pantel Zolty, *And All Your Children Shall Be Learned* (Northvale, N.J.: J. Aronson, 1993), 263–97.

329 Secular tilt. Toronto Board of Jewish Education, "Revised Affiliation Requirements," adopted 29 May 1984, provided courtesy of Rabbi Irwin Witty.

329 "I remember at one Board of Education meeting. . . ." Interview by author, 19 February 1995.

330 "In my son's generation. . . ." Interview by author, New York City, 24 May 1995.

330 "It wasn't a tough sell. . . ." Interview by author, 19 February 1995.

331 "Most developers didn't even know . . . the most brilliant man I ever met." Interview by author, Toronto, 22 June 1995.

331 Details of the Shell lease and bond issue. Instruments A-213067 and A-2130608, Land Registry Office, Toronto.

332 "Paul always used to tell me. . . ." Interview by author.

332 Texaco Canada and Bell Telephone financings. Instruments A-239492 and A-239493, and A-244048 and A-244049, respectively, Land Registry Office, Toronto.

332 "We were doing a huge amount. . . ." Interview by author.

332 "They thought maybe it . . ." Interview by author.

332 "They are a first-class. . . ." Bennett, "Canadian Realty Firms Make Waves in U.S. with Major Projects," 1.

332 "They were still known . . ." Walter Stewart, *Too Big to Fail* (Toronto: McClelland & Stewart, 1993), 43–44.

333 The doubling of annual spending on office construction. Lorimer, *The Developers,* 159.

334 The eight properties included in the second mortgage were 480 University Avenue, 99 Carlingview Drive, 1000 Lawrence Avenue West, 58 Prince Andrew

Place, 48 Prince Andrew Place, 100 Wingold Avenue, 75 Wynford Drive, and 73 Samor Road. Instrument A-219971, Land Registry Office, Toronto.

335 "I had Olympia & York checked. . . ." Interview by author, Toronto, 26 September 1994.

335 Reichmann's dealings with Engel. Tom Engel, telephone interview by author, 17 November 1994.

335 "People were flabbergasted. . . ." Interview by author, Toronto, 26 June 1992.

335 Terms of the *Star* purchase. Instruments 65566 E.S. and 65567 E.S., Land Registry Office, Toronto.

336 "Each of us could submit a single bid . . ." Powell, *Risk, Ruin and Riches*, 35.

336 Campeau as favorite in the press. "Star Building 25-Storey Complex," *Toronto Telegram*, 17 June 1969, 3.

336 "The thing that really appealed. . . ." Interview by author.

336 "There's the challenge of starting . . ." "New Star Building to Pace Waterfront, Developer Predicts," *Toronto Daily Star*, 17 June 1969, 2.

336 Paul sharing a laugh with Honderich. "Agreement Signed for New Star Tower," *Toronto Daily Star*, 22 October 1969, 46.

337 "Olympia & York did everything. . . ." Interview by author.

337 "I remember it like yesterday. . . ." Interview by author, London, 23 November 1993.

337 "His death shocked everyone. . . ." Interview by author, 26 September 1993.

338 "Her only daughter. . . ." Interview by author.

338 "Some nights there was a queue. . . ." Interview by author.

338 "Each person that received money. . . ." Telephone interview by author, London, 27 September 1993.

339 Heller's death certificate. General Register Office, London, QDX 120808.

339 "A surprising number of them disassociated. . . ." Telephone interview by author, London, 27 September 1993.

339 "That Lippa . . ." Interview by author, London.

339 Willie Stern's shrewdly orchestrated entry into merchant banking would go for naught when his debt-bloated empire came crashing down in the great London property collapse of 1973–74. First Bank of Maryland took possession of the remnants of Lippa Heller's firm and liquidated them. The total tab for First Maryland's disastrous foray into the City amounted to $11 million—twenty times its initial investment. When it came to humiliation, though, the Marylanders had nothing on Stern, who from 1979 to 1985 held the dubious distinction of being listed in the *Guinness Book of World Records* as the largest personal bankrupt in history, with debts totaling £142,978,413. This would stand as the largest bankruptcy of any sort in British history until the multibillion-dollar deficit the Reichmanns ran up at Canary Wharf made even Stern's failure seem like small change.

339 "Paul, who struck me as the leader. . . ." Interview by author, London, 18 September 1993.

340 "At one point . . ." Telephone interview by author, London, 25 November 1993.

340 Sale of 18 percent to First Bank of Maryland and expansion plans. "First National Bank of Maryland Buys 18 Percent of Heller & Co., London," *American Banker,* 16 June 1970.

340 "If the Heller bank had survived. . . ." Interview by author.

340 Loans and loan guarantees advanced to Amalgamated Food. See Annual Returns of Heller & Partners Ltd. (1968 and 1969), City Finance for Commerce Ltd. (1970); and First Maryland Ltd. (1971), Companies House, London and Cardiff. Also "In the Matter of City Finance for Commerce Limited," Chancery Division, High Court of Justice, London.

340 Amalgamated Food forced into receivership. "Receiver Appointed for Artic-Kartiv," *Jerusalem Post,* 8 March 1971.

341 "Certain questionable loans. . . ." First Maryland Bancorp 10-K for 1976, 31.

341 *First Maryland vs. Peat Marwick Mitchell.* First Maryland Bancorp 10-K for 1974, 24.

341 First Maryland sued by City Finance For Commerce. Ibid.

341 "My sister never forgave him." Interview by author, 29 October 1995.

Chapter 26

343 "Custodians of the free enterprise ethic." Newman, *Canadian Establishment,* vol. 1, 97f.

343 "Everybody and his dog . . . with that corner." Interview by author, Toronto, 30 September, 1994.

344 "Our site was really not that big . . . a crucial factor." Ibid.

345 "When I did Global House. . . ." Interview by author, 19 February 1995.

345 Edward Durell Stone's corporate following. The architect's best-known buildings included the John F. Kennedy Center for the Performing Arts in Washington, the Huntington Hartford Gallery of Modern Art in New York, the General Motors Building in New York, and the Standard Oil (Indiana) Building in Chicago. See Paul Goldberger, "Edward Durell Stone Services Will Be Held Tomorrow," *New York Times,* 8 August 1978, 10.

345 "They were at all the design meetings . . . for people to use." Charles Wilkins, "The Vertical City," *Canadian Geographic,* October/November 1991, 50.

345 "The concept of large office towers. . . ." Olympia & York Development, First Canadian Place report, 10 June 1974, 11, Toronto Public Library, Metro Affairs branch.

346 Sarcastic two-thousand-foot height limit. John Sewell, telephone interview by author, 11 January 1995.

346 Press reaction to bylaw. See, for example, Edmund Faltermayer, "Toronto, the New Great City," *Fortune,* September 1974, 137.

347 Developer reaction to bylaw. Jon Caulfield, *The Tiny Perfect Mayor* (Toronto: J. Lorimer, 1974), 100–101.

347 Olympia & York as a target of antidevelopment forces. See, for example, James Lorimer, "The Property Industry and the Media," in *A Citizen's Guide to City Politics* (Toronto: James Lewis & Samuel, 1972).

347 "Who made downtown land. . . ." Caulfield, *The Tiny Perfect Mayor,* 102.

348 "We desperately need your help. . . ." Toronto City Council Minutes of 1974, vol. 2, appendix A, 1399–1400.

348 The Council's request "to begin negotiations with the consortium." Ibid., 1401.

348 For Olympia & York's own analysis of the harmful effects of retaining the Provincial Bank Building, see Toronto City Council Minutes of 1974, vol. 3, appendix A, 4191.

348 Toronto as the construction capital of North America. Faltermeyer, "Toronto, the New Great City," 137. See also "Toronto Keeps Building Despite Voters' Anti–High Rise Stand," *Engineering News Record,* 12 April 1973, 70.

349 "You can't imagine the chaos. . . . They left me alone, basically." Interview by author, Toronto, 27 September 1994.

349 "I was particularly . . ." "His Swan Song a Record-Breaker," *Real Estate Weekly,* 2.

350 "Both of them understood. . . ." Interview by author.

350 "Convince every subcontract. . . ." *Olympia & York Development, First Bank Tower,* a twenty-two-minute film produced by the company in 1976 and written and narrated by Roberts.

350 "If the job had . . ." Interview by author.

350 Labor savings of 1.3 million man hours and other project details. *First Bank Tower.*

351 "Keith Roberts was an . . ." Interview by author, 29 October 1995.

351 "The Reichmanns had a lot of property. . . ." Interview by author.

352 "Crombie's style. . . ." Caulfield, *Tiny Perfect Mayor,* 111.

352 "The mayor was a friend. . . ." Interview by author, 19 February 1995.

352 "When I look at the skyline. . . ." Caulfield, *Tiny Perfect Mayor,* 102.

352 "Lectured at me. . . ." Interview by author.

353 "I'd meet with Paul. . . ." Telephone interview by author, 27 January 1995.

353 "We knew when crunch time. . . ." Interview by author.

354 The mid-1970s decline of the Toronto office market. See Gary Weiss and Sonita Horvitch, "Toronto," *National Real Estate Investor,* October 1977, 123.

355 "Middle is more comfortable." Goldenberg, "The Unknown Empire," 22.

355 "Half the money in Ontario. . . ." Tully, "The Bashful Billionaires of Olympia & York," 80.

Chapter 27

353 "To us, O & Y wasn't just a company. . . ." Interview by author, Toronto, 20 June 1995.

356 Ownership structure of Olympia & York. Paul Reichmann, interview by author, 19 February 1995.

357 "The standard of giving. . . ." Ibid.

357 "It was us responding. . . ." Ibid.

358 "The Reichmanns' giving. . . ." Interview by author.

358 Israeli yeshiva enrollments. Abraham Levy, *The Sephardim: A Problem of Survival* (London: Abraham Levy, 1972), 47.

359 "The time that Paul devoted . . . knows the problems from firsthand." Interview by author.

359 "Because it was unusual . . . twenty other people, too." Interview by author, 29 October 1995.

360 Witty's request on behalf of Steinsaltz. Irwin Witty and Paul Reichmann, interviews by author, 29 October 1995.

360 "People say that . . ." Landau, *Piety and Power*, 47.

360 Witty's visit with Modern Orthodox rabbi. Irwin Witty and Paul Reichmann, interviews by author, 29 October 1995.

360 "In business we have to . . ." Dianne Maley, "Reichmann Helps Build Bridge to Soviets," *Toronto Globe & Mail*, 2 July 1989, B1.

361 The rise and fall of Siedenfeld. Interviews by author of Moses Lasry, Edmund Tennenhaus, and Mr. and Mrs. Mordecai Neustadt, Brooklyn, 23 September 1995.

361 Purchase of Old Bridge land. Indenture 19014-1, 18 December 1973, Middlesex County Deed Room, New Brunswick, N.J. See also "Canadian Interests Buy Big Jersey Tract," *New York Times*, 20 January 1974.

361 "I made the mistake. . . ." Interview by author, 29 October 1995.

361 "I would say that Paul. . . ." Interview by author.

362 Details of the Old Bridge venture. Rachelle Garbarine, "Olympia & York's Troubled Superproject," *New York Times*, 17 August 1986, 10R.

362 On Neumann's woes, see Peter Grant, "Troubled Developer Reemerges," *Crain's New York Business*, 11 November 1991, 3.

362 "It was more to help . . . still paying for monthly." Interview by author, 29 October 1995.

362 "My father always used to ask. . . ." Interview by author, 24 May 1995.

363 Lea Reichmann's exchange with Samuel Reichmann. Lea Reichmann, interview by author, Toronto, 20 November 1994.

363–64 Circumstances of Samuel's death. Edward, Louis, Paul, and Lea Reichmann, interview by author.

364 Samuel's death certificate. Obtained from the Registrar General of Ontario, registration number 1975-05-25620.

364 "When my father-in-law died. . . ." Interview by author.

364 "My father-in-law was a great man." Interview by author, Queens, N.Y., 8 August 1994.

364 "As a child. . . ." Interview by author.

364 "Is regarded as a proof. . . ." Birnbaum, *Encyclopedia of Jewish Concepts*, s.v. "Death."

364 "Our whole family . . ." Interview by author, 19 February 1995.

364 The financing of Beit Shmaya. Ibid.

365 The terms of Samuel's will. The last will and testament of Samuel Reichmann, 17 February 1972, Office of the Registrar of the Surrogate Court, Judicial District of York, Toronto.

365 The purchase of 1 Forest Wood. Transfer 699090 (North York), Land Registry Office, Toronto.

366 "We were hoping Eva. . . ." Interview by author, 24 May 1995.

366 "She was not much involved . . . the same problem." Interview by author, 19 February 1995.

366 "My late father . . ." Tully, "The Bashful Billionaires of Olympia & York," 89.

Chapter 28

368 "Being Canadian opens doors. . . ." Colin Stephens of Design International Limited, quoted in Diane Francis, "Our New Export: Revitalized Cities," *Canadian Business*, August 1980, 44.

369 "New York, because . . ." "Canada's Secretive Reichmanns," *Business Week*, 6 March 1978, 58.

369 "As soon as I heard. . . ." Interview by author.

369 "You needed very little imagination. . . ." Vianney Carriere, "Billion-Dollar Men," *Toronto Globe & Mail*, 27 June 1981, 1.

369 "The biggest crapshooter. . . ." Richard Kahan, chairman of the Battery Park City Authority, quoted in Peter Hellman, "Manhattan Transfer," *Saturday Night*, April 1983, 46.

370 "Paul knew perfectly well. . . ." Interview by author.

370 "I asked Albert . . . This is my Las Vegas.' " Ibid.

370 "A shrewd player . . . ability of a card shark." Andrew Sarlos, *Fireworks* (Toronto: Key Porter Books, 1993), 185.

370 "I don't think. . . ." Interview by author, 19 February 1995.

371 "The great names were Tishman. . . ." Jerry Adler, *High Rise* (New York: HarperCollins, 1993), 15.

371 "The position of these families. . . ." Tom Schachtman, *Skyscraper Dreams* (Boston: Little Brown, 1991), 252–62.

371 "The only beautiful building. . . ." Ibid., 199.

372 "We went home one Friday. . . ." Geoffrey Smith, "The One That Got Away," *Forbes*, 1 April 1977, 59.

372 "Some close to Ross. . . ." Connie Bruck, *Master of the Game* (New York: Simon & Schuster, 1994), 104.

373 Sixty-one new office towers. Carter Horsely, "Builders' Year: The Long Sleep," *New York Times*, 15 February 1976, VIII-1.

373 "A giant step . . ." *National Kinney Annual Report for 1973,* 2, New York Public Library.

374 "They were crappy buildings." Interview by author.

374 "They weren't trophies . . . problematic today." Interview by author, New York City, 3 March 1995.

374 "Exceedingly fair price . . . on that basis alone." Telephone interview by author, 9 February 1995.

375 "I called in my treasurer . . . a good chance." "Sam Lefrak: Real Estate Bargain Hunter," *Business Week,* 31 May 1976, 53.

375 Joseph Fried, "Office Renting Here Called Good Omen," *New York Times,* 25 March 1976, 39.

375 "The opportunity of acquiring. . . ." *Business Week,* "Sam Lefrak: Real Estate Bargain Hunter," 53.

375 "Competition is fierce . . . exhausted the supply." Ibid.

375 "I found both Reichmann brothers. . . ." Interview by author, New York City, 8 June 1992.

376 "He was really pressing. . . ." Interview by author, 19 February 1995.

376 "Recent studies . . . very viable." "European Purchase," *New York Times,* 31 October 1976.

376 "I don't buy anticipation. . . ." Powell, *Risk, Ruin and Riches,* 37.

376 September 21 meeting. Affidavit of Edward Minskoff, 63, *Ficor, Inc. and Edward J. Minskoff vs. National Kinney Corp. et al.,* Supreme Court, New York County.

376 "You look at a pair of Orthodox guys. . . ." Hellman, "Manhattan Transfer," 47.

376 Heights and sizes of the Uris buildings. Memo prepared for author by Joel Simon of Olympia & York, 8 September 1996.

377 "I asked Paul why. . . ." Interview by author.

377 "We felt that New York. . . ." Hellman, "Manhattan Transfer," 47.

378 "A boom in New York rents. . . ." Tully, "The Bashful Billionaires of Olympia & York," 86.

378 Premature November announcement. "National Kinney Reaches Accord to Sell Buildings," *Wall Street Journal,* 12 November 1976, 7.

378 Sale officially announced. "National Kinney to Sell Buildings to Canada Firm," *Wall Street Journal,* 14 March 1977, 2.

378 "I cannot understand. . . ." Reichmann to Frankel, 27 June 1977, Exhibit A in plaintiff's brief in *Ficor, Inc. and Edward J. Minskoff vs. National Kinney Corp. et al.,* Supreme Court, New York County.

378 "I think there was a period . . . depressing its stock price." Interview by author, 19 February 1995.

379 Increase in average rent to $30 a square foot and decline of vacancy rate toward zero. Ibid.

379 "That would have put us . . ." Hellman, "Manhattan Transfer," 47.

379 On 245 Park leases at $60 a square foot, see ibid.

379 "There have been two great deals. . . ." Albert Scardino, "Building a Manhattan Empire," *New York Times,* 18 April 1987, I-27.

Chapter 29

380 "We could never tell. . . ." Meyer Frucher, interview by author, New York City, 30 July 1992.

380 "In my twenties . . . when I was a student." Interview by author, 19 February 1995.

381 "Hegel said. . . ." Interview by author.

381 Lea's confrontational teasing. As witnessed by the author during interviews.

381 Paul's telephone manner. As witnessed by the author during interviews.

381 "Paul has a hell of a way. . . ." Interview by author, London, 21 September 1993.

381 "Don't worry . . ." Newman, *The Acquisitors,* 278.

382 "It wasn't easy . . . especially in real estate." Interview by author, New York City, 22 March 1994.

382 "The standing of Olympia & York. . . ." Interview by author, 29 October 1995.

382 "Paul worked very, very hard. . . ." Interview by author.

382–83 Details of Mulholland's career. Alexander Ross, "Bill Mulholland's Biggest Turnaround," *Canadian Business,* November 1978, 46; and Rod McQueen, "The Man with the Midas Touch," in *The Moneyspinners* (Toronto: Macmillan of Canada, 1983), 93.

383 "Paul Reichmann had an easy, charming way. . . ." Interview by author.

383 "They wanted their own design. . . ." Interview by author, New York City, 26 February 1996.

384 "After two and a half years. . . ." Interview by author.

384 The argument over being shortchanged. Plaintiff's complaint and minutes of settlement, *Bank of Montreal vs. Olympia & York Development,* Supreme Court of Ontario, Toronto, file 24182/84.

384 "A good many millions of dollars." Interview by author.

384 The 302 Bay incident. William Mulholland and a source within Olympia & York, interviews by author.

384 "I said, 'He has an excellent . . .' " Interview by author, New York City, 15 October 1996.

385 "You had to be on your toes. . . ." Interview by author.

385 "That is rubbish. . . ." Interview by author, 15 October 1996.

386 "Many people I knew . . ." Interview by author, 29 October 1995.

387 The terms of Fruchthandler's deal. Deposition given by Paul Reichmann, 5 June 1985, *Edward J. Minskoff vs. Ficor, Inc. and Jan T. Hyde,* Supreme Court of New York, County of New York, index no. 21699/83.

387 "I went to get advice. . . ." Interview by author.

387 "Ron Sosklone is. . . ." Interview by author, 19 February 1995.

388 "The city was our training ground . . . with less momentum." Judy Steed, "Battery of Talent Takes on N.Y.," *Toronto Globe & Mail*, 14 January 1984, 10.

388 "I think anyone who does the job well. . . ." Ibid.

389 "If I want a replacement. . . ." Ibid.

389 "There are certain talents. . . ." Cited in Plaintiff's Affidavit in Opposition to Summons, 12 July 1985, 69, *Minskoff vs. Ficor*, Supreme Court of New York.

389 The sale of half of Fruchthandler's interest. Deposition of Paul Reichmann, 5 June 1985, 44; Defendant's Post-Trial Brief, 29 September, 1989, 16–17; and Fame Associates Partnership Agreement, 12 July 1985. *Minskoff vs. Ficor*, Supreme Court of New York.

389 "I wanted to be president. . . ." Interview by author.

389 Minskoff's $26 million profit. Defendant's Post-Trial Brief, 29 September 1989, 36, *Minskoff vs. Ficor*, Supreme Court of New York.

390 "I didn't detect any backlash. . . ." Interview by author, New York City, 28 October 1992.

390 "Going into Lou Siegel's. . . ." Interview by author.

391 "The Reichmanns in New York. . . ." Interview by author, New York City, 9 June 1992.

391 Olympia & York's winning bid. "Penn Central Seeks to Sell Real Estate for $40.3 Million," *Wall Street Journal*, 10 February 1978, 10.

391 "When I called Sam. . . ." Interview by author. New York City, 2 November 1992.

391 Recovery of the New York market. Schachtman, *Skyscraper Dreams*, 294.

392 "He walked slowly. . . ." Interview by author.

392 Details of the 466 Lexington project. Carter Horsley, "$90 Million Renovation at Lexington and 46th," *New York Times*, 20 April 1979, B1; and "An Atrium for Public in Midtown," *New York Times*, 19 August 1981, 16.

392 "Working with the Reichmanns . . . 'can't work on Saturdays?' " Interview by author.

393 The Koch administration's development subsidies. Schachtman, *Skyscraper Dreams*, 293–94.

393 "We wanted 466 Lex renovated. . . ." Interview by author.

393 The disapproval of Olympia & York's abatement application and the responses of Solomon and Reichmann. Glenn Fowler, "New York Holds Up $90 Million Project," *New York Times*, 31 May 1979, 1.

393 Details of compromise. "Agency Supports Tax Cuts to Aid Midtown Plans," *New York Times*, 15 August 1979, B1.

394 The building at 237 Park Avenue had no less than five names and addresses. All four sides say "237 Park Ave." Three sides also bear additional labels: one is marked 11 E. 45th St., one is 466 Lexington, and one is 100 E. 46th. All four sides also have signs saying "Park Avenue Atrium." See Randall Smith, "A

Fancy Address in New York City May Just Be Fanciful," *Wall Street Journal*, 27 May 1983, 1.

Chapter 30

395 "We have not had one disagreement. . . ." Carriere, "Billion-Dollar Men," 1.

395 "In major negotiations. . . ." Susan Goldenberg, "A Reichmann Touch in Real Estate," *New York Times*, 17 August 1980, C-1.

395 "More or less interchangeable." Goldenberg, "The Unknown Empire," 14.

395 "We work well together. . . ." Jeffrey Robinson, "From the Ground Up," *Barron's*, 21 November 1983, 52.

395 The Minskoff suit was settled out of court, with Minskoff collecting $2 million from National Kinney.

395 "Paul Reichmann testified. . . ." Deposition of Samuel N. Greenspoon of Eaton, Van Winkle & Greenspoon, 3–4, *Ficor, Inc. and Edward Minskoff vs. National Kinney Corp. et al.*, New York Supreme Court, New York County.

396 "Albert is a good man. . . ." Interview by author.

397 "There's no genius required. . . ." Maley, "The Philosopher King," 56.

397 "Paul's deals . . . rein each other in." Interview by author.

398 "Accustomed as I was. . . ." Powell, *Risk, Ruin and Riches*, 248.

399 On the Shapiros' history, see David Wilkinson, "Paul and Albert and Ralph and David," *Canadian Business*, November 1989; and Albert Warson, "The Reichmanns' Best Partners File for a Friendly Divorce," *Canadian Business*, November 1992, 21.

399 The terms of the Shapiros' partnership with Olympia & York. Interview by author of a source within Olympia & York.

399 The recasting of the Shapiro arrangement. "In my view. . . ." Ibid.

400 Biography of Zeev Vered. Examination of Zeev Vered, 29 November 1994, 4–7 and 15–16, *Albert Reichmann vs. Zeev Vered and Ron Engineering and Construction (International) Ltd.*, Ontario Court (General Division), Toronto, court file 94-CQ-52726.

400 Early projects of Olympia & York and Vered. Ibid., 8–9, 11–14. Also examination of Albert Reichmann, 3 March 1995, 3–6.

400 On the $7 million profit, see "Olympia, York Unit Makes Profit on Sale," *Toronto Globe & Mail*, 30 June 1982.

401 Oskar Brecher's Cadillac Fairview career. Interview by author of Bernard Ghert.

401 Details of Olympia & York's investment in American Landmark. Source within Olympia & York, interview by author.

401 David Chase's career. See Katarzyna Wandycz, "Solidarity's Partner," *Forbes*, 27 May 1991, 168, and "Low Profile, High Finance World of Chase Enterprises," *Broadcasting*, 20 August 1990, 32.

401 Chase as one of the 400 richest Americans, *Forbes*, 27 October 1986, 228. *Forbes* subsequently raised its estimate of Chase's net worth to $300 million but dropped him abruptly from the 400 in 1992.

402 Paul's visit to the sandbox. John Zuccotti, interview by author, New York City, 9 February 1994.

402 Battery Park City's woeful history. See James Grant, "Castles of Sand?" *Barron's*, 26 May 1980, 7.

402 "Pedestrians would be shunted . . ." Brendan Gill, "The Skyline," *New Yorker*, 20 August 1990, 73.

402–3 Kahan's background and view of Battery Park City as "last great urban laboratory." Ibid., 77.

403 "They didn't know from . . ." Interview by author.

403 "This was because. . . ." Powell, *Risk, Ruin and Riches*, 40–41.

403 "From a developer's point of view. . . ." Hewland Productions, *The Men Who Built Canary Wharf*, an hour-long documentary that aired in Britain in 1989.

403 Advantage of $5 to $8 a square foot. Paul Reichmann, interview by the author, 19 February 1995.

403 Downtown Manhattan's rebound. "Real Estate Perks Up in Lower Manhattan as Shortage of Office Space Looms There," *Wall Street Journal*, 4 November 1980, 46.

404 "We concluded . . . offering special deals." Interview by author, 19 February 1995.

404 George Klein, of Park Towers Realty, was a son of Stephen Klein of the chocolate-making family that Samuel and Renée Reichmann had befriended during their long sojourn in Vienna before the war and that played an important supporting role in the Reichmanns' rescue and relief campaign in Tangier. Although Paul's generation of Reichmanns remained on friendly terms socially with their Klein contemporaries, Olympia & York and Park Tower Realty never collaborated on a real estate project.

404 "We are only interested. . . ." Reichmann to Kahan, 22 October 1980, attached as an exhibit to the plaintiff's complaint in *Minskoff vs. Ficor*, Supreme Court of New York.

405 Present value of Olympia & York's proposal and other bids. Exhibit B to a memorandum by Richard Kahan to the BPCA board, 12 November 1980, and publicly available at the BPCA office, New York City.

405 Reichmann's meeting with Kahan. Hellman, "Manhattan Transfer," 44.

405 "We sat in the room . . . 'I just did.' " Hewland Productions, *The Men Who Built Canary Wharf.*

405 "I reached essentially the same conclusions. . . ." Powell, *Risk, Ruin and Riches*, 43.

405 Selection of Olympia & York. "Battery Park City Job Is Awarded to Toronto Firm," *Wall Street Journal*, 14 November 1980, 12; and Robert McFadden, "Battery Park City Builder Picked," *New York Times*, 14 November 1980, II-3.

405 Solow's complaints. Carter Horsley, "Battery Park City Bidding Faulted," *New York Times*, 30 November/80, VIII-1.

406 "Started dealing from . . ." Schachtman, *Skyscraper Dreams*, 317.

406 The Christmas Eve trip from New Haven. Powell, *Risk, Ruin and Riches*, 117.

407 Pelli's very formal presentation. Foster, *The Master Builders*, 47.

407 "One is immediately struck. . . ." John Pastier, "The Evolution of an Architect," in *Cesar Pelli: Buildings and Projects 1965–1990* (New York: Rizzoli, 1990), 13.

407 "Cesar Pelli's design. . . ." Hewland Productions, *The Men Who Built Canary Wharf.*

407 Olympia & York's design unveiled. Joyce Purnick, "Plans Disclosed for Office Core at Battery Park," *New York Times*, 14 May 1981, B1.

408 "The classical or Art Deco . . ." Ada Louis Huxtable, "A New 'Rockefeller Center' Planned for Battery Park," *New York Times*, 24 May 1981, D25.

408 "The finest group of skyscrapers. . . ." Paul Goldberger, "A Dramatic Counterpoint for Trade Center," *New York Times*, 14 May 1981, B1.

408 "A coordinated and architecturally first-rate . . . monumental penny-ante operation." Huxtable, "A New 'Rockefeller Center' Planned for Battery Park," D25. See also Andrea Oppenheimer Dean and Allen Freeman, "The Rockefeller Center of the '80s?" in *American Architecture of the 1980s* (Washington, D.C.: American Institute of Architects Press, 1990), 219–24.

408 "The whole effect . . ." Schachtman, *Skyscraper Dreams*, 154. Critical opinion of Rockefeller Center began to reverse itself in 1936 when the influential French architect Le Corbusier visited New York and praised Rockefeller Center as a "machine-age temple [that] affirms to the world the dignity of the new times by its useful and noble halls."

409 Although the Rockefeller family never undertook another development of the scale of Rockefeller Center, two of John D.'s sons played seminal roles in conceiving the Battery Park City project. David Rockefeller organized a group called the Downtown–Lower Manhattan Association, which pushed hard during the early 1960s for various redevelopment schemes in the financial district, including some derived from the landfill from the World Trade Center. Governor Nelson Rockefeller, David's older and equally pro-development brother, championed the legislation that established the Battery Park City Authority in 1968.

Chapter 31

411 Cash flow of $230 million. Paul Reichmann quoted in Tully, "The Bashful Billionaires of Olympia & York," 89.

412 "They believe that inflation. . . ." Susan Goldenberg, *Men of Property* (Toronto: Personal Library, 1981), 64.

412 "A new common wisdom. . . ." William Greider, *Secrets of the Temple* (New York: Simon & Schuster, 1987), 16.

412 "In real estate you . . ." Carriere, "Billion-Dollar Men," 1.

412 "The fact that . . ." Interview by author, 3 March 1994.

413 "We want to become. . . ." Leonard Zehr, "Canada's Rich and Reticent Reichmanns Plan to Use Property Profits to Diversify," *Wall Street Journal*, 21 May 1981, B1.

414 The oft-told tale of the Bronfman disinheritance. See, for example, Newman, *Bronfman Dynasty*; Patricia Best and Ann Shortell, *The Brass Ring* (Toronto: Random House, 1988); and Philip Siekman, "The Bronfmans: An Instinct for Dynasty," *Fortune*, December 1966, 176.

414 Peter Bronfman's odd habits. Newman, *The Acquisitors*, 287.

414 "It would regard . . ." Jack Willoughby, "Bid by Olympia and York May Mean Fight over Trizec," *Toronto Globe & Mail*, 22 February 1979, B6.

414 "There has been a very mistaken notion. . . ." Foster, *The Master Builders*, 69.

415 "I guess he got to his room. . . ." Ibid., 70.

415 "Whenever we reached . . ." Goldenberg, "A Reichmann Touch in Real Estate, C-1.

415 Stealing the headlines. Roderick McQueen, "Joining the Towers That Be," *Maclean's*, 26 March 1979, 42.

415 "I always thought those Bronfmans were smart. . . ." Ibid.

416 "The heart of Edper." Best and Shortell, *Brass Ring*, 5.

416 "South Africa is a country. . . ." Ibid., 53.

416 On the 152 companies, $120 billion in assets. Ibid., 2.

416 "The Bronfmans entrusted. . . ." Ibid., 95.

416 "A Jesuitical approach to business. . . ." Best and Shortell, *Brass Ring*, 122.

417 "He preferred to be. . . ." Ibid.

418 "I don't see why. . . ." According to Campeau's testimony in an Ontario Securities Commission hearing into the Royal Trust affair, quoted by McQueen, *The Moneyspinners*, 41.

418 "There was no reason . . ." Patricia Best and Ann Shortell, *A Matter of Trust* (Markham, Ont.: Viking, 1985), 82.

419 "Went running around . . ." Foster, *The Master Builders*, 75.

419 "The Reichmanns said . . ." Zehr, "Canada's Rich and Reticent Reichmanns," B1.

419 "We like them. . . ." McQueen, *The Moneyspinners*, 51.

419 "He came to us. . . ." Foster, *The Master Builders*, 75.

420 The OSC hearing attracted much press coverage in Canada. See especially Anthony Wittingham, "The White Knight Rides Within," *Maclean's*, 13 October 1980, 46. It included a photo of Paul Reichmann, captioned "not a member of 'the Club.' "

420 Half of the 300 largest companies on the Toronto stock exchange being controlled by nine families. "Other northern lights," *U.S. News & World Report*, 14 March 1988, 38.

421 Brinco stake. "Brinco States Details for Olympia & York's Purchase of Control," *Wall Street Journal,* 25 September 1980, 25.

421 "Thanked them and . . ." Foster, *The Master Builders,* 88.

422 The $1 billion bid for Hudson's Bay is discussed in "Conoco Rejects Offer from Olympia & York for Hudson's Bay Oil," *Wall Street Journal,* 1 June 1981, 20.

422 Reichmann's "brief chat" with Wilder. Foster, *The Master Builders,* 159–60. (This incident apparently was first reported by Newman in *The Acquisitors,* but the Reichmann in question was misidentified as Albert.)

422 "Reacted to the bidding." Zehr, "Canada's Rich and Reticent Reichmanns," B1.

423 Decline in the value of Abitibi and other stockholdings. Tully, "The Bashful Billionaires of Olympia & York."

Chapter 32

424 "Sense of awe . . . handed him for comment." Carriere, "Billion-Dollar Men," 1.

425 Albert's photo phobia at Oakdale. Newman, *The Acquisitors,* 269.

425 Publicity "can't be avoided. . . ." Zehr, "Canada's Rich and Reticent Reichmanns," B1.

426 "Thinly veiled revulsion . . . around this city." Carriere, "Billion-Dollar Men," 1.

426 "Paul had a completely compartmentalized life. . . ." Interview by author.

427 "I used to ask Paul. . . ." Interview by author, Toronto, 1994.

427 "Basically, I did . . ." Interview by author, 19 February 1995.

427 Separation of home and office. Ironically, when Albert's son, Philip, became a senior executive of Olympia & York, he adopted his Uncle Paul's approach. "I don't have business meetings in the house," he said. "I don't bring home models of buildings." Gord McLaughlin, "The Reichmanns Rise Again," *Financial Post Magazine,* April 1994, 21.

427 "The business wasn't highlighted. . . ." Interview by author.

427 "The Reichmanns are the . . ." Interview by author.

427 "Startled . . . dawned on me." Interview by author.

427 "Honesty, modesty and philanthropy. . . ." Landau, *Piety and Power,* 271.

428 "My sons outwardly. . . ." Interview by author, 29 October 1995.

428 "Ciphers and nonentities." Interview by author, 1993.

429 "My children's generation. . . ." Interview by author, 16 August 1994.

430 "My son was never . . ." Interview by author, 24 May 1995.

430 The rise and fall of Edward's textile venture. Ibid.

430 "When my son is learning. . . ." Ibid.

431 "None of my brothers. . . ." Interview by author.

431 "It became an American company." Ibid.

431 "I didn't grow up. . . ." Interview by author, Toronto, 21 June 1995.

431 Paul Jacobs is the son of Harold M. Jacobs, a past president of the Union of Orthodox Jewish Congregations of America and the founder of Precision Ware, a kitchenware company. See Ronald Sullivan, "Harold M. Jacobs, 81: Civic and Religious Leader," *New York Times*, 19 May 1995, 29.

432 "We looked around but. . . ." Interview by author, Toronto, 21 June 1995.

432 "I'm sure if we had wanted. . . ." Interview by author.

432 "We were able . . . the development business." Ibid.

433 "Of the six of us. . . ." Interview by author, 24 May 1995.

433 On the flight of the yeshiva students from Lithuania to Shanghai, see David Kranzler, *Japanese, Nazis and Jews* (New York: Yeshiva University Press, 1976). Sugihara's story is recounted by Carey Goldberg, "The Honors Come Late for a Japanese Schindler," *New York Times*, 8 November 1995, B1.

433 "She was quite happy. . . ." Interview by author.

434 "Eva's kids may be. . . ." Interview by author, 1992.

434 "It was very frustrating . . . never seriously considered it." Interview by author.

435 "Our first meeting. . . ." Interview by author, Toronto, 20 June 1995.

436 "You get a little bored . . . best sounding board I had." Hauer served as a sounding board not only for Philip but for another of Paul's sons-in-law, Henry Brackfield, who joined Olympia & York in the late 1980s. Brackfield married Libby Reichmann, the youngest of Paul's daughters.

436 "Expected David to get everything. . . ." Bryan Burrough, "An Unorthodox Death," *Vanity Fair*, January 1996, 81.

437 "I went to my father. . . ." Allison Kaplan Sommer, "Plugged In," *Jerusalem Post*, 20 May 1994, 12.

437 "It was good. . . ." Interview by author.

437 Olympia Floor's financial performance. A source within the company, interview by author, Toronto, 1994.

437 "Albert and even Paul. . . ." Interview by author.

437 "Ralph is not an easy man. . . ." Interview by author.

438 "I didn't want to believe her." Interview by author, 24 May 1995.

438 "He was so direct . . . longer than she did." Ibid.

439 "My sister remained . . ." Ibid.

439 "All she had to do was look. . . ." Telephone interview by author, 31 May 1995.

439 "The first thing my mother-in-law. . . ." Ibid.

439 Eva's death. The *Jewish Tribune* (London) published a brief but heartfelt obituary on 24 January 1985: "This week the tragic news reached us that Maedi is no more. Stemming from the elite of Orthodox Jewry in Hungary, she possessed the courage, enthusiasm, charm and determination which, with matching intelligence, stood her—and all of us—in good stead for so many years. . . . One can never cease to marvel at the spirit which under difficult circumstances rose above the sudden and tragic loss of her husband Lippa. . . . Singlehandedly, she carried on to

prove both mother and father to her large family of children, while "31 The Park" continued as an admirable 'achsania,' not only for family and friends, but even more, for all Torah causes."

439 "A very delicate situation." Interview by author, 24 May 1995.

Chapter 33

441 Terms of the City Investing deal. "City Investing to Sell Its Headquarters to Olympia & York," *Wall Street Journal*, 15 September 1981, 20.

441 "I credit the Reichmanns. . . ." Hellman, "Manhattan Transfer," 50.

442 "The only one we could think of . . . from Toronto to see us." Interview by author, New York City, 7 October 1992.

442 Sandy Weill's stature in financial services. See Tim Carrington, *The Year They Sold Wall Street* (New York: Houghton Mifflin, 1985); and Jon Friedman and John Meehan, *House of Cards* (New York: G. P. Putnam's Sons, 1992).

442 "Paul doesn't do anything. . . ." Interview by author.

443 Robinson's call to Reichmann. James Robinson, interview by author, New York City, 13 June 1995.

443 "The point is. . . ." Interview by author, New York City, 1992.

443 Terms of the American Express transaction. Frank Prial, "A Tenant Signs $2 Billion Lease for Battery Park," *New York Times*, 24 March 1995, 1; Daniel Hertzberg and Randall Smith, "Sale of Building by American Express Co. Set," *Wall Street Journal*, 24 March 1982, 48.

443 Playful photo. See Douglas Martin, "A Canadian Family Becomes Key Force in City Real Estate," *New York Times*, 24 March 1982, D4.

443 "This is monopoly . . . builder or lender." Randall Smith, "Real-Estate Giant Olympia & York Says It Is in Solid Shape Despite Skeptics' Doubts," *Wall Street Journal*, 14 May 1982, 46.

444 Terms of revised AmEx deal. "American Express to Buy New Tower, Rather Than Lease," *Wall Street Journal*, 17 June 1983, 6.

444 "A very successful developer . . ." Interview by author, 9 February 1994.

444 "We agreed on . . ." Randall Smith, "American Express Confirms Plan to Own Headquarters, Not Lease It from Olympia," *Wall Street Journal*, 15 December 1982, 12.

444 "He is very tough. . . ." Ann Walmsley, "A Family's Way to Wealth," *Maclean's*, 24 October 1988, 16.

445 "There really is no one. . . ." Neil Barsky, "Paul Reichmann Scales Real Estate's Heights, Including Sears Tower," *Wall Street Journal*, 5 September 1989, 1.

445 The big Aetna mortgage. Sharon Reier, "Is Commercial Real Estate Ready for Securitization?" *Institutional Investor*, November 1985, 210.

445 "Olympia & York was . . ." Interview by author, New York City, 17 July 1992.

445 "Paul was one of three people. . . ." Ibid.

446 "It took me a while . . . powerful intellect." Ibid.

446 The crafting of the $1 billion bond issue is recounted by Powell, *Risk, Ruin and Riches,* 156–65.

446 "I had a real tug of war. . . ." Interview by author.

447 The financial structure of the securities is authoritatively laid out in James Meager, " 'Megadeal' Week: O&Y's $1 Billion Loan," *Barron's,* 26 March 1984, 60.

447 The largest commercial mortgage. "A Whopper of a Mortgage," *Institutional Investor,* December 1984, 196.

447 120 subcontractors, 4,000 workers. Powell, *Risk, Ruin and Riches,* 286.

447 On Pelli's views on art versus commerce, see Paul Goldberger's introduction to *Cesar Pelli: Buildings and Projects 1965–1990,* 6–8.

448 "Gilt-and-marble . . . grandeur." Gill, "The Skyline," 70.

448 "They're extraordinarily polite. . . ." Powell, *Risk, Ruin and Riches,* 228–29.

448 "You could tell Pelli. . . ." Interview by author.

449 "Because the change . . ." Powell, *Risk, Ruin and Riches,* 119.

449 Shift from Canadian to Italian marble. Ibid., 291–92.

449 Terms of the Merrill Lynch deal. James Brooke, "Battery Park Complex Attracts Giant Tenant," *New York Times,* 28 August 1984, 1.

449 The favorable economics of Olympia & York's role as general contractor. Dianne Maley, "N.Y. Towers Reflect O & Y's Style," *Toronto Globe & Mail,* 15 October 1985, B1.

450 On mob influence in New York construction in the 1980s, see Selwyn Raab, "High-Pay Construction Reported Raising Housing and Office Rents," *New York Times,* 13 June 1985, II-5.

450 Morrison's pay records. Exhibit attached to the hearing transcript of 13 June 1985, Commission of Investigation, State of New York, obtained by the author under the Freedom of Information Act.

450 Morrison's travel itinerary. Selwyn Raab, " '84 Pay for New York Construction Job: $308,651," *New York Times,* 12 June 1985. 1.

451 The eleven featherbed positions. Exhibit attached to the hearing transcript of 13 June 1985, Commission of Investigation.

451 "I didn't write the rules. . . ." Selwyn Raab, "Extra Pay Called a Cost of Building in City," *New York Times,* 14 June 1985, II-1.

452 "I always had the feeling. . . ." Interview by author.

452 "This was something . . ." Interview by author, 29 October 1995.

452 "I built that company. . . ." Interview by author. When Minskoff finally resigned under pressure in 1987, few of his colleagues were sorry to see him go. That Minskoff lasted long enough to capitalize on his carried interest in Olympia & York's property portfolio was in itself an achievement, considering that he had nearly gotten himself fired right off the bat. Minskoff had joined Olympia & York in September 1981 but continued to own a majority interest in the real estate brokerage Ficor until June 1982. Unbeknownst to Paul Reichmann or anyone else at Olympia & York,

Minskoff in early 1982 retained Ficor to help secure mortgage financing for Tower A of the World Financial Center and another Olympia & York project. This arrangement ended when Reichmann walked into a meeting with Teachers Insurance one day to find Jan Hyde of Ficor. Reichmann was asked about this incident in a deposition taken in a bitter lawsuit pitting Minskoff against Hyde. Reichmann's testimony was summarized as follows: "He testified that when he learned the Ficor was involved in the financings, he was 'amazed' and discussed whether Minskoff 'should leave the company or not.' The source of Mr. Reichmann's amazement was not only that he learned that Minskoff anticipated receiving an interest in O & Y's fee to Ficor, but even more due 'to the fact that financing had been negotiated by myself with another employee.' " Appendices to Defendants' Post-Trial Brief, 166, *Minskoff vs. Ficor Inc. and Jan Hyde*, Supreme Court of New York. Although Reichmann did not fire Minskoff, he did insist that he sever his tie with Ficor.

453 "With all the other developers. . . ." Interview by author

453 "Olympia & York basically saved the authority . . . more like 8 million." Ibid.

453 Bell Gouinlock's lack of lease. Robert Canning, interview by author.

454 "Nobody else in the industry. . . ." Interview by author.

454 "Half the time. . . ." Interview by author, New York City, 1992.

454 The awkward orientation session. Stewart, *Too Big to Fail*, 71.

455 "Paul makes all the decisions. . . ." Maley, "The Philosopher King," 63.

Chapter 34

456 Olympia & York's purchase of Cadillac Fairview stock. Robert Cole, "Olympia Buys Stake in Cadillac," *New York Times*, 9 June 1984, B1.

456 "We didn't like the idea. . . ." Interview by author.

457 "It wasn't even considered for five minutes." Dianne Maley and Bruce Little, "Gulf Canada's Reorganization to Save $500 Million in Taxes," *Toronto Globe & Mail*, B1.

457 Olympia & York's extraction of huge tax break. Ibid.

457 Derivation and mechanics of the "Little Egypt Bump." Foster, *The Master Builders*, 130.

458 "Cleverly worked the press. . . ." Ibid., 135.

458 "The Gulf deal was straightforward. . . ." Terri Thompson and Edith Terry, "What the Reichmanns Plan Next for Their Real Estate Billions," *Business Week*, 28 October 1985, 97.

458 "I am dazzled. . . ." Ibid.

459 "All of us at my table. . . ." Interview by author.

459 Ralph's omission from invitations. Sample invitation provided by Olympia & York U.S.A.

459 Frucher's conversation with Reneé. Sandy Frucher, interview by author, New York City, 28 September 1995.

459 Governor Cuomo's exchange with Albert. Sandy Frucher and Philip Reichmann, interviews by author.

459 "A soaring triumph. . . ." Promotional video of the opening ceremonies produced by Olympia & York U.S.A., 1985.

460 "This is that part of the city. . . ." Ibid.

460 "Ah, ladies and gentlemen. . . ." Ibid.

460 "First and foremost. . . ." Ibid.

460 "I know I shouldn't make. . . ." Pat Brennan, "New York Celebrates Opening of Reichmanns' Giant Project," *Toronto Star,* 18 October 1985.

460 "The tragedy of government deficits . . . as we have come here." Larry Black, "Toronto Developer Urges Freer Trade at N.Y. Opening," *St. Catherine's Standard,* 18 October 1985.

461 The gong-ringing snafu. Olympia & York video.

461 "He was in awe. . . ." Interview by author, 29 October 1995.

461 "It came in right on budget. . . ." Interview by author.

461 Statistics on World Financial Center leases. Winston Williams, "Finally, the Debut of Wall Street West," *New York Times,* 25 August 1984, VI-1; and "Almost Leased Up," *New York Times,* 25 August 1985, VIII-1.

461–62 Design defects of World Financial Center retail space. Tom Koslowski, interviews by author.

462 Losses of $30 million. A source within Olympia & York, interview by author.

462 "Philip perceived himself. . . ." Ibid.

462 "Each tower was . . ." Interview by author, New York City, 28 September 1995.

462 Vacancy rates in O & Y's buildings as half that of the Manhattan average. Margaret Philip, "Reichmanns Battling New York Real Estate Slump," *Toronto Globe & Mail,* 24 June 1991, B1.

463 "Prominent imprint. . . ." Thompson and Terry, "What the Reichmanns Plan Next for Their Real Estate Billions," 97.

463 Impact of large-scale public works. To Reichmann's delight, World Financial Center was roundly hailed not only for its aesthetics but as a triumph of sophistication in urban planning. "In a time when intelligent thinking about the long-term shape of this city has all but vanished amid high-gloss mega-visions, there is tangible proof that smart urban design can work—aesthetically, socially and financially." Carter Wiseman, "The Next Great Place," *New York* magazine, 16 June 1986, 34. See also Martin Gottlieb, "Battery Project Reflects Changing City Priorities," *New York Times,* 18 October 1985, B1; and Bonnie Angelo, "Where the Skyline Meets the Shore," *Time* magazine, 23 October 1989, 83.

463 "The most important to be built. . . ." Martin Gottlieb, "Palms and a Pavilion for Battery Park City," *New York Times,* 11 August 1984, 25.

463 "Go take a close look. . . ." Interview by author.

463 "Kings of Officeland," *Economist,* 22 July 1989, 17.

464 Olympia & York's oil price projections. Foster, *The Master Builders*, 146.

464 "Can you imagine. . . ." Ibid., 148.

464 "With another $50 million. . . . It is nothing given." Maley and Little, "Gulf Canada's Reorganization to Save $500 Million in Taxes," 22 October 1985, B1.

465 Cohen's handling of the Gulf Canada tax matter is recounted by McQuaig, *Behind Closed Doors*, 294–98.

465 Cohen's marital history and career in Ottawa. Ibid. 281–94.

465 "Criticism hits things. . . ." Vivian Smith, "Molson Cos. Pops a Corker, Tough and Teflon, into Its No. 1 Spot," *Toronto Globe & Mail*, 7 November 1988, B6.

465 "The department was. . . ." McQuaig, *Behind Closed Doors*, 294.

466 "If ever the next generation. . . ." Thompson and Terry, "What the Reichmanns Plan Next," 97.

466 "The question in this business . . . we will be the most active." Edith Terry, "The Reichmann Touch: Facing the Toughest Test Yet," *Business Week*, 23 March 1987, 97.

466 The Downing ambush. Foster, *Towers of Debt*, 122.

467 "Significantly understates . . . hasty decision." Leonard Zehr, "Hiram Walker's Directors Turn Down $1.22 Billion Offer by Gulf Canada," *Wall Street Journal*, 27 March 1988, 14.

467 "To find out why Walker. . . ." Foster, *Towers of Debt*, 146–47.

467 "When under attack. . . ." Ibid., 152.

467 Walker's acceptance of O & Y offer, with conditions. Leonard Zehr, "Hiram Walker Board Endorses Takeover Proposed by Gulf Canada for $38 a Share," *Wall Street Journal*, 18 April 1986, 6.

468 Reichmann's web of prevarication and contradiction. See Foster, *Towers of Debt*, 164–79.

468 "Despite Mr. Reichmann's. . . ." Ibid., 180–81.

468 Reichmann's outburst and his visitors' reaction. Ibid., 181–83.

469 The *As It Happens* interview. Ibid., 186.

469 The peace pact with Allied-Lyons. Dennis Slocum, "Reichmanns Set to Acquire 10 Percent Stake in Allied-Lyons," *Toronto Globe & Mail*, 25 November 1987, B1.

470 "They have a different style. . . ." Foster, *Towers of Debt*, 188.

470 "My brother and I goofed. . . ." Dianne Maley, "Reichmanns Not out of the Game, Despite Competing Bid for Walker," *Toronto Globe & Mail*, 11 April 1986, A1.

471 "In part, this was . . ." Interview by author, Toronto, 1992.

471 "We were amazed. . . ." Foster, *The Master Builders*, 147.

471 "When I say that Paul. . . ." Sarlos, *Fireworks*, 185.

Chapter 35

473 "There is a vibrant ultra-Orthodox pocket. . . ." Interview by author, Toronto, 6 October 1994.

474 The Reichmanns were related to the Dushinskys by marriage. Renée's late sister, Klára, had been married to Samuel Dushinsky, a brother of Rabbi Israel Dushinsky.

474 Synagogue preferences. Paul Reichmann objected to the description of the Boat Shul as "the Reichmann synagogue" in a deposition taken in the Reichmanns' libel case against *Toronto Life*: "An Orthodox Jew, those who have a background in Jewish studies as well, would choose a synagogue by a measure that is strictly to do with the level of the community in scholarly aspect. So this is why you find that in our family each one belongs to a different community. The synagogue and Rabbi quoted here [the Boat Shul] is the one that Albert belongs to. I belong to another one because there are young men there who are together in the group because of a certain scholastic level. Ralph is at a different place. . . . That's why you have groups of 20, 30, rather than thousands as you would have in bigger, more modern synagogues because the purpose in the synagogue would be for praying, while in these synagogues the purpose is a combination of prayer and studies. So that intellectual level determines." Examination of Paul Reichmann, 27 September 1989, 234–35, *Reichmann et al. vs. Toronto Life et al.*, Supreme Court of Ontario.

474 "Rabbi Sofer tried. . . ." Telephone interview by author, Toronto, 26 April 1994. The hiring of Rabbi Sofer did not signal a Reichmann conversion to Hasidism. Like many Oberlanders of their generation, the brothers believed that the greater zealousness of the Hasidic rabbinate made it the purest repository of Torah traditionalism.

474 "Rabbi Sofer was not brought here. . . ." Interview by author, Toronto, 18 August 1995.

475 History of disunity in the Orthodox community. See Stephen Speisman, *The Jews of Toronto* (Toronto: McClelland & Stewart, 1979), 283–99.

475 Forty Orthodox congregations. Edmond Lipsitz, ed., *Ontario Jewish Resource Directory* (Willowdale: Canadian Jewish Congress, 1989), 53–56.

475 Explanation of eruv. Birnbaum, *Encyclopedia of Jewish Concepts*, s.v. "eruv."

475 Rabbi Price's history. See Leila Speisman, "Rabbi Abraham Price Dies at 94," *Canadian Jewish News*, 7 April 1994, 4.

476 The Sofer-Price meeting. Irwin Witty and Dr. Liebel Zoberman, interviews by author, Toronto, 15 August 1995.

476 Rabbi Price's response. Liebel Zoberman, interview by author.

476 Deliberations of the Vaad HaRabbonim. David Birkan, "To. Eruv Decision Hoped for by Rosh Hashana," *Canadian Jewish News*, 27 August 1987, 3.

476 The consternation caused by the eruv controversy spilled over into the Jewish community at large, even prompting an implicitly anti-Sofer editorial in the *Canadian Jewish News*: "The campaign to discredit the eruv has sown both confusion and discord among those elements of Toronto Jewry who respect, honor and observe Jewish law." "Eruv Challenge," *Canadian Jewish News*, 9 July 1987, 8.

477 "The Reichmanns were held in the greatest respect. . . ." Interview by author, Toronto, 29 April 1994.

477 "My custom is to wear a beret. . . ." Telephone interview by author, Toronto, 31 July 1995.

477 "The Reichmanns will accept. . . ." Interview by author.

477 "Olympia & York's strength. . . ." Interview by author, 19 February 1995.

478 1,000 beneficiaries, mostly in Israel. Examination of Paul Reichmann, 27 September 1989, 230–31, *Renée Reichmann et al vs. Toronto Life et al.*, Supreme Court of Ontario.

478 The Reichmann newlywed fund. Landau, *Piety and Power,* 279.

478 "Medical care is . . ." Interview by author, 19 February 1995.

478 "Maintain their own worldwide network." Landau, *Piety and Power,* 44–45.

478 "The impact of the Reichmanns' refusal. . . ." Telephone interview by author, 2 September 1994.

478 Data on Reichmann contributions to Bais Yaakov High School. Bernard Shoub, director of school financing for the Jewish Board of Education, interview by author, Toronto, 11 October 1994.

479 "It became a bit of a game of chicken. . . ." Interview by author, 19 February 1995. Later, the Jewish Board of Education implemented a new tuition policy that had the effect of providing a substantial indirect subsidy to the Bais Yaakov schools. Under a new "shared tuition policy," needy families with more than one child attending schools received a group discount. While the policy applied to all Jewish families receiving assistance, the strictly Orthodox qualified disproportionately for the program, having less family income and more children on average.

479 "It was not a formal pledge . . . a dead end anyway." Telephone interview by author, 21 February 1995.

479 Cressy's audience with Albert. Gordon Cressy, telephone interview by author, 29 February 1996. *Bronfman Dynasty* contains a mangled account of Tubby Cole's solicitation of the Reichmanns. "Cole's first step," wrote Peter Newman, "was to invite Paul Reichmann for daily squash games at the York Racquets Club. They became friends, and eventually Reichmann said that he and his family had been reconsidering their stand and would like to become more closely allied to the Toronto community by making a sizable UJA donation. Would Tubby recommend a proper amount? Cole was hoping to raise $19 million in the annual campaign (the largest amount ever in a year when Israel wasn't involved in an open war with its neighbors). He was making rapid calculations when Reichmann asked, 'How much do the Bronfmans give in Montreal?' Told that it was about $1.5 million a year, Reichmann promptly pledged $1.75 million on behalf of his family, promising a total of $7 million over the next five years." Would that this anecdote were true, for the notion of the formal, resolutely unathletic Paul Reichmann playing squash with a man named Tubby is irresistible. But when Newman's account was read to him, Paul Reichmann gave a quizzical smile and said that he has never met Tubby Cole, never played squash, and never set foot inside the York Racquets Club. "Perhaps it's time for me to take up the game, though," he said, in rueful ref-

erence to the extra weight he was carrying around his middle. Although Albert was indeed friendly with Cole, he was not a squash-player either.

480 Forty houses bought for $20 million. Properties owned by the extended Reichmann family in the mid-1990s included 34 Alexandra Wood, 40 Alexandra Wood, 350 Cortleigh, 371 Cortleigh, 1 Forest Wood, 25 Forest Wood, 29 Forest Wood, 31 Forest Wood, 33 Forest Wood, 409 Glencairn, 415 Glencairn, 460 Glencairn, 391 Glengrove, 393 Glengrove, 395 Glengrove, 226 Hillhurst, 231 Hillhurst, 294 Hillhurst, 392 Hillhurst, 413 Lytton, 98 Prue, 214 Strathallan, 237 Strathallan, 239 Strathallan and 241 Strathallan. Land Registry Office, Toronto. This list does not include the dwellings of Heller family members nor those occupied by school boarders and teachers.

480 Steven and Shirley Reichmann's holdings. Transfers TB 140459, TB892147, TB836487, TB386182, Land Registry Office, Toronto.

480 $2.2 million for Henry's house (350 Cortleigh Boulevard). Transfer TB637667, Land Registry Office, Toronto.

480 Close encounter with security man in parked car. Interview by author, Toronto, 1994.

481 The account of the Lindros-Reichmann clash is drawn from Extract of Clause 6 of the Legislation and Intergovernmental Affairs Committee report 15, 20 June 1994, North York City Council.

481 "Unquestionably, the building is close. . . ." Mary Gooderham, "Lindroses Take Reichmann to Court over Bathhouse," *Toronto Globe & Mail*, 8 July 1994, A6.

482 "Albert never said no. . . ." Interview by author.

482 Albert's $1,000 dare. Ibid.

482 "It's going to go . . ." Mary Gooderham, "North York Reverses Stand in Reichmann Row," *Toronto Globe & Mail*, 21 July 1994, A8.

482 Paul paid $885,000 for two adjoining lots. Transfers TB186484 and TB247513, Land Registry Office, Toronto.

482 "Landscaping is the family specialty." Interview by author.

482 Lea's forceful direction of the remodeling project. Paul Reichmann, interview by author, 19 February 1995.

482–83 $1 million landscaping. See lien TB59472 and release TB604223, Land Registry Office, Toronto.

484 "She was very Swiss. . . ." Burrough, "An Unorthodox Death," 78.

484 $900,000 for 413 Lytton Blvd. Transfer TB439267, Land Registry Office, Toronto.

484 Rachele's anonymous visit; David Turner's phone call. Joan Foy, telephone interview by author, 19 July 1995.

484 "Don't try to hold up a Reichmann. . . ." Ibid.

484 David's variance and plans. Jack Lakey, "Residents Fume over 'Monster' Hole," *Toronto Star*, 8 September 1989.

484 "David told me. . . ." Interview by author.

485 "Whenever there were problems . . . for damages." Ibid.

485 Schonberger's letter. Lakey, "Residents Fume over 'Monster' Hole."

485 Sale for $1.675 million. Transfer 641131, Land Registry Office, Toronto.

485 "The Reichmanns really tried to appease . . . house by house." Interview by author.

Chapter 36

488 "An extremely fine gentleman." Interview by author 29 October 1995.

488 "There are no superlatives. . . ." Interview by Margo Sugarman for author, Jerusalem, July 1995.

488 "The whole thing was highly politicized. . . ." Interview by author, 29 October 1995.

488 Clal consisted of Bank Leumi, Discount Bank, and Bank Hapoalim.

488 Reichmanns' attempts to buy Bank Tefahot. See Shlomo Maoz, "Struggle to Buy Bank Tefahot as Talks with Canadian Start," *Jerusalem Post*, 5 June 1978, 1; Shlomo Moaz, "Tefahot Shares May Go to Canadians," *Jerusalem Post*, 15 June 1978, 2; Shlomo Maoz, "Clal, IIC Must Be Protected in Sale of Tefahot—Ehrlich," *Jerusalem Post*, 13 July 1978, 7; and Joseph Morgenstern, "Tefahot Sale to Toronto's Reichmann Brothers Okayed," *Jerusalem Post*, 14 July 1978, 8.

489 Reichmanns' aborted interest in Ararat. Macabee Dean, "Ararat Insurance Floats IL53m. Share Emission," *Jerusalem Post*, 20 August 1979.

489 "There was an intent and a will . . ." Interview by author, 29 October 1995.

489 "When Begin came in. . . ."·Interview by author, 24 May 1995.

489 "His projects are really something. . . ." Interview by Jill Hamburg for author, Jerusalem, September 1992.

489 $1.7 million for villa. Edward Reichmann, interview by author, 24 May 1995.

489 Financial details of Academy House project. Ibid.

490 "I'm basically a city center man. . . ." David Rosenberg, "Reichmann Makes a Bet on Downtown," *Jerusalem Post*, 20 May 1987, 8.

490 The economics of the Mill project. Ibid.

490 Edward's $2 million purchase of the "Valero hole." "Canadian Buys Central Jerusalem Plot," *Jerusalem Post*, 9 April 1987.

490 "His solution . . . modern and well-maintained equipment." David Rosenberg, "Building on Experience," *Jerusalem Post*, 12 January 1990, 15.

490 $25 million investment. Interview by author, 24 May 1995.

491 Olympia & York's cash distributions to Eva, Edward, and Louis. Paul Reichmann, interview by author, 29 October 1995.

491 Discovery and return of Edward's pack of receipts. Michael Hausman, interview by Jill Hamburg for author, Jerusalem, September 1992.

491 "The pack amounted to. . . ." Ibid.

492 $634,000 debt. Confession of judgment, 22 February 1983, *Banque de Montreal vs. Edward Reichmann,* Superior Court, Montreal, case number 500-05-009020-817.

492 $171,000 claim against Edward and Albert. *Canadian Imperial Bank of Commerce vs. A & E Reichmann Ltd. and Albert Reichmann,* Superior Court, Montreal.

492 Edward's refusal to acknowledge second round of failures. Interview by author, August 6 1994.

492 "He'll sit in the back . . ." Interview by Hamburg.

492 "As far as the religious vote. . . ." Interview by author, 24 May 1995.

492–93 On the history of relations between Orthodox and secular Israelis, see Landau, *Piety and Power,* 110–29, 292–344; Avishai Margalit, "Israel: The Rise of the Ultra-Orthodox," *New York Review of Books,* 9 November 1989, 38; and Noah J. Efron, "Trembling with Fear: How Secular Israelis See the Ultra-Orthodox, and Why," *Tikkun,* September 1991, 15.

493 Ultra-Orthodox violence against Kollek and others. See Abraham Rabinovich, "Rampaging Rabbis," *New Republic,* 14 September 1987, 24.

493 On the internecine political conflicts within Israeli ultra-Orthodoxy see Landau, *Piety and Power,* 79–92.

494 "We are Rav Schach's men." Interview by author, 24 May 1995.

494 "It so happens. . . ." Interview by author, 29 October 1995.

494 "Whenever Rabbi Schach needed funds. . . ." Patrick Martin, "Reichmann Woes Felt in Israeli Election," 6 June 1992.

494 "His idea. . . ." Interview by author, 29 October 1995.

494 The Reichmanns contributed $35 million of $100 million raised. Ibid.

494 Frenzy caused by rumors about rescue fund. See Haim Shapiro, "Yeshivot in Rush for Reichmann Funds," *Jerusalem Post,* 5 February 1987, 4; Haim Shapiro, "The Givers and Takers," *Jerusalem Post,* 20 February 1987, 8; and Yehuda Schwartz, "Israeli Yeshivot to Receive $100 Million for Rescue Fund."

495 "Rav Schach wasn't involved. . . ." Interview by author, 29 October 1995.

495 "Toward Palestinians. . . ." Margalit, "Israel: The Rise of the Ultra-Orthodox," 44.

495 Ariel contribution. Robert I. Friedman, *Zealots for Zion* (New York: Random House, 1992), 70.

495 Attacks on Bidya. Ibid., 66.

495 Rabin's yeshiva-trained killer. See John Kifner, "Belief to Blood: The Making of Rabin's Killer," *New York Times,* 19 November 1995, 1.

496 "We did help greatly in many situations. . . ." Interview by author, 26 February 1996.

496 "I was never interested in publicity. . . ." Rosenberg, "Reichmann Makes a Bet on Downtown."

496 "It used to be. . . ." Patrick Martin, "Diamond Created New Jewel," *Toronto Globe & Mail,* 28 June 1993.

497 "He told us he had this fabulous project. . . ." Interview by author, Toronto, 20 June 1995.

497 Terms of the City Hall project. See Reichmann's Submissions, 4 April 1995, 2, *Albert Reichmann vs. Zeev Vered and Ron Engineering and Construction (International) Ltd.*, Ontario Court of Justice (General Division).

497 Terms of Vered's arrangement with Reichmann. Ibid., 3–4.

498 The Israeli architect firms hired by Diamond were Kolker, Kolker Epstein Architects; Meltzer Igra Architects; and Bugog Figueiredo Krendel Architects.

498 Design of City Hall Square. See "Jerusalem City Hall Square," *Canadian Architect*, July 1990, 18.

498 "We needed a place for demonstrations. . . ." Martin, "Diamond Creates New Jewel."

498 Letter urging the Reichmanns to withdraw from the City Hall project. In addition to Rabbi Schach, those who signed it were Yosef Shalom Eliashiz, Shlomo Zalman Auerbach, and Yitzak Weiss, head of the Eda Haredit rabbinical court.

498 Albert's meeting with the rabbis and conversation with Paul. Cross-examination of Albert Reichmann, 13 March 1995, 11–13, *Albert Reichmann vs. Zeev Vered and Ron Engineering and Construction (International) Ltd.*

499 "The best [developers] in the world." Charles Hoffman and Andy Court, "Kollek, Toronto Billionaires Lay Cornerstone for $65m. Civic Centre," *Jerusalem Post*, 24 June 1988, 1.

499 "The Vereds drove everyone crazy. . . ." Interview by author, 1995.

V   BABEL ON THE RIVER THAMES

Chapter 37

503 "One reason I was surprised. . . ." Interview by author, 29 October 1995.

503 "Paul is not interested. . . ." Interview by author.

504 "Things would take five or six times. . . ." Wheatley, "Men at Wharf," L13.

505 On the meteoric, intertwined rise of Lipton and Bradman, see Alastair Ross Goobey, *Bricks & Mortals* (London: Century Business, 1992), 44–84.

505 The City Corporation as landlord. See Godfrey Hodgson, "The City Shapes Its Future," *Financial Times*, 15 March 1986, 1.

505 Highest rents in the world. Amy Borrus, "The City of London Spawns a Suburb," *Business Week*, 13 January 1986, 111.

506 Development of outlying areas. See Jason Nisse, "Beyond the Square Mile," *Banker*, November 1986, 1.

506 History of Isle of Dogs. See Eve Hostettler, *An Outline History of the Isle of Dogs* (London: Island History Trust, n.d.); and S. K. Al Naib, *London Docklands: Past, Present and Future* (London: Ashmead Press, 1990).

506 "An evil plexus. . . ." Arthur Morrison as quoted by John Brennan, "A Far from Inevitable Rebirth," *Financial Times* (London), 12 May 1989, 38.

506 The abandonment of the docks and its effects. Ibid.

507 The formation of London Docklands Development Corp. See Docklands Consultative Committee, *The Docklands Experiment* (London: Docklands Consultative Committee, 1990); and Peter Turlick, planning director of the LDDC, interview by author, 7 September 1993.

507 "Romantic dreamer with both feet. . . ." and sleeping on a camp bed. Peter Turlick, interview by author.

507 "Creating a new economy. . . ." Michael Ver Meulen, "The Rise of Canary Wharf," *Institutional Investor,* November 1986, 287.

507 Isle of Dogs as a commercial cul de sac. Brian Edwards, *London Docklands: Urban Design in an Age of Deregulation* (Oxford: Butterworth Architecture, 1992), 59.

508 Isle of Dogs enterprise zone. Docklands Consultative Committee, "The Docklands Experiment," 19.

508 Two hundred companies, 5,700 workers; LDDC expenditure of £140 million, private investment of £800 million. Brennan, "A Far from Inevitable Rebirth," 38.

508 "The loading bays. . . ." Hewland Productions, *The Men Who Built Canary Wharf.*

509 "I looked at Mike. . . ." Ver Meulen, "The Rise of Canary Wharf," 280.

509 "The only way you'll get your traders. . . ." Hewland Productions, *The Men Who Built Canary Wharf.*

509 "Cloud cuckooland." Peter Turlick, interview by author.

509 Ownership of Canary Wharf Development. "Report of the Canary Wharf Development Company Ltd. for 1986" (Companies House, London), 2.

509 Details of Skidmore's plan. Charles Knevitt, "Canary Wharf Wings Skyward," London *Times,* 24 March 1987, 2.

509 "I think we all blinked. . . ." Hewland Productions, *The Men Who Built Canary Wharf.*

509 "I wouldn't think twice. . . ." Paul Cheeseright, "The Developer Who Looks a Decade Ahead," *Financial Times,* 15 January 1990, 34.

510 "The Brits are scared. . . ." Ver Meulen, "The Rise of Canary Wharf," 280.

510 Travelstead's visit to Guildhall. Michael Cassidy, telephone interview by author, London, 15 September 1993.

510 "The effect on the room. . . ." Ibid.

510 "There's going to be a dramatic boom. . . ." Hodgson, "The City Shapes Its Future," 1.

510 "After half a dozen . . ." Ibid.

510 "We're going to change the marketplace. . . ." Ver Meulen, "The Rise of Canary Wharf," 287.

510 "Travelstead was a hype merchant. . . ." Interview by author, London, 1993.

511 "There were just . . ." Interview by author.

511 Olympia & York's initial proposal to Travelstead and Dennis's chance meeting with First Boston executive. Foster, *Towers of Debt*, 196.

511 Reichmann's call to Davis. Paul Reichmann, interview by author, 29 October 1995.

512 Henley Centre's projections. Hodgson, "The City Shapes Its Future," 1.

512 "Wildly optimistic." Ibid.

512 Jones Lang Wooton study. Ibid.

512 "It's like selling shoes in Africa. . . ." Martin Mayer, *Markets* (New York: W. W. Norton & Co., 1988), 199.

512 "The British economy has been transformed. . . ." Text of speech made in London, 9 March 1988, issued in press release form by Olympia & York.

512 "The best, strongest single market. . . ." Harvey Shapiro, "Olympia & York's American Empire," *Institutional Investor,* February 1986, 153.

513 "Each time I go to London. . . ." Dianne Maley, "O & Y Upgrading Its Plans for Canary Wharf Project," *Toronto Globe & Mail,* 21 March 1988, B1.

513 "I was staggered. . . ." Rodney Tyler, "Canary Wharf: The Untold Story," a promotional pamphlet produced by Olympia & York, 4.

514 "Out of all of it . . ." Interview by author, 29 October 1995.

514 Two-hundred-year lease at £400,000 an acre. Report issued by the National Audit Office, May 1988, as cited by the Docklands Consultative Committee, "All That Glitters: A Critical Assessment of Canary Wharf," May 1992, 19. In 1989 a committee of the House of Commons criticized the terms of LDDC's land deal with Olympia & York as overly generous in a report on the various urban development corporations created by the Thatcher government. The Public Accounts Committee argued that the LDDC should have insisted on a share of the profits from Canary Wharf in exchange for its cut-rate land price. Of course, this argument was rendered politically moot when the project produced gargantuan losses for Olympia & York, instead of the lush profits foreseen in 1989.

514 Half the going rate in the City. Paul Reichmann, interview by author, 29 October 1995.

514 "I asked them all. . . ." Ibid. According to Tim Bell, Olympia & York's London public relations counsel, the typical executive queried by Reichmann did not respond negatively per se. "The British don't say no," Bell explained. "They say, 'I wouldn't rule it out,' which means no." Interview by author.

515 Net worth of $10 billion. Information Circular, 9 November 1992, for special meeting of the creditors of Olympia & York Development, Ontario Court of Justice (General Division), Toronto.

515 "I was dead against . . . to do a Canary Wharf." Interview by author.

515 "As I became more interested. . . ." Interview by author, 29 October 1995.

515 "Albert was a lot less. . . ." Interview by author.

516 Terms of Olympia & York's purchase. Olympia & York Canary Wharf Limited, Accounts (for the period ending 31 August 1987), 8 and 11, Companies

House, London. As noted on page 12 of this report, Travelstead and a few of his colleagues had also profited personally through his ownership of a limousine service and a design consultancy that received £730,000 in payments.

516 Press reaction. Matthew Bond, "Reichmann Uncages Canary Wharf," *Sunday Telegraph,* 19 July 1987; Judi Bevan, "Quiet Man Will Make Canary Sing," *Sunday Times,* 19 July 1987, 61.

517 "We will fund it ourselves." D'arcy Jenish, "Capital Developments," *Maclean's* magazine, 24 August 1987, 28.

517 "We have never made. . . ." "The eleventh hour rescue of the Isle of Dogs' Canary Wharf elicited sighs all round—some rueful but most relieved," *Estate Times,* pt. 2, 23 July 1987, 9.

Chapter 38

518 Lord Young's premature pile-driving. Mary Brasier, "Canary Wharf Gets Off to a Hurried Start," *Guardian,* 5 November 1987.

519 "Leo was pissed off. . . ." Interview by author.

519 "At one point when Paul was away. . . ." Ibid.

519 Details of the deal with Allied-Lyon. Dennis Slocumb, "Reichmanns Set to Acquire 10% Stake in Allied-Lyons," *Toronto Globe & Mail,* 25 November 1987, B1.

520 Olympia & York's open-market purchases upped its controlling position in Gulf to 72.5 percent from 68 percent, and in Abitibi to 78 percent from 73 percent.

520 Southern Pacific Santa Fe's merger tribulations. See Judith Valente and Daniel Machalaba, "Plan to Join Santa Fe, Southern Pacific Faces a Possible Final Blow," *Wall Street Journal,* 29 June 1987, 1.

520 $465 million for 6.2 percent stake. Leonard Zehr and Judith Valente, "Olympia & York Has 6.18% Stake in Rail Concern," *Wall Street Journal,* 24 September 1987, 5.

521 Reichmann's outmaneuvering of Dingman. Frederick Rose, "How Henley's Chief Lost a Long Struggle to Take Over Santa Fe," *Wall Street Journal,* 29 July 1987, 1.

521 "Distance[d] himself . . ." Ibid.

521 "I trust them. . . ." Judith Valente and Gary Lamphier, "Santa Fe Southern's New Ally," *Wall Street Journal,* 17 February 1988, 6.

521 "Is like a general partner . . ." Ibid.

521–22 Campeau's attributes and oddities. See especially Phil Patton, "The Man Who Bought Bloomingdale's," *New York Times Magazine,* 17 July 1988, 16; and John Rothchild, *Going for Broke* (New York: Simon & Schuster, 1991).

522 "Blindsided by a trainload of clowns" (Thomas Macioce) and "a living water torture" (Peter Buchanan). Foster, *Towers of Debt,* 214.

522 Campeau's real estate rise. See Susan Goldenberg, "Campeau Corporation," in *Men of Property,* 163–89; and Michael Babad and Catherine Mulroney, *Campeau: The Building of an Empire* (Toronto: Doubleday Canada, 1989).

523 "He knew could be gruff. . . ." Rothchild, *Going for Broke*, 98.

522 "Paul Reichmann didn't aspire to be any role model . . ." Foster, *Towers of Debt*, 215.

523 Carol Loomis, "The Biggest Looniest Deal Ever," *Fortune*, 18 June 1990, 48.

524 "Very extraordinary . . . a great future." Martin Mittelstaedt, "O&Y Breaks Silence on Campeau Deal, Claiming 'Great Future' for Federated," *Toronto Globe & Mail*, B1.

524 "It's a bizarre feeling. . . ." Interview by author.

524 "I have read enough about anti-Semitism. . . ." Examination of Paul Reichmann, 3 August 1989, 122–23, *Reichmann et al. vs. Toronto Life et al.*, Supreme Court of Ontario.

524 "Our view is the family. . . ." Jan Wong, "Apart from That, How Was the Issue?" *Toronto Globe & Mail*, 11 December 1987, B1.

524 "A murderous piece. . . ." Conrad Black, *A Life in Progress* (Toronto: Key Porter Books, 1993), 490.

526 "The difficult thing. . . ." Interview by author, New York City, 20 November 1995.

527 "By suddenly slapping. . . ." Wong, "Apart from That, How Was the Issue?" B1.

527 Heaps's wartime exploits. See Leo Heaps, *Escape from Arnem* (Toronto: Macmillan, 1945); and Alan Barnes, "War Hero Leo Heaps Wrote Books about Battle," *Toronto Star*, 22 June 1995.

527 "The one man who might have brought cohesion. . . ." Cornelius Ryan, *A Bridge Too Far* (London: Hamilton, 1974), 247.

527 "It was driven. . . ." R. E. Urquart, *Arnem* (London: Cassell, 1958), 59.

528 Biography of his father. Leo Heaps, *The Rebel in the House* (Markham, Ont.: Fitzhenry & Whiteside Ltd., 1984).

528 "After they'd laid down their guns. . . ." Ron Lowman, "Museum Rejects War Hero's Gift of Medals," *Toronto Star*, 28 March 1982.

528 Heaps as sleuthing collector. See Terry Kirkman and Judy Heviz, "Peddling Our Heritage, Piece by Piece," *Montreal Star*, 1 May 1971.

528 "My father was someone. . . ." Telephone interview by author, 22 July 1995.

528 "Adversity was his fuel . ." Interview by author.

528 Enfant terrible of the courts. On 18 November 1990, the *Toronto Star* ran a photo of Heaps playing tennis in a ski jacket and toque, preparing "for the first Arctic Challenge Tennis Tournament at his Kew Gardens club."

529 "Antisocial night." Adrian Heaps, interview by author.

529 "He accused me of stealing . . . his own righteous indignation." Telephone interview by author, 25 July 1995.

529 On Heaps's battle with McClelland & Stewart, see John Partridge, "The Players Make Book War an Industry Good Read," *Toronto Globe & Mail*, 6 August 1987, B1.

529 "What they've done . . ." Wong, "Apart from That, How Was the Issue?" B1.

529 "If the decision were monetary. . . ." Dianne Maley, "The Philosopher King," 56.

530 The Reichmanns sued the *Toronto Sun* over a column by Diane Francis lauding Dewar and her article: "The Reclusive Reichmanns," *Toronto Sun*, 18 October 1987, C2.

530 The disqualification of Dewar's article by awards program and response. See Rudy Platiel, "Story on Reichmanns Rejected," *Toronto Globe & Mail*, 20 February 1988, A13; and Alexandra Radkewycz, "Decision to Reject Story Called Dangerous Move," *Toronto Globe & Mail*, 22 February 1988.

530 Libel chill. See especially Martin Krossel, "Libel: Canada's Cold Wave," *Columbia Journalism Review*, July 1988, 10.

530 Chronology of the Reichmanns' dealings with Heaps. Statement of Claim, 10 March 1988, 10–17, *Albert Reichmann et al. vs. The Globe and Mail Division of Canadian Newspapers Company Limited et al.*, Supreme Court of Ontario, Toronto, court file No. 26901/88.

531 "He said that we should tell . . ." Telephone interview by author, 17 July 1995.

531 "Our instruction. . . ." Interview by author, New York City, 20 November 1995.

531 Invoice for $844,625. Exhibit 2216 in *Reneé Reichmann et al. vs. Toronto Life et al.*

531 Details of the Kroll investigation. Sources within the Kroll organization, interviews by author.

Chapter 39

533 "The center reminds me. . . ." Walmsley, "A Family's Way to Wealth," 46.

534 "Michael's combination of skill. . . ." Interview by author, 29 October 1995.

534 "I asked him, 'What would you like. . . .' " Interview by author, London, 9 September 1993.

535 "There's never been a project . . . crews swarming over it." Interview by author.

535 "We have realized. . . ." Maley, "O & Y Upgrading Its Plans for Canary Wharf Project," B1.

535 "The business capital . . . location of their expansion." Barsky, "Paul Reichmann Scales Real Estate's Heights, Including Sears Tower," 1.

535 "The difference between East London. . . ." Matthew Bond, "Why Reichmann Is Celebrating a Jubilee at Canary Wharf," *Sunday Telegraph* (London), 19 November 1989, 32.

536 "But for the restraints. . . ." Text of speech made in London, 9 March 1988.

536 "This is not a risky project. . . ." Maley, "O & Y Upgrading Its Plans for Canary Wharf Project," B1.

536 "The fact that I had never been wrong. . . ." Interview by author, 29 October 1995.

536 "Paul told me. . . ." Interview by author, 31 May 1995.

536 "The only question. . . ." Jim Gardner, *Chartered Surveyor Weekly*, 3 December 1987.

537 "When I saw the size. . . ." Interview by author.

537 *Financial Times* caricature. Bernard Simon and Vanessa Houlder, "Long View from the Top of Canary Wharf," *Financial Times* (London), 19 February 1991, 19.

537 "It is ludicrously thin-skinned. . . ." David Rosenberg, "Drawing Hasty Conclusions," *Jewish Chronicle*, 1 March 1991.

537 "Let us build ourselves. . . ." Gen. 11: 4–9.

538 "It is probable that they were neither so foolish. . . ." Quoted by Birnbaum, *Encyclopedia of Jewish Concepts*, s.v. "Tower of Babel."

538 Reichmann's conversation with reporter. Hellman, "Manhattan Transfer," 51.

538 Future capital of Greater Germany. In public, Reichmann never made explicit mention of Berlin, leaving it to Michael Dennis, as in this quote from James Buchan, "A High Risk Business," *Independent (The Review)*, 16 December 1990, 2: "You know of another city in Europe, with a lot of developable land in the east, pointing to an emerging market? . . . Docklands is not going to boom for 5 years but for 25 years, and it's got only one competitor: Berlin."

539 "Is a challenge of creativity. . . ." Lever, "Born-Again Anglophile of Docklands," 23.

539 "A literal translation. . . ." Maley, "The Philosopher King," 63.

539 "I can't tell you the agony. . . ." Tyler, "Canary Wharf: The Untold Story," 9.

539 "To make places . . ." Ibid., 8.

540 "American heroic urbanism. . . ." Edwards, *London Docklands*, 158.

540 Eight-hundred-foot tower. Olympia & York would have preferred a tower of 850 feet but was required to knock off 50 feet by the Civil Aviation Authority, which contended that the tower otherwise would interfere with the flight path to the new Docklands airport.

540 "Paul and Michael were suspicious. . . ." Interview by author.

540 "The required flair or dignity." Edward Greenspon, "Reichmann Revisions Mollify Objections to Canary Wharf," *Toronto Globe & Mail*, 30 March 1988, B3.

541 "The scale and complexity. . . ." Edwards, *London Docklands*, 74.

541 "I can't think of anything. . . ." Tyler, "Canary Wharf: The Untold Story," 7.

541 "The layout is simplistic and banal . . ." Andrew Philips, "The Reichmanns' Bold New Venture," *Maclean's* magazine, 27 June 1988, 47.

541 "It's every bit as bad. . . ." Hugh Pearman, "Turquoise Tower Gives London a New Skyline," London *Times*, 2 September 1990, 22.

542 "Canary Wharf Is Being Built. . . ." Hugh Pearman and Jo Revill, "Charles in Trouble for Prejudging Inquiry," London *Times*, 10 October 1988, A2. When the book version of *A Vision of Britain* was published a year later, Prince Charles fired

another broadside at Pelli's tower, predicting that this "out-of-scale obelisk . . . may become the tomb of modernist dogma. The tragedy is that it will cast its shadow over generations of Londoners who have suffered enough from towers of architectural arrogance." Pelli was aghast but held his return fire until he was interviewed for a 1991 documentary film on Canary Wharf. Prince Charles's antipathy toward skyscrapers was well established when he had accepted an invitation to stop by Olympia & York's London offices in 1988 for an eighty-minute briefing, which was filmed in its entirety by the Prince's own camera crew. Even so, Pelli had come away from the royal visit thinking Charles well disposed to the project on balance. "I thought, and everybody in the group thought, that he was very supportive of the project," recalled Pelli, who said he had asked members of the Prince's entourage what use would be made of the footage they were shooting. "I was assured that these [were] for the private archives of the Prince. So I never expected that this was going to be in public or I would have been a little more guarded in what I said. . . . It just was not a very princely thing to have done." Hewland Productions, *The Men Who Built Canary Wharf.*

542 "The architecture plays it. . . ." Charles Jencks, *Post-Modern Triumphs in London* (London: Academy Editions, 1991), 44.

542 "We must remember. . . ." Tyler, "Canary Wharf: The Untold Story," 17.

542 "Most thoughtful and wonderful touch." Transcript of Mrs. Thatcher's Speech in Response to Paul Reichmann at Banqueting House, 11 May 1988, issued as an Olympia & York press release.

543 "My ambition was open-ended. . . ." Interview by author, 19 February 1995.

543 "Both Paul and Albert were intrigued. . . ." Interview by author, New York City, 10 January 1996.

543 "Abrasive political scuffler." E. J. Dionne Jr., "Furor over Nominee," *New York Times*, 28 March 1981, B26.

544 "I was laser-focused . . ." Interview by author, 10 January 1996.

544 At the time, Paramount Communications was still known as Gulf + Western Industries Inc.

544 For details of the Paramount project, see Albert Scardino, "12-Block Office-Entertainment Center Planned on West Side," *New York Times*, 6 April 1987, B1.

544 "This was one we really wanted." Interview by author, New York City, 28 September 1995.

545 "I asked the Japanese. . . ." Interview by author, New York City, 28 September 1995.

545 On Teleport Town, see Edith Terry, "O & Y Eyes Tokyo Bay," *Toronto Globe & Mail*, 2 April 1991, B1.

Chapter 40

547 "It seemed to me. . . ." Interview by author.

547 Losses of $500 million to $700 million. Sources within Olympia & York, interviews by author.

547 Losses of $200 million to $250 million in Florida. Ibid.

548 $125 million deficit in condo conversion. Ibid.

548 The Miami Center project was publicly hyped by Larry Adams, an Olympia & York Southeast executive, as "the largest privately owned contiguous development in North America." The complex, he predicted, "will move the center of Miami. It will become the new image of downtown." Bruce Gates, "Reich-manns Target Miami for Facelift," *Financial Post* (Toronto), 14 September 1987, 1.

548 O & Y's troubles in Orlando. See Alex Finkelstein, "GE Takes Olympia Place," *Orlando Business Journal*, 11 March 1994, 6: "Olympia Place has struggled under an insurmountable debt load almost since obtaining its first loan. . . . Only 30 percent of the 4.3-million-square-foot project was ever leased."

548 The building's not turning an operating profit. Sources within Olympia & York, interviews by author.

548 $240 million tied up in condos. A source within Olympia & York, interview by author.

548 "Albert is very smart. . . ." Interview by author.

549 "Albert is a real . . ." Interview by author.

549 Terms of out-of-court settlement. Sources within Olympia & York, interviews by author.

550 On the history of the Jews under the Soviet Union, see Geoffrey Hosking, *A History of the Soviet Union* (London: Fontana, 1990), 255–59.

551 Jewish emigration figures. Seth Mydans, "New Tactics Almost Halt Exit of Soviet Jews," *New York Times*, 14 November 1984, 1.

551 State Department report. Cited by Wendy Eisen, *Count Us In* (Toronto: Burgher Books, 1995), 205.

551 "The vast majority of Jews. . . ." Yaacov Roi, "The Role of the Synagogue and Religion in the Jewish National Awakening," 112, in *Jewish Culture and Identity in the Soviet Union* (New York: New York University Press, 1991).

551 Emergence of a Hasidic underground. Ibid., 124.

551 On the underground activities of the Vaad Hatzalah Nichei Israel in the USSR, see "The Files Declassified," *Coalition* (New York), March 1989, 13.

552 "He seemed to know nothing. . . ." Telephone interview by author, 26 September 1995.

552 Reichmann's letter-writing campaign and recruitment of Carney. Ibid.

552 "Yes, he'd done things. . . ." Interview by author, Brooklyn, 23 September 1995.

553 "Joe Clark mentioned. . . ." Maley, "Reichmann Helps Build Bridge to Soviets," *Toronto Globe & Mail*, B1.

553 Shultz's seder diplomacy. David Shipler, "Shultz Visits Embassy Seder for Noted Soviet Dissidents," *New York Times*, 14 April 1987, 1.

554 "Perestroika had taken hold. . . ." Interview by author, Toronto, 18 August 1995.

554 "For the refuseniks. . . ." Interview by author.

554 On Essas, see Miriam Stark Zakon, *Silent Revolution* (Brooklyn: Mesorah Publications, 1992).

555 "Don't be blinded. . . ." Eisen, *Count Us In*, 242.

555 "Most of these things. . . ." Interview by author.

555 "Most of those present. . . ." David Landau, "Soviet Jews Test the Limits of 'Glasnost,' " *Jerusalem Post*, 1 December 1987.

556 History of Hungarian Jews under Communism. See especially Charles Hoffman, *Gray Dawn* (New York: HarperCollins, 1992), 1–12, 74–118.

557 Fixler's dealings with Reichmann. Herman Fixler, interview by author and Mihaly Benkő, Budapest, 20 February 1996.

557 Palmer's background. Henry Kamm, "How to Disarm Hungary (Hamburgers? Tennis?)" *New York Times*, 4 October 1989, 4.

557 On Hungarian resistance to Wallenberg memorial, see Hoffman, *Gray Dawn*, 86.

558 "Mr. Palmer was very interested. . . ." Telephone interview by author, 22 January 1996.

558 Edward reproached by Israeli foreign office. Ibid.

558 The description of Beled is based on author's own visit to the town on 24 February 1996; and Edward Reichmann, interview by author, 22 January 1996.

558 Destruction of the graveyard; search for Jewish treasure. Vilmos Hajós (formerly Hoffman), interview by Mihaly Benkő, Győr, 1 March 1996. Hajós grew up in Beled, survived deportation to Auschwitz, and returned to the village after World War II.

559 Grosz's trip to Canada. Sarlos, *Fireworks*, 245–46.

559 The Tengleman investment. Ibid., 248–49.

559 On First Hungary Fund and the Sarlos-Soros connection in general, see Arthur Johnson, "Hungary's Capitalist Revolution," *Financial Times of Canada*, 21 November, 1988, 18.

559 Albert's reason for not investing in First Hungary fund. Andy Sarlos, interview by author.

559 Moskovits biography. David Moskovits, interview by author, 8 November 1992; and press release by the American Endowment for Hungarian Jewry, n.d.

560 "To foster the ideals of freedom. . . ." "Fact Sheet," 2 August 1991, Endowment for Democracy in Eastern Europe.

560 Endowment for Democracy as largest financial contributor. Herman Fixler, interview by author and Benkő.

560 Annotated list of Endowment projects. "Fact Sheet," 2–3.

560 "My sole attachment. . . . 'What am I doing here?' " Interview by author, 20 November 1994.

Chapter 41

562 "Without the inspiration. . . ." Hewland Productions, *The Men Who Built Canary Wharf*.

562 "When I learned about this project. . . ." Transcript of Mrs. Thatcher's Speech in Response to Paul Reichmann at Banqueting Hall, 11 May 1988.

563 "Mr. Big." "Where Derelict Land Is a Greenfield Site," *Economist*, 13 February 1988, 67.

563 "A most charming man. . . ." Interview by author 29 October 1995.

563 Meeting at MacAlpine's townhouse between Reichmann and Lord Young. Stanley Honeyman, interview by author.

563 "I told him that otherwise. . . ." Ibid.

564 Thatcher down on one knee. Paul Reichmann, interview by author, 29 October 1995.

564 "I think Paul was especially intriguing. . . ." Interview by author, London, 3 September 1993.

564 "It was the Jewish belief. . . ." Hugo Young, *One of Us* (London: Macmillan, 1987), 422. On Mrs. Thatcher's philo-Semitism generally, see Geoffrey Alderman, *Modern British Jewry* (Oxford: Claredon Press, 1992).

564 "A valuable source-book." Ibid., 423. The Jakobovitses and the Reichmanns shared common history as well as a common economic philosophy. Lady Jakobovits, the former Emilie Munk, was the daughter of the rabbi whose synagogue Samuel and Renée Reichmann had attended during their two years in Paris. In London, Eva Reichmann Heller had been one of "Lady J's" closest friends.

564 Brian Griffith at the Chelsea Flower Show. Amiel, "The Man Who Made the Canary Fly." Griffith's concluding remark—"It could only have happened. . . ."— does not appear in Amiel's article but was related by Paul Reichmann in an interview with the author, 29 October 1995.

565 "If I might add a quotation. . . ." Speech at Banqueting Hall, 11 May 1988.

565 Meetings between Paul Reichmann and Margaret Thatcher. Paul Reichmann, interview by author, 29 October 1995.

565 "Mrs. Thatcher would not . . ." Interview by author.

565 "There was great enthusiasm. . . ." Interview by author, London, 24 September 1993.

565 Reichmann's fondness for anecdote about Thatcher rebuke. John Zuccotti, interview by author, 3 March 1994.

566 "Canary Wharf's close identification. . . ." Interview by author.

566 "With Canary Wharf at its heart. . . ." Michael Leapman, *London's River* (London: Pavilion Books, 1991), 153. This book was published "in association with" Olympia & York, and Sir Roy Strong, the company's Canary Wharf design consultant, wrote the foreword.

566 Net decrease of 4,000 jobs. Stewart, *Too Big to Fail*, 157.

566 "We're not here to . . ." Ibid., 163.

567 "The Japanese bankers. . . ." Ibid., 164–65.

567 "This thing was going to go ahead. . . ." Ibid., 172.

567 "The people from . . ." Ibid., 175.

568 "I was appalled. . . ." Interview by author.

568 "To people like me. . . ." Interview by author.

569 "Olympia & York consistently . . ." Ibid.

569 On the difficult logistics of Canary Wharf construction, see Angela Long, "Finding Ways of Building Office Blocks on Water," London *Times*, 14 May 1989, D14.

569 "I have never worked on a site. . . ." Ibid.

570 On the use of the Thames in building Canary Wharf. See Peter Reina, "Canary Wharf Starts Foundations," *Engineering News Record*, 24 November 1988, 14.

570 Aker's cement plant. Ibid.

570 Outbidding Disney for trees. Foster, *Towers of Debt*, 203.

570–71 On the management structure of the construction project, see Peter Reina, "Giant Canary Wharf Keeps on Singing, Despite Some Blues," *Engineering News Record*, 18 March 1991, 22.

571 The reluctance of subcontractors. Ibid.: Richard Griffiths "now doubts whether U.K. subcontractors had the corporate culture for CM (Construction Management). 'There is a fear of risk,' he says. And Griffiths adds the project's scale, especially the tower's, overawed would-be subcontractors."

571 "A wall of noise." Ross Fisher, "Digging In at Canary Wharf," *Canadian Business*, February 1990, 28.

571 "I never mind doing a U-turn. . . ." Foster, *Towers of Debt*, 206.

572 The critical mass provision. Paul Reichmann, interview by author, 29 October 1995.

572 O & Y's pricing strategy. Ibid.

573 "Marano was Olympia & York's bypass. . . ." Interview by author, London, 23 September 1993.

573 "I used to wheel Paul in. . . ." Interview by author, London, 24 November 1993.

574 Reichmann "didn't realize. . . ." Buchan, "High-Risk Business," 2.

574 "Londoners are used to living in villages. . . ." Interview by author, 15 September 1993.

574 "Paul never understood one thing. . . . Dreamers don't like to be awakened." Interview by author.

575 Investment in Stanhope. Paul Cheesewright, "Olympia & York Takes Big Stake in Stanhope," *Financial Times*, 12 May 1989, 8.

575 "Olympia & York certainly knew . . ." Interview by author.

575 "My first impression. . . ." Interview by author.

575 Reichmann's view of Lipton as England's best developer. Paul Reichmann, interview by author, 29 October 1995.

575 Cohen tour of Canary Wharf and exchange with Dennis. Peter Cohen, interview by author.

575 Talks with four banks. Paul Reichmann, interview by author, 29 October 1995.

576 "We thought at the time . . . a grave error." Ibid.

Chapter 42

577 $2.2 billion invested. Olympia & York Canary Wharf Ltd., Accounts (for the 14 months ended 31 October 1989), 4–6, Companies House, London.

577 No effort to recruit minority partners. Paul Reichmann, interview by author, 20 October 1995.

577 Change in ownership of the U.S. firm. Information circular, 9 November 1995, 31–32, special meeting of creditors of Olympia & York Development, Ontario Court of Justice. As part of this transaction, the family also took ownership of 2 million shares of Landmark Land and a 90 percent interest in a subsidiary of Olympia & York's American company called Baden Real Estate, which essentially was a dumping ground for the bad land deals the brothers had done in the United States over the years, including the New Jersey parcel they had acquired in bailing out Isiah Siedenfeld in 1973. In taking the bulk of these money-losing investments off the books of the U.S. company, the Reichmanns boosted its borrowing capacity.

577 Hiring of Lazard Frères and Swiss Banking Corp. Paul Reichmann, interview by author, 20 October 1995.

578 "Professionalization" and "discipline of inquiry." John Zuccotti, interview by author.

578 "Paul would be the first . . . seemed like reasonable offers to me." Ibid.

578 Japanese offer for the Aetna Center and Reichmann's rejection. Robert Canning, interview by author.

579 Twenty-five-fold increase in Trizec. Eric Reguly, "Reichmanns Return to Property Roots," *Financial Post*, 22 September 1990, 1.

579 $100 million trading profit. "Most people would consider it. . . ." Barsky, "Paul Reichmann Scales Real Estate's Heights," 1.

579 Figures on First Canadian Place. Offering circular, 16 September 1988, Olympia & York First Canadian Place Limited, 12.

580 Terms and conditions of the Jumbo Loan. Foster, *Towers of Debt*, 247–48.

580 On the Baltic independence movements, see Hoskings, *A History of the Soviet Union*, 472–73.

580 Vilnius as a Jewish center. Anatol Lieven, *The Baltic Revolution* (New Haven: Yale University Press, 1993), 139–58.

581 One remaining synagogue. Carmela Raiz, *Blue Star over Red Square* (Jerusalem: Feldheim, 1994), 154.

581 SOS to Rabbi Mandel. Ibid., 250–51.

581 Background of Ronnie Greenwald. Craig Whitney, *Spy Trader* (New York: Times Books, 1993), 193–94.

581 Greenwald's first meeting with Albert. Ronnie Greenwald, interview by author, New York City, 20 September 1995.

582 Appointments with the mayor of Moscow and head of Avto. Fax to Albert Reichmann from Ronald Greenwald, 16 February 1989, copy provided to the author by Greenwald.

582 "I thought him to be rather sad. . . ." Steve Lieberman, "Gilman, Local Rabbi Help Free Refusenik," *Rockland County Journal-News,* 9 March 1990, A1.

582 "I explained to him. . . ." Interview by author.

582 Assurances given Reichmann concerning Raiz. Memorandum to Simas Velonskis from Ronnie Greenwald, 28 December 1988, provided to the author by Greenwald.

583 Wiesel's appearance at the cultural center. Esther B. Fein, "Lasting Faith of Soviet Jews Moves Wiesel," *New York Times,* 13 February 1989, A1.

583 Opening of Moscow yeshiva. Ari Goldman, "Moscow to Get Academy of Jewish Learning," *New York Times,* 19 February 1989, 25.

583 Sharp increase in Jewish emigration. Joel Brinkley, "Soviet Jews Leave at a Record Pace, Many for Israel," *New York Times,* 14 December 1989, 1.

583 Repainting of the Vilnius airport. Raiz, *Blue Star over Red Square,* 265–66.

583 Establishment of the agricultural joint venture. Protocol of agreements between Albert International Corp., USA; Olympia and York Developments Ltd., Canada; and Lithuanian State Agro-Industrial Committee, 18 May 1989, signed by S. Velonskis, A. Reichmann, and G. Konopliovas. Copy provided to the author by Greenwald.

583–84 The Raizes' confrontation with KGB agent. Raiz, *Blue Star over Red Square,* 128.

584 "We could tell . . . to ponder our fate." Ibid., 267,

584 Albert's Yom Kippur phone call. Ronnie Greenwald, interview by author.

585 "I'd be at the stage. . . ." Interview by author.

585 "The press viewed. . . ." Interview by author.

585 "We knew that if. . . ." Interview by author, London, 27 September 1993.

585 Docklands roadworks improvements. See Gareth David and Philip Beresford, "Docklands Pleads for Fast Roads," London *Times,* 28 February 1988, D8.

585 The Limehouse Link's high cost. David Nicholson-Lord, "The Golden Link Road That Is Splitting Limehouse," London *Times,* 26 December 1988, 4. The tab would have risen to at least £325 million, or £4,586 an inch, if one included, as seems appropriate, the £105 million spent to acquire and demolish houses in its path.

585 On the Travelstead consortium's role in the plan to upgrade the DLR, see ver Meulen, "The Rise of Canary Wharf," 284.

586 O & Y's £67 million obligation. John Ardill, "Docklands Adds a Little Reality to the Megahype," *Guardian,* 21 July 1987, 21.

586 "I went to see Paul . . . overaffected by cash." Interview by author.

586 Relegation of the Jubilee proposal to back burner. The Department of Transport, British Rail Networth SouthEast, London Regional Transport, London Underground Ltd., Central London Rail Study, Central London Rail Study, January 1989, 23.

586 "Had an entrée . . ." Stewart, *Too Big to Fail,* 184.

587 "It is sometimes argued. . . ." Cecil Parkinson, *Right at the Center* (London: Weidenfeld and Nicolson, 1992), 291.

587 "We were able to improve the terms. . . ." Ibid., 290.

587 Announcement of compromise agreement on Jubilee project. Edward Greenspon, "Olympia & York to Finance Part of London Tube," *Toronto Globe & Mail*, 17 November 1989, B1.

587 "The Jubilee Line was . . ." Bond, "Why Reichmann Is Celebrating a Jubilee at Canary Wharf," 23.

588 Albert's leadership of the Canada-USSR Business Council. Maley, "Reichmann Helps Build Bridge to Soviets," B1.

588 Ceremonial photograph taken at Moscow lunch. *Toronto Globe & Mail*, 23 November 1989.

588 Raiz's appeal to Mulroney and Reichmann's reception at yeshiva. Stephen Handelman, "PM Promises 'Better Days' to Refuseniks," *Toronto Star*, 23 November 1989.

588 Premature Soviet announcement of Moscow tower. Jeff Sallot, "Reichmann Firm to Build Skyscraper in Moscow," *Toronto Globe & Mail*, 6 November 1989, A1.

589 "They're saying, 'Make it taller. . . .' " Peter Gorrie, "O & Y to Start Soviet Tower in a Year," *Toronto Star*, 21 February 1990, D1.

589 Largest Canadian trade delegation ever. Edward Balababa, telephone interview by author, 20 October 1993.

589 "The Berlin Wall fell. . . ." Ibid.

589 Gryfe and Koshitsky's audience with Albert. Mark Gryfe, interview by author.

589 The terms of agreement with the UJA. Ibid.

590 On conditions in Ladispoli, see Clyde Haberman, "For Stranded Jews, 'When' Is Now 'If,' " *New York Times*, 11 December 1988.

590–91 Japanese government pressure on prospective bidders for Sears Tower. See Neil Barsky, "Sears Narrows Tower Bidding to 4 Contenders," *Wall Street Journal*, 22 June 1989, A5.

591 In addition to Olympia & York, the other finalists were JMB Realty in partnership with Trammell Crow Co.; LaSalle Partners with Prudential Insurance Co. of America; and Aldrich, Easter and Waltech, Inc.

591 Reichmann's withdrawal from the Sears bidding. Neil Barksy, "Sears Hits Snag in Talks to Sell Tallest Tower," *Wall Street Journal*, 13 September 1989, A3.

591 Circumstances leading to Olympia & York's $75 million loan to Campeau. Rothchild, *Going for Broke*, 240.

591 The Reichmanns' dominant role in Campeau's restructuring. Jacquie McNish, "O & Y Calls the Shots in Campeau Affairs after Life-saving Loan," *Toronto Globe & Mail*, 27 September 1989, B1; and Ann Walmsley, "The Price of a Reprieve," *Maclean's* magazine, 2 October 1989, 36.

592 Details of the Reichmann plan to restructure Campeau. Rothchild, *Going for Broke*, 252–53.

592 "The Reichmann reputation. . . ." Ibid., 253.

592 "Clearly the Reichmanns are doing. . . ." Jacquie McNish, "Bankers Dismayed that O & Y Left Campeau Talks," *Toronto Globe & Mail*, 16 January 1990, B1.

592 "Up until Campeau. . . ." Interview by author.

592 Sale of one-third interest in World Financial Center. Affidavit of Manfred J. Walt, 7–8, *Battery Park Holdings, Inc. et al. vs. O & Y (U.S.) Development Company, L.P., et al.*, Supreme Court of the State of New York, index no. 31782/92.

592 "Was done in an extremely short . . . Bronfman-controlled entity." Affidavit of Joel M. Simon, 12–13, *Battery Park Holdings, Inc. et al. vs. O & Y (U.S.) Development Company, L.P., et al.*

593 "Did not participate. . . ." Eight-page Olympia & York U.S.A. memorandum, headed "Background," n.d.

593 "Represented that the investment . . . within three to six months." Walt affidavit, 6–7, *Battery Park Holdings, Inc. et al. vs. O & Y (U.S.) Development Company, L.P., et al.*

593 Audit requirement of Jumbo Loan. Foster, *Towers of Debt*, 248.

593 Negative reaction of U.S. management and auditors to World Financial Center sale. Simon affidavit, background memo; and John Zuccotti, interview by author.

593 "Assurances were given. . . ." Simon affidavit, 13–14.

Chapter 43

595 Symptoms of Renée's declining health. Edward Reichmann, interview by author, New York City, 29 October 1995.

595 Renée's obituaries. Phil Fine, "Family Matriarch Remembered for Charitable Works," *Canadian Jewish News*, 22 February 1990; "Mother of Developers Supported Many Charities," *Toronto Globe & Mail*, 16 February 1990; "Renée Reichmann Assisted War Victims," *Toronto Star*, 15 February 1990.

595 "Toronto International Airport. . . ." Herman Landau, interview by author, Toronto, 26 April 1994.

596 "I was very worried. . . ." Raiz, *Blue Star over Red Square*, 298.

596 "I searched for the right words. . . ." Ibid., 242–43.

596 "When we were sitting shivah. . . ." Edward Reichmann, 25 February 1990, provided to the author by Reichmann.

596 Details of Renée's estate. Registrar, Surrogate Court Judicial District of York, file 21497. Daphne and Marcel Gestetner were the adult children of Aaron Gestetner, a longtime Olympia & York employee who had been raised by the Reichmanns in Tangier after his parents had perished in Auschwitz.

596 Sale of 160 Dalemount. Transfer TB721753, Land Registry Office, Toronto.

596 "There was never any distribution. . . ." Interview by author.

597 "It became a moot issue." Interview by author, 29 October 1995.

597 "One of the commandments. . . ." Interview by author.

597 Birth of Renée. Ibid.

597 "I'm sure if Paul had asked. . . ." Interview by author.

597 Warsaw phone call. Greenwald, interview by author.

597 Bush's list of refuseniks headed by the Raizes. Remarks to Members of the Jewish Community, 21 December 1989, White House press office.

598 Schifter's impromptu selection of Raiz. Raiz, *Blue Star over Red Square*, 342.

598 On the mounting political agitation in Lithuania, see Ernest Mandel, *Beyond Perestroika* (London: Verso, 1989), 240–42; and Francis X. Clines, "Nationalists Victorious in Lithuanian Election," *New York Times*, 26 February 1990, 10.

598 Schneur's phone call to Dinkins and Dinkins's surprise announcement. Raiz, *Blue Star over Red Square*, 351.

598 "Until I hear from Zev. . . ." Ibid., 352.

598 Greenwald's conversation with Zev Raiz. Greenwald, interview by author.

598 Greenwald's conversation with Reichmann. Ibid.

599 "I am glad to inform you. . . ." Brazauskas to Reichmann, 7 March 1990, copy provided by Greenwald.

599 Gilman's photo and statement. Lieberman, "Gilman, Local Rabbi Help Free Refusenik," A1.

599 Moynihan's press release, 8 March 1990. Copy provided by Greenwald.

599 Lithuania's defiant standoff with USSR. Mandel, *Beyond Perestroika*, 241.

600 Greenwald's conversation with Raiz and Raiz's departure. Greenwald, interview by author.

600 Kremlin ultimatum. "Lithuania Rejects Moscow's Demand," *New York Times*, 18 March 1990, 15.

600 "No one could anticipate. . . ." Raiz, *Blue Star over Red Square*, 362–63.

600 Escalating diplomatic and military maneuvering. See Francis X. Clines, "Soviet Insurgents Voted into Power in the 3 Main Cities," *New York Times*, 20 March 1990, A1; and Clines, "Gorbachev Tells the Lithuanians to Turn In Arms," 22 March 1990, A1.

600 "Both of them said. . . ." Interview by author.

601 Greenwald's conversation with Reichmann in airport. Ibid.

601 Jankauskas's intervention. Greenwald, interview by author.

601 "Despite the poor reception. . . ." Raiz, *Blue Star over Red Square*, 365.

601 "How far is it. . . ." Ibid., 357.

601 "I feel as if . . ." Herb Keinon, "After 18-Year Wait, Refusenik Arrives in Israel," *Jerusalem Post*, 21 March 1990.

601 "I assumed after I left. . . ." Greenwald to Reichmann, 20 March 1990, copy provided by Greenwald.

602 Malev suspends flight to Israel. Celestine Bohlen, "Hungary Halts Emigré Flights after Muslim Threat," *New York Times*, 22 March 1990, A18.

602 "We are making every effort. . . ." Joel Brinkley, "Soviets to Curb Jews' Flights to Israel," *New York Times*, 24 March 1990, 1.

602 "Everyone agreed to cooperate. . . ." Sarlos, *Fireworks*, 183.

602 Malev resumes flights. Celestine Bohlen, "Hungarians Will Again Fly Soviet Jews to Israel," *New York Times*, 29 March 1990, A13.

603 Paul's sacking of Ellis Don MacAlpine. Andrew Taylor, "Docklands Tower Managers Replaced," *Financial Times*, 29 March 1990, 1.

603 "Keith resisted. . . ." Interview by author, 29 October 1995.

603 Reworking of the Morgan agreement. Statement of Claim, 28 January 1992, *Morgan Stanley Properties Limited vs. Rochmoor Limited and Olympia and York Developments Limited*, High Court of Justice, Chancery Division, London.

604 "Breakthrough lease." Edward Greenspon, "Olympia & York Lures Merrill Lynch to Canary Wharf Project," 10 March 1989, B17.

604 Texaco lease. "Texaco's London Offices to Move to New Project," *Wall Street Journal*, 21 September 1989, A18.

604 "It was supposed to be a secret. . . ." Interview by author.

604 On the decline of the London property market, see Goobey, *Bricks and Mortals*, 201–8; and Fiametta Rocco, "London Property: The Next Crash?" *Institutional Investor*, October 1989, 315.

604 "Is in danger . . ." "Unreal Estate," *Economist*, 21 October 1989, 94.

604 Reichmann's purchase of Rosehaugh stock. Paul Cheeseright, "Tentacles Spread from Canary Wharf," *Financial Times*, 6 April 1990, 29.

605 "Signalling a striking vote. . . ." Vanessa Houlder, "Docklands: Will It Stay a Cut-price Ghost Town?" *Financial Times*, 11 January 1992, 1.

605 Last-minute leasing blitz. Paul Cheeseright, "Oglivy & Mather Opts for Canary Wharf," *Financial Times*, 25 April 1990, 8; "Canary Wharf Move" [Skidmore Owings], *Financial Times*, 4 May 1990, 8; Matthew Bond, "Amex European Base Goes to Canary Wharf," London *Times*, 26 June 1990, 21; and David Lascelles, "One Gain and One Loss for Canary Wharf," *Financial Times* 26 June 1990, 10.

605 "We in New York saved the day . . ." Interview by author, 28 September 1995.

605 £30 million fit-out allowance. Affidavit of Paul A. Seader, 18 June 1992, 5, *In the Matter of a Plan of Arrangement for Olympia & York Developments et al.*, Ontario Court of Justice (General Division), court file B125/92.

605 £25 million a year. A source within Olympia & York, interview by author.

606 *Daily Telegraph* lease. Matthew Bond, "Telegraph Moving to Canary Wharf," London *Times*, 11 July 1990, 23; and Bond, "O & Y Carrot Carries £40m Price Tag," London *Times*, 6 April 1990.

606 Surge in Jewish emigration. Eisen, *Count Us In*, 268.

606 On Pamyat and resurgent anti-Semitism, see David Remnick, *Lenin's Tomb* (New York: Random House, 1993), 87–100.

607 Albert's declining to contribute to "Operation Exodus." Mark Gryfe, interview by author.

607 "They felt I was naive. . . ." Maley, "Reichmann Helps Build Bridge to Soviets," B1.

607 Reichmann's contributions. Philip Reichmann, Mordecai Neustadt, and Ronnie Greenwald, interviews by author. Also see "Largest Effort for Torah in 70 Years as Schlichim Fan Out over USSR," *Coalition*, September 1990.

607 Formation of the Union of Jewish Religious Communities. Charles Hoffman, "Revival of the Dead," *Jerusalem Report*, 4 July 1991, 31.

607 Reichmann's role in reforming the Great Synagogue. Ibid.; and Israel Singer and Mordecai Neustadt, interviews by author.

607 "In Moscow, the Jews. . . ." Interview by author.

607 Rabbi Goldschmidt's founding new institutions. "New Yeshiva and Women's Seminary Open in Moscow," *Coalition*, March 1991, 3.

608 "Gorbachev supported . . . forms of co-operation." "Gorbachev Blesses Reichmann Tower Plan," *Montreal Gazette*, 24 May 1990.

608 "If you stand in a lobby. . . ." Celestine Bohlen, "U.S. Envoy in Hungary Quits to Handle Investment in East," *New York Times*, 26 January 1990, A1.

608 CEDC's purchase of stake in bank (Hungarian General Banking and Trust Co.). Stuart Auerbach, "Lauder Group Buys Bank in Hungary," *Washington Post*, 26 January 1990, F4.

608 Budapest project. Allan Thompson, "Reichmanns to Build New Office in Budapest," *Toronto Star*, 10 January 1992, B1.

608 $5 million for 17 percent. Affidavit of Otto Blau, 16 June 1992, 2–4, *In the Matter of a Plan of Arrangement for Olympia & York Developments et al.*, Ontario Court of Justice (General Division).

608 Dedication of the Budapest school. "Hungarian Officials, Budapest Jewry Celebrate Pioneering School," *Coalition*, January 1991.

609 "My father gets absolutely. . . ." Interview by author, 16 August 1995.

609 Unpopularity of state-run Jewish school in Budapest. Hoffman, *Gray Dawn*, 65.

609 "Finally, we told the government. . . ." Interview by author, New York City, 16 November 1992.

609 "It would have cost me. . . ." Interview by author.

609 Costs of school project. Nicholas Comfort, "Budapest's Jews Face Classroom Revolution," *European*, 6 September 1991.

609 Intramural wrangling over the Budapest school. Hoffman, *Gray Dawn*, 95–97; Richard Roth and David Gold, interviews by author; and Herman Fixler, interview by author and Benkő.

Chapter 44

611 Annual doubling of vacancy rate and the global overbuilding trend. James Grant, "C-SPAN–Over Here," in *Minding Mr. Market* (New York: Farrar Straus Giroux, 1993), 102–3.

611 "Have rarely overlent so extensively. . . ." Ibid., 103. Grant testified before the House Banking Committee on 30 July 1992.

611 New York vacancy rates and rents. Margaret Philip, "Reichmanns Battling New York Real Estate Slump," *Toronto Globe & Mail*, 24 June 1991, B1.

612 55 Water Street's problematic prospects. Ibid.

612 Rising vacancy rates in Toronto. Margaret Philip, "O & Y Lowers Standards in Real Estate Battle," *Toronto Globe & Mail*, 26 April 1991, B4.

612 "a startling admission . . ." Ibid.

612 On the high cost of O & Y's stock market woes, see Reguly, "Reichmann Return to Property Roots," 1; and James Norman, "Property Rich, Cash Poor," *Forbes*, 11 November 1990, 43–44.

612 The company's assets exceeding its liabilities. As of 31 January 1991, Olympia & York Developments showed positive shareholders' equity of $2.1 billion on its books. Offering Circular, *In the Matter of a Plan of Arrangement for Olympia & York Developments et al.*, 42.

613 Reichmann's judgment. Paul Reichmann, interview by author, 29 October 1996.

613 On the final round of Canary Wharf financing, see "Pie in the Sky or a Dream Come True?" *Accountancy*, September 1991, 20–21.

614 Asset sales and use of proceeds. Offering Circular, *In the Matter of a Plan of Arrangement for Olympia & York Developments et al.*, 35–41.

614 Reichmann wanting higher prices. John Zuccotti and two investment bankers associated with O & Y, interviews by author.

614 Reichmann family purchase of O & Y assets. Offering Circular, *In the Matter of a Plan of Arrangement for Olympia & York Developments et al.*, 44–48. Other assets purchased by the family included an office building at 5140 Yonge Street in Toronto, the Queen's Quay shopping mall in Toronto, the Charlottetown Mall on Prince Edward Island, and Place des Quatres Bourgeois in Quebec.

614 "From a family point of view. . . ." Interview by author, 26 February 1996.

614 In 1993, a federal judge in Alexandria, Virginia, appended an embarrassing postscript to the Reichmanns' condo conversion follies in sentencing Scott and Gary Nordheimer to twenty-four and twenty-seven months, respectively, in prison. Albert's ex-partners pleaded guilty to three counts of wire fraud as part of a scheme to entice investors into a condo conversion project in Utah. The brothers were convicted of forging signatures on forty bogus purchase agreements from nonexistent buyers, creating the illusion of $1.7 million in condo sales.

614–15 Chase's lobbying of Albert and Albert's $10 million loan. Sources within Olympia & York, interviews by author.

615 "I think the problem in Florida. . . ." Ibid.

615 O & Y's withdrawal from the Jerusalem project. Statement of Defence, 30 August 1994, 5–7, and Reichmann's Submissions, 4 April 1995, 3–5, *Albert Reichmann vs. Zeev Vered and Ron Engineering and Construction*, Ontario Court of Justice.

615 Settlement in libel case. Peter Cheney, "Toronto Life, Reichmanns Settle Libel Suit out of Court," *Toronto Star*, 2 February 1991, A3.

616 "Had gone on long enough. . . ." Interview by author, 26 February 1996.

616 "I'm ambivalent. . . ." Ibid.

616 Leo Heaps, "Empire of the Sons," *Esquire* (British edition only), September 1992, 63.

616 *Esquire* piece as filled with errors. To cite a single paragraph on page 65, Samuel Reichmann was born in 1898, not 1910, in Beled, not Csorna; the founder of the Gestetner stencil duplicating company was David, not Sigmund, Gestetner, and David Gestetner emigrated to England in the 1880s, not the 1930s.

617 "Paul's demeanor was just so different. . . ." Interview by author, Toronto, 1992.

617 Bankers' tendency to be overawed by favorable publicity. Oskar Lustig, interview by author.

617 Olympia & York's complex corporate structure. See Offering Circular, *In the Matter of a Plan of Arrangement for Olympia & York Developments et al.*, 20.

618 "The one thing that Paul. . . ." Interview by author.

618 "Our future growth will be. . . ." James Graff and Adam Corelli, "Time for No Debt and Cash Reserves," *Time* (Canadian edition), 5 November 1990, 62.

618 "Rubbish." Neil Barsky, "Olympia & York Finds That It Isn't Immune to Real-Estate Crunch," *Wall Street Journal*, 15 October 1991, 1.

618 "Children who don't know. . . ." Richard Hylton, "Reshaping a Real Estate Dynasty," *New York Times*, 28 November 1990, D-1.

618–19 Promise of a third-party purchase by mid-1990. Walt affidavit, 6–7, *Park Holdings, Inc. et al. vs. O & Y (U.S.) Development Company, L. P., et al.*

619 Formal notice. Cockwell to Reichmann, 29 August 1990, exhibit attached to the Walt affidavit. Ibid.

619 Reichmann purchase of 50 percent with $140 million loan. Walt affidavit, 10. The lender was Hees International Bancorp, the parent company of Carena Development.

619 Reichmann's refusal to acknowledge transaction. "Background" memorandum, n.d., 4, Olympia & York U.S.A.

619 Edper's IRS report. Ibid.

619–20 Showdown with Sanya. Offering Circular, *In the Matter of a Plan of Arrangement for Olympia & York Developments et al.*, 101–2.

620 Olympia & York as better off husbanding cash. Paul Reichmann, interview by author, 26 February 1996.

620 Olympia & York as unable to make the $100 million payment. John Zuccotti, interview by author, 22 March 1994.

620 Morgan loan. Neil Barsky, "Olympia & York Arranges Loan to Refinance," *Wall Street Journal*, 25 June 1991, A10.

621 "It was always to do tomorrow." Interview by author, 19 February 1995.

621 "The precipitous end. . . ." Interview by author.

621 Day of prayer in Israel. Peter Hirschberg, "When Charity Ends," *Jerusalem Report*, 1 July 1993, 14.

622 Impact of lost Reichmann funding. See ibid. and Steven Chase, "Reichmann's Plight Has Charities Hurting," *Toronto Globe & Mail*, 15 June 1992, B1.

622 "Even with me. . . ." Interview by author, 16 August 1995.

622 "The Reichmanns had always. . . ." Interview by author.

622 Morgan Stanley's proprietary bus service. Vanessa Houlder, "Public Transport to Canary Wharf Shunned by Bank," *Financial Times*, 25 November 1991, 5.

623 "From the marbled canyons. . . ." "In the Balance," *Economist*, 22 June 1991, 55.

623 Reichmann's portfolio. A source close to Reichmann, interview by author.

623 O & Y's new willingness to dicker. See Arthur Johnson, "Tenants Wanted, Will Negotiate Terms," *Report on Business* Magazine, August 1990, 40; and Andrew Davidson, "Special Offers Fail to Fill Canary Wharf," London *Times*, 23 September 1990, 4.

623 "The horrors of the recession. . . ." "In the Balance," 22 June 1991, 55.

623 Reichmann asks Major's help. Philip Stephens, "Developer of Canary Wharf in Plea to PM," *Financial Times*, 23 July 1991, 16.

623 "Major's attitude. . . ." Interview by author, 29 October 1995.

623 Heseltine's proposal. Andrew Lorenz and Andrew Grice, "DoE May Move to Docklands," London *Times*, 17 March 1991, 2.

624 "I think Paul could have financed. . . ." Interview by author.

624 £50 million mortgage. "O & Y Completes Sale and Leaseback Deal," London *Times*, 16 August 1991, 20.

624 Morgan's exercise of option. Statement of Claim, 28 January 1992, 4. *Morgan Stanley Properties Limited vs. Rochmoor Limited and Olympia and York Developments Limited*, High Court of Justice.

624 "In a touching, almost naive way. . . ." Anthony Bianco, "Magnificent Obsession," *Vanity Fair*, October 1992, 238.

624 "In Singapore. . . ." Interview by author, 28 September 1995.

624 "When I can't sleep. . . ." Interview by author, 26 February 1996.

624 "He was not the same Paul. . . ." Interview by author.

625 Terms of sale of 60 Broad to Li Ka-Shing. Neil Barsky, "Olympia & York Sells 49% Stake in New York Site," *Wall Street Journal*, 21 October 1991, B11.

625 "I wanted to be sure. . . ." Interview by author, 29 October 1995.

625 "What we kept getting back. . . ." Interview by author.

625–26 New Year's Eve negotiations. Ibid.

Chapter 45

627 "This thing is dying. . . ." Jacquie McNish and Madelaine Drohan, "U.K. Court Decision Leads to O & Y's Filing," *Toronto Globe & Mail*, 15 May 1992, 1.

627 Reichmann's taste for short-term financing. See Jacquie McNish, Margaret Philip and Brian Milner, "O & Y's Hard Times Stem from Shift to Short-term Debt," *Toronto Globe & Mail*, 4 April 1992, B1.

628 Three commercial paper issues. Dominion Bond Rating Service report no. 11458.

628 "The lack of any financial information. . . ." Ibid.

628 "The question is. . . ." Peter Foster, "How Deep Are Their Pockets?" *Canadian Business*, October 1991, 38.

628 Reichmann's request of the Gang of Four. John Zuccotti, interview by author, 22 March 1994.

628 "He could have closed. . . ." Jacquie McNish, "How Banks Flubbed O & Y," *Toronto Globe & Mail*, 4 December 1992, 1.

628 Aborted February 28 closing. Ibid.

629 Rushing the day's receipts. Dominion Bond Rating Service report no. 11460.

630 Commerce's $1.2 billion exposure leading the list. McNish, "How Banks Flubbed O & Y," 1.

630 $126 million Gang of Four loan, plus $30 million from CIBC. Offering Circular, *In the Matter of a Plan of Arrangement for Olympia & York Developments et al.*, 96–97.

630 $89 million Canary Wharf loan. Ibid., 98.

631 "On an extremely confidential basis . . . definitely disappear." Quoted by Stewart, *Too Big to Fail*, 231.

631 Terms of proposed government-backed financing. Jacquie McNish and Margaret Philip, "No Stone Unturned in Quest for Cash," *Toronto Globe & Mail*, 21 April 1992, B1.

631 The $165 million needed from the parent company. John Zuccotti, interview by author, 22 March 1994.

631 "John didn't show his anger. . . ." Interview by author.

632 "Everything he could. . . ." McNish, "How Banks Flubbed O & Y," 1.

632 Conversation between Zuccotti and Johnson. John Zuccotti and Tom Johnson, interviews by author, New York City, 21 July 1992 and 10 August 1992.

633 Reichmann's belated admission. See, for example, Neil Barsky, "Olympia & York Plans a Huge Restructuring Involving Many Banks," *Wall Street Journal*, 23 March 1992, 1.

633 "I couldn't read anything. . . ." Interview by author.

633 Miller's antic history. Foster, *Towers of Debt*, 269.

633 "Nothing changes as far as the top. . . ." Stewart, *Too Big to Fail*, 232.

634 "Olympia & York needed someone . . ." Interview by author, 26 February 1996.

634 "I read in the papers. . . ." Margaret Philip and Brian Milner, "O & Y Debt Crisis Squad Taking Another Week for Homework," *Toronto Globe & Mail*, 3 April 1992, B1.

634 "If, like some banks. . . ." Barsky, "Olympia & York Plans a Huge Restructuring Involving Many Banks," 1.

634 "Our view was. . . ." Neil Barsky, "Johnson's Exit from O&Y Signalled Firm's Hardball Strategy with Banks," *Wall Street Journal*, 17 April 1992, B8.

634 Reichmann stonewalling Johnson. Tom Johnson, a senior Toronto banker, and sources within O & Y, interviews by author.

635 Postponement of April 3 meeting. Neil Barsky and Larry Greenberg, "Olympia & York Meeting With Bankers Is Delayed; Firm Moves to Pay Some Debt," *Wall Street Journal*, 3 April 1992, A5.

635 Hill & Knowlton joining the fray. Jacquie McNish and Margaret Philip, "O & Y president hires PR firm," *Toronto Globe & Mail*, 11 April 1992, B1.

635 Albert and Ralph taking a stand. Tom Johnson, Philip Reichmann, and sources within Olympia & York, interview by author.

635 Negotiations between Reichmann and Johnson. Paul Reichmann and Tom Johnson, interview by author. See also Margaret Philip, Jacquie McNish, Brian Milner, and Alan Freeman, "O & Y's New Boss Having Second Thoughts," *Toronto Globe & Mail*, 9 April 1992, B1; Neil Barsky, "New President of Ailing Olympia & York Said Unhappy and May Step Down," *Wall Street Journal*, 9 April 1992, A3.

635 "I rationalized my stand as follows . . ." Interview by author, 22 March 1994.

636 Another factor weighing against sacking Zuccotti was his five-year employment contract (expiring in 1995), which Paul Reichmann had guaranteed personally to the tune of $1 million a year. If Reichmann sacked him, he might have ended up digging into his own pocket to pay him off.

636 "He wasn't happy about it but. . . ." Interview by author.

636 April 13 meeting. Brian Milner and Margaret Philip, "O & Y Opens Books to Bankers," *Toronto Globe & Mail*, 14 April 1992, A1.

636 "Has very substantial equity . . . a disaster for all concerned." Clyde Farnsworth, "Olympia Asks for More Time," *New York Times*, 14 April 1992, D1.

636 O & Y's financial report and hostile banker reaction. Neil Barsky and Larry Greenberg, "Bankers Complain About Firm's Secrecy as Olympia & York Meets with Lenders," *Wall Street Journal*, 15 April 1992, A5.

637 Meeting of Jumbo Loan lenders, including the "insider trading" analogy. McNish, "How Banks Flubbed O & Y," 1.

638 April 15 meeting. Ibid.

638 April 20 meeting. Ibid.

639 Granting of the lights-on loan. See Offering Circular, *In the Matter of a Plan of Arrangement for Olympia & York Developments*, 97.

639 Default on First Canadian Place bonds. Margaret Philip, "O & Y Misses Critical Interest Payment," *Toronto Globe & Mail*, 5 May 1992, B7.

639 "After decades of total family. . . ." Madelaine Drohan, Jacquie McNish, and Margaret Philip, "O & Y Offers Bankers Stock If They Forgo Debt Payments," *Toronto Globe & Mail*, 8 May 1992, B1.

640 "Olympia & York brought Canary Wharf down. . . ." Interview by author, 29 October 1995.

640 "He is the smartest. . . ." Interview by author.

640 "It felt to all of us. . . ." Interview by author.

640 "By the end of 1991. . . ." Interview by author, 29 October 1995.

640 Buxton's call to Flood. Ibid.

641 £5 million advance. Offering Circular, *In the Matter of a Plan of Arrangement for Olympia & York Developments*, 98.

641 May 7 meeting. Jacquie McNish, "The Day the Banks Said No," *Toronto Globe & Mail*, 5 December 1992, 1.

641 Hopes of bailout dashed. Alan Freeman and Jacquie McNish, "Ottawa, Ontario Refuse to Help Out Troubled O & Y," *Toronto Globe & Mail*, 5 May 1992, B1.

641 "Kept glaring at . . ." McNish, "The Day the Banks Said No," 1.

641 The token loan. Offering Circular, *In the Matter of a Plan of Arrangement for Olympia & York Developments*, 99.

641 Ruling on 25 Cabot Square. Jacquie McNish and Madelaine Drohan, "U.K. Court Decision Leads to O & Y's Filing," *Toronto Globe & Mail*, 15 May 1992, B1. Also see Offering Circular, *In the Matter of a Plan of Arrangement for Olympia & York Developments*, 48.

642 Largest Canadian bankruptcy. Richard Hylton, "Real Estate Giant in Canada Enters Bankruptcy Filing," *New York Times*, 15 May 1992, A1. Adding insult to injury, Representative Henry Gonzalez, chairman of the Banking Committee of the U. S. House of Representatives, compared the Reichmanns to Donald Trump, the egomaniacal New York developer who had gotten himself into serious financial trouble in 1991. "I look on this as a sort of a high-level Donald Trump operation," Gonzalez said. "These old boys are just more sophisticated and worked on a much broader international scale, but essentially the same." Brian Milner and Margaret Philip, "O & Y Puts on Brave Face to Mask Predicament," *Toronto Globe & Mail*, 16 May 1992, B1.

642 Zuccotti's threat to resign over tax issue. Todd Purdum, "Olympia Tax to Be Paid on Property," *New York Times*, 22 May 1992, B3.

642 "I've spent too much of my life. . . ." Interview by author. Zuccotti and Frucher worked out a plan under which the U.S. company was allowed to stretch out the $75 million payment over six months in return for immediate payment of a penalty to the city.

642 The last-ditch attempt to secure a British government bailout. Philip Stephens, "The Olympia & York Insolvency; Shoring up a Thatcher Memorial," *Financial Times*, 16 May 1992, 11.

642 "An ill-conceived act . . . architectural folly." Madelaine Drohan, "Canary Wharf Poses Tough Political Choice," *Toronto Globe & Mail*, 19 May 1992.

642–43 Circumstances of Canary Wharf's entry into administration. See Robert Peston, "Banks Abandon Canary Wharf," *Financial Times*, 29 May 1992, 1.

Chapter 46

644 "It was an instinctive thing. . . ." Interview by author, 29 October 1995.

644 "Olympia & York is continuing. . . ." Milner and Philip, "O & Y Puts on Brave Face to Mask Predicament," B1.

644 "Why are they doing this. . . ." Neil Barsky, "How O & Y's Miscues Led Creditor Banks to End Forbearance," *Wall Street Journal*, 1 June 1992, 1.

645 "It would have been relatively easy. . . ." Interview by author, 26 February 1996.

645 $2 billion loss (for the fiscal year ending January 31, 1992). Offering Circular, *In the Matter of a Plan of Arrangement for Olympia & York Developments*, C-2.

645 "The value of the development. . . ." Ibid., C-1. The *Financial Times* reported that two large British companies—Hanson and P & O—that looked at acquiring Canary Wharf out of bankruptcy separately decided that the complex was worth only about one-fifth of what it had cost Olympia & York to build. Roland Rudd, Vanessa Houlder, Ivo Dawnay, and Michael Smith, "Hanson and P & O Would Make Canary Wharf Offers Under £600m," *Financial Times*, 2 June 1991, 11.

645 "It is set in eight square miles. . . ." "Canary Wharf's Real Problem," *Economist*, 23 May 1992, 61.

645 "I was amazed. . . ." Interview by author.

646 Reichmann's £350 million offer and its rejection. Lew Ranieri and Paul Reichmann, interviews by author, 26 February 1996. See also Stephanie Strom, "Group Cuts Offer for London Development," *New York Times*, 28 August 1992, D4, and Richard Stevenson, "Bankers Reject Sole Canary Wharf Bid," *New York Times*, 24 September 1992, D3.

646 O & Y's provisional restructuring plan. Clyde Farnsworth, "Olympia Proposes Debt Delay," 21 August 1992, D1.

646 "It's a crap shoot. . . ." Brenda Dalglish, "A Final Gamble," *Maclean's* magazine, 31 August 1992, 29.

647 "A lot of bankers. . . ." Jacquie McNish, "Reports of Secret Stake Infuriate O & Y Bankers," *Toronto Globe & Mail*, 19 September 1992, B1.

647 "I've told fifty people . . . twitch of conscience." Kimberly Noble and Jacquie McNish, "Edper Reveals O & Y Stake," *Toronto Globe & Mail*, 18 September 1992, B1.

647 "To the question. . . ." Interview by author.

647 "That we shall be satisfied. . . ." Kelfer to David Ferguson, 25 September 1992, exhibit in *Battery Park Holdings, Inc. et al. vs. O & Y (U.S.) Development Company, L.P., et al.*

647 "It is completely unacceptable. . . ." Ferguson to Kelfer, 29 September 1996, Ibid.

647 Reichmanns' sale of BPHI stake. Bernard Simon, "Reichmanns sell secret stake in NY development," *Financial Times*, 2 October 1992, 30.

648 "Paul didn't raise his voice. . . ." Interview by author.

648 The second reorganization plan. Deirdre McMurdy, "Turning the Tables," *Maclean's* magazine, 9 November 1992, 99.

648 "Olympia & York's proposal. . . . this is ridiculous." Foster, *Towers of Debt*, 293.

648 The Reichmanns surrender control. Brian Milner and Margaret Philip, "O & Y's Creditors Sure to Accept Plan," *Toronto Globe & Mail*, 20 November 1992, B1.

648 For the details of the court-approved reorganization plan, see Larry Greenberg, "Creditors Are Set to Dismantle Olympia & York," *Wall Street Journal*, 11 January 1993, A3; and Margaret Philip, "O & Y Plan Protects Reichmanns," *Toronto Globe & Mail*, 17 December 1992, B9.

648–49 The next generation acquires O & Y Properties. Janet McFarland, "New O & Y First Step to an Empire?" *Financial Post*, 20 November, 1993, 11. See also Harry Cornelius, "Bold Caution," *Relocation Toronto*, Summer 1994, 9; and Leonard Zehr, "O & Y Properties Flexes Its Muscles," *Toronto Globe & Mail*, 29 May 1995, B1.

649 "We needed to find . . ." Interview by author, 20 June 1995.

649 "We spent many hours debating. . . ." McLaughlin, "The Reichmanns Rise Again," 14.

650 "People were aware. . . ." Interview by author.

650 "The Salinas administration. . . ." Interview by author, 19 February 1995.

650 Fundamentals of the Mexican market. Ibid.; and Paul Carroll, "Reichmann and Soros Plan to Construct 3 Real-Estate Projects in Mexico City," *Wall Street Journal*, 11 November 1993, A10.

650 For background on the Santa Fe project, see Anthony DePalma, "A Glittering Vision of Suburbia Supplants a Dump," *New York Times*, 23 June 1993, A4.

651 $400 million fortune (in Canadian dollars). Neil Barsky, "Reichmann Family Said to Still Hold $300 Million Fortune,"*Wall Street Journal*, 13 November 1992, A4.

651 $131 million repayment. Offering Circular, *In the Matter of a Plan of Arrangement for Olympia & York Developments*, 4.

651 The family's having $100 million at most. Sarlos, *Fireworks*, 199.

651 Paul's $15 million mortgage. Charge CA328622, Land Registry Office. Reichmann let almost two years elapse between borrowing the money and filing the forms making the requisite public disclosure of the loan.

651 "No other investor. . . ." Gary Weiss, "The Man Who Moves Markets," *Business Week*, 23 August 1993, 50.

652 The $1 billion profit in sterling speculation. Michael Lewis, "The Speculator," *New Republic*, 10 January 1994, 28.

652 Paul's twenty-investor list. Paul Reichmann, interview by author, 19 February 1995.

652 "I am basically looking. . . ." Kurt Eichenwald, "Reichmann Joins Soros in New Fund," *New York Times*, 9 February 1993, D4. On formation of the fund, see

also George Anders, "Reichmann to Manage Real Estate Fund Set Up by Soros," *Wall Street Journal*, 8 February 1993, C1.

652 Paul's predominant ownership within the family. Paul Reichmann, interview by author, 19 February 1995.

652 Formation of Reichmann Asia. Ron Soskolne, interview by author.

653 "We're interested in becoming. . . ." Ibid.

653 The Travelers transaction. Jeanne Pinder, "Soros Real Estate Fund in $634 Million Purchase," *New York Times*, 9 September 1993, D1.

653 Reichmann versus Marks. Paul Reichmann, interview by author, 19 February 1995. See also Leslie Eaton, "Trouble for Soros-Reichmann team," *New York Times*, 25 September 1994, III-11.

654 Schwartz replacing Marks. Bernard Simon, "Reichmann Recruits Soros Aide," *Financial Times*, 5 July 1994, 32.

654 Reichmann's Mexican press conference. See "Reichmann's US$1 B deals," *Financial Post*, 16 October 1993, 3.

654 "With Santa Fe. . . ." Interview by author.

654 "Will be a landmark. . . ." Drew Fagan, "Reichmanns Look to China, Latin America," *Toronto Globe & Mail*, 23 June 1994, B1.

655 "The idea was to create. . . ." Interview by author, 19 February 1995.

655 "Canary Wharf with enchiladas on the side." Stewart, *Too Big to Fail*, 267.

655 "Building there on a spec . . ." Fagan, "Reichmanns Look to China, Latin America," B1.

655 On the joint venture with Empresas ICA, see Drew Fagan, "Reichmanns Cut Mexican Deal," *Toronto Globe & Mail*, 18 February 1994, B1.

656 The purchase of Central Park Lodges. John Saunders, "Trizec Sells Nursing Home Chain," *Toronto Globe & Mail*, 27 October 1994, B2. See also *J. Silver Holdings v. George Kuhl, Meadowcroft Holdings . . . Paul Reichmann, Barry Reichmann, Eli Koenig, Abraham Fruchthandler, et al.*, Ontario Court (General Division), Toronto, court file 95-CQ-60150CM.

656 The Reichmann-Bronfman investment in NHC Communications. Scott Anderson, "High-profile Shareholders Leave NHC," *Financial Post*, 16 December 1995, 7.

656 David's O & Y stock bought by his father. Paul Reichmann, interview by author, 26 February 1996.

656 David's having at least $200 million. Burrough, "An Unorthodox Death," 82.

657 "He didn't know anything. . . ." Ibid., 83.

657 "They respected my ambition. . . ." Allison Kaplan Sommer, "Plugged In," *Jerusalem Post*, 20 May 1994, 12.

657 "She wanted him away from the family . . ." Burrough, "An Unorthodox Death," 82.

657 "It's like telecommunications was this pond . . ." Sommer, "Plugged In," 12.

657 The formation of the alliance with IDB. Joshua Shuman, "US Firm to Invest $10m in Darcom," *Jerusalem Post*, 22 June 1993.

658 "I believe . . ." Sommer, "Plugged In," 12.

658 David's disappearance and institutionalization. Burrough, "An Unorthodox Death," 127–28.

658–59 Buganim's account of Reichmann's last hours and the tangled aftermath of his death. Ibid., 129, 132.

659 "Had leadership qualities . . ." Ibid.

660 "It was clear to me. . . ." Interview by author, 19 February 1995.

660 "For the time being. . . ." Interview by author, 19 February 1995.

660 The unhappiness of Quantum's investors. Mitchell Pacelle, "Soros Seeks Large Investor to Buy Out Holders of His U.S. Real Estate Fund," *Wall Street Journal*, 28 April 1995, A4.

661 "I have a good relationship with Soros. . . ." Interview by author, 19 February 1995.

661 "There is no reason. . . ." Ibid.

661 Quantum's lagging performance. Gary Weiss, "Soros: Anatomy of a Comeback," *Business Week*, 25 September 1995, 100.

661 "Over the last two weeks. . . ." Interview by author, 19 February 1995.

661 Canary Wharf's emergence from administration. Patricia Tehan, "Banks Agree to £1.1bn Canary Wharf Rescue," London *Times*, 11 September 1993, 1.

662 The improved leasing outlook at the Wharf. Kyle Pope, "Canary Wharf Climbs Out of the Pits," *Wall Street Journal*, 20 June 1994, A7; and Richard Stevenson, "From Debacle to Desirable," *New York Times*, 18 July 1995, D1.

662 The termination of partnership with Soros. Richard Siklos, "Reichmann Sells Interest in Quantum Realty Trust," *Financial Post*, 29 September 1995, 3.

662 Soros's sale to Goldman. "Goldman Unit Buys Stake in Firm," *Chicago Tribune*, 18 November 1995, C-1.

662 Banker's tip and Reichmann's first meeting with Prince Alaweed. Paul Reichmann, interview by author, 26 February 1996.

663 "Reichmann knows how to manage. . . ." Paula Dwyer, "The Reichmann Reconquest," *Business Week*, 23 October 1995, 54.

663 "Reichmann's an Orthodox Jew. . . ." John Rossant, "The Prince," *Business Week*, 25 September 1995, 89.

663 Prince Alaweed joins Reichmann. Larry Greenberg, "Saudi Prince Joins Reichmann in Bid to Reacquire Canary Wharf Complex," *Wall Street Journal*, 8 August 1995, A5.

663 Final terms of Reichmann repurchase. Patrick Harverson, "Consortium Complex Canary Wharf Deal," 28 December 1995, 11.

664 "Regaining Canary Wharf . . . not kidding myself." Interview by author, 29 October 1995.

Selected Bibliography

BOOKS

Abella, Irving. *None Is Too Many.* Toronto: Lester & Orpen Dennys, 1982.

Adler, Jacques. *The Jews of Paris and the Final Solution.* New York: Oxford University Press, 1987.

Adler, Jerry. *High Rise.* New York: HarperCollins Publishers, 1993.

Al Naib, S. K. *London Docklands: Past, Present and Future.* London: Ashmead Press, 1990.

Alderman, Geoffrey. *Modern British Jewry.* Oxford: Clarendon Press, 1992.

Alexy, Trudy. *The Mezuzah in the Madonna's Foot.* New York: Simon & Schuster, 1993.

Aronsfeld, Caeser. *Ghosts of 1492.* New York: Conference on Jewish Social Studies, 1979.

Avni, Haim. *Spain, the Jews and Franco.* Philadelphia: Jewish Publication Society of America, 1982.

Babad, Michael, and Catherine Mulroney. *Campeau: The Building of an Empire.* Toronto: Doubleday Canada, 1989.

Basch, Antonín. *The Danube Basin and the German Economic Sphere.* New York: Columbia University Press, 1943.

Bauer, Yehuda. *American Jewry and the Holocaust.* Detroit, Mich.: Wayne State University Press, 1981.

Beckerman, Ruth. *Die Mazzesinsel.* Vienna: Locker, 1984.

Ben-Tov, Arieh. *Facing the Holocaust in Budapest.* Boston: Dordrecht, 1988.

Berend, Ivan, and Gyorgi Ránki. *The Development of the Manufacturing Industry.* Budapest: Akadémia Kiado, 1960.

———. *East Central Europe in the Nineteenth and Twentieth Centuries.* Budapest: Akadémia Kiado, 1977.

Berkley, George. *Vienna and Its Jews.* Cambridge, Mass.: Abt Books, 1987.

Bermant, Chaim. *Lord Jakobovits.* London: Weidenfeld and Nicolson, 1990.

Best, Patricia, and Ann Shortell. *A Matter of Trust.* Markham, Ont.: Viking, 1985.

———. *The Brass Ring.* Toronto: Random House, 1988.

Birnbaum, Philip. *Encyclopedia of Jewish Concepts.* New York: Hebrew, 1993.

Black, Conrad. *A Life in Progress.* Toronto: Key Porter Books, 1993.

Bowles, Paul. *Let It All Come Down.* London: John Lehmann Ltd., 1952.

Braham, Randolph. *The Politics of Genocide.* New York: Columbia University Press, 1981.

Brenner, Reeve Robert. *The Faith and Doubt of Holocaust Survivors.* New York: Free Press, 1990.

Brown, Brendan. *The Flight of International Capital.* London: Croom Helm, 1987.

Bullock, Alan. *Hitler and Stalin.* New York: Alfred A. Knopf, 1992.

Bunin, Amos. *A Fire in His Soul.* Jerusalem; New York: Feldheim, 1981.

Caulfield, Jon. *The Tiny Perfect Mayor.* Toronto: J. Lorimer, 1974.

Childs, J. Rives. *Foreign Service Farewell.* Charlottesville: University of Virginia Press, 1969.

———. *Let the Credit Go.* New York: K. S. Giniger, 1983.

———. *Vignettes.* New York: Vantage Press, 1977.

Clare, George. *Last Waltz in Vienna.* London: Macmillan, 1980.

Clemente, Josep. *Historia de la Cruz Roja Española.* Madrid: La Cruz Roja Española, 1986.

Cohen, Richard. *The Burden of Conscience.* Bloomington: Indiana University Press, 1987.

Conway, John. *Debts to Pay.* Toronto: James Lorimer, 1992.

Coon, Carleton. *Adventures and Discoveries.* Englewood Cliffs, N.J.: Prentice-Hall, 1981.

Copetas, A. Craig. *Metal Men.* New York: G. P. Putnam's Sons, 1985.

Dansky, Miriam. *Gateshead.* Southfield, Mich.: Targan Press, 1992.

Dean, Andrea Oppenheimer, and Allen Freeman. "The Rockefeller Center of the '80s?" In *American Architecture of the 1980s.* Washington, D.C.: American Institute of Architects Press, 1990.

Don, Yehuda, and V. Karody. *A Social and Economic History of Central European Jewry.* New Brunswick, N.J.: Transactions, 1990.

Edwards, Brian. *London Docklands: Urban Design in an Age of Deregulation.* Oxford: Butterworth Architecture, 1992.

Edwards, Tudor. *The Blue Danube.* London: Hale, 1973.

Eisen, Wendy. *Count Us In.* Toronto: Burgher Books, 1995.

Finger, Seymour (ed.). *American Jewry During the Holocaust.* New York: American Jewish Commission on the Holocaust, 1983.

Finlayson, Iain. *Tangier: City of the Dream.* Hammersmith: HarperCollins, 1992.

Foster, Peter. *The Master Builders.* Toronto: Key Porter Books, 1986.

———. *Towers of Debt.* London: Hodder and Stoughton, 1993.

Fraenkel, Josef. *The Jews of Austria.* London: Vallentine, Mitchell, 1967.

Freidenreich, Harriet. *Jewish Politics in Vienna, 1918–1938.* Bloomington: Indiana University Press, 1991.

Friedenson, Joseph, and David Kranzler. *Heroine of Rescue.* Brooklyn: Mesorah, 1984.

Fuchs, Abraham. *The Unheeded Cry.* Brooklyn: Mesorah, 1984.

García, Figueras. *Spain, Franco and the Jews.* Madrid, 1988.

Garfinkle, Max. *The Jews of Morocco.* New York: Zionist Youth Council, 1956.

Gilbert, Martin. *The Holocaust.* New York: Holt, Rinehart and Winston, 1985.

Gluskin, Ira. *The Cadillac Fairview Corporation Limited.* Toronto: Royal Commission on Corporate Concentration, 1976.

Goldenberg, Susan. *Men of Property.* Toronto: Personal Library, 1981.

Goobey, Alastair Ross. *Bricks and Mortals.* London: Century Business, 1992.

Good, David. *The Economic Rise of the Hapsburg Empire, 1750–1914.* Berkeley: University of California Press, 1984.

Green, Michelle. *The Dream at the End of the World.* New York: HarperCollins, 1991.

Gutman, Yisrael, and Efraim Zuroff (eds.). *Rescue Attempts During the Holocaust.* Jerusalem: Yad Vashem, 1977.

Hall, Luella. *The United States and Morocco, 1776–1956.* Metuchen, N.J., Scarecow Press, 1971.

Hamilton, Thomas. *Appeasement's Child.* New York: A. A. Knopf, 1943.

Heaps, Leo. *Escape from Arnem.* Toronto: Macmillan, 1945.

Heilman, Samuel. *Defenders of the Faith.* New York: Schocken Books, 1992.

———, and Steven Cohen. *Cosmopolitans and Parochials.* Chicago: University of Chicago Press, 1989.

Helmreich, William. *The World of the Yeshiva.* New York: Free Press, 1982.

Hills, George. *Franco: The Man and His Nation.* London: Hale, 1967.

Hoffman, Charles. *Gray Dawn.* New York: HarperCollins, 1992.

Hosking, Geoffrey. *A History of the Soviet Union.* London: Fontana, 1990.

Hostettler, Eve. *An Outline History of the Isle of Dogs.* London: Island History Trust, n.d.

Hyman, Paula. *From Dreyfus to Vichy.* New York: Columbia University Press, 1979.

International Committee of the Red Cross. "The Work of the International Committee of the Red Cross for Civilian Detainees in German Concentration Camps From 1939 to 1945." Geneva: IRCR, 1975.

———. "Relief for Prisoners of War and Civilian Detainees." Geneva: ICRC, 1944.

Jackson, Robert. *The Fall of France.* London: Barker, 1975.

Johnson, Paul. *A History of the Jews.* New York: Harper & Row, 1987.

Katz, Jacob. "Toward a Biography of the Hatam Sofer." In *From East and West: Jews in a Changing Europe,* ed. Frances Malino and David Sorkin. Oxford: Basil Blackwell, 1990.

———. *The "Shabbas Goy."* Philadelphia: Jewish Publication Society, 1989.

Kranzler, David. *Thy Brother's Blood.* Brooklyn: Mesorah, 1987.

———, and Eliezer Gevirtz. *To Save a World.* Vol. 1. Lakewood, N.J.: C.I.S., 1991.

Landau, David. *Piety and Power.* London: Martin Secker & Warburg, 1993.

Landau, Rom. *Portrait of Tangiers.* London: Hale, 1952.

Laredo, Isaac. *Memorias de un viejo Tangerino.* Madrid: C. Barmajo, 1935.

Laskier, Michel. *The Alliance Israélite Universelle and the Jewish Communities of Morocco, 1862–1962.* Albany: State University of New York Press, 1983.

———. *North African Jewry in the Twentieth Century.* New York: New York University Press, 1994.

Leapman, Michael. *London's River.* London: Pavilion Books, 1991.

Lederer, Zdenek. *Ghetto Theresienstadt.* New York: Fertig, 1983.

Levai, Jeno. *Black Book on the Martyrdom of Hungarian Jewry.* Zurich: Central European Times, 1945.

Levy, Arnold. *The Story of Gateshead Yeshiva.* Taunton-Somerset: Wessex Press, 1952.

Lieven, Anatol. *The Baltic Revolution.* New Haven, Conn.: Yale University Press, 1993.

Lipschitz, Chaim. *Franco, Spain, the Jews and the Holocaust.* New York: Ktav, 1984.

Lipsitz, Edmond, ed. *Ontario Jewish Resource Directory.* Willowdale, Ont.: Canadian Jewish Congress, 1989.

Lorimer, James. *The Developers.* Toronto: J. Lorimer, 1978.

Lottman, Herbert. *The Fall of Paris.* London: Sinclair-Stevenson, 1992.

McCagg, William. *Jewish Nobles and Geniuses in Modern Hungary.* New York: Columbia University Press, 1972.

McKenna, Brian, and Susan Purcell. *Drapeau.* Toronto: Clarke Irwin, 1980.

McNaught, Kenneth. *The Penguin History of Canada.* London: Penguin Books, 1988.

McQuaig, Linda. *Behind Closed Doors.* Toronto: Viking, 1987.

Mandel, Ernest. *Beyond Perestroika.* London: Verso, 1989.

Marrus, Michael. *The Unwanted.* New York: Oxford University Press, 1985.

———. *Samuel Bronfman.* Hanover, N.H.: Brandeis University Press, 1991.

May, Harry. *Francisco Franco: The Jewish Connection.* Washington, D.C.: University Press of America, 1978.

Medlicott, William. *The Economic Blockade.* London: Her Majesty's Stationery Office, 1952–59.

Ministerio de Asuntos Exteriores. *Tanger: Bajo la Accion Protectora de España el Conflicto Mundial.* Madrid, 1946.

Moore, Wilbert. *Economic Demography of Eastern and Southern Europe.* Geneva: League of Nations, 1945.

Newman, Peter. *The Canadian Establishment.* Vol. 1. Toronto: McClelland & Stewart, 1975.

———. *The Canadian Establishment.* Vol. 2: *The Acquisitors.* Toronto: McClelland & Stewart, 1989.

North York: Realizing the Dream. Burlington, Ont.: Windsor Publications, 1988.

Nyiri, János. *Battlefields and Playgrounds.* London: Macmillan, 1989.

Parkinson, Cecil. *Right at the Center.* London: Weidenfeld and Nicolson, 1992.

Patai, Raphael. *The Vanished Worlds of Jewry.* New York: Macmillan, 1980.

Pauley, Bruce. *From Prejudice to Persecution.* Chapel Hill: University of North Carolina Press, 1992.

Payne, Stanley. *The Franco Regime, 1936–1975.* Madison, Wisc.: University of Wisconsin Press, 1987.

Penkower, Monty. *The Jews Were Expendable.* Urbana: University of Illinois Press, 1983.

Poll, Solomon. *The Hasidic Community of Williamsburg.* New York: Free Press of Glencoe, 1962.

Pons, Dominique. *Les Riches Heures de Tanger.* Paris: La Table Ronde, 1990.

Powell, Jim. *Risk, Ruin and Riches.* New York: Macmillan, 1986.

Proudfoot, William. *The Origin of Stencil Duplicating.* London: Hutchison, 1972.

Raiz, Carmela. *Blue Star over Red Square.* Jerusalem: Feldheim, 1994.

Reichmann, Marika. *Eszti's Story.* Brooklyn: Tova Press, 1995.

Remnick, David. *Lenin's Tomb.* New York: Random House, 1993.

Richardson, Gerald. *Crime Zone.* London: J. Long, 1959.

Richter, Charles. *The Vienna Kehileth: Adas Yereim 25 Years Journal.* New York: Adas Yereim, 1967.

Roi, Yaacov. "The Role of the Synagogue and Religion in the Jewish National Awakening." In *Jewish Culture and Identity in the Soviet Union.* New York: New York University Press, 1991.

Rosenberg, Stuart. *The Jewish Community in Canada.* Toronto: McClelland & Stewart, 1970–71.

Rothchild, John. *Going for Broke.* New York: Simon & Schuster, 1991.

Rothkirchen, Livia. "The Role of Czech and Slovak Jewish Leadership in the Field of Rescue Work." In *Rescue Attempts During the Holocaust.* Jerusalem: Yad Vashem, 1977.

Sachar, Howard. *A History of the Jews in America.* New York: Alfred A. Knopf, 1992.

Sarlos, Andrew. *Fireworks.* Toronto: Key Porter Books, 1993.

Schachtman, Tom. *Skyscraper Dreams.* Boston: Little, Brown, 1991.

Schwertfeger, Ruth. *Women of Theresienstadt.* New York: St. Martin's Press, 1989.

Serels, M. Mitchell. *A History of the Jews of Tangier.* New York: Sepher-Hermon Press, 1991.

Shelley, Lore. *Secretaries of Death.* New York: Shengold, 1986.

Shirer, William. *The Collapse of the Third Republic.* New York: Simon & Schuster, 1969.

Smith, Bradley. *The Shadow Warriors.* New York: Basic Books, 1983.

Smith, R. Harris. *OSS, The Secret History of America's First Central Intelligence Agency.* Berkeley: University of California Press, 1972.

Speisman, Stephen. *The Jews of Toronto.* Toronto: McClelland & Stewart, 1979.

Steinsaltz, Adin. *The Essential Talmud.* London: Weidenfeld and Nicolson, 1976.

Stewart, Walter. *Too Big to Fail.* Toronto: McClelland & Stewart, 1993.

Stuart, Graham. *The International City of Tangier.* Stanford: University of California Press, 1955.

Szulc, Tad. *The Secret Alliance.* New York: Farrar, Straus & Giroux, 1991.

Tamari, Meir. *In the Marketplace.* Southfield, Mich.: Targum Press, 1991.

Tartakower, Arieh, and Kurt Grossman. *The Jewish Refugee.* New York: Institute of Jewish Affairs, 1944.

Tyler, Rodney. *Canary Wharf: The Untold Story.* London: Olympia & York, 1990.

U.S. War Department. *War Report of the OSS.* New York: Walker, 1976.

Wagschal, Rabbi S. *Torah Guide for the Businessman.* Jerusalem: Feldheim, 1990.

Weinberg, David. *A Community on Trial.* Chicago: University of Chicago Press, 1977.

Wharton-Tigar, Edward. *Burning Bright.* England: Metal Bulletin Books, 1987.

Whealey, Robert. *Hitler and Spain.* Lexington: University Press of Kentucky, 1989.

Whitaker, Reg. *Double Standard.* Toronto: Lester & Orpen Dennys, 1987.

Vaidon, Lawdon. *Tangier: A Different Way.* Metuchen, N.J.: Scarecrow Press, 1977.

Walters, E. Garrison. *The Other Europe.* Syracuse, N.Y.: Syracuse University Press, 1988.

Whitney, Craig. *Spy Trader.* New York: Times Books, 1993.

Wyman, David. *The Abandonment of the Jews.* New York: Pantheon Books, 1984.

Yahil, Leni. *The Holocaust.* New York: Oxford University Press, 1990.

Zakon, Miriam Stark. *Silent Revolution.* Brooklyn: Mesorah, 1992.

Zeckendorf, William, with Edward McCreary. *The Autobiography of William Zeckendorf.* New York: Holt, Rinehart and Winston, 1970.

Zuccotti, Susan. *The Holocaust, the French, and the Jews.* New York: Basic Books, 1993.

ARTICLES

"Agreement Signed for New Star Tower." *Toronto Daily Star,* 22 October 1969.

Amiel, Barbara. "The Man Who Made the Canary Fly." London *Times,* 28 March 1990.

Appleyard, Bryan. "Office Boys Who Made Good." London *Times,* 31 August 1989.

Babad, Abraham. "Gateshead." *Jewish Life,* March 1953, 27.

Barsky, Neil. "Paul Reichmann Scales Real Estate's Heights, Including Sears Tower." *Wall Street Journal,* 5 September 1989.

———. "Olympia & York Finds That It Isn't Immune to Real-Estate Crunch." *Wall Street Journal,* 25 October 1991.

———. "How O & Y's Miscues Led Creditor Banks to End Forbearance." *Wall Street Journal,* 1 June 1992.

———. "Olympia & York Plans a Huge Restructuring Involving Many Banks." *Wall Street Journal,* 23 March 1992.

———. "Olympia & York Bets on a Radical Proposal for Debt Revamping." *Wall Street Journal,* 13 April 1992.

———. "Johnson's Exit from O&Y Signalled Firm's Hardball Strategy with Banks." *Wall Street Journal,* 17 April 1992.

Bartlett, Sarah. "Holding Vast Space and Vast Debt." *New York Times,* 29 April 1992.

Bennett, Amanda. "Canadian Realty Firms Make Waves in U.S. with Major Projects." *Wall Street Journal,* 24 April 1978.

Berkovits, Rabbi Berel. "The Jerusalem of England." *Jewish Chronicle,* 19 June 1987.

Bess, Demaree. "Uncle Sam Sponsors a Smugglers' Paradise." *Saturday Evening Post,* 16 April 1949.

Bevan, Judi. "Quiet Man Will Make Canary Sing." *Sunday Times,* 19 July 1987.

Bianco, Anthony. "Magnificent Obsession." *Vanity Fair,* October 1992.

Bohlen, Celestine. "U. S. Envoy in Hungary Quits to Handle Investment in East." *New York Times,* 26 January 1990.

Bond, Matthew. "Why Reichmann Is Celebrating a Jubilee at Canary Wharf." *Sunday Telegraph* (London), 19 November 1989.

Borrus, Amy. "The City of London Spawns a Suburb." *Business Week,* 13 January 1986.

Bowles, Paul. "View from Tangier: The Spreading Arab Tide." *Nation,* 30 June 1956.

Brennan, John. "A Far From Inevitable Rebirth." *Financial Times* (London), 12 May 1989.

Brooke, James. "Battery Park Complex Attracts Giant Tenant." *New York Times,* 28 August 1984.

Bucham, James. "A High Risk Business." *Independent,* 16 December 1990.

Burck, Gilbert. "Man in a $100-Million Jam." *Fortune,* July 1960.

Burrough, Bryan. "Sam Lefrak: Real Estate Bargain Hunter." *Business Week,* 31 May 1976.

———. "Canada's Secretive Reichmanns." *Business Week,* 6 March 1978.

———. "The Reichmann Brothers: Real Estate Development's Hottest Team." *Business Week,* 15 August, 1983.

———. "An Unorthodox Death." *Vanity Fair,* January 1996.

"Canadian Cities Rebuild on a Three-Layer Plan." *Business Week,* 12 March 1966.

"Canary Wharf's Real Problem." *Economist,* 23 May 1992.

Carriere, Vianney. "Billion-Dollar Men." *Toronto Globe & Mail,* 27 June 1981.

Chase, Steven. "Reichmann's Plight Has Charities Hurting." *Toronto Globe & Mail,* 15 June 1992.

Cheeseright, Paul. "The Developer Who Looks a Decade Ahead." *Financial Times,* 15 January 1990.

———. "Tentacles Spread from Canary Wharf." *Financial Times,* 6 April 1990.

Chisholm, Patricia. "Big Dollar Battle." *Maclean's,* 24 October 1988.

———. "Hungarian Officials, Budapest Jewry Celebrate Pioneering School." *Coalition,* January 1991.

"Cleaning up Morocco." *Time,* 2 November 1959.

Comfort, Nicholas. "Budapest's Jews Face Classroom Revolution." *European,* 6 September 1991.

"Crémazie Project Under Way." *Montreal Star,* 10 July 1962.

Davidson, Andrew. "Special Offers Fail to Fill Canary Wharf." London *Times,* 23 September 1990.

Dewar, Elaine. "The Mysterious Reichmanns." *Toronto Life,* November, 1987.

Docklands Consultative Commitee. "All That Glitters: A Critical Assessment of Canary Wharf." May 1992.

Drohan, Madelaine. "The Shock of the New." *Toronto Globe & Mail,* 10 August 1991.

———. "Canary Wharf Poses Tough Political Choice." *Toronto Globe & Mail,* 19 May 1992.

———. "O & Y Officer Still Singing Praises of Canary Wharf." *Toronto Globe & Mail,* 1 June 1992.

Dwyer, Paula. "The Reichmann Reconquest." *Business Week,* 23 October 1995.

Eaton, Leslie. "Trouble for Soros-Reichmann team." *New York Times,* 25 September 1994.

Efron, Noah J. "Trembling with Fear: How Secular Israelis See the Ultra-Orthodox, and Why." *Tikkun,* September 1991.

Egan, Jack. "The 'New Rothschilds.' " *U.S. News & World Report,* 14 March 1988.

Eichenwald, Kurt. "Reichmann Joins Soros in New Fund." *New York Times,* 9 February 1993.

"The Empire Builders." *Maclean's,* 6 April 1992.

Fagan, Drew. "Reichmanns Look to China, Latin America." *Toronto Globe & Mail,* 23 June 1994.

Faltermayer, Edmund. "Toronto, the New Great City." *Fortune,* September 1974.

Fennell, Tom. "The Roots of Power." *Maclean's,* 10 October 1988.

"The Files Declassified." *Coalition* (New York), March 1989.

Fisher, Ross. "Digging In at Canary Wharf." *Canadian Business,* February 1990.

Fleming, James. "The Reichmanns Recharge the Battery." *Maclean's,* 5 April 1982.

Foster, Peter. "How Deep Are Their Pockets?" *Canadian Business,* October 1991.

———. "The $18-Billion Miscalculation." *Canadian Business,* June 1992.

Fowler, Glenn. "New York Holds Up $90 Million Project." *New York Times,* 31 May 1979.

Francis, Diane. "Our New Export: Revitalized Cities." *Canadian Business,* August 1980.

Freeman, Alan, and Jacquie McNish. "Place Crémazie Called Success Story of '64, With 2 New Wings Scheduled to Open May 1." *Toronto Globe & Mail,* 17 April 1964.

———. "Reichmanns' Circular Tower Didn't Get off Ground." *Toronto Globe & Mail,* 24 December, 1988.

———. "Ottawa, Ontario Refuse to Help Out Troubled O & Y." *Toronto Globe & Mail,* 5 May 1992.

Gill, Brendan. "The Skyline." *New Yorker,* 20 August 1990.

Goldberger, Paul. "A Dramatic Counterpoint for Trade Center." *New York Times*, 14 May 1981.

Goldenberg, Susan. "A Reichmann Touch in Real Estate." *New York Times*, 17 August 1980.

———. "The Unknown Empire." *Financial Post Magazine*, September 1981.

Gorrie, Peter. "O & Y to Start Soviet Tower in a Year." *Toronto Star*, 21 February 1990.

Gottlieb, Martin. "Battery Project Reflects Changing City Priorities." *New York Times*, 18 October 1985.

Graff, James, and Adam Corelli. "Time for No Debt and Cash Reserves." *Time* (Canadian edition), 5 November 1990.

Greenspon, Edward. "Reichmann Revisions Mollify Objections to Canary Wharf." *Toronto Globe & Mail*, 30 March 1988.

———. "Residents of London Docklands Cool to Largesse of Reichmanns." *Toronto Globe & Mail*, 5 July 1989.

———. "Canary Wharf Depends as Much on New Attitudes as New Buildings." *Toronto Globe & Mail*, 13 April 1990.

Greenspon, Edward, and Harvey Enchin. "O & Y Myth Meets Match." *Toronto Globe & Mail*, 16 May 1992.

Handelman, Stephen. "PM Promises 'Better Days' to Refuseniks." *Toronto Star*, 23 November 1989.

Harris, Marjorie. "Sidney and George's Billion-Dollar Baby." *Quest* (Toronto edition), February 1977.

Hellman, Peter. "Manhattan Transfer." *Saturday Night*, April 1983.

Hertzberg, Daniel, and Randall Smith. "Sale of Building by American Express Co. Set." *Wall Street Journal*, 24 March 1982.

Hirschberg, Peter. "When Charity Ends." *Jerusalem Report*, 1 July 1993.

Hodgson, Godfrey. "The City Shapes Its Future." *Financial Times*, 15 March 1986.

Hoffman, Charles. "Revival of the Dead." *Jerusalem Report*, 4 July 1991.

Horsley, Carter. "$90 Million Renovation at Lexington and 46th." *New York Times*, 20 April 1979.

Horsman, Matthew. "Reichmann Clings to Canary Wharf Vision." *Financial Post*, 22 September 1990.

Houlder, Vanessa. "Docklands: Will It Stay a Cut-price Ghost Town?" *Financial Times*, 11 January 1992.

———. "The People's Jury Is Out." *Financial Times*, 20 March 1992.

———. "Olympia & York Files for Protection." *Financial Times*, 15 May 1992.

———. "A Price on Its High-rise Head." *Financial Times*, 5 June 1992.

Houlder, Vanessa, Robert Simon, Bernard Simon, and Alan Friedman. "Olympia & York: Debt Shakes a $20bn Edifice to Its Foundations." *Financial Times*, 30 March 1992.

Hylton, Richard. "Reshaping a Real Estate Dynasty." *New York Times*, 28 November 1990.

———. "The Man Who Blew $10 Billion." *Fortune*, 17 May 1993.

Huxtable, Ada Louise. "A New 'Rockefeller Center' Planned for Battery Park." *New York Times*, 24 May 1981.

"In the Balance." *Economist*, 22 June 1991.

Ipsen, Erik. "Call It Albatross Wharf." *Institutional Investor*, November 1990.

Jenish, D'arcy. "Capital Developments." *Maclean's*, 24 August 1987.

Johnson, Arthur. "The Reichmanns' London Gamble." *Business*, July 1988.

———. "Hungary's Capitalist Revolution." *Financial Times of Canada*, 21 November 1988, 18.

———. "Tenants Wanted, Will Negotiate Terms." *Report on Business*, August 1990.

Kahn, H. "Tanger, Ville de Tora." *Kountrass*, January–February 1993.

Keinon, Herb. "After 18-Year Wait, Refusenik Arrives in Israel." *Jerusalem Post*, 21 March 1990.

"Kings of Officeland." *Economist*, 22 July 1989.

Knecht, Bruce. "Canary Wharf: What Went Wrong?" *Barron's*, 1 June 1992.

Kranzler, David. "Renée Reichmann and the Tangier Rescue Connection." *Jewish Observer*, February 1991.

Krossel, Martin. "Libel: Canada's Cold Wave." *Columbia Journalism Review*, July 1988.

Landau, David. "Soviet Jews Test the Limits of 'Glasnost.' " *Jerusalem Post*, 1 December 1987.

Lechasseur, Marc. "Le nord de la ville de Montréal se développe." *Le Petit Journal* (Montreal), 15 July 1962.

Lehrman, Hal. "Typically, Depressed Tangier Gets a Lift Thanks to Neighboring Morocco's Troubles." *Wall Street Journal*, 6 September 1955.

Lever, Lawrence. "Born-Again Anglophile of Docklands." London *Times*, 9 May 1988.

Lieberman, Steven. "Gilman, Local Rabbi Help Free Refusenik." *Rockland County Journal-News* (N.Y.), 9 March 1990.

Light, Larry. "Even the Reichmanns Are Feeling the Pinch." *Business Week*, 8 October 1990.

Long, Angela. "Finding Ways of Building Office Blocks on Water." London *Times*, 14 May 1989.

McFadden, Robert. "Battery Park City Builder Picked." *New York Times*, 14 November 1980.

McFarland, Janet. "New O & Y First Step to an Empire?" *Financial Post*, 20 November, 1993, 11.

McLaughlin, Gord. "The Reichmanns Rise Again." *Financial Post Magazine*, April 1994.

McMurdry, Deirdre. "O & Y Holdings Worth at Least $6.6 Billion." *Financial Post*, 13 April 1990.

———. "A Family Affair." *Maclean's*, 6 April 1992.

———. "A Patriarch at Bay." *Maclean's*, 15 June 1992.

McNish, Jacquie. "O & Y Calls the Shots in Campeau Affairs after Life-Saving Loan." *Toronto Globe & Mail*, 27 September 1989.

———. "Reports of Secret Stake Infuriate O & Y Bankers." *Toronto Globe & Mail*, 19 September 1992.

———. "How Banks Flubbed O & Y." *Toronto Globe & Mail*, 4 December 1992.

———. "The Day the Banks Said No." *Toronto Globe & Mail*, 5 December 1992.

McNish, Jacquie, and Madelaine Drohan. "U.K. Court Decision Leads to O & Y's Filing." *Toronto Globe & Mail*, 15 May 1992.

McNish, Jacquie, and Edward Greenspon. "Reichmann Sale Scares Buyers." *Toronto Globe & Mail*, 21 September 1990.

McNish, Jacquie, and Margaret Philip. "No Stone Unturned in Quest for Cash." *Toronto Globe & Mail*, 21 April 1992.

McNish, Jacquie, Margaret Philip, and Brian Milner. "O & Y's Hard Times Stem from Shot to Short-term Debt." *Toronto Globe & Mail*, 4 April 1992.

McQueen, Roderick. "Joining the Towers That Be." *Maclean's*, 26 March 1979.

Maier, Thomas, and Elizabeth Sanger. "The Leaning Tower." *Newsday*, 3 May 1992.

Maley, Dianne. "N.Y. Towers Reflect O & Y's Style." *Toronto Globe & Mail*, 15 October 1985.

———. "Reichmanns Not Out of the Game, Despite Competing Bid for Walker." *Toronto Globe & Mail*, 11 April 1986.

———. "O & Y Upgrading Its Plans for Canary Wharf Project." *Toronto Globe & Mail*, 21 March 1988.

———. "The Philosopher King." *Report on Business*, December 1988.

———. "Reichmann Helps Build Bridge to Soviets." *Toronto Globe & Mail*, 2 July 1989.

Maley, Dianne, and Bruce Little. "Gulf Canada's Reorganization to Save $500 Million in Taxes." *Toronto Globe & Mail*, 22 October 1985.

Margalit, Avishai. "Israel: The Rise of the Ultra-Orthodox." *New York Review of Books*, 9 November 1989.

Martin, Douglas. "A Canadian Family Becomes Key Force in City Real Estate." *New York Times*, 24 March 1982.

———. "Olympia & York's Sharp Rise." *New York Times*, 30 May 1985.

Martin, Patrick. "Reichmann Woes Felt in Israeli Election." *Toronto Globe & Mail*, 6 June 1992.

Mason, Todd, and Elizabeth Weiner. "The Reichmanns." *Business Week*, 29 January 1990.

Meyer, Ernie. "The Second Wallenberg." *Jerusalem Post*, 29 September 1989.

Milligan, John. "Blind Faith." *Institutional Investor*, September 1992.

Negley, Harrison. "Why They Love Us in Tangier." *Collier's Magazine*, 16 May 1953.

"Les Néo-Canadiens tiennent pour légitimes et fondées les aspirations du Quebec." *Le Devoir* (Montreal), 30 October 1963.

"New Office-Shopping Complex, Place Crémazie, Opened Here." *Montreal Gazette*, 30 October 1963.

"New Star Building to Pace Waterfront, Developer Predicts." *Toronto Daily Star,* 17 June 1969.

Noble, Kimberly, and Jacquie McNish. "Edper Reveals O & Y Stake." *Toronto Globe & Mail,* 18 September 1992.

Norman, James. "Property Rich, Cash Poor." *Forbes,* 11 November 1990.

Olins, Rufus. "Bumpy Ride to Canary Wharf." London *Times,* 8 September 1991.

Olive, David. "Canada's Top Private Companies." *Canadian Business,* November 1983.

———. "Owe & Why." *Report on Business* magazine, August 1992.

Palmer, Jay. "Will London's Canary Wharf Lay an Egg?" *Barron's,* 1 October 1990.

Partridge, John. "The Players Make Book War an Industry Good Read." *Toronto Globe & Mail,* 6 August 1987.

Philip, Margaret. "O & Y Losing Tenants in Toronto." *Toronto Globe & Mail,* 21 September 1990.

———. "Reichmanns Battling New York Real Estate Slump." *Toronto Globe & Mail,* 24 June 1991.

Philip, Margaret, and Jacquie McNish. "A Tale of Two Buildings." *Toronto Globe & Mail,* 18 April 1992.

Philip, Margaret, Jacquie McNish, Brian Milner, and Alan Freeman. "O & Y's New Boss Having Second Thoughts." *Toronto Globe & Mail,* 9 April 1992.

Philips, Andrew. "The Reichmanns' Bold New Venture." *Maclean's,* 27 June 1988.

———. "Building Pains." *Maclean's,* 8 April 1991.

"Pie in the Sky or a Dream Come True?" *Accountancy,* September 1991.

Pope, Kyle. "Canary Wharf Climbs Out of the Pits." *Wall Street Journal,* 20 June 1994.

Prévost, Arthur. Le "Les gratte-ciel à l'assaut du nord de Montréal." *Le Petit Journal,* 3 November 1963.

Prial, Frank. "A Tenant Signs $2 Billion Lease for Battery Park." *New York Times,* 24 March 1995.

Prokesch, Steven. "3 Named to Administer Olympia London Project." *New York Times,* 29 May 1992.

Purnick, Joyce. "Plans Disclosed for Office Core at Battery Park." *New York Times,* 14 May 1981.

Raab, Selwyn. "'84 Pay for New York Construction Job: $308,651." *New York Times,* 12 June 1985.

Rabinovich, Abraham. "Rampaging Rabbis." *New Republic,* 14 September 1987.

Reguly, Eric. "New Generation Tries Its Wings." *Financial Post,* 22 September 1990.

———. "Reichmanns Return to Property Roots." *Financial Post,* 22 September 1990.

Reina, Peter. "Giant Canary Wharf Keeps on Singing, Despite Some Blues." *Engineering News Record,* 18 March 1991.

"A Reputation for Integrity." *Jewish Post,* 27 March 1980.

Robinson, Jeffrey. "From the Ground Up." *Barron's,* 21 November 1983.

Rocco, Fiametta. "London Property: The Next Crash?" *Institutional Investor,* October 1989.

Rose, Frederick. "How Henley's Chief Lost a Long Struggle to Take Over Santa Fe." *Wall Street Journal,* 29 July 1987.

Rosenberg, David. "Reichman [sic] Makes a Bet on Downtown." *Jerusalem Post,* 20 May 1987.

———. "Building on Experience." *Jerusalem Post,* 12 January 1990.

———. "Drawing Hasty Conclusions." *Jewish Chronicle,* 1 March 1991.

Sallot, Jeff. "Reichmann Firm to Build Skyscraper in Moscow." *Toronto Globe & Mail,* 6 November 1989.

Scardino, Albert. "Building a Manhattan Empire." *New York Times,* 18 April 1987.

Schlamm, William S. "Tangier." *Fortune,* August, 1950.

Shapiro, Haim. "The Givers and Takers." *Jerusalem Post,* 20 February 1987.

Shapiro, Harry. "Olympia & York's American Empire." *Institutional Investor,* February 1986.

Shaw, Paul. "Gateshead." *Jewish Chronicle,* 2 September 1977 (supplement).

Siekman, Philip. "The Bronfmans: An Instinct for Dynasty." *Fortune,* December 1966.

Simon, Bernard, and Vanessa Houlder. "Long View from the Top of Canary Wharf." *Financial Times,* 19 February 1991.

Simpkins, Raoul. "Banking in Tangier." *Atlantic Monthly,* December, 1950.

Smith, Geoffrey. "The One That Got Away." *Forbes,* 1 April 1977.

Smith, Randall. "Real-Estate Giant Olympia & York Says It Is in Solid Shape Despite Skeptics' Doubts." *Wall Street Journal,* 14 May 1982.

Smith, Vivian. "Molson Cos. Pops a Corker, Tough and Teflon, into Its No. 1 Spot." *Toronto Globe & Mail,* 24 October 1988.

Sommer, Allison Kaplan. "Plugged In." *Jerusalem Post,* 20 May 1994.

Steed, Judy. "Battery of Talent Takes on N.Y." *Toronto Globe & Mail,* 14 January 1984.

Stephens, Philip. "The Olympia & York Insolvency; Shoring Up a Thatcher Memorial." *Financial Times,* 16 May 1992.

Stevenson, Richard. "From Debacle to Desirable." *New York Times,* 18 July 1995.

Stewart, Walter. "Good and Rich." *Weekend Magazine,* 13 October 1979.

Taberner, John. "The Phony Gold Rush." *American Mercury,* December 1952.

Temple, Peter. "An Empire Built on Property." *Accountancy,* August 1989.

Terry, Edith. "The Reichmann Touch: Facing the Toughest Test Yet." *Business Week,* 23 March 1987.

Thompson, Allan. "Reichmanns to Build New Office in Budapest." *Toronto Star,* 10 January 1992.

Thompson, Terri, and Edith Terry. "What the Reichmanns Plan Next for Their Real Estate Billions." *Business Week,* 28 October 1985.

Tifft, Susan. "Giving London a Lift." *Time,* 18 April 1988.

———. "Man at Work." *Time,* 6 January 1991.

Toman, Barbara. "Second 'City,' Rising on London's Docks, Faces Risky Future." *Wall Street Journal*, 6 November 1989.

Tully, Shawn. "The Bashful Billionaires of Olympia & York." *Fortune*, 14 June 1982.

"Unreal Estate." *Economist*, 21 October 1989.

Ver Meulen, Michael. "The Rise of Canary Wharf." *Institutional Investor*, November 1986.

Walmsley, Ann. "A Family's Way to Wealth." *Maclean's*, 24 October 1988.

———. "The Price of a Reprieve." *Maclean's*, 2 October 1989.

Warson, Albert. "The Reichmanns' Best Partners File for a Friendly Divorce." *Canadian Business*, November 1992.

Wechsberg, Joseph. "Anything Goes." *New Yorker*, April 1952.

Wertenschlag, Yossef. "La Dette de Reconnaissance au Caudillo." *Kountrass*, no. 32, January–February 1992.

Westell, Dan. "Golden Touch Turns to Stone." *Toronto Globe & Mail*, 17 April 1991.

Wheatley, Keith. "Men at Wharf." London *Times*, 2 October 1988.

"When a City Really Sets Out to Rebuild." *U.S. News & World Report*, 22 August 1966.

"Where Derelict Land Is a Greenfield Site." *Economist*, 13 February 1988.

Wilkinson, David. "Paul and Albert and Ralph and David." *Canadian Business*, November 1989.

Willoughby, Jack. "Reichmanns of Olympia and York Can Act Swiftly, Secretively on a Deal." *Toronto Globe & Mail*, 5 May 1979.

Wiseman, Carter. "The Next Great Place." *New York* magazine, 16 June 1986.

Wong, Jan. "Reichmanns Set to Spend, but Shopping List's a Secret." *Toronto Globe & Mail*, 25 September 1987.

———. "Apart from That, How Was the Issue?" *Toronto Globe & Mail*, 11 December 1987.

Wood, Chris. "On the Ropes." *Maclean's*, 25 May 1992.

Yehuda, Tzvi Zev Ben. "Eli Reichmann: From Tangiers to Jerusalem. *Jewish Press*, 3 May 1991 (pt. 1) and 10 May 1991 (pt. 2).

Zehr, Leonard. "Canada's Rich and Reticent Reichmanns Plan to Use Property Profits to Diversify." *Wall Street Journal*, 21 May 1981.

Zukosky, Jerome. "He Wheels His Way to Real Estate Empire but Piles Up Debt, Too." *Wall Street Journal*, 9 February 1959.

LEGAL PROCEEDINGS

Albert Reichmann et al. vs. the Globe and Mail Division of Canadian Newspapers Company Limited et al., Supreme Court of Ontario, Toronto, court file no. 26901/88.

Albert Reichmann vs. Zeev Vered and Ron Engineering and Construction (International) Ltd., Ontario Court (General Division), Toronto, court file 94-CQ-52726.

Amelia Rose vs. Minister of Revenue, Federal Court of Canada, cited in Dominion Tax Cases 1971, 5481-6.

Bank of Montreal vs. Olympia & York Development, Supreme Court of Ontario, Toronto, file 24182/84.

Banque de Montreal vs. Edward Reichmann, Superior Court, Montreal, case 500-05-009020-817.

Battery Park Holdings, Inc. et al. vs. O & Y (U.S.) Development Company, L.P., et al., Supreme Court of the State of New York, index no. 31782/92.

Canadian Imperial Bank of Commerce vs. A & E Reichmann Ltd. and Albert Reichmann, Superior Court, Montreal.

D & D Holdings Inc. vs. the Minister of National Revenue, Tax Review Board case 71-147.

Edouard Reichmann, Tibor Pivko and Louis Reichmann vs. the Minister of National Revenue, Tax Review Board cases 71-837, 71-836, and 71-838.

Edward J. Minskoff vs. Ficor, Inc. and Jan T. Hyde, Supreme Court of New York, County of New York, index number 21699/83.

Edward J. Minskoff vs. National Kinney Corp. et al., Supreme Court of New York, New York County.

In the Matter of a Plan of Arrangement for Olympia & York Developments et al., Ontario Court of Justice (General Division), court file B125/92.

Joseph Bergman vs. Louis Reichman and Maple Leaf Ceramic Industries, Superior Court, Montreal.

Louis Reichmann, Edouard Reichmann and Tibor Pivko vs. Her Majesty the Queen, Federal Court of Canada, Trial Division cases T-1103-73, T-1104-73, T-1104-74.

Maple Leaf Ceramic Industries (1967) Ltd. vs. Edouard Reichmann, Court of Appeals, Montreal.

Morgan Stanley Properties Limited vs. Rochmoor Limited and Olympia and York Developments Limited, High Court of Justice, Chancery Division, London.

Olympia Floor & Wall Tile (Quebec) Ltd. vs. Minister of National Revenue, Tax Appeal Board, cited in 1967 Dominion Tax Cases.

Olympia Floor & Wall Tile (Quebec) Ltd. vs. Minister of National Revenue, Exchequer Court of Canada, cited in 1970 Dominion Tax Cases.

ARCHIVES

Archivo Historico Nacional, Madrid.

Agudath Israel, New York City.

Allgemeines Verweltungsarchiv (General Administrative Archive), Vienna.

American Jewish Joint Distribution Committee, New York City.

Bureau de la Division d'Enregistrement, Montreal.

Canadian Jewish Congress, Montreal.

Casier Central des Etrangers, Paris.
Companies House, London.
Franklin D. Roosevelt Library, Hyde Park., N.Y.
Hungarian State Archives, Sopron.
Land Registry Office, Toronto.
National Archives (U.S.), Washington, D.C.
Ontario Securities Commission, Toronto.
Public Records Office, London.
Securities and Exchange Commission, Washington, D.C.
Yad Vashem, Jerusalem.
Yeshiva University, New York City.

UNPUBLISHED WORKS

David, Charles. "The DG I Knew."
Kranzler, David. Interview with Eva Heller Gutwirth, 1 May 1983.
Reichmann, Edward. Memoir.

TELEVISION AND VIDEO

Hewland Productions, *The Men Who Built Canary Wharf,* an hour-long documentary that aired in Britain in 1981.
Olympia & York Development, First Bank Tower, a 22-minute film produced by the company in 1976 and written and narrated by Roberts.

Index

Taylor, Allan, 632
Teitelbaum, Rabbi Moses, 5, 8
Tengelman Group, 559
Tennenhaus, Edmund, 204
Texaco Canada, 332
Texaco Incorporated, 604
Thatcher, Margaret:
  and Canary Wharf, 503, 507, 508, 511,
    512–14, 518, 542, 562–66, 568,
    585, 587
  and Docklands, 516, 565
  election lost by, 565, 566, 623
  philo-Semitism of, 564
Three Star Construction Limited:
  bailout of, 315–21, 365, 492
  and Chabanel, 274–75, 288, 290, 314
  and Côte des Lieses Industrial Park,
    313–14, 319–20
  financing of, 273, 276, 311–15
  formation of, 270–75
  growth of, 278
  in industrial development, 270, 274,
    288
  net worth of, 294
  and Place Crémazie, 290–94, 311,
    313–15, 317, 319–20
  and Tour Laurier, 294–95, 311, 312,
    317, 319
  and Zimmermans, 271–72
Tibbalds, Francis, 541
Tisch, Lawrence, 646, 662, 663
Tishman, Robert, 404
Tishman Realty and Construction Corporation, 371, 373
Tiso, Josef, 63
Tokai Bank, 580
Tokyo Teleport Town, 544–45
Toledano, Samuel, 227
Toledano family, 94, 359
Torah:
  on bribes, 451
  on death and the medical profession, 43
  given to Moses, 203
  on rescue (pidyon shevuyim), 102–3
  on secular law, 190
  sefer, 362–63
  study of, 11, 24, 202, 303, 329, 428,
    435
  on wealth, 10–11
  on women's roles, 40, 116
  see also Talmud
Toronto:
  Board of Jewish Education, 329, 360,
    473, 478–79

building height in, 346–47, 351–52,
  388
as Canada's business capital, 239
eruv of, 475–76
financial district of, 333–37, 348–49,
  354
First Bank Tower in, 344–46, 347, 349,
  354–55, 365
First Canadian Place in, *see* First Cana-
  dian Place
Glenwood area of, 479–80
Global House in, 333, 334, 345
Louis Reichmann in, 236–37, 239
MINT in, 333–34
North York area of, *see* North York
Olympia & York in, 258, 259
Olympia Tile in, 236–37
Orthodox Jews in, 246–48, 473–76
Paul Reichmann in, 239, 246–47,
  327–28
politics in, 345–48, 351–54
Ralph Reichmann in, 237–38, 239,
  246–47
Reichmann homes in, 246, 327–28,
  479–86
Samuel and Renée Reichmann in, 239,
  244, 246, 248
Schlome Emune Israel in, 246
Talmud Torah Ets Chaim in, 246
United Way of, 479
York Center in, 334–37
Toronto Daily Star, 334, 336
Toronto-Dominion Bank, and MINT,
  333–34
Toronto-Dominion Center, 333, 343
Toronto Industrial Leaseholds (TIL), 259,
  298
Toronto Life, 524–27, 529–30, 532,
  615–16
Toronto Star Limited building, 334–37,
  344, 347, 354
Toronto Stock Exchange, 384
Toronto Sun, 526–27, 530
Tour Laurier, 294–95, 311, 312, 317,
  319
Tovar, Duke of (Figueroa), 114–15
Travelers Corporation, 653
Travelstead, Gouch Ware, 508–12, 516,
  534, 563, 566–67, 585
Treitel, Mauric, 271–72
Trizec Corporation, 368, 451, 580
  and Edper, 387, 414, 417–19, 423,
    456, 647, 656
  and English Property, 414, 417, 503

ABOUT THE AUTHOR

ANTHONY BIANCO is a senior writer at *Business Week* and the author of *Rainmaker.* He lives in Brooklyn, New York.